THE NEW AMERICAN BIBLE
CONCISE CONCORDANCE

THE NEW AMERICAN BIBLE
CONCISE CONCORDANCE

John R. Kohlenberger III

EDITOR

NEW YORK · OXFORD

OXFORD UNIVERSITY PRESS

OXFORD
UNIVERSITY PRESS

Oxford   New York
Auckland   Bangkok   Buenos Aires   Cape Town   Chennai
Dar es Salaam   Delhi   Hong Kong   Istanbul   Karachi   Kolkata
Kuala Lumpur   Madrid   Melbourne   Mexico City   Mumbai
Nairobi   São Paulo   Shanghai   Taipei   Tokyo   Toronto

Published by Oxford University Press, Inc.
198 Madison Avenue, New York, NY 10016

www.oup.com

Oxford is a registered trademark of Oxford University Press

Design and Typesetting by Blue Heron Bookcraft
Battle Ground, Washington

Printed in the United States of America
5   7   9   8   6

INTRODUCTION

A concordance is an index to a book. It is usually arranged in alphabetical order and shows the location of each word in the book. In addition, it often supplies several words of the context in which each word is found.

The New American Bible Concise Concordance (NABCC) is an selective concordance to the New American Bible. It covers all 73 books contained in the NAB. However, it does not exhaustively index all the words of the NAB. Rather, more than 40,000 references to nearly 6,000 key words provide access to texts most significant to personal and professional Bible research.

FEATURES OF THE NAB CONCISE CONCORDANCE

The *NABCC* indexes the Bible in two formats: (1) traditional concordance entries and (2) capsule biographies.

CONCORDANCE ENTRIES

Below is a traditional concordance entry:

> **LOVE** → BELOVED, LOVED, LOVER, LOVERS, LOVES,
> LOVING
>
> Ge 29:20 a few days because of his **l** for her.

Headings:

The heading consists of:

(1) the indexed word: **LOVE**;

(2) the list of related words following an arrow (→).

The *NABCC* indexes 5,874 words. Since contexts represent words spelled exactly as the entry headword, the key word is abbreviated and bold. If an indexed word occurs more than once in a context, it is abbreviated as many times as necessary within the context, as under the heading HOLY:

> Isa   6: 3 "**H, h, h** is the LORD of hosts!"
> Rev   4: 8 "**H, h, h,** is the Lord God almighty,

Related words point to other spellings and forms of the headword (LOVED, LOVING) as well as cognate terms (BELOVED). Rather than listing all related words after each headword, the editor chose one indexed word to act as the "group heading." All related words are listed after the group heading, and each of the related word headings points back to the group heading. In the example above, LOVE serves as the group heading for six related words.

Context Lines:

The context lines consist of:

    (1) the book-chapter-verse reference;

    (2) the context for the indexed word.

37,266 context lines represent 38,317 occurrences of the 5,874 headwords. Books of the Bible are abbreviated according to the table on page viii. The book abbreviation is listed on each context line. Context lines are listed in the canonical order of the New American Bible.

Taken by themselves, context lines can and do misrepresent the teaching of Scripture by taking statements out of the larger context. "There is no God" is a context taken straight from Psalm 14:1. Of course the Bible does not teach this; it is what "Fools say in their hearts"! Similarly, a context for Leviticus 24:16 might read, "the LORD shall be put to death" while the text actually says, "One who blasphemes the name of the LORD shall be put to death."

Great care has been taken by the editor and programmer of the *NABCC* to create contexts that are informative and accurate. But the reader should always check word contexts by looking them up in the NAB itself. "The Wicked Bible," a KJV edition of 1631, accidentally omitted the word "not" from the seventh commandment, for which the printers were fined 300 pounds sterling! Though there are no longer such fines for misleading contexts, the editor and publisher are still deeply concerned that the *NABCC* be used discerningly.

CAPSULE BIOGRAPHIES

435 prominent personalities are given capsule biographies:

    SIMON →=PETER, =SIMEON

    1. See Peter.
    2. Apostle, called the Zealot (Mt 10:4; Mk 3:18; Lk 6:15; Acts
  1:13).
    3. Samaritan sorcerer (Acts 8:9-24).

It is easier to represent and to locate key events in an individual's life in such an entry rather than by using context lines—especially in the entry on Jesus. As in the example above, different individuals of the same name are distinguished by separately numbered biographies. These entries index over 2,100 biblical texts.

SPECIAL SYMBOLS AND TYPOGRAPHY

When a person or place is known by more than one name in the biblical text, the cross-reference indicates this by using the equal sign (=):

    SIMON →=PETER, =SIMEON

The equal sign does *not* mean that Peter is always the same individual as Simon, for there are twelve men named Simon in the NAB.

Special typefaces. There are two headings apiece for GOD, LORD, and LORD'S. *LORD and *LORD'S represent the proper name of God, *Yahweh,* which is typeset in the NAB as "LORD" and "LORD's." This distinguishes "LORD" from "Lord" and "lord" (which are indexed under the heading LORD), and "LORD's" from "Lord's" and "lord's" (indexed under LORD'S). In contexts where the Hebrew words for "Lord" (*Adonay*) and "LORD" (*Yahweh*) appear as a compound name, the NAB translates Lord GOD. Therefore the heading *GOD is used for "GOD" and GOD for "God" and "god."

Some words are set in italic type in the NAB. These include *Selah* and *maskil* throughout the Psalms and *Abba* in Romans 8:15. These typefaces are reflected in the context lines, as under the headings CRY and ETHAN:

Rom 8:15   through which we **c**, "*Abba*, Father!"

Ps   89: 1   A *maskil* of **E** the Ezrahite.

Brackets. In the preface to the revised edition of the New Testament, the translators note, "The editors of the Greek text placed square brackets around words or portions of words of which the authenticity is questionable because the evidence of textual witnesses is inconclusive. The same has been done in the translation insofar as it is possible to reproduce this convention in English." Whenever square brackets appear in the NAB text, they also appear in the context line, as under the heading ABOMINABLE:

Ez   7:20   of them their **a** images [their idols].
Rv   21:27   nor any[one] who does **a** things

Books of One Chapter. Five books have only one chapter: Obadiah, Philemon, 2 John, 3 John, and Jude. Therefore some reference books refer only to the verse number (e.g., Jude 1). In the *NABCC* all contexts from these books refer to chapter 1 in addition to the verse number (e.g., Jude 1:1).

Prologue to Sirach. The book of Sirach (or Ecclesiasticus) has a three-paragraph prologue or foreword preceding chapter 1. The abbreviation "Pr" is used as the "chapter" number of the prologue; the numbers 1, 2, and 3 are used as "verse" designations for the three paragraphs, as under the heading HEBREW:

Sir   Pr: 2   originally in **H** are not as effective

The Shorter Ending of Mark. The NAB is one of the few translations to include the "shorter ending" of Mark. However, it places this ending at the end of Mark 16, following the traditional "longer ending," verses 9 to 20. Rather than index this passage as part of verse 20, the letter "S" is used as the verse designation for the "shorter ending," as under the heading ETERNAL:

Mk   16: S   proclamation of **e** salvation. Amen.]

ABBREVIATIONS

Books of the Bible

1 Chr	1 Chronicles	Eccl	Ecclesiastes	Mi	Micah
1 Cor	1 Corinthians	Eph	Ephesians	Mk	Mark
1 Jn	1 John	Est	Esther	Mt	Matthew
1 Kgs	1 Kings	Ex	Exodus	Na	Nahum
1 Mc	1 Maccabees	Ez	Ezekiel	Neh	Nehemiah
1 Pt	1 Peter	Ezr	Ezra	Nm	Numbers
1 Sm	1 Samuel	Gal	Galatians	Ob	Obadiah
1 Thes	1 Thessalonians	Gn	Genesis	Phil	Philippians
1 Tm	1 Timothy	Hb	Habakkuk	Phlm	Philemon
2 Chr	2 Chronicles	Heb	Hebrews	Prv	Proverbs
2 Cor	2 Corinthians	Hg	Haggai	Ps(s)	Psalms
2 Jn	2 John	Hos	Hosea	Rev	Revelation
2 Kgs	2 Kings	Is	Isaiah	Rom	Romans
2 Mc	2 Maccabees	Jas	James	Ru	Ruth
2 Pt	2 Peter	Jb	Job	Sg	Song of Songs
2 Sm	2 Samuel	Jdt	Judith	Sir	Sirach
2 Thes	2 Thessalonians	Jer	Jeremiah	Tb	Tobit
2 Tm	2 Timothy	Jgs	Judges	Ti	Titus
3 Jn	3 John	Jl	Joel	Wis	Wisdom
Acts	Acts of the Apostles	Jn	John	Zec	Zechariah
Am	Amos	Jon	Jonah	Zep	Zephaniah
Bar	Baruch	Jos	Joshua		
Col	Colossians	Jude	Jude		
Dn	Daniel	Lam	Lamentations		
Dt	Deuteronomy	Lk	Luke		
		Lv	Leviticus		
		Mal	Malachi		

Other Abbreviations

Pr	Prologue to Sirach
S	Shorter Ending of Mark

THE NEW AMERICAN BIBLE
CONCISE CONCORDANCE

A

AARON
Genealogy of (Ex 6:16-20; Jos 21:4, 10; 1 Chr 5:29-41). Priesthood of (Ex 28:1; Nm 17; Heb 5:1-4; 7), vestments of (Ex 28; 39), consecration of (Ex 29), ordination of (Lv 8). Spokesman for Moses (Ex 4:14-16, 27-31; 7:1-2). Supported Moses' hands in battle (Ex 17:8-13). Built golden calf (Ex 32; Dt 9:20). Spoke against Moses (Nm 12). Priesthood opposed (Nm 16); staff budded (Nm 17). Forbidden to enter the promised land (Nm 20:1-12). Death of (Nm 20:22-29; 33:38-39). Praise of (Sir 45:6-22).

ABADDON → =APOLLYON
Jb	28:22	A and Death say, "Only by rumor
Rv	9:11	whose name in Hebrew is A

ABANDON → ABANDONED
Dt	4:31	God, he will not a and destroy you,
Jos	10: 6	at Gilgal: "Do not a your servants.
1 Chr	28: 9	but if you a him, he will cast you
2 Chr	15: 2	but if you a him, he will a you.
Tb	4: 3	do not a her as long as she lives.
Ps	94:14	your people, nor a your very own.
Acts	2:27	because you will not a my soul

ABANDONED → ABANDON
Jgs	2:13	Because they had thus a him
2 Chr	12: 5	'You have a me, and therefore I have
Sir	49: 4	They a the law of the Most High,
Is	54: 7	For a brief moment I a you,
Acts	2:31	neither was he a to the netherworld

ABBA
Mk	14:36	he said, "A, Father, all things are
Rom	8:15	through which we cry, "A, Father!"
Gal	4: 6	our hearts, crying out, "A, Father!"

ABDON
A judge of Israel (Jgs 12:13-15).

ABEDNEGO → =AZARIAH
Deported to Babylon with Daniel (Dn 1:1-6). Name changed from Azariah (Dn 1:7). Refused defilement by food (Dn 1:8-20). Refused idol worship (Dn 3:1-18); saved from furnace (Dn 3:19-97).

ABEL
Second son of Adam (Gn 4:2). Offered acceptable sacrifice (Gn 4:4; Heb 11:4; 12:24). Murdered by Cain (Gn 4:8; Mt 23:35; Lk 11:51; 1 Jn 3:12).

ABHOR → ABHORRED, ABHORS
Dt	7:26	and a it utterly as a thing that is
Dt	23: 8	But do not a the Edomite, since he
Ps	119:163	Falsehood I hate and a;
Am	5:10	and a him who speaks the truth.
Am	6: 8	God of hosts: I a the pride of Jacob,
Mi	3: 9	of Israel! You who a what is just,

ABHORRED → ABHOR
Ps	106:40	with his people, a his own heritage.

ABHORS → ABHOR
Ps	5: 7	Murderers and deceivers the LORD a.

ABIATHAR
High priest in days of Saul and David (1 Sm 22; 2 Sm 15; 1 Kgs 1-2; Mk 2:26). Escaped Saul's slaughter of priests (1 Sm 22:18-23). Supported David in Absalom's revolt (2 Sm 15:24-29). Supported Adonijah (1 Kgs 1:7-42); deposed by Solomon (1 Kgs 2:22-35; cf. 1 Sm 2:31-35).

ABIB
The month of the Exodus and Passover (Ex 13:4; 23:15; 34:18; Dt: 16:1).

ABIDE → ABODE
Ps	15: 1	LORD, who may a in your tent?
Ps	91: 1	High, who a in the shadow
Wis	3: 9	the faithful shall a with him in love:

ABIGAIL
1. Sister of David (1 Chr 2:16-17).
2. Wife of Nabal (1 Sm 25:30); pled for his life with David (1 Sm 25:14-35). Became David's wife after Nabal's death (1 Sm 25:36-43); bore him Kileab (2 Sm 3:3) also known as Daniel (1 Chr 3:1).

ABIHU
Son of Aaron (Ex 6:23; 24:1, 9); killed for offering illicit fire (Lv 10; Nm 3:2-4; 1 Chr 24:1-2).

ABIJAH
1. Second son of Samuel (1 Chr 6:13); a corrupt judge (1 Sm 8:1-5).
2. An Aaronic priest (1 Chr 24:10; Lk 1:5).
3. Son of Jeroboam I of Israel; died as prophesied by Ahijah (1 Kgs 14:1-18).
4. Son of Rehoboam, also called Abijam; king of Judah who fought Jeroboam I attempting to reunite the kingdom (1 Kgs 14:31-15:8; 2 Chr 12:16-14:1; Mt 1:7).

ABILITY → ABLE
Mt	25:15	third, one—to each according to his a.
Acts	11:29	according to a, each should send

ABIMELECH
1. King of Gerar who took Abraham's wife Sarah, believing her to be his sister (Gn 20). Later made a covenant with Abraham (Gn 21:22-33).
2. King of Gerar who took Isaac's wife Rebe-kah, believing her to be his sister (Gn 26:1-11). Later made a covenant with Isaac (Gn 26:12-31).
3. Son of Gideon (Jgs 8:31). Attempted to make himself king (Jgs 9).

ABIRAM
Sided with Dathan in rebellion against Moses and Aaron (Nm 16; 26:9; Dt 11:6; Sir 45:18).

ABISHAG
Shunammite virgin; attendant of David in his old age (1 Kgs 1:1-15; 2:17-22).

ABISHAI
Son of Zeruiah, David's sister (1 Sm 26:6; 1 Chr 2:16). One of David's chief warriors (1 Chr 11:15-21): against Edom (1 Chr 18:12-13), Ammon (2 Sm 10), Absalom (2 Sm 18), Sheba (2 Sm 20). Wanted to kill Saul (1 Sm 26), killed Abner (2 Sm 2:18-27; 3:22-39), wanted to kill Shimei (2 Sm 16:5-13; 19:16-23).

ABLAZE
Jas	3: 5	small a fire can set a huge forest a.

ABLE → ABILITY, ENABLES
Ex	18:25	He picked out a men from all Israel
Nm	14:16	'The LORD was not a to bring this
Dt	7:24	No man will be a to stand
1 Kgs	3: 9	who is a to govern this vast people
2 Chr	2: 5	Yet who is really a to build him
2 Chr	32:15	or kingdom has been a to save his
Jdt	11:18	of them will be a to withstand you.
1 Mc	3:53	How shall we be a to resist them
Dn	5:16	if you are a to read the writing
Dn	6:21	you serve so constantly been a
Acts	5:39	you will not be a to destroy them;
Acts	15:10	our ancestors nor we have been a
Rom	4:21	had promised he was also a to do.
Rom	8:39	nor any other creature will be a
Rom	14: 4	for the Lord is a to make him stand.
2 Cor	1: 4	that we may be a to encourage those
2 Cor	9: 8	God is a to make every grace
Eph	3:20	to him who is a to accomplish far
Eph	6:11	you may be a to stand firm against
2 Tm	1:12	that he is a to guard what has been
Heb	2:18	he is a to help those who are being
Heb	4:12	and a to discern reflections
Heb	5: 2	He is a to deal patiently
Heb	7:25	he is always a to save those who
Heb	11:19	that God was a to raise even
Jas	3: 2	a to bridle his whole body also.
Jas	4:12	lawgiver and judge who is a to save
Jude	1:24	To the one who is a to keep you
Rv	5: 3	or under the earth was a to open

ABNER
Cousin of Saul and commander of his army (1 Sm 14:50; 17:55-57; 26). Made Ish-Bosheth king after Saul (2 Sm 2:8-10), but later

defected to David (2 Sm 3:6-21). Killed Asahel (2 Sm 2:18-32), for which he was killed by Joab and Abishai (2 Sm 3:22-39).

ABODE → ABIDE
Jer   31:23   you, holy mountain, a of justice!"

ABOLISH → ABOLISHED, ABOLISHING
Mt   5:17   I have come not to a but to fulfill.

ABOLISHED → ABOLISH
1 Mc   6:59   which we a, that they became angry
2 Mc   2:22   laws that were in danger of being a,

ABOLISHING → ABOLISH
Dn   11:31   a the daily sacrifice and setting

ABOMINABLE → ABOMINATION
2 Chr 28: 3   by fire according to the a practice
2 Chr 33: 2   following the a practices
2 Mc   6: 5   covered with a offerings prohibited
Sir   15:13   A wickedness the LORD hates,
Ez   7:20   of them their a images [their idols].
Rv   21:27   nor any[one] who does a things

ABOMINATION → ABOMINABLE, ABOMINATIONS
Lv   18:22   with a woman; such a thing is an a.
1 Mc   6: 7   they had pulled down the A
Prv   6:16   hates, yes, seven are an a to him;
Prv   11: 1   False scales are an a to the LORD,
Prv   11:20   in heart are an a to the LORD,
Prv   12:22   Lying lips are an a to the LORD,
Dn   9:27   temple wing shall be the horrible a
Dn   11:31   and setting up the horrible a.
Dn   12:11   and the horrible a is set up,
Lk   16:15   of human esteem is an a in the sight

ABOMINATIONS → ABOMINATION
Ezr   9: 1   of the land and their a [Canaanites,
Prv   26:25   him not, for seven a are in his heart.
Is   66: 3   and taken pleasure in their own a,
Ez   7: 3   you the consequences of all your a.
Ez   8: 6   But you shall see still greater a!
Ez   44: 7   broken my covenant by all your a.
Rv   17: 5   of harlots and of the a of the earth."

ABOUND → ABOUNDING
Rom   6: 1   we persist in sin that grace may a?
Rom   15:13   so that you may a in hope
2 Cor   3: 9   of righteousness will a much more
1 Thes   3:12   and a in love for one another

ABOUNDING → ABOUND
Ps   103: 8   LORD, slow to anger, a in kindness.
Ps   145: 8   slow to anger and a in love.
Col   2: 7   you were taught, a in thanksgiving.

ABOVE
Dt   4:39   the LORD is God in the heavens a
Jdt   13:18   God, a all the women on earth;
Ps   8: 2   set your majesty a the heavens!
Ps   18:49   have exalted me a my adversaries,
Ps   57: 6   your glory appear a all the earth.
Sir   32:13   A all, give praise to your Creator,
Is   6: 2   Seraphim were stationed a
Is   40:22   He sits enthroned a the vault
Ez   1:26   A the firmament over their heads
Ez   10:19   of the God of Israel was up a them.
Mt   10:24   No disciple is a his teacher, no slave a his master.
Jn   3: 7   told you, 'You must be born from a.'
Jn   3:31   The one who comes from a is a all.
Jn   8:23   what is below; I belong to what is a.
Eph   1:21   far a every principality, authority,
Eph   4:10   who ascended far a all the heavens,
Phil   2: 9   him the name that is a every name,
Col   3: 2   Think of what is a, not of what is
2 Thes   2: 4   exalts himself a every so-called god
Jas   1:17   and every perfect gift is from a,
Jas   3:17   But the wisdom from a is first of all
1 Pt   4: 8   A all, let your love for one another

ABRAHAM → =ABRAM
Abram, son of Terah (Gn 11:26-27), husband of Sarah (Gn 11:29).
Covenant relation with the LORD (Gn 12:1-3; 13:14-17; 15; 17;

22:15-18; Ex 2:24; Neh 9:8; Ps 105; Mi 7:20; Lk 1:68-75; Rom 4; Heb 6:13-15).
Called from Ur, via Haran, to Canaan (Gn 12:1; Acts 7:2-4; Heb 11:8-10). Moved to Egypt, nearly lost Sarah to Pharoah (Gn 12:10-20). Divided the land with Lot; settled in Hebron (Gn 13). Saved Lot from four kings (Gn 14:1-16); blessed by Melchizedek (Gn 14:17-20; Heb 7:1-20). Declared righteous by faith (Gn 15:6; 1 Mc 2:52; Rom 4:3; Gal 3:6-9). Fathered Ishmael by Hagar (Gn 16).
Name changed from Abram (Gn 17:5; Neh 9:7). Circumcised (Gn 17; Rom 4:9-12). Entertained three visitors (Gn 18); promised a son by Sarah (Gn 18:9-15; 17:16). Questioned destruction of Sodom and Gomorrah (Gn 18:16-33). Moved to Gerar; nearly lost Sarah to Abimelech (Gn 20). Fathered Isaac by Sarah (Gn 21:1-7; Acts 7:8; Heb 11:11-12); sent away Hagar and Ishmael (Gn 21:8-21; Gal 4:22-30). Covenant with Abimelech (Gn 21:22-32). Tested by offering Isaac (Gn 22; Heb 11:17-19; Jas 2:21-24). Sarah died; bought field of Ephron for burial (Gn 23). Secured wife for Isaac (Gn 24). Fathered children by Keturah (Gn 25:1-6; 1 Chr 1:32-33). Death (Gn 25:7-11).
Called servant of God (Gn 26:24), friend of God (2 Chr 20:7; Is 41:8; Jas 2:23), prophet (Gn 20:7), father of Israel (Ex 3:15; Is 51:2; Mt 3:9; Jn 8:39-58). Praised (Sir 44:19-23).

ABRAM → =ABRAHAM
Gn   17: 5   No longer shall you be called A;

ABSALOM
Son of David by Maacah (2 Sm 3:3; 1 Chr 3:2). Killed Amnon for rape of his sister Tamar; banished by David (2 Sm 13). Returned to Jerusalem; received by David (2 Sm 14). Rebelled against David (2 Sm 15-17). Killed (2 Sm 18).

ABSENT
1 Cor   5: 3   although a in body but present
Col   2: 5   For even if I am a in the flesh, yet I

ABSTAIN → ABSTAINS, ABSTINENCE
Acts   15:29   to a from meat sacrificed to idols,
Acts   21:25   that they a from meat sacrificed

ABSTAINS → ABSTAIN
Rom   14: 3   eats must not despise the one who a,

ABSTINENCE → ABSTAIN
1 Tm   4: 3   and require a from foods that God

ABUNDANCE → ABUNDANT, ABUNDANTLY
Jb   36:31   nations, and gives them food in a.
Lam   3:32   takes pity, in the a of his mercies;
2 Cor   9: 8   you may have an a for every good
1 Pt   1: 2   may grace and peace be yours in a.
2 Pt   1: 2   be yours in a through knowledge
Jude   1: 2   peace, and love be yours in a.

ABUNDANT → ABUNDANCE
Ps   51: 3   in your a compassion blot out my
Ez   31: 7   roots were turned toward a water.

ABUNDANTLY → ABUNDANCE
Jn   10:10   might have life and have it more a.

ABUSE → ABUSED, ABUSIVE
Heb   10:33   you were publicly exposed to a

ABUSED → ABUSE
Jgs   19:25   a her all night until the following

ABUSIVE → ABUSE
Sir   23:15   who has the habit of a language
2 Tm   3: 2   haughty, a, disobedient to their

ABYSS
Sir   1: 3   the depths of the a: who can explore
Lk   8:31   not to order them to depart to the a.
Rom   10: 7   or "Who will go down into the a?"
Rv   9: 1   the key for the passage to the a.
Rv   11: 7   the beast that comes up from the a
Rv   17: 8   It will come up from the a
Rv   20: 1   in his hand the key to the a

ACACIA
Ex   25:10   "You shall make an ark of a wood,
Ex   25:23   shall also make a table of a wood,
Ex   26:15   make boards of a wood as walls
Ex   27: 1   "You shall make an altar of a wood,

ACCEPT → ACCEPTABLE, ACCEPTANCE, ACCEPTED, ACCEPTING, ACCEPTS

Jb	42: 8	for his prayer I will a, not to punish
Ps	119:108	A my freely offered praise; LORD,
Ez	20:40	there I will a them, and there I will
Ez	43:27	Then I will a you, says the Lord
Zep	3: 7	you will a correction"; She should
Mal	1:10	neither will I a any sacrifice
Mt	11:14	And if you are willing to a it, he is
Mt	19:11	"Not all can a [this] word, but only
Jn	1:11	but his own people did not a him.
Jn	5:41	"I do not a human praise;
Jn	5:43	of my Father, but you do not a me;
Jn	6:60	"This saying is hard; who can a it?"
Acts	22:18	they will not a your testimony

ACCEPTABLE → ACCEPT

Lv	1: 4	that it may be a to make atonement
Prv	21: 3	is more a to the LORD than sacrifice
Is	58: 5	call this a fast, a day a to the LORD?
2 Cor	6: 2	Behold, now is a very a time;
Phil	4:18	"a fragrant aroma," an a sacrifice,
1 Pt	2: 5	to offer spiritual sacrifices a to God

ACCEPTANCE → ACCEPT

Rom	11:15	what will their a be but life
1 Tm	1:15	is trustworthy and deserves full a:
1 Tm	4: 9	is trustworthy and deserves full a.

ACCEPTED → ACCEPT

Jb	42: 9	the LORD a the intercession of Job.
Lk	4:24	no prophet is a in his own native
2 Cor	11: 4	different gospel from the one you a,

ACCEPTING → ACCEPT

3 Jn	1: 7	and are a nothing from the pagans.

ACCEPTS → ACCEPT

Jn	3:32	heard, but no one a his testimony.

ACCESS

Rom	5: 2	through whom we have gained a
Eph	2:18	through him we both have a in one
Eph	3:12	and confidence of a through faith

ACCOMPLISH → ACCOMPLISHED, ACCOMPLISHES

Is	60:22	the LORD, will swiftly a these things
Eph	3:20	is able to a far more than all we ask

ACCOMPLISHED → ACCOMPLISH

Rom	15:18	what Christ has a through me

ACCOMPLISHES → ACCOMPLISH

Eph	1:11	the One who a all things according

ACCORDANCE → ACCORDING

Mk	12:14	the way of God in a with the truth.
1 Cor	15: 3	for our sins in a with the scriptures;
1 Cor	15: 4	raised on the third day in a

ACCORDING → ACCORDANCE

Ex	26:30	You shall erect the Dwelling a
2 Chr	6:30	render to everyone a to his conduct,
Prv	26: 4	Answer not the fool a to his folly,
Prv	26: 5	Answer the fool a to his folly,
Sir	16:12	he judges men, each a to his deeds.
Sir	50:22	and fashions them a to his will!
Ez	7: 3	and judge you a to your conduct
Mt	9:29	it be done for you a to your faith."
Jn	19: 7	and a to that law he ought to die,
Rom	2: 6	who will repay everyone a to his
Rom	8: 4	who live not a to the flesh but a
Rom	8:13	For if you live a to the flesh,
2 Tm	1: 9	not a to our works but a to his own
2 Tm	2: 5	except by competing a to the rules.
Heb	2: 4	gifts of the holy Spirit a to his will.
Heb	5: 6	a to the order of Melchizedek."
Jas	2: 8	if you fulfill the royal law a
1 Jn	5:14	that if we ask anything a to his will,
2 Jn	1: 6	we walk a to his commandments;
Rv	20:12	The dead were judged a to their
Rv	22:12	I will give to each a to his deeds.

ACCOUNT → ACCOUNTABLE

Mt	12:36	of judgment people will render an a
Rom	14:12	each of us shall give an a of himself
Heb	4:13	him to whom we must render an a.

ACCOUNTABLE → ACCOUNT

Rom	3:19	and the whole world stand a to God,

ACCURATELY

Acts	18:25	spoke and taught a about Jesus,

ACCURSED → CURSE

Wis	14: 8	but the handmade idol is a, and its
Mt	25:41	you a, into the eternal fire prepared
Rom	9: 3	I could wish that I myself were a
1 Cor	16:22	does not love the Lord, let him be a.
Gal	1: 8	preached to you, let that one be a!
2 Pt	2:14	are trained in greed. A children!
Rv	22: 3	Nothing a will be found there

ACCUSATION → ACCUSE

1 Tm	5:19	not accept an a against a presbyter

ACCUSE → ACCUSATION, ACCUSED, ACCUSER, ACCUSERS, ACCUSES

Dt	19:16	the stand against a man to a him
Zec	3: 1	stood at his right hand to a him.
Mt	12:10	sabbath?" so that they might a him.
Rom	2:15	their conflicting thoughts a or even

ACCUSED → ACCUSE

Mk	15: 3	The chief priests a him of many
Acts	22:30	why he was being a by the Jews,
Ti	1: 6	believing children who are not a

ACCUSER → ACCUSE

Ps	109: 6	an a to stand by his right hand,
Rv	12:10	For the a of our brothers is cast out,

ACCUSERS → ACCUSE

Ps	109:20	the LORD bring all this upon my a,

ACCUSES → ACCUSE

Rv	12:10	who a them before our God day

ACCUSTOMED → CUSTOM

Jer	13:23	able to do good, a to evil as you are.
Mt	27:15	of the feast the governor was a

ACHAN

Sin at Jericho caused defeat at Ai; stoned (Jos 7; 22:20; 1 Chr 2:7).

ACHIEVE

Jb	5:12	so that their hands a no success;

ACHIOR

Ammonite mercenary (Jdt 5:5-6:20); converted to Judaism after Judith's victory (Jdt 14:5-10).

ACHISH

King of Gath before whom David feigned insanity (1 Sm 21:11-16). Later "ally" of David (2 Sm 27-29).

ACHOR

Jos	7:26	the place is called the Valley of A
Hos	2:17	the valley of A as a door of hope.

ACKNOWLEDGE → ACKNOWLEDGED, ACKNOWLEDGES

Tb	12: 6	a the many good things he has done
Mt	10:32	others I will a before my heavenly
Lk	12: 8	Son of Man will a before the angels
Rom	1:28	since they did not see fit to a God,
3 Jn	1: 9	loves to dominate, does not a us.

ACKNOWLEDGED → ACKNOWLEDGE

Lk	7:29	of John, a the righteousness of God;

ACKNOWLEDGES → ACKNOWLEDGE

Mt	10:32	Everyone who a me before others I
Lk	12: 8	everyone who a me before others

ACQUIT

Ex	23: 7	to death, nor shall you a the guilty.

ACT → ACTED, ACTION, ACTIVE, ACTS

Ex	21:13	but caused his death by an a of God,
Ps	37: 5	to the LORD; trust that God will a
Ps	119:126	It is time for the LORD to a;

Dn 9:19 be attentive and a without delay,
Jn 8: 4 the very a of committing adultery.

ACTED → ACT
Ez 20: 9 but I a for my name's sake, that it
Acts 3:17 that you a out of ignorance, just as
1 Tm 1:13 been mercifully treated because I a

ACTION → ACT
Dn 11:32 to their God shall take strong a.

ACTIVE → ACT
Jas 2:22 faith was a along with his works,

ACTS → ACT
Ex 6: 6 arm and with mighty a of judgment.
Ex 7: 4 great a of judgment I will bring
Ps 71:15 day after day your a of deliverance,
Mt 7:24 a on them will be like a wise man
Jas 1:25 who forgets but a doer who a,

ADAM
1. First man (Gn 1:26-2:25; Tb 8:6; Rom 5:14; 1 Tm 2:13). Sin of (Gn 3; Rom 5:12-21). Children of (Gn 4:1-5:5). Death of (Gn 5:5; Rom 5:12-21; 1 Cor 15:22).
2. Town (Jos 3:16).

ADAR
Month in which temple was rebuilt (Ezr 6:15); celebration of Purim (Est 3:7; 9:1-21); of victory over Nicanor (1 Mc 7:43-49).

ADD → ADDED, ADDING, ADDS
Dt 4: 2 you shall not a to what I command
2 Kgs 20: 6 I will a fifteen years to your life.
Prv 30: 6 A nothing to his words, lest he
Mt 6:27 you by worrying a a single moment
Lk 12:25 of you by worrying a a moment
Rv 22:18 them, God will a to him the plagues

ADDED → ADD
Acts 2:41 three thousand persons were a
Acts 2:47 And every day the Lord a to their
Acts 5:14 of men and women, were a to them.
Gal 3:19 It was a for transgressions,

ADDER
Prv 23:32 like a serpent, or like a poisonous a.

ADDING → ADD
Dt 13: 1 neither a to it nor subtracting
Eccl 7:27 a one thing to another that I might

ADDRESSED
Lk 23:20 Again Pilate a them, still wishing
Acts 21:40 all was quiet he a them in Hebrew.
Heb 12: 5 forgotten the exhortation a to you

ADDS → ADD
Rv 22:18 if anyone a to them, God will add

ADJURE
Song 5: 8 I a you, daughters of Jerusalem,
Mk 5: 7 I a you by God, do not torment me!"
Acts 19:13 "I a you by the Jesus whom Paul

ADMAH
Dt 29:22 and Gomorrah, A and Zeboiim,
Hos 11: 8 How could I treat you as A, or make

ADMONISH → ADMONITION
1 Cor 4:14 but to a you as my beloved children.
Col 3:16 you teach and a one another,
1 Thes 5:12 you in the Lord and who a you,

ADMONITION → ADMONISH
Prv 15: 5 The fool spurns his father's a,

ADONIJAH
1. Son of David by Haggith (2 Sm 3:4; 1 Chr 3:2). Attempted to be king after David; killed at Solomon's order (1 Kgs 1-2).
2. Levite; teacher of the Law (2 Chr 17:8).

ADOPT → ADOPTED, ADOPTION
Acts 16:21 are not lawful for us Romans to a

ADOPTED → ADOPT
2 Chr 7:22 Egypt, and they a strange gods
Acts 7:21 Pharaoh's daughter a him

ADOPTION → ADOPT
Rom 8:23 within ourselves as we wait for a,
Rom 9: 4 Israelites; theirs the a, the glory,
Gal 4: 5 the law, so that we might receive a.
Eph 1: 5 he destined us for a to himself

ADORNED → ADORNMENT
2 Kgs 9:30 she shadowed her eyes, a her hair,
Ez 16:11 I a you with jewelry: I put bracelets
Lk 21: 5 how the temple was a with costly
Rv 17: 4 purple and scarlet and a with gold,
Rv 21: 2 God, prepared as a bride a for her

ADORNMENT → ADORNED
Ex 28: 2 the glorious a of your brother Aaron
Prv 3:22 to your soul, and an a for your neck.
1 Pt 3: 3 Your a should not be an external one:

ADULLAM
1 Sm 22: 1 Gath and escaped to the cave of A.
1 Chr 11:15 cave of A while the Philistines were
Mi 1:15 Even to A shall go the glory

ADULTERER → ADULTERY
Jb 24:15 The eye of the a watches

ADULTERERS → ADULTERY
Jer 23:10 With a the land is filled; on their
Mal 3: 5 Against the sorcerers, a,
1 Cor 6: 9 nor idolaters nor a nor boy
Heb 13: 4 God will judge the immoral and a.

ADULTERESS → ADULTERY
Lv 20:10 and the a shall be put to death.
Prv 2:16 from the a with her smooth words,
Prv 23:27 a deep ditch, and the a a narrow pit;
Hos 3: 1 beloved of a paramour, an a;
Rom 7: 3 she is not an a if she consorts

ADULTERIES → ADULTERY
Jer 3: 8 for all the a rebellious Israel had
Ez 23:43 I said: "Oh, this woman jaded with a!

ADULTERY → ADULTERER, ADULTERERS, ADULTERESS, ADULTERIES
Ex 20:14 "You shall not commit a.
Dt 5:18 'You shall not commit a.
Prv 6:32 But he who commits a is a fool;
Jer 3: 9 committing a with stone and wood.
Ez 23:37 They committed a with their idols;
Hos 2: 4 her, her a from between her breasts,
Mt 5:27 it was said, 'You shall not commit a.'
Mt 5:28 lust has already committed a
Mt 5:32 a divorced woman commits a.
Mt 15:19 evil thoughts, murder, a, unchastity,
Mt 19: 9 and marries another commits a."
Mt 19:18 you shall not commit a; you shall
Mk 7:22 a, greed, malice, deceit,
Mk 10:11 another commits a against her;
Mk 10:12 and marries another, she commits a."
Mk 10:19 you shall not commit a; you shall
Lk 16:18 and marries another commits a,
Lk 18:20 'You shall not commit a; you shall
Jn 8: 3 a woman who had been caught in a
Rom 2:22 who forbid a, do you commit a?
Rom 13: 9 "You shall not commit a; you shall
Jas 2:11 "You shall not commit a," also said,
Jas 2:11 Even if you do not commit a
2 Pt 2:14 Their eyes are full of a

ADVANCE → ADVANCED
1 Pt 1:11 it testified in a to the sufferings

ADVANCED → ADVANCE
Gn 18:11 and Sarah were old, a in years,

ADVANTAGE
Eccl 3:19 and man has no a over the beast;
Eccl 6: 8 what a has the wise man over
Eccl 7:12 the a of knowledge is that wisdom
Rom 3: 1 What a is there then in being a Jew?
1 Cor 10:24 No one should seek his own a,
Jude 1:16 as they fawn over people to gain a.

ADVERSARIES → ADVERSARY
2 Sm	22:49	Above my a you exalt me
Na	1: 2	LORD brings vengeance on his a,
Heb	10:27	fire that is going to consume the a.

ADVERSARY → ADVERSARIES
1 Kgs	11:14	then raised up an a to Solomon:
1 Tm	5:14	so as to give the a no pretext

ADVICE
Nm	31:16	who on Balaam's a prompted
2 Chr	10:13	Ignoring the a the elders had given
Tb	4:18	lightly of any a that can be useful.
Prv	8:14	Mine are counsel and a; Mine is
Prv	12:15	eyes, but he who listens to a is wise.
Prv	20:18	Plans made after a succeed;
Sir	37:11	pay no attention to any a they give.

ADVOCATE
Jn	14:16	and he will give you another A to be
Jn	14:26	The A, the holy Spirit
Jn	15:26	the A comes whom I will send you
Jn	16: 7	not go, the A will not come to you.
1 Jn	2: 1	sin, we have an A with the Father,

AENEAS
Paralytic healed by Peter (Acts 9:33-34).

AFFAIRS
Ps	112: 5	who conduct their a with justice.

AFFECTION
Gn	43:30	he was so overcome with a for his
Rom	12:10	love one another with mutual a;
2 Pt	1: 7	devotion with mutual a, mutual a

AFFLICT → AFFLICTED, AFFLICTING, AFFLICTION, AFFLICTIONS
2 Sm	7:10	continue to a them as they did

AFFLICTED → AFFLICT
Ps	9:13	does not forget the cry of the a.
Ps	25:16	pity on me, for I am alone and a.
Ps	119:107	I am very much a, LORD; give me
Is	53: 4	as one smitten by God and a.
2 Cor	1: 6	If we are a, it is for your
2 Cor	4: 8	We are a in every way, but not

AFFLICTING → AFFLICT
Lam	3:33	He has no joy in a or grieving
2 Thes	1: 6	afflictions those who are a you,

AFFLICTION → AFFLICT
Dt	16: 3	bread, the bread of a, that you may
Dt	26: 7	and he heard our cry and saw our a,
Jb	36:15	the unfortunate through their a,
Ps	25:18	Put an end to my a and suffering;
2 Cor	1: 4	who encourages us in our every a,
2 Cor	4:17	this momentary light a is producing
2 Cor	7: 4	all the more because of all our a.

AFFLICTIONS → AFFLICT
Acts	7:10	and rescued him from all his a.
2 Cor	6: 4	much endurance, in a, hardships,
Col	1:24	what is lacking in the a of Christ

AFFORD
Lv	5: 7	he cannot a an animal of the flock,
Lv	5:11	is unable to a even two turtledoves
Lv	12: 8	however, she cannot a a lamb,

AFRAID → FEAR
Gn	3:10	but I was a, because I was naked,
Gn	21:17	Don't be a; God has heard the boy's
Ex	2:14	Then Moses became a and thought,
Ex	3: 6	face, for he was a to look at God.
Ex	20:20	"Do not be a, for God has come
Ex	34:30	they were a to come near him.
Dt	2: 4	Though they are a of you, be very
Dt	20: 3	Be not weakhearted or a; be neither
Jos	10:25	to them, "Do not be a or dismayed,
1 Kgs	19: 3	Elijah was a and fled for his life,
1 Chr	13:12	David was now a of God, and he
Ps	27: 1	is my life's refuge; of whom am I a?
Ps	56: 4	when I am a, in you I place my

Prv	3:24	you lie down, you need not be a,
Mt	1:20	do not be a to take Mary your wife
Mt	10:31	So do not be a; you are worth more
Mt	14:27	"Take courage, it is I; do not be a."
Mt	28: 5	to the women in reply, "Do not be a!
Mt	28:10	Jesus said to them, "Do not be a.
Lk	1:13	said to him, "Do not be a, Zechariah,
Lk	1:30	said to her, "Do not be a, Mary,
Lk	2:10	The angel said to them, "Do not be a;
Lk	12:32	Do not be a any longer, little flock,
Jn	14:27	not let your hearts be troubled or a.
Acts	9:26	but they were all a of him,
Acts	27:24	and said, 'Do not be a, Paul. You are
Rom	13: 4	be a, for it does not bear the sword
Heb	13: 6	[and] I will not be a. What can
2 Pt	2:10	they are not a to revile glorious

AFTERNOON → NOON
Mk	15:33	the whole land until three in the a.
Acts	10: 3	One a about three o'clock, he saw

AGABUS
A Christian prophet (Acts 11:28; 21:10).

AGAG → AGAGITE
King of Amalekites; not killed by Saul (1 Sm 15).

AGAGITE → AGAG
Est	8: 3	the harm done by Haman the A,

AGAIN
Gn	8:21	"Never a will I doom the earth
Dt	30: 9	God, will a take delight in your
2 Chr	33: 8	I will not a allow Israel's feet
Jb	14:14	a man has died, were he to live a,
Ps	42: 6	for God, whom I shall praise a,
Ps	78:41	A and a they tested God,
Ps	85: 7	Please give us life a, that your
Jer	12:15	I will pity them a and bring them
Jer	31: 4	A I will restore you, and you shall
Ez	37:22	Never a shall they be two nations,
Ez	37:22	never a shall they be divided
Zec	1:17	the LORD will a comfort Zion,
Jn	14: 3	I will come back a and take you
Rom	11:23	for God is able to graft them in a.
Heb	5:12	have someone teach you a the basic
Heb	6: 1	laying the foundation all over a:
Heb	6: 6	to bring them to repentance a,

AGE → AGED, AGES
Gn	21: 2	bore Abraham a son in his old a,
Gn	37: 3	for he was the child of his old a;
Mt	13:39	The harvest is the end of the a,
Mt	28:20	you always, until the end of the a."
Lk	18:30	return in this present a and eternal life in the a to come."
Gal	1: 4	us from the present evil a in accord
1 Tm	6:17	rich in the present a not to be proud
Ti	2:12	justly, and devoutly in this a,

AGED → AGE
Lv	19:32	"Stand up in the presence of the a,
Sir	25: 5	How becoming to the a is wisdom,

AGES → AGE
Tb	13: 1	because his kingdom lasts for all a.
Rom	16:25	of the mystery kept secret for long a
1 Cor	2: 7	God predetermined before the a
Eph	2: 7	in the a to come he might show
Eph	3: 9	of the mystery hidden from a past
Col	1:26	the mystery hidden from a
1 Tm	1:17	To the king of a, incorruptible,

AGREE → AGREEMENT
Mt	18:19	you, if two of you a on earth
Mk	14:56	him, but their testimony did not a.
2 Cor	13:11	one another, a with one another,
1 Tm	6: 3	does not a with the sound words

AGREEMENT → AGREE
Dt	26:17	Today you are making this a
2 Cor	6:16	What a has the temple of God

AGRIPPA
Descendant of Herod; king before whom Paul argued his case in Caesarea (Acts 25:13-26:32).

AGUR
Prv   30: 1   The words of **A**, son of Jakeh

AHAB
1. Son of Omri; king of Israel (1 Kgs 16:28-22:40), husband of Jezebel (1 Kgs 16:31). Promoted Baal worship (1 Kgs 16:31-33); opposed by Elijah (1 Kgs 17:1; 18; 21), a prophet (1 Kgs 20:35-43), Micaiah (1 Kgs 22:1-28). Defeated Ben-Hadad (1 Kgs 20). Killed for failing to kill Ben-Hadad and for murder of Naboth (1 Kgs 20:35-21:40).
2. A false prophet (Jer 29:21-22).

AHASUERUS →=ARTAXERXES
King of Persia (Ezr 4:6), husband of Esther. Deposed Vashti; replaced her with Esther (Est 1-2). Sealed Haman's edict to annihilate the Jews (Est 3). Received Esther without having called her (Est 5:1-8). Honored Mordecai (Est 6). Hanged Haman (Est 7). Issued edict allowing Jews to defend themselves (Est 8). Promoted Mordecai (Est 8:1-2, 15; 9:4; 10). Called Artaxerxes in the Additions to Esther.

AHAZ
Son of Jotham; king of Judah, (2 Kgs 16; 2 Chr 28; Mt 1:9). Idolatry of (2 Kgs 16:3-4, 10-18; 2 Chr 28:1-4, 22-25). Defeated by Aram and Israel (2 Kgs 16:5-6; 2 Chr 28:5-15). Sought help from Assyria rather than the LORD (2 Kgs 16:7-9; 2 Chr 28:16-21; Is 7).

AHAZIAH
1. Son of Ahab; king of Israel (1 Kgs 22:52-2 Kgs 1:18; 2 Chr 20:35-37). Made an unsuccessful alliance with Jehoshaphat (2 Chr 20:35-37). Died for seeking Baal rather than the LORD (2 Kgs 1).
2. Son of Jehoram; king of Judah (2 Kgs 8:25-29; 9:14-29), also called Jehoahaz (2 Chr 21:17-22:9; 25:23). Killed by Jehu while visiting Joram (2 Kgs 9:14-29; 2 Chr 22:1-9).

AHEAD
Nm   22:26   The angel of the LORD then went **a**,
Dt   1:22   'Let us send men **a** to reconnoiter
Jos   24:12   I sent the hornets **a** of you
Mt   11:10   I am sending my messenger **a**
Jn   1:15   after me ranks **a** of me because he
1 Cor 11:21   each one goes **a** with his own
Phil   3:13   but straining forward to what lies **a**,

AHIJAH
1. Priest during Sauls reign (1 Sm 14:3,18).
2. Prophet of Shiloh (1 Kgs 11:29-39; 14:1-18).

AHIKAM
Father of Gedaliah (2 Kgs 25:22), protector of Jeremiah (Jer 26:24).

AHIMAAZ
1. Father-in-law of Saul (1 Sm 14:50).
2. Son of Zadok, the high priest, loyal to David (2 Sm 15:27,36; 17:17-20; 18:19-33).

AHIMELECH
1. Priest who helped David in his flight from Saul (1 Sm 21-22).
2. One of David's warriors (1 Sm 26:6).

AHINOAM
1. Wife of Saul (1 Sm 14:50).
2. Wife of David (1 Sm 25:43; 30:5; 1 Chr 3:1).

AHITHOPHEL
One of David's counselors who sided with Absalom (2 Sm 15:12, 31-37; 1 Chr 27:33-34); committed suicide when his advice was ignored (2 Sm 16:15-17:23).

AI
Gn   12: 8   Bethel to the west and **A** to the east.
Jos   7: 4   they were defeated by those at **A**,
Jos   8:26   the doom on all the inhabitants of **A**.

AIJALON
Jos   10:12   Gibeon, O moon, in the valley of **A**!

AIM →AIMLESSLY
Ps   21:13   you will **a** at them with your bow.
1 Tm   1: 5   The **a** of this instruction is love

AIMLESSLY →AIM
1 Cor   9:26   Thus I do not run **a**; I do not fight as

AIR
Dn   3:80   All you birds of the **a**,
Acts   22:23   cloaks and flinging dust into the **a**,
1 Cor 14: 9   For you will be talking to the **a**.
Eph   2: 2   the ruler of the power of the **a**,
1 Thes 4:17   the clouds to meet the Lord in the **a**.
Rv   16:17   poured out his bowl into the **a**.

AKELDAMA
Acts   1:19   'A,' that is, Field of Blood.

ALABASTER
Mt   26: 7   up to him with an **a** jar of costly
Mk   14: 3   a woman came with an **a** jar
Lk   7:37   Bringing an **a** flask of ointment,

ALARM →ALARMED
Nm   10: 5   When you sound the first **a**,
Jer   4:19   sound of the trumpet, the **a** of war.
Jl   2: 1   sound the **a** on my holy mountain!

ALARMED →ALARM
Mk   13: 7   and reports of wars do not be **a**;
2 Thes   2: 2   or to be **a** either by a "spirit,"

ALCIMUS
A high priest in the time of the Maccabees (1 Mc 7:5-25; 9; 2 Mc 14).

ALERT
Mk   13:33   Be **a**! You do not know

ALEXANDER
1 Mc   1: 1   After **A** the Macedonian,
1 Mc   10: 1   the year one hundred and sixty, **A**,
Acts   19:33   Some of the crowd prompted **A**,
1 Tm   1:20   among them Hymenaeus and **A**,
2 Tm   4:14   **A** the coppersmith did me a great

ALIEN →ALIENS
Ex   12:19   be he a resident **a** or a native,
Ex   22:20   shall not molest or oppress an **a**,
Lv   19:34   You shall treat the **a** who resides
Lv   23:22   shall leave for the poor and the **a**. I,
Dt   24:17   shall not violate the rights of the **a**

ALIENATED
Eph   4:18   **a** from the life of God because

ALIENS →ALIEN
Gn   15:13   that your descendants shall be **a**
Ex   23: 9   since you were once **a** yourselves
1 Pt   2:11   I urge you as **a** and sojourners

ALIKE →LIKE
Nm   15:15   the LORD you and the alien are **a**,
Ps   14: 3   have gone astray; all **a** are perverse.
Eccl   11: 6   or whether both **a** will turn out well.
Rom   14: 5   another person considers all days **a**.

ALIVE →LIVE
Gn   6:19   that you may keep them **a** with you.
Gn   16:13   and remained **a** after my vision?"
Lv   16:10   he shall set **a** before the LORD,
Nm   16:30   and swallows them **a** down
2 Sm   12:18   "When the child was **a**, we spoke
Ps   55:16   let them go down **a** to Sheol,
Prv   1:12   up, as the nether world does, **a**,
Lk   24:23   who announced that he was **a**.
Acts   1: 3   He presented himself **a** to them
Acts   9:41   and the widows, he presented her **a**.
Rom   7: 9   commandment came, sin became **a**;
1 Thes 4:17   Then we who are **a**, who are left,
Rv   1:18   but now I am **a** forever and ever.
Rv   3: 1   you have the reputation of being **a**,
Rv   19:20   The two were thrown **a**

ALL
Gn   2: 3   rested from **a** the work he had done
Gn   3:20   became the mother of **a** the living.
Gn   6:13   to put an end to **a** mortals on earth;
Gn   6:13   destroy them and **a** life on earth.
Gn   7:21   **A** creatures that stirred on earth

Gn	11: 6	a speaking the same language,
Gn	12: 3	A the communities of the earth
Gn	13:15	a the land that you see I will give
Gn	45: 9	God has made me lord of a Egypt;
Gn	46: 6	and a his descendants migrated
Ex	3:15	this is my title for a generations;
Ex	12:12	executing judgment on a the gods
Ex	20: 1	Then God delivered a these
Ex	24: 4	wrote down a the words of the Lord
Ex	24: 7	answered, "A that the Lord has said,
Ex	33:19	"I will make a my beauty pass before
Lv	20:22	"Be careful to observe a my statutes
Nm	3:13	When I slew the first-born
Nm	3:13	I made a the first-born in Israel
Nm	11:29	Would that a the people of the Lord
Nm	11:29	might bestow his spirit on them a!"
Nm	27:16	the God of the spirits of a mankind,
Dt	6: 5	with a your heart, and with a your soul, and with a your strength.
Dt	10:12	with a your heart and a your soul,
Dt	11:13	with a your heart and a your soul,
Dt	28: 2	a these blessings will come
Dt	28:15	a these curses shall come upon you
Jos	8:34	were read aloud a the words
Jos	21:44	the Lord brought a their enemies
1 Sm	12:20	true you have committed a this evil;
2 Sm	5: 1	A the tribes of Israel came to David
1 Kgs	5:10	Solomon surpassed a the Cedemites
2 Kgs	17:16	and worshiped a the host of heaven,
Est	2:15	the admiration of a who saw her.
Est	3: 6	he sought to destroy a the Jews,
Est	4:13	you alone of a the Jews will escape.
Jb	1:22	In a this Job did not sin, nor did he
Jb	2:10	Through a this, Job said nothing
Ps	8: 2	is your name through a the earth!
Ps	8: 7	hands, put a things at their feet;
Ps	34: 2	I will bless the Lord at a times;
Ps	34:21	God watches over a their bones;
Ps	47: 8	God is king over a the earth;
Ps	57: 6	your glory appear above a the earth.
Ps	72:17	may a the nations regard him as
Ps	96: 5	the gods of the nations a do nothing,
Ps	135: 5	our Lord is greater than a gods.
Ps	145: 9	The Lord is good to a,
Ps	145:17	You, Lord, are just in a your ways, faithful in a your works.
Prv	3: 5	Trust in the Lord with a your heart,
Prv	3:17	ways, and a her paths are peace;
Prv	8:36	himself; a who hate me love death."
Eccl	1: 2	of vanities! A things are vanity!
Eccl	9: 2	in that there is the same lot for a,
Song	8: 7	Were one to offer a he owns
Wis	12:15	are just, you govern a things justly;
Wis	16: 7	he saw, but by you, the savior of a.
Sir	1: 1	A wisdom comes from the Lord
Sir	7:29	With a your soul, fear God,
Is	2: 2	A nations shall stream toward it;
Is	25: 8	the tears from a faces; The reproach
Is	44: 9	Idol makers a amount to nothing,
Is	53: 6	We had a gone astray like sheep,
Is	53: 6	Lord laid upon him the guilt of us a.
Jer	3:17	there a nations will be gathered
Jer	10:16	he is the creator of a things; Israel is
Jer	29:13	you seek me with a your heart,
Jer	31:34	A, from least to greatest, shall know
Ez	36:33	I purify you from a your crimes,
Jl	3: 1	out my spirit upon a mankind.
Jl	4: 2	I will assemble a the nations
Mt	6:29	a his splendor was clothed like one
Mt	6:33	and a these things will be given you
Mt	12:15	followed him, and he cured them a,
Mt	28:18	"A power in heaven and on earth has
Mk	7:19	(Thus he declared a foods clean.)
Mk	7:23	A these evils come from within
Mk	10:27	A things are possible for God."
Mk	14:36	Father, a things are possible to you.
Lk	10:27	with a your heart, with a your
Jn	1: 3	A things came to be through him,
Jn	1: 7	so that a might believe through him.

Jn	1:16	his fullness we have a received,
Jn	16:13	of truth, he will guide you to a truth.
Jn	17:21	so that they may a be one, as you,
Acts	2: 4	And they were a filled with the holy
Acts	2:17	upon a flesh. Your sons and your
Acts	2:44	A who believed were together
Acts	2:44	and had a things in common;
Acts	10:44	fell upon a who were listening
Rom	2:12	A who sin outside the law will
Rom	2:12	and a who sin under the law will be
Rom	3:23	a have sinned and are deprived
Rom	5:12	and thus death came to a, inasmuch as a sinned—
Rom	6:10	death, he died to sin once and for a;
Rom	10:12	the same Lord is Lord of a,
Rom	14:10	For we shall a stand before
1 Cor	9:22	I have become a things to a, to save
1 Cor	12:12	and a the parts of the body,
1 Cor	12:29	Are a apostles? Are a prophets? Are a teachers? Do a work mighty deeds? Do a have gifts of healing? Do a speak in tongues? Do a interpret?
1 Cor	15:22	For just as in Adam a die, so too in Christ shall a be brought
1 Cor	15:28	to him, so that God may be a in a.
1 Cor	15:51	We shall not a fall asleep, but we will a be changed,
2 Cor	5:14	to the conviction that one died for a; therefore, a have died.
Eph	1:22	And he put a things beneath his feet
Eph	1:22	gave him as head over a things
Eph	1:23	the one who fills a things in every
Eph	4: 6	one God and Father of a, who is over a and through a
Phil	4: 7	that surpasses a understanding will
Col	1:15	God, the firstborn of a creation.
Col	1:16	a things were created through him
Col	1:19	in him a the fullness was pleased
Col	2: 3	whom are hidden a the treasures
Col	3:11	slave, free; but Christ is a in a.
1 Thes	5:18	In a circumstances give thanks,
1 Tm	4:10	who is the savior of a,
1 Tm	6:10	love of money is the root of a evils,
2 Tm	3:12	a who want to live religiously
2 Tm	3:16	A scripture is inspired by God and is
Ti	1:15	To the clean a things are clean,
Heb	1: 2	whom he made heir of a things
Heb	1: 3	who sustains a things by his mighty
Heb	8:11	for a shall know me, from least
Heb	9:26	now once for a he has appeared
1 Pt	1:24	for: "A flesh is like grass, and a its
1 Pt	5: 7	Cast a your worries upon him
2 Pt	3: 9	that a should come to repentance.
Rv	4:11	for you created a things;
Rv	15: 4	are holy. A the nations will come
Rv	21: 5	said, "Behold, I make a things new."

ALLEGORY

Gal	4:24	Now this is an a. These women

ALLELUIA

Tb	13:18	all her houses shall cry out, "A!"
Rv	19: 1	"A! Salvation, glory, and might
Rv	19: 3	"A! Smoke will rise from her
Rv	19: 4	on the throne, saying, "Amen. A."
Rv	19: 6	"A! The Lord has established his

ALLOW → ALLOWED

Lk	4:41	and did not a them to speak because
Acts	16: 7	the Spirit of Jesus did not a them,

ALLOWED → ALLOW

Mt	19: 8	your hearts Moses a you to divorce
Acts	28:16	Paul was a to live by himself,

ALLURE

Hos	2:16	So I will a her; I will lead her

ALLY

2 Mc	8:24	With the Almighty as their a,

ALMIGHTY → MIGHT

Gn	17: 1	to him and said: "I am God the A.
Gn	35:11	to him: "I am God A; be fruitful

Ex	6: 3	As God the **A** I appeared
Nm	24: 4	Of one who sees what the **A** sees,
Ru	1:20	for the **A** has made it very bitter
Jdt	16: 5	"But the LORD **A** thwarted them,
Jb	6: 4	For the arrows of the **A** pierce me,
Jb	11: 7	vie with the perfection of the **A**?
Jb	21:15	What is the **A** that we should serve
Jb	33: 4	the breath of the **A** keeps me alive.
Ps	91: 1	who abide in the shadow of the **A**,
Is	13: 6	as destruction from the **A** it comes.
Bar	3: 1	"LORD **A**, God of Israel,
Jl	1:15	and it comes as ruin from the **A**.
Rv	1: 8	who was and who is to come, the **a**."
Rv	4: 8	"Holy, holy, holy is the Lord God **a**,
Rv	19: 6	his reign, [our] God, the **a**.
Rv	21:22	for its temple is the Lord God **a**

ALMOND → ALMONDS
Ex	25:33	shaped like a blossoms,

ALMONDS → ALMOND
Nm	17:23	as well, and even bore ripe **a**!

ALMS → ALMSGIVING
Tb	4:16	you have left over, give away as **a**;
Tb	4:16	and do not begrudge the **a** you give.
Tb	12: 8	It is better to give **a** than to store
Sir	7:10	and neglect not the giving of **a**.
Mt	6: 2	When you give **a**, do not blow
Lk	12:33	Sell your belongings and give **a**.
Acts	3: 2	to beg for **a** from the people who

ALMSGIVING → ALMS
Tb	4:10	**A** frees one from death, and keeps

ALONE → LONELY
Gn	2:18	"It is not good for the man to be **a**.
Ex	18:18	heavy for you; you cannot do it **a**.
Dt	6: 4	The LORD is our God, the LORD **a**!
Dt	8: 3	that not by bread **a** does man live,
1 Kgs	19:10	I **a** am left, and they seek to take my
Tb	8: 6	'It is not good for the man to be **a**;
Ps	51: 6	Against you **a** have I sinned; I have
Ps	62: 2	My soul rests in God **a**, from whom
Ps	136: 4	Who **a** has done great wonders,
Ps	148:13	for his name **a** is exalted,
Eccl	4:11	How can one **a** keep warm?
Is	2:11	and the LORD **a** will be exalted,
Dn	13:14	when they could meet her **a**.
Mt	4: 4	'One does not live by bread **a**,
Mk	2: 7	Who but God **a** can forgive sins?"
Mk	10:18	No one is good but God **a**.
Jn	16:32	own home and you will leave me **a**.
Jn	16:32	But I am not **a**, because the Father
Rom	11: 3	and I **a** am left, and they are seeking
Jas	2:24	by works and not by faith **a**.
Rv	15: 4	For you **a** are holy. All the nations

ALOUD → LOUD
Rv	1: 3	Blessed is the one who reads **a**

ALPHA
Rv	1: 8	"I am the **A** and the Omega,"
Rv	21: 6	I [am] the **A** and the Omega,
Rv	22:13	I am the **A** and the Omega, the first

ALREADY
Mt	17:12	but I tell you that Elijah has **a** come,
Jn	3:18	not believe has **a** been condemned,
Jn	19:33	to Jesus and saw that he was **a** dead,
Phil	3:12	It is not that I have **a** taken hold of it
Phil	3:12	or have **a** attained perfect maturity,
2 Thes	2: 7	mystery of lawlessness is **a** at work
2 Tm	2:18	[the] resurrection has **a** taken place
1 Jn	2: 8	away, and the true light is **a** shining.

ALTAR → ALTARS
Gn	8:20	Then Noah built an **a** to the LORD,
Gn	8:20	bird, he offered holocausts on the **a**.
Gn	12: 7	So Abram built an **a** there
Gn	13:18	There he built an **a** to the LORD.
Gn	22: 9	Abraham built an **a** there
Gn	22: 9	put him on top of the wood on the **a**.

Gn	26:25	So he built an **a** there and invoked
Gn	35: 1	and build an **a** there to the God who
Ex	17:15	Moses also built an **a** there,
Ex	20:24	"An **a** of earth you shall make
Ex	24: 4	at the foot of the mountain an **a**
Ex	27: 1	"You shall make an **a** of acacia
Ex	30: 1	burning incense you shall make an **a**
Ex	32: 5	Aaron built an **a** before the calf
Ex	37:25	The **a** of incense was made
Ex	38: 1	The **a** of holocausts was made
Lv	8:11	of this oil seven times on the **a**,
Lv	9:24	and the remnants of the fat on the **a**.
Dt	27: 5	an **a** made of stones that no iron tool
Jos	8:30	Later Joshua built an **a** to the LORD,
Jos	22:10	the Jordan a conspicuously large **a**.
Jgs	6:24	So Gideon built there an **a**
Jgs	13:20	LORD ascended in the flame of the **a**.
Jgs	21: 4	next day the people built an **a** there
1 Sm	7:17	Israel and built an **a** to the LORD.
1 Sm	14:35	Saul built an **a** to the LORD—this was the first time he built an **a**
2 Sm	24:25	David built an **a** there to the LORD,
1 Kgs	3: 4	its **a** Solomon offered a thousand
1 Kgs	12:33	Jeroboam ascended the **a** he built
1 Kgs	13: 2	"O **a**, **a**, the LORD says, 'A child shall
1 Kgs	16:32	Ahab erected an **a** to Baal
1 Kgs	18:30	he repaired the **a** of the LORD
2 Kgs	16:10	When he saw the **a** in Damascus,
1 Chr	21:26	then built an **a** there to the LORD,
2 Chr	4: 1	made a bronze **a** twenty cubits long,
2 Chr	4:19	the golden **a**, the tables
2 Chr	15: 8	to restore the **a** of the LORD
2 Chr	32:12	yourselves before one **a** only,
2 Chr	33:16	He restored the **a** of the LORD,
Ezr	3: 2	about rebuilding the **a** of the God
Neh	10:35	to be burnt on the **a** of the LORD,
Jdt	4:12	The **a**, too, they draped in sackcloth;
1 Mc	1:54	upon the **a** of holocausts,
1 Mc	1:59	on the **a** erected over the **a**
1 Mc	2:24	forward and killed him upon the **a**.
1 Mc	4:45	defiled it; so they tore down the **a**.
1 Mc	4:47	built a new **a** like the former one.
1 Mc	4:56	celebrated the dedication of the **a**
2 Mc	1:19	took some of the fire from the **a**
2 Mc	1:32	brilliance cast from a light on the **a**.
Ps	43: 4	That I may come to the **a** of God,
Ps	51:21	bullocks will be offered on your **a**.
Ps	118:27	branches up to the horns of the **a**.
Sir	35: 5	just man's offering enriches the **a**
Is	6: 6	he had taken with tongs from the **a**.
Is	60: 7	be acceptable offerings on my **a**,
Lam	2: 7	The Lord has disowned his **a**,
Ez	8:16	between the vestibule and the **a**,
Ez	40:47	The **a** stood in front of the temple.
Ez	47: 1	side of the temple, south of the **a**.
Jl	1:13	wail, O ministers of the **a**! Come,
Am	2: 8	they recline beside any **a**;
Am	9: 1	saw the Lord standing beside the **a**,
Mal	1: 7	By offering polluted food on my **a**!
Mt	5:24	leave your gift there at the **a**,
Mt	23:18	say, 'If one swears by the **a**, it means
Mt	23:18	if one swears by the gift on the **a**,
Lk	11:51	Zechariah who died between the **a**
Acts	17:23	I even discovered an **a** inscribed,
1 Cor	10:18	the sacrifices participants in the **a**?
Heb	13:10	We have an **a** from which those
Jas	2:21	he offered his son Isaac upon the **a**?
Rv	6: 9	I saw underneath the **a** the souls
Rv	8: 3	angel came and stood at the **a**,
Rv	11: 1	the temple of God and the **a**,

ALTARS → ALTAR
Ex	34:13	Tear down their **a**; smash their
Nm	3:31	the **a**, the utensils
Nm	23: 1	"Build me seven **a**, and prepare
Dt	7: 5	Tear down their **a**, smash their
Jgs	2: 2	and you were to pull down their **a**.
2 Kgs	23:20	upon the **a** all the priests of the high
2 Chr	33: 3	torn down, erected **a** for the Baals,

ALTER

2 Chr	34: 4	the **a** of the Baals were destroyed;
1 Mc	2:45	about and tore down the pagan **a**;
Is	36: 7	places and **a** Hezekiah removed,
Ez	6: 5	their bones all around your **a**.
Hos	8:11	Ephraim made many **a** to expiate
Hos	8:11	sin, his **a** became occasions of sin.

ALTER

Ps	89:35	the promise of my lips I will not **a**.

ALWAYS

Dt	5:29	that they might **a** be of such a mind,
Dt	14:23	you may learn **a** to fear the LORD,
Ps	16: 8	I keep the LORD **a** before me;
Ps	103: 9	God does not **a** rebuke, nurses no
Prv	5:19	Her love will invigorate you **a**,
Prv	6:21	them fastened over your heart **a**,
Prv	23:17	zealous for the fear of the LORD **a**;
Is	57:16	not accuse forever, nor **a** be angry;
Mt	26:11	The poor you will **a** have with you; but you will not **a** have me.
Mt	28:20	I am with you **a**, until the end
Lk	18: 1	to pray **a** without becoming weary.
Jn	6:34	to him, "Sir, give us this bread **a**."
Jn	11:42	I know that you **a** hear me;
2 Cor	2:14	who **a** leads us in triumph in Christ
2 Cor	5: 6	So we are **a** courageous,
2 Cor	6:10	as sorrowful yet **a** rejoicing; as poor
Phil	4: 4	Rejoice in the Lord **a**. I shall say it
1 Thes	5:15	**a** seek what is good [both] for each
1 Thes	5:16	Rejoice **a**.
Phlm	1: 4	I give thanks to my God **a**,
Heb	7:25	he is **a** able to save those who
1 Pt	3:15	**A** be ready to give an explanation

AMALEK → AMALEKITE, AMALEKITES

Ex	17: 8	**A** came and waged war against
Ex	17:14	out the memory of **A** from under
Nm	24:20	First of the peoples was **A**, but his
Dt	25:17	Bear in mind what **A** did to you
1 Sm	15: 3	attack **A**, and deal with him and all
1 Sm	15: 8	He took Agag, king of **A**, alive,
1 Sm	28:18	carry out his fierce anger against **A**,

AMALEKITE → AMALEK

2 Sm	1: 8	'Who are you?' and I replied, 'An **A**.'

AMALEKITES → AMALEK

Nm	14:43	For there the **A** and Canaanites face

AMASA

Nephew of David (1 Chr 2:17). Commander of Absalom's forces (2 Sm 17:24-27). Returned to David (2 Sm 19:14). Killed by Joab (2 Sm 20:4-13).

AMAZED → AMAZEMENT

Mt	8:27	The men were **a** and said, "What sort
Mt	9:33	The crowds were **a** and said,
Mt	15:31	The crowds were **a** when they saw
Mk	6: 6	He was **a** at their lack of faith.
Mk	15: 5	further answer, so that Pilate was **a**.
Rv	17: 8	the world shall be **a** when they see

AMAZEMENT → AMAZED

Acts	3:10	and they were filled with **a**

AMAZIAH

1. Son of Joash; king of Judah (2 Kgs 14; 2 Chr 25). Defeated Edom (2 Kgs 14:7; 2 Chr 25:5-13); defeated by Israel for worshiping Edom's gods (2 Kgs 14:8-14; 2 Chr 25:14-24).
2. Idolatrous priest who opposed Amos (Am 7:10-17).

AMBASSADOR → AMBASSADORS

Eph	6:20	for which I am an **a** in chains,

AMBASSADORS → AMBASSADOR

2 Cor	5:20	So we are **a** for Christ, as if God

AMBITION

Phil	1:17	proclaim Christ out of selfish **a**,
Jas	3:14	and selfish **a** in your hearts, do not
Jas	3:16	where jealousy and selfish **a** exist,

AMBUSH

Jos	8: 2	as booty. Set an **a** behind the city."

AMEN

Jgs	20:29	Israel set men in **a** around Gibeah.
2 Chr	20:22	hymn, the LORD laid an **a** against
Prv	12: 6	words of the wicked are a deadly **a**,

AMEN

Dt	27:15	And all the people shall answer, 'A!'
1 Chr	16:36	Let all the people say, A! Alleluia.
Neh	5:13	the whole assembly answered, "A,"
Neh	8: 6	hands raised high, answered, "A, a!"
Tb	8: 8	They said together, "A, a,"
Jdt	13:20	And all the people answered, "A! A!"
Ps	89:53	be the LORD forever! A and a!
Rom	1:25	creator, who is blessed forever. A.
Rom	9: 5	is over all be blessed forever. A.
Rom	11:36	things. To him be glory forever. A.
1 Cor	14:16	of the uninstructed say the "A" to your
2 Cor	1:20	the A from us also goes through him
Rv	3:14	" 'The A, the faithful and true witness,
Rv	5:14	four living creatures answered, "A,"
Rv	19: 4	who sat on the throne, saying, "A.
Rv	22:20	says, "Yes, I am coming soon." A!

AMENDS

Lv	26:41	and they make **a** for their guilt,

AMMI

Hos	2: 3	Say to your brothers, "A,"

AMMONITE → AMMONITES

Dt	23: 4	No **A** or Moabite may ever be
Neh	2:10	and Tobiah the **A** slave had heard
Neh	13: 1	it was found written there that "no **A**
Neh	13:23	Jews who had married Ashdodite, **A**,
Jdt	6: 5	you, Achior, you **A** mercenary,

AMMONITES → AMMONITE

Gn	19:38	He is the ancestor of the **A** of today.
Dt	2:19	As you come opposite the **A**, do not
Jgs	11: 4	time later, the **A** warred on Israel.
2 Sm	10: 1	time later the king of the **A** died,
1 Kgs	11: 5	and Milcom, the idol of the **A**,
Jer	49: 6	the lot of the **A**, says the LORD.
Ez	25: 2	turn toward the **A** and prophesy
Ez	25:10	I will hand her over, along with the **A**,

AMNON

Firstborn of David (2 Sm 3:2; 1 Chr 3:1). Killed by Absalom for raping his sister Tamar (2 Sm 13).

AMON

1. Son of Manasseh; king of Judah (2 Kgs 21:18-26; 1 Chr 3:14; 2 Chr 33:21-25).
2. Ruler of Samaria under Ahab (1 Kgs 22:26; 2 Chr 18:25).

AMORITE → AMORITES

Gn	14:13	at the terebinth of Mamre the **A**,
Ez	16: 3	your father was an **A** and your

AMORITES → AMORITE

Gn	15:16	the **A** will not have reached its full
Ex	34:11	"I will drive out before you the **A**,
Nm	21:31	had settled in the land of the **A**,
Jgs	6:10	gods of the **A** in whose land you are
1 Sm	7:14	was peace between Israel and the **A**.
Am	2: 9	I who destroyed the **A** before them,

AMOS

1. Prophet from Tekoa (Tb 2:6; Am 1:1; 7:10-17).
2. Ancestor of Jesus (Lk 3:25).

AMRAM

Ex	6:20	**A** married his aunt Jochebed,
1 Chr	5:29	The children of **A** were Aaron,

AMULETS

Is	3:20	cinctures, perfume boxes, and **a**;

ANAK → ANAKIM

Jos	15:13	(Arba was the father of A), that is,

ANAKIM → ANAK

Nm	13:28	Besides, we saw descendants of the **A** there.
Dt	1:28	besides, they saw the **A** there.'
Jos	11:22	so that no **A** were left in the land

ANANIAS
1. Husband of Sapphira; died for lying to God (Acts 5:1-11).
2. Disciple who baptized Saul (Acts 9:10-19).
3. High priest at Paul's arrest (Acts 22:30-24:1).

ANATHOTH
Jer 32: 7 "Buy for yourself my field in A,

ANCESTOR →ANCESTORS
Rom 4: 1 found, our a according to the flesh?

ANCESTORS →ANCESTOR
Ps 22: 5 In you our a trusted; they trusted
Ps 106: 6 We have sinned like our a; we have
Lk 11:48 give consent to the deeds of your a,
Jn 4:20 Our a worshiped on this mountain;
Jn 6:31 Our a ate manna in the desert, as it
Acts 5:30 The God of our a raised Jesus,
Heb 1: 1 ways to our a through the prophets;

ANCHOR
Heb 6:19 This we have as an a of the soul,

ANCIENT
Ps 24: 7 rise up, you a portals, that the king
Ps 68:34 rides the heights of the a heavens,
Prv 22:28 Remove not the a landmark
Is 58:12 The a ruins shall be rebuilt for your
Dn 7: 9 and the A One took his throne.
Dn 7:13 When he reached the A One
Dn 7:22 until the A One arrived;
Mi 5: 1 origin is from of old, from a times.
Rv 12: 9 The huge dragon, the a serpent,
Rv 20: 2 He seized the dragon, the a serpent,

ANDREW
Apostle; brother of Simon Peter (Mt 4:18; 10:2; Mk 1:16-18, 29;
3:18; 13:3; Lk 6:14; Jn 1:35-44; 6:8-9; 12:22; Acts 1:13).

ANEW →NEW
Wis 19: 6 kinds, was being made over a,
1 Pt 1:23 You have been born a,

ANGEL →ANGELS, ARCHANGEL
Gn 48:16 The A who has delivered me
Ex 3: 2 There an a of the LORD appeared
Ex 14:19 The a of God, who had been leading
Ex 23:20 I am sending an a before you,
Ex 32:34 told you. My a will go before you.
Ex 33: 2 I will send an a before you
Nm 20:16 sent an a who led us out of Egypt.
Nm 22:22 the a of the LORD stationed himself
Jgs 2: 1 An a of the LORD went
Jgs 6:12 the a of the LORD appeared to him
Jgs 6:22 that it had been the a of the LORD,
Jgs 6:22 I have seen the a of the LORD face
Jgs 13: 3 An a of the LORD appeared
2 Sm 14:17 my lord the king is like an a of God,
2 Sm 19:28 my lord the king is like an a of God.
2 Sm 24:16 when the a stretched forth his hand
2 Sm 24:16 the a causing the destruction among
1 Kgs 13:18 an a told me in the word of the LORD
1 Kgs 19: 5 then an a touched him and ordered
2 Kgs 1: 3 the a of the LORD said to Elijah
2 Kgs 19:35 night the a of the LORD went forth
1 Chr 21:15 also sent an a to destroy Jerusalem;
Tb 5: 4 he found the a Raphael standing
Tb 5: 4 not know that this was an a of God.
Tb 12:22 done when the a of God appeared
1 Mc 7:41 your a went out and killed
2 Mc 11: 6 tears to send a good a to save Israel.
Jb 33:23 If then there be for him an a,
Ps 34: 8 The a of the LORD, who encamps
Ps 35: 5 the a of the LORD driving them on.
Is 37:36 The a of the LORD went forth
Is 63: 9 It was not a messenger or an a,
Dn 3:49 the a of the Lord went down
Dn 3:95 who sent his a to deliver
Dn 6:23 My God has sent his a and closed
Dn 13:59 "for the a of God waits with a sword
Dn 14:34 when an a of the Lord told him,
Hos 12: 5 He contended with the a
Zec 1:11 they answered the a of the LORD

Zec 3: 1 the high priest standing before the a
Mt 1:20 the a of the Lord appeared to him
Mt 2:13 the a of the Lord appeared to Joseph
Mt 28: 2 for an a of the Lord descended
Lk 1:11 the a of the Lord appeared to him,
Lk 1:26 the a Gabriel was sent from God
Lk 2: 9 The a of the Lord appeared to them
Lk 22:43 to strengthen him an a from heaven
Jn 12:29 others said, "An a has spoken to him."
Acts 5:19 the a of the Lord opened the doors
Acts 6:15 his face was like the face of an a.
Acts 7:30 an a appeared to him in the desert
Acts 8:26 the a of the Lord spoke to Philip,
Acts 10: 3 plainly in a vision an a of God come
Acts 12: 7 Suddenly the a of the Lord stood
Acts 27:23 For last night an a of the God
2 Cor 11:14 even Satan masquerades as an a
Gal 1: 8 an a from heaven should preach
Gal 4:14 rather you received me as an a
Rv 1: 1 by sending his a to his servant John,
Rv 2: 1 "To the a of the church in Ephesus,
Rv 5: 2 I saw a mighty a who proclaimed
Rv 7: 2 I saw another a come
Rv 8: 3 Another a came and stood
Rv 9:11 They had as their king the a
Rv 14: 6 Then I saw another a flying high
Rv 16: 2 The first a went and poured out his
Rv 19:17 I saw an a standing on the sun.
Rv 22:16 sent my a to give you this testimony

ANGELS →ANGEL
Gn 19: 1 The two a reached Sodom'
Tb 11:14 and blessed be all his holy a.
Jb 4:18 and with his a he can find fault.
Ps 91:11 For God commands the a to guard
Ps 103:20 Bless the LORD, all you a;
Ps 148: 2 Praise him, all you a; give praise,
Wis 16:20 your people with food of a
Mt 4: 6 will command his a concerning you'
Mt 4:11 a came and ministered to him.
Mt 13:39 of the age, and the harvesters are a.
Mt 16:27 come with his a in his Father's glory,
Mt 18:10 that their a in heaven always look
Mt 24:36 one knows, neither the a of heaven,
Mt 25:41 fire prepared for the devil and his a.
Mt 26:53 with more than twelve legions of a?
Mk 1:13 beasts, and the a ministered to him.
Mk 8:38 in his Father's glory with the holy a."
Mk 12:25 but they are like the a in heaven.
Mk 13:32 one knows, neither the a in heaven,
Lk 2:15 When the a went away from them
Lk 4:10 will command his a concerning you,
Lk 12: 8 Man will acknowledge before the a
Lk 15:10 there will be rejoicing among the a
Lk 16:22 he was carried away by a
Lk 20:36 no longer die, for they are like a;
Jn 1:51 opened and the a of God ascending
Jn 20:12 and saw two a in white sitting there,
Acts 7:53 the law as transmitted by a, but you
Acts 23: 8 say that there is no resurrection or a
Rom 8:38 nor life, nor a, nor principalities,
1 Cor 4: 9 world, to a and human beings alike.
1 Cor 6: 3 you not know that we will judge a?
1 Cor 11:10 on her head, because of the a.
Gal 3:19 it was promulgated by a at the hand
Col 2:18 in self-abasement and worship of a,
2 Thes 1: 7 from heaven with his mighty a,
1 Tm 3:16 spirit, seen by a,
1 Tm 5:21 and the elect a to keep these rules
Heb 1: 4 as far superior to the a as the name
Heb 1: 6 "Let all the a of God worship him."
Heb 1: 7 Of the a he says: "He makes his a
Heb 2: 2 announced through a proved firm,
Heb 2: 7 for a little while lower than the a;
Heb 2: 7 while" was made "lower than the a,"
Heb 12:22 and countless a in festal gathering,
Heb 13: 2 have unknowingly entertained a.
1 Pt 1:12 things into which a longed to look.
1 Pt 3:22 hand of God, with a, authorities,

2 Pt	2: 4	if God did not spare the **a** when they
Jude	1: 6	The **a** too, who did not keep to their
Rv	1:20	the seven stars are the **a** of the seven
Rv	3: 5	presence of my Father and of his **a**.
Rv	5:11	many **a** who surrounded the throne
Rv	7: 1	this I saw four **a** standing at the four
Rv	8: 2	the seven **a** who stood before God
Rv	9:14	"Release the four **a** who are bound
Rv	12: 7	and his **a** battled against the dragon.
Rv	12: 7	The dragon and its **a** fought back,
Rv	15: 1	seven **a** with the seven last plagues,
Rv	21:12	gates where twelve **a** were stationed

ANGER → ANGRY

Gn	27:45	[until your brother's **a** against you
Ex	34: 6	slow to **a** and rich in kindness
Nm	14:18	The Lord is slow to **a** and rich
Nm	22:22	now the **a** of God flared up at him
Nm	25: 3	the Lord's **a** flared up against Israel.
Dt	9:19	I dreaded the fierce **a** of the Lord
Dt	29:27	and tremendous **a** the Lord uprooted
Jos	7: 1	the **a** of the Lord flared up against
Jos	7:26	Then the **a** of the Lord relented.
Jos	23:16	them, the **a** of the Lord will flare
Jgs	14:19	he went off to his own family in **a**,
1 Kgs	16:13	the God of Israel, to **a** by their idols.
Neh	9:17	slow to **a** and rich in mercy; you did
Ps	6: 2	Do not reprove me in your **a**, Lord,
Ps	30: 6	For divine **a** lasts but a moment;
Ps	37: 8	Give up your **a**, abandon your
Ps	78:38	and again he turned back his **a**,
Ps	86:15	slow to **a**, most loving and true.
Ps	90: 7	Truly we are consumed by your **a**,
Ps	95:11	Therefore I swore in my **a**:
Ps	103: 8	slow to **a**, abounding in kindness.
Ps	103: 9	always rebuke, nurses no lasting **a**,
Ps	145: 8	slow to **a** and abounding in love.
Prv	12:16	The fool immediately shows his **a**,
Prv	15: 1	wrath, but a harsh word stirs up **a**.
Prv	19:11	good sense in a man to be slow to **a**,
Prv	29:11	The fool gives vent to all his **a**;
Prv	30:33	the stirring of **a** brings forth blood.
Sir	30:24	Envy and **a** shorten one's life,
Is	48: 9	sake of my name I restrain my **a**,
Is	63: 6	trampled down the peoples in my **a**,
Lam	4:11	The Lord has spent his **a**,
Dn	9:16	let your **a** and your wrath be turned
Hos	11: 9	I will not give vent to my blazing **a**,
Jl	2:13	is he, slow to **a**, rich in kindness,
Jon	4: 2	God, slow to **a**, rich in clemency,
Mi	7:18	Who does not persist in **a** forever,
Na	1: 3	The Lord is slow to **a**, yet great
Mk	3: 5	Looking around at them with **a**
Eph	4:26	do not let the sun set on your **a**,
Eph	6: 4	do not provoke your children to **a**,
Col	3: 8	away: **a**, fury, malice, slander,
1 Tm	2: 8	holy hands, without **a** or argument.

ANGRY → ANGER

1 Kgs	11: 9	therefore, became **a** with Solomon,
Ps	2:12	Lest God be **a** and you perish from the way
Ps	79: 5	Will you be **a** forever? Will your
Prv	25:23	tongue an **a** countenance.
Jer	3:12	Lord, I will not remain **a** with you;
Jon	4: 4	asked, "Have you reason to be **a**?"
Zec	1: 2	The Lord was indeed **a** with your
Mt	5:22	whoever is **a** with his brother will
Lk	15:28	He became **a**, and when he refused
Jn	7:23	are you **a** with me because I made
Eph	4:26	Be **a** but do not sin; do not let
Rv	12:17	Then the dragon became **a**

ANGUISH

Jb	7:11	I will speak in the **a** of my spirit;
Is	8:23	**A** has taken wing, dispelled is
Zep	1:15	is that day, a day of **a** and distress,
Jn	16:21	is in **a** because her hour has arrived;
Rom	9: 2	sorrow and constant **a** in my heart.

ANIMAL → ANIMALS

Ex	22:18	who lies with an **a** shall be put

Lv	18:23	not have carnal relations with an **a**,
Lv	20:15	a man has carnal relations with an **a**,
Lv	20:15	put to death, and the **a** shall be slain.
Dt	14: 6	Any **a** that has hoofs you may eat.
Ps	50:10	For every **a** of the forest is mine,
Lk	10:34	Then he lifted him up on his own **a**,
Heb	12:20	"If even an **a** touches the mountain,

ANIMALS → ANIMAL

Gn	1:25	God made all kinds of wild **a**,
Gn	2:19	out of the ground various wild **a**
Gn	3: 1	of all the **a** that the Lord God had
Gn	3:14	from all the **a** and from all the wild
Gn	7: 2	and of the unclean **a**, one pair,
Gn	8:19	and all the **a**, wild and tame,
Gn	9: 2	come upon all the **a** of the earth
Dt	14: 4	These are the **a** you may eat: the ox,
Ps	147: 9	Who gives **a** their food and ravens
Is	40:16	nor its **a** be enough for holocausts.
Acts	11: 6	saw the four-legged **a** of the earth,
Jude	1:10	know by nature like irrational **a**.

ANNA

1. Wife of Tobit (Tb 1:20; 2:1, 11).
2. Prophetess who spoke about the child Jesus (Lk 2:36-38).

ANNAS

High priest A.D. 6-15 (Lk 3:2; Jn 18:13, 24; Acts 4:6).

ANNUL

Gal	3:17	does not **a** a covenant previously

ANOINT → ANOINTED, ANOINTING

Ex	28:41	**A** and ordain them,
Ex	30:26	oil you shall **a** the meeting tent
Ex	30:30	and his sons you shall also **a**
1 Sm	9:16	whom you are to **a** as commander
1 Sm	15: 1	to **a** you king over his people Israel.
1 Kgs	1:34	the prophet are to **a** him king
1 Kgs	19:16	Then you shall **a** Jehu.
2 Kgs	9: 3	the Lord: I **a** you king over Israel.'
Ps	23: 5	watch; You **a** my head with oil;
Mk	16: 1	so that they might go and **a** him.
Lk	7:46	You did not **a** my head with oil,

ANOINTED → ANOINT

Gn	31:13	where you **a** a memorial stone
Lv	4: 3	if it is the **a** priest who thus sins
1 Sm	2:10	his king and exalt the horn of his **a**!"
1 Sm	10: 1	the Lord has **a** you commander over
1 Sm	16:13	a him in the midst of his brothers;
1 Sm	26: 9	who can lay hands on the Lord's **a**
2 Sm	1:14	your hand to desecrate the Lord's **a**?"
2 Sm	2: 4	and **a** David king of the Judahites.
2 Sm	5: 3	Lord, and they **a** him king of Israel.
2 Sm	19:22	for this. He cursed the Lord's **a**."
1 Kgs	1:39	of oil from the tent and **a** Solomon.
1 Chr	16:22	"Touch not my **a**, and to my prophets
2 Chr	6:42	God, reject not the plea of your **a**,
Ps	2: 2	together against the Lord and his **a**:
Ps	18:51	and shown kindness to your **a**,
Ps	89:21	with my holy oil I have **a** him.
Ps	105:15	"Do not touch my **a**, to my prophets
Is	61: 1	because the Lord has **a** me; He has
Dn	9:24	ratified, and a most holy will be **a**.
Dn	9:26	weeks an **a** shall be cut down
Hb	3:13	to save your **a** one. You crush
Zec	4:14	"These are the two **a** who stand
Mk	6:13	they **a** with oil many who were sick
Lk	4:18	because he has **a** me to bring glad
Lk	7:46	oil, but she **a** my feet with ointment.
Jn	1:41	the Messiah" (which is translated **A**).
Jn	12: 3	nard and **a** the feet of Jesus
Acts	10:38	how God **a** Jesus of Nazareth
2 Cor	1:21	you in Christ and who **a** us is God;
Heb	1: 9	therefore God, your God, **a** you

ANOINTING → ANOINT

Ex	30:25	and blend them into sacred **a** oil,
1 Jn	2:27	the **a** that you received from him
1 Jn	2:27	his **a** teaches you about everything

ANOTHER → ANOTHER'S

Prv	27: 2	Let a praise you—not your own
Eccl	7:27	adding one thing to a that I might
Is	48:11	My glory I will not give to a.
Lk	19:44	a within you because you did not
Jn	4:37	verified that 'One sows and a reaps.'
Jn	5:43	yet if a comes in his own name,
Jn	13:34	a new commandment: love one a.
Jn	13:34	you, so you also should love one a.
Jn	14:16	he will give you a Advocate to be
Jn	18:15	Peter and a disciple followed Jesus.
Rom	12:10	love one a with mutual affection;
Rom	12:10	anticipate one a in showing honor.
1 Cor	7: 5	but then return to one a,
1 Cor	12: 9	to a faith by the same Spirit; to a
1 Cor	16:20	Greet one a with a holy kiss.
Gal	1: 7	(not that there is a). But there are
Eph	4: 2	bearing with one a through love,
Eph	4:25	for we are members one of a.
Eph	4:32	[And] be kind to one a,
Eph	4:32	forgiving one a as God has forgiven
Col	3:16	you teach and admonish one a,
1 Thes	4:18	console one a with these words.
Heb	10:24	consider how to rouse one a to love
Jas	4:11	Do not speak evil of one a, brothers.
1 Pt	1:22	love one a intensely from a [pure]
1 Pt	4: 8	let your love for one a be intense,
1 Jn	3:11	beginning: we should love one a,
1 Jn	3:23	love one a just as he commanded
Rv	20:12	Then a scroll was opened, the book

ANOTHER'S → ANOTHER

Jn	13:14	you ought to wash one a feet.
Gal	6: 2	Bear one a burdens, and so

ANSWER → ANSWERED, ANSWERS

1 Kgs	18:26	to noon, saying, "A us, Baal!"
1 Kgs	18:37	A me, LORD! A me, that this people
Jb	30:20	I cry to you, but you do not a me;
Ps	4: 2	A when I call, my saving God.
Ps	20:10	the king; a when we call upon you.
Ps	38:16	for you; O Lord, my God, a me.
Prv	15: 1	A mild a calms wrath, but a harsh
Prv	26: 5	A the fool according to his folly,
Is	46: 7	they cry out to it, it cannot a;
Is	58: 9	you shall call, and the LORD will a,
Is	65:24	Before they call, I will a; while they
Mt	22:46	No one was able to a him a word,
Mt	27:14	But he did not a him one word,
Lk	23: 9	him at length, but he gave him no a.

ANSWERED → ANSWER

1 Chr	21:26	he a him by sending down fire
Ps	118:21	I thank you for you a me; you have

ANSWERS → ANSWER

1 Kgs	18:24	The God who a with fire is God."
Prv	18:13	He who a before he hears — his is

ANT → ANTS

Prv	6: 6	Go to the a, O sluggard, study her

ANTICHRIST → ANTICHRISTS

1 Jn	2:18	as you heard that the a was coming,
1 Jn	2:22	the Father and the Son, this is the a.
1 Jn	4: 3	This is the spirit of the a that, as you
2 Jn	1: 7	such is the deceitful one and the a.

ANTICHRISTS → ANTICHRIST

1 Jn	2:18	so now many a have appeared.

ANTIOCH

Acts	11:26	it was in A that the disciples were
Acts	13: 1	were in the church at A prophets
Gal	2:11	And when Kephas came to A,

ANTIOCHUS

Antiochus IV Epiphanes, king of the Syrian Greeks B.C.E. 175-164 (1 Mc 1:10-19). Plundered the temple in Jerusalem (1 Mc 1:20-28). Attempted to force the Hellenization of the Jewish people (1 Mc 1:41-53), including defiling the altar and holy place (1 Mc 1:54-63). His policies sparked the Maccabean revolt.

ANTIPAS

Rv	2:13	in me, not even in the days of A,

ANTS → ANT

Prv	30:25	A—a species not strong, yet they

ANXIETIES → ANXIETY

1 Cor	7:32	I should like you to be free of a.

ANXIETY → ANXIETIES, ANXIOUS

Prv	12:25	A in a man's heart depresses it,

ANXIOUS → ANXIETY

1 Cor	7:32	An unmarried man is a

ANYTHING → THING

Gn	18:14	Is a too marvelous for the LORD
Jer	32:27	all mankind! Is a impossible to me?
Mt	18:19	of you agree on earth about a
Mk	2:12	"We have never seen a like this."
Jn	1:46	"Can a good come from Nazareth?"
Jn	14:14	If you ask a of me in my name,
Jn	16:23	you will not question me about a.
2 Cor	13: 8	we cannot do a against the truth,

APART

Rom	1: 1	and set a for the gospel of God,
Rom	3:21	God has been manifested a

APOLLOS

Christian from Alexandria, learned in the Scriptures; instructed by Aquila and Priscilla (Acts 18:24-28). Ministered at Corinth (Acts 19:1; 1 Cor 1:12; 3; Ti 3:13).

APOLLYON → =ABADDON

Rv	9:11	Hebrew is Abaddon and in Greek A.

APOSTASY

1 Mc	2:15	of enforcing the a came to the city

APOSTLE → APOSTLES, APOSTLES', APOSTLESHIP, SUPERAPOSTLES

Rom	1: 1	called to be an a and set apart
Rom	11:13	then as I am the a to the Gentiles,
1 Cor	1: 1	called to be an a of Christ Jesus
1 Cor	9: 1	Am I not an a? Have I not seen
1 Cor	15: 9	not fit to be called an a, because I
2 Cor	12:12	of an a were performed among you
1 Tm	2: 7	and a (I am speaking the truth, I am
2 Tm	1:11	I was appointed preacher and a
Heb	3: 1	Jesus, the a and high priest of our
1 Pt	1: 1	Peter, an a of Jesus Christ,
2 Pt	1: 1	a slave and a of Jesus Christ,

APOSTLES → APOSTLE

See also Andrew, Bartholomew, Barnabas, James, John, Judas, Matthew, Matthias, Nathanael, Paul, Peter, Philip, Simon, Thaddaeus, Thomas.

Mt	10: 2	names of the twelve a are these:
Mk	3:14	named a] that they might be
Lk	6:13	Twelve, whom he also named a:
Lk	11:49	'I will send to them prophets and a;
Acts	1:26	he was counted with the eleven a.
Acts	2:42	devoted themselves to the teaching of the a
Acts	2:43	and signs were done through the a.
Acts	4:33	great power the a bore witness
Acts	4:35	put them at the feet of the a,
Acts	5:18	laid hands upon the a and put them
Acts	8: 1	of Judea and Samaria, except the a.
Acts	14:14	The a Barnabas and Paul tore their
Rom	16: 7	they are prominent among the a
1 Cor	12:28	in the church to be, first, a; second,
1 Cor	15: 9	For I am the least of the a, not fit
2 Cor	11:13	For such people are false a,
2 Cor	11:13	who masquerade as a of Christ.
Eph	2:20	built upon the foundation of the a
Eph	3: 5	has now been revealed to his holy a
Eph	4:11	And he gave some as a, others as
Jude	1:17	by the a of our Lord Jesus Christ,
Rv	2: 2	tested those who call themselves a
Rv	21:14	names of the twelve a of the Lamb.

APOSTLES' → APOSTLE

Acts	8:18	conferred by the laying on of the a hands,

APOSTLESHIP → APOSTLE
Rom   1: 5   we have received the grace of a,
1 Cor   9: 2   you are the seal of my a in the Lord.

APPALLED
Jer   50:13   who passes by Babylon will be a
Ez   19: 7   The land and all in it were a
Ez   32:10   Many peoples shall be a at you,

APPEAL → APPEALING
Acts   25:11   hand me over to them. I a to Caesar."
1 Pt   3:21   an a to God for a clear conscience,

APPEALING → APPEAL
2 Cor   5:20   Christ, as if God were a through us.

APPEAR → APPEARANCE, APPEARANCES, APPEARED, APPEARING, APPEARS
Gn   1: 9   basin, so that the dry land may a."
Ex   23:15   of Egypt. No one shall a before me
Sir   35: 4   A not before the LORD
Mt   24:30   of the Son of Man will a in heaven,
Lk   19:11   of God would a there immediately.
2 Cor   5:10   we must all a before the judgment
Heb   9:24   he might now a before God on our
Heb   9:28   sins of many, will a a second time,

APPEARANCE → APPEAR
Nm   9:15   on the a of fire over the Dwelling.
1 Sm   16: 7   "Do not judge from his a or from his
1 Sm   16: 7   because man sees the a but the LORD
Sir   19:25   One can tell a man by his a;
Is   52:14   and his a beyond that of mortals—
Is   53: 2   nor a that would attract us to him.
Jl   2: 4   Their a is that of horses; like steeds
Mt   28: 3   His a was like lightning and his
Lk   12:56   how to interpret the a of the earth
2 Cor   5:12   who boast of external a rather than
2 Tm   1:10   through the a of our savior
2 Tm   4: 8   to all who have longed for his a.
Rv   9: 7   The a of the locusts was like

APPEARANCES → APPEAR
Jn   7:24   Stop judging by a, but judge justly."

APPEARED → APPEAR
Gn   12: 7   The LORD a to Abram and said,
Gn   12: 7   there to the LORD who had a to him.
Gn   17: 1   old, the LORD a to him and said:
Gn   18: 1   The LORD a to Abraham
Gn   26: 2   The LORD a to him and said: "Do not
Gn   35: 9   God a to him again and blessed
Ex   3: 2   There an angel of the LORD a to him
Ex   6: 3   As God the Almighty I a
Ex   16:10   the glory of the LORD a in the cloud!
Nm   14:10   of the LORD a at the meeting tent
Nm   16:19   the LORD a to the entire community,
Nm   20: 6   the glory of the LORD a to them,
Jgs   6:12   the angel of the LORD a to him
Jgs   13: 3   angel of the LORD a to the woman
1 Kgs   9: 2   the LORD a to him a second time, as he had a to him in Gibeon.
2 Chr   1: 7   That night God a to Solomon
Ps   102:17   LORD has rebuilt Zion and a in glory,
Dn   5: 5   the fingers of a human hand a,
Mt   1:20   the angel of the Lord a to him
Mt   2:13   the angel of the Lord a to Joseph
Mt   2:19   the angel of the Lord a in a dream
Mk   9: 4   Elijah a to them along with Moses,
Lk   1:11   the angel of the Lord a to him,
Lk   22:43   him an angel from heaven a to him.
Lk   24:34   been raised and has a to Simon!"
Acts   2: 3   there a to them tongues as of fire,
1 Cor   15: 5   that he a to Kephas,
Ti   2:11   For the grace of God has a,
Heb   9:26   now once for all he has a at the end
Rv   12: 1   A great sign a in the sky, a woman

APPEARING → APPEAR
Acts   1: 3   a to them during forty days

APPEARS → APPEAR
Mal   3: 2   And who can stand when he a?

Jas   4:14   are a puff of smoke that a briefly

APPETITE → APPETITES
Prv   6:30   to satisfy his a when he is hungry;
Prv   16:26   The laborer's a labors for him,

APPETITES → APPETITE
Rom   16:18   our Lord Christ but their own a,

APPLE → APPLES
Dt   32:10   guarding them as the a of his eye.
Ps   17: 8   Keep me as the a of your eye;
Prv   7: 2   my teaching as the a of your eye;
Song   2: 3   As an a tree among the trees
Song   8: 5   Under the a tree I awakened you;
Zec   2:12   Whoever touches you touches the a

APPLES → APPLE
Prv   25:11   Like golden a in silver settings
Song   2: 5   refresh me with a, for I am faint
Song   7: 9   the fragrance of your breath like a,

APPLIED → APPLY
Eccl   1:17   yet when I a my mind to know
Eccl   8:16   When I a my heart to know wisdom
1 Cor   4: 6   I have a these things to myself

APPLY → APPLIED
Prv   22:17   and a your heart to my doctrine;
Prv   23:12   A your heart to instruction, and your

APPOINT → APPOINTED, APPOINTS
1 Sm   8: 5   your example, a a king over us,
Is   60:17   iron; I will a peace your governor,
Hos   2: 2   They shall a for themselves one head
Ti   1: 5   and a presbyters in every town, as I

APPOINTED → APPOINT
Ex   31: 6   As his assistant I have a Oholiab,
1 Sm   13:14   has a him commander of his people,
Neh   5:14   that King Artaxerxes a me governor
Est   9:31   for their a time, these days of Purim
Dn   8:19   for at the a time, there will be
Dn   11:27   because the a end is not yet.
Mk   3:16   [he a the twelve:] Simon, whom he
Lk   10: 1   this the Lord a seventy[-two] others
Jn   15:16   but I who chose you and a you to go
Acts   3:20   send you the Messiah already a
Heb   9:27   Just as it is a that human beings die

APPOINTS → APPOINT
Heb   7:28   For the law a men subject
Heb   7:28   was taken after the law, a a son,

APPORTION → PORTION
Nm   33:54   You shall a the land among

APPROACH → APPROACHED, APPROACHES
Lv   18: 6   "None of you shall a a close relative
Heb   4:16   So let us confidently a the throne
Heb   7:25   save those who a God through him,

APPROACHED → APPROACH
Lk   22:47   a crowd a and in front was one

APPROACHES → APPROACH
Nm   17:28   Every time anyone a the Dwelling

APPROVED
Rom   16:10   Greet Apelles, who is a in Christ.
2 Cor   10:18   who recommends himself who is a,

AQUILA
Husband of Priscilla; co-worker with Paul, instructor of Apollos (Acts 18; Rom 16:3; 1 Cor 16:19; 2 Tm 4:19).

ARAB → ARABIA, ARABS
Neh   2:19   and Geshem the A mocked us

ARABAH
Dt   3:17   Chinnereth to the Salt Sea of the A,
Jos   11:16   the A, as well as the mountain
Ez   47: 8   eastern district down upon the A,

ARABIA → ARAB
2 Chr   9:14   All the kings of A also,
Gal   1:17   I went into A and then returned

Gal 4:25 represents Sinai, a mountain in **A**;

ARABS →ARAB
Neh 4: 1 Tobiah, the **A**, the Ammonites,
1 Mc 5:39 they have also hired **A** to help them,
Acts 2:11 Cretans and **A**, yet we hear them

ARAM →ARAMAIC, ARAMEAN, ARAMEANS
Gn 10:23 The descendants of **A**: Uz, Hul,
Gn 24:10 to the city of Nahor in **A** Naharaim.
Nm 23: 7 From **A** has Balak brought me here,
Jgs 3: 8 king of **A** Naharaim, whom they served
Jgs 10: 6 the gods of **A**, the gods of Sidon,
1 Kgs 19:15 shall anoint Hazael as king of **A**.
2 Kgs 13: 3 king of **A**, and of Ben-hadad,
2 Chr 16: 7 "Because you relied on the king of **A**

ARAMAIC →ARAM
2 Kgs 18:26 "Please speak to your servants in **A**;
Ezr 4: 7 The document was written in **A**
2 Mc 15:36 month, called Adar in **A**, the eve
Is 36:11 "Please speak to your servants in **A**;
Dn 2: 4 Chaldeans answered the king [**A**]:

ARAMEAN →ARAM
Gn 31:20 Jacob had hoodwinked Laban the **A**
Dt 26: 5 was a wandering **A** who went down

ARAMEANS →ARAM
2 Sm 8: 6 and the **A** became subjects,
2 Kgs 7: 6 the army of the **A** to hear the sound
2 Kgs 8:28 where the **A** wounded Joram.

ARARAT
Gn 8: 4 came to rest on the mountains of **A**.
2 Kgs 19:37 sword and fled into the land of **A**.
Tb 1:21 escaped into the mountains of **A**.
Jer 51:27 kingdoms, **A**, Minni, and Ashkenaz;

ARAUNAH →=ORNAN
2 Sm 24:16 the threshing floor of **A** the Jebusite.

ARBA
Jos 14:15 for **A**, the greatest among

ARBITRATOR
Lk 12:14 appointed me as your judge and **a**?"

ARCHANGEL →ANGEL
1 Thes 4:16 of command, with the voice of an **a**
Jude 1: 9 Yet the **a** Michael, when he argued

ARCHELAUS
Mt 2:22 heard that **A** was ruling over Judea

ARCHER →ARCHERS
Prv 26:10 Like an **a** wounding all who pass by

ARCHERS →ARCHER
Gn 49:23 and attacking, the **a** opposed him;
1 Sm 31: 3 around Saul, and the **a** hit him;
2 Chr 35:23 Then the **a** shot King Josiah,
Jdt 2:15 and twelve thousand mounted **a**,
1 Mc 9:11 the **a** came on ahead of the army,
Jer 50:29 Call up against Babylon **a**, all who

ARCHIPPUS
  Co-worker of Paul (Col 4:17; Phlm 2).

ARCHITE
2 Sm 16:16 David's friend Hushai the **A** came

ARCHITECT
Heb 11:10 whose **a** and maker is God.

ARCHIVES
Ezr 5:17 be made in the royal **a** of Babylon
1 Mc 14:23 copy of their words in the public **a**,

AREOPAGUS
Acts 17:19 him and led him to the **A** and said,
Acts 17:22 Paul stood up at the **A** and said:
Acts 17:34 Dionysius, a member of the Court of the **A**,

ARGUE →ARGUING, ARGUMENT, ARGUMENTS
Mk 8:11 forward and began to **a** with him,

ARGUING →ARGUE
Mk 9:14 them and scribes **a** with them.

ARGUMENT →ARGUE
Lk 9:46 An **a** arose among the disciples
1 Tm 2: 8 up holy hands, without anger or **a**.

ARGUMENTS →ARGUE
Acts 2:40 He testified with many other **a**,
2 Cor 10: 4 destroying fortresses. We destroy **a**
Col 2: 4 one may deceive you by specious **a**.

ARIEL
Is 29: 1 Woe to **A**, **A**, the city where David

ARIMATHEA
Jn 19:38 Joseph of **A**, secretly a disciple

ARIOCH
Dn 2:15 from the king?" When **A** told him,

ARISE →RISE
Nm 10:35 "**A**, O LORD, that your enemies may
Song 2:10 "**A**, my beloved, my beautiful one,
Dn 7:17 which shall **a** on the earth.
Dn 12: 1 "At that time there shall **a** Michael,
Mi 4:13 **A** and thresh, O daughter Zion;
Mt 24:11 Many false prophets will **a**

ARISEN →RISE
Dt 34:10 then no prophet has **a** in Israel like
Lk 9: 8 "One of the ancient prophets has **a**."

ARISES →RISE
1 Mc 14:41 high priest until a true prophet **a**.

ARISTARCHUS
  Companion of Paul (Acts 19:29; 20:4; 27:2; Col 4:10; Phlm
  1:24).

ARK
Gn 6:14 "Make yourself an **a** of gopherwood,
Gn 7: 1 "Go into the **a**, you and all your
Gn 8:16 "Go out of the **a**, together with your
Ex 25:10 "You shall make an **a** of acacia
Ex 25:16 In the **a** you are to put
Ex 37: 1 Bezalel made the **a** of acacia wood,
Ex 40:20 and put them in the **a**; he placed
Nm 3:31 of whatever pertained to the **a**,
Nm 10:35 Whenever the **a** set out,
Dt 10: 5 the tablets in the **a** I had made.
Jos 3: 3 "When you see the **a** of the covenant
Jgs 20:27 the LORD (for the **a** of the covenant
1 Sm 3: 3 of the LORD where the **a** of God was.
1 Sm 4:11 The **a** of God was captured, and Eli's
1 Sm 5: 2 They then took the **a** of God
1 Sm 6: 3 to send away the **a** of the God
1 Sm 7: 2 From the day the **a** came to rest
2 Sm 6:17 The **a** of the LORD was brought
1 Kgs 8: 9 There was nothing in the **a**
1 Chr 13: 9 out his hand to steady the **a**,
2 Chr 35: 3 "Put the holy **a** in the house built
2 Mc 2: 4 and the **a** should accompany him
Ps 132: 8 place, you and your majestic **a**.
Jer 3:16 "The **a** of the covenant of the LORD!"
Lk 17:27 to the day that Noah entered the **a**,
Heb 9: 4 and the **a** of the covenant entirely
Heb 11: 7 with reverence built an **a**
1 Pt 3:20 Noah during the building of the **a**,
Rv 11:19 the **a** of his covenant could be seen

ARM →ARMED, ARMIES, ARMOR, ARMOR-BEARER, ARMS,
ARMY
Ex 6: 6 rescue you by my outstretched **a**
Dt 4:34 his strong hand and outstretched **a**,
Dt 7:19 outstretched **a** with which the LORD,
1 Kgs 8:42 hand and your outstretched **a**),
2 Chr 32: 8 For he has only an **a** of flesh, but we
Jb 40: 9 Have you an **a** like that of God,
Ps 44: 1 It was your right hand, your own **a**,
Ps 89:14 Mighty your **a**, strong your hand,
Song 8: 6 as a seal on your **a**; For stern as
Is 40:10 who rules by his strong **a**; Here is
Is 52:10 The LORD has bared his holy **a**

Is	53: 1	To whom has the **a** of the Lord been
Jer	27: 5	power, with my outstretched **a**;
Zec	11:17	May the sword fall upon his **a**
Zec	11:17	Let his a wither away entirely,
Lk	1:51	He has shown might with his **a**,
1 Pt	4: 1	**a** yourselves also with the same

ARMED → ARM
Prv	6:11	and want like an **a** man.
Lk	11:21	a strong man fully **a** guards his

ARMIES → ARM
1 Sm	17:36	because he has insulted the **a**
Ps	60:12	Do you no longer march with our **a**?
Lk	21:20	you see Jerusalem surrounded by **a**,
Rv	19:14	The **a** of heaven followed him,

ARMOR → ARM
1 Sm	31: 9	head and stripped him of his **a**,
1 Kgs	20:11	for the man who is buckling his **a**
1 Chr	10:10	His **a** they put in the house of their
Wis	5:17	He shall take his zeal for **a** and he
Rom	13:12	darkness [and] put on the **a** of light;
Eph	6:11	Put on the **a** of God so that you may
Eph	6:13	put on the **a** of God, that you may

ARMOR-BEARER → ARM, BEAR
1 Sm	31: 4	Then Saul said to his **a**, "Draw your
1 Sm	31: 4	But his **a**, badly frightened,

ARMS → ARM
Gn	49:24	stiff, as their **a** were unsteady,
Jgs	15:14	ropes around his **a** became as flax
Jgs	16:12	snapped them off his **a** like thread.
2 Sm	22:35	till my **a** could bend a bow of brass.
Ps	10:15	Break the **a** of the wicked
Ps	37:17	The **a** of the wicked will be broken;
Prv	31:17	with strength, and sturdy are her **a**.
Song	5:14	His **a** are rods of gold
Is	40:11	flock; in his **a** he gathers the lambs,
Dn	2:32	its chest and **a** were silver, its belly
Dn	10: 6	his **a** and feet looked like burnished
Hos	11: 3	to walk, who took them in my **a**;

ARMY → ARM
Ex	14:17	glory through Pharaoh and all his **a**,
Ex	15: 4	and **a** he hurled into the sea;
Jgs	8:12	throwing the entire **a** into panic.
Ps	27: 3	Though an **a** encamp against me,
Ps	33:16	A king is not saved by a mighty **a**,
Ez	38:15	a great horde and a mighty **a**?
Jl	2:11	at the head of his **a**; For immense
Rv	19:19	riding the horse and against his **a**.

ARNON
Nm	21:13	for the **A** forms Moab's boundary
Jos	12: 1	from the River **A** to Mount Hermon,
Jer	48:20	Publish it at the **A**, Moab is ruined!

AROMA
2 Cor	2:15	For we are the **a** of Christ for God

AROUND
Jos	6: 4	seventh day march **a** the city seven
Ps	3: 4	But you, Lord, are a shield **a** me;
Ps	48:13	Go about Zion, walk all **a** it,
Prv	3: 3	leave you; bind them **a** your neck;
Is	11: 5	Justice shall be the band **a** his waist,
Ez	1:18	their rims were full of eyes all **a**.
Ez	10:12	four wheels were full of eyes all **a**.
Lk	2: 9	the glory of the Lord shone **a** them,
Jn	13: 4	took a towel and tied it **a** his waist.
1 Pt	5: 8	the devil is prowling **a** like a roaring
Rv	4: 3	**A** the throne was a halo as brilliant
Rv	7:11	All the angels stood **a** the throne

AROUSED
Ez	38:18	the Lord God, my fury shall be **a**.

ARPAD
Is	36:19	are the gods of Hamath and **A**?
Jer	49:23	and **A** are covered with shame,

ARPHAXAD
Jdt	1: 1	that time **A** ruled over the Medes

ARRAYED
Jb	6: 4	the terrors of God are **a** against me.

ARREST → ARRESTED
Mt	21:46	they were attempting to **a** him,
Mk	14: 1	scribes were seeking a way to **a** him
Acts	12: 3	Jews he proceeded to **a** Peter also.

ARRESTED → ARREST
Mt	14: 3	Now Herod had **a** John,
Mt	26:50	they laid hands on Jesus and **a** him.

ARROGANCE → ARROGANT, ARROGANTLY
1 Sm	2: 3	nor let **a** issue from your mouths.
1 Mc	1:24	after he had spoken with great **a**
Prv	8:13	to hate evil;] Pride, **a**, the evil way,
Sir	10: 7	Odious to the Lord and to men is **a**,
Is	9: 8	those who say in **a** and pride

ARROGANT → ARROGANCE
Ps	73: 3	Because I was envious of the **a**
Ps	101: 5	Haughty eyes and **a** hearts I cannot
Prv	21:24	**A** is the name for the man
Dn	7:11	the first of the **a** words
Ti	1: 7	be blameless, not **a**, not irritable,

ARROGANTLY → ARROGANCE
Dn	7: 8	a man, and a mouth that spoke **a**.

ARROW → ARROWS
1 Sm	20:36	said to the boy, "Run and fetch the **a**."
2 Kgs	9:24	so that the **a** went through his heart
2 Kgs	13:17	exclaimed, "The Lord's **a** of victory!
Ps	91: 5	the night nor the **a** that flies by day,
Prv	25:18	a club, or a sword, or a sharp **a**,
Is	49: 2	He made me a polished **a**, in his
Jer	9: 7	A murderous **a** is his tongue,

ARROWS → ARROW
Ex	19:13	be stoned to death or killed with **a**.
Dt	32:42	I will make my **a** drunk with blood,
1 Sm	20:20	day of the month I will shoot **a**,
2 Kgs	13:15	"Take a bow and some **a**," Elisha said
Jb	6: 4	the **a** of the Almighty pierce me,
Ps	38: 3	Your **a** have sunk deep in me;
Ps	64: 4	ready their bows for **a** of poison
Ps	64: 8	But God will shoot **a** at them
Ps	127: 4	Like **a** in the hand of a warrior
Prv	26:18	scattering firebrands and deadly **a**
Eph	6:16	to quench all [the] flaming **a**

ART → ARTISAN, ARTISANS, ARTS
Acts	17:29	stone by human **a** and imagination.

ARTAXERXES → =AHASUERUS
1. King of Persia; allowed rebuilding of temple under Ezra (Ezr 4; 7), and of walls of Jerusalem under his cupbearer Nehemiah (Neh 2; 5:14; 13:6).
2. See Ahasuerus.

ARTEMIS
Acts	19:27	of the great goddess **A** will be of no

ARTISAN → ART
Hos	8: 6	The work of an **a**, no god at all,

ARTISANS → ART
Jer	10: 9	purple— all of them the work of **a**.
Hos	13: 2	all of them the work of **a**. "To these,"

ARTS → ART
Ex	7:11	did likewise by their magic **a**.
Ex	8:14	bring forth gnats by their magic **a**,

ASA
King of Judah (1 Kgs 15:8-24; 1 Chr 3:10; 2 Chr 14-16). Godly reformer (2 Chr 15); in later years defeated Israel with help of Aram, not the Lord (1 Kgs 15:16-22; 2 Chr 16).

ASAHEL
1. Nephew of David, one of his warriors (2 Sm 23:24; 1 Chr 2:16; 11:26; 27:7). Killed by Abner (2 Sm 2); avenged by Joab (2 Sm 3:22-39).
2. Levite; teacher (2 Chr 17:8).

ASAPH
1. Recorder to Hezekiah (2 Kgs 18:18, 37; Is 36:3, 22).
2. Levitical musician (1 Chr 6:24; 15:17-19; 16:4-7, 37), seer (2 Chr 29:30). Sons of (1 Chr 25; 2 Chr 5:12; 20:14; 29:13; 35:15; Ezr 2:41; 3:10; Neh 7:44; 11:17; 12:27-47). Psalms of (2 Chr 29:30; Ps 50; 73-83).

ASCEND → ASCENDED, ASCENDING, ASCENTS
Ps	139: 8	If I a to the heavens, you are there;
Is	14:14	I will a above the tops of the clouds;

ASCENDED → ASCEND
Jgs	13:20	the angel of the Lᴏʀᴅ a in the flame
Jn	20:17	for I have not yet a to the Father.
Eph	4: 8	"He a on high and took prisoners

ASCENDING → ASCEND
Jn	1:51	the angels of God a and descending
Jn	6:62	of Man a to where he was before?

ASCENTS → ASCEND
Songs of ascents (Ps 120-134).

ASH → ASHES
1 Sm	2: 8	from the a heap he lifts up the poor,
Ps	113: 7	dust, lifts the poor from the a heap,
Lam	4: 5	in purple now cling to the a heaps.

ASHAMED → SHAME
Ezr	9: 6	I am too a and confounded to raise
Is	29:22	Jacob shall have nothing to be a of,
Ez	43:10	[that they may be a of their sins],
Zec	13: 4	every prophet shall be a to prophesy
Mk	8:38	Whoever is a of me and of my
Mk	8:38	the Son of Man will be a
Rom	1:16	For I am not a of the gospel. It is
Rom	6:21	the things of which you are now a?
2 Tm	1: 8	So do not be a of your testimony
Heb	2:11	he is not a to call them "brothers,"
Heb	11:16	God is not a to be called their God,

ASHDOD
Jos	13: 3	lords of the Philistines in Gaza, A,
1 Sm	5: 1	transferred it from Ebenezer to A.

ASHER
Son of Jacob by Zilpah (Gn 30:13; 35:26; 46:17; Ex 1:4; 1 Chr 2:2). Tribe of blessed (Gn 49:20; Dt 33:24-25), numbered (Nm 1:40-41; 26:44-47), allotted land (Jos 10:24-31; Ez 48:2), failed to fully possess (Jgs 1:31-32), failed to support Deborah (Jgs 5:17), supported Gideon (Jgs 6:35; 7:23) and David (1 Chr 12:37), 12,000 from (Rv 7:6).

ASHERAH → ASHERAHS, ASTARTE
1 Kgs	18:19	four hundred prophets of A who eat
2 Chr	15:16	made an outrageous object for A;

ASHERAHS → ASHERAH
Jgs	3: 7	and serving the Baals and the A,

ASHES → ASH
Gn	18:27	Lord, though I am but dust and a!
1 Kgs	13: 5	the a from it were strewn
Jdt	4:11	with a strewn on their heads,
Est	4: 1	put on sackcloth and a, and walked
1 Mc	3:47	they sprinkled a on their heads
Jb	42: 6	have said, and repent in dust and a.
Ps	102:10	I eat a like bread, mingle my drink
Sir	17:27	while all men are dust and a.
Is	44:20	He is chasing—a thing that cannot save
Is	61: 3	a diadem instead of a, To give them
Jer	6:26	roll in the a. Mourn as for an only
Dn	9: 3	with fasting, sackcloth, and a.
Dn	14:14	his servants to bring some a,
Jon	3: 6	with sackcloth, and sat in the a.
Mt	11:21	have repented in sackcloth and a.

ASHIMA
2 Kgs	17:30	Nergal; the men of Hamath made A;

ASHKELON
Jgs	1:18	with its territory, A with its territory,
2 Sm	1:20	herald it not in the streets of A,
Zec	9: 5	A shall see it and be afraid;

ASHTAROTH → ASTARTE
Jgs	2:13	abandoned him and served Baal and the A,
1 Sm	7: 4	Israelites put away their Baals and A,
1 Sm	12:10	the Lᴏʀᴅ and worshiping Baals and A;

ASIA
Acts	2: 9	and Cappadocia, Pontus and A,
Acts	16: 6	the message in the province of A.
Rom	16: 5	who was the firstfruits in A
1 Cor	16:19	churches of A send you greetings.
Rv	1: 4	John, to the seven churches in A:

ASIDE → SIDE
Ex	32: 8	They have soon turned a
Dt	28:14	not turning a to the right

ASK → ASKED, ASKING, ASKS
Ex	3:13	if they a me, 'What is his name?'
Ex	12:26	When your children a you,
Dt	4:32	"A now of the days of old,
Dt	32: 7	A your father and he will inform
Dt	32: 7	a your elders and they will tell you:
Jos	4: 6	your children a you what these
Jgs	13:18	"Why do you a my name, which is
Ps	2: 8	Only a it of me, and I will make
Prv	30: 7	Two things I a of you, deny them
Is	7:11	A for a sign from the Lᴏʀᴅ,
Jer	6:16	earliest roads, a the pathways of old
Mt	6: 8	what you need before you a him.
Mt	7: 7	"A and it will be given to you;
Mk	6:23	"I will grant you whatever you a
Mk	11:24	tell you, all that you a for in prayer,
Lk	11:13	the holy Spirit to those who a him?"
Jn	14:14	If you a anything of me in my
Jn	15: 7	a for whatever you want and it will
Jn	16:24	a and you will receive, so that your
1 Cor	14:35	they should a their husbands
Eph	3:20	accomplish far more than all we a
Jas	1: 5	he should a God who gives to all
Jas	4: 3	You a but do not receive,
Jas	4: 3	because you a wrongly, to spend it
1 Jn	3:22	receive from him whatever we a,
1 Jn	5:14	if we a anything according to his

ASKED → ASK
Ps	21: 5	He a life of you; you gave it to him,
Ps	106:15	So he gave them what they a
Is	65: 1	to respond to those who a me not,
Jn	16:24	Until now you have not a anything
Jn	19:38	a Pilate if he could remove the body

ASKING → ASK
Mt	20:22	"You do not know what you are a.
Rom	10:20	to those who were not a for me."

ASKS → ASK
Lk	11:10	For everyone who a, receives;

ASLEEP → SLEEP
Jon	1: 5	hold of the ship, and lay there fast a.
Mt	8:24	swamped by waves; but he was a.
Mt	28:13	and stole him while we were a.'
Mk	14:37	When he returned he found them a.
Mk	14:37	He said to Peter, "Simon, are you a?
Jn	11:11	"Our friend Lazarus is a, but I am

ASS
Gn	16:12	He shall be a wild a of a man,
Nm	22:30	But the a said to Balaam, "Am I not
Dt	22:10	plow with an ox and an a harnessed
Jgs	15:15	Near him saw the fresh jawbone of an a;
Hos	8: 9	to Assyria— a wild a off on its own—
Zec	9: 9	Meek, and riding on an a, on a colt, the foal of an a.
Mt	21: 5	meek and riding on an a,

ASSEMBLE → ASSEMBLED, ASSEMBLY
Is	48:14	All of you a and listen: Who among
Jl	2:16	the congregation; A the elders,
Zep	3: 8	to a the kingdoms, In order to pour
Rv	16:14	of the whole world to a them

ASSEMBLED → ASSEMBLE
Nm	16:19	Korah had **a** all his band against
Rv	16:16	then **a** the kings in the place that is

ASSEMBLY → ASSEMBLE
Ex	12:16	first day you shall hold a sacred **a**,
2 Chr	29:28	The entire **a** prostrated itself,
Neh	8: 2	priest brought the law before the **a**,
Ps	149: 1	song, a hymn in the **a** of the faithful.
Jl	1:14	a fast, call an **a**; Gather the elders,
Jl	2:15	proclaim a fast, call an **a**;
Lk	23: 1	Then the whole **a** of them arose
Heb	12:23	and the **a** of the firstborn enrolled
Jas	2: 2	in fine clothes comes into your **a**,

ASSHUR
Gn	10:22	Elam, **A**, Arpachshad,

ASSIGN → ASSIGNED
Nm	4:19	go in and **a** to each of them his task
Ez	47:23	resident, there you shall **a** him his

ASSIGNED → ASSIGN
1 Cor	3: 5	just as the Lord **a** each one.
1 Cor	7:17	should live as the Lord has **a**, just as

ASSIST → ASSISTANCE
1 Tm	5:16	widowed relatives, she must **a** them;

ASSISTANCE → ASSIST
1 Cor	12:28	deeds; then gifts of healing, **a**,

ASSOCIATE → ASSOCIATED
Sir	37:12	Instead, **a** with a religious man,
Zec	13: 7	against the man who is my **a**,
Acts	10:28	for a Jewish man to **a** with, or visit,
Rom	12:16	not be haughty but **a** with the lowly;
1 Cor	5: 9	in my letter not to **a** with immoral
1 Cor	5:11	to you not to **a** with anyone named

ASSOCIATED → ASSOCIATE
Eph	5: 7	So do not be **a** with them.

ASSURED
Col	2: 2	richness of fully **a** understanding,
Col	4:12	and fully **a** in all the will of God.

ASSYRIA → ASSYRIAN, ASSYRIANS
2 Kgs	15:29	deporting the inhabitants to **A**.
2 Kgs	18:11	The king of **A** then deported the Israelites to **A**
2 Kgs	19:10	not be handed over to the king of **A**.
Is	10: 5	Woe to **A**! My rod in anger,
Is	36: 1	king of **A**, went on an expedition
Is	37:37	the king of **A**, broke camp and went
Jer	50:18	as once I punished the king of **A**;
Hos	14: 4	**A** will not save us, nor shall we
Na	3:18	shepherds slumber, O king of **A**,
Zec	10:10	and gather them from **A**. I will bring

ASSYRIAN → ASSYRIA
Jdt	2:14	generals and officers of the **A** army.

ASSYRIANS → ASSYRIA
Jdt	15: 6	swept down on the camp of the **A**,
Sir	48:21	God struck the camp of the **A**
Ez	23: 5	after her lovers, the **A**,

ASTARTE → ASHERAH, ASHTAROTH
1 Sm	31:10	put his armor in the temple of **A**,
1 Kgs	11: 5	By adoring **A**, the goddess

ASTONISHED
Lk	2:48	they were **a**, and his mother said

ASTOUNDED
Lk	24:22	from our group, however, have **a** us:
Acts	10:45	who had accompanied Peter were **a**

ASTRAY → STRAY
Nm	5:12	If a man's wife goes **a** and becomes
Dt	30:17	but are led **a** and adore and serve
Ps	14: 3	All have gone **a**; all alike are
Ps	58: 4	from the womb, they have gone **a**.
Ps	119:67	Before I was afflicted I went **a**,
Prv	10:17	he who disregards reproof goes **a**.
Prv	20: 1	none who goes **a** for it is wise.

Sir	31: 5	he who pursues wealth is led **a** by it.
Is	53: 6	We had all gone **a** like sheep,
Jer	23:13	by Baal and led my people Israel **a**.
Am	2: 4	fathers followed have led them **a**,
Mt	18:12	sheep and one of them goes **a**,
1 Pt	2:25	For you had gone **a** like sheep,
2 Pt	2:15	they have gone **a**,

ASUNDER
Ps	107:14	and gloom and broke their chains **a**.
Is	24:19	The earth will burst **a**, the earth will

ATE → EAT
Gn	3: 6	she took some of its fruit and **a** it;
Gn	3: 6	who was with her, and he **a** it.
Gn	3:13	serpent tricked me into it, so I **a** it."
Gn	27:25	Jacob served it to him, and Isaac **a**;
Gn	41: 4	the ugly, gaunt cows **a** up the seven
Ex	16:35	The Israelites **a** this manna for forty
Ex	16:35	they **a** manna until they reached
Nm	25: 2	and the people **a** of the sacrifices
Ru	2:14	some roasted grain and she **a** her fill
2 Sm	9:11	so Meribbaal **a** at David's table like
2 Kgs	6:29	So we boiled my son and **a** him.
Ps	78:25	All **a** a meal fit for heroes; food he
Ez	3: 3	I **a** it, and it was as sweet as honey
Dn	14:27	and when the dragon **a** them,
Mt	14:20	They all **a** and were satisfied.
Mt	15:37	They all **a** and were satisfied.
Mk	6:42	They all **a** and were satisfied.
Lk	9:17	They all **a** and were satisfied.
Jn	6:58	Unlike your ancestors who **a**
1 Cor	10: 3	All **a** the same spiritual food,

ATHALIAH
Granddaughter of Omri; wife of Jehoram and mother of Ahaziah; encouraged their evil ways (2 Kgs 8:18, 27; 2 Chr 22:2). At death of Ahaziah she made herself queen, killing all his sons but Joash (2 Kgs 11:1-3; 2 Chr 22:10-12); killed six years later when Joash revealed (2 Kgs 11:4-16; 2 Chr 23:1-15).

ATHENS
Acts	17:16	Paul was waiting for them in **A**,

ATHLETE
1 Cor	9:25	Every **a** exercises discipline
2 Tm	2: 5	an **a** cannot receive the winner's

ATONEMENT → ATONES
Ex	29:36	day as a sin offering, to make **a**.
Ex	29:36	purge the altar in making **a** for it;
Ex	30:10	a year Aaron shall perform the **a** rite
Ex	32:30	may be able to make **a** for your sin."
Lv	4:31	Thus the priest shall make **a**
Lv	5: 6	priest shall then make **a** for his sin.
Lv	5:18	then make **a** for the fault which was
Lv	5:26	the latter shall make **a** for him
Lv	23:28	because it is the Day of **A**, when **a** is
Nm	8:21	and made **a** for them to purify them.
Nm	35:33	land can have no **a** for the blood shed
1 Chr	6:34	of holies and of making **a** for Israel,
Neh	10:34	sin offerings to make **a** for Israel,
Sir	35: 3	LORD, and to avoid injustice is an **a**.

ATONES → ATONEMENT
Sir	3: 3	He who honors his father **a** for sins;

ATTACK → ATTACKED, ATTACKING, ATTACKS
1 Sm	15: 3	now, **a** Amalek, and deal with him
1 Sm	24: 8	would not permit them to **a** Saul.

ATTACKED → ATTACK
1 Mc	2:38	and soldiers **a** them on the sabbath,

ATTACKING → ATTACK
Ps	109: 3	surround me, **a** me without cause.

ATTACKS → ATTACK
1 Mc	2:41	fight against anyone who **a** us
Lk	11:22	when one stronger than he **a**

ATTAIN → ATTAINED
Prv	8:12	and judicious knowledge I **a**.
Phil	3:11	if somehow I may **a** the resurrection

ATTAINED →ATTAIN
Phil   3:16 with regard to what we have **a**,

ATTEMPTED
Heb 11:29 when the Egyptians **a** it they were

ATTENDANT
Lk   4:20 he handed it back to the **a** and sat

ATTENTION →ATTENTIVE
1 Tm 4: 1 faith by paying **a** to deceitful spirits
Ti   1:14 instead of paying **a** to Jewish myths
3 Jn 1:10 I will draw **a** to what he is doing,

ATTENTIVE →ATTENTION
2 Chr 6:40 and your ears **a** to the prayer of this
Neh   1:11 may your ear be **a** to my prayer
Ps 130: 2 May your ears be **a** to my cry
Prv   4:20 My son, to my words be **a**, to my
2 Pt 1:19 You will do well to be **a** to it,

ATTIRE
Jdt 10: 3 the festive **a** she had worn while her
Est D: 1 and arrayed herself in her royal **a**.

AUGUSTUS
Lk   2: 1 from Caesar **A** that the whole world

AUTHOR
Acts 3:15 The **a** of life you put to death,

AUTHORITIES →AUTHORITY
Lk 12:11 synagogues and before rulers and **a**,
Jn   7:26 Could the **a** have realized that he is
Jn 12:42 even among the **a**, believed in him,
Acts 16:19 the public square before the local **a**.
Rom 13: 1 be subordinate to the higher **a**,
Rom 13: 6 for the **a** are ministers of God,
Eph   3:10 principalities and **a** in the heavens.
Ti   3: 1 the control of magistrates and **a**,
1 Pt 3:22 with angels, **a**, and powers subject

AUTHORITY →AUTHORITIES
Mt   7:29 for he taught them as one having **a**,
Mt   9: 6 the Son of Man has **a** on earth
Mk   1:27 is this? A new teaching with **a**.
Mk 11:28 what **a** are you doing these things?
Mk 11:28 Or who gave you this **a** to do them?"
Lk   4:32 teaching because he spoke with **a**.
Lk   5:24 the Son of Man has **a** on earth
Lk   7: 8 For I too am a person subject to **a**,
Acts 1: 7 Father has established by his own **a**.
Rom 13: 1 for there is no **a** except from God,
Rom 13: 2 whoever resists **a** opposes what God
1 Cor 7: 4 wife does not have **a** over her own
1 Cor 7: 4 does not have **a** over his own body,
1 Cor 11:10 a woman should have a sign of **a**
1 Cor 15:24 sovereignty and every **a** and power.
2 Cor 10: 8 boast a little too much of our **a**,
Eph   1:21 far above every principality, **a**,
1 Tm 2:12 to teach or to have **a** over a man.
Ti   2:15 Exhort and correct with all **a**. Let no
Rv   2:26 end, I will give **a** over the nations.
Rv 12:10 and the **a** of his Anointed.
Rv 13: 4 the dragon because it gave its **a**

AUTUMN
Jude 1:12 fruitless trees in late **a**, twice dead

AVENGE →VENGEANCE
Nm 31: 2 "**A** the Israelites on the Midianites,
Jgs 16:28 for my two eyes I may **a** myself
2 Kgs 9: 7 master; thus will I **a** the blood of my
1 Mc 2:67 and you shall **a** the wrongs of your
Jl   4:21 I will **a** their blood, and not leave it
Rv   6:10 **a** our blood on the inhabitants

AVENGED →VENGEANCE
Gn   4:24 If Cain is **a** sevenfold, then Lamech
Rv 19: 2 He has **a** on her the blood of his

AVENGER →VENGEANCE
Nm 35:12 of asylum from the **a** of blood,
Jos 20: 3 flee for asylum from the **a** of blood.
Ps   8: 3 your foes, to silence enemy and **a**.

1 Thes 4: 6 the Lord is an **a** in all these things,

AVENGES →VENGEANCE
Dt 32:43 For he **a** the blood of his servants

AVENGING →VENGEANCE
1 Sm 25:33 blood and from **a** myself personally.
Na   1: 2 A jealous and **a** God is the LORD,

AVERTED
Jdt 13:20 and you **a** our disaster,

AVOID →AVOIDS
1 Tm 6:20 to you. **A** profane babbling
2 Tm 2:16 **A** profane, idle talk, for such people
Ti   3: 9 **A** foolish arguments, genealogies,

AVOIDS →AVOID
Prv 16: 6 by the fear of the LORD man **a** evil.
Prv 16:17 path of the upright **a** misfortune;

AWAKE →AWAKEN, AWAKENED, AWOKE
Jgs   5:12 **A, a**, Deborah! **a, a**,
Ps 44:24 **A**! Why do you sleep, O Lord?
Ps 57: 9 **A**, my soul; **a**, lyre and harp! I will
Is   51: 9 **A, a**, put on strength, O arm
Is   52: 1 **A, a**! Put on your strength, O Zion;
Dn 12: 2 sleep in the dust of the earth shall **a**;
Zec 13: 7 **A**, O sword, against my shepherd,
Mt 24:42 Therefore, stay **a**! For you do not
Eph   5:14 Therefore, it says: "**A**, O sleeper,
1 Thes 5:10 so that whether we are **a** or asleep

AWAKEN →AWAKE
Jn 11:11 is asleep, but I am going to **a** him."

AWAKENED →AWAKE
1 Kgs 18:27 Perhaps he is asleep and must be **a**."
Song 8: 5 Under the apple tree I **a** you;

AWARE
Mk   5:30 **a** at once that power had gone

AWAY
Nm 22:33 she turned **a** from me these three
1 Sm 7: 4 So the Israelites put **a** their Baals
Jb   1:21 LORD gave and the LORD has taken **a**;
Prv   3: 7 fear the LORD and turn **a** from evil;
Eccl 3: 6 a time to keep, and a time to cast **a**.
Jon 1: 3 to flee to Tarshish **a** from the LORD.
Zep 1: 2 I will completely sweep **a** all things
Zep 3:15 he has turned **a** your enemies;
Hg   1: 9 what you brought home, I blew **a**.
Mt   4:10 this, Jesus said to him, "Get **a**, Satan!
Mk 13:31 Heaven and earth will pass **a**, but my words will
          not pass **a**.
Lk   8:13 for a time and fall **a** in time of trial.
Lk 24: 2 They found the stone rolled **a**
Jn   1:29 who takes **a** the sin of the world.
Jn 14:28 'I am going **a** and I will come back
1 Cor 7:31 in its present form is passing **a**.
2 Cor 5:17 the old things have passed **a**;
Heb   2: 1 so that we may not be carried **a**.
Heb   6: 6 and then have fallen **a**, to bring
2 Pt 3:10 then the heavens will pass **a**
1 Jn 2: 8 for the darkness is passing **a**,
1 Jn 2:17 and its enticement are passing **a**.
Rv   7:17 and God will wipe **a** every tear
Rv 21: 1 and the former earth had passed **a**,

AWE →AWESOME
1 Kgs 3:28 had given, they were in **a** of him,
Is   29:23 and be in **a** of the God of Israel.
Mal   2: 5 me, and stood in **a** of my name.
Mt   9: 8 saw this they were struck with **a**
Lk   5:26 and, struck with **a**, they said,
Acts 2:43 **A** came upon everyone, and many
Rom 11:20 not become haughty, but stand in **a**.
Heb 12:28 pleasing to God in reverence and **a**.

AWESOME →AWE
Gn 28:17 he cried out: "How **a** is this shrine!
Dt   7:21 in your midst, is a great and **a** God.
Dt 10:17 mighty and **a**, who has no favorites,

Dt	28:58	the glorious and **a** name of the LORD,
Neh	1: 5	great and **a** God, you who preserve
Neh	9:32	and **a** God, you who in your mercy
Jb	37:22	surrounding God's **a** majesty!
Ps	65: 6	You answer us with **a** deeds
Ps	66: 3	Say to God: "How **a** your deeds!
Ps	66: 5	of God, **a** in the deeds done for us.
Ps	68:36	**A** is God in his holy place, the God
Ps	76: 8	So terrible and **a** are you; who can
Ps	76:12	all present bring gifts to this **a** God,
Ps	89: 8	and more **a** than all who sit there!
Ps	99: 3	them praise your great and **a** name:
Ps	111: 9	forever; holy and **a** is your name.
Is	64: 2	While you wrought **a** deeds we
Dn	9: 4	great and **a** God, you who keep your

AWL
Ex	21: 6	he shall pierce his ear with an **a**,
Dt	15:17	you shall take an **a** and thrust it

AWOKE → AWAKE
1 Kgs	3:15	When Solomon **a** from his dream,
Ps	78:65	Then the Lord **a** as from sleep,
Mt	1:24	When Joseph **a**, he did as the angel

AXE
Is	10:15	Will the **a** boast against him who hews
Mt	3:10	Even now the **a** lies at the root

AZARIAH → =ABEDNEGO, =UZZIAH
1. King of Judah; see Uzziah (2 Kgs 15:1-7).
2. Prophet (2 Chr 15:1-8).
3. Opponent of Jeremiah (Jer 43:2).
4. Jewish exile; see Abednego (Dn 1:6-19).

AZAZEL
Lv	16: 8	one is for the LORD and which for **A**.

AZEKAH
Jos	10:10	harassing them as far as **A**

B

BAAL → BAALS
Nm	25: 3	submitted to the rites of **B** of Peor,
Dt	4: 3	that followed the **B** of Peor;
Jgs	2:13	him and served **B** and the Ashtaroth,
Jgs	8:33	making **B** of Berith their god
1 Kgs	16:32	Ahab erected an altar to **B** in the temple of **B**
		which he built
1 Kgs	18:25	Elijah then said to the prophets of **B**,
1 Kgs	19:18	those who have not knelt to **B**
2 Kgs	3: 2	He did away with the pillar of **B**,
2 Kgs	10:28	out the worship of **B** from Israel.
2 Chr	23:17	the people went to the temple of **B**
Ps	106:28	joined in the rites of **B** of Peor,
Jer	2: 8	The prophets prophesied by **B**,
Jer	19: 5	their sons in fire as holocausts to **B**:
Hos	2:18	"My husband," and never again "My **b**."
Hos	13: 1	but he sinned through **B** and died.
Rom	11: 4	men who have not knelt to **B**."

BAALS → BAAL
Jgs	3: 7	and serving the **B** and the Asherahs,
Jgs	10:10	our God and have served the **B**."
1 Sm	7: 4	So the Israelites put away their **B**
2 Chr	17: 3	and he did not consult the **B**.
2 Chr	34: 4	the altars of the **B** were destroyed;
Hos	2:19	from her mouth the names of the **B**,

BAALZEBUB
2 Kgs	1: 2	inquire of **B**, the god of Ekron,

BAASHA
King of Israel (1 Kgs 15:16-16:7; 2 Chr 16:1-6).

BABBLER
Prv	20:19	so have nothing to do with a **b**!

BABEL → BABYLON
Gn	11: 9	That is why it was called **B**,

BABES
Ps	8: 3	Out of the mouths of **b** and infants

BABYLON → BABEL, BABYLONIANS
2 Kgs	24:15	He deported Jehoiachin to **B**,
1 Chr	9: 1	in captivity to **B** because of its
2 Chr	36:18	princes, all these he brought to **B**.
2 Chr	36:20	the sword he carried captive to **B**,
Ezr	7: 6	this Ezra came up from **B**.
Ps	137: 1	By the rivers of **B** we sat mourning
Ps	137: 8	Fair **B**, you destroyer, happy those
Is	13: 1	An oracle concerning **B**; a vision
Is	14: 4	taunt-song against the king of **B**:
Is	21: 9	says, 'Fallen, fallen is **B**, And all
Is	47: 1	dust, O virgin daughter **B**;
Jer	25:11	shall be enslaved to the king of **B**:
Jer	50: 1	which the LORD spoke against **B**,
Jer	51:37	**B** shall become a heap of ruins,
Jer	52:11	had him brought to **B** and kept
Bar	2:24	or serve the king of **B**, and you
Bar	6: 1	you are being led captive to **B**
Dn	2:48	ruler of the whole province of **B**
Dn	2:48	prefect over all the wise men of **B**.
Dn	14:36	he set him down in **B** above the den.
1 Pt	5:13	chosen one at **B** sends you greeting,
Rv	14: 8	"Fallen, fallen is **B** the great,
Rv	17: 5	which is a mystery, "**B** the great,
Rv	18: 2	"Fallen, fallen is **B** the great. She has

BABYLONIANS → BABYLON
Dn	14: 3	The **B** had an idol called Bel,

BACCHIDES
1 Mc	7: 8	Then the king chose **B**,
1 Mc	9:11	the army of **B** moved out of camp

BACK → BACKS
Gn	8:11	the evening the dove came **b** to him,
Gn	19:26	But Lot's wife looked **b**, and she was
Ru	1:11	"Go **b**, my daughters!" said Naomi.
2 Sm	12:23	Can I bring him **b** again? I shall go
Ps	114: 5	you fled? Jordan, that you turned **b**?
Ps	137: 7	happy those who pay you **b** the evil
Is	38: 8	So the sun came **b** the ten steps it
Is	38:17	When you cast behind your **b** all my
Is	49: 5	That Jacob may be brought **b** to him
Is	55:12	in peace you shall be brought **b**;
Jer	29:14	bring you **b** to the place
Mt	28: 2	approached, rolled **b** the stone,
Heb	10:39	are not among those who draw **b**

BACKS → BACK
Neh	9:26	they cast your law behind their **b**,
Prv	19:29	and blows for the **b** of fools.

BAD → WORSE
Gn	37: 2	he brought his father **b** reports
Prv	20:14	"**B**, **b**!" says the buyer; but once he
Jer	24: 2	other basket contained very **b** figs, so **b** they could
		not be eaten.
Mt	7:17	fruit, and a rotten tree bears **b** fruit.
1 Cor	15:33	"**B** company corrupts good morals."

BAG → BAGGAGE, BAGS
1 Sm	17:49	David put his hand into the **b**
Hg	1: 6	earned them for a **b** with holes in it.
Lk	10: 4	Carry no money **b**, no sack,

BAGGAGE → BAG
1 Sm	10:22	answered, "He is hiding among the **b**."
Ez	12: 7	I brought out my **b** as though it were

BAGS → BAG
Mi	6:11	balances, **b** of false weights?

BAKE → BAKED, BAKER
Ex	16:23	You may either **b** or boil the manna,

BAKED → BAKE
Ex	12:39	they **b** it into unleavened loaves.
Lv	2: 4	the cereal offering you present is **b**

BAKER → BAKE
Gn	40: 1	and **b** gave offense to their lord,

BALAAM
Prophet who attempted to curse Israel (Nm 22-24; Dt 23:5-6; 2 Pt

2:15; Jude 11; Rv 2:14). Killed in Israel's vengeance on Midianites (Nm 31:8; Jos 13:22).

BALAK
Moabite king who hired Balaam to curse Israel (Nm 22-24; Jos 24:9; Mi 6:5).

BALANCE
Prv	16:11	**B** and scales belong to the LORD;
Sir	6:15	price, no sum can **b** his worth.
Sir	28:25	and gold, so **b** and weigh your words.
Is	40:12	in scales and the hills in a **b**?

BALDHEAD →HEAD
2 Kgs	2:23	"Go up, **b**," they shouted, "go up, **b**!"

BALL
Is	22:18	roll you up and toss you like a **b**

BALM
Jer	8:22	Is there no **b** in Gilead, no physician
Jer	46:11	Go up to Gilead, and take **b**,

BAND →BANDS
1 Sm	10: 5	city, you will meet a **b** of prophets,

BANDAGE →BANDAGED
1 Kgs	20:38	himself with a **b** over his eyes.

BANDAGED →BANDAGE
Lk	10:34	wine over his wounds and **b** them.

BANDITS
Hos	7: 1	thieves break in, **b** plunder abroad.

BANDS →BAND
Hos	11: 4	with human cords, with **b** of love;

BANK →BANKS
Gn	41:17	I was standing on the **b** of the Nile,
Ex	2: 3	it among the reeds on the river **b**.
Ex	7:15	and present yourself by the river **b**,
2 Kgs	2:13	and stood at the **b** of the Jordan.
Mt	25:27	not then have put my money in the **b**
Mk	5:13	two thousand rushed down a steep **b**

BANKS →BANK
Jos	3:15	overflows all its **b** during the entire
1 Chr	12:16	it was overflowing both its **b**
Ez	47:12	Along both **b** of the river, fruit trees

BANNERS
Ps	20: 6	raise the **b** in the name of our God.

BANQUET →BANQUETS
Jdt	12:10	the fourth day Holofernes gave a **b**
Est	5: 5	to the **b** Esther had prepared.
Est	6:14	off to the **b** Esther had prepared.
Song	2: 4	He brings me into the **b** hall
Lk	5:29	Levi gave a great **b** for him in his
Lk	14:13	when you hold a **b**, invite the poor,

BANQUETS →BANQUET
Mk	12:39	and places of honor at **b**.

BAPTISM →BAPTIZE
Mt	3: 7	and Sadducees coming to his **b**,
Mt	21:25	Where was John's **b** from? Was it
Mk	1: 4	in the desert proclaiming a **b**
Mk	10:38	be baptized with the **b** with which I
Mk	10:39	and with the **b** with which I am
Mk	11:30	Was John's **b** of heavenly
Lk	3: 3	proclaiming a **b** of repentance
Lk	7:29	were baptized with the **b** of John,
Lk	12:50	There is a **b** with which I must be
Lk	20: 4	was John's **b** of heavenly
Acts	1:22	from the **b** of John until the day
Acts	10:37	after the **b** that John preached,
Acts	13:24	by proclaiming a **b** of repentance
Acts	18:25	although he knew only the **b**
Acts	19: 3	They replied, "With the **b** of John."
Acts	19: 4	baptized with a **b** of repentance,
Rom	6: 4	with him through **b** into death,
Eph	4: 5	one Lord, one faith, one **b**;
Col	2:12	You were buried with him in **b**,
1 Pt	3:21	This prefigured **b**, which saves you

BAPTISMS →BAPTIZE
Heb	6: 2	instruction about **b** and laying

BAPTIST →BAPTIZE
Mt	3: 1	In those days John the **B** appeared,
Mt	11:11	been none greater than John the **B**;
Mt	14: 8	on a platter the head of John the **B**."
Mt	16:14	"Some say John the **B**, others Elijah,

BAPTIZE →BAPTISM, BAPTISMS, BAPTIST, BAPTIZED, BAPTIZING
Mt	3:11	He will **b** you with the holy Spirit
Mk	1: 8	he will **b** you with the holy Spirit."
Lk	3:16	He will **b** you with the holy Spirit
Jn	1:26	John answered them, "I **b** with water;
Jn	1:33	the one who sent me to **b** with water
1 Cor	1:17	For Christ did not send me to **b**

BAPTIZED →BAPTIZE
Mt	3: 6	were being **b** by him in the Jordan
Mt	3:13	to John at the Jordan to be **b** by him.
Mt	3:14	"I need to be **b** by you, and yet you
Mt	3:16	After Jesus was **b**, he came
Mk	1: 5	were being **b** by him in the Jordan
Mk	1: 8	I have **b** you with water; he will
Mk	1: 9	and was **b** in the Jordan by John.
Mk	10:38	be **b** with the baptism with which I am **b**?"
Mk	10:39	with the baptism with which I am **b**, you will be **b**;
Mk	16:16	believes and is **b** will be saved;
Lk	3: 7	who came out to be **b** by him,
Lk	3:12	Even tax collectors came to be **b**
Lk	3:21	After all the people had been **b**
Lk	3:21	also had been **b** and was praying,
Lk	7:29	and who were **b** with the baptism
Lk	7:30	of the law, who were not **b** by him,
Lk	12:50	is a baptism with which I must be **b**,
Jn	3:23	there, and people came to be **b**,
Acts	1: 5	for John **b** with water, but in a few
Acts	2:38	"Repent and be **b**, every one of you,
Acts	2:41	who accepted his message were **b**,
Acts	8:12	men and women alike were **b**.
Acts	8:13	after being **b**, became devoted
Acts	8:16	they had only been **b** in the name
Acts	8:36	What is to prevent my being **b**?"
Acts	8:38	down into the water, and he **b** him.
Acts	9:18	his sight. He got up and was **b**,
Acts	10:48	He ordered them to be **b** in the name
Acts	11:16	'John **b** with water but you will be **b**
Acts	16:15	she and her household had been **b**,
Acts	16:33	he and all his family were **b** at once.
Acts	18: 8	who heard believed and were **b**.
Acts	19: 3	He said, "How were you **b**?"
Acts	19: 4	then said, "John **b** with a baptism
Acts	19: 5	they were **b** in the name of the Lord
Acts	22:16	and have yourself **b** and your sins
Rom	6: 3	we who were **b** into Christ Jesus were **b** into his death?
1 Cor	1:13	Or were you **b** in the name of Paul?
1 Cor	1:14	[to God] that I **b** none of you except
1 Cor	1:15	no one can say you were **b** in my
1 Cor	1:16	(I **b** the household of Stephanas
1 Cor	1:16	not know whether I **b** anyone else.)
1 Cor	10: 2	all of them were **b** into Moses
1 Cor	12:13	in one Spirit we were all **b** into one
1 Cor	15:29	having themselves **b** for the dead?
Gal	3:27	of you who were **b** into Christ have

BAPTIZING →BAPTIZE
Mt	28:19	**b** them in the name of the Father,
Jn	1:28	the Jordan, where John was **b**.
Jn	1:31	the reason why I came **b** with water
Jn	3:23	was also **b** in Aenon near Salim,
Jn	3:26	here he is **b** and everyone is coming
Jn	4: 1	and **b** more disciples than John
Acts	10:47	the water for **b** these people,

BAR →BARS
Jgs	16: 3	and tore them loose, **b** and all.
Neh	7: 3	they shall shut and **b** the doors.

BAR-JESUS →=ELYMAS
Acts	13: 6	met a magician named **B** who was

BARABBAS
Prisoner released by Pilate instead of Jesus (Mt 27:16-26; Mk 15:7-15; Lk 23:18-19; Jn 18:40).

BARAK
Judge who fought with Deborah against Canaanites (Jgs 4-5; 1 Sm 12:11; Heb 11:32).

BARBARIAN
2 Mc	2:21	land, put to flight the **b** hordes,
Col	3:11	circumcision and uncircumcision, **b**,

BARBS
Nm	33:55	to remain will become as **b** in your

BARE →BARED, BAREFOOT
Ps	18:16	the world's foundations lay **b**,

BARED →BARE
Is	52:10	The Lord has **b** his holy arm
Ez	4: 7	**b** arm you shall prophesy against it.

BAREFOOT →BARE, FOOT
Is	20: 3	naked and **b** for three years as a sign
Mi	1: 8	I lament and wail, I go **b** and naked;

BARGAINED
Hos	8: 9	off on its own— Ephraim **b** for lovers.

BARLEY
Ex	9:31	Now the flax and the **b** were ruined,
Ru	1:22	at the beginning of the **b** harvest.
2 Kgs	7: 1	and two seahs of **b** for a shekel,
Jdt	8: 2	had died at the time of the **b** harvest.
Jn	6: 9	is a boy here who has five **b** loaves
Rv	6: 6	three rations of **b** cost a day's pay.

BARN →BARNS
Mt	13:30	but gather the wheat into my **b**." ' "
Lk	12:24	they have neither storehouse nor **b**,

BARNABAS →=JOSEPH
Disciple, originally Joseph (Acts 4:36), prophet (Acts 13:1), apostle (Acts 14:14). Brought Paul to apostles (Acts 9:27), Antioch (Acts 11:22-29; Gal 2:1-13), on the first missionary journey (Acts 13-14). Together at Jerusalem Council, they separated over John Mark (Acts 15). Later co-workers (1 Cor 9:6; Col 4:10).

BARNS →BARN
Dt	28: 8	upon you, on your **b** and on all your
Ps	144:13	May our **b** be full with every kind
Prv	3:10	will your **b** be filled with grain,
Mt	6:26	they gather nothing into **b**, yet your
Lk	12:18	do: I shall tear down my **b** and build

BARREN
Gn	11:30	Sarai was **b**; she had no child.
Gn	29:31	fruitful, while Rachel remained **b**.
Ex	23:26	no woman in your land will be **b**
Jgs	13: 2	His wife was **b** and had borne no
1 Sm	2: 5	The **b** wife bears seven sons,
Prv	30:16	The nether world, and the **b** womb;
Is	49:21	I was bereft and **b**
Is	54: 1	cry, you **b** one who did not bear,
Lk	1: 7	because Elizabeth was **b** and both
Lk	23:29	'Blessed are the **b**, the wombs

BARS →BAR
Ex	26:26	Also make **b** of acacia wood:
Nm	3:36	of the Dwelling, its **b**, columns,
Ps	147:13	Who has strengthened the **b** of your
Lam	2: 9	he has removed and broken her **b**.

BARSABBAS →=JOSEPH, =JUDAS, =JUSTUS
Acts	1:23	two, Joseph called **B**, who was
Acts	15:22	Judas, who was called **B**, and Silas,

BARTHOLOMEW →=NATHANAEL?
Apostle (Mt 10:3; Mk 3:18; Lk 6:14; Acts 1:13). Possibly also called Nathanael (Jn 1:45-49; 21:2).

BARTIMAEUS
Blind man healed by Jesus (Mk 10:46-52).

BARUCH
Jeremiah's secretary (Jer 32:12-16; 36; 43:1-6; 45:1-2). Book of Baruch ascribed to him (Bar 1:1, 3, 8).

BARZILLAI
1. Gileadite who aided David during Absalom's revolt (2 Sm 17:27; 19:31-39).
2. Son-in-law of 1. (Ezr 2:61; Neh 7:63).

BASE →BASED
Ex	29:12	shall pour out at the **b** of the altar.
2 Kgs	18:19	On what do you **b** this confidence

BASED →BASE
Phil	3: 9	of my own **b** on the law

BASHAN
Nm	21:33	king of **B**, advanced against them
Jos	13:30	Og, king of **B**, and all the villages
Jos	22: 7	Moses had assigned land in **B**;
Ps	22:13	fierce bulls of **B** encircle me.
Am	4: 1	you cows of **B**, You who oppress
Mi	7:14	Let them feed in **B** and Gilead,
Zec	11: 2	Wail, you oaks of **B**,

BASIC
Heb	5:12	teach you again the **b** elements
Heb	6: 1	let us leave behind the **b** teaching

BASIN →BASINS
Jn	13: 5	he poured water into a **b** and began

BASINS →BASIN
1 Kgs	7:38	Ten bronze **b** were then made,

BASKET →BASKETS
Ex	2: 3	she took a papyrus **b**, daubed it
Jer	24: 2	One **b** contained excellent figs,
Jer	24: 2	the other **b** contained very bad figs,
Am	8: 1	God showed me: a **b** of ripe fruit.
Mt	5:15	and then put it under a bushel **b**; it is
Acts	9:25	in the wall, lowering him in a **b**.
2 Cor	11:33	lowered in a **b** through a window

BASKETS →BASKET
Mk	6:43	up twelve wicker **b** full of fragments
Mk	8: 8	up the fragments left over—seven **b**.
Mk	8:19	how many wicker **b** full

BATCH
Rom	11:16	are holy, so is the whole **b** of dough;
1 Cor	5: 7	you may become a fresh **b** of dough,
Gal	5: 9	A little yeast leavens the whole **b**

BATHE →BATHED, BATHING
Ex	2: 5	came down to the river to **b**,
Ps	58:11	and **b** their feet in the blood
Dn	13:15	She decided to **b**, for the weather
Lk	7:38	began to **b** his feet with her tears.

BATHED →BATHE
Song	5: 3	I then to put it on? I have **b** my feet,
Ez	16: 9	Then I **b** you with water,
Jn	13:10	"Whoever has **b** has no need except

BATHING →BATHE
2 Sm	11: 2	From the roof he saw a woman **b**,
Jdt	12: 8	After **b**, she besought the Lord,

BATHSHEBA
Wife of Uriah who committed adultery with and became wife of David (2 Sm 11; Ps 51), mother of Solomon (2 Sm 12:24; 1 Kgs 1-2; 1 Chr 3:5).

BATTLE →BATTLES
Ex	13:18	In **b** array the Israelites marched
Jos	4:13	for **b** passed over before the Lord
1 Sm	17:47	For the **b** is the Lord's, and he shall
1 Sm	31: 3	The **b** raged around Saul,
2 Sm	1:25	in the thick of the **b**, slain upon your
1 Kgs	22:30	"I will disguise myself and go into **b**,
2 Chr	20:15	for the **b** is not yours but God's.
Ps	24: 8	warrior, the Lord, mighty in **b**.
Eccl	9:11	the swift, nor the **b** by the valiant,
1 Cor	14: 8	sound, who will get ready for **b**?
Rv	16:14	them for the **b** on the great day
Rv	20: 8	and Magog, to gather them for **b**;

BATTLES →BATTLE
1 Sm	8:20	to lead us in warfare and fight our **b**."

1 Sm 18:17 and fight the **b** of the LORD."
1 Sm 25:28 your lordship is fighting the **b**
2 Chr 32: 8 God, to help us and to fight our **b**."

BEAM
Ezr 6:11 a **b** is to be taken from his house,

BEAR → ARMOR-BEARER, BEARING, BEARS, BIRTH,
BIRTHDAY, BIRTHRIGHT, BORE, BORN, BORNE,
CHILDBEARING, CUPBEARER, FIRSTBORN, NEWBORN,
REBIRTH, STILLBORN
Gn 4:13 "My punishment is too great to **b**.
Gn 17:19 your wife Sarah is to **b** you a son,
Ex 28:12 Thus Aaron shall **b** their names
Jgs 13: 3 yet you will conceive and **b** a son.
1 Sm 17:36 has killed both a lion and a **b**,
Jb 9: 9 He made the **B** and Orion,
Is 7:14 and **b** a son, and shall name him
Is 11: 7 cow and the **b** shall be neighbors,
Is 53:11 many, and their guilt he shall **b**.
Jer 30: 6 see: since when do men **b** children?
Ez 47:12 Every month they shall **b** fresh fruit,
Dn 7: 5 The second was like a **b**; it was
Am 5:19 and a **b** should meet him; Or as
Mt 1:23 shall be with child and **b** a son,
Mt 7:18 A good tree cannot **b** bad fruit,
Mt 7:18 nor can a rotten tree **b** good fruit.
Lk 1:13 wife Elizabeth will **b** you a son,
Jn 15: 2 branch in me that does not **b** fruit,
Jn 15: 8 that you **b** much fruit and become
Jn 15:16 to go and **b** fruit that will remain,
Acts 15:10 nor we have been able to **b**?
Rom 7: 4 order that we might **b** fruit for God.
1 Cor 15:49 **b** the image of the heavenly one.
Gal 6: 2 **B** one another's burdens, and so you

BEARD → BEARDS
Ezr 9: 3 plucked hair from my head and **b**,
Is 50: 6 cheeks to those who plucked my **b**;
Jer 48:37 been made bald, every **b** shaved;

BEARDS → BEARD
2 Sm 10: 4 after shaving off half their **b**

BEARING → BEAR
Eph 4: 2 **b** with one another through love,
Col 1: 6 as in the whole world it is **b** fruit
Col 1:10 in every good work **b** fruit
Col 3:13 **b** with one another and forgiving

BEARS → BEAR
Dn 9:18 and the city which **b** your name.
1 Cor 13: 7 It **b** all things, believes all things,

BEAST → BEASTS
Is 35: 9 nor **b** of prey go up to be met
Dn 7: 6 this I looked and saw another **b**,
Dn 7: 6 To this **b** dominion was given.
Rv 11: 7 the **b** that comes up from the abyss
Rv 13: 1 I saw a **b** come out of the sea
Rv 13: 2 The **b** I saw was like a leopard,
Rv 13:11 I saw another **b** come
Rv 13:18 can calculate the number of the **b**,
Rv 16: 2 on those who had the mark of the **b**
Rv 17: 3 on a scarlet **b** that was covered
Rv 19:20 The **b** was caught and with it
Rv 19:20 who had accepted the mark of the **b**
Rv 20: 4 who had not worshiped the **b** or its

BEASTS → BEAST
Dn 7: 3 which emerged four immense **b**,
Mk 1:13 He was among wild **b**,

BEAT → BEATEN, BEATING, BEATINGS
Prv 23:35 me not; they **b** me, but I felt it not;
Is 2: 4 They shall **b** their swords
Jl 4:10 **B** your plowshares into swords,
Mi 4: 3 They shall **b** their swords
Lk 10:30 They stripped and **b** him and went
Acts 22:19 and **b** those who believed in you.

BEATEN → BEAT
Ex 5:16 Look how your servants are **b**! It is

Acts 16:22 and ordered them to be **b** with rods.
2 Cor 11:25 Three times I was **b** with rods,
1 Pt 2:20 if you are patient when **b** for doing

BEATING → BEAT
Lk 22:63 custody were ridiculing and **b** him.

BEATINGS → BEAT
2 Cor 6: 5 **b**, imprisonments, riots, labors,

BEAUTIFUL → BEAUTY
Gn 12:11 "I know well how **b** a woman you
Gn 12:14 Egyptians saw how **b** the woman
Gn 29:17 but Rachel was well formed and **b**.
Jos 7:21 I saw a **b** Babylonian mantle,
2 Sm 11: 2 a woman bathing, who was very **b**.
2 Sm 13: 1 son Absalom had a **b** sister named
2 Sm 14:27 named Tamar, who was a **b** woman.
1 Kgs 1: 3 for a **b** girl throughout the territory
1 Kgs 1: 4 who was very **b**, nursed the king
Tb 6:12 is sensible, courageous, and very **b**;
Jdt 10: 4 Thus she made herself very **b**,
Jdt 10:14 appeared wondrously **b** to them,
Jdt 11:21 of the world to the other looks so **b**
Est 2: 2 "Let **b** young virgins be sought
Est 2: 3 bring together all **b** young virgins
2 Mc 3:26 strikingly **b**, and splendidly attired,
Jb 42:15 women were as **b** as the daughters
Prv 11:22 is a **b** woman with a rebellious
Song 1:15 Ah, you are **b**, my beloved, ah,
Song 1:16 Ah, you are **b**, my lover— yes,
Song 4: 1 Ah, you are **b**, my beloved, ah,
Song 6: 4 You are as **b** as Tirzah,
Is 52: 7 How **b** upon the mountains
Jer 3:19 land, a heritage most **b** among
Ez 16:13 You were exceedingly **b**,
Ez 31: 7 It became **b** and stately in its spread
Ez 31: 9 I made it **b**, with much foliage,
Dn 13: 2 who married a very **b**
Dn 13:31 Susanna, very delicate and **b**,
Mt 23:27 which appear **b** on the outside,
Acts 3: 2 temple called "the **B** Gate" every day
Acts 3:10 to sit begging at the **B** Gate
Acts 7:20 was born, and he was extremely **b**.
Rom 10:15 "How **b** are the feet of those who
Heb 11:23 they saw that he was a **b** child,

BEAUTY → BEAUTIFUL
2 Sm 14:25 so be praised for his **b** as Absalom,
Jdt 10: 7 were very much astounded at her **b**
Jdt 10:19 They marveled at her **b**,
Jdt 10:23 all marveled at the **b** of her face.
Jdt 16: 6 the **b** of her countenance disabled
Jdt 16: 9 and her **b** captivated his mind.
Est 1:11 that he might display her **b**
Est D: 5 glowed with the perfection of her **b**
1 Mc 1:26 the **b** of the women was disfigured.
1 Mc 2:12 We see our sanctuary and our **b**
Ps 27: 4 To gaze on the LORD's **b**, to visit his
Ps 45:12 that the king might desire your **b**.
Ps 50: 2 Zion God shines forth, perfect in **b**.
Prv 6:25 Lust not in your heart after her **b**,
Prv 31:30 Charm is deceptive and **b** fleeting;
Wis 8: 2 bride and was enamored of her **b**.
Wis 13: 3 in their **b** they thought them gods,
Wis 13: 3 original source of **b** fashioned them.
Wis 13: 5 greatness and the **b** of created things
Sir 9: 8 gaze not upon the **b** of another's wife—
Sir 9: 8 Through woman's **b** many perish,
Sir 26:16 the **b** of a virtuous wife is
Sir 36:22 A woman's **b** makes her husband's
Sir 40:22 Charm and **b** delight the eye,
Sir 43: 9 The **b**, the glory, of the heavens are
Is 3:24 a sackcloth skirt. Then, instead of **b**:
Is 28: 1 the fading blooms of his glorious **b**,
Is 28: 4 The fading blooms of his glorious **b**
Ez 16:14 among the nations for your **b**,
Ez 16:15 you were captivated by your own **b**,
Ez 16:25 yourself to use your **b** obscenely,
Ez 27: 3 you said, "I am a ship, perfect in **b**."
Ez 27: 4 placed you, perfected your **b**.

Ez	27:11	walls, and made perfect your **b**.
Ez	28:12	of complete wisdom and perfect **b**.
Ez	28:17	haughty of heart because of your **b**;
Ez	31: 8	in the garden of God matched its **b**.
Ez	32:19	"Whom do you excel in **b**?
Dn	13:32	so as to sate themselves with her **b**.
Dn	13:56	said to him, "**b** has seduced you,
Zec	9:17	what wealth is theirs, and what **b**!
Jas	1:11	the **b** of its appearance vanishes.
1 Pt	3: 4	in the imperishable **b** of a gentle

BECAME → BECOME

Gn	2: 7	of life, and so man **b** a living being.
Ex	15:25	into the water, the water **b** fresh.
Dt	26: 5	But there he **b** a nation great,
2 Kgs	17:15	they pursued, they themselves **b**:
1 Chr	11: 9	David **b** more and more powerful,
Dn	2:35	struck the statue **b** a great mountain
Hos	9:10	they **b** as abhorrent as the thing they
Mt	17: 2	sun and his clothes **b** white as light.
Lk	6:16	and Judas Iscariot, who **b** a traitor.
Jn	1:14	And the Word **b** flesh and made his
1 Cor	9:20	To the Jews I **b** like a Jew to win
1 Cor	9:20	under the law I **b** like one under
2 Cor	8: 9	for your sake he **b** poor although he
Heb	5: 9	he **b** the source of eternal salvation

BECOME → BECAME

Gn	2:24	and the two of them **b** one body.
Gn	9:15	waters shall never again **b** a flood
Ps	118:22	rejected has **b** the cornerstone.
Mt	19: 5	wife, and the two shall **b** one flesh'?
Mk	12:10	rejected has **b** the cornerstone;
Lk	4: 3	command this stone to **b** bread."
Jn	1:12	him he gave power to **b** children
Acts	4:11	which has **b** the cornerstone.'
1 Cor	9:22	I have **b** all things to all, to save
Eph	5:31	wife, and the two shall **b** one flesh."
Heb	2:17	he had to **b** like his brothers in every
Heb	7:22	**b** the guarantee of an [even] better
1 Pt	2: 7	rejected has **b** the cornerstone,"

BED → BEDS, SICKBED

Gn	47:31	Israel bowed at the head of the **b**.
Gn	48: 2	rallied his strength and sat up in **b**.
1 Kgs	1:47	the king in his **b** worshiped God,
Jdt	13: 4	Judith stood by Holofernes' **b**
Ps	63: 7	When I think of you upon my **b**,
Prv	26:14	on its hinges, the sluggard, on his **b**!
Song	3: 1	On my **b** at night I sought him
Is	28:20	For the **b** shall be too short
Dn	7: 1	Daniel had a dream as he lay in **b**,
Mt	8:14	saw his mother-in-law lying in **b**
Lk	11: 7	my children and I are already in **b**.
Lk	17:34	there will be two people in one **b**;
Acts	9:34	Get up and make your **b**."
Heb	13: 4	the marriage **b** be kept undefiled,

BEDS → BED

Ps	4: 5	upon your **b** ponder in silence.
Ps	36: 5	In their **b** they hatch plots; they set

BEE → BEES

Sir	11: 3	Least is the **b** among winged things,
Is	7:18	and for the **b** in the land of Assyria.

BEER-LAHAI-ROI

Gn	16:14	That is why the well is called **B**. It is

BEER-SHEBA

Gn	21:31	This is why the place is called **B**;
Gn	26:33	hence the name of the city, **B**, to this
1 Sm	3:20	Israel from Dan to **B** came to know
2 Sm	24:15	of the people from Dan to **B** died.]
1 Kgs	5: 5	or under his fig tree from Dan to **B**,

BEES → BEE

Dt	1:44	against you and, like **b**, chased you,
Jgs	14: 8	found a swarm of **b** and honey
Ps	118:12	They surrounded me like **b**;

BEFALL → BEFALLEN, BEFALLS

Dt	31:29	evil will **b** you in some future age

Ps	91:10	No evil shall **b** you, no affliction

BEFALLEN → BEFALL

Jer	44:23	this evil has **b** you at the present

BEFALLS → BEFALL

Eccl	2:14	I knew that one lot **b** both of them.
Sir	2: 4	Accept whatever **b** you, in crushing
Am	3: 6	If evil **b** a city, has not the LORD

BEFORE

Gn	18:22	LORD remained standing **b** Abraham.
Gn	27: 4	give you my special blessing **b** I die."
Ex	4:21	that you perform **b** Pharaoh all
Ex	23:15	shall appear **b** me empty-handed.
Ex	33: 2	Jebusites, I will send an angel **b** you
Nm	17:22	laid the staffs down **b** the LORD
Dt	1:30	who goes **b** you, will himself fight
Dt	7:22	dislodge these nations **b** you little
Dt	11:26	"I set **b** you here, this day, a blessing
Dt	30:15	then, I have today set **b** you life
1 Sm	4: 7	to us! This has never happened **b**.
Jb	26: 6	Naked **b** him is the nether world,
Ps	16: 8	I keep the LORD always **b** me;
Ps	37: 7	Be still **b** the LORD; wait for God.
Ps	97: 5	mountains melt like wax **b** the LORD,
Ps	97: 7	things; all gods bow down **b** you.
Ps	139: 4	Even **b** a word is on my tongue,
Prv	8:23	poured forth, at the first, **b** the earth.
Prv	16:18	Pride goes **b** disaster, and a haughty spirit **b** a fall.
Prv	18:12	**B** his downfall a man's heart is
Prv	18:12	but humility goes **b** honors.
Prv	18:13	He who answers **b** he hears — his is
Sir	1: 4	**B** all things else wisdom was
Sir	18:19	**B** you are judged, seek merit
Is	43:10	that it is I. **B** me no god was formed,
Is	48: 5	**b** they took place I let you hear
Is	49:16	name; your walls are ever **b** me.
Is	53: 7	or a sheep **b** the shearers, he was
Is	65:24	**B** they call, I will answer;
Jer	1: 5	**B** I formed you in the womb I knew
Jer	1: 5	**b** you were born I dedicated you,
Mal	3: 1	to prepare the way **b** me;
Mal	3:23	**B** the day of the LORD comes,
Mt	5:16	your light must shine **b** others,
Mt	6: 8	what you need **b** you ask him.
Mt	7: 6	or throw your pearls **b** swine.
Mt	11:10	he will prepare your way **b** you.'
Mt	24:38	In [those] days **b** the flood,
Lk	12: 8	who acknowledges me **b** others
Lk	12: 8	Man will acknowledge **b** the angels
Lk	22:61	said to him, "**B** the cock crows today,
Jn	1:15	of me because he existed **b** me.' "
Jn	8:58	I say to you, **b** Abraham came to be,
Jn	10: 8	All who came [**b** me] are thieves
Jn	13:19	on I am telling you **b** it happens,
Jn	17: 5	I had with you **b** the world began.
Acts	2:25	'I saw the Lord ever **b** me, with him
Acts	8:32	and as a lamb **b** its shearer is silent,
Rom	14:10	shall all stand **b** the judgment seat
Col	1:17	He is **b** all things, and in him all
Ti	1: 2	does not lie, promised **b** time began,
Heb	12: 2	that lay **b** him he endured the cross,
1 Pt	1:20	He was known **b** the foundation
Rv	7: 9	They stood **b** the throne and **b**

BEG → BEGGAR, BEGGED, BEGGING

Lk	16: 3	to dig and I am ashamed to **b**.
Jn	9: 8	this the one who used to sit and **b**?"

BEGAN → BEGIN

Gn	4:26	that time men **b** to invoke the LORD
Lk	3:23	When Jesus **b** his ministry he was
Lk	14:30	'This one **b** to build but did not have

BEGGAR → BEG

Sir	40:28	My son, live not the life of a **b**,
Jn	9: 8	had seen him earlier as a **b** said,

BEGGED → BEG

Mk	6:56	**b** him that they might touch only

BEGGING →BEG
Ps 37:25 abandoned or their children **b** bread.

BEGIN →BEGAN, BEGINNING, BEGUN
1 Pt 4:17 time for the judgment to **b**

BEGINNING →BEGIN
Gn	1: 1	In the **b**, when God created
Ps	111:10	fear of the LORD is the **b** of wisdom;
Prv	1: 7	of the LORD is the **b** of knowledge;
Prv	4: 7	The **b** of wisdom is: get wisdom;
Prv	9:10	The **b** of wisdom is the fear
Eccl	3:11	ever discovering, from **b** to end,
Eccl	7: 8	is the end of speech than its **b**;
Is	40:21	Was it not foretold you from the **b**?
Is	46:10	At the **b** I foretell the outcome;
Mt	19: 8	wives, but from the **b** it was not so.
Mt	24: 8	All these are the **b** of the labor
Mt	24:21	such as has not been since the **b**
Mk	1: 1	The **b** of the gospel of Jesus Christ
Lk	1: 2	who were eyewitnesses from the **b**
Jn	1: 1	In the **b** was the Word,
Jn	8:44	He was a murderer from the **b**
Jn	15:27	you have been with me from the **b**.
Acts	1:22	**b** from the baptism of John until
Col	1:18	He is the **b**, the firstborn
Heb	7: 3	without **b** of days or end of life,
1 Jn	1: 1	What was from the **b**, what we have
1 Jn	3: 8	the devil has sinned from the **b**.
2 Jn	1: 6	as you heard from the **b**,
Rv	21: 6	and the Omega, the **b** and the end.
Rv	22:13	first and the last, the **b** and the end."

BEGOTTEN
Acts	13:33	are my son; this day I have **b** you.'
Heb	1: 5	are my son; this day I have **b** you"?
Heb	5: 5	are my son; this day I have **b** you";

BEGUILE
Jdt 16: 8 and put on a linen robe to **b** him.

BEGUN →BEGIN
Dt 3:24 you have **b** to show to your servant

BEHALF
Jb	36: 2	are still words to be said on God's **b**.
Jer	7:16	not in their **b** a pleading prayer!
Dn	9:20	my God, on **b** of his holy mountain—
Jn	5:32	is another who testifies on my **b**,
Jn	5:32	testimony he gives on my **b** is true.
Jn	8:14	"Even if I do testify on my own **b**,
Heb	6:20	has entered on our **b** as forerunner,

BEHAVE →BEHAVING, BEHAVIOR
1 Tm 3:15 you should know how to **b**

BEHAVING →BEHAVE
1 Cor 7:36 thinks he is **b** improperly toward his

BEHAVIOR →BEHAVE
Ti 2: 3 should be reverent in their **b**,

BEHEADED →HEAD
Lk	9: 9	But Herod said, "John I **b**.
Rv	20: 4	of those who had been **b** for their

BEHEMOTH
Jb 40:15 See, besides you I made **B**,

BEHIND
Ps	50:17	you cast my words **b** you!
Ps	139: 5	**B** and before you encircle me
Is	38:17	When you cast **b** your back all my
Ez	3:12	and I heard **b** me the noise of a loud
Mt	16:23	turned and said to Peter, "Get **b** me,
Lk	2:43	the boy Jesus remained **b**
Lk	8:44	came up **b** him and touched
Phil	3:13	forgetting what lies **b** but straining
Heb	6: 1	let us leave **b** the basic teaching
Rv	1:10	and heard **b** me a voice as loud as

BEHOLD
Nm	23: 9	from the heights I **b** him. Here is
Nm	24:17	not now; I **b** him, though not near:
Jb	19:27	own eyes, not another's, shall **b** him,

BEING →BEINGS
Gn	2: 7	life, and so man became a living **b**.
1 Sm	28:13	"I see a preternatural **b** rising
Ps	51: 8	in my inmost **b** teach me wisdom.
1 Cor	15:45	became a living **b**," the last Adam
Heb	1: 3	the very imprint of his **b**, and who

BEINGS →BEING
Mt 9: 8 given such authority to human **b**.

BEL
Babylonian deity (Is 46:1; Jer 50:2; 51:44; Bar 6:40; Dan 14:3-28).

BELIAR
2 Cor 6:15 What accord has Christ with **B**?

BELIEF →BELIEVE
2 Mc	15:11	a kind of vision, worthy of **b**.
2 Thes	2:13	by the Spirit and **b** in truth.

BELIEVE →BELIEF, BELIEVED, BELIEVER, BELIEVERS, BELIEVES, BELIEVING
Gn	45:26	dumbfounded; he could not **b** them.
Ex	4: 1	"suppose they will not **b** me,
Ex	4: 5	will take place so that they may **b**,"
Ex	4: 8	"If they will not **b** you, nor heed
Ex	4: 9	they will not **b** even these two signs,
Nm	14:11	How long will they refuse to **b**
1 Kgs	10: 7	"Though I did not **b** the report until I
2 Chr	9: 6	"Yet I did not **b** the report until I
2 Chr	32:15	Do not **b** him! Since no other god
Tb	2:14	Yet I would not **b** her; and told her
Tb	10: 7	mother do not **b** they will ever see
Tb	14: 4	for I **b** God's word which was
Tb	14: 4	**b** that whatever God has spoken will
Jb	9:16	I could not **b** that he would hearken
Ps	27:13	I **b** I shall enjoy the LORD's goodness
Ps	78:32	they did not **b** in his wonders.
Is	43:10	chosen To know and **b** in me
Jer	12: 6	Do not **b** them, even if they are
Lam	4:12	The kings of the earth did not **b**,
Mt	9:28	to them, "Do you **b** that I can do this?"
Mt	18: 6	one of these little ones who **b** in me
Mt	21:25	to us, "Then why did you not **b** him?"
Mt	21:32	of righteousness, you did not **b** him;
Mt	21:32	later change your minds and **b** him.
Mt	24:23	Messiah!' or, 'There he is!' do not **b** it.
Mt	24:26	'He is in the inner rooms,' do not **b** it.
Mt	27:42	the cross now, and we will **b** in him.
Mk	1:15	at hand. Repent, and **b** in the gospel."
Mk	9:24	cried out, "I do **b**, help my unbelief!"
Mk	9:42	of these little ones who **b** [in me]
Mk	11:24	**b** that you will receive it and it shall
Mk	11:31	say, '[Then] why did you not **b** him?'
Mk	13:21	Look, there he is!' do not **b** it.
Mk	15:32	the cross that we may see and **b**."
Mk	16:11	been seen by her, they did not **b**.
Mk	16:13	but they did not **b** them either.
Mk	16:16	saved; whoever does not **b** will be
Mk	16:17	signs will accompany those who **b**:
Lk	1:20	because you did not **b** my words,
Lk	8:12	their hearts that they may not **b**
Lk	8:13	they **b** only for a time and fall away
Lk	20: 5	he will say, 'Why did you not **b** him?'
Lk	22:67	to them, "If I tell you, you will not **b**,
Lk	24:11	nonsense and they did not **b** them.
Lk	24:25	of heart to **b** all that the prophets
Jn	1: 7	so that all might **b** through him.
Jn	1:50	"Do you **b** because I told you that I
Jn	3:12	earthly things and you do not **b**, how will you **b** if I tell you
Jn	3:18	but whoever does not **b** has already
Jn	4:21	Jesus said to her, "**B** me, woman,
Jn	4:42	"We no longer **b** because of your
Jn	4:48	signs and wonders, you will not **b**."
Jn	5:38	because you do not **b** in the one
Jn	5:44	How can you **b**, when you accept
Jn	5:47	But if you do not **b** his writings, how will you **b** my words?"
Jn	6:29	God, that you **b** in the one he sent."

Jn	6:30	do, that we may see and **b** in you?
Jn	6:36	you have seen [me], you do not **b**.
Jn	6:64	there are some of you who do not **b**."
Jn	6:64	beginning the ones who would not **b**
Jn	6:69	We have come to **b** and are
Jn	7: 5	For his brothers did not **b** in him.
Jn	8:24	For if you do not **b** that I AM,
Jn	8:45	I speak the truth, you do not **b** me.
Jn	8:46	the truth, why do you not **b** me?
Jn	9:18	Now the Jews did not **b** that he had
Jn	9:35	said, "Do you **b** in the Son of Man?"
Jn	9:36	"Who is he, sir, that I may **b** in him?"
Jn	9:38	He said, "I do **b**, Lord," and he
Jn	10:25	them, "I told you and you do not **b**.
Jn	10:26	But you do not **b**, because you are
Jn	10:37	my Father's works, do not **b** me;
Jn	10:38	them, even if you do not **b** me,
Jn	11:15	that I was not there, that you may **b**.
Jn	11:26	in me will never die. Do you **b** this?"
Jn	11:27	I have come to **b** that you are
Jn	11:42	that they may **b** that you sent me."
Jn	11:48	leave him alone, all will **b** in him,
Jn	12:36	you have the light, **b** in the light,
Jn	12:37	their presence they did not **b** in him,
Jn	12:39	For this reason they could not **b**,
Jn	13:19	it happens you may **b** that I AM.
Jn	14:10	Do you not **b** that I am in the Father
Jn	14:11	**B** me that I am in the Father
Jn	14:11	**b** because of the works themselves.
Jn	14:29	so that when it happens you may **b**.
Jn	16: 9	sin, because they do not **b** in me;
Jn	16:30	Because of this we **b** that you came
Jn	16:31	answered them, "Do you **b** now?
Jn	17:20	those who will **b** in me through their
Jn	17:21	the world may **b** that you sent me.
Jn	19:35	so that you also may [come to] **b**.
Jn	20:25	my hand into his side, I will not **b**."
Jn	20:27	and do not be unbelieving, but **b**."
Jn	20:29	to **b** because you have seen me?
Jn	20:31	you may [come to] **b** that Jesus is
Acts	13:41	you will never **b** even if someone
Acts	15:11	we **b** that we are saved through
Acts	16:31	"**B** in the Lord Jesus and you
Acts	19: 4	telling the people to **b** in the one
Acts	26:27	Agrippa, do you **b** the prophets? I know you **b**."
Acts	28:24	he had said, while others did not **b**.
Rom	3:22	faith in Jesus Christ for all who **b**.
Rom	4:11	of all the uncircumcised who **b**,
Rom	4:24	who **b** in the one who raised Jesus
Rom	6: 8	we **b** that we shall also live
Rom	10: 9	**b** in your heart that God raised him
Rom	10:14	how can they **b** in him of whom
1 Cor	11:18	among you, and to a degree I **b** it;
2 Cor	4:13	spoke," we too **b** and therefore speak,
Gal	3:22	might be given to those who **b**.
Eph	1:19	greatness of his power for us who **b**,
1 Thes	4:14	For if we **b** that Jesus died and rose,
2 Thes	2:11	power so that they may **b** the lie,
1 Tm	1:16	those who would come to **b** in him
1 Tm	4: 3	with thanksgiving by those who **b**
1 Tm	4:10	of all, especially of those who **b**.
Heb	11: 6	anyone who approaches God must **b**
Jas	2:19	You **b** that God is one. You do well. Even the demons **b**
1 Pt	1: 8	you do not see him now yet **b**
1 Jn	3:23	we should **b** in the name of his Son,
1 Jn	4:16	and to **b** in the love God has for us.
1 Jn	5:10	Whoever does not **b** God has made
1 Jn	5:13	you who **b** in the name of the Son
Jude	1: 5	later destroyed those who did not **b**.

BELIEVED → BELIEVE

Ex	4:31	The people **b**, and when they heard
Ex	14:31	they feared the LORD and **b** in him
Jdt	14:10	of Israel had done, **b** firmly in him.
Ps	106:12	Then they **b** his words and sang
Dn	13:41	The assembly **b** them, since they
Jon	3: 5	when the people of Nineveh **b** God;
Mk	16:14	they had not **b** those who saw him

Lk	1:45	Blessed are you who **b** that what
Jn	3:18	because he has not **b** in the name
Jn	4:50	The man **b** what Jesus said to him
Jn	5:46	For if you had **b** Moses, you would have **b** me, because he
Jn	7:48	or the Pharisees **b** in him?
Jn	8:31	said to those Jews who **b** in him,
Jn	12:38	"Lord, who has **b** our preaching,
Jn	12:42	among the authorities, **b** in him,
Jn	17: 8	and they have **b** that you sent me.
Jn	20: 8	at the tomb first, and he saw and **b**.
Jn	20:29	those who have not seen and have **b**."
Acts	2:44	All who **b** were together and had all
Acts	8:13	Even Simon himself **b** and,
Acts	22:19	and beat those who **b** in you.
Rom	4: 3	"Abraham **b** God, and it was credited
Rom	4:17	in whom he **b**, who gives life
Rom	4:18	He **b**, hoping against hope, that he
Rom	10:14	on him in whom they have not **b**?
Rom	10:16	who has **b** what we heard from us?"
2 Cor	4:13	is written, "I **b**, therefore I spoke,"
Gal	3: 6	Thus Abraham "**b** God, and it was
Eph	1:13	and have **b** in him, were sealed
2 Thes	1:10	on that day among all who have **b**, for our testimony to you was **b**.
2 Thes	2:12	that all who have not **b** the truth
1 Tm	3:16	Gentiles, **b** in throughout the world,
2 Tm	3:14	to what you have learned and **b**,
Heb	4: 3	For we who **b** enter into [that] rest,
Jas	2:23	fulfilled that says, "Abraham **b** God,

BELIEVER → BELIEVE

Acts	16: 1	of a Jewish woman who was a **b**,
2 Cor	6:15	Or what has a **b** in common

BELIEVERS → BELIEVE

Acts	5:14	Yet more than ever, **b** in the Lord,
Acts	10:45	The circumcised **b** who had
Acts	11: 2	the circumcised **b** confronted him,
Acts	15: 5	Pharisees who had become **b** stood
Acts	17:34	some did join him, and became **b**.
Acts	19: 2	the holy Spirit when you became **b**?"
Acts	19:18	who had become **b** came forward
Acts	21:20	how many thousands of **b** there are
1 Thes	1: 7	a model for all the **b** in Macedonia
1 Thes	2:10	we behaved toward you **b**.
1 Tm	6: 2	whose masters are **b** must not take

BELIEVES → BELIEVE

Prv	14:15	The simpleton **b** everything,
Sir	34: 2	wind, is the one who **b** in dreams.
Mk	11:23	but **b** that what he says will happen,
Mk	16:16	Whoever **b** and is baptized will be
Jn	3:15	everyone who **b** in him may have
Jn	3:16	everyone who **b** in him might not
Jn	3:36	Whoever **b** in the Son has eternal
Jn	5:24	**b** in the one who sent me has eternal
Jn	6:35	whoever **b** in me will never thirst.
Jn	6:40	and **b** in him may have eternal life,
Jn	6:47	to you, whoever **b** has eternal life.
Jn	7:38	Whoever **b** in me, as scripture says:
Jn	11:25	whoever **b** in me, even if he dies,
Jn	11:26	lives and **b** in me will never die.
Jn	12:44	"Whoever **b** in me **b** not only in me
Jn	12:46	everyone who **b** in me might not
Jn	14:12	whoever **b** in me will do the works
Acts	10:43	everyone who **b** in him will receive
Rom	9:33	whoever **b** in him shall not be put
Rom	10:10	For one **b** with the heart and so is
Rom	10:11	"No one who **b** in him will be put
Rom	14: 2	One person **b** that one may eat
1 Cor	13: 7	It bears all things, **b** all things,
1 Pt	2: 6	whoever **b** in it shall not be put
1 Jn	5: 1	Everyone who **b** that Jesus is
1 Jn	5: 5	the one who **b** that Jesus is the Son

BELIEVING → BELIEVE

Jn	12:11	away and **b** in Jesus because of him.
Rom	15:13	fill you with all joy and peace in **b**,
1 Jn	5:10	not **b** the testimony God has given

BELL → BELLS
Ex   28:34   first a gold **b**, then a pomegranate,

BELLS → BELL
Zec   14:20   shall be upon the **b** of the horses,

BELLY
Gn   3:14   On your **b** shall you crawl, and dirt
Lv   11:42   Whether it crawls on its **b**,
Jgs   3:21   thigh, and thrust it into Eglon's **b**.
Prv   13:25   but the **b** of the wicked suffers want.
Jon   2: 1   in the **b** of the fish three days
Jon   2: 2   the **b** of the fish Jonah said this
Mt   12:40   was in the **b** of the whale three days

BELONG → BELONGED, BELONGS
Dt   10:14   the highest heavens, **b** to the Lord,
Ps   47:10   For the rulers of the earth **b** to God,
Jn   10:16   sheep that do not **b** to this fold.
Jn   15:19   because you do not **b** to the world,
Jn   17:14   because they do not **b** to the world any more than
                 I **b**
Rom   1: 6   who are called to **b** to Jesus Christ;
Rom   7: 4   so that you might **b** to another,
Rom   8: 9   Spirit of Christ does not **b** to him.
1 Cor   1:12   each of you is saying, "I **b** to Paul," or "I **b** to
                 Apollos," or "I **b** to Kephas," or "I **b** to Christ."
1 Cor 12:15   "Because I am not a hand I do not **b**
1 Cor 12:15   it does not for this reason **b** any less
1 Cor 15:23   his coming, those who **b** to Christ;
Gal   3:29   And if you **b** to Christ, then you are

BELONGED → BELONG
Jn   15:19   If you **b** to the world, the world
Acts   9: 2   men or women who **b** to the Way,

BELONGS → BELONG
Ps   22:29   For kingship **b** to the Lord, the ruler
Ps   62:12   I have heard: Power **b** to God;
Mt   19:14   of heaven **b** to such as these."
Jn   18:37   Everyone who **b** to the truth listens
2 Cor 10: 7   consider that as he **b** to Christ, so do
Col   2:17   to come; the reality **b** to Christ.

BELOVED → LOVE
Dt   33:12   said: "Benjamin is the **b** of the Lord,
2 Sm   1:23   Saul and Jonathan, **b** and cherished,
Neh   13:26   and though he was **b** of his God
Tb   3:10   'You had only one **b** daughter,
Tb   10:13   "My child and **b** kinsman,
Tb   10:   13 your mother, and Sarah is your **b**.
Ps   127: 2   all this God gives to his **b** in sleep.
Song   2:10   "Arise, my **b**, my beautiful one,
Song   5: 2   "Open to me, my sister, my **b**,
Sir   46:13   B of his people, dear to his Maker,
Jer   11:15   What right has my **b** in my house,
Jer   12: 7   heritage; The **b** of my soul I deliver
Dn   3:35   us, for the sake of Abraham, your **b**,
Dn   9:23   to announce, because you are **b**.
Dn   10:11   "Daniel, **b**," he said to me,
Dn   10:19   "Fear not, **b**, you are safe;
Mt   3:17   "This is my **b** Son, with whom I am
Mt   12:18   chosen, my **b** in whom I delight;
Mt   17: 5   "This is my **b** Son, with whom I am
Mk   1:11   the heavens, "You are my **b** Son;
Mk   9: 7   came a voice, "This is my **b** Son.
Mk   12: 6   He had one other to send, a **b** son.
Lk   3:22   from heaven, "You are my **b** Son;
Lk   20:13   I shall send my **b** son; maybe they
Acts   15:25   to you along with our **b** Barnabas
Rom   1: 7   to all the **b** of God in Rome,
Rom   9:25   and her who was not **b** I will call "**b**."
Rom   11:28   they are **b** because of the patriarchs.
Rom   12:19   B, do not look for revenge but leave
Rom   16: 5   Greet my **b** Epaenetus, who was
Rom   16: 8   Greet Ampliatus, my **b** in the Lord.
Rom   16: 9   in Christ, and my **b** Stachys.
Rom   16:12   Greet the **b** Persis, who has worked
1 Cor   4:14   to admonish you as my **b** children.
1 Cor   4:17   who is my **b** and faithful son
1 Cor 15:58   Therefore, my **b** brothers, be firm,
2 Cor   7: 1   Since we have these promises, **b**,

2 Cor 12:19   and all for building you up, **b**.
Eph   1: 6   his grace that he granted us in the **b**.
Eph   5: 1   be imitators of God, as **b** children,
Phil   2:12   my **b**, obedient as you have always
Phil   4: 1   this way stand firm in the Lord, **b**.
Col   1: 7   it from Epaphras our **b** fellow slave,
Col   1:13   us to the kingdom of his **b** Son,
Col   3:12   holy and **b**, heartfelt compassion,
Col   4: 7   Tychicus, my **b** brother,
Col   4: 9   a trustworthy and **b** brother, who is
Col   4:14   Luke the **b** physician sends
1 Tm   6: 2   their work are believers and are **b**.
Phlm   1:16   a brother, **b** especially to me,
Heb   6: 9   But we are sure in your regard, **b**,
Jas   1:16   Do not be deceived, my **b** brothers:
Jas   2: 5   Listen, my **b** brothers. Did not God
1 Pt   2:11   B, I urge you as aliens
1 Pt   4:12   B, do not be surprised that a trial
2 Pt   1:17   my **b**, with whom I am well pleased."
2 Pt   3: 1   This is now, **b**, the second letter I
2 Pt   3: 8   But do not ignore this one fact, **b**,
2 Pt   3:14   Therefore, **b**, since you await these
2 Pt   3:15   as salvation, as our **b** brother Paul,
2 Pt   3:17   Therefore, **b**, since you are
1 Jn   2: 7   B, I am writing no new
1 Jn   3: 2   B, we are God's children now;
1 Jn   3:21   B, if [our] hearts do not condemn
1 Jn   4: 1   B, do not trust every spirit but test
1 Jn   4: 7   B, let us love one another,
1 Jn   4:11   B, if God so loved us, we also must
3 Jn   1: 1   to the **b** Gaius whom I love in truth.
3 Jn   1: 2   B, I hope you are prospering
3 Jn   1: 5   B, you are faithful in all you do
3 Jn   1:11   B, do not imitate evil but imitate
Jude   1: 1   **b** in God the Father and kept safe
Jude   1: 3   B, although I was making every
Jude   1:17   But you, **b**, remember the words
Jude   1:20   But you, **b**, build yourselves
Rv   20: 9   of the holy ones and the **b** city.

BELOW
Jos   2:11   in heaven above and on earth **b**.
Jn   8:23   "You belong to what is **b**, I belong
Acts   2:19   and signs on the earth **b**: blood, fire,

BELSHAZZAR
King of Babylon in days of Daniel (Bar 1:11-12; Dn 5).

BELT → BELTS
1 Sm   18: 4   and his sword, his bow and his **b**.
Is   11: 5   and faithfulness a **b** upon his hips.
Dn   10: 5   a **b** of fine gold around his waist.
Mk   1: 6   with a leather **b** around his waist.
Acts   21:11   took Paul's **b**, bound his own feet

BELTESHAZZAR → =DANIEL
Dn   1: 7   Daniel to **B**, Hananiah to Shadrach,

BELTS → BELT
Mk   6: 8   food, no sack, no money in their **b**.

BEN-HADAD
1. King of Syria in time of Asa (1 Kgs 15:18-20; 2 Chr 16:2-4).
2. King of Syria in time of Ahab (1 Kgs 20; 2 Kgs 6:24; 8:7-15).
3. King of Syria in time of Jehoahaz (2 Kgs 13:3, 24-25; Jer 49:27;
Am 1:4).

BEN-HINNOM
2 Kgs   23:10   defiled Topheth in the Valley of **B**,
2 Chr   28: 3   offered sacrifice in the Valley of **B**,
Jer   32:35   places to Baal in the Valley of **B**,

BEN-ONI → =BENJAMIN
Gn   35:18   the point of death—she called him **B**;

BENAIAH
A commander of Davids army (2 Sm 8:18; 20:23; 23:20-30);
loyal to Solomon (1 Kgs 1:8-2:46; 4:4).

BENCH
Jn   19:13   on the judge's **b** in the place called

BEND → BENT
2 Sm   22:35   till my arms could **b** a bow of brass.

Phil	2:10	every knee should **b**, of those

BENEATH

| Dt | 5: 8 | below or in the waters **b** the earth; |

BENEFACTOR → BENEFACTORS

Est	E:13	our savior and constant **b**,
2 Mc	4: 2	government the man who was a **b**
Rom	16: 2	for she has been a **b** to many

BENEFACTORS → BENEFACTOR

| Est | E: 3 | begin plotting against their own **b**. |
| Lk | 22:25 | over them are addressed as '**B**'; |

BENEFICIAL → BENEFIT

| 1 Cor | 6:12 | for me," but not everything is **b**. |
| 1 Cor | 10:23 | is lawful," but not everything is **b**. |

BENEFIT → BENEFICIAL

| Gal | 5: 2 | Christ will be of no **b** to you. |

BENJAMIN → =BEN-ONI, BENJAMINITE

Twelfth son of Jacob by Rachel (Gn 35:16-24; 46:19-21; 1 Chr 2:2). Jacob refused to send him to Egypt, but relented (Gn 42-45). Tribe of blessed (Gn 49:27; Dt 33:12), numbered (Nm 1:37; 26:41), allotted land (Jos 18:11-28; Ez 48:23), failed to fully possess (Jgs 1:21), nearly obliterated (Jgs 20-21), sided with Ish-Bosheth (2 Sm 2), but turned to David (1 Chr 12:2, 30). 12,000 from (Rv 7:8).

BENJAMINITE → BENJAMIN

Jgs	3:15	up for them a savior, the **B** Ehud,
1 Sm	9:21	"Am I not a **B**, of one of the smallest
2 Sm	19:17	son of Gera, the **B** from Bahurim,
Est	2: 5	son of Shimei, son of Kish, a **B**,

BENT → BEND

Lk	13:11	a spirit; she was **b** over,
Jn	8: 6	Jesus **b** down and began to write
Jn	20: 5	he **b** down and saw the burial cloths
Rom	11:10	see, and keep their backs **b** forever."

BEOR

| Nm | 22: 5 | Balaam, son of **B**, at Pethor |
| Nm | 31: 8 | Balaam, son of **B**, with the sword. |

BERACAH

| 2 Chr | 20:26 | since been called the Valley of **B**. |

BEREAVES

| Lam | 1:20 | In the streets the sword **b**, at home |

BERNICE

| Acts | 25:13 | **B** arrived in Caesarea on a visit |

BEROEA

| Acts | 17:10 | Paul and Silas to **B** during the night. |

BERYL

| Rv | 21:20 | the eighth, the ninth topaz, |

BESIDES

Wis	12:13	is there any god **b** you who have
Is	45:21	**b** whom there is no other God?
Dn	14:41	Daniel, and there is no other **b** you!"

BESIEGED → SIEGE

| 2 Kgs | 17: 5 | Samaria, which he **b** for three years. |

BEST → GOOD

Gn	45:18	I will assign you the **b** land
Nm	18:29	and from the **b** parts, you are
Dt	33:21	He saw that the **b** should be his
Mi	7: 4	The **b** of them is like a brier,

BESTOW → BESTOWER, BESTOWING

| Prv | 4: 9 | a glorious crown will she **b** on you." |

BESTOWER → BESTOW

| Is | 23: 8 | thing against Tyre, the **b** of crowns, |

BESTOWING → BESTOW

| Ex | 20: 6 | but **b** mercy down to the thousandth |
| Dt | 5:10 | but **b** mercy, down to the thousandth |

BETHANY

Mt	26: 6	when Jesus was in **B** in the house
Mk	11:12	they were leaving **B** he was hungry.
Jn	1:28	happened in **B** across the Jordan,

| Jn | 11: 1 | Lazarus from **B**, the village of Mary |

BETHEL → =LUZ

Gn	12: 8	pitching his tent with **B** to the west
Gn	28:19	He called that site **B**,
Gn	31:13	the God who appeared to you in **B**,
Gn	35: 7	an altar and named the place **B**,
Gn	35: 8	was buried under the oak below **B**,
Jos	8: 9	position to the west of Ai, toward **B**.
Jgs	20:18	moved on to **B** and consulted God.
1 Sm	7:16	passing through **B**,
1 Kgs	12:29	And he put one in **B**, the other
1 Kgs	13:11	man of God had done that day in **B**.
2 Kgs	2: 2	"The LORD has sent me on to **B**."
2 Kgs	10:29	as regards the golden calves at **B**
2 Kgs	23:15	Likewise the altar which was at **B**,
Tb	2: 6	by the prophet Amos against **B**:
Am	4: 4	Come to **B** and sin, to Gilgal,
Am	7:10	the priest of **B**, sent word

BETHLEHEM → BETHLEHEM-EPHRATHAH, EPHRATH

Gn	35:19	on the road to Ephrath [that is, **B**].
Ru	1: 1	so a man from **B** of Judah departed
Ru	1:19	went on together till they reached **B**.
Ru	4:11	in Ephrathah and win fame in **B**.
1 Sm	17:12	Jesse, who was from **B** in Judah.
2 Sm	23:15	the cistern that is by the gate of **B**!"
Mt	2: 1	When Jesus was born in **B** of Judea,
Mt	2: 6	'And you, **B**, land of Judah,
Mt	2:16	the massacre of all the boys in **B**
Lk	2:15	to **B** to see this thing that has taken
Jn	7:42	of David's family and come from **B**,

BETHLEHEM-EPHRATHAH → BETHLEHEM

| Mi | 5: 1 | But you, **B**, too small to be among |

BETHPHAGE

| Mt | 21: 1 | came to **B** on the Mount of Olives, |

BETHSAIDA

| Mt | 11:21 | Woe to you, **B**! For if the mighty |
| Jn | 1:44 | Now Philip was from **B**, the town |

BETHSHAN

| 1 Sm | 31:10 | impaled his body on the wall of **B**. |

BETHUEL

| Gn | 22:23 | **B** became the father of Rebekah. |
| Gn | 24:24 | "I am the daughter of **B** the son |

BETRAY → BETRAYER, BETRAYING

Mt	24:10	they will **b** and hate one another.
Mt	26:21	I say to you, one of you will **b** me."
Jn	13:11	For he knew who would **b** him;

BETRAYER → BETRAY

| Mk | 14:42 | up, let us go. See, my **b** is at hand." |

BETRAYING → BETRAY

| Lk | 22:48 | are you **b** the Son of Man |

BETROTH → BETROTHED

| Dt | 28:30 | Though you **b** a wife, another man |

BETROTHED → BETROTH

Dt	20: 7	Is there anyone who has **b** a woman
Mt	1:18	When his mother Mary was **b** to Joseph,
Lk	1:27	to a virgin **b** to a man named Joseph,

BETTER → GOOD

1 Sm	15:22	LORD? Obedience is **b** than sacrifice,
Tb	3: 6	It is **b** for me to die than to live,
Tb	12: 8	but **b** than either is almsgiving
Tb	12: 8	righteousness is **b** than abundance
Tb	12: 8	It is **b** to give alms than to store
Ps	37:16	**B** the poverty of the just
Ps	63: 4	For your love is **b** than life; my lips
Ps	118: 8	**B** to take refuge in the LORD
Prv	3:14	her profit is **b** than profit in silver,
Prv	3:14	and **b** than gold is her revenue;
Prv	8:11	[For Wisdom is **b** than corals,
Prv	8:19	My fruit is **b** than gold, yes,
Prv	12: 9	**B** a lowly man who supports
Prv	15:16	**B** a little with fear of the LORD
Prv	15:17	**B** a dish of herbs where love is

Prv	16: 8	B a little with virtue, than a large
Prv	16:16	How much b to acquire wisdom
Prv	16:19	It is b to be humble with the meek
Prv	16:32	A patient man is b than a warrior,
Prv	17: 1	B a dry crust with peace
Prv	19: 1	B a poor man who walks in his
Prv	21: 9	It is b to dwell in a corner
Prv	21:19	It is b to dwell in a wilderness
Prv	25:24	It is b to dwell in a corner
Prv	27: 5	B is an open rebuke than a love
Prv	27:10	B is a neighbor near at hand than
Prv	28: 6	B a poor man who walks in his
Eccl	2:24	There is nothing b for man than
Eccl	3:12	there is nothing b than to be glad
Eccl	3:22	there is nothing b for a man than
Eccl	4: 3	b off than both is the yet unborn,
Eccl	4: 6	B is one handful with tranquility
Eccl	4: 9	Two are b than one: they get a good
Eccl	4:13	B is a poor but wise youth than
Eccl	5: 4	You had b not make a vow than
Eccl	6: 9	"What the eyes see is b than what
Eccl	7: 1	good name is b than good ointment,
Eccl	7: 2	It is b to go to the house
Eccl	7: 3	Sorrow is b than laughter,
Eccl	7: 5	It is b to hearken to the wise man's
Eccl	7: 8	B is the end of speech than its
Eccl	7: 8	b is the patient spirit than the lofty
Eccl	9: 4	a live dog is b off than a dead lion.
Eccl	9:16	I had said, "Wisdom is b than force,"
Sir	16: 3	For one can be b than a thousand;
Sir	23:27	That nothing is b than the fear
Sir	40:20	but b than either, conjugal love.
Sir	40:23	but b than either, a prudent wife.
Sir	40:26	but b than either, fear of God.
Sir	40:28	life of a beggar, b to die than to beg;
Dn	1:20	found them ten times b than all
Jon	4: 3	for it is b for me to die than to live."
Mt	5:29	It is b for you to lose one of your
Mt	18: 6	it would be b for him to have a great
Mt	19:10	with his wife, it is b not to marry."
Mt	26:24	It would be b for that man if he had
Mk	14:21	It would be b for that man if he had
Lk	10:42	Mary has chosen the b part and it
Jn	11:50	do you consider that it is b for you
1 Cor	7: 9	for it is b to marry than to be
Phil	1:23	be with Christ, [for] that is far b.
Heb	6: 9	of b things related to salvation,
Heb	7:19	other hand, a b hope is introduced,
Heb	7:22	guarantee of an [even] b covenant.
Heb	8: 6	as he is mediator of a b covenant, enacted on b promises.
Heb	9:23	by b sacrifices than these.
Heb	10:34	knowing that you had a b
Heb	11:16	But now they desire a b homeland,
Heb	11:35	in order to obtain a b resurrection.
Heb	11:40	God had foreseen something b
1 Pt	3:17	For it is b to suffer for doing good,
2 Pt	2:21	it would have been b for them not

BETWEEN

Gn	3:15	I will put enmity b you
Gn·	3:15	and b your offspring and hers;
Gn	9:13	serve as a sign of the covenant b me
Gn	16: 5	May the LORD decide b you and me!"
Gn	17: 2	B you and me I will establish my
Gn	17:11	be the mark of the covenant b you
Gn	31:44	I; the LORD shall be a witness b us."
Ex	8:19	make this distinction b my people
Ex	31:17	B me and the Israelites it is to be
Jgs	11:10	"The LORD is witness b us that we
1 Sm	7:12	placed it b Mizpah and Jeshanah;
Is	2: 4	He shall judge b the nations,
Is	5: 3	Judah, judge b me and my vineyard:
Ez	20:12	them my sabbaths to be a sign b me
Ez	34:17	I will judge b one sheep and another, b rams and goats.
Mi	4: 3	He shall judge b many peoples
Lk	11:51	of Zechariah who died b the altar
Rom	10:12	For there is no distinction b Jew

Phil	1:23	I am caught b the two. I long
1 Tm	2: 5	one mediator b God and the human

BEWARE

Eccl	12:12	As to more than these, my son, b.
Mt	7:15	"B of false prophets, who come
Phil	3: 2	B of the dogs!
Phil	3: 2	B of the mutilation!

BEWITCHED

Gal	3: 1	Who has b you, before whose eyes

BEYOND

Gn	31:52	neither may I pass b this mound
Gn	31:52	your territory nor may you pass b it
Jos	24: 2	dwelt b the River and served other
Ps	147: 5	in power, with wisdom b measure.
Sir	6:15	A faithful friend is b price, no sum
Sir	8:13	Go not surety b your means;
Is	52:14	him— so marred was his look b
Is	52:14	and his appearance b that of mortals—
1 Cor	4: 6	from us not to go b what is written,
1 Cor	10:13	not let you be tried b your strength;
2 Cor	4:17	weight of glory b all comparison,
2 Cor	10:16	may preach the gospel even b you,

BEZALEL
Judahite craftsman in charge of building the tabernacle (Ex 31:1-11; 35:30-39:31).

BIG

Lv	8:23	and on the b toe of his right foot.
Lv	14:14	hand, and the b toe of his right foot.

BILDAD
One of Job's friends (Jb 2:11; 8; 18; 25; 42:9).

BILHAH
Servant of Rachel, mother of Jacob's sons Dan and Naphtali (Gn 30:1-7; 35:25; 46:23-25).

BILL

Dt	24: 1	he writes out a b of divorce
Dt	24: 3	handing her a written b of divorce;
Is	50: 1	the LORD: Where is the b of divorce
Mt	5:31	divorces his wife must give her a b
Mt	19: 7	man give the woman a b of divorce
Mk	10: 4	permitted him to write a b of divorce

BILLOWS

Jon	2: 4	breakers and your b passed over me.

BIND →BINDS, BOUND

Dt	6: 8	B them at your wrist as a sign
Dt	11:18	B them at your wrist as a sign,
Prv	3: 3	b them around your neck;
Prv	7: 3	B them on your fingers, write them
Ez	34:16	the injured I will b up, the sick I
Mt	16:19	Whatever you b on earth shall be
Mt	18:18	whatever you b on earth shall be

BINDS →BIND

Jb	5:18	For he wounds, but he b up;
Ps	147: 3	brokenhearted, b up their wounds,
Is	30:26	the day the LORD b up the wounds

BIRD →BIRD'S, BIRDS

Gn	7:14	of the earth, and every kind of b.
Lv	20:25	the uncleanness of any beast or b
Dt	4:17	or of any b that flies in the sky,
Ps	11: 1	me, "Flee like a b to the mountains!
Ps	124: 7	like a b from the fowler's snare;
Prv	6: 5	as a b from the hand of the fowler.
Prv	7:23	Like a b that rushes into a snare,
Prv	27: 8	Like a b that is far from its nest
Is	46:11	I call from the east a b of prey,
Rv	18: 2	a cage for every unclean b, [a cage

BIRD'S →BIRD

Dt	22: 6	chance upon a b nest with young birds

BIRDS →BIRD

Gn	1:21	teems, and all kinds of winged b.
Gn	1:22	and let the b multiply on the earth."
Gn	7: 3	and of all the unclean b, one pair,
Dt	14:11	"You may eat all clean b.

Eccl	10:20	Because the **b** of the air may carry
Jer	7:33	will be food for the **b** of the sky
Ez	17:23	**B** of every kind shall dwell beneath
Mt	6:26	Look at the **b** in the sky; they do not
Mt	8:20	dens and **b** of the sky have nests,
Mt	13: 4	the path, and **b** came and ate it up.
Acts	10:12	and reptiles and the **b** of the sky.
Rom	1:23	or of **b** or of four-legged animals
Rv	19:21	all the **b** gorged themselves on their

BIRTH →BEAR

Dt	32:18	forgot the God who gave you **b**.
Ps	22:11	the womb; since **b** you are my God.
Ps	58: 4	wicked have been corrupt since **b**;
Ps	71: 6	On you I depend since **b**; from my
Eccl	7: 1	the day of death than the day of **b**.
Is	26:18	writhed in pain, giving **b** to wind;
Jer	2:27	and to a stone, "You gave me **b**."
Mt	1:18	Now this is how the **b** of Jesus
Lk	1:14	and many will rejoice at his **b**,
Lk	1:57	have her child she gave **b** to a son.
Jn	9: 1	by he saw a man blind from **b**.
Acts	3: 2	a man crippled from **b** was carried
Acts	14: 8	man, lame from **b**, who had never
1 Cor	1:26	powerful, not many were of noble **b**.
Jas	1:15	sin reaches maturity it gives **b**
Jas	1:18	He willed to give us **b** by the word
1 Pt	1: 3	his great mercy gave us a new **b**
Rv	12: 5	She gave **b** to a son, a male child,

BIRTHDAY →BEAR, DAY

Mt	14: 6	But at a **b** celebration for Herod,

BIRTHRIGHT →BEAR, RIGHT

Gn	25:34	his way. Esau cared little for his **b**.
Gn	27:36	First he took away my **b**, and now
1 Chr	5: 1	of his father his **b** was given
1 Chr	5: 2	though the **b** had been Joseph's.)
Heb	12:16	who sold his **b** for a single meal.

BISHOP

1 Tm	3: 1	the office of **b** desires a noble task.
1 Tm	3: 2	a **b** must be irreproachable,
Ti	1: 7	For a **b** as God's steward must be

BIT →BITE, BITS

2 Kgs	19:28	and my **b** in your mouth, and make
Ps	32: 9	with **b** and bridle their temper is

BITE →BIT, BITES, BITING, BITTEN

Sir	21: 2	that will **b** you if you go near it;
Jer	8:17	when they **b** you, says the LORD.
Am	9: 3	the serpent there to **b** them;

BITES →BITE

Prv	23:32	but in the end it **b** like a serpent,

BITING →BITE

Gal	5:15	if you go on **b** and devouring one another,

BITS →BIT

Jas	3: 3	If we put **b** into the mouths

BITTEN →BITE

Nm	21: 8	anyone who has been **b** looks at it,

BITTER →BITTERLY, BITTERNESS

Ex	1:14	making life **b** for them with hard
Ex	12: 8	with unleavened bread and **b** herbs.
Ex	15:23	the water, because it was too **b**.
Nm	5:24	may go into her with all its **b** curse.
Ru	1:13	my lot is too **b** for you,
Ru	1:20	the Almighty has made it very **b** for me.
Prv	5: 4	in the end she is as **b** as wormwood,
Prv	27: 7	who is hungry, any **b** thing is sweet.
Eccl	7:26	More **b** than death I find the woman
Is	5:20	who change **b** into sweet, and sweet into **b**!
Zep	1:14	the LORD! **b**, then, the warrior's cry.
Rv	8:11	this water, because it was made **b**.

BITTERLY →BITTER

Lk	22:62	He went out and began to weep **b**.

BITTERNESS →BITTER

Prv	14:10	The heart knows its own **b**,

Eph	4:31	All **b**, fury, anger, shouting,

BITUMEN

Gn	11: 3	bricks for stone, and **b** for mortar.
Gn	14:10	Valley of Siddim was full of **b** pits;
Ex	2: 3	basket, daubed it with **b** and pitch,

BLACK →BLACKNESS

Zec	6: 2	horses, the second chariot **b** horses,
Mt	5:36	make a single hair white or **b**.
Rv	6: 5	and there was a **b** horse, and its
Rv	6:12	sun turned as **b** as dark sackcloth

BLACKNESS →BLACK

Jb	3: 5	upon it, the **b** of night affright it!

BLACKSMITHS

Zec	2: 3	Then the LORD showed me four **b**.

BLAMELESS

Gn	6: 9	Noah, a good man and **b** in that age,
Gn	17: 1	Walk in my presence and be **b**.
Est	E:13	and of Esther, our **b** royal consort,
1 Mc	4:42	He chose **b** priests,
Jb	1: 1	In the land of Uz there was a **b**
Jb	1: 8	one on earth like him, **b** and upright,
Ps	19:14	Then shall I be **b**, innocent of grave
Ps	37:18	LORD watches over the days of the **b**;
Ps	51: 6	sentence, **b** when you condemn.
Ps	119: 1	Happy those whose way is **b**,
Prv	28:10	[And **b** men will gain prosperity.]
Wis	10: 5	just man, kept him **b** before God,
Wis	10:15	holy people and **b** race—it was she
Wis	18:21	For the **b** man hastened to be their
Sir	11:10	is avid for wealth will not be **b**?
Ez	28:15	**B** you were in your conduct
Phil	1:10	be pure and **b** for the day of Christ,
Phil	2:15	that you may be **b** and innocent,
Phil	3: 6	based on the law I was **b**.
1 Thes	3:13	to be **b** in holiness before our God
1 Thes	5:23	be preserved **b** for the coming
Ti	1: 6	on condition that a man be **b**,
Ti	1: 7	a bishop as God's steward must be **b**,

BLASPHEME →BLASPHEMED, BLASPHEMER, BLASPHEMES, BLASPHEMIES, BLASPHEMING, BLASPHEMOUS, BLASPHEMY

Acts	26:11	in an attempt to force them to **b**;
1 Tm	1:20	over to Satan to be taught not to **b**.
Jas	2: 7	Is it not they who **b** the noble name

BLASPHEMED →BLASPHEME

Lv	24:11	and cursed and **b** the LORD's name.
Ez	20:27	In this way also your fathers **b** me,
Mt	26:65	tore his robes and said, "He has **b**!

BLASPHEMER →BLASPHEME

Sir	3:16	A **b** is he who despises his father;
1 Tm	1:13	I was once a **b** and a persecutor

BLASPHEMES →BLASPHEME

Lv	24:16	whoever **b** the name of the LORD
Mk	3:29	whoever **b** against the holy Spirit
Lk	12:10	but the one who **b** against the holy

BLASPHEMIES →BLASPHEME

Tb	1:18	because of the **b** he had uttered.
1 Mc	7:38	Remember their **b**, and do not let
2 Mc	8: 4	and the **b** uttered against his name;
2 Mc	10:35	angered over such **b**,
Mk	3:28	and all **b** that people utter will be
Lk	5:21	"Who is this who speaks **b**?
Rv	13: 6	its mouth to utter **b** against God,

BLASPHEMING →BLASPHEME

1 Sm	3:13	he knew his sons were **b** God,
Mt	9: 3	said to themselves, "This man is **b**."
Rv	13: 6	**b** his name and his dwelling

BLASPHEMOUS →BLASPHEME

2 Mc	10: 4	and not hand them over to **b**
2 Mc	13:11	to be subjected again to **b** Gentiles.
Acts	6:11	heard him speaking **b** words against
Rv	13: 1	and on its heads **b** name[s].

Rv   17: 3   that was covered with **b** names,

BLASPHEMY → BLASPHEME
Mt   12:31   sin and **b** will be forgiven people,
Mt   12:31   but **b** against the Spirit will not be
Mt   26:65   You have now heard the **b**;
Mk   14:64   You have heard the **b**. What do you
Jn   10:33   you for a good work but for **b**. You,

BLAST → BLASTS
Ex   19:16   and a very loud trumpet **b**,
Jos   6: 5   they give a long **b** on the ram's horns
2 Sm   22:16   at the **b** of the wind of his wrath.
Jb   4: 9   and by the **b** of his wrath they are

BLASTS → BLAST
Lv   23:24   with the trumpet **b** as a reminder;
Rv   8:13   the trumpet **b** that the three angels

BLAZING
Ez   21: 3   The **b** flame shall not be quenched,
Heb   12:18   which could be touched and a **b** fire

BLEACH
Mk   9: 3   as no fuller on earth could **b** them.

BLEATING
1 Sm   15:14   is the meaning of this **b** of sheep

BLEMISH → BLEMISHES
Ex   12: 5   be a year-old male and without **b**.
Lv   1: 3   herd, it must be a male without **b**.
Nm   19: 2   a red heifer that is free from every **b**
2 Sm   14:25   who was without **b** from the sole
Eph   5:27   she might be holy and without **b**.
Phil   2:15   of God without **b** in the midst
2 Pt   3:14   found without spot or **b** before him,

BLEMISHES → BLEMISH
Jude   1:12   These are **b** on your love feasts,

BLESS → BLESSED, BLESSEDNESS, BLESSES, BLESSING,
     BLESSINGS
Gn   12: 2   and I will **b** you; I will make your
Gn   12: 3   I will **b** those who **b** you and curse
Gn   17:16   I will **b** her, and I will give you
Gn   17:16   Him also will I **b**; he shall give rise
Gn   17:20   I am heeding you: I hereby **b** him.
Gn   22:17   I will **b** you abundantly and make
Gn   26: 3   and I will be with you and **b** you;
Gn   26:24   I will **b** you and multiply your
Gn   27:34   "Father, **b** me too!" he begged.
Gn   28: 3   May God Almighty **b** you and make
Gn   32:27   "I will not let you go until you **b** me."
Gn   48: 9   said his father, "that I may **b** them."
Ex   20:24   name I will come to you and **b** you.
Ex   23:25   then I will **b** your food and drink,
Nm   6:24   The Lord **b** you and keep you!
Nm   22: 6   know that whoever you **b** is blessed
Nm   24: 1   the Lord was pleased to **b** Israel,
Dt   1:11   over, and **b** you as he promised!
Dt   7:13   He will love and **b** and multiply
Dt   7:13   he will **b** the fruit of your womb
Dt   8:10   eaten your fill, you must **b** the Lord,
Dt   14:29   may **b** you in all that you undertake.
Dt   15: 4   will **b** you abundantly in the land he
Dt   23:21   may **b** you in all your undertakings.
Dt   24:19   may **b** you in all your undertakings.
Dt   26:15   and **b** your people Israel and the soil
Dt   30:16   God, will **b** you in the land you are
Dt   33:11   **B**, O Lord, his possessions
Jgs   5: 2   deeds by the people who **b** the Lord,
Ru   2: 4   and they replied, "The Lord **b** you!"
1 Sm   2:20   Eli would **b** Elkanah and his wife,
2 Sm   7:29   **b** the house of your servant that it
2 Sm   21: 3   that you may **b** the inheritance
1 Chr   4:10   that you may truly **b** me and extend
1 Chr   16:43   David returned to **b** his household.
1 Chr   29:20   "Now **b** the Lord your God!"
Neh   9: 5   said, "Arise, **b** the Lord, your God,
Tb   4:19   At all times **b** the Lord God, and ask
Tb   8:15   praise you; let them **b** you forever!
Ps   5:13   For you, Lord, **b** the just;

Ps   16: 7   I **b** the Lord who counsels me;
Ps   26:12   in assemblies I will **b** the Lord.
Ps   28: 9   your people, **b** your inheritance;
Ps   29:11   may the Lord **b** his people
Ps   34: 2   I will **b** the Lord at all times;
Ps   62: 5   in lies; they **b** with their mouths,
Ps   63: 5   I will **b** you as long as I live; I will
Ps   66: 8   **B** our God, you peoples;
Ps   67: 2   God be gracious to us and **b** us;
Ps   68:27   In your choirs, **b** God; **b** the Lord,
Ps   96: 2   Sing to the Lord, **b** his name;
Ps   100: 4   Give thanks to God, **b** his name;
Ps   103: 1   **B** the Lord, my soul; all my being, **b** his holy
                name!
Ps   103: 2   **B** the Lord, my soul; do not forget
Ps   103:20   **B** the Lord, all you angels,
Ps   103:21   **B** the Lord, all you hosts,
Ps   103:22   **B** the Lord, all creatures,
Ps   104: 1   **B** the Lord, my soul! Lord, my God,
Ps   104:35   be no more. **B** the Lord, my soul!
Ps   109:28   Though they curse, may you **b**;
Ps   115:12   Lord remembers us and will **b** us, will **b** the house
                of Israel,
Ps   115:18   It is we who **b** the Lord, both now
Ps   118:26   We **b** you from the Lord's house.
Ps   128: 5   May the Lord **b** you from Zion;
Ps   129: 8   We **b** you in the name of the Lord!"
Ps   132:15   I will **b** Zion with meat; its poor I
Ps   134: 1   Come, **b** the Lord, all you servants
Ps   135:19   House of Israel, **b** the Lord!
Ps   135:19   House of Aaron, **b** the Lord!
Ps   135:20   House of Levi, **b** the Lord!
Ps   135:20   You who fear the Lord, **b** the Lord!
Ps   145: 2   Every day I will **b** you; I will praise
Ps   145:10   O Lord and your faithful **b** you.
Ps   145:21   all flesh will **b** your holy name
Sir   39:35   and **b** the name of the Holy One.
Jer   31:23   "May the Lord **b** you, holy mountain,
Dn   3:57   **B** the Lord, all you works
Hg   2:19   yet borne. From this day, I will **b**!
Lk   6:28   **b** those who curse you,
Acts   3:26   sent him to **b** you by turning each
Rom   12:14   **B** those who persecute [you],
1 Cor   4:12   When ridiculed, we **b**;
1 Cor   10:16   The cup of blessing that we **b**, is it
Heb   6:14   "I will indeed **b** you and multiply"
Jas   3: 9   With it we **b** the Lord and Father,

BLESSED → BLESS
Gn   1:22   and God **b** them, saying, "Be fertile,
Gn   2: 3   So God **b** the seventh day and made
Gn   5: 2   he **b** them and named them "man."
Gn   9: 1   God **b** Noah and his sons and said
Gn   9:26   "**B** be the Lord, the God of Shem!
Gn   14:19   "**B** be Abram by God Most High,
Gn   24: 1   the Lord had **b** him in every way.
Gn   39: 5   the Lord **b** the Egyptian's house
Gn   48:20   So when he **b** them that day
Ex   20:11   why the Lord has **b** the sabbath day
Ex   39:43   Lord had commanded, he **b** them.
Lv   9:22   hands over the people and **b** them.
Nm   22: 6   I know that whoever you bless is **b**
Nm   24: 9   **B** is he who blesses you,
Dt   7:14   You will be **b** above all peoples;
Dt   12: 7   the Lord, your God, has **b** you.
Dt   16:15   has **b** you in all your crops and in all
Dt   28: 3   "May you be **b** in the city, and **b**
Dt   33:13   he said: "**B** by the Lord is his land
Jos   22: 6   Joshua then **b** them and sent them
Jgs   5:24   **B** among women be Jael, **b** among
Jgs   13:24   boy grew up and the Lord **b** him;
Ru   2:19   he who took notice of you be **b**!"
1 Sm   25:33   **B** be your good judgment and **b** be
1 Sm   26:25   to David: "**B** are you, my son David!
2 Sm   22:47   And **b** be my Rock! Extolled be my
1 Kgs   1:48   '**B** be the Lord, the God of Israel,
1 Kgs   2:45   But King Solomon shall be **b**,
1 Chr   16: 2   he **b** the people in the name
1 Chr   17:27   O Lord, who **b** it, it is **b** forever."

2 Chr	2:11	"**B** be the Lord, the God of Israel,
2 Chr	31:10	over, for the Lord has **b** his people.
Neh	9: 5	blessing, "**B** is your glorious name,
Tb	3:11	"**B** are you, O Lord, merciful God!
Tb	3:11	Forever **b** and honored is your holy
Tb	8:15	"**B** are you, O God, with every holy
Jdt	13:17	saying with one accord, "**B** are you,
Jb	1:21	away; **b** be the name of the Lord!"
Jb	42:12	Thus the Lord **b** the latter days
Ps	18:47	The Lord lives! **B** be my rock!
Ps	28: 6	**B** be the Lord, who has heard
Ps	31:22	**B** be the Lord, who has shown me
Ps	41:14	**B** be the Lord, the God of Israel,
Ps	66:20	**B** be God, who did not refuse me
Ps	68:20	**B** be the Lord day by day, God,
Ps	72:17	May his name be **b** forever; as long
Ps	72:19	**B** be his glorious name forever;
Ps	89:53	**B** be the Lord forever!
Ps	106:48	**B** be the Lord, the God of Israel,
Ps	113: 2	**B** be the name of the Lord both now
Ps	118:26	**B** is he who comes in the name
Ps	135:21	**B** from Zion the Lord,
Ps	144: 1	Of David. **B** be the Lord, my rock,
Prv	22: 9	The kindly man will be **b**, for he
Is	30:18	justice: **b** are all who wait for him!
Jer	17: 7	**B** is the man who trusts in the Lord,
Dn	2:20	"**B** be the name of God forever
Mt	5: 3	"**B** are the poor in spirit, for theirs is
Mt	5: 4	**B** are they who mourn, for they will
Mt	5: 5	**B** are the meek, for they will inherit
Mt	5: 6	**B** are they who hunger and thirst
Mt	5: 7	**B** are the merciful, for they will be
Mt	5: 8	**B** are the clean of heart, for they
Mt	5: 9	**B** are the peacemakers, for they will
Mt	5:10	**B** are they who are persecuted
Mt	5:11	**B** are you when they insult you
Mt	11: 6	**b** is the one who takes no offense
Mk	10:16	Then he embraced them and **b** them,
Mk	11: 9	**B** is he who comes in the name
Lk	1:42	said, "Most **b** are you among women,
Lk	1:42	and **b** is the fruit of your womb.
Lk	1:48	from now on will all ages call me **b**.
Lk	6:20	he said: "**B** are you who are poor,
Lk	6:21	**B** are you who are now hungry,
Lk	6:21	**B** are you who are now weeping,
Lk	6:22	**B** are you when people hate you,
Jn	12:13	**B** is he who comes in the name
Jn	13:17	this, **b** are you if you do it.
Jn	20:29	**B** are those who have not seen
Acts	3:25	the families of the earth shall be **b**.'
Acts	20:35	'It is more **b** to give than to receive.' "
Rom	1:25	than the creator, who is **b** forever.
Rom	4: 7	"**B** are they whose iniquities are
Rom	9: 5	God who is over all be **b** forever.
Gal	3: 8	you shall all the nations be **b**."
Eph	1: 3	**B** be the God and Father of our Lord
Eph	1: 3	who has **b** us in Christ with every
1 Tm	6:15	that the **b** and only ruler will make
Ti	2:13	as we await the **b** hope,
Heb	7: 7	a lesser person is **b** by a greater.
Jas	1:12	**B** is the man who perseveres
Jas	5:11	Indeed we call **b** those who have
1 Pt	3:14	because of righteousness, **b** are you.
1 Pt	4:14	for the name of Christ, **b** are you,
Rv	1: 3	**B** is the one who reads aloud and **b**
Rv	14:13	**B** are the dead who die in the Lord
Rv	16:15	**B** is the one who watches and keeps
Rv	19: 9	**B** are those who have been called
Rv	20: 6	**B** and holy is the one who shares
Rv	22: 7	**B** is the one who keeps
Rv	22:14	**B** are they who wash their robes so

BLESSEDNESS →BLESS
Rom	4: 6	David declares the **b** of the person

BLESSES →BLESS
Nm	24: 9	Blessed is he who **b** you, and cursed
Prv	3:33	but the dwelling of the just he **b**;

BLESSING →BLESS
Gn	12: 2	name great, so that you will be a **b**.
Gn	26: 4	the nations of the earth shall find **b**—
Gn	27: 4	give you my special **b** before I die."
Gn	27:36	and now he has taken away my **b**."
Gn	27:36	"Haven't you saved a **b** for me?"
Ex	32:29	bring a **b** upon yourselves this day."
Nm	23:20	a **b** which I cannot restrain.
Dt	11:26	you here, this day, a **b** and a curse:
Dt	23: 6	turned his curse into a **b** for you,
Dt	28: 8	The Lord will affirm his **b**
Dt	28: 8	**b** you in the land that the Lord,
Dt	33: 1	This is the **b** which Moses, the man
Jos	8:33	for the **b** of the people of Israel
2 Sm	7:29	by your **b** the house of your servant
Neh	13: 2	our God turned the curse into a **b**."
Tb	8:15	O God, with every holy and pure **b**!
Tb	12: 6	by **b** and extolling his name in song.
Ps	3: 9	the Lord! Your **b** for your people!
Prv	10:22	It is the Lord's **b** that brings wealth,
Sir	11:22	God's **b** is the lot of the just man,
Sir	34:17	the eyes, gives health and life and **b**.
Is	44: 3	and my **b** upon your descendants.
Ez	34:26	rains that shall be a **b** to them.
Jl	2:14	and leave behind him a **b**,
Zec	8:13	will I save you that you may be a **b**;
Mal	3:10	to pour down **b** upon you without
Mk	14:22	he took bread, said the **b**, broke it,
Rom	15:29	come in the fullness of Christ's **b**.
1 Cor	10:16	The cup of **b** that we bless, is it not
1 Cor	14:16	you pronounce a **b** [with] the spirit,
Gal	3:14	that the **b** of Abraham might be
Eph	1: 3	every spiritual **b** in the heavens,
Heb	6: 7	whom it is cultivated receives a **b**
Heb	12:17	he wanted to inherit his father's **b**,
Heb	12:17	even though he sought the **b**
Jas	3:10	From the same mouth come **b**
1 Pt	3: 9	a **b**, because to this you were called, that you might inherit a **b**.
Rv	5:12	and strength, honor and glory and **b**."
Rv	7:12	"Amen. **B** and glory,

BLESSINGS →BLESS
Gn	48:20	the people of Israel pronounce **b**;
Gn	49:26	the **b** of fresh grain and blossoms,
Gn	49:26	The **b** of the everlasting mountains,
Lv	25:21	I will bestow such **b** on you
Dt	21: 5	to him and to give **b** in his name,
Dt	27:12	to pronounce **b** over the people,
Dt	28: 2	all these **b** will come upon you
Dt	30: 1	set before you, the **b** and the curses,
Jos	8:34	of the law, the **b** and the curses,
Ps	21: 7	make him the pattern of **b** forever,
Ps	24: 5	They will receive **b** from the Lord,
Prv	10: 6	**B** are for the head of the just,
Sir	40:27	The fear of God is a paradise of **b**;
Rom	15:27	come to share in their spiritual **b**,
Rom	15:27	also to serve them in material **b**.

BLEW →BLOW
Ex	15:10	When your wind **b**, the sea covered
Tb	11:11	holding him firmly, **b** into his eyes.
Hg	1: 9	what you brought home, I **b** away.
Mt	7:25	the winds **b** and buffeted the house.
Rv	8: 7	When the first one **b** his trumpet,

BLIGHT
Dt	28:22	drought, with **b** and searing wind,
1 Kgs	8:37	or if **b** comes, or mildew, or a locust
Am	4: 9	I struck you with **b** and searing
Hg	2:17	with **b**, searing wind, and hail,

BLIND →BLINDED, BLINDFOLDED, BLINDNESS, BLINDS
Ex	4:11	sight to one and makes another **b**?
Lv	19:14	a stumbling block in front of the **b**,
Lv	21:18	he who is **b**, or lame, or who has
Lv	22:22	One that is **b** or crippled or maimed,
Dt	27:18	'Cursed be he who misleads a **b** man
2 Sm	5: 8	"The **b** and the lame shall not enter
Jb	29:15	I was eyes to the **b**, and feet
Ps	146: 8	the Lord gives sight to the **b**.

Is	35: 5	will the eyes of the **b** be opened,
Is	42: 7	To open the eyes of the **b**, to bring
Is	42:19	Who is **b** but my servant, or deaf
Is	56:10	My watchmen are **b**, all of them
Mal	1: 8	you offer a **b** animal for sacrifice,
Mt	9:27	there, two **b** men followed [him],
Mt	11: 5	the **b** regain their sight, the lame
Mt	15:14	alone; they are **b** guides [of the **b**].
Mt	15:14	If a **b** person leads a **b** person,
Mt	23:16	"Woe to you, **b** guides, who say,
Mk	10:46	Bartimaeus, a **b** man, the son
Lk	6:39	"Can a **b** person guide a **b** person?
Lk	14:13	poor, the crippled, the lame, the **b**;
Jn	9: 1	by he saw a man **b** from birth.
Jn	9:25	One thing I do know is that I was **b**
Rom	2:19	that you are a guide for the **b**
2 Pt	1: 9	Anyone who lacks them is **b**
Rv	3:17	pitiable, poor, **b**, and naked.

BLINDED →BLIND

Jn	12:40	"He **b** their eyes and hardened their
2 Cor	4: 4	of this age has **b** the minds

BLINDFOLDED →BLIND

Mk	14:65	They **b** him and struck him and said
Lk	22:64	They **b** him and questioned him,

BLINDNESS →BLIND

Dt	28:28	you with madness, **b** and panic,

BLINDS →BLIND

Ex	23: 8	a bribe, for a bribe **b** even the most
Dt	16:19	for a bribe **b** the eyes even

BLOCK

Lv	19:14	or put a stumbling **b** in front
Is	44:19	of the rest, or worship a **b** of wood?"
Ez	3:20	I place a stumbling **b** before him,
Sir	31: 7	It is a stumbling **b** to those who are
Rom	11: 9	a stumbling **b** and a retribution
Rom	14:13	resolve never to put a stumbling **b**
1 Cor	1:23	crucified, a stumbling **b** to Jews
1 Cor	8: 9	in no way becomes a stumbling **b**
Rv	2:14	to put a stumbling **b** before

BLOOD →BLOODSHED, BLOODTHIRSTY

Gn	4:10	Your brother's **b** cries out to me
Gn	9: 6	If anyone sheds the **b** of man,
Gn	9: 6	by man shall his **b** be shed;
Ex	4:25	said, "You are a spouse of **b** to me."
Ex	7:17	hold, and it shall be changed into **b**.
Ex	12:13	the **b** will mark the houses where
Ex	12:13	Seeing the **b**, I will pass over you;
Ex	24: 8	he took the **b** and sprinkled it
Ex	24: 8	"This is the **b** of the covenant
Lv	1: 5	shall offer up its **b** by splashing it
Lv	3:17	shall not partake of any fat or any **b**."
Lv	17:11	the life of a living body is in its **b**,
Lv	17:14	the life of every living body is in its **b**,
Lv	17:14	not partake of the **b** of any meat.
Nm	35:19	of **b** may execute the murderer,
Nm	35:33	have no atonement for the **b** shed
Dt	12:23	that you do not partake of the **b**; for **b** is life,
1 Sm	14:32	ground and eating the flesh with **b**.
1 Kgs	21:19	the dogs licked up the **b** of Naboth,
1 Kgs	21:19	the dogs shall lick up your **b**, too.' "
1 Kgs	22:38	the dogs licked up his **b** and harlots
2 Kgs	9:33	of her **b** spurted against the wall
1 Mc	1:24	great arrogance and shed much **b**.
Ps	50:13	of bulls or drink the **b** of goats?
Ps	72:14	for precious is their **b** in his sight.
Ps	78:44	God changed their rivers to **b**;
Ps	106:38	Shedding innocent **b**, the **b** of their
Prv	6:17	and hands that shed innocent **b**;
Sir	34:22	he sheds **b** who denies the laborer
Is	1:11	In the **b** of calves, lambs and goats
Is	9: 4	every cloak rolled in **b**, will be
Is	34: 6	The Lord has a sword filled with **b**,
Is	66: 3	offering, like offering swine's **b**;
Jl	3: 3	**b**, fire, and columns of smoke;
Jl	3: 4	and the moon to **b**, At the coming
Zec	9:11	for the **b** of your covenant with me,

Mt	23:30	them in shedding the prophets' **b**.'
Mt	26:28	for this is my **b** of the covenant,
Mt	27: 6	treasury, for it is the price of **b**."
Mt	27: 8	even today is called the Field of B.
Mt	27:24	"I am innocent of this man's **b**.
Mk	14:24	them, "This is my **b** of the covenant,
Lk	11:51	from the **b** of Abel to the **b**
Lk	11:51	will be charged with their **b**!
Lk	22:20	cup is the new covenant in my **b**,
Lk	22:44	sweat became like drops of **b** falling
Jn	6:53	of the Son of Man and drink his **b**,
Jn	19:34	immediately **b** and water flowed
Acts	1:19	'Akeldama,' that is, Field of B.
Acts	2:20	and the moon to **b**,
Acts	15:20	meat of strangled animals, and **b**.
Acts	18: 6	to them, "Your **b** be on your heads!
Acts	20:26	I am not responsible for the **b** of any
Rom	3:25	by his **b**, to prove his righteousness
Rom	5: 9	since we are now justified by his **b**,
1 Cor	10:16	a participation in the **b** of Christ?
1 Cor	11:25	cup is the new covenant in my **b**.
Eph	1: 7	him we have redemption by his **b**,
Eph	2:13	become near by the **b** of Christ.
Eph	6:12	our struggle is not with flesh and **b**
Col	1:20	making peace by the **b** of his cross
Heb	9: 7	year, not without **b** that he offers
Heb	9:12	not with the **b** of goats and calves but with his own **b**,
Heb	9:20	"This is 'the **b** of the covenant
Heb	9:22	almost everything is purified by **b**,
Heb	9:22	of **b** there is no forgiveness.
Heb	10: 4	it is impossible that the **b** of bulls
Heb	12: 4	resisted to the point of shedding **b**.
Heb	12:24	and the sprinkled **b** that speaks more
Heb	13:12	consecrate the people by his own **b**.
Heb	13:20	by the **b** of the eternal covenant,
1 Pt	1:19	with the precious **b** of Christ as
1 Jn	1: 7	the **b** of his Son Jesus cleanses us
1 Jn	5: 6	one who came through water and **b**,
1 Jn	5: 6	by water alone, but by water and **b**.
1 Jn	5: 8	and the **b**, and the three are of one
Rv	1: 5	has freed us from our sins by his **b**,
Rv	5: 9	with your **b** you purchased for God
Rv	6:10	avenge our **b** on the inhabitants
Rv	6:12	and the whole moon became like **b**.
Rv	7:14	them white in the **b** of the Lamb.
Rv	11: 6	have power to turn water into **b**
Rv	12:11	conquered him by the **b** of the Lamb
Rv	14:20	**b** poured out of the wine press
Rv	16: 4	of water. These also turned to **b**.
Rv	16: 6	For they have shed the **b** of the holy
Rv	16: 6	you [have] given them **b** to drink;
Rv	17: 6	was drunk on the **b** of the holy ones
Rv	17: 6	on the **b** of the witnesses to Jesus.
Rv	18:24	In her was found the **b** of prophets
Rv	19:13	a cloak that had been dipped in **b**,

BLOODSHED →BLOOD, SHED

Lv	17: 4	shall be judged guilty of **b**;
Is	5: 7	He looked for judgment, but see, **b**!
Ez	9: 9	the land is filled with **b**, the city
Hos	4: 2	in their lawlessness, **b** follows **b**.
Hb	2:12	Woe to him who builds a city by **b**,

BLOODTHIRSTY →BLOOD

Ps	55:24	the pit of destruction. These **b** liars
Ps	59: 3	from evildoers; from the **b** save me.
Ps	139:19	and the **b** would depart from me!
Prv	29:10	**B** men hate the honest man,

BLOSSOM →BLOSSOMS

Is	27: 6	Israel shall sprout and **b**,
Hos	14: 6	of Israel: he shall **b** like the lily;
Hb	3:17	For though the fig tree **b** not

BLOSSOMS →BLOSSOM

Ex	25:33	shaped like almond **b**, each with its
Nm	17:23	but **b** as well, and even bore ripe

BLOT →BLOTTED

Ex	17:14	I will completely **b** out the memory

Dt	9:14	and **b** out their name from under
Ps	51: 3	your abundant compassion **b** out my
Jer	18:23	**b** not out their sin in your sight!

BLOTTED →BLOT

Dt	25: 6	that his name may not be **b**
Ps	9: 6	their name you **b** out for all time.

BLOW →BLEW, BLOWING, BLOWS

Song	4:16	south wind! **b** upon my garden
Ez	33: 6	and fails to **b** the warning trumpet,
Jl	2: 1	**B** the trumpet in Zion,
Rv	7: 1	so that no wind could **b** on land
Rv	8: 6	seven trumpets prepared to **b** them.

BLOWING →BLOW

Jos	6:13	of the ark of the Lord, **b** their horns.
2 Chr	23:13	of the land rejoicing and **b** trumpets,
Tb	6: 9	**b** into his eyes right on the cataracts,
Lk	12:55	the wind is **b** from the south you say

BLOWS →BLOW

Is	40: 7	the breath of the Lord **b** upon it.
Jn	3: 8	The wind **b** where it wills, and you

BLUSH

Is	1:29	**b** for the groves which you chose.
Jer	6:15	they know not how to **b**. Hence they
Jer	8:12	they know not how to **b**. Hence they

BOANERGES

Mk	3:17	James, whom he named **B**, that is,

BOAST →BOASTED, BOASTFUL, BOASTING, BOASTS

Ps	75: 5	So I say to the boastful: "Do not **b**!"
Prv	27: 1	**B** not of tomorrow, for you know
Rom	2:23	You who **b** of the law, do you
Rom	5: 3	but we even **b** of our afflictions,
Rom	11:18	do not **b** against the branches. If you do **b**,
		consider that you do not
1 Cor	1:31	boasts, should **b** in the Lord."
1 Cor	13: 3	hand my body over so that I may **b**,
2 Cor	1:14	that we are your **b** as you also are
2 Cor	5:12	giving you an opportunity to **b**
2 Cor	5:12	those who **b** of external appearance
2 Cor	10: 8	even if I should **b** a little too much
2 Cor	10:17	boasts, should **b** in the Lord."
2 Cor	11:30	If I must **b**, I will **b** of the things
Gal	6:14	may I never **b** except in the cross
Eph	2: 9	is not from works, so no one may **b**.
Phil	2:16	so that my **b** for the day of Christ

BOASTED →BOAST

Ps	44: 9	In God we have **b** all the day long;

BOASTFUL →BOAST

Ps	75: 5	So I say to the **b**: "Do not boast!"
Rom	1:30	haughty, **b**, ingenious in their

BOASTING →BOAST

1 Cor	4: 7	why are you **b** as if you did not
1 Cor	5: 6	Your **b** is not appropriate. Do you
Jas	4:16	now you are **b** in your arrogance. All such **b** is evil.

BOASTS →BOAST

Prv	20:14	but once he has gone his way, he **b**.
1 Cor	1:31	"Whoever **b**, should boast
2 Cor	10:17	"Whoever **b**, should boast

BOAT →BOATS

Sir	33: 2	is tossed about like a **b** in a storm.
Mt	4:21	They were in a **b**, with their father
Mt	8:23	He got into a **b** and his disciples
Mt	13: 2	around him that he got into a **b**
Mt	14:13	withdrew in a **b** to a deserted place
Mt	14:29	Peter got out of the **b** and began
Lk	5: 3	and taught the crowds from the **b**.
Jn	21: 6	the net over the right side of the **b**

BOATS →BOAT

Lk	5: 7	filled both **b** so that they were

BOAZ

Wealthy Bethlehemite who showed favor to Ruth (Ru 2), married

her (Ru 4). Ancestor of David (Ru 4:18-22; 1 Chr 2:12-15), Jesus (Mt 1:5-16; Lk 3:23-32).

BODIES →BODY

Nm	14:29	in the desert shall your dead **b** fall.
1 Chr	10:12	man, recovered the **b** of Saul and his
Is	66:14	and your **b** flourish like the grass;
Dn	3:94	the fire had had no power over the **b**
Mt	27:52	the **b** of many saints who had fallen
Rom	1:24	the mutual degradation of their **b**.
Rom	8:23	adoption, the redemption of our **b**.
Rom	12: 1	to offer your **b** as a living sacrifice,
1 Cor	6:15	not know that your **b** are members
Eph	5:28	love their wives as their own **b**.
Heb	10:22	and our **b** washed in pure water.

BODILY →BODY

Lk	3:22	upon him in **b** form like a dove.
Col	2: 9	the whole fullness of the deity **b**,

BODY →BODIES, BODILY

Ps	16: 9	rejoices; my **b** also dwells secure,
Ez	1:23	of them had two covering his **b**.]
Mi	6: 7	the fruit of my **b** for the sin of my
Mt	6:22	"The lamp of the **b** is the eye. If your
Mt	10:28	not be afraid of those who kill the **b**
Mt	10:28	destroy both soul and **b** in Gehenna.
Mt	26:26	said, "Take and eat; this is my **b**."
Mt	27:58	Pilate and asked for the **b** of Jesus;
Mk	14:22	them, and said, "Take it; this is my **b**."
Lk	11:34	The lamp of the **b** is your eye.
Lk	11:34	your whole **b** is filled with light,
Lk	11:34	it is bad, then your **b** is in darkness.
Lk	12: 4	not be afraid of those who kill the **b**
Lk	12:23	food and the **b** more than clothing.
Lk	22:19	"This is my **b**, which will be given
Lk	24: 3	they did not find the **b** of the Lord
Jn	2:21	speaking about the temple of his **b**.
Rom	6: 6	our sinful **b** might be done away
Rom	7:24	will deliver me from this mortal **b**?
Rom	8:10	although the **b** is dead because
Rom	12: 4	For as in one **b** we have many parts,
1 Cor	5: 3	although absent in **b** but present
1 Cor	6:13	the Lord, and the Lord is for the **b**;
1 Cor	6:18	a person commits is outside the **b**,
1 Cor	6:18	person sins against his own **b**.
1 Cor	6:19	not know that your **b** is a temple
1 Cor	6:20	Therefore glorify God in your **b**.
1 Cor	7: 4	not have authority over her own **b**,
1 Cor	7: 4	not have authority over his own **b**,
1 Cor	9:27	No, I drive my **b** and train it,
1 Cor	10:16	a participation in the **b** of Christ?
1 Cor	11:24	said, "This is my **b** that is for you.
1 Cor	12:12	As a **b** is one though it has many
1 Cor	12:12	and all the parts of the **b**,
1 Cor	12:12	many, are one **b**, so also Christ.
1 Cor	12:13	we were all baptized into one **b**,
1 Cor	12:15	not a hand I do not belong to the **b**,"
1 Cor	12:15	this reason belong any less to the **b**.
1 Cor	15:44	is sown a natural **b**; it is raised a spiritual **b**.
1 Cor	15:44	If there is a natural **b**, there is
2 Cor	4:10	about in the **b** the dying of Jesus,
2 Cor	5: 8	we would rather leave the **b** and go
2 Cor	12: 2	fourteen years ago (whether in the **b** or out of the **b** I do not know,
Gal	6:17	I bear the marks of Jesus on my **b**.
Eph	1:23	which is his **b**, the fullness
Eph	2:16	God, in one **b**, through the cross,
Eph	4: 4	one **b** and one Spirit, as you were
Eph	4:12	for building up the **b** of Christ,
Eph	5:30	because we are members of his **b**.
Phil	1:20	Christ will be magnified in my **b**,
Phil	3:21	He will change our lowly **b**
Phil	3:21	with his glorified **b** by the power
Col	1:18	He is the head of the **b**, the church.
Col	1:24	of Christ on behalf of his **b**,
1 Thes	5:23	and **b**, be preserved blameless
Heb	10: 5	desire, but a **b** you prepared for me;
Jas	2:26	just as a **b** without a spirit is dead,
1 Pt	2:24	our sins in his **b** upon the cross,

Jude   1: 9   in a dispute over the **b** of Moses,

BOIL →BOILED, BOILING, BOILS
Ex   23:19 "You shall not **b** a kid in its mother's
Is   38:21 figs to be taken and applied to the **b**,

BOILED →BOIL
Lam   4:10   women **b** their own children,

BOILING →BOIL
Jer   1:13   "I see a **b** cauldron," I replied,

BOILS →BOIL
Ex   9: 9   Egypt and cause festering **b** on man
Dt   28:27 LORD will strike you with Egyptian **b**

BOLDLY →BOLDNESS
Acts   9:28   spoke out **b** in the name of the Lord.
Acts   14: 3 period, speaking out **b** for the Lord,

BOLDNESS →BOLDLY
Acts   4:13   Observing the **b** of Peter and John
Acts   4:29   to speak your word with all **b**,
Eph   3:12   in whom we have **b** of speech

BOND →BONDS
Eph   4: 3   of the spirit through the **b** of peace:
Col   3:14   love, that is, the **b** of perfection.

BONDS →BOND
Ps   116:16 maidservant; you have loosed my **b**.
Is   52: 2 Loose the **b** from your neck,

BONE →BONES
Gn   2:23   "This one, at last, is **b** of my bones
Ez   37: 7 bones came together, **b** joining **b**.

BONES →BONE
Gn   50:25 you must bring my **b** up with you
Ex   12:46 You shall not break any of its **b**.
Ex   13:19 Moses also took Joseph's **b** along,
Jos   24:32 The **b** of Joseph,
2 Kgs   13:21 came in contact with the **b** of Elisha,
Ps   22:15 life drains away; all my **b** grow soft.
Ps   22:18 that I can count all my **b**. They stare
Ps   34:21 God watches over all their **b**;
Prv   14:30 to the body, but jealousy rots the **b**.
Sir   28:17 a blow from the tongue smashes **b**;
Jer   20: 9 imprisoned in my **b**; I grow weary
Ez   37: 4 Prophesy over these **b**, and say
Ez   37: 4 Dry **b**, hear the word of the LORD!
Mt   23:27 inside are full of dead men's **b**

BOOK →BOOKS
Ex   24: 7 Taking the **b** of the covenant,
Ex   32:33 against me will I strike out of my **b**.
Dt   29:19 curse mentioned in this **b** will alight
Jos   1: 8   Keep this **b** of the law on your lips.
Jos   10:13 this not recorded in the **B** of Jashar?
Jos   23: 6 that is written in the **b** of the law
2 Kgs   22: 8 "I have found the **b** of the law
2 Kgs   22: 8 Hilkiah gave the **b** to Shaphan,
Neh   8: 8   read plainly from the **b** of the law
Ps   69:29 Strike them from the **b** of the living;
Is   34:16 Look in the **b** of the LORD and read:
Dn   12: 1 who is found written in the **b**.
Mk   12:26 you not read in the **B** of Moses,
Jn   20:30 that are not written in this **b**.
Acts   1: 1   In the first **b**, Theophilus, I dealt
Phil   4: 3   whose names are in the **b** of life.
Rv   3: 5   erase his name from the **b** of life
Rv   13: 8 of the world in the **b** of life,
Rv   17: 8 have not been written in the **b** of life
Rv   20:12 scroll was opened, the **b** of life was thrown
Rv   20:15 written in the **b** of life was thrown
Rv   21:27 are written in the Lamb's **b** of life.
Rv   22: 7 the prophetic message of this **b**.
Rv   22:18 hears the prophetic words in this **b**:
Rv   22:18 him the plagues described in this **b**,

BOOKS →BOOK
Eccl   12:12 making of many **b** there is no end,
Dn   7:10   convened, and the **b** were opened.
Jn   21:25 whole world would contain the **b**

BOOTHS
Lv   23:34 month is the LORD's feast of **B**,
Dt   16:13 "You shall celebrate the feast of **B**
2 Chr   8:13   feast of Weeks and the feast of **B**.
Ezr   3: 4   kept the feast of **B** in the manner
Neh   8:14   must dwell in **b** during the feast
1 Mc   10:21 hundred and sixty at the feast of **B**,
2 Mc   1: 9   celebrate the feast of **B** in the month
Zec   14:16 and to celebrate the feast of **B**.

BOOTY
Nm   14: 3 and little ones will be taken as **b**.
Nm   14:31 who you said would be taken as **b**,
Dt   1:39   who you said would become **b**,
Prv   1:13   gain, we shall fill our houses with **b**;

BORDER →BORDERS
2 Chr   9:26   and down to the **b** of Egypt.

BORDERS →BORDER
Ex   16:35 ate manna until they reached the **b**
Ps   147:14 Brought peace to your **b**, and filled

BORE →BEAR
Gn   6: 4   daughters of man, who **b** them sons.
Gn   16:15 Hagar **b** Abram a son, and Abram
Ex   19: 4 and how I **b** you up on eagle wings
Nm   17:23 as well, and even **b** ripe almonds!
Is   53: 4 Yet it was our infirmities that he **b**,
Mt   8:17   our infirmities and **b** our diseases."
1 Pt   2:24   He himself **b** our sins in his body

BORN →BEAR
Gn   17:17 "Can a child be **b** to a man who is
Ex   1:22   every boy that is **b** to the Hebrews,
Jb   14: 1 Man **b** of woman is short-lived
Prv   17:17 a brother is **b** for the time of stress.
Eccl   3: 2   A time to be **b**, and a time to die;
Is   9: 5   For a child is **b** to us, a son is given
Is   66: 8 or a nation be **b** in a single moment?
Jer   1: 5   before you were **b** I dedicated you,
Mt   1:16   Of her was **b** Jesus who is called
Mt   2: 1   When Jesus was **b** in Bethlehem
Mk   14:21 for that man if he had never been **b**."
Lk   1:35   the child to be **b** will be called holy,
Lk   2:11   of David a savior has been **b** for you
Lk   7:28   I tell you, among those **b** of women,
Jn   1:13   who were **b** not by natural
Jn   3: 3   of God without being **b** from above."
Jn   3: 5   of God without being **b** of water
Jn   3: 7   you, 'You must be **b** from above.'
Jn   3: 8   with everyone who is **b** of the Spirit."
Jn   18:37 For this I was **b** and for this I came
Rom   9:11   before they had yet been **b** or had
1 Cor   15: 8 as to one **b** abnormally, he appeared
Gal   4: 4   God sent his Son, **b** of a woman,
1 Pt   1:23   You have been **b** anew,

BORNE →BEAR
Gn   21: 7 Yet I have **b** him a son in his old

BORROW →BORROWED, BORROWER
Dt   15: 6 to many nations, and **b** from none;
Dt   28:12 to many nations, and **b** from none.
2 Kgs   4: 3   "b vessels from all your neighbors—as
Ps   37:21 The wicked **b** but do not repay;
Mt   5:42   your back on one who wants to **b**.

BORROWED →BORROW
Neh   5: 4   pay the king's tax we have **b** money

BORROWER →BORROW
Prv   22: 7 and the **b** is the slave of the lender.
Sir   29: 6 and insults the **b** pays him back,
Is   24: 2 The lender as the **b**, the creditor as

BOSOM
Prv   6:27   Can a man take fire to his **b**, and his

BOTHER →BOTHERING
Lk   11: 7 in reply from within, 'Do not **b** me;

BOTHERING →BOTHER
Lk   18: 5 this widow keeps **b** me I shall

BOTTOM
Am	9: 3	in the **b** of the sea, I will command
Mk	15:38	was torn in two from top to **b**.

BOUGHS
Lv	23:40	branches of palms and **b** of myrtles
Ez	31: 6	In its **b** nested all the birds

BOUGHT →BUY
Gn	33:19	he had pitched his tent he **b**
Gn	50:13	Abraham had **b** for a burial ground
2 Sm	24:24	So David **b** the threshing floor
Neh	5: 8	we **b** back our fellow Jews who had

BOUND →BIND, BOUNDARY
Nm	30: 5	or the pledge to which she **b** herself
Jgs	16:21	Gaza and **b** him with bronze fetters,
2 Kgs	25: 7	Zedekiah, **b** him with fetters,
Jer	39: 7	and **b** him in chains to bring him
Dn	3:21	They were **b** and cast
Mt	16:19	bind on earth shall be **b** in heaven;
Mt	18:18	bind on earth shall be **b** in heaven,
Mk	15: 1	They **b** Jesus, led him away,
Lk	13:16	whom Satan has **b** for eighteen
Rom	7: 2	Thus a married woman is **b** by law
1 Cor	7:15	or sister is not **b** in such cases;
1 Cor	7:39	A wife is **b** to her husband as long
Rv	9:14	"Release the four angels who are **b**

BOUNDARIES →BOUNDARY
Nm	34:12	be yours, with the **b** that surround it."
Dt	32: 8	He set up the **b** of the peoples
Ez	47:13	These are the **b** within which you

BOUNDARY →BOUND, BOUNDARIES
Nm	34: 3	"Your southern **b** shall be
Ez	47:15	This is the **b** of the land on the north

BOUNTIFULLY →BOUNTY
2 Cor	9: 6	whoever sows **b** will also reap **b**.

BOUNTY →BOUNTIFULLY
1 Kgs	10:13	given her from Solomon's royal **b**.
Ps	65:12	You adorn the year with your **b**;
Wis	16:25	it was serving your all-nourishing **b**

BOW →BOWED, BOWS, BOWSTRINGS
Gn	9:13	I set my **b** in the clouds to serve as
Gn	27:29	may your mother's sons **b** down
Gn	49: 8	of your father shall **b** down to you.
Ex	20: 5	you shall not **b** down before them
Dt	5: 9	you shall not **b** down before them
Dt	26:10	you shall **b** down in his presence.
1 Sm	18: 4	and his sword, his **b** and his belt.
2 Sm	22:35	till my arms could bend a **b** of brass.
1 Kgs	22:34	however, drew his **b** at random,
2 Kgs	13:15	"Take a **b** and some arrows,"
Est	3: 2	would kneel and **b** down to Haman,
Est	3: 2	would not kneel and **b** down.
Ps	44: 7	Not in my **b** do I trust, nor does my
Ps	95: 6	Enter, let us **b** down in worship;
Ps	97: 7	things; all gods **b** down before you.
Ps	138: 2	I **b** low toward your holy temple;
Ez	1:28	Like the **b** which appears
Hos	1: 7	by war, by sword or **b**, by horses
Zec	9:13	For I will bend Judah as my **b**, I will
Rv	6: 2	a white horse, and its rider had a **b**.

BOWED →BOW
Gn	37: 7	around my sheaf and **b** down to it."
Gn	47:31	Then Israel **b** at the head of the bed.
Ex	12:27	Then the people **b** down in worship,
Ex	34: 8	Moses at once **b** down to the ground
Jdt	10: 8	of Jerusalem." Judith **b** down to God.
Jdt	13:17	They **b** down and worshiped God,
Ps	38: 7	I am stooped and deeply **b**; all day I
Ps	145:14	and raises up all who are **b** down.
Ps	146: 8	raises up those who are **b** down;

BOWELS
2 Chr	21:15	pains from a disease in your **b**,
2 Mc	9: 5	with excruciating pains in his **b**

BOWL →BOWLS
Dt	28: 5	your grain bin and your kneading **b**!
Dt	28:17	your grain bin and your kneading **b**!
Eccl	12: 6	and the golden **b** is broken,
Song	7: 3	Your navel is a round **b** that should
Rv	16: 2	and poured out his **b** on the earth.

BOWLS →BOWL
Ezr	1:10	golden **b**, thirty; silver **b**,
Jer	52:19	the fire holders, the **b**, the pots,
Jer	52:19	the sacrificial **b** which were of gold
Rv	5: 8	harp and gold **b** filled with incense,
Rv	16: 1	pour out the seven **b** of God's fury
Rv	21: 9	angels who held the seven **b** filled

BOWS →BOW
1 Sm	2: 4	The **b** of the mighty are broken,
Ps	37:15	own hearts; their **b** will be broken.
Is	46: 1	Bel **b** down, Nebo stoops, their idols

BOWSTRINGS →BOW
Jgs	16: 7	seven fresh **b** which have not dried,"

BOY →BOYS
Gn	22:12	"Do not lay your hand on the **b**,"
Gn	44:22	lord, 'The **b** cannot leave his father;
Ex	1:22	into the river every **b** that is born
Jgs	13: 5	for this **b** is to be consecrated
Mt	17:18	and from that hour the **b** was cured.
Lk	2:43	the **b** Jesus remained behind
Jn	6: 9	"There is a **b** here who has five

BOYS →BOY
Ex	1:18	acted thus, allowing the **b** to live?"
1 Mc	2:46	any uncircumcised **b** whom they

BOZRAH
Is	34: 6	For the Lord has a sacrifice in B,
Jer	49:13	B shall become an object of horror

BRACELETS
Gn	24:22	two gold **b** weighing ten shekels,
Jdt	10: 4	feet, and put on her anklets, **b**, rings,
Is	3:19	the pendants, **b**, and veils;
Ez	16:11	I put **b** on your arms, a necklace

BRAIDED
1 Tm	2: 9	not with **b** hairstyles and gold

BRAMBLES
Lk	6:44	nor do they gather grapes from **b**.

BRANCH →BRANCHES
Nm	13:23	where they cut down a **b**
1 Mc	13:37	crown and the palm **b** that you sent.
Is	4: 2	The **b** of the Lord will be luster
Jer	1:11	"I see a **b** of the watching-tree,"
Mal	3:19	fire, leaving them neither root nor **b**,
Jn	15: 2	He takes away every **b** in me
Jn	15: 4	Just as a **b** cannot bear fruit on its

BRANCHES →BRANCH
Gn	2:10	there it divides and becomes four **b**.
Gn	40:10	and on the vine were three **b**. It had
Ex	25:32	Six **b** are to extend from the sides
Ex	25:32	the lampstand, three **b** on one side,
Lv	23:40	**b** of palms and boughs of myrtles
2 Sm	18: 9	as the mule passed under the **b**
Neh	8:15	country and bring in **b** of olive trees,
1 Mc	13:51	waving of palm **b**, the music
Ps	118:27	Join in procession with leafy **b**
Ez	17: 6	Thus it became a vine, produced **b**
Lk	13:19	'the birds of the sky dwelt in its **b**.' "
Jn	12:13	they took palm **b** and went
Jn	15: 5	I am the vine, you are the **b**.
Rom	11:21	if God did not spare the natural **b**,
Rv	7: 9	and holding palm **b** in their hands.

BRAND
Am	4:11	you were like a **b** plucked
Zec	3: 2	Is not this man a **b** snatched

BREACH →BREACHED, BREACHES
Jgs	21:15	Lord had made a **b** among the tribes
Ps	106:23	Withstood him in the **b** to turn back

Ps	144:14	May there be no **b** in the walls,
Ez	22:30	stand in the **b** before me to keep me

BREACHED →BREACH

2 Kgs	25: 4	the city walls were **b**. Then the king

BREACHES →BREACH

Am	9:11	I will wall up its **b**, raise up its

BREAD

Gn	3:19	of your face shall you get **b** to eat,
Gn	14:18	of Salem, brought out **b** and wine,
Ex	12: 8	its roasted flesh with unleavened **b**
Ex	12:17	this custom of the unleavened **b**.
Ex	16: 4	"I will now rain down **b** from heaven
Ex	23:15	keep the feast of Unleavened **B**.
Ex	23:15	you must eat unleavened **b** for seven
Lv	7:13	include loaves of leavened **b** along
Dt	8: 3	that not by **b** alone does man live,
Dt	16: 3	You shall not eat leavened **b** with it.
Dt	16: 3	unleavened **b**, the **b** of affliction,
Dt	29: 5	**b** was not your food, nor wine
Jgs	7:13	a round loaf of barley **b** was rolling
1 Sm	21: 5	"I have no ordinary **b** on hand, only holy **b**;
1 Kgs	17: 6	Ravens brought him **b** and meat
1 Kgs	22:27	and feed him scanty rations of **b**
Ps	37:25	or their children begging **b**.
Ps	53: 5	devour my people as they devour **b**;
Ps	80: 6	You have fed them the **b** of tears,
Prv	6:26	may be scarcely a loaf of **b**,
Prv	9:17	and **b** gotten secretly is pleasing!"
Prv	20:17	The **b** of deceit is sweet to a man,
Eccl	9: 7	eat your **b** with joy and drink your
Eccl	11: 1	Cast your **b** upon the waters;
Wis	16:20	and furnished them **b** from heaven,
Sir	15: 3	him with the **b** of understanding,
Sir	23:17	The rake to whom all **b** is sweet
Is	55: 2	spend your money for what is not **b**;
Am	8:11	land: Not a famine of **b**, or thirst
Ob	1: 7	Those who eat your **b** lay snares
Mt	4: 3	these stones become loaves of **b**."
Mt	6:11	Give us today our daily **b**;
Mt	15:33	"Where could we ever get enough **b**
Mt	16: 5	disciples had forgotten to bring **b**.
Mt	26:26	Jesus took **b**, said the blessing,
Mk	2:26	ate the **b** of offering that only
Lk	4: 4	'One does not live by **b** alone.' "
Lk	11: 3	Give us each day our daily **b**
Lk	22:19	Then he took the **b**,
Lk	24:35	to them in the breaking of the **b**.
Jn	6:33	For the **b** of God is
Jn	6:35	said to them, "I am the **b** of life;
Jn	6:41	"I am the **b** that came down
Jn	6:48	I am the **b** of life.
Jn	6:51	I am the living **b** that came down
Jn	6:51	the **b** that I will give is my flesh
Jn	21:13	and took the **b** and gave it to them,
Acts	2:42	to the breaking of the **b**
1 Cor	5: 8	with the unleavened **b** of sincerity
1 Cor	10:16	The **b** that we break, is it not
1 Cor	11:23	night he was handed over, took **b**,
1 Cor	11:26	For as often as you eat this **b**

BREADTH

Gn	13:17	through its length and **b**, for to you I
Eph	3:18	with all the holy ones what is the **b**

BREAK →BREAKING, BREAKS, BROKE, BROKEN, BROKENHEARTED, DAYBREAK

Ex	12:46	You shall not **b** any of its bones.
Ex	19:21	not to **b** through toward the Lord
Ex	34:20	not redeem it, you must **b** its neck.
Jgs	2: 1	I would never **b** my covenant
Ps	3: 8	you will **b** the teeth of the wicked.
Ps	10:15	**B** the arms of the wicked
Prv	25:15	and a soft tongue will **b** a bone.
Is	42: 3	A bruised reed he shall not **b**,
Ez	17:15	Can he **b** a covenant and still go
Mt	6:19	destroys, and thieves **b** in and steal.
Mt	12:20	A bruised reed he will not **b**,
Mt	15: 3	why do you **b** the commandment

Jn	19:33	dead, they did not **b** his legs,
Acts	20: 7	week when we gathered to **b** bread,
Rom	2:25	the law; but if you **b** the law,
1 Cor	10:16	The bread that we **b**, is it not
Rv	5: 2	to open the scroll and **b** its seals?"

BREAKFAST

Jn	21:12	Jesus said to them, "Come, have **b**."

BREAKING →BREAK

Dt	31:20	despising me and **b** my covenant;
Ez	16:59	despised your oath, **b** a covenant.
Acts	2:42	life, to the **b** of the bread
Rom	2:23	do you dishonor God by **b** the law?

BREAKS →BREAK

Ps	46:10	earth, **b** the bow, splinters the spear,
Mt	5:19	whoever **b** one of the least of these

BREAST →BREASTPIECE, BREASTPLATE, BREASTPLATES, BREASTS

Ex	29:26	take the **b** of Aaron's ordination ram
Lv	7:30	together with the **b**, which is to be
Nm	6:20	with the **b** of the wave offering
Ps	22:10	made me safe at my mother's **b**.
Lk	18:13	to heaven but beat his **b** and prayed,

BREASTPIECE →BREAST, PIECE

Ex	28:15	"The **b** of decision you shall
Ex	28:30	this **b** of decision you shall put
Lv	8: 8	He then set the **b** on him,

BREASTPLATE →BREAST

Wis	5:18	He shall don justice for a **b** and shall
Is	59:17	He put on justice as his **b**, salvation,
Eph	6:14	clothed with righteousness as a **b**,
1 Thes	5: 8	putting on the **b** of faith and love

BREASTPLATES →BREAST

Rv	9: 9	and they had chests like iron **b**.
Rv	9:17	and yellow **b**, and the horses' heads

BREASTS →BREAST

Gn	49:25	The blessings of **b** and womb,
Song	4: 5	Your **b** are like twin fawns,
Is	32:12	Beat your **b** for the pleasant fields,
Is	66:11	with delight at her abundant **b**!
Ez	23: 3	bosoms and fondled their virginal **b**.
Na	2: 8	Moaning like doves, beating their **b**.
Lk	11:27	you and the **b** at which you nursed."
Lk	23:29	bore and the **b** that never nursed.'

BREATH →BREATHED, BREATHING

Gn	2: 7	blew into his nostrils the **b** of life,
Gn	6:17	in which there is the **b** of life;
Jb	27: 3	and the **b** of God is in my nostrils,
Ps	39:12	All mortals are but a **b**.
Eccl	12: 7	the life **b** returns to God who gave
Is	40: 7	when the **b** of the Lord blows
Jer	10:14	molded a fraud, without **b** of life.
Lam	4:20	one of the Lord, our **b** of life,
Acts	17:25	he who gives to everyone life and **b**
2 Thes	2: 8	will kill with the **b** of his mouth
Rv	11:11	a **b** of life from God entered them.

BREATHED →BREATH

Mk	15:37	Jesus gave a loud cry and **b** his last.
Jn	20:22	this, he **b** on them and said to them,

BREATHING →BREATH

Acts	9: 1	still **b** murderous threats against

BRIBE →BRIBES

Ex	23: 8	Never take a **b**, for a **b** blinds even
Dt	16:19	You shall not take a **b**; for a **b** blinds
1 Sm	12: 3	From whom have I accepted a **b**
Eccl	7: 7	man, and a **b** corrupts the heart.
Mi	3:11	Her leaders render judgment for a **b**,

BRIBES →BRIBE

1 Sm	8: 3	sought illicit gain and accepted **b**,
Prv	15:27	house, but he who hates **b** will live.
Is	5:23	To those who acquit the guilty for **b**,
Ez	22:12	in you who take **b** to shed blood.

BRICK → BRICKS
Ex	1:14	with hard work in mortar and **b**

BRICKS → BRICK
Gn	11: 3	They used **b** for stone, and bitumen

BRIDE → BRIDEGROOM
Song	4: 8	Come from Lebanon, my **b**,
Is	49:18	like a **b** you shall fasten them
Is	62: 5	as a bridegroom rejoices in his **b**
Jer	2: 2	how you loved me as a **b**,
Jn	3:29	who has the **b** is the bridegroom;
Rv	19: 7	come, his **b** has made herself ready.
Rv	21: 2	prepared as a **b** adorned for her
Rv	21: 9	I will show you the **b**, the wife
Rv	22:17	The Spirit and the **b** say, "Come."

BRIDEGROOM → BRIDE
Ps	19: 6	it comes forth like a **b** from his
Jer	25:10	the voice of the **b** and the voice
Bar	2:23	the voice of the **b** and the voice
Mt	9:15	guests mourn as long as the **b** is
Mt	9:15	will come when the **b** is taken away
Mt	25: 1	lamps and went out to meet the **b**.
Mk	2:20	will come when the **b** is taken away
Jn	3:29	The one who has the bride is the **b**;

BRIDLE
Ps	32: 9	bit and **b** their temper is curbed,
Is	30:28	a **b** on the jaws of the peoples
Jas	3: 2	man, able to **b** his whole body also.
Rv	14:20	of a horse's **b** for two hundred miles.

BRIEF → BRIEFLY
Is	54: 7	For a **b** moment I abandoned you,

BRIEFLY → BRIEF
Heb	13:22	for I have written to you rather **b**.

BRIER → BRIERS
Mi	7: 4	The best of them is like a **b**,

BRIERS → BRIER
Is	7:24	for all the country shall be **b**

BRIGHT → BRIGHTER, BRIGHTNESS
Mt	17: 5	a **b** cloud cast a shadow over them,
Rv	19: 8	to wear a **b**, clean linen garment."
Rv	22:16	of David, the **b** morning star."

BRIGHTER → BRIGHT
Acts	26:13	a light from the sky, **b** than the sun,

BRIGHTNESS → BRIGHT
Is	59: 9	for **b**, but we walk in gloom!
Is	60:19	light by day, Nor the **b** of the moon
Ez	1: 4	with flashing fire [enveloped in **b**],
Am	5:20	and not light, gloom without any **b**?
Acts	22:11	see nothing because of the **b**

BRIM
Jn	2: 7	So they filled them to the **b**.

BRING → BRINGING, BRINGS, BROUGHT
Gn	6:17	to **b** the flood [waters] on the earth,
Gn	6:19	living creatures you shall **b** two
Gn	28:15	you go, and **b** you back to this land.
Lv	1: 2	you wishes to **b** an animal offering
Nm	20: 5	only to **b** us to this wretched place
Dt	24: 4	you shall not **b** such guilt
2 Sm	12:23	I fast? Can I **b** him back again?
2 Kgs	22:16	I will **b** upon this place and upon its
Ps	25:17	my heart; **b** me out of my distress.
Prv	25: 8	seen **b** not forth hastily against
Eccl	11: 9	all this God will **b** you to judgment.
Eccl	12:14	Because God will **b** to judgment
Is	60:17	In place of bronze I will **b** gold,
Jer	24: 6	and **b** them back to this land,
Ez	5:17	and I will **b** the sword upon you. I,
Zec	3: 8	Yes, I will **b** my servant the Shoot.
Zec	4: 7	He shall **b** out the capstone amid
Mt	10:34	I have come to **b** peace
Mt	10:34	I have come to **b** not peace
Lk	4:18	me to **b** glad tidings to the poor.
Rom	8:33	Who will **b** a charge against God's

Rom	10: 6	heaven?" (that is, to **b** Christ down)
Rom	10:15	of those who **b** [the] good news!"
1 Cor	8: 8	Now food will not **b** us closer
2 Jn	1:10	to you and does not **b** this doctrine,
Rv	21:24	of the earth will **b** their treasure.

BRINGING → BRING
Nm	14: 3	Why is the LORD **b** us into this land
Dt	8: 7	God, is **b** you into a good country,
1 Kgs	21:21	I am **b** evil upon you: I will destroy
Lk	18:15	People were **b** even infants to him
Heb	2:10	exist, in **b** many children to glory,
2 Pt	2: 1	**b** swift destruction on themselves.

BRINGS → BRING
Sir	26: 2	A worthy wife **b** joy to her husband.
Is	52: 7	the feet of him who **b** glad tidings,
Mt	12:35	A good person **b** forth good
Mt	12:35	an evil person **b** forth evil
Lk	11:26	and **b** back seven other spirits more
Jas ·	5:20	know that whoever **b** back a sinner

BROKE → BREAK
Ex	32:19	**b** them on the base of the mountain.
Ex	34: 1	on the former tablets that you **b**.
Dt	32:51	because both of you **b** faith with me
2 Kgs	23:14	He **b** to pieces the pillars, cut down
2 Kgs	25:13	LORD, the Chaldeans **b** into pieces;
Jer	31:32	for they **b** my covenant and I had
Ez	17:19	my covenant which he **b**, I swear
Mt	14:19	he said the blessing, **b** the loaves,
Mt	26:26	said the blessing, **b** it, and giving it
Mk	14:22	said the blessing, **b** it, and gave it
1 Cor	11:24	he had given thanks, **b** it and said,

BROKEN → BREAK
Gn	17:14	his people; he has **b** my covenant."
1 Sm	4:18	man and heavy, he died of a **b** neck.
2 Kgs	18:21	fact a **b** reed which pierces the hand
Ps	34:21	all their bones; not a one shall be **b**.
Ps	51:19	My sacrifice, God, is a **b** spirit;
Ps	51:19	do not spurn a **b**, humbled heart.
Prv	18:14	but a **b** spirit who can bear?
Eccl	4:12	A three-ply cord is not easily **b**.
Eccl	12: 6	and the golden bowl is **b**,
Wis	4: 5	Their twigs shall be **b** off untimely,
Jer	33:21	with my servant David also be **b**,
Ez	44: 7	thus you have **b** my covenant by all
Jn	7:23	that the law of Moses may not be **b**,
Jn	19:36	fulfilled: "Not a bone of it will be **b**."
Rom	11:20	They were **b** off because

BROKENHEARTED → BREAK, HEART
Ps	34:19	The LORD is close to the **b**,
Ps	109:16	poor and brought death to the **b**.
Ps	147: 3	Heals the **b**, binds up their wounds,
Is	61: 1	to heal the **b**, To proclaim liberty

BRONZE
Gn	4:22	of all who forge instruments of **b**
Ex	26:11	make fifty **b** clasps and put them
Ex	27: 2	You shall then plate it with **b**.
Ex	27:10	columns and twenty pedestals of **b**;
Ex	30:18	shall make a **b** laver with a **b** base.
Nm	17: 4	Eleazar the priest had the **b** censers
Nm	21: 9	Moses accordingly made a **b** serpent
Dt	28:23	sky over your heads will be like **b**
1 Sm	17: 5	He had a **b** helmet on his head
1 Sm	17: 5	and wore a **b** corselet of scale armor
1 Kgs	7:15	Two hollow **b** columns were cast,
1 Kgs	7:27	Ten stands were also made of **b**,
2 Kgs	16:14	The **b** altar that stood before
2 Kgs	25:13	they carried away the **b** to Babylon.
1 Mc	14:48	should be engraved on **b** tablets,
Ps	18:35	my arms to bend even a bow of **b**.
Is	60:17	In place of **b** I will bring gold,
Is	60:17	In place of wood, **b**,
Ez	1: 7	with a gleam like burnished **b**.
Dn	2:32	were silver, its belly and thighs **b**,
Dn	7:19	with its iron teeth and **b** claws,
Dn	10: 6	and feet looked like burnished **b**,
Dn	14: 7	"it is only clay inside and **b** outside;

Zec 6: 1 and the mountains were of **b**.

BROOD
Nm 32:14 now here you are, a **b** of sinners,
Mt 3: 7 he said to them, "You **b** of vipers!
Mt 12:34 You **b** of vipers, how can you say
Mt 23:33 You serpents, you **b** of vipers,
Lk 13:34 a hen gathers her **b** under her wings,

BROOK →BROOKS
Jer 15:18 become for me a treacherous **b**,

BROOKS →BROOK
Jer 31: 9 them; I will lead them to **b** of water,

BROOM
1 Kgs 19: 4 until he came to a **b** tree and sat
Is 14:23 sweep it with the **b** of destruction,

BROTH
Jgs 6:19 meat in a basket and the **b** in a pot,
Is 65: 4 flesh, with carrion **b** in their dishes,

BROTHER →BROTHER'S, BROTHER-IN-LAW, BROTHERS
Gn 4: 8 Cain said to his **b** Abel, "Let us go
Gn 4: 8 Cain attacked his **b** Abel and killed
Gn 20:13 we come to, say that I am your **b**.' "
Gn 27:35 "Your **b** came here by a ruse
Gn 27:41 father comes, I will kill my **b** Jacob."
Gn 32:12 I pray, from the hand of my **b** Esau!
Gn 42:20 back to me with your youngest **b**
Gn 43:30 affection for his **b** that he was
Gn 45: 4 "I am your **b** Joseph, whom you once
Ex 7: 1 and Aaron your **b** shall act as your
Dt 13: 7 "If your own full **b**, or your son
Dt 25: 5 but her husband's **b** shall go to her
2 Sm 13:12 But she answered him, "No, my **b**!
Song 8: 1 Oh, that you were my **b**,
Am 1:11 Because he pursued his **b**
Ob 1:10 of violence to your **b** Jacob,
Mt 5:22 is angry with his **b** will be liable
Mt 5:22 and whoever says to his **b**, 'Raqa,'
Mt 5:24 first and be reconciled with your **b**,
Mt 10:21 **B** will hand over **b** to death,
Mk 3:35 does the will of God is my **b**
Lk 20:28 'If someone's **b** dies leaving a wife
Lk 20:28 and raise up descendants for his **b**.'
Rom 14:15 If your **b** is being hurt by what you
Rom 14:21 that causes your **b** to stumble.
1 Cor 5:11 to associate with anyone named a **b**,
Phlm 1:16 slave, a **b**, beloved especially to me,
Jas 2:15 If a **b** or sister has nothing to wear
1 Jn 2:10 Whoever loves his **b** remains
1 Jn 3:15 who hates his **b** is a murderer,
1 Jn 3:17 who has worldly means sees a **b**
1 Jn 4:20 God," but hates his **b**, he is a liar;
1 Jn 4:20 does not love a **b** whom he has seen
1 Jn 5:16 If anyone sees his **b** sinning,

BROTHER'S →BROTHER
Gn 4: 9 "I do not know. Am I my **b** keeper?"
Lv 20:21 If a man marries his **b** wife and
Dt 25: 7 does not care to marry his **b** wife,
Mk 6:18 lawful for you to have your **b** wife."

BROTHER-IN-LAW →BROTHER
Gn 38: 8 in fulfillment of your duty as **b**,

BROTHERS →BROTHER
Gn 9:25 lowest of slaves shall he be to his **b**."
Gn 27:29 Be master of your **b**, and may your
Gn 37:11 So his **b** were wrought up against
Gn 42:13 "were twelve **b**, sons of a certain man
Lv 25:48 be redeemed by one of his own **b**,
Jgs 9: 5 and slew his **b**, the seventy sons
2 Chr 21:13 because you have murdered your **b**
1 Mc 3:25 Judas and his **b** began to be feared,
Mt 5:47 And if you greet your **b** only,
Mt 12:49 said, "Here are my mother and my **b**.
Mt 19:29 who has given up houses or **b**
Mt 20:24 they became indignant at the two **b**.
Mk 3:33 "Who are my mother and [my] **b**?"
Mk 12:20 Now there were seven **b**. The first

Lk 21:16 even be handed over by parents, **b**,
Lk 22:32 back, you must strengthen your **b**."
Jn 7: 5 For his **b** did not believe in him.
2 Cor 11:26 at sea, dangers among false **b**;
1 Thes 4:10 for all the **b** throughout Macedonia.
1 Thes 5:26 Greet all the **b** with a holy kiss.
1 Tm 5: 1 as a father. Treat younger men as **b**,
Heb 2:11 he is not ashamed to call them "**b**,"
Heb 2:17 to become like his **b** in every way,

BROUGHT →BRING
Gn 2:19 he **b** them to the man to see what he
Gn 2:22 the man. When he **b** her to the man,
Gn 15: 7 "I am the LORD who **b** you from Ur
Ex 3: 8 a strong hand the LORD **b** you
Ex 32: 1 as for the man Moses who **b** us
Nm 21: 5 "Why have you **b** us up from Egypt
Jgs 2: 1 "It was I who **b** you up from Egypt
Ru 1:21 the LORD has **b** me back destitute.
Ru 1:21 the Almighty has **b** evil upon me?"
2 Chr 36:18 princes, all these he **b** to Babylon.
Ezr 1: 7 the house of the LORD **b** forth
Ezr 6: 5 **b** to Babylon are to be sent back:
Ps 30: 4 LORD, you **b** me up from Sheol;
Ps 105:43 He **b** his people out with joy,
Prv 8:25 place, before the hills, I was **b** forth;
Ez 11: 1 **b** me to the east gate of the temple.
Dn 5:13 Daniel was **b** into the presence
Jon 2: 7 But you **b** up my life from the pit,
Mt 4:24 they **b** to him all who were sick
Mk 6:28 He **b** in the head on a platter
Mk 8:22 they **b** to him a blind man
Mk 15:22 They **b** him to the place of Golgotha
1 Tm 6: 7 For we **b** nothing into the world,
Heb 13:20 who **b** up from the dead the great

BRUISED
Is 42: 3 A **b** reed he shall not break,
Mt 12:20 A **b** reed he will not break,

BRUTE
Ps 73:22 I was like a **b** beast in your

BUCKET
Is 40:15 the nations count as a drop of the **b**,
Jn 4:11 you do not even have a **b**

BUCKLER
Ps 35: 2 Take up the shield and **b**;

BUDDED
Gn 40:10 It had barely **b** when its blossoms

BUGLE
1 Cor 14: 8 if the **b** gives an indistinct sound,

BUILD →BUILDER, BUILDERS, BUILDING, BUILDINGS, BUILDS, BUILT, REBUILD, REBUILT
Gn 11: 4 let us **b** ourselves a city and a tower
Ex 20:25 for me, do not **b** it of cut stone,
Nm 23: 1 said to Balak, "**B** me seven altars,
Dt 6:10 fine, large cities that you did not **b**,
Dt 27: 5 you shall also **b** to the LORD,
2 Sm 7: 5 Should you **b** me a house to dwell
Ps 127: 1 Unless the LORD **b** the house,
Ps 127: 1 they labor in vain who **b**.
Eccl 3: 3 a time to tear down, and a time to **b**.
Is 57:14 **B** up, **b** up, prepare the way,
Is 62:10 the people; **B** up, **b** up the highway,
Jer 18: 9 I promise to **b** up and plant a nation
Mi 3:10 Who **b** up Zion with bloodshed,
Zep 1:13 They will **b** houses, but shall not
Hg 1: 8 bring timber, and **b** the house That I
Zec 6:12 he shall **b** the temple of the LORD.
Mt 16:18 upon this rock I will **b** my church,
Mt 23:29 You **b** the tombs of the prophets
Mk 14:58 three days I will **b** another not made
Acts 20:32 word of his that can **b** you
1 Thes 5:11 one another and **b** one another up,
Jude 1:20 yourselves up in your most holy

BUILDER →BUILD
1 Cor 3:10 to me, like a wise master **b** I laid

BUILDERS → BUILD

1 Kgs	5:32	Solomon's and Hiram's **b**,
Ezr	3:10	When the **b** had laid the foundation
Ps	118:22	The stone the **b** rejected has become
Mt	21:42	The stone that the **b** rejected
Mk	12:10	The stone that the **b** rejected
Lk	20:17	The stone which the **b** rejected
Acts	4:11	by you, the **b**, which has become
1 Pt	2: 7	"The stone which the **b** rejected

BUILDING → BUILD

Jos	22:16	rebelled against him by **b** an altar
1 Kgs	9: 1	Solomon finished **b** the temple
Ezr	4: 1	the exiles were **b** a temple
Neh	2:18	They replied, "Let us be up and **b**!"
Mi	7:11	It is the day for **b** your walls;
Lk	6:48	That one is like a person **b** a house,
Rom	15: 2	our neighbor for the good, for **b** up.
1 Cor	3: 9	you are God's field, God's **b**.
1 Cor	14:26	Everything should be done for **b** up.
2 Cor	5: 1	destroyed, we have a **b** from God,
2 Cor	10: 8	which the Lord gave for **b** you up
2 Cor	12:19	and all for **b** you up, beloved.
Eph	4:12	for **b** up the body of Christ,

BUILDINGS → BUILD

Mk	13: 1	teacher, what stones and what **b**!"

BUILDS → BUILD

Prv	14: 1	Wisdom **b** her house, but Folly tears
Sir	21: 8	He who **b** his house with another's
Jer	22:13	Woe to him who **b** his house
1 Cor	3:10	each one must be careful how he **b**
1 Cor	3:12	If anyone **b** on this foundation
1 Cor	8: 1	inflates with pride, but love **b** up.
1 Cor	10:23	is lawful," but not everything **b** up.
1 Cor	14: 4	speaks in a tongue **b** himself up,
1 Cor	14: 4	up, but whoever prophesies **b**

BUILT → BUILD

Gn	8:20	Then Noah **b** an altar to the LORD,
Gn	12: 7	So Abram **b** an altar there
Gn	22: 9	him, Abraham **b** an altar there
Gn	26:25	So he **b** an altar there and invoked
Gn	35: 7	There he **b** an altar and named
Ex	17:15	Moses also **b** an altar there,
Ex	32: 5	Aaron **b** an altar before the calf
Jos	8:30	Later Joshua **b** an altar to the LORD,
Jos	22:11	of Manasseh had **b** an altar
Jgs	6:24	So Gideon **b** there an altar
1 Sm	7:17	Israel and **b** an altar to the LORD.
1 Sm	14:35	Saul **b** an altar to the LORD—this was the first time he **b** an altar
2 Sm	24:25	David **b** an altar there to the LORD,
1 Mc	4:47	be a new altar like the former one.
Ps	122: 3	Jerusalem, **b** as a city, walled round
Prv	9: 1	Wisdom has **b** her house, she has set
Prv	24: 3	By wisdom is a house **b**,
Is	5: 2	Within it he **b** a watchtower,
Hos	10: 1	fruit, the more altars he **b**; The more
Mt	7:24	be like a wise man who **b** his house
Mk	12: 1	it, dug a wine press, and **b** a tower.
Lk	6:49	act is like a person who **b** a house
1 Cor	3:14	that someone **b** upon the foundation,
1 Cor	14:17	very well, but the other is not **b** up.
Eph	2:20	**b** upon the foundation
Col	2: 7	rooted in him and **b** upon him
Heb	11: 7	seen, with reverence **b** an ark
1 Pt	2: 5	let yourselves be **b** into a spiritual

BULL → BULLS

Ex	29: 1	priests. Procure a young **b** and two
Lv	1: 5	then slaughter the **b** before the LORD,
Lv	4: 3	unblemished **b** as a sin offering

BULLS → BULL

1 Chr	29:21	a thousand **b**, a thousand rams,
Ezr	6:17	they offered one hundred **b**,
Ps	22:13	Many **b** surround me; fierce
Ps	50:13	Do I eat the flesh of **b** or drink
Heb	10: 4	it is impossible that the blood of **b**

BURDEN → BURDENED, BURDENS, BURDENSOME

Gn	49:15	He bent his shoulder to the **b**
Ex	18:22	Thus, your **b** will be lightened,
Nm	11:11	with me that you **b** me with all this
Ps	38: 5	me, a **b** beyond my strength.
Is	10:27	day, His **b** shall be taken from your
Jer	23:33	asks you, "What is the **b** of the LORD?"
Jer	23:33	"You are the **b**, and I cast you off,
Mt	11:30	For my yoke is easy, and my **b** light."
Acts	15:28	you any **b** beyond these necessities,
2 Cor	11: 9	I did not **b** anyone, for the brothers
2 Cor	12:14	And I will not be a **b**, for I want not
2 Thes	3: 8	worked, so as not to **b** any of you.
Rv	2:24	on you I will place no further **b**,

BURDENED → BURDEN

Is	43:24	Instead, you **b** me with your sins,
1 Tm	5:16	the church is not to be **b**, so that it

BURDENS → BURDEN

Wis	9:15	For the corruptible body **b** the soul
Lk	11:46	You impose on people **b** hard
Gal	6: 2	Bear one another's **b**, and so you will

BURDENSOME → BURDEN

1 Jn	5: 3	And his commandments are not **b**,

BURIAL → BURY

Gn	23: 6	dead in the choicest of our **b** sites.
Gn	23: 6	us would deny you his **b** ground
Gn	49:30	Ephron the Hittite for a **b** ground.
Dt	34: 6	day no one knows the place of his **b**.
Mt	26:12	body, she did it to prepare me for **b**.

BURIED → BURY

Gn	15:15	you shall be **b** at a contented old
Ru	1:17	you die I will die, and there be **b**.
Acts	2:29	David that he died and was **b**,
Rom	6: 4	We were indeed **b** with him through
1 Cor	15: 4	that he was **b**; that he was raised
Col	2:12	You were **b** with him in baptism,

BURN → BURNED, BURNING, BURNS, BURNT

Ex	21:25	**b** for **b**, wound for wound,
Lk	3:17	his barn, but the chaff he will **b**

BURNED → BURN

Gn	38:24	her out," cried Judah; "she shall be **b**."
Ex	3: 3	sight, and see why the bush is not **b**."
Lv	20:14	the two women as well shall be **b**
Lv	21: 9	her father also, shall be **b** to death.
Nm	11: 3	the fire of the LORD **b** among them.
2 Kgs	23:20	and **b** human bones upon them.
Jer	36:29	You **b** that scroll, saying, "Why did
Mt	13:40	are collected and **b** [up] with fire,
Jn	15: 6	them into a fire and they will be **b**.
1 Cor	3:15	But if someone's work is **b** up,
Heb	6: 8	it will soon be cursed and finally **b**.
Rv	8: 7	A third of the land was **b** up,

BURNING → BURN

Lv	6: 2	the fire is to be kept **b** on the altar.
Ps	79: 5	Will your rage keep **b** like fire?
Ps	140:11	May God rain **b** coals upon them,
Ez	1:13	creatures something like **b** coals
Dn	7: 9	flames of fire, with wheels of **b** fire.
Lk	24:32	not our hearts **b** [within us] while he
Jn	5:35	He was a **b** and shining lamp,
Acts	7:30	Sinai in the flame of a **b** bush.
Rom	12:20	so doing you will heap **b** coals
Rv	8: 8	like a large **b** mountain was hurled

BURNISHED

1 Kgs	7:45	of the LORD were of **b** bronze.
Ez	1: 7	sparkled with a gleam like **b** bronze.
Dn	10: 6	arms and feet looked like **b** bronze,

BURNS → BURN

Sir	23:16	not to be quenched till it **b** itself out:
Is	44:16	Half of it he **b** in the fire, and on its

BURNT → BURN

Ps	51:18	a **b** offering you would not accept.
Ps	66:15	you and **b** offerings of rams; I will

Mk	12:33	is worth more than all **b** offerings

BURST → BURSTS

Gn	7:11	fountains of the great abyss **b** forth,
Jb	32:19	pressure, my bosom is ready to **b**.
Dn	14:27	the dragon ate them, he **b** asunder.
Lk	5:37	the new wine will **b** the skins, and it
Lk	6:48	the river **b** against that house
Acts	1:18	headlong, he **b** open in the middle,

BURSTS → BURST

Jer	23:19	that **b** upon the heads of the wicked.

BURY → BURIAL, BURIED

Gn	23: 4	ground, that I may **b** my dead wife."
Gn	50: 7	So Joseph left to **b** his father;
2 Kgs	9:10	of Jezreel, so that no one can **b** her.' "
Mt	8:22	me, and let the dead **b** their dead."
Lk	9:60	him, "Let the dead **b** their dead.

BUSH → THORNBUSH

Ex	3: 2	to him in fire flaming out of a **b**.
Mk	12:26	in the passage about the **b**, how God
Lk	20:37	known in the passage about the **b**,
Acts	7:35	angel who appeared to him in the **b**.

BUSHEL

Mt	5:15	and then put it under a **b** basket; it is

BUSINESS

Jas	4:13	spend a year there doing **b**,

BUSYBODIES

1 Tm	5:13	idlers but gossips and **b** as well,

BUY → BOUGHT, BUYER, BUYING, BUYS

2 Sm.	24:21	"To **b** the threshing floor from you,
Jer	13: 1	me: Go **b** yourself a linen loincloth;
Jer	19: 1	LORD: Go, **b** a potter's earthen flask.
Jer	32: 7	"B for yourself my field in Anathoth,
Mt	27: 7	**b** the potter's field as a burial place
Jn	6: 5	"Where can we **b** enough food
Rv	3:18	I advise you to **b** from me gold
Rv	3:18	**b** ointment to smear on your eyes so
Rv	13:17	so that no one could **b** or sell except

BUYER → BUY

Dt	28:68	slaves, but there will be no **b**."
Prv	20:14	says the **b**; but once he has gone his

BUYING → BUY

Mt	21:12	those engaged in selling and **b** there.
Lk	17:28	were eating, drinking, **b**, selling,

BUYS → BUY

Mt	13:44	sells all that he has and **b** that field.

BYWORD → WORD

2 Chr	7:20	proverb and a **b** among all peoples.
Jb	17: 6	and I am made a **b** of the people;
Ps	44:15	You make us a **b** among the nations;
Ez	23:10	Thus she became a **b** for women,

C

CAESAR

Mt	22:17	lawful to pay the census tax to C
Mk	12:17	"Repay to C what belongs to C
Jn	19:12	release him, you are not a Friend of C.
Acts	17: 7	in opposition to the decrees of C
Acts	25:11	over to them. I appeal to C."

CAESAREA

Mt	16:13	of C Philippi he asked his disciples,
Acts	10: 1	Now in C there was a man named
Acts	12:19	left Judea to spend some time in C.
Acts	25: 4	Paul was being held in custody in C

CAIAPHAS

High priest at trial of Jesus (Mt 26:3, 57; Lk 3:2; Jn 11:49; 18:13-28); at trial of disciples (Acts 4:6).

CAIN

Firstborn of Adam (Gn 4:1), murdered brother Abel (Gn 4:1-25; Heb 11:4; 1 Jn 3:12; Jude 11).

CAKE → CAKES

1 Kgs	17:13	first make me a little **c** and bring it
Hos	7: 8	Ephraim is a hearth **c** unturned.

CAKES → CAKE

Ex	29: 2	flour make unleavened **c** mixed
Ex	29:23	of bread, one of the **c** made with oil,
Nm	11: 8	which tasted like **c** made with oil.
Jgs	6:21	touched the meat and unleavened **c**.
Jdt	10: 5	grain, fig **c**, bread and cheese;
Jer	7:18	dough to make **c** for the queen
Jer	44:19	that we baked for her **c** in her image
Dn	14:27	he boiled together and made into **c**.
Hos	3: 1	other gods and are fond of raisin **c**.

CALAMITIES → CALAMITY

1 Sm	10:19	you from all your evils and **c**,

CALAMITY → CALAMITIES

Prv	22: 8	He who sows iniquity reaps **c**,
Dn	9:13	of Moses, this **c** came full upon us.

CALCULATE

Rv	13:18	who understands can **c** the number

CALEB

Judahite who spied out Canaan (Nm 13:6); allowed to enter land because of faith (Nm 13:30-14:38; Dt 1:36; 1 Mc 2:56; Sir 46:7-9). Given Hebron (Jos 14:6-15:19).

CALF → CALVES

Ex	32: 4	a graving tool, made a molten **c**.
Lv	9: 2	"Take a **c** for a sin offering and a ram
Dt	9:16	making for yourselves a molten **c**!
Neh	9:18	made for themselves a molten **c**,
Is	11: 6	The **c** and the young lion shall
Jer	31:18	I was an untamed **c**. If you allow
Hos	8: 5	Cast away your **c**, O Samaria!
Lk	15:23	Take the fattened **c** and slaughter it.
Acts	7:41	So they made a **c** in those days,

CALL → CALLED, CALLING, CALLS, SO-CALLED

Gn	2:19	man to see what he would **c** them;
Gn	30:13	"Women **c** me fortunate."
Dt	4:26	I **c** heaven and earth this day
Ru	1:20	said to them, "Do not **c** me Naomi.
1 Sm	3: 5	"I did not **c** you," Eli said.
1 Kgs	18:24	You shall **c** on your gods, and I will **c** on the LORD.
Ps	4: 2	Answer when I **c**, my saving God.
Ps	28: 1	To you, LORD, I **c**; my Rock, do not
Ps	50:15	Then **c** on me in time of distress;
Ps	61: 3	From the brink of Sheol I **c**;
Ps	116:13	and **c** on the name of the LORD.
Ps	145:18	are near to all who **c** upon you, to all who **c** upon you in truth.
Prv	1:28	"Then they **c** me, but I answer not;
Prv	8: 1	Does not Wisdom **c**,
Is	5:20	Woe to those who **c** evil good,
Is	55: 6	be found, **c** him while he is near.
Is	60:14	They shall **c** you "City of the LORD,"
Is	65:24	Before they **c**, I will answer;
Jer	33: 3	C to me, and I will answer you;
Lam	3:21	But I will **c** this to mind, as my
Hos	2:18	LORD, She shall **c** me "My husband,"
Jon	1: 6	Rise up, **c** upon your God!
Zep	3: 9	That they all may **c** upon the name
Zec	13: 9	They shall **c** upon my name, and I
Mt	9:13	I did not come to **c** the righteous
Mt	23: 9	C no one on earth your father;
Mk	10:18	him, "Why do you **c** me good?
Lk	6:46	"Why do you **c** me, 'Lord, Lord,'
Jn	13:13	You **c** me 'teacher' and 'master,'
Jn	15:15	I no longer **c** you slaves,
Acts	10:15	clean, you are not to **c** profane."
Rom	9:25	not my people I will **c** 'my people,"
Rom	9:25	was not beloved I will **c** "beloved."
Rom	10:12	of all, enriching all who **c** upon him.
1 Cor	1: 2	all those everywhere who **c**
1 Thes	4: 7	For God did not **c** us to impurity
2 Tm	2:22	along with those who **c** on the Lord
Heb	2:11	is not ashamed to **c** them "brothers,"
2 Pt	1:10	be all the more eager to make your **c**

CALLED →CALL

Gn	1: 5	God c the light "day," and the darkness he c "night."
Gn	1: 8	God c the dome "the sky."
Gn	1:10	God c the dry land "the earth,"
Gn	1:10	the basin of the water he c "the sea."
Gn	2:19	whatever the man c each of them
Gn	2:23	This one shall be c 'woman,'
Gn	3: 9	The LORD God then c to the man
Gn	21:17	God's messenger c to Hagar
Gn	22:11	the LORD's messenger c to him
Gn	35:10	shall no longer be c Jacob, but Israel
Ex	3: 4	God c out to him from the bush,
Ex	16:31	The Israelites c this food manna.
Ex	19: 3	Then the LORD c to him and said,
1 Sm	3: 4	The LORD c to Samuel,
2 Sm	22: 7	In my distress I c upon the LORD
1 Kgs	18:26	c on Baal from morning to noon,
1 Chr	21:26	When he c upon the LORD,
Ps	116: 4	Then I c on the name of the LORD,
Prv	1:24	"Because I c and you refused,
Is	1:26	After that you shall be c
Is	42: 6	have c you for the victory of justice,
Is	43: 1	I have c you by name: you are mine.
Is	49: 1	peoples. The LORD c me from birth,
Is	56: 7	For my house shall be c a house
Is	65:12	Since I c and you did not answer,
Lam	3:55	I c upon your name, O LORD,
Hos	11: 1	loved him, out of Egypt I c my son.
Mt	1:16	born Jesus who is c the Messiah.
Mt	2:15	fulfilled, "Out of Egypt I c my son."
Mt	2:23	fulfilled, "He shall be c a Nazorean."
Mt	5: 9	for they will be c children of God.
Mt	5:19	do so will be c least in the kingdom
Mt	5:19	commandments will be c greatest
Mt	23: 8	As for you, do not be c 'Rabbi.'
Lk	1:32	and will be c Son of the Most High,
Lk	1:35	the child to be born will be c holy,
Lk	1:76	will be c prophet of the Most High,
Lk	15:19	I no longer deserve to be c your son;
Jn	15:15	I have c you friends, because I have
Jn	19:17	to what is c the Place of the Skull,
Rom	1: 1	c to be an apostle and set apart
Rom	1: 6	who are c to belong to Jesus Christ;
Rom	1: 7	of God in Rome, c to be holy.
Rom	8:28	who are c according to his purpose.
Rom	8:30	And those he predestined he also c;
Rom	8:30	and those he c he also justified,
1 Cor	1: 9	by him you were c to fellowship
1 Cor	1:24	but to those who are c,
1 Cor	7:15	such cases; God has c you to peace.
1 Cor	7:17	assigned, just as God c each one.
1 Cor	7:24	God in the state in which he was c.
Gal	5:13	For you were c for freedom,
Eph	4: 4	also c to the one hope of your call;
Col	3:15	which you were also c in one body.
2 Thes	2:14	c you through our gospel to possess
1 Tm	6:12	you were c when you made
2 Tm	1: 9	He saved us and c us to a holy life,
Heb	9:15	those who are c may receive
Heb	11:16	is not ashamed to be c their God,
Jas	2:23	and he was c "the friend of God."
1 Pt	1:15	but, as he who c you is holy,
1 Pt	2: 9	the praises" of him who c you
1 Pt	3: 9	because to this you were c, that you
1 Pt	5:10	of all grace who c you to his eternal
2 Pt	1: 3	of him who c us by his own glory
1 Jn	3: 1	we may be c the children of God.
Jude	1: 1	to those who are c, beloved in God
Rv	12: 9	who is c the Devil and Satan,
Rv	17:14	and those with him are c, chosen,
Rv	19:11	its rider was [c] "Faithful and True."
Rv	19:13	his name was c the Word of God.

CALLING →CALL

1 Sm	3: 8	that the LORD was c the youth.
Is	40:26	numbers them, c them all by name.
Mt	27:47	it said, "This one is c for Elijah."
Mk	10:49	"Take courage; get up, he is c you."

Acts	22:16	sins washed away, c upon his name.'
1 Cor	1:26	Consider your own c, brothers.
Phil	3:14	goal, the prize of God's upward c,
Heb	3: 1	sharing in a heavenly c,

CALLS →CALL

Ps	42: 8	Here deep c to deep in the roar
Prv	9: 3	She has sent out her maidens; she c
Is	64: 6	There is none who c upon your
Hos	7: 7	fallen; none of them c upon me.
Jl	3: 5	who c on the name of the LORD;
Mt	22:45	If David c him 'lord,' how can he be
Jn	10: 3	as he c his own sheep by name
Acts	2:21	everyone shall be saved who c on
Rom	4:17	and c into being what does not exist.
Rom	10:13	For "everyone who c on the name
1 Thes	2:12	of the God who c you into his
1 Thes	5:24	The one who c you is faithful,
2 Tm	2:19	"Let everyone who c upon the name
Rv	2:20	Jezebel, who c herself a prophetess,

CALM

Mk	4:39	wind ceased and there was great c.

CALVES →CALF

1 Kgs	12:28	the king made two c of gold
2 Kgs	10:29	as regards the golden c at Bethel
Hos	13: 2	they say, "offer sacrifice." Men kiss c!
Mi	6: 6	with holocausts, with c a year old?
Mal	3:20	you will gambol like c
Heb	9:12	not with the blood of goats and c

CAME →COME

Gn	7: 6	the flood waters c upon the earth.
Gn	11: 5	The LORD c down to see the city
Gn	15: 1	this word of the LORD c to Abram
Gn	20: 3	God c to Abimelech in a dream one
Ex	13: 3	day on which you c out of Egypt,
Ex	32:24	it into the fire, and this calf c out."
Lv	9:24	Fire c forth from the LORD's presence
Nm	11:25	The LORD then c down in the cloud
Nm	11:25	and as the spirit c to rest on them,
Nm	12: 5	the LORD c down in the column
Nm	16:35	the LORD c forth which consumed
Nm	24: 2	tribe, the spirit of God c upon him,
Jgs	3:10	The spirit of the LORD c upon him,
Jgs	11:29	spirit of the LORD c upon Jephthah.
1 Sm	3:10	the LORD c and revealed his
1 Sm	19: 9	the LORD c upon Saul as he was
1 Sm	19:23	the spirit of God c upon him also,
2 Kgs	1:10	And fire c down from heaven
2 Chr	15: 1	son of Oded, c the spirit of God.
2 Chr	20:14	spirit of the LORD c upon Jahaziel,
Ps	18:10	He parted the heavens and c down,
Eccl	5:15	evil, that he goes just as he c.
Dn	3:93	and Abednego c out of the fire.
Mt	7:25	the floods c, and the winds blew
Mk	1:11	And a voice c from the heavens,
Jn	1: 3	All things c to be through him,
Jn	1: 3	and without him nothing c to be.
Jn	1:11	He c to what was his own, but his
Jn	1:17	and truth c through Jesus Christ.
Jn	6:41	"I am the bread that c down
Jn	6:51	I am the living bread that c down
Jn	10:10	I c so that they might have life
Acts	19: 6	them, the holy Spirit c upon them,
Rom	5:12	and thus death c to all, inasmuch as
1 Cor	11:12	For just as woman c from man,
1 Tm	1:15	Christ Jesus c into the world to save
1 Jn	5: 6	This is the one who c through water
Rv	2: 8	who once died but c to life,
Rv	20: 4	They c to life and they reigned
Rv	20: 9	But fire c down from heaven

CAMEL →CAMEL'S, CAMELS

Mt	19:24	easier for a c to pass through the eye
Mt	23:24	out the gnat and swallow the c!
Mk	10:25	for a c to pass through [the] eye
Lk	18:25	easier for a c to pass through the eye

CAMEL'S →CAMEL

Mk	1: 6	John was clothed in c hair,

CAMELS → CAMEL
Gn	24:14	and let me give water to your **c**, too,'

CAMP → ENCAMP, ENCAMPS
Ex	16:13	quail came up and covered the **c**.
Ex	16:13	morning a dew lay all about the **c**,
Ex	33: 7	go to this meeting tent outside the **c**.
Lv	24:14	"Take the blasphemer outside the **c**,
Nm	9:17	tent, the Israelites would break **c**;
Nm	9:17	came to rest, they would pitch **c**.
Nm	11:26	and they prophesied in the **c**.
Dt	23:15	journeys along within your **c**
Dt	23:15	at your mercy, your **c** must be holy;
1 Sm	4: 7	said, "Gods have come to their **c**."
Heb	13:13	Let us then go to him outside the **c**,

CAN → CANNOT
Gn	17:17	"**C** a child be born to a man who is
Gn	17:17	Or **c** Sarah give birth at ninety?"
Gn	41:15	are told a dream you **c** interpret it."
Nm	23: 8	How **c** I curse whom God has not
Nm	35:33	the land **c** have no atonement
Jb	4:17	"**C** a man be righteous as against
Jb	4:17	**C** a mortal be blameless against his
Jb	11: 7	**C** you penetrate the designs of God?
Jb	34:29	tranquil, who then **c** condemn?
Jb	38:35	**C** you send forth the lightnings
Jb	40: 9	**c** you thunder with a voice like his?
Jb	42: 2	I know that you **c** do all things,
Jb	42: 2	no purpose of yours **c** be hindered.
Ps	19:13	Who **c** detect heedless failings?
Ps	22:18	that I **c** count all my bones.
Ps	56: 5	What **c** mere flesh do to me?
Ps	139: 7	Where **c** I hide from your spirit?
Ps	139: 7	From your presence, where **c** I flee?
Prv	20: 6	but who **c** find one worthy of trust?
Eccl	7:13	Who **c** make straight what he has
Sir	15:15	If you choose you **c** keep
Is	43:13	There is none who **c** deliver
Is	43:13	who **c** countermand what I do?
Jer	18: 6	**C** I not do to you, house of Israel,
Ez	37: 3	of man, **c** these bones come to life?
Dn	2: 9	there **c** be but one decree for you.
Dn	5:16	heard that you **c** interpret dreams
Jl	2:11	exceedingly terrible; who **c** bear it?
Mal	3: 2	And who **c** stand when he appears?
Mt	5:13	its taste, with what **c** it be seasoned?
Mt	6:24	"No one **c** serve two masters. He will
Mk	2: 7	Who but God alone **c** forgive sins?"
Lk	18:26	this said, "Then who **c** be saved?"
Jn	3: 4	"How **c** a person once grown old be
Jn	3: 9	and said to him, "How **c** this happen?"
Jn	6:44	No one **c** come to me unless
Jn	10:29	and no one **c** take them
Jn	15: 5	without me you **c** do nothing.
Rom	9:19	fault? For who **c** oppose his will?"
Heb	13: 6	be afraid. What **c** anyone do to me?"
Jas	2:14	have works? **C** that faith save him?
Jas	3: 8	no human being **c** tame the tongue.
Rv	13: 4	"Who **c** compare with the beast or who **c** fight against it?"

CANA
Jn	2: 1	third day there was a wedding in **C**

CANAAN → CANAANITE, CANAANITES
Gn	9:18	Japheth. (Ham was the father of **C**.)
Gn	9:25	"Cursed be **C**! The lowest of slaves
Gn	13:12	Abram stayed in the land of **C**,
Gn	42: 5	was famine in the land of **C** also,
Ex	6: 4	to give them the land of **C**, the land
Nm	13: 2	men to reconnoiter the land of **C**,
Nm	33:51	across the Jordan into the land of **C**,
Nm	34: 2	to you as your heritage—the land of **C**
Dt	32:49	and view the land of **C**, which I am
1 Chr	16:18	"To you will I give the land of **C**
Ps	106:38	they sacrificed to the idols of **C**,
Dn	13:56	"Offspring of **C**, not of Judah,"
Acts	13:19	seven nations in the land of **C**,

CANAANITE → CANAAN
Gn	28: 1	"You shall not marry a **C** woman!
Mt	15:22	a **C** woman of that district came

CANAANITES → CANAAN
Gn	10:18	the clans of the **C** spread out,
Gn	12: 6	(The **C** were then in the land.)
Ex	3: 8	the country of the **C**, Hittites,
Ex	33: 2	Driving out the **C**, Amorites,
Jos	16:10	they did not drive out the **C** living
Jos	17:12	cities, the **C** persisted in this region.
Jgs	1: 1	be first among us to attack the **C**
Jgs	1:27	The **C** kept their hold in this district.
Jgs	3: 5	Israelites were living among the **C**,

CANDACE
Acts	8:27	a court official of the **C**, that is,

CANNOT → CAN
Ex	33:20	But my face you **c** see, for no man
Nm	23:20	a blessing which I **c** restrain.
2 Sm	5: 6	David was told, "You **c** enter here:
1 Kgs	8:27	the highest heavens **c** contain you,
Jb	23: 8	or to the west, I **c** perceive him;
Jb	37:23	The Almighty! we **c** discover him,
Eccl	1:15	What is crooked **c** be made straight,
Eccl	1:15	and what is missing **c** be supplied.
Song	8: 7	Deep waters **c** quench love,
Sir	9:10	for the new one **c** equal him. A new
Is	45:20	idols and pray to gods that **c** save.
Mt	5:14	city set on a mountain **c** be hidden.
Mt	16: 3	you **c** judge the signs of the times.]
Mt	27:42	"He saved others; he **c** save himself.
Mk	3:24	against itself, that kingdom **c** stand.
Lk	16:13	You **c** serve God and mammon."
Jn	7:34	[me], and where I am you **c** come."
Jn	13:33	'Where I go you **c** come,' so now I
Jn	15: 4	Just as a branch **c** bear fruit on its
Jn	16:12	to tell you, but you **c** bear it now.
Rom	8: 8	who are in the flesh **c** please God.
1 Cor	10:21	You **c** drink the cup of the Lord
1 Cor	10:21	You **c** partake of the table
1 Cor	15:50	blood **c** inherit the kingdom of God,

CANOPY
Ps	18:12	his **c**, heavy thunderheads.
Jer	43:10	sunk, and stretch his **c** over them.

CAPERNAUM
Mt	4:13	and went to live in **C** by the sea,
Mt	11:23	And as for you, **C**: 'Will you be
Jn	4:46	official whose son was ill in **C**.
Jn	6:59	teaching in the synagogue in **C**.

CAPITALS
Ex	36:38	with their hooks as well as their **c**
1 Kgs	7:16	were also two **c** cast in bronze,

CAPTAIN
2 Kgs	1: 9	the king sent a **c** with his company
Jon	1: 6	The **c** came to him and said,

CAPTIVATED → CAPTURE
Jdt	16: 9	and her beauty **c** his mind.

CAPTIVE → CAPTURE
2 Kgs	24:16	led **c** to Babylon all seven thousand
1 Mc	1:32	took **c** the women and children,
Ps	106:46	from all who held them **c**.
Song	7: 6	purple; a king is held **c** in its tresses.
Is	52: 2	from your neck, O **c** daughter Zion!
Rom	7:23	taking me **c** to the law of sin
2 Cor	10: 5	take every thought **c** in obedience
Eph	4: 8	on high and took prisoners **c**;

CAPTIVES → CAPTURE
Ps	68:19	you took **c**, received slaves as
Is	61: 1	To proclaim liberty to the **c**
Lk	4:18	has sent me to proclaim liberty to **c**
2 Tm	3: 6	make **c** of women weighed down by sins,

CAPTIVITY → CAPTURE
Dt	28:41	remain with you, but will go into **c**.
Ezr	3: 8	had come from the **c** to Jerusalem,

CAPTORS
Ezr	8:35	those who had returned from the **c**,
Neh	1: 2	the remnant preserved after the **c**,
Jer	15: 2	whoever is marked for **c**, to **c**.
Rv	13:10	Anyone destined for **c** goes into **c**.

CAPTORS →CAPTURE
1 Kgs	8:50	and grant them mercy before their **c**,
Ps	137: 3	There our **c** asked us for the words
Is	14: 2	making captives of its **c** and ruling

CAPTURE →CAPTIVATED, CAPTIVE, CAPTIVES, CAPTIVITY, CAPTORS, CAPTURED
1 Sm	23:26	and his men in order to **c** them,

CAPTURED →CAPTURE
1 Sm	4:11	The ark of God was **c**, and Eli's two

CARAVAN →CARAVANS
Gn	37:25	they saw a **c** of Ishmaelites coming

CARAVANS →CARAVAN
Jgs	5: 6	in the days of slavery **c** ceased;

CARCASS →CARCASSES
Jgs	14: 9	scooped the honey from the lion's **c**.

CARCASSES →CARCASS
Gn	15:11	of prey swooped down on the **c**,

CARCHEMISH
2 Chr	35:20	up to fight at **C** on the Euphrates,

CARE →CARED, CAREFUL, CARELESS, CARES
Dt	6:12	take **c** not to forget the LORD,
Ps	8: 5	mere mortals that you **c** for them?
1 Tm	3: 5	how can he take **c** of the church
Heb	2: 6	the son of man that you **c** for him?
Jas	1:27	to **c** for orphans and widows in their

CARED →CARE
Dt	32:10	He shielded them and **c** for them,

CAREFUL →CARE
Dt	2: 4	they are afraid of you, be very **c**
Dt	5:32	"Be **c**, therefore, to do as the LORD,
Dt	12:28	Be **c** to heed all these
Dt	24: 8	of leprosy you shall be **c** to observe
Jgs	13: 4	be **c** to take no wine or strong drink
2 Kgs	10:31	But Jehu was not **c** to observe
2 Kgs	17:37	You must be **c** to observe forever
2 Kgs	21: 8	that they are **c** to observe all I have
1 Chr	22:13	if you are **c** to observe the precepts
2 Chr	33: 8	provided they are **c** to observe all
Ez	18: 9	and is **c** to observe my ordinances,
Ez	18:19	and has been **c** to observe all my
Ez	20:19	and be **c** to keep my ordinances;
Ez	36:27	statutes, **c** to observe my decrees.
Ti	3: 8	in God be **c** to devote themselves

CARELESS →CARE
Mt	12:36	for every **c** word they speak.

CARES →CARE
Ps	94:19	When **c** increase within me,
Ps	142: 5	no escape for me; no one **c** for me.
Eccl	5: 2	For nightmares come with many **c**,
1 Pt	5: 7	upon him because he **c** for you.

CARGO
Jon	1: 5	they threw its **c** into the sea.
Acts	27:18	the next day they jettisoned some **c**,

CARMEL
1 Sm	25: 2	of Maon who had property in **C**;
1 Kgs	18:20	the prophets assemble on Mount **C**.
Na	1: 4	Withered are Bashan and **C**,

CARNELIAN
Ex	28:17	row, a **c**, a topaz and an emerald;
Rv	4: 3	sparkled like jasper and **c**.
Rv	21:20	the sixth **c**, the seventh chrysolite,

CAROUSING
1 Pt	4: 3	orgies, **c**, and wanton idolatry.

CARPENTER →CARPENTER'S, CARPENTERS
Is	44:13	The **c** stretches a line and marks

Mk	6: 3	Is he not the **c**, the son of Mary,

CARPENTER'S →CARPENTER
Mt	13:55	Is he not the **c** son?

CARPENTERS →CARPENTER
1 Chr	14: 1	to David along with masons and **c**,
2 Chr	24:12	masons and **c** to restore the temple,
Ezr	3: 7	Then they hired stonecutters and **c**,

CARRIED →CARRY
Ex	4:20	The staff of God he **c** with him.
Dt	1:31	your God, **c** you, as a man carries
Jer	10: 5	They must be **c** about, for they
Jn	20:15	if you **c** him away, tell me where
Heb	13: 9	Do not be **c** away by all kinds
Rv	17: 3	he **c** me away in spirit to a deserted

CARRIES →CARRY
Dt	1:31	as a man **c** his child, all along your
Is	40:24	and the stormwind **c** them away like

CARRY →CARRIED, CARRIES, CARRYING
Ex	13:19	they would **c** his bones away
Nm	1:50	It is they who shall **c** the Dwelling
Dt	10: 8	of Levi to **c** the ark of the covenant
1 Chr	15: 2	"No one may **c** the ark of God except
1 Chr	15: 2	the LORD chose them to **c** the ark
Is	46: 4	and I who will **c** you to safety.
Mt	3:11	I am not worthy to **c** his sandals.
Mt	27:32	pressed into service to **c** his cross.
Lk	14:27	Whoever does not **c** his own cross

CARRYING →CARRY
Jos	6: 6	seven of the priests **c** ram's horns
Is	40:11	the lambs, **C** them in his bosom,
Lk	22:10	city, a man will meet you **c** a jar
Jn	19:17	**c** the cross himself he went
2 Cor	4:10	always **c** about in the body

CART
1 Sm	6:11	placed the ark of the LORD on the **c**,
1 Chr	13: 7	Uzzah and Ahio were guiding the **c**,

CARVED
1 Kgs	6:29	and the outer rooms had **c** figures

CASE →CASES
Jos	20: 4	shall plead his **c** before the elders,
Prv	18:17	man who pleads his **c** first seems
Prv	25: 9	Discuss your **c** with your neighbor,
Is	41:21	Present your **c**, says the LORD;
Jer	12: 1	so, I must discuss the **c** with you.
Acts	25:14	Festus referred Paul's **c** to the king,

CASES →CASE
Ex	18:26	for the people in all ordinary **c**.
Ex	18:26	The more difficult **c** they referred
Ex	18:26	but all the lesser **c** they settled

CAST →CASTING, CASTS, DOWNCAST
Lv	16: 8	he shall **c** lots to determine
Jos	18: 6	**c** lots for you here before the LORD,
1 Sm	14:42	said, "**C** lots between me and my son
1 Kgs	7:15	Two hollow bronze columns were **c**,
Est	3: 7	or lot, was **c** in Haman's presence,
Est	9:24	to destroy them and had **c** the pur,
Ps	22:19	them; for my clothing they **c** lots.
Ps	55:23	**C** your care upon the LORD, who will
Ps	71: 9	Do not **c** me aside in my old age;
Prv	16:33	When the lot is **c** into the lap,
Is	38:17	When you **c** behind your back
Jer	7:15	I will **c** you away from me, as I **c**
Jl	4: 3	Over my people they have **c** lots;
Ob	1:11	and **c** lots over Jerusalem, you too
Jon	1: 7	let us **c** lots to find out on whose
Jon	1: 7	So they **c** lots, and thus singled
Jn	19:24	**c** lots for it to see whose it will be,"
Jn	19:24	and for my vesture they **c** lots."
Jn	21: 6	"**C** the net over the right side
1 Pt	5: 7	**C** all your worries upon him

CASTING →CAST
Mt	4:18	brother Andrew, **c** a net into the sea;

CASTLE
Mt 27:35 they divided his garments by c lots;
Mk 1:16 his brother Andrew c their nets

CASTLE
Prv 18:19 and a friend is like the bars of a c.

CASTRATE
Gal 5:12 you might also c themselves!

CASTS →CAST
Ps 147: 6 but c the wicked to the ground.

CATAPULTS
1 Mc 6:51 c and mechanical bows for shooting

CATARACTS
Tb 2:10 droppings settled in my eyes, causing c.
Tb 11:13 both hands to peel off the c.

CATCH →CATCHES, CATCHING, CAUGHT
Song 2:15 C us the foxes, the little foxes
Lk 5: 4 water and lower your nets for a c."
Lk 11:54 for they were plotting to c him

CATCHES →CATCH
1 Cor 3:19 "He c the wise in their own ruses,"

CATCHING →CATCH
Lk 5:10 from now on you will be c men."

CATERPILLAR →CATERPILLARS
Ps 78:46 He gave their harvest to the c,

CATERPILLARS →CATERPILLAR
2 Chr 6:28 blight, or mildew, or locusts, or c;

CATTLE
Gn 1:25 all kinds of c, and all kinds
Gn 2:20 The man gave names to all the c,
Ps 104:14 You raise grass for the c and plants

CAUGHT →CATCH
Gn 22:13 he spied a ram c by its horns
Ex 22: 6 if c, must make twofold restitution.
Dt 24: 7 "If a any man is c kidnaping a fellow
2 Sm 18: 9 terebinth, his hair c fast in the tree.
Prv 6: 2 lips, c by the words of your mouth;
Sir 27:26 it, and he who lays a snare is c in it,
Lk 5: 5 hard all night and have c nothing;
Jn 8: 3 brought a woman who had been c
2 Cor 12: 2 was c up to the third heaven.
1 Thes 4:17 will be c up together with them

CAUSE →CAUSED, CAUSES
1 Kgs 8:45 and petition, and defend their c.
Ps 9: 5 You upheld my right and my c,
Ps 35: 7 Without c they set their snare
Ps 35: 7 without c they dug a pit for me.
Ps 45: 5 In the c of truth and justice
Ps 74:22 Arise, God, defend your c;
Ps 109: 3 me, attacking me without c.
Ps 119:86 Help me! I am pursued without c.
Ps 119:154 Take up my c and redeem me;
Prv 24:28 your neighbor without just c,
Jer 11:20 for to you I have entrusted my c!
Jer 51:36 Surely I will defend your c, I will
Lk 17: 2 for him to c one of these little ones
Jn 15:25 fulfilled, 'They hated me without c.'
1 Cor 8:13 that I may not c my brother to sin.
1 Jn 2:10 there is nothing in him to c a fall.

CAUSED →CAUSE
1 Kgs 14:16 committed and c Israel to commit."
2 Kgs 23:15 who c Israel to sin—this same altar

CAUSES →CAUSE
Mt 5:29 If your right eye c you to sin, tear it
Mt 5:30 And if your right hand c you to sin,
Mt 5:32 the marriage is unlawful) c her
Mt 18: 8 If your hand or foot c you to sin,

CAUTIOUS
Prv 14:16 The wise man is c and shuns evil;

CAVE →CAVES
Gn 19:30 lived with his two daughters in a c.
Gn 23: 9 to sell me the c of Machpelah

Gn 25: 9 buried him in the c of Machpelah,
Gn 49:29 my fathers in the c that lies
Gn 50:13 buried him in the c in the field
Jos 10:16 had fled, hid in a c at Makkedah.
1 Sm 22: 1 and escaped to the c of Adullam.
1 Sm 24: 4 he found a c, which he entered
1 Kgs 19: 9 There he came to a c, where he took
Ps 57: 1 when he fled from Saul into a c.
Ps 142: 1 of David, when he was in the c.
Jn 11:38 It was a c, and a stone lay across it.

CAVERNS
Is 2:21 They go into c in the rocks

CAVES →CAVE
Jgs 6: 2 on the mountains, the c for refuge,
1 Sm 13: 6 hid themselves in c, in thickets,
2 Mc 6:11 in nearby c to observe the sabbath
Is 2:19 Men will go into c in the rocks
Heb 11:38 in c and in crevices in the earth.
Rv 6:15 free person hid themselves in c

CEASE →CEASED
Gn 8:22 and day and night shall not c."
Prv 22:10 discord goes out; strife and insult c.
Jer 31:36 Then shall the race of Israel c
1 Cor 13: 8 to nothing; if tongues, they will c;

CEASED →CEASE
1 Mc 9:73 Then the sword c in Israel.
Ps 77: 9 Has God's love c forever?
Lam 5:15 The joy of our hearts has c,

CEDAR →CEDARS
2 Sm 7: 2 "Here I am living in a house of c,
1 Kgs 7: 7 it was paneled with c from floor
2 Chr 25:18 a message to the c of the Lebanon,
Ezr 3: 7 that they might ship c trees
Jb 40:17 He carries his tail like a c;
Ps 92:13 tree, shall grow like a c of Lebanon.
Song 8: 9 we will reinforce it with a c plank."
Sir 24:13 "Like a c on Lebanon I am raised
Is 41:19 I will plant in the desert the c,
Ez 17: 3 Lebanon. He took the crest of the c,
Ez 31: 3 Behold, a cypress [c] in Lebanon,

CEDARS →CEDAR
Jgs 9:15 and devour the c of Lebanon.'
1 Kgs 5:24 to provide Solomon with all the c
Ps 29: 5 The voice of the Lord cracks the c;
Ps 29: 5 the Lord splinters the c of Lebanon,
Is 37:24 I cut down its lofty c, its choice

CELEBRATE →CELEBRATED
Ex 5: 1 that they may c a feast to me
Ex 12:14 all your generations shall c
Ex 12:48 among you wish to c the Passover
Lv 23: 4 you shall c at their proper time
Nm 29:12 you shall c a pilgrimage feast
Dt 16:15 days you shall c this pilgrim feast
Neh 12:27 to Jerusalem to c a joyful dedication
Na 2: 1 peace! C your feasts, O Judah,
Lk 15:23 Then let us c with a feast,
Lk 15:32 But now we must c and rejoice,
1 Cor 5: 8 Therefore let us c the feast,

CELEBRATED →CELEBRATE
1 Mc 4:56 eight days they c the dedication

CELL
Acts 12: 7 by him and a light shone in the c.
Acts 16:24 he put them in the innermost c

CENSER →CENSERS
2 Chr 26:19 who was holding a c for burning
Ez 8:11 each of them with his c in his hand,
Rv 8: 3 stood at the altar, holding a gold c.

CENSERS →CENSER
Lv 10: 1 Nadab and Abihu took their c and,
Nm 16:18 So they all took their c, and laying
Nm 17: 3 these sinners have consecrated the c
1 Mc 1:22 the bowls, the golden c, the curtain,

CENSUS
Ex 30:12 you take a c of the Israelites who
Nm   1: 2 "Take a c of the whole community
Nm 26: 2 "Take a c, by ancestral houses,

CENTER
Rv   7:17 in the c of the throne will shepherd

CENTURION → CENTURIONS
Mt   8: 5 a c approached him and appealed
Mt 27:54 The c and the men with him who
Mk 15:39 the c who stood facing him saw
Lk 23:47 The c who witnessed what had
Acts 10: 1 a c of the Cohort called the Italica,
Acts 22:25 Paul said to the c on duty, "Is it
Acts 27: 1 prisoners over to a c named Julius

CENTURIONS → CENTURION
Acts 23:17 called one of the c and requested,

CEPHAS → =PETER
  Name given to the apostle Peter (Jn 1:42; 1 Cor 1:12; 3:22; 9:5; 15:5; Gal 1:18; 2:9, 11, 14).

CHAFF
Jb   21:18 and like c which the storm snatches
Ps   1: 4 They are like c driven by the wind.
Ps. 35: 5 Make them like c before the wind,
Jer 13:24 I will scatter them like c that flies
Dn   2:35 fine as the c on the threshing floor
Hos 13: 3 away, Like c storm-driven
Zep   2: 2 driven away, like c that passes on;
Mt   3:12 his barn, but the c he will burn
Lk   3:17 his barn, but the c he will burn

CHAIN → CHAINED, CHAINS
Gn   41:42 and put a gold c about his neck.
Mk   5: 3 him any longer, even with a c.
Rv   20: 1 the key to the abyss and a heavy c.

CHAINED → CHAIN
2 Tm 2: 9 But the word of God is not c.

CHAINS → CHAIN
Ex   28:14 as well as two c of pure gold,
Ex   28:14 fasten the cordlike c to the filigree
1 Kgs 6:21 gold, and looped it with golden c.
Lam   3: 7 and weighed me down with c;
Mk   5: 4 been bound with shackles and c,
Mk   5: 4 the c had been pulled apart by him
Acts 12: 7 The c fell from his wrists.
Acts 16:26 and the c of all were pulled loose.
Acts 28:20 hope of Israel that I wear these c."
Eph   6:20 for which I am an ambassador in c,
Col   4:18 Remember my c. Grace be
Heb 11:36 even c and imprisonment,
2 Pt   2: 4 them to the c of Tartarus
Jude 1: 6 he has kept in eternal c, in gloom,

CHALDEA → CHALDEAN, CHALDEANS, CHALDEES
Jer 50:10 C shall be their plunder, and all her
Ez   23:16 she sent messengers to them in C.
Hb   1: 6 I am raising up C, that bitter

CHALDEAN → CHALDEA
Ezr   5:12 them into the power of the C,
Dn   5:30 same night Belshazzar, the C king,

CHALDEANS → CHALDEA
Gn   11:31 brought them out of Ur of the C,
Gn   15: 7 of the C to give you this land as
2 Chr 36:17 up against them the king of the C,
Jdt   5: 7 who were born in the land of the C.
Is   47: 5 sit in silence, O daughter of the C,
Jer 50:35 A sword upon the C, says the Lord.
Bar   1: 2 the time when the C took Jerusalem
Ez   1: 3 of the C by the river Chebar.—There
Dn   1: 4 the language and literature of the C;
Dn   5:11 enchanters, C, and astrologers,

CHALDEES → CHALDEA
Neh   9: 7 who brought him out from Ur of the C,

CHAMBER → CHAMBERS
Jb   37: 9 Out of its c comes forth the tempest;

Am   9: 6 I have built heaven, my upper c,

CHAMBERS → CHAMBER
1 Chr 9:26 had charge of the c and treasures
1 Chr 23:28 courts, the c, and the preservation
Tb   6:14 her husbands died in their bridal c.
Song 1: 4 Bring me, O king, to your c.

CHAMPION
1 Sm 17: 4 A c named Goliath of Gath came

CHANGE → CHANGED, CHANGERS, CHANGES
Nm   23:19 human, that he should c his mind.
Jer 13:23 Can the Ethiopian c his skin?
Mal   3: 6 Surely I, the Lord, do not c, nor do
Mt   21:32 you did not later c your minds
Heb   7:12 When there is a c of priesthood,
Heb   7:12 there is necessarily a c of law as
Jas   1:17 no alteration or shadow caused by c.

CHANGED → CHANGE
Gn   31: 7 me and c my wages time after time.
Jer   2:11 But my people have c their glory
Lk   9:29 While he was praying his face c
1 Cor 15:51 all fall asleep, but we will all be c,
Heb   1:12 and like a garment they will be c.

CHANGERS → CHANGE
Mt   21:12 overturned the tables of the money c
Mk   11:15 overturned the tables of the money c

CHANGES → CHANGE
Dn   2:21 He causes the c of the times

CHANNELS
Is   8: 7 It shall rise above all its c,

CHARACTER
Rom   5: 4 endurance, proven c, and proven c,

CHARGE → CHARGED, CHARGES
Gn   39: 4 he put him in c of his household
Nm   4:16 shall be in c of the oil for the light,
Nm   4:16 He shall be in c of the whole
Nm   9:23 ever heeding the c of the Lord, as he
Dt   11: 1 therefore, and always heed his c:
Ps   50:21 I accuse you, I lay the c before you."
Mt   24:47 to you, he will put him in c of all his
Mk   15:26 of the c against him read, "The King
Rom   8:33 will bring a c against God's chosen
1 Cor 9:18 I offer the gospel free of c so as not
2 Cor 11: 7 the gospel of God to you without c?
Phlm 1:18 or owes you anything, c it to me.

CHARGED → CHARGE
Dn   13:43 which these wicked men have c me."

CHARGES → CHARGE
Lk   23:14 the c you have brought against him,
Acts 25: 7 brought many serious c against him,

CHARIOT → CHARIOTS
Gn   41:43 had him ride in the c of his vizier,
Ex   14:25 he so clogged their c wheels
Jgs   4:15 himself dismounted from his c
1 Kgs 7:33 were constructed like c wheels;
2 Kgs 2:11 a flaming c and flaming horses
1 Chr 28:18 for what would suggest a c throne:
Ps 104: 3 You make the clouds your c;
Sir 48: 9 whirlwind, in a c with fiery horses.
Zec   6: 2 The first c had red horses,
Zec   6: 2 horses, the second c black horses,
Acts 8:28 Seated in his c, he was reading

CHARIOTS → CHARIOT
Ex   14:28 it covered the c and the charioteers
Ex   15:19 thus because Pharaoh's horses and c
Jos 11: 4 with a multitude of horses and c.
Jos 17:18 if, despite their strength and iron c,
Jgs   4: 3 his nine hundred iron c he sorely
2 Sm 8: 4 only enough for a hundred c.
2 Kgs 6:17 horses and fiery c around Elisha.
2 Chr 1:17 would then bring up c from Egypt
2 Chr 1:14 he had one thousand four hundred c
Jdt   7:20 camp, infantry, c, and cavalry,

1 Mc	1:17	a strong force, with c and elephants,
Ps	20: 8	Some rely on c, others on horses,
Is	36: 9	And yet you rely on Egypt for c
Jl	2: 5	As with the rumble of c they leap
Na	2: 4	Fiery steel are the c on the day
Hg	2:22	I will overthrow the c and their
Zec	6: 1	and saw four c coming
Rv	9: 9	of many horse-drawn c racing

CHARITABLE

Tb	1:16	I performed many c works

CHARM →CHARMED, CHARMER

Prv	31:30	C is deceptive and beauty fleeting;
Jer	8:17	snakes, Against which no c will work

CHARMED →CHARM

Eccl	10:11	bites because it has not been c,

CHARMER →CHARM

Sir	12:13	Who pities a snake c when he is

CHASED

Dt	1:44	like bees, c you, cutting you down

CHASM

Lk	16:26	us and you a great c is established

CHASTE

2 Cor	11: 2	present you as a c virgin to Christ.
Ti	2: 5	to be self-controlled, c,

CHASTENED →CHASTISE

Jb	33:19	Or a man is c on his bed by pain

CHASTISE →CHASTENED

Jer	30:11	I will c you as you deserve,

CHATTER

Sir	21:16	A fool's c is like a load on a journey,

CHEATED

Gn	31: 7	yet your father c me and changed

CHEBAR

Ez	1: 1	was among the exiles by the river C,
Ez	10:15	creatures I had seen by the river C.

CHEEK →CHEEKS

1 Kgs	22:24	up and slapped Micaiah on the c,
Jb	16:10	They smite me on the c insultingly;
Lam	3:30	Let him offer his c to be struck,
Mi	4:14	With the rod they strike on the c
Mt	5:39	strikes you on [your] right c,
Lk	6:29	the person who strikes you on one c,

CHEEKS →CHEEK

Song	1:10	Your c lovely in pendants,
Song	5:13	His c like beds of spice
Is	50: 6	me, my c to those who plucked my
Lam	1: 2	tears upon her c, With not one
Hos	11: 4	who raises an infant to his c; Yet,

CHEERFUL →CHEERFULNESS, CHEERS

Sir	35: 8	contribution show a c countenance,
Zec	8:19	c festivals for the house of Judah;
2 Cor	9: 7	compulsion, for God loves a c giver.

CHEERFULNESS →CHEERFUL

Rom	12: 8	if one does acts of mercy, with c.

CHEERS →CHEERFUL

Jgs	9:13	'Must I give up my wine that c gods

CHEESE

2 Sm	17:29	butter and c from the flocks
Jb	10:10	out as milk, and thicken me like c?

CHEMOSH

Nm	21:29	You are ruined, O people of C!
1 Kgs	11: 7	then built a high place to C, the idol
2 Kgs	23:13	horror, of C, the Moabite horror,
Jer	48: 7	be captured. C shall go into exile,

CHERETHITES

2 Sm	15:18	As all the C and Pelethites,
1 Kgs	1:38	and the C and Pelethites went down,
Ez	25:16	I will cut off the C and wipe

CHERISHED

Ps	66:18	Had I c evil in my heart, the Lord

CHERUB →CHERUBIM

Ex	25:19	them so that one c springs direct
Ps	18:11	Mounted on a c he flew,
Ez	28:14	With the C I placed you; you were
Ez	41:18	cherubim. Each c had two faces:

CHERUBIM →CHERUB

Gn	3:24	and he stationed the c and the fiery
Ex	25:18	Make two c of beaten gold
Ex	26: 1	yarn, with c embroidered on them.
Nm	7:89	from between the two c; and it
1 Sm	4: 4	hosts, who is enthroned upon the c.
2 Sm	6: 2	of hosts enthroned above the c.
1 Kgs	6:23	In the sanctuary were two c,
2 Kgs	19:15	God of Israel, enthroned upon the c!
1 Chr	13: 6	name "LORD enthroned upon the c."
2 Chr	3: 7	and he engraved c upon the walls.
2 Chr	3:11	The wings of the c spanned twenty cubits:
Ps	80: 2	throne upon the c reveal yourself
Ps	99: 1	God is enthroned on the c, the earth
Is	37:16	God of Israel, enthroned upon the c!
Ez	10: 1	above the c what appeared to be
Ez	10: 4	glory of the LORD rose from over the c
Ez	41:18	the figures of c and palmtrees:
Ez	41:18	a palmtree between every two c.
Heb	9: 5	Above it were the c of glory

CHEST →CHESTS

2 Kgs	12:10	The priest Jehoiada then took a c,
Dn	2:32	gold, its c and arms were silver,
Zec	13: 6	"What are these wounds on your c?"
Rv	1:13	robe, with a gold sash around his c.

CHESTS →CHEST

Rv	15: 6	with a gold sash around their c.

CHEW →CHEWS

Dt	14: 7	of the following that only c the cud

CHEWS →CHEW

Lv	11: 3	it is cloven-footed and c the cud.

CHIEF

Gn	39:21	by making the c jailer well-disposed
Gn	40: 2	the c cupbearer and the c baker,
Gn	41: 9	Then the c cupbearer spoke
1 Sm	21: 8	and he was Saul's c henchman.
Dn	5:11	father, made him c of the magicians,
Dn	10:13	one of the c princes, came to help
Mt	20:18	will be handed over to the c priests
Mt	27: 6	The c priests gathered
Mk	15: 3	The c priests accused him of many
Acts	9:14	he has authority from the c priests
Acts	26:10	I received from the c priests,
1 Pt	5: 4	when the c Shepherd is revealed,

CHILD →CHILD'S, CHILDBEARING, CHILDHOOD, CHILDISH, CHILDLESS, CHILDREN, CHILDREN'S, GRANDCHILDREN

Gn	17:17	"Can a c be born to a man who is
Ex	2: 3	and putting the c in it, placed it
Dt	1:31	as a man carries his c, all along your
Jgs	11:34	She was an only c: he had neither
Ru	4:16	Naomi took the c, placed him on her
1 Sm	1:22	her husband, "Once the c is weaned,
1 Sm	1:27	I prayed for this c, and the LORD
2 Sm	12:16	David besought God for the c.
Tb	3:15	he has no other c to make his heir,
Ps	131: 2	Like a weaned c on its mother's lap,
Eccl	6: 3	the c born dead is more fortunate
Sir	30: 9	Pamper your c and he will be
Is	7:14	the virgin shall be with c, and bear
Is	9: 5	For a c is born to us, a son is given
Is	11: 6	with a little c to guide them.
Is	49:15	tenderness for the c of her womb?
Jer	4:31	anguish of a mother with her first c—
Jer	6:26	Mourn as for an only c with bitter
Hos	11: 1	When Israel was a c I loved him,
Mt	1:18	with c through the holy Spirit.
Mt	2:11	on entering the house they saw the c

Mt	18: 2	He called a **c** over, placed it in their
Mk	5:39	The **c** is not dead but asleep."
Mk	10:15	of God like a **c** will not enter it."
Lk	1:80	The **c** grew and became strong
Lk	2:40	The **c** grew and became strong,
Lk	9:48	"Whoever receives this **c** in my name
1 Cor	13:11	When I was a **c**, I used to talk as a **c**, think as a **c**, reason as a **c**;
Gal	4: 7	So you are no longer a slave but a **c**, and if a **c** then also an heir,
Heb	11:23	they saw that he was a beautiful **c**,
Rv	12: 4	to devour her **c** when she gave birth.

CHILD'S →CHILD

Ex	2: 8	went and called the **c** own mother.

CHILDBEARING →CHILD, BEAR

Gn	3:16	"I will intensify the pangs of your **c**;

CHILDHOOD →CHILD

Prv	29:21	a man pampers his servant from **c**,

CHILDISH →CHILD

1 Cor	13:11	I became a man, I put aside **c** things.

CHILDLESS →CHILD

Gn	15: 2	if I keep on being **c** and have as my
1 Sm	15:33	"As your sword has made women **c**,
1 Sm	15:33	your mother be **c** among women."
Sir	16: 3	rather die **c** than have godless

CHILDREN →CHILD

Gn	3:16	in pain shall you bring forth **c**.
Gn	21: 7	added, "that Sarah would nurse **c**!
Gn	30: 1	that she failed to bear **c** to Jacob,
Ex	2: 6	and said, "It is one of the Hebrews' **c**."
Ex	12:26	When your **c** ask you, 'What does
Ex	20: 5	on the **c** of those who hate me,
Dt	4: 9	but teach them to your **c** and to your children's **c**;
Dt	6: 7	Drill them into your **c**.
Dt	11:19	Teach them to your **c**,
Dt	14: 1	"You are **c** of the LORD, your God.
Dt	24:16	shall not be put to death for their **c**, nor **c** for their fathers;
Dt	32:46	which you must impress on your **c**,
Jos	4: 6	your **c** ask you what these stones
1 Sm	1: 2	Peninnah had **c**, but Hannah was
Ezr	10:44	away, both the women and their **c**.
Neh	13:24	Of their **c**, half spoke Ashdodite,
1 Mc	1:60	had had their **c** circumcised were
Ps	34:12	Come, **c**, listen to me; I will teach
Ps	37:25	abandoned or their **c** begging bread.
Ps	78: 5	ancestors, they were to teach their **c**;
Ps	103:13	As a father has compassion on his **c**,
Prv	7:24	So now, O **c**, listen to me,
Prv	14:26	even for one's **c** he will be a refuge.
Prv	17: 6	and the glory of **c** is their parentage.
Prv	20: 7	justice, happy are his **c** after him!
Prv	31:28	Her **c** rise up and praise her;
Eccl	6: 3	Should a man have a hundred **c**
Sir	4:11	Wisdom instructs her **c**
Is	1: 4	evil race, corrupt **c**! They have
Is	30: 1	Woe to the rebellious **c**,
Is	54:13	great shall be the peace of your **c**.
Jer	4:22	know me not; Senseless **c** they are,
Jer	31:15	Rachel mourns her **c**, she refuses
Ez	23:37	they immolated the **c** they had borne
Hos	1: 2	Go, take a harlot wife and harlot's **c**,
Hos	2: 6	I will have no pity on her **c**, for they are the **c** of harlotry.
Jl	1: 3	Tell it to your **c**, and your **c** to their **c**, and their **c**
Zec	10: 7	Their **c** shall see it and be glad,
Mal	3:24	the hearts of the fathers to their **c**,
Mal	3:24	the hearts of the **c** to their fathers,
Mt	2:18	Rachel weeping for her **c**, and she
Mt	3: 9	you, God can raise up **c** to Abraham
Mt	5: 9	for they will be called **c** of God.
Mt	7:11	how to give good gifts to your **c**,
Mt	13:38	the good seed the **c** of the kingdom.
Mt	13:38	The weeds are the **c** of the evil one,
Mt	15:26	food of the **c** and throw it to the dogs."
Mt	18: 3	unless you turn and become like **c**,

Mt	19:14	Jesus said, "Let the **c** come to me,
Mt	27:25	blood be upon us and upon our **c**."
Mk	10:14	said to them, "Let the **c** come to me;
Mk	10:30	sisters and mothers and **c** and lands,
Mk	13:12	**c** will rise up against parents
Lk	18:16	"Let the **c** come to me and do not
Jn	1:12	he gave power to become **c** of God.
Jn	8:39	"If you were Abraham's **c**, you would
Acts	2:39	and to your **c** and to all those far off,
Rom	8:14	by the Spirit of God are **c** of God.
Rom	8:16	with our spirit that we are **c** of God,
Rom	9: 8	it is not the **c** of the flesh who are the **c** of God,
Rom	9:26	there they shall be called **c**
2 Cor	12:14	**C** ought not to save for their parents, but parents for their **c**.
Gal	3:26	through faith you are all **c** of God
Gal	4:28	like Isaac, are **c** of the promise.
Eph	2: 3	and we were by nature **c** of wrath,
Eph	5: 8	light in the Lord. Live as **c** of light,
Eph	6: 1	**C**, obey your parents [in the Lord],
Eph	6: 4	do not provoke your **c** to anger,
Phil	2:15	**c** of God without blemish
Col	3:20	**C**, obey your parents in everything,
Col	3:21	do not provoke your **c**, so they may
1 Thes	2: 7	as a nursing mother cares for her **c**.
1 Tm	3: 4	keeping his **c** under control
1 Tm	3:12	and must manage their **c** and their
1 Tm	5:10	that she has raised **c**,
1 Tm	5:14	marry, have **c**, and manage a home,
Ti	1: 6	believing **c** who are not accused
Ti	2: 4	to love their husbands and **c**,
Heb	2:13	I and the **c** God has given me."
1 Pt	1:14	Like obedient **c**, do not act
1 Jn	3: 1	that we may be called the **c** of God.
1 Jn	3:10	the **c** of God and the **c** of the devil
2 Jn	1: 1	Lady and to her **c** whom I love
3 Jn	1: 4	to hear that my **c** are walking

CHILDREN'S →CHILD

Prv	13:22	leaves an inheritance to his **c** children,
Jer	31:29	and the **c** teeth are set on edge,"
Ez	18: 2	thus their **c** teeth are on edge"?

CHISLEV

Neh	1: 1	the month **C** of the twentieth year,
1 Mc	1:54	On the fifteenth day of the month **C**,
1 Mc	4:59	the twenty-fifth day of the month **C**.
Zec	7: 1	on the fourth day of **C**, the ninth

CHOICE →CHOOSE

Prv	8:10	and knowledge rather than **c** gold.
Prv	10:20	Like **c** silver is the just man's
Jer	2:21	I had planted you, a **c** vine of fully

CHOKE →CHOKED

Mt	13:22	the lure of riches **c** the word and it

CHOKED →CHOKE

Mk	4: 7	the thorns grew up and **c** it and it
Lk	8: 7	and the thorns grew with it and **c** it.
Lk	8:14	they are **c** by the anxieties

CHOOSE →CHOICE, CHOOSES, CHOSE, CHOSEN

Dt	30:19	**C** life, then, that you and your
1 Kgs	18:25	"**C** one young bull and prepare it
Prv	3:31	lawless man and **c** none of his ways:
Sir	15:15	If you **c** you can keep
Is	7:15	to reject the bad and **c** the good.
Zec	2:16	land, and he will again **c** Jerusalem.
Jn	6:70	them, "Did I not **c** you twelve? Yet is

CHOOSES →CHOOSE

Nm	16: 7	the LORD then **c** is the holy one.
Dt	12:14	the LORD **c** from among your tribes;
Is	14: 1	has pity on Jacob and again **c** Israel

CHORAZIN

Mt	11:21	"Woe to you, **C**! Woe to you,
Lk	10:13	"Woe to you, **C**! Woe to you,

CHOSE →CHOOSE

Gn	13:11	**c** for himself the whole Jordan Plain
Dt	4:37	your fathers he **c** their descendants

1 Sm	2:28	I c them out of all the tribes
Neh	9: 7	are the God who c Abram,
Ps	47: 5	Who c a land for our heritage,
Ps	78:68	God c the tribe of Judah,
Ps	78:70	He c David his servant, took him
Ez	20: 5	The day I c Israel, I swore
Mk	13:20	for the sake of the elect whom he c,
Lk	6:13	and from them he c Twelve,
Jn	15:16	It was not you who c me, but I who c you and appointed you
Acts	6: 5	so they c Stephen, a man filled
Acts	15:40	But Paul c Silas and departed
1 Cor	1:27	God c the foolish of the world
1 Cor	1:27	and God c the weak of the world
Eph	1: 4	as he c us in him,
2 Thes	2:13	because God c you as the firstfruits

CHOSEN → CHOOSE

Dt	7: 6	he has c you from all the nations
Dt	18: 5	has c him and his sons out of all
Jos	24:22	that you have c to serve the Lord."
Jgs	10:14	and cry out to the gods you have c;
1 Sm	8:18	against the king whom you have c
1 Kgs	8:44	toward the city you have c
Neh	1: 9	which I have c as the dwelling place
Ps	89: 4	made a covenant with my c one;
Ps	105: 6	offspring of Jacob the c one!
Ps	119:30	The way of loyalty I have c; I have
Is	41: 8	Jacob, whom I have c,
Is	42: 1	my c one with whom I am pleased,
Is	43:10	my servants whom I have c
Hg	2:23	for I have c you, says the Lord
Zec	3: 2	Lord who has c Jerusalem rebuke
Mt	12:18	"Behold, my servant whom I have c,
Mt	22:14	Many are invited, but few are c."
Lk	9:35	a voice that said, "This is my c Son;
Lk	10:42	Mary has c the better part and it will
Lk	23:35	him save himself if he is the c one,
Jn	15:19	and I have c you out of the world,
Acts	1: 2	to the apostles whom he had c.
Acts	9:15	this man is a c instrument of mine
Rom	11: 5	time there is a remnant, c by grace.
Col	3:12	as God's c ones, holy and beloved,
1 Thes	1: 4	loved by God, how you were c.
1 Pt	2: 6	a cornerstone, c and precious,
1 Pt	2: 9	But you are "a c race, a royal
Rv	17:14	and those with him are called, c,

CHRIST → CHRIST'S, CHRISTIAN, CHRISTIANS, MESSIAH

Mk	1: 1	of the gospel of Jesus C [the Son
Jn	1:17	and truth came through Jesus C.
Acts	3: 6	the name of Jesus C the Nazorean,
Acts	4:10	of Jesus C the Nazorean whom you
Acts	9:34	to him, "Aeneas, Jesus C heals you.
Rom	1: 4	from the dead, Jesus C our Lord.
Rom	3:22	faith in Jesus C for all who believe.
Rom	5: 1	with God through our Lord Jesus C.
Rom	5: 6	For C, while we were still helpless,
Rom	5: 8	while we were still sinners C died
Rom	5:11	of God through our Lord Jesus C,
Rom	5:17	life through the one person Jesus C.
Rom	6: 4	just as C was raised from the dead
Rom	6:23	is eternal life in C Jesus our Lord.
Rom	7: 4	to the law through the body of C,
Rom	8: 1	for those who are in C Jesus.
Rom	8: 9	have the Spirit of C does not belong
Rom	8:17	heirs of God and joint heirs with C,
Rom	8:35	will separate us from the love of C?
Rom	10: 4	For C is the end of the law
Rom	12: 5	are one body in C and individually
Rom	13:14	But put on the Lord Jesus C,
Rom	14: 9	For this is why C died and came
Rom	15: 3	For C did not please himself; but,
Rom	15: 5	another, in keeping with C Jesus,
Rom	15: 7	then, as C welcomed you,
Rom	16:18	such people do not serve our Lord C
1 Cor	1: 2	have been sanctified in C Jesus,
1 Cor	1: 7	the revelation of our Lord Jesus C.
1 Cor	1:13	Is C divided? Was Paul crucified
1 Cor	1:17	For C did not send me to baptize

1 Cor	1:17	the cross of C might not be emptied
1 Cor	1:23	but we proclaim C crucified,
1 Cor	1:30	due to him that you are in C Jesus,
1 Cor	2: 2	I was with you except Jesus C,
1 Cor	2:16	him?" But we have the mind of C.
1 Cor	3:11	one that is there, namely, Jesus C.
1 Cor	5: 7	For our paschal lamb, C, has been
1 Cor	6:15	that your bodies are members of C?
1 Cor	8: 6	and one Lord, Jesus C,
1 Cor	8:12	they are, you are sinning against C.
1 Cor	10: 4	them, and the rock was the C.
1 Cor	11: 1	Be imitators of me, as I am of C.
1 Cor	11: 3	to know that C is the head of every
1 Cor	11: 3	of his wife, and the head of C.
1 Cor	15: 3	received: that C died for our sins
1 Cor	15:14	And if C has not been raised,
1 Cor	15:22	so too in C shall all be brought
1 Cor	15:57	victory through our Lord Jesus C.
2 Cor	1: 5	to us, so through C does our
2 Cor	2:14	who always leads us in triumph in C
2 Cor	3: 3	be a letter of C administered by us,
2 Cor	3:14	because through C it is taken away.
2 Cor	4: 4	light of the gospel of the glory of C,
2 Cor	4: 5	ourselves but Jesus C as Lord,
2 Cor	4: 6	of God on the face of [Jesus] C.
2 Cor	5:10	before the judgment seat of C,
2 Cor	5:14	For the love of C impels us,
2 Cor	5:17	whoever is in C is a new creation:
2 Cor	6:15	What accord has C with Beliar?
2 Cor	10: 1	the gentleness and clemency of C,
2 Cor	11: 2	present you as a chaste virgin to C.
2 Cor	11:13	who masquerade as apostles of C.
Gal	1: 7	and wish to pervert the gospel of C.
Gal	2:16	the law but through faith in Jesus C,
Gal	2:16	we may be justified by faith in C
Gal	3:28	for you are all one in C Jesus.
Gal	5: 1	For freedom C set us free; so stand
Gal	6: 2	and so you will fulfill the law of C.
Eph	1: 3	who has blessed us in C with every
Eph	2: 5	life with C (by grace you have been
Eph	2:10	created in C Jesus for the good
Eph	2:12	were at that time without C,
Eph	2:20	C Jesus himself as the capstone.
Eph	3: 8	Gentiles the inscrutable riches of C,
Eph	3:17	and that C may dwell in your hearts
Eph	4:13	to the extent of the full stature of C,
Eph	4:15	way into him who is the head, C,
Eph	4:32	as God has forgiven you in C.
Eph	5: 2	as C loved us and handed himself
Eph	5:21	one another out of reverence for C.
Eph	5:23	of his wife just as C is head
Eph	5:25	even as C loved the church
Phil	1: 6	complete it until the day of C Jesus.
Phil	1:18	or in truth, C is being proclaimed?
Phil	1:21	For to me life is C, and death is
Phil	1:23	to depart this life and be with C,
Phil	1:27	in a way worthy of the gospel of C,
Phil	1:29	for the sake of C, not only
Phil	2: 5	attitude that is also yours in C Jesus,
Phil	2:11	tongue confess that Jesus C is Lord,
Phil	3: 7	to consider a loss because of C.
Phil	3:18	as enemies of the cross of C.
Phil	4:19	with his glorious riches in C Jesus.
Col	1: 4	have heard of your faith in C Jesus
Col	1:27	it is C in you, the hope for glory.
Col	1:28	may present everyone perfect in C.
Col	2: 2	of the mystery of God, C,
Col	2: 6	as you received C Jesus the Lord,
Col	2:17	to come; the reality belongs to C.
Col	3: 1	where C is seated at the right hand
Col	3: 3	your life is hidden with C in God.
Col	3:15	the peace of C control your hearts,
Col	3:16	Let the word of C dwell in you
1 Thes	4:16	and the dead in C will rise first.
1 Thes	5: 9	salvation through our Lord Jesus C,
1 Thes	5:18	the will of God for you in C Jesus.
2 Thes	2: 1	to the coming of our Lord Jesus C
2 Thes	2:14	the glory of our Lord Jesus C.
1 Tm	1:15	C Jesus came into the world to save

1 Tm	1:16	C Jesus might display all his
1 Tm	2: 5	race, C Jesus, himself human,
1 Tm	4: 6	will be a good minister of C Jesus,
1 Tm	6:14	the appearance of our Lord Jesus C
2 Tm	1: 9	on us in C Jesus before time began,
2 Tm	1:10	appearance of our savior C Jesus,
2 Tm	2: 1	in the grace that is in C Jesus.
2 Tm	2: 3	me like a good soldier of C Jesus.
2 Tm	2: 8	Remember Jesus C,
2 Tm	2:10	the salvation that is in C Jesus,
2 Tm	3:12	in C Jesus will be persecuted.
2 Tm	3:15	salvation through faith in C Jesus.
Ti	2:13	great God and of our savior Jesus C,
Phlm	1: 6	good there is in us that leads to C.
Phlm	1:20	in the Lord. Refresh my heart in C.
Heb	3: 6	C was faithful as a son placed over
Heb	3:14	We have become partners of C
Heb	5: 5	it was not C who glorified himself
Heb	6: 1	behind the basic teaching about C
Heb	9:11	when C came as high priest
Heb	9:24	For C did not enter into a sanctuary
Heb	9:28	so also C, offered once to take away
Heb	10:10	of the body of Jesus C once for all.
Heb	13: 8	Jesus C is the same yesterday,
1 Pt	1: 2	with the blood of Jesus C:
1 Pt	1:11	Spirit of C within them indicated
1 Pt	1:11	to the sufferings destined for C
1 Pt	1:19	with the precious blood of C as
1 Pt	2:21	because C also suffered for you,
1 Pt	3:15	sanctify C as Lord in your hearts.
1 Pt	3:18	For C also suffered for sins once,
1 Pt	3:21	through the resurrection of Jesus C,
1 Pt	4: 1	since C suffered in the flesh,
1 Pt	4:14	you are insulted for the name of C,
2 Pt	1: 1	a slave and apostle of Jesus C,
2 Pt	1:16	and coming of our Lord Jesus C,
2 Pt	3:18	of our Lord and savior Jesus C.
1 Jn	2: 1	Father, Jesus C the righteous one.
1 Jn	2:22	Whoever denies that Jesus is the C.
1 Jn	3:23	Jesus C, and love one another just
1 Jn	4: 2	acknowledges Jesus C come
1 Jn	5: 1	Jesus is the C is begotten by God,
1 Jn	5: 6	blood, Jesus C, not by water alone,
1 Jn	5:20	one who is true, in his Son Jesus C.
2 Jn	1: 7	not acknowledge Jesus C as coming
2 Jn	1: 9	of the C does not have God;
Jude	1: 1	a slave of Jesus C and brother
Jude	1: 1	the Father and kept safe for Jesus C:
Jude	1: 4	our only Master and Lord, Jesus C.
Jude	1:17	by the apostles of our Lord Jesus C,
Rv	1: 1	The revelation of Jesus C,
Rv	1: 5	and from Jesus C, the faithful
Rv	20: 4	they reigned with C for a thousand
Rv	20: 6	they will be priests of God and of C,

CHRIST'S → CHRIST

Eph	4: 7	of us according to the measure of C gift.

CHRISTIAN → CHRIST

Acts	26:28	will soon persuade me to play the C."
1 Pt	4:16	suffer as a C should not be ashamed

CHRISTIANS → CHRIST

Acts	11:26	that the disciples were first called C.

CHRYSOLITE

Ez	28:13	topaz, and beryl, c, onyx,
Rv	21:20	the seventh c, the eighth beryl,

CHURCH → CHURCHES

Mt	16:18	and upon this rock I will build my c,
Mt	18:17	refuses to listen to them, tell the c.
Mt	18:17	If he refuses to listen even to the c,
Acts	5:11	great fear came upon the whole c
Acts	8: 1	persecution of the c in Jerusalem,
Acts	8: 3	was trying to destroy the c;
Acts	12: 1	members of the c to harm them.
Acts	14:23	presbyters for them in each c and,
Acts	15: 4	they were welcomed by the c,
Acts	20:28	which you tend the c of God that he
Rom	16: 5	greet also the c at their house.

1 Cor	4:17	I teach them everywhere in every c.
1 Cor	6: 4	people of no standing in the c?
1 Cor	10:32	to Jews or Greeks or the c of God,
1 Cor	11:18	you meet as a c there are divisions
1 Cor	12:28	God has designated in the c to be,
1 Cor	14: 4	whoever prophesies builds up the c.
1 Cor	14:12	of them for building up the c.
1 Cor	14:35	for a woman to speak in the c.
1 Cor	15: 9	because I persecuted the c of God.
Gal	1:13	how I persecuted the c of God
Eph	1:22	him as head over all things to the c,
Eph	3:10	now be made known through the c
Eph	3:21	to him be glory in the c
Eph	5:23	wife just as Christ is head of the c,
Eph	5:25	even as Christ loved the c
Phil	3: 6	in zeal I persecuted the c,
Col	1:18	He is the head of the body, the c.
Col	1:24	behalf of his body, which is the c,
1 Tm	3: 5	can he take care of the c of God?
1 Tm	3:15	which is the c of the living God,
Jas	5:14	summon the presbyters of the c,
3 Jn	1: 9	I wrote to the c, but Diotrephes,
Rv	2: 1	"To the angel of the c in Ephesus,

CHURCHES → CHURCH

Acts	15:41	Cilicia bringing strength to the c.
Acts	16: 5	Day after day the c grew stronger
1 Cor	7:17	I give this order in all the c.
1 Cor	11:16	such a custom, nor do the c of God.
1 Cor	14:34	women should keep silent in the c,
2 Cor	11: 8	I plundered other c by accepting
1 Thes	2:14	become imitators of the c of God
2 Thes	1: 4	you in the c of God regarding your
Rv	1: 4	John, to the seven c in Asia:
Rv	1:20	stars are the angels of the seven c,
Rv	1:20	seven lampstands are the seven c.
Rv	2: 7	to hear what the Spirit says to the c.
Rv	22:16	to give you this testimony for the c.

CILICIA

Jdt	2:25	He seized the territory of C, and cut
Acts	15:41	C bringing strength to the churches.
Acts	21:39	of Tarsus in C, a citizen of no mean

CIRCLE → ENCIRCLE

Jos	6:11	the ark of the LORD c the city,
Jb	26:10	has marked out a c on the surface

CIRCUMCISE → CIRCUMCISED, CIRCUMCISION

Gn	17:11	C the flesh of your foreskin,
Dt	10:16	C your hearts, therefore, and be no
Dt	30: 6	will c your hearts and the hearts
Jos	5: 2	c the Israelite nation for the second
Lk	1:59	on the eighth day to c the child,
Jn	7:22	you c a man on the sabbath.
Acts	21:21	telling them not to c their children

CIRCUMCISED → CIRCUMCISE

Gn	17:10	every male among you shall be c.
Gn	17:26	and his son Ishmael were c;
Gn	21: 4	was eight days old, Abraham c him,
Gn	34:15	by having every male among you c.
Jos	5: 3	c the Israelites at Gibeath-haaraloth,
Jdt	14:10	He had the flesh of his foreskin c,
1 Mc	1:60	had had their children c were put
1 Mc	2:46	forcibly c any uncircumcised boys
2 Mc	6:10	for having c their children were
Acts	10:45	The c believers who had
Acts	11: 2	Jerusalem the c believers confronted
Acts	15: 1	"Unless you are c according
Acts	16: 3	Paul had him c, for they all knew
Rom	3:30	and will justify the c on the basis
Rom	4: 9	this blessedness apply only to the c,
1 Cor	7:18	someone called after he had been c?
1 Cor	7:18	person called? He should not be c.
Gal	2: 3	was a Greek, was compelled to be c,
Gal	2: 7	uncircumcised, just as Peter to the c,
Gal	6:13	having themselves c observe
Gal	6:13	they only want you to be c so
Phil	3: 5	C on the eighth day, of the race
Col	2:11	were also c with a circumcision not

CIRCUMCISION →CIRCUMCISE

Ex	4:26	spouse of blood," in regard to the c.
1 Mc	1:15	covered over the mark of their c
Acts	7: 8	Then he gave him the covenant of c,
Rom	2:25	C, to be sure, has value if you
Rom	2:25	your c has become uncircumcision.
Rom	2:29	and c is of the heart, in the spirit,
1 Cor	7:19	C means nothing,
Gal	5: 6	neither c nor uncircumcision counts
Eph	2:11	by those called the c, which is done
Phil	3: 3	For we are the c, we who worship
Col	2:11	with a c not administered by hand,
Col	2:11	carnal body, with the c of Christ.

CIRCUMSTANCES

Phil	4:12	indeed how to live in humble c;
1 Thes	5:18	In all c give thanks, for this is

CISTERN →CISTERNS

2 Kgs	18:31	and drink the water of his own c,
Prv	5:15	Drink water from your own c,
Jer	38: 6	There was no water in the c,

CISTERNS →CISTERN

Dt	6:11	garner, with c that you did not dig,
Neh	9:25	with all good things, c already dug,
Jer	2:13	They have dug themselves c, broken c, that hold no water.

CITADEL →CITADELS

1 Mc	1:33	strong towers, and it became their c.
1 Mc	4:41	men to attack those in the c,

CITADELS →CITADEL

Ps	48:14	the ramparts, examine its c, that you

CITIES →CITY

Gn	13:12	while Lot settled among the c
Gn	19:25	He overthrew those c and the whole
Ex	1:11	for Pharaoh the supply c of Pithom
Lv	25:32	levitical c the Levites shall always
Nm	35:11	select for yourselves c to serve as c
Dt	6:10	fine, large c that you did not build,
Jos	20: 2	the Israelites to designate the c
Ps	69:36	rescue Zion, rebuild the c of Judah.
Is	6:11	he replied: Until the c are desolate,
Is	64: 9	Your holy c have become a desert,
Jer	4:16	shouting their war cry against the c
Zec	1:17	My c shall again overflow
Lk	19:17	small matter; take charge of ten c.'
2 Pt	2: 6	if he condemned the c of Sodom
Rv	16:19	three parts, and the gentile c fell.

CITIZEN →CITIZENS, CITIZENSHIP

Acts	21:39	in Cilicia, a c of no mean city;
Acts	22:25	to scourge a man who is a Roman c
Acts	23:27	I learned that he was a Roman c.

CITIZENS →CITIZEN

Acts	16:38	they heard that they were Roman c.
Eph	2:19	you are fellow c with the holy ones

CITIZENSHIP →CITIZEN

Acts	22:28	"I acquired this c for a large sum
Phil	3:20	But our c is in heaven, and from it

CITY →CITIES

Gn	4:17	Cain also became the founder of a c,
Gn	11: 4	let us build ourselves a c
Gn	18:24	were fifty innocent people in the c;
Gn	19:14	"the LORD is about to destroy the c."
Dt	28: 3	"May you be blessed in the c,
Dt	28:16	"May you be cursed in the c,
Jos	6:16	for the LORD has given you the c
Jgs	16: 3	seized the doors of the c gate
2 Sm	5: 9	which was called the C of David;
1 Kgs	8:44	toward the c you have chosen
1 Chr	11: 7	thenceforth was called the C
Neh	11: 1	the holy c, while the other nine
1 Mc	1:31	He plundered the c and set fire to it,
1 Mc	2:31	king who were in the C of David,
Ps	46: 5	of the river gladden the c of God,
Ps	48: 2	in the c of our God: The holy

Ps	60:11	will bring me to the fortified c?
Ps	122: 3	Jerusalem, built as a c, walled round
Ps	127: 1	Unless the LORD guard the c, in vain
Prv	11:10	the just prosper, the c rejoices;
Prv	31:23	husband is prominent at the c gates
Prv	31:31	her works praise her at the c gates.
Is	1:21	adulteress, the faithful c, so upright!
Is	1:26	be called c of justice, faithful c.
Is	62:12	"Frequented," a c that is not forsaken.
Jer	34: 2	I am handing this c over to the king
Jer	34:22	LORD, and bring them back to this c.
Lam	1: 1	the once crowded c! Widowed is
Ez	4: 1	you, and draw on it a c [Jerusalem].
Ez	11: 3	The c is the kettle, and we are
Dn	9:24	for your people and for your holy c:
Am	5: 3	GOD: The c that marched
Jon	1: 2	"Set out for the great c of Nineveh,
Jon	3: 2	"Set out for the great c of Nineveh,
Jon	4:11	the great c, in which there are more
Na	3: 1	Woe to the bloody c, all lies,
Hb	2:12	to him who builds a c by bloodshed,
Zep	2:15	Is this the exultant c that dwelt
Zec	8: 3	shall be called the faithful c,
Zec	14: 2	half of the c shall go into exile,
Mt	4: 5	the devil took him to the holy c,
Mt	5:14	A c set on a mountain cannot be
Lk	2: 4	to the c of David that is called
Lk	19:41	near, he saw the c and wept over it,
Acts	18:10	for I have many people in this c."
Heb	11:10	forward to the c with foundations,
Heb	12:22	Zion and the c of the living God,
Heb	13:14	For here we have no lasting c,
Rv	3:12	and the name of the c of my God,
Rv	11: 2	who will trample the holy c
Rv	16:19	The great c was split into three
Rv	17:18	you saw represents the great c
Rv	18:10	"Alas, alas, great c, Babylon,
Rv	20: 9	of the holy ones and the beloved c.
Rv	21: 2	I also saw the holy c, a new
Rv	21:22	I saw no temple in the c, for its

CLAIM →CLAIMED, CLAIMING

Neh	2:20	be neither share nor c nor memorial

CLAIMED →CLAIM

Acts	4:32	no one c that any of his possessions

CLAIMING →CLAIM

Acts	5:36	c to be someone important,
Rom	1:22	While c to be wise, they became

CLAN →CLANS

Nm	27: 4	his c merely because he had no son?

CLANS →CLAN

Gn	36:15	The following are the c of Esau's
Nm	1: 2	Israelites, by c and ancestral houses,
Mi	5: 1	small to be among the c of Judah,

CLAP →CLAPPED

Ps	47: 2	All you peoples, c your hands;
Ps	98: 8	Let the rivers c their hands,
Is	55:12	the countryside shall c their hands.
Lam	2:15	who pass by c their hands at you;
Ez	6:11	C your hands, stamp your feet,
Na	3:19	news of you c their hands over you;

CLAPPED →CLAP

Ez	25: 6	GOD: Because you c your hands

CLASPS

Ex	26: 6	Then make fifty c of gold,
Ex	36:13	Then fifty c of gold were made,

CLAUDIUS

Acts	11:28	the world, and it happened under C.
Acts	18: 2	Priscilla because C had ordered all
Acts	23:26	"C Lysias to his excellency

CLAWS

Dn	7:19	with its iron teeth and bronze c,

CLAY

Jb	10: 9	that you fashioned me from c!

Jb	33: 6	been taken from the same **c** by God.
Wis	15: 7	class the worker in **c** is the judge.
Sir	33:13	Like **c** in the hands of a potter, to be
Is	29:16	were taken to be the **c**: As though
Is	41:25	red earth, as the potter treads the **c**.
Is	45: 9	Dare the **c** say to its modeler,
Is	64: 7	we are the **c** and you the potter:
Jer	18: 6	like **c** in the hand of the potter,
Dn	14: 7	said; "it is only **c** inside and bronze
Rom	9:21	the potter have a right over the **c**,
2 Tm	2:20	and silver but also of wood and **c**,

CLEAN →CLEANSE, CLEANSED, CLEANSES, CLEANSING

Gn	7: 2	Of every **c** animal, take with you
Lv	10:10	between what is **c** and what is
Lv	20:25	the **c** animals from the unclean,
Lv	20:25	and the **c** birds from the unclean,
Dt	14:11	"You may eat all **c** birds.
2 Kgs	5:10	flesh will heal, and you will be **c**."
Ps	24: 4	"The **c** of hand and pure of heart,
Ps	73:13	in vain that I have kept my heart **c**,
Prv	20: 9	can say, "I have made my heart **c**,
Eccl	9: 2	the bad, for the **c** and the unclean,
Wis	15: 7	the vessels that serve for **c** purposes
Ez	36:25	I will sprinkle **c** water upon you
Zec	3: 5	also said, "Put a **c** miter on his head."
Mt	8: 2	if you wish, you can make me **c**."
Mt	27:59	body, Joseph wrapped it [in] **c** linen
Mk	7:19	(Thus he declared all foods **c**.)
Jn	13:10	his feet washed, for he is **c** all over; so you are **c**, but not all."
Acts	10:15	"What God has made **c**, you are not
Rom	14:20	Everything is indeed **c**, but it is
Heb	10:22	our hearts sprinkled **c** from an evil

CLEANSE →CLEAN

2 Chr	29:15	to **c** the LORD's house in keeping
Jb	9:30	with snow and **c** my hands with lye,
Ps	51: 4	all my guilt; from my sin **c** me.
Sir	38:10	be just, **c** your heart of every sin;
Jer	33: 8	I will **c** them of all the guilt they
Ez	36:25	and from all your idols I will **c** you.
Mt	10: 8	raise the dead, **c** lepers,
2 Cor	7: 1	let us **c** ourselves from every
Jas	4: 8	**C** your hands, you sinners,
1 Jn	1: 9	and **c** us from every wrongdoing.

CLEANSED →CLEAN

Neh	13:30	Thus I **c** them of all foreign
Mt	8: 3	His leprosy was **c** immediately.
Mt	11: 5	walk, lepers are **c**, the deaf hear,
Lk	4:27	yet not one of them was **c**, but only
Heb	10: 2	once **c**, would no longer have had

CLEANSES →CLEAN

2 Tm	2:21	If anyone **c** himself of these things,
1 Jn	1: 7	of his Son Jesus **c** us from all sin.

CLEANSING →CLEAN

Mk	1:44	for your **c** what Moses prescribed;
Lk	5:14	for your **c** what Moses prescribed;
Eph	5:26	**c** her by the bath of water
2 Pt	1: 9	forgetful of the **c** of his past sins.

CLEAR →CLEARED, CLEARLY

Nm	15:34	there was no **c** decision as to what
Ps	19: 9	The command of the LORD is **c**,
Mt	3:12	He will **c** his threshing floor
Acts	23: 1	a perfectly **c** conscience before God
1 Tm	3: 9	of the faith with a **c** conscience.
2 Tm	1: 3	a **c** conscience as my ancestors did,
Heb	13:18	that we have a **c** conscience,
1 Pt	3:16	keeping your conscience **c**, so that,
Rv	21:11	stone, like jasper, **c** as crystal.
Rv	21:18	the city was pure gold, **c** as glass.

CLEARED →CLEAR

Ps	80:10	You **c** the ground; it took root
Is	5: 2	He spaded it, **c** it of stones,

CLEARLY →CLEAR

Mk	8:25	his eyes a second time and he saw **c**;
Lk	6:42	you will see **c** to remove the splinter

CLEFT →CLEFTS

Jer	13: 4	there hide it in a **c** of the rock.

CLEFTS →CLEFT

Song	2:14	"O my dove in the **c** of the rock,
Ob	1: 3	you who dwell in the **c** of the rock,

CLEVERLY

2 Pt	1:16	We did not follow **c** devised myths

CLIMB →CLIMBED

Song	7: 9	I said: I will **c** the palm tree, I will
Am	9: 2	Though they **c** to the heavens,

CLIMBED →CLIMB

Lk	19: 4	and **c** a sycamore tree in order to see

CLING →CLINGS, CLUNG

Ps	119:31	I **c** to your decrees, LORD; do not let

CLINGS →CLING

Gn	2:24	father and mother and **c** to his wife,
Ps	63: 9	My soul **c** fast to you; your right
Heb	12: 1	of every burden and sin that **c** to us

CLOAK →CLOAKS

Ex	22:25	take your neighbor's **c** as a pledge,
Dt	22:12	of the **c** that you wrap around you.
Ru	3: 9	the corner of your **c** over me,
Ez	16: 8	I spread the corner of my **c** over you
Mt	5:40	your tunic, hand him your **c** as well.
Mt	9:21	"If only I can touch his **c**, I shall be
Heb	1:12	You will roll them up like a **c**,

CLOAKS →CLOAK

Ex	12:34	in their **c** on their shoulders.
Mk	11: 8	Many people spread their **c**
Acts	22:23	and throwing off their **c** and flinging

CLOSED →CLOSER

Gn	2:21	his ribs and **c** up its place with flesh.
Gn	20:18	God had tightly **c** every womb
Lk	12: 3	have whispered behind **c** doors will

CLOSER →CLOSED

1 Cor	8: 8	Now food will not bring us **c** to God.

CLOTH →CLOTHS, SACKCLOTH

Nm	4: 6	on top of this spread an all-violet **c**.
Dt	22:17	spread out the **c** before the elders
Mt	9:16	cloak with a piece of unshrunken **c**,
Mk	14:51	nothing but a linen **c** about his body.
Acts	16:14	a dealer in purple **c**, from the city

CLOTHE →CLOTHED, CLOTHES, CLOTHING

Ps	132:16	I will **c** its priests with blessing;
Ps	132:18	His foes I will **c** with shame,
1 Pt	5: 5	**c** yourselves with humility in your

CLOTHED →CLOTHE

Gn	3:21	garments, with which he **c** them.
Lv	8: 7	with the sash, **c** him with the robe,
1 Sm	17:38	Then Saul **c** David in his own tunic,
2 Chr	6:41	LORD God, be **c** with salvation,
Ps	30:12	sackcloth and **c** me with gladness.
Ps	104: 1	You are **c** with majesty and glory,
Ps	132: 9	Your priests will be **c** with justice;
Is	61:10	For he has **c** me with a robe
Zec	3: 5	head and **c** him with the garments.
Lk	24:49	the city until you are **c** with power
2 Cor	5: 2	to be further **c** with our heavenly
Gal	3:27	into Christ have **c** yourselves
Rv	12: 1	in the sky, a woman **c** with the sun,

CLOTHES →CLOTHE

Gn	37:29	Joseph was not in it, he tore his **c**,
Gn	44:13	At this, they tore their **c**. Then,
Dt	29: 4	Your **c** did not fall from you
Mt	17: 2	sun and his **c** became white as light.
Lk	12:28	If God so **c** the grass in the field
1 Tm	2: 9	or pearls, or expensive **c**,
Jas	2: 2	and a poor person in shabby **c**

CLOTHING →CLOTHE

Ex	3:22	articles and for **c** to put on your sons
Ex	12:35	articles of silver and gold and for **c**.

Ex	21:10	food, her **c**, or her conjugal rights.
Ps	22:19	among them; for my **c** they cast lots.
Ps	102:27	Like **c** you change them and they
Sir	29:21	prime needs are water, bread, and **c**,
Dn	7: 9	his throne. His **c** was snow bright,
Mt	3: 4	John wore **c** made of camel's hair
Mt	7:15	who come to you in sheep's **c**,
1 Tm	6: 8	If we have food and **c**, we shall be

CLOTHS →CLOTH
Lk	24:12	down, and saw the burial **c** alone;

CLOUD →CLOUDS
Ex	13:21	of a column of **c** to show them
Ex	16:10	glory of the LORD appeared in the **c**!
Ex	19: 9	"I am coming to you in a dense **c**,
Ex	24:18	into the midst of the **c** as he went
Ex	40:34	Then the **c** covered the meeting tent,
Lv	16: 2	myself in a **c** above the propitiatory,
Nm	9:15	erected, the **c** covered the Dwelling,
Dt	1:33	you a resting place—by day in the **c**,
1 Kgs	8:10	the **c** filled the temple of the LORD
1 Kgs	18:44	"There is a **c** as small as a man's hand
Neh	9:19	The column of **c** did not cease
Ps	105:39	He spread a **c** as a cover, and made
Is	19: 1	See, the LORD is riding on a swift **c**
Ez	1: 4	North, a huge **c** with flashing fire
Ez	10: 4	the temple was filled with the **c**,
Hos	6: 4	Your piety is like a morning **c**,
Mk	9: 7	Then a **c** came, casting a shadow
Mk	9: 7	then from the **c** came a voice,
Lk	21:27	of Man coming in a **c** with power
Acts	1: 9	and a **c** took him from their sight.
1 Cor	10: 2	were baptized into Moses in the **c**
Heb	12: 1	by so great a **c** of witnesses, let us
Rv	10: 1	down from heaven wrapped in a **c**,
Rv	11:12	in a **c** as their enemies looked on.
Rv	14:14	I looked and there was a white **c**,
Rv	14:14	on the **c** one who looked like a son

CLOUDS →CLOUD
Gn	9:13	my bow in the **c** to serve as a sign
Jgs	5: 4	while the **c** sent down showers.
1 Kgs	18:45	the sky grew dark with **c** and wind,
Jb	38:37	Who counts the **c** in his wisdom?
Ps	36: 6	to heaven; your fidelity, to the **c**.
Ps	68: 5	exalt the rider of the **c**.
Ps	77:18	The **c** poured down their rains;
Ps	104: 3	You make the **c** your chariot;
Prv	25:14	Like **c** and wind when no rain
Is	14:14	will ascend above the tops of the **c**;
Dn	3:73	Lightnings and **c**, bless the Lord;
Dn	7:13	on the **c** of heaven; When he
Jl	2: 2	gloom, a day of **c** and somberness!
Na	1: 3	path, and **c** are the dust at his feet;
Zep	1:15	and gloom, A day of thick black **c**,
Mt	24:30	Man coming upon the **c** of heaven
Mt	26:64	and 'coming on the **c** of heaven.' "
1 Thes	4:17	them in the **c** to meet the Lord
Jude	1:12	They are waterless **c** blown
Rv	1: 7	Behold, he is coming amid the **c**,

CLUB →CLUBS
Prv	25:18	Like a **c**, or a sword, or a sharp
Dn	14:26	kill this dragon without sword or **c**."

CLUBS →CLUB
Mk	14:43	and **c** who had come from the chief

CLUNG →CLING
2 Kgs	3: 3	but he still **c** to the sin
Acts	3:11	As he **c** to Peter and John,

CLUSTER →CLUSTERS
Nm	13:23	a branch with a single **c** of grapes
Mi	7: 1	been gleaned; There is no **c** to eat,

CLUSTERS →CLUSTER
Rv	14:18	and cut the **c** from the earth's vines,

CO-WORKER →WORK
Rom	16:21	Timothy, my **c**, greets you; so do

CO-WORKERS →WORK
3 Jn	1: 8	so that we may be **c** in the truth.

COALS
Ps	11: 6	the wicked fiery **c** and brimstone,
Ps	18: 9	his mouth; it kindled **c** into flame.
Ps	140:11	May God rain burning **c** upon them,
Prv	6:28	Or can a man walk on live **c**, and his
Prv	25:22	For live **c** you will heap on his head,
Ez	1:13	creatures something like burning **c**
Ez	10: 2	with burning **c** from among
Rom	12:20	by so doing you will heap burning **c**

COAST →COASTLANDS
Nm	34: 6	shall have the Great Sea with its **c**;

COASTLANDS →COAST, LAND
Is	42: 4	the **c** will wait for his teaching.
Is	66:19	the distant **c** that have never heard

COCK
Jn	13:38	the **c** will not crow before you deny
Jn	18:27	And immediately the **c** crowed.

COFFIN
Gn	50:26	and laid to rest in a **c** in Egypt.

COHORT
Mk	15:16	and assembled the whole **c**.
Acts	10: 1	centurion of the **C** called the Italica,
Acts	27: 1	named Julius of the **C** Augusta.

COIN →COINS
Mt	17:27	you will find a **c** worth twice
Mt	22:19	Show me the **c** that pays the census
Lk	15: 9	me because I have found the **c** that I

COINS →COIN
Lk	15: 8	"Or what woman having ten **c**
Lk	21: 2	poor widow putting in two small **c**.
Jn	2:15	spilled the **c** of the money-changers

COLD
Gn	8:22	seedtime and harvest, **c** and heat,
Ps	147:17	before such **c** the waters freeze.
Zec	14: 6	that day there shall no longer be **c**
Mt	10:42	whoever gives only a cup of **c** water
Mt	24:12	the love of many will grow **c**.
Rv	3:16	neither hot nor **c**, I will spit you

COLLECT →COLLECTION, COLLECTOR, COLLECTORS
Mt	13:30	"First **c** the weeds and tie them

COLLECTION →COLLECT
1 Cor	16: 1	in regard to the **c** for the holy ones,

COLLECTOR →COLLECT
Mt	10: 3	Thomas and Matthew the tax **c**;
Lk	5:27	saw a tax **c** named Levi sitting
Lk	18:10	a Pharisee and the other was a tax **c**.
Lk	19: 2	who was a chief tax **c**

COLLECTORS →COLLECT
Mt	5:46	Do not the tax **c** do the same?
Mt	9:10	many tax **c** and sinners came and sat
Mt	11:19	a friend of tax **c** and sinners.'
Mt	17:24	the **c** of the temple tax approached
Mt	21:32	but tax **c** and prostitutes did.

COLONY
Acts	16:12	of Macedonia and a Roman **c**.

COLT
Zec	9: 9	on an ass, on a **c**, the foal of an ass.
Mt	21: 5	ass, and on a **c**, the foal of a beast
Jn	12:15	king comes, seated upon an ass's **c**."

COME →CAME, COMES, COMING, OUTCOME
Gn	15:16	the others shall **c** back here;
Gn	38:16	he said, "**C**, let me have intercourse
Ex	3: 5	God said, "**C** no nearer!
Ex	19:11	the third day the LORD will **c** down
Ex	24: 1	himself was told, "**C** up to the LORD,
Dt	28: 2	all these blessings will **c** upon you
Dt	28:45	"All these curses will **c** upon you,
1 Sm	4: 7	said, "Gods have **c** to their camp."

Ps	14: 7	Oh, that from Zion might **c**
Ps	17: 2	From you let my vindication **c**;
Ps	88: 3	Let my prayer **c** before you;
Ps	91:10	you, no affliction **c** near your tent.
Ps	119:41	Let your love **c** to me, LORD,
Ps	121: 1	From where will my help **c**?
Ps	144: 5	LORD, incline your heavens and **c**;
Prv	2: 6	from his mouth **c** knowledge
Prv	24:34	Then will poverty **c** upon you like
Song	2:13	beloved, my beautiful one, and **c**!
Is	1:18	**C** now, let us set things right,
Is	13: 5	They **c** from a far-off country,
Is	41:22	Let them **c** near and foretell to us
Is	41:22	or declare to us the things to **c**!
Is	55: 1	you who are thirsty, **c** to the water!
Is	55: 1	**C**, without paying and without cost,
Is	59:20	He shall **c** to Zion a redeemer
Hos	3: 5	They shall **c** trembling to the LORD
Mi	6: 6	With what shall I **c** before the LORD,
Hb	2: 3	it, it will surely **c**, it will not be late.
Zec	10: 4	From him shall **c** leader and chief,
Zec	14: 5	shall **c**, and all his holy ones
Mt	2: 2	rising and have **c** to do him homage."
Mt	5:17	think that I have **c** to abolish the law
Mt	5:17	I have **c** not to abolish but to fulfill.
Mt	6:10	your kingdom **c**, your will be done,
Mt	10:34	think that I have **c** to bring peace
Mt	10:34	I have **c** to bring not peace
Mt	11:14	it, he is Elijah, the one who is to **c**.
Mt	12:28	the kingdom of God has **c** upon you.
Mt	15:19	For from the heart **c** evil thoughts,
Mt	17:12	I tell you that Elijah has already **c**,
Mt	19:14	Jesus said, "Let the children **c** to me,
Mt	24: 5	For many will **c** in my name,
Mt	27:40	God, [and] **c** down from the cross!"
Mk	13:33	do not know when the time will **c**.
Lk	5:32	I have not **c** to call the righteous
Lk	7:20	ask, 'Are you the one who is to **c**,
Jn	2: 4	affect me? My hour has not yet **c**."
Jn	6:37	the Father gives me will **c** to me,
Jn	12:23	"The hour has **c** for the Son of Man
Jn	14: 3	I will **c** back again and take you
Gal	4: 4	But when the fullness of time had **c**,
Col	2:17	These are shadows of things to **c**;
Heb	10: 9	he says, "Behold, I **c** to do your will."
1 Pt	2: 4	**C** to him, a living stone,
2 Pt	3: 9	but that all should **c** to repentance.
1 Jn	4: 2	acknowledges Jesus Christ **c**
Rv	1: 4	is and who was and who is to **c**,
Rv	3: 3	are not watchful, I will **c** like a thief,
Rv	3: 3	at what hour I will **c** upon you.
Rv	4: 1	"**C** up here and I will show you what
Rv	4: 8	was, and who is, and who is to **c**."
Rv	22:17	The Spirit and the bride say, "**C**." Let the hearer say, "**C**."
Rv	22:20	coming soon." Amen! **C**, Lord Jesus!

COMES →COME

Dt	8: 3	by every word that **c** forth
2 Sm	7:12.	when your time **c** and you rest
1 Chr	16:33	before the LORD, for he **c**: he **c**
Jb	3:25	and what I shrink from **c** upon me.
Ps	30: 6	At dusk weeping **c** for the night;
Ps	62: 2	alone, from whom **c** my salvation.
Ps	118:26	is he who **c** in the name of the LORD,
Ps	121: 2	My help **c** from the LORD, the maker
Prv	11: 2	When pride **c**, disgrace **c**;
Is	40:10	Here **c** with power the Lord GOD,
Mt	4: 4	but by every word that **c** forth
Mk	7:20	"But what **c** out of a person, that is
Mk	11: 9	Blessed is he who **c** in the name
Lk	18: 8	But when the Son of Man **c**, will he
Lk	19:38	"Blessed is the king who **c**
Jn	3:31	The one who **c** from above is
Jn	6:33	is that which **c** down from heaven
Jn	10:10	A thief **c** only to steal and slaughter
Jn	14: 6	No one **c** to the Father except
Jn	15:26	the Advocate **c** whom I will send
Jn	16:13	But when he **c**, the Spirit of truth,

Acts	1: 8	when the holy Spirit **c** upon you,
Rom	10:17	Thus faith **c** from what is heard,
Rom	10:17	what is heard **c** through the word
Gal	2:21	for if justification **c** through the law,
Gal	3:18	if the inheritance **c** from the law,
Phil	3: 9	that which **c** through faith in Christ,
2 Jn	1:10	If anyone **c** to you and does not
Rv	3:12	which **c** down out of heaven
Rv	11: 7	the beast that **c** up from the abyss

COMFORT →COMFORTED, COMFORTERS, COMFORTING, COMFORTS

Jb	2:11	to give him sympathy and **c**.
Jb	7:13	When I say, "My bed shall **c** me,
Jb	21:34	How then can you offer me vain **c**,
Ps	71:21	Restore my honor; turn and **c** me,
Ps	119:50	This is my **c** in affliction;
Ps	119:76	May your love **c** me in accord
Ps	119:82	your promise. When will you **c** me?
Eccl	4: 1	of the victims with none to **c** them!
Is	22: 4	Do not try to **c** me for the ruin
Is	40: 1	**C**, give **c** to my people, says your
Is	51: 3	Yes, the LORD shall **c** Zion and have
Is	51:19	and sword! Who is there to **c** you?
Is	57:18	I will give full **c** to them
Is	61: 2	by our God, to **c** all who mourn;
Is	66:13	so will I **c** you; in Jerusalem you shall find your **c**.
Lam	2:13	example can I show you for your **c**,
Zec	1:17	the LORD will again **c** Zion,
Col	4:11	God, and they have been a **c** to me.

COMFORTED →COMFORT

Ru	2:13	you have **c** me, your servant,
1 Chr	7:22	his kinsmen had come and **c** him,
Est	D: 8	and **c** her with reassuring words.
Jb	42:11	**c** him for all the evil which the LORD
Ps	119:52	your edicts of old I am **c**, LORD.
Mt	5: 4	they who mourn, for they will be **c**.
Lk	16:25	but now he is **c** here, whereas you
Acts	20:12	alive and were immeasurably **c**.

COMFORTERS →COMFORT

Jb	16: 2	Wearisome **c** are you all!
Ps	69:21	was none, for **c**, but found none.

COMFORTING →COMFORT

Zec	1:13	me, the LORD replied with **c** words.

COMFORTS →COMFORT

Is	66:13	As a mother **c** her son, so will I

COMING →COME

Ez	43: 2	of the God of Israel **c** from the east.
Dn	7:13	saw One like a son of man **c**,
Jl	2: 1	tremble, for the day of the LORD is **c**;
Mal	3: 2	who will endure the day of his **c**?
Mal	3:19	the day is **c**, blazing like an oven,
Mk	13:26	see 'the Son of Man **c** in the clouds'
Jn	1:27	the one who is **c** after me,
Jn	4:25	"I know that the Messiah is **c**,
Jn	17:13	But now I am **c** to you. I speak this
1 Thes	1:10	who delivers us from the **c** wrath.
1 Thes	4:15	who are left until the **c** of the Lord,
2 Thes	2: 1	to the **c** of our Lord Jesus Christ
Jas	5: 8	because the **c** of the Lord is at hand.
2 Pt	1:16	and **c** of our Lord Jesus Christ,
2 Pt	3: 4	"Where is the promise of his **c**?
2 Pt	3:12	hastening the **c** of the day of God,
1 Jn	2:18	you heard that the antichrist was **c**,
Rv	1: 7	Behold, he is **c** amid the clouds,
Rv	3:11	I am **c** quickly. Hold fast to what
Rv	16:15	("Behold, I am **c** like a thief."
Rv	21: 2	**c** down out of heaven from God,
Rv	21:10	me the holy city Jerusalem **c** down
Rv	22: 7	"Behold, I am **c** soon." Blessed is
Rv	22:20	testimony says, "Yes, I am **c** soon."

COMMAND →COMMANDED, COMMANDERS, COMMANDMENT, COMMANDMENTS, COMMANDS

Ex	7: 2	You shall tell him all that I **c** you.
Dt	1:26	and after defying the **c** of the LORD,
Dt	4: 2	not add to what I **c** you nor subtract

Dt	13: 1	"Every c that I enjoin on you,
Jos	1: 9	I c you: be firm and steadfast!
2 Mc	7:30	I will not obey the king's c. I obey
Prv	8:29	waters should not transgress his c;
Jer	1: 7	whatever I c you, you shall speak.
Jer	1:17	all that I c you. Be not crushed
Jer	7:23	Walk in all the ways that I c you,
Jer	11: 4	to my voice and do all that I c you.
Jer	26: 2	whatever I c them, tell them,
Dn	3:95	they disobeyed the royal c
Mt	4: 3	c that these stones become loaves
Mt	4: 6	'He will c his angels concerning you'
Jn	10:18	This c I have received from my
Jn	15:14	my friends if you do what I c you.
1 Cor	7: 6	of concession, however, not as a c.
2 Cor	8: 8	I say this not by way of c, but to test

COMMANDED →COMMAND

Gn	7: 5	Noah did just as the LORD had c him.
Ex	7: 6	Aaron did as the LORD had c them.
Ex	40:32	the altar, as the LORD c Moses.
Lv	8:36	that the LORD had c through Moses.
Dt	6:24	the LORD c us to observe all these
Dt	18:20	that I have not c him to speak,
Jos	1:16	"We will do all you have c us,"
Jos	22: 2	the servant of the LORD, c you,
2 Kgs	21: 8	careful to observe all I have c them,
2 Chr	33: 8	careful to observe all that I c them,
Ps	33: 9	came to be, c, and it stood in place.
Ps	78: 5	in Israel: What he c our ancestors,
Ps	148: 5	name; for the LORD c and they were
Is	13: 3	I have c my dedicated soldiers,
Am	2:12	and c the prophets not to prophesy.
Mt	28:20	to observe all that I have c you.
Jn	14:31	that I do just as the Father has c me.
1 Jn	3:23	and love one another just as he c us.
2 Jn	1: 4	in the truth just as we were c

COMMANDERS →COMMAND

Nm	31:14	the clan and company c, who were

COMMANDMENT →COMMAND

Mt	22:36	which c in the law is the greatest?"
Mt	22:38	This is the greatest and the first c.
Mk	7: 8	You disregard God's c but cling
Mk	12:31	is no other c greater than these."
Lk	23:56	on the sabbath according to the c.
Jn	13:34	I give you a new c: love one
Rom	7: 8	sin, finding an opportunity in the c,
Rom	7: 9	but when the c came, sin became
Rom	7:10	the c that was for life turned
Rom	7:11	sin, seizing an opportunity in the c,
Rom	7:12	and the c is holy and righteous
Rom	13: 9	and whatever other c there may be,
Eph	6: 2	This is the first c with a promise,
1 Tm	6:14	to keep the c without stain
Heb	7:18	a former c is annulled because of its
Heb	9:19	When every c had been proclaimed
1 Jn	2: 7	I am writing no new c to you
1 Jn	2: 7	The old c is the word that you have
1 Jn	3:23	And his c is this: we should believe
2 Jn	1: 5	not as though I were writing a new c

COMMANDMENTS →COMMAND

Gn	26: 5	me, keeping my mandate (my c,
Ex	20: 6	those who love me and keep my c.
Ex	34:28	the words of the covenant, the ten c.
Lv	26: 3	and are careful to observe my c,
Lv	26:14	heed me and do not keep all these c,
Dt	4:13	the ten c, which he wrote on two
Dt	5:10	those who love me and keep my c.
Dt	6: 1	"These then are the c, the statutes
Dt	7: 9	those who love him and keep his c,
Dt	7:11	therefore carefully observe the c,
Dt	10: 4	the ten c which he spoke to you
Dt	11:13	you truly heed my c which I enjoin
Dt	11:27	for obeying the c of the LORD,
Dt	28:13	as long as you obey the c
Dt	30:16	If you obey the c of the LORD,
Jos	22: 5	keep his c; remain loyal to him;
Jgs	3: 4	they would obey the c the LORD had

2 Kgs	17:16	They disregarded all the c
Ezr	9:10	For we have abandoned your c,
Neh	1: 5	who love you and keep your c,
Tb	3: 4	and disobeyed your c. So you
Eccl	12:13	Fear God and keep his c, for this is
Sir	15:15	If you choose you can keep the c;
Dn	9: 4	who love you and observe your c!
Mt	5:19	breaks one of the least of these c
Mt	19:17	wish to enter into life, keep the c."
Mt	22:40	the prophets depend on these two c."
Mk	10:19	You know the c: 'You shall not kill;
Lk	1: 6	observing all the c and ordinances
Lk	18:20	You know the c, 'You shall not
Jn	14:15	"If you love me, you will keep my c.
Jn	15:10	If you keep my c, you will remain
Jn	15:10	just as I have kept my Father's c
Rom	13: 9	The c, "You shall not commit
1 Cor	7:19	what matters is keeping God's c.
Eph	2:15	abolishing the law with its c
1 Jn	2: 3	that we know him is to keep his c.
1 Jn	5: 2	when we love God and obey his c.
1 Jn	5: 3	that we keep his c. And his c are not burdensome,
2 Jn	1: 6	that we walk according to his c;
Rv	12:17	those who keep God's c and bear
Rv	14:12	the holy ones who keep God's c

COMMANDS →COMMAND

Ex	25:22	I will tell you all the c that I wish
Ps	91:11	For God c the angels to guard you
Mk	1:27	He c even the unclean spirits
Lk	8:25	who c even the winds and the sea,

COMMEMORATED

Est	9:28	These days were to be c and kept

COMMEND →COMMENDED

Eccl	8:15	Therefore I c mirth, because there is
Lk	23:46	into your hands I c my spirit";
2 Cor	3: 1	we beginning to c ourselves again?
2 Cor	4: 2	of the truth we c ourselves

COMMENDED →COMMEND

Jb	29:11	those who saw me c me.
Lk	16: 8	the master c that dishonest steward

COMMIT →COMMITS, COMMITTED, COMMITTING

Ex	20:14	"You shall not c adultery.
Dt	5:18	'You shall not c adultery.
1 Kgs	14:16	committed and caused Israel to c."
2 Kgs	17:21	LORD, causing them to c a great sin.
Ps	37: 5	C your way to the LORD;
Jer	7: 9	and murder, c adultery and perjury,
Mt	5:27	it was said, 'You shall not c adultery.'
Mt	5:32	unlawful) causes her to c adultery,
Mt	19:18	you shall not c adultery; you shall
Mk	10:19	you shall not c adultery; you shall
Lk	18:20	'You shall not c adultery; you shall
Rom	2:22	forbid adultery, do you c adultery?
Rom	13: 9	"You shall not c adultery; you shall
Jas	2:11	"You shall not c adultery," also said,
Rv	2:22	plunge those who c adultery

COMMITS →COMMIT

Prv	6:32	But he who c adultery is a fool;
Mt	5:32	a divorced woman c adultery.
Mt	19: 9	and marries another c adultery."
Mk	10:11	marries another c adultery against
Mk	10:12	and marries another, she c adultery."
Lk	16:18	wife and marries another c adultery,
Lk	16:18	from her husband c adultery.
Jn	8:34	everyone who c sin is a slave of sin.
1 Cor	6:18	other sin a person c is outside
1 Jn	3: 4	Everyone who c sin c lawlessness,

COMMITTED →COMMIT

Jgs	20: 6	the monstrous crime they had c
2 Kgs	17:22	Jeroboam in all the sins he c,
2 Kgs	24: 3	for the sins Manasseh had c in all
1 Mc	2: 6	that were being c in Judah
Mt	5:28	lust has already c adultery with her
Rom	3:25	the forgiveness of sins previously c,
Jas	5:15	If he has c any sins, he will be

1 Pt   2:22   "He **c** no sin, and no deceit was

COMMITTING → COMMIT
Jer   3: 9   **c** adultery with stone and wood.
Jn   8: 4   caught in the very act of **c** adultery.

COMMON
2 Chr 1:15 and gold as **c** in Jerusalem as stones,
2 Chr 9:27 The king made silver as **c**
Prv   22: 2 Rich and poor have a **c** bond:
Prv 29:13 and the oppressor have a **c** bond:
Acts 2:44 together and had all things in **c**;
Acts 4:32 own, but they had everything in **c**.

COMMUNITY
Ex   12: 3 Tell the whole **c** of Israel:
Lv   4:13 "If the whole **c** of Israel
Nm   1: 2 a census of the whole **c** of the Israelites,
Ps   22:23 in the **c** I will praise you:

COMPANION → COMPANIONS
Jb   30:29 brother of jackals, **c** to the ostrich.
Prv 13:20 but the **c** of fools will fare badly.
Mal   2:14 though she is your **c**, your betrothed

COMPANIONS → COMPANION
Ps   38:12 Friends and **c** shun my pain;
Sir   9:16 Have just men for your table **c**;
Dn   2:13 Daniel and his **c** were also sought
Acts 4:13 they recognized them as the **c**
Heb 1: 9 the oil of gladness above your **c**";

COMPANY
Ex   6:26 from the land of Egypt, **c** by **c**."
Ex   12:51 the Israelites out of Egypt **c** by **c**.
Ps   14: 5 to fear; God is with the **c** of the just.
Ps   26: 5 I hate the **c** of evildoers;
1 Cor 15:33 astray: "Bad **c** corrupts good morals."

COMPARE → COMPARED
Prv   3:15 your choice possessions can **c**
Prv   8:11 no choice possession can **c** with her.
Is   46: 5 Whom would you **c** me with,
Lam   2:13 To what can I liken or **c** you,
Mt   11:16 "To what shall I **c** this generation?
Lk   7:31 to what shall I **c** the people of this
Lk   13:20 what shall I **c** the kingdom of God?
2 Cor 10:12 and **c** themselves with one another,

COMPARED → COMPARE
Bar   3:36 our God; no other is to be **c** to him:
Rom 8:18 nothing **c** with the glory to be

COMPASSION → COMPASSIONATE
2 Kgs 13:23 them with **c** because of his covenant
2 Chr 36:15 for he had **c** on his people and his
1 Mc 3:44 to pray and implore mercy and **c**.
2 Mc 7: 6 and he truly has **c** on us, as Moses
Ps   77:10 mercy, in anger withheld **c**?"
Ps   79: 8 may your **c** come quickly,
Ps   103:13 As a father has **c** on his children,
Ps   103:13 so the Lord has **c** on the faithful.
Jer   13:14 I will show no **c**, I will not spare
Ez   16: 5 **c** to do any of these things for you.
Hos 13:14 world! My eyes are closed to **c**.
Mi   7:19 And will again have **c** on us,
Lk   15:20 sight of him, and was filled with **c**.
Phil 2: 1 in the Spirit, any **c** and mercy,
Col   3:12 and beloved, heartfelt **c**, kindness,

COMPASSIONATE → COMPASSION
Ex   22:26 to me, I will hear him; for I am **c**.
Sir   2:11 **C** and merciful is the Lord;
Lam   4:10 The hands of **c** women boiled their
Jas   5:11 because "the Lord is **c** and merciful."

COMPEL → COMPELLED, COMPULSION
Gal   2:14 how can you **c** the Gentiles to live
Gal   6:12 the flesh who are trying to **c** you

COMPELLED → COMPEL
Gal   2: 3 a Greek, was **c** to be circumcised,

COMPETING
2 Tm 2: 5 crown except by **c** according

COMPLACENT
Is   32: 9 O **c** ladies, rise up and hear my

COMPLAIN → COMPLAINED, COMPLAINING, COMPLAINT
Jb   7:11 I will **c** in the bitterness of my soul.
Lam   3:39 Why should any living man **c**,

COMPLAINED → COMPLAIN
Nm   11: 1 Now the people **c** in the hearing
Acts 6: 1 the Hellenists **c** against the Hebrews

COMPLAINING → COMPLAIN
1 Pt   4: 9 hospitable to one another without **c**.

COMPLAINT → COMPLAIN
Jb   10: 1 I will give myself up to **c**; I will
Ps   142: 3 Before God I pour out my **c**,
Sir   35:14 widow when she pours out her **c**;
Hb   2: 1 what answer he will give to my **c**.

COMPLETE → COMPLETELY
Jn   15:11 be in you and your joy might be **c**.
Jn   16:24 receive, so that your joy may be **c**.
2 Cor 10: 6 once your obedience is **c**.
Phil 2: 2 **c** my joy by being of the same
Ti   2:10 but exhibiting **c** good faith, so as
Jas   1: 4 so that you may be perfect and **c**,
1 Jn   1: 4 this so that our joy may be **c**.
2 Jn   1:12 to face so that our joy may be **c**.

COMPLETELY → COMPLETE
2 Chr 12:12 him so that it did not destroy him **c**;
Jer   14:19 Have you cast Judah off **c**? Is Zion

COMPREHEND → COMPREHENDED
Eph   3:18 may have strength to **c** with all

COMPREHENDED → COMPREHEND
Jb   38:18 Have you **c** the breadth of the earth?

COMPULSION → COMPEL
2 Cor 9: 7 without sadness or **c**, for God loves

CONCEALING → CONCEALS
Gn   37:26 killing our brother and **c** his blood?

CONCEALS → CONCEALING
Prv 10:11 the mouth of the wicked **c** violence.
Prv 12:23 A shrewd man **c** his knowledge,
Prv 25: 2 God has glory in what he **c**,
Prv 28:13 He who **c** his sins prospers not,

CONCEIT → CONCEITED
2 Cor 12:20 slander, gossip, **c**, and disorder.

CONCEITED → CONCEIT
Gal   5:26 Let us not be **c**, provoking one
1 Tm 3: 6 so that he may not become **c**
1 Tm 6: 4 is **c**, understanding nothing, and has
2 Tm 3: 4 reckless, **c**, lovers of pleasure rather

CONCEIVE → CONCEIVED
Jb   15:35 They **c** malice and bring forth
Ps   7:15 Sinners **c** iniquity;
Is   33:11 you **c** dry grass, bring forth stubble;
Lk   1:31 you will **c** in your womb and bear

CONCEIVED → CONCEIVE
1 Sm 2:21 Lord favored Hannah so that she **c**
Ps   51: 7 a sinner, even as my mother **c** me.
Is   8: 3 prophetess and she **c** and bore a son.
Mt   1:20 that this child has been **c** in her.
Lk   1:24 After this time his wife Elizabeth **c**,

CONCERN → CONCERNED
Gn   39: 8 "my master does not **c** himself
Phil 4:10 at last you revived your **c** for me.

CONCERNED → CONCERN
Jon   4:10 "You are **c** over the plant which cost
1 Cor 9: 9 out the grain." Is God **c** about oxen,
Phil 4:10 of course, **c** about me but lacked

CONCESSION
1 Cor 7: 6 This I say by way of **c**, however,

CONCUBINE → CONCUBINES
Gn	35:22	and lay with Bilhah, his father's c.
Jgs	19:25	the husband seized his c and thrust
2 Sm	3: 7	been intimate with my father's c?"

CONCUBINES → CONCUBINE
2 Sm	5:13	David took more c and wives
2 Sm	16:21	"Have relations with your father's c,
1 Kgs	11: 3	princely rank and three hundred c,

CONDEMN → CONDEMNATION, CONDEMNED, CONDEMNING, CONDEMNS, SELF-CONDEMNED
Jb	9:20	right, my own mouth might c me;
Jb	34:17	or will you c the supreme Just One,
Jb	34:29	remains tranquil, who then can c?
Jb	40: 8	Would you c me that you may be
Ps	94:21	the just and c the innocent to death?
Dn	13:48	To c a woman of Israel without
Mt	12:41	arise with this generation and c it,
Mt	12:42	arise with this generation and c it,
Mt	20:18	and they will c him to death,
Mk	10:33	and they will c him to death
Lk	11:31	this generation and she will c them,
Lk	11:32	arise with this generation and c it,
Jn	3:17	Son into the world to c the world,
Jn	8:11	Then Jesus said, "Neither do I c you.
Rom	2: 1	you judge another you c yourself,
Rom	8:34	Who will c? It is Christ [Jesus] who
Rom	14:22	is the one who does not c himself
1 Jn	3:20	in whatever our hearts c, for God is
1 Jn	3:21	if [our] hearts do not c us, we have

CONDEMNATION → CONDEMN
Mk	12:40	They will receive a very severe c."
Jn	5:29	deeds to the resurrection of c.
Rom	5:16	was the judgment that brought c;
Rom	5:18	as through one transgression c came
Rom	8: 1	now there is no c for those who are
2 Cor	3: 9	if the ministry of c was glorious,
1 Tm	5:12	will incur c for breaking their first
Jas	5:12	mean "No," that you may not incur c.
2 Pt	2: 3	from of old their c has not been idle
Jude	1: 4	long ago were designated for this c,

CONDEMNED → CONDEMN
1 Mc	1:57	law, was c to death by royal decree.
Ps	34:22	those who hate the just are c.
Ps	34:23	no one is c whose refuge is God.
Ps	37:33	power, nor let them be c when tried.
Dn	13:41	the people, and they c her to death.
Mt	12: 7	you would not have c these innocent
Mt	12:37	and by your words you will be c."
Mt	27: 3	seeing that Jesus had been c,
Mk	14:64	They all c him as deserving to die.
Mk	16:16	whoever does not believe will·be c.
Lk	6:37	condemning and you will not be c.
Lk	23:41	we have been c justly,
Jn	3:18	believes in him will not be c,
Jn	3:18	does not believe has already been c,
Jn	8:10	where are they? Has no one c you?"
Jn	16:11	the ruler of this world has been c.
Rom	3: 7	why am I still being c as a sinner?
Rom	8: 3	the sake of sin, he c sin in the flesh,
Rom	14:23	whoever has doubts is c if he eats,
1 Cor	11:32	that we may not be c along
2 Thes	2:12	approved wrongdoing may be c.
Heb	11: 7	Through this he c the world
Jas	5: 6	You have c; you have murdered
2 Pt	2: 6	and if he c the cities of Sodom

CONDEMNING → CONDEMN
Dn	13:53	unjust sentences, c the innocent,
Acts	13:27	by c him they fulfilled the oracles

CONDEMNS → CONDEMN
Jb	15: 6	Your own mouth c you, not I;
Prv	17:15	the wicked, he who c the just,

CONDUCT
Tb	4:14	and discipline yourself in all your c.
Ps	112: 5	who c their affairs with justice.
Prv	21: 8	but the c of the innocent is right.

Eccl	6: 8	in knowing how to c himself in life?
Sir	37:17	The root of all c is the mind;
Ez	22:31	I have brought down their c
Rom	13: 3	are not a cause of fear to good c,
Col	4: 5	C yourselves wisely toward
1 Pt	1:15	in every aspect of your c,
1 Pt	3: 1	without a word by their wives' c

CONFESS → CONFESSED, CONFESSES, CONFESSING, CONFESSION
Lv	5: 5	of these cases shall c the sin he has
Lv	16:21	he shall c over it all the sinful faults
Lv	26:40	"Thus they will have to c that they
Nm	5: 7	he shall c the wrong he has done,
Ps	32: 5	I said, "I c my faults to the LORD,"
Rom	10: 9	if you c with your mouth that Jesus
Phil	2:11	and every tongue c that Jesus Christ
Heb	13:15	is, the fruit of lips that c his name.
Jas	5:16	c your sins to one another and pray

CONFESSED → CONFESS
Neh	9: 2	stood forward and c their sins

CONFESSES → CONFESS
Prv	28:13	he who c and forsakes them obtains
Rom	10:10	and one c with the mouth and so is
1 Jn	2:23	whoever c the Son has the Father as

CONFESSING → CONFESS
Neh	1: 6	c the sins which we of Israel have
Dn	9:20	c my sin and the sin of my people

CONFESSION → CONFESS
Neh	9: 3	fourth part they made their c
2 Cor	9:13	for your obedient c of the gospel
1 Tm	6:12	when you made the noble c
1 Tm	6:13	under Pontius Pilate for the noble c,
Heb	3: 1	the apostle and high priest of our c,
Heb	4:14	Son of God, let us hold fast to our c.
Heb	10:23	to our c that gives us hope, for he

CONFIDENCE → CONFIDENT
2 Kgs	18:19	what do you base this c of yours?
Jb	4: 6	Is not your peity a source of c,
Jb	8:14	His c is but a gossamer thread and
Prv	3:26	For the LORD will be your c, and will
Prv	11:13	but a trustworthy man keeps a c.
Is	36: 4	what do you base this c of yours?
Mi	7: 5	a friend, have no c in a companion;
2 Cor	3: 4	Such c we have through Christ
2 Cor	7:16	because I have c in you in every
2 Cor	8:22	because of his great c in you.
Eph	3:12	and c of access through faith in him.
Phil	3: 3	Jesus and do not put our c in flesh,
Phil	3: 4	I myself have grounds for even
Heb	3: 6	if [only] we hold fast to our c
Heb	10:19	of Jesus we have c of entrance
Heb	10:35	do not throw away your c; it will
Heb	13: 6	Thus we may say with c: "The Lord
1 Jn	2:28	when he appears we may have c

CONFIDENT → CONFIDENCE
Jb	6:20	disappointed, though they were c;
2 Cor	10: 7	Whoever is c of belonging to Christ
Phil	1: 6	I am c of this, that the one who
Phil	3: 4	If anyone else thinks he can be c

CONFINED
Gn	40: 3	(the same jail where Joseph was c).

CONFIRM → CONFIRMATION, CONFIRMED
2 Sm	7:25	c for all time the prophecy you have
Rom	15: 8	to c the promises to the patriarchs,

CONFIRMATION → CONFIRM
Phil	1: 7	in the defense and c of the gospel.

CONFIRMED → CONFIRM
1 Kgs	8:26	my father David, your servant, be c.

CONFLICTING → CONFLICTS
Rom	2:15	witness and their c thoughts accuse

CONFLICTS → CONFLICTING
Jas	4: 1	where do the c among you come

CONFORMED
Rom 8:29 predestined to be **c** to the image

CONFOUNDED
Ps 35: 4 against me be turned back and **c**.
Acts 9:22 and **c** [the] Jews who lived

CONFRONT
Ps 17:13 O Lord, **c** and cast them down;

CONFUSE → CONFUSED, CONFUSION
Gn 11: 7 go down and there **c** their language,
Ps 55:10 Lord, check and **c** their scheming.

CONFUSED → CONFUSE
Gn 11: 9 because there the Lord **c** the speech

CONFUSION → CONFUSE
1 Sm 7:10 into such **c** that they were defeated
Neh 4: 2 and thus to throw us into **c**.
Mi 7: 4 has come; now is the time of your **c**.
Acts 19:29 The city was filled with **c**,

CONIAH → =JEHOIACHIN
Jer 22:28 Is this man **C** a vessel despised,

CONQUER → CONQUERED, CONQUEROR, CONQUERS
Rom 8:37 in all these things we **c** overwhelmingly
Rv 11: 7 wage war against them and **c** them
Rv 13: 7 against the holy ones and **c** them,
Rv 17:14 but the Lamb will **c** them, for he is

CONQUERED → CONQUER
Jn 16:33 but take courage, I have **c** the world."
Heb 11:33 who by faith **c** kingdoms, did what
1 Jn 2:13 because you have **c** the evil one.
1 Jn 4: 4 and you have **c** them, for the one
Rv 12:11 They **c** him by the blood

CONQUEROR → CONQUER
Mi 1:15 Yet must I bring to you the **c**,

CONQUERS → CONQUER
1 Jn 5: 4 is begotten by God **c** the world.
1 Jn 5: 4 victory that **c** the world is our faith.

CONSCIENCE → CONSCIENCES
1 Sm 25:31 this as a qualm or burden on your **c**,
Acts 23: 1 a perfectly clear **c** before God
Acts 24:16 strive to keep my **c** clear before God
Rom 2:15 while their **c** also bears witness
Rom 9: 1 my **c** joins with the holy Spirit
Rom 13: 5 of the wrath but also because of **c**.
1 Cor 8: 7 to idols, their **c**, which is weak,
1 Cor 8:10 idol, may not his **c** too, weak as it is,
1 Cor 10:25 raising questions on grounds of **c**,
1 Cor 10:27 raising questions on grounds of **c**.
1 Cor 10:28 attention to it and on account of **c**;
1 Cor 10:29 be determined by someone else's **c**?
2 Cor 1:12 of our **c** that we have conducted
2 Cor 4: 2 ourselves to everyone's **c** in the sight
1 Tm 1: 5 heart, a good **c**, and a sincere faith.
1 Tm 1:19 by having faith and a good **c**.
1 Tm 1:19 Some, by rejecting **c**, have made
1 Tm 3: 9 mystery of the faith with a clear **c**.
2 Tm 1: 3 with a clear **c** as my ancestors did,
Heb 9: 9 cannot perfect the worshiper in **c**
Heb 10:22 hearts sprinkled clean from an evil **c**
Heb 13:18 are confident that we have a clear **c**,
1 Pt 3:16 keeping your **c** clear, so that,
1 Pt 3:21 but an appeal to God for a clear **c**,

CONSCIENCES → CONSCIENCE
Dn 13: 9 They suppressed their **c**; they would
1 Cor 8:12 your brothers and wound their **c**,
1 Tm 4: 2 hypocrisy of liars with branded **c**.
Ti 1:15 their minds and their **c** are tainted.
Heb 9:14 cleanse our **c** from dead works

CONSCRIPTED
1 Kgs 5:27 King Solomon **c** thirty thousand

CONSECRATE → CONSECRATED
Ex 13: 2 "**C** to me every first-born that opens

CONSECRATED → CONSECRATE
Lv 8:15 the blood at its base when he **c** it.
1 Kgs 9: 3 I have **c** this temple which you have
2 Chr 7:16 **c** this house that my name may be

CONSENT
Phlm 1:14 want to do anything without your **c**,

CONSEQUENCES
Nm 9:13 That man shall bear the **c** of his sin.

CONSIDER → CONSIDERED
Jb 37:14 and **c** the wondrous works of God!
Eccl 7:13 **C** the work of God. Who can make
Is 43:18 past, the things of long ago **c** not;
Lam 2:20 "Look, O Lord, and **c**: whom have
Heb 10:24 We must **c** how to rouse one
Heb 12: 3 **C** how he endured such opposition
Jas 1: 2 **C** it all joy, my brothers, when you

CONSIDERED → CONSIDER
Prv 17:28 a fool, if he keeps silent, is **c** wise;

CONSIST
Lk 12:15 one's life does not **c** of possessions."

CONSISTENT
Ti 2: 1 you must say what is **c** with sound

CONSOLATION → CONSOLATIONS, CONSOLED
Jb 6:10 Then I should still have **c** and could
Jb 21: 2 and let that be the **c** you offer.
Lk 2:25 and devout, awaiting the **c** of Israel,
Lk 6:24 rich, for you have received your **c**.

CONSOLATIONS → CONSOLE
Jb 15:11 Are the **c** of God not enough

CONSOLED → CONSOLE
Mt 2:18 and she would not be **c**, since they

CONSPIRACY → CONSPIRE
2 Sm 15:12 So the **c** gained strength,

CONSPIRE → CONSPIRACY
1 Sm 22:13 Saul asked him, "Why did you **c** against me

CONSTANTLY
Acts 10: 2 Jewish people and pray to God **c**.

CONSTRUCTED → CONSTRUCTION
Heb 9: 2 For a tabernacle was **c**, the outer

CONSTRUCTION → CONSTRUCTED
Ex 38:24 used in the entire **c** of the sanctuary,
Jn 2:20 "This temple has been under **c**

CONSULT → CONSULTED, CONSULTS
Is 40:14 Whom did he **c** to gain knowledge?
Ez 20: 3 Lord God: Have you come to **c** me?
Hos 4:12 They **c** their piece of wood,

CONSULTED → CONSULT
1 Kgs 12: 8 **c** the young men who had grown
Ez 20: 3 not allow myself to be **c** by you,

CONSULTS → CONSULT
Dt 18:11 nor one who **c** ghosts and spirits

CONSUME → CONSUMED, CONSUMING
Nm 16:21 this band, that I may **c** them at once."
Dt 5:25 Surely this great fire will **c** us. If we
Ps 21:10 Then the Lord's anger will **c** them,
Eccl 10:12 win favor, but the fool's lips **c** him.
Is 26:11 prepared for your enemies **c** them.
Is 43: 2 burned; the flames shall not **c** you.
Jn 2:17 "Zeal for your house will **c** me."
Heb 10:27 that is going to **c** the adversaries.

CONSUMED → CONSUME
Ex 3: 2 the bush, though on fire, was not **c**.
Lv 9:24 Lord's presence and **c** the holocaust
Nm 11: 1 and **c** the outskirts of the camp.
Nm 16:35 came forth which **c** the two hundred
1 Kgs 18:38 fire came down and **c** the holocaust,
2 Kgs 1:10 came down from heaven and **c** him
2 Chr 7: 1 from heaven and **c** the holocaust
Ps 90: 7 Truly we are **c** by your anger,

Is	1:28	who desert the LORD shall be c.
Lam	4:11	in Zion that has c her foundations.
Zep	3: 8	my jealousy shall all the earth be c.
Gal	5:15	that you are not c by one another.
Rv	20: 9	down from heaven and c them.

CONSUMING →CONSUME
Heb   12:29   For our God is a c fire.

CONTAIN
1 Kgs	8:27	the highest heavens cannot c you,
2 Chr	2: 5	the highest heavens cannot c him?
2 Chr	6:18	the highest heavens cannot c you,
Jn	21:25	the whole world would c the books

CONTEMPT
1 Mc	1:39	sabbaths to shame, her honor to c.
Ps	107:40	But he poured out c on princes,
Ps	123: 3	us favor, for we have our fill of c.
Prv	18: 3	With wickedness comes c,
Mk	9:12	suffer greatly and be treated with c?
1 Cor	11:22	Or do you show c for the church
Heb	6: 6	themselves and holding him up to c.

CONTEND →CONTENDED
| Jb | 9: 3 | Should one wish to c with him, |
| Jude | 1: 3 | to encourage you to c for the faith |

CONTENDED →CONTEND
Dt   33: 8   and you c with him at the waters

CONTENT →CONTENTMENT
Jos	7: 7	Would that we had been c to dwell
Sir	26: 4	Be he rich or poor, his heart is c,
Sir	29:23	or much, be c with what you have,
2 Cor	12:10	Therefore, I am c with weaknesses,
1 Tm	6: 8	clothing, we shall be c with that.
Heb	13: 5	money but be c with what you have,

CONTENTMENT →CONTENT
1 Tm   6: 6   religion with c is a great gain.

CONTINUAL →CONTINUE
Prv   15:15   but a lighthearted man has a c feast.

CONTINUALLY →CONTINUE
Tb	14: 2	giving alms and c blessing God
Lk	24:53	they were c in the temple praising
Heb	13:15	let us c offer God a sacrifice

CONTINUE →CONTINUAL, CONTINUALLY, CONTINUED
Ps	36:11	C your kindness toward your
Ps	89:37	His dynasty will c forever,
2 Cor	1:10	of death, and he will c to rescue us;
Heb	13: 1	Let mutual love c.

CONTINUED →CONTINUE
Gn	7:17	The flood c upon the earth for forty
Acts	6: 7	The word of God c to spread,
Acts	12:24	But the word of God c to spread
Acts	14: 7	where they c to proclaim the good

CONTRADICTED
Acts   13:45   with violent abuse c what Paul said.

CONTRARY
Acts	18:13	people to worship God c to the law."
Rom	3:31	On the c, we are supporting the law.
Rom	11:24	tree, and grafted, c to nature,

CONTRIBUTE →CONTRIBUTED
Rom   12:13   C to the needs of the holy ones,

CONTRIBUTED →CONTRIBUTE
| Mk | 12:44 | they have all c from their surplus |
| Mk | 12:44 | from her poverty, has c all she had, |

CONTRITE
Dn   3:39   But with c heart and humble spirit

CONTROL →SELF-CONTROL, SELF-CONTROLLED
Gn   45: 1   Joseph could no longer c himself

CONTROVERSIES
Acts   26: 3   in all the Jewish customs and c.

CONVERSATION
Sir   9:15   let all your c be about the law

CONVERSION →CONVERT
Acts   15: 3   telling of the c of the Gentiles,

CONVERT →CONVERSION, CONVERTED, CONVERTS
| Mt | 23:15 | traverse sea and land to make one c, |
| 1 Tm | 3: 6 | He should not be a recent c, |

CONVERTED →CONVERT
Tb   14: 6   the nations of the world shall be c

CONVERTS →CONVERT
| Tb | 1: 8 | and to c who were living |
| Acts | 13:43 | worshipers who were c to Judaism |

CONVICT →CONVICTED, CONVICTION
Jude   1:15   and to c everyone for all the godless

CONVICTED →CONVICT
| Dn | 13:61 | their own words Daniel had c them |
| Jas | 2: 9 | are c by the law as transgressors. |

CONVICTION →CONVICT
1 Thes   1: 5   in the holy Spirit and [with] much c.

CONVINCE →CONVINCED
Acts	18: 4	attempting to c both Jews
Acts	28:23	trying to c them about Jesus
2 Tm	4: 2	c, reprimand, encourage through all

CONVINCED →CONVINCE
Acts	28:24	Some were c by what he had said,
Rom	4:21	and was fully c that what he had
Rom	8:38	For I am c that neither death,

COOL
| Jgs | 3:20 | he sat alone in his c upper room, |
| Lk | 16:24 | his finger in water and c my tongue, |

COPPER
Mt   10: 9   gold or silver or c for your belts;

COPY
| Dt | 17:18 | he shall have a c of this law made |
| Heb | 9:24 | made by hands, a c of the true one, |

CORD →CORDS
Gn	38:18	"Your seal and c, and the staff you
Nm	15:38	each corner tassel with a violet c.
Jos	2:18	land, tie this scarlet c in the window
Eccl	4:12	A three-ply c is not easily broken.
Eccl	12: 6	Before the silver c is snapped

CORDS →CORD
2 Sm	22: 6	The c of the nether world enmeshed
Hos	11: 4	I drew them with human c,
Jn	2:15	He made a whip out of c and drove

CORIANDER
| Ex | 16:31 | It was like c seed, but white, and it |
| Nm | 11: 7 | Manna was like c seed and had |

CORINTH →CORINTHIANS
Acts	18: 1	this he left Athens and went to C.
1 Cor	1: 2	to the church of God that is in C,
2 Cor	1: 1	to the church of God that is in C,

CORINTHIANS →CORINTH
| Acts | 18: 8 | many of the C who heard believed |
| 2 Cor | 6:11 | We have spoken frankly to you, C; |

CORNELIUS
    Roman to whom Peter preached; first Gentile Christian (Acts 10).

CORNER →CORNERS, CORNERSTONE
Prv	7:12	and at every c she lurks in ambush—
Prv	21: 9	better to dwell in a c of the housetop
Acts	26:26	his notice; this was not done in a c.

CORNERS →CORNER
Dt	22:12	cords on the four c of the cloak
Ez	7: 2	come upon the four c of the land!
Mt	6: 5	on street c so that others may see
Acts	10:11	lowered to the ground by its four c.
Rv	7: 1	standing at the four c of the earth,
Rv	20: 8	the nations at the four c of the earth,

CORNERSTONE →CORNER, STONE
Jb   38: 6   pedestals sunk, and who laid the c,

Ps	118:22	builders rejected has become the c.
Is	28:16	A precious c as a sure foundation;
Mt	21:42	has become the c; by the Lord has
Mk	12:10	builders rejected has become the c;
Lk	20:17	builders rejected has become the c'?
Acts	4:11	builders, which has become the c.'
1 Pt	2: 6	in Zion, a c, chosen and precious,

CORPSE

Lv	22: 4	become unclean by contact with a c,
Mt	24:28	Wherever the c is, there the vultures

CORRECTING →CORRECTION

2 Tm	2:25	c opponents with kindness. It may

CORRECTION →CORRECTING, CORRECTS

Jer	2:30	children; the c they did not take.
Jer	5: 3	laid them low, but they refused c;
Zep	3: 2	accepts no c; In the LORD she has not
Zep	3: 7	you will accept c"; She should not
2 Tm	3:16	refutation, for c, and for training

CORRECTS →CORRECT

Prv	9: 7	He who c an arrogant man earns

CORRESPONDS

Gal	4:25	it c to the present Jerusalem, for she

CORRUPT →CORRUPTED, CORRUPTION, CORRUPTS

Gn	6:11	In the eyes of God the earth was c
Ps	14: 1	Their deeds are loathsome and c;
Acts	2:40	yourselves from this c generation."

CORRUPTED →CORRUPT

Eph	4:22	of life, c through deceitful desires,
Rv	19: 2	who c the earth with her harlotry.

CORRUPTION →CORRUPT

Acts	2:31	netherworld nor did his flesh see c.
Acts	13:35	not suffer your holy one to see c.'
2 Pt	1: 4	escaping from the c that is

CORRUPTS →CORRUPT

Eccl	7: 7	a wise man, and a bribe c the heart.

COST →COSTLY

Nm	17: 3	the censers at the c of their lives.
1 Chr	21:24	up holocausts that c me nothing."
Lk	14:28	and calculate the c to see if there is

COSTLY →COST

Mt	26: 7	an alabaster jar of c perfumed oil,

COTS

Acts	5:15	and laid them on c and mats so

COUCH →COUCHES

Est	7: 8	had thrown himself on the c

COUCHES →COUCH

Am	6: 4	stretched comfortably on their c,

COUNCIL

Ps	82: 1	God rises in the divine c,
Ps	89: 8	dreaded in the c of the holy ones,
Jer	23:18	who has stood in the c of the LORD,
Mk	15:43	a distinguished member of the c,

COUNSEL →COUNSELOR, COUNSELORS, COUNSELS

2 Sm	15:34	undo for me the c of Ahithophel.
2 Sm	17:23	saw that his c was not acted upon,
Tb	4:18	"Seek c from every wise man, and do
Jb	12:13	might; his are c and understanding.
Ps	73:24	With your c you guide me,
Ps	107:11	scorned the c of the Most High,
Prv	12:20	but those who c peace have joy.
Prv	15:22	Plans fail when there is no c,
Wis	9:17	Or who ever knew your c,
Sir	25: 4	and a knowledge of c to those
Is	11: 2	A spirit of c and of strength, a spirit
Is	28:29	wonderful is his c and great his

COUNSELOR →COUNSEL

Sir	37: 7	Every c points out a way, but somE
Is	40:13	LORD, or has instructed him as his c?
Rom	11:34	of the Lord or who has been his c?"

COUNSELORS →COUNSEL

Jb	12:17	He sends c away barefoot,
Ps	119:24	are my delight; they are my c.
Prv	11:14	people falls; security lies in many c.
Prv	24: 6	the victory is due to a wealth of c.

COUNSELS →COUNSEL

Ps	16: 7	I bless the LORD who c me;

COUNT →COUNTED, COUNTING, COUNTS

Gn	15: 5	"Look up at the sky and c the stars,
Dt	16: 9	You shall c off seven weeks,
Ps	22:18	that I can c all my bones. They stare
Ps	90:12	Teach us to c our days aright,
Ps	139:18	Were I to c, they would outnumber
Rv	7: 9	which no one could c, from every

COUNTED →COUNT

Gn	13:16	your descendants too might be c.
Nm	23:10	Who has ever c the dust of Jacob,
Mt	10:30	all the hairs of your head are c.

COUNTENANCE

Jdt	16: 6	by the beauty of her c disabled him.
Sir	13:25	sign of a good heart is a cheerful c;

COUNTERFEITS

Wis	15: 9	and takes pride in modeling c.

COUNTING →COUNT

2 Cor	5:19	not c their trespasses against them

COUNTRIES →COUNTRY

Ez	11:16	their only sanctuary in the c
Ez	20:34	gather you from the c over

COUNTRY →COUNTRIES, COUNTRYSIDE

Lk	15:13	a distant c where he squandered his

COUNTRYSIDE →COUNTRY

Mk	1: 5	People of the whole Judean c

COUNTS →COUNT

Gal	5: 6	circumcision nor uncircumcision c

COURAGE →COURAGEOUS

2 Sm	7:27	your servant now finds the c
Ezr	7:28	I herefore took c and, with the hand
Tb	5:10	healing in store for you; so take c!"
Tb	7:17	place of your grief. C, my daughter."
Hg	2: 4	But now take c, Zerubbabel,
Hg	2: 4	and take c, Joshua, high priest,
Hg	2: 4	And take c, all you people
Jn	16:33	but take c, I have conquered
Acts	23:11	Lord stood by him and said, "Take c.
Acts	27:22	I urge you now to keep up your c;
Acts	27:25	Therefore, keep up your c, men;

COURAGEOUS →COURAGE

1 Mc	2:64	be c and strong in keeping the law,
1 Cor	16:13	firm in the faith, be c, be strong.

COURIERS

2 Chr	30: 6	Accordingly the c, with the letters
Est	3:15	The c set out in haste at the king's
Est	8:10	by mounted c riding thoroughbred

COURSE

Ps	19: 6	like an athlete joyfully runs its c.

COURT →COURTS, COURTYARD

Ex	27: 9	also make a c for the Dwelling.
Nm	3:26	the hangings of the c, the curtain
1 Kgs	7: 8	living quarters were in another c,
Ez	10: 3	entered, the cloud filled the inner c,
Dn	7:10	The c was convened, and the books
Mt	5:25	while on the way to c with him.
1 Cor	6: 6	brother goes to c against brother,
Jas	2: 6	themselves not haul you off to c?

COURTS →COURT

1 Chr	28: 6	who shall build my house and my c,
Ps	65: 5	to dwell in your c. May we be filled
Ps	84:11	Better one day in your c
Ps	96: 8	Bring gifts and enter his c;
Ps	100: 4	with praise, its c with thanksgiving.

COURTYARD →COURT
Mk 14:66 While Peter was below in the **c**,

COUSIN
Est 2: 7 to Hadassah, that is, Esther, his **c**;
Col 4:10 as does Mark the **c** of Barnabas

COVENANT →COVENANTS
Gn 6:18 But with you I will establish my **c**;
Gn 9: 9 I am now establishing my **c**
Gn 15:18 that the LORD made a **c** with Abram,
Gn 17: 2 you and me I will establish my **c**,
Ex 2:24 was mindful of his **c** with Abraham,
Ex 6: 5 as slaves, I am mindful of my **c**.
Ex 19: 5 hearken to my voice and keep my **c**,
Ex 23:32 You shall not make a **c** with them
Ex 24: 7 Taking the book of the **c**, he read it
Ex 34:28 on the tablets the words of the **c**,
Lv 26:42 I will remember my **c** with Jacob, my **c** with Isaac, and my **c** with Abraham;
Dt 4:13 He proclaimed to you his **c**,
Dt 28:69 the **c** which the LORD ordered Moses
Jos 3: 6 the priests to take up the ark of the **c**
Jgs 2: 1 I would never break my **c** with you,
1 Kgs 8: 1 the ark of the LORD's **c** from the City
1 Kgs 8:21 the ark in which is the **c** of the LORD,
1 Kgs 8:23 you keep your **c** of kindness
2 Kgs 23: 2 book of the **c** that had been found
1 Chr 16:15 He remembers forever his **c**
2 Chr 34:30 book of the **c** that had been found
Ezr 10: 3 enter into a **c** before our God
Neh 1: 5 you who preserve your **c** of mercy
Neh 9:32 who in your mercy preserve the **c**,
Jdt 9:13 planned dire things against your **c**,
1 Mc 1:15 and abandoned the holy **c**;
1 Mc 1:57 was found with a scroll of the **c**,
1 Mc 2:27 and who stands by the **c** follow
Ps 25:14 to the faithful; the **c** instructs them.
Ps 44:18 you, nor been disloyal to your **c**.
Ps 78:37 they were not faithful to his **c**.
Ps 89: 4 I have made a **c** with my chosen
Ps 105: 8 He remembers forever his **c**,
Ps 111: 5 fear you, mindful of your **c** forever.
Ps 132:12 If your sons observe my **c**, the laws
Sir 28: 7 of the Most High's **c**, and overlook
Is 28:15 say, "We have made a **c** with death,
Is 42: 6 and set you as a **c** of the people,
Is 61: 8 a lasting **c** I will make with them.
Jer 31:31 I will make a new **c** with the house
Jer 32:40 I will make with them an eternal **c**,
Ez 16:60 set up an everlasting **c** with you.
Ez 17:15 Can he break a **c** and still go free?
Ez 37:26 I will make with them a **c** of peace;
Ez 37:26 it shall be an everlasting **c**,
Dn 11:28 his mind set against the holy **c**;
Hos 6: 7 they, in their land, violated the **c**;
Mal 2: 4 because I have a **c** with Levi,
Mal 3: 1 of the **c** whom you desire. Yes, he is
Mt 26:28 for this is my blood of the **c**,
Mk 14:24 "This is my blood of the **c**,
Lk 1:72 and to be mindful of his holy **c**
Lk 22:20 "This cup is the new **c** in my blood,
Acts 7: 8 he gave him the **c** of circumcision;
Rom 11:27 and this is my **c** with them when I
1 Cor 11:25 "This cup is the new **c** in my blood.
2 Cor 3: 6 qualified us as ministers of a new **c**,
2 Cor 3:14 unlifted when they read the old **c**,
Gal 3:17 not annul a **c** previously ratified
Heb 7:22 the guarantee of an [even] better **c**.
Heb 8: 8 I will conclude a new **c**
Heb 9:15 reason he is mediator of a new **c**:
Heb 12:24 the mediator of a new **c**,
Heb 13:20 sheep by the blood of the eternal **c**,
Rv 11:19 the ark of his **c** could be seen

COVENANTS →COVENANT
Wis 12:21 whose fathers you gave the sworn **c**
Rom 9: 4 glory, the **c**, the giving of the law,
Gal 4:24 These women represent two **c**.
Eph 2:12 and strangers to the **c** of promise,

COVER →COVERED, COVERING, COVERS
Gn 6:14 it, and **c** it inside and out with pitch.
Ex 33:22 will **c** you with my hand until I have
Nm 4: 5 **c** the ark of the commandments
Hos 10: 8 shall cry out to the mountains, "**C** us!"
Mal 2:13 you do: the altar of the LORD you **c**
Lk 23:30 'Fall upon us!' and to the hills, '**C** us!'
Jas 5:20 death and will **c** a multitude of sins.

COVERED →COVER
Gn 1: 2 and darkness **c** the abyss,
Ex 14:28 it **c** the chariots and the charioteers
Ex 16:13 quail came up and **c** the camp.
Ex 24:15 gone up, a cloud **c** the mountain.
Ex 40:34 Then the cloud **c** the meeting tent,
Nm 9:15 erected, the cloud **c** the Dwelling,
Jon 3: 8 and beast shall be **c** with sackcloth
Rom 4: 7 are forgiven and whose sins are **c**.

COVERING →COVER
Ex 35:11 with its tent, its **c**, its clasps,
Mal 2:16 And **c** one's garment with injustice,
1 Cor 11:15 hair has been given [her] for a **c**?

COVERS →COVER
Prv 10:12 up disputes, but love **c** all offenses.
Is 11: 9 of the LORD, as water **c** the sea.
Hb 2:14 the LORD's glory as water **c** the sea.
1 Pt 4: 8 because love **c** a multitude of sins.

COVET →COVETOUSNESS
Ex 20:17 "You shall not **c** your neighbor's
Ex 34:24 there will be no one to **c** your land
Dt 5:21 'You shall not **c** your neighbor's
Dt 7:25 Do not **c** the silver or gold on them,
Mi 2: 2 They **c** fields, and seize them;
Rom 7: 7 I did not know what it is to **c** except
Rom 13: 9 you shall not **c**," and whatever other
Jas 4: 2 You **c** but do not possess. You kill

COVETOUSNESS →COVET
Rom 7: 8 produced in me every kind of **c**.

COW →COWS
Is 11: 7 The **c** and the bear shall be

COWARDICE →COWARDS
2 Tm 1: 7 For God did not give us a spirit of **c**

COWARDS →COWARDICE
Rv 21: 8 But as for **c**, the unfaithful, the depraved,

COWS →COW
Gn 41: 2 up out of the Nile came seven **c**,
1 Sm 6: 7 take two milch **c** that have not borne
Am 4: 1 of Samaria, you **c** of Bashan,

CRAFT →CRAFTINESS, CRAFTY
Ex 31: 3 and knowledge in every **c**:

CRAFTINESS →CRAFT
Lk 20:23 Recognizing their **c** he said to them,

CRAFTY →CRAFT
Jb 15: 5 and you choose to speak like the **c**.
Sir 11:29 for many are the snares of the **c** one;
2 Cor 12:16 yet I was **c** and got the better of you

CRAGS
Nm 23: 9 For from the top of the **c** I see him,

CRAVED →CRAVING
Ps 78:18 hearts, demanding the food they **c**.
Ps 78:29 he gave them what they had **c**.

CRAVES →CRAVING
Prv 13: 4 The soul of the sluggard **c** in vain,

CRAVING →CRAVED, CRAVES, CRAVINGS
Prv 10: 3 but the **c** of the wicked he thwarts.

CRAVINGS →CRAVING
Ps 106:14 the desert they gave way to their **c**,

CREATE →CREATED, CREATION, CREATOR
Ps 51:12 A clean heart **c** for me, God;
Is 4: 5 Then will the LORD **c**,

Is	45: 7	I form the light, and c the darkness,
Is	65:17	Lo, I am about to c new heavens
Is	65:18	in what I c; For I c Jerusalem to be
Eph	2:15	that he might c in himself one new

CREATED →CREATE

Gn	1: 1	when God c the heavens
Gn	1:21	God c the great sea monsters and all
Gn	1:27	God c man in his image; in the divine image he c him; male and female he c them.
Gn	5: 1	When God c man, he made him
Gn	5: 2	he c them male and female.
Gn	6: 7	the earth the men whom I have c,
Dt	4:32	ever since God c man
Dt	32: 6	Is he not your father who c you?
Ps	89:13	Zaphon and Amanus you c;
Ps	89:48	is my life, how frail the race you c!
Ps	104:30	send forth your breath, they are c,
Ps	148: 5	LORD commanded and they were c,
Sir	1: 4	all things else wisdom was c;
Is	40:26	and see who has c these: He leads
Is	41:20	this, the Holy One of Israel has c it.
Is	42: 5	who c the heavens and stretched
Is	43: 1	who c you, O Jacob, and formed
Is	43: 7	as mine, whom I c for my glory,
Is	45: 8	spring up! I, the LORD, have c this.
Is	45:12	and c mankind upon it; It was my
Is	54:16	Lo, I have c the craftsman
Is	54:16	It is I also who have c the destroyer
Jer	31:22	The LORD has c a new thing
Ez	21:35	In the place where you were c,
Ez	28:13	were made, on the day you were c.
Ez	28:15	from the day you were c, Until evil
Mal	2:10	Has not the one God c us?
1 Cor	11: 9	nor was man c for woman,
Eph	2:10	c in Christ Jesus for the good works
Eph	3: 9	ages past in God who c all things,
Eph	4:24	c in God's way in righteousness
Col	1:16	in him were c all things in heaven
Col	1:16	all things were c through him
1 Tm	4: 3	foods that God c to be received
1 Tm	4: 4	For everything c by God is good,
Heb	1: 2	through whom he c the universe,
Heb	12:27	to [the] removal of shaken, c things,
Rv	4:11	for you c all things; because of your
Rv	10: 6	who c heaven and earth and sea

CREATION →CREATE

Gn	2: 3	from all the work he had done in c.
Tb	8: 5	Let the heavens and all your c
Mk	10: 6	But from the beginning of c,
Mk	13:19	the beginning of God's c until now,
Rom	1:20	Ever since the c of the world,
Rom	8:19	For c awaits with eager expectation
Rom	8:20	for c was made subject to futility,
Rom	8:21	that c itself would be set free
Rom	8:22	We know that all c is groaning
2 Cor	5:17	So whoever is in Christ is a new c:
Col	1:15	invisible God, the firstborn of all c.
Heb	9:11	that is, not belonging to this c,
2 Pt	3: 4	as it was from the beginning of c."
Rv	3:14	the source of God's c, says this:

CREATOR →CREATE

Jdt	9:12	heaven and earth, C of the waters,
2 Mc	1:24	LORD God, c of all things,
2 Mc	7:23	since it is the C of the universe who
2 Mc	13:14	the outcome to the C of the world,
Eccl	12: 1	Remember your C in the days
Sir	4: 6	you, his C will hear his prayer.
Sir	24: 8	the C of all gave me his command,
Is	40:28	God, c of the ends of the earth.
Is	43:15	One, the c of Israel, your King.
Rom	1:25	the creature rather than the c, who is
Col	3:10	for knowledge, in the image of its c.
1 Pt	4:19	over to a faithful c as they do good.

CREATURE →CREATURES

Gn	9:10	with every living c that was
Lv	11:43	with any swarming c through being
Rom	1:25	and worshiped the c rather than

Rv	4: 7	The first c resembled a lion,
Rv	5:13	Then I heard every c in heaven

CREATURES →CREATURE

Gn	1:20	teem with an abundance of living c,
Gn	1:24	bring forth all kinds of living c:
Ps	104:24	them all; the earth is full of your c.
Wis	9: 2	man to rule the c produced by you,
Ez	1: 5	figures resembling four living c
Ez	10:15	Such were the living c I had seen
Jas	1:18	may be a kind of firstfruits of his c.
Rv	4: 6	there were four living c covered
Rv	5: 6	and the four living c and the elders,
Rv	8: 9	a third of the c living in the sea
Rv	19: 4	and the four living c fell down

CREDIT →CREDITOR, CREDITORS

Lk	6:33	good to you, what c is that to you?
1 Pt	2:20	But what c is there if you are patient

CREDITOR →CREDIT

Dt	15: 2	Every c shall relax his claim
Lk	7:41	people were in debt to a certain c;

CREDITORS →CREDIT

Is	50: 1	Or to which of my c have I sold
Hb	2: 7	Shall not your c rise suddenly?

CREEPING

Gn	1:24	cattle, c things, and wild animals
Ez	8:10	the figures of all kinds of c things

CRETANS →CRETE

Acts	2:11	converts to Judaism, C and Arabs,
Ti	1:12	once said, "C have always been liars,

CRETE →CRETANS

Acts	27:12	a port in C facing west-northwest,
Ti	1: 5	this reason I left you in C so

CRIED →CRY

Ex	2:23	and c out because of their slavery.
Ex	14:10	In great fright they c
Nm	20:16	when we c to the LORD, he heard our
Jos	24: 7	Because they c out to the LORD,
Jgs	3: 9	But when the Israelites c
Jgs	4: 3	But the Israelites c out to the LORD;
Jgs	6: 6	so the Israelites c out to the LORD.
Jgs	10:12	Yet when you c out to me, and I
Jdt	7:19	The Israelites c to the LORD,
Jb	29:12	For I rescued the poor who c
Ps	18: 7	called out: LORD! I c out to my God.
Ps	22: 6	To you they c out and they escaped;
Ps	107:13	In their distress they c to the LORD,
Jon	1: 5	and each one c to his god.
Jon	1:14	Then they c to the LORD:
Mt	14:30	beginning to sink, he c out, "Lord,
Mt	27:46	about three o'clock Jesus c

CRIES →CRY

Prv	1:20	Wisdom c aloud in the street,
Prv	8: 3	city, in the entryways she c aloud:
Heb	5: 7	supplications with loud c and tears

CRIME →CRIMINAL, CRIMINALS

Gn	50:17	therefore, forgive the c that we,

CRIMINAL →CRIME

Jn	18:30	"If he were not a c, we would not
2 Tm	2: 9	even to the point of chains, like a c.

CRIMINALS →CRIME

Lk	23:32	both c, were led away with him

CRIMSON →CRIMSONED

Gn	38:28	taking a c thread, tied it on his hand,
Is	1:18	Though they be c red, they may

CRIMSONED →CRIMSON

Is	63: 1	Edom, in c garments, from Bozrah—

CRIPPLED

2 Sm	9: 3	still Jonathan's son, whose feet are c."
Lk	14:13	invite the poor, the c, the lame,
Acts	14: 8	At Lystra there was a c man,

CRITICIZE
Sir 11: 7 find no fault; examine first, then c.

CROOKED
Dt 32: 5 children, a perverse and c race!
2 Sm 22:27 but toward the c you are astute.
Ps 125: 5 But those who turn aside to c ways
Prv 2:15 Whose ways are c, and devious
Prv 8: 8 mouth, no one of them is wily or c;
Eccl 1:15 What is c cannot be made straight,
Eccl 7:13 make straight what he has made c?
Is 59: 8 paths; Their ways they have made c,
Phil 2:15 without blemish in the midst of a c

CROP → CROPS
2 Tm 2: 6 farmer ought to have the first share of the c.

CROPS → CROP
Heb 6: 7 and brings forth c useful to those

CROSS → CROSSED, CROSSING, CROSSROADS
Nm 32: 5 Do not make us c the Jordan."
Dt 4:22 you will c over and take possession
Dt 30:13 'Who will c the sea to get it for us
Dt 31: 3 your God, who will c before you;
Jos 3:14 struck their tents to c the Jordan,
Mt 10:38 whoever does not take up his c
Mt 16:24 take up his c, and follow me.
Mt 27:32 pressed into service to carry his c.
Mk 15:30 by coming down from the c."
Lk 14:27 Whoever does not carry his own c
Jn 19:17 carrying the c himself he went
Jn 19:25 by the c of Jesus were his mother
1 Cor 1:17 the c of Christ might not be emptied
1 Cor 1:18 The message of the c is foolishness
Gal 5:11 block of the c has been abolished.
Gal 6:14 in the c of our Lord Jesus Christ,
Eph 2:16 through the c, putting that enmity
Phil 2: 8 obedient to death, even death on a c.
Phil 3:18 as enemies of the c of Christ.
Col 1:20 making peace by the blood of his c
Col 2:14 it from our midst, nailing it to the c;
Heb 12: 2 lay before him he endured the c,

CROSSED → CROSS
Dt 12:10 But after you have c the Jordan
Jos 4: 7 of the Lord when it c the Jordan.'
2 Kgs 2: 8 and both c over on dry ground.

CROSSING → CROSS
Gn 48:14 But Israel, c his hands, put out his
Dt 4:22 in this country without c the Jordan;

CROSSROADS → CROSS, ROAD
Prv 8: 2 road, at the c she takes her stand;

CROW → CROWED, CROWS
Jn 13:38 the cock will not c before you deny me

CROWD → CROWDS
Ex 12:38 A c of mixed ancestry also went
Mt 21: 8 The very large c spread their cloaks
Mk 8: 2 heart is moved with pity for the c,
Mk 14:43 accompanied by a c with swords
Jn 7:31 many of the c began to believe

CROWDS → CROWD
Mt 4:25 And great c from Galilee,
Mt 7:28 words, the c were astonished at his
Lk 3: 7 He said to the c who came out to be
Acts 8: 6 the c paid attention to what was said
Acts 14:19 Iconium arrived and won over the c.
Acts 17:13 cause a commotion and stir up the c.

CROWED → CROW
Mt 26:74 the man." And immediately a cock c.

CROWN → CROWNED, CROWNS
Ps 21: 4 placed on his head a c of pure gold.
Prv 4: 9 a glorious c will she bestow on you."
Prv 12: 4 A worthy wife is the c of her
Prv 14:24 The c of the wise is resourcefulness;
Prv 16:31 Gray hair is a c of glory; it is gained
Prv 17: 6 Grandchildren are the c of old men,

Prv 27:24 nor even a c from age to age.
Is 62: 3 You shall be a glorious c
Zec 6:11 gold you shall take, and make a c;
Zec 9:16 For they are the jewels in a c
Mt 27:29 Weaving a c out of thorns,
Mk 15:17 purple and, weaving a c of thorns,
Jn 19: 2 the soldiers wove a c out of thorns
Jn 19: 5 out, wearing the c of thorns
Phil 4: 1 my joy and c, in this way stand firm
1 Thes 2:19 c to boast of in the presence of our
2 Tm 4: 8 on the c of righteousness awaits me,
Jas 1:12 been proved he will receive the c
1 Pt 5: 4 you will receive the unfading c
Rv 2:10 and I will give you the c of life.
Rv 3:11 so that no one may take your c.
Rv 6: 2 He was given a c, and he rode forth
Rv 12: 1 and on her head a c of twelve stars.
Rv 14:14 man, with a gold c on his head

CROWNED → CROWN
Jdt 15:13 the other women c themselves
Ps 8: 6 a god, c them with glory and honor.
Song 3:11 with which his mother has c him
Sir 45:26 the Lord who has c you with glory!
Heb 2: 7 you c him with glory and honor,
Heb 2: 9 but we do see Jesus "c with glory

CROWNS → CROWN
Is 23: 8 against Tyre, the bestower of c,
Rv 4: 4 and with gold c on their heads.
Rv 4:10 They throw down their c before
Rv 9: 7 heads they wore what looked like c

CROWS → CROW
Lk 22:34 before the cock c this day, you will

CRUCIFIED → CRUCIFY
Mt 20:19 to be mocked and scourged and c,
Mt 26: 2 of Man will be handed over to be c."
Mt 27:22 They all said, "Let him be c!"
Mt 27:23 shouted the louder, "Let him be c!"
Mt 27:26 he handed him over to be c.
Mt 27:35 After they had c him, they divided
Mt 27:38 Two revolutionaries were c
Mt 27:44 The revolutionaries who were c
Mt 28: 5 that you are seeking Jesus the c.
Mk 15:15 scourged, handed him over to be c.
Mk 15:24 Then they c him and divided his
Mk 15:25 in the morning when they c him.
Mk 15:27 him they c two revolutionaries with
Mk 15:32 Those who were c with him
Mk 16: 6 You seek Jesus of Nazareth, the c.
Lk 23:33 they c him and the criminals there,
Lk 24: 7 be handed over to sinners and be c,
Lk 24:20 to a sentence of death and c him.
Jn 19:16 he handed him over to them to be c.
Jn 19:18 There they c him, and with him two
Jn 19:20 where Jesus was c was near the city;
Jn 19:23 When the soldiers had c Jesus,
Jn 19:32 the other one who was c with Jesus.
Jn 19:41 where he had been c there was
Acts 2:36 Messiah, this Jesus whom you c."
Acts 4:10 Christ the Nazorean whom you c,
Rom 6: 6 that our old self was c with him,
1 Cor 1:13 Christ divided? Was Paul c for you?
1 Cor 1:23 but we proclaim Christ c,
1 Cor 2: 2 you except Jesus Christ, and him c.
1 Cor 2: 8 they would not have c the Lord
2 Cor 13: 4 For indeed he was c
Gal 2:19 for God. I have been c with Christ;
Gal 3: 1 Christ was publicly portrayed as c?
Gal 5:24 Christ [Jesus] have c their flesh
Gal 6:14 which the world has been c to me,
Rv 11: 8 where indeed their Lord was c.

CRUCIFY → CRUCIFIED
Mt 23:34 some of them you will kill and c,
Mt 27:31 clothes, and led him off to c him.
Mk 15:13 They shouted again, "C him."
Mk 15:14 only shouted the louder, "C him."
Mk 15:20 clothes, and led him out to c him.

Lk	23:21	continued their shouting, "C him!
Jn	19: 6	saw him they cried out, "C him,
Jn	19: 6	"Take him yourselves and c him.
Jn	19:10	you and I have power to c you?"
Jn	19:15	him away, take him away! C him!"
Jn	19:15	said to them, "Shall I c your king?"

CRUEL

Is	13: 9	c, with wrath and burning anger;

CRUMBS

Ps	147:17	Hail is dispersed like c; before such

CRUSH →CRUSHED, CRUSHES

Jdt	9:10	c their pride by the hand
1 Mc	3:22	He himself will c them before us;
Jb	6: 9	that God would decide to c me,
Ps	89:24	I will c his foes before him,
Is	53:10	was pleased to c him in infirmity.]
Rom	16:20	of peace will quickly c Satan under

CRUSHED →CRUSH

Jgs	5:26	She hammered Sisera, c his head;
Ps	34:19	saves those whose spirit is c.
Ps	51:10	let the bones you have c rejoice.
Ps	74:14	You c the heads of Leviathan,
Ps	89:11	You c Rahab with a mortal blow;
Is	53: 5	for our offenses, c for our sins,

CRUSHES →CRUSH

Jdt	16: 2	For the LORD is God; he c warfare,

CRY →CRIED, CRIES, CRYING

Ex	2:23	As their c for release went
Ex	3: 9	So indeed the c of the Israelites has
Jgs	10:14	c out to the gods you have chosen,
1 Mc	4:10	So now let us c to Heaven
Ps	5: 3	Hear my c for help, my king,
Ps	28: 2	of my pleading when I c to you,
Ps	34:16	eyes for the just and ears for their c.
Ps	55: 2	who bent down and heard my c,
Ps	88: 3	before you; incline your ear to my c.
Prv	21:13	shuts his ear to the c of the poor
Is	40: 6	A voice says, "C out!" I answer, "What shall I c out?"
Jer	4:31	The c of daughter Zion gasping,
Lam	2:18	C out to the Lord; moan, O daughter
Hb	1: 2	How long, O LORD? I c for help
Hb	2:11	For the stone in the wall shall c out,
Mk	15:37	Jesus gave a loud c and breathed his
Rom	8:15	through which we c, "Abba, Father!"

CRYING →CRY

Ps	69: 4	I am weary with c out; my throat is
Mt	3: 3	"A voice of one c out in the desert,
Mk	1: 3	A voice of one c out in the desert:
Gal	4: 6	of his Son into our hearts, c out,

CRYSTAL

Ez	1:22	seeming like glittering c,
Rv	4: 6	that resembled a sea of glass like c.
Rv	21:11	stone, like jasper, clear as c.
Rv	22: 1	sparkling like c,

CUBS

2 Sm	17: 8	as a bear in the wild robbed of her c.
Prv	17:12	Face a bear robbed of her c,

CUCUMBERS

Nm	11: 5	cost in Egypt, and the c, the melons,

CUD

Lv	11: 3	it is cloven-footed and chews the c.
Dt	14: 6	it is cloven-footed and chews the c.

CULTIVATED

Rom	11:24	into a c one, how much more will
Heb	6: 7	for whom it is c receives a blessing

CUMMIN

Mt	23:23	pay tithes of mint and dill and c,

CUNNING

2 Cor	11: 3	the serpent deceived Eve by his c,

CUP →CUPBEARER, CUPS

Gn	40:11	Pharaoh's c was in my hand; so I
2 Sm	12: 3	and drank from his c and slept in his
1 Kgs	7:26	and its brim resembled that of a c,
Ps	23: 5	my head with oil; my c overflows.
Ps	75: 9	Yes, a c is in the LORD's hand,
Is	51:22	from your hand the c of staggering;
Jer	25:15	Take this c of foaming wine
Lam	4:21	To you also shall the c be passed;
Ez	23:31	of your sister, I will hand you her c.
Hb	2:16	On you shall revert the c
Mt	10:42	And whoever gives only a c of cold
Mt	20:22	Can you drink the c that I am going
Mt	23:25	You cleanse the outside of c
Mt	23:26	cleanse first the inside of the c,
Mt	26:27	Then he took a c, gave thanks,
Mt	26:39	is possible, let this c pass from me;
Mk	9:41	Anyone who gives you a c of water
Mk	10:38	Can you drink the c that I drink
Mk	14:23	Then he took a c, gave thanks,
Mk	14:36	Take this c away from me, but not
Lk	11:39	you cleanse the outside of the c
Lk	22:17	Then he took a c, gave thanks,
Lk	22:20	"This c is the new covenant in my
Lk	22:42	willing, take this c away from me;
Jn	18:11	Shall I not drink the c
1 Cor	10:16	The c of blessing that we bless, is it
1 Cor	10:21	You cannot drink the c of the Lord and also the c of demons.
1 Cor	11:25	"This c is the new covenant in my
1 Cor	11:27	drinks the c of the Lord unworthily
Rv	14:10	full strength into the c of his wrath,
Rv	17: 4	in her hand a gold c that was filled
Rv	18: 6	her c pour double what she poured.

CUPBEARER →BEAR, CUP

Gn	40: 1	the royal c and baker gave offense
Gn	41: 9	Then the chief c spoke up and said
Neh	1:11	with this man"—for I was c to the king.
Tb	1:22	Ahiqar had been chief c,

CUPS →CUP

Ex	25:33	one branch there are to be three c,
1 Mc	1:22	offering table, the c and the bowls,
Mk	7: 4	the purification of c and jugs

CURDS

Gn	18: 8	Then he got some c and milk,
Is	7:15	He shall be living on c and honey

CURE →CURED, CURING

2 Kgs	5: 3	"he would c him of his leprosy."
Mt	8: 7	said to him, "I will come and c him."
Mk	3: 2	if he would c him on the sabbath so
Lk	9: 1	over all demons and to c diseases,

CURED →CURE

Tb	12: 3	back safe and sound; he c my wife;
Tb	12: 3	money back with me; and he c you.
Mt	8:16	spirits by a word and c all the sick,
Mt	12:15	followed him, and he c them all,
Lk	6:18	tormented by unclean spirits were c.
Acts	5:16	unclean spirits, and they were all c.
Acts	28: 9	the island came to Paul and were c.

CURING →CURE

Mt	4:23	and c every disease and illness
Mt	9:35	and c every disease and illness.
Lk	9: 6	news and c diseases everywhere.

CURSE →ACCURSED, CURSED, CURSES, CURSING

Gn	12: 3	you and c those who c you.
Gn	27:13	"Let any c against you, son,
Ex	22:27	God, nor c a prince of your people.
Nm	5:18	hold the bitter water that brings a c.
Nm	22: 6	come and c this people for us;
Nm	22: 6	and whoever you c is cursed."
Nm	22:12	with them and do not c this people,
Dt	11:26	here, this day, a blessing and a c:
Dt	11:28	a c if you do not obey
Dt	21:23	since God's c rests on him who
Dt	23: 6	turned his c into a blessing for you,

Jos	24: 9	Balaam, son of Beor, to c you;
2 Sm	16: 9	should this dead dog c my lord
Neh	10:30	the sanction of a c take this oath
Neh	13: 2	but they hired Balaam to c them,
Neh	13: 2	though our God turned the c
Jb	2: 9	to your innocence? C God and die."
Ps	62: 5	mouths, but inwardly they c.
Ps	109:28	Though they c, may you bless;
Prv	3:33	The c of the LORD is on the house
Sir	4: 5	eyes, give no man reason to c you;
Is	24: 6	Therefore a c devours the earth,
Lam	3:65	of heart, as your c upon them;
Mal	2: 2	of hosts, I will send a c upon you
Mal	2: 2	and of your blessing I will make a c.
Mk	14:71	He began to c and to swear, "I do not
Lk	6:28	bless those who c you,
Rom	12:14	[you], bless and do not c them.
Gal	3:10	on works of the law are under a c;
Gal	3:13	ransomed us from the c of the law by becoming a c for us,
Jas	3: 9	it we c human beings who are made

CURSED →CURSE

Gn	3:17	"C be the ground because of you!
Gn	9:25	he said: "C be Canaan! The lowest
Gn	27:29	to you. C be those who curse you,
Nm	22: 6	blessed and whoever you curse is c."
Nm	23: 8	can I curse whom God has not c?
Nm	24: 9	you, and c is he who curses you!
Dt	27:15	'C be the man who makes a carved
Dt	27:16	'C be he who dishonors his father
Dt	27:17	'C be he who moves his neighbor's
Dt	27:18	'C be he who misleads a blind man
Dt	27:19	'C be he who violates the rights
Dt	27:20	'C be he who has relations with his
Dt	27:21	'C be he who has relations with any
Dt	27:22	'C be he who has relations with his
Dt	27:23	'C be he who has relations with his
Dt	27:24	'C be he who slays his neighbor
Dt	27:25	'C be he who accepts payment
Dt	27:26	'C be he who fails to fulfill any
Dt	28:16	"May you be c in the city, and c
Jos	6:26	C before the LORD be the man who
1 Sm	17:43	the Philistine c David by his gods
2 Sm	16: 7	Shimei was saying as he c: "Away,
2 Sm	19:22	for this. He c the LORD's anointed."
1 Kgs	21:13	"Naboth has c God and king."
Jb	3: 1	Job opened his mouth and c his day.
Jer	11: 3	C be the man who does not observe
Jer	17: 5	C is the man who trusts in human
Mal	1:14	C is the deceiver, who has in his
Mk	11:21	The fig tree that you c has withered."
Gal	3:10	"C be everyone who does not
Gal	3:13	"C be everyone who hangs on a tree,"
Heb	6: 8	it will soon be c and finally burned.

CURSES →CURSE

Ex	21:17	"Whoever c his father or mother
Lv	24:15	Anyone who c his God shall bear
Nm	24: 9	you, and cursed is he who c you!
Dt	28:15	all these c shall come upon you
Dt	30: 1	the blessings and the c, are fulfilled
Jos	8:34	the blessings and the c, exactly as
2 Chr	34:24	all the c written in the book that has
Prv	20:20	If one c his father or mother,
Prv	30:11	is a group of people that c its father,
Sir	21:27	a godless man c his adversary, he really c himself.

CURSING →CURSE

Ps	109:18	May c clothe him like a robe; may it
Rom	3:14	their mouths are full of bitter c.
Jas	3:10	same mouth come blessing and c.

CURTAIN →CURTAINS

1 Mc	1:22	golden censers, the c, the crowns,

CURTAINS →CURTAIN

1 Mc	4:51	on the table and hung up the c.

CUSH →CUSHITE

Gn	2:13	that winds all through the land of C.
Gn	10: 6	Ham: C, Mizraim, Put and Canaan.

CUSHITE →CUSH

Nm	12: 1	he had contracted with a C woman.
2 Sm	18:21	Then Joab said to a C, "Go,
Jer	38: 7	Now Ebed-melech, a C, a courtier

CUSTODY

Lv	24:12	who kept him in c till a decision
Nm	15:34	But they kept him in c, for there
Acts	4: 3	and put them in c until the next day,
Acts	24:23	centurion that he should be kept in c

CUSTOM →ACCUSTOMED, CUSTOMS

Ru	4: 7	it used to be the c in Israel that,
1 Mc	1:14	according to the Gentile c.
Mk	10: 1	as was his c, he again taught them.
Lk	4:16	to his c into the synagogue
Jn	18:39	But you have a c that I release one
Jn	19:40	according to the Jewish burial c.
Acts	17: 2	Following his usual c, Paul joined
1 Cor	11:16	we do not have such a c, nor do

CUSTOMS →CUSTOM

1 Mc	1:42	each abandoning his particular c.
Acts	16:21	are advocating c that are not lawful

CUT →CUTTING

Gn	15:10	other; but the birds he did not c up.
Gn	17:14	such a one shall be c off from his
Ex	34:13	and c down their sacred poles.
Jgs	21: 6	of the tribes of Israel has been c off.
1 Sm	17:51	dispatched him and c off his head.
1 Sm	24: 5	and stealthily c off an end of Saul's
2 Chr	15:16	Asa c this down, smashed it,
Jdt	13: 8	twice in the neck and c off his head.
Ps	37: 9	Those who do evil will be c off,
Prv	2:22	the wicked will be c off
Prv	10:31	the perverse tongue will be c off.
Prv	23:18	and your hope will not be c off.
Is	14:22	and c off from Babylon name
Is	53: 8	When he was c off from the land
Jer	34:18	like the calf which they c in two,
Ez	37:11	our hope is lost, and we are c off."
Dn	9:26	an anointed shall be c down
Mt	3:10	not bear good fruit will be c down
Mk	9:43	your hand causes you to sin, c it off.
Jn	18:26	the one whose ear Peter had c off,
Acts	2:37	heard this, they were c to the heart,
Rom	11:22	otherwise you too will be c off.
1 Cor	11: 6	she may as well have her hair c off.
1 Cor	11: 6	for a woman to have her hair c off

CUTTING →CUT

Mt	26:51	high priest's servant, c off his ear.

CYMBAL →CYMBALS

1 Cor	13: 1	a resounding gong or a clashing c.

CYMBALS →CYMBAL

2 Sm	6: 5	harps, tambourines, sistrums and c.
1 Chr	15:16	and c, to make a loud sound
2 Chr	5:12	in fine linen, with c, harps and lyres,
2 Chr	29:25	Levites in the LORD's house with c,
Ezr	3:10	there with the c to praise the LORD
Neh	12:27	hymns and the music of c, harps,
Ps	150: 5	Give praise with crashing c, praise him with sounding c.

CYPRESS

Is	55:13	of the thornbush, the c shall grow,
Hos	14: 9	"I am like a verdant c tree"—

CYPRUS

Acts	13: 4	Seleucia and from there sailed to C.

CYRENIAN

Mt	27:32	they met a C named Simon; this man

CYRUS
Persian king who allowed exiles to return (2 Chr 36:22-Ezr 1:8), to rebuild temple (Ezr 5:13-6:14), as appointed by the LORD (Is 44:28-45:13).

D

DAGON
Jgs	16:23	offer a great sacrifice to their god **D**
1 Sm	5: 2	and brought it into the temple of **D**, placing it beside **D**.
1 Chr	10:10	they impaled on the temple of **D**.

DAILY → DAY
Mt	6:11	Give us today our **d** bread;
Lk	9:23	take up his cross **d** and follow me.
Lk	11: 3	Give us each day our **d** bread

DAMASCUS
2 Sm	8: 5	the Arameans of **D** came to the aid
2 Kgs	8: 7	Elisha came to **D** at a time
2 Kgs	16:10	When he saw the altar in **D**,
Is	7: 8	**D** is the capital of Aram, and Rezin
Is	17: 1	Oracle on **D**: Lo, **D** shall cease to be
Am	1: 3	For three crimes of **D**, and for four,
Acts	9: 3	as he was nearing **D**, a light
Acts	22: 6	"On that journey as I drew near to **D**,

DAN
1. Son of Jacob by Bilhah (Gn 30:4-6; 35:25; 46:23). Tribe of blessed (Gn 49:16-17; Dt 33:22), numbered (Nm 1:39; 26:43), allotted land (Jos 19:40-48; Ez 48:1), failed to fully possess (Jgs 1:34-35), failed to support Deborah (Jgs 5:17), possessed Laish/Dan (Jgs 18).

2. Northernmost city in Israel (Gn 14:14; Jgs 18; 20:1).

DANCE → DANCERS, DANCES, DANCING
Jdt	15:12	her and performed a **d** in her honor.
Ps	87: 7	So all sing in their festive **d**:
Ps	149: 3	Let them praise his name in festive **d**,
Ps	150: 4	Give praise with tambourines and **d**.
Eccl	3: 4	a time to mourn, and a time to **d**.
Jer	31:13	the virgins shall make merry and **d**,
Lam	5:15	our **d** has turned into mourning;
Mt	11:17	but you did not **d**, we sang a dirge
Mt	14: 6	performed a **d** before the guests
Mk	6:22	performed a **d** that delighted Herod
Lk	7:32	the flute for you, but you did not **d**.

DANCERS → DANCE
Jgs	21:23	of them from their raid on the **d**,

DANCES → DANCE
1 Sm	21:12	During their **d** do they not sing,
1 Sm	29: 5	of whom they sing during their **d**,

DANCING → DANCE
Ex	15:20	out after her with tambourines, **d**;
Ex	32:19	the camp, he saw the calf and the **d**.
Jgs	11:34	playing the tambourines and **d**.
1 Sm	18: 6	singing and **d**, with tambourines,
2 Sm	6:14	came **d** before the LORD with abandon,
2 Sm	6:16	leaping and **d** before the LORD,
2 Sm	6:21	"I was **d** before the LORD.
1 Chr	15:29	she saw King David leaping and **d**,
Ps	30:12	You changed my mourning into **d**;
Lk	15:25	he heard the sound of music and **d**.

DANGER → DANGERS
Lk	8:23	were taking in water and were in **d**.
Acts	19:40	is, we are in **d** of being charged

DANGERS → DANGER
2 Cor	11:26	in **d** from rivers, **d** from robbers,

DANIEL → =BELTESHAZZAR
1. Hebrew exile to Babylon, name changed to Belteshazzar (Dn 1:6-7). Refused to eat unclean food (Dn 1:8-21). Interpreted Nebuchadnezzar's dreams (Dn 2; 4), writing on the wall (Dn 5). Thrown into lion's den (Dn 6; 14:30-42). Visions of (Dn 7-12). Saves Susanna (Dn 13:45-64). Destroys idol and temple of Bel (Dn 14:1-22). Destroys a dragon (Dn 14:23-28).

2. Son of David (1 Chr 3:1).

DARE → DARED
Mt	22:46	did anyone **d** to ask him any more
Acts	7:32	trembling, did not **d** to look at it.
1 Cor	6: 1	a case against another **d** to bring it

DARED → DARE
Mk	12:34	And no one **d** to ask him any more
Jn	21:12	none of the disciples **d** to ask him,
Acts	5:13	None of the others **d** to join them,

DARIUS
1. King of Persia (Ezr 4:5), allowed rebuilding of temple (Ezr 5-6).

2. Mede who conquered Babylon (Dn 6:1).

DARK → DARKENED, DARKENS, DARKNESS
Gn	15:17	When the sun had set and it was **d**,
Jos	2: 5	At **d**, when it was time for the gate
Ps	23: 4	Even when I walk through a **d** valley,
Ps	35: 6	Make their way slippery and **d**,
Ps	139:12	Darkness is not **d** for you, and night
2 Pt	1:19	it, as to a lamp shining in a **d** place,

DARKENED → DARK
Jl	2:10	The sun and the moon are **d**,
Jl	4:15	Sun and moon are **d**, and the stars
Mt	24:29	the sun will be **d**, and the moon will
Rom	1:21	and their senseless minds were **d**.
Eph	4:18	**d** in understanding,
Rv	9: 2	the air were **d** by the smoke

DARKENS → DARK
Am	5: 8	and **d** day into night; Who summons

DARKNESS → DARK
Gn	1: 2	and **d** covered the abyss,
Gn	1: 4	then separated the light from the **d**.
Gn	15:12	a deep, terrifying **d** enveloped him.
Ex	10:22	there was dense **d** throughout
Dt	5:23	the voice from the midst of the **d**,
Jos	24: 7	he put **d** between your people
2 Sm	22:29	God, you brighten the **d** about me.
Tb	5:10	but must remain in **d**, like the dead
Jb	12:22	The recesses of the **d** he discloses;
Ps	18:12	He made **d** the cover about him;
Ps	18:29	my God brightens the **d** about me.
Ps	91: 6	Nor the pestilence that roams in **d**,
Ps	97: 2	Cloud and **d** surround the Lord;
Ps	112: 4	They shine through the **d**, a light
Ps	139:12	as the day. **D** and light are but one.
Prv	4:19	The way of the wicked is like **d**;
Eccl	2:13	as light has the advantage over **d**.
Is	5:20	who change **d** into light, and light into **d**,
Is	9: 1	The people who walked in **d**
Is	42:16	I will turn **d** into light before them,
Is	45: 7	I form the light, and create the **d**,
Is	58:10	light shall rise for you in the **d**,
Jer	13:16	the light you look for turns to **d**,
Jl	3: 4	The sun will be turned to **d**,
Am	5:18	LORD mean for you? **D** and not light!
Am	5:20	Will not the day of the LORD be **d**
Na	1: 8	and his enemies he pursues with **d**.
Zep	1:15	desolation, a day of **d** and gloom,
Mt	4:16	the people who sit in **d** have seen
Mt	6:23	And if the light in you is **d**, how great will the **d** be.
Mt	22:13	feet, and cast him into the **d** outside,
Lk	1:79	to shine on those who sit in **d**
Lk	11:34	it is bad, then your body is in **d**.
Lk	23:44	**d** came over the whole land until
Jn	1: 5	the light shines in the **d**, and the **d**
Jn	3:19	but people preferred **d** to light,
Jn	8:12	follows me will not walk in **d**,
Jn	12:35	so that **d** may not overcome you.
Acts	2:20	The sun shall be turned to **d**,
Rom	2:19	the blind and a light for those in **d**,
Rom	13:12	throw off the works of **d** [and] put
2 Cor	4: 6	"Let light shine out of **d**," has shone
2 Cor	6:14	fellowship does light have with **d**?
Eph	5: 8	For you were once **d**, but now you
Eph	5:11	no part in the fruitless works of **d**;
Col	1:13	He delivered us from the power of **d**
1 Thes	5: 5	We are not of the night or of **d**.
Heb	12:18	blazing fire and gloomy **d** and storm
1 Pt	2: 9	out of **d** into his wonderful light.
2 Pt	2:17	the gloom of **d** has been reserved.

1 Jn	1: 5	light, and in him there is no **d** at all.
1 Jn	2: 8	for the **d** is passing away,
1 Jn	2: 9	yet hates his brother, is still in the **d**.
Jude	1:13	of **d** has been reserved forever.
Rv	16:10	Its kingdom was plunged into **d**,

DASH →DASHED

2 Kgs	8:12	you will **d** their little children
Jdt	16: 4	sword, **D** my babes to the ground,
Lk	4:11	lest you **d** your foot against a stone.' "

DASHED →DASH

Is	13:16	Their infants shall be **d** to pieces
Na	3:10	even her little ones were **d** to pieces

DATHAN

Involved in Korah's rebellion against Moses and Aaron (Nm 16:1-27; 26:9; Dt 11:6; Ps 106:17; Sir 45:18).

DAUGHTER →DAUGHTER-IN-LAW, DAUGHTERS, DAUGHTERS-IN-LAW

Gn	24:24	"I am the **d** of Bethuel the son
Gn	29:10	Rachel, the **d** of his uncle Laban,
Gn	34: 3	attracted to Dinah, **d** of Jacob,
Gn	38: 2	There he met the **d** of a Canaanite
Ex	2: 5	Pharaoh's **d** came down to the river
Ex	21: 7	"When a man sells his **d** as a slave,
Nm	27: 8	let his heritage pass on to his **d**;
Jgs	11:34	he had neither son nor **d** besides her.
Ru	2: 2	Naomi said to her, "Go, my **d**,"
Ru	3:10	said, "May the LORD bless you, my **d**!
1 Sm	18:20	Now Saul's **d** Michal loved David,
2 Sm	6:16	David, Saul's **d** Michal looked down
1 Kgs	11: 1	many foreign women besides the **d**
Jdt	10:12	"I am a **d** of the Hebrews, and I am
Est	2: 7	had taken her as his own **d**.
Ps	9:15	salvation in the gates of **d** Zion.
Is	47: 1	dust, O virgin **d** Babylon;
Is	47: 1	dethroned, O **d** of the Chaldeans.
Is	52: 2	from your neck, O captive **d** Zion!
Is	62:11	Say to **d** Zion, your savior comes!
Jer	6: 2	and delicate **d** Zion, you are ruined!
Jer	46:11	balm, O virgin **d** Egypt! No use
Lam	2: 1	has detested **d** Zion! He has cast
Ez	16:45	you are the true **d** of the mother who
Mi	7: 6	the **d** rises up against her mother,
Zep	3:14	Shout for joy, O **d** Zion!
Zep	3:14	with all your heart, O **d** Jerusalem!
Zec	9: 9	Rejoice heartily, O **d** Zion,
Zec	9: 9	shout for joy, O **d** Jerusalem!
Mt	9:18	him, and said, "My **d** has just died.
Mt	14: 6	the **d** of Herodias performed a dance
Mt	15:28	her **d** was healed from that hour.
Mk	5:35	arrived and said, "Your **d** has died;
Mk	7:29	The demon has gone out of your **d**."
Lk	12:53	a mother against her **d** and a **d**
Heb	11:24	be known as the son of Pharaoh's **d**;

DAUGHTER-IN-LAW →DAUGHTER

Gn	11:31	and his **d** Sarai, the wife of his son
Gn	38:16	and not realizing that she was his **d**,
Ru	1:22	Naomi returned with the Moabite **d**,
Ru	4:15	his mother is the **d** who loves you.
1 Chr	2: 4	Judah's **d** Tamar bore him Perez
Mi	7: 6	The **d** against her mother-in-law,
Mt	10:35	and a **d** against her mother-in-law;

DAUGHTERS →DAUGHTER

Gn	6: 4	had intercourse with the **d** of man,
Gn	19:36	both of Lot's **d** became pregnant
Gn	29:16	Now Laban had two **d**; the older
Ex	2:16	seven **d** of a priest of Midian came
Nm	27: 1	son of Joseph, had **d** named Mahlah,
Nm	36:10	The **d** of Zelophehad obeyed
Dt	7: 3	neither giving your **d** to their sons nor taking their **d** for your
Dt	12:31	their sons and **d** to their gods.
Ru	1: 8	"Go back, my **d**!" said Naomi.
Ezr	9:12	then, give your **d** to their sons
Ezr	9:12	do not take their **d** for your sons.
Neh	5: 5	to reduce our sons and **d** to slavery,
Jb	42:15	women were as beautiful as the **d**

Ps	144:12	youth, Our **d**, like carved columns,
Prv	30:15	The two **d** of the leech are, "Give,
Song	1: 5	as dark—but lovely, O **d** of Jerusalem—
Sir	7:24	If you have **d**, keep them chaste,
Ez	23: 2	two women, **d** of the same mother,
Jl	3: 1	Your sons and **d** shall prophesy,
Lk	23:28	to them and said, "**D** of Jerusalem,
Acts	2:17	sons and your **d** shall prophesy,
Acts	21: 9	He had four virgin **d** gifted
2 Cor	6:18	and you shall be sons and **d** to me,

DAUGHTERS-IN-LAW →DAUGHTER

Ru	1: 8	Naomi said to her two **d**, "Go back,

DAVID

Son of Jesse (Ru 4:17-22; 1 Chr 2:13-15), ancestor of Jesus (Mt 1:1-17; Lk 3:31). Wives and children (1 Sm 18; 25:39-44; 2 Sm 3:2-5; 5:13-16; 11:27; 1 Chr 3:1-9).

Anointed king by Samuel (1 Sm 16:1-13). Musician to Saul (1 Sm 16:14-23; 18:10). Killed Goliath (1 Sm 17). Relation with Jonathan (1 Sm 18:1-4; 19-20; 23:16-18; 2 Sm 1). Disfavor of Saul (1 Sm 18:6-23:29). Spared Saul's life (1 Sm 24; 26). Among Philistines (1 Sm 21:11-16; 27-30). Lament for Saul and Jonathan (2 Sm 1).

Anointed king of Judah (2 Sm 2:1-11). Conflict with house of Saul (2 Sm 2-4). Anointed king of Israel (2 Sm 5:1-4; 1 Chr 11:1-3). Conquered Jerusalem (2 Sm 5:6-10; 1 Chr 11:4-9). Brought ark to Jerusalem (2 Sm 6; 1 Chr 13; 15-16). The LORD promised eternal dynasty (2 Sm 7; 1 Chr 17; Ps 132). Showed kindness to Mephibosheth (2 Sm 9). Adultery with Bathsheba, murder of Uriah (2 Sm 11-12). Son Amnon raped daughter Tamar; killed by Absalom (2 Sm 13). Absalom's revolt (2 Sm 14-17); death (2 Sm 18). Sheba's revolt (2 Sm 20). Victories: Philistines (2 Sm 5:17-25; 21:15-22; 1 Chr 14:8-17; 20:4-8), Ammonites (2 Sm 10; 1 Chr 19), various (2 Sm 8; 1 Chr 18). Mighty men (2 Sm 23:8-39; 1 Chr 11-12). Punished for numbering army (2 Sm 24; 1 Chr 21). Appointed Solomon king (1 Kgs 1:28-2:9). Prepared for building of temple (1 Chr 22-29). Last words (2 Sm 23:1-7). Death (1 Kgs 2:10-12; 1 Chr 29:28).

Psalmist (Mt 22:43-45), musician (Am 6:5), prophet (2 Sm 23:2-7; Acts 1:16; 2:30).

Psalms of: 2 (Acts 4:25), 3-32, 34-41, 51-65, 68-70, 86, 95 (Heb 4:7), 101, 103, 108-110, 122, 124, 131, 133, 138-145.

DAWN →DAWNS

Jb	38:12	morning and shown the **d** its place
Ps	57: 9	lyre and harp! I will wake the **d**.
Song	6:10	is this that comes forth like the **d**,
Sir	24:30	I send my teachings forth shining like the **d**,
Is	14:12	O morning star, son of the **d**!
Is	58: 8	light shall break forth like the **d**,
Is	62: 1	vindication shines forth like the **d**
Hos	6: 3	as certain as the **d** is his coming,
Zep	3: 5	renders judgment unfailingly, at **d**.

DAWNS →DAWN

Ps	97:11	Light **d** for the just; gladness,
2 Pt	1:19	until day **d** and the morning star

DAY →BIRTHDAY, DAILY, DAY'S, DAYBREAK, DAYLIGHT, DAYS

Gn	1: 5	God called the light "**d**,"
Gn	1: 5	and morning followed—the first **d**.
Gn	1: 8	and morning followed—the second **d**.
Gn	1:13	and morning followed—the third **d**.
Gn	1:19	and morning followed—the fourth **d**.
Gn	1:23	and morning followed—the fifth **d**.
Gn	1:31	and morning followed—the sixth **d**.
Gn	2: 2	on the seventh **d** God was finished
Gn	8:22	Summer and winter, and **d** and night
Ex	12:17	celebrate this **d** throughout your
Ex	13:21	Thus they could travel both **d**
Ex	16:30	the people rested on the seventh **d**.
Ex	20: 8	to keep holy the sabbath **d**.
Ex	40: 2	"On the first **d** of the first month you
Nm	14:14	and you go before them by **d**
Dt	1:33	find you a resting place—by **d**
Dt	34: 6	to this **d** no one **d** no one knows
Jos	1: 8	Recite it by **d** and by night, that you
Jos	10:14	or since was there a **d** like this,
2 Kgs	7: 9	This is a **d** of good news, and we are

1 Chr	16:23	announce his salvation, **d** after **d**.
Neh	8:10	Lord. Do not be saddened this **d**,
Neh	8:18	the book of the law of God **d** after **d**,
Tb	12:18	So continue to thank him every **d**
1 Mc	4:54	on that very **d** it was reconsecrated
1 Mc	7:48	observed that **d** as a great festival.
2 Mc	15:36	never to let this **d** pass unobserved,
2 Mc	15:36	in Aramaic, the eve of Mordecai's **D**.
Ps	1: 2	God's law they study **d** and night.
Ps	19: 3	One **d** to the next conveys
Ps	37:13	at them, knowing their **d** is coming.
Ps	84:11	Better one **d** in your courts
Ps	96: 2	announce his salvation **d** after **d**.
Ps	118:24	This is the **d** the Lord has made;
Ps	119:97	teaching, Lord! I study it all **d** long.
Ps	119:164	Seven times a **d** I praise you
Prv	11: 4	Wealth is useless on the **d** of wrath,
Prv	27: 1	not what any **d** may bring forth.
Eccl	7: 1	the **d** of death than the **d** of birth.
Sir	5: 8	the Lord, put it not off from **d** to **d**;
Is	2:12	For the Lord of hosts will have his **d**
Is	13: 9	Lo, the **d** of the Lord comes, cruel,
Is	49: 8	on the **d** of salvation I help you,
Is	60:19	the sun be your light by **d**,
Is	66: 8	a country be brought forth in one **d**,
Jer	30: 7	How mighty is that **d**— none like it!
Jer	46:10	But this is the **d** of the Lord God
Jer	50:31	For your **d** has come, the time
Ez	4: 6	one **d** for each year I have allotted
Ez	7: 7	The time has come, near is the **d**:
Ez	30: 2	says the Lord God: Cry, Oh, the **d**!
Dn	6:14	three times a **d** he offers his prayer."
Jl	1:15	Alas, the **d**! for near is the **d**
Jl	3: 4	At the coming of the **d** of the Lord, the great and terrible **d**.
Am	3:14	On the **d** when I punish Israel
Am	5:20	Will not the **d** of the Lord be
Mi	7: 4	The **d** announced by your
Hb	3:16	beneath me. I await the **d** of distress
Zep	1:14	Near is the great **d** of the Lord,
Zec	2:15	themselves to the Lord on that **d**,
Zec	14: 1	a **d** shall come for the Lord
Zec	14: 7	There shall be one continuous **d**,
Zec	14: 7	known to the Lord, not **d** and night,
Mal	3: 2	But who will endure the **d** of his
Mal	3:23	Before the **d** of the Lord comes, the great and terrible **d**,
Mt	10:15	on the **d** of judgment than
Mt	12:36	the **d** of judgment people will render
Mt	20:19	and he will be raised on the third **d**."
Mt	24:38	to the **d** that Noah entered the ark.
Mt	25:13	you know neither the **d** nor the hour.
Mt	28: 1	as the first **d** of the week was
Lk	1:59	the eighth **d** to circumcise the child,
Lk	11: 3	Give us each **d** our daily bread
Lk	17:24	so will the Son of Man be [in his **d**].
Lk	24:46	and rise from the dead on the third **d**
Jn	6:40	and I shall raise him [on] the last **d**."
Acts	2:20	the great and splendid **d** of the Lord,
Acts	2:46	Every **d** they devoted themselves
Acts	5:42	And all **d** long, both at the temple
Acts	17:31	because he has established a **d**
Rom	2: 5	wrath for yourself for the **d** of wrath
Rom	14: 5	considers one **d** more important
1 Cor	5: 5	may be saved on the **d** of the Lord.
1 Cor	15: 4	raised on the third **d** in accordance
1 Cor	15:31	Every **d** I face death; I swear it
2 Cor	4:16	our inner self is being renewed **d** by **d**.
2 Cor	6: 2	on the **d** of salvation I helped you."
2 Cor	6: 2	behold, now is the **d** of salvation.
2 Cor	11:25	I passed a night and a **d** on the deep;
Eph	4:30	were sealed for the **d** of redemption.
Eph	6:13	be able to resist on the evil **d** and,
Phil	1: 6	to complete it until the **d** of Christ
1 Thes	5: 2	the **d** of the Lord will come like
1 Thes	5: 8	But since we are of the **d**, let us be
2 Thes	2: 2	the effect that the **d** of the Lord is
Heb	7:27	to offer sacrifice **d** after **d**,
2 Pt	3: 8	the Lord one **d** is like a thousand

2 Pt	3: 8	and a thousand years like one **d**.
2 Pt	3:10	the **d** of the Lord will come like
1 Jn	4:17	the **d** of judgment because as he is,
Jude	1: 6	for the judgment of the great **d**.
Rv	1:10	caught up in spirit on the Lord's **d**
Rv	6:17	because the great **d** of their wrath
Rv	8:12	The **d** lost its light for a third
Rv	16:14	on the great **d** of God the almighty.
Rv	20:10	There they will be tormented **d**
Rv	21:25	During the **d** its gates will never be

DAY'S → DAY

Nm	11:31	distance of a **d** journey all around the camp.
1 Kgs	19: 4	and went a **d** journey into the desert,
Jon	3: 4	had gone but a single **d** walk announcing,
Acts	1:12	near Jerusalem, a sabbath **d** journey away.
Rv	6: 6	"A ration of wheat costs a **d** pay,

DAYBREAK → DAY, BREAK

Lk	4:42	At **d**, Jesus left and went

DAYLIGHT → DAY, LIGHT

Am	8: 9	the earth with darkness in broad **d**.

DAYS → DAY

Gn	1:14	the fixed times, the **d** and the years,
Gn	3:14	shall you eat all the **d** of your life.
Gn	3:17	eat its yield all the **d** of your life.
Gn	7: 4	Seven **d** from now I will bring rain down on the earth for forty
Ex	24:18	there he stayed for forty **d** and forty
Ex	34:28	there with the Lord for forty **d**
Nm	13:25	the land for forty **d** they returned.
Nm	14:34	Forty **d** you spent in scouting
Dt	17:19	read it all the **d** of his life that he
Dt	32: 7	Think back on the **d** of old,
Jgs	17: 6	In those **d** there was no king
Jgs	21:25	In those **d** there was no king
1 Sm	17:16	morning and evening for forty **d**
1 Kgs	19: 8	he walked forty **d** and forty nights
Tb	4: 5	Perform good works all the **d**
Jdt	16:24	of Israel mourned for seven **d**.
1 Mc	4:56	For eight **d** they celebrated
Ps	21: 5	gave it to him, length of **d** forever.
Ps	23: 6	will pursue me all the **d** of my life;
Ps	34:13	life, takes delight in prosperous **d**?
Ps	39: 6	You have given my **d** a very short
Ps	90:12	Teach us to count our **d** aright,
Ps	103:15	Our **d** are like the grass; like flowers
Ps	128: 5	you from Zion, all the **d** of your life
Prv	9:11	For by me your **d** will be multiplied
Prv	31:12	and not evil, all the **d** of her life.
Eccl	9: 9	all the **d** of the fleeting life that is
Eccl	12: 1	your Creator in the **d** of your youth,
Eccl	12: 1	before the evil **d** come
Dn	12:11	thousand two hundred and ninety **d**.
Dn	12:12	three hundred and thirty-five **d**.
Hos	3: 5	Lord and to his bounty, in the last **d**.
Jl	3: 2	in those **d**, I will pour out my spirit.
Mt	4: 2	He fasted for forty **d** and forty
Mk	1:13	remained in the desert for forty **d**,
Mk	10:34	death, but after three **d** he will rise."
Lk	4: 2	for forty **d**, to be tempted
Lk	4: 2	He ate nothing during those **d**,
Lk	19:43	For the **d** are coming upon you
Acts	1: 3	appearing to them during forty **d**
Acts	2:17	'It will come to pass in the last **d**,'
Eph	5:16	opportunity, because the **d** are evil.
2 Tm	3: 1	will be terrifying times in the last **d**.
Heb	1: 2	in these last **d**, he spoke to us
2 Pt	3: 3	in the last **d** scoffers will come
Rv	11: 3	those twelve hundred and sixty **d**,
Rv	11:11	But after the three and a half **d**,
Rv	12: 6	of for twelve hundred and sixty **d**.

DAZZLING

Mk	9: 3	and his clothes became **d** white,
Lk	24: 4	two men in **d** garments appeared
Acts	10:30	a man in **d** robes stood before me

DEACONS

1 Tm	3: 8	Similarly, **d** must be dignified,

1 Tm	3:10	against them, let them serve as **d**.
1 Tm	3:12	**D** may be married only once
1 Tm	3:13	serve well as **d** gain good standing

DEAD → DEATH, DIE, DIED, DIES, DYING

Ex	12:30	there was not a house without its **d**.
Nm	17:13	there between the living and the **d**,
Dt	18:11	spirits or seeks oracles from the **d**.
1 Kgs	3:22	one is my son, the **d** one is yours."
Ps	115:17	The **d** do not praise the LORD,
Eccl	9: 4	a live dog is better off than a **d** lion.
Is	8:19	gods, apply to the **d** on behalf
Is	26:19	But your **d** shall live, their corpses
Mt	8:22	me, and let the **d** bury their **d**."
Mt	9:24	The girl is not **d** but sleeping."
Mt	10: 8	the sick, raise the **d**, cleanse lepers,
Mt	11: 5	the deaf hear, the **d** are raised,
Mt	14: 2	He has been raised from the **d**;
Mt	28: 7	'He has been raised from the **d**,
Mk	12:27	He is not God of the **d**
Lk	15:24	because this son of mine was **d**,
Lk	16:31	if someone should rise from the **d**.' "
Lk	20:37	the **d** will rise even Moses made
Lk	24: 5	seek the living one among the **d**?
Lk	24:46	and rise from the **d** on the third day
Jn	5:21	For just as the Father raises the **d**
Jn	11:44	The **d** man came out, tied hand
Jn	20: 9	that he had to rise from the **d**.
Jn	21:14	after being raised from the **d**.
Rom	6: 4	was raised from the **d** by the glory
Rom	6:11	of yourselves as [being] **d** to sin
Rom	14: 9	that he might be Lord of both the **d**
1 Cor	15:12	is preached as raised from the **d**,
1 Cor	15:12	say there is no resurrection of the **d**?
1 Cor	15:29	themselves baptized for the **d**?
Eph	2: 1	You were **d** in your transgressions
Eph	5:14	and arise from the **d**, and Christ will
Phil	3:11	attain the resurrection from the **d**.
Col	1:18	beginning, the firstborn from the **d**,
Col	2:13	when you were **d** [in] transgressions
1 Thes	4:16	and the **d** in Christ will rise first.
2 Tm	4: 1	who will judge the living and the **d**,
Heb	11:19	was able to raise even from the **d**,
Jas	2:26	just as a body without a spirit is **d**, so also faith without works is **d**.
1 Pt	4: 5	ready to judge the living and the **d**.
Rv	1: 5	the firstborn of the **d** and ruler
Rv	1:18	Once I was **d**, but now I am alive
Rv	11:18	and the time for the **d** to be judged,
Rv	14:13	Blessed are the **d** who die
Rv	20:12	The **d** were judged according

DEAF

Ex	4:11	and makes another **d** and dumb?
Lv	19:14	You shall not curse the **d**, or put
Is	29:18	On that day the **d** shall hear
Is	35: 5	opened, the ears of the **d** be cleared;
Is	42:19	or **d** like the messenger I send?
Mk	7:32	to him a **d** man who had a speech
Lk	7:22	lepers are cleansed, the **d** hear,

DEAL → DEALT

Ex	1:10	let us **d** shrewdly with them to stop
Ez	16:59	I will **d** with you according to what
Heb	5: 2	He is able to **d** patiently

DEALT → DEAL

Ex	1:20	Therefore God **d** well

DEAR

Ps	102:15	Its stones are **d** to your servants;

DEATH → DEAD

Ex	21:12	man a mortal blow must be put to **d**.
Ex	21:15	father or mother shall be put to **d**.
Ex	21:16	him when caught, shall be put to **d**.
Ex	21:17	father or mother shall be put to **d**.
Ex	22:18	lies with an animal shall be put to **d**.
Ex	31:14	desecrates it shall be put to **d**.
Ex	31:15	on the sabbath day shall be put to **d**.
Nm	23:10	May I die the **d** of the just, may my
Nm	35:16	is a murderer and shall be put to **d**.

Dt	13: 6	or that dreamer shall be put to **d**,
Dt	17: 6	is required for putting a person to **d**;
Dt	30:19	I have set before you life and **d**,
Ru	1:17	aught but **d** separates me from you!"
2 Chr	23:15	the palace, they put her to **d** there.
2 Chr	25: 4	"Fathers shall not be put to **d** for their
2 Chr	25: 4	own guilt shall a man be put to **d**."
Jb	3:21	They wait for **d** and it comes not;
Ps	13: 4	light to my eyes lest I sleep in **d**,
Ps	18: 5	The breakers of **d** surged round
Ps	22:16	palate; you lay me in the dust of **d**.
Ps	49:15	where **d** will be their shepherd.
Ps	89:49	What mortal can live and not see **d**?
Ps	116:15	of the LORD is the **d** of his faithful.
Prv	5: 5	Her feet go down to **d**, to the nether
Prv	8:36	himself; all who hate me love **d**."
Prv	10: 2	nothing, but virtue saves from **d**.
Prv	14:12	a man, but the end of it leads to **d**!
Prv	16:25	a man, but the end of it leads to **d**!
Prv	18:21	**D** and life are in the power
Eccl	7: 1	the day of **d** than the day of birth.
Song	8: 6	For stern as **d** is love, relentless as
Wis	1:12	Court not **d** by your erring way
Sir	4:28	Even to the **d** fight for truth,
Sir	15:17	Before man are life and **d**,
Is	28:15	"We have made a covenant with **d**,
Is	53:12	Because he surrendered himself to **d**
Jer	26:16	"This man does not deserve **d**; it is
Ez	18:23	pleasure from the **d** of the wicked?
Ez	18:32	in the **d** of anyone who dies,
Ez	33:11	pleasure in the **d** of the wicked man,
Dn	3:88	and saved us from the power of **d**;
Dn	13:28	determined to put Susanna to **d**.
Dn	13:62	they put them to **d**. Thus was
Hos	13:14	Where are your plagues, O **d**!
Hb	2: 5	and is insatiable as **d**, Who gathers
Mt	10:21	Brother will hand over brother to **d**,
Mt	10:21	parents and have them put to **d**.
Mt	16:28	who will not taste **d** until they see
Mk	10:33	and they will condemn him to **d**
Jn	5:24	but has passed from **d** to life.
Jn	8:51	keeps my word will never see **d**."
Jn	11:13	But Jesus was talking about his **d**,
Acts	2:24	releasing him from the throes of **d**,
Rom	5:12	and through sin, **d**, and thus **d** came
Rom	6: 3	Jesus were baptized into his **d**?
Rom	6:23	For the wages of sin is **d**,
Rom	8:13	the spirit you put to **d** the deeds
1 Cor	15:21	For since **d** came through a human
1 Cor	15:26	The last enemy to be destroyed is **d**,
1 Cor	15:55	Where, O **d**, is your victory? Where, O **d**, is your sting?"
2 Cor	2:16	to the latter an odor of **d** that leads to **d**,
2 Cor	3: 7	Now if the ministry of **d**,
Phil	2: 8	becoming obedient to **d**, even **d**
Col	1:22	in his fleshly body through his **d**,
2 Tm	1:10	who destroyed **d** and brought life
Heb	2:14	through **d** he might destroy the one who has the power of **d**,
Jas	5:20	of his way will save his soul from **d**
1 Jn	3:14	that we have passed from **d** to life
1 Jn	3:14	does not love remains in **d**.
Rv	1:18	I hold the keys to **d**
Rv	2:11	not be harmed by the second **d**." '
Rv	6: 8	Its rider was named **D**, and Hades
Rv	9: 6	that time these people will seek **d**
Rv	9: 6	long to die but **d** will escape them.
Rv	20: 6	The second **d** has no power over
Rv	20:14	Then **D** and Hades were thrown
Rv	20:14	(This pool of fire is the second **d**.)
Rv	21: 4	and there shall be no more **d**
Rv	21: 8	and sulfur, which is the second **d**."

DEBATE → DEBATER

Acts	15: 2	no little dissension and **d** by Paul
Acts	15: 7	After much **d** had taken place,

DEBATER → DEBATE

1 Cor	1:20	scribe? Where is the **d** of this age?

DEBAUCHERIES → DEBAUCHERY
Na 3: 4 For the many **d** of the harlot,

DEBAUCHERY → DEBAUCHERIES
2 Mc 6: 4 Gentiles filled the temple with **d**
Eph 5:18 in which lies **d**, but be filled

DEBIR
Jos 12:13 **D**, Geder,
Jgs 1:11 against the inhabitants of **D**,

DEBORAH
1. Prophetess who led Israel to victory over Canaanites (Jgs 4-5).
2. Rebekah's nurse (Gn 35:8).

DEBT → DEBTOR, DEBTORS, DEBTS
1 Sm 22: 2 who were in difficulties or in **d**,
Neh 10:32 year, as well as every kind of **d**.
1 Mc 10:43 or because of any other **d**, shall be
Mt 18:30 in prison until he paid back the **d**.
Mt 18:32 you your entire **d** because you
Mt 18:34 he should pay back the whole **d**.
Lk 7:43 whose larger **d** was forgiven."

DEBTOR → DEBT
Is 24: 2 the borrower, the creditor as the **d**.

DEBTORS → DEBT
Mt 6:12 us our debts, as we forgive our **d**;
Lk 16: 5 called in his master's **d** one by one.
Rom 8:12 brothers, we are not **d** to the flesh,

DEBTS → DEBT
Dt 15: 1 you shall have a relaxation of **d**,
1 Mc 15: 8 All **d**, present or future,
Prv 22:26 of those who become surety for **d**;
Mt 6:12 and forgive us our **d**, as we forgive

DECAPOLIS
Mt 4:25 from Galilee, the **D**, Jerusalem,

DECAYS
Sir 10: 9 even during life man's body **d**;

DECEIT → DECEITFUL, DECEITFULLY, DECEIVE, DECEIVED, DECEIVERS, DECEIVES
Dt 32: 4 A faithful God, without **d**, how just
Jb 27: 4 falsehood, nor my tongue utter **d**!
Ps 32: 2 no guilt, in whose spirit is no **d**.
Ps 101: 7 No one who practices **d** can hold
Prv 26:24 in his inmost being he maintains **d**;
Mk 7:22 greed, malice, **d**, licentiousness,
Acts 13:10 full of every sort of **d** and fraud.
1 Pt 2:22 and no **d** was found in his mouth."

DECEITFUL → DECEIT
Ps 35:20 in the land they fashion **d** speech.
Zep 3:13 be found in their mouths a **d** tongue;
2 Cor 11:13 people are false apostles, **d** workers,
Eph 4:14 in the interests of **d** scheming.
1 Tm 4: 1 faith by paying attention to **d** spirits

DECEITFULLY → DECEIT
1 Mc 1:30 spoke to them **d** in peaceful terms,
Prv 12:17 of, but a lying witness speaks **d**.

DECEIVE → DECEIT
2 Kgs 18:29 'Do not let Hezekiah **d** you, since he
Jer 37: 9 LORD: Do not **d** yourselves
Rom 16:18 flattering speech they **d** the hearts
1 Cor 3:18 Let no one **d** himself. If anyone
Eph 5: 6 Let no one **d** you with empty
Col 2: 4 that no one may **d** you by specious
2 Thes 2: 3 Let no one **d** you in any way.
1 Jn 1: 8 "We are without sin," we **d** ourselves,
1 Jn 3: 7 Children, let no one **d** you.
Rv 20: 8 to **d** the nations at the four corners

DECEIVED → DECEIT
Dn 14: 7 "Do not be **d**, O king," he said; "it is
Ob 1: 3 The pride of your heart has **d** you:
Jn 7:47 them, "Have you also been **d**?
Rom 7:11 **d** me and through it put me to death.
1 Cor 6: 9 Do not be **d**; neither fornicators nor
2 Cor 11: 3 as the serpent **d** Eve by his cunning,

1 Tm 2:14 Adam was not **d**, but the woman was **d** and transgressed.
2 Tm 3:13 from bad to worse, deceivers and **d**.
Jas 1:16 Do not be **d**, my beloved brothers:

DECEIVERS → DECEIT
Ti 1:10 idle talkers and **d**,
2 Jn 1: 7 Many **d** have gone

DECEIVES → DECEIT
Prv 26:19 Is the man who **d** his neighbor,

DECIDE → DECIDED, DECISION, DECISIONS
Is 11: 3 he judge, nor by hearsay shall he **d**,
Acts 24:22 comes down, I shall **d** your case."

DECIDED → DECIDE
Lk 1: 3 I too have **d**, after investigating

DECISION → DECIDE
Lv 24:12 him in custody till a **d** from the LORD
Prv 16:33 its **d** depends entirely on the LORD.
Jl 4:14 day of the LORD in the valley of **d**.
Zep 3: 8 For it is my **d** to gather together

DECISIONS → DECIDE
Nm 27:21 out for him the **d** of the Urim

DECLARE → DECLARED
Jn 16:14 from what is mine and **d** it to you.

DECLARED → DECLARE
Mk 7:19 latrine?" (Thus he **d** all foods clean.)

DECREASE
Ps 107:38 many, and their livestock did not **d**.
Jer 29: 6 you must increase in number, not **d**.
Jn 3:30 He must increase; I must **d**."

DECREE → DECREED, DECREES
Ezr 5: 3 "Who issued the **d** for you to build
Est 3: 9 let a **d** be issued to destroy them;
1 Mc 1:57 was condemned to death by royal **d**.
Ps 2: 7 I will proclaim the **d** of the LORD,
Ps 81: 6 Who made it a **d** for Joseph when he
Dn 2:13 When the **d** was issued that the wise
Lk 2: 1 In those days a **d** went
Rom 1:32 Although they know the just **d**

DECREED → DECREE
1 Kgs 22:23 LORD himself has **d** evil against you."
Ps 122: 4 of the LORD, As it was **d** for Israel,
Is 10:22 will return; their destruction is **d**
Dn 9:24 "Seventy weeks are **d** for your people

DECREES → DECREE
Dt 11: 1 his statutes, **d** and commandments.
Dt 30:16 statutes and **d**, you will live
2 Kgs 23: 3 and **d** with their whole hearts
Ps 119: 2 Happy those who observe God's **d**,
Ps 119:24 Your **d** are my delight; they are my
Ps 119:99 teachers, because I ponder your **d**.
Is 10: 1 statutes and who write oppressive **d**,
Acts 17: 7 act in opposition to the **d** of Caesar

DEDICATED → DEDICATION
Nm 18: 6 **d** to the LORD for the service
1 Kgs 7:51 he brought in the **d** offerings of his
1 Kgs 8:63 all the Israelites **d** the temple

DEDICATION → DEDICATED
Nm 7:10 For the **d** of the altar also,
2 Chr 7: 9 they had celebrated the **d** of the altar
Ezr 6:16 other returned exiles—celebrated the **d**
Neh 12:27 At the **d** of the wall of Jerusalem,
1 Mc 4:56 eight days they celebrated the **d**
Dn 3: 2 be summoned to the **d** of the statue
Jn 10:22 The feast of the **D** was then taking

DEED → DO
Sir 3: 8 In word and **d** honor your father
Jer 32:10 I had written and sealed the **d**,
Mk 6: 5 able to perform any mighty **d** there,
Lk 24:19 who was a prophet mighty in **d**
Col 3:17 in word or in **d**, do everything

DEEDS → DO

Dt	3:24	on earth can perform **d** as mighty as
Dt	11: 7	eyes you have seen all these great **d**
Ezr	9:13	that has come upon us for our evil **d**
Ps	9: 2	I will declare all your wondrous **d**.
Ps	26: 7	recounting all your wondrous **d**.
Ps	28: 4	Repay them for their **d**, for the evil
Ps	45: 5	right hand show you wondrous **d**.
Ps	65: 6	us with awesome **d** of justice,
Ps	66: 3	Say to God: "How awesome your **d**!
Ps	71:17	day I proclaim your wondrous **d**.
Ps	75: 2	declare your wonderful **d**. You said:
Ps	77:12	I will remember the **d** of the Lord;
Ps	78: 4	and mighty **d** of the Lord,
Ps	145: 6	power and attest to your great **d**.
Sir	16:12	judges men, each according to his **d**.
Is	63: 7	recall, the glorious **d** of the Lord,
Jer	50:29	Repay her for her **d**; as she has
Lam	3:64	O Lord, according to their **d**;
Hos	5: 4	Their **d** do not allow them to return
Mt	13:58	work many mighty **d** there because
Lk	10:13	the mighty **d** done in your midst had
Acts	2:22	to you by God with mighty **d**,
Rom	8:13	you put to death the **d** of the body,
1 Cor	12:28	then, mighty **d**; then gifts of healing,
Col	1:21	hostile in mind because of evil **d**
2 Tm	4:14	will repay him according to his **d**.
Rv	18: 6	Pay her back double for her **d**.
Rv	19: 8	linen represents the righteous **d**

DEEP → DEEPEST, DEPTH, DEPTHS

Gn	2:21	So the Lord God cast a **d** sleep
Gn	15:12	Abram, and a **d**, terrifying darkness
1 Sm	26:12	Lord had put them into a **d** slumber.
Ps	36: 7	your judgments, like the mighty **d**;
Ps	42: 8	Here **d** calls to **d** in the roar of your
Prv	22:14	mouth of the adulteress is a **d** pit;
Prv	23:27	For the harlot is a **d** ditch,
Is	7:11	let it be **d** **d** as the nether world,
Is	29:10	a spirit of **d** sleep. He has shut your
Ez	23:32	so wide and **d**, which holds so
Dn	2:22	He reveals **d** and hidden things
Jon	2: 4	For you cast me into the **d**,
Lk	5: 4	"Put out into **d** water and lower your
Acts	20: 9	sinking into a **d** sleep as Paul talked
Rv	2:24	of the so-called **d** secrets of Satan:

DEEPEST → DEEP

Tb	4:19	he casts him down to the **d** recesses

DEER

Ps	42: 2	As the **d** longs for streams of water,

DEFEAT

Dt	7: 2	them up to you and you **d** them,

DEFECT

Nm	19: 2	is free from every blemish and **d**
Dt	15:21	or blind or has any other serious **d**,
Dt	17: 1	flock an animal with any serious **d**;
Dn	1: 4	young men without any **d**,

DEFEND → DEFENDED, DEFENSE, DEFENSES

Est	8:11	to group together and **d** their lives,
Jb	13:15	I will **d** my conduct before him.
Ps	72: 4	he may **d** the oppressed among
Prv	31: 9	is just, **d** the needy and the poor!
Is	1:17	hear the orphan's plea, **d** the widow.
Is	1:23	The fatherless they **d** not,
Jer	5:28	justice they do not **d** By advancing
Jer	51:36	Surely I will **d** your cause, I will

DEFENDED → DEFEND

Est	9:16	also mustered and **d** themselves,

DEFENSE → DEFEND

Ps	35:23	Awake, be vigilant in my **d**, in my
Lk	21:14	not to prepare your **d** beforehand,
Acts	22: 1	I am about to say to you in my **d**."
Phil	1:16	I am here for the **d** of the gospel;

DEFENSES → DEFEND

Ps	60: 3	God, you rejected us, broke our **d**;

DEFERRED

Prv	13:12	Hope **d** makes the heart sick,

DEFILE → DEFILED, DEFILES

Nm	35:34	Do not **d** the land in which you live
Jdt	9: 8	**d** the tent where your glorious name
Ez	20: 7	do not **d** yourselves with the idols
Dn	1: 8	was resolved not to **d** himself
Mt	15:20	These are what **d** a person,
Mt	15:20	with unwashed hands does not **d**."
Mk	7:15	one from outside can **d** that person;
Mk	7:15	come out from within are what **d**."
Jude	1: 8	nevertheless also **d** the flesh,

DEFILED → DEFILE

Gn	34: 5	Shechem had **d** his daughter Dinah;
1 Mc	1:37	the sanctuary; they **d** the sanctuary.
Ps	79: 1	they have **d** your holy temple,
Ez	22: 4	idols you made you have become **d**;
Ez	23:13	I saw that she had **d** herself.
Rv	14: 4	These are they who were not **d**

DEFILES → DEFILE

Mt	15:11	is not what enters one's mouth that **d**
Mt	15:11	out of the mouth is what **d** one."

DEFRAUD

Lv	19:13	"You shall not **d** or rob your
Mk	10:19	you shall not **d**; honor your father

DEFY

1 Sm	17:10	"I **d** the ranks of Israel today.

DEGENERATE

Dt	32: 5	he been treated by his **d** children,

DEGRADING

Rom	1:26	handed them over to **d** passions.

DEITY

Col	2: 9	the whole fullness of the **d** bodily,

DELAY → DELAYED, DELAYS

Ps	40:18	and deliverer; my God, do not **d**!
Ps	70: 6	help and deliverer. Lord, do not **d**!
Eccl	5: 3	a vow to God, **d** not its fulfillment.
Sir	35:19	God indeed will not **d**, and like
Dn	9:19	be attentive and act without **d**,
Heb	10:37	to come shall come; he shall not **d**.
Rv	10: 6	in them, "There shall be no more **d**.

DELAYED → DELAY

Mt	25: 5	Since the bridegroom was long **d**,
Lk	12:45	himself, 'My master is **d** in coming,'

DELAYS → DELAY

Hb	2: 3	not disappoint; If it **d**, wait for it,

DELICACIES

Prv	23: 3	Do not desire his **d**; they are

DELIGHT → DELIGHTS

Dt	28:63	"Just as the Lord once took **d**
Dt	28:63	so will he now take **d** in ruining
Dt	30: 9	will again take **d** in your prosperity,
Dt	30: 9	even as he took **d** in your fathers',
1 Sm	15:22	"Does the Lord so **d** in holocausts
Jb	22:26	For then you shall **d** in the Almighty
Jb	27:10	Will he then **d** in the Almighty
Ps	16: 3	Accursed are all who **d** in them.
Ps	37: 4	Find your **d** in the Lord who will
Ps	40: 9	To do your will is my **d**; my God,
Ps	68:31	scatter the nations that **d** in war.
Ps	112: 1	who greatly **d** in God's commands.
Ps	119:16	In your laws I take **d**; I will never
Ps	119:24	Your decrees are my **d**; they are my
Ps	119:35	of your commands, for that is my **d**.
Ps	119:47	I **d** in your commands, which I
Ps	119:70	as for me, your teaching is my **d**.
Ps	119:77	may live, for your teaching is my **d**.
Ps	119:92	Had your teaching not been my **d**,
Ps	119:143	upon me, your commands are my **d**.
Ps	119:174	Lord; your teaching is my **d**.
Ps	147:10	God takes no **d** in the strength
Prv	2:14	Who **d** in doing evil,

Prv	8:30	and I was his **d** day by day,
Prv	8:31	and I found **d** in the sons of men.
Prv	11: 1	the Lord, but a full weight is his **d**.
Prv	29:17	comfort, and give **d** to your soul.
Song	2: 3	I **d** to rest in his shadow,
Sir	40:20	Wine and music **d** the soul,
Is	11: 3	his **d** shall be the fear of the Lord.
Is	13:17	of silver and take no **d** in gold.
Is	55: 2	eat well, you shall **d** in rich fare.
Is	58:13	If you call the sabbath a **d**,
Is	62: 4	But you shall be called "My **D**,"
Is	65:18	to be a joy and its people to be a **d**;
Is	66:11	That you may nurse with **d** at her
Jer	31:20	the child in whom I **d**? Often as I
Ez	24:16	away from you the **d** of your eyes,
Ez	24:21	of your pride, the **d** of your eyes,
Ez	24:25	glorious joy, the **d** of their eyes,
Mk	12:37	[The] great crowd heard this with **d**.
Rom	7:22	For I take **d** in the law of God,

DELIGHTS → DELIGHT

Ps	5: 5	You are not a god who **d** in evil;
Ps	35:27	Lord who **d** in the peace of his loyal
Ps	111: 2	to be treasured for all their **d**.
Sir	26:13	A gracious wife **d** her husband,
Mi	7:18	forever, but **d** rather in clemency,

DELILAH
Philistine who betrayed Samson (Jgs 16:4-22).

DELIVER → DELIVERANCE, DELIVERED, DELIVERER,
    DELIVERS

Ps	22: 9	relied on the Lord—let him **d** you;
Is	50: 2	Have I not the strength to **d**? Lo,
Jer	1: 8	because I am with you to **d** you,
Mt	27:43	let him **d** him now if he wants him.

DELIVERANCE → DELIVER

Est	4:14	and **d** will come to the Jews
1 Mc	4:25	Thus Israel had a great **d** that day.
Ps	53: 7	Zion might come the **d** of Israel,
Jon	2:10	I will pay: **d** is from the Lord.
Phil	1:19	this will result in **d** for me through

DELIVERED → DELIVER

1 Mc	2:60	was **d** from the jaws of lions.
Ps	33:16	nor a warrior **d** by great strength.
Ps	34: 5	me, **d** me from all my fears.
Dn	3:88	he has **d** us from the nether world,
Dn	3:88	raging flame and **d** us from the fire.

DELIVERER → DELIVER

2 Sm	22: 2	"O Lord, my rock, my fortress, my **d**,
Ps	18: 3	Lord, my rock, my fortress, my **d**,
Ps	40:18	You are my help and **d**; my God,
Ps	70: 6	You are my help and **d**. Lord, do not
Ps	144: 2	my stronghold, my **d**, My shield,
Rom	11:26	"The **d** will come out of Zion, he will

DELIVERS → DELIVER

Ps	41: 2	misfortune strikes, the Lord **d** them.

DEMAND → DEMANDED, DEMANDING

1 Cor	1:22	For Jews **d** signs and Greeks look

DEMANDED → DEMAND

Lk	12:20	this night your life will be **d** of you;
Lk	12:48	still more will be **d** of the person
Lk	22:31	behold Satan has **d** to sift all of you

DEMANDING → DEMAND

Ps	78:18	their hearts, **d** the food they craved.

DEMAS
Associate of Paul (Col 4:14; 2 Tm 4:10; Phlm 24).

DEMETRIUS

1 Mc	10: 2	When King **D** heard of it,
Acts	19:24	a silversmith named **D** who made
3 Jn	1:12	**D** receives a good report from all,

DEMOLISH

Nm	33:52	images, and **d** all their high places.

DEMON → DEMONIAC, DEMONIACS, DEMONIC, DEMONS

Tb	3: 8	the wicked **d** Asmodeus killed them
Tb	3:17	drive the wicked **d** Asmodeus
Tb	6: 8	a woman who is afflicted by a **d**
Tb	6:14	said that it was a **d** who killed them.
Tb	6:16	not give another thought to this **d**,
Tb	6:18	As soon as the **d** smells the odor
Tb	8: 3	The **d**, repelled by the odor
Mt	9:33	when the **d** was driven out the mute
Mt	11:18	they said, 'He is possessed by a **d**.'
Mt	15:22	My daughter is tormented by a **d**."
Mt	17:18	him and the **d** came out of him,
Mk	7:26	she begged him to drive the **d**
Mk	7:29	may go. The **d** has gone out of your
Mk	7:30	child lying in bed and the **d** gone.
Lk	4:33	man with the spirit of an unclean **d**,
Lk	4:35	the **d** threw the man down in front
Lk	7:33	you said, 'He is possessed by a **d**.'
Lk	8:29	by the **d** into deserted places.)
Lk	9:42	the **d** threw him to the ground
Lk	11:14	was driving out a **d** [that was] mute,
Jn	10:21	surely a **d** cannot open the eyes

DEMONIAC → DEMON

Mt	9:32	out, a **d** who could not speak was
Mt	12:22	brought to him a **d** who was blind

DEMONIACS → DEMON

Mt	8:28	two **d** who were coming
Mt	8:33	what had happened to the **d**.

DEMONIC → DEMON

Rv	16:14	These were **d** spirits who performed

DEMONS → DEMON

Dt	32:17	They offered sacrifice to **d**,
Bar	4: 7	with sacrifices to **d**, to no-gods;
Bar	4:35	**d** shall dwell in her from that time
Mt	7:22	Did we not drive out **d** in your
Mt	8:16	many who were possessed by **d**,
Mt	8:31	The **d** pleaded with him, "If you
Mt	9:34	"He drives out **d** by the prince of **d**."
Mt	10: 8	the dead, cleanse lepers, drive out **d**.
Mt	12:24	"This man drives out **d** only
Mt	12:24	power of Beelzebul, the prince of **d**."
Mt	12:27	And if I drive out **d** by Beelzebul,
Mt	12:28	the Spirit of God that I drive out **d**,
Mk	1:32	all who were ill or possessed by **d**.
Mk	1:34	and he drove out many **d**,
Mk	1:39	driving out **d** throughout the whole
Mk	3:15	and to have authority to drive out **d**.
Mk	3:22	"By the prince of **d** he drives out **d**."
Mk	6:13	They drove out many **d**, and they
Mk	9:38	we saw someone driving out **d**
Mk	16: 9	out of whom he had driven seven **d**.
Mk	16:17	in my name they will drive out **d**,
Lk	4:41	And **d** also came out from many,
Lk	8: 2	from whom seven **d** had gone out,
Lk	8:27	who was possessed by **d** met him.
Lk	8:30	because many **d** had entered him.
Lk	8:33	The **d** came out of the man
Lk	8:35	the man from whom the **d** had come
Lk	8:38	man from whom the **d** had come
Lk	9: 1	and authority over all **d** and to cure
Lk	9:49	we saw someone casting out **d**
Lk	10:17	even the **d** are subject to us because
Lk	11:15	the prince of **d**, he drives out **d**."
Lk	11:18	it is by Beelzebul that I drive out **d**.
Lk	11:19	I, then, drive out **d** by Beelzebul,
Lk	11:20	finger of God that [I] drive out **d**,
Lk	13:32	I cast out **d** and I perform healings
1 Cor	10:20	[they sacrifice] to **d**, not to God,
1 Cor	10:20	you to become participants with **d**.
1 Cor	10:21	of the Lord and also the cup of **d**.
Jas	2:19	Even the **d** believe that and tremble.
Rv	9:20	to give up the worship of **d**
Rv	18: 2	She has become a haunt for **d**.

DEMONSTRATION

1 Cor	2: 4	but with a **d** of spirit and power,

DEN

Is	11: 8	The baby shall play by the cobra's **d**,
Jer	7:11	become in your eyes a **d** of thieves?
Dn	6: 8	he shall be cast into a **d** of lions.
Dn	14:31	They threw Daniel into a lions' **d**,
Na	2:12	the young lions' **d**, Where the lion
Mt	21:13	but you are making it a **d** of thieves."
Mk	11:17	But you have made it a **d** of thieves."
Lk	19:46	but you have made it a **d** of thieves.' "

DENARIUS

Mk	12:15	testing me? Bring me a **d** to look at."
Lk	20:24	"Show me a **d**; whose image

DENIED → DENY

Mt	26:70	But he **d** it in front of everyone,
Jn	18:25	are you?" He **d** it and said, "I am not."
1 Tm	5: 8	family members has **d** the faith
Rv	3: 8	my word and have not **d** my name.

DENIES → DENY

Sir	14: 4	What he **d** himself he collects
Mt	10:33	But whoever **d** me before others,
Lk	12: 9	whoever **d** me before others will be
1 Jn	2:22	Whoever **d** that Jesus is the Christ.
1 Jn	2:22	Whoever **d** the Father and the Son,
1 Jn	2:23	No one who **d** the Son has

DENOUNCE → DENOUNCED

Nm	23: 7	for me on Jacob, come and **d** Israel."

DENOUNCED → DENOUNCE

Nm	23: 8	denounce whom the LORD has not **d**?

DENY → DENIED, DENIES, DENYING

Mt	16:24	to come after me must **d** himself,
Mt	26:34	crows, you will **d** me three times."
Mk	8:34	to come after me must **d** himself,
Lk	9:23	he must **d** himself and take up his
Acts	4:16	through them, and we cannot **d** it.
2 Tm	2:12	But if we **d** him he will **d** us.
2 Tm	2:13	faithful, for he cannot **d** himself.
Ti	1:16	God, but by their deeds they **d** him.
2 Pt	2: 1	even **d** the Master who ransomed
Jude	1: 4	and who **d** our only Master

DENYING → DENY

Is	59:13	Transgressing, and **d** the LORD,

DEPART → DEPARTED, DEPARTURE

Gn	49:10	The scepter shall never **d**
2 Sm	12:10	the sword shall never **d** from your
Is	52:11	D, **d**, come forth from there,
Mt	25:41	say to those on his left, 'D from me,
Phil	1:23	I long to **d** this life and be

DEPARTED → DEPART

1 Sm	16:14	spirit of the LORD had **d** from Saul,

DEPARTURE → DEPART

2 Tm	4: 6	and the time of my **d** is at hand.
2 Pt	1:15	remember these things after my **d**.

DEPEND → DEPENDS

Jdt	9:11	nor does your power **d**

DEPENDS → DEPEND

Rom	4:16	For this reason, it **d** on faith,
Rom	9:16	So it **d** not upon a person's will

DEPRAVED

2 Pt	2:10	follow the flesh with its **d** desire

DEPRIVE

1 Cor	7: 5	Do not **d** each other, except perhaps

DEPTH → DEEP

Rom	8:39	nor **d**, nor any other creature will be
Rom	11:33	the **d** of the riches and wisdom
Eph	3:18	breadth and length and height and **d**,

DEPTHS → DEEP

Ex	15: 5	they sank into the **d** like a stone.
Ps	86:13	rescued me from the **d** of Sheol.
Ps	130: 1	Out of the **d** I call to you, LORD;
Prv	9:18	in the **d** of the nether world are her

1 Cor	2:10	everything, even the **d** of God.

DESCENDANT → DESCENDANTS, DESCENDED, DESCENDING

Lv	21:21	No **d** of Aaron the priest who has
2 Tm	2: 8	raised from the dead, a **d** of David:

DESCENDANTS → DESCENDANT

Gn	9: 9	with you and your **d** after you
Gn	15:18	"To your **d** I give this land,
Ex	28:43	ordinance for him and for his **d**.
Dt	4:37	love of your fathers he chose their **d**
Ps	112: 2	Their **d** shall be mighty in the land,
Is	44: 3	and my blessing upon your **d**.
Lk	1:55	to Abraham and to his **d** forever."
Acts	2:30	set one of his **d** upon his throne,
Rom	9: 7	of Abraham because they are his **d**;

DESCENDED → DESCENDANT

Lk	3:22	the holy Spirit **d** upon him in bodily
Rom	1: 3	**d** from David according to the flesh,
Eph	4: 9	also **d** into the lower [regions]

DESCENDING → DESCENDANT

Mt	3:16	saw the Spirit of God **d** like a dove
Mk	1:10	the Spirit, like a dove, **d** upon him.
Jn	1:51	ascending and **d** on the Son of Man."

DESERT → DESERTED, DESERTS

Dt	32:10	a wasteland of howling **d**.
Ps	78:17	against the Most High in the **d**.
Ps	106:14	In the **d** they gave way to their
Is	35: 6	Streams will burst forth in the **d**,
Is	40: 3	out: In the **d** prepare the way

DESERTED → DESERT

Mk	8: 4	to satisfy them here in this **d** place?"
2 Tm	4:10	**d** me and went to Thessalonica,

DESERTS → DESERT

Is	51: 3	Her **d** he shall make like Eden,
Heb	11:38	They wandered about in **d**

DESERVE → DESERVED, DESERVES, DESERVING

1 Sm	26:16	you people **d** death because you
1 Kgs	2:26	Though you **d** to die, I will not put
Ps	94: 2	earth; give the proud what they **d**.
Jer	26:16	"This man does not **d** death; it is
Rom	1:32	all who practice such things **d** death,
Rv	2:23	give each of you what your works **d**.
Rv	16: 6	blood to drink; it is what they **d**."

DESERVED → DESERVE

Ezr	9:13	made less of our sinfulness than it **d**

DESERVES → DESERVE

Dt	25: 2	if the latter **d** stripes, the judge shall
Mt	26:66	They said in reply, "He **d** to die!"
Lk	10: 7	you, for the laborer **d** his payment.
Acts	26:31	is doing nothing [at all] that **d** death
1 Tm	5:18	threshing," and, "A worker **d** his pay."

DESERVING → DESERVE

Mk	14:64	They all condemned him as **d** to die.
Acts	23:29	law and not of any charge **d** death
Acts	25:25	that he had done nothing **d** death,

DESIRE → DESIRED, DESIRES

Dt	5:21	'You shall not **d** your neighbor's
1 Sm	9:20	Whom does Israel **d** ardently if not
2 Sm	23: 5	all my salvation and my every **d**?
Ps	21: 3	You have granted him his heart's **d**;
Ps	40:15	in disgrace those who **d** my ruin.
Ps	70: 3	in disgrace those who **d** my ruin.
Prv	10:24	but the **d** of the just will be granted.
Prv	11:23	The **d** of the just ends only in good;
Prv	24: 1	evil men, and **d** not to be with them;
Sir	6:37	and the wisdom you **d** he will grant.
Is	26: 8	and your title are the **d** of our souls;
Hos	6: 6	For it is love that I **d**, not sacrifice,
Mt	9:13	meaning of the words, 'I **d** mercy,
Mt	12: 7	knew what this meant, 'I **d** mercy,
Rom	10: 1	my heart's **d** and prayer to God
Heb	11:16	But now they **d** a better homeland,

Jas	1:14	is lured and enticed by his own **d**.
Jas	1:15	Then **d** conceives and brings forth

DESIRED →DESIRE

Eccl	2:10	that my eyes **d** did I deny them,
Lk	22:15	"I have eagerly **d** to eat this Passover

DESIRES →DESIRE

Ps	140: 9	do not grant the **d** of the wicked;
Sir	18:30	your lusts, but keep your **d** in check.
Lk	5:39	has been drinking old wine **d** new,
Jn	8:44	willingly carry out your father's **d**.
Rom	13:14	no provision for the **d** of the flesh.
Eph	2: 3	among them in the **d** of our flesh,
1 Tm	3: 1	the office of bishop **d** a noble task.
1 Tm	6: 9	into many foolish and harmful **d**,
2 Tm	3: 6	down by sins, led by various **d**,
2 Tm	4: 3	following their own **d** and insatiable
1 Pt	1:14	with the **d** of your former ignorance
1 Pt	2:11	worldly **d** that wage war against
1 Pt	4: 2	of one's life in the flesh on human **d**,
2 Pt	2:18	licentious **d** of the flesh those who

DESOLATE →DESOLATING, DESOLATION

Ex	23:29	else the land will become so **d**
1 Mc	1:39	sanctuary was as **d** as a wilderness;
1 Mc	4:38	They found the sanctuary **d**,
Mt	23:38	your house will be abandoned, **d**.
Rv	17:16	they will leave her **d** and naked;

DESOLATING →DESOLATE

Mt	24:15	you see the **d** abomination spoken
Mk	13:14	you see the **d** abomination standing

DESOLATION →DESOLATE

Na	2:11	Emptiness, **d**, waste; melting hearts
Lk	21:20	armies, know that its **d** is at hand.

DESPAIR →DESPAIRED

2 Cor	4: 8	perplexed, but not driven to **d**;

DESPAIRED →DESPAIR

2 Cor	1: 8	strength, so that we **d** even of life.

DESPISE →DESPISED, DESPISES, DESPISING

Prv	1: 7	wisdom and instruction fools **d**.
Prv	23:22	**d** not your mother when she is old.
Mt	6:24	be devoted to one and **d** the other.
Lk	16:13	be devoted to one and **d** the other.

DESPISED →DESPISE

2 Sm	6:16	the Lord, and she **d** him in her heart.
Ps	22: 7	by everyone, **d** by the people.
Ps	106:24	Next they **d** the beautiful land;
Prv	12: 8	but one with a warped mind is **d**.
Eccl	9:16	yet the wisdom of the poor man is **d**
Mal	1: 6	ask, "How have we **d** your name?"
1 Cor	1:28	chose the lowly and **d** of the world,

DESPISES →DESPISE

Prv	15:32	who rejects admonition **d** his own

DESPISING →DESPISE

Dt	31:20	**d** me and breaking my covenant;

DESTINE →DESTINED, DESTINY

Is	65:12	You I will **d** for the sword; you shall

DESTINED →DESTINE

Jer	43:11	with exile, everyone **d** for exile;
Lk	2:34	this child is **d** for the fall and rise
Acts	13:48	All who were **d** for eternal life came
Eph	1: 5	he **d** us for adoption to himself
Eph	1:11	**d** in accord with the purpose
1 Thes	3: 3	know that we are **d** for this.
1 Pt	1:11	to the sufferings **d** for Christ

DESTINY →DESTINE

Is	65:11	and fill cups of blended wine for **D**,

DESTITUTE

Prv	31: 8	dumb, and for the rights of the **d**;

DESTROY →DESTROYED, DESTROYER, DESTROYING, DESTROYS, DESTRUCTION, DESTRUCTIVE

Gn	6:13	So I will **d** them and all life

Gn	18:28	Will you **d** the whole city because
Dt	6:15	he **d** you from the face of the land;
2 Kgs	8:19	the Lord was unwilling to **d** Judah,
2 Kgs	13:23	He was unwilling to **d** them
1 Chr	21:15	also sent an angel to **d** Jerusalem;
Est	3: 6	he sought to **d** all the Jews,
Ps	145:20	love you, but all the wicked you **d**.
Is	65:25	None shall hurt or **d** on all my holy
Jer	1:10	to tear down, to **d** and to demolish,
Hos	11: 9	I will not **d** Ephraim again; For I am
Mt	2:13	to search for the child to **d** him."
Mt	10:28	of the one who can **d** both soul
Mk	14:58	'I will **d** this temple made with hands
Lk	4:34	Have you come to **d** us? I know
Jn	10:10	only to steal and slaughter and **d**;
1 Cor	1:19	"I will **d** the wisdom of the wise,
1 Cor	3:17	temple, God will **d** that person;
Jas	4:12	judge who is able to save or to **d**.
1 Jn	3: 8	God was revealed to **d** the works
Rv	11:18	and to **d** those who **d** the earth."

DESTROYED →DESTROY

Gn	9:11	again shall all bodily creatures be **d**
Gn	19:29	when God **d** the Cities of the Plain,
Dt	28:20	until your are speedily **d** and perish
Jos	24: 8	and I **d** them [the two kings
1 Mc	1:30	and **d** many of the people in Israel.
Ps	37:38	But all sinners will be **d**; the future
Dn	2:44	up a kingdom that shall never be **d**
Dn	6:27	his kingdom shall not be **d**, and his
Dn	14:28	"he has **d** Bel, killed the dragon,
Lk	17:27	and the flood came and **d** them all.
1 Cor	15:24	when he has **d** every sovereignty
1 Cor	15:26	The last enemy to be **d** is death,
2 Cor	4: 9	abandoned; struck down, but not **d**;
2 Cor	5: 1	should be **d**, we have a building
2 Pt	2:12	their destruction they will also be **d**,
Jude	1: 5	of Egypt later **d** those who did not

DESTROYER →DESTROY

Ex	12:23	not let the **d** come into your houses
Jer	6:26	For sudden upon us comes the **d**.
1 Cor	10:10	did, and suffered death by the **d**.
Heb	11:28	that the **D** of the firstborn might not

DESTROYING →DESTROY

Ps	106:23	to turn back his **d** anger.

DESTROYS →DESTROY

Prv	1:32	them, the smugness of fools **d** them.
1 Cor	3:17	If anyone **d** God's temple, God will

DESTRUCTION →DESTROY

Sir	36: 8	and your people's oppressors meet **d**.
Is	10:22	them will return; their **d** is decreed
Is	13: 6	as **d** from the Almighty it comes.
Is	14:23	I will sweep it with the broom of **d**,
Hb	2:17	the **d** of the beasts shall terrify you;
Mt	7:13	and the road broad that leads to **d**,
Rom	9:22	the vessels of wrath made for **d**?
1 Cor	5: 5	man to Satan for the **d** of his flesh,
Phil	1:28	This is proof to them of **d**,
Phil	3:19	Their end is **d**. Their God is their
1 Tm	6: 9	which plunge them into ruin and **d**.
2 Pt	2: 1	bringing swift **d** on themselves.
2 Pt	2: 3	been idle and their **d** does not sleep.
2 Pt	3: 7	of judgment and of **d** of the godless.
2 Pt	3:16	and unstable distort to their own **d**,
Rv	17: 8	from the abyss and is headed for **d**.
Rv	17:11	to the seven and is headed for **d**.

DESTRUCTIVE →DESTROY

2 Pt	2: 1	who will introduce **d** heresies

DETAIL

Heb	9: 5	not the time to speak of these in **d**.

DETERMINED

Ru	1:18	for she saw she was **d** to go
Jb	38: 5	Who **d** its size; do you know?
Jer	44:11	of Israel: I have **d** evil against you;
Dn	11:36	ready, for what is **d** must take place.

DEVIATED
1 Tm	1: 6	Some people have **d** from these

DEVIL
Wis	2:24	by the envy of the **d**, death entered
Mt	4: 1	the desert to be tempted by the **d**.
Mt	4: 5	the **d** took him to the holy city,
Mt	4: 8	the **d** took him up to a very high
Mt	4:11	Then the **d** left him and, behold,
Mt	13:39	the enemy who sows them is the **d**.
Mt	25:41	the eternal fire prepared for the **d**
Lk	4: 2	forty days, to be tempted by the **d**.
Lk	4: 3	The **d** said to him, "If you are
Lk	4: 6	The **d** said to him, "I shall give
Lk	4:13	the **d** had finished every temptation,
Lk	8:12	but the **d** comes and takes away
Jn	6:70	twelve? Yet is not one of you a **d**?"
Jn	8:44	You belong to your father the **d**
Jn	13: 2	The **d** had already induced Judas,
Acts	10:38	healing all those oppressed by the **d**,
Acts	13:10	"You son of the **d**, you enemy of all
Eph	4:27	and do not leave room for the **d**.
Eph	6:11	firm against the tactics of the **d**.
Heb	2:14	the power of death, that is, the **d**,
Jas	4: 7	Resist the **d**, and he will flee
1 Pt	5: 8	Your opponent the **d** is prowling
1 Jn	3: 8	Whoever sins belongs to the **d**, because the **d** has sinned
1 Jn	3: 8	to destroy the works of the **d**.
1 Jn	3:10	the children of the **d** are made plain;
Jude	1: 9	with the **d** in a dispute over the body
Rv	2:10	the **d** will throw some of you
Rv	12: 9	who is called the **D** and Satan,
Rv	12:12	for the **D** has come down to you
Rv	20: 2	serpent, which is the **D** or Satan,
Rv	20:10	The **D** who had led them astray was

DEVIOUS
Prv	2:15	ways are crooked, and **d** their paths;
Prv	14: 2	he who is **d** in his ways spurns him.

DEVISED
2 Pt	1:16	We did not follow cleverly **d** myths

DEVOID
Jude	1:19	on the natural plane, **d** of the Spirit.

DEVOTE → DEVOTED, DEVOTION
2 Chr	31: 4	they might **d** themselves entirely
Mi	4:13	You shall **d** their spoils to the LORD,
Ti	3: 8	in God be careful to **d** themselves
Ti	3:14	learn to **d** themselves to good works

DEVOTED → DEVOTE
1 Mc	4:42	blameless priests, **d** to the law;
Mt	6:24	or be **d** to one and despise the other.
Acts	2:42	They **d** themselves to the teaching
1 Cor	16:15	that they have **d** themselves

DEVOTION → DEVOTE
Jer	2: 2	I remember the **d** of your youth,

DEVOUR → DEVOURED, DEVOURING, DEVOURS
2 Chr	7:13	I command the locust to **d** the land,
Dn	14:32	so that they would **d** Daniel.
Hos	13: 8	I will **d** them on the spot like a lion,
Mk	12:40	They **d** the houses of widows and,
1 Pt	5: 8	lion looking for [someone] to **d**.
Rv	12: 4	to **d** her child when she gave birth.

DEVOURED → DEVOUR
Gn	37:20	could say that a wild beast **d** him.
Jer	30:16	Yet all who devour you shall be **d**,

DEVOURING → DEVOUR
Ps	18: 9	a **d** fire poured from his mouth;
Ps	50: 3	will not be silent! **D** fire precedes,
Gal	5:15	you go on biting and **d** one another,

DEVOURS → DEVOUR
2 Sm	11:25	for the sword **d** now here and now
Jer	46:10	The sword **d**, is sated,

DEVOUT
Is	57: 1	it to heart; **D** men are swept away,
Lk	2:25	This man was righteous and **d**,
Acts	10: 2	**d** and God-fearing along with his
Acts	10: 7	and a **d** soldier from his staff,
Acts	22:12	Ananias, a **d** observer of the law,

DEW
Gn	27:28	of the **d** of the heavens
Ex	16:13	In the morning a **d** lay all
Dt	32: 2	my discourse permeate like the **d**,
Jgs	6:37	If **d** comes on the fleece alone,
2 Sm	1:21	may there be neither **d** nor rain
Jb	38:28	or who has begotten the drops of **d**?
Prv	19:12	but his favor, like **d** on the grass.
Is	26:19	the dust. For your **d** is a **d** of light,
Dn	3:64	Every shower and **d**, bless the Lord;
Hos	6: 4	like the **d** that early passes away.
Hos	14: 6	I will be like the **d** of Israel: he shall
Hg	1:10	heavens withheld from you their **d**,
Zec	8:12	and the heavens shall give their **d**;

DIADEM → DIADEMS
Ex	39:30	The plate of the sacred **d** was made
Is	62: 3	LORD, a royal **d** held by your God.

DIADEMS → DIADEM
Rv	12: 3	and on its heads were seven **d**.
Rv	13: 1	on its horns were ten **d**, and on its
Rv	19:12	and on his head were many **d**.

DICTATED
Jer	36:18	"Jeremiah **d** all these words to me,"

DIE → DEAD
Gn	2:17	from it you are surely doomed to **d**."
Gn	3: 3	eat it or even touch it, lest you **d**.' "
Gn	3: 4	woman: "You certainly will not **d**!
Ex	11: 5	Every first-born in this land shall **d**,
Ex	14:11	bring us out here to **d** in the desert?
Nm	23:10	May I **d** the death of the just,
Ru	1:17	Wherever you **d** I will **d**, and there
Tb	3: 6	It is better for me to **d** than to live,
Jb	2: 9	your innocence? Curse God and **d**."
Jb	12: 2	folk, and with you wisdom shall **d**!
Ps	118:17	I shall not **d** but live and declare
Prv	5:23	He will **d** from lack of discipline,
Prv	10:21	many, but fools **d** for want of sense.
Prv	15:10	astray; he who hates reproof will **d**.
Prv	23:13	beat him with the rod, he will not **d**.
Eccl	3: 2	A time to be born, and a time to **d**;
Sir	8: 7	man dies; remember, we are all to **d**.
Sir	40:28	of a beggar, better to **d** than to beg;
Is	22:13	"Eat and drink, for tomorrow we **d**!"
Is	66:24	Their worm shall not **d**, nor their
Jer	31:30	his own fault only shall anyone **d**:
Ez	3:18	that wicked man shall **d** for his sin,
Ez	18: 4	mine; only the one who sins shall **d**.
Ez	18:31	Why should you **d**, O house
Ez	33: 8	wicked man that he shall surely **d**,
Jon	4: 3	it is better for me to **d** than to live."
Mt	26:35	"Even though I should have to **d**
Jn	6:50	so that one may eat it and not **d**.
Jn	8:21	for me, but you will **d** in your sin.
Jn	11:26	and believes in me will never **d**.
Jn	11:50	that one man should **d** instead
Jn	12:33	the kind of death he would **d**.
Jn	18:14	one man should **d** rather than
Jn	21:23	that that disciple would not **d**.
Rom	5: 7	with difficulty does one **d** for a just
Rom	14: 8	and if we **d**, we **d** for the Lord;
1 Cor	15:22	For just as in Adam all **d**, so too
1 Cor	15:32	eat and drink, for tomorrow we **d**."
Heb	9:27	that human beings **d** once,
Rv	9: 6	they will long to **d** but death will
Rv	14:13	Blessed are the dead who **d**

DIED → DEAD
Nm	14: 2	"Would that we had **d** in the land
Nm	17:14	to those who **d** because of Korah.
2 Sm	24:15	people from Dan to Beer-sheba **d**.]
1 Kgs	3:19	This woman's son **d** during
1 Chr	10:13	Thus Saul **d** because of his rebellion
Lk	16:22	When the poor man **d**, he was

Lk	16:22	The rich man also **d** and was buried,
Jn	6:58	your ancestors who ate and still **d**,
Rom	5: 6	yet **d** at the appointed time
Rom	5: 8	while we were still sinners Christ **d**
Rom	6: 2	How can we who **d** to sin yet live
Rom	6: 8	If, then, we have **d** with Christ,
Rom	6:10	death, he **d** to sin once and for all;
Rom	14: 9	For this is why Christ **d** and came
1 Cor	8:11	the brother for whom Christ **d**.
1 Cor	15: 3	that Christ **d** for our sins
2 Cor	5:15	He indeed **d** for all, so that those
Gal	2:19	For through the law I **d** to the law,
Col	2:20	If you **d** with Christ to the elemental
Col	3: 3	For you have **d**, and your life is
1 Thes	4:14	For if we believe that Jesus **d**
1 Thes	5:10	who **d** for us, so that whether we are
2 Tm	2:11	If we have **d** with him we shall
Heb	11:13	All these **d** in faith. They did not
Rv	8: 9	of the creatures living in the sea **d**,
Rv	8:11	Many people **d** from this water,
Rv	16: 3	every creature living in the sea **d**.

DIES →DEAD

Dt	25: 5	and one of them **d** without a son,
Eccl	2:16	the wise man **d** as well as the fool!
Eccl	3:19	the one **d** as well as the other.
Sir	14:18	blood: one **d** and another is born.
Mt	22:24	'If a man **d** without children,
Jn	12:24	of wheat falls to the ground and **d**,
Jn	12:24	but if it **d**, it produces much fruit.
Rom	7: 2	but if her husband **d**, she is released
1 Cor	7:39	But if her husband **d**, she is free
1 Cor	15:36	sow is not brought to life unless it **d**.

DIFFER →DIFFERENCE, DIFFERENT, DIFFERS

Rom	12: 6	Since we have gifts that **d** according

DIFFERENCE →DIFFER

Ez	22:26	nor teach the **d** between the unclean
Ez	44:23	to them the **d** between the clean

DIFFERENT →DIFFER

Lv	19:19	animals with others of a **d** species;
Lv	19:19	of yours with two **d** kinds of seed;
Lv	19:19	a garment woven with two **d** kinds
Nm	14:24	my servant Caleb has a **d** spirit
Sir	39: 1	How **d** the man who devotes
Dn	7: 3	beasts, each **d** from the others.
Dn	7: 7	fourth beast, **d** from all the others,
Dn	7:19	very terrible and **d** from the others,
Dn	7:23	on earth, **d** from all the others;
Dn	7:24	them, **D** from those before him,
2 Cor	11: 4	if you receive a **d** spirit from the one
2 Cor	11: 4	or a **d** gospel from the one you
Gal	1: 6	[the] grace [of Christ] for a **d** gospel

DIFFERS →DIFFER

1 Cor	15:41	For star **d** from star in brightness.

DIFFICULT

Ez	3: 5	Not to a people with **d** speech
Dn	2:11	What you demand, O king, is too **d**;

DIG →DIGS, DUG

Ez	8: 8	man, he ordered, **d** through the wall.

DIGNITY

Est	4:14	this that you obtained the royal **d**?"
Prv	31:25	She is clothed with strength and **d**,
1 Tm	2: 2	tranquil life in all devotion and **d**.

DIGS →DIG

Ex	21:33	"When a man uncovers or **d** a cistern
Prv	26:27	He who **d** a pit falls into it;
Eccl	10: 8	He who **d** a pit may fall into it,
Sir	27:26	As he who **d** a pit falls into it,

DILIGENCE →DILIGENT

Rom	12: 8	if one is over others, with **d**; if one

DILIGENT →DILIGENCE, DILIGENTLY

Prv	10: 4	but the hand of the **d** enriches.
Prv	12:24	The **d** hand will govern,
Prv	12:27	but the wealth of the **d** man is great.

Prv	13: 4	but the **d** soul is amply satisfied.
Prv	21: 5	The plans of the **d** are sure of profit,

DILIGENTLY →DILIGENT

Mt	2: 8	said, "Go and search **d** for the child.

DIM

Gn	48:10	(Now Israel's eyes were **d** from age,
Lam	5:17	are sick, at this our eyes grow **d**:

DINAH

Only daughter of Jacob, by Leah (Gn 30:21; 46:15). Raped by Shechem; avenged by Simeon and Levi (Gn 34).

DINE →DINNER

Lk	11:37	a Pharisee invited him to **d** at his

DINNER →DINE

Lk	14:12	"When you hold a lunch or a **d**,

DIONYSIUS

Acts	17:34	Among them were **D**, a member

DIONYSUS

2 Mc	6: 7	the festival of **D** was celebrated,
2 Mc	14:33	erect here a splendid temple to **D**."

DIOTREPHES

3 Jn	1: 9	but **D**, who loves to dominate,

DIP →DIPPED

Lk	16:24	Send Lazarus to **d** the tip of his

DIPPED →DIP

Gn	37:31	a goat, **d** the tunic in its blood.
Mt	26:23	"He who has **d** his hand into the dish
Rv	19:13	a cloak that had been **d** in blood,

DIRECT →DIRECTED, DIRECTIONS, DIRECTS

Jdt	12: 8	to **d** her way for the triumph of his
Jer	10:23	nor is it for him to **d** his step.
2 Thes	3: 5	May the Lord **d** your hearts

DIRECTED →DIRECT

Is	40:13	Who has **d** the spirit of the LORD,
Acts	7:44	the One who spoke to Moses **d** him
Ti	1: 5	presbyters in every town, as I **d** you,

DIRECTIONS →DIRECT

Ez	1:17	in any of the four **d** they faced,
Ez	10:11	their four **d** without veering as they

DIRECTS →DIRECT

Prv	16: 9	his course, but the LORD **d** his steps.

DIRT

2 Sm	1: 2	his clothes torn and **d** on his head.
1 Pt	3:21	It is not a removal of **d**

DISAGREEMENT

Acts	15:39	So sharp was their **d** that they

DISAPPEARING

Heb	8:13	and has grown old is close to **d**.

DISAPPOINT →DISAPPOINTED

Rom	5: 5	and hope does not **d**,

DISAPPOINTED →DISAPPOINT

Sir	2:10	hoped in the LORD and been **d**?

DISASTER

Ez	7: 5	Thus says the Lord GOD: **D** upon **d**!

DISCERN →DISCERNING, DISCERNMENT

Jb	6:30	or cannot my taste **d** falsehood?

DISCERNING →DISCERN

Gn	41:33	Pharaoh seek out a wise and **d** man
Gn	41:39	one can be as wise and **d** as you are.
1 Cor	11:29	eats and drinks without **d** the body,

DISCERNMENT →DISCERN

1 Cor	12:10	to another **d** of spirits; to another

DISCIPLE →DISCIPLES, DISCIPLES'

Mt	10:24	No **d** is above his teacher, no slave
Lk	14:26	his own life, he cannot be my **d**.
Lk	14:27	and come after me cannot be my **d**.
Lk	14:33	all his possessions cannot be my **d**.

Jn	9:28	him and said, "You are that man's **d**;
Jn	19:26	and the **d** there whom he loved,
Jn	19:38	secretly a **d** of Jesus for fear
Jn	20: 2	to the other **d** whom Jesus loved,
Jn	21: 7	So the **d** whom Jesus loved said
Jn	21:20	saw the **d** following whom Jesus
Jn	21:24	It is this **d** who testifies to these
Acts	9:10	There was a **d** in Damascus named
Acts	16: 1	there was a **d** named Timothy,

DISCIPLES → DISCIPLE

Is	8:16	sealed instruction kept among my **d**.
Mt	9:10	came and sat with Jesus and his **d**.
Mt	10: 1	he summoned his twelve **d** and gave
Mt	12: 2	your **d** are doing what is unlawful
Mt	26:56	Then all the **d** left him and fled.
Mt	28:19	and make **d** of all nations,
Mk	3: 7	withdrew toward the sea with his **d**.
Mk	6:29	When his **d** heard about it,
Mk	7: 5	him, "Why do your **d** not follow
Mk	9:18	I asked your **d** to drive it out,
Mk	14:14	I may eat the Passover with my **d**?" '
Lk	6:13	day came, he called his **d** to himself,
Lk	11: 1	us to pray just as John taught his **d**."
Lk	22:45	from prayer and returned to his **d**,
Jn	2:11	and his **d** began to believe in him.
Jn	6:66	many [of] his **d** returned to their
Jn	8:31	in my word, you will truly be my **d**,
Jn	9:28	man's disciple; we are **d** of Moses!
Jn	12:16	His **d** did not understand this at first,
Jn	13:35	all will know that you are my **d**,
Jn	15: 8	bear much fruit and become my **d**.
Jn	18:17	"You are not one of this man's **d**,
Jn	20:20	The **d** rejoiced when they saw
Jn	20:30	of [his] **d** that are not written in this
Acts	6: 1	as the number of **d** continued
Acts	9: 1	murderous threats against the **d**
Acts	11:26	the **d** were first called Christians.
Acts	13:52	The **d** were filled with joy
Acts	14:22	strengthened the spirits of the **d**
Acts	18:23	bringing strength to all the **d**.

DISCIPLES' → DISCIPLE

Jn	13: 5	and began to wash the **d** feet

DISCIPLINARIAN → DISCIPLINE

Gal	3:24	the law was our **d** for Christ, that we
Gal	3:25	come, we are no longer under a **d**.

DISCIPLINE → DISCIPLINARIAN, DISCIPLINED, DISCIPLINES

Dt	4:36	he let you hear his voice to **d** you;
Dt	11: 2	who must now understand the **d**
Prv	3:11	The **d** of the LORD, my son,
Prv	5:23	He will die from lack of **d**,
Prv	6:23	a way to life are the reproofs of **d**;
Prv	22:15	the rod of **d** will drive it far
Sir	6:18	son, from your youth embrace **d**;
Heb	12: 5	son, do not disdain the **d** of the Lord
Heb	12: 7	Endure your trials as "**d**"; God treats
Heb	12: 7	is there whom his father does not **d**?
Heb	12: 8	If you are without **d**, in which all
Heb	12:11	all **d** seems a cause not for joy

DISCIPLINED → DISCIPLINE

1 Cor	11:32	we are being **d** so that we may not
Heb	12:10	They **d** us for a short time as

DISCIPLINES → DISCIPLINE

Dt	8: 5	God, **d** you even as a man **d** his son.
2 Mc	6:16	Although he **d** us with misfortunes,
Sir	30: 2	He who **d** his son will benefit
Heb	12: 6	for whom the Lord loves, he **d**;

DISCLOSE → DISCLOSED

Prv	25: 9	but another man's secret do not **d**;
1 Cor	3:13	come to light, for the Day will **d** it.

DISCLOSED → DISCLOSE

1 Cor	14:25	the secrets of his heart will be **d**,

DISCORD

Prv	6:14	is always plotting evil, sows **d**.
Prv	6:19	and he who sows **d** among brothers.

Sir	28: 9	and sows **d** among those at peace.

DISCOURAGE → DISCOURAGED

Nm	32: 7	Why do you wish to **d** the Israelites

DISCOURAGED → DISCOURAGE

Nm	32: 9	so **d** the Israelites that they would
2 Sm	17: 2	upon him when he is weary and **d**,
1 Mc	4:27	he heard it he was disturbed and **d**,
2 Cor	4: 1	the mercy shown us, we are not **d**.
2 Cor	4:16	Therefore, we are not **d**;

DISCOURSE

Sir	6:35	Be eager to hear every godly **d**;
Sir	8: 8	Spurn not the **d** of the wise,

DISCREDITED

Ti	2: 5	that the word of God may not be **d**.

DISCUSSED → DISCUSSIONS

Lk	6:11	**d** together what they might do

DISCUSSING → DISCUSSIONS

Lk	24:17	"What are you **d** as you walk along?"

DISCUSSIONS → DISCUSSED, DISCUSSING

Acts	18:19	and held **d** with the Jews.

DISEASE → DISEASES

2 Chr	16:12	Asa contracted a serious **d** in his
2 Chr	21:15	bowels issue forth because of the **d**,
Ps	106:15	and sent among them a wasting **d**.
Mt	4:23	curing every **d** and illness among
Mt	9:35	and curing every **d** and illness.
Mt	10: 1	to cure every **d** and every illness.

DISEASES → DISEASE

Ex	15:26	any of the **d** with which I afflicted
Dt	7:15	of the malignant **d** that you know
Dt	28:60	afflict you with all the **d** of Egypt
Mt	4:24	all who were sick with various **d**
Mt	8:17	away our infirmities and bore our **d**."
Mk	1:34	many who were sick with various **d**,
Mk	3:10	those who had **d** were pressing
Lk	4:40	sick with various **d** brought them
Lk	6:18	hear him and to be healed of their **d**;
Lk	7:21	that time he cured many of their **d**,
Lk	9: 1	over all demons and to cure **d**,
Lk	9: 6	news and curing **d** everywhere.
Acts	19:12	their **d** left them and the evil spirits

DISGRACE → DISGRACED

Jdt	14:18	Hebrew woman has brought **d**
1 Mc	4:58	the **d** of the Gentiles was removed.
Ps	44:16	All day long my **d** is before me;
Prv	6:33	and his **d** will not be wiped away;
Prv	11: 2	When pride comes, **d** comes;
Prv	18: 3	contempt, and with **d** comes scorn.
Sir	3:11	**d** for her children, a mother's shame.
Is	4: 1	be given us, put an end to our **d**!"
Lam	5: 1	has befallen us, look, and see our **d**:
Lk	1:25	fit to take away my **d** before others."
1 Tm	3: 7	so that he may not fall into **d**,

DISGRACED → DISGRACE

Ps	71:24	ruin will have been shamed and **d**.

DISGUISE → DISGUISED

1 Kgs	14: 2	and **d** yourself so that none will

DISGUISED → DISGUISE

1 Sm	28: 8	So he **d** himself, putting on other

DISGUSTED

Ez	23:17	by them, she became **d** with them.

DISH

2 Kgs	21:13	Jerusalem clean as one wipes a **d**,
Prv	19:24	sluggard loses his hand in the **d**;
Lk	11:39	the outside of the cup and the **d**,

DISHEARTENED → HEART

Ez	13:22	Because you have **d** the upright man

DISHONEST

Ex	18:21	trustworthy men who hate **d** gain,
Lk	16: 8	master commended that **d** steward

Lk 16:10 the person who is **d** in very small matters is also **d** in great ones.

DISHONOR → DISHONORED, DISHONORS
1 Mc 1:40 Her **d** was as great as her glory had
Lam 2: 2 He has brought to the ground in **d**
Jn 8:49 I honor my Father, but you **d** me.
Acts 5:41 worthy to suffer **d** for the sake
Rom 2:23 do you **d** God by breaking the law?
2 Cor 6: 8 through glory and **d**,

DISHONORED → DISHONOR
Jas 2: 6 But you **d** the poor person. Are not

DISHONORS → DISHONOR
Dt 27:16 'Cursed be he who **d** his father or his
Sir 26:26 And the man who **d** his marriage bed

DISLIKED
Sir 42: 9 when she is married, lest she be **d**;

DISMAYED
Dt 31: 8 forsake you. So do not fear or be **d**."
Jos 1: 9 Do not fear nor be **d**, for the LORD,
Jos 8: 1 to Joshua, "Do not be afraid or **d**.
1 Sm 17:11 were **d** and terror-stricken.

DISMISS
Sir 7:19 **D** not a sensible wife; a gracious

DISOBEDIENCE → DISOBEY
Rom 5:19 just as through the **d** of one person
Rom 11:30 received mercy because of their **d**,
Rom 11:32 For God delivered all to **d**, that he
2 Cor 10: 6 and we are ready to punish every **d**,
Heb 2: 2 and **d** received its just recompense,
Heb 4: 6 news did not enter because of **d**,
Heb 4:11 fall after the same example of **d**.

DISOBEDIENT → DISOBEY
Bar 1:19 day, we have been **d** to the LORD,
Lk 1:17 the **d** to the understanding
Acts 26:19 I was not **d** to the heavenly vision.
Rom 10:21 long I stretched out my hands to a **d**
Eph 2: 2 spirit that is now at work in the **d**.
Eph 5: 6 wrath of God is coming upon the **d**.
Col 3: 6 of God is coming [upon the **d**].
2 Tm 3: 2 haughty, abusive, **d** to their parents,
Ti 1:16 They are vile and **d** and unqualified
Ti 3: 3 we ourselves were once foolish, **d**,
Heb 3:18 his rest," if not to those who were **d**?
Heb 11:31 the harlot did not perish with the **d**,

DISOBEY → DISOBEDIENCE, DISOBEDIENT, DISOBEYING, DISOBEYS
Est 3: 3 "Why do you **d** the king's order?"

DISOBEYING → DISOBEY
Lv 26:27 you still persist in **d** and defying me,
1 Pt 2: 8 They stumble by **d** the word, as is

DISOBEYS → DISOBEY
Jn 3:36 whoever **d** the Son will not see life,

DISORDER
1 Cor 14:33 since he is not the God of **d**
2 Cor 12:20 slander, gossip, conceit, and **d**.
Jas 3:16 there is **d** and every foul practice.

DISPERSE → DISPERSED, DISPERSION
Ps 106:27 the nations, **d** them in foreign lands.
Ez 12:15 when I **d** them among the nations

DISPERSED → DISPERSE
Is 11:12 The **d** of Judah he shall assemble
Jn 11:52 into one the **d** children of God.

DISPERSION → DISPERSE
Jn 7:35 not going to the **d** among the Greeks
Jas 1: 1 Christ, to the twelve tribes in the **d**,
1 Pt 1: 1 sojourners of the **d** in Pontus,

DISPLAY → DISPLAYED
Ez 39:21 Thus I will **d** my glory among
1 Tm 1:16 Christ Jesus might **d** all his patience

DISPLAYED → DISPLAY
Ps 78:43 When he **d** his wonders in Egypt,

DISPLEASED → DISPLEASING
2 Sm 11:27 the LORD was **d** with what David had
Prv 24:18 Lest the LORD see it, be **d** with you,

DISPLEASING → DISPLEASED
Jon 4: 1 But this was greatly **d** to Jonah,

DISPOSSESS → DISPOSSESSED
Dt 11:23 and you will **d** nations greater

DISPOSSESSED → DISPOSSESS
Ob 1:17 possession of those that **d** them.

DISPUTES
Prv 18:18 The lot puts an end to **d**, and is

DISQUALIFIED → DISQUALIFY
1 Cor 9:27 to others, I myself should be **d**.

DISQUALIFY → DISQUALIFIED
Col 2:18 Let no one **d** you,

DISREGARDED
Is 40:27 LORD, and my right is **d** by my God"?

DISREPUTE
1 Cor 4:10 you are held in honor, but we in **d**.

DISSENSION → DISSENSIONS
Acts 15: 2 Because there arose no little **d**

DISSENSIONS → DISSENSION
Rom 16:17 to watch out for those who create **d**
Gal 5:20 fury, acts of selfishness, **d**, factions,

DISSOLVED
2 Pt 3:10 and the elements will be **d** by fire,

DISTANCE → DISTANT
Ex 2: 4 sister stationed herself at a **d** to find
Ex 20:21 Still the people remained at a **d**,
Dt 32:52 may indeed view the land at a **d**,
Mk 14:54 at a **d** into the high priest's courtyard
Mk 15:40 also women looking on from a **d**.

DISTANT → DISTANCE
Jer 4:16 are coming from the **d** land,

DISTINCTION → DISTINCTIONS
Ex 8:19 will make this **d** between my people
Acts 15: 9 He made no **d** between us and them,
Rom 3:22 all who believe. For there is no **d**;
Rom 10:12 For there is no **d** between Jew

DISTINCTIONS → DISTINCTION
Jas 2: 4 you not made **d** among yourselves

DISTINGUISH → DISTINGUISHED
Lv 10:10 be able to **d** between what is sacred

DISTINGUISHED → DISTINGUISH
Lk 14: 8 A more **d** guest than you may have

DISTRESS → DISTRESSED
Dt 4:30 In your **d**, when all these things
Jgs 2:15 would do, till they were in great **d**.
2 Sm 22: 7 In my **d** I called upon the LORD
2 Chr 15: 4 in their **d** they turned to the LORD,
Neh 9:37 as they please. We are in great **d**!"
Ps 18: 7 In my **d** I called out: LORD! I cried
Ps 25:17 of my heart; bring me out of my **d**.
Ps 81: 8 In **d** you called and I rescued you;
Ps 107: 6 In their **d** they cried to the LORD,
Ps 120: 1 answered me when I called in my **d**:
Prv 1:27 when **d** and anguish befall you.
Is 25: 4 a refuge to the needy in **d**;
Is 37: 3 'This is a day of **d**, of rebuke,
Jer 30: 7 At time of **d** for Jacob, though he
Ob 1:12 Speak not haughtily on the day of **d**!
Jon 2: 3 Out of my **d** I called to the LORD,
Rom 2: 9 and **d** will come upon every human
Rom 8:35 Will anguish, or **d**, or persecution,

DISTRESSED → DISTRESS
Mk 14:33 and began to be troubled and **d**.

DISTRIBUTE → DISTRIBUTED, DISTRIBUTION
Mk | 8: 6 | and gave them to his disciples to d,
Lk | 18:22 | that you have and d it to the poor,

DISTRIBUTED → DISTRIBUTE
Acts | 4:35 | they were d to each according

DISTRIBUTION → DISTRIBUTE
Acts | 6: 1 | were being neglected in the daily d.

DISTURBANCE → DISTURBED
Acts | 19:23 | that time a serious d broke
Acts | 24:18 | in the temple without a crowd or d.

DISTURBED → DISTURBANCE
Acts | 15:24 | teachings and d your peace of mind,

DIVIDE → DIVIDED, DIVIDING, DIVISION, DIVISIONS
Ps | 22:19 | they d my garments among them;
Is | 53:12 | and he shall d the spoils

DIVIDED → DIVIDE
Gn | 10:25 | for in his time the world was d;
Ex | 14:21 | When the water was thus d,
Neh | 9:11 | The sea you d before them, on dry
Is | 63:12 | Who d the waters before them,
Dn | 2:41 | mean that it shall be a d kingdom,
Dn | 5:28 | your kingdom has been d and given
Mt | 12:25 | "Every kingdom d against itself will
Mk | 6:41 | also d the two fish among them all.
Mk | 15:24 | d his garments by casting lots
Lk | 11:18 | And if Satan is d against himself,
1 Cor | 1:13 | Is Christ d? Was Paul crucified

DIVIDING → DIVIDE
Eph | 2:14 | broke down the d wall of enmity,

DIVINATION → DIVINE
Gn | 44: 5 | drinks and which he uses for d.
1 Sm | 15:23 | For a sin like d is rebellion,
2 Kgs | 17:17 | practiced fortune-telling and d,
Sir | 34: 5 | D, omens and dreams all are unreal;
Ez | 13:23 | see false visions and practice d,

DIVINE → DIVINATION, DIVINERS
Ex | 31: 3 | I have filled him with a d spirit
Ps | 82: 1 | God rises in the d council,
2 Pt | 1: 3 | His d power has bestowed on us
2 Pt | 1: 4 | may come to share in the d nature,

DIVINERS → DIVINE
Is | 44:25 | who make fools of d; I turn wise
Jer | 29: 8 | prophets and d who are among you;
Mi | 3: 7 | and the d confounded; They shall
Zec | 10: 2 | nonsense, the d have false visions:

DIVISION → DIVIDE
Lk | 12:51 | earth? No, I tell you, but rather d.
Jn | 7:43 | So a d occurred in the crowd

DIVISIONS → DIVIDE
1 Cor | 1:10 | and that there be no d among you,
1 Cor | 11:18 | as a church there are d among you,
Jude | 1:19 | These are the ones who cause d;

DIVORCE → DIVORCED, DIVORCES
Dt | 22:19 | he may not d her as long as he lives.
Dt | 22:29 | he may not d her as long as he lives.
Dt | 24: 1 | therefore he writes out a bill of d
Dt | 24: 3 | by handing her a written bill of d;
Is | 50: 1 | Where is the bill of d with which I
Jer | 3: 8 | her away and gave her a bill of d,
Mal | 2:16 | For I hate d, says the LORD, the God
Mt | 5:31 | his wife must give her a bill of d.'
Mt | 19: 3 | a man to d his wife for any cause
Mt | 19: 7 | the man give the woman a bill of d
Mt | 19: 8 | Moses allowed you to d your wives,
Mk | 10: 2 | lawful for a husband to d his wife?"
Mk | 10: 4 | permitted him to write a bill of d
1 Cor | 7:11 | a husband should not d his wife.
1 Cor | 7:12 | living with him, he should not d her;
1 Cor | 7:13 | her, she should not d her husband.

DIVORCED → DIVORCE
Lv | 21: 7 | nor a woman who has been d by her

Lv | 21:14 | or a woman who has been d
Lv | 22:13 | daughter is widowed or d and,
Nm | 30:10 | vow of a widow or of a d woman,
Ez | 44:22 | wives either widows or d women,
Mt | 5:32 | marries a d woman commits
Lk | 16:18 | and the one who marries a woman d

DIVORCES → DIVORCE
Mt | 5:31 | 'Whoever d his wife must give her
Mt | 5:32 | you, whoever d his wife (unless
Mt | 19: 9 | you, whoever d his wife (unless
Mk | 10:11 | "Whoever d his wife and marries
Mk | 10:12 | if she d her husband and marries
Lk | 16:18 | "Everyone who d his wife

DO → DEED, DEEDS, DOER, DOERS, DOES, DOING, DONE, EVILDOERS, WRONGDOER, WRONGDOING
Gn | 4: 7 | If you d well, you can hold up your
Gn | 18:25 | Far be it from you to d such a thing,
Ex | 19: 8 | the LORD has said, we will d."
Ps | 37: 3 | Trust in the LORD and d good
Ps | 143:10 | Teach me to d your will, for you are
Sir | 12: 1 | If you d good, know for whom you
Sir | 12: 1 | for what he hates he does not d.
Jer | 22: 3 | the LORD: D what is right and just.
Mt | 23: 3 | d and observe all things whatsoever
Mt | 23: 3 | you, but d not follow their example.
Mt | 23: 3 | they preach but they d not practice.
Mk | 3: 4 | "Is it lawful to d good on the sabbath rather than to d evil,
Lk | 6:31 | D to others as you would have them d
Jn | 6:28 | "What can we d to accomplish
Jn | 7:17 | to d his will shall know whether my
Acts | 16:30 | "Sirs, what must I d to be saved?"
Acts | 22:10 | I asked, 'What shall I d, sir?'
Rom | 7:15 | What I d, I d not understand. For I d not d what I want, but I d
Col | 3:17 | d everything in the name
1 Pt | 3:11 | must turn from evil and d good,

DOCTRINE → DOCTRINES
2 Tm | 4: 3 | people will not tolerate sound d but,
Ti | 1: 9 | be able both to exhort with sound d
Ti | 2: 1 | say what is consistent with sound d,
Ti | 2:10 | as to adorn the d of God our savior

DOCTRINES → DOCTRINE
Mt | 15: 9 | teaching as d human precepts.' "
Mk | 7: 7 | teaching as d human precepts.'
1 Tm | 1: 3 | certain people not to teach false d

DOE
Prv | 5:19 | your lovely hind, your graceful d.

DOEG
Edomite; Saul's chief shepherd; murdered 85 priests at Nob (1 Sm 21:8; 22:6-23; Ps 52).

DOER → DO
Jas | 4:11 | law, you are not a d of the law

DOERS → DO
Jas | 1:22 | Be d of the word and not hearers

DOES → DO
Ps | 135: 6 | wishes he d in heaven and on earth,
Eccl | 3:14 | whatever God d will endure forever;
Zep | 3: 5 | within her is just, who d no wrong;
Mk | 3:35 | [For] whoever d the will of God is
Jn | 5:19 | for what he d, his son will do also.
Rom | 10: 5 | "The one who d these things will live
3 Jn | 1:11 | Whoever d what is good is of God;
3 Jn | 1:11 | whoever d what is evil has never

DOG → DOGS
Jgs | 7: 5 | up the water as a d does with its
1 Sm | 17:43 | "Am I a d that you come against me
1 Sm | 24:15 | pursuing? A dead d, or a single flea!
Prv | 26:11 | As the d returns to his vomit,
Eccl | 9: 4 | a live d is better off than a dead
2 Pt | 2:22 | "The d returns to its own vomit,"

DOGS → DOG
Ex | 22:30 | you shall not eat; throw it to the d.

1 Kgs	21:19	the **d** shall lick up your blood, too.' "
2 Kgs	9:10	**D** shall devour Jezebel
Ps	22:17	Many **d** surround me; a pack
Is	56:11	They are relentless **d**, they know not
Mt	7: 6	"Do not give what is holy to **d**,
Mt	15:26	of the children and throw it to the **d**."
Phil	3: 2	Beware of the **d**!
Rv	22:15	Outside are the **d**, the sorcerers,

DOING → DO
Mk	11:28	authority are you **d** these things?
1 Pt	3:17	For it is better to suffer for **d** good,

DOME
Gn	1: 6	"Let there be a **d** in the middle

DOMESTIC
Gn	7:14	every kind of **d** animal, every kind

DOMINATED → DOMINION
1 Cor	6:12	me," but I will not let myself be **d**

DOMINION → DOMINATED, DOMINIONS
Gn	1:26	Let them have **d** over the fish
Jb	25: 2	**D** and awesomeness are his
Dn	7:14	He received **d**, glory, and kingship;
Dn	7:14	serve him. His **d** is an everlasting **d**
Zec	9:10	His **d** shall be from sea to sea,
Eph	1:21	and **d**, and every name that is named

DOMINIONS → DOMINION
Dn	7:27	all **d** shall serve and obey him."
Col	1:16	invisible, whether thrones or **d**

DONE → DO
Gn	4:10	Lord then said: "What have you **d**!
Est	6: 6	him, "What should be **d** for the man
Jb	21:31	what he has **d** who will repay him?
Ps	71:19	heaven. You have **d** great things;
Ps	98: 1	Lord, who has **d** marvelous deeds,
Ps	105: 5	Recall the wondrous deeds he has **d**,
Eccl	1: 9	what has been **d**, that will be **d**.
Jer	50:29	her deeds; as she has **d**, do to her,
Jl	2:21	for the Lord has **d** great things.
Ob	1:15	As you have **d**, so shall it be **d**
Mi	6: 3	O my people, what have I **d** to you,
Mt	6:10	come, your will be **d**, on earth as
Mt	26:42	my drinking it, your will be **d**!"
Lk	19:17	He replied, 'Well **d**, good servant!
Lk	23:41	but this man has **d** nothing criminal."
Rv	16:17	from the throne, saying, "It is **d**."

DOOM → DOOMED
Dt	32:35	and their **d** is rushing upon them!
Ps	81:16	tremble, their **d** sealed forever.

DOOMED → DOOM
Ps	79:11	by your great power free those **d**
Ps	102:21	prisoners, to release those **d** to die."
Zec	14:11	Never again shall she be **d**;

DOOR → DOORPOST, DOORPOSTS, DOORS
Gn	4: 7	not, sin is a demon lurking at the **d**:
Gn	19: 9	in closer to break down the **d**.
Dt	15:17	thrust it through his ear into the **d**,
Jgs	19:22	the house and beat on the **d**.
Prv	5: 8	approach not the **d** of her house,
Prv	9:14	She sits at the **d** of her house
Prv	26:14	The **d** turns on its hinges,
Dn	14:11	shut the **d** and seal it with your ring.
Mt	6: 6	close the **d**, and pray to your Father
Mt	7: 7	and the **d** will be opened to you.
Acts	14:27	how he had opened the **d** of faith
1 Cor	16: 9	because a **d** has opened for me wide
2 Cor	2:12	although a **d** was opened for me
Col	4: 3	that God may open a **d** to us
Rv	3: 8	I have left an open **d** before you,
Rv	3:20	" '"Behold, I stand at the **d** and knock.
Rv	3:20	hears my voice and opens the **d**,
Rv	4: 1	had a vision of an open **d** to heaven,

DOORPOST → DOOR
Ex	21: 6	at the door or **d**, he shall pierce his

DOORPOSTS → DOOR
Ex	12: 7	apply it to the two **d** and the lintel

DOORS → DOOR
Jgs	16: 3	seized the **d** of the city gate
1 Kgs	6:31	**d** of olive wood were made;
Neh	3: 1	They timbered it and set up its **d**,
Jn	20:26	came, although the **d** were locked,
Acts	5:19	the Lord opened the **d** of the prison,
Acts	16:26	all the **d** flew open, and the chains

DORCAS → =TABITHA
Disciple, also known as Tabitha, whom Peter raised from the dead (Acts 9:36-43).

DOUBLE → DOUBLE-TONGUED
Dt	21:17	giving him a **d** share of whatever he
1 Sm	1: 5	a **d** portion to Hannah because he
2 Kgs	2: 9	"May I receive a **d** portion of your
Is	40: 2	hand of the Lord **d** for all her sins.
Is	61: 7	Since their shame was **d**
Is	61: 7	They shall have a **d** inheritance
1 Tm	5:17	who preside well deserve **d** honor,
Rv	18: 6	Pay her back **d** for her deeds.

DOUBLE-TONGUED → DOUBLE, TONGUE
Sir	28:13	Cursed be gossips and the **d**,

DOUBT → DOUBTED, DOUBTING, DOUBTS
Mt	14:31	"O you of little faith, why did you **d**?"
Mk	11:23	sea,' and does not **d** in his heart

DOUBTED → DOUBT
Mt	28:17	him, they worshiped, but they **d**.

DOUBTING → DOUBT
Jas	1: 6	not **d**, for the one who doubts is like

DOUBTS → DOUBT
Rom	14:23	whoever has **d** is condemned if he
Jas	1: 6	for the one who **d** is like a wave

DOUGH
Ex	12:39	Since the **d** they had brought
1 Cor	5: 6	that a little yeast leavens all the **d**?
Gal	5: 9	yeast leavens the whole batch of **d**.

DOVE → DOVES
Gn	8: 8	Then he sent out a **d**, to see
Ps	55: 7	I say, "If only I had wings like a **d**
Song	5: 2	my beloved, my **d**, my perfect one!
Hos	7:11	Ephraim is like a **d**,
Mk	1:10	like a **d**, descending upon him.

DOVES → DOVE
Song	4: 1	Your eyes are **d** behind your veil.
Is	59:11	like **d** we moan without ceasing.
Ez	7:16	to the mountains like the **d**
Mt	10:16	shrewd as serpents and simple as **d**.
Mt	21:12	seats of those who were selling **d**

DOWN → DOWNCAST, DOWNFALL
Gn	11: 5	The Lord came **d** to see the city
Gn	18:21	that I must go **d** and see whether
Gn	46: 3	Do not be afraid to go **d** to Egypt,
Ex	3: 8	Therefore I have come **d** to rescue
Ex	19:11	the third day the Lord will come **d**
Nm	11:25	The Lord then came **d** in the cloud
2 Sm	22:10	inclined the heavens and came **d**,
Neh	9:13	On Mount Sinai you came **d**,
Ps	18:17	He reached **d** from on high
Ps	113: 6	looking **d** on heaven and earth?
Prv	5: 5	Her feet go **d** to death, to the nether
Eccl	3: 3	a time to tear **d**, and a time to build.
Dn	8:10	so that it cast **d** to earth some
Mk	15:30	by coming **d** from the cross."
Lk	4: 9	of God, throw yourself **d** from here,
Jn	6:41	the bread that came **d** from heaven,"
Jn	10:11	A good shepherd lays **d** his life
1 Jn	3:16	know love was that he laid **d** his life
1 Jn	3:16	so we ought to lay **d** our lives
Rv	3:12	which comes **d** out of heaven
Rv	12: 9	whole world, was thrown **d** to earth,
Rv	12: 9	and its angels were thrown **d** with it.

Rv	21: 2	coming **d** out of heaven from God,
Rv	21:10	the holy city Jerusalem coming **d**

DOWNCAST → DOWN, CAST
2 Cor   7: 6   who encourages the **d**,

DOWNFALL → DOWN, FALL
Prv   29:16   but their **d** the just will behold.
Sir   25: 7   he who lives to see his enemies' **d**.

DRAG → DRAGGED, DRAGGING
Ps   28: 3   Do not **d** me off with the wicked,

DRAGGED → DRAG
Acts   14:19   Paul and **d** him out of the city,

DRAGGING → DRAG
Jn   21: 8   yards, **d** the net with the fish.
Acts   8: 3   house after house and **d** out men

DRAGON → DRAGONS
Is   27: 1   he will slay the **d** that is in the sea.
Is   51: 9   Rahab, you who pierced the **d**?
Dn   14:23   There was a great **d**
Rv   12: 3   it was a huge red **d**, with seven
Rv   13: 2   To it the **d** gave its own power
Rv   16:13   frogs come from the mouth of the **d**,
Rv   20: 2   He seized the **d**, the ancient serpent,

DRAGONS → DRAGON
Est   F: 4   The two **d** are myself and Haman.
Ps   74:13   the heads of the **d** on the waters.

DRANK → DRINK
Gn   9:21   When he **d** some of the wine,
Jgs   15:19   Samson **d** till his spirit returned
Jdt   12:20   by her, **d** a great quantity of wine,
Jer   51: 7   earth drunk; The nations **d** its wine,
Mk   14:23   it to them, and they all **d** from it.
1 Cor   10: 4   and all **d** the same spiritual drink,
1 Cor   10: 4   for they **d** from a spiritual rock

DRAW → DREW
Gn   24:11   when women go out to **d** water,
Ex   2:16   a priest of Midian came to **d** water
1 Sm   31: 4   "**D** your sword and run me through,
Is   12: 3   With joy you will **d** water
Jn   2: 8   "**D** some out now and take it
Jn   4: 7   woman of Samaria came to **d** water.
Jn   12:32   earth, I will **d** everyone to myself."
Jas   4: 8   **D** near to God, and he will **d** near

DREAD → DREADED
Gn   9: 2   **D** fear of you shall come upon all
Dt   31: 6   have no fear or **d** of them, for it is
Jos   2: 9   that a **d** of you has come upon us,
1 Sm   11: 7   In **d** of the LORD, the people turned

DREADED → DREAD
Ex   1:12   The Egyptians, then, **d** the Israelites

DREAM → DREAMER, DREAMERS, DREAMS
Gn   20: 3   came to Abimelech in a **d** one night
Gn   28:12   Then he had a **d**: a stairway
Gn   31:11   In the **d** God's messenger called
Gn   37: 5   Once Joseph had a **d**, which he told
Gn   37: 6   "Listen to this **d** I had.
Gn   40: 5   night, each **d** with its own meaning.
Gn   41: 1   of two years, Pharaoh had a **d**.
Jgs   7:13   "I had a **d**," he said, "that a round loaf
1 Kgs   3: 5   appeared to Solomon in a **d** at night.
Est   F: 2   I recall the **d** I had about these very
Jer   23:28   prophet who has a **d** recount his **d**;
Dn   2: 1   King Nebuchadnezzar had a **d**
Dn   2: 3   "I had a **d** which will allow my spirit
Dn   7: 1   Daniel had a **d** as he lay in bed,
Jl   3: 1   your old men shall **d** dreams,
Mt   1:20   of the Lord appeared to him in a **d**
Mt   2:12   having been warned in a **d** not
Mt   2:13   the Lord appeared to Joseph in a **d**
Mt   2:19   the Lord appeared in a **d** to Joseph
Mt   2:22   because he had been warned in a **d**,
Mt   27:19   suffered much in a **d** today because
Acts   2:17   your old men shall **d** dreams.

DREAMER → DREAM
Gn   37:19   another: "Here comes that master **d**!

DREAMERS → DREAM
Jer   27: 9   to your diviners and **d**, to your
Jude   1: 8   these **d** nevertheless also defile

DREAMS → DREAM
Nm   12: 6   to him, in **d** will I speak to him;
1 Sm   28: 6   whether in **d** or by the Urim
Sir   34: 7   For **d** have led many astray,
Jl   3: 1   your old men shall dream **d**,
Acts   2:17   visions, your old men shall dream **d**.

DREGS
Ps   75: 9   they will drain it even to the **d**;
Is   51:17   Who drained to the **d** the bowl

DRESSED
Jdt   10: 7   in looks and differently **d**, they were
Lk   7:25   Someone **d** in fine garments?
Rv   3: 4   they will walk with me **d** in white,
Rv   4: 4   **d** in white garments and with gold

DREW → DRAW
Ex   2:10   she said, "I **d** him out of the water."
Ps   18:17   **d** me out of the deep waters.
Ps   40: 3   **D** me out of the pit of destruction,
Jer   38:13   they **d** him up with the ropes

DRIED → DRY
Jos   5: 1   that the LORD had **d** up the waters
Is   51:10   Was it not you who **d** up the sea,
Rv   16:12   Its water was **d** up to prepare

DRIES → DRY
Prv   17:22   a depressed spirit **d** up the bones.
Na   1: 4   and all the rivers he **d** up.

DRINK → DRANK, DRINKING, DRINKS, DRUNK,
DRUNKARD, DRUNKARDS, DRUNKENNESS
Gn   24:14   'Take a **d**, and let me give water
Ex   15:23   where they could not **d** the water,
Ex   17: 1   was no water for the people to **d**.
Ex   32: 6   Then they sat down to eat and **d**,
Ex   32:20   the water and made the Israelites **d**.
Nm   6: 3   abstain from wine and strong **d**; he may neither **d** wine vinegar.
Nm   20: 5   Here there is not even water to **d**!"
Jgs   7: 5   everyone who kneels down to **d**."
Jgs   13: 4   strong **d** and to eat nothing unclean.
2 Sm   23:15   that someone would give me a **d**
Tb   4:15   Do not **d** wine till you become
Jdt   12:17   said to her, "**D** and be merry with us!"
Ps   50:13   of bulls or **d** the blood of goats?
Ps   80: 6   made them **d** tears in abundance.
Prv   5:15   **D** water from your own cistern,
Prv   31: 7   When they **d**, they will forget their
Eccl   2:24   better for man than to eat and **d**
Eccl   9: 7   and **d** your wine with a merry heart,
Sir   15: 3   give him the water of learning to **d**.
Is   22:13   You eat meat and **d** wine: "Eat and **d**,
Jer   8:14   he has given us poison to **d**,
Jer   25:15   to whom I will send you **d** it.
Jer   35: 2   the rooms, and give them wine to **d**.
Ez   23:32   The cup of your sister you shall **d**,
Dn   1:12   us vegetables to eat and water to **d**.
Am   2:12   you gave the nazirites wine to **d**,
Hb   2:15   a flood of your wrath to **d**,
Mt   20:22   Can you **d** the cup that I am going to **d**?"
Mt   26:27   them, saying, "**D** from it, all of you,
Mt   27:34   they gave Jesus wine to **d** mixed
Mt   27:34   he had tasted it, he refused to **d**.
Lk   1:15   He will **d** neither wine nor strong **d**.
Lk   12:19   many years, rest, eat, **d**, be merry!"'
Lk   22:18   this time on I shall not **d** of the fruit
Jn   4: 7   Jesus said to her, "Give me a **d**."
Jn   18:11   Shall I not **d** the cup that the Father
Rom   14:17   of God is not a matter of food and **d**,
1 Cor   10: 4   and all drank the same spiritual **d**,
1 Cor   10:21   You cannot **d** the cup of the Lord
1 Cor   12:13   we were all given to **d** of one Spirit.
1 Cor   15:32   "Let us eat and **d**, for tomorrow we

Col	2:16	on you in matters of food and **d**
Heb	9:10	only in matters of food and **d**
Rv	14: 8	that made all the nations **d** the wine
Rv	14:10	will also **d** the wine of God's fury,
Rv	16: 6	you [have] given them blood to **d**;

DRINKING → DRINK

Est	5: 6	During the **d** of the wine, the king
Est	7: 2	day, during the **d** of the wine,
Jb	1:13	**d** wine in the house of their eldest
Is	5:22	Woe to the champions at **d** wine,
Mt	11:19	The Son of Man came eating and **d**
Lk	17:27	they were eating and **d**,
1 Tm	5:23	Stop **d** only water, but have a little

DRINKS → DRINK

Jn	4:13	"Everyone who **d** this water will be
Jn	6:54	and **d** my blood has eternal life,
1 Cor	11:27	or **d** the cup of the Lord unworthily

DRIP → DRIPPINGS

Prv	5: 3	lips of an adulteress **d** with honey,
Jl	4:18	the mountains shall **d** new wine,
Am	9:13	grapes shall **d** down the mountains,

DRIPPINGS → DRIP

Ps	19:11	also than honey or **d** from the comb.

DRIVE → DRIVEN, DRIVING, DROVE

Ex	6: 1	arm, he will **d** them from his land."
Ex	23:30	I will **d** them out little by little
Nm	33:52	**d** out all the inhabitants of the land
Jos	23:13	will no longer **d** these nations
Mk	11:15	the temple area he began to **d**

DRIVEN → DRIVE

Jos	23: 9	At your approach the LORD has **d**
Jn	12:31	the ruler of this world will be **d** out.
Jas	1: 6	is like a wave of the sea that is **d**

DRIVING → DRIVE

Lv	20:23	of the nations whom I am **d**
Ps	35: 5	the angel of the LORD **d** them on.
Acts	26:24	Paul; much learning is **d** you mad."

DROP → DROPPINGS, DROPS

Dt	28:40	for your olives will **d** off unripe.
Is	40:15	the nations count as a **d**

DROPPINGS → DROP

Tb	2:10	till their warm **d** settled in my eyes,

DROPS → DROP

Lk	22:44	his sweat became like **d** of blood

DROSS

Ps	119:119	Like **d** you regard all the wicked
Prv	25: 4	Remove the **d** from silver, and it
Is	1:22	Your silver is turned to **d**, your wine
Is	1:25	and refine your **d** in the furnace,
Ez	22:18	of Israel has become **d** for me.

DROUGHT

Dt	28:22	fiery **d**, with blight and searing
Sir	35:24	distress as rain clouds in time of **d**.
Jer	14: 1	came to Jeremiah concerning the **d**:
Jer	17: 8	In the year of **d** it shows no distress,
Hg	1:11	And I called for a **d** upon the land

DROVE → DRIVE

Jos	24:18	our approach the LORD **d** out [all
Mt	21:12	**d** out all those engaged in selling
Mk	1:12	At once the Spirit **d** him

DROWNED

Mt	18: 6	and to be **d** in the depths of the sea.
Lk	8:33	steep bank into the lake and was **d**.
Heb	11:29	Egyptians attempted it they were **d**.

DROWSY

Mt	25: 5	they all became **d** and fell asleep.

DRUNK → DRINK

Gn	9:21	he became **d** and lay naked inside
Dt	32:42	I will make my arrows **d** with blood,
1 Sm	1:13	not be heard. Eli, thinking her **d**,

1 Sm	25:36	was merry because he was very **d**.
2 Sm	11:13	drank with David, who made him **d**.
Sir	31:28	are wine **d** freely at the proper time.
Is	29: 9	stay blind! Be **d**, but not from wine,
Jn	2:10	and then when people have **d** freely,
Acts	2:15	These people are not **d**, as you
1 Cor	11:21	goes hungry while another gets **d**.
Eph	5:18	And do not get **d** on wine,
1 Thes	5: 7	and those who are **d** get **d** at night.
Rv	17: 6	that the woman was **d** on the blood
Rv	18: 3	For all the nations have **d** the wine

DRUNKARD → DRINK

Dt	21:20	listen to us; he is a glutton and a **d**.'
Prv	23:21	For the **d** and the glutton come
Is	19:14	does, as a **d** staggers in his vomit.
Is	24:20	The earth will reel like a **d**, and it
Mt	11:19	he is a glutton and a **d**, a friend
1 Cor	5:11	a slanderer, a **d**, or a robber,
1 Tm	3: 3	not a **d**, not aggressive, but gentle,

DRUNKARDS → DRINK

Ps	107:27	They reeled, staggered like **d**;
Jl	1: 5	Wake up, you **d**, and weep; wail,
Mt	24:49	servants, and eat and drink with **d**,
1 Cor	6:10	the greedy nor **d** nor slanderers nor

DRUNKENNESS → DRINK

Tb	4:15	nor let **d** accompany you on your
Jer	13:13	am filling with **d** all the inhabitants
Lk	21:34	drowsy from carousing and **d**
Rom	13:13	the day, not in orgies and **d**,
1 Pt	4: 3	debauchery, evil desires, **d**, orgies,

DRUSILLA

Acts	24:24	later Felix came with his wife **D**,

DRY → DRIED, DRIES

Gn	1: 9	basin, so that the **d** land may appear."
Gn	7:22	Everything on **d** land
Ex	14:16	may pass through it on **d** land.
Jos	3:17	all Israel crossed over on **d** ground,
Jgs	6:37	while all the ground is **d**, I shall
2 Kgs	2: 8	and both crossed over on **d** ground.
Ps	66: 6	He changed the sea to **d** land;
Ps	95: 5	The sea and **d** land belong to God,
Ez	37: 4	**D** bones, hear the word of the LORD!
Na	1: 4	He rebukes the sea and leaves it **d**,
Heb	11:29	the Red Sea as if it were **d** land,

DUE

Lv	10:13	This is your **d** from the oblations
1 Chr	16:29	to the LORD the glory **d** his name!
Mal	1: 6	father, where is the honor **d** to me?
Rom	1:27	their own persons the **d** penalty
Rom	13: 7	taxes to whom taxes are **d**, toll to whom toll is **d**, respect to whom respect is **d**, honor to whom honor is **d**.
1 Pt	5: 6	that he may exalt you in **d** time.

DUG → DIG

Ps	57: 7	down; They have **d** a pit before me.
Mt	21:33	hedge around it, **d** a wine press in it,

DULL

Is	6:10	to **d** their ears and close their eyes;
Is	59: 1	to save, nor his ear too **d** to hear.

DUNG

Mal	2: 3	and I will strew **d** in your faces, The **d** of your feasts,

DUNGEON

Gn	40:15	I should have been put into a **d**."
Is	42: 7	and from the **d**, those who live

DUST

Gn	13:16	make your descendants like the **d**
Gn	28:14	These shall be as plentiful as the **d**
Nm	23:10	Who has ever counted the **d**
1 Sm	2: 8	He raises the needy from the **d**;
Jb	42: 6	have said, and repent in **d** and ashes.
Ps	22:16	palate; you lay me in the **d** of death.
Ps	72: 9	before him, his enemies lick the **d**.

Ps	90: 3	But humans you return to d, saying,
Ps	103:14	formed, remembers that we are d.
Eccl	3:20	both were made from the d, and to the d they both return.
Is	65:25	ox [but the serpent's food shall be d].
Mi	7:17	shall lick the d like the serpent,
Na	1: 3	and clouds are the d at his feet;
Mt	10:14	and shake the d from your feet
Acts	13:51	So they shook the d from their feet
Rv	18:19	They threw d on their heads

DUTIES →DUTY

Nm	8:26	are to regulate the d of the Levites."

DUTY →DUTIES

Gn	38: 8	of your d as brother-in-law,
Dt	25: 5	perform the d of a brother-in-law

DWELL →DWELLING, DWELLINGS, DWELLS

Ex	25: 8	for me, that I may d in their midst.
1 Kgs	6:13	I will d in the midst of the Israelites
Ps	23: 6	life; I will d in the house of the LORD
Is	57:15	One: On high I d, and in holiness,
Zec	2:15	and he will d among you, and you
Acts	7:48	Yet the Most High does not d
2 Cor	12: 9	the power of Christ may d with me.
Eph	3:17	Christ may d in your hearts through
Col	1:19	all the fullness was pleased to d,
Col	3:16	the word of Christ d in you richly,
Rv	12:12	and you who d in them. But woe
Rv	21: 3	He will d with them and they will

DWELLING →DWELL

Ex	25: 9	This D and all its furnishings
Ex	38:21	the various amounts used on the D, the D of the commandments,
Ex	40:18	It was Moses who erected the D.
Ex	40:34	the glory of the LORD filled the D.
Lv	8:10	Moses anointed and consecrated the D,
Lv	26:11	I will set my D among you, and will
Nm	1:50	give the Levites charge of the D
Dt	12:11	chooses as the d place for his name
1 Kgs	8:30	Listen from your heavenly d
1 Chr	6:33	services of the D of the house of God.
Ez	37:27	My d shall be with them; I will
Jl	4:17	God, d on Zion, my holy mountain;
Jn	14: 2	house there are many d places.
Eph	2:22	being built together into a d place
Rv	13: 6	and his d and those who dwell

DWELLINGS →DWELL

Ps	49:12	their d through all generations,

DWELLS →DWELL

1 Kgs	8:27	it indeed be that God d among men
Is	8:18	LORD of hosts who d on Mount Zion.
Jl	4:21	it unpunished. The LORD d in Zion.
Jn	14:10	The Father who d in me is doing his
Rom	7:17	I who do it, but sin that d in me.
Rom	8: 9	if only the Spirit of God d in you.
1 Cor	3:16	and that the Spirit of God d in you?
Col	2: 9	in him d the whole fullness
1 Tm	6:16	who d in unapproachable light,

DYING →DEAD

2 Cor	6: 9	as d and behold we live;

E

EACH

Gn	49:28	gave to e of them an appropriate
Ex	12: 3	a lamb, one apiece for e household.
Nm	1: 4	there shall be a man from e tribe,
Nm	17:17	Mark e man's name on his staff;
Is	6: 2	above; e of them had six wings:
Ez	10:14	E had four faces: the first face was
Lk	11: 3	Give us e day our daily bread
Acts	2: 6	were confused because e one heard
Rom	14:12	e of us shall give an account
1 Cor	7: 7	but e has a particular gift from God,
1 Cor	12: 7	To e individual the manifestation
1 Pt	4:10	As e one has received a gift, use it
Rv	2:23	I will give e of you what your works

Rv	4: 8	creatures, e of them with six wings,
Rv	6:11	E of them was given a white robe,
Rv	21:21	e of the gates made from a single
Rv	22: 2	twelve times a year, once e month;

EAGER →EAGERLY

Rom	8:19	with e expectation the revelation
2 Pt	1:10	be all the more e to make your call

EAGERLY →EAGER

Lk	22:15	"I have e desired to eat this Passover

EAGLE →EAGLE'S, EAGLES

Ex	19: 4	how I bore you up on e wings
Dt	14:12	the e, the vulture, the osprey,
Dt	32:11	As an e incites its nestlings forth
Prv	30:19	The way of an e in the air, the way
Jer	48:40	Behold, like an e he soars,
Jer	49:16	you build your nest high as the e,
Ez	1:10	finally each had the face of an e.
Ez	17: 3	The great e, with great wings,
Rv	4: 7	the fourth looked like an e in flight.
Rv	8:13	heard an e flying high overhead cry
Rv	12:14	given the two wings of the great e,

EAGLE'S →EAGLE

Ps	103: 5	your youth is renewed like the e.
Dn	7: 4	like a lion, but with e wings.

EAGLES →EAGLE

Is	40:31	they will soar as with e' wings;

EAR →EARRINGS, EARS

Ex	21: 6	he shall pierce his e with an awl,
Dt	15:17	awl and thrust it through his e
2 Kgs	19:16	Incline your e, O LORD, and listen!
Neh	1:11	LORD, may your e be attentive to my
Jb	12:11	Does not the e judge words
Ps	116: 2	Who turned an e to me on the day I
Prv	2: 2	Turning your e to wisdom,
Prv	25:12	is a wise reprover to an obedient e.
Eccl	1: 8	nor is the e filled with hearing.
Is	59: 1	to save, nor his e too dull to hear.
Is	64: 3	No e has ever heard, no eye ever
Dn	9:18	Give e, O my God, and listen;
Mk	14:47	priest's servant, and cut off his e.
Lk	22:51	he touched the servant's e and healed
1 Cor	2: 9	has not seen, and e has not heard,

EARLY

Dt	11:14	land, the e rain and the late rain,
Ps	127: 2	It is vain for you to rise e and put
Prv	27:14	with a loud voice in the e morning,
Hos	6: 4	like the dew that e passes away.
Jl	2:23	the e and the late rain as before.
Lk	24:22	were at the tomb e in the morning
Jas	5: 7	patient with it until it receives the e

EARNED

Hg	1: 6	And he who e wages e them

EARNEST →EARNESTNESS

Rv	3:19	chastise. Be e, therefore, and repent.

EARNESTNESS →EARNEST

2 Cor	7:11	behold what e this godly sorrow has

EARRINGS →EAR, RING

Ex	35:22	them, brought brooches, e, rings,

EARS →EAR

Gn	41: 5	He saw seven e of grain,
Dt	29: 3	or eyes to see, or e to hear.
Ps	34:16	eyes for the just and e for their cry.
Ps	115: 6	They have e but do not hear,
Prv	26:17	who seizes a passing dog by the e
Wis	15:15	to snuff the air, Nor e to hear,
Is	6:10	to dull their e and close their eyes;
Is	35: 5	opened, the e of the deaf be cleared;
Jer	6:10	See! their e are uncircumcised,
Bar	2:31	will give them hearts, and heedful e;
Mt	11:15	Whoever has e ought to hear.
Mk	8:18	eyes and not see, e and not hear?
Acts	7:51	uncircumcised in heart and e,

Acts	28:27	they will not hear with their e;
1 Pt	3:12	and his e turned to their prayer,
Rv	2: 7	" ' "Whoever has e ought to hear what
Rv	13: 9	Whoever has e ought to hear these

EARTH → EARTHEN, EARTHLY, EARTHQUAKE, EARTHQUAKES

Gn	1: 1	God created the heavens and the e,
Gn	1: 2	the e was a formless wasteland,
Gn	1:28	multiply; fill the e and subdue it.
Gn	4:12	a restless wanderer on the e."
Gn	6:11	In the eyes of God the e was corrupt
Gn	6:17	to bring the flood [waters] on the e,
Gn	6:17	of life; everything on e shall perish.
Gn	7:24	maintained their crest over the e
Gn	9:13	the covenant between me and the e.
Gn	12: 3	All the communities of the e
Gn	14:19	High, the creator of heaven and e;
Gn	24: 3	the God of heaven and the God of e,
Gn	28:14	be as plentiful as the dust of the e,
Gn	28:14	nations of the e shall find blessing.
Ex	19: 5	people, though all the e is mine.
Dt	5: 8	or on the e below or in the waters beneath the e;
Jos	3:13	the Lord of the whole e,
1 Kgs	8:27	that God dwells among men on e?
1 Chr	16:23	Sing to the LORD, all the e,
1 Chr	16:30	Tremble before him, all the e;
Jdt	2: 5	the great king, the lord of all the e:
Jdt	13:18	God, above all the women on e;
Jb	26: 7	suspends the e over nothing at all;
Ps	8: 2	is your name through all the e!
Ps	24: 1	The e is the LORD's and all it holds,
Ps	46: 7	voice thunders and the e trembles.
Ps	47: 3	awe, the great king over all the e,
Ps	73:25	None beside you delights me on e.
Ps	90: 2	the e and the world brought forth,
Ps	97: 1	The LORD is king; let the e rejoice;
Ps	108: 6	your glory appear above all the e.
Prv	8:26	While as yet the e and the fields
Sir	40:11	All that is of e returns to e, and what
Is	6: 3	"All the e is filled with his glory!"
Is	24:20	The e will reel like a drunkard,
Is	37:16	God over all the kingdoms of the e.
Is	37:16	have made the heavens and the e.
Is	40:22	enthroned above the vault of the e,
Is	51: 6	the e wears out like a garment
Is	55: 9	high as the heavens are above the e,
Is	65:17	and a new e; The things of the past
Is	66: 1	are my throne, the e is my footstool.
Jer	10:10	Before whose anger the e quakes,
Jer	23:24	both heaven and e? says the LORD.
Jer	33:25	have given no laws to heaven and e,
Dn	2:39	which shall rule over the whole e.
Dn	3:74	Let the e bless the Lord,
Dn	12: 2	in the dust of the e shall awake;
Jl	3: 3	in the heavens and on the e, blood,
Am	9: 5	of hosts. I melt the e with my touch,
Hb	2:20	silence before him, all the e!
Hg	2: 6	I will shake the heavens and the e,
Hg	2:21	I will shake the heavens and the e;
Zec	14: 9	shall become king over the whole e;
Mt	5:13	"You are the salt of the e. But if salt
Mt	5:18	until heaven and e pass away,
Mt	5:35	nor by the e, for it is his footstool;
Mt	6:10	will be done, on e as in heaven.
Mt	16:19	you bind on e shall be bound
Mt	16:19	you loose on e shall be loosed
Mt	24:35	Heaven and e will pass away,
Mt	28:18	and on e has been given to me.
Lk	2:14	on e peace to those on whom his
Lk	5:24	of Man has authority on e to forgive
Jn	12:32	And when I am lifted up from the e,
Acts	2:19	and signs on the e below: blood,
Acts	4:24	maker of heaven and e and the sea
Acts	7:49	are my throne, the e is my footstool.
1 Cor	10:26	for "the e and its fullness are
1 Cor	15:47	The first man was from the e,
Eph	1:10	things in Christ, in heaven and on e.
Eph	3:15	family in heaven and on e is named,

Phil	2:10	in heaven and on e and under the e,
Heb	1:10	O Lord, you established the e,
Heb	12:26	"I will once more shake not only e
2 Pt	3:13	and a new e in which righteousness
Rv	5: 3	on e or under the e was able to open
Rv	6: 8	authority over a quarter of the e,
Rv	8: 7	which was hurled down to the e.
Rv	12:12	But woe to you, e and sea,
Rv	20:11	The e and the sky fled from his
Rv	21: 1	I saw a new heaven and a new e.
Rv	21: 1	and the former e had passed away,

EARTHEN → EARTH

Lam	4: 2	Now worth no more than e jars
2 Cor	4: 7	we hold this treasure in e vessels,

EARTHLY → EARTH

Jn	3:12	If I tell you about e things and you
2 Cor	5: 1	For we know that if our e dwelling,
Phil	3:19	minds are occupied with e things.
Col	3: 5	then, the parts of you that are e:
Jas	3:15	not come down from above but is e,

EARTHQUAKE → EARTH, QUAKE

1 Kgs	19:11	the LORD was not in the e.
Est	A: 4	noise and tumult, thunder and e—
Is	29: 6	With thunder, e, and great noise,
Mt	28: 2	And behold, there was a great e;
Acts	16:26	there was suddenly such a severe e
Rv	6:12	sixth seal, and there was a great e;
Rv	11:13	At that moment there was a great e,
Rv	16:18	and peals of thunder, and a great e.

EARTHQUAKES → EARTH, QUAKE

Mt	24: 7	famines and e from place to place.

EASIER → EASY

Mt	9: 5	Which is e, to say, 'Your sins are
Lk	16:17	It is e for heaven and earth to pass
Lk	18:25	For it is e for a camel to pass

EAST

Gn	2: 8	in the e, and he placed there
Ex	14:21	a strong e wind throughout the night
Ps	103:12	As far as the e is from the west,
Ez	11:23	the mountain which is to the e of the city.
Ez	43: 2	the God of Israel coming from the e.
Hos	13:15	an e wind shall come, a wind
Jon	4: 8	arose, God sent a burning e wind;
Zec	14: 4	shall be cleft in two from e to west
Mt	2: 1	behold, magi from the e arrived
Mt	8:11	many will come from the e
Rv	16:12	the way for the kings of the E.

EASY → EASIER

Mt	11:30	For my yoke is e, and my burden

EAT → ATE, EATEN, EATER, EATING, EATS

Gn	2:16	"You are free to e from any
Gn	2:17	From that tree you shall not e;
Gn	3:19	shall you get bread to e, Until you
Gn	3:22	and thus e of it and live forever."
Gn	9: 4	lifeblood still in it you shall not e.
Ex	12:11	"This is how you are to e it:
Ex	12:20	Nothing leavened may you e;
Ex	12:16	evening twilight you shall e flesh,
Ex	32: 6	Then they sat down to e and drink,
Lv	11: 4	you shall not e any of the following
Dt	14: 4	These are the animals you may e:
2 Sm	9: 7	and you shall always e at my table."
1 Mc	1:62	hearts not to e anything unclean;
Ps	22:27	The poor will e their fill; those who
Ps	50:13	Do I e the flesh of bulls or drink
Eccl	2:24	is nothing better for man than to e
Eccl	5:17	it is well for a man to e and drink
Is	11: 7	rest; the lion shall e hay like the ox.
Is	55: 1	come, receive grain and e; Come,
Is	65:25	and the lion shall e hay like the ox
Jer	19: 9	I will have them e the flesh of their
Jer	19: 9	they shall e one another's flesh
Lam	2:20	Must women e their offspring,
Ez	3: 1	Son of man, e what is before you;
Dn	1:12	Give us vegetables to e and water

Mt	15: 2	[their] hands when they e a meal."
Mt	26:26	it to his disciples said, "Take and e;
Mk	2:26	only the priests could lawfully e,
Mk	14:14	room where I may e the Passover
Lk	10: 8	you, e what is set before you,
Lk	12:19	up for many years, rest, e, drink,
Lk	12:29	do not seek what you are to e
Jn	4:32	"I have food to e of which you do not
Jn	6:31	gave them bread from heaven to e.' "
Jn	6:53	unless you e the flesh of the Son
Acts	10:13	him, "Get up, Peter. Slaughter and e."
Rom	14: 2	believes that one may e anything,
Rom	14:15	brother is being hurt by what you e,
1 Cor	5:11	not even to e with such a person.
1 Cor	8:13	I will never e meat again, so that I
1 Cor	10:25	E anything sold in the market,
1 Cor	10:31	So whether you e or drink,
1 Cor	11:26	For as often as you e this bread
2 Thes	3:10	to work, neither should that one e.
Rv	2: 7	the victor I will give the right to e

EATEN →EAT
Gn	3:11	You have e, then, from the tree
Ez	4:14	never have I e carrion flesh
Dn	14:12	you do not find that Bel has e it all
Acts	10:14	For never have I e anything profane
Acts	12:23	to God, and he was e by worms
Rv	10:10	but when I had e it, my stomach

EATER →EAT
Jgs	14:14	"Out of the e came forth food,

EATING →EAT
Tb	1:11	I refrained from e that kind of food.
Lk	7:34	The Son of Man came e
Rom	14:20	to become a stumbling block by e;
1 Cor	8: 4	So about the e of meat sacrificed

EATS →EAT
Ex	12:15	Whoever e leavened bread
Lv	7:18	anyone who e of it shall have his
Prv	31:27	and e not her food in idleness.
Lk	15: 2	welcomes sinners and e with them."
Jn	6:51	whoever e this bread will live
1 Cor	11:27	Therefore whoever e the bread

EBAL
Dt	11:29	Gerizim, the curse on Mount E.
Jos	8:30	the God of Israel, on Mount E,

EBED-MELECH
An Ethiopian eunuch; saved Jeremiah from the cistern (Jer 38:1-13; 39:16).

EBENEZER
1 Sm	4: 1	to engage them in battle and camped at E,
1 Sm	5: 1	transferred it from E to Ashdod.
1 Sm	7:12	he named it E, explaining, "To this

EBER
Ancestor of Abraham (Gn 11:14-17), of Jesus (Lk 3:35).

ECBATANA
Ezr	6: 2	and in E, the stronghold
Tb	3: 7	On the same day, at E in Media,
Jdt	1: 1	ruled over the Medes in E.

EDEN
Gn	2: 8	the LORD God planted a garden in E,
Is	51: 3	Her deserts he shall make like E,
Ez	28:13	In E, the garden of God, you were,
Jl	2: 3	garden of E is the land before them,

EDGE →TWO-EDGED
Jos	3: 8	when they reach the e of the waters."
Jer	31:29	and the children's teeth are set on e,"

EDICT
Heb	11:23	they were not afraid of the king's e.

EDOM → =ESAU, EDOMITE, EDOMITES
Gn	25:30	(That is why he was called E.)
Gn	36: 1	the descendants of Esau [that is, E].
Nm	20:18	But E answered him, "You shall not
1 Kgs	11:16	they had killed off every male in E.

Ps	60:10	upon E I cast my sandal. I will
Is	63: 1	Who is this that comes from E,
Jer	49: 7	Concerning E, thus says the LORD
Lam	4:21	rejoice and are glad, O daughter E,
Ez	25:12	Because E has taken vengeance
Am	1:11	For three crimes of E, and for four,
Ob	1: 1	Of E we have heard a message
Mal	1: 4	If E says, "We have been crushed

EDOMITE →EDOM
1 Sm	22: 9	Then Doeg the E, who was standing
Ps	52: 1	when Doeg the E went and told

EDOMITES →EDOM
2 Sm	8:13	having slain eighteen thousand E
1 Chr	18:13	all the E became David's subjects.

EDUCATED
Acts	22: 3	of Gamaliel I was e strictly in our

EFFECT →EFFECTIVE
Heb	9:17	For a will takes e only at death;

EFFECTIVE →EFFECT
Phlm	1: 6	in the faith may become e

EFFORT
2 Pt	1: 5	make every e to supplement your
2 Pt	1:15	make every e to enable you always

EGG →EGGS
Lk	11:12	a scorpion when he asks for an e?

EGGS →EGG
Dt	22: 6	nest with young birds or e in it,
Is	59: 5	They hatch adders' e, and weave
Is	59: 5	Whoever eats their e will die, if one

EGLAH
A wife of David (2 Sm 3:5; 1 Chr 3:3).

EGLON
1. King of Moab killed by Ehud (Jgs 3:12-30).
2. City in Canaan (Jos 10).

EGYPT →EGYPTIAN, EGYPTIANS
Gn	12:10	land; so Abram went down to E
Gn	26: 2	"Do not go down to E, but continue
Gn	37:28	out of the cistern and took him to E.
Gn	41:41	in charge of the whole land of E."
Gn	42: 3	emergency supply of grain from E.
Gn	45: 9	God has made me lord of all E;
Gn	45:20	the whole land of E shall be yours.' "
Gn	46: 6	all his descendants migrated to E.
Gn	47:27	Thus Israel settled in the land of E,
Ex	1: 8	of Joseph, came to power in E.
Ex	3:11	and lead the Israelites out of E?"
Ex	7: 3	that I will work in the land of E,
Ex	12:12	this same night I will go through E,
Ex	12:40	had stayed in E was four hundred
Ex	12:41	of the LORD left the land of E on this
Ex	32: 1	who brought us out of the land of E,
Nm	11:18	Oh, how well off we were in E!'
Nm	14: 4	appoint a leader and go back to E."
Nm	24: 8	It is God who brought him out of E,
Dt	6:21	were once slaves of Pharaoh in E,
Dt	6:21	us out of E with his strong hand
Dt	16:12	that you too were once slaves in E,
Jos	15:47	as far as the Wadi of E and the coast
1 Kgs	11:40	in E, where he remained until
1 Kgs	14:25	king of E, attacked Jerusalem.
2 Chr	35:20	Neco, king of E, came up to fight
2 Chr	36: 3	The king of E deposed him
Neh	9:18	God who brought you up out of E,'
Ps	78:51	He struck all the firstborn of E,
Ps	80: 9	You brought a vine out of E;
Is	19: 1	Oracle on E: See, the LORD is riding
Jer	42:19	remnant of Judah; do not go to E!
Jer	44: 1	of Judah who were living in E,
Jer	46: 2	Concerning E. Against the army
Lam	5: 6	To E we submitted, and to Assyria,
Ez	29: 2	king of E, and prophesy against him and against all E.
Ez	30: 4	Then a sword shall come upon E,

Hos	11: 1	loved him, out of E I called my son.
Mt	2:15	fulfilled, "Out of E I called my son."
Heb	11:27	By faith he left E, not fearing
Rv	11: 8	the symbolic names "Sodom" and "E,"

EGYPTIAN →EGYPT

Gn	16: 1	an E maidservant named Hagar.
Ex	1:19	women are not like the E women.
Ex	2:11	he saw an E striking a Hebrew,
Ex	14:24	cloud upon the E force a glance
Dt	11: 4	what he did to the E army
Acts	7:24	man by striking down the E.

EGYPTIANS →EGYPT

Ex	1:12	The E, then, dreaded the Israelites
Ex	3:22	Thus you will despoil the E."
Ex	12:36	Thus did they despoil the E.
Ex	14: 4	the E will know that I am the LORD."
Ex	15:26	with which I afflicted the E; for I,
Nm	14:13	the LORD: "Are the E to hear of this?
Ez	16:26	You played the harlot with the E,
Acts	7:22	[in] all the wisdom of the E and was
Heb	11:29	when the E attempted it they were

EHUD
Left-handed judge who delivered Israel from Moabite king, Eglon (Jgs 3:12-30).

EIGHT →EIGHTH

Gn	17:12	you, when he is e days old, shall be
Gn	21: 4	When his son Isaac was e days old,
2 Kgs	22: 1	Josiah was e years old when he
1 Pt	3:20	ark, in which a few persons, e in all,

EIGHTEEN

Lk	13:11	who for e years had been crippled

EIGHTH →EIGHT

Lv	12: 3	On the e day, the flesh of the boy's
Lv	23:39	the e day shall be days of complete
Lv	25:22	When you sow in the e year,
Lk	1:59	When they came on the e day
Phil	3: 5	Circumcised on the e day,
Rv	17:11	but exists no longer is an e king,

EIGHTY

Ex	7: 7	Moses was e years old and Aaron
2 Sm	19:36	I am now e years old. Can I
Ps	90:10	of our years, or e, if we are strong;

EIGHTY-FIVE

Jos	14:10	and although I am now e years old,

EITHER

Sir	40:18	but better than e, attaining wisdom.
Sir	40:26	but better than e, fear of God.
Lk	16:13	He will e hate one and love
Rv	3:15	I wish you were e cold or hot.

EKRON

Jos	13: 3	Ashdod, Ashkelon, Gath and E);
1 Sm	5:10	The ark of God was next sent to E;
1 Sm	6:17	one for Gath, and one for E.
2 Kgs	1: 2	the god of E, whether I shall recover
Am	1: 8	I will turn my hand against E,

EL

Gn	33:20	and invoked "E, the God of Israel."

EL-BERITH

Jgs	9:46	into the crypt of the temple of E.

ELAH
1. Son of Baasha; king of Israel (1 Kgs 16:6-14).
2. Valley in which David fought Goliath (1 Sm 17:2, 19; 21:9).

ELAM

1 Chr	1:17	The descendants of Shem were E,
Jer	49:34	of the LORD against E came

ELDAD

Nm	11:27	"E and Medad are prophesying

ELDER →ELDERS

Is	3: 2	and prophet, fortuneteller and e,
Ez	16:46	Your e sister was Samaria with her

ELDERS →ELDER

Ex	3:16	and assemble the e of the Israelites,
Ex	24: 1	and seventy of the e of Israel.
Dt	25: 7	she shall go up to the e at the gate
Jos	24: 1	summoning their e, their leaders,
Jgs	2: 7	of those e who outlived Joshua
Ru	4: 2	picked out ten of the e of the city
Ps	105:22	by his word, to teach his e wisdom
Prv	31:23	as he sits with the e of the land.
Is	3:14	with his people's e and princes: It is
Ez	8:11	stood seventy of the e of the house
Dn	13:50	To Daniel the e said, "Come,
Dn	13:61	They rose up against the two e,
Mt	15: 2	break the tradition of the e? They do
Mt	27:12	accused by the chief priests and e,
Mk	7: 3	hands, keeping the tradition of the e.
Lk	9:22	greatly and be rejected by the e,
Acts	4: 5	their leaders, e, and scribes were
Acts	23:14	They went to the chief priests and e
Acts	24: 1	Ananias came down with some e
Acts	25:15	the e of the Jews brought charges
Rv	4: 4	thrones on which twenty-four e sat,
Rv	4:10	the twenty-four e fall down before
Rv	5: 6	the four living creatures and the e,
Rv	7:11	and around the e and the four living
Rv	11:16	The twenty-four e who sat on their
Rv	14: 3	the four living creatures and the e.
Rv	19: 4	The twenty-four e and the four

ELEAZAR
1. Third son of Aaron (Ex 6:23-25). Succeeded Aaron as high priest (Nm 20:26; Dt 10:6). Allotted land to tribes (Jos 14:1). Death (Jos 24:33).
2. Father of the writer of Sirach (Sir 50:27).
3. Brother of Judas Maccabeus (1 Mc 2:5; 6:43-46).

ELECT →ELECTION

Wis	3: 9	holy ones, and his care is with his e.
Mt	24:22	sake of the e they will be shortened.
Mt	24:24	if that were possible, even the e.
Mt	24:31	they will gather his e from the four
Mk	13:20	the sake of the e whom he chose,
Mk	13:22	mislead, if that were possible, the e.
Mk	13:27	gather [his] e from the four winds,
Rom	11: 7	it did not attain, but the e attained it;
1 Tm	5:21	and the e angels to keep these rules

ELECTION →ELECT

Rom	11:28	but in respect to e, they are beloved
2 Pt	1:10	eager to make your call and e firm,

ELEMENTAL →ELEMENTS

Gal	4: 3	were enslaved to the e powers
Gal	4: 9	to the weak and destitute e powers?
Col	2: 8	according to the e powers
Col	2:20	Christ to the e powers of the world,

ELEMENTS →ELEMENTAL

Wis	7:17	the universe and the force of its e,
Heb	5:12	someone teach you again the basic e
2 Pt	3:10	and the e will be dissolved by fire,
2 Pt	3:12	in flames and the e melted by fire.

ELEPHANT →ELEPHANTS

1 Mc	6:46	He ran right under the e and stabbed

ELEPHANTS →ELEPHANT

1 Mc	1:17	with chariots and e, and with a large

ELEVEN

Gn	32:23	two maidservants and his e children,
Gn	37: 9	e stars were bowing down to me."
Ex	26: 8	E such sheets are to be made
Dt	1: 2	it is a journey of e days from Horeb
Mt	28:16	The e disciples went to Galilee,
Lk	24: 9	announced all these things to the e
Lk	24:33	they found gathered together the e
Acts	1:26	he was counted with the e apostles.
Acts	2:14	Then Peter stood up with the E,

ELI →ELOI
1. High priest in youth of Samuel (1 Sm 1-4). Blessed Hannah (1 Sm 1:12-18); raised Samuel (1 Sm 2:11-26). Prophesied against

because of wicked sons (1 Sm 2:27-36). Death of Eli and sons (1 Sm 4:11-22).
2. "Eli, Eli, lema sabachthani?" (Mt 27:46).

ELIAKIM → =JEHOIAKIM
1. Original name of king Jehoiakim (2 Kgs 23:34; 2 Chr 36:4).
2. Hezekiah's palace administrator (2 Kgs 18:17-37; 19:2; Is 36:1-22; 37:2).

ELIASHIB
Neh   3: 1 E the high priest and his priestly

ELIEZER
1. Servant of Abraham (Gn 15:2).
2. Son of Moses (Ex 18:4; 1 Chr 23:15-17).

ELIHU
A friend of Job (Jb 32-37).

ELIJAH
Prophet; predicted famine in Israel (1 Kgs 17:1; Jas 5:17). Fed by ravens (1 Kgs 17:2-6). Raised Sidonian widow's son (1 Kgs 17:7-24). Defeated prophets of Baal at Carmel (1 Kgs 18:16-46). Ran from Jezebel (1 Kgs 19:1-9). Prophesied death of Azariah (2 Kgs 1). Succeeded by Elishah (1 Kgs 19:19-21; 2 Kgs 2:1-18). Taken to heaven in whirlwind (2 Kgs 2:11-12; 1 Mc 2:58; Sir 48:1-12).
Return prophesied (Mal 3:23-24); equated with John the Baptist (Mt 17:9-13; Mk 9:9-13; Lk 1:17). Appeared with Moses in transfiguration of Jesus (Mt 17:1-8; Mk 9:1-8).

ELIM
Ex   15:27 Then they came to E, where there
Nm   33: 9 they came to E, where there were

ELIMELECH
Ru   1: 3 E, the husband of Naomi, died,
Ru   4: 9 from Naomi all the holdings of E,

ELIPHAZ
1. Firstborn of Esau (Gn 36).
2. A friend of Job (Jb 4-5; 15; 22; 42:7, 9).

ELISHA
Prophet; successor of Elijah (1 Kgs 19:16-21; Sir 48:12-14); inherited his mantle (2 Kgs 2:1-18). Purified bad water (2 Kgs 2:19-22). Cursed young men (2 Kgs 2:23-25). Aided Israel's defeat of Moab (2 Kgs 3). Provided widow with oil (2 Kgs 4:1-7). Raised Shunammite woman's son (2 Kgs 4:8-37). Purified food (2 Kgs 4:38-41). Fed 100 men (2 Kgs 4:42-44). Healed Naaman's leprosy (2 Kgs 5). Made axhead float (2 Kgs 6:1-7). Captured Arameans (2 Kgs 6:8-23). Political adviser to Israel (2 Kgs 6:24-8:6; 9:1-3; 13:14-19), Aram (2 Kgs 8:7-15). Death (2 Kgs 13:20).

ELIZABETH
Mother of John the Baptist (Lk 1:5-58).

ELKANAH
Husband of Hannah, father of Samuel (1 Sm 1-2).

ELOI → ELI
Mk   15:34 Jesus cried out in a loud voice, "E, E,

ELON
Judge of Israel (Jgs 12:11-12).

ELOQUENT
Ex   4:10 I have never been e,
Acts 18:24 a native of Alexandria, an e speaker,

ELSE
Ex   4:13 you please, Lord, send someone e!"
Acts   4:12 is no salvation through anyone e,

ELYMAS → =BAR-JESUS
Acts 13: 8 E the magician (for that is what his

EMBALMED
Gn   50: 2 his father. When they e Israel,
Gn   50:26 He was e and laid to rest in a coffin

EMBRACE → EMBRACED, EMBRACES
Prv   4: 8 will bring you honors if you e her;
Eccl   3: 5 a time to e, and a time to be far

EMBRACED → EMBRACE
Gn   48:10 close to him, he kissed and e them.

EMBRACES → EMBRACE
Prv   5:20 and accept the e of an adulteress?

EMBROIDERED
Ez   16:10 I clothed you with an e gown,
Ez   26:16 robes, and strip off their e garments.

EMERALD
Ex   28:17 row, a carnelian, a topaz and an e;
Rv   4: 3 was a halo as brilliant as an e.
Rv   21:19 the third chalcedony, the fourth e,

EMMANUEL → =IMMANUEL
Mt   1:23 and they shall name him E,"

EMMAUS
Lk   24:13 miles from Jerusalem called E,

EMPTIED → EMPTY
Neh   5:13 may he thus be shaken out and e!"
1 Cor 1:17 cross of Christ might not be e of its
Phil   2: 7 Rather, he e himself,

EMPTY → EMPTIED, EMPTY-HANDED
2 Kgs 4: 3 your neighbors—as many e vessels as
Lk   1:53 things; the rich he has sent away e.
Eph   5: 6 one deceive you with e arguments,
Col   2: 8 that no one captivate you with an e,

EMPTY-HANDED → EMPTY, HAND
Gn   31:42 would now have sent me away e.
Ex   3:21 when you leave, you will not go e.
Ex   23:15 No one shall appear before me e.
Dt   15:13 so, you shall not send him away e,
Ru   3:17 come back to my mother-in-law e!"
Sir   35: 4 Appear not before the Lord e, for all
Mk   12: 3 him, beat him, and sent him away e.

ENABLES → ABLE
Phil   3:21 body by the power that e him

ENCAMP → CAMP
Ps   27: 3 Though an army e against me,
Is   29: 3 I will e like David against you;

ENCAMPS → CAMP
Ps   34: 8 angel of the Lord, who e with them,

ENCHANTERS
Dn   1:20 the magicians and e in his kingdom.
Dn   5: 7 The king shouted for the e,

ENCIRCLE → CIRCLE
Ps   22:13 fierce bulls of Bashan e me.

ENCOURAGE → ENCOURAGED, ENCOURAGEMENT, ENCOURAGES, ENCOURAGING
Dt   1:38 E him, for he is to give Israel its
Dt   3:28 Joshua, and e and strengthen him,
2 Sm 11:25 on the city and destroy it.' E him."
Eph   6:22 us and that he may e your hearts.
Col   4: 8 us and that he may e your hearts,
1 Thes 3: 2 strengthen and e you in your faith,
1 Thes 5:11 e one another and build one another
2 Tm   4: 2 e through all patience and teaching.

ENCOURAGED → ENCOURAGE
2 Chr 35: 2 e them in the service of the Lord's
Ez   13:22 have e the wicked man not to turn
Acts 16:40 where they saw and e the brothers,
Acts 18:27 the brothers e him and wrote
Acts 27:36 They were all e, and took some food
Rom   1:12 I may be mutually e by one another's
1 Cor 14:31 so that all may learn and all be e.
Col   2: 2 that their hearts may be e as they are
Heb   6:18 taken refuge might be strongly e

ENCOURAGEMENT → ENCOURAGE
1 Mc 12: 9 we have for our e the sacred books
Acts   4:36 (which is translated "son of e"),
Acts 20: 2 he provided many words of e
Rom   15: 4 by the e of the scriptures we might
Rom   15: 5 and e grant you to think in harmony
1 Cor 14: 3 for their building up, e, and solace.
Phil   2: 1 If there is any e in Christ,
Phlm   1: 7 much joy and e from your love,

ENCOURAGES → ENCOURAGE
Is   41: 7 The craftsman e the goldsmith,

ENCOURAGING →ENCOURAGE
1 Mc	5:53	and e the people the whole way,
2 Mc	15: 9	By e them with words from the law
Acts	20: 1	after e them, he bade them farewell
1 Thes	2:12	exhorting and e you and insisting

END →ENDS
Gn	6:13	decided to put an e to all mortals
Ex	12:41	At the e of four hundred and thirty
Dt	8:16	also make you prosperous in the e.
Prv	5: 4	the e she is as bitter as wormwood,
Prv	5:11	And you groan in the e, when your
Prv	14:12	a man, but the e of it leads to death!
Prv	14:13	sad and the e of joy may be sorrow.
Prv	16:25	a man, but the e of it leads to death!
Prv	20:21	outset will in the e not be blessed.
Eccl	3:11	from beginning to e, the work
Eccl	7: 8	Better is the e of speech than its
Eccl	12:12	making of many books there is no e,
Sir	21: 9	of tow; they will e in a flaming fire.
Ez	7: 2	An e! The e has come upon the four
Dn	6:27	and his dominion shall be without e.
Dn	8:17	that the vision refers to the e time."
Dn	9:26	Then the e shall come like a torrent;
Dn	9:26	until the e there shall be war,
Dn	12:13	rise for your reward at the e of days."
Mt	10:22	endures to the e will be saved.
Mt	13:39	The harvest is the e of the age,
Mt	24:13	perseveres to the e will be saved.
Mt	24:14	nations, and then the e will come.
Mt	28:20	you always, until the e of the age."
Lk	21: 9	but it will not immediately be the e."
Jn	13: 1	world and he loved them to the e.
Rom	6:21	For the e of those things is death.
Rom	10: 4	For Christ is the e of the law
1 Cor	15:24	then comes the e, when he hands
Phil	3:19	Their e is destruction. Their God is
Heb	3:14	of the reality firm until the e,
1 Pt	4: 7	The e of all things is at hand.
Rv	2:26	who keeps to my ways until the e,
Rv	21: 6	the Omega, the beginning and the e.
Rv	22:13	the last, the beginning and the e."

ENDOR
1 Sm	28: 7	is a woman in E who is a medium."

ENDOWED
Ex	28: 3	expert workmen whom I have e

ENDS →END
Ps	2: 8	your possession the e of the earth.
Ps	67: 8	the e of the earth may revere our
Prv	30: 4	marked out all the e of the earth?
Sir	11:28	for by how he e, a man is known.
Is	40:28	creator of the e of the earth. He does
Mi	5: 3	shall reach to the e of the earth;
Lk	11:31	she came from the e of the earth
Acts	13:47	of salvation to the e of the earth.' "
Rom	10:18	their words to the e of the world."

ENDURANCE →ENDURE
Rom	5: 3	knowing that affliction produces e,
2 Cor	6: 4	God, through much e, in afflictions,
Ti	2: 2	sound in faith, love, and e.
Heb	10:36	You need e to do the will of God
2 Pt	1: 6	self-control with e, e with devotion,
Rv	1: 9	and the e we have in Jesus,
Rv	13:10	Such is the faithful e of the holy

ENDURE →ENDURANCE, ENDURED, ENDURES, ENDURING
Jb	20:21	Therefore his prosperity shall not e,
Ps	72:17	as long as the sun, may his name e.
Ps	104:31	May the glory of the Lord e forever;
Prv	12:19	Truthful lips e forever, the lying
Jer	10:10	whose wrath the nations cannot e;
Mal	3: 2	who will e the day of his coming?
1 Cor	4:12	we bless; when persecuted, we e;
Heb	12: 7	E your trials as "discipline";

ENDURED →ENDURE
Rom	9:22	power, has e with much patience
2 Tm	3:11	and Lystra, persecutions that I e.

Heb	12: 2	that lay before him he e the cross,
Heb	12: 3	Consider how he e such opposition

ENDURES →ENDURE
1 Chr	16:41	"because his kindness e forever,"
1 Mc	4:24	he is good, for his mercy e forever."
Ps	136: 1	is so good; God's love e forever;
Sir	40:17	off, and justice e forever.
Bar	4: 1	the law that e forever; All who cling
Dn	3:89	he is good, for his mercy e forever.
Jn	6:27	for the food that e for eternal life,
1 Cor	13: 7	things, hopes all things, e all things.
2 Cor	9: 9	poor; his righteousness e forever."

ENDURING →ENDURE
Ps	19:10	fear of the Lord is pure, e forever.
Dn	6:27	"For he is the living God, e forever;

ENEMIES →ENEMY
Ex	1:10	war they too may join our e to fight
Ex	23:22	I will be an enemy to your e
Dt	6:19	thrusting all your e out of your way.
Jos	21:44	Lord brought all their e under their
Jgs	2:14	the power of their e round
2 Sm	7: 1	him rest from his e on every side,
Jdt	8:35	you to take vengeance upon our e!"
Est	9: 5	The Jews struck down all their e
Est	9: 5	they did to their e as they pleased.
Est	9:22	the Jews obtained rest from their e
1 Mc	4:36	"Now that our e have been crushed,
Ps	23: 5	as my e watch; You anoint my head
Ps	110: 1	while I make your e your footstool."
Prv	16: 7	he makes even his e be at peace
Is	59:18	He repays his e their deserts,
Mi	7: 6	a man's e are those of his household.
Mt	5:44	love your e, and pray for those who
Mk	12:36	until I place your e under your feet." '
Lk	6:35	love your e and do good to them,
Lk	20:43	till I make your e your footstool." '
Acts	2:35	until I make your e your footstool." '
Rom	5:10	if, while we were e, we were
Rom	11:28	gospel, they are e on your account;
1 Cor	15:25	he has put all his e under his feet.
Phil	3:18	conduct themselves as e of the cross
Heb	1:13	until I make your e your footstool"?
Heb	10:13	he waits until his e are made his

ENEMY →ENEMIES, ENMITY
Ex	15: 6	hand, O Lord, has shattered the e.
Ex	23:22	I will be an e to your enemies
Dt	33:27	He drove the e out of your way
1 Sm	18:29	the more [and was his e ever after].
2 Sm	22:18	He rescued me from my mighty e,
Est	3:10	the Agagite, the e of the Jews.
Est	7: 6	"The e oppressing us is this wicked
Ps	8: 3	your foes, to silence e and avenger.
Ps	18:18	He rescued me from my mighty e,
Ps	74:10	How long, O God, shall the e jeer?
Prv	27: 6	greetings of an e one prays against.
Jer	30:14	I struck you as an e would strike,
Lam	2: 5	The Lord has become an e, he has
Mi	2: 8	late my people has risen up as an e:
Mt	5:43	love your neighbor and hate your e.'
Mt	13:39	the e who sows them is the devil.
Lk	10:19	and upon the full force of the e
1 Cor	15:26	The last e to be destroyed is death,
Jas	4: 4	of the world makes himself an e

ENGEDI
1 Sm	24: 1	there and stayed in the refuges behind E.

ENGRAVE →ENGRAVED, ENGRAVES
Zec	3: 9	I will e its inscription, says the Lord

ENGRAVED →ENGRAVE
Ex	32:16	on them that were e by God himself.
Jer	17: 1	iron stylus, E with a diamond point

ENGRAVES →ENGRAVE
Ex	28:11	As a gem-cutter e a seal, so shall

ENJOY →ENJOYMENT
Eccl	9: 9	E life with the wife whom you love,

Heb 11:25 of God rather than **e** the fleeting

ENJOYMENT →ENJOY
1 Tm 6:17 provides us with all things for our **e**.

ENLARGE →LARGE
Is 54: 2 E the space for your tent,

ENLARGES →LARGE
Dt 19: 8 your God, **e** your territory, as he

ENLIGHTENED →LIGHT
Eph 1:18 May the eyes of [your] hearts be **e**,
Heb 6: 4 case of those who have once been **e**
Heb 10:32 after you had been **e**, you endured

ENLIGHTENING →LIGHT
Ps 19: 9 of the LORD is clear, **e** the eye.

ENLIGHTENS →LIGHT
Jn 1: 9 which **e** everyone, was coming

ENMITY →ENEMY
Gn 3:15 I will put **e** between you
Jas 4: 4 of the world means **e** with God?

ENOCH
1. Son of Cain (Gn 4:17-18).
2. Descendant of Seth; walked with God and taken by him (Gn 5:18-24; Heb 11:5). Prophet (Jude 14).

ENOUGH
Dt 1: 6 'You have stayed long **e** at this
Prv 30:15 never satisfied, four never say, "E!"

ENRICHED →RICH
Prv 11:25 confers benefits will be amply **e**,
1 Cor 1: 5 in him you were **e** in every way,
2 Cor 9:11 You are being **e** in every way for all

ENROLL
Nm 1: 3 Aaron shall **e** in companies all

ENSIGNS
Nm 2: 2 under the **e** of their ancestral

ENSLAVE →SLAVE
Gal 2: 4 in Christ Jesus, that they might **e** us—

ENSNARED →SNARE
Dt 7:25 it for yourselves, lest you be **e** by it;

ENTANGLED
2 Pt 2:20 again become **e** and overcome

ENTER →ENTERED, ENTERING, ENTERS, ENTRANCE, ENTRY
Ex 40:35 Moses could not **e** the meeting tent,
Nm 20:24 he shall not **e** the land I am giving
Dt 1:37 and said, 'Not even you shall **e** there,
Ps 95:11 anger: "They shall never **e** my rest."
Ps 100: 4 E the temple gates with praise,
Ps 118:20 LORD's own gate, where the victors **e**.
Prv 4:14 The path of the wicked **e** not,
Jl 4: 2 I will **e** into judgment with them
Mt 5:20 you will not **e** into the kingdom
Mt 7:13 "E through the narrow gate;
Mt 7:21 Lord,' will **e** the kingdom of heaven,
Mt 18: 3 you will not **e** the kingdom
Mt 18: 8 better for you to **e** into life maimed
Mt 19:17 If you wish to **e** into life,
Mk 10:15 of God like a child will not **e** it."
Mk 10:23 who have wealth to **e** the kingdom
Lk 13:24 "Strive to **e** through the narrow gate,
Lk 24:26 these things and **e** into his glory?"
Jn 3: 5 no one can **e** the kingdom of God
Acts 14:22 many hardships to **e** the kingdom
Heb 3:11 "They shall not **e** into my rest." ' "
Heb 4: 3 "They shall not **e** into my rest,' "
Heb 4:11 let us strive to **e** into that rest,
Rv 15: 8 that no one could **e** it until the seven
Rv 21:27 but nothing unclean will **e** it,
Rv 21:27 Only those will **e** whose names are

ENTERED →ENTER
2 Chr 26:16 He **e** the temple of the LORD to make
Ez 43: 4 as the glory of the LORD **e** the temple
Lk 9:34 frightened when they **e** the cloud.

Lk 22: 3 Then Satan **e** into Judas, the one
Jn 13:27 he took the morsel, Satan **e** him.
Acts 11: 8 or unclean has ever **e** my mouth.'
Heb 6:20 where Jesus has **e** on our behalf as
Heb 9:12 he **e** once for all into the sanctuary,
Rv 11:11 a breath of life from God **e** them.

ENTERING →ENTER
Heb 4: 1 on our guard while the promise of **e**

ENTERS →ENTER
Jn 10: 2 whoever **e** through the gate is
Jn 10: 9 Whoever **e** through me will be

ENTERTAINED
Heb 13: 2 it some have unknowingly **e** angels.

ENTHRONED →THRONE
1 Sm 4: 4 hosts, who is **e** upon the cherubim.
2 Sm 6: 2 LORD of hosts **e** above the cherubim.
2 Kgs 19:15 God of Israel, **e** upon the cherubim!
1 Chr 13: 6 the name "LORD **e** upon the cherubim."
Ps 22: 4 Yet you are **e** as the Holy One;
Ps 29:10 The LORD sits **e** above the flood!
Ps 55:20 God, who sits **e** forever, will hear
Ps 99: 1 God is **e** on the cherubim, the earth
Ps 102:13 But you, LORD, are **e** forever;
Ps 123: 1 I raise my eyes, to you **e** in heaven.
Is 37:16 God of Israel, **e** upon the cherubim!

ENTICE →ENTICED, ENTICES
Prv 1:10 My son, should sinners **e** you,

ENTICED →ENTICE
Jb 31: 9 heart has been **e** toward a woman,
Jb 31:27 And had my heart been secretly **e**
Jas 1:14 he is lured and **e** by his own desire.

ENTICES →ENTICE
Dt 13: 7 **e** you secretly to serve other gods,

ENTIRE
Acts 2: 2 it filled the **e** house in which they
Gal 5: 3 he is bound to observe the **e** law.

ENTRANCE →ENTER
Ex 26:36 the **e** of the tent make a variegated
Mk 16: 3 stone for us from the **e** to the tomb?"

ENTRAP →TRAP
Mt 22:15 and plotted how they might **e** him

ENTREAT →ENTREATED
1 Kgs 13: 6 "E the LORD, your God," he said,

ENTREATED →ENTREAT
1 Kgs 13: 6 So the man of God **e** the LORD,

ENTRUST →TRUST
2 Tm 2: 2 me through many witnesses **e**

ENTRUSTED →TRUST
Lk 12:48 required of the person **e** with much,
Rom 3: 2 they were **e** with the utterances
Rom 6:17 of teaching to which you were **e**.
1 Cor 9:17 I have been **e** with a stewardship.
Gal 2: 7 that I had been **e** with the gospel
1 Thes 2: 4 by God to be **e** with the gospel,
1 Tm 1:11 God, with which I have been **e**.
1 Tm 6:20 guard what has been **e** to you.
2 Tm 1:12 to guard what has been **e** to me until
Ti 1: 3 which I was **e** by the command

ENTRY →ENTER
2 Pt 1:11 **e** into the eternal kingdom of our

ENVOY
Prv 13:17 a trustworthy **e** is a healing remedy.

ENVY
Prv 3:31 E not the lawless man and choose
Wis 2:24 But by the **e** of the devil,
Sir 9:11 E not a sinner's fame, for you know
Ez 31: 9 the **e** of all Eden's trees in the garden
Mk 7:22 deceit, licentiousness, **e**, blasphemy,
Rom 1:29 full of **e**, murder, rivalry, treachery,
Gal 5:21 occasions of **e**, drinking bouts,

Phil	1:15	some preach Christ from **e**
1 Tm	6: 4	From these come **e**, rivalry, insults,
Ti	3: 3	living in malice and **e**,
1 Pt	2: 1	insincerity, **e**, and all slander;

EPAPHRAS
Associate of Paul (Col 1:7; 4:12; Phlm 23).

EPAPHRODITUS
Associate of Paul (Phil 2:25; 4:18).

EPHAH

| Ex | 16:36 | [An omer is one tenth of an **e**.] |
| Ez | 45:10 | an honest **e**, and an honest liquid |

EPHESIANS → EPHESUS

| Acts | 19:28 | to shout, "Great is Artemis of the **E**!" |

EPHESUS → EPHESIANS

Acts	18:19	When they reached **E**, he left them
Acts	19: 1	to **E** where he found some disciples.
Acts	20:17	of the church at **E** summoned.
1 Cor	15:32	If at **E** I fought with beasts,
Eph	1: 1	the holy ones who are [in **E**] faithful
Rv	2: 1	"To the angel of the church in **E**,

EPHOD

Ex	28: 6	"The **e** they shall make of gold
Lv	8: 7	with the robe, placed the **e** on him,
Jgs	8:27	Gideon made an **e** out of the gold
Jgs	17: 5	also made an **e** and household idols,
1 Chr	15:27	David was also wearing a linen **e**.
Hos	3: 4	pillar, without **e** or household idols.

EPHPHATHA

| Mk | 7:34 | and groaned, and said to him, "**E**!" |

EPHRAIM
1. Second son of Joseph (Gn 41:52; 46:20). Blessed as firstborn by Jacob (Gn 48). Tribe of numbered (Nm 1:33; 26:37), blessed (Dt 33:17), allotted land (Jos 16:4-9; Ez 48:5), failed to fully possess (Jos 16:10; Jgs 1:29).
2. A term for the Northern Kingdom of Israel (Is 7:17; Hos 5).

EPHRATH → BETHLEHEM, EPHRATHAH

| Gn | 35:19 | was buried on the road to **E** [that is, |

EPHRATHAH → EPHRATH

| Ru | 4:11 | May you do well in **E** and win fame |

EPHRON
Hittite who sold Abraham a field (Gn 23).

EPICUREAN

| Acts | 17:18 | Even some of the **E** and Stoic |

EPIPHANES

| 1 Mc | 1:10 | offshoot, Antiochus **E**, son of King |

EQUAL → EQUALITY

Jb	28:17	Gold or crystal cannot **e** it, nor can
Sir	9:10	for the new one cannot **e** him.
Is	40:25	To whom can you liken me as an **e**?
Is	46: 5	you compare me with, as an **e**,
Jn	5:18	father, making himself **e** to God.

EQUALITY → EQUAL

| Phil | 2: 6 | of God, did not regard **e** with God |

EQUIP → EQUIPPED

| Eph | 4:12 | to **e** the holy ones for the work |

EQUIPPED → EQUIP

| 2 Tm | 3:17 | competent, **e** for every good work. |

ER

| Gn | 38: 6 | named Tamar for his first-born, **E**. |

ERASTUS
Associate(s) of Paul (Acts 19:22; Rom 16:23; 2 Tm 4:20).

ERECT → ERECTED

| Ex | 26:30 | You shall **e** the Dwelling according |
| Heb | 8: 5 | he was about to **e** the tabernacle. |

ERECTED → ERECT

1 Kgs	16:32	Ahab **e** an altar to Baal
2 Kgs	21: 3	He **e** altars to Baal, and also set
1 Mc	1:54	the king **e** the horrible abomination

ERROR

2 Pt	2:18	escaped from people who live in **e**.
2 Pt	3:17	be led into the **e** of the unprincipled
Jude	1:11	to Balaam's **e** for the sake of gain,

ESAU → =EDOM
Firstborn of Isaac, twin of Jacob (Gn 25:21-26). Also called Edom (Gn 25:30). Sold Jacob his birthright (Gn 25:29-34); lost blessing (Gen 27). Married Hittites (Gn 26:34), Ishmaelites (Gn 28:6-9). Reconciled to Jacob (Gen 33). Genealogy (Gn 36). The LORD chose Jacob over Esau (Mal 1:2-3), but gave Esau land (Dt 2:2-12). Descendants eventually obliterated (Ob 1-21; Jer 49:7-22).

ESCAPE → ESCAPED, ESCAPES

2 Sm	15:14	or none of us will **e** from Absalom.
Jb	11:20	**E** shall be cut off from them,
Ps	68:21	**e** from death is in the LORD God's
Ps	89:49	Who can **e** the power of Sheol?
Sir	16:13	A criminal does not **e** with his
Jer	11:11	misfortune which they cannot **e**.
Ez	17:15	Can he who does such things **e**?
Dn	13:22	if I refuse, I cannot **e** your power.
Rom	2: 3	that you will **e** the judgment
1 Thes	5: 3	woman, and they will not **e**.
Heb	2: 3	how shall we **e** if we ignore so great
Heb	12:25	they did not **e** when they refused

ESCAPED → ESCAPE

1 Sm	22: 1	Gath and **e** to the cave of Adullam.
Ps	124: 7	We **e** with our lives like a bird
Jn	10:39	but he **e** from their power.
Heb	11:34	raging fires, **e** the devouring sword;
2 Pt	2:20	they, having **e** the defilements

ESCAPES → ESCAPE

| Sir | 42:20 | does he lack; no single thing **e** him. |

ESHCOL

| Nm | 13:23 | They also reached the Wadi **E**, |

ESTABLISH → ESTABLISHED

Gn	6:18	But with you I will **e** my covenant;
Dt	28: 9	he will **e** you as a people sacred
1 Kgs	9: 5	I will **e** your throne of sovereignty
1 Chr	28: 7	I will **e** his kingdom forever, if he
Ps	89: 5	and **e** your throne through all ages."
Rom	10: 3	to **e** their own [righteousness],
Heb	10: 9	takes away the first to **e** the second.

ESTABLISHED → ESTABLISH

Gn	9:17	the covenant I have **e** between me
Ex	6: 4	I also **e** my covenant with them,
Ps	89: 3	For you said, "My love is **e** forever;
Ps	103:19	The LORD's throne is **e** in heaven;
Prv	8:27	"When he **e** the heavens I was there,
Is	2: 2	shall be **e** as the highest mountain
Is	54:14	In justice shall you be **e**,
Jer	10:12	power, **e** the world by his wisdom,
2 Pt	1:12	and are **e** in the truth you have.

ESTEEMED

| Acts | 5:13 | to join them, but the people **e** them. |

ESTHER → HADASSAH
Jewess, originally named Hadassah, who lived in Persia; cousin of Mordecai (Est 2:7). Chosen queen of Xerxes (Est 2:8-18). Persuaded by Mordecai to foil Haman's plan to exterminate the Jews (Est 3-4). Revealed Haman's plans to Xerxes, resulting in Haman's death (Est 7), the Jews' preservation (Est 8-9), Mordecai's exaltation (Est 8:15; 9:4; 10). Decreed celebration of Purim (Est 9:18-32). See also the Additions to Esther.

ESTRANGED

| Ez | 14: 5 | Israel, who have become **e** from me |

ETERNAL → ETERNITY

Gn	49:26	the delights of the **e** hills. May they
2 Mc	1:25	and **e**, Israel's savior from all evil,
Wis	7:26	For she is the refulgence of **e** light,
Wis	17: 2	as exiles from the **e** providence.
Dn	13:42	"O **e** God, you know what is hidden
Hb	3: 6	The **e** mountains are shattered,
Mt	18: 8	or two feet to be thrown into **e** fire.
Mt	19:16	what good must I do to gain **e** life?"

Mt	19:29	times more, and will inherit e life.
Mt	25:41	into the e fire prepared for the devil
Mt	25:46	these will go off to e punishment,
Mt	25:46	but the righteous to e life."
Mk	10:17	what must I do to inherit e life?"
Mk	10:30	and e life in the age to come.
Mk	16: S	proclamation of e salvation. Amen.]
Lk	10:25	what must I do to inherit e life?"
Lk	16: 9	will be welcomed into e dwellings.
Lk	18:18	what must I do to inherit e life?"
Lk	18:30	age and e life in the age to come."
Jn	3:15	believes in him may have e life."
Jn	3:16	not perish but might have e life.
Jn	3:36	believes in the Son has e life,
Jn	4:14	spring of water welling up to e life."
Jn	4:36	and gathering crops for e life,
Jn	5:24	in the one who sent me has e life
Jn	5:39	think you have e life through them;
Jn	6:27	for the food that endures for e life,
Jn	6:40	and believes in him may have e life,
Jn	6:47	to you, whoever believes has e life.
Jn	6:54	flesh and drinks my blood has e life,
Jn	6:68	You have the words of e life.
Jn	10:28	I give them e life, and they shall
Jn	12:25	this world will preserve it for e life.
Jn	12:50	that his commandment is e life.
Jn	17: 2	he may give e life to all you gave
Jn	17: 3	Now this is e life, that they should
Acts	13:46	yourselves as unworthy of e life,
Acts	13:48	who were destined for e life came
Rom	1:20	his invisible attributes of e power
Rom	2: 7	e life to those who seek glory,
Rom	5:21	e life through Jesus Christ our Lord.
Rom	6:22	sanctification, and its end is e life.
Rom	6:23	of God is e life in Christ Jesus our
Rom	16:26	to the command of the e God,
2 Cor	4:17	us an e weight of glory beyond all
2 Cor	4:18	is transitory, but what is unseen is e.
2 Cor	5: 1	not made with hands, e in heaven.
Gal	6: 8	the spirit will reap e life
Eph	3:11	This was according to the e purpose
2 Thes	1: 9	These will pay the penalty of e ruin,
1 Tm	6:12	Lay hold of e life, to which you
1 Tm	6:16	To him be honor and e power.
2 Tm	2:10	Christ Jesus, together with e glory.
Ti	1: 2	in the hope of e life that God,
Ti	3: 7	and become heirs in hope of e life.
Heb	5: 9	he became the source of e salvation
Heb	6: 2	of the dead and e judgment.
Heb	9:12	blood, thus obtaining e redemption.
Heb	9:14	who through the e spirit offered
Heb	9:15	receive the promised e inheritance.
Heb	13:20	by the blood of the e covenant,
1 Pt	5:10	to his e glory through Christ [Jesus]
2 Pt	1:11	entry into the e kingdom of our
1 Jn	1: 2	it and proclaim to you the e life
1 Jn	2:25	the promise that he made us: e life.
1 Jn	3:15	no murderer has e life remaining
1 Jn	5:11	God gave us e life, and this life is
1 Jn	5:13	you may know that you have e life,
1 Jn	5:20	Christ. He is the true God and e life.
Jude	1: 6	he has kept in e chains, in gloom,
Jude	1: 7	undergoing a punishment of e fire.
Jude	1:21	Lord Jesus Christ that leads to e life.

ETERNITY → ETERNAL

Sir	1: 2	rain, the days of e: who can number
Sir	1: 4	and prudent understanding, from e.
Sir	42:21	he is from all e one and the same,
2 Pt	3:18	be glory now and to the day of e.

ETHAN

1 Kgs	5:11	all other men—than E the Ezrahite,
1 Chr	15:19	and E, sounded brass cymbals.
Ps	89: 1	A *maskil* of E the Ezrahite.

ETHIOPIA → ETHIOPIAN, ETHIOPIANS

Jdt	1:10	of Egypt as far as the borders of E.
Est	1: 1	provinces from India to E —
Ps	87: 4	the Lord. Philistia, E, Tyre, of them

Is	18: 1	insects, beyond the rivers of E,
Ez	30: 4	and anguish shall be in E,

ETHIOPIAN → ETHIOPIA

Acts	8:27	Now there was an E eunuch, a court
Jer	13:23	Can the E change his skin?

ETHIOPIANS → ETHIOPIA

Am	9: 7	Are you not like the E to me, O men

EUNICE
Mother of Timothy (2 Tm 1:5).

EUNUCH → EUNUCHS

Est	2:14	the care of the royal e Shaashgaz,
Is	56: 3	Nor let the e say, "See, I am a dry
Acts	8:27	Now there was an Ethiopian e,

EUNUCHS → EUNUCH

Is	56: 4	To the e who observe my sabbaths

EUODIA

Phil	4: 2	I urge E and I urge Syntyche

EUPHRATES

Gn	2:14	of Asshur. The fourth river is the E.
Gn	15:18	of Egypt to the Great River [the E],
Dt	11:24	from the E River to the Western
2 Kgs	24: 7	the wadi of Egypt to the E River.
Rv	9:14	at the banks of the great river E."
Rv	16:12	his bowl on the great river E.

EUTYCHUS

Acts	20: 9	and a young man named E who was

EVANGELIST → EVANGELISTS

Acts	21: 8	we went to the house of Philip the e,
2 Tm	4: 5	perform the work of an e;

EVANGELISTS → EVANGELIST

Eph	4:11	others as e, others as pastors

EVE

Gn	3:20	The man called his wife E,
Gn	4: 1	man had relations with his wife E,
Tb	8: 6	Adam and you gave him his wife E
2 Cor	11: 3	as the serpent deceived E by his
1 Tm	2:13	For Adam was formed first, then E.

EVENING → EVENINGS

Gn	1: 5	"night." Thus e came, and morning
Gn	8:11	In the e the dove came back to him,
Gn	24:11	Near e, at the time when women go
Eccl	11: 6	and at e let not your hand be idle:
Zec	14: 7	for in the e time there shall be light.

EVENINGS → EVENING

Dn	8:14	"For two thousand three hundred e
Dn	8:26	The vision of the e

EVER → EVERLASTING, FOREVER

Ex	11: 6	has never been, nor will e be again.
Ex	15:18	The Lord shall reign forever and e.
Dt	4:32	e since God created man
Ps	25:15	My eyes are e upon the Lord,
Ps	111: 8	Established forever and e, to be
Jer	31:36	If e these natural laws give way
Dn	7:18	kingship, to possess it forever and e."
Mi	4: 5	of the Lord, our God, forever and e.
Jn	1:18	No one has e seen God. The only
Gal	1: 5	to whom be glory forever and e.
Eph	3:21	to all generations, forever and e.
Phil	4:20	God and Father, glory for e and e.
1 Tm	1:17	God, honor and glory forever and e.
2 Tm	4:18	To him be glory forever and e.
Heb	1: 8	throne, O God, stands forever and e;
Heb	13:21	to whom be glory forever [and e].
1 Pt	4:11	glory and dominion forever and e.
1 Jn	4:12	No one has e seen God. Yet, if we
Rv	1: 6	be glory and power forever [and e].
Rv	1:18	but now I am alive forever and e,
Rv	4: 9	the throne, who lives forever and e,
Rv	7:12	be to our God forever and e. Amen."
Rv	10: 6	by the one who lives forever and e,
Rv	11:15	and he will reign forever and e."

Rv	14:11	them will rise forever and e,
Rv	20:10	day and night forever and e.
Rv	22: 5	and they shall reign forever and e.

EVERLASTING → EVER, LAST

Gn	9:16	and recall the e covenant that I have
Gn	17: 7	throughout the ages as an e pact,
Gn	17:13	shall be in your flesh as an e pact.
Gn	17:19	my covenant with him as an e pact,
1 Chr	16:17	statute, for Israel as an e covenant,
1 Mc	6:44	and win an e name for himself.
Ps	78:66	to flight; e shame he dealt them.
Ps	105:10	for Jacob, an e covenant for Israel:
Ps	106:48	Lord, the God of Israel, from e to e!
Sir	15: 6	he will find, an e name inherit.
Is	33:14	of us can live with the e flames?"
Is	35:10	crowned with e joy; They will meet
Is	51:11	crowned with e joy; They will meet
Is	55: 3	will renew with you the e covenant,
Is	55:13	renown, an e imperishable sign.
Is	61: 7	in their land, e joy shall be theirs.
Jer	25: 9	of horror, of ridicule, of e reproach.
Jer	50: 5	Lord with covenant e, never to be
Ez	16:60	I will set up an e covenant with you.
Ez	37:26	it shall be an e covenant with them,
Dn	3:00	his kingdom is an e kingdom,
Dn	7:14	His dominion is an e dominion
Dn	7:27	Whose kingdom shall be e:
Dn	9:24	E justice will be introduced,
Dn	12: 2	others shall be an e horror

EVERY → EVERYONE, EVERYTHING, EVERYWHERE

Gn	1:29	I give you e seed-bearing plant all
Gn	1:29	e tree that has seed-bearing fruit
Gn	7: 4	of the earth e moving creature that I
Gn	7:23	The Lord wiped out e living thing
Ex	11: 5	E first-born in this land shall die,
Dt	8: 3	by e word that comes forth
Tb	12:18	So continue to thank him e day;
Ps	7:12	judge, who rebukes in anger e day.
Ps	50:10	For e animal of the forest is mine,
Ps	145: 2	E day I will bless you; I will praise
Prv	30: 5	E word of God is tested; he is
Eccl	3: 1	time for e affair under the heavens.
Eccl	12:14	God will bring to judgment e work,
Sir	6:35	Be eager to hear e godly discourse;
Is	40: 4	E valley shall be filled in,
Is	45:23	To me e knee shall bend; by me e
Jer	2:20	On e high hill, under e green tree,
Ez	21:12	when it comes e heart shall fail,
Ez	21:12	helpless, e spirit shall be daunted,
Mt	4: 4	but by e word that comes forth
Mt	7:17	Just so, e good tree bears good fruit,
Mt	9:35	and curing e disease and illness.
Mt	12:25	"E kingdom divided against itself
Lk	4:13	the devil had finished e temptation,
Jn	15: 2	He takes away e branch in me
Rom	3:19	so that e mouth may be silenced
Rom	14:11	Lord, e knee shall bend before me,
Rom	14:11	e tongue shall give praise to God."
1 Cor	15:24	he has destroyed e sovereignty and e authority
2 Cor	10: 5	take e thought captive in obedience
Eph	1: 3	in Christ with e spiritual blessing
Eph	1:21	far above e principality, authority,
Eph	1:21	e name that is named not only
Phil	2:10	name of Jesus e knee should bend,
Phil	2:11	and e tongue confess that
1 Thes	5:22	Refrain from e kind of evil.
2 Tm	3:17	equipped for e good work.
Heb	12: 1	let us rid ourselves of e burden
1 Jn	4: 1	do not trust e spirit but test
Rv	1: 7	and e eye will see him, even those
Rv	7:17	and God will wipe away e tear
Rv	21: 4	He will wipe e tear from their eyes,

EVERYONE → EVERY, ONE

Ex	35:21	e, as his heart suggested and his
Ez	20:11	which e must keep, to have life
Dn	12: 1	e who is found written in the book.
Jl	3: 5	Then e shall be rescued who calls

Mt	7: 8	For e who asks, receives;
Mt	7:21	"Not e who says to me, 'Lord, Lord,'
Lk	11: 4	for we ourselves forgive e in debt
Jn	1: 9	which enlightens e, was coming
Jn	3:16	so that e who believes in him might
Acts	2:21	be that e shall be saved who calls on
Rom	10:13	For "e who calls on the name
1 Cor	10:33	just as I try to please e in every way,
1 Tm	2: 4	who wills e to be saved and to come
1 Jn	3: 4	E who commits sin commits
1 Jn	4: 7	e who loves is begotten by God

EVERYTHING → EVERY, THING

Gn	1:31	God looked at e he had made,
Gn	6:17	of life; e on earth shall perish.
Ex	19: 8	together, "E the Lord has said,
Ps	150: 6	Let e that has breath give praise
Eccl	3: 1	There is an appointed time for e,
Eccl	3:11	He has made e appropriate to its
Lk	1: 3	investigating e accurately anew,
Jn	6:37	E that the Father gives me will
Jn	14:26	send in my name—he will teach you e
Acts	4:32	his own, but they had e in common.
Rom	14:20	E is indeed clean, but it is wrong
1 Cor	2:10	For the Spirit scrutinizes e,
1 Cor	10:31	you do, do e for the glory of God.
Col	3:17	do e in the name of the Lord Jesus,
1 Thes	5:21	Test e; retain what is good.
1 Tm	4: 4	For e created by God is good,
2 Pt	1: 3	has bestowed on us e that makes

EVERYWHERE → EVERY, WHERE

Lk	9: 6	good news and curing diseases e.
Acts	17:30	he demands that all people e repent

EVIDENCE

Nm	35:30	The e of a single witness is not
Dt	22:15	of the girl shall take the e of her
2 Thes	1: 5	This is e of the just judgment

EVIL → EVILDOERS, EVILS

Gn	6: 5	conceived was ever anything but e,
Gn	44: 4	'Why did you repay good with e?
Ex	32:22	how prone the people are to e.
Nm	32:13	that had done e in the sight
Dt	1:35	man of this e generation shall look
Dt	13: 6	Thus shall you purge the e
Dt	28:20	perish for the e you have done
1 Sm	12:20	true you have committed all this e;
1 Sm	16:14	he was tormented by an e spirit sent
1 Sm	18:10	[The next day an e spirit from God
1 Sm	19: 9	an e spirit from the Lord came
1 Kgs	11: 6	Solomon did e in the sight
1 Kgs	16:25	But Omri did e in the Lord's sight
2 Kgs	15:24	He did e in the sight of the Lord,
Tb	6: 8	is afflicted by a demon or e spirit,
Tb	12: 7	and e will not find its way to you.
Jb	1: 1	Job, who feared God and avoided e.
Jb	1: 8	fearing God and avoiding e?"
Jb	2: 3	fearing God and avoiding e? He still
Jb	28:28	and avoiding e is understanding.
Ps	5: 5	You are not a god who delights in e;
Ps	28: 4	for the e that they do. For the work
Ps	34:14	Keep your tongue from e, your lips
Ps	34:15	Turn from e and do good;
Ps	37:27	Turn from e and do good, that you
Ps	51: 6	I have done such e in your sight
Ps	97:10	The Lord loves those who hate e,
Ps	141: 4	Do not let my heart incline to e,
Prv	3: 7	fear the Lord and turn away from e;
Prv	4:27	to left, keep your foot far from e.
Prv	8:13	[The fear of the Lord is to hate e;]
Prv	11:19	but he who pursues e does so to his
Prv	11:27	he who pursues e will have e befall
Prv	14:16	wise man is cautious and shuns e;
Prv	14:22	Do not those who plot e go astray?
Prv	16: 6	the fear of the Lord man avoids e.
Prv	17:13	If a man returns e for good, from his house e will not depart.
Prv	20:30	E is cleansed away by bloody
Prv	24:20	For the e man has no future,

Prv	28: 5	E men understand nothing
Sir	7: 1	Do no e, and e will not overtake
Is	5:20	Woe to those who call e good, and good e,
Is	13:11	I will punish the world for its e
Jer	4:14	Cleanse your heart of e,
Jer	18: 8	I have threatened turns from its e,
Jer	18:10	nation does what is e in my eyes,
Ez	33:11	Turn, turn from your e ways!
Am	5:13	silent at this time, for it is an e time.
Am	5:14	Seek good and not e, that you may
Jon	3: 8	every man shall turn from his e way
Mi	3: 2	who hate what is good, and love e?
Hb	1:13	pure are your eyes to look upon e,
Zec	8:17	none of you plot e against another
Mt	6:13	test, but deliver us from the e one.
Mt	12:35	an e person brings forth e out of a store of e.
Mt	13:38	weeds are the children of the e one,
Mt	15:19	For from the heart come e thoughts,
Mk	7:21	from their hearts, come e thoughts,
Jn	3:19	to light, because their works were e.
Jn	17:15	that you keep them from the e one.
Rom	2: 9	every human being who does e,
Rom	3: 8	we should do e that good may come
Rom	7:19	I want, but I do the e I do not want.
Rom	7:21	I want to do right, e is at hand.
Rom	12: 9	hate what is e, hold on to what is
Rom	12:17	Do not repay anyone e for e;
Rom	12:21	Do not be conquered by e but conquer e with good.
Rom	16:19	is good, and simple as to what is e;
1 Cor	10: 6	so that we might not desire e things,
1 Cor	14:20	In respect to e be like infants,
Eph	5:16	opportunity, because the days are e.
Eph	6:12	with the e spirits in the heavens.
Eph	6:16	[the] flaming arrows of the e one.
Col	1:21	hostile in mind because of e deeds
Col	3: 5	passion, e desire, and the greed
1 Thes	5:22	Refrain from every kind of e.
2 Thes	3: 3	you and guard you from the e one.
Heb	5:14	by practice to discern good and e.
Jas	1:13	is not subject to temptation to e,
Jas	2: 4	and become judges with e designs?
Jas	3: 8	It is a restless e, full of deadly
Jas	4:16	arrogance. All such boasting is e.
1 Pt	2:16	using freedom as a pretext for e,
1 Pt	3: 9	Do not return e for e, or insult
1 Pt	3:10	must keep the tongue from e
1 Pt	3:17	be the will of God, than for doing e.
1 Jn	2:13	you have conquered the e one.
1 Jn	2:14	and you have conquered the e one.
1 Jn	3:12	Cain who belonged to the e one
1 Jn	3:12	Because his own works were e,
1 Jn	5:18	and the e one cannot touch him.
1 Jn	5:19	is under the power of the e one.
2 Jn	1:11	greets him shares in his e works.
3 Jn	1:11	do not imitate e but imitate good.
3 Jn	1:11	does what is e has never seen God.

EVILDOERS → DO, EVIL

Jb	34: 8	Keeps company with e and goes
Jb	34:22	so dense that e can hide in it.
Ps	14: 4	Will these e never learn?
Ps	26: 5	I hate the company of e;
Ps	34:17	The LORD's face is against e to wipe
Ps	36:13	There make the e fall; thrust them
Ps	53: 5	Will these e never learn?
Ps	64: 3	the malicious crowd, the mob of e.
Ps	94: 4	go on boasting, all these e?
Ps	94:16	Who will stand up for me against e?
Ps	141: 9	set for me, from the snares of e.
Prv	10:29	honestly, but to e, their downfall.
Prv	21:15	is a joy for the just, but terror for e.
Prv	24:19	Be not provoked with e, nor envious
Is	31: 2	and against those who help e.
Mal	3:15	for indeed e prosper, and even
Mt	7:23	knew you. Depart from me, you e.'
Lk	13:27	are from. Depart from me, all you e!'
1 Pt	2:12	so that if they speak of you as e,

EVILS → EVIL

Jer	2:13	Two e have my people done:
1 Tm	6:10	love of money is the root of all e,

EWE

2 Sm	12: 3	at all except one little e lamb that he

EXACT

Est	4: 7	as well as the e amount of silver

EXALT → EXALTED, EXALTING, EXALTS

Jos	3: 7	"Today I will begin to e you
1 Sm	2:10	king and e the horn of his anointed!"
Tb	13: 6	and e the King of the ages.
Tb	13: 7	"As for me, I e my God, and my
Ps	34: 4	with me; let us e his name together.
Prv	4: 8	Extol her, and she will e you;
Sir	1:27	E not yourself lest you fall
Dn	3:57	praise and e him above all forever.
Jas	4:10	before the Lord and he will e you.
1 Pt	5: 6	God, that he may e you in due time.

EXALTED → EXALT

Nm	24: 7	and his royalty shall be e.
Jos	4:14	day the LORD e Joshua in the sight
2 Sm	5:12	and had e his rule for the sake of his
1 Chr	14: 2	his kingdom was greatly e
1 Chr	29:11	you are e as head over all.
1 Chr	29:25	the LORD e Solomon greatly
Neh	9: 5	and e above all blessing and praise."
Jb	24:24	They are e for a while,
Ps	18:47	be my rock! E be God, my savior!
Ps	18:49	Truly you have e me above my
Ps	46:11	am God! I am e among the nations, e on the earth."
Ps	89:25	through my name his horn will be e.
Ps	89:43	You have e the right hand of his
Ps	97: 9	all the earth, e far above all gods.
Ps	99: 2	on Zion, e above all the peoples.
Ps	138: 2	For you have e over all your name
Ps	148:13	for his name alone is e,
Prv	11:11	of the righteous the city is e,
Is	2:11	and the LORD alone will be e,
Is	2:17	And the LORD alone will be e,
Is	5:16	of hosts shall be e by his judgment,
Is	12: 4	deeds, proclaim how e is his name.
Is	33: 5	The LORD is e, enthroned on high;
Is	33:10	now will I be e, now be lifted up.
Is	52:13	he shall be raised high and greatly e.
Jer	17:12	of glory, e from the beginning,
Hos	13: 1	for he was e in Israel; but he sinned
Mt	23:12	whoever humbles himself will be e.
Lk	14:11	one who humbles himself will be e."
Lk	18:14	one who humbles himself will be e."
Acts	2:33	E at the right hand of God,
Acts	5:31	God e him at his right hand as
Phil	2: 9	Because of this, God greatly e him

EXALTING → EXALT

Dn	11:36	e himself and making himself

EXALTS → EXALT

1 Sm	2: 7	makes rich, he humbles, he also e.
Prv	14:34	Virtue e a nation, but sin is
Sir	7:11	be mindful of him who e
Lk	14:11	For everyone who e himself will be
Lk	18:14	for everyone who e himself will be
2 Thes	2: 4	e himself above every so-called god

EXAMINATION → EXAMINE

Dn	13:48	a woman of Israel without e

EXAMINE → EXAMINATION, EXAMINED

Sir	11: 7	find no fault; e first, then criticize.
Lam	3:40	Let us search and e our ways
1 Cor	11:28	A person should e himself, and so
2 Cor	13: 5	E yourselves to see whether you are

EXAMINED → EXAMINE

Acts	17:11	e the scriptures daily to determine

EXAMPLE → EXAMPLES

Jgs	2:17	did not follow their e of obedience

Jdt	8:24	let us set an **e** for our kinsmen.
1 Cor	10:11	things happened to them as an **e**,
1 Tm	1:16	display all his patience as an **e**
1 Tm	4:12	but set an **e** for those who believe,
Jas	5:10	Take as an **e** of hardship
1 Pt	2:21	leaving you an **e** that you should
2 Pt	2: 6	making them an **e** for the godless
Jude	1: 7	vice, serve as an **e** by undergoing

EXAMPLES → EXAMPLE
1 Cor	10: 6	These things happened as **e** for us,
1 Pt	5: 3	to you, but be **e** to the flock.

EXCEL → EXCELLENCE, EXCELLENT
Gn	49: 4	as water, you shall no longer **e**,
2 Cor	8: 7	Now as you **e** in every respect,
2 Cor	8: 7	may you **e** in this gracious act also.

EXCELLENCE → EXCEL
Phil	4: 8	if there is any **e** and if there is

EXCELLENT → EXCEL
1 Cor	12:31	I shall show you a still more **e** way.
Ti	3: 8	these are **e** and beneficial to others.
Heb	1: 4	has inherited is more **e** than theirs.
Heb	8: 6	so much more **e** a ministry as he is

EXCEPT
Nm	14:30	swore to settle you, **e** Caleb,
2 Sm	22:32	"For who is God **e** the Lord? Who is
1 Kgs	12:20	loyal to David's house **e** the tribe
1 Kgs	15: 5	**e** in the case of Uriah the Hittite.
Mt	11:27	No one knows the Son **e** the Father,
Mt	11:27	no one knows the Father **e** the Son
Lk	11:29	will be given it, **e** the sign of Jonah.
Jn	3:13	to heaven **e** the one who has come
Jn	6:46	has seen the Father **e** the one who is
Jn	14: 6	comes to the Father **e** through me.
Jn	17:12	none of them was lost **e** the son

EXCESSIVE
2 Cor	2: 7	may be overwhelmed by **e** pain.

EXCHANGED
Ps	106:20	They **e** their glorious God
Rom	1:23	**e** the glory of the immortal God
Rom	1:25	They **e** the truth of God for a lie
Rom	1:26	Their females **e** natural relations

EXCLUDE → EXCLUDED
Lk	6:22	and when they **e** and insult you,

EXCLUDED → EXCLUDE
2 Chr	26:21	for he was **e** from the house

EXCUSE
Jn	15:22	as it is they have no **e** for their sin.
Rom	1:20	As a result, they have no **e**;
Rom	2: 1	you are without **e**, every one of you

EXECUTED → EXECUTES
Nm	33: 4	gods, too, the Lord **e** judgments.

EXECUTES → EXECUTED
Dt	10:18	who **e** justice for the orphan

EXERCISES
1 Cor	9:25	Every athlete **e** discipline in every

EXHIBITED
1 Cor	4: 9	God has **e** us apostles as the last

EXHORT → EXHORTATION
Ti	2:15	**E** and correct with all authority.

EXHORTATION → EXHORT
Acts	13:15	you has a word of **e** for the people,
Acts	15:31	it, they were delighted with the **e**.

EXILE → EXILED, EXILES
2 Kgs	25:11	led into **e** the last of the people
Ezr	6:21	had returned from the **e** partook of it
Tb	13: 6	In the land of my **e** I praise him,
Ps	144:14	walls, no **e**, no outcry in our streets.
Is	5:13	Therefore my people go into **e**,
Jer	13:19	All Judah is banished in universal **e**.
Jer	48: 7	Chemosh shall go into **e**, his priests

Jer	49: 3	For Milcom goes into **e**
Lam	1: 3	Judah has fled into **e**

EXILED → EXILE
Sir	47:24	caused them to be **e** from their land.

EXILES → EXILE
Ezr	6:19	The **e** kept the Passover
Jer	24: 5	favor Judah's **e** whom I sent away
Ez	11:25	I told the **e** everything the Lord had shown me.

EXIST → EXISTED, EXISTS
Rom	4:17	and calls into being what does not **e**.
1 Cor	8: 6	all things are and for whom we **e**,
Heb	2:10	and through whom all things **e**,

EXISTED → EXIST
2 Pt	3: 5	the fact that the heavens **e** of old

EXISTS → EXIST
Heb	11: 6	God must believe that he **e**

EXODUS
Heb	11:22	spoke of the **E** of the Israelites

EXORCISTS
Acts	19:13	some itinerant Jewish **e** tried

EXPECTATION → EXPECTING
Prv	10:28	but the **e** of the wicked
Lk	3:15	Now the people were filled with **e**,

EXPECTING → EXPECTATION
Lk	6:35	to them, and lend **e** nothing back;

EXPENSIVE
1 Tm	2: 9	ornaments, or pearls, or **e** clothes,

EXPERIENCE
Sir	25: 6	The crown of old men is wide **e**;
Gal	3: 4	Did you **e** so many things in vain?—if

EXPIATE → EXPIATED, EXPIATION
Heb	2:17	before God to **e** the sins of the people.

EXPIATED → EXPIATE
Prv	16: 6	By kindness and piety guilt is **e**,
Dn	9:24	sin will end, guilt will be **e**,

EXPIATION → EXPIATE
Rom	3:25	whom God set forth as an **e**, through faith,
1 Jn	2: 2	He is **e** for our sins, and not for
1 Jn	4:10	sent his Son as **e** for our sins.

EXPLAIN → EXPLAINED
2 Chr	9: 2	Solomon that he could not **e** to her.
Dn	5:12	how to interpret dreams, **e** enigmas,
Mt	13:36	"**E** to us the parable of the weeds
Mt	15:15	him in reply, "**E** [this] parable to us."
Heb	5:11	and it is difficult to **e**, for you have

EXPLAINED → EXPLAIN
Jgs	14:17	she **e** the riddle to her countrymen.
Mk	4:34	his own disciples he **e** everything
Acts	18:26	and **e** to him the Way [of God] more

EXPLOIT
2 Pt	2: 3	In their greed they will **e** you

EXPOSE → EXPOSED
Mt	1:19	yet unwilling to **e** her to shame,
Eph	5:11	works of darkness; rather **e** them,

EXPOSED → EXPOSE
Ez	23:29	so that your indecent nakedness is **e**.
Jn	3:20	so that his works might not be **e**.
Eph	5:13	everything **e** by the light becomes
Heb	10:33	times you were publicly **e** to abuse
Rv	16:15	not go naked and people see him **e**.)

EXTOL
Jb	36:24	Remember, you should **e** his work,
Song	1: 4	we **e** your love; it is beyond wine:

EXTORTION
Ps	62:11	Do not trust in **e**; in plunder put no
Ez	22:29	The people of the land practice **e**
Lk	3:14	"Do not practice **e**, do not falsely accuse

EXTRAORDINARY
Acts 19:11 So e were the mighty deeds God

EXULT → EXULTS
Song 1: 4 With you we rejoice and e,
Hb 3:18 in the LORD and e in my saving God.

EXULTS → EXULT
1 Sm 2: 1 she said: "My heart e in the LORD,

EYE → EYES, EYEWITNESSES
Ex 21:24 e for e, tooth for tooth,
Lv 24:20 Limb for limb, e for e,
Dt 19:21 Life for life, e for e, tooth for tooth,
Ps 17: 8 Keep me as the apple of your e;
Ps 94: 9 The one who formed the e not see?
Prv 7: 2 my teaching as the apple of your e;
Prv 30:17 The e that mocks a father, or scorns
Eccl 1: 8 The e is not satisfied with seeing
Sir 31:13 No creature is greedier than the e:
Is 64: 3 ear has ever heard, no e ever seen,
Zec 2:12 you touches the apple of my e.
Mt 5:29 If your right e causes you to sin,
Mt 5:38 'An e for an e and a tooth for a tooth.'
Mt 6:22 "The lamp of the body is the e.
Mt 7: 3 the splinter in your brother's e,
Mt 7: 3 the wooden beam in your own e?
Mt 18: 9 And if your e causes you to sin,
Mk 10:25 to pass through [the] e of [a] needle
1 Cor 2: 9 "What e has not seen, and ear has not
1 Cor 12:17 If the whole body were an e,
1 Cor 15:52 in the blink of an e, at the last
Rv 1: 7 and every e will see him, even those

EYES → EYE
Gn 3: 7 the e of both of them were opened,
Nm 15:39 the desires of your hearts and e.
Nm 22:31 removed the veil from Balaam's e,
Nm 33:55 will become as barbs in your e
Dt 11:12 his e are upon it continually
Dt 16:19 a bribe blinds the e even of the wise
Dt 29: 3 or e to see, or ears to hear.
Dt 34: 4 I have let you feast your e upon it,
Jos 23:13 for your sides and thorns for your e,
Jgs 16:28 my two e I may avenge myself once
1 Kgs 10: 7 I came and saw with my own e,
2 Kgs 6:17 "O LORD, open his e, that he may see."
2 Kgs 9:30 she shadowed her e, adorned her
2 Chr 16: 9 The e of the LORD roam over
Tb 2:10 warm droppings settled in my e,
Tb 6: 9 on the e of a man who has cataracts,
Jb 31: 1 I have made an agreement with my e
Ps 13: 4 Give light to my e lest I sleep
Ps 25:15 My e are ever upon the LORD,
Ps 36: 2 their e are closed to the fear of God.
Ps 66: 7 Whose e are fixed upon the nations.
Ps 115: 5 but do not speak, e but do not see.
Ps 118:23 been done; it is wonderful in our e.
Ps 119:18 Open my e to see clearly
Ps 119:37 Avert my e from what is worthless;
Ps 121: 1 I raise my e toward the mountains.
Ps 123: 1 ascents. To you I raise my e, to you
Ps 123: 2 Yes, like the e of a servant
Ps 123: 2 So our e are on the LORD our God,
Ps 139:16 Your e foresaw my actions; in your
Ps 141: 8 My e are upon you, O GOD;
Prv 3: 7 Be not wise in your own e,
Prv 4:25 Let your e look straight ahead
Prv 6:17 Haughty e, a lying tongue,
Prv 15: 3 The e of the LORD are in every place,
Prv 17:24 the e of a fool are on the ends
Prv 22:12 The e of the LORD safeguard
Prv 23:29 for nothing? Who have black e?
Prv 26: 5 lest he become wise in his own e.
Eccl 2:10 that my e desired did I deny them,
Song 4: 1 you are beautiful! Your e are doves
Is 1:15 out your hands, I close my e to you;
Is 6: 5 yet my e have seen the King,
Is 6:10 to dull their ears and close their e;
Is 6:10 Else their e will see, their ears hear,
Is 33:17 Your e will see a king in his

Is 42: 7 To open the e of the blind, to bring
Jer 8:23 of water, my e a fountain of tears,
Lam 3:48 My e run with streams of water
Ez 1:18 their rims were full of e all around.
Ez 24:16 from you the delight of your e,
Dn 7: 8 This horn had e like a man,
Dn 10: 6 his e were like fiery torches,
Hb 1:13 Too pure are your e to look
Zec 4:10 These seven facets are the e
Zec 12:4 the house of Judah I will open my e,
Mt 9:30 And their e were opened.
Mt 13:15 they have closed their e, lest they see with their e and hear
Mt 21:42 done, and it is wonderful in our e'?
Mk 8:25 he laid hands on his e a second time
Lk 10:23 "Blessed are the e that see what you
Lk 24:31 With that their e were opened
Jn 9:10 him, "[So] how were your e opened?"
Jn 10:21 surely a demon cannot open the e
Jn 12:40 "He blinded their e and hardened
Acts 9: 8 when he opened his e he could see
Acts 28:27 they have closed their e, so they may not see with their e
Rom 11:10 let their e grow dim so that they
Eph 1:18 May the e of [your] hearts be
Heb 4:13 exposed to the e of him to whom we
1 Pt 3:12 For the e of the Lord are
1 Jn 1: 1 what we have seen with our e,
1 Jn 2:16 lust, enticement for the e,
Rv 1:14 and his e were like a fiery flame.
Rv 2:18 whose e are like a fiery flame
Rv 4: 6 four living creatures covered with e
Rv 5: 6 He had seven horns and seven e;
Rv 7:17 wipe away every tear from their e."
Rv 19:12 His e were [like] a fiery flame,
Rv 21: 4 He will wipe every tear from their e,

EYEWITNESSES → EYE, WITNESS
Lk 1: 2 just as those who were e
2 Pt 1:16 but we had been e of his majesty.

EZEKIEL
Priest called to be prophet to the exiles (Sir 49:8; Ez 1-3). Symbolically acted out destruction of Jerusalem (Ez 4-5; 12; 24).

EZION-GEBER
1 Kgs 9:26 Solomon also built a fleet at E,
2 Chr 20:36 to Tarshish; the fleet was built at E.

EZRA
Priest and teacher of the Law who led a return of exiles to Israel to reestablish temple and worship (Ezr 7-8). Corrected intermarriage of priests (Ezr 9-10). Read Law at celebration of Feast of Tabernacles (Neh 8). Participated in dedication of Jerusalem's walls (Neh 12).

F

FACE → FACES
Gn 32:31 "Because I have seen God f to f,"
Ex 3: 6 Moses hid his f, for he was afraid
Ex 33:11 LORD used to speak to Moses f to f,
Ex 33:20 But my f you cannot see, for no man
Ex 34:30 radiant the skin of his f had become,
Nm 6:25 The LORD let his f shine upon you,
Nm 12: 8 f to f I speak to him, plainly and not
Dt 5: 4 The LORD spoke with you f to f
Dt 31:17 them and hide my f from them,
Dt 34:10 Moses, whom the LORD knew f to f.
Jgs 6:22 seen the angel of the LORD f to f!"
2 Kgs 14: 8 challenge, "Come, let us meet f to f."
2 Chr 25:17 "Come, let us meet each other f to f."
2 Chr 30: 9 he will not turn away his f from you
Ezr 9: 6 confounded to raise my f to you,
Jdt 10:23 all marveled at the beauty of her f.
Est 7: 8 the f of Haman was covered over.
Jb 1:11 he will blaspheme you to your f."
Ps 4: 7 LORD, show us the light of your f!"
Ps 13: 2 How long will you hide your f
Ps 27: 8 "Come," says my heart, "seek God's f"; your f, LORD, do I seek!

Ps	31:17	Let your f shine on your servant;
Ps	51:11	Turn away your f from my sins;
Ps	67: 2	bless us; may God's f shine upon us,
Ps	80: 4	restore us; Let your f shine upon us,
Ps	104:29	When you hide your f, they are lost.
Ps	119:135	Let your f shine upon your servant;
Eccl	8: 1	A man's wisdom illumines his f,
Sir	45: 5	f to f, he gave him the commandments,
Is	8:17	who is hiding his f from the house
Is	50: 7	I have set my f like flint,
Is	54: 8	for a moment I hid my f from you;
Jer	32: 4	They shall meet and speak f to f,
Ez	1:10	each of the four had the f of a man,
Ez	1:10	on the right side was the f of a lion,
Ez	1:10	and on the left side the f of an ox,
Ez	1:10	finally each had the f of an eagle.
Ez	10:14	the first f was that of an ox,
Ez	39:23	me, and I hid my f from them
Ez	39:29	No longer will I hide my f
Dn	10: 6	chrysolite, his f shone like lightning,
Mt	17: 2	his f shone like the sun and his
Mt	18:10	upon the f of my heavenly Father.
Mt	26:67	they spat in his f and struck him,
Lk	9:29	While he was praying his f changed
Acts	6:15	saw that his f was like the f
1 Cor	13:12	as in a mirror, but then f to f.
2 Cor	3: 7	intently at the f of Moses because
2 Cor	4: 6	of God on the f of [Jesus] Christ.
2 Cor	10: 1	I who am humble when f to f
1 Pt	3:12	but the f of the Lord is against
2 Jn	1:12	to speak f to f so that our joy may be
3 Jn	1:14	you soon, when we can talk f to f.
Rv	1:16	and his f shone like the sun at its
Rv	4: 7	the third had a f like that of a human
Rv	10: 1	his f was like the sun and his feet
Rv	22: 4	They will look upon his f, and his

FACES →FACE

Ex	25:20	but with their f looking toward
Ps	34: 6	and your f may not blush for shame.
Ps	83:17	Cover their f with shame, till they
Is	6: 2	with two they veiled their f,
Ez	1: 6	but each had four f and four wings,
Ez	10:14	Each had four f: the first face was
Ez	41:18	cherubim. Each cherub had two f:
Rv	9: 7	of gold; their f were like human f,

FACT

2 Pt	3: 5	They deliberately ignore the f

FACTIONS

1 Cor	11:19	there have to be f among you
Gal	5:20	acts of selfishness, dissensions, f,

FAIL →FAILED, FAILINGS, FAILS

Nm	15:22	through inadvertence you f to carry
Dt	31: 6	he will never f you or forsake you."
1 Chr	28:20	He will not f you or abandon you
Ez	47:12	shall not fade, nor their fruit f.
Lk	22:32	that your own faith may not f;
2 Cor	13: 5	you?—unless, of course, you f the test.

FAILED →FAIL

Rom	9: 6	it is not that the word of God has f.
2 Cor	13: 6	you will discover that we have not f.

FAILINGS →FAIL

Rom	15: 1	to put up with the f of the weak

FAILS →FAIL

Ps	143: 7	for my spirit f me. Do not hide your
Is	58:11	like a spring whose water never f.

FAINT

Ps	142: 4	My spirit is f within me, but you
Song	2: 5	me with apples, for I am f with love.
Is	40:31	grow weary, walk and not grow f.

FAIR →FAIRLY

Hos	10:11	upon her f neck; Ephraim was to be
Mt	16: 2	'Tomorrow will be f, for the sky is

FAIRLY →FAIR

Ps	58: 2	O gods; do you judge mortals f?

Col	4: 1	treat your slaves justly and f,

FAITH →FAITHFUL, FAITHFULLY, FAITHFULNESS, FAITHLESS

Nm	5: 6	him, thus breaking f with the LORD,
Dt	32:51	of you broke f with me among
Jgs	9:15	anoint me king over you in good f,
Jgs	9:16	then, if you have acted in good f
Jgs	9:19	you have acted in good f
1 Mc	10:27	to keep f with us, and we will
Ps	116:10	I kept f, even when I said, "I am
Ps	146: 6	that is in them, Who keeps f forever,
Sir	27:17	your friend, keep f with him;
Is	7: 9	a nation. Unless your f is firm
Is	26: 2	a nation that is just, one that keeps f.
Hb	2: 4	just man, because of his f, shall live.
Mt	6:30	provide for you, O you of little f?
Mt	8:10	no one in Israel have I found such f.
Mt	8:26	are you terrified, O you of little f?"
Mt	9: 2	When Jesus saw their f, he said
Mt	9:22	daughter! Your f has saved you."
Mt	9:29	be done for you according to your f."
Mt	14:31	him, "O you of little f, why did you
Mt	15:28	in reply, "O woman, great is your f!
Mt	16: 8	"You of little f, why do you conclude
Mt	17:20	to them, "Because of your little f.
Mt	17:20	if you have f the size of a mustard
Mt	21:21	you, if you have f and do not waver,
Mt	21:22	you ask for in prayer with f,
Mk	2: 5	When Jesus saw their f, he said
Mk	4:40	terrified? Do you not have f?"
Mk	5:34	her, "Daughter, your f has saved you.
Mk	10:52	"Go your way; your f has saved you."
Mk	11:22	said to them in reply, "Have f in God.
Lk	5:20	When he saw their f, he said,
Lk	7: 9	even in Israel have I found such f."
Lk	7:50	the woman, "Your f has saved you;
Lk	8:25	he asked them, "Where is your f?"
Lk	8:48	her, "Daughter, your f has saved you;
Lk	12:28	provide for you, O you of little f?
Lk	17: 5	said to the Lord, "Increase our f."
Lk	17: 6	"If you have f the size of a mustard
Lk	17:19	up and go; your f has saved you."
Lk	18: 8	Man comes, will he find f on earth?"
Lk	18:42	"Have sight; your f has saved you."
Lk	22:32	prayed that your own f may not fail;
Acts	3:16	And by f in his name, this man,
Acts	6: 5	a man filled with f and the holy
Acts	6: 7	were becoming obedient to the f.
Acts	11:24	filled with the holy Spirit and f.
Acts	13: 8	turn the proconsul away from the f.
Acts	14: 9	saw that he had the f to be healed,
Acts	14:22	exhorted them to persevere in the f,
Acts	14:27	how he had opened the door of f
Acts	15: 9	for by f he purified their hearts.
Acts	16: 5	day the churches grew stronger in f
Acts	20:21	God and to f in our Lord Jesus.
Acts	24:24	to him speak about f in Christ Jesus.
Acts	26:18	who have been consecrated by f
Rom	1: 5	to bring about the obedience of f,
Rom	1: 8	of you, because your f is heralded
Rom	1:12	encouraged by one another's f,
Rom	1:17	the righteousness of God from f to f;
Rom	1:17	one who is righteous by f will live."
Rom	3:22	of God through f in Jesus Christ
Rom	3:25	expiation, through f, by his blood,
Rom	3:26	justify the one who has f in Jesus.
Rom	3:27	No, rather on the principle of f.
Rom	3:28	a person is justified by f apart
Rom	3:30	the circumcised on the basis of f and the uncircumcised through f.
Rom	3:31	we then annulling the law by this f?
Rom	4: 5	his f is credited as righteousness.
Rom	4: 9	Now we assert that "f was credited
Rom	4:11	received through f while he was
Rom	4:12	follow the path of f that our father
Rom	4:13	the righteousness that comes from f.
Rom	4:14	f is null and the promise is void.
Rom	4:16	those who follow the f of Abraham,
Rom	4:19	He did not weaken in f when he

Rom	4:20	he was empowered by f and gave	1 Tm	1:19	by having f and a good conscience.
Rom	5: 1	since we have been justified by f,	1 Tm	1:19	have made a shipwreck of their f,
Rom	9:30	is, righteousness that comes from f;	1 Tm	2: 7	teacher of the Gentiles in f
Rom	9:32	Because they did it not by f, but as	1 Tm	2:15	provided women persevere in f
Rom	10: 6	that comes from f says, "Do not say	1 Tm	3: 9	of the f with a clear conscience.
Rom	10: 8	is, the word of f that we preach),	1 Tm	3:13	confidence in their f in Christ Jesus.
Rom	10:17	Thus f comes from what is heard,	1 Tm	4: 1	away from the f by paying attention
Rom	11:20	but you are there because of f. So do	1 Tm	4: 6	nourished on the words of the f
Rom	12: 3	to the measure of f that God has	1 Tm	4:12	speech, conduct, love, f, and purity.
Rom	12: 6	if prophecy, in proportion to the f;	1 Tm	5: 8	family members has denied the f
Rom	14: 1	Welcome anyone who is weak in f,	1 Tm	6:10	desire for it have strayed from the f
Rom	14:22	Keep the f [that] you have	1 Tm	6:11	righteousness, devotion, f, love,
Rom	14:23	if he eats, because this is not from f; for whatever	1 Tm	6:12	Compete well for the f. Lay hold
		is not from f is sin.	1 Tm	6:21	people have deviated from the f.
Rom	16:26	to bring about the obedience of f,	2 Tm	1: 5	as I recall your sincere f that first
1 Cor	2: 5	so that your f might rest not	2 Tm	1:13	in the f and love that are in Christ
1 Cor	12: 9	to another f by the same Spirit;	2 Tm	2:18	and are upsetting the f of some.
1 Cor	13: 2	if I have all f so as to move	2 Tm	2:22	desires and pursue righteousness, f,
1 Cor	13:13	So f, hope, love remain, these three;	2 Tm	3: 8	depraved mind, unqualified in the f.
1 Cor	15:14	is our preaching; empty, too, your f.	2 Tm	3:10	way of life, purpose, f, patience,
1 Cor	15:17	has not been raised, your f is vain;	2 Tm	3:15	salvation through f in Christ Jesus.
1 Cor	16:13	stand firm in the f, be courageous,	2 Tm	4: 7	finished the race; I have kept the f.
2 Cor	1:24	Not that we lord it over your f;	Ti	1: 1	sake of the f of God's chosen ones
2 Cor	1:24	your joy, for you stand firm in the f.	Ti	1: 4	my true child in our common f:
2 Cor	4:13	then, we have the same spirit of f,	Ti	1:13	so that they may be sound in the f,
2 Cor	5: 7	for we walk by f, not by sight.	Ti	2: 2	self-controlled, sound in f, love,
2 Cor	8: 7	in every respect, in f, discourse,	Ti	3:15	Greet those who love us in the f.
2 Cor	10:15	as your f increases, our influence	Phlm	1: 5	and the f you have in the Lord Jesus
2 Cor	13: 5	to see whether you are living in f.	Phlm	1: 6	in the f may become effective
Gal	1:23	is now preaching the f he once tried	Heb	4: 2	they were not united in f with those
Gal	2:16	law but through f in Jesus Christ,	Heb	6: 1	from dead works and f in God,
Gal	2:16	we may be justified by f in Christ	Heb	6:12	those who, through f and patience,
Gal	2:20	I live by f in the Son of God who	Heb	10:38	But my just one shall live by f,
Gal	3: 8	God would justify the Gentiles by f,	Heb	10:39	among those who have f and will
Gal	3:11	one who is righteous by f will live."	Heb	11: 1	F is the realization of what is hoped
Gal	3:12	But the law does not depend on f;	Heb	11: 3	By f we understand that the universe
Gal	3:14	the promise of the Spirit through f.	Heb	11: 4	By f Abel offered to God a sacrifice
Gal	3:22	sin, that through f in Jesus Christ	Heb	11: 5	By f Enoch was taken up so that he
Gal	3:23	Before f came, we were held	Heb	11: 6	without f it is impossible to please
Gal	3:23	confined for the f that was to be	Heb	11: 7	By f Noah, warned about what was
Gal	3:24	that we might be justified by f.	Heb	11: 7	righteousness that comes through f.
Gal	3:25	But now that f has come, we are no	Heb	11: 8	By f Abraham obeyed when he was
Gal	3:26	For through f you are all children	Heb	11: 9	By f he sojourned in the promised
Gal	5: 5	the Spirit, by f, we await the hope	Heb	11:11	By f he received power to generate,
Gal	5: 6	but only f working through love.	Heb	11:13	All these died in f. They did not
Gal	6:10	who belong to the family of the f.	Heb	11:17	By f Abraham, when put to the test,
Eph	1:15	hearing of your f in the Lord Jesus	Heb	11:20	By f regarding things still to come
Eph	2: 8	you have been saved through f,	Heb	11:21	By f Jacob, when dying,
Eph	3:12	of access through f in him.	Heb	11:22	By f Joseph, near the end of his life,
Eph	3:17	may dwell in your hearts through f;	Heb	11:23	By f Moses was hidden by his
Eph	4: 5	one Lord, one f, one baptism;	Heb	11:24	By f Moses, when he had grown up,
Eph	4:13	until we all attain to the unity of f	Heb	11:27	By f he left Egypt, not fearing
Eph	6:16	all circumstances, hold f as a shield,	Heb	11:28	By f he kept the Passover
Eph	6:23	and love with f, from God	Heb	11:29	By f they crossed the Red Sea as
Phil	1:25	for your progress and joy in the f,	Heb	11:30	By f the walls of Jericho fell
Phil	1:27	together for the f of the gospel,	Heb	11:31	By f Rahab the harlot did not perish
Phil	2:17	the sacrificial service of your f,	Heb	11:33	who by f conquered kingdoms,
Phil	3: 9	which comes through f in Christ,	Heb	11:39	though approved because of their f,
Col	1: 4	have heard of your f in Christ Jesus	Heb	12: 2	Jesus, the leader and perfecter of f.
Col	1:23	provided that you persevere in the f,	Heb	13: 7	their way of life and imitate their f.
Col	2: 5	and the firmness of your f in Christ.	Jas	1: 3	of your f produces perseverance.
Col	2: 7	in the f as you were taught,	Jas	1: 6	But he should ask in f, not doubting,
Col	2:12	with him through f in the power	Jas	2: 5	are poor in the world to be rich in f
1 Thes	1: 3	calling to mind your work of f	Jas	2:14	if someone says he has f but does
1 Thes	1: 8	every place your f in God has gone	Jas	2:14	have works? Can that f save him?
1 Thes	3: 2	and encourage you in your f,	Jas	2:17	So also f of itself, if it does not have
1 Thes	3: 5	I sent to learn about your f, for fear	Jas	2:18	say, "You have f and I have works."
1 Thes	3: 6	bringing us the good news of your f	Jas	2:18	Demonstrate your f to me without
1 Thes	3: 7	and affliction, through your f.	Jas	2:18	I will demonstrate my f to you
1 Thes	3:10	to remedy the deficiencies of your f.	Jas	2:20	that f without works is useless?
1 Thes	5: 8	putting on the breastplate of f	Jas	2:22	You see that f was active along
2 Thes	1: 3	because your f flourishes ever more,	Jas	2:22	and f was completed by the works.
2 Thes	1: 4	and f in all your persecutions	Jas	2:24	by works and not by f alone.
2 Thes	1:11	good purpose and every effort of f,	Jas	2:26	so also f without works is dead.
2 Thes	3: 2	wicked people, for not all have f.	Jas	5:15	prayer of f will save the sick person,
1 Tm	1: 2	to Timothy, my true child in f:	1 Pt	1: 5	of God are safeguarded through f,
1 Tm	1: 1	of God that is to be received by f.	1 Pt	1: 7	so that the genuineness of your f,
1 Tm	1: 5	a good conscience, and a sincere f.	1 Pt	1: 9	as you attain the goal of [your] f,
1 Tm	1:14	along with the f and love that are	1 Pt	1:21	so that your f and hope are in God.

1 Pt	5: 9	steadfast in f, knowing that your
2 Pt	1: 1	those who have received a f of equal
2 Pt	1: 5	to supplement your f with virtue,
1 Jn	5: 4	that conquers the world is our f.
Jude	1: 3	contend for the f that was once
Jude	1:20	yourselves up in your most holy f;
Rv	2:13	and have not denied your f in me,
Rv	2:19	your works, your love, f, service,
Rv	14:12	commandments and their f in Jesus.

FAITHFUL → FAITH

Dt	7: 9	the f God who keeps his merciful
Dt	32: 4	his ways! A f God, without deceit,
1 Sm	2: 9	guard the footsteps of his f ones,
1 Sm	2:35	I will choose a f priest who shall do
2 Chr	6:41	may your f ones rejoice in good
2 Chr	31:20	upright and f before the LORD.
Neh	9: 8	you had found his heart f in your
1 Mc	2:52	Was not Abraham found f in trial,
1 Mc	3:13	an assembly of f men ready for war.
1 Mc	7: 8	in the kingdom, and f to the king.
2 Mc	1: 2	his covenant with his f servants,
Ps	4: 4	the LORD works wonders for the f;
Ps	12: 2	the f have vanished from the human
Ps	16:10	nor let your f servant see the pit.
Ps	30: 5	Sing praise to the LORD, you f;
Ps	31: 6	you will redeem me, LORD, f God.
Ps	31:24	Love the LORD, all you f. The LORD
Ps	32: 6	Thus should all your f pray in time
Ps	37:28	and does not abandon the f.
Ps	50: 5	"Gather my f ones before me,
Ps	52:11	I will proclaim before the f that your
Ps	78: 8	whose spirit was not f to God,
Ps	79: 2	the flesh of your f for the beasts
Ps	85: 9	To his people, to the f, to those who
Ps	89:20	to your f ones you said: "I have set
Ps	97:10	protects the lives of the f,
Ps	101: 6	I look to the f of the land; they alone
Ps	116:15	eyes of the LORD is the death of his f.
Ps	132: 9	justice; your f will shout for joy."
Ps	132:16	blessing; its f shall shout for joy.
Ps	145:10	thanks, O LORD and your f bless you.
Ps	145:13	in every word, and f in every work.
Ps	148:14	to the glory of all the f, of Israel,
Ps	149: 1	a hymn in the assembly of the f.
Ps	149: 5	Let the f rejoice in their glory,
Ps	149: 9	them— such is the glory of all God's f.
Prv	25:13	is a f messenger for the one who
Wis	3: 9	the f shall abide with him in love:
Sir	6:14	A f friend is a sturdy shelter; he who
Sir	6:15	A f friend is beyond price, no sum
Sir	6:16	A f friend is a life-saving remedy,
Sir	34: 8	is found in the mouth of the f man.
Sir	39:13	Listen, my f children: open up your
Is	1:21	adulteress, the f city, so upright!
Is	1:26	shall be called city of justice, f city.
Is	25: 1	wonderful plans of old, f and true.
Is	49: 7	Because of the LORD who is f,
Hos	12: 1	God, against the Holy One, who is f.
Mi	7: 2	The f are gone from the earth,
Zec	8: 3	Jerusalem shall be called the f city,
Mt	24:45	then, is the f and prudent servant,
Lk	12:42	is the f and prudent steward whom
Acts	11:23	them all to remain f to the Lord
1 Cor ·	1: 9	God is f, and by him you were
1 Cor	4:17	is my beloved and f son in the Lord;
1 Cor	10:13	God is f and will not let you be tried
2 Cor	1:18	As God is f, our word to you is not
Eph	1: 1	are [in Ephesus] f in Christ Jesus:
Col	1: 2	and f brothers in Christ in Colossae:
1 Thes	5:24	The one who calls you is f, and he
2 Thes	3: 3	But the Lord is f; he will strengthen
1 Tm	3:11	but temperate and f in everything.
2 Tm	2: 2	to f people who will have the ability
2 Tm	2:13	he remains f, for he cannot deny
Heb	2:17	f high priest before God to expiate
Heb	3: 2	who was f to the one who appointed
Heb	3: 2	just as Moses was "f in [all] his
Heb	3: 5	Moses was "f in all his house" as

Heb	3: 6	Christ was f as a son placed over his
1 Pt	4:19	over to a f creator as they do good.
1 Pt	5:12	whom I consider a f brother,
1 Jn	1: 9	he is f and just and will forgive our
Rv	1: 5	and from Jesus Christ, the f witness,
Rv	2:10	Remain f until death, and I will give
Rv	2:13	in the days of Antipas, my f witness,
Rv	3:14	" 'The Amen, the f and true witness,
Rv	17:14	with him are called, chosen, and f."
Rv	19:11	its rider was [called] "F and True."

FAITHFULLY → FAITH

1 Sm	12:24	and worship him f with your whole
2 Chr	31:15	who f made the distribution to their
2 Chr	34:12	The men worked f at their tasks;
Sir	7:20	Mistreat not a servant who f serves,
Is	61: 8	I will give them their recompense f,

FAITHFULNESS → FAITH

1 Sm	26:23	each man for his justice and f.
Ps	26: 3	my eyes; I walk guided by your f.
Ps	30:10	give you thanks or declare your f?
Ps	54: 7	my foes; in your f, destroy them.
Ps	57:11	to the heavens; your f, to the skies.
Ps	71:22	with the lyre for your f, my God,
Ps	91: 4	refuge; God's f is a protecting shield.
Ps	92: 3	in the morning, your f in the night,
Ps	100: 5	whose f lasts through every age.
Ps	108: 5	to the heavens; your f, to the skies.
Ps	115: 1	glory because of your f and love.
Ps	119:138	in justice and in surpassing f.
Ps	143: 1	in your f listen to my pleading;
Is	11: 5	his waist, and f a belt upon his hips.
Is	38:19	declare to their sons, O God, your f.
Lam	3:23	each morning, so great is his f.
Mi	7:20	You will show f to Jacob, and grace
Zec	8: 8	will be their God, with f and justice.
Gal	5:22	patience, kindness, generosity, f,

FAITHLESS → FAITH

Ps	119:158	I view the f with loathing,
Mt	17:17	reply, "O f and perverse generation,
Rom	1:31	They are senseless, f, heartless,

FALL → DOWNFALL, FALLEN, FALLING, FALLS, FELL

Nm	14:29	the desert shall your dead bodies f.
1 Chr	21:13	But I prefer to f into the hand
Ps	35: 8	let them f into the pit they have dug.
Ps	37:24	May stumble, but they will never f,
Ps	91: 7	Though a thousand f at your side,
Prv	16:18	and a haughty spirit before a f.
Eccl	4:10	For if he should f, he has no one
Eccl	10: 8	He who digs a pit may f into it,
Sir	28:23	who forsake the LORD will f victims
Is	40:30	weary, and youths stagger and f,
Jer	6:15	they shall be among those who f;
Dn	11:35	some shall f, so that the rest may be
Hos	10: 8	us!" and to the hills, "F upon us!"
Mk	4:17	of the word, they quickly f away.
Lk	10:18	have observed Satan f like lightning
Lk	23:30	to say to the mountains, 'F upon us!'
Acts	5:15	at least his shadow might f on one
Rom	9:33	and a rock that will make them f,
Rom	11:11	I ask, did they stumble so as to f?
1 Cor	10:12	secure should take care not to f.
Heb	10:31	It is a fearful thing to f
1 Pt	2: 8	and a rock that will make them f."
Rv	6:16	"F on us and hide us from the face

FALLEN → FALL

2 Sm	1:19	how can the warriors have f!
Sir	28:18	Many have f by the edge
Is	14:12	How have you f from the heavens,
Is	21: 9	calls out and says, 'F, f is Babylon,
Am	9:11	I will raise up the f hut of David;
Acts	15:16	and rebuild the f hut of David;
Gal	5: 4	by law; you have f from grace.
Heb	6: 6	and then have f away, to bring them
Rv	9: 1	I saw a star that had f from the sky
Rv	14: 8	saying: "F, f is Babylon the great,
Rv	17:10	five have already f, one still lives,

Rv   18: 2   voice: "**F**, **f** is Babylon the great.

FALLING →FALL
Sir   34:16   against stumbling, a help against **f**.
Lk   22:44   like drops of blood **f** on the ground.]
1 Tm   6: 9   want to be rich are **f** into temptation

FALLS →FALL
Prv   11:14   For lack of guidance a people **f**;
Prv   26:27   He who digs a pit **f** into it;
Eccl   4:10   If the one **f**, the other will lift up his
Mt   13:21   of the word, he immediately **f** away.
Lk   20:18   Everyone who **f** on that stone will
Lk   20:18   it will crush anyone on whom it **f**."
Jn   12:24   a grain of wheat **f** to the ground

FALSE →FALSEHOOD, FALSELY, FALSIFYING
Ex   20:16   shall not bear **f** witness against your
Ex   23: 1   "You shall not repeat a **f** report.
Dt   19:18   find that the witness is a **f** witness
Prv   14: 5   not lie, but a **f** witness utters lies.
Prv   19: 5   The **f** witness will not go
Prv   21:28   The **f** witness will perish, but he
Prv   25:18   man who bears **f** witness against his
Mt   7:15   "Beware of **f** prophets, who come
Mt   15:19   theft, **f** witness, blasphemy.
Mt   24:11   Many **f** prophets will arise
Mt   24:24   **F** messiahs and **f** prophets will arise,
Mk   10:19   you shall not bear **f** witness;
Mk   13:22   **F** messiahs and **f** prophets will arise
Lk   6:26   you, for their ancestors treated the **f**
Lk   18:20   you shall not bear **f** witness;
Acts   6:13   They presented **f** witnesses who
Acts   13: 6   who was a Jewish **f** prophet.
2 Cor   11:13   For such people are **f** apostles,
2 Cor   11:26   at sea, dangers among **f** brothers;
2 Pt   2: 1   also **f** prophets among the people,
2 Pt   2: 1   there will be **f** teachers among you,
1 Jn   4: 1   because many **f** prophets have gone
Rv   16:13   and from the mouth of the **f** prophet.
Rv   19:20   it the **f** prophet who had performed
Rv   20:10   the beast and the **f** prophet were.

FALSEHOOD →FALSE
Jb   31: 5   If I have walked in **f** and my foot
Ps   119:163   **F** I hate and abhor; your teaching I
Prv   30: 8   Put **f** and lying far from me, give me
Is   28:15   in **f** we have found a hiding place,"—
Rom   3: 7   redounds to his glory through my **f**,
Eph   4:25   putting away **f**, speak the truth,

FALSELY →FALSE
Lv   19:12   You shall not swear **f** by my name,
Jer   5:31   The prophets prophesy **f**,
Mt   5:11   evil against you [**f**] because of me.

FALSIFYING →FALSE
2 Cor   4: 2   deceitfully or **f** the word of God,

FAME →FAMOUS
Jos   6:27   his **f** spread throughout the land.
1 Chr   14:17   Thus David's **f** was spread abroad
2 Chr   9: 1   of Sheba heard of Solomon's **f**,
1 Mc   3:26   His **f** reached the king, and all
Is   66:19   that have never heard of my **f**,
Mk   1:28   His **f** spread everywhere throughout

FAMILIES →FAMILY
Ex   1:21   feared God, he built up **f** for them.
Jos   14: 1   and the heads of **f** in the tribes
Ps   107:41   their **f** increased like their flocks.
Am   3: 2   more than all the **f** of the earth;
Acts   3:25   your offspring all the **f** of the earth
Ti   1:11   as they are upsetting whole **f**

FAMILY →FAMILIES
Lk   2: 4   he was of the house and **f** of David,
Acts   16:33   and all his **f** were baptized at once.
Gal   6:10   who belong to the **f** of the faith.
Eph   3:15   from whom every **f** in heaven
1 Tm   5: 4   their religious duty to their own **f**
1 Tm   5: 8   especially **f** members has denied

FAMINE →FAMINES
Gn   12:10   There was **f** in the land; so Abram
Gn   26: 1   There was a **f** in the land (distinct
Gn   41:27   ears; they are seven years of **f**.
Gn   42: 5   since there was **f** in the land
Gn   43: 1   Now the **f** in the land grew more
Ru   1: 1   the judges there was a **f** in the land;
2 Kgs   4:38   to Gilgal, there was a **f** in the land.
2 Kgs   6:25   of the seige the **f** in Samaria was so
2 Chr   6:28   When there is **f** in the land,
1 Mc   6:54   for the **f** was too much for them.
Jb   5:20   In **f** he will deliver you from death,
Ps   37:19   in days of **f** they will have plenty.
Sir   39:29   time, are fire and hail, **f**, disease,
Jer   14:15   and **f** shall not befall this land":
Am   8:11   when I will send **f** upon the land:
Am   8:11   Not a **f** of bread, or thirst for water,
Lk   4:25   and a severe **f** spread over the entire
Acts   11:28   would be a severe **f** all over
Rom   8:35   or persecution, or **f**, or nakedness,
Rv   18: 8   pestilence, grief, and **f**; she will be

FAMINES →FAMINE
Lk   21:11   will be powerful earthquakes, **f**,

FAMISHED
Gn   25:29   stew, Esau came in from the open, **f**.

FAMOUS →FAME
1 Kgs   1:47   God make Solomon more **f** than you

FAN
Jer   15: 7   I winnowed them with the **f** in every
Mt   3:12   His winnowing **f** is in his hand.

FAR
Gn   18:25   **F** be it from you to do such a thing,
Jos   24:16   "**F** be it from us to forsake the Lord
1 Sm   12:23   **f** be it from me to sin against
Ps   22:12   Do not stay **f** from me, for trouble is
Ps   103:12   As **f** as the east is from the west, so **f**
Ps   119:155   Salvation is **f** from sinners
Prv   5: 8   Keep your way **f** from her,
Prv   31:10   wife, her value is **f** beyond pearls.
Is   29:13   though their hearts are **f** from me,
Is   57:19   Peace, peace to the **f** and the near,
Jer   23:23   says the Lord, and not a God **f** off?
Mk   7: 6   lips, but their hearts are **f** from me;
Mk   12:34   "You are not **f** from the kingdom

FARMER
2 Tm   2: 6   The hardworking **f** ought to have
Jas   5: 7   See how the **f** waits for the precious

FASHION →FASHIONED
Jb   31:15   not the same One **f** us before our

FASHIONED →FASHION
Jb   10: 9   remember that you **f** me from clay!
Ps   119:73   Your hands made me and **f** me;

FAST →FASTED, FASTING, FASTS
Dt   10:20   hold **f** to him and swear by his
Dt   11:22   ways exactly, and holding **f** to him,
Dt   13: 5   him and holding **f** to him alone.
Dt   30:20   his voice, and holding **f** to him.
2 Chr   20: 3   He proclaimed a **f** for all Judah.
Ezr   8:21   Then I proclaimed a **f**,
Est   4:16   **f** on my behalf, not eating
Ps   139:10   me, your right hand hold me **f**.
Prv   4: 4   me: "Let your heart hold **f** my words:
Is   56: 4   me and hold **f** to my covenant,
Is   58: 5   ashes? Do you call this a **f**, a day
Jl   1:14   Proclaim a **f**, call an assembly;
Jon   3: 5   they proclaimed a **f** and all of them,
Mt   6:16   "When you **f**, do not look gloomy
Mt   9:14   do we and the Pharisees **f** [much], but your
                 disciples do not **f**?"
Lk   18:12   I **f** twice a week, and I pay tithes
2 Thes   2:15   hold **f** to the traditions that you were
1 Tm   3: 9   holding **f** to the mystery of the faith
Heb   4:14   God, let us hold **f** to our confession.
Rv   3:11   Hold **f** to what you have, so that no

FASTED →FAST
1 Kgs	21:27	He f, slept in the sackcloth,
Ezr	8:23	So we f, and prayed to our God
Jdt	8: 6	She f all the days of her
1 Mc	3:47	That day they f and wore sackcloth;
Zec	7: 5	was it really for me that you f?
Mt	4: 2	He f for forty days and forty nights,

FASTING →FAST
Tb	12: 8	Prayer and f are good, but better
Ps	35:13	afflicted myself with f, sobbed my
Dn	9: 3	in earnest prayer, with f, sackcloth,
Mt	6:16	they may appear to others to be f.
Acts	13: 2	were worshiping the Lord and f,
Acts	14:23	with prayer and f, commended them

FASTS →FAST
| Sir | 34:26 | So with a man who f for his sins, |

FAT →FATLING, FATLINGS, FATTED, FATTENED
Lv	3:16	All the f belongs to the LORD.
Lv	7:23	You shall not eat the f of any ox
Jgs	3:17	king of Moab, who was very f,
Ez	34:20	Now will I judge between the f
Dn	14:27	Then Daniel took some pitch, f,

FATE
| Nm | 16:29 | merely suffering the f common |

FATHER →FATHER'S, FATHER-IN-LAW, FATHERLESS, FATHERS
Gn	2:24	That is why a man leaves his f
Gn	17: 4	to become the f of a host of nations.
Gn	19:32	let us ply our f with wine
Gn	19:32	that we may have offspring by our f."
Gn	26:24	"I am the God of your f Abraham.
Gn	27:38	But Esau urged his f, "Have you only that one blessing, f?
Gn	31: 5	the God of my f has been with me.
Gn	46: 3	said: "I am God, the God of your f.
Ex	20:12	"Honor your f and your mother,
Ex	21:15	Whoever strikes his f or mother
Ex	21:17	"Whoever curses his f or mother
Ex	22:16	If her f refuses to give her to him,
Dt	5:16	'Honor your f and your mother,
Dt	21:18	son who will not listen to his f
Dt	26: 5	'My f was a wandering Aramean
Dt	32: 6	Is he not your f who created you?
Jgs	17:10	"Be f and priest to me, and I will give
Jgs	18:19	with us and be our f and priest. Is it
2 Sm	7:14	I will be a f to him, and he shall be
1 Kgs	2:12	seated on the throne of his f David,
1 Chr	17:13	I will be a f to him, and he shall be
1 Chr	22:10	and I will be a f to him, and I will
1 Chr	28: 6	for my son, and I will be a f to him.
Jb	38:28	Has the rain a f; or who has
Ps	27:10	Even if my f and mother forsake
Ps	68: 6	F of the fatherless,
Ps	89:27	He shall cry to me, 'You are my f,
Ps	103:13	As a f has compassion on his
Prv	10: 1	A wise son makes his f glad,
Prv	17:25	A foolish son is vexation to his f,
Prv	19:26	He who mistreats his f, or drives
Prv	20:20	If one curses his f or mother,
Prv	23:22	Listen to your f who begot you,
Prv	23:24	The f of a just man will exult
Prv	28:24	He who defrauds f or mother
Wis	2:16	the just and boasts that God is his F.
Sir	3: 3	He who honors his f atones for sins;
Sir	3:16	blasphemer is he who despises his f;
Is	8: 4	the child knows how to call his f
Is	45:10	Woe to him who asks a f, "What are
Is	63:16	You, LORD, are our f, our redeemer
Jer	2:27	to a piece of wood, "You are my f,"
Jer	3:19	would call me, "My F," I thought,
Jer	31: 9	For I am a f to Israel, Ephraim is my
Ez	16: 3	your f was an Amorite and your
Ez	18:19	son charged with the guilt of his f?"
Mi	7: 6	For the son dishonors his f,
Mal	1: 6	A son honors his f, and a servant
Mal	1: 6	If then I am a f, where is the honor
Mal	2:10	Have we not all the one F? Has not
Mt	3: 9	to yourselves, 'We have Abraham as our f."
Mt	5:16	deeds and glorify your heavenly F.
Mt	6: 9	you are to pray: Our F in heaven,
Mt	6:14	your heavenly F will forgive you.
Mt	6:15	neither will your F forgive your
Mt	6:26	yet your heavenly F feeds them.
Mt	10:37	"Whoever loves f or mother more
Mt	11:27	been handed over to me by my F.
Mt	11:27	No one knows the Son except the F,
Mt	11:27	no one knows the F except the Son
Mt	15: 4	said, 'Honor your f and your mother,'
Mt	15: 4	'Whoever curses f or mother shall
Mt	18:10	upon the face of my heavenly F.
Mt	19: 5	this reason a man shall leave his f
Mt	19:19	honor your f and your mother';
Mt	19:29	brothers or sisters or f or mother
Mt	23: 9	Call no one on earth your f; you have but one F in heaven.
Mt	28:19	baptizing them in the name of the F,
Mk	14:36	"Abba, F, all things are possible
Lk	6:36	just as [also] your F is merciful.
Lk	9:59	let me go first and bury my f."
Lk	11: 2	say: F, hallowed be your name,
Lk	12:30	your F knows that you need them.
Lk	12:53	a f will be divided against his son and a son against his f,
Lk	14:26	comes to me without hating his f
Lk	15:12	So the f divided the property
Lk	16:24	And he cried out, 'F Abraham,
Lk	18:20	honor your f and your mother.' "
Lk	23:34	[Then Jesus said, "F, forgive them,
Jn	3:35	The F loves the Son and has given
Jn	4:23	true worshipers will worship the F
Jn	4:23	indeed the F seeks such people
Jn	5:17	them, "My F is at work until now,
Jn	5:18	but he also called God his own f,
Jn	5:20	For the F loves his Son and shows
Jn	6:44	me unless the F who sent me draw
Jn	6:46	has seen the F except the one who is from God; he has seen the F.
Jn	8:19	they said to him, "Where is your f?"
Jn	8:19	"You know neither me nor my F.
Jn	8:28	but I say only what the F taught me.
Jn	8:41	You are doing the works of your f!
Jn	8:41	illegitimate. We have one F, God."
Jn	8:44	You belong to your f the devil
Jn	8:44	because he is a liar and the f of lies.
Jn	10:17	This is why the F loves me,
Jn	10:30	The F and I are one."
Jn	10:38	[and understand] that the F is in me and I am in the F."
Jn	12:27	I say? 'F, save me from this hour'?
Jn	14: 6	comes to the F except through me.
Jn	14: 9	has seen me has seen the F.
Jn	14: 9	How can you say, 'Show us the F'?
Jn	14:11	Believe me that I am in the F and the F is in me,
Jn	14:21	loves me will be loved by my F,
Jn	14:28	rejoice that I am going to the F; for the F is greater than I.
Jn	15: 9	As the F loves me, so I also love
Jn	15:23	Whoever hates me also hates my F.
Jn	20:17	for I have not yet ascended to the F.
Jn	20:17	'I am going to my F and your F,
Jn	20:21	As the F has sent me, so I send you."
Acts	1: 4	"the promise of the F
Rom	4:16	Abraham, who is the f of all of us,
Rom	8:15	through which we cry, "Abba, F!"
1 Cor	4:15	for I became your f in Christ Jesus
2 Cor	1: 3	God and F of our Lord Jesus Christ,
2 Cor	1: 3	the F of compassion and God of all
2 Cor	6:18	and I will be a f to you, and you
Gal	4: 6	into our hearts, crying out, "Abba, F!"
Eph	5:31	this reason a man shall leave [his] f
Eph	6: 2	"Honor your f and mother." This is
Phil	2:11	is Lord, to the glory of God the F.
1 Thes	2:11	one of you as a f treats his children,
1 Tm	5: 1	older man, but appeal to him as a f.
Heb	1: 5	"I will be a f to him, and he shall be

Heb	12: 9	all the more to the F of spirits
Jas	1:17	coming down from the F of lights,
1 Jn	1: 3	for our fellowship is with the F
1 Jn	2:15	the love of the F is not in him.
1 Jn	2:22	Whoever denies the F and the Son,
1 Jn	3: 1	See what love the F has bestowed
2 Jn	1: 9	remains in the teaching has the F
Rv	3: 5	his name in the presence of my F
Rv	3:21	and sit with my F on his throne.

FATHER'S → FATHER

Gn	12: 1	and from your f house to a land
Gn	27:34	On hearing his f words, Esau
Gn	31:19	appropriated her f household idols.
Gn	49: 4	for you climbed into your f bed
Dt	23: 1	"A man shall not marry his f wife,
2 Sm	16:21	relations with your f concubines,
Est	4:14	you and your f house will perish.
Prv	4: 1	Hear, O children, a f instruction,
Lk	2:49	know that I must be in my F house?"
Jn	1:14	the glory as of the F only Son,
Jn	1:18	The only Son, God, who is at the F side,
Jn	2:16	stop making my F house a marketplace."
Jn	10:29	no one can take them out of the F hand.
Jn	14: 2	In my F house there are many dwelling
Rv	14: 1	his F name written on their foreheads.

FATHER-IN-LAW → FATHER

Ex	18: 8	told his f of all that the LORD had
Jn	18:13	He was the f of Caiaphas, who was

FATHERLESS → FATHER

Lam	5: 3	We have become orphans, f;

FATHERS → FATHER

Is	49:23	Kings shall be your foster f,
1 Cor	4:15	yet you do not have many f, for I
Eph	6: 4	F, do not provoke your children
Col	3:21	F, do not provoke your children,
1 Jn	2:13	I am writing to you, f, because you

FATLING → FAT

2 Sm	6:13	six steps, he sacrificed an ox and a f.

FATLINGS → FAT

Ps	66:15	Holocausts of f I will offer you

FATTED → FAT

Prv	15:17	love is than a f ox and hatred with it.

FATTENED → FAT

Jas	5: 5	you have f your hearts for the day

FAULT → FAULTLESS, FAULTS

1 Sm	29: 3	I have no f to find with him
Sir	11: 7	Before investigating, find no f;
Mt	18:15	tell him his f between you and him
Rom	9:19	"Why [then] does he still find f?

FAULTLESS → FAULT

Heb	8: 7	For if that first covenant had been f,

FAULTS → FAULT

Ps	19:13	Cleanse me from my unknown f.

FAVOR → FAVORED, FAVORITE, FAVORITISM

Gn	6: 8	But Noah found f with the LORD.
Ex	33:12	and also, 'You have found f with me.'
Ex	34: 9	he said, "If I find f with you, O LORD,
Lv	26: 9	I will look with f upon you,
Nm	11:15	please do me the f of killing me
Jgs	6:17	"If I find f with you, give me a sign
Est	7: 3	"If I have found f with you, O king,
1 Mc	4:10	Heaven in the hope that he will f us,
Ps	5:13	surround them with f like a shield.
Ps	30: 6	a moment; divine f lasts a lifetime.
Ps	90:17	May the f of the Lord our God be
Prv	8:35	finds life, and wins f from the LORD;
Prv	13:15	Good sense brings f, but the way
Prv	18:22	it is a f he receives from the LORD.
Prv	19: 6	Many curry f with a noble; all are
Eccl	9:11	by the shrewd, nor f by the experts;
Is	49: 8	In a time of f I answer you,
Is	61: 2	announce a year of f from the LORD

Dn	1: 9	Though God had given Daniel the f
Zec	11: 7	one of which I called "F,"
Lk	1:30	for you have found f with God.
Lk	2:14	peace to those on whom his f rests."
Lk	2:40	and the f of God was upon him.
Lk	2:52	and age and f before God and man.
Acts	7:10	He granted him f and wisdom
Acts	7:46	who found f in the sight of God
2 Cor	1:15	so that you might receive a double f,

FAVORED → FAVOR

Ps	85: 2	You once f, LORD, your land,
Lk	1:28	coming to her, he said, "Hail, f one!

FAVORITE → FAVOR

2 Sm	23: 1	Jacob, f of the Mighty One of Israel.

FAVORITISM → FAVOR

Sir	4:22	Show no f to your own discredit;

FAWNS

Gn	49:21	loose, which brings forth lovely f.
Song	4: 5	Your breasts are like twin f,

FEAR → AFRAID, FEARED, FEARFUL, FEARING, FEARS, GOD-FEARING

Gn	9: 2	Dread f of you shall come upon all
Ex	9:30	I know, do not yet f the LORD God."
Ex	20:20	to test you and put his f upon you,
Dt	2:25	This day I will begin to put a f
Dt	6:13	The LORD, your God, shall you f;
Dt	10:12	ask of you but to f the LORD,
Dt	31:12	it, and so f the LORD, your God,
Jos	2:24	the land are overcome with f of us."
Jos	4:24	and that you may f the LORD,
1 Sm	12:14	If you f the LORD and worship him,
1 Sm	12:24	But you must f the LORD
2 Sm	23: 3	in justice, that rules in the f of God,
1 Kgs	8:43	may f you as do your people Israel,
2 Chr	19: 7	let the f of the LORD be upon you.
2 Chr	26: 5	lived, who taught him to f God;
Est	8:17	were seized with a f of the Jews.
Jb	6:14	though he have forsaken the f
Ps	2:11	Serve the LORD with f;
Ps	15: 4	but honors those who f the LORD;
Ps	19:10	The f of the LORD is pure,
Ps	23: 4	I f no harm for you are at my side;
Ps	27: 1	whom do I f? The LORD is my life's
Ps	33: 8	Let all the earth f the LORD; let all
Ps	34: 8	with them, delivers all who f God.
Ps	34:10	F the LORD, you holy ones;
Ps	34:12	I will teach you the f of the LORD.
Ps	46: 3	Thus we do not f, though earth be
Ps	55:20	their ways; they have no f of God.
Ps	90:11	Your wrath matches the f it inspires.
Ps	91: 5	You shall not f the terror
Ps	111:10	The f of the LORD is the beginning
Ps	118: 4	Let those who f the LORD say,
Ps	119:63	I am the friend of all who f you,
Ps	145:19	the desire of those who f you;
Prv	1: 7	The f of the LORD is the beginning
Prv	1:29	and chose not the f of the LORD;
Prv	2: 5	will you understand the f
Prv	3: 7	f the LORD and turn away from evil;
Prv	8:13	[The f of the LORD is to hate evil;]
Prv	9:10	of wisdom is the f of the LORD,
Prv	10:27	The f of the LORD prolongs life,
Prv	14:27	The f of the LORD is a fountain
Prv	15:33	The f of the LORD is training
Prv	16: 6	by the f of the LORD man avoids evil.
Prv	19:23	The f of the LORD is an aid to life;
Prv	22: 4	reward of humility and f of the LORD
Prv	29:25	The f of man brings a snare, but he
Eccl	8:12	shall be well with those who f God,
Eccl	12:13	all is heard: F God and keep his
Sir	7:29	With all your soul, f God, revere his
Sir	40:26	but better than either, f of God.
Is	8:12	and f not, nor stand in awe of what they f.
Is	11: 3	his delight shall be the f of the LORD.
Is	33: 6	the f of the LORD is her treasure.
Is	35: 4	Be strong, f not! Here is your God,

Is	41:10	F not, I am with you; be not
Is	41:13	It is I who say to you, "F not, I will
Is	43: 1	F not, for I have redeemed you;
Is	43: 5	F not, for I am with you;
Is	51: 7	at heart: F not the reproach of men,
Is	54:14	far from the f of oppression,
Jer	5:22	Should you not f me, says the LORD,
Jer	30:10	my servant Jacob, f not,
Mi	6: 9	[It is wisdom to f your name!] Hear,
Zep	3:15	you have no further misfortune to f.
Lk	12: 5	I shall show you whom to f.
Lk	18: 4	that I neither f God nor respect any
Jn	19:38	a disciple of Jesus for f of the Jews,
Jn	20:19	the disciples were, for f of the Jews,
Acts	5:11	great f came upon the whole church
Rom	8:15	a spirit of slavery to fall back into f,
Rom	13: 3	rulers are not a cause of f to good
Rom	13: 3	you wish to have no f of authority?
2 Cor	5:11	since we know the f of the Lord,
Phil	2:12	work out your salvation with f
Heb	2:15	free those who through f of death
1 Pt	3:14	be afraid or terrified with f of them,
1 Jn	4:18	There is no f in love, but perfect love drives out f because f has to do
Jude	1:23	fire; on others have mercy with f,
Rv	14: 7	voice, "F God and give him glory,
Rv	15: 4	Who will not f you, Lord, or glorify

FEARED →FEAR

Ex	1:21	And because the midwives f God,
Ex	14:31	they f the LORD and believed in him
Jb	1: 1	Job, who f God and avoided evil.
Hg	1:12	the people f because of the LORD.
Mk	6:20	Herod f John, knowing him to be

FEARFUL →FEAR

Heb	10:27	but a f prospect of judgment

FEARING →FEAR

Dt	8: 6	by walking in his ways and f him.
Col	3:22	but in simplicity of heart, f the Lord.

FEARS →FEAR

Jdt	16:16	one who f the LORD is forever great.
Ps	34: 5	me, delivered me from all my f.
Prv	31:30	the woman who f the LORD is to be
Eccl	7:18	he who f God will win through at all
Sir	1:11	He who f the LORD will have
Sir	15: 1	He who f the LORD will do this;
Jer	17: 8	It f not the heat when it comes,
2 Cor	7: 5	way—external conflicts, internal f.
1 Jn	4:18	so one who f is not yet perfect

FEAST →FEASTING, FEASTS

Ex	5: 1	may celebrate a f to me in the desert."
Ex	23:14	you shall celebrate a pilgrim f to me.
1 Mc	1:45	to profane the sabbaths and f days,
Ps	36: 9	We f on the rich food of your house;
Prv	15:15	a lighthearted man has a continual f.
Is	25: 6	A f of rich food and choice wines,
1 Cor	5: 8	Therefore let us celebrate the f, not

FEASTING →FEAST

Est	9:17	and made it a day of f and rejoicing.
Est	9:19	of Adar as a day of rejoicing and f,
Prv	17: 1	than a house full of f with strife.

FEASTS →FEAST

1 Mc	1:39	her f were turned into mourning,
Jb	1: 4	His sons used to take turns giving f,
Hos	2:13	her f, her new moons, her sabbaths,
Am	8:10	I will turn your f into mourning
Na	2: 1	Celebrate your f, O Judah, fulfill
Jude	1:12	These are blemishes on your love f,

FED →FEED

Dt	8:16	and f you in the desert with manna,
Ps	80: 6	You have f them the bread of tears,
1 Cor	3: 2	I f you milk, not solid food,

FEEBLE

Is	35: 3	Strengthen the hands that are f,

FEED →FED, FEEDS

1 Kgs	17: 4	commanded ravens to f you there."
Jn	21:15	He said to him, "F my lambs."
Jn	21:17	[Jesus] said to him, "F my sheep.
Rom	12:20	"if your enemy is hungry, f him; if he

FEEDS →FEED

Is	40:11	Like a shepherd he f his flock; in his
Mt	6:26	yet your heavenly Father f them.

FEEL

Ps	115: 7	They have hands but do not f,

FEET →FOOT

Ex	3: 5	Remove the sandals from your f,
Ex	12:11	sandals on your f and your staff
Ex	24:10	Under his f there appeared to be
Ex	30:21	they must wash their hands and f,
Dt	8: 4	nor did your f swell these forty
Ru	3: 8	to find a woman lying at his f.
2 Sm	22:34	Who made my f swift as those
Ps	8: 7	your hands, put all things at their f:
Ps	22:17	So wasted are my hands and f
Ps	40: 3	of the swamp, Set my f upon rock,
Ps	56:14	death, kept my f from stumbling,
Ps	66: 9	alive and not allowed our f to slip.
Ps	73: 2	my balance; my f all but slipped,
Ps	115: 7	but do not feel, f but do not walk,
Ps	119:105	Your word is a lamp for my f,
Prv	1:16	[For their f run to evil, they hasten
Prv	4:26	Survey the path for your f, and let
Prv	5: 5	Her f go down to death,
Prv	6:18	schemes, f that run swiftly to evil,
Is	6: 2	with two they veiled their f,
Is	52: 7	are the f of him who brings glad
Ez	34:18	to foul the remainder with your f?
Dn	2:33	iron, its f partly iron and partly tile.
Na	1: 3	path, and clouds are the dust at his f;
Hb	3:19	he makes my f swift as those
Zec	14: 4	That day his f shall rest
Mt	10:14	and shake the dust from your f.
Mt	22:44	I place your enemies under your f" '?
Lk	1:79	to guide our f into the path of peace."
Lk	7:38	stood behind him at his f weeping
Lk	7:38	began to bathe his f with her tears.
Lk	8:35	had come out sitting at his f. He was
Lk	24:39	Look at my hands and my f, that it
Jn	13: 5	began to wash the disciples' f
Acts	4:35	and put them at the f of the apostles.
Acts	5: 2	and put it at the f of the apostles.
Rom	3:15	Their f are quick to shed blood;
Rom	10:15	"How beautiful are the f of those
Rom	16:20	quickly crush Satan under your f.
1 Cor	12:21	nor again the head to the f, "I do not
1 Cor	15:25	has put all his enemies under his f.
Eph	1:22	he put all things beneath his f
Eph	6:15	and your f shod in readiness
1 Tm	5:10	washed the f of the holy ones,
Heb	2: 8	subjecting all things under his f."
Heb	12:13	Make straight paths for your f,
Rv	1:15	His f were like polished brass
Rv	12: 1	with the moon under her f,

FELIX

Governor before whom Paul was tried (Acts 23:23-24:27).

FELL →FALL

Gn	15:12	about to set, a trance f upon Abram,
1 Sm	4:18	Eli f backward from his chair
1 Sm	31: 4	took his own sword and f upon it.
Mt	7:25	The rain f, the floods came,
Mk	4: 8	And some seed f on rich soil
Jn	18: 6	turned away and f to the ground.
Acts	5: 5	he f down and breathed his last,
Heb	11:30	of Jericho f after being encircled
Rv	1:17	I f down at his feet as though dead.
Rv	5:14	the elders f down and worshiped.
Rv	6:13	the sky f to the earth like unripe figs
Rv	8:10	a large star burning like a torch f
Rv	8:10	It f on a third of the rivers

FELLOW → FELLOWSHIP
Ex	2:13	are you striking your f Hebrew?"
Mt	18:31	when his f servants saw what had
Rv	22: 9	I am a f servant of yours and of your

FELLOWSHIP → FELLOW
1 Cor	1: 9	by him you were called to f with his
2 Cor	6:14	Or what f does light have
2 Cor	13:13	the f of the holy Spirit be with all
1 Jn	1: 3	so that you too may have f with us; for our f is with the Father
1 Jn	1: 6	If we say, "We have f with him,"
1 Jn	1: 7	then we have f with one another,

FEMALE
Gn	1:27	male and f he created them.
Gn	5: 2	he created them male and f.
Gn	6:19	one male and one f, that you may
Mt	19: 4	the Creator 'made them male and f'
Mk	10: 6	'God made them male and f.
Gal	3:28	free person, there is not male and f;

FERTILE
Is	5: 1	friend had a vineyard on a f hillside;

FERVENTLY → FERVOR
Jdt	4:12	one accord they cried out f
Acts	12: 5	the church was f being made to God

FERVOR → FERVENTLY
Jdt	4: 9	of Israel cried to God with great f

FESTAL → FESTIVAL
Zec	3: 4	·and clothe him in f garments."
Heb	12:22	and countless angels in f gathering,

FESTIVAL → FESTAL, FESTIVALS
Col	2:16	with regard to a f or new moon or sabbath.

FESTIVALS → FESTIVAL
Lv	23: 2	The following are the f of the LORD,
Neh	10:34	moons, and f, for the holy offerings,
Is	1:14	Your new moons and f I detest;

FESTUS
Governor who sent Paul to Caesar (Acts 25-26).

FEVER
Dt	28:22	will strike you with wasting and f,
Mk	1:30	mother-in-law lay sick with a f.
Lk	4:39	her, rebuked the f, and it left her.
Jn	4:52	told him, "The f left him yesterday,
Acts	28: 8	father of Publius was sick with a f

FEW
Gn	47: 9	F and hard have been these years
1 Chr	16:19	When they were f in number,
1 Mc	3:18	for many to be overcome by a f;
1 Mc	3:18	deliverance by many or by f;
Ps	105:12	When they were f in number,
Eccl	5: 1	earth; therefore let your words be f.
Sir	32: 8	brief, but say much in those f words,
Mt	7:14	to life. And those who find it are f.
Mt	22:14	Many are invited, but f are chosen."
Lk	10: 2	is abundant but the laborers are f;
Lk	13:23	"Lord, will only a f people be saved?"

FIELD → FIELDS
Gn	4: 8	brother Abel, "Let us go out in the f."
Gn	23:17	Thus Ephron's f in Machpelah,
Gn	49:30	the cave in the f of Machpelah,
Gn	49:30	the f that Abraham bought
Lv	19: 9	that you reap the f to its very edge,
Ru	2: 3	The f she entered to glean
Ps	50:11	the creatures of the f belong to me.
Ps	103:15	like flowers of the f we blossom.
Prv	24:30	I passed by the f of the sluggard,
Prv	31:16	She picks out a f to purchase;
Is	5: 8	to house, who connect f with f,
Is	40: 6	their glory like the flower of the f.
Jer	32: 7	"Buy for yourself my f in Anathoth,
Mt	6:30	If God so clothes the grass of the f,
Mt	13:38	the f is the world, the good seed
Mt	13:44	is like a treasure buried in a f,
Mt	13:44	sells all that he has and buys that f.

Mt	24:40	Two men will be out in the f;
Mt	27: 8	why that f even today is called the F
1 Cor	3: 9	you are God's f, God's building.

FIELDS → FIELD
Neh	5: 3	"We are forced to pawn our f,
Ps	144:13	by tens of thousands in our f;
Mi	2: 2	They covet f, and seize them;
Lk	2: 8	in that region living in the f
Jn	4:35	up and see the f ripe for the harvest.

FIERCE
Gn	49: 7	Cursed be their fury so f, and their

FIERY → FIRE
Dn	3:49	drove the f flames

FIFTY
Gn	18:24	there were f innocent people
Jn	8:57	"You are not yet f years old and you

FIG → FIGS
Gn	3: 7	so they sewed f leaves together
Jgs	9:10	Then the trees said to the f tree,
1 Kgs	5: 5	vine or under his f tree from Dan
Prv	27:18	He who tends a f tree eats its fruit,
Hos	9:10	Like the first fruits of the f tree in its
Mi	4: 4	or under his own f tree, undisturbed;
Na	3:12	All your fortresses are but f trees,
Hb	3:17	For though the f tree blossom not
Zec	3:10	another under your vines and f trees."
Mt	21:19	immediately the f tree withered.
Mt	24:32	"Learn a lesson from the f tree.
Lk	13: 6	a person who had a f tree planted
Jn	1:48	you, I saw you under the f tree."
Jas	3:12	Can a f tree, my brothers,

FIGHT → FIGHTING, FIGHTS, FOUGHT
Ex	14:14	The LORD himself will f for you;
Dt	1:30	before you, will himself f for you,
Neh	4:14	join us there; our God will f with us."
1 Mc	2:40	do not f against the Gentiles for our
Sir	4:28	Even to the death f for truth,
Jer	21: 5	and I myself will f against you
Zec	14: 3	go forth and f against those nations,
1 Tm	1:18	Through them may you f a good f

FIGHTING → FIGHT
Ex	2:13	and now two Hebrews were f! So he
Ex	14:25	because the LORD was f for them
Acts	5:39	even find yourselves f against God."

FIGHTS → FIGHT
Jos	23:10	your God, himself who f for you,

FIGS → FIG
2 Kgs	20: 7	ordered a poultice of f to be brought
Jer	24: 1	of f placed before the temple
Na	3:12	trees, bearing early f That fall,
Mk	11:13	but leaves; it was not the time for f.
Lk	6:44	For people do not pick f
Jas	3:12	produce olives, or a grapevine f?
Rv	6:13	the earth like unripe f shaken loose

FIGURE → FIGURES
Dt	4:16	an idol to represent any f, whether it
Jn	10: 6	Although Jesus used this f

FIGURES → FIGURE
Jn	16:25	"I have told you this in f of speech.
Jn	16:25	I will no longer speak to you in f

FILL → FILLED, FILLS, FULL, FULLNESS, FULLY
Gn	1:28	multiply; f the earth and subdue it.
Gn	9: 1	fertile and multiply and f the earth.
Dt	31:20	they have eaten their f and grown
Ps	81:11	wide your mouth that I may f it.'
Jer	23:24	Do I not f both heaven and earth?
Ez	10: 2	f both your hands with burning
Hg	2: 7	And I will f this house with glory,
Jn	2: 7	told them, "F the jars with water."
Rom	15:13	May the God of hope f you with all
Eph	4:10	heavens, that he might f all things.

FILLED →FILL

Ex	1: 7	strong that the land was f with them.
Ex	31: 3	I have f him with a divine spirit
Ex	35:31	has f him with a divine spirit of skill
Ex	40:34	the glory of the LORD f the Dwelling.
1 Kgs	8:11	the LORD's glory had f the temple
2 Kgs	3:17	yet this wadi will be f with water
2 Chr	5:14	since the LORD's glory f the house
2 Chr	7: 1	the glory of the LORD f the house.
Ps	71: 8	My mouth shall be f with your
Ps	72:19	may all the earth be f with the LORD's
Ps	107: 9	f the hungry with good things.
Sir	2:16	those who love him are f with his
Sir	39: 6	he will be f with the spirit
Is	6: 4	and the house was f with smoke.
Ez	10: 4	the temple was f with the cloud,
Ez	43: 5	that the temple was f with the glory
Dn	2:35	mountain and f the whole earth.
Na	2:13	lionesses; He f his dens with prey,
Hb	2:14	But the earth shall be f
Lk	1:15	He will be f with the holy Spirit
Lk	1:41	and Elizabeth, f with the holy Spirit,
Lk	1:67	his father, f with the holy Spirit,
Lk	2:40	and became strong, f with wisdom;
Jn	6:26	you ate the loaves and were f.
Jn	12: 3	the house was f with the fragrance
Acts	2: 4	they were all f with the holy Spirit
Acts	4: 8	Then Peter, f with the holy Spirit,
Acts	4:31	they were all f with the holy Spirit
Acts	5: 3	why has Satan f your heart so
Acts	7:55	But he, f with the holy Spirit,
Acts	9:17	sight and be f with the holy Spirit."
Acts	13: 9	as Paul, f with the holy Spirit,
Acts	13:52	The disciples were f with joy
Eph	5:18	debauchery, but be f with the Spirit,
Rv	8: 5	f it with burning coals
Rv	15: 8	the temple became so f

FILLS →FILL

Eph	1:23	of the one who f all things in every

FILTH →FILTHY

Is	4: 4	away the f of the daughters of Zion,
Mt	23:27	men's bones and every kind of f.

FILTHY →FILTH

Is	28: 8	are covered with f vomit, with no
Zec	3: 3	before the angel, clad in f garments.
Rv	22:11	still act wickedly, and the f still be f.

FIND →FINDS, FOUND

Gn	18:26	"If I f fifty innocent people in the city
Ex	33:13	I may continue to f favor with you.
Dt	4:29	you shall indeed f him when you
Jb	23: 3	Oh, that today I might f him, that I
Ps	132: 5	Till I f a home for the LORD,
Prv	2: 5	the knowledge of God you will f;
Prv	4:22	they are life to those who f them,
Prv	8:17	love, and those who seek me f me.
Prv	20: 6	but who can f one worthy of trust?
Prv	24:14	If you f it, you will have a future,
Eccl	12:10	sought to f pleasing sayings,
Sir	11: 7	Before investigating, f no fault;
Jer	6:16	thus you will f rest for your souls.
Jer	29:13	you look for me, you will f me. Yes,
Dn	6: 5	and satraps tried to f grounds
Mt	7: 7	seek and you will f;
Mt	11:29	and you will f rest for yourselves.
Mt	16:25	loses his life for my sake will f it.
Mt	22: 9	invite to the feast whomever you f.'
Lk	11: 9	seek and you will f;
Lk	18: 8	Man comes, will he f faith on earth?"
Lk	23: 4	the crowds, "I f this man not guilty."
Lk	24: 3	they did not f the body of the Lord
Jn	10: 9	come in and go out and f pasture.
Acts	23: 9	"We f nothing wrong with this man.
Rom	9:19	"Why [then] does he still f fault?

FINDS →FIND

Prv	8:35	For he who f me f life, and wins
Prv	18:22	He who f a wife f happiness; it is

Prv	31:10	When one f a worthy wife, her value
Sir	25:10	He who f wisdom is great indeed,
Mt	7: 8	and the one who seeks, f;
Mt	13:46	When he f a pearl of great price,
Lk	11:10	and the one who seeks, f;
Lk	12:37	servants whom the master f vigilant
Lk	15: 4	go after the lost one until he f it?
Lk	15: 8	searching carefully until she f it?

FINE

Lk	7:25	Someone dressed in f garments?
1 Pt	3: 3	jewelry, or dressing in f clothes,

FINGER →FINGERS

Ex	8:15	to Pharaoh, "This is the f of God."
Ex	31:18	tablets inscribed by God's own f.
Dt	9:10	by God's own f, with a copy of all
2 Chr	10:10	'My little f is thicker than my father's
Mt	23: 4	they will not lift a f to move them.
Lk	11:20	if it is by the f of God that [I] drive
Lk	16:24	to dip the tip of his f in water
Jn	8: 6	to write on the ground with his f.
Jn	20:25	and put my f into the nailmarks

FINGERS →FINGER

2 Sm	21:20	large stature with six f on each hand
Ps	8: 4	your heavens, the work of your f,
Prv	7: 3	Bind them on your f, write them
Dn	5: 5	the f of a human hand appeared,

FINISH →FINISHED

Lk	14:30	but did not have the resources to f.'
Acts	20:24	if only I may f my course

FINISHED →FINISH

Gn	2: 2	the seventh day God was f
Gn	24:15	He had scarcely f these words
Ex	40:33	Thus Moses f all the work.
Dt	32:45	Moses had f speaking all these
1 Kgs	8:54	When Solomon f offering this entire
Ezr	6:14	They f the building according
Neh	6:15	The wall was f on the twenty-fifth
Jn	19:30	had taken the wine, he said, "It is f."
2 Tm	4: 7	competed well; I have f the race;
Rv	11: 7	When they have f their testimony,

FINS

Dt	14: 9	whatever has both f and scales you

FIRE →FIERY

Gn	19:24	the LORD rained down sulphurous f
Ex	3: 2	appeared to him in f flaming
Ex	3: 2	though on f, was not consumed.
Ex	13:21	of a column of f to give them light.
Ex	19:18	for the LORD came down upon it in f.
Ex	40:38	f was seen in the cloud by the whole
Lv	9:24	F came forth from the LORD's
Lv	10: 2	F therefore came forth
Nm	11: 1	that the f of the LORD burned among
Nm	16:35	f from the LORD came forth
Dt	4:12	spoke to you from the midst of the f.
Dt	4:24	is a consuming f, a jealous God.
Jgs	6:21	Thereupon a f came
1 Kgs	18:38	The LORD's f came down
1 Kgs	19:12	but the LORD was not in the f.
1 Kgs	19:12	the f there was a tiny whispering
2 Kgs	1:10	"may f come down from heaven
2 Kgs	16: 3	and even immolated his son by f,
2 Chr	7: 1	f came down from heaven
2 Chr	28: 3	immolated his sons by f according
2 Chr	33: 6	who immolated his sons by f
Neh	1: 3	its gates have been gutted with f."
Ps	50: 3	not be silent! Devouring f precedes,
Ps	89:47	Must your wrath smolder like f?
Prv	6:27	Can a man take f to his bosom,
Sir	2: 5	For in f gold is tested, and worthy
Is	5:24	as the tongue of f licks up stubble,
Is	10:17	The Light of Israel will become a f,
Is	30:27	his tongue is like a consuming f;
Is	66:24	not die, nor their f be extinguished;
Jer	23:29	Is not my word like f, says the LORD,
Jer	36:23	entire roll was consumed in the f.

Ez	1:13	burning coals of f could be seen;
Dn	3:92	walking in the f, and the fourth
Dn	7: 9	His throne was flames of f, with wheels of burning f.
Am	4:11	like a brand plucked from the f;
Zec	2: 9	be for her an encircling wall of f,
Zec	3: 2	man a brand snatched from the f?"
Mal	3: 2	For he is like the refiner's f, or like
Mt	3:11	you with the holy Spirit and f.
Mt	18: 8	two feet to be thrown into eternal f.
Mt	25:41	the eternal f prepared for the devil
Mk	9:43	Gehenna, into the unquenchable f.
Mk	9:48	not die, and the f is not quenched.'
Mk	9:49	"Everyone will be salted with f.
Lk	3:16	you with the holy Spirit and f.
Lk	12:49	"I have come to set the earth on f,
Jn	15: 6	throw them into a f and they will be
Acts	2: 3	appeared to them tongues as of f,
1 Cor	3:13	It will be revealed with f, and the f
Heb	10:27	a flaming f that is going to consume
Heb	12:29	For our God is a consuming f.
Jas	3: 6	The tongue is also a f. It exists
Jas	3: 6	the entire course of our lives on f, itself set on f by Gehenna.
1 Pt	1: 7	perishable even though tested by f,
2 Pt	3:10	the elements will be dissolved by f,
Jude	1: 7	a punishment of eternal f.
Jude	1:23	by snatching them out of the f;
Rv	8: 7	came hail and f mixed with blood,
Rv	9:17	and out of their mouths came f,
Rv	11: 5	f comes out of their mouths
Rv	15: 2	like a sea of glass mingled with f.
Rv	20:14	were thrown into the pool of f.
Rv	20:14	(This pool of f is the second death.)

FIRM → FIRMLY

Is	7: 9	Unless your faith is f you shall not be f!
1 Cor	16:13	on your guard, stand f in the faith,
2 Cor	1:24	your joy, for you stand f in the faith.
Gal	5: 1	so stand f and do not submit again
Phil	1:27	that you are standing f in one spirit,
Phil	4: 1	in this way stand f in the Lord,
1 Thes	3: 8	now live, if you stand f in the Lord.
2 Thes	2:15	stand f and hold fast to the traditions
Heb	3:14	of the reality f until the end,

FIRMLY → FIRM

1 Kgs	2:12	with his sovereignty f established,

FIRST → FIRSTBORN, ONE

Gn	1: 5	and morning followed—the f day.
Gn	9:20	soil, was the f to plant a vineyard.
Gn	13: 4	site where he had f built the altar;
Ex	12: 2	you shall reckon it the f month
Ex	23:19	The choicest f fruits of your soil you
Ex	40:17	On the f day of the f month
Prv	3: 9	with f fruits of all your produce;
Prv	18:17	man who pleads his case f seems
Sir	11: 7	no fault; examine f, then criticize.
Is	41: 4	I, the LORD, am the f,
Is	44: 6	of hosts: I am the f and I am the last;
Is	48:12	I, it is I who am the f,
Dn	7: 4	The f was like a lion,
Mt	5:24	go f and be reconciled with your
Mt	6:33	But seek f the kingdom [of God]
Mt	7: 5	the wooden beam from your eye f;
Mt	8:21	let me go f and bury my father."
Mt	19:30	But many who are f will be last, and the last will be f.
Mt	22:38	greatest and the f commandment.
Mk	9:11	scribes say that Elijah must come f?"
Mk	9:35	"If anyone wishes to be f, he shall be
Mk	10:31	But many that are f will be last, and [the] last will be f."
Mk	10:44	to be f among you will be the slave
Mk	13:10	the gospel must f be preached to all
Mk	16: 2	had risen, on the f day of the week,
Lk	11:26	of that person is worse than the f."
Jn	8: 7	you who is without sin be the f
Acts	11:26	disciples were f called Christians.

Rom	1:16	believes: for Jew f, and then Greek.
1 Cor	12:28	has designated in the church to be, f,
1 Cor	15:45	too, it is written, "The f man, Adam,
2 Cor	8: 5	they gave themselves f to the Lord
Eph	1:12	his glory, we who f hoped in Christ.
Eph	6: 2	This is the f commandment
1 Thes	4:16	and the dead in Christ will rise f.
1 Tm	2:13	For Adam was formed f, then Eve.
Heb	8:13	he declares the f one obsolete.
Heb	10: 9	He takes away the f to establish
Jas	3:17	wisdom from above is f of all pure,
2 Pt	2:20	last condition is worse than their f.
1 Jn	4:19	We love because he f loved us.
Rv	1:17	not be afraid. I am the f and the last,
Rv	2: 4	you have lost the love you had at f.
Rv	4: 7	The f creature resembled a lion,
Rv	8: 7	When the f one blew his trumpet,
Rv	9:12	The f woe has passed, but there are
Rv	13:12	all the authority of the f beast in its
Rv	13:12	its inhabitants worship the f beast,
Rv	20: 5	were over. This is the f resurrection.
Rv	22:13	and the Omega, the f and the last,

FIRSTBORN, FIRST-BORN → BEAR, FIRST

Gn	27:19	"I am Esau, your f. I did as you told
Gn	48:18	the other one is the f; lay your right
Ex	4:22	Israel is my son, my f.
Ex	11: 5	from the f of Pharaoh on the throne to the f of the slave-girl at the handmill, as well as all the f of the animals.
Ex	12:29	At midnight the LORD slew every f
Ex	13: 2	"Consecrate to me every f that opens
Ex	34:20	The f among your sons you shall redeem.
Nm	3:41	in place of all the f of the Israelites,
Dt	21:17	he shall recognize as his f the son of
Jos	6:26	He shall lose his f when he lays its
1 Kgs	16:34	He lost his f son, Abiram, when he
Ps	78:51	He struck all the f of Egypt,
Ps	89:28	I myself make him f, Most High
Sir	36:11	Israel, whom you named your f.
Ez	20:26	by their immolation of every f,
Mi	6: 7	Shall I give my f for my crime,
Zec	12:10	over him as one grieves over a f.
Lk	2: 7	and she gave birth to her f son.
Rom	8:29	that he might be the f among many
Col	1:15	invisible God, the f of all creation.
Col	1:18	the beginning, the f from the dead,
Heb	12:23	and the assembly of the f enrolled
Rv	1: 5	the f of the dead and ruler

FISH → FISHERMEN

Gn	1:26	Let them have dominion over the f
Ex	7:18	The f in the river shall die,
Nm	11: 5	We remember the f we used to eat
Tb	8: 3	repelled by the odor of the f,
Tb	11: 8	Smear the f gall on them.
Ez	47: 9	and there shall be abundant f,
Jon	2: 1	But the LORD sent a large f,
Jon	2: 1	in the belly of the f three days
Jon	2: 2	belly of the f Jonah said this prayer
Mt	7:10	or a snake when he asks for a f?
Mt	14:17	and two f are all we have here."
Mk	8: 7	They also had a few f. He said
Lk	5: 6	they caught a great number of f
Jn	6: 9	has five barley loaves and two f;
Jn	21:11	of one hundred fifty-three large f.

FISHERMEN → FISH, MAN

Mk	1:16	their nets into the sea; they were f.

FIT → FITTING

Lk	9:62	to what was left behind is f

FITTING → FIT

Ps	147: 1	in song; how sweet to give f praise.
Heb	2:10	For it was f that he, for whom

FIVE

1 Sm	6: 4	"F golden hemorrhoids and f golden
1 Sm	6:16	this, the f Philistine lords returned
1 Sm	17:40	David selected f smooth stones
1 Mc	2: 2	He had f sons: John, who was called

Is	30:17	if f threaten you, you shall flee,
Mt	14:19	Taking the f loaves and the two fish,
Mt	16: 9	do you not remember the f loaves for the f thousand,
Mt	25: 2	F of them were foolish and f were
Mt	25:15	To one he gave f talents; to another,
Jn	4:18	For you have had f husbands,
1 Cor	14:19	church I would rather speak f words
Rv	9: 5	only to torment them for f months;
Rv	17:10	f have already fallen, one still lives,

FIX
Am	9: 4	I will f my gaze upon them

FLAME → FLAMES, FLAMING
Jgs	13:20	LORD ascended in the f of the altar.
Is	10:17	Israel's Holy One a f, That burns
Acts	7:30	Sinai in the f of a burning bush.
Rv	1:14	and his eyes were like a fiery f.
Rv	2:18	whose eyes are like a fiery f
Rv	19:12	His eyes were [like] a fiery f,

FLAMES → FLAME
Ps	106:18	fire blazed; f consumed the wicked.
Dn	3:22	the f devoured the men who threw
Dn	3:49	drove the fiery f out of the furnace,
Lk	16:24	for I am suffering torment in these f.'

FLAMING → FLAME
Ex	3: 2	appeared to him in fire f out of a bush.
Eph	6:16	quench all [the] f arrows of the evil

FLASH → FLASHED, FLASHES, FLASHING
Ps	144: 6	F forth lightning and scatter my
Ez	21:15	to f lightning has it been burnished.

FLASHED → FLASH
Ps	77:18	your arrows f back and forth.
Acts	9: 3	from the sky suddenly f around him.

FLASHES → FLASH
Lk	17:24	For just as lightning f and lights
Rv	4: 5	From the throne came f of lightning,
Rv	8: 5	rumblings, f of lightning,
Rv	11:19	temple. There were f of lightning,
Rv	16:18	Then there were lightning f,

FLASHING → FLASH
Dt	32:41	I will sharpen my f sword, and my

FLASK
2 Kgs	9: 1	loins, take this f of oil with you,
2 Kgs	9: 3	From the f you have, pour oil on his

FLATTERING → FLATTERS
Prv	26:28	enemy, and the f mouth works ruin.

FLATTERS → FLATTERING
Prv	29: 5	The man who f his neighbor

FLAX
Jos	2: 6	them among her stalks of f spread
Jgs	15:14	ropes around his arms became as f
Prv	31:13	She obtains wool and f and makes

FLED → FLEE
Ex	2:15	But Moses f from him and stayed
2 Sm	4: 4	and his nurse took him up and f.
2 Sm	19:10	But now he has f from the country
Ps	3: 1	when he f from his son Absalom.
Ps	57: 1	when he f from Saul into a cave.
Ps	114: 3	The sea beheld and f; the Jordan
Mk	14:50	And they all left him and f.
Rv	12: 6	The woman herself f into the desert
Rv	16:20	Every island f, and mountains
Rv	20:11	and the sky f from his presence

FLEE → FLED
Gn	19:17	outside, he was told: "F for your life!
Gn	27:43	f at once to my brother Laban
Tb	6:18	off, he will f and never again show
Ps	11: 1	me, "F like a bird to the mountains!
Ps	68: 2	those who hate God will f.
Ps	139: 7	From your presence, where can I f?
Sir	21: 2	F from sin as from a serpent

Is	30:17	if five threaten you, you shall f,
Jer	46: 6	The swift cannot f, nor the hero
Jer	51: 6	F out of Babylon; let each one save
Jon	1: 3	Jonah made ready to f to Tarshish
Zec	2:10	F from the land of the north,
Lk	3: 7	Who warned you to f
Jas	4: 7	the devil, and he will f from you.

FLEECE
Jgs	6:37	I am putting this woolen f
Jgs	6:37	If dew comes on the f alone,

FLEETING
Sir	41:11	Man's body is a f thing,

FLESH → FLESHPOTS
Gn	2:23	and f of my f; This one shall be
Gn	17:13	be in your f as an everlasting pact.
Lv	11: 8	Their f you shall not eat, and their
1 Sm	17:44	I will leave your f for the birds
2 Chr	32: 8	For he has only an arm of f, but we
Jb	19:26	And from my f I shall see God;
Ps	50:13	Do I eat the f of bulls or drink
Ps	73:26	Though my f and my heart fail,
Sir	17:26	How obscure then the thoughts of f and blood!
Sir	41: 4	Thus God has ordained for all f;
Sir	44:20	his own f he incised the ordinance,
Is	31: 3	God, their horses are f, not spirit;
Jer	17: 5	who seeks his strength in f,
Ez	37: 6	upon you, make f grow over you,
Ez	44: 7	uncircumcised both in heart and f,
Mal	2:15	make one being, with f and spirit:
Mt	16:17	For f and blood has not revealed this
Mt	19: 5	and the two shall become one f?
Mt	26:41	spirit is willing, but the f is weak."
Lk	24:39	because a ghost does not have f
Jn	1:14	And the Word became f and made
Jn	3: 6	What is born of f is f and what is
Jn	6:51	that I will give is my f for the life
Jn	6:63	gives life, while the f is of no avail.
Acts	2:17	spirit upon all f. Your sons and your
Rom	7: 5	For when we were in the f,
Rom	8: 3	weakened by the f, was powerless
Rom	8: 3	own Son in the likeness of sinful f
Rom	8: 3	of sin, he condemned sin in the f,
Rom	8: 4	who live not according to the f
Rom	8: 9	But you are not in the f;
Rom	8:13	For if you live according to the f,
1 Cor	6:16	"the two," it says, "will become one f."
1 Cor	15:39	Not all f is the same, but there is one
1 Cor	15:50	f and blood cannot inherit
2 Cor	12: 7	a thorn in the f was given to me,
Gal	3: 3	are you now ending with the f?
Gal	5:17	the f has desires against the Spirit, and the Spirit against the f;
Gal	5:19	Now the works of the f are obvious:
Eph	2: 3	following the wishes of the f
Eph	5:31	and the two shall become one f."
Eph	6:12	For our struggle is not with f
Phil	1:22	If I go on living in the f, that means
Phil	3: 4	for confidence even in the f.
Phil	3: 4	else thinks he can be confident in f,
Col	1:24	and in my f I am filling up what is
1 Tm	3:16	Who was manifested in the f,
Heb	5: 7	In the days when he was in the f,
1 Pt	1:24	for: "All f is like grass, and all its
1 Jn	4: 2	Jesus Christ come in the f belongs
2 Jn	1: 7	Jesus Christ as coming in the f;
Jude	1: 8	nevertheless also defile the f,
Rv	19:18	to eat the f of kings, the f of military
Rv	19:18	and the f of all, free and slave,

FLESHPOTS → FLESH, POT
Ex	16: 3	as we sat by our f and ate our fill

FLEW → FLY
Ps	18:11	Mounted on a cherub he f,
Is	6: 6	Then one of the seraphim f to me,

FLIES → FLY
Ex	8:17	I will loose swarms of f upon you
Ps	91: 5	night nor the arrow that f by day,

Ps   105:31 spoke and there came swarms of f,

FLIGHT →FLY
Dt   32:30 or two men put ten thousand to f,
Mt   24:20 Pray that your f not be in winter

FLINT
Ex   4:25 Zipporah took a piece of f and cut
Jos   5: 2 "Make f knives and circumcise
Is   50: 7 I have set my face like f,

FLOATED
Gn   7:18 but the ark f on the surface

FLOCK →FLOCKS
Gn   4: 4 one of the best firstlings of his f.
Ex   2:17 defended them and watered their f.
Ex   3: 1 Meanwhile Moses was tending the f
Ps   77:21 You led your people like a f
Ps   78:52 them through the desert like a f.
Ps   80: 2 guide of the f of Joseph! From your
Song   4: 1 Your hair is like a f of goats
Song   6: 6 Your teeth are like a f of ewes
Is   40:11 Like a shepherd he feeds his f; in his
Jer   31:10 he guards them as a shepherd his f.
Am   7:15 LORD took me from following the f,
Zec   11: 7 shepherd of the f to be slaughtered
Mt   26:31 the sheep of the f will be dispersed';
Lk   2: 8 keeping the night watch over their f.
Lk   12:32 little f, for your Father is pleased
Jn   10:16 voice, and there will be one f,
Acts 20:28 over the whole f of which the holy
1 Cor 9: 7 Or who shepherds a f without using
1 Pt   5: 2 Tend the f of God in your midst,
1 Pt   5: 3 to you, but be examples to the f.

FLOCKS →FLOCK
Jer   10:21 and all their f were scattered.

FLOGGED
Acts   5:40 they had them f, ordered them

FLOOD →FLOODS
Gn   7: 7 ark because of the waters of the f.
Gn   9:15 waters shall never again become a f
Ps   29:10 The LORD sits enthroned above the f!
Mt   24:38 In [those] days before the f,
Lk   6:48 when the f came, the river burst
2 Pt   2: 5 he brought a f upon the godless

FLOODS →FLOOD
Song   8: 7 quench love, nor f sweep it away.
Mt   7:25 The rain fell, the f came,

FLOOR
Dt   15:14 and threshing f and wine press,
Jgs   6:37 woolen fleece on the threshing f.
Ru   3: 3 and go down to the threshing f.
1 Chr 21:15 by the threshing f of Ornan
Dn   14:19 "Look at the f," he said;
Mt   3:12 He will clear his threshing f

FLOUR
Nm   7:13 both filled with fine f mixed with oil
Lk   13:21 of wheat f until the whole batch

FLOURISH
Ps   72: 7 That abundance may f in his days,
Ps   92: 8 Though the wicked f like grass
Ps   92:13 The just shall f like the palm tree,

FLOW →FLOWING
Lv   12: 7 be clean again after her f of blood.
Ps   78:16 He made streams f from crags,
Jl   4:18 and the hills shall f with milk;
Zec   14: 8 living waters shall f from Jerusalem,
Jn   7:38 living water will f from within him.' "

FLOWER →FLOWERS
Jb   14: 2 Like a f that springs up and fades,
Is   40: 7 The grass withers, the f wilts,
Jas   1:10 he will pass away "like the f
1 Pt   1:24 all its glory like the f of the field;
1 Pt   1:24 the grass withers, and the f wilts;

FLOWERS →FLOWER
1 Kgs 6:18 in the form of gourds and open f;
Ps   103:15 grass; like f of the field we blossom.

FLOWING →FLOW
Ex   3: 8 land, a land f with milk and honey,
Ex   33: 3 to the land f with milk and honey.
Nm   16:14 bringing us to a land f with milk
Jos   5: 6 he would not let them see the land f
Jer   32:22 oath, a land f with milk and honey.
Ez   20: 6 them, a land f with milk and honey,
Ez   47: 1 I saw water f out from beneath
Rv   22: 1 f from the throne of God

FLUTE →FLUTES
1 Mc   3:45 and the f and the harp were silent.
Mt   11:17 'We played the f for you, but you did
1 Cor 14: 7 produce sound, such as f or harp,

FLUTES →FLUTE
1 Sm   10: 5 by lyres, tambourines, f and harps.

FLY →FLEW, FLIES, FLIGHT, FLYING
Gn   1:20 earth let birds f beneath the dome
Rv   12:14 so that she could f to her place

FLYING →FLY
Zec   5: 1 my eyes again and saw a scroll f.
Rv   14: 6 I saw another angel f high overhead,

FOAL
Zec   9: 9 on an ass, on a colt, the f of an ass.
Mt   21: 5 on a colt, the f of a beast of burden.' "

FOAM →FOAMING, FOAMS
Ps   46: 4 Though its waters rage and f
Mk   9:20 began to roll around and f at the mouth.

FOAMING →FOAM
Ps   75: 9 the LORD's hand, f wine, fully spiced.
Jude   1:13 the sea, f up their shameless deeds,

FOAMS →FOAM
Lk   9:39 and it convulses him until he f

FOE →FOES
Ex   23:22 to your enemies and a f to your foes.
Ps   60:13 Give us aid against the f;
Ps   78:42 day he redeemed them from the f,
Lam   1: 5 gone away, captive before the f.

FOES →FOE
Ex   23:22 to your enemies and a foe to your f.
Lv   26:17 enemies and lorded over by your f.
Ps   3: 2 How many are my f, LORD!
Ps   44: 6 Through you we batter our f;
Lam   1: 5 Her f are uppermost, her enemies

FOLD →FOLDING, FOLDS
Ps   50: 9 from your house, no goats from your f.
Jn   10:16 sheep that do not belong to this f.

FOLDING →FOLD
Prv   6:10 slumber, a little f of the arms to rest—
Prv   24:33 slumber, a little f of the arms to rest—

FOLDS →FOLD
Neh   5:13 also shook out the f of my garment,

FOLLOW →FOLLOWED, FOLLOWING, FOLLOWS
Ex   16: 4 see whether they f my instructions
Dt   6:14 You shall not f other gods, such as
Jgs   2:17 did not f their example of obedience
1 Sm   8: 3 His sons did not f his example
1 Kgs 18:21 If the LORD is God, f him; if Baal,
1 Mc   1:44 ordering them to f customs foreign
Ez   13: 3 who f their own spirit and have seen
Mt   8:19 I will f you wherever you go."
Mt   8:22 But Jesus answered him, "F me,
Mt   16:24 himself, take up his cross, and f me.
Lk   9:23 and take up his cross daily and f me.
Lk   9:61 And another said, "I will f you, Lord,
Jn   10: 4 and the sheep f him, because they
Jn   10: 5 But they will not f a stranger;
Jn   10:27 voice; I know them, and they f me.
Jn   12:26 Whoever serves me must f me,

Jn	13:36	I am going, you cannot f me now, though you will f later."
Jn	21:19	had said this, he said to him, "F me."
1 Tm	5:15	have already turned away to f Satan.
1 Pt	2:21	that you should f in his footsteps.
2 Pt	1:16	We did not f cleverly devised myths
Rv	14: 4	the ones who f the Lamb wherever

FOLLOWED →FOLLOW

Nm	32:11	they have not f me unreservedly,
Jgs	2:12	they f the other gods of the various
Jer	9:13	f rather the hardness of their hearts
Mt	9: 9	And he got up and f him.
Mk	1:18	Then they left their nets and f him.
Mk	14:54	Peter f him at a distance
Lk	18:28	given up our possessions and f you."
Lk	18:43	received his sight and f him,
Rv	13: 3	the whole world f after the beast.

FOLLOWING →FOLLOW

Nm	32:15	If you turn away from f him, he will
1 Kgs	11:10	him this very act of f strange gods,
Sir	5: 2	in f the desires of your heart.
Lk	22:54	high priest; Peter was f at a distance.
Eph	2: 2	you once lived f the age of this
Eph	2: 2	f the ruler of the power of the air,
2 Pt	2:15	gone astray, f the road of Balaam,

FOLLOWS →FOLLOW

Jn	8:12	Whoever f me will not walk

FOLLY →FOOL

Prv	9:13	The woman F is fickle,
Prv	13:16	prudence, but the fool peddles f.
Prv	14: 1	F tears hers down with her own hands.
Prv	14:18	The adornment of simpletons is f,
Prv	14:24	the diadem of fools is f.
Prv	14:29	the quick-tempered man displays f
Prv	15:14	but the mouth of fools feeds on f.
Prv	16:22	but f brings chastisement on fools.
Prv	19: 3	A man's own f upsets his way,
Prv	22:15	F is close to the heart of a child,
Prv	26: 4	not the fool according to his f,
Prv	26: 5	Answer the fool according to his f,
Eccl	1:17	madness and f, I learned that this
Eccl	2:13	has the advantage over f as much as
Eccl	10: 1	than wisdom or wealth is a little f!
Sir	20:30	Better the man who hides his f than
Mk	7:22	envy, blasphemy, arrogance, f.

FOOD →FOODS

Gn	1:30	I give all the green plants for f."
Gn	3: 6	saw that the tree was good for f,
Nm	21: 5	desert, where there is no f or water?
Tb	1:11	refrained from eating that kind of f.
1 Mc	1:63	than to be defiled with unclean f
Ps	42: 4	My tears have been my f day
Ps	78:18	hearts, demanding the f they craved.
Ps	104:27	to you to give them f in due time.
Ps	111: 5	You gave f to those who fear you,
Ps	136:25	And gives f to all flesh, God's love
Ps	146: 7	the oppressed, gives f to the hungry.
Prv	12:11	He who tills his own land has f
Prv	23: 3	his delicacies; they are deceitful f.
Prv	31:15	and distributes f to her household.
Is	65:25	ox [but the serpent's f shall be dust].
Dn	1: 8	not to defile himself with the king's f
Mt	3: 4	His f was locusts and wild honey.
Mt	6:25	Is not life more than f and the body
Jn	4:32	"I have f to eat of which you do not
Jn	4:34	"My f is to do the will of the one who
Jn	6:27	Do not work for f that perishes
Jn	6:27	for the f that endures for eternal life,
Jn	6:55	For my flesh is true f, and my blood
1 Cor	3: 2	not solid f, because you were unable
1 Cor	6:13	"F for the stomach and the stomach and the stomach for f,"
1 Cor	8: 8	Now f will not bring us closer
1 Cor	10: 3	All ate the same spiritual f,
1 Tm	6: 8	If we have f and clothing, we shall
Heb	5:14	But solid f is for the mature,

Jas	2:15	to wear and has no f for the day,

FOODS →FOOD

Mk	7:19	(Thus he declared all f clean.)
1 Tm	4: 3	require abstinence from f that God

FOOL →FOLLY, FOOL'S, FOOLISH, FOOLISHLY, FOOLISHNESS, FOOLS

Ps	49:11	the f and the senseless pass away
Prv	10:18	he who spreads accusations is a f.
Prv	14:16	the f is reckless and sure of himself.
Prv	15: 5	The f spurns his father's admonition,
Prv	17:12	her cubs, but never a f in his folly!
Prv	18: 2	The f takes no delight
Prv	19:10	Luxury is not befitting a f;
Prv	20: 3	strife, while every f starts a quarrel.
Prv	26: 4	Answer not the f according to his
Prv	26: 7	A proverb in the mouth of a f
Prv	26:11	his vomit, so the f repeats his folly.
Prv	27:22	Though you should pound the f
Prv	29:11	The f gives vent to all his anger;
Prv	29:20	More can be hoped for from a f!
Sir	31:30	and more wine is a snare for the f;
Hos	9: 7	"The prophet is a f, the man
Mt	5:22	says, 'You f,' will be liable to fiery
Lk	12:20	'You f, this night your life will be

FOOL'S →FOOL

Prv	18: 6	The f lips lead him into strife,
Sir	21:16	A f chatter is like a load on a journey,

FOOLISH →FOOL

Dt	32: 6	O stupid and f people? Is he not
Prv	10: 1	but a f son is a grief to his mother.
Prv	17:25	A f son is vexation to his father,
Sir	42: 8	chastisement of the silly and the f,
Is	44:25	back and make their knowledge f.
Jer	5:21	to this, f and senseless people
Mt	25: 2	Five of them were f and five were
Lk	24:25	he said to them, "Oh, how f you are!
1 Cor	1:20	made the wisdom of the world f?
1 Cor	1:27	God chose the f of the world
Ti	3: 3	For we ourselves were once f,
1 Pt	2:15	silence the ignorance of f people.

FOOLISHLY →FOOL

2 Chr	16: 9	You have acted f in this matter,

FOOLISHNESS →FOOL

1 Cor	1:18	of the cross is f to those who are
1 Cor	1:21	the will of God through the f
1 Cor	1:23	block to Jews and f to Gentiles,
1 Cor	1:25	the f of God is wiser than human
1 Cor	2:14	God, for to him it is f, and he cannot
1 Cor	3:19	wisdom of this world is f in the eyes
2 Cor	11: 1	would put up with a little f from me!

FOOLS →FOOL

Ps	14: 1	Of David. F say in their hearts,
Ps	53: 2	F say in their hearts, "There is no
Ps	94: 8	You f, when will you be wise?
Prv	1: 7	wisdom and instruction f despise.
Prv	1:32	the smugness of f destroys them.
Prv	3:35	of wise men, but f inherit shame.
Prv	10:21	many, but f die for want of sense.
Prv	13:19	the soul, but f hate to turn from evil.
Prv	13:20	the companion of f will fare badly.
Prv	14:24	the diadem of f is folly.
Prv	16:22	but folly brings chastisement on f.
Eccl	5: 3	For God has no pleasure in f;
Eccl	7: 4	but the heart of f is in the house
Eccl	7: 5	than to hearken to the song of f;
Mt	23:17	Blind f, which is greater, the gold,
Rom	1:22	claiming to be wise, they became f
1 Cor	4:10	We are f on Christ's account, but you
2 Cor	11:19	For you gladly put up with f,

FOOT →BAREFOOT, FEET, FOOTHOLD, FOOTSTOOL

Ex	21:24	for tooth, hand for hand, f for f,
Dt	11:24	place where you set f shall be yours:
Jos	1: 3	to you every place where you set f.
Ps	26:12	My f stands on level ground;
Ps	91:12	lest you strike your f against a stone.

Ps	94:18	When I say, "My f is slipping,"
Ps	121: 3	God will not allow your f to slip;
Prv	1:15	hold back your f from their path!
Prv	3:23	your way; your f will never stumble;
Prv	4:27	nor to left, keep your f far from evil.
Prv	25:17	Let your f be seldom in your
Is	1: 6	From the sole of the f to the head
Mt	18: 8	If your hand or f causes you to sin,
Lk	4:11	lest you dash your f against a stone.' "
1 Cor	12:15	If a f should say, "Because I am not
Rv	10: 2	He placed his right f on the sea and his left f on the land,

FOOTHOLD →FOOT
Ps	69: 3	where there is no f. I have gone

FOOTSTOOL →FOOT
1 Chr	28: 2	LORD, the f for the feet of our God;
Ps	99: 5	bow down before his f; holy is God!
Ps	110: 1	while I make your enemies your f."
Is	66: 1	the earth is my f. What kind
Lam	2: 1	Unmindful of his f on the day of his
Mt	5:35	nor by the earth, for it is his f;
Acts	7:49	the earth is my f. What kind
Heb	1:13	until I make your enemies your f"?
Heb	10:13	until his enemies are made his f.

FORBEARANCE
Rom	3:26	through the f of God—to prove his

FORBID
Rom	2:22	You who f adultery, do you commit
1 Cor	14:39	and do not f speaking in tongues,
1 Tm	4: 3	They f marriage and require

FORCE →FORCED
Gn	34: 2	he seized her and lay with her by f.
Acts	26:11	an attempt to f them to blaspheme;

FORCED →FORCE
Ex	1:11	to oppress them with f labor.
1 Kgs	9:15	This is an account of the f labor
Phlm	1:14	that the good you do might not be f

FORDS
Jos	2: 7	along the way to the f of the Jordan,

FOREHEAD →FOREHEADS
Ex	13: 9	hand and as a reminder on your f;
Ex	28:38	this plate must always be over his f,
Dt	6: 8	let them be as a pendant on your f.
Dt	11:18	and let them be a pendant on your f.
1 Sm	17:49	and struck the Philistine on the f.
Rv	17: 5	On her f was written a name,

FOREHEADS →FOREHEAD
Ez	9: 4	an X on the f of those who moan
Rv	7: 3	put the seal on the f of the servants
Rv	9: 4	not have the seal of God in their f.
Rv	13:16	image on their right hands or their f,
Rv	14: 1	his Father's name written on their f.
Rv	20: 4	nor had accepted its mark on their f
Rv	22: 4	face, and his name will be on their f.

FOREIGN →FOREIGNER, FOREIGNERS
Gn	35: 2	"Get rid of the f gods that you have
1 Kgs	11: 1	loved many f women besides
2 Chr	33:15	He removed the f gods and the idol
Ps	81:10	There must be no f god among you;
Acts	17:18	sounds like a promoter of f deities,"

FOREIGNER →FOREIGN
Ex	12:43	the Passover. No f may partake of it.
Dt	17:15	a f, who is no kin of yours, you may
Dt	23:21	You may demand interest from a f,
1 Kgs	8:41	"To the f, likewise, who is not
Lk	17:18	but this f returned to give thanks
1 Cor	14:11	I shall be a f to one who speaks it, and one who speaks it a f to me.

FOREIGNERS →FOREIGN
Mt	27: 7	potter's field as a burial place for f.
1 Cor	14:21	and by the lips of f I will speak

FOREKNEW →KNOW
Rom	8:29	For those he f he also predestined
Rom	11: 2	not rejected his people whom he f.

FOREKNOWLEDGE →KNOW
Jdt	9: 6	and your judgment is made with f.
Acts	2:23	up by the set plan and f of God,

FOREMOST
1 Tm	1:15	to save sinners. Of these I am the f.

FORERUNNER →RUN
Heb	6:20	Jesus has entered on our behalf as f,

FORESAW →SEE
Acts	2:31	he f and spoke of the resurrection

FORESKIN →FORESKINS
Gn	17:14	flesh of his f has not been cut away,
Ex	4:25	of flint and cut off her son's f and,

FORESKINS →FORESKIN
1 Sm	18:25	the bride than the f of one hundred
Jer	4: 4	remove the f of your hearts, O men

FOREST
1 Kgs	7: 2	He built the hall called the F
1 Chr	16:33	Then shall all the trees of the f exult
Ps	50:10	For every animal of the f is mine,
Jas	3: 5	small a fire can set a huge f ablaze.

FORETOLD →TELL
2 Kgs	17:23	his sight as he had f through all his
2 Kgs	24:13	of the LORD, as the LORD had f.
Sir	49: 6	streets desolate, As JEREMIAH had f;
Is	43: 9	this, or f to us the earlier things?

FOREVER →EVER
Gn	3:22	life also, and thus eat of it and live f."
Gn	6: 3	"My spirit shall not remain in man f,
Ex	3:15	"This is my name f; this is my title
Dt	29:28	concern us and our descendants f,
2 Sm	7:13	I will make his royal throne firm f.
2 Sm	7:26	Your name will be f great,
1 Kgs	2:33	be the peace of the LORD f for David,
1 Kgs	9: 3	I confer my name upon it f, and my
1 Chr	16:15	He remembers f his covenant
1 Chr	16:41	"because his kindness endures f,"
1 Chr	17:24	may be great and abide f,
2 Chr	5:13	for his mercy endures f," the building
2 Chr	33: 7	of Israel I shall place my name f.
Ezr	3:11	for his kindness to Israel endures f";
Tb	3:11	F blessed and honored is your holy
Tb	3:11	may all your works f bless you.
1 Mc	4:24	he is good, for his mercy endures f."
Ps	9: 8	The LORD rules f, has set up a throne
Ps	19:10	enduring f. The statutes of the LORD
Ps	28: 9	inheritance; feed and sustain them f!
Ps	29:10	the flood! The LORD reigns as king f!
Ps	33:11	But the plan of the LORD stands f,
Ps	44: 9	your name we will praise f.
Ps	44:24	O Lord? Rise up! Do not reject us f!
Ps	72:19	Blessed be his glorious name f;
Ps	73:26	the rock of my heart, my portion f.
Ps	74:10	Shall the foe revile your name f?
Ps	77: 9	Has God's love ceased f?
Ps	79:13	will give thanks to you f; through all
Ps	81:16	would tremble, their doom sealed f.
Ps	86:12	glorify your name f, Lord my God.
Ps	89: 2	promises of the LORD I will sing f,
Ps	92: 9	for you, LORD, are f on high.
Ps	100: 5	LORD, Whose love endures f,
Ps	102:13	But you, LORD, are enthroned f;
Ps	104:31	May the glory of the LORD endure f;
Ps	107: 1	who is good, whose love endures f!"
Ps	110: 4	"Like Melchizedek you are a priest f."
Ps	111: 3	work, your wise design endures f.
Ps	112: 6	the just shall be remembered f.
Ps	117: 2	the LORD is faithful f. Hallelujah!
Ps	118: 1	who is good, whose love endures f.
Ps	119:111	Your decrees are my heritage f;
Ps	119:152	that you have established them f.
Ps	136: 1	is so good; God's love endures f;

Ps	146: 6	that is in them, Who keeps faith **f**,
Prv	10:25	but the just man is established **f**.
Prv	27:24	For wealth lasts not **f**, nor even
Eccl	3:14	whatever God does will endure **f**;
Wis	5:15	But the just live **f**, and in the LORD is
Sir	40:17	off, and justice endures **f**.
Is	26: 4	Trust in the LORD **f**! For the LORD is
Is	40: 8	wilts, the word of our God stands **f**."
Is	51: 6	My salvation shall remain **f** and my
Is	51: 8	But my justice shall remain **f**
Is	59:21	from now on and **f**, says the LORD.
Jer	3:12	I will not continue my wrath **f**.
Jer	33:11	LORD is good; his mercy endures **f**."
Lam	5:19	You, O LORD, are enthroned **f**;
Bar	3: 3	for you are enthroned **f**, while we are perishing **f**.
Dn	2:44	an end to them, and it shall stand **f**.
Dn	3:57	praise and exalt him above all **f**.
Dn	6:27	"For he is the living God, enduring **f**;
Hos	2:21	I will espouse you to me **f**: I will
Jn	6:51	whoever eats this bread will live **f**;
Rom	9: 5	God who is over all be blessed **f**.
Rom	16:27	through Jesus Christ be glory **f**
Heb	5: 6	"You are a priest **f**
Heb	7:17	"You are a priest **f**
Heb	7:24	but he, because he remains **f**,
Heb	13: 8	is the same yesterday, today, and **f**.
1 Pt	1:25	but the word of the Lord remains **f**."
1 Jn	2:17	does the will of God remains **f**.
2 Jn	1: 2	dwells in us and will be with us **f**.
Rv	1:18	dead, but now I am alive **f** and ever.
Rv	4: 9	on the throne, who lives **f** and ever,
Rv	11:15	and he will reign **f** and ever."
Rv	20:10	tormented day and night **f** and ever.
Rv	22: 5	and they shall reign **f** and ever.

FOREWARNED →WARN

2 Pt	3:17	since you are **f**, be on your guard

FORFEIT →FORFEITS

Mk	8:36	gain the whole world and **f** his life?
Lk	9:25	whole world yet lose or **f** himself?

FORFEITS →FORFEIT

Prv	20: 2	he who incurs his anger **f** his life.

FORGAVE →FORGIVE

Ps	78:38	But God is merciful and **f** their sin;
Ps	85: 3	You **f** the guilt of your people,
Mt	18:27	let him go and **f** him the loan.
Mt	18:32	I **f** you your entire debt because you

FORGET →FORGETFUL, FORGETS, FORGETTING, FORGOT, FORGOTTEN

Gn	41:51	"God has made me **f** entirely
Dt	6:12	take care not to **f** the LORD,
2 Kgs	17:38	I made with you, you must not **f**;
1 Mc	1:49	so that they might **f** the law
Ps	9:18	depart, all the nations that **f** God.
Ps	10:12	Raise your arm! Do not **f** the poor!
Ps	50:22	"Understand this, you who **f** God,
Ps	78: 7	in God, And not **f** the works of God,
Ps	103: 2	soul; do not **f** all the gifts of God,
Ps	119:93	I will never **f** your precepts;
Ps	137: 5	If I **f** you, Jerusalem, may my right
Prv	3: 1	My son, **f** not my teaching,
Prv	4: 5	Do not **f** or turn aside
Prv	31: 5	Lest in drinking they **f** what the law
Is	49:15	Can a mother **f** her infant,
Is	49:15	Even should she **f**, I will never **f**
Jer	2:32	Does a virgin **f** her jewelry, a bride

FORGETFUL →FORGET

2 Pt	1: 9	**f** of the cleansing of his past sins.

FORGETS →FORGET

Jb	8:13	is the end of everyone who **f** God,

FORGETTING →FORGET

Phil	3:13	**f** what lies behind but straining

FORGIVE →FORGAVE, FORGIVEN, FORGIVENESS, FORGIVES, FORGIVING

Gn	50:17	therefore, **f** the crime that we,

Ex	10:17	But now, do **f** me my sin once more,
Ex	32:32	If you would only **f** their sin! If you
Jos	24:19	who will not **f** your transgressions
1 Sm	25:28	Please **f** the transgression of your
1 Kgs	8:34	and **f** the sin of your people Israel,
1 Kgs	8:36	heaven and **f** the sin of your servant
1 Kgs	8:39	your heavenly dwelling place and **f**.
1 Kgs	8:50	**F** your people their sins and all
2 Chr	6:25	and **f** the sin of your people Israel,
2 Chr	6:27	and **f** the sin of your servants
2 Chr	6:30	your heavenly dwelling place, and **f**.
2 Chr	6:39	**F** your people who have sinned
Sir	5: 6	his mercy; my many sins he will **f**."
Sir	28: 2	**F** your neighbor's injustice;
Sir	34:19	many sacrifices does he **f** their sins.
Jer	18:23	plans to slay me. **F** not their crime,
Jer	31:34	LORD, for I will **f** their evildoing
Jer	33: 8	and rebelled against me, I will **f**.
Jer	36: 3	so that I may **f** their wickedness
Am	7: 2	in the land, I said: **F**, O Lord GOD!
Mt	6:12	and **f** us our debts, as we **f** our
Mt	6:14	If you **f** others their transgressions,
Mt	6:14	your heavenly Father will **f** you.
Mt	6:15	But if you do not **f** others,
Mt	6:15	your Father **f** your transgressions.
Mt	9: 6	has authority on earth to **f** sins"—he
Mt	18:21	against me, how often must I **f** him?
Mk	2: 7	Who but God alone can **f** sins?"
Mk	2:10	Man has authority to **f** sins on earth"—
Mk	11:25	**f** anyone against whom you have
Mk	11:25	in turn **f** you your transgressions.
Lk	5:21	Who but God alone can **f** sins?"
Lk	5:24	earth to **f** sins"—he said to the man who
Lk	6:37	**F** and you will be forgiven.
Lk	11: 4	and **f** us our sins for we ourselves **f**
Lk	17: 3	rebuke him; and if he repents, **f** him.
Lk	17: 4	'I am sorry,' you should **f** him."
Lk	23:34	"Father, **f** them, they know not what
Jn	20:23	Whose sins you **f** are forgiven them,
2 Cor	2: 7	so that on the contrary you should **f**
2 Cor	2:10	Whomever you **f** anything, so do I.
2 Cor	12:13	not burden you? **F** me this wrong!
1 Jn	1: 9	just and will **f** our sins and cleanse

FORGIVEN →FORGIVE

Lv	4:20	for them, and they will be **f**.
Lv	19:22	has committed, and it will be **f** him.
Nm	15:25	thus they will be **f** the inadvertence
Ps	32: 1	fault is removed, whose sin is **f**.
Mt	9: 5	to say, 'Your sins are **f**,' or to say,
Mt	12:31	sin and blasphemy will be **f** people,
Mt	12:31	against the Spirit will not be **f**.
Mk	2: 9	paralytic, 'Your sins are **f**,' or to say,
Lk	6:37	Forgive and you will be **f**.
Lk	7:47	tell you, her many sins have been **f**;
Lk	7:47	But the one to whom little is **f**,
Rom	4: 7	are they whose iniquities are **f**
Eph	4:32	one another as God has **f** you
Col	3:13	as the Lord has **f** you, so must you
Jas	5:15	has committed any sins, he will be **f**.
1 Jn	2:12	because your sins have been **f**

FORGIVENESS →FORGIVE

Ps	130: 4	But with you is **f** and so you are
Sir	5: 5	Of **f** be not overconfident,
Dn	9: 9	our God, are compassion and **f**!
Mt	26:28	on behalf of many for the **f** of sins.
Mk	1: 4	of repentance for the **f** of sins.
Mk	3:29	the holy Spirit will never have **f**,
Lk	1:77	salvation through the **f** of their sins,
Lk	3: 3	of repentance for the **f** of sins,
Lk	24:47	for the **f** of sins, would be preached
Acts	5:31	grant Israel repentance and **f** of sins.
Acts	10:43	in him will receive **f** of sins through
Acts	13:38	that through him **f** of sins is being
Acts	26:18	so that they may obtain **f** of sins
Eph	1: 7	by his blood, the **f** of transgressions,
Col	1:14	we have redemption, the **f** of sins.
Heb	9:22	the shedding of blood there is no **f**.
Heb	10:18	Where there is **f** of these, there is no

FORGIVES →FORGIVE
Sir	2:11	he f sins, he saves in time of trouble.
Sir	16:11	him who remits and f,
Mt	18:35	you, unless each of you f his brother
Lk	7:49	"Who is this who even f sins?"

FORGIVING →FORGIVE
Ex	34: 7	and f wickedness and crime and sin;
Nm	14:18	kindness, f wickedness and crime;
Ps	86: 5	Lord, you are kind and f,
Ps	99: 8	them; you were a f God, though you
Eph	4:32	f one another as God has forgiven

FORGOT →FORGET
Dt	32:18	You f the God who gave you birth.
1 Sm	12: 9	But they f the Lord their God;
Ps	78:11	They f his works, the wondrous
Ps	106:13	But they soon f all he had done;
Ps	106:21	They f the God who saved them,
Jer	23:27	just as their fathers f my name
Hos	2:15	after her lovers, f me, says the Lord.

FORGOTTEN →FORGET
Ps	9:19	The needy will never be f, nor will
Ps	44:21	If we had f the name of our God,
Ps	77:10	Has God f mercy, in anger withheld
Sir	35: 6	most pleasing, never will it ever be f.
Is	17:10	For you have f God, your savior,
Is	49:14	has forsaken me; my Lord has f me."
Jer	2:32	Yet my people have f me
Hos	8:14	Israel has f his maker and built
Mt	16: 5	the disciples had f to bring bread.
Heb	12: 5	f the exhortation addressed to you as

FORM →FORMED, FORMLESS
Dt	4:15	"You saw no f at all on the day
Ez	1: 5	looked like this: their f was human,
Lk	3:22	upon him in bodily f like a dove.
Jn	5:37	never heard his voice nor seen his f,
Acts	14:11	have come down to us in human f."
1 Cor	7:31	in its present f is passing away.
Phil	2: 6	Who, though he was in the f of God,

FORMED →FORM
Gn	2: 7	the Lord God f man out of the clay
Ps	94: 9	The one who f the eye not see?
Ps	139:13	You f my inmost being; you knit me
Is	43: 1	you, O Jacob, and f you, O Israel:
Is	43:10	Before me no god was f,
Is	44: 2	help, who f you from the womb:
Is	49: 5	who f me as his servant
Jer	1: 5	Before I f you in the womb I knew
Am	4:13	Him who f the mountains, and created
Gal	4:19	in labor until Christ be f in you!
1 Tm	2:13	For Adam was f first, then Eve.
2 Pt	3: 5	of old and earth was f out of water

FORMER
1 Mc	4:47	and built a new altar like the f one.
Eph	4:22	put away the old self of your f way

FORMLESS →FORM
Gn	1: 2	the earth was a f wasteland,
Wis	11:17	the universe from f matter, to send

FORNICATORS
1 Cor	6: 9	neither f nor idolaters nor adulterers

FORSAKE →FORSAKEN, FORSAKES, FORSAKING
Dt	31: 6	he will never fail you or f you."
Jos	1: 5	I will not leave you nor f you.
Jos	24:16	from us to f the Lord for the service
Ps	27:10	Even if my father and mother f me,
Ps	94:14	You, Lord, will not f your people,
Ps	138: 8	Never f the work of your hands!
Prv	4: 6	F her not, and she will preserve
Prv	27:10	friend and your father's friend f not;
Is	55: 7	Let the scoundrel f his way,
Jer	17:13	all who f you shall be in disgrace;
Heb	13: 5	"I will never f you or abandon you."

FORSAKEN →FORSAKE
Jdt	9:11	the protector of the f, the savior

Is	1: 4	children! They have f the Lord,
Is	49:14	But Zion said, "The Lord has f me;
Dn	14:38	"you have not f those who love you."
Mt	27:46	God, my God, why have you f me?"

FORSAKES →FORSAKE
Prv	2:17	Who f the companion of her youth

FORSAKING →FORSAKE
Hos	4:12	they commit harlotry, f their God.

FORTH
Ps	50: 2	From Zion God shines f,

FORTIFIED →FORTRESS
Nm	13:28	and the towns are f and very strong.
Dt	9: 1	having large cities f to the sky,

FORTRESS →FORTIFIED
2 Sm	22: 2	Lord, my rock, my f, my deliverer,
Ps	59:10	for you I watch; you, God, are my f,
Ps	71: 3	for you are my rock and f.

FORTUNE →FORTUNE-TELLING
Is	65:11	You who spread a table for F

FORTUNE-TELLING →FORTUNE, TELL
Acts	16:16	profit to her owners through her f.

FORTY
Gn	7: 4	rain down on the earth for f days and f nights,
Gn	18:29	"What if only f are found there?"
Ex	16:35	Israelites ate this manna for f years,
Ex	24:18	and there he stayed for f days and f
Nm	14:34	F days you spent in scouting
Nm	14:34	f years shall you suffer for your
Dt	25: 3	F stripes may be given him, but no
Jos	14: 7	I was f years old when the servant
1 Sm	4:18	He had judged Israel for f years.
2 Sm	5: 4	king, and he reigned for f years:
1 Kgs	19: 8	he walked f days and f nights
2 Chr	9:30	Jerusalem over all Israel for f years.
Neh	9:21	F years in the desert you sustained
Ez	29:12	most deserted of cities for f years;
Am	2:10	you through the desert for f years,
Jon	3: 4	"F days more and Nineveh shall be
Mt	4: 2	He fasted for f days and f nights,
Lk	4: 2	for f days, to be tempted
2 Cor	11:24	Jews I received f lashes minus one.
Heb	3:17	whom was he "provoked for f years"?

FOUGHT →FIGHT
Jos	10:42	Lord, the God of Israel, f for Israel.
1 Cor	15:32	If at Ephesus I f with beasts,
Rv	12: 7	The dragon and its angels f back,

FOUND →FIND
Gn	6: 8	But Noah f favor with the Lord.
Ex	12:19	seven days no leaven may be f
Ex	33:12	and also, 'You have f favor with me.'
2 Kgs	22: 8	"I have f the book of the law
1 Chr	28: 9	him, he will let himself be f by you;
1 Mc	1:56	of the law which they f they tore
Prv	10:13	lips of the intelligent is f wisdom,
Eccl	7:27	Behold, this have I f, says Qoheleth,
Is	55: 6	Seek the Lord while he may be f,
Is	65: 1	to be f by those who sought me not.
Jer	15:16	When I f your words, I devoured
Dn	1:19	of them, none was f equal to Daniel,
Dn	5:27	on the scales and f wanting;
Dn	12: 1	everyone who is f written
Mt	1:18	she was f with child through
Lk	1:30	for you have f favor with God.
Lk	7: 9	not even in Israel have I f such faith."
Lk	15: 6	me because I have f my lost sheep.'
Lk	15: 9	me because I have f the coin that I
Lk	15:24	again; he was lost, and has been f.'
Rom	10:20	"I was f [by] those who were not
Phil	2: 7	and f human in appearance,
Rv	5: 4	tears because no one was f worthy
Rv	20:15	whose name was not f written

FOUNDATION →FOUNDATIONS, FOUNDED
Ezr	3: 6	though the f of the temple

Ps	97: 2	and right are the f of his throne.
Is	28:16	A precious cornerstone as a sure f;
Lk	14:29	after laying the f and finding
Rom	15:20	so that I do not build on another's f,
1 Cor	3:10	like a wise master builder I laid a f,
1 Cor	3:11	no one can lay a f other than the one
Eph	2:20	built upon the f of the apostles
2 Tm	2:19	God's solid f stands, bearing this
Heb	6: 1	without laying the f all over again:

FOUNDATIONS →FOUNDATION

1 Kgs	6:37	The f of the Lᴏʀᴅ's temple were laid
Ps	82: 5	darkness, and all the world's f shake.
Ps	137: 7	said: "Level it, level it down to its f!"
Is	54:11	carnelians, and your f in sapphires;
Heb	11:10	looking forward to the city with f,

FOUNDED →FOUNDATION

Ps	78:69	like the earth which he f forever.
Prv	3:19	The Lᴏʀᴅ by wisdom f the earth,

FOUNTAIN →FOUNTAINS

Ps	36:10	For with you is the f of life,
Prv	10:11	A f of life is the mouth of the just,
Prv	13:14	teaching of the wise is a f of life,
Prv	14:27	The fear of the Lᴏʀᴅ is a f of life,
Prv	16:22	Good sense is a f of life to its
Song	4:12	an enclosed garden, a f sealed.
Jer	8:23	spring of water, my eyes a f of tears,
Bar	3:12	You have forsaken the f of wisdom!
Jl	4:18	A f shall issue from the house
Zec	13: 1	Jerusalem, a f to purify from sin

FOUNTAINS →FOUNTAIN

Gn	7:11	that All the f of the great abyss burst

FOUR →FOURTH

Gn	2:10	it divides and becomes f branches.
1 Kgs	18:19	as well as the f hundred and fifty
1 Kgs	18:19	the f hundred prophets of Asherah
Prv	30:15	never satisfied, f never say, "Enough!"
Prv	30:18	for me, yes, f I cannot understand:
Prv	30:21	yes, under f it cannot bear up:
Prv	30:24	F things are among the smallest
Prv	30:29	yes, f are stately in their carriage:
Is	11:12	from the f corners of the earth.
Ez	1: 5	figures resembling f living creatures
Ez	10: 9	I also saw f wheels beside them,
Ez	10:14	Each had f faces: the first face was
Dn	1:17	To these f young men God gave
Dn	7: 3	which emerged f immense beasts,
Dn	8: 8	and in its place came up f others, facing the f winds of heaven.
Zec	2: 3	the Lᴏʀᴅ showed me f blacksmiths.
Zec	6: 5	reply, "These are the f winds
Mt	15:38	who ate were f thousand men,
Mk	8:20	the seven loaves for the f thousand,
Jn	4:35	'In f months the harvest will be here'?
Rv	4: 6	there were f living creatures covered
Rv	9:14	"Release the f angels who are bound

FOURTEEN

Mt	1:17	Abraham to David is f generations;
Mt	1:17	the Babylonian exile, f generations;
Mt	1:17	exile to the Messiah, f generations.
2 Cor	12: 2	f years ago (whether in the body

FOURTH →FOUR

Gn	15:16	In the f time-span the others shall
Ex	20: 5	down to the third and f generation;
Dn	3:92	and the f looks like a son of God."

FOWLER

Prv	6: 5	or as a bird from the hand of the f.

FOX →FOXES

Neh	3:35	Any f that attacked it would breach
Lk	13:32	replied, "Go and tell that f, 'Behold,

FOXES →FOX

Jgs	15: 4	left and caught three hundred f.
Song	2:15	Catch us the f, the little f
Lk	9:58	"F have dens and birds of the sky

FRAGRANCE →FRAGRANT

Jn	12: 3	was filled with the f of the oil.

FRAGRANT →FRAGRANCE

Ex	25: 6	anointing oil and for the f incense;
Ex	30: 7	"On it Aaron shall burn f incense.
Eph	5: 2	offering to God for a f aroma.
Phil	4:18	through Epaphroditus, "a f aroma,"

FRANKINCENSE →INCENSE

Is	60: 6	bearing gold and f, and proclaiming
Mt	2:11	and offered him gifts of gold, f,

FREE →FREED, FREEDOM, FREELY

Ps	146: 7	hungry. The Lᴏʀᴅ sets prisoners f;
Lk	13:12	you are set f of your infirmity."
Jn	8:32	the truth, and the truth will set you f."
Jn	8:36	frees you, then you will truly be f.
1 Cor	12:13	slaves or f persons, and we were all
Gal	3:28	there is neither slave nor f person,
Gal	5: 1	For freedom Christ set us f; so stand
Eph	6: 8	he does, whether he is slave or f.
Heb	13: 5	Let your life be f from love
1 Pt	2:16	Be f, yet without using freedom as

FREED →FREE

Rv	1: 5	has f us from our sins by his blood,

FREEDOM →FREE

Rom	8:21	in the glorious f of the children
1 Cor	7:21	even if you can gain your f,
2 Cor	3:17	the Spirit of the Lord is, there is f.
Gal	5: 1	For f Christ set us free; so stand
1 Pt	2:16	yet without using f as a pretext
2 Pt	2:19	They promise them f, though they

FREELY →FREE

Hos	14: 5	I will love them f; for my wrath is

FRENZY

1 Sm	19:20	in a prophetic f, they too fell

FRESH

Ez	47: 8	the salt waters, which it makes f.

FRIEND →FRIENDLY, FRIENDS, FRIENDSHIP

Dt	13: 7	wife, or your intimate f, entices you
2 Sm	16:17	"Is this your devotion to your f? Why did you not go with your f?"
2 Chr	20: 7	descendants of Abraham, your f?
Ps	41:10	Even the f who had my trust,
Prv	17:17	He who is a f is always a f,
Prv	18:24	a true f is more loyal than a brother.
Prv	27: 6	a f may be accepted as well meant,
Prv	27:10	Your own f and your father's f
Song	5:16	Such is my lover, and such my f,
Sir	7:18	Barter not a f for money, nor a dear
Sir	9:10	Discard not an old f, for the new
Sir	9:10	equal him. A new f is like new wine
Sir	25: 9	Happy is he who finds a f and he
Sir	27:17	Cherish your f, keep faith with him;
Is	41: 8	chosen, offspring of Abraham my f—
Mt	11:19	a f of tax collectors and sinners.'
Jn	19:12	him, you are not a F of Caesar.
Jas	2:23	and he was called "the f of God."

FRIENDLY →FRIEND

Sir	12: 9	is successful even his enemy is f;

FRIENDS →FRIEND

Jb	2:11	when three of Job's f heard of all
Jb	42:10	of Job, after he had prayed for his f;
Prv	16:28	and a talebearer separates bosom f.
Sir	6: 5	A kind mouth multiplies f,
Sir	12: 8	prosperity we cannot know our f;
Sir	37: 1	there are f who are f in name only.
Lam	1: 2	ones; Her f have all betrayed her
Jn	15:13	this, to lay down one's life for one's f.
Jn	15:14	You are my f if you do what I
3 Jn	1:15	The f greet you; greet the f there

FRIENDSHIP →FRIEND

Wis	7:14	who gain this treasure win the f

FRIGHTEN
Dt	28:26	the field, with no one to f them off.
Neh	6: 9	They were all trying to f us,

FROGS
Ex	7:27	a plague of f over all your territory.
Rv	16:13	saw three unclean spirits like f come

FRONT
Ex	14:19	also, leaving the f, took up its place
Ex	32:15	written on both sides, f and back;
Ez	2:10	It was covered with writing f
Rv	4: 6	creatures covered with eyes in f

FROST
Zec	14: 6	there shall no longer be cold or f.

FRUIT → FRUITFUL, FRUITS
Gn	1:11	and every kind of f tree on earth
Gn	3: 3	it is only about the f of the tree
Gn	3: 6	So she took some of its f and ate it;
Dt	28: 4	"Blessed be the f of your womb,
Dt	28:53	you will eat the f of your womb,
Jgs	9:11	up my sweetness and my good f,
Ps	1: 3	that yields its f in season; Its leaves
Ps	92:15	They shall bear f even in old age,
Prv	8:19	My f is better than gold, yes,
Prv	11:30	The f of virtue is a tree of life,
Prv	12:14	the f of his words a man has his fill
Prv	27:18	He who tends a fig tree eats its f,
Is	27: 6	covering all the world with f.
Jer	17: 8	it shows no distress, but still bears f.
Ez	47:12	f trees of every kind shall grow;
Ez	47:12	leaves shall not fade, nor their f fail.
Am	8: 1	God showed me: a basket of ripe f.
Mt	3: 8	Produce good f as evidence of your
Mt	3:10	that does not bear good f will be cut
Mt	7:17	every good tree bears good f, and a rotten tree bears bad f.
Lk	6:44	every tree is known by its own f.
Lk	13: 6	when he came in search of f on it
Jn	15: 2	branch in me that does not bear f,
Jn	15: 2	he prunes so that it bears more f.
Jn	15:16	to go and bear f that will remain,
Rom	7: 4	order that we might bear f for God.
Col	1:10	in every good work bearing f
Heb	13:15	the f of lips that confess his name.
Rv	22: 2	that produces f twelve times a year,

FRUITFUL → FRUIT
Gn	35:11	God Almighty; be f and multiply.
Ex	1: 7	the Israelites were f and prolific.
Ps	128: 3	Like a f vine your wife within your
Phil	1:22	the flesh, that means f labor for me.

FRUITS → FRUIT
Lv	2:14	cereal offering of first f to the LORD,
Lv	23:17	offering of your first f to the LORD,
Nm	28:26	"On the day of first f, on your feast
1 Mc	3:49	vestments, the first f, and the tithes;
Prv	3: 9	with first f of all your produce;
Jer	2: 3	was Israel, the first f of his harvest;
Hos	9:10	Like the first f of the fig tree in its
Mt	7:16	By their f you will know them.
Lk	3: 8	Produce good f as evidence of your

FRUSTRATES → FRUSTRATION
Jb	5:12	He f the plans of the cunning,
Ps	33:10	of nations, f the designs of peoples.

FRUSTRATION → FRUSTRATES
Dt	28:20	f in every enterprise you undertake,

FUEL
Is	9:18	and the people are like f for fire;
Ez	21:37	You shall be f for the fire,

FULFILL → FULFILLED
Nm	23:19	and not act, to decree and not f?
2 Chr	10:15	f the prophecy the LORD had uttered
Ps	119:166	LORD, and I f your commands.
Eccl	5: 3	in fools; f what you have vowed.
Jer	33:14	when I will f the promise I made
Mt	1:22	f what the Lord had said through

Mt	3:15	fitting for us to f all righteousness."
Mt	5:17	I have come not to abolish but to f.
Mt	8:17	to f what had been said by Isaiah
Mt	12:17	to f what had been spoken through
Mt	13:35	to f what had been said through
Jn	18: 9	This was to f what he had said,
Gal	6: 2	and so you will f the law of Christ.
Jas	2: 8	if you f the royal law according

FULFILLED → FULFILL
Jos	23:15	made to you as has been f for you,
Prv	13:12	sick, but a wish f is a tree of life.
Mt	2:15	said through the prophet might be f,
Mt	2:17	was f what had been said through
Mt	2:23	through the prophets might be f,
Mt	4:14	Isaiah the prophet might be f:
Mt	13:14	Isaiah's prophecy is f in them,
Mt	21: 4	through the prophet might be f:
Mt	26:54	how would the scriptures be f
Mt	26:56	writings of the prophets may be f."
Mt	27: 9	was f what had been said through
Mk	14:49	but that the scriptures may be f."
Lk	1: 1	events that have been f among us,
Lk	4:21	"Today this scripture passage is f
Lk	21:24	until the times of the Gentiles are f.
Lk	24:44	the prophets and psalms must be f."
Jn	12:38	Isaiah the prophet spoke might be f:
Jn	13:18	But so that the scripture might be f,
Jn	15:25	word written in their law might be f,
Jn	17:12	order that the scripture might be f.
Jn	18:32	word of Jesus might be f that he said
Jn	19:24	of scripture might be f [that says]:
Jn	19:28	order that the scripture might be f,
Jn	19:36	the scripture passage might be f:
Acts	1:16	to be f which the holy Spirit spoke
Rom	8: 4	decree of the law might be f in us,
Rom	13: 8	one who loves another has f the law.
Jas	2:23	Thus the scripture was f that says,
Rv	10: 7	mysterious plan of God shall be f,

FULL → FILL
Jb	14: 1	is short-lived and f of trouble,
Ps	127: 5	are they whose quivers are f.
Eccl	1: 7	yet never does the sea become f.
Is	1:15	listen. Your hands are f of blood!
Ez	10:12	of the four wheels were f of eyes all
Mt	23:25	but inside they are f of plunder
Jn	1:14	only Son, f of grace and truth.
Eph	4:13	the extent of the f stature of Christ,
Jas	3:17	f of mercy and good fruits,
2 Jn	1: 8	for but may receive a f recompense.

FULLNESS → FILL
Dt	33:16	With the best of the earth and its f,
Jn	1:16	From his f we have all received,
1 Cor	10:26	for "the earth and its f are the Lord's."
Gal	4: 4	But when the f of time had come,
Eph	1:23	the f of the one who fills all things
Eph	3:19	may be filled with all the f of God.
Col	1:19	him all the f was pleased to dwell,
Col	2: 9	him dwells the whole f of the deity
Col	2:10	and you share in this f in him,

FULLY → FILL
Lk	6:40	but when f trained, every disciple
Rom	4:21	was f convinced that what he had
Rom	14: 5	Let everyone be f persuaded in his
1 Cor	13:12	then I shall know f as I am f known.

FURNACE
Gn	19:28	the land rising like fumes from a f.
Ps	21:10	you will drive them into a f.
Sir	31:26	As the f probes the work
Is	48:10	tested you in the f of affliction.
Dn	3: 6	be instantly cast into a white-hot f."
Dn	3:49	went down into the f with Azariah
Dn	3:49	drove the fiery flames out of the f,
Mt	13:42	will throw them into the fiery f,
Rv	1:15	like polished brass refined in a f,
Rv	9: 2	passage like smoke from a huge f.

FURNISHED
Mk   14:15   will show you a large upper room f

FURY
Sir   40: 5   terror of death, f and strife.
Hb   3:12   earth, in f you trample the nations.
Rom   2: 8   f to those who selfishly disobey
Rv   16:19   the cup filled with the wine of his f
Rv   19:15   in the wine press the wine of the f

FUTILE → FUTILITY
1 Pt   1:18   were ransomed from your f conduct,

FUTILITY → FUTILE
Rom   8:20   for creation was made subject to f,
Eph   4:17   Gentiles do, in the f of their minds;

FUTURE
Prv   23:18   For you will surely have a f,
Prv   24:20   For the evil man has no f, the lamp
Jer   29:11   plans to give you a f full of hope.
Jer   31:17   There is hope for your f,
1 Cor 3:22   life or death, or the present or the f:
1 Tm   6:19   treasure a good foundation for the f,

G

GABBATHA
Jn   19:13   Stone Pavement, in Hebrew, G.

GABRIEL
  Angel who interpreted Daniel's visions (Dn 8:16-26; 9:20-27);
announced births of John (Lk 1:11-20), Jesus (Lk 1:26-38).

GAD
  1. Son of Jacob by Zilpah (Gn 30:9-11; 35:26; 1 Chr 2:2). Tribe of
blessed (Gn 49:19; Dt 33:20-21), numbered (Nm 1:25; 26:18),
allotted land east of the Jordan (Nm 32; 34:14; Jos 18:7; 22), west
(Ez 48:27-28), 12,000 from (Rv 7:5).
  2. Prophet; seer of David (1 Sm 22:5; 2 Sm 24:11-19; 1 Chr
29:29).

GADARENES
Mt   8:28   side, to the territory of the G,

GAIN → GAINED
Gn   24:60   may your descendants g possession
1 Sm   8: 3   sought illicit g and accepted bribes,
Ps   90:12   that we may g wisdom of heart.
Prv   1: 5   man will g sound guidance,
Prv   1:19   unlawful g takes away the life
Prv   4: 1   that you may g understanding!
Prv   28:16   who hates ill-gotten g prolongs his
Sir   6: 7   When you g a friend, first test him,
Mk   8:36   is there for one to g the whole world
Lk   9:25   one to g the whole world yet lose
1 Cor 13: 3   but do not have love, I g nothing.
Phil   1:21   to me life is Christ, and death is g.
Phil   3: 8   so much rubbish, that I may g Christ
1 Tm   3:13   well as deacons g good standing
1 Tm   6: 5   religion to be a means of g.
1 Tm   6: 6   with contentment is a great g.
Ti   1: 7   aggressive, not greedy for sordid g,
Ti   1:11   for sordid g what they should not.
Jude   1:11   to Balaam's error for the sake of g,

GAINED → GAIN
Prv   16:31   of glory; it is g by virtuous living.
Eccl   2:11   wind, with nothing g under the sun.

GAIUS
Rom   16:23   G, who is host to me
3 Jn   1: 1   to the beloved G whom I love

GALATIA → GALATIANS
1 Pt   1: 1   of the dispersion in Pontus, G,

GALATIANS → GALATIA
Gal   3: 1   O stupid G! Who has bewitched

GALILEAN → GALILEE
Mt   26:69   "You too were with Jesus the G."
Mk   14:70   are one of them; for you too are a G."
Lk   22:59   too was with him, for he also is a G."
Lk   23: 6   this Pilate asked if the man was a G;
Acts   5:37   him came Judas the G at the time

GALILEANS → GALILEE
Lk   13: 1   about the G whose blood Pilate had
Jn   4:45   into Galilee, the G welcomed him,
Acts   2: 7   these people who are speaking G?

GALILEE → GALILEAN, GALILEANS
Tb   1: 5   all the mountains of G as well as
1 Mc   5:15   of Gentile G had joined forces
Mt   3:13   Jesus came from G to John
Mt   4:15   the Jordan, G of the Gentiles,
Mt   21:11   the prophet, from Nazareth in G."
Mt   26:32   up, I shall go before you to G."
Mt   28:10   Go tell my brothers to go to G,
Lk   23:49   who had followed him from G
Jn   2: 1   there was a wedding in Cana in G,
Jn   7:41   "The Messiah will not come from G,

GALL
Tb   11: 8   Smear the fish g on them.
Jb   16:13   he pours out my g upon the ground.
Mt   27:34   Jesus wine to drink mixed with g.

GALLIO
  Proconsul of Achaia, who refused to hear complaints against Paul
(Acts 18:12-17).

GAMALIEL
  Prominent Pharisee (Acts 5:34-39); teacher of Paul (Acts 22:5).

GAME
Gn   25:28   Esau, because he was fond of g;
Gn   27: 3   the country to hunt some g for me.

GAMES
2 Mc   4:18   When the quinquennial g were held

GANGRENE
2 Tm   2:17   and their teaching will spread like g.

GAPS
Neh   4: 1   progressing—for the g were beginning

GARDEN → GARDENER, GARDENS
Gn   2: 8   the Lord God planted a g in Eden,
Gn   2:15   and settled him in the g of Eden,
Gn   3:23   banished him from the g of Eden,
Gn   13:10   like the Lord's own g, or like Egypt.
Song   4:12   You are an enclosed g, my sister,
Song   4:12   an enclosed g, a fountain sealed.
Is   58:11   and you shall be like a watered g,
Ez   28:13   In Eden, the g of God, you were,
Ez   31: 9   of all Eden's trees in the g of God.
Dn   13:15   she entered the g as usual, with two
Jn   19:41   he had been crucified there was a g, and in the g a
              new tomb,

GARDENER → GARDEN
Lk   13: 7   he said to the g, 'For three years now
Jn   20:15   She thought it was the g and said

GARDENS → GARDEN
Jer   31:12   themselves shall be like watered g,
Am   4: 9   wind; your many g and vineyards,

GARMENT → GARMENTS
Neh   5:13   I also shook out the folds of my g,
Ps   102:27   they all wear out like a g;
Sir   14:17   All flesh grows old, like a g;
Is   51: 6   the earth wears out like a g and its

GARMENTS → GARMENT
Gn   3:21   wife the Lord God made leather g,
2 Sm 13:31   rent his g, and then lay
2 Sm 13:31   standing by him also rent their g.
Jdt   10: 3   laid aside the g of her widowhood,
Prv   31:24   She makes g and sells them,
Is   52: 1   O Zion; Put on your glorious g,
Is   63: 1   Edom, in crimsoned g, from Bozrah—

GATE → GATES
Dt   21:19   the elders at the g of his home city,
Jos   2: 5   it was time for the g to be shut,
Ru   4:11   All those at the g,
Est   2:19   was passing his time at the king's g,
Jb   29: 7   I went forth to the g of the city
Ps   69:13   They who sit at the g gossip

Ps	118:20	This is the LORD's own g,
Mt	7:13	"Enter through the narrow g;
Mt	7:13	for the g is wide and the road broad
Jn	10: 2	enters through the g is the shepherd
Jn	10: 7	say to you, I am the g for the sheep.
Jn	10: 9	I am the g. Whoever enters through
Acts	3: 2	at the g of the temple called "the Beautiful G"
Heb	13:12	Jesus also suffered outside the g,

GATES →GATE

Gn	24:60	possession of the g of their enemies!"
Dt	6: 9	of your houses and on your g.
Neh	1: 3	and its g have been gutted with fire."
1 Mc	4:38	the altar desecrated, the g burnt,
Ps	24: 7	Lift up your heads, O g; rise up,
Ps	87: 2	Loves the g of Zion more than any
Ps	100: 4	Enter the temple g with praise,
Ps	118:19	Open the g of victory; I will enter
Is	60:11	Your g shall stand open constantly;
Is	60:18	walls "Salvation" and your g "Praise."
Is	62:10	Pass through, pass through the g,
Lam	4:12	foe could enter the g of Jerusalem.
Ez	48:31	there shall be three g: the gate
Mt	16:18	the g of the netherworld shall not
Rv	21:12	twelve g where twelve angels were
Rv	21:21	The twelve g were twelve pearls,
Rv	21:21	each of the g made from a single
Rv	21:25	During the day its g will never be
Rv	22:14	life and enter the city through its g.

GATH

1 Sm	5: 8	The men of G replied, "Let them
1 Sm	17: 4	champion named Goliath of G came
1 Sm	21:11	Saul, going to Achish, king of G.
2 Sm	1:20	"Tell it not in G, herald it not
Mi	1:10	Publish it not in G, weep not at all;

GATHER →GATHERED, GATHERS

Ex	16: 4	to go out and g their daily portion;
Dt	30: 4	will the LORD, your God, g you;
Ru	2: 7	She asked leave to g the gleanings
Neh	1: 9	the world, I will g them from there,
Ps	106:47	g us from among the nations
Is	11:12	and g the outcasts of Israel;
Jer	23: 3	I myself will g the remnant of my
Zep	2: 1	G, g yourselves together, O nation
Zep	3:20	and at that time I will g you; For I
Zec	14: 2	And I will g all the nations against
Mt	12:30	and whoever does not g with me
Mt	13:30	but g the wheat into my barn." ' "
Mt	23:37	yearned to g your children together,
Mt	25:26	plant and g where I did not scatter?
Mk	13:27	g [his] elect from the four winds,
Lk	3:17	and to g the wheat into his barn,
Lk	11:23	and whoever does not g with me
Lk	13:34	to g your children together as a hen
Lk	17:37	is, there also the vultures will g."
Jn	11:52	to g into one the dispersed children
Rv	19:17	"Come here. G for God's great feast,
Rv	20: 8	and Magog, to g them for battle;

GATHERED →GATHER

Gn	1: 9	"Let the water under the sky be g
Ex	16:18	he who had g a large amount did not
Ex	16:18	he who had g a small amount did
Ex	16:18	They so g that everyone had enough
Nm	11:32	one who got the least g ten homers
Jer	3:17	there all nations will be g together
Mt	18:20	or three are g together in my name,
Rv	19:19	their armies g to fight against

GATHERS →GATHER

Ps	147: 2	Jerusalem, g the dispersed of Israel,
Is	56: 8	GOD, who g the dispersed of Israel:
Jer	31:10	Israel, now g them together.
Mt	23:37	as a hen g her young under her

GAVE →GIVE

Gn	2:20	The man g names to all the cattle,
Gn	3: 6	and she also g some to her husband,
Gn	14:20	Abram g him a tenth of everything.
Gn	28: 4	your descendants the blessing he g

Gn	35:12	The land I once g to Abraham
Ex	31:18	he g him the two tablets
Dt	3:12	I g Reuben and Gad the territory
Dt	9:10	till the LORD g me the two tablets
Dt	26: 9	he g us this land flowing with milk
Jos	11:23	Joshua g it to Israel as their
Jos	15:13	had commanded, Joshua g Caleb,
Jos	21:44	the LORD g them peace on every
Jos	24:13	"I g you a land which you had not
Jgs	3: 6	g their own daughters to their sons
1 Sm	27: 6	That same day Achish g him Ziklag,
2 Sm	12: 8	I g you your lord's house and your
2 Sm	12: 8	I g you the house of Israel
1 Kgs	5: 9	God g Solomon wisdom
1 Kgs	5:26	g Solomon wisdom as he promised
Neh	9:15	heaven you g them in their hunger,
Neh	9:20	and you g them water in their thirst.
Neh	9:22	You g them kingdoms and peoples,
Jb	1:21	The LORD g and the LORD has taken
Jb	42:10	the LORD even g to Job twice as
Ps	69:22	for my thirst they g me vinegar.
Eccl	12: 7	life breath returns to God who g it.
Ez	3: 2	mouth and he g me the scroll to eat.
Dn	1:17	four young men God g knowledge
Mt	25:35	I was hungry and you g me food,
Mt	25:35	I was thirsty and you g me drink,
Mt	25:42	I was hungry and you g me no food,
Mt	25:42	I was thirsty and you g me no drink,
Mk	6: 7	and g them authority over unclean
Mk	11:28	Or who g you this authority to do
Jn	1:12	who did accept him he g power
Jn	3:16	the world that he g his only Son,
Jn	17: 4	the work that you g me to do.
Jn	17: 6	name to those whom you g me
Acts	11:17	God g them the same gift he g to us
2 Cor	8: 5	they g themselves first to the Lord
Eph	4: 8	prisoners captive; he g gifts to men."
Eph	4:11	And he g some as apostles, others as
1 Tm	2: 6	who g himself as ransom for all.
Ti	2:14	who g himself for us to deliver us
1 Jn	5:11	God g us eternal life, and this life is
Rv	11:13	and g glory to the God of heaven.
Rv	13: 2	To it the dragon g its own power
Rv	20:13	The sea g up its dead; then Death and Hades g up their dead.

GAZA

Jgs	16: 1	Once Samson went to G, where he
1 Sm	6:17	one for G, one for Ashkelon,
Am	1: 6	For three crimes of G, and for four,

GAZE

Sir	9: 8	g not upon the beauty of another's
Rv	11: 9	nation will g on their corpses

GAZELLE

2 Sm	2:18	fleet of foot as a g in the open field,
Song	2: 9	My lover is like a g or a young stag.
Song	7: 4	like twin fawns, the young of a g.

GEDALIAH
Governor of Judah appointed by Nebuchadnezzar (2 Kgs 25:22-26; Jer 39-41).

GEHAZI
Servant of Elisha (2 Kgs 4:12-5:27; 8:4-5).

GEHENNA

Mt	5:22	'You fool,' will be liable to fiery G.
Mt	5:29	to have your whole body thrown into G.
Mt	5:30	to have your whole body go into G.
Mt	10:28	can destroy both soul and body in G.
Mt	18: 9	two eyes to be thrown into fiery G.
Mt	23:15	you make him a child of G twice as
Mt	23:33	can you flee from the judgment of G?
Mk	9:43	into G into the unquenchable fire.
Mk	9:45	with two feet to be thrown into G.
Mk	9:47	with two eyes to be thrown into G,
Lk	12: 5	has the power to cast into G;
Jas	3: 6	on fire, itself set on fire by G.

GEMS
Ex 25: 7 other **g** for mounting on the ephod

GENEALOGIES →GENEALOGY
1 Tm 1: 4 with myths and endless **g**,
Ti 3: 9 Avoid foolish arguments, **g**,

GENEALOGY →GENEALOGIES
Mt 1: 1 The book of the **g** of Jesus Christ,

GENERATION →GENERATIONS
Ex 1: 6 his brothers and that whole **g** died.
Ex 20: 6 mercy down to the thousandth **g**,
Ex 34: 7 third and fourth **g** for their fathers'
Nm 32:13 until the whole **g** that had done evil
Dt 1:35 'Not one man of this evil **g** shall look
Jgs 2:10 a later **g** arose that did not know
1 Mc 2:61 And so, consider this from **g** to **g**,
Ps 78: 4 we recite them to the next **g**,
Ps 102:19 Let this be written for the next **g**,
Ps 112: 2 in the land, a **g** upright and blessed.
Ps 145: 4 One **g** praises your deeds to the next
Is 34:17 forever, and dwell there from **g** to **g**.
Jl 1: 3 and their children to the next **g**.
Mt 12:39 evil and unfaithful **g** seeks a sign,
Mt 17:17 "O faithless and perverse **g**,
Mt 23:36 these things will come upon this **g**.
Mt 24:34 this **g** will not pass away until all
Mk 9:19 "O faithless **g**, how long will I be
Mk 13:30 this **g** will not pass away until all
Lk 7:31 shall I compare the people of this **g**?
Lk 11:29 he said to them, "This **g** is an evil **g**;
Lk 11:50 in order that this **g** might be charged
Lk 21:32 this **g** will not pass away until all
Acts 2:40 "Save yourselves from this corrupt **g**."
Phil 2:15 midst of a crooked and perverse **g**,
Heb 3:10 of this I was provoked with that **g**

GENERATIONS →GENERATION
Ex 12:17 this day throughout your **g** as
Ex 30:21 his descendants throughout their **g**."
Ex 31:13 you and me throughout the **g**,
Ex 40:15 priesthood throughout all future **g**."
1 Chr 16:15 he made binding for a thousand **g**—
Jb 8: 8 If you inquire of the former **g**,
Ps 33:11 forever, wise designs through all **g**.
Ps 45:18 your name renowned through all **g**;
Ps 48:14 citadels, that you may tell future **g**:
Ps 90: 1 have been our refuge through all **g**.
Ps 102:12 forever; your renown is for all **g**.
Ps 105: 8 the pact imposed for a thousand **g**,
Ps 119:90 Through all **g** your truth endures;
Ps 145:13 your dominion for all **g**. The LORD is
Ps 146:10 your God, Zion, through all **g**!
Sir 2:10 Study the **g** long past
Is 41: 4 who has called forth the **g** since
Is 51: 8 forever and my salvation, for all **g**.
Dn 3:100 his dominion endures through all **g**.
Mt 1:17 Abraham to David is fourteen **g**;
Mt 1:17 to the Babylonian exile, fourteen **g**;
Mt 1:17 exile to the Messiah, fourteen **g**.
Eph 3: 5 other **g** as it has now been revealed
Eph 3:21 church and in Christ Jesus to all **g**,
Col 1:26 hidden from ages and from **g** past.

GENEROSITY →GENEROUS
Sir 37:11 to a miser about **g**, to a cruel man
Rom 12: 8 if one contributes, in **g**; if one is
2 Cor 8: 2 in a wealth of **g** on their part.
2 Cor 9:11 enriched in every way for all **g**,
2 Cor 9:13 the **g** of your contribution to them
Gal 5:22 patience, kindness, **g**, faithfulness,

GENEROUS →GENEROSITY, GENEROUSLY
Sir 14: 5 To whom will he be **g** who is stingy
Sir 35: 7 In **g** spirit pay homage to the LORD.
Mt 20:15 Are you envious because I am **g**?'
1 Tm 6:18 good works, to be **g**, ready to share,

GENEROUSLY →GENEROUS
Sir 35: 9 to you, **g**, according to your means.
Acts 10: 2 to give alms **g** to the Jewish people

Jas 1: 5 should ask God who gives to all **g**

GENTILE →GENTILES
1 Mc 1:14 according to the G custom.
Mt 18:17 treat him as you would a G or a tax
Gal 2:14 are living like a G and not like

GENTILES →GENTILE
1 Mc 1:11 an alliance with the G all around us;
1 Mc 2:12 And the G have defiled them!
1 Mc 4:54 day on which the G had defiled it,
1 Mc 13:41 the yoke of the G was removed
Mt 4:15 beyond the Jordan, Galilee of the G,
Lk 2:32 a light for revelation to the G,
Lk 21:24 be taken as captives to all the G;
Lk 21:24 underfoot by the G until the times of the G are fulfilled.
Lk 22:25 "The kings of the G lord it over them
Acts 9:15 of mine to carry my name before G,
Acts 10:45 have been poured out on the G also,
Acts 11: 1 the G too had accepted the word
Acts 11:18 life-giving repentance to the G too."
Acts 13:46 of eternal life, we now turn to the G.
Acts 13:47 us, 'I have made you a light to the G,
Acts 14:27 opened the door of faith to the G.
Acts 15:19 to stop troubling the G who turn
Acts 18: 6 From now on I will go to the G."
Acts 22:21 I shall send you far away to the G.' "
Acts 26:20 and then to the G, I preached
Acts 28:28 of God has been sent to the G;
Rom 2:14 the G who do not have the law
Rom 3:29 Does he not belong to G, too? Yes, also to G,
Rom 9:24 from the Jews but also from the G.
Rom 11:11 salvation has come to the G, so as
Rom 11:12 number is enrichment for the G,
Rom 11:13 Now I am speaking to you G.
Rom 11:13 then as I am the apostle to the G,
Rom 15: 9 so that the G might glorify God
Rom 15: 9 I will praise you among the G
Rom 15:27 for if the G have come to share
1 Cor 1:23 block to Jews and foolishness to G,
2 Cor 11:26 dangers from G, dangers in the city,
Gal 1:16 that I might proclaim him to the G,
Gal 3: 8 God would justify the G by faith,
Eph 3: 6 that the G are coheirs,
Eph 3: 8 to the G the inscrutable riches
Eph 4:17 you must no longer live as the G do,
Col 1:27 glory of this mystery among the G;
1 Tm 2: 7 teacher of the G in faith and truth.
2 Tm 4:17 and all the G might hear it. And I

GENTLE →GENTLENESS, GENTLY
1 Thes 2: 7 Rather, we were **g** among you,
1 Tm 3: 3 aggressive, but **g**, not contentious,
Jas 3:17 pure, then peaceable, **g**, compliant,
1 Pt 3: 4 in the imperishable beauty of a **g**

GENTLENESS →GENTLE
Est D: 8 God changed the king's anger to **g**.
2 Cor 10: 1 Paul, urge you through the **g**
Gal 5:23 **g**, self-control. Against such there is
Eph 4: 2 with all humility and **g**,
1 Tm 6:11 faith, love, patience, and **g**.
1 Pt 3:16 but do it with **g** and reverence,

GENTLY →GENTLE
Jb 15:11 and speech that deals **g** with you?

GENUINENESS
2 Cor 8: 8 to test the **g** of your love by your
1 Pt 1: 7 so that the **g** of your faith,

GERAR
Gn 20: 2 king of G, sent and took Sarah.
Gn 26: 6 So Isaac settled in G.

GERASENES
Lk 8:26 they sailed to the territory of the G,

GERIZIM
Dt 27:12 on Mount G to pronounce blessings
Jos 8:33 Half of them were facing Mount G

GERSHOM
Son of Moses (Ex 2:22; 1 Chr 23:15).

GERSHON →GERSHONITES
Gn   46:11 sons of Levi: **G**, Kohath and Merari.
1 Chr 23: 6 of Levi: **G**, Kohath, and Merari.

GERSHONITES →GERSHON
Nm   3:21 these were the clans of the **G**.
Jos   21: 6 The **G** obtained thirteen cities by lot

GESHEM
Neh   6: 1 Tobiah, **G** the Arab, and our other

GESHUR
2 Sm 13:38 and stayed in **G** for three years.

GET
Gn   24: 4 my kindred to **g** a wife for my son
Dt   30:12 will go up in the sky to **g** it for us
Prv   4: 5 "**G** wisdom, **g** understanding! Do not
Mt 16:23 and said to Peter, "**G** behind me,
Mk   6: 2 said, "Where did this man **g** all this?
Mk 13:16 field must not return to **g** his cloak.

GETHSEMANE
Mt 26:36 came with them to a place called **G**,
Mk 14:32 Then they came to a place named **G**,

GEZER
Jos 16:10 drive out the Canaanites living in **G**,
1 Chr 14:16 Philistine army from Gibeon to **G**.

GHOST →GHOSTS
Mt 14:26 "It is a **g**," they said, and they cried
Lk 24:39 because a **g** does not have flesh

GHOSTS →GHOST
Dt 18:11 nor one who consults **g** and spirits

GIANT →GIANTS
1 Mc 3: 3 and put on his breastplate like a **g**.
Sir 47: 4 As a youth he slew the **g** and wiped

GIANTS →GIANT
Wis 14: 6 the proud **g** were being destroyed,
Bar 3:26 In it were born the **g**,

GIBEAH
Jgs 19:12 not Israelites, but will go on to **G**.
1 Sm 10:26 Saul also went home to **G**,
Hos 10: 9 war was not to reach them in **G**.

GIBEON →GIBEONITES
Jos 10:12 Stand still, O sun, at **G**, O moon,
2 Sm 2:13 out and met them at the pool of **G**.
1 Kgs 3: 5 In **G** the LORD appeared to Solomon

GIBEONITES →GIBEON
2 Sm 21: 1 his family because he put the **G**

GIDEON →=JERUBBAAL
Judge, also called Jerubbaal; freed Israel from Midianites (Jgs 6-8;
Heb 11:32). Given sign of fleece (Jgs 8:36-40).

GIFT →GIFTS
Nm 18: 7 I give you the priesthood as a **g**.
Prv 18:16 A man's **g** clears the way for him,
Prv 21:14 A secret **g** allays anger,
Eccl 3:13 fruit of all his labor is a **g** of God.
Eccl 5:18 fruits of his toil, has a **g** from God.
Sir 18:16 the word means more than the **g**;
Mt 5:23 if you bring your **g** to the altar,
Mt 8: 4 offer the **g** that Moses prescribed;
Jn 4:10 "If you knew the **g** of God and who
Acts 2:38 you will receive the **g** of the holy
Acts 8:20 that you could buy the **g** of God
Acts 11:17 God gave them the same **g** he gave
Rom 1:11 you some spiritual **g** so that you
Rom 5:15 the **g** is not like the transgression.
Rom 6:23 the **g** of God is eternal life in Christ
1 Cor 7: 7 each has a particular **g** from God,
2 Cor 9:15 be to God for his indescribable **g**!
Eph 2: 8 is not from you; it is the **g** of God;
Eph 4: 7 to the measure of Christ's **g**.
Phil 4:17 It is not that I am eager for the **g**;

1 Tm 4:14 Do not neglect the **g** you have,
2 Tm 1: 6 stir into flame the **g** of God that you
Heb 6: 4 tasted the heavenly **g** and shared
Jas 1:17 and every perfect **g** is from above,
1 Pt 3: 7 we are joint heirs of the **g** of life,
1 Pt 4:10 As each one has received a **g**, use it
Rv 21: 6 the thirsty I will give a **g**
Rv 22:17 the one who wants it receive the **g**

GIFTS →GIFT
Ezr 1: 6 many precious **g** besides all their
Est 9:22 to one another and **g** to the poor.
Ps 76:12 May all present bring **g** to this
Mt 2:11 treasures and offered him **g** of gold,
Lk 11:13 how to give good **g** to your children,
Rom 11:29 For the **g** and the call of God are
Rom 12: 6 Since we have **g** that differ
1 Cor 12: 1 Now in regard to spiritual **g**,
1 Cor 12: 4 are different kinds of spiritual **g**
1 Cor 12:28 deeds; then **g** of healing, assistance,
1 Cor 12:30 Do all have **g** of healing? Do all
1 Cor 12:31 eagerly for the greatest spiritual **g**.
1 Cor 14: 1 but strive eagerly for the spiritual **g**,
Eph 4: 8 prisoners captive; he gave **g** to men."
Heb 2: 4 of the **g** of the holy Spirit according
Heb 9: 9 in which **g** and sacrifices are offered

GIHON
Gn 2:13 name of the second river is the **G**;
2 Chr 32:30 the upper outflow of water from **G**

GILBOA
1 Chr 10: 8 where they had fallen on Mount **G**.

GILEAD →GILEADITE
Nm 32:29 shall give them **G** as their property
Jgs 11: 1 Jephthah, born to **G** of a harlot.
2 Sm 2: 9 where he made him king over **G**,
1 Chr 27:21 for the half-tribe of Manasseh in **G**,
Jer 8:22 Is there no balm in **G**, no physician
Jer 46:11 Go up to **G**, and take balm, O virgin
Hos 6: 8 **G** is a city of evildoers,
Mi 7:14 Let them feed in Bashan and **G**,

GILEADITE →GILEAD
Jgs 11: 1 was a chieftain, the **G** Jephthah,
2 Sm 19:32 Barzillai the **G** also came down

GILGAL
Jos 4:20 At **G** Joshua set up the twelve
Jos 5: 9 Therefore the place is called **G**
Jgs 2: 1 the LORD went up from **G** to Bochim
1 Sm 7:16 **G** and Mizpah and judging Israel

GIRD →GIRDED
1 Sm 2: 4 while the tottering **g** on strength.
Ps 45: 4 **G** your sword upon your hip,

GIRDED →GIRD
1 Kgs 18:46 who **g** up his clothing and ran
Ps 18:33 This God who **g** me with might,
Ps 93: 1 the LORD is robed, **g** with might.

GIRGASHITES
Dt 7: 1 nations before you—the Hittites, **G**,

GIRL →GIRLS
Gn 24:16 The **g** was very beautiful, a virgin,
Ex 1:16 but if it is a **g**, she may live."
2 Kgs 5: 2 the land of Israel in a raid a little **g**,
Tb 6:12 Now the **g** is sensible, courageous,
Est 2: 7 The **g** was beautifully formed
Mk 5:41 which means, "Little **g**, I say to you,
Mk 6:22 The king said to the **g**, "Ask of me

GIRLS →GIRL
Zec 8: 5 boys and **g** playing in her streets.

GIVE →GAVE, GIVEN, GIVER, GIVES, GIVING, LAWGIVER, LIFE-GIVING
Gn 9: 3 I **g** them all to you as I did the green
Gn 12: 7 your descendants I will **g** this land."
Gn 28:22 Of everything you **g** me, I will
Ex 13: 5 to your fathers he would **g** you,
Ex 17: 2 and said, "**G** us water to drink."

Ex	30:15	The rich need not **g** more, nor shall the poor **g** less,
Nm	6:26	upon you kindly and **g** you peace!
Nm	11:13	Where can I get meat to **g** to all this
Dt	15:10	When you **g** to him, **g** freely and not
Jos	1: 6	you may **g** this people possession
1 Sm	1:11	you **g** your handmaid a male child,
1 Sm	1:11	I will **g** him to the LORD for as long
1 Kgs	3: 5	of me and I will **g** it to you."
2 Chr	1:10	**G** me, therefore,
Neh	9: 6	To all of them you **g** life,
Tb	4:16	"**G** to the hungry some of your bread,
Tb	4:16	you have left over, **g** away as alms;
Tb	4:16	and do not begrudge the alms you **g**.
Tb	12: 9	Those who regularly **g** alms shall
Jb	2: 4	that a man has will he **g** for his life.
Ps	13: 4	**G** light to my eyes lest I sleep
Ps	30:13	God, forever will I **g** you thanks.
Prv	23:26	My son, **g** me your heart, and let
Prv	25:21	enemy be hungry, **g** him food to eat, if he be thirsty, **g** him to drink;
Prv	30: 8	me, **g** me neither poverty nor riches;
Prv	30:15	two daughters of the leech are, "**G, G**."
Prv	31:31	**G** her a reward of her labors, and let
Is	7:14	Lord himself will **g** you this sign:
Is	42: 8	my name; my glory I **g** to no other,
Ez	36:26	I will **g** you a new heart and place
Hos	9:14	**G** them, O LORD! **g** them what?
Hos	11: 8	How could I **g** you up, O Ephraim,
Mt	5:42	**G** to the one who asks of you,
Mt	6: 2	When you **g** alms, do not blow
Mt	6:11	**G** us today our daily bread;
Mt	7: 6	"Do not **g** what is holy to dogs,
Mt	7:11	know how to **g** good gifts to your
Mt	7:11	your heavenly Father **g** good things
Mt	10: 8	received; without cost you are to **g**.
Mt	16:19	I will **g** you the keys to the kingdom
Mk	8:37	What could one **g** in exchange
Mk	10:45	to **g** his life as a ransom for many."
Lk	6:38	**G** and gifts will be given to you;
Lk	11: 3	**G** us each day our daily bread
Lk	11:13	know how to **g** good gifts to your
Lk	11:13	Father in heaven **g** the holy Spirit
Jn	4:14	the water I shall **g** will never thirst;
Jn	6:52	"How can this man **g** us [his] flesh
Jn	10:28	I **g** them eternal life, and they shall
Jn	13:34	I **g** you a new commandment:
Jn	14:16	he will **g** you another Advocate
Jn	14:27	leave with you; my peace I **g** to you.
Jn	14:27	Not as the world gives do I **g** it
Jn	17: 2	so that he may **g** eternal life to all
Acts	3: 6	gold, but what I do have I **g** you:
Acts	20:35	said, 'It is more blessed to **g** than
Rom	8:32	also **g** us everything else along
1 Cor	13: 3	If I **g** away everything I own,
Gal	6: 9	reap our harvest, if we do not **g** up.
Heb	13:17	you and will have to **g** an account,
Rv	2: 7	To the victor I will **g** the right to eat
Rv	2:10	and I will **g** you the crown of life.
Rv	2:17	To the victor I shall **g** some
Rv	2:17	also **g** a white amulet upon which is
Rv	2:26	I will **g** authority over the nations.
Rv	2:28	to him I will **g** the morning star.
Rv	3:21	I will **g** the victor the right to sit
Rv	14: 7	"Fear God and **g** him glory, for his

GIVEN → GIVE

Ex	16:15	which the LORD has **g** you to eat.
Dt	1:21	God, has **g** this land over to you.
Dt	26:11	the LORD, your God, has **g** you.
Ps	115:16	to the LORD, but the earth is **g** to us.
Sir	35: 9	to the Most High as he has **g** to you,
Is	9: 5	a child is born to us, a son is **g** us;
Dn	2:37	the God of heaven has **g** dominion
Am	9:15	From the land I have **g** them, say I,
Mt	6:33	these things will be **g** you besides.
Mt	7: 7	"Ask and it will be **g** to you;
Mt	22:30	they neither marry nor are **g**
Mt	25:29	more will be **g** and he will grow

Mk	4:25	To the one who has, more will be **g**;
Mk	8:12	no sign will be **g** to this generation."
Lk	6:38	Give and gifts will be **g** to you;
Lk	22:19	is my body, which will be **g** for you;
Jn	1:17	while the law was **g** through Moses,
Jn	3:27	except what has been **g** him
Acts	5:32	God has **g** to those who obey him."
Rom	5: 5	the holy Spirit that has been **g** to us.
Rom	11:35	"Or who has **g** him anything that he
1 Cor	11:24	and after he had **g** thanks, broke it
2 Cor	5: 5	who has **g** us the Spirit as a first
2 Cor	12: 7	a thorn in the flesh was **g** to me,
Eph	4: 7	grace was **g** to each of us according
1 Jn	4:13	in us, that he has **g** us of his Spirit.
1 Jn	5:20	has **g** us discernment to know
Rv	6: 2	He was **g** a crown, and he rode forth

GIVER → GIVE

2 Cor	9: 7	for God loves a cheerful **g**.

GIVES → GIVE

Ex	4:11	"Who **g** one man speech and makes
Ex	4:11	Or who **g** sight to one and makes
Ps	119:130	light, **g** understanding to the simple.
Ps	136:25	And **g** food to all flesh, God's love
Prv	2: 6	For the LORD **g** wisdom, from his
Prv	14:30	A tranquil mind **g** life to the body,
Prv	21:26	day, but the just man **g** unsparingly.
Prv	28:27	He who **g** to the poor suffers no
Prv	29: 4	justice a king **g** stability to the land;
Eccl	2:26	man he sees fit he **g** wisdom
Eccl	2:26	the sinner he **g** the task of gathering
Sir	34:17	eyes, **g** health and life and blessing.
Sir	35: 2	he **g** alms he presents his sacrifice
Is	40:29	He **g** strength to the fainting;
Mt	10:42	whoever **g** only a cup of cold water
Jn	5:21	the Father raises the dead and **g** life,
Jn	6:32	my Father **g** you the true bread
Jn	6:37	that the Father **g** me will come
Jn	6:63	It is the spirit that **g** life,
Jn	14:27	Not as the world **g** do I give it
Rom	4:17	who **g** life to the dead and calls
1 Cor	15:57	to God who **g** us the victory through
2 Cor	3: 6	brings death, but the Spirit **g** life.
1 Thes	4: 8	who [also] **g** his holy Spirit to you.
Jas	4: 6	proud, but **g** grace to the humble."

GIVING → GIVE

Mt	24:38	marrying and **g** in marriage,
Phil	4:15	shared with me in an account of **g**
Jas	1:17	all good **g** and every perfect gift is

GLAD → GLADDEN, GLADNESS

1 Chr	16:31	Let the heavens be **g** and the earth
Ps	14: 7	Jacob may rejoice, and Israel be **g**
Ps	16: 9	Therefore my heart is **g**, my soul
Ps	32:11	Be **g** in the LORD and rejoice,
Ps	34: 3	that the poor may hear and be **g**.
Ps	40:17	rejoice and be **g** in you. May those
Ps	48:12	Mount Zion is **g**! The cities
Ps	53: 7	Jacob may rejoice and Israel be **g**
Ps	67: 5	May the nations be **g** and shout
Ps	69:33	"See, you lowly ones, and be **g**;
Ps	70: 5	rejoice and be **g** in you. May those
Ps	90:15	Make us **g** as many days as you
Ps	96:11	Let the heavens be **g** and the earth
Ps	97: 1	rejoice; let the many islands be **g**.
Ps	97: 8	Zion hears and is **g**, and the cities
Ps	118:24	made; let us rejoice in it and be **g**.
Ps	149: 2	Let Israel be **g** in their maker,
Prv	10: 1	A wise son makes his father **g**,
Prv	15:13	A **g** heart lights up the face,
Prv	15:20	A wise son makes his father **g**,
Prv	17: 5	he who is **g** at calamity will not go
Prv	29: 3	loves wisdom makes his father **g**,
Eccl	10:19	and wine makes the living **g**,
Is	25: 9	and be **g** that he has saved us!"
Is	66:10	Jerusalem and be **g** because of her,
Lam	4:21	Though you rejoice and are **g**,
Zec	10: 7	Their children shall see it and be **g**,
Mt	5:12	Rejoice and be **g**, for your reward

Jn	8:56	to see my day; he saw it and was **g**.
Jn	11:15	I am **g** for you that I was not there,
Acts	2:26	Therefore my heart has been **g**

GLADDEN →GLAD

Ps	86: 4	**G** the soul of your servant; to you,
Ps	104:15	and wine to **g** our hearts,

GLADNESS →GLAD

Est	9:22	these days with feasting and **g**,
Ps	51:10	Let me hear sounds of joy and **g**;
Ps	100: 2	worship the LORD with cries of **g**;
Is	16:10	joy and **g**, In the vineyards there is
Is	35:10	They will meet with joy and **g**,
Is	51: 3	Joy and **g** shall be found in her,
Is	51:11	They will meet with joy and **g**,
Is	61: 3	To give them oil of **g** in place
Jer	7:34	of joy, the cry of **g**, the voice
Jer	16: 9	place the cry of joy and the cry of **g**,
Jer	25:10	the song of joy and the song of **g**,
Jer	33:11	of joy, the cry of **g**, the voice
Jl	1:16	the house of our God, joy and **g**?
Zep	3:17	He will rejoice over you with **g**,
Zec	8:19	become occasions of joy and **g**,
Lk	1:14	And you will have joy and **g**,
Heb	1: 9	the oil of **g** above your companions";

GLASS

Rv	4: 6	resembled a sea of **g** like crystal.
Rv	15: 2	something like a sea of **g** mingled
Rv	21:18	the city was pure gold, clear as **g**.
Rv	21:21	was of pure gold, transparent as **g**.

GLAZED

Prv	26:23	Like a **g** finish on earthenware

GLEAM

Ps	132:18	but on him my crown shall **g**."
Hb	3:11	at the **g** of your flashing spear.

GLEAN →GLEANED, GLEANER, GLEANING, GLEANINGS

Ru	2: 2	**g** ears of grain in the field of anyone

GLEANED →GLEAN

Ru	2:17	She **g** in the field until evening,
Mi	7: 1	as when the vines have been **g**;

GLEANER →GLEAN

Sir	33:16	keep vigil, like a **g** after the vintage;

GLEANING →GLEAN

Is	24:13	with a **g** when the vintage is done.

GLEANINGS →GLEAN

Ob	1: 5	you, would they not leave some **g**?

GLOAT

Ps	22:18	my bones. They stare at me and **g**;
Rv	11:10	of the earth will **g** over them and be

GLOOM

Jb	3: 5	May darkness and **g** claim it,
Ps	107:10	Some lived in darkness and **g**,
Is	8:23	for there is no **g** where but now
Jl	2: 2	is near, a day of darkness and of **g**,
Am	5:20	not light, **g** without any brightness?
Zep	1:15	a day of darkness and **g**, A day

GLORIFIED →GLORY

Is	60: 9	Holy One of Israel, who has **g** you.
Mt	9: 8	**g** God who had given such authority
Mk	2:12	They were all astounded and **g** God,
Lk	5:26	seized them all and they **g** God, and,
Lk	7:16	all, and they **g** God, exclaiming,
Jn	7:39	because Jesus had not yet been **g**.
Jn	11: 4	the Son of God may be **g** through it."
Jn	12:16	Jesus had been **g** they remembered
Jn	12:23	come for the Son of Man to be **g**.
Jn	12:28	"I have **g** it and will glorify it again."
Jn	13:31	"Now is the Son of Man **g**, and God is **g** in him.
Jn	13:32	[If God is **g** in him,] God will
Jn	14:13	that the Father may be **g** in the Son.
Jn	15: 8	By this is my Father **g**, that you bear
Jn	17: 4	I **g** you on earth by accomplishing
Jn	17:10	is mine, and I have been **g** in them.

Acts	3:13	has **g** his servant Jesus whom you
Rom	8:17	so that we may also be **g** with him.
Rom	8:30	and those he justified he also **g**.
Gal	1:24	So they **g** God because of me.
2 Thes	1:10	comes to be **g** among his holy ones
2 Thes	1:12	of our Lord Jesus may be **g** in you,
2 Thes	3: 1	Lord may speed forward and be **g**,
1 Pt	4:11	God may be **g** through Jesus Christ,

GLORIFIES →GLORY

Jn	8:54	but it is my Father who **g** me,

GLORIFY →GLORY

Ps	86:12	**g** your name forever, Lord my God.
Jn	8:54	"If I **g** myself, my glory is worth
Jn	12:28	Father, **g** your name." Then a voice
Jn	12:28	have glorified it and will **g** it again."
Jn	13:32	God will also **g** him in himself, and he will **g** him at once.
Jn	16:14	He will **g** me, because he will take
Jn	17: 1	son, so that your son may **g** you,
Jn	17: 5	Now **g** me, Father, with you,
Jn	21:19	what kind of death he would **g** God.
Rom	15: 6	you may with one voice **g** the God
Rom	15: 9	the Gentiles might **g** God for his
1 Cor	6:20	Therefore **g** God in your body.
1 Pt	2:12	and **g** God on the day of visitation.
1 Pt	4:16	but **g** God because of the name.
Rv	15: 4	or **g** your name? For you alone are

GLORIFYING →GLORY

Lk	2:20	**g** and praising God for all they had
Lk	5:25	lying on, and went home, **g** God.
2 Cor	9:13	you are **g** God for your obedient

GLORIOUS →GLORY

Ex	28: 2	For the **g** adornment of your brother
Ex	28:40	for the **g** adornment of Aaron's sons
Dt	28:58	to revere the **g** and awesome name
Neh	9: 5	"Blessed is your **g** name, and exalted
Jdt	16:13	O LORD, great are you and **g**,
1 Mc	2: 9	her **g** ornaments have been carried
Ps	66: 2	sing of his **g** name; give him **g**
Ps	72:19	Blessed be his **g** name forever;
Ps	87: 3	**G** things are said of you, O city
Ps	145:12	power, the **g** splendor of your rule.
Is	11:10	seek out, for his dwelling shall be **g**.
Is	28: 1	the fading blooms of his **g** beauty,
Is	28: 4	The fading blooms of his **g** beauty
Is	42:21	justice to make his law great and **g**,
Is	63:12	Whose **g** arm was the guide
Is	63:15	from your holy and **g** palace!
Jer	48:17	the strong staff is broken, the **g** rod!
Col	1:11	in accord with his **g** might, for all
1 Tm	1:11	according to the **g** gospel
Jas	2: 1	the faith in our **g** Lord Jesus Christ.
1 Pt	1: 8	with an indescribable and **g** joy,
2 Pt	2:10	are not afraid to revile **g** beings,
Jude	1: 8	scorn lordship, and revile **g** beings.

GLORIOUSLY →GLORY

Ex	15: 1	to the LORD, for he is **g** triumphant;

GLORY →GLORIFIED, GLORIFIES, GLORIFY, GLORIFYING, GLORIOUS, GLORIOUSLY

Ex	14: 4	I will receive **g** through Pharaoh
Ex	14:17	I will receive **g** through Pharaoh
Ex	14:18	when I receive **g** through Pharaoh
Ex	16: 7	in the morning you will see the **g**
Ex	16:10	lo, the **g** of the LORD appeared
Ex	24:16	The **g** of the LORD settled
Ex	24:17	the Israelites the **g** of the LORD was
Ex	29:43	it will be made sacred by my **g**.
Ex	33:18	Moses said, "Do let me see your **g**!"
Ex	33:22	When my **g** passes I will set you
Ex	40:34	tent, and the **g** of the LORD filled
Lv	9:23	the **g** of the LORD was revealed to all
Nm	14:10	the **g** of the LORD appeared
Nm	14:21	and the LORD's **g** that fills the whole
Nm	14:22	of all the men who have seen my **g**
Nm	16:19	the **g** of the LORD appeared
Nm	17: 7	it and the **g** of the LORD appeared.

Nm	20: 6	the g of the LORD appeared to them,
Dt	5:24	has indeed let us see his g and his
Jos	7:19	g and honor by telling me what you
1 Sm	4:21	saying, "Gone is the g from Israel,"
1 Sm	15:29	The G of Israel neither retracts nor
2 Sm	1:19	"Alas! the g of Israel, Saul,
1 Kgs	8:11	since the LORD's g had filled
1 Chr	16:10	G in his holy name; rejoice,
1 Chr	16:24	Tell his g among the nations;
1 Chr	16:28	give to the LORD g and praise;
1 Chr	29:11	majesty, splendor, and g. For all
2 Chr	5:14	since the LORD's g filled the house
2 Chr	7: 1	the g of the LORD filled the house.
Tb	12:15	and serve before the G of the Lord."
Jdt	15: 9	saying: "You are the g of Jerusalem,
1 Mc	1:40	was as great as her g had been,
Jb	29:20	My g is fresh within me, and my
Ps	3: 4	my g, you keep my head high.
Ps	8: 6	crowned them with g and honor.
Ps	19: 2	The heavens declare the g of God;
Ps	24: 7	portals, that the king of g may enter.
Ps	26: 8	dwell, the tenting-place of your g.
Ps	29: 1	give to the LORD g and might;
Ps	29: 3	the God of g thunders, the LORD,
Ps	29: 9	All in his palace say, "G!"
Ps	57: 6	may your g appear above all
Ps	63: 3	sanctuary to see your power and g.
Ps	72:19	the earth be filled with the LORD's g.
Ps	96: 3	Tell God's g among the nations;
Ps	96: 8	give to the LORD the g due his name!
Ps	97: 6	God's justice; all peoples see his g.
Ps	102:16	all the kings of the earth, your g,
Ps	104:31	May the g of the LORD endure
Ps	108: 6	may your g appear above all
Ps	138: 5	"How great is the g of the LORD!"
Ps	149: 9	such is the g of all God's faithful.
Prv	19:11	it is his g to overlook an offense.
Prv	20:29	The g of young men is their
Prv	25: 2	God has g in what he conceals,
Wis	7:25	effusion of the g of the Almighty;
Is	6: 3	"All the earth is filled with his g!"
Is	35: 2	They will see the g of the LORD,
Is	40: 5	the g of the LORD shall be revealed,
Is	42: 8	is my name; my g I give to no other,
Is	42:12	Let them give g to the LORD,
Is	43: 7	whom I created for my g, whom I
Is	48:11	My g I will not give to another.
Is	60:19	forever, your God shall be your g.
Is	66:18	they shall come and see my g.
Is	66:19	heard of my fame, or seen my g;
Is	66:19	they shall proclaim my g among
Jer	2:11	But my people have changed their g
Bar	5: 4	of justice, the g of God's worship.
Ez	1:28	of the likeness of the g of the LORD.
Ez	3:23	I saw that the g of the LORD was
Ez	3:23	like the g I had seen by the river
Ez	8: 4	I saw there the g of the God of Israel,
Ez	10: 4	the g of the LORD rose from over
Ez	10: 4	was bright with the g of the LORD.
Ez	10:18	the g of the LORD left the threshold
Ez	43: 2	and there I saw the g of the God
Ez	43: 2	and the earth shone with his g.
Ez	43: 5	was filled with the g of the LORD.
Ez	44: 4	I looked I saw the g of the LORD
Dn	2:37	and strength, power and g;
Dn	7:14	He received dominion, g,
Hos	4: 7	me, exchanging their g for shame.
Hb	2:14	with the knowledge of the LORD's g
Hb	3: 3	Covered are the heavens with his g,
Zec	2: 9	and I will be the g in her midst."
Zec	12: 7	that the g of the house of David
Mal	2: 2	to give g to my name, says the LORD
Mt	16:27	with his angels in his Father's g,
Mt	24:30	of heaven with power and great g.
Mt	25:31	the Son of Man comes in his g,
Mk	8:38	his Father's g with the holy angels."
Mk	10:37	in your g we may sit one at your
Mk	13:26	the clouds' with great power and g,
Lk	2: 9	and the g of the Lord shone around
Lk	2:14	"G to God in the highest and on earth
Lk	2:32	and g for your people Israel."
Lk	9:26	ashamed of when he comes in his g
Lk	9:32	they saw his g and the two men
Lk	19:38	in heaven and g in the highest."
Lk	21:27	in a cloud with power and great g.
Lk	24:26	these things and enter into his g?"
Jn	1:14	and we saw his g, the g as
Jn	2:11	in Galilee and so revealed his g,
Jn	7:18	speaks on his own seeks his own g,
Jn	7:18	whoever seeks the g of the one who
Jn	8:50	I do not seek my own g; there is one
Jn	8:54	myself, my g is worth nothing;
Jn	11: 4	but is for the g of God, that the Son
Jn	11:40	if you believe you will see the g
Jn	12:41	Isaiah said this because he saw his g
Jn	17: 5	with the g that I had with you before
Jn	17:22	have given them the g you gave me,
Jn	17:24	they may see my g that you gave
Acts	7: 2	The God of g appeared to our father
Acts	7:55	to heaven and saw the g of God
Rom	1:23	exchanged the g of the immortal
Rom	2: 7	eternal life to those who seek g,
Rom	2:10	But there will be g, honor,
Rom	3: 7	to his g through my falsehood,
Rom	3:23	and are deprived of the g of God.
Rom	4:20	by faith and gave g to God
Rom	5: 2	we boast in hope of the g of God.
Rom	8:18	compared with the g to be revealed
Rom	9: 4	the adoption, the g, the covenants,
Rom	9:23	the riches of his g to the vessels
Rom	11:36	things. To him be g forever. Amen.
Rom	16:27	through Jesus Christ be g forever
1 Cor	2: 7	before the ages for our g,
1 Cor	2: 8	not have crucified the Lord of g.
1 Cor	10:31	do, do everything for the g of God.
1 Cor	11:15	if a woman has long hair it is her g,
2 Cor	1:20	also goes through him to God for g.
2 Cor	3: 7	because of its g that was going
2 Cor	3:10	to have no g in this respect because of the g that surpasses it.
2 Cor	3:18	unveiled face on the g of the Lord,
2 Cor	3:18	into the same image from g to g,
2 Cor	4: 4	light of the gospel of the g of Christ,
2 Cor	4: 6	light the knowledge of the g of God
2 Cor	4:15	to overflow for the g of God.
2 Cor	4:17	weight of g beyond all comparison,
Eph	1:12	might exist for the praise of his g,
Eph	1:14	possession, to the praise of his g.
Eph	3:13	afflictions for you; this is your g.
Eph	3:21	to him be g in the church
Phil	1:11	comes through Jesus Christ for the g
Phil	2:11	is Lord, to the g of God the Father.
Phil	3:19	stomach; their g is in their "shame."
Phil	4:20	God and Father, g for ever and ever.
Col	1:27	of the g of this mystery among
Col	1:27	it is Christ in you, the hope for g.
Col	3: 4	you too will appear with him in g.
1 Thes	2:12	calls you into his kingdom and g.
1 Thes	2:20	For you are our g and joy.
2 Thes	2:14	to possess the g of our Lord Jesus
1 Tm	1:17	God, honor and g forever and ever.
1 Tm	3:16	throughout the world, taken up in g.
2 Tm	2:10	Christ Jesus, together with eternal g.
2 Tm	4:18	To him be g forever and ever.
Heb	1: 3	who is the refulgence of his g,
Heb	2: 7	you crowned him with g and honor,
Heb	2: 9	we do see Jesus "crowned with g
Heb	2:10	in bringing many children to g,
Heb	3: 3	he is worthy of more "g" than Moses,
Heb	9: 5	of g overshadowing the place
Heb	13:21	to whom be g forever [and ever].
1 Pt	1: 7	may prove to be for praise, g,
1 Pt	1:24	all its g like the flower of the field;
1 Pt	4:11	to whom belong g and dominion
1 Pt	4:13	that when his g is revealed you may
1 Pt	4:14	for the Spirit of g and of God rests
1 Pt	5: 1	has a share in the g to be revealed.
1 Pt	5: 4	receive the unfading crown of g.

1 Pt	5:10	his eternal **g** through Christ [Jesus]
2 Pt	1: 3	of him who called us by his own **g**
2 Pt	1:17	**g** from God the Father
2 Pt	1:17	came to him from the majestic **g**,
2 Pt	3:18	To him be **g** now and to the day
Jude	1:25	through Jesus Christ our Lord be **g**,
Rv	1: 6	to him be **g** and power forever
Rv	4: 9	the living creatures give **g**
Rv	4:11	to receive **g** and honor and power,
Rv	5:12	strength, honor and **g** and blessing."
Rv	5:13	be blessing and honor, **g** and might,
Rv	7:12	"Amen. Blessing and **g**,
Rv	11:13	and gave **g** to the God of heaven.
Rv	14: 7	"Fear God and give him **g**, for his
Rv	15: 8	filled with the smoke from God's **g**
Rv	16: 9	they did not repent or give him **g**.
Rv	19: 1	Salvation, **g**, and might belong
Rv	19: 7	and give him **g**. For the wedding
Rv	21:23	for the **g** of God gave it light, and its

GLUTTON →GLUTTONS

Prv	23:21	drunkard and the **g** come to poverty,
Sir	31:20	sleep, and restless tossing for the **g**!
Mt	11:19	'Look, he is a **g** and a drunkard,
Lk	7:34	'Look, he is a **g** and a drunkard,

GLUTTONS →GLUTTON

Prv	28: 7	but the **g**' companion disgraces his
Ti	1:12	liars, vicious beasts, and lazy **g**."

GNASH →GNASHED, GNASHES

Ps	112:10	they will **g** their teeth and waste
Lam	2:16	They hiss and **g** their teeth.

GNASHED →GNASH

Ps	35:16	mocked me, **g** their teeth against me.

GNASHES →GNASH

Jb	16: 9	he **g** his teeth against me.

GNAT →GNATS

Mt	23:24	who strain out the **g** and swallow

GNATS →GNAT

Ex	8:12	be turned into **g** throughout the land
Ps	105:31	of flies, **g** through all their country.

GO →GOES, GOING, GONE

Gn	4: 8	Abel, "Let us **g** out in the field."
Gn	7: 1	"G into the ark, you and all your
Gn	11: 7	Let us then **g** down and there
Gn	18:21	that I must **g** down and see whether
Gn	46: 4	Not only will I **g** down to Egypt
Ex	3:19	allow you to **g** unless he is forced.
Ex	5: 1	Let my people **g**, that they may
Ex	12:31	G and worship the LORD as you said.
Ex	13:15	stubbornly refused to let us **g**,
Ex	33: 3	But I myself will not **g** up in your
Nm	13:30	"We ought to **g** up and seize the land,
Dt	1:26	"But you refused to **g** up,
Jos	1: 9	God, is with you wherever you **g**."
Ru	1:16	for wherever you **g** I will **g**,
Ps	122: 1	"Let us **g** to the house of the LORD."
Prv	6: 6	G to the ant, O sluggard, study her
Is	2: 3	from Zion shall **g** forth instruction,
Ez	1:12	wherever the spirit wished to **g**,
Mi	4: 2	from Zion shall **g** forth instruction,
Zec	14: 3	the LORD shall **g** forth and fight
Mt	5:41	one mile, **g** with him for two miles.
Mt	6: 6	you pray, **g** to your inner room,
Mt	28:19	G, therefore, and make disciples
Lk	9:57	"I will follow you wherever you **g**."
Jn	6:68	him, "Master, to whom shall we **g**?
Jn	14: 3	if I **g** and prepare a place for you,

GOADS

Eccl	12:11	The sayings of the wise are like **g**;

GOAL

Phil	3:14	I continue my pursuit toward the **g**,

GOAT →GOATS, GOATS'

Gn	37:31	and after slaughtering a **g**,
Ex	26: 7	"Also make sheets woven of **g** hair,

Lv	16: 9	The **g** that is determined by lot
Nm	7:16	one **g** for a sin offering;
Tb	2:12	gave her a young **g** for the table.
Lk	15:29	you never gave me even a young **g**

GOATS →GOAT

Nm	7:17	five **g**, and five yearling lambs
Ps	50:13	of bulls or drink the blood of **g**?
Ez	34:17	and another, between rams and **g**.
Mt	25:32	separates the sheep from the **g**.
Heb	9:12	not with the blood of **g** and calves
Heb	10: 4	blood of bulls and **g** take away sins.

GOATS' →GOAT

Nm	31:20	every article of cloth, leather, **g** hair,

GOD →GOD'S, GOD-FEARING, GODDESS, GODLESS, GODLINESS, GODLY, GODS

Gn	1: 1	when **G** created the heavens
Gn	1: 3	Then **G** said, "Let there be light,"
Gn	1: 7	G made the dome, and it separated
Gn	1: 9	Then **G** said, "Let the water under
Gn	1:11	Then **G** said, "Let the earth bring
Gn	1:21	G saw how good it was,
Gn	1:22	and **G** blessed them, saying,
Gn	1:25	G made all kinds of wild animals,
Gn	1:26	Then **G** said: "Let us make man
Gn	1:27	G created man in his image;
Gn	1:28	G blessed them, saying: "Be fertile
Gn	1:31	G looked at everything he had
Gn	2: 3	So **G** blessed the seventh day
Gn	2: 4	when the LORD **G** made the earth
Gn	2: 7	the LORD **G** formed man
Gn	2: 8	Then the LORD **G** planted a garden
Gn	2:16	The LORD **G** gave man this order:
Gn	2:22	The LORD **G** then built
Gn	3: 1	"Did **G** really tell you not to eat
Gn	3: 5	G knows well that the moment you
Gn	3: 8	sound of the LORD **G** moving
Gn	3: 9	The LORD **G** then called to the man
Gn	3:13	The LORD **G** then asked the woman,
Gn	3:14	Then the LORD **G** said to the serpent:
Gn	3:21	his wife the LORD **G** made leather
Gn	3:23	The LORD **G** therefore banished him
Gn	5: 1	When **G** created man, he made him in the likeness of **G**;
Gn	5:24	Then Enoch walked with **G**, and he was no longer here, for **G** took him.
Gn	6:12	G saw how corrupt the earth had
Gn	8: 1	then **G** remembered Noah and all
Gn	9: 1	G blessed Noah and his sons
Gn	9: 6	For in the image of **G** has man been
Gn	9:16	that I have established between **G**
Gn	14:18	and being a priest of **G** Most High,
Gn	14:19	"Blessed be Abram by **G** Most High,
Gn	16:13	saying, "You are the **G** of Vision";
Gn	17: 1	him and said: "I am the Almighty.
Gn	17: 7	pact, to be your **G** and the **G** of your
Gn	19:29	G overthrew the cities where Lot
Gn	21: 2	at the set time that **G** had stated.
Gn	21: 6	said, "G has given me cause to laugh,
Gn	21:17	G heard the boy's cry, and God's
Gn	21:20	G was with the boy as he grew up.
Gn	21:22	"G is with you in everything you do.
Gn	21:33	by name the LORD, **G** the Eternal.
Gn	22: 1	events, **G** put Abraham to the test.
Gn	22: 8	"G himself will provide the sheep
Gn	22:12	now how devoted you are to **G**,
Gn	25:11	Abraham, **G** blessed his son Isaac,
Gn	26:24	"I am the **G** of your father Abraham.
Gn	28:17	is nothing else but an abode of **G**,
Gn	30: 2	"Can I take the place of **G**, who has
Gn	31:13	I am the **G** who appeared to you
Gn	31:42	But **G** saw my plight and the fruits
Gn	31:50	G will be witness between you
Gn	32:31	"Because I have seen **G** face to face,"
Gn	33:11	G has been generous toward me,
Gn	35: 1	an altar there to the **G** who appeared
Gn	35: 5	a terror from **G** fell upon the towns
Gn	35:10	G said to him: "You whose name is

Gn	35:11	G also said to him: "I am G
Gn	41:38	so endowed with the spirit of G?"
Gn	41:51	"G has made me forget entirely
Gn	41:52	"G has made me fruitful in the land
Gn	46: 2	There G, speaking to Israel
Gn	48:15	The G who has been my shepherd
Gn	50:19	no fear. Can I take the place of G?
Gn	50:20	harm to me, G meant it for good,
Gn	50:24	G will surely take care of you
Ex	1:17	The midwives, however, feared G;
Ex	3: 4	G called out to him from the bush,
Ex	3: 6	I am the G of your father,"
Ex	3: 6	he continued, "the G of Abraham, the G of Isaac,
		the G of Jacob."
Ex	3: 6	face, for he was afraid to look at G.
Ex	3:12	you will worship G on this very
Ex	3:14	G replied, "I am who am." Then he
Ex	3:18	The Lord, the G of the Hebrews,
Ex	4:27	they met at the mountain of G,
Ex	6: 7	and you shall have me as your G.
Ex	7: 1	I have made you as G to Pharaoh,
Ex	8: 6	there is none like the Lord, our G.
Ex	8:15	to Pharaoh, "This is the finger of G."
Ex	10:16	the Lord, your G, and against you.
Ex	13:19	that, when G should come to them,
Ex	14:19	The angel of G, who had been
Ex	15: 2	my savior. He is my G, I praise him;
Ex	16:12	know that I, the Lord, am your G."
Ex	17: 9	hill with the staff of G in my hand."
Ex	18: 4	he said, "My father's G is my helper;
Ex	18: 5	encamped near the mountain of G,
Ex	19: 3	Moses went up the mountain to G.
Ex	20: 1	Then G delivered all these
Ex	20: 2	am your G, who brought you
Ex	20: 5	I, the Lord, your G, am a jealous G,
Ex	20: 7	name of the Lord, your G, in vain.
Ex	20:10	is the sabbath of the Lord, your G.
Ex	20:12	the Lord, your G, is giving you.
Ex	20:19	but let not G speak to us, or we shall
Ex	22:19	"Whoever sacrifices to any g,
Ex	22:27	"You shall not revile G, nor curse
Ex	23:19	to the house of the Lord, your G.
Ex	24:10	and they beheld the G of Israel.
Ex	29:46	their G, might dwell among them.
Ex	34: 6	a merciful and gracious G,
Ex	34:14	You shall not worship any other g,
Ex	34:14	'the Jealous One'; a jealous G is he.
Nm	15:40	and be holy to your G.
Nm	16:22	"O G, G of the spirits of all mankind,
Nm	22: 9	Then G came to Balaam and said,
Nm	22:18	to the command of the Lord, my G.
Nm	22:38	I can speak only what G puts in my
Nm	23:19	G is not man that he should speak
Nm	25:13	he was zealous on behalf of his G
Nm	27:16	the G of the spirits of all mankind,
Dt	1:21	your G, has given this land over
Dt	1:32	would not trust the Lord, your G,
Dt	3:22	the Lord, your G, will fight for you.'
Dt	3:24	For what g in heaven or on earth
Dt	4: 7	our G, is to us whenever we call
Dt	4:24	Lord, your G, is a consuming fire, a jealous G.
Dt	4:29	too you shall seek the Lord, your G;
Dt	4:31	the Lord, your G, is a merciful G,
Dt	4:39	that the Lord is G in the heavens
Dt	5: 9	I, the Lord, your G, am a jealous G,
Dt	5:11	name of the Lord, your G, in vain.
Dt	5:12	the Lord, your G, commanded you.
Dt	5:14	is the sabbath of the Lord, your G.
Dt	5:15	your G, brought you from there
Dt	5:16	the Lord, your G, is giving you.
Dt	5:24	man can still live after G has spoken
Dt	5:26	of the living G speaking
Dt	6: 2	fear the Lord, your G, and keep,
Dt	6: 4	The Lord is our G, the Lord alone!
Dt	6: 5	Lord, your G, with all your heart,
Dt	6:13	The Lord, your G, shall you fear;
Dt	6:16	not put the Lord, your G, to the test,
Dt	7: 6	a people sacred to the Lord, your G;
Dt	7: 9	that the Lord, your G, is G indeed,
Dt	7:21	Lord, your G, who is in your midst, is a great and
		awesome G.
Dt	8: 5	your G, disciplines you even as
Dt	8:11	the Lord, your G, by neglecting his
Dt	8:18	your G, who gives you the power
Dt	10:12	your G, ask of you but to fear
Dt	10:14	your G, as well as the earth
Dt	10:17	the Lord, your G, is the G of gods,
Dt	10:21	your G, who has done for you those
Dt	11: 1	"Love the Lord, your G, therefore,
Dt	11:13	your G, with all your heart and all
Dt	12:12	Lord, your G, with your sons
Dt	12:28	in the sight of the Lord, your G.
Dt	13: 4	Lord, your G, is testing you to learn
Dt	14: 1	are children of the Lord, your G.
Dt	14: 2	your G, who has chosen you
Dt	15: 6	Lord, your G, will bless you as he
Dt	15:19	your G, all the male firstlings
Dt	16:11	your G, chooses as the dwelling
Dt	16:17	Lord, your G, has bestowed on you.
Dt	16:22	such as the Lord, your G, detests.
Dt	18:13	sincere toward the Lord, your G.
Dt	18:15	Lord, your G, raise up for you
Dt	19: 9	your G, and ever walking in his
Dt	23: 6	your G, would not listen to Balaam
Dt	23:15	your G, journeys along within your
Dt	23:22	Lord, your G, you shall not delay
Dt	25:16	an abomination to the Lord, your G.
Dt	26: 5	your G, 'My father was a wandering
Dt	27: 5	your G, an altar made of stones
Dt	28: 1	your G, and are careful to observe
Dt	28:15	Lord, your G, and are not careful
Dt	29:12	as his people and he may be your G,
Dt	30: 2	your G, and heed his voice with all
Dt	30: 4	will the Lord, your G, gather you;
Dt	30: 6	your G, will circumcise your hearts
Dt	30:16	your G, will bless you in the land
Dt	30:20	the Lord, your G, heeding his voice,
Dt	31: 6	your G, who marches with you;
Dt	32: 3	proclaim the greatness of our G!
Dt	32: 4	A faithful G, without deceit,
Dt	32:18	You forgot the G who gave you
Dt	32:39	"Learn then that I, I alone, am G,
Dt	32:39	and there is no g beside me.
Jos	1: 9	your G, is with you wherever you
Jos	1:13	your G, will permit you to settle
Jos	14: 8	completely loyal to the Lord, my G.
Jos	14:14	loyal to the Lord, the G of Israel.
Jos	22: 5	love the Lord, your G; follow him
Jos	22:22	The Lord, the G of gods,
Jos	22:34	among them that the Lord is G.
Jos	23: 3	your G, himself who fought for you.
Jos	23: 8	your G, as you have been to this
Jos	23:11	however, to love the Lord, your G.
Jos	23:14	your G, made to you has remained
Jos	23:15	the Lord, your G, has given you.
Jos	24:19	to serve the Lord, for he is a holy G;
Jgs	1: 7	As I have done, so has G repaid me."
Jgs	5: 5	of the Lord, the G of Israel.
Jgs	6:20	The angel of G said to him,
Jgs	6:31	altar has been destroyed is a g,
Jgs	8:33	Baals, making Baal of Berith their g
Jgs	13: 6	husband, "A man of G came to me;
Jgs	13: 6	the appearance of an angel of G,
Jgs	16:23	a great sacrifice to their g Dagon
Jgs	16:23	"Our g has delivered into our power
Jgs	16:28	O G, this last time that for my two
Jgs	20:27	the covenant of G was there in those
Ru	1:16	be my people, and your G my G.
1 Sm	2: 2	Lord; there is no Rock like our G.
1 Sm	2: 3	For an all-knowing G is the Lord, a G who judges
		deeds.
1 Sm	3: 3	lamp of G was not yet extinguished,
1 Sm	3: 3	of the Lord where the ark of G was.
1 Sm	4:11	The ark of G was captured, and Eli's
1 Sm	5:11	"Send away the ark of G of Israel.
1 Sm	10: 9	Samuel, G gave him another heart.
1 Sm	11: 6	the spirit of G rushed upon him
1 Sm	12:12	the Lord your G is your king.

1 Sm	16:15	evil spirit from **G** is tormenting you.
1 Sm	17:36	insulted the armies of the living **G**."
1 Sm	17:45	the **G** of the armies of Israel
1 Sm	17:46	land shall learn that Israel has a **G**.
1 Sm	19:23	the spirit of **G** came upon him also,
1 Sm	28:15	me and **G** has abandoned me.
1 Sm	30: 6	renewed trust in the L<small>ORD</small> his **G**,
2 Sm	6: 7	**G** struck him on that spot, and he died there before **G**.
2 Sm	7:23	which **G** has led, redeeming it as his
2 Sm	7:27	L<small>ORD</small> of hosts, **G** of Israel, who said
2 Sm	14:14	though **G** does not bring back life,
2 Sm	14:17	lord the king is like an angel of **G**,
2 Sm	21:14	out, **G** granted relief to the land.
2 Sm	22: 3	my **G**, my rock of refuge!
2 Sm	22:32	"For who is **G** except the L<small>ORD</small>? Who is a rock save our **G**?
2 Sm	22:33	The **G** who girded me with strength
2 Sm	22:47	Extolled be my **G**, Rock of my
1 Kgs	2: 3	your **G**, following his ways
1 Kgs	5: 9	**G** gave Solomon wisdom
1 Kgs	5:19	my **G**, as the L<small>ORD</small> predicted to my
1 Kgs	8:23	"L<small>ORD</small>, **G** of Israel, there is no **G** like
1 Kgs	8:27	indeed be that **G** dwells among men
1 Kgs	8:60	of the earth may know the L<small>ORD</small> is **G**
1 Kgs	8:61	our **G**, observing his statutes
1 Kgs	10:24	him the wisdom which **G** had put
1 Kgs	11: 4	his **G**, as the heart of his father
1 Kgs	11:33	Chemosh, **g** of Moab, and Milcom, **g** of the Ammonites;
1 Kgs	15:30	provoked the L<small>ORD</small>, the **G** of Israel,
1 Kgs	18:21	If the L<small>ORD</small> is **G**, follow him; if Baal,
1 Kgs	18:24	The **G** who answers with fire is **G**."
1 Kgs	18:36	said, "L<small>ORD</small>, **G** of Abraham, Isaac,
1 Kgs	18:36	this day that you are **G** in Israel
1 Kgs	18:39	prostrate and said, "The L<small>ORD</small> is **G**!
1 Kgs	20:28	Aram has said the L<small>ORD</small> is a **g** of mountains, not a **g** of plains,
2 Kgs	1: 2	of Baalzebub, the **g** of Ekron,
2 Kgs	5:15	that there is no **G** in all the earth,
2 Kgs	17: 7	their **G**, who had brought them
2 Kgs	19: 4	sent to taunt the living **G**, and will
2 Kgs	19:15	You alone are **G** over all
2 Kgs	19:19	know that you alone, O L<small>ORD</small>, are **G**."
1 Chr	12:19	your **G** it is who helps you."
1 Chr	13: 2	and is so decreed by the L<small>ORD</small> our **G**,
1 Chr	16:35	And say, "Save us, O **G**, our savior,
1 Chr	17:20	like you and there is no **G** but you,
1 Chr	17:24	as L<small>ORD</small> of hosts, **G** of Israel, may be
1 Chr	21: 8	Then David said to **G**, "I have sinned
1 Chr	21:15	**G** also sent an angel to destroy
1 Chr	22:19	souls to seeking the L<small>ORD</small> your **G**.
1 Chr	22:19	to build the sanctuary of the L<small>ORD</small> **G**,
1 Chr	28: 2	the footstool for the feet of our **G**;
1 Chr	28: 9	know the **G** of your father and serve
1 Chr	28:20	for the L<small>ORD</small> **G**, my **G**, is with you.
1 Chr	29: 1	for man, but for the L<small>ORD</small> **G**.
1 Chr	29: 2	stored up for the house of my **G**,
1 Chr	29:10	be, O L<small>ORD</small>, **G** of Israel our father,
1 Chr	29:13	our **G**, we give you thanks and we
1 Chr	29:18	O L<small>ORD</small>, **G** of our fathers Abraham,
2 Chr	1: 7	That night **G** appeared to Solomon
2 Chr	2: 3	and festivals of the L<small>ORD</small>, our **G**:
2 Chr	2: 4	our **G** is greater than all other gods.
2 Chr	5:14	L<small>ORD</small>'s glory filled the house of **G**.
2 Chr	6:14	"L<small>ORD</small>, **G** of Israel, there is no **g** like
2 Chr	6:18	"Can it indeed be that **G** dwells
2 Chr	13:12	See, **G** is with us, at our head,
2 Chr	15: 3	For a long time Israel had no true **G**,
2 Chr	15:12	seek the L<small>ORD</small>, the **G** of their fathers,
2 Chr	18:13	"I will say what my **G** tells me."
2 Chr	19: 3	have been determined to seek **G**."
2 Chr	19: 7	L<small>ORD</small>, our **G**, there is no injustice,
2 Chr	20: 6	"L<small>ORD</small>, **G** of our fathers, are you not the **G** in heaven,
2 Chr	20:20	your **G**, and you will be found firm.
2 Chr	25: 8	It is **G** who has the power
2 Chr	26: 5	seek **G** as long as Zechariah lived, who taught him to fear **G**;
2 Chr	30: 9	your **G**, and he will not turn away
2 Chr	30:19	who has resolved to seek **G**, the L<small>ORD</small>, the **G** of his fathers,
2 Chr	31:21	for the service of the house of **G**
2 Chr	31:21	was to do the will of his **G**.
2 Chr	32:15	Since no other **g** of any other nation
2 Chr	32:17	to deride the L<small>ORD</small>, the **G** of Israel,
2 Chr	32:17	neither shall Hezekiah's **g** save his
2 Chr	32:31	the land, **G** forsook him to test him,
2 Chr	33:12	he began to appease the L<small>ORD</small>, his **G**.
2 Chr	34:33	in Israel to serve the L<small>ORD</small>, their **G**.
Ezr	1: 3	go up, and may his **G** be with him!
Ezr	2:68	offerings for the house of **G**,
Ezr	6:16	of this house of **G** with joy.
Ezr	7: 9	the favoring hand of his **G** was
Ezr	7:18	conformably to the will of your **G**.
Ezr	7:23	for the house of the **G** of heaven,
Ezr	8:22	"The favoring hand of our **G** is
Ezr	8:31	The hand of our **G** remained
Ezr	9: 6	I said: "My **G**, I am too ashamed
Ezr	9: 6	O my **G**, for our wicked deeds are
Ezr	9: 9	but in our servitude our **G** has not
Ezr	9: 9	life to raise again the house of our **G**
Ezr	10: 3	a covenant before our **G** to dismiss
Ezr	10: 3	fear the commandments of our **G**.
Neh	1: 5	"O L<small>ORD</small>, **G** of heaven,
Neh	1: 5	great and awesome **G**, you who
Neh	4:14	us there; our **G** will fight with us."
Neh	5:15	because I feared **G**, did not act thus.
Neh	8: 8	from the book of the law of **G**,
Neh	8:18	book of the law of **G** day after day,
Neh	9: 5	"Arise, bless the L<small>ORD</small>, your **G**,
Neh	9:17	But you are a **G** of pardons,
Neh	9:31	for you are a kind and merciful **G**.
Neh	9:32	therefore, O our **G**, great, mighty,
Neh	10:30	to follow the law of **G** which was
Neh	10:40	will not neglect the house of our **G**.
Neh	13: 2	though our **G** turned the curse
Neh	13:11	"Why is the house of **G** abandoned?"
Neh	13:26	though he was beloved of his **G** and **G** had made him king over all
Neh	13:31	this in my favor, O my **G**!
Tb	3:11	are you, O Lord, merciful **G**!
Tb	4:19	At all times bless the Lord **G**,
Jdt	3: 8	people and tribe invoke him as a **g**.
Jdt	6: 2	because their **G** protects them?
Jdt	6: 2	What **g** is there beside
Jdt	6: 2	Their **G** will not save them;
Jdt	8:20	since we acknowledge no other **g**
Jb	1: 1	Job, who feared **G** and avoided evil.
Jb	1:22	he say anything disrespectful of **G**.
Jb	2:10	We accept good things from **G**;
Jb	4:17	a man be righteous as against **G**?
Jb	5:17	is the man whom **G** reproves!
Jb	8: 3	Does **G** pervert judgment, and does
Jb	8:20	**G** will not cast away the upright;
Jb	9: 2	can a man be justified before **G**?
Jb	11: 7	Can you penetrate the designs of **G**?
Jb	19:26	And from my flesh I shall see **G**;
Jb	20:29	the heritage appointed him by **G**.
Jb	21:19	May **G** not store up the man's misery
Jb	21:22	Can anyone teach **G** knowledge, seeing that
Jb	22:12	Does not **G**, in the heights
Jb	22:13	Yet you say, "What does **G** know?
Jb	31: 6	Let **G** weigh me in the scales
Jb	31:14	then should I do when **G** rose up;
Jb	32:13	**G** may vanquish him but not man!"
Jb	33: 6	taken from the same clay by **G**.
Jb	33:14	For **G** does speak, perhaps once,
Jb	33:26	He shall pray and **G** will favor him;
Jb	34:10	far be it from **G** to do wickedness;
Jb	34:23	time to come before **G** in judgment.
Jb	36: 5	**G** rejects the obstinate in heart;
Jb	36:26	**G** is great beyond our knowledge;
Jb	40: 2	who would correct **G** give answer!
Ps	5: 3	my king, my **G**! To you I pray,
Ps	5: 5	You are not a **g** who delights in evil;
Ps	7:11	A shield before me is **G** who saves
Ps	7:12	**G** is a just judge, who rebukes

Ps	14: 5	G is with the company of the just.
Ps	18: 3	deliverer, My G, my rock of refuge,
Ps	18:22	LORD; I was not disloyal to my G.
Ps	18:29	my G brightens the darkness
Ps	18:32	Truly, who is G except the LORD? Who but our G is the rock?
Ps	18:33	This G who girded me with might,
Ps	18:47	my rock! Exalted be G, my savior!
Ps	19: 2	The heavens declare the glory of G;
Ps	22: 2	My G, my G, why have you
Ps	22:11	womb; since birth you are my G.
Ps	27: 9	do not forsake me, G my savior!
Ps	29: 3	the waters; the G of glory thunders,
Ps	31: 6	will redeem me, LORD, faithful G.
Ps	31:15	in you, LORD; I say, "You are my G."
Ps	33:12	the nation whose G is the LORD,
Ps	35:23	in my cause, my G and my Lord.
Ps	40: 4	a hymn to our G. Many shall look
Ps	40: 9	my G, your law is in my heart!"
Ps	42: 2	so my soul longs for you, O G.
Ps	42: 3	My being thirsts for G, the living G.
Ps	42: 3	can I go and see the face of G?
Ps	42: 9	the night, praise to the G of my life.
Ps	42:12	Wait for G, whom I shall praise
Ps	43: 4	That I may come to the altar of G, to G, my joy, my delight.
Ps	44: 9	G we have boasted all the day long;
Ps	45: 7	Your throne, O g, stands forever;
Ps	45: 8	therefore G, your G, has anointed
Ps	46: 2	G is our refuge and our strength;
Ps	46: 6	G is in its midst; it shall not be
Ps	46: 6	G will help it at break of day.
Ps	46:11	"Be still and confess that I am G!
Ps	47: 2	hands; shout to G with joyful cries.
Ps	47: 7	Sing praise to G, sing praise;
Ps	47: 8	G is king over all the earth;
Ps	48:10	O G, within your temple we ponder
Ps	48:15	"Yes, so mighty is G, our G who
Ps	49: 8	redeem oneself, pay to G a ransom.
Ps	50: 2	From Zion G shines forth,
Ps	50: 3	Our G comes and will not be silent!
Ps	51: 3	Have mercy on me, G, in your
Ps	51:12	A clean heart create for me, G;
Ps	51:19	My sacrifice, G, is a broken spirit;
Ps	51:19	G, do not spurn a broken,
Ps	53: 2	"There is no G." Their deeds are
Ps	53: 3	G looks down from heaven
Ps	53: 3	one is wise, if even one seeks G.
Ps	54: 6	G is present as my helper; the Lord
Ps	55:20	G, who sits enthroned forever,
Ps	55:20	their ways; they have no fear of G.
Ps	56: 5	G, I praise your promise; in you I
Ps	56:14	That I may walk before G
Ps	57: 4	May G send help from heaven
Ps	57: 4	May G send fidelity and love.
Ps	57: 8	My heart is steadfast, G, my heart is
Ps	59:18	G, are my fortress, my loving G.
Ps	62: 2	My soul rests in G alone,
Ps	62: 8	My safety and glory are with G,
Ps	62: 9	Trust G at all times, my people!
Ps	62:12	One thing G has said; two things I
Ps	62:12	I have heard: Power belongs to G;
Ps	63: 2	O G, you are my G— for you I long!
Ps	65: 6	deeds of justice, O G our savior,
Ps	66: 1	Shout joyfully to G, all you
Ps	66: 3	Say to G: "How awesome your
Ps	66: 5	Come and see the works of G,
Ps	66:16	Come and hear, all you who fear G,
Ps	66:20	Blessed be G, who did not refuse
Ps	68: 5	Sing to G, praise the divine name;
Ps	68: 5	Rejoice before this G whose name
Ps	68:21	Our G is a G who saves;
Ps	68:27	In your choirs, bless G;
Ps	68:36	Awesome is G in his holy place, the G of Israel,
Ps	69: 6	G, you know my folly; my faults are
Ps	70: 2	Graciously rescue me, G!
Ps	70: 5	help always say, "G be glorified!"
Ps	70: 6	afflicted and poor. G, come quickly!
Ps	71:17	G, you have taught me from my
Ps	71:18	do not forsake me, G, That I may
Ps	71:19	things; O G, who is your equal?
Ps	71:22	for your faithfulness, my G,
Ps	73:17	Till I entered the sanctuary of G
Ps	73:26	fail, G is the rock of my heart,
Ps	76:12	and keep vows to the LORD your G.
Ps	76:12	bring gifts to this awesome G,
Ps	77:14	Your way, O G, is holy; what g is as great as our G?
Ps	77:15	alone are the G who did wonders;
Ps	78:19	They spoke against G, and said,
Ps	78:19	"Can G spread a table in the desert?
Ps	78:59	G heard and grew angry; he rejected
Ps	79: 9	Help us, G our savior, for the glory
Ps	81: 2	Sing joyfully to G our strength;
Ps	82: 1	G rises in the divine council,
Ps	84: 3	and flesh cry out for the living G.
Ps	84:11	the threshold of the house of my G
Ps	84:12	For a sun and shield is the LORD G,
Ps	86:12	your name forever, Lord my G.
Ps	86:15	Lord, are a merciful and gracious G,
Ps	87: 3	are said of you, O city of G!
Ps	89: 8	A G dreaded in the council
Ps	90: 2	from eternity to eternity you are G.
Ps	91: 2	and fortress, my G in whom I trust."
Ps	94: 1	LORD, avenging G, avenging G,
Ps	94:22	my G, the rock where I find refuge,
Ps	95: 3	For the LORD is the great G,
Ps	95: 7	For this is our G, whose people we
Ps	99: 8	you were a forgiving G, though you
Ps	99: 9	mountain; holy is the LORD, our G.
Ps	100: 3	Know that the LORD is G, our maker
Ps	106:21	They forgot the G who saved them,
Ps	108: 2	My heart is steadfast, G; my heart is
Ps	108: 6	on high over the heavens, G;
Ps	113: 5	the LORD, our G enthroned on high,
Ps	115: 3	Our G is in heaven; whatever G
Ps	116: 5	and just; yes, our G is merciful.
Ps	123: 2	So our eyes are on the LORD our G,
Ps	136: 2	Praise the G of gods; God's love
Ps	136:26	Praise the G of heaven, God's love
Ps	139:17	to me are your designs, O G;
Ps	139:23	Probe me, G, know my heart;
Ps	143:10	for you are my G. May your kind
Ps	145: 1	I will extol you, my G and king;
Ps	147: 1	good to celebrate our G in song;
Ps	150: 1	Praise G in his holy sanctuary;
Prv	2: 5	the knowledge of G you will find;
Prv	3: 4	and good esteem before G and man.
Prv	25: 2	G has glory in what he conceals,
Prv	30: 5	Every word of G is tested; he is
Eccl	1:13	A thankless task G has appointed
Eccl	2:26	be given to whatever man G sees fit.
Eccl	3:11	to end, the work which G has done.
Eccl	3:14	that whatever G does will endure
Eccl	5: 1	G is in heaven and you are on earth;
Eccl	5: 3	When you make a vow to G,
Eccl	5: 3	For G has no pleasure in fools;
Eccl	5:18	Any man to whom G gives riches
Eccl	5:18	fruits of his toil, has a gift from G.
Eccl	7:18	he who fears G will win through
Eccl	8:12	shall be well with those who fear G,
Eccl	11: 5	So you know not the work of G
Eccl	12: 7	life breath returns to G who gave it.
Eccl	12:13	all is heard: Fear G and keep his
Sir	4:28	the LORD your G will battle for you.
Sir	32:14	He who would find G must accept
Wis	2:18	if the just one be the son of G,
Is	5:16	G the Holy shall be shown holy
Is	7:11	for a sign from the LORD, your G;
Is	12: 2	G indeed is my savior; I am
Is	17:10	For you have forgotten G,
Is	25: 9	"Behold our G, to whom we looked
Is	29:23	and be in awe of the G of Israel.
Is	30:18	For the LORD is a G of justice:
Is	35: 4	Here is your G, he comes
Is	37:16	"O LORD of hosts, G of Israel,
Is	37:16	You alone are G over all
Is	40: 1	comfort to my people, says your G.
Is	40: 3	the wasteland a highway for our G!

Jn	5:44	praise that comes from the only **G**?
Jn	6:29	"This is the work of **G**, that you
Jn	6:33	For the bread of **G** is
Jn	6:69	that you are the Holy One of **G**."
Jn	7:17	whether my teaching is from **G**
Jn	8:42	"If **G** were your Father, you would
Jn	8:42	me, for I came from **G** and am here;
Jn	8:47	belongs to **G** hears the words of **G**;
Jn	8:47	because you do not belong to **G**."
Jn	11:40	believe you will see the glory of **G**?"
Jn	13: 3	that he had come from **G** and was returning to **G**,
Jn	13:31	glorified, and **G** is glorified in him.
Jn	14: 1	You have faith in **G**; have faith
Jn	17: 3	the only true **G**, and the one whom
Jn	20:17	your Father, to my **G** and your **G**.' "
Jn	20:28	said to him, "My Lord and my **G**!"
Jn	20:31	the Son of **G**, and that through this
Acts	1: 3	speaking about the kingdom of **G**.
Acts	2:22	to you by **G** with mighty deeds,
Acts	2:22	which **G** worked through him
Acts	2:24	But **G** raised him up, releasing him
Acts	2:33	Exalted at the right hand of **G**,
Acts	2:36	that **G** has made him both Lord
Acts	3:15	but **G** raised him from the dead;
Acts	4:31	speak the word of **G** with boldness.
Acts	5: 4	lied not to human beings, but to **G**."
Acts	5:29	"We must obey **G** rather than men."
Acts	5:31	**G** exalted him at his right hand as
Acts	5:32	as is the holy Spirit that **G** has given
Acts	5:39	But if it comes from **G**, you will not
Acts	5:39	find yourselves fighting against **G**."
Acts	6: 7	The word of **G** continued to spread,
Acts	7:55	and saw the glory of **G** and Jesus
Acts	8:21	your heart is not upright before **G**.
Acts	10:46	in tongues and glorifying **G**.
Acts	11: 9	answered, 'What **G** has made clean,
Acts	12:24	the word of **G** continued to spread
Acts	13:32	that what **G** promised our ancestors
Acts	14:22	to enter the kingdom of **G**."
Acts	15:10	are you now putting **G** to the test
Acts	17:23	altar inscribed, 'To an Unknown **G**.'
Acts	17:30	**G** has overlooked the times
Acts	20:27	to you the entire plan of **G**.
Acts	20:32	now I commend you to **G**
Acts	24:16	keep my conscience clear before **G**
Acts	28: 6	and began to say that he was a **g**.
Rom	1: 4	established as Son of **G** in power
Rom	1:16	It is the power of **G** for the salvation
Rom	1:17	it is revealed the righteousness of **G**
Rom	1:18	wrath of **G** is indeed being revealed
Rom	1:24	**G** handed them over to impurity
Rom	1:26	**G** handed them over to degrading
Rom	2:11	There is no partiality with **G**.
Rom	2:16	**G** will judge people's hidden works
Rom	3: 4	**G** must be true, though every
Rom	3:19	world stand accountable to **G**,
Rom	3:23	and are deprived of the glory of **G**.
Rom	3:29	Does **G** belong to Jews alone?
Rom	4: 3	"Abraham believed **G**, and it was
Rom	4: 6	whom **G** credits righteousness apart
Rom	4:17	He is our father in the sight of **G**,
Rom	5: 1	**G** through our Lord Jesus Christ,
Rom	5: 8	But **G** proves his love for us
Rom	6:22	sin and have become slaves of **G**,
Rom	6:23	the gift of **G** is eternal life in Christ
Rom	7: 4	order that we might bear fruit for **G**.
Rom	8: 7	of the flesh is hostility toward **G**;
Rom	8: 7	it does not submit to the law of **G**,
Rom	8: 8	are in the flesh cannot please **G**.
Rom	8:17	heirs, heirs of **G** and joint heirs
Rom	8:28	for good for those who love **G**,
Rom	8:31	If **G** is for us, who can be against
Rom	10: 9	in your heart that **G** raised him
Rom	11: 2	**G** has not rejected his people whom
Rom	11: 2	he pleads with **G** against Israel?
Rom	11:22	the kindness and severity of **G**:
Rom	11:32	For **G** delivered all to disobedience,
Rom	13: 1	there is no authority except from **G**,
Rom	13: 1	exist have been established by **G**.

Rom	14:12	give an account of himself [to **G**].
Rom	16:20	the **G** of peace will quickly crush
1 Cor	1:18	are being saved it is the power of **G**.
1 Cor	1:20	Has not **G** made the wisdom
1 Cor	1:24	Christ the power of **G** and the wisdom of **G**.
1 Cor	1:27	**G** chose the foolish of the world
1 Cor	1:27	**G** chose the weak of the world
1 Cor	2: 9	what **G** has prepared for those who
1 Cor	2:11	what pertains to **G** except the Spirit of **G**.
1 Cor	3: 6	watered, but **G** caused the growth.
1 Cor	3:16	Do you not know that you are the temple of **G**, and that the Spirit of **G** dwells in you?
1 Cor	3:17	temple, **G** will destroy that person;
1 Cor	3:17	for the temple of **G**, which you are,
1 Cor	6:20	Therefore glorify **G** in your body.
1 Cor	7: 7	each has a particular gift from **G**,
1 Cor	7:15	cases; **G** has called you to peace.
1 Cor	8: 3	But if one loves **G**, one is known
1 Cor	8: 8	food will not bring us closer to **G**.
1 Cor	10:13	**G** is faithful and will not let you be
1 Cor	10:31	do, do everything for the glory of **G**.
1 Cor	12:24	**G** has so constructed the body as
1 Cor	14:25	so he will fall down and worship **G**,
1 Cor	14:25	declaring, "**G** is really in your midst."
1 Cor	14:33	since he is not the **G** of disorder
1 Cor	15:24	he hands over the kingdom to his **G**
1 Cor	15:28	to him, so that **G** may be all in all.
1 Cor	15:34	For some have no knowledge of **G**;
2 Cor	1: 9	but in **G** who raises the dead.
2 Cor	2:14	But thanks be to **G**, who always
2 Cor	3: 5	our qualification comes from **G**,
2 Cor	4: 2	or falsifying the word of **G**,
2 Cor	4: 4	in whose case the **g** of this age has
2 Cor	4: 4	of Christ, who is the image of **G**.
2 Cor	4: 7	the surpassing power may be of **G**
2 Cor	5: 5	prepared us for this very thing is **G**,
2 Cor	5:19	**G** was reconciling the world
2 Cor	5:20	as if **G** were appealing through us.
2 Cor	5:20	behalf of Christ, be reconciled to **G**.
2 Cor	5:21	become the righteousness of **G**
2 Cor	6:16	we are the temple of the living **G**;
2 Cor	6:16	and I will be their **G** and they shall
2 Cor	9: 7	for **G** loves a cheerful giver.
2 Cor	10:13	to the limits **G** has apportioned us,
Gal	2: 6	**G** shows no partiality)—those
Gal	6: 7	**G** is not mocked, for a person will
Eph	2: 8	is not from you; it is the gift of **G**;
Eph	2:10	the good works that **G** has prepared
Eph	2:22	a dwelling place of **G** in the Spirit.
Eph	4: 6	one **G** and Father of all, who is over
Eph	5: 1	So be imitators of **G**, as beloved
Eph	6: 6	doing the will of **G** from the heart,
Phil	2: 6	though he was in the form of **G**,
Phil	2: 6	regard equality with **G** something
Phil	2: 9	of this, **G** greatly exalted him
Phil	2:13	For **G** is the one who, for his good
Phil	3:19	Their **G** is their stomach; their glory
Phil	4: 7	the peace of **G** that surpasses all
Phil	4:19	My **G** will fully supply whatever
Col	3: 1	is seated at the right hand of **G**.
1 Thes	2: 4	as we were judged worthy by **G**
1 Thes	2: 4	but rather **G**, who judges our hearts.
1 Thes	4: 7	For **G** did not call us to impurity
1 Thes	4: 9	yourselves have been taught by **G**
1 Thes	5: 9	For **G** did not destine us for wrath,
2 Thes	1: 8	on those who do not acknowledge **G**
1 Tm	1:17	the only **G**, honor and glory forever
1 Tm	2: 5	For there is one **G**. There is also one mediator between **G**
1 Tm	4: 4	everything created by **G** is good,
2 Tm	1: 6	flame the gift of **G** that you have
Ti	1: 2	in the hope of eternal life that **G**,
Ti	2:13	of the glory of the great **G**
Heb	1: 1	**G** spoke in partial and various ways
Heb	3: 4	but the founder of all is **G**.
Heb	4: 4	**G** rested on the seventh day from all
Heb	4:12	Indeed, the word of **G** is living
Heb	6:10	For **G** is not unjust so as to overlook
Heb	6:18	which it was impossible for **G** to lie,

Heb	7:19	through which we draw near to G.
Heb	7:25	those who approach G through him,
Heb	10: 7	I come to do your will, O G.'"
Heb	10:31	to fall into the hands of the living G.
Heb	11: 5	no more because G had taken him."
Heb	11: 5	he was attested to have pleased G.
Heb	11: 6	who approaches G must believe
Heb	11:16	G is not ashamed to be called their G,
Heb	12: 7	as "discipline"; G treats you as sons.
Heb	12:29	For our G is a consuming fire.
Heb	13:15	let us continually offer G a sacrifice
Jas	1:13	say, "I am being tempted by G"; for G
Jas	1:27	undefiled before G and the Father is
Jas	2:19	You believe that G is one. You do
Jas	2:23	"Abraham believed G, and it was
Jas	2:23	and he was called "the friend of G."
Jas	4: 4	of the world means enmity with G?
Jas	4: 4	makes himself an enemy of G.
Jas	4: 6	it says: "G resists the proud,
Jas	4: 8	Draw near to G, and he will draw
1 Pt	1:21	him believe in G who raised him
1 Pt	1:21	so that your faith and hope are in G.
1 Pt	1:23	the living and abiding word of G,
1 Pt	3:18	that he might lead you to G.
1 Pt	4: 2	human desires, but on the will of G.
1 Pt	4:11	let it be with the words of G;
1 Pt	4:11	be with the strength that G supplies,
1 Pt	4:11	that in all things G may be glorified
1 Pt	4:17	to begin with the household of G;
1 Pt	4:17	who fail to obey the gospel of G?
1 Pt	5: 5	another, for: "G opposes the proud
2 Pt	1:21	spoke under the influence of G.
2 Pt	2: 4	if G did not spare the angels
1 Jn	1: 5	G is light, and in him there is no
1 Jn	2:14	and the word of G remains in you,
1 Jn	2:17	does the will of G remains forever.
1 Jn	3: 1	we may be called the children of G.
1 Jn	3: 9	who is begotten by G commits sin,
1 Jn	3: 9	sin because he is begotten by G.
1 Jn	3:10	the children of G and the children
1 Jn	3:10	to act in righteousness belongs to G,
1 Jn	3:20	for G is greater than our hearts
1 Jn	4: 2	how you can know the Spirit of G:
1 Jn	4: 2	come in the flesh belongs to G,
1 Jn	4: 7	one another, because love is of G;
1 Jn	4: 7	who loves is begotten by G and knows G.
1 Jn	4: 8	is without love does not know G, for G is love.
1 Jn	4: 9	this way the love of G was revealed
1 Jn	4: 9	sent his only Son into the world
1 Jn	4:11	if G so loved us, we also must love
1 Jn	4:12	No one has ever seen G.
1 Jn	4:12	love one another, G remains in us,
1 Jn	4:15	that Jesus is the Son of G, G remains in him and he in G.
1 Jn	4:16	to believe in the love G has for us.
1 Jn	4:16	G is love, and whoever remains in love remains in G and G
1 Jn	4:20	says, "I love G," but hates his brother,
1 Jn	5: 2	we love the children of G when we love G
1 Jn	5: 3	For the love of G is this, that we
1 Jn	5: 4	begotten by G conquers the world.
1 Jn	5:10	believing the testimony G has given
1 Jn	5:11	G gave us eternal life, and this life
1 Jn	5:18	that no one begotten by G sins;
1 Jn	5:18	the one begotten by G he protects,
2 Jn	1: 9	of the Christ does not have G;
3 Jn	1:11	Whoever does what is good is of G;
3 Jn	1:11	does what is evil has never seen G."
Jude	1: 4	grace of our G into licentiousness
Jude	1:21	Keep yourselves in the love of G
Rv	2:18	" 'The Son of G, whose eyes are like
Rv	3: 1	one who has the seven spirits of G
Rv	4: 5	which are the seven spirits of G.
Rv	4: 8	holy, holy is the Lord G almighty,
Rv	6: 9	witness they bore to the word of G.
Rv	7: 2	holding the seal of the living G.
Rv	7:10	"Salvation comes from our G, who is
Rv	7:12	might be to our G forever and ever.
Rv	7:17	G will wipe away every tear

Rv	11:16	on their thrones before G prostrated
Rv	12: 5	Her child was caught up to G
Rv	13: 6	to utter blasphemies against G,
Rv	14: 7	voice, "Fear G and give him glory,
Rv	15: 3	are your works, Lord G almighty.
Rv	15: 7	gold bowls filled with the fury of G,
Rv	16:14	on the great day of G the almighty.
Rv	17:17	For G has put it into their minds
Rv	17:17	the words of G are accomplished.
Rv	18:20	G has judged your case against her."
Rv	19: 1	glory, and might belong to our G,
Rv	19: 6	his reign, [our] G, the almighty.
Rv	19: 9	words are true; they come from G."
Rv	19:13	his name was called the Word of G.
Rv	21: 3	G himself will always be with them
Rv	21:11	It gleamed with the splendor of G.
Rv	21:23	for the glory of G gave it light,
Rv	22: 5	for the Lord G shall give them light,

*GOD →*LORD [This is the proper name of God, *Yahweh*, and is GOD in the NAB.]

Gn	15: 2	"O Lord G, what good will your gifts
Jgs	6:22	Lord, G, that I have seen the angel
Jgs	16:28	and said, "O Lord G, remember me!
2 Sm	7:18	I, Lord G, and who are the members
Ps	71:16	O G, I will tell of your singular
Ps	73:28	to make the Lord G my refuge.
Is	25: 8	forever. The Lord G will wipe away
Is	40:10	the Lord G, who rules by his strong
Is	50: 9	See, the Lord G is my help;
Is	61: 1	The spirit of the Lord G is upon me,
Is	61:11	So will the Lord G make justice
Jer	32:17	Lord G, you have made heaven
Hb	3:19	G, my Lord, is my strength;
Zep	1: 7	in the presence of the Lord G!

GOD'S →GOD

Dt	21:23	since G curse rests on him who
2 Chr	20:15	for the battle is not yours but G.
1 Cor	2: 7	Rather we speak G wisdom,
1 Cor	3: 9	For we are G co-workers; you are G field, G building.
1 Cor	9:21	law—though I am not outside G law
2 Tm	2:19	G solid foundation stands,
Ti	1: 7	For a bishop as G steward must be
Heb	4:10	And whoever enters into G rest,
1 Pt	2:10	but now you are G people; you "had
1 Jn	3: 2	Beloved, we are G children now;
Rv	3:14	the source of G creation, says this:
Rv	11:19	G temple in heaven was opened,
Rv	14:10	will also drink the wine of G fury,

GOD-FEARING →FEAR, GOD

Jdt	8:31	But now, G woman that you are,
Jb	1: 9	said, "Is it for nothing that Job is G?
Acts	10:22	an upright and G man,

GODDESS →GOD

1 Kgs	11: 5	Astarte, the g of the Sidonians,
1 Kgs	11:33	Astarte, g of the Sidonians,
2 Mc	1:13	of the g Nanea through a deceitful
Acts	19:27	of the great g Artemis will be of no
Acts	19:37	nor have they insulted our g.

GODLESS →GOD

Jb	8:13	shall the hope of the g man perish.
Sir	27:11	the g man, like the moon, is inconstant.
1 Tm	1: 9	lawless and unruly, the g and sinful,
2 Pt	3: 7	and of destruction of the g.

GODLINESS →GOD

2 Mc	12:45	those who had gone to rest in g,

GODLY →GOD

Sir	6:35	Be eager to hear every g discourse;
Sir	44:10	Yet these also were g men
Mal	2:15	that one require but g offspring?
2 Cor	7: 9	for you were saddened in a g way,
2 Cor	7:10	For g sorrow produces a salutary
2 Cor	7:11	what earnestness this g sorrow has

GODS →GOD

Gn	35: 4	to Jacob all the foreign g in their

Ex	12:12	judgment on all the g of Egypt—I,
Ex	15:11	Who is like to you among the g,
Ex	20: 3	shall not have other g besides me.
Dt	5: 7	shall not have other g besides me.
Dt	7:25	images of their g you shall destroy
Dt	13: 3	urging you to follow other g,
Jos	24:14	the g your fathers served beyond
Jgs	2:17	to the worship of other g. They were
1 Sm	4: 7	said, "G have come to their camp."
1 Sm	17:43	the Philistine cursed David by his g
1 Kgs	20:23	to him: "Their g are g of mountains.
2 Kgs	17: 7	and because they venerated other g.
1 Chr	16:26	all the g of the nations are things
2 Chr	2: 4	our God is greater than all other g.
Jdt	3: 8	to destroy all the g of the earth,
Est	C:18	because we worshiped their g.
1 Mc	5:68	and burned the statues of their g;
Ps	82: 6	I declare: "G though you be,
Ps	89: 7	Who is like the LORD among the g?
Ps	97: 7	things; all g bow down before you.
Ps	135: 5	great, our Lord is greater than all g.
Ps	136: 2	Praise the God of g; God's love
Wis	12:24	error, taking for g the worthless
Is	8:19	not a people inquire of their g,
Jer	2:11	Does any other nation change its g?— yet they are not g at all!
Jer	10:11	Let the g that did not make heaven
Jer	16:20	Can man make for himself g? These are not g.
Dn	5: 4	they praised their g of gold
Zep	2:11	when he makes all the g of earth
Jn	10:34	in your law, 'I said, "You are g" '?
Acts	19:26	saying that g made by hands are not g at all.
1 Cor	8: 5	even though there are so-called g
1 Cor	8: 5	to be sure, many "g" and many "lords"),

GOES →GO

Nm	5:12	If a man's wife g astray and becomes
Prv	16:18	Pride g before disaster,
Prv	18:12	but humility g before honors.
Is	42:13	The LORD g forth like a hero,
Mt	26:24	The Son of Man indeed g, as it is
Rv	14: 4	follow the Lamb wherever he g.

GOG

Ez	38: 2	turn toward G [the land of Magog],
Ez	38:18	the day when G invades the land
Rv	20: 8	corners of the earth, G and Magog,

GOING →GO

Jn	8:21	"I am g away and you will look
Jn	8:21	Where I am g you cannot come."
Jn	13:36	to him, "Master, where are you g?"
Jn	13:36	"Where I am g, you cannot follow
Jn	16:10	because I am g to the Father

GOLAN

Dt	4:43	G in Bashan for the Manassehites.

GOLD →GOLDEN, GOLDSMITH, GOLDSMITHS

Ex	3:22	house guest for silver and g articles
Ex	12:35	Egyptians for articles of silver and g
Ex	20:23	silver nor gods of g shall you make
Ex	25:17	then make a propitiatory of pure g,
Ex	25:31	lampstand of pure beaten g —its shaft
Ex	28: 6	ephod they shall make of g thread
Ex	32:31	making a god of g for themselves!
Dt	17:17	a vast amount of silver and g.
Jos	7:21	a bar of g fifty shekels in weight;
1 Kgs	6:21	interior of the temple with pure g.
1 Kgs	20: 3	'Your silver and g are mine,
2 Chr	9:13	The g that Solomon received each
Ezr	1: 6	in every way, with silver, g, goods,
Tb	12: 8	to give alms than to store up g;
1 Mc	1:23	and took away the g and silver
Jb	22:25	Almighty himself shall be your g
Jb	23:10	me, I should come forth as g.
Jb	28:15	Solid g cannot purchase it, nor can
Jb	31:24	Had I put my trust in g or called fine g my security;
Ps	19:11	More desirable than g, than a hoard of purest g,
Ps	115: 4	Their idols are silver and g,
Ps	119:127	commands more than the finest g.

Prv	3:14	and better than g is her revenue;
Prv	8:19	My fruit is better than g, yes, than pure g,
Prv	22: 1	and high esteem, than g and silver.
Wis	3: 6	As g in the furnace, he proved them,
Sir	2: 5	For in fire g is tested, and worthy
Sir	30:15	More precious than g is health
Sir	31: 5	The lover of g will not be free
Is	60:17	In place of bronze I will bring g,
Dn	2:32	The head of the statue was pure g,
Hg	2: 8	Mine is the silver and mine the g,
Zec	4: 2	"I see a lampstand all of g,
Zec	6:11	Silver and g you shall take,
Mt	2:11	treasures and offered him gifts of g,
Acts	3: 6	"I have neither silver nor g, but what
1 Pt	1: 7	faith, more precious than g that is
Rv	3:18	to buy from me g refined by fire so
Rv	9: 7	wore what looked like crowns of g;
Rv	21:18	while the city was pure g, clear as
Rv	21:21	the street of the city was of pure g,

GOLDEN →GOLD

1 Mc	1:21	sanctuary and took away the g altar,
Eccl	12: 6	and the g bowl is broken,
Dn	3: 5	worship the g statue which King

GOLDSMITH →GOLD

Is	46: 6	they hire a g to make it into a god

GOLDSMITHS →GOLD

Bar	6:45	produced by woodworkers and g,

GOLGOTHA

Mt	27:33	to a place called G (which means
Mk	15:22	the place of G (which is translated
Jn	19:17	Place of the Skull, in Hebrew, G.

GOLIATH

Philistine giant killed by David (1 Sm 17; 21:9; Sir 47:4).

GOMER

Hos	1: 3	So he went and took G, the daughter

GOMORRAH

Gn	13:10	LORD had destroyed Sodom and G.)
Gn	18:20	against Sodom and G is so great,
Gn	19:24	G [from the LORD out of heaven].
Dt	29:22	grass, destroyed like Sodom and G,
Is	1: 9	as Sodom, we should be like G.
Jer	23:14	all like Sodom, its citizens like G.
Mt	10:15	G on the day of judgment than
Rom	9:29	Sodom and have been made like G."
Jude	1: 7	Sodom, G, and the surrounding

GONE →GO

Is	53: 6	We had all g astray like sheep,
Mk	5:30	once that power had g out from him,
1 Pt	3:22	who has g into heaven and is
1 Jn	4: 1	because many false prophets have g
2 Jn	1: 7	Many deceivers have g

GONG

1 Cor	13: 1	I am a resounding g or a clashing

GOOD →BEST, BETTER, GOODNESS, GOODS

Gn	1: 4	God saw how g the light was.
Gn	1:10	"the sea." God saw how g it was.
Gn	1:12	its seed in it. God saw how g it was.
Gn	1:18	the darkness. God saw how g it was.
Gn	1:21	God saw how g it was,
Gn	1:25	of the earth. God saw how g it was.
Gn	1:31	he had made, and he found it very g.
Gn	2: 9	delightful to look at and g for food,
Gn	2: 9	the tree of the knowledge of g
Gn	2:17	except the tree of knowledge of g
Gn	2:18	"It is not g for the man to be alone.
Gn	3: 6	saw that the tree was g for food,
Gn	3:22	knowing what is g and what is bad!
Gn	50:20	God meant it for g, to achieve his
Ex	3: 8	lead them out of that land into a g
Dt	6:18	right and g in the sight of the LORD,
Jos	23:15	to exterminate you from this g land
1 Sm	25:21	nothing. He has repaid g with evil.
2 Sm	14:17	angel of God, evaluating g and bad.
2 Chr	7: 3	"for he is g, for his mercy endures

2 Chr	31:20	He did what was g,
Neh	2:18	And they undertook the g work
Neh	9:20	"Your g spirit you bestowed
Tb	8: 6	'It is not g for the man to be alone;
1 Mc	4:24	"for he is g, for his mercy endures
Jb	2:10	We accept g things from God;
Ps	34: 9	Learn to savor how g the LORD is;
Ps	34:15	Turn from evil and do g; seek peace
Ps	37: 3	Trust in the LORD and do g that you
Ps	37:27	Turn from evil and do g, that you
Ps	52:11	the faithful that your name is g.
Ps	73: 1	How g God is to the upright,
Ps	84:12	The LORD withholds no g thing
Ps	103: 5	Fills your days with g things;
Ps	109: 5	They repay me evil for g,
Ps	119:68	You are g and do what is g;
Ps	133: 1	How g it is, how pleasant,
Ps	145: 9	The LORD is g to all,
Ps	147: 1	How g to celebrate our God in song;
Prv	3: 4	will you win favor and g esteem
Prv	3:27	Refuse no one the g on which he
Prv	11:27	who seeks the g commands favor,
Prv	13:22	The g man leaves an inheritance
Prv	14:22	those intent on g gain kindness
Prv	15: 3	keeping watch on the evil and the g.
Prv	15:23	a word in season, how g it is!
Prv	15:30	heart; g news invigorates the bones.
Prv	19: 2	knowledge even zeal is not g;
Prv	22: 1	A g name is more desirable than
Prv	31:12	She brings him g, and not evil,
Eccl	12:14	hidden qualities, whether g or bad.
Sir	2: 9	fear the LORD, hope for g things,
Sir	12: 1	If you do g, know for whom you are
Sir	26: 3	A g wife is a generous gift
Sir	39:27	For the g all these are g,
Sir	41:13	days, but a g name, for days without
Is	5:20	Woe to those who call evil g, and g
Is	40: 9	Jerusalem, herald of g news!
Is	52: 7	Announcing peace, bearing news,
Jer	6:16	Which is the way to g, and walk it;
Jer	13:23	As easily would you be able to do g,
Jer	32:39	to their own g and that of their
Lam	3:26	It is g to hope in silence
Ez	34:14	In g pastures will I pasture them,
Ez	34:14	shall lie down on g grazing ground,
Dn	3:99	It has seemed g to me to publish
Hos	8: 3	Israel have thrown away what is g;
Am	5:14	Seek g and not evil, that you may
Mi	6: 8	have been told, O man, what is g,
Na	2: 1	the bearer of g news,
Mt	5:13	It is no longer g for anything
Mt	5:45	his sun rise on the bad and the g,
Mt	7:11	know how to give g gifts to your
Mt	7:11	your heavenly Father give g things
Mt	7:17	Just so, every g tree bears g fruit,
Mt	12:35	A g person brings forth g
Mt	13:24	to a man who sowed g seed in his
Mt	13:48	down to put what is g into buckets.
Mt	25:21	done, my g and faithful servant.
Mk	3: 4	to do g on the sabbath rather than
Mk	10:18	him, "Why do you call me g? No one is g but God alone.
Lk	2:10	I proclaim to you g news of great
Lk	3: 9	does not produce g fruit will be cut
Lk	6:27	do g to those who hate you,
Lk	6:35	love your enemies and do g to them,
Lk	6:43	"A g tree does not bear rotten fruit,
Lk	6:43	nor does a rotten tree bear g fruit.
Lk	7:22	poor have the g news proclaimed
Lk	8: 8	And some seed fell on g soil,
Lk	14:34	"Salt is g, but if salt itself loses its
Lk	18:19	him, "Why do you call me g? No one is g but God alone.
Lk	19:17	He replied, 'Well done, g servant!
Jn	1:46	to him, "Can anything g come
Jn	2:10	him, "Everyone serves g wine first,
Jn	2:10	you have kept the g wine until now."
Jn	10:11	I am the g shepherd. A g shepherd
Jn	10:14	I am the g shepherd, and I know

Acts	8:12	Philip as he preached the g news
Rom	7:12	is holy and righteous and g.
Rom	7:16	not want, I concur that the law is g.
Rom	7:18	I know that g does not dwell in me,
Rom	7:18	ready at hand, but doing the g is not.
Rom	8:28	all things work for g for those who
Rom	10:15	of those who bring [the] g news!"
Rom	12: 2	what is g and pleasing and perfect.
Rom	12: 9	what is evil, hold on to what is g;
Rom	12:21	by evil but conquer evil with g.
Rom	13: 4	for it is a servant of God for your g.
Rom	16:19	want you to be wise as to what is g,
1 Cor	15:33	"Bad company corrupts g morals."
2 Cor	9: 8	an abundance for every g work.
Gal	6:10	the opportunity, let us do g to all,
Eph	2:10	in Christ Jesus for the g works
Eph	6: 8	the Lord for whatever g he does,
Phil	1: 6	the one who began a g work in you
Phil	2:13	for his g purpose, works in you both
Col	1:10	in every g work bearing fruit
1 Thes	5:21	Test everything; retain what is g.
2 Thes	2:17	strengthen them in every g deed
1 Tm	1: 5	from a pure heart, a g conscience,
1 Tm	1: 8	We know that the law is g,
1 Tm	1:18	them may you fight a g fight
1 Tm	4: 4	For everything created by God is g,
1 Tm	6:18	Tell them to do g, to be rich in g
2 Tm	2: 3	me like a g soldier of Christ Jesus.
2 Tm	3:17	equipped for every g work.
Ti	2: 3	to drink, teaching what is g,
Ti	2: 7	yourself as a model of g deeds
Ti	2:14	as his own, eager to do what is g.
Heb	5:14	are trained by practice to discern g
Heb	10: 1	has only a shadow of the g things
Heb	10:24	one another to love and g works.
Heb	13:16	Do not neglect to do g and to share
1 Pt	2: 3	you have tasted that the Lord is g.
1 Pt	3:17	For it is better to suffer for doing g,
3 Jn	1: 2	in every respect and are in g health,
3 Jn	1:11	do not imitate evil but imitate g.
3 Jn	1:11	Whoever does what is g is of God;

GOODNESS →GOOD

Ps	23: 6	Only g and love will pursue me
Ps	27:13	I believe I shall enjoy the LORD's g
Ti	1: 8	hospitable, a lover of g, temperate,

GOODS →GOOD

Sir	34:18	who offers in sacrifice ill-gotten g!

GOPHERWOOD

Gn	6:14	"Make yourself an ark of g,

GORGED

Rv	19:21	all the birds g themselves on their

GORGIAS

1 Mc	4: 1	Now G took five thousand infantry
1 Mc	5:59	But G and his men came

GOSHEN

Gn	45:10	You will settle in the region of G,
Ex	8:18	make an exception of the land of G:

GOSPEL

Mk	8:35	sake and that of the g will save it.
Rom	1: 1	and set apart for the g of God,
Rom	1:16	For I am not ashamed of the g. It is
Rom	15:16	the priestly service of the g of God,
1 Cor	1:17	me to baptize but to preach the g,
1 Cor	9:12	place an obstacle to the g of Christ.
1 Cor	9:14	those who preach the g should live by the g.
1 Cor	9:16	If I preach the g, this is no reason
2 Cor	4: 3	And even though our g is veiled,
2 Cor	4: 4	not see the light of the g of the glory
2 Cor	9:13	confession of the g of Christ
2 Cor	11: 4	or a different g from the one you
Gal	1: 6	grace [of Christ] for a different g
Eph	1:13	of truth, the g of your salvation,
Eph	3: 6	in Christ Jesus through the g.
Eph	6:15	shod in readiness for the g of peace.
Phil	1: 7	defense and confirmation of the g.

Phil	1:27	in a way worthy of the **g** of Christ,
Col	1:23	the hope of the **g** that you heard,
1 Thes	2: 4	by God to be entrusted with the **g**,
2 Thes	1: 8	those who do not obey the **g** of our
2 Tm	1: 8	hardship for the **g** with the strength
Phlm	1:13	in my imprisonment for the **g**,
1 Pt	4: 6	this is why the **g** was preached even

GOSSIP →GOSSIPS
| Sir | 19: 6 | Never repeat **g**, and you will not be |
| 2 Cor | 12:20 | selfishness, slander, **g**, conceit, |

GOSSIPS →GOSSIP
Sir	28:13	Cursed be **g**
Rom	1:29	treachery, and spite. They are **g**
1 Tm	5:13	not only idlers but **g** and busybodies

GOURDS
| 1 Kgs | 6:18 | temple was carved in the form of **g** |
| 2 Kgs | 4:39 | he picked a clothful of wild **g**. |

GOVERN →GOVERNOR, GOVERNORS
| 1 Kgs | 3: 9 | who is able to **g** this vast people |

GOVERNOR →GOVERN
Gn	42: 6	It was Joseph, as **g** of the country,
Neh	5:14	King Artaxerxes appointed me **g**
Neh	12:26	in the time of Nehemiah the **g**
Hg	2:21	this to Zerubbabel, the **g** of Judah;
Mal	1: 8	Present it to your **g**; see if he will
Mt	27: 2	handed him over to Pilate, the **g**.
Lk	3: 1	when Pontius Pilate was **g** of Judea,

GOVERNORS →GOVERN
| Mk | 13: 9 | You will be arraigned before **g** |

GRACE →GRACIOUS
Wis	3: 9	Because **g** and mercy are with his
Jn	1:14	Father's only Son, full of **g** and truth.
Jn	1:16	have all received, **g** in place of **g**,
Jn	1:17	**g** and truth came through Jesus
Acts	6: 8	Stephen, filled with **g** and power,
Acts	11:23	he arrived and saw the **g** of God,
Acts	13:43	to remain faithful to the **g** of God.
Acts	14: 3	word about his **g** by granting signs
Acts	14:26	been commended to the **g** of God
Acts	15:11	we are saved through the **g**
Acts	15:40	by the brothers to the **g** of the Lord.
Acts	18:27	who had come to believe through **g**.
Acts	20:24	witness to the gospel of God's **g**.
Rom	1: 5	him we have received the **g**
Rom	1: 7	**G** to you and peace from God our
Rom	3:24	by his **g** through the redemption
Rom	5: 2	faith] to this **g** in which we stand,
Rom	5:15	how much more did the **g** of God
Rom	5:17	who receive the abundance of **g**
Rom	5:20	**g** overflowed all the more,
Rom	5:21	in death, **g** also might reign through
Rom	6: 1	we persist in sin that **g** may abound?
Rom	6:14	are not under the law but under **g**.
Rom	6:15	are not under the law but under **g**?
Rom	11: 5	there is a remnant, chosen by **g**.
Rom	11: 6	But if by **g**, it is no longer because
Rom	11: 6	otherwise **g** would no longer be **g**.
Rom	12: 3	by the **g** given to me I tell everyone
Rom	12: 6	differ according to the **g** given to us,
Rom	15:15	because of the **g** given me by God
Rom	16:20	The **g** of our Lord Jesus be
1 Cor	1: 3	**G** to you and peace from God our
1 Cor	1: 4	account for the **g** of God bestowed
1 Cor	3:10	According to the **g** of God given
1 Cor	15:10	But by the **g** of God I am what I am,
1 Cor	15:10	his **g** to me has not been ineffective.
1 Cor	16:23	The **g** of the Lord Jesus be
2 Cor	1: 2	**g** to you and peace from God our
2 Cor	1:12	human wisdom but by the **g** of God.
2 Cor	4:15	so that the **g** bestowed in abundance
2 Cor	6: 1	to you not to receive the **g** of God
2 Cor	8: 1	of the **g** of God that has been given
2 Cor	9:14	because of the surpassing **g** of God
2 Cor	12: 9	to me, "My **g** is sufficient for you,
2 Cor	13:13	The **g** of the Lord Jesus Christ

Gal	1: 3	**g** to you and peace from God our
Gal	1: 6	called you by [the] **g** [of Christ]
Gal	1:15	apart and called me through his **g**,
Gal	2: 9	they recognized the **g** bestowed
Gal	2:21	I do not nullify the **g** of God;
Gal	5: 4	by law; you have fallen from **g**.
Gal	6:18	The **g** of our Lord Jesus Christ be
Eph	1: 2	**g** to you and peace from God our
Eph	1: 6	the glory of his **g** that he granted us
Eph	1: 7	in accord with the riches of his **g** ·
Eph	2: 5	Christ (by **g** you have been saved),
Eph	2: 7	riches of his **g** in his kindness to us
Eph	2: 8	by **g** you have been saved through
Eph	3: 2	of God's **g** that was given to me
Eph	3: 7	gift of God's **g** that was granted me
Eph	3: 8	all the holy ones, this **g** was given,
Eph	4: 7	**g** was given to each of us according
Eph	4:29	it may impart **g** to those who hear.
Eph	6:24	**G** be with all who love our Lord
Phil	1: 2	**g** to you and peace from God our
Phil	1: 7	who are all partners with me in **g**,
Phil	4:23	The **g** of the Lord Jesus Christ be
Col	1: 2	**g** to you and peace from God our
Col	1: 6	came to know the **g** of God in truth;
Col	4:18	my chains. **G** be with you.
1 Thes	1: 1	Jesus Christ: **g** to you and peace.
1 Thes	5:28	The **g** of our Lord Jesus Christ be
2 Thes	1: 2	**g** to you and peace from God [our]
2 Thes	1:12	in accord with the **g** of our God
2 Thes	2:16	and good hope through his **g**,
2 Thes	3:18	The **g** of our Lord Jesus Christ be
1 Tm	1: 2	**g**, mercy, and peace from God
1 Tm	1:14	Indeed, the **g** of our Lord has been
1 Tm	6:21	from the faith. **G** be with all of you.
2 Tm	1: 2	**g**, mercy, and peace from God
2 Tm	1: 9	the **g** bestowed on us in Christ Jesus
2 Tm	2: 1	be strong in the **g** that is in Christ
2 Tm	4:22	your spirit. **G** be with all of you.
Ti	1: 4	**g** and peace from God the Father
Ti	2:11	For the **g** of God has appeared,
Ti	3: 7	that we might be justified by his **g**
Ti	3:15	us in the faith. **G** be with all of you.
Phlm	1: 3	**G** to you and peace from God our
Phlm	1:25	The **g** of the Lord Jesus Christ be
Heb	2: 9	by the **g** of God he might taste death
Heb	4:16	confidently approach the throne of **g**
Heb	4:16	mercy and to find **g** for timely help.
Heb	10:29	and insults the spirit of **g**?
Heb	12:15	no one be deprived of the **g** of God,
Heb	13: 9	to have our hearts strengthened by **g**
Heb	13:25	**G** be with all of you.
Jas	4: 6	But he bestows a greater **g**;
Jas	4: 6	proud, but gives **g** to the humble."
1 Pt	1: 2	Christ: may **g** and peace be yours
1 Pt	1:10	who prophesied about the **g** that was
1 Pt	1:13	completely on the **g** to be brought
1 Pt	4:10	as good stewards of God's varied **g**.
1 Pt	5:10	The God of all **g** who called you
1 Pt	5:12	that this is the true **g** of God.
2 Pt	1: 2	may **g** and peace be yours
2 Pt	3:18	grow in **g** and in the knowledge
2 Jn	1: 3	**G**, mercy, and peace will be with us
Jude	1: 4	who pervert the **g** of our God
Rv	1: 4	**g** to you and peace from him who is
Rv	22:21	The **g** of the Lord Jesus be with all.

GRACEFUL
| Prv | 5:19 | your lovely hind, your **g** doe. |
| Sir | 24:16 | my branches so bright and so **g**. |

GRACIOUS →GRACE
Gn	43:29	said to him, "May God be **g** to you,
Ex	34: 6	a merciful and **g** God, slow to anger
Nm	6:25	shine upon you, and be **g** to you!
Neh	9:17	of pardons, **g** and compassionate,
2 Mc	10:26	they begged him to be **g** to them,
2 Mc	14: 9	the same **g** consideration that you
Ps	26:11	blame; redeem me, be **g** to me!
Ps	31:10	Be **g** to me, LORD, for I am
Ps	67: 2	May God be **g** to us and bless us;

Ps	86:15	Lord, are a merciful and **g** God,
Ps	103: 8	Merciful and **g** is the LORD,
Ps	111: 4	deeds; **g** and merciful is the LORD.
Ps	112: 4	they are **g**, merciful, and just.
Ps	116: 5	**G** is the LORD and just; yes, our God
Ps	119:132	Turn to me and be **g**, your edict
Ps	135: 3	is good! Sing to God's name; it is **g!**
Ps	145: 8	The LORD is **g** and merciful,
Prv	11:16	A **g** woman wins esteem, but she
Sir	6: 5	and **g** lips prompt friendly greetings.
Is	30:19	He will be **g** to you when you cry
Jl	2:13	your God. For **g** and merciful is he,
Jon	4: 2	I knew that you are a **g** and merciful
Mt	11:26	Father, such has been your **g** will.
Lk	4:22	and were amazed at the **g** words
Lk	10:21	Father, such has been your **g** will.
Col	4: 6	Let your speech always be **g**,

GRAFT → GRAFTED

Rom	11:23	for God is able to **g** them in again.

GRAFTED → GRAFT

Rom	11:17	were **g** in their place and have come

GRAIN → GRAINS

Gn	41: 5	He saw seven ears of **g**,
Gn	41:57	to Joseph to obtain rations of **g**,
Dt	25: 4	an ox when it is treading out **g**.
Ru	2: 2	go and glean ears of **g** in the field
Jl	2:19	I will send you **g**, and wine, and oil,
Mk	2:23	he was passing through a field of **g**
Mk	2:23	a path while picking the heads of **g**.
Lk	6: 1	going through a field of **g** on a sabbath,
1 Cor	9: 9	an ox while it is treading out the **g**."

GRAINS → GRAIN

Is	48:19	those born of your stock like its **g**,

GRANDCHILDREN → CHILD

Prv	17: 6	**G** are the crown of old men,
1 Tm	5: 4	But if a widow has children or **g**,

GRANDMOTHER → MOTHER

2 Tm	1: 5	faith that first lived in your **g** Lois

GRANT → GRANTED

Ps	85: 8	LORD, your love; **g** us your salvation.
Ps	140: 9	do not **g** the desires of the wicked;
Sir	45:26	May he **g** you wisdom of heart

GRANTED → GRANT

1 Sm	1:27	child, and the LORD **g** my request.
Est	7: 2	ask, Queen Esther, shall be **g** you.
Prv	10:24	but the desire of the just will be **g**.
Jn	6:65	me unless it is **g** him by my Father."
Phil	1:29	For to you has been **g**, for the sake

GRAPE → GRAPES, GRAPEVINE

Nm	6: 3	or any kind of **g** juice, nor eat either

GRAPES → GRAPE

Gn	40:11	so I took the **g**, pressed them
Nm	13:23	with a single cluster of **g** on it,
Dt	32:32	Poisonous are their **g** and bitter their
Is	5: 2	Then he looked for the crop of **g**, but what it yielded was wild **g**.
Jer	31:29	"The fathers ate unripe **g**,
Ez	18: 2	"Fathers have eaten green **g**,
Mi	6:15	no oil, and the **g**, yet drink no wine.
Mt	7:16	Do people pick **g** from thornbushes,
Rv	14:18	the earth's vines, for its **g** are ripe."

GRAPEVINE → GRAPE, VINE

Jas	3:12	brothers, produce olives, or a **g** figs?

GRASPED

Jgs	16:29	Samson **g** two middle columns

GRASS

Ps	37: 2	Like **g** they wither quickly;
Ps	103:15	Our days are like the **g**; like flowers
Ps	104:14	You raise **g** for the cattle and plants
Prv	19:12	but his favor, like dew on the **g**.
Is	40: 6	"All mankind is **g**, and all their glory
Mt	6:30	If God so clothes the **g** of the field,

1 Pt	1:24	"All flesh is like **g**, and all its glory
1 Pt	1:24	flower of the field; the **g** withers,
Rv	8: 7	a third of the trees and all green **g**.

GRASSHOPPERS

Nm	13:33	we felt like mere **g**, and so we must
Is	40:22	and its inhabitants are like **g**;

GRATIFY

Gal	5:16	you will certainly not **g** the desire

GRATITUDE

Col	3:16	spiritual songs with **g** in your hearts

GRAVE → GRAVES

Nm	19:16	who touches a human bone or a **g**,
Ps	49:15	Straight to the **g** they descend,
Ps	88:12	Is your love proclaimed in the **g**,
Is	53: 9	A **g** was assigned him among

GRAVEL

Prv	20:17	his mouth will be filled with **g**.
Lam	3:16	He has broken my teeth with **g**,

GRAVES → GRAVE

Ps	5:10	Their throats are open **g**; on their
Ez	37:12	I will open your **g** and have you rise
Lk	11:44	You are like unseen **g** over
Rom	3:13	Their throats are open **g**;

GRAY → GRAYING

Ps	71:18	Now that I am old and **g**, do not
Prv	16:31	**G** hair is a crown of glory; it is
Prv	20:29	and the dignity of old men is **g** hair.

GRAYING → GRAY

Sir	6:18	will you find wisdom with **g** hair.

GREAT → GREATER, GREATEST, GREATNESS

Gn	1:16	God made the two **g** lights,
Gn	6: 5	the LORD saw how **g** was man's
Gn	12: 2	"I will make of you a **g** nation, and I
Gn	12: 2	I will make your name **g**,
Gn	15: 1	I will make your reward very **g**."
Gn	15:18	to the **G** River [the Euphrates],
Gn	21:18	for I will make of him a **g** nation."
Gn	46: 3	for there I will make you a **g** nation.
Ex	32:10	Then I will make of you a **g** nation."
Ex	32:11	the land of Egypt with such **g** power
Dt	4:32	Did anything so **g** ever happen
Dt	7:21	midst, is a **g** and awesome God.
Dt	10:17	the LORD of lords, the **g** God,
Jos	7: 9	What will you do for your **g** name?"
Jgs	16: 5	find out the secret of his **g** strength,
2 Sm	7: 9	make you famous like the **g** ones
2 Sm	7:22	And so— "**G** are you, Lord GOD!
2 Sm	22:36	and your help has made me **g**.
1 Chr	16:25	For **g** is the LORD and highly to be
1 Chr	17:19	purpose, you have done this **g** thing.
Neh	1: 5	of heaven, **g** and awesome God,
Neh	8: 6	Ezra blessed the LORD, the **g** God,
Tb	11:14	God, and praised be his **g** name,
Jdt	2: 5	"Thus says the **g** king, the lord of all
Jdt	16:13	O LORD, **g** are you and glorious,
Jdt	16:16	one who fears the LORD is forever **g**.
1 Mc	4:25	Thus Israel had a **g** deliverance
Ps	18:36	you stooped to make me **g**.
Ps	25:11	pardon my guilt, though it is **g**.
Ps	47: 3	awe, the **g** king over all the earth,
Ps	48: 3	of Zaphon, the city of the **g** king.
Ps	77:14	holy; what god is as **g** as our God?
Ps	95: 3	For the LORD is the **g** God, the **g**
Ps	145: 3	**G** is the LORD and worthy of high
Prv	22: 1	is more desirable than **g** riches,
Sir	17:24	How **g** the mercy of the LORD,
Sir	25:10	He who finds wisdom is **g** indeed,
Jer	10: 6	one is like you, O LORD, **g** are you,
Jer	27: 5	the earth, by my **g** power, with my
Jer	32:19	**g** in counsel, mighty in deed,
Lam	3:23	morning, so **g** is his faithfulness.
Ez	17: 3	The **g** eagle, with **g** wings,
Dn	2:45	The **g** God has revealed to the king
Dn	9: 4	Lord, **g** and awesome God, you who

Dn	14:23	There was a **g** dragon
Jl	2:11	For **g** is the day of the LORD,
Na	1: 3	is slow to anger, yet **g** in power,
Zep	1:14	Near is the **g** day of the LORD,
Mal	1:11	my name is **g** among the nations;
Mal	3:23	LORD comes, the **g** and terrible day,
Mt	4:16	have seen a **g** light, on those
Mt	13:46	When he finds a pearl of **g** price,
Mt	20:26	to be **g** among you shall be your
Mk	13:26	coming in the clouds' with **g** power
Lk	2:10	you good news of **g** joy that will be
Lk	6:23	your reward will be **g** in heaven.
Lk	6:35	your reward will be **g** and you will
Lk	21:27	in a cloud with power and **g** glory.
Eph	1:19	with the exercise of his **g** might,
Eph	2: 4	because of the **g** love he had for us,
1 Tm	3:16	Undeniably **g** is the mystery
1 Tm	6: 6	with contentment is a **g** gain.
Ti	2:13	of the glory of the **g** God and of our
Heb	2: 3	if we ignore so **g** a salvation?
Heb	10:21	since we have "a **g** priest over
Heb	12: 1	we are surrounded by so **g** a cloud
Heb	13:20	the dead the **g** shepherd of the sheep
1 Pt	1: 3	in his **g** mercy gave us a new birth
Jude	1: 6	for the judgment of the **g** day.
Rv	6:17	because the **g** day of their wrath has
Rv	7:14	have survived the time of **g** distress;
Rv	14: 8	"Fallen, fallen is Babylon the **g**,
Rv	16:14	the battle on the **g** day of God
Rv	17: 1	the **g** harlot who lives near the many
Rv	18:10	"Alas, alas, **g** city, Babylon,

GREATER →GREAT

Gn	1:16	lights, the **g** one to govern the day,
2 Chr	2: 4	for our God is **g** than all other gods.
Mt	11:11	there has been none **g** than John
Mt	12: 6	something **g** than the temple is here.
Mk	12:31	other commandment **g** than these."
Lk	11:31	there is something **g** than Solomon
Lk	11:32	and there is something **g** than Jonah
Jn	1:50	You will see **g** things than this."
Jn	14:12	I do, and will do **g** ones than these,
Jn	15:13	No one has **g** love than this, to lay
Jn	15:20	you, 'No slave is **g** than his master.'
Heb	11:26	of the Anointed **g** wealth than
1 Jn	3:20	for God is **g** than our hearts
1 Jn	4: 4	is in you is **g** than the one who is
1 Jn	5: 9	the testimony of God is surely **g**.

GREATEST →GREAT

Mt	18: 4	himself like this child is the **g**
Mt	22:38	This is the **g** and the first
Mt	23:11	The **g** among you must be your
Lk	9:48	all of you is the one who is the **g**."
Lk	22:24	of them should be regarded as the **g**.
1 Cor	13:13	three; but the **g** of these is love.

GREATNESS →GREAT

Dt	3:24	to show to your servant your **g**
Dt	32: 3	Oh, proclaim the **g** of our God!
Ez	38:23	I will prove my **g** and holiness
Eph	1:19	and what is the surpassing **g** of his

GREECE →GREEK, GREEKS

1 Mc	1: 1	in his place, having first ruled in G.
Dn	10:20	I leave, the prince of G will come;

GREED →GREEDY

Lk	12:15	"Take care to guard against all **g**,
Eph	5: 3	or **g** must not even be mentioned
Col	3: 5	evil desire, and the **g** that is idolatry.
2 Pt	2: 3	In their **g** they will exploit you
2 Pt	2:14	and their hearts are trained in **g**.

GREEDY →GREED

Prv	15:27	He who is **g** of gain brings ruin
Prv	28:25	The **g** man stirs up disputes, but he
1 Cor	5:11	if he is immoral, **g**, an idolater,
1 Cor	6:10	thieves nor the **g** nor drunkards nor
Eph	5: 5	no immoral or impure or **g** person,
1 Tm	3: 8	to drink, not **g** for sordid gain,
Ti	1: 7	aggressive, not **g** for sordid gain,

GREEK →GREECE

2 Mc	4:10	his countrymen into the G way
Jn	19:20	written in Hebrew, Latin, and G.
Acts	16: 1	a believer, but his father was a G.
Acts	17:12	a few of the influential G women
Acts	21:37	you?" He replied, "Do you speak G?
Rom	1:16	believes: for Jew first, and then G.
Gal	3:28	There is neither Jew nor G, there is
Col	3:11	Here there is not G and Jew,

GREEKS →GREECE

1 Mc	6: 2	of Macedon, the first king of the G.
Dn	8:21	The he-goat is the king of the G,
Jn	12:20	there were some G among those
Acts	18: 4	to convince both Jews and G.
Acts	20:21	and G to repentance before God
1 Cor	1:22	signs and G look for wisdom,
1 Cor	12:13	whether Jews or G, slaves or free

GREEN

Gn	1:30	I give all the **g** plants for food."
Gn	9: 3	them all to you as I did the **g** plants.
Ps	23: 2	In **g** pastures you let me graze;
Jer	17: 8	its leaves stay **g**; In the year
Mk	6:39	sit down in groups on the **g** grass.

GREET →GREETING, GREETINGS

Mt	5:47	And if you **g** your brothers only,
1 Cor	16:20	All the brothers **g** you. G one

GREETING →GREET

Lk	1:29	what sort of **g** this might be.
1 Cor	16:21	write you this **g** in my own hand.
Col	4:18	The **g** is in my own hand, Paul's.
2 Thes	3:17	This **g** is in my own hand, Paul's.

GREETINGS →GREET

Mt	23: 7	**g** in marketplaces, and the

GREW →GROW

Gn	21:20	God was with the boy as he **g** up.
Jgs	13:24	The boy **g** up and the LORD blessed
1 Sm	2:21	while young Samuel **g**
1 Sm	3:19	Samuel **g** up, and the LORD was
2 Sm	3: 1	in which David **g** stronger,
Is	53: 2	He **g** up like a sapling before him,
Lk	1:80	The child **g** and became strong
Lk	2:40	The child **g** and became strong,

GRIEF →GRIEVE, GRIEVED, GRIEVOUS

Prv	10: 1	a foolish son is a **g** to his mother.
Jer	8:18	My **g** is incurable, my heart within

GRIEVE →GRIEF

Eph	4:30	And do not **g** the holy Spirit of God,
1 Thes	4:13	so that you may not **g** like the rest,

GRIEVED →GRIEF

Gn	6: 6	on the earth, and his heart was **g**.
Is	63:10	But they rebelled, and **g** his holy

GRIEVOUS →GRIEF

Eccl	5:12	This is a **g** evil which I have seen

GRIND →GRINDING

Jb	31:10	Then may my wife **g** for another,

GRINDING →GRIND

Is	3:15	**g** down the poor when they look
Mt	8:12	there will be wailing and **g** of teeth."
Mt	13:42	there will be wailing and **g** of teeth.
Mt	13:50	there will be wailing and **g** of teeth.
Mt	22:13	there will be wailing and **g** of teeth.'
Mt	24:51	there will be wailing and **g** of teeth.
Mt	25:30	there will be wailing and **g** of teeth.'
Lk	13:28	there will be wailing and **g** of teeth
Lk	17:35	will be two women **g** meal together;

GROAN →GROANED, GROANING

Prv	29: 2	when the wicked rule, the people **g**.
Rom	8:23	**g** within ourselves as we wait
2 Cor	5: 2	For in this tent we **g**, longing to be
2 Cor	5: 4	For while we are in this tent we **g**

GROANED → GROAN
Ex   2:23   Still the Israelites g and cried

GROANING → GROAN
Ex   2:24   he heard their g and was mindful
Ex   6: 5   I have heard the g of the Israelites,
Rom   8:22   all creation is g in labor pains even

GROPE
Dt   28:29 midday you will g like a blind man
Is   59:10 Like blind men we g along the wall,
Acts 17:27 even perhaps g for him and find

GROUND → GROUNDED, GROUNDS
Gn   2: 7   formed man out of the clay of the g
Gn   3:17   eat, "Cursed be the g because of you!
Ex   3: 5   the place where you stand is holy g.
Jos   3:17   all Israel crossed over on dry g,
Jgs   6:37   while all the g is dry, I shall know
1 Sm 5: 3   lying prone on the g before the ark
2 Kgs 2: 8   and both crossed over on dry g.
Ps   26:12 My foot stands on level g;
Ps   147: 6 poor, but casts the wicked to the g.
Mt   10:29 falls to the g without your Father's
Mt   13: 5 Some fell on rocky g, where it had
Mt   25:25 off and buried your talent in the g.
Mk   4:31   that, when it is sown in the g,
Lk   22:44 like drops of blood falling on the g.]
Jn   8: 6   to write on the g with his finger.

GROUNDED → GROUND
Eph   3:17   faith; that you, rooted and g in love,

GROUNDS → GROUND
Dn   6: 5   find g for accusation against Daniel

GROUP → GROUPS
2 Sm 2:13   one g on one side of the pool

GROUPS → GROUP
Mk   6:39   to have them sit down in g

GROVES
Dt   6:11   and olive g that you did not plant;

GROW → GREW, GROWING, GROWN, GROWTH
Gn   2: 9   the LORD God made various trees g
Nm   6: 5   let the hair of his head g freely.
Jgs   16:22 to g as soon as it was shaved off.
Ps   92:13 tree, shall g like a cedar of Lebanon.
Ez   47:12 fruit trees of every kind shall g;
Mt   6:28   from the way the wild flowers g.
Eph   4:15   we should g in every way into him
1 Pt 2: 2   through it you may g into salvation,
2 Pt 3:18   But g in grace and in the knowledge

GROWING → GROW
1 Sm 2:26   young Samuel was g in stature
Col   1: 6   world it is bearing fruit and g,
Col   1:10   fruit and g in the knowledge of God,

GROWL
Ex   11: 7 their animals not even a dog shall g,
Jdt   11:19 and not even a dog will g at you.

GROWN → GROW
Ex   2:11   after Moses had g up, when he
2 Chr 10:10 The young men who had g
Heb   11:24 when he had g up, refused to be

GROWTH → GROW
1 Cor 3: 7   but only God, who causes the g.
Eph   4:16   brings about the body's g and builds
Col   2:19   achieves the g that comes

GRUDGE
Gn   50:15 has been nursing a g against us
Lv   19:18 and cherish no g against your fellow
Mk   6:19   Herodias harbored a g against him

GRUMBLE → GRUMBLED
Lk   19: 7 all saw this, they began to g, saying,

GRUMBLED → GRUMBLE
Mt   20:11 on receiving it they g against

GUARANTEE → GUARANTEED
Heb   7:22   become the g of an [even] better

GUARANTEED → GUARANTEE
Rom   4:16   and the promise may be g to all his

GUARD → GUARDED, GUARDIAN, GUARDIANS,
      GUARDING, GUARDS, SAFEGUARD
Gn   3:24   to g the way to the tree of life.
1 Sm 2: 9   He will g the footsteps of his
Ps   91:11 the angels to g you in all your ways.
Ps   141: 3 Set a g, LORD, before my mouth,
Prv   2:11   over you, understanding will g you;
Sir   6:13   be on your g with your friends.
Sir   32:23 Whatever you do, be on your g,
Is   52:12 and your rear g is the God of Israel.
Mt   27:66 a seal to the stone and setting the g.
Lk   12:15 "Take care to g against all greed,
Phil 4: 7   all understanding will g your hearts
2 Thes 3: 3 you and g you from the evil one.
1 Tm 6:20   g what has been entrusted to you.
2 Tm 1:12   is able to g what has been entrusted
2 Tm 1:14   G this rich trust with the help

GUARDED → GUARD
Jn   17:12 and I g them, and none of them was

GUARDIAN → GUARD
1 Pt 2:25   to the shepherd and g of your souls.

GUARDIANS → GUARD
Gal   4: 2   he is under the supervision of g

GUARDING → GUARD
Prv   2: 8   G the paths of justice,

GUARDS → GUARD
Prv   13: 6 Virtue g one who walks honestly,
Mt   28: 4 The g were shaken with fear of him

GUEST → GUESTS
Mk   14:14 "Where is my g room where I may

GUESTS → GUEST
Prv   9:18   depths of the nether world are her g!
Mt   9:15   "Can the wedding g mourn as long as
Lk   5:34   make the wedding g fast while

GUIDANCE → GUIDE
Prv   11:14 For lack of g a people falls;

GUIDE → GUIDANCE, GUIDED, GUIDES
Ps   31: 4 for your name's sake lead and g me.
Ps   67: 5 you g the nations upon the earth.
Ps   73:24 With your counsel you g me,
Is   58:11 Then the LORD will g you always
Lk   1:79   to g our feet into the path of peace."
Lk   6:39   a blind person g a blind person?
Jn   16:13 of truth, he will g you to all truth.

GUIDED → GUIDE
Ps   78:72 heart; with skilled hands he g them.

GUIDES → GUIDE
Prv   11: 3 The honesty of the upright g them;
Mt   15:14 they are blind g [of the blind].
Mt   23:16 "Woe to you, blind g, who say,
Mt   23:24 Blind g, who strain out the gnat

GUILT → GUILTY
Gn   44:16 God has uncovered your servant's g.
Lv   5:15   to the LORD as his g offering
Lv   5:15   As his g offering he shall bring
1 Sm 6: 4   "What g offering should be our
Ezr   9: 6   and our g reaches up to heaven.
Ps   32: 5 my sin to you; my g I did not hide.
Ps   32: 5 and you took away the g of my sin.
Prv   14: 9 G lodges in the tents of the arrogant,
Jer   2:22   stain of your g is still before me,
Hos   5:15   until they pay for their g and seek
Zec   3: 9   I will take away the g of the land

GUILTY → GUILT
Ex   23: 7 to death, nor shall you acquit the g.
Ex   34: 7 yet not declaring the g guiltless,
Nm   14:18 yet not declaring the guiltless g,

Ps	51: 7	True, I was born **g**, a sinner, even as
Is	5:23	those who acquit the **g** for bribes,
Dn	13:53	and freeing the **g**, although the Lord
Na	1: 3	Lᴏʀᴅ never leaves the **g** unpunished.
Mk	3:29	but is **g** of an everlasting sin."

GUSHED
Ps	78:20	he struck the rock, water **g** forth,
Ps	105:41	He split the rock and water **g** forth;

GYMNASIUM
1 Mc	1:14	Thereupon they built a **g**
2 Mc	4: 9	were given authority to establish a **g**

H

HABAKKUK
Prophet to Judah (Hb 1:1; 3:1). In Bel and the Dragon (Dn 14:33-39).

HABIT
Nm	22:30	in the **h** of treating you this way

HAD →HAVE
Ex	16:18	so gathered that everyone **h** enough
Nm	11: 4	"Would that we **h** meat for food!
Jgs	1:19	plain, because they **h** iron chariots.
1 Sm	2:12	they **h** respect neither for the Lᴏʀᴅ
Jb	42:10	to Job twice as much as he **h** before.
Ps	55: 7	I say, "If only I **h** wings like a dove
Is	5: 1	vineyard. My friend **h** a vineyard
Ez	1: 6	but each **h** four faces and four
Ez	10:14	Each **h** four faces: the first face was
Ez	41:18	cherubim. Each cherub **h** two faces
Mk	10:22	sad, for he **h** many possessions.
Acts	1:16	the scripture **h** to be fulfilled
Acts	2:44	and **h** all things in common;
Acts	14: 9	saw that he **h** the faith to be healed,
2 Cor	8:15	"Whoever **h** much did not have
2 Cor	8:15	whoever **h** little did not have less."
Rv	13:11	it **h** two horns like a lamb's

HADAD
Edomite adversary of Solomon (1 Kgs 11:14-25).

HADADEZER
2 Sm	8: 3	Next David defeated H,

HADASSAH →=ESTHER
Est	2: 7	He was foster father to H, that is,

HADES
Rv	6: 8	Death, and H accompanied him.
Rv	20:13	Death and H gave up their dead.
Rv	20:14	H were thrown into the pool of fire.

HAGAR
Servant of Sarah, wife of Abraham, mother of Ishmael (Gn 16:1-6; 25:12). Driven away by Sarah while pregnant (Gn 16:5-16); after birth of Isaac (Gn 21:9-21; Gal 4:21-31).

HAGGAI
Post-exilic prophet who encouraged rebuilding of the temple (Ezr 5:1; 6:14; Hg 1-2).

HAIL →HAILSTONES
Ex	9:19	shelter shall die when the **h** comes
Ex	9:26	the Israelites dwelt, was there no **h**.
Ps	78:47	He killed their vines with **h**,
Ps	147:17	H is dispersed like crumbs;
Sir	39:29	time, are fire and **h**, famine, disease,
Jn	19: 3	and they came to him and said, "H,
Rv	8: 7	there came **h** and fire mixed
Rv	16:21	**h** because this plague was so severe.

HAILSTONES →HAIL
Jos	10:11	from these **h** than the Israelites slew
Ez	13:11	**h** shall fall, and a stormwind shall
Rv	16:21	Large **h** like huge weights came

HAIR →HAIRS, HAIRY
Ex	26: 7	"Also make sheets woven of goat **h**,
Jgs	16:22	the **h** of his head began to grow as
Jgs	20:16	sling a stone at a **h** without missing.
2 Sm	14:26	because his **h** became too heavy
Prv	16:31	Gray **h** is a crown of glory; it is

Prv	20:29	and the dignity of old men is gray **h**.
Sir	6:18	you find wisdom with graying **h**.
Dn	7: 9	the **h** on his head as white as wool;
Dn	14:27	Daniel took some pitch, fat, and **h**;
Mt	3: 4	wore clothing made of camel's **h**
Lk	7:44	her tears and wiped them with her **h**.
Lk	21:18	but not a **h** on your head will be
Jn	11: 2	oil and dried his feet with her **h**;
Jn	12: 3	of Jesus and dried them with her **h**;
1 Cor	11: 6	she may as well have her **h** cut off.
1 Cor	11:14	that if a man wears his **h** long it is
1 Cor	11:15	a woman has long **h** it is her glory,
1 Pt	3: 3	one: braiding the **h**, wearing gold
Rv	1:14	The **h** of his head was as white as
Rv	9: 8	and they had **h** like women's **h**.

HAIRS →HAIR
Ps	40:13	They are more than the **h** of my
Mt	10:30	Even all the **h** of your head are
Lk	12: 7	Even the **h** of your head have all

HAIRY →HAIR
Gn	27:11	"But my brother Esau is a **h** man,"

HALAH
2 Kgs	18:11	to Assyria and settled them in H,

HALF →HALF-TRIBE
Gn	15:10	placed each **h** opposite the other;
Ex	24: 6	Moses took **h** of the blood and put it
Ex	24: 6	the other **h** he splashed on the altar.
Jos	8:33	H of them were facing Mount Gerizim and **h** Mount Ebal.
2 Sm	10: 4	after shaving off **h** their beards
1 Kgs	3:25	and give **h** to one woman and **h**
1 Kgs	10: 7	that they were not telling me the **h**.
Neh	4:10	only **h** my able men took a hand
Neh	13:24	their children, **h** spoke Ashdodite,
Est	5: 3	Even if it is **h** of my kingdom,
Is	44:19	"H of the wood I burned in the fire,
Ez	16:51	Samaria did not commit **h** your sins!
Mk	6:23	of me, even to **h** of my kingdom."
Lk	19: 8	"Behold, **h** of my possessions, Lord,
Rv	8: 1	in heaven for about **h** an hour.
Rv	11:11	But after the three and a **h** days,

HALF-TRIBE →HALF, TRIBE
Jos	4:12	Gadites, and **h** of Manasseh, armed,

HALL
Dn	5:10	she entered the banquet **h** and said,
Mt	22:10	and the **h** was filled with guests.
Acts	19: 9	in the lecture **h** of Tyrannus.

HALLOWED
Mt	6: 9	Father in heaven, **h** be your name,
Lk	11: 2	say: Father, **h** be your name,

HALO
Rv	4: 3	Around the throne was a **h** as brilliant
Rv	10: 1	in a cloud, with a **h** around his head;

HAM
Son of Noah (Gn 5:32; 1 Chr 1:4), father of Canaan (Gn 9:18; 10:6-20; 1 Chr 1:8-16). Saw Noah's nakedness (Gn 9:20-27).

HAMAN
Agagite nobleman honored by Xerxes (Est 3:1-2). Plotted to exterminate the Jews because of Mordecai (Est 3:3-15). Forced to honor Mordecai (Est 5-6). Plot exposed by Esther (Est 5:1-8; 7:1-8). Hanged (Est 7:9-10). See also Additions to Esther.

HAMATH
2 Sm	8: 9	Toi, king of H, heard that David had
2 Kgs	14:28	and turned back H from Israel,
2 Kgs	18:34	Where are the gods of H

HAMMERS
Jer	10: 4	With nails and **h** they are fastened,

HAMOR
Gn	34: 2	son of H the Hivite, who was chief

HAMSTRING →HAMSTRUNG
Jos	11: 6	You must **h** their horses and burn

HAMSTRUNG →HAMSTRING

Jos	11: 9	he h their horses and burned their
1 Chr	18: 4	horses, David h all but one hundred.

HANAMEL

Jer	32: 7	H, son of your uncle Shallum,

HANANEL

Neh	3: 1	the rebuilding to the Tower of H.
Jer	31:38	the Tower of H to the Corner Gate.

HANANI

Neh	7: 2	Over Jerusalem I placed H,

HANANIAH →=SHADRACH

1. False prophet; adversary of Jeremiah (Jer 28).
2. Original name of Shadrach (Dn 1:6-19; 2:17).

HAND →EMPTY-HANDED, HANDED, HANDFUL, HANDS, LEFT-HANDED

Gn	3:22	to put out his h to take fruit
Gn	4:11	your brother's blood from your h.
Gn	16:12	of a man, his h against everyone,
Gn	16:12	and everyone's h against him;
Gn	22:12	"Do not lay your h on the boy,"
Gn	24: 2	"Put your h under my thigh,
Gn	47:29	put your h under my thigh as a sign
Gn	48:14	put out his right h and laid it
Gn	48:14	his left h on the head of Manasseh,
Ex	4: 6	to him, "Put your h in your bosom."
Ex	4: 6	to his surprise his h was leprous,
Ex	6: 1	Forced by my mighty h, he will
Ex	13: 3	a strong h that the LORD brought you
Ex	15: 6	your right h, O LORD, has shattered
Ex	21:24	tooth for tooth, h for h, foot for foot,
Ex	33:22	with my h until I have passed by.
Dt	4:34	with his strong h and outstretched
Dt	19:21	tooth for tooth, h for h, and foot
Dt	32:39	and from my h there is no rescue.
1 Sm	24:11	'I will not raise a h against my lord,
2 Sm	1:14	to put forth your h to desecrate
1 Kgs	8:42	your mighty h and your outstretched
1 Kgs	13: 4	the h he stretched forth against him
1 Kgs	18:44	a cloud as small as a man's h rising
2 Chr	6:15	by your own h you have brought it
2 Chr	32:15	shall your god save you from my h!"
2 Chr	32:22	from the h of Sennacherib,
Ezr	7: 9	for the favoring h of his God was
Neh	2: 8	for the favoring h of my God was
Neh	4:11	each did his work with one h
Jdt	9:10	their pride by the h of a woman.
Jdt	13:15	him down by the h of a woman.
Jb	40: 4	I put my h over my mouth.
Ps	32: 4	night your h was heavy upon me;
Ps	37:24	fall, for the LORD holds their h.
Ps	44: 4	It was your right h, your own arm,
Ps	45:10	gold comes to stand at your right h.
Ps	63: 9	fast to you; your right h upholds me.
Ps	74:11	Why draw back your right h,
Ps	75: 9	Yes, a cup is in the LORD's h,
Ps	80:18	help be with the man at your right h,
Ps	91: 7	ten thousand at your right h,
Ps	95: 4	Whose h holds the depths
Ps	109:31	God stands at the right h of the poor
Ps	110: 1	"Take your throne at my right h,
Ps	137: 5	Jerusalem, may my right h wither.
Ps	139:10	Even there your h will guide me,
Ps	145:16	You open wide your h and satisfy
Prv	3:16	Long life is in her right h, in her left
Prv	19:24	The sluggard loses his h in the dish;
Prv	21: 1	the king's heart in the h of the Lord;
Eccl	2:24	this, I realized, is from the h of God.
Eccl	9:10	Anything you can turn your h to,
Sir	7:32	To the poor man also extend your h,
Is	1:25	I will turn my h against you,
Is	5:25	he raises his h to strike them;
Is	5:25	back, and his h is still outstretched.
Is	11: 8	the child lay his h on the adder's lair.
Is	40:12	Who has cupped in his h the waters
Is	41:13	who grasp your right h; It is I who
Is	44: 5	And this one shall write on his h,

Is	48:13	my right h spread out the heavens.
Jer	22:24	are a signet ring on my right h,
Jer	31:32	them by the h to lead them forth
Jer	51: 7	a golden cup in the h of the LORD
Lam	3: 3	me alone he brings back his h
Ez	1: 3	the h of the LORD came upon me.
Ez	2: 9	then I saw a h stretched out to me,
Dn	5: 5	the fingers of a human h appeared,
Dn	10:10	But then a h touched me, raising me
Am	7: 7	standing by a wall, plummet in h.
Jon	4:11	who cannot distinguish their right h
Hb	2:16	the cup from the LORD's right h,
Mt	3:12	His winnowing fan is in his h.
Mt	5:30	if your right h causes you to sin,
Mt	6: 3	not let your left h know what your
Mt	12:10	a man there who had a withered h.
Mt	18: 8	If your h or foot causes you to sin,
Mt	22:44	"Sit at my right h until I place your
Mt	26:64	seated at the right h of the Power'
Mk	1:31	grasped her h, and helped her up.
Mk	3: 1	a man there who had a withered h.
Mk	5:41	He took the child by the h and said
Mk	9:43	If your h causes you to sin, cut it
Mk	12:36	"Sit at my right h until I place your
Mk	14:62	seated at the right h of the Power
Lk	5:13	Jesus stretched out his h,
Lk	9:62	"No one who sets a h to the plow
Lk	20:42	said to my lord, "Sit at my right h
Lk	22:69	be seated at the right h of the power
Jn	10:28	No one can take them out of my h.
Jn	20:27	bring your h and put it into my side,
Acts	2:34	said to my Lord, "Sit at my right h
Acts	7:55	Jesus standing at the right h of God,
Rom	8:34	who also is at the right h of God,
1 Cor	12:15	I am not a h I do not belong
Eph	1:20	him at his right h in the heavens,
Col	3: 1	is seated at the right h of God.
Heb	1:13	"Sit at my right h until I make your
Heb	8: 1	his seat at the right h of the throne
Heb	10:12	seat forever at the right h of God;
1 Pt	3:22	heaven and is at the right h of God,
Rv	1:16	In his right h he held seven stars.
Rv	5: 1	in the right h of the one who sat

HANDED →HAND

Mt	26: 2	Man will be h over to be crucified."
Mt	27:26	he h him over to be crucified.
Acts	3:13	his servant Jesus whom you h over
Rom	4:25	who was h over for our
1 Cor	15: 3	For I h on to you of first

HANDFUL →HAND

Eccl	4: 6	Better is one h with tranquility

HANDLE

Col	2:21	"Do not h! Do not taste! Do not

HANDS →HAND

Gn	5:29	from our work and the toil of our h."
Gn	27:22	the voice is Jacob's, the h are Esau's."
Gn	37:22	was to rescue him from their h
Ex	29:10	his sons shall lay their h on its head.
Ex	32:15	of the commandments in his h,
1 Sm	5: 4	his head and h broken off and lying
1 Sm	26: 9	who can lay h on the LORD's anointed
2 Sm	18:12	pieces of silver in my two h,
2 Kgs	11:12	him, clapping their h and shouting,
2 Kgs	22:17	to which they turn their h, my anger
1 Mc	2:48	the law from the h of the Gentiles
Ps	18:25	the cleanness of my h in his sight.
Ps	22:17	So wasted are my h and feet
Ps	47: 2	All you peoples, clap your h;
Ps	63: 5	I will lift up my h, calling on your
Ps	90:17	Prosper the work of our h! Prosper the work of our h!
Ps	115: 7	They have h but do not feel,
Ps	138: 8	Never forsake the work of your h!
Prv	21:25	slays him, for his h refuse to work.
Prv	31:13	flax and makes cloth with skillful h.
Prv	31:20	She reaches out her h to the poor,
Sir	33:13	Like clay in the h of a potter, to be

Sir	33:13	So are men in the **h** of their Creator,
Is	5:12	not, the work of his **h** they see not.
Is	35: 3	Strengthen the **h** that are feeble,
Is	37:19	not gods but the work of human **h**,
Is	45:12	It was my **h** that stretched
Is	49:16	of my **h** I have written your name;
Is	55:12	of the countryside shall clap their **h**.
Is	64: 7	we are all the work of your **h**.
Is	65: 2	I have stretched out my **h** all the day
Jer	26:14	As for me, I am in your **h**;
Ez	1: 8	Human **h** were under their wings,
Dn	3:17	white-hot furnace and from your **h**,
Hos	14: 4	to the work of our **h**; for in you
Mi	7: 3	Their **h** succeed at evil; the prince
Zec	8:13	do not fear, but let your **h** be strong.
Mal	1:10	I accept any sacrifice from your **h**,
Mk	7: 5	instead eat a meal with unclean **h**?"
Mk	10:16	blessed them, placing his **h** on them.
Lk	23:46	into your **h** I commend my spirit";
Lk	24:40	he showed them his **h** and his feet.
Jn	20:27	"Put your finger here and see my **h**,
Acts	6: 6	who prayed and laid **h** on them.
Acts	8:18	by the laying on of the apostles' **h**,
Acts	13: 3	they laid **h** on them and sent them
Acts	19: 6	And when Paul laid [his] **h** on them,
Acts	28: 8	laid his **h** on him and healed him.
Rom	10:21	I stretched out my **h** to a disobedient
1 Cor	15:24	when he **h** over the kingdom to his
1 Thes	4:11	and to work with your [own] **h**,
1 Tm	2: 8	lifting up holy **h**, without anger
1 Tm	4:14	word with the imposition of **h**
2 Tm	1: 6	through the imposition of my **h**.
Heb	6: 2	about baptisms and laying on of **h**,
Heb	10:31	to fall into the **h** of the living God.
1 Jn	1: 1	and touched with our **h**
Rv	13:16	a stamped image on their right **h**
Rv	20: 4	its mark on their foreheads or **h**.

HANDSOME

Gn	39: 6	Now Joseph was strikingly **h**
1 Sm	16:12	a youth **h** to behold and making
1 Sm	17:42	and **h** in appearance, he held him
1 Kgs	1: 6	Adonijah was also very **h**, and next
Dn	1: 4	young men without any defect, **h**,

HANG → HANGED, HANGING, HUNG

Jdt	14: 1	and **h** it on the parapet of your wall.
Est	7: 9	The king answered, "**H** him on it."

HANGED → HANG

2 Sm	17:23	concerning his family, he **h** himself.
Est	2:23	both of them were **h** on a gibbet.
Est	7:10	So they **h** Haman on the gibbet
Mt	27: 5	and went off and **h** himself.

HANGING → HANG

Acts	10:39	put him to death by **h** him on a tree.

HANNAH

Wife of Elkanah, mother of Samuel (1 Sm 1). Prayer at dedication of Samuel (1 Sm 2:1-10). Blessed (1 Sm 2:18-21).

HAPPEN → HAPPENED, HAPPENING

Gn	49: 1	I may tell you what is to **h** to you
Ex	2: 4	to find out what would **h** to him.
Dn	10:14	make you understand what shall **h**
Mk	10:32	to tell them what was going to **h**
Jn	18: 4	that was going to **h** to him,

HAPPENED → HAPPEN

1 Sm	4: 7	"Woe to us! This has never **h** before.
Jl	1: 2	Has the like of this **h** in your days,

HAPPENING → HAPPEN

1 Pt	4:12	if something strange were **h** to you.

HAPPINESS → HAPPY

Sir	8:19	to no man, and banish not your **h**.
Lam	3:17	of peace, I have forgotten what **h** is;

HAPPY → HAPPINESS

1 Kgs	10: 8	**H** are your men, **h** these servants
Tb	13:16	**H** for me if a remnant of my
Est	5: 9	That day Haman left **h** and in good

Jb	5:17	**H** is the man whom God reproves!
Ps	1: 1	**H** those who do not follow
Ps	2:11	**H** are all who take refuge in God!
Ps	32: 1	**H** the sinner whose fault is
Ps	33:12	**H** the nation whose God is the LORD,
Ps	34: 9	**h** are those who take refuge in him.
Ps	40: 5	**H** those whose trust is the LORD,
Ps	41: 2	**H** those concerned for the lowly
Ps	84:13	hosts, **h** are those who trust in you!
Ps	112: 1	**H** are those who fear the LORD,
Ps	119: 2	**H** those who observe God's decrees,
Ps	128: 1	ascents. **H** are all who fear the LORD,
Ps	137: 8	**h** those who pay you back the evil
Prv	3:13	**H** the man who finds wisdom,
Prv	8:34	**H** the man watching daily at my
Sir	14: 1	**H** the man whose mouth brings him no grief,
Sir	14:20	**H** the man who meditates
Sir	25: 9	**H** is he who finds a friend and he
Sir	26: 1	**H** the husband of a good wife,
Sir	34:15	**H** the soul that fears the LORD!
Is	56: 2	**H** is the man who does this, the son
Jon	4: 6	Jonah was very **h** over the plant.

HARAN

Gn	11:27	Nahor and **H**, and **H** became
Gn	11:31	son of **H**, and his daughter-in-law

HARD → HARDEN, HARDENED, HARDENING, HARDENS, HARDER, HARDSHIPS

Ex	1:14	for them with **h** work in mortar
Mt	19:23	it will be **h** for one who is rich
Rom	16:12	who has worked **h** in the Lord.
2 Pt	3:16	In them there are some things **h**

HARDEN → HARD

Ps	95: 8	Do not **h** your hearts as at Meribah,
Heb	3: 8	'**H** not your hearts as at the rebellion
Heb	4: 7	hear his voice: "**H** not your hearts.' "

HARDENED → HARD

Mk	8:17	or comprehend? Are your hearts **h**?
Jn	12:40	and **h** their heart, so that they might
Rom	11: 7	the elect attained it; the rest were **h**,
Heb	3:13	of you may grow **h** by the deceit

HARDENING → HARD

Rom	11:25	a **h** has come upon Israel in part,

HARDENS → HARD

Rom	9:18	he wills, and he **h** whom he wills.

HARDER → HARD

Jer	5: 3	They set their faces **h** than stone,
1 Cor	15:10	I have toiled **h** than all of them;

HARDSHIPS → HARD

2 Cor	6: 4	in afflictions, **h**, constraints,
2 Cor	12:10	weaknesses, insults, **h**, persecutions,

HAREM

Est	2: 9	her maids to the best place in the **h**.

HARM → HARMED, HARMFUL

Gn	31: 7	did not let him do me any **h**.
Gn	48:16	who has delivered me from all **h**,
Gn	50:20	Even though you meant **h** to me,
1 Sm	26:21	I will not **h** you again, because you
1 Chr	16:22	and to my prophets do no **h**."
Neh	6: 2	They were planning to do me **h**.
Prv	12:21	No **h** befalls the just, but the wicked
1 Pt	3:13	Now who is going to **h** you if you
Rv	9:19	like snakes, with heads that inflict **h**.
Rv	11: 5	If anyone wants to **h** them,

HARMED → HARM

Rv	2:11	The victor shall not be **h**

HARMFUL → HARM

2 Kgs	4:41	there was no longer anything **h**
2 Mc	15:39	Just as it is **h** to drink wine alone
1 Tm	6: 9	and into many foolish and **h** desires,

HARP → HARPISTS, HARPS

Ps	33: 2	Give thanks to the LORD on the **h**;
Ps	108: 3	Awake, my soul; awake, lyre and **h**!

Ps	150: 3	the horn, praise him with **h** and lyre.
Is	5:12	With **h** and lyre, timbrel and flute,
Rv	5: 8	Each of the elders held a **h** and gold

HARPISTS →HARP

Rv	14: 2	like that of **h** playing their harps.
Rv	18:22	No melodies of **h** and musicians,

HARPS →HARP

1 Sm	10: 5	by lyres, tambourines, flutes and **h**.
1 Chr	15:16	to play on musical instruments, **h**,
1 Chr	25: 1	to the accompaniment of lyres and **h**
Neh	12:27	hymns and the music of cymbals, **h**,
1 Mc	4:54	it was reconsecrated with songs, **h**,
Ps	137: 2	of that land we hung up our **h**.
Rv	15: 2	They were holding God's **h**,

HARSH

Prv	15: 1	wrath, but a **h** word stirs up anger.
Jude	1:15	all the **h** words godless sinners have

HARVEST

Gn	8:22	lasts, seedtime and **h**, cold and heat,
Ex	23:16	the feast of the grain **h** with the first
Prv	10: 5	a son who slumbers during **h**,
Prv	20: 4	when he looks for the **h**, it is not
Jer	8:20	"The **h** has passed, the summer is
Jl	4:13	for the **h** is ripe; Come and tread,
Mt	9:37	"The **h** is abundant but the laborers
Mt	13:39	The **h** is the end of the age,
Lk	10: 2	"The **h** is abundant but the laborers
Lk	10: 2	so ask the master of the **h** to send out laborers for his **h**.
Jn	4:35	'In four months the **h** will be here'?
Jn	4:35	up and see the fields ripe for the **h**.
2 Cor	9:10	increase the **h** of your righteousness.
Rv	14:15	"Use your sickle and reap the **h**,
Rv	14:15	because the earth's **h** is fully ripe."

HAS →HAVE

2 Chr	25: 8	It is God who **h** the power
Jb	1:12	all that he **h** is in your power;
Jb	42: 7	concerning me, as **h** my servant Job.
Is	34: 8	For the LORD **h** a day of vengeance,
Jer	23:28	let him who **h** my word speak my
Mt	8:20	the Son of Man **h** nowhere to rest
Mt	9: 6	the Son of Man **h** authority on earth
Mk	3:30	had said, "He **h** an unclean spirit."
Jn	3:36	believes in the Son **h** eternal life,
Jn	4:44	testified that a prophet **h** no honor
Jn	15:13	No one **h** greater love than this,
Rom	6: 9	death no longer **h** power over him.
1 Cor	7: 7	each **h** a particular gift from God,
1 Cor	7:13	if any woman **h** a husband who is
1 Cor	11:15	a woman **h** long hair it is her glory,
1 Jn	2:23	who denies the Son **h** the Father,
1 Jn	2:23	confesses the Son **h** the Father as
1 Jn	5:12	Whoever possesses the Son **h** life;
Rv	20: 6	The second death **h** no power over

HASIDEANS

1 Mc	2:42	they were joined by a group of **H**,
1 Mc	7:13	The **H** were the first among
2 Mc	14: 6	"Those Jews called **H**, led by Judas

HASTE →HASTENING, HASTILY

Dt	16: 3	in frightened **h** you left the land

HASTENING →HASTE

2 Pt	3:12	and **h** the coming of the day of God,

HASTILY →HASTE

Prv	25: 8	seen bring not forth **h** against

HATE →HATED, HATES, HATING, HATRED

Ex	18:21	men who **h** dishonest gain, and set
2 Chr	18: 7	but I **h** him, for he prophesies not
Ps	5: 6	before you. You **h** all who do evil;
Ps	45: 8	You love justice and **h** wrongdoing;
Ps	97:10	The LORD loves those who **h** evil,
Ps	119:104	insight; therefore I **h** all false ways.
Ps	119:163	Falsehood I **h** and abhor;
Ps	129: 5	in disgrace, all who **h** Zion.
Ps	139:21	Do I not **h**, LORD, those who **h** you?

Prv	8:13	[The fear of the LORD is to **h** evil;]
Prv	8:13	way, and the perverse mouth I **h**.
Prv	9: 8	not an arrogant man, lest he **h** you;
Prv	25:17	than enough of you, and **h** you.
Prv	29:10	Bloodthirsty men **h** the honest man,
Eccl	3: 8	A time to love, and a time to **h**;
Sir	7:15	**H** not laborious tasks, nor farming,
Is	61: 8	is right, I **h** robbery and injustice;
Jer	44: 4	commit this horrible deed which I **h**,
Am	5:15	**H** evil and love good, and let justice
Mal	2:16	For I **h** divorce, says the LORD,
Mt	5:43	your neighbor and **h** your enemy.'
Lk	6:22	Blessed are you when people **h** you,
Lk	6:27	do good to those who **h** you,
Lk	16:13	He will either **h** one and love
Jn	7: 7	The world cannot **h** you, but it hates
Rom	7:15	do what I want, but I do what I **h**.
Rom	12: 9	**h** what is evil, hold on to what is

HATED →HATE

Gn	37: 4	they **h** him so much that they would
Prv	1:29	Because they **h** knowledge,
Mal	1: 3	yet I loved Jacob, but **h** Esau;
Mt	10:22	You will be **h** by all because of my
Jn	15:18	hates you, realize that it **h** me first.
Rom	9:13	is written: "I loved Jacob but **h** Esau."
Heb	1: 9	loved justice and **h** wickedness;

HATES →HATE

Prv	6:16	There are six things the LORD **h**, yes,
Prv	13: 5	Anything deceitful the just man **h**,
Sir	15:11	away"; for what he **h** he does not do.
Sir	15:13	Abominable wickedness the LORD **h**,
Sir	33: 2	He who **h** the law is without
Jn	15:19	out of the world, the world **h** you.
Jn	15:23	Whoever **h** me also **h** my Father.
Eph	5:29	For no one **h** his own flesh

HATING →HATE

2 Tm	3: 3	licentious, brutal, **h** what is good,
Ti	3: 3	hateful ourselves and **h** one another.

HATRED →HATE

Ps	139:22	With fierce **h** I hate them, enemies I
Prv	10:12	**H** stirs up disputes, but love covers
Prv	15:17	love is than a fatted ox and **h** with it.

HAUGHTY

Ps	18:28	you save; **h** eyes you bring low.
Prv	6:17	**H** eyes, a lying tongue, and hands
Prv	16:18	disaster, and a **h** spirit before a fall.
Rom	12:16	do not be **h** but associate

HAUNT

Rv	18: 2	She has become a **h** for demons.

HAVE →HAD, HAS, HAVING

Gn	1:26	Let them **h** dominion over the fish
Gn	18:10	year, and Sarah will then **h** a son."
Gn	27:38	father, "**H** you only that one blessing,
Ex	16:12	the morning you shall **h** your fill
Ex	20: 3	You shall not **h** other gods besides
Dt	5: 7	You shall not **h** other gods besides
Jos	22:25	and Gad **h** no share in the LORD.'
Jb	40: 9	**H** you an arm like that of God,
Ps	73:25	Whom else **h** I in the heavens?
Ps	115: 5	They **h** mouths but do not speak,
Ps	119:99	I **h** more understanding than all my
Jer	2:28	are the altars you **h** set up for Baal.
Jer	5:21	Who **h** eyes and see not, who **h** ears and hear not.
Mal	2:10	**H** we not all the one Father?
Mt	3: 9	'We **h** Abraham as our father." For I
Mt	21:21	you, if you **h** faith and do not waver,
Mk	10:21	sell what you **h**, and give
Mk	10:21	and you will **h** treasure in heaven;
Mk	14: 7	The poor you will always **h**
Mk	14: 7	them, but you will not always **h** me.
Jn	3:16	not perish but might **h** eternal life.
Jn	4:32	"I **h** food to eat of which you do not
Jn	8:12	darkness, but will **h** the light of life."
Jn	16:12	"I **h** much more to tell you, but you
Jn	16:33	In the world you will **h** trouble,

Acts	3: 6	said, "I **h** neither silver nor gold, but what I do **h** I give you:
Rom	5: 1	we **h** peace with God through our
Rom	8: 9	Whoever does not **h** the Spirit
Rom	12: 6	Since we **h** gifts that differ
1 Cor	2:16	him?" But we **h** the mind of Christ.
1 Cor	13: 1	but do not **h** love, I am a resounding
2 Cor	8:15	"Whoever had much did not **h** more,
2 Cor	8:15	whoever had little did not **h** less."
Eph	1: 7	him we **h** redemption by his blood,
Eph	2:18	for through him we both **h** access
Heb	4:14	since we **h** a great high priest who
Heb	6:19	This we **h** as an anchor of the soul,
1 Jn	2:20	you **h** the anointing that comes
1 Jn	5:12	the Son of God does not **h** life.
Rv	22:14	wash their robes so as to **h** the right

HAVILAH

Gn	2:11	winds through the whole land of **H**,

HAVING → HAVE

Mt	7:29	he taught them as one **h** authority,

HAY

1 Cor	3:12	precious stones, wood, **h**, or straw,

HAZAEL

1 Kgs	19:15	you shall anoint **H** as king of Aram.
2 Kgs	8: 9	**H** went to visit him,

HAZOR

Jos	11:11	was left alive. **H** itself he burned.
Jer	49:33	**H** shall become a haunt of jackals,

HEAD → BALD-HEAD, BEHEADED, HEADLONG, HEADS, HOTHEADED

Gn	3:15	He will strike at your **h**, while you
Gn	28:18	stone that he had put under his **h**,
Gn	48:18	lay your right hand on his **h**!"
Nm	6: 5	let the hair of his **h** grow freely.
Dt	28:13	The LORD will make you the **h**,
Jgs	16:17	"No razor has touched my **h**, for I
1 Sm	1:11	and no razor shall ever touch his **h**."
1 Sm	9: 2	he stood **h** and shoulders
1 Sm	17:51	he dispatched him and cut off his **h**.
Jdt	13: 8	twice in the neck and cut off his **h**.
1 Mc	7:47	they cut off Nicanor's **h** and his right
Ps	23: 5	watch; You anoint my **h** with oil;
Ps	133: 2	Like precious ointment on the **h**,
Prv	1: 9	diadem will they be for your **h**;
Prv	10: 6	Blessings are for the **h** of the just,
Is	59:17	salvation, as the helmet on his **h**;
Jer	8:23	that my **h** were a spring of water,
Dn	2:32	The **h** of the statue was pure gold,
Dn	7: 9	the hair on his **h** as white as wool;
Mt	8:20	of Man has nowhere to rest his **h**."
Mk	6:28	He brought in the **h** on a platter
Jn	19: 2	out of thorns and placed it on his **h**,
1 Cor	11: 3	that Christ is the **h** of every man,
1 Cor	11: 3	and a husband the **h** of his wife,
1 Cor	11: 3	and God the **h** of Christ.
1 Cor	11: 4	with his **h** covered brings shame upon his **h**.
1 Cor	11: 5	with her **h** unveiled brings shame upon her **h**,
1 Cor	12:21	need you," nor again the **h** to the feet,
Eph	1:22	gave him as **h** over all things
Eph	5:23	the husband is **h** of his wife just as Christ is **h**
Col	1:18	He is the **h** of the body, the church.
Rv	1:14	of his **h** was as white as white wool
Rv	10: 1	in a cloud, with a halo around his **h**;
Rv	12: 1	on her **h** a crown of twelve stars.
Rv	14:14	with a gold crown on his **h**
Rv	19:12	and on his **h** were many diadems.

HEADLONG → HEAD

Acts	1:18	and falling **h**, he burst open

HEADS → HEAD

Neh	3:36	back their derision upon their own **h**
1 Mc	3:47	they sprinkled ashes on their **h**
Ps	22: 8	and jeer; they shake their **h** at me:
Ps	24: 7	Lift up your **h**, O gates; rise up,
Ez	11:21	down their conduct upon their **h**,
Dn	7: 6	those of a bird, and it had four **h**.

Mt	27:39	by reviled him, shaking their **h**
Mk	2:23	make a path while picking the **h**
Lk	21:28	erect and raise your **h** because your
Acts	18: 6	to them, "Your blood be on your **h**!
Rv	4: 4	and with gold crowns on their **h**.
Rv	12: 3	dragon, with seven **h** and ten horns,
Rv	12: 3	and on its **h** were seven diadems.
Rv	17: 9	The seven **h** represent seven hills

HEAL → HEALED, HEALING, HEALS, HEALTH

Nm	12:13	LORD, "Please, not this! Pray, **h** her!"
Dt	32:39	I who inflict wounds and **h** them,
2 Kgs	20: 5	I will **h** you. In three days you shall
2 Kgs	20: 8	is the sign that the LORD will **h** me
Tb	3:17	So Raphael was sent to **h** them both:
Tb	12:14	God commissioned me to **h** you
Ps	6: 3	weak; **h** me, LORD, for my bones are
Ps	41: 5	**h** me, I have sinned against you.
Eccl	3: 3	A time to kill, and a time to **h**;
Sir	38: 9	but pray to God, who will **h** you:
Is	19:22	he shall be won over and **h** them.
Is	57:18	but I will **h** them and lead them;
Is	57:19	says the LORD; and I will **h** them.
Jer	17:14	**H** me, LORD, that I may be healed;
Jer	30:17	of your wounds I will **h** you,
Jer	33: 6	I will **h** them, and reveal to them
Jer	51: 9	"We have tried to **h** Babylon, but she
Lam	2:13	is your downfall; who can **h** you?
Hos	5:13	But he cannot **h** you nor take away
Hos	6: 1	is he who has rent, but he will **h** us;
Hos	7: 1	when I would **h** Israel, The guilt
Hos	14: 5	I will **h** their defection, I will love
Zec	11:16	seek the strays, nor **h** the injured,
Mt	13:15	and be converted, and I **h** them.'
Lk	9: 2	kingdom of God and to **h** [the sick].
Jn	4:47	him to come down and **h** his son,
Jn	12:40	be converted, and I would **h** them."
Acts	4:30	you stretch forth [your] hand to **h**,
Acts	28:27	and be converted, and I **h** them.'

HEALED → HEAL

Lv	13:18	had a boil on his skin which later **h**,
Lv	13:37	grown on it, the disease has been **h**;
Lv	14: 3	sore of leprosy has **h** in the leper,
Lv	14:48	since the infection has been **h**.
1 Sm	6: 3	Then you will be **h**, and will learn
2 Kgs	8:29	Jezreel to be **h** of the wounds
2 Kgs	9:15	to be **h** of the wounds the Arameans
2 Chr	22: 6	be **h** of the wounds he had received
Ps	30: 3	I cried out to you and you **h** me.
Is	6:10	and they will turn and be **h**.
Is	53: 5	us whole, by his stripes we were **h**.
Jer	15:18	wound incurable, refusing to be **h**?
Jer	17:14	Heal me, LORD, that I may be **h**;
Jer	51: 8	her wounds, in case she can be **h**.
Jer	51: 9	but she cannot be **h**. Leave her,
Mt	8: 8	the word and my servant will be **h**.
Mt	8:13	at that very hour [his] servant was **h**.
Mt	14:36	and as many as touched it were **h**.
Mt	15:28	her daughter was **h** from that hour.
Mk	5:29	that she was **h** of her affliction.
Mk	6:56	and as many as touched it were **h**.
Lk	6:18	him and to be **h** of their diseases;
Lk	6:19	came forth from him and **h** them all.
Lk	7: 7	the word and let my servant be **h**.
Lk	8:47	how she had been **h** immediately.
Lk	9:11	he **h** those who needed to be cured.
Lk	9:42	the unclean spirit, **h** the boy,
Lk	14: 4	after he had **h** him, dismissed him.
Lk	17:15	realizing he had been **h**, returned,
Lk	22:51	touched the servant's ear and **h** him.
Jn	5:13	The man who was **h** did not know
Acts	14: 9	saw that he had the faith to be **h**,
Heb	12:13	is lame may not be dislocated but **h**.
Jas	5:16	for one another, that you may be **h**.
1 Pt	2:24	By his wounds you have been **h**.
Rv	13: 3	but this mortal wound was **h**.
Rv	13:12	whose mortal wound had been **h**.

HEALING → HEAL

Tb	5:10	God has **h** in store for you; so take
Jb	5:18	he smites, but his hands give **h**.
Prv	12:18	but the tongue of the wise is **h**.
Prv	13:17	a trustworthy envoy is a **h** remedy.
Sir	21: 3	when it cuts, there can be no **h**.
Sir	28: 3	fellows and expect **h** from the LORD?
Jer	8:15	for a time of **h**, but terror comes
Jer	14:19	for a time of **h**, but terror comes
Jer	30:13	for your running sore, no **h** for you.
Ez	30:21	and **h** remedies that it may be strong
Mal	3:20	the sun of justice with its **h** rays;
Lk	5:17	of the Lord was with him for **h**.
Acts	4:22	of **h** had been done was over forty
Acts	10:38	**h** all those oppressed by the devil,
1 Cor	12: 9	another gifts of **h** by the one Spirit;
1 Cor	12:28	deeds; then gifts of **h**, assistance,
1 Cor	12:30	Do all have gifts of **h**? Do all speak

HEALS → HEAL

Ps	103: 3	pardons all your sins, **h** all your ills,
Ps	147: 3	the brokenhearted, binds up their
Acts	9:34	to him, "Aeneas, Jesus Christ **h** you.

HEALTH → HEAL

Tb	5:16	In good **h** we shall leave you,
Tb	5:16	in good **h** we shall return to you,
Tb	5:21	Our son will leave in good **h** and come back to us in good **h**.
Tb	7: 1	Good **h** to you, and welcome!"
2 Mc	9:19	and best wishes for their **h**
2 Mc	11:28	we desire. We too are in good **h**.
Wis	7:10	Beyond **h** and comeliness I loved
Sir	30:15	More precious than gold is **h**
Sir	34:17	eyes, gives **h** and life and blessing.
Is	38:16	You have given me **h** and life;
Jer	30:17	For I will restore you to **h**; of your
Lk	7:10	they found the slave in good **h**.
Acts	3:16	it has given him this perfect **h**,
3 Jn	1: 2	in every respect and are in good **h**,

HEAP

1 Sm	2: 8	from the ash **h** he lifts up the poor,
Prv	25:22	live coals you will **h** on his head,
Rom	12:20	so doing you will **h** burning coals

HEAR → HEARD, HEARERS, HEARING, HEARS

Nm	14:13	"Are the Egyptians to **h** of this?
Dt	1:17	is too hard for you and I will **h** it.'
Dt	4:36	the heavens he let you **h** his voice
Dt	5: 1	all Israel and said to them, "**H**,
Dt	6: 3	**H** then, Israel, and be careful
Dt	6: 4	"**H**, O Israel! The LORD is our God,
Dt	9: 1	"**H**, O Israel! You are now
Dt	20: 3	'**H**, O Israel! Today you are going
Dt	31:13	know it yet, must **h** it and learn it,
Jos	7: 9	other inhabitants of the land **h** of it,
2 Kgs	19:16	**H** the words of Sennacherib
2 Chr	7:14	I will **h** them from heaven
Jb	20: 3	rebuke which puts me to shame I **h**,
Jb	26:14	and how faint is the word we **h**!
Jb	31:35	Oh, that I had one to **h** my case,
Ps	30:11	**H**, O LORD, have mercy on me;
Ps	51:10	Let me **h** sounds of joy
Ps	94: 9	the one who shaped the ear not **h**?
Ps	135:17	They have ears but **h** not; no breath
Eccl	7:21	is spoken lest you **h** your servant
Is	1:10	**H** the word of the LORD,
Is	21: 3	labor; I am to bewildered to **h**,
Is	29:18	On that day the deaf shall **h**
Is	59: 1	to save, nor his ear too dull to **h**.
Jer	5:21	see not, who have ears and **h** not.
Bar	1: 3	to **h** it, as well as all the people who
Ez	33: 7	when you **h** me say anything,
Ez	37: 4	Dry bones, **h** the word of the LORD!
Mi	6: 2	**H**, O mountains, the plea
Mt	11: 5	the deaf **h**, the dead are raised,
Mt	13:17	and to **h** what you **h** but did not **h** it.
Mk	12:29	replied, "The first is this: '**H**, O Israel!
Lk	7:22	the deaf **h**, the dead are raised,
Jn	5:25	the dead will **h** the voice of the Son

Jn	5:25	of God, and those who **h** will live.
Acts	13: 7	and wanted to **h** the word of God.
Acts	13:44	whole city gathered to **h** the word
Acts	17:32	"We should like to **h** you on this
Rom	10:14	how can they **h** without someone
Heb	3: 7	that today you would **h** his voice,
Rv	9:20	which cannot see or **h** or walk.

HEARD → HEAR

Gn	3: 8	When they **h** the sound of the LORD
Gn	21:17	God **h** the boy's cry, and God's
Ex	2:24	he **h** their groaning and was mindful
Ex	6: 5	now that I have **h** the groaning
Nm	12: 2	us also?" And the LORD **h** this.
Nm	14:27	I have **h** the grumblings
Dt	4:32	happen before? Was it ever **h** of?
Jos	24:27	for it has **h** all the words
2 Sm	7:22	but you, just as we have **h** it told.
1 Kgs	5:14	the earth who had **h** of his wisdom.
1 Kgs	10: 1	Sheba, having **h** of Solomon's fame,
Jb	42: 5	I had **h** of you by word of mouth,
Ps	18: 7	From his temple he **h** my voice;
Ps	62:12	two things I have **h**: Power belongs
Ps	78:59	God **h** and grew angry; he rejected
Sir	3: 5	children, and when he prays he is **h**.
Is	40:21	Have you not **h**? Was it not foretold
Is	40:28	or have you not **h**? The LORD is
Is	66: 8	Who ever **h** of such a thing, or saw
Jer	18:13	who has ever **h** the like?
Lam	3:56	You **h** me call, "Let not your ear
Ez	10: 5	of the cherubim could be **h** as far as
Dn	10:12	before God, your prayer was **h**.
Dn	12: 8	I **h**, but I did not understand; so I
Dn	13:44	The Lord **h** her prayer.
Mt	2: 3	When King Herod **h** this, he was
Mt	5:21	"You have **h** that it was said to your
Mt	5:27	"You have **h** that it was said,
Mt	5:33	"Again you have **h** that it was said
Mt	5:38	"You have **h** that it was said, 'An eye
Mt	5:43	"You have **h** that it was said,
Mk	6: 2	many who **h** him were astonished.
Mk	14:64	You have **h** the blasphemy. What do
Lk	12: 3	in the darkness will be **h** in the light,
Jn	8:26	what I **h** from him I tell the world."
Acts	2: 6	because each one **h** them speaking
Rom	10:14	in him of whom they have not **h**?
1 Cor	2: 9	eye has not seen, and ear has not **h**,
2 Cor	12: 4	into Paradise and **h** ineffable things,
2 Tm	1:13	sound words that you **h** from me,
Heb	4: 2	word that they **h** did not profit them,
2 Pt	1:18	We ourselves **h** this voice come
1 Jn	1: 3	what we have seen and **h**
1 Jn	3:11	this is the message you have **h**
2 Jn	1: 6	as you **h** from the beginning,
Rv	1:10	**h** behind me a voice as loud as
Rv	22: 8	I, John, who **h** and saw these things,

HEARERS → HEAR

Jas	1:22	doers of the word and not **h** only,

HEARING → HEAR

Nm	11: 1	complained in the **h** of the LORD;
Dt	13:12	And all Israel, **h** of it, shall fear
Dt	19:20	The rest, on **h** of it, shall fear,
Sir	4: 8	Give a **h** to the poor man, and return
Am	8:11	but for **h** the word of the LORD.
Lk	4:21	passage is fulfilled in your **h**."
1 Cor	12:17	were an eye, where would the **h** be? If the whole body were **h**,

HEARS → HEAR

Ps	69:34	For the LORD **h** the poor, does not
Prv	15:29	but the prayer of the just he **h**.
Sir	21:15	When an intelligent man **h** words
Is	30:19	as soon as he **h** he will answer you.
Jn	5:24	whoever **h** my word and believes
Jn	8:47	belongs to God **h** the words of God;
1 Jn	5:14	according to his will, he **h** us.
Rv	22:18	warn everyone who **h** the prophetic

HEART → BROKENHEARTED, DISHEARTENED, HEART'S, HEARTLESS, HEARTS, WHOLEHEARTED

Gn	6: 6	on the earth, and his **h** was grieved.
Ex	28:30	may be over Aaron's **h** whenever he
Ex	35:21	as his **h** suggested and his spirit
Dt	4:29	search after him with your whole **h**
Dt	6: 5	with all your **h**, and with all your
Dt	10:12	with all your **h** and all your soul
Dt	11:13	with all your **h** and all your soul,
Dt	13: 4	you really love him with all your **h**
Dt	26:16	to observe them with all your **h**
Dt	30: 2	heed his voice with all your **h**
Dt	30: 6	with all your **h** and all your soul
Dt	30:10	with all your **h** and all your soul.
Jos	22: 5	serve him with your whole **h**
1 Sm	10: 9	Samuel, God gave him another **h**.
1 Sm	12:20	worship him with your whole **h**.
1 Sm	12:24	him faithfully with your whole **h**;
1 Sm	13:14	sought out a man after his own **h**
1 Sm	16: 7	but the LORD looks into the **h**."
2 Sm	6:16	LORD, and she despised him in her **h**.
1 Kgs	2: 4	faithful to me with their whole **h**
1 Kgs	8:48	if with their whole **h** and soul they
1 Kgs	9: 3	eyes and my **h** shall be there always.
1 Kgs	11: 4	his **h** was not entirely with the LORD,
1 Kgs	14: 8	and followed me with his whole **h**,
1 Kgs	15:14	yet Asa's **h** was entirely
1 Chr	28: 9	and serve him with a perfect **h**
2 Chr	6:38	with their whole **h** and with their
2 Chr	7:16	and my **h** also shall be there always.
2 Chr	15:12	fathers, with all their **h** and soul;
2 Chr	15:17	yet Asa's **h** was undivided as long as
2 Chr	22: 9	sought the LORD with his whole **h**."
2 Chr	34:31	statutes with his whole **h** and soul,
2 Chr	36:13	hardened his **h** rather than return
1 Mc	1: 3	him, and his **h** became proud
1 Mc	2:24	his **h** was moved and his just fury
Jb	22:22	and lay up his words in your **h**.
Jb	31: 7	and my **h** has followed my eyes,
Jb	37: 1	At this my **h** trembles and leaps
Ps	7:11	me is God who saves the honest **h**
Ps	9: 2	will praise you, LORD, with all my **h**;
Ps	16: 9	Therefore my **h** is glad, my soul
Ps	19:15	the thoughts of my **h** before you,
Ps	20: 5	Grant what is in your **h**, fulfill
Ps	26: 2	and try me; search my **h** and mind.
Ps	28: 7	in whom my **h** trusted and found
Ps	28: 7	So my **h** rejoices; with my song I
Ps	44:22	who knows the secrets of the **h**?
Ps	51:12	A clean **h** create for me, God;
Ps	51:19	do not spurn a broken, humbled **h**.
Ps	66:18	Had I cherished evil in my **h**,
Ps	73: 1	Lord, to those who are clean of **h**!
Ps	73:26	Though my flesh and my **h** fail,
Ps	73:26	God is the rock of my **h**, my portion
Ps	81:13	So I gave them over to hardness of **h**;
Ps	90:12	that we may gain wisdom of **h**.
Ps	97:11	just; gladness, for the honest of **h**.
Ps	108: 2	My **h** is steadfast, God; my **h** is
Ps	109:22	in need; my **h** is pierced within me.
Ps	111: 1	I will praise the LORD with all my **h**
Ps	119: 2	who seek the LORD with all their **h**.
Ps	119:10	With all my **h** I seek you; do not let
Ps	119:11	In my **h** I treasure your promise,
Ps	119:34	teaching, to keep it with all my **h**.
Ps	119:36	Direct my **h** toward your decrees
Ps	119:58	I entreat you with all my **h**:
Ps	119:69	observe your precepts with all my **h**.
Ps	119:111	forever; they are the joy of my **h**.
Ps	119:112	My **h** is set on fulfilling your laws;
Ps	119:145	I call with all my **h**, O LORD;
Ps	119:161	but my **h** reveres only your word.
Ps	138: 1	I thank you, LORD, with all my **h**;
Ps	139:23	Probe me, God, know my **h**; try me,
Ps	141: 4	Do not let my **h** incline to evil,
Prv	2: 2	inclining your **h** to understanding;
Prv	3: 5	Trust in the LORD with all your **h**,
Prv	4: 4	me: "Let your **h** hold fast my words:
Prv	4:21	your sight, keep them within your **h**;

Prv	4:23	With closest custody, guard your **h**,
Prv	6:21	them fastened over your **h** always,
Prv	6:25	Lust not in your **h** after her beauty,
Prv	7: 3	write them on the tablet of your **h**.
Prv	12:25	Anxiety in a man's **h** depresses it,
Prv	13:12	Hope deferred makes the **h** sick,
Prv	14:13	Even in laughter the **h** may be sad
Prv	15:13	A glad **h** lights up the face,
Prv	15:30	cheerful glance brings joy to the **h**;
Prv	17:22	A joyful **h** is the health of the body,
Prv	20: 9	can say, "I have made my **h** clean,
Prv	21: 1	Like a stream is the king's **h**
Prv	22:11	The LORD loves the pure of **h**;
Prv	22:15	Folly is close to the **h** of a child,
Prv	23:15	My son, if your **h** be wise, my own **h** also will rejoice;
Prv	23:17	Let not your **h** emulate sinners,
Prv	23:26	My son, give me your **h**, and let
Prv	24:17	he stumbles, let not your **h** exult,
Prv	27:19	so does one human **h** from another.
Eccl	2:10	my **h** rejoiced in the fruit of all my
Eccl	5: 1	let not your **h** be quick to make
Eccl	7: 7	man, and a bribe corrupts the **h**.
Eccl	9: 7	and drink your wine with a merry **h**,
Song	4: 9	You have ravished my **h**, my sister,
Song	5: 2	I was sleeping, but my **h** kept vigil;
Song	8: 6	Set me as a seal on your **h**,
Sir	2: 2	Be sincere of **h** and steadfast,
Sir	21: 6	who fears the LORD repents in his **h**.
Is	51: 7	you people who have my teaching at **h**:
Is	66:14	you see this, your **h** shall rejoice,
Jer	3:15	over you shepherds after my own **h**,
Jer	4:14	Cleanse your **h** of evil, O Jerusalem,
Jer	9:25	of Israel, are uncircumcised in **h**.
Jer	17: 9	than all else is the human **h**,
Jer	17:10	and test the **h**, To reward everyone
Jer	24: 7	return to me with their whole **h**.
Jer	29:13	when you seek me with all your **h**,
Jer	32:39	One **h** and one way I will give them,
Jer	32:41	in this land, with all my **h** and soul.
Ez	11:19	I will give them a new **h** and put
Ez	11:19	I will remove the stony **h** from their
Ez	11:19	and replace it with a natural **h**,
Ez	18:31	make for yourselves a new **h**
Ez	28: 2	Because you are haughty of **h**,
Ez	36:26	I will give you a new **h** and place
Ez	44: 7	uncircumcised both in **h** and flesh,
Dn	3:39	with contrite **h** and humble spirit
Hos	11: 8	Zeboiim? My **h** is overwhelmed,
Jl	2:12	return to me with your whole **h**,
Zep	3:14	Be glad and exult with all your **h**,
Mal	2: 2	And if you do not lay it to **h**, to give
Mt	5: 8	Blessed are the clean of **h**, for they
Mt	5:28	adultery with her in his **h**.
Mt	6:21	treasure is, there also will your **h** be.
Mt	11:29	me, for I am meek and humble of **h**;
Mt	12:34	fullness of the **h** the mouth speaks.
Mt	13:15	Gross is the **h** of this people,
Mt	15:19	For from the **h** come evil thoughts,
Mt	18:35	you forgives his brother from his **h**."
Mt	22:37	with all your **h**, with all your soul,
Mk	11:23	does not doubt in his **h** but believes
Mk	12:30	the Lord your God with all your **h**,
Lk	2:19	things, reflecting on them in her **h**.
Lk	2:51	mother kept all these things in her **h**.
Lk	6:45	of goodness in his **h** produces good,
Lk	6:45	fullness of the **h** the mouth speaks.
Lk	8:15	it with a generous and good **h**,
Lk	10:27	with all your **h**, with all your being,
Lk	12:34	treasure is, there also will your **h** be.
Lk	24:25	How slow of **h** to believe all
Acts	2:46	meals with exultation and sincerity of **h**,
Acts	4:32	of believers was of one **h** and mind,
Acts	5: 3	why has Satan filled your **h** so
Acts	8:21	for your **h** is not upright before God.
Acts	15: 8	who knows the **h**, bore witness
Acts	16:14	and the Lord opened her **h** to pay
Acts	28:27	Gross is the **h** of this people;
Rom	2:29	and circumcision is of the **h**,

Rom	10: 8	in your mouth and in your **h**" (that is,
Rom	10: 9	in your **h** that God raised him
1 Cor	14:25	secrets of his **h** will be disclosed,
2 Cor	2: 4	and anguish of **h** I wrote to you
Eph	6: 5	in sincerity of **h**, as to Christ,
Eph	6: 6	doing the will of God from the **h**,
Phil	1: 7	because I hold you in my **h**,
1 Tm	1: 5	instruction is love from a pure **h**,
2 Tm	2:22	call on the Lord with purity of **h**.
Phlm	1:12	him, that is, my own **h**, back to you.
Heb	3:12	may have an evil and unfaithful **h**,
Heb	4:12	reflections and thoughts of the **h**.
Heb	10:22	let us approach with a sincere **h**
Heb	12: 5	or lose **h** when reproved by him;
1 Pt	1:22	another intensely from a [pure] **h**.

HEART'S → HEART

| Ps | 37: 4 | the LORD who will give you your **h** desire. |
| Rom | 10: 1 | my **h** desire and prayer to God |

HEARTLESS → HEART

| Rom | 1:31 | are senseless, faithless, **h**, ruthless. |

HEARTS → HEART

Dt	29:17	who would now turn away their **h**
Dt	30:14	in your mouths and in your **h**;
Jos	24:23	you and turn your **h** to the LORD,
1 Sm	10:26	by warriors whose **h** the LORD had
1 Kgs	8:39	You who alone know the **h** of all
2 Kgs	23: 3	and decrees with their whole **h**
1 Chr	29:18	and direct their **h** toward you.
1 Mc	1:62	and resolved in their **h** not to eat
Jb	1: 5	and blasphemed God in their **h**."
Ps	7:10	of justice, who tries **h** and minds.
Ps	33:15	The one who fashioned the **h**
Ps	95: 8	Do not harden your **h** as at Meribah,
Ps	104:15	and wine to gladden our **h**,
Prv	17: 3	gold, but the tester of **h** is the LORD.
Prv	21: 2	but it is the LORD who proves **h**.
Eccl	9: 3	madness is in their **h** during life;
Sir	48:10	To turn back the **h** of fathers toward
Is	29:13	though their **h** are far from me,
Is	57:15	to revive the **h** of the crushed.
Jer	4: 4	remove the foreskins of your **h**,
Jer	17: 1	upon the tablets of their **h**.
Jer	31:33	them, and write it upon their **h**;
Bar	2:31	I will give them **h**, and heedful ears;
Lam	5:15	The joy of our **h** has ceased,
Ez	14: 3	of their idols fresh in their **h**,
Ez	24:25	the pride of their **h**, their sons and
Mal	3:24	To turn the **h** of the fathers to their
Mal	3:24	the **h** of the children to their fathers,
Mt	15: 8	lips, but their **h** are far from me;
Mk	6:52	the contrary, their **h** were hardened.
Mk	7: 6	lips, but their **h** are far from me;
Lk	1:17	turn the **h** of fathers toward children
Lk	16:15	of others, but God knows your **h**;
Lk	24:32	"Were not our **h** burning [within us]
Jn	14: 1	"Do not let your **h** be troubled.
Jn	14:27	Do not let your **h** be troubled
Acts	1:24	Lord, who know the **h** of all,
Acts	15: 9	for by faith he purified their **h**.
Rom	2:15	of the law are written in their **h**,
Rom	5: 5	into our **h** through the holy Spirit
2 Cor	1:22	Spirit in our **h** as a first installment.
2 Cor	3: 2	written on our **h**, known and read
2 Cor	3: 3	but on tablets that are **h** of flesh.
2 Cor	4: 6	has shone in our **h** to bring to light
Eph	1:18	the eyes of [your] **h** be enlightened,
Eph	3:17	may dwell in your **h** through faith;
Phil	4: 7	all understanding will guard your **h**
Col	3:15	the peace of Christ control your **h**,
Col	3:16	with gratitude in your **h** to God.
1 Thes	2: 4	but rather God, who judges our **h**.
1 Thes	3:13	so as to strengthen your **h**, to be
2 Thes	2:17	encourage your **h** and strengthen
Phlm	1: 7	because the **h** of the holy ones have
Heb	3: 8	'Harden not your **h** as
Heb	8:10	and I will write them upon their **h**.
Heb	10:16	"I will put my laws in their **h**, and I

Heb	10:22	with our **h** sprinkled clean
Jas	4: 8	and purify your **h**, you of two
1 Pt	3:15	sanctify Christ as Lord in your **h**.
2 Pt	1:19	and the morning star rises in your **h**.
2 Pt	2:14	and their **h** are trained in greed.
1 Jn	3:20	in whatever our **h** condemn, for God is greater than our **h**
Rv	2:23	to know that I am the searcher of **h**

HEAT → HEATED

Gn	8:22	cold and **h**, Summer and winter,
Ps	19: 7	to the other; nothing escapes its **h**.
Dn	3:66	Fire and **h**, bless the Lord;
Rv	16: 9	were burned by the scorching **h**

HEATED → HEAT

| Dn | 3:19 | to be **h** seven times more than usual |

HEAVEN → HEAVENLY, HEAVENS

Gn	14:19	High, the creator of **h** and earth;
Gn	21:17	messenger called to Hagar from **h**:
Gn	22:11	messenger called to him from **h**,
Gn	24: 3	the God of **h** and the God of earth,
Ex	16: 4	"I will now rain down bread from **h**
Ex	20:22	that I have spoken to you from **h**.
Dt	3:24	For what god in **h** or on earth can
Dt	4:26	I call **h** and earth this day to witness
Dt	26:15	then, from **h**, your holy abode,
Dt	31:28	so may call **h** and earth to witness
Jos	2:11	God, is God in **h** above and on earth
1 Kgs	8:23	there is no God like you in **h**
1 Kgs	22:19	with the whole host of **h** standing
2 Kgs	1:10	And fire came down from **h**
2 Kgs	2: 1	take Elijah up to **h** in a whirlwind,
2 Chr	6:14	there is no god like you in **h**
2 Chr	7:14	I will hear them from **h** and pardon
Ezr	7:12	of the law of the God of **h** (then,
Jdt	5: 8	with divine worship the God of **h**,
1 Mc	2:58	zeal for the law, was taken up to **h**.
1 Mc	3:50	And they cried aloud to **H**:
Jb	16:19	now, behold, my witness is in **h**,
Ps	121: 2	the LORD, the maker of **h** and earth.
Prv	30: 4	Who has gone up to **h** and come
Jer	23:24	Do I not fill both **h** and earth?
Dn	2:19	vision, and he blessed the God of **h**:
Dn	7:13	on the clouds of **h**; When he
Dn	14: 5	but only the living God who made **h**
Mt	3: 2	for the kingdom of **h** is at hand!"
Mt	4:17	for the kingdom of **h** is at hand."
Mt	5:12	for your reward will be great in **h**.
Mt	5:19	be called least in the kingdom of **h**.
Mt	5:19	called greatest in the kingdom of **h**.
Mt	6: 9	Our Father in **h**, hallowed be your
Mt	6:10	your will be done, on earth as in **h**.
Mt	6:20	But store up treasures in **h**,
Mt	7:21	will enter the kingdom of **h**,
Mt	7:21	who does the will of my Father in **h**.
Mt	16:19	you the keys to the kingdom of **h**.
Mt	16:19	bind on earth shall be bound in **h**;
Mt	16:19	loose on earth shall be loosed in **h**."
Mt	18: 3	you will not enter the kingdom of **h**.
Mt	18:18	bind on earth shall be bound in **h**,
Mt	18:18	loose on earth shall be loosed in **h**.
Mt	19:14	the kingdom of **h** belongs to such as
Mt	19:21	and you will have treasure in **h**.
Mt	19:23	is rich to enter the kingdom of **h**.
Mt	23:13	kingdom of **h** before human beings.
Mt	24:35	**H** and earth will pass away, but my
Mt	26:64	and 'coming on the clouds of **h**.' "
Mt	28:18	"All power in **h** and on earth has
Mk	8:11	from him a sign from **h** to test him.
Mk	10:21	and you will have treasure in **h**;
Mk	13:31	**H** and earth will pass away, but my
Mk	14:62	and coming with the clouds of **h**.' "
Lk	3:21	and was praying, **h** was opened
Lk	9:54	to call down fire from **h** to consume
Lk	10:20	your names are written in **h**."
Lk	12:33	an inexhaustible treasure in **h**
Lk	15: 7	**h** over one sinner who repents than
Lk	18:22	and you will have a treasure in **h**.

141

Lk	19:38	Peace in **h** and glory in the highest."
Lk	21:33	**H** and earth will pass away, but my
Lk	24:51	from them and was taken up to **h**.
Jn	3:13	the one who has come down from **h**,
Jn	6:31	'He gave them bread from **h** to eat.' "
Jn	6:38	because I came down from **h** not
Jn	12:28	Then a voice came from **h**, "I have
Acts	1:11	as you have seen him going into **h**."
Acts	7:55	looked up intently to **h** and saw
Rom	10: 6	your heart, 'Who will go up into **h**?"
1 Cor	15:47	earthly; the second man, from **h**.
2 Cor	12: 2	was caught up to the third **h**.
Eph	1:10	things in Christ, in **h** and on earth.
Phil	2:10	of those in **h** and on earth and under
Phil	3:20	But our citizenship is in **h**,
Col	1: 5	of the hope reserved for you in **h**.
Col	1:16	in him were created all things in **h**
Col	4: 1	that you too have a Master in **h**.
1 Thes	1:10	and to await his Son from **h**,
1 Thes	4:16	will come down from **h**,
Heb	9:24	one, but **h** itself, that he might now
Heb	12:23	of the firstborn enrolled in **h**,
1 Pt	1: 4	and unfading, kept in **h** for you
1 Pt	3:22	who has gone into **h** and is
2 Pt	1:18	voice come from **h** while we were
Rv	4: 1	I had a vision of an open door to **h**,
Rv	5:13	I heard every creature in **h**
Rv	11:19	Then God's temple in **h** was opened,
Rv	12: 7	Then war broke out in **h**;
Rv	19: 1	loud voice of a great multitude in **h**,
Rv	19:14	The armies of **h** followed him,
Rv	21: 1	Then I saw a new **h** and a new earth.
Rv	21: 2	coming down out of **h** from God,
Rv	21:10	coming down out of **h** from God.

HEAVENLY → HEAVEN

Mt	5:48	just as your **h** Father is perfect.
Lk	2:13	there was a multitude of the **h** host
2 Cor	5: 2	further clothed with our **h** habitation
2 Tm	4:18	will bring me safe to his **h** kingdom.
Heb	3: 1	sharing in a **h** calling,
Heb	6: 4	tasted the **h** gift and shared
Heb	9:23	for the copies of the **h** things to be
Heb	12:22	of the living God, the **h** Jerusalem,

HEAVENS → HEAVEN

Gn	1: 1	when God created the **h**
Gn	2: 1	Thus the **h** and the earth and all
Gn	28:12	with its top reaching to the **h**;
Dt	10:14	The **h**, even the highest **h**,
Dt	28:12	you his rich treasure house of the **h**,
Dt	33:26	who rides the **h** in his power,
2 Sm	22:10	He inclined the **h** and came down,
1 Kgs	8:27	If the **h** and the highest **h** cannot
2 Kgs	19:15	You have made the **h** and the earth.
Neh	9: 6	you made the **h**, the highest **h**
Jb	38:33	you know the ordinances of the **h**;
Jb	41: 3	come off safe— Who under all the **h**?
Ps	8: 4	When I see your **h**, the work of your
Ps	19: 2	The **h** declare the glory of God;
Ps	33: 6	the LORD's word the **h** were made;
Ps	57: 6	Show yourself over the **h**, God;
Ps	73:25	Whom else have I in the **h**?
Ps	102:26	the **h** are the work of your hands.
Ps	103:11	As the **h** tower over the earth,
Ps	108: 5	For your love towers to the **h**;
Ps	115:16	The **h** belong to the LORD,
Ps	136: 5	Who skillfully made the **h**,
Ps	148: 1	Praise the LORD from the **h**;
Prv	3:19	established the **h** by understanding;
Eccl	3: 1	a time for every affair under the **h**.
Is	1: 2	Hear, O **h**, and listen, O earth,
Is	14:12	How have you fallen from the **h**,
Is	45: 8	descend, O **h**, like dew from above,
Is	51: 6	Though the **h** grow thin like smoke,
Is	55: 9	As high as the **h** are above the earth,
Is	65:17	Lo, I am about to create new **h**
Is	66: 1	says the LORD: The **h** are my throne,
Jer	10:11	the earth, and from beneath these **h**!
Jer	31:37	If the **h** on high can be measured,

Ez	1: 1	by the river Chebar, the **h** opened,
Jl	3: 3	I will work wonders in the **h**
Mt	3:16	the **h** were opened [for him], and he
Acts	7:49	'The **h** are my throne, the earth is my
Acts	7:56	I see the **h** opened and the Son
Eph	4:10	who ascended far above all the **h**,
Heb	4:14	priest who has passed through the **h**,
Heb	7:26	from sinners, higher than the **h**.
2 Pt	3: 5	ignore the fact that the **h** existed
2 Pt	3:10	the **h** will pass away with a mighty
Rv	19:11	Then I saw the **h** opened, and there

HEAVIER → HEAVY

Prv	27: 3	a fool's provocation is **h** than both.

HEAVY → HEAVIER

Ex	18:18	The task is too **h** for you;
1 Kgs	12: 4	"Your father put on us a **h** yoke.
Ps	88: 8	Your wrath lies **h** upon me; all your
Sir	30:13	your son, make **h** his yoke, lest his
Is	47: 6	old men you laid a very **h** yoke.
Mt	23: 4	They tie up **h** burdens [hard

HEBREW → HEBREWS, HEBREWS'

Gn	14:13	brought the news to Abram the **H**,
Gn	41:12	There with us was a **H** youth,
Ex	1:19	"The **H** women are not like
Ex	2:11	he saw an Egyptian striking a **H**,
Ex	21: 2	When you purchase a **H** slave, he is
Sir	Pr: 2	originally in **H** are not as effective
Jer	34: 9	Everyone was to free his **H** slaves,
Jon	1: 9	"I am a **H**," Jonah answered them;
Jn	19:20	and it was written in **H**, Latin,
Acts	21:40	was quiet he addressed them in **H**.
Phil	3: 5	of Benjamin, a **H** of **H** parentage,

HEBREWS → HEBREW

Ex	3:18	the God of the **H**, has sent us word.
Ex	9: 1	says the LORD, the God of the **H**:
Jdt	10:12	"I am a daughter of the **H**, and I am
2 Cor	11:22	Are they **H**? So am I. Are they

HEBREWS' → HEBREW

Ex	2: 6	said, "It is one of the **H** children."

HEBRON → =MAMRE

Gn	13:18	terebinth of Mamre, which is at **H**.
Gn	23: 2	(that is, **H**) in the land of Canaan,
Jos	14:13	and gave him **H** as his heritage.
Jos	20: 7	**H**) in the mountain region of Judah.
Jos	21:13	city of asylum for homicides at **H**,
Jgs	16: 3	to the top of the ridge opposite **H**.
2 Sm	2:11	and six months in **H** as king
2 Sm	3: 2	Sons were born to David in **H**:
1 Chr	2:43	The sons of **H** were Korah,
1 Chr	11: 1	all Israel gathered about David in **H**,

HEDGE

Is	5: 5	Take away its **h**, give it to grazing,
Hos	2: 8	I will **h** in her way with thorns
Mi	7: 4	the most upright like a thorn **h**.

HEED → HEEDING, HEEDS

Eccl	7:21	Do not give **h** to every word that is

HEEDING → HEED

Dt	7:12	"As your reward for **h** these decrees

HEEDS → HEED

Prv	10: 8	A wise man **h** commands,
Prv	10:17	path to life is his who **h** admonition,
Prv	13:18	but he who **h** reproof is honored.
Prv	15: 5	but prudent is he who **h** reproof.

HEEL

Gn	3:15	your head, while you strike at his **h**."
Gn	25:26	came out next, gripping Esau's **h**;
Jb	18: 9	A trap seizes him by the **h**,
Jn	13:18	my food has raised his **h** against me.'

HEIFER

Gn	15: 9	him, "Bring me a three-year-old **h**,
Nm	19: 2	procure for you a red **h** that is free
Jgs	14:18	"If you had not plowed with my **h**,

HEIGHT → HIGH
Nm	23: 3	He went out on the barren h,
Sir	1: 3	Heaven's h, earth's breadth, the depths
Rom	8:39	nor h, nor depth, nor any other
Eph	3:18	breadth and length and h and depth,
Rv	21:16	miles in length and width and h.

HEIGHTS → HIGH
Ps	18:34	as a deer's, set me safe on the h,
Ps	148: 1	the heavens; give praise in the h.
Hb	3:19	and enables me to go upon the h.

HEIR → HEIRS
Gn	15: 4	"No, that one shall not be your h; your own issue shall be your h."
Lk	20:14	said to one another, 'This is the h.
Gal	4: 7	a child, and if a child then also an h,
Heb	1: 2	whom he made h of all things

HEIRS → HEIR
Rom	4:14	who adhere to the law are the h,
Rom	8:17	then h, h of God and joint h
Gal	3:29	h according to the promise.
Ti	3: 7	become h in hope of eternal life.
Heb	11: 9	and Jacob, h of the same promise;
Jas	2: 5	h of the kingdom that he promised
1 Pt	3: 7	since we are joint h of the gift

HELD → HOLD
Col	2:19	and h together by its ligaments
Rv	1:16	In his right hand he h seven stars.
Rv	6: 5	and its rider h a scale in his hand.
Rv	10: 2	In his hand he h a small scroll

HELDAI
Zec	6:14	temple of the Lord in favor of H,

HELIODORUS
2 Mc	3:40	was how the matter concerning H

HELLENISTS
Acts	6: 1	grow, the H complained against
Acts	9:29	also spoke and debated with the H,

HELMET
Ps	108: 9	Ephraim is the h for my head,
Wis	5:18	shall wear sure judgment for a h;
Is	59:17	salvation, as the h on his head;
Eph	6:17	And take the h of salvation
1 Thes	5: 8	and the h that is hope for salvation.

HELP → HELPED, HELPER, HELPERS, HELPLESS, HELPS
Gn	4: 1	a man with the h of the Lord."
Ex	23: 5	h him, rather, to raise it up.
1 Chr	12:23	to David's h until there was a vast
2 Chr	28:16	time King Ahaz sent an appeal for h
Neh	6:16	our God's h that this work had been
Jdt	6:21	called upon the God of Israel for h.
Ps	22:20	my strength, come quickly to h me.
Ps	33:20	the Lord, who is our h and shield.
Ps	40:18	You are my h and deliverer;
Ps	46: 2	an ever-present h in distress.
Ps	79: 9	H us, God our savior, for the glory
Ps	108:13	the foe; worthless is human h.
Ps	115: 9	the Lord, who is their h and shield.
Ps	121: 1	From where will my h come?
Ps	146: 5	Happy those whose h is Jacob's
Sir	2: 6	Trust God and he will h you;
Sir	29: 9	Because of the precept, h the needy,
Is	41:10	I will strengthen you, and h you,
Lam	1: 7	and she had no one to h her;
Mk	9:24	out, "I do believe, h my unbelief!"
Acts	16: 9	"Come over to Macedonia and h us."
Acts	26:22	I have enjoyed God's h to this very
Heb	2:18	able to h those who are being tested.
Heb	4:16	and to find grace for timely h.

HELPED → HELP
1 Sm	7:12	"To this point has the Lord h us."
Lk	1:54	He has h Israel his servant,
2 Cor	6: 2	and on the day of salvation I h you."

HELPER → HELP
Ps	30:11	have mercy on me; Lord, be my h."

Sir	40:24	A brother, a h, for times of stress;
Heb	13: 6	"The Lord is my h, [and] I will not

HELPLESS → HELP
Ps	10:14	To you the h can entrust their cause;

HELPS → HELP
Ps	37:40	The Lord h and rescues them,

HEM
Lk	19:43	you and h you in on all sides.

HEMAN
1 Chr	15:19	The chanters, H, Asaph, and Ethan,
Ps	88: 1	singing; a *maskil* of H the Ezrahite.

HEMORRHAGES
Lk	8:43	a woman afflicted with h for twelve

HEN
Mt	23:37	as a h gathers her young under her
Lk	13:34	together as a h gathers her brood

HERALD
Is	40: 9	Jerusalem, h of good news!
2 Pt	2: 5	Noah, a h of righteousness,

HERBS
Ex	12: 8	with unleavened bread and bitter h.
Nm	9:11	with unleavened bread and bitter h,

HERD → HERDS
Mt	8:31	us out, send us into the h of swine."

HERDS → HERD
Dt	8:13	have increased your h and flocks,
Dt	12: 6	the firstlings of your h and flocks.
2 Sm	12: 4	h to prepare a meal for the wayfarer

HERE
Ex	3: 4	Moses!" He answered, "H I am."
1 Sm	3: 4	to Samuel, who answered, "H I am."
Ps	40: 8	so I said, "H I am; your commands
Prv	9: 4	"Let whoever is simple turn in h;
Is	6: 8	go for us?" "H I am;" I said; "send me!"
Is	40: 9	the cities of Judah: H is your God!
Mt	12:42	something greater than Solomon h.
Mt	24:23	to you then, 'Look, h is the Messiah!'
Mk	16: 6	He has been raised; he is not h.
Rv	4: 1	"Come up h and I will show you
Rv	11:12	heaven say to them, "Come up h."

HERITAGE
Jdt	9:12	God of the h of Israel,
Ps	119:111	Your decrees are my h forever;

HERMON
Dt	3: 8	from the Wadi Arnon to Mount H
Ps	133: 3	Like dew of H coming down

HEROD → HERODIANS
1. King of Judea who tried to kill Jesus (Mt 2; Lk 1:5).
2. Son of 1. Tetrarch of Galilee who arrested and beheaded John the Baptist (Mt 14:1-12; Mk 6:14-29; Lk 3:1, 19-20; 9:7-9); tried Jesus (Lk 23:6-15).
3. Grandson of 1. King of Judea who killed James (Acts 12:2); arrested Peter (Acts 12:3-19). Death (Acts 12:19-23).

HERODIANS → HEROD
Mt	22:16	disciples to him, with the H, saying,
Mk	3: 6	took counsel with the H against him
Mk	12:13	and H to him to ensnare him in his

HERODIAS
Wife of Herod the Tetrarch who persuaded her daughter to ask for John the Baptist's head (Mt 14:1-12; Mk 6:14-29; Lk 3:19).

HEROES
Gn	6: 4	They were the h of old, the men

HESHBON
Nm	21:26	Now H was the capital of Sihon,
Dt	3: 6	king of H, so also here we doomed

HEWN
Is	51: 1	to the rock from which you were h,
Mk	15:46	in a tomb that had been h

HEZEKIAH
King of Judah (Sir 48:17-25). Restored the temple and worship (2 Chr 29-31). Sought the LORD for help against Assyria (2 Kgs 18-19; 2 Chr 32:1-23; Is 36-37). Illness healed (2 Kgs 20:1-11; 2 Chr 32:24-26; Is 38). Judged for showing Babylonians his treasures (2 Kgs 20:12-21; 2 Chr 32:31; Is 39).

HEZRON
Ru	4:18	of Perez: Perez was the father of H,
Mt	1: 3	Perez became the father of H,

HID →HIDE
Gn	3: 8	his wife h themselves from the LORD
Ex	2: 2	child, she h him for three months.
Ex	3: 6	Moses h his face, for he was afraid
Jos	6:17	because she h the messengers we
1 Kgs	18:13	of the LORD—that I h a hundred
2 Chr	22:11	h the child from Athaliah's sight,
2 Mc	1:19	h it secretly in the hollow of a dry
Is	49: 2	arrow, in his quiver he h me.
Is	54: 8	for a moment I h my face from you;
Ez	39:23	me, and I h my face from them

HIDDEN →HIDE
Jos	2: 6	and h them among her stalks of flax
Jos	7:22	to the tent and found them h there,
2 Kgs	11: 3	For six years he remained h
Jb	28:11	streams, and brings h things to light.
Ps	69: 6	folly; my faults are not h from you.
Ps	142: 4	I walk they have h a trap for me.
Prv	2: 4	and like h treasures search her out:
Prv	27: 5	rebuke than a love that remains h.
Is	40:27	Israel, "My way is h from the LORD,
Dn	2:22	He reveals deep and h things
Mt	13:35	I will announce what has lain h
Mk	4:22	there is nothing h except to be made
Lk	10:21	for although you have h these things
Lk	18:34	the word remained h from them
1 Cor	2: 7	wisdom, mysterious, h, which God
1 Cor	4: 5	bring to light what is h in darkness
Eph	3: 9	plan of the mystery h from ages past
Col	1:26	the mystery h from ages
Col	2: 3	in whom are h all the treasures
Col	3: 3	your life is h with Christ in God.
Rv	2:17	I shall give some of the h manna;

HIDE →HID, HIDDEN
Gn	18:17	"Shall I h from Abraham what I am
Ex	2: 3	When she could h him no longer,
Dt	31:17	them and h my face from them,
Ps	13: 2	How long will you h your face
Ps	17: 8	h me in the shadow of your wings
Ps	27: 5	For God will h me in his shelter
Sir	4:23	time, and h not away your wisdom;
Is	53: 3	those from whom men h their faces,
Ez	39:29	No longer will I h my face
Rv	6:16	h us from the face of the one who

HIGH →HEIGHT, HEIGHTS, HIGHER, HIGHEST, HIGHLY, HIGHWAY
Gn	14:18	and being a priest of God Most H,
Gn	14:22	God Most H, the creator of heaven
1 Kgs	3: 2	were sacrificing on the h places,
1 Kgs	11: 7	then built a h place to Chemosh,
1 Kgs	12:31	built temples on the h places
Ps	7: 8	sit on your throne h above them,
Ps	21: 8	firm through the love of the Most H.
Ps	46: 5	the holy dwelling of the Most H.
Ps	82: 6	offspring of the Most H all of you,
Ps	91: 1	dwell in the shelter of the Most H,
Ps	113: 5	the LORD, our God enthroned on h,
Wis	5:15	thought of them is with the Most H.
Sir	35: 9	Give to the Most H as he has given
Is	14:14	clouds; I will be like the Most H!"
Jer	2:20	On every h hill, under every green
Mt	4: 8	took him up to a very h mountain,
Mt	17: 1	and led them up a h mountain
Mk	5: 7	me, Jesus, Son of the Most H God?
Mk	14:53	They led Jesus away to the h priest,
Jn	18:22	the way you answer the h priest?"
Acts	23: 4	"Would you revile God's h priest?"

Eph	4: 8	it says: "He ascended on h and took
Heb	2:17	and faithful h priest before God
Heb	7: 1	of Salem and priest of God Most H,"
Heb	7:26	that we should have such a h priest:

HIGHER →HIGH
Dt	28:43	alien residing among you will rise h and h above you,

HIGHEST →HIGH
1 Kgs	8:27	the h heavens cannot contain you,
Mt	21: 9	name of the Lord; hosanna in the h."
Lk	2:14	"Glory to God in the h and on earth
Lk	19:38	Peace in heaven and glory in the h."

HIGHLY →HIGH
Rom	12: 3	of himself more h than one ought

HIGHWAY →HIGH, WAY
Is	40: 3	in the wasteland a h for our God!

HILKIAH
2 Kgs	22:10	the priest H had given him a book,
2 Chr	34:14	H the priest found the book

HILL →HILLS
Ex	17: 9	on top of the h with the staff of God
1 Kgs	16:24	then bought the h of Samaria
Is	40: 4	mountain and h shall be made low;
Lk	3: 5	mountain and h shall be made low.

HILLS →HILL
Ps	114: 6	You h, like lambs of the flock?
Prv	8:25	before the h, I was brought forth;
Is	2: 2	and raised above the h. All nations
Hos	10: 8	us!" and to the h, "Fall upon us!"
Jl	4:18	and the h shall flow with milk;
Am	9:13	and all the h shall run with it.
Lk	23:30	upon us!' and to the h, 'Cover us!'

HINDER →HINDERED, HINDRANCE
Acts	11:17	who was I to be able to h God?"

HINDERED →HINDER
1 Pt	3: 7	so that your prayers may not be h.

HINDRANCE →HINDER
Acts	28:31	and without h he proclaimed
Rom	14:13	block or h in the way of a brother.

HINGES
Prv	26:14	The door turns on its h,

HIP
Gn	32:26	him, he struck Jacob's h at its socket,

HIRAM →=HURAM, =HURAM-ABI
King of Tyre; helped David build his palace (2 Sm 5:11-12; 1 Chr 14:1); helped Solomon build the temple (1 Kgs 5; 2 Chr 2) and his navy (1 Kgs 9:10-27; 2 Chr 8).

HIRE →HIRED, HIRES
Mt	20: 1	dawn to h laborers for his vineyard.

HIRED →HIRE
Dt	23: 5	and because Moab h Balaam,
1 Mc	5:39	they have also h Arabs to help them,
Lk	15:15	So he h himself out to one
Jn	10:12	A h man, who is not a shepherd

HIRES →HIRE
Prv	26:10	pass by is he who h a drunken fool.

HITTITE →HITTITES
Gn	23:10	Hittites. So Ephron the H replied
Gn	27:46	also should marry a H woman,
2 Sm	11: 3	[Joab's armor-bearer] Uriah the H."
2 Sm	11:17	and among them Uriah the H died.
Ez	16: 3	an Amorite and your mother a H.

HITTITES →HITTITE
Gn	25:10	Abraham had bought from the H;
Dt	20:17	You must doom them all—the H,
Ezr	9: 1	their abominations [Canaanites, H,
Neh	9: 8	the land of the Canaanites, H,

HIVITE →HIVITES
Gn	34: 2	son of Hamor the H, who was chief

HIVITES →HIVITE
Ex	23:28	I will send hornets to drive the **H**,
Jos	9: 7	the men of Israel replied to the **H**,

HOBAB
Nm	10:29	Moses said to his brother-in-law **H**,
Jgs	4:11	the descendants of **H**,

HOLD →HELD, HOLDING, HOLDS
Ps	73:23	you take **h** of my right hand.
Ps	139:10	guide me, your right hand **h** me fast.
Prv	4: 4	me: "Let your heart **h** fast my words:
Sir	21:14	jar— no knowledge at all can it **h**.
Zec	8:23	take **h** of every Jew by the edge
Acts	7:60	"Lord, do not **h** this sin against them";
1 Cor	15: 2	if you **h** fast to the word I preached
Phil	2:16	as you **h** on to the word of life,
Col	1:17	and in him all things **h** together.
2 Thes	2:15	**h** fast to the traditions that you were
1 Tm	6:12	Lay **h** of eternal life, to which you
Heb	3:14	Christ if only we **h** the beginning
Heb	4:14	God, let us **h** fast to our confession.
Heb	10:23	Let us **h** unwaveringly to our

HOLDING →HOLD
Ex	9: 2	to let them go and persist in **h** them,
Dt	13: 5	serving him and **h** fast to him alone.
Jn	20:17	Jesus said to her, "Stop **h** on to me,
Col	2:19	and not **h** closely to the head,
1 Tm	3: 9	**h** fast to the mystery of the faith

HOLDS →HOLD
Ps	37:24	never fall, for the LORD **h** their hand.
Prv	3:18	her, and he is happy who **h** her fast.
Rv	2: 1	" 'The one who **h** the seven stars

HOLE →HOLES
Ps	7:16	They open a **h** and dig it deep,

HOLES →HOLE
Hg	1: 6	earned them for a bag with **h** in it.

HOLIES →HOLY
Heb	9: 3	the tabernacle called the Holy of **H**,

HOLINESS →HOLY
Ex	15:11	is like to you, magnificent in **h**?
Ps	89:36	By my **h** I swore once for all: I will
Ps	93: 5	**h** belongs to your house, LORD,
Wis	9: 3	To govern the world in **h**
Ez	20:41	you I will manifest my **h** in the sight
Ez	36:23	I will prove the **h** of my great name,
Ez	38:23	I will prove my greatness and **h**
Am	4: 2	The Lord GOD has sworn by his **h**:
Lk	1:75	in **h** and righteousness before him
Rom	1: 4	the spirit of **h** through resurrection
2 Cor	7: 1	making **h** perfect in the fear of God.
Eph	4:24	way in righteousness and **h** of truth.
1 Thes	4: 7	did not call us to impurity but to **h**.
1 Tm	2:15	persevere in faith and love and **h**,
Heb	12:10	in order that we may share his **h**.
Heb	12:14	that **h** without which no one will see
2 Pt	3:11	be, conducting yourselves in **h**

HOLLOW
Ex	27: 8	altar itself in the form of a **h** box,

HOLOCAUST →HOLOCAUSTS
Gn	22: 2	you shall offer him up as a **h**
Gn	22: 8	"God himself will provide the sheep for the **h**."
Ex	18:12	father-in-law of Moses, brought a **h**
Ex	29:18	altar, since it is a **h**, a sweet-smelling
Lv	1: 3	"If his **h** offering is from the herd,
Jgs	6:26	offer it as a **h** on the wood
Jgs	13:16	you may offer a **h** to the LORD."
2 Chr	7: 1	fire came down from heaven and consumed the **h**
Ez	46:13	He shall offer as a daily **h** to the LORD

HOLOCAUSTS →HOLOCAUST
Gn	8:20	he offered **h** on the altar.
Ex	10:25	"You must also grant us sacrifices and **h**
Ex	40: 6	Put the altar of **h** in front of
Dt	12: 6	there you shall bring your **h** and sacrifices,
Jos	8:31	On this altar they offered **h**

Jos	22:26	not for **h** or for sacrifices,
1 Sm	15:22	"Does the LORD so delight in **h**
1 Kgs	3: 4	its altar Solomon offered a thousand **h**.
1 Kgs	10: 5	the **h** he offered in the temple
Ezr	3: 2	to offer on it the **h** prescribed
Ezr	8:35	offered as **h** to the God of Israel
Jdt	16:18	they offered their **h**, free-will
1 Mc	1:45	to prohibit **h**, sacrifices, and libations
1 Mc	1:54	the horrible abomination upon the altar of **h**,
1 Mc	4:56	and joyfully offered **h** and sacrifices
Jb	1: 5	and offering **h** for every one of them.
Ps	40: 7	**H** and sin-offerings you do not require;
1 Mc	4:44	what ought to be done with the altar of **h**
Is	40:16	nor its animals be enough for **h**.
Jer	6:20	Your **h** find no favor with me,
Ez	43:18	set up for the offering of **h** upon it
Hos	6: 6	and knowledge of God rather than **h**.
Mi	6: 6	Shall I come before him with **h**,
Heb	10: 6	**h** and sin offerings you took no delight in.

HOLOFERNES
Assyrian general (Jdt 2:4). Beguiled and beheaded by Judith (Jdt 10-13).

HOLY →HOLIES, HOLINESS
Ex	3: 5	place where you stand is **h** ground.
Ex	19: 6	me a kingdom of priests, a **h** nation.
Ex	20: 8	to keep **h** the sabbath day.
Ex	26:33	which divides the **h** place from the **h**
Lv	11:44	shall make and keep yourselves **h**, because I am **h**.
Lv	19: 2	Be **h**, for I, the LORD, your God, am **h**.
Nm	16: 7	the LORD then chooses is the **h** one.
Dt	5:12	keep **h** the sabbath day as the LORD,
Dt	23:15	your mercy, your camp must be **h**;
Dt	26:15	from heaven, your **h** abode,
Jos	5:15	on which you are standing is **h**."
Jos	24:19	to serve the LORD, for he is a **h** God;
1 Sm	2: 2	There is no **H** One like the LORD;
1 Sm	6:20	stand in the presence of this **H** One?
2 Kgs	4: 9	"I know that he is a **h** man of God.
1 Chr	16:10	Glory in his **h** name; rejoice,
1 Chr	16:35	we may give thanks to your **h** name
1 Chr	29: 3	all that I stored up for the **h** house,
2 Chr	3: 8	made the room of the **h** of holies.
2 Chr	30:27	reached heaven, God's **h** dwelling.
Ezr	9: 2	thus they have desecrated the **h** race
Neh	11: 1	to reside in Jerusalem, the **h** city,
Tb	11:14	and blessed be all his **h** angels. May his **h** name be praised
1 Mc	1:15	and abandoned the **h** covenant;
Jb	6:10	the commands of the **H** One.
Ps	2: 6	my king on Zion, my **h** mountain."
Ps	5: 8	I can worship in your **h** temple
Ps	11: 4	The LORD is in his **h** temple;
Ps	22: 4	you are enthroned as the **H** One;
Ps	24: 3	LORD? Who can stand in his **h** place?
Ps	30: 5	give thanks to God's **h** name.
Ps	33:21	rejoice; in your **h** name we trust.
Ps	47: 9	nations; God sits upon his **h** throne.
Ps	77:14	Your way, O God, is **h**; what god is
Ps	78:54	He brought them to his **h** land,
Ps	89: 6	in the assembly of the **h** ones.
Ps	89:19	the **H** One of Israel, our king!
Ps	99: 3	great and awesome name: **h** is God!
Ps	99: 9	bow down before his **h** mountain;
Ps	105: 3	Glory in his **h** name; rejoice.
Ps	111: 9	**h** and awesome is your name.
Prv	9:10	of the **H** One is understanding.
Wis	3:19	grace and mercy are with his **h** ones
Wis	6:10	who keep the **h** precepts hallowed shall be found **h**,
Is	1: 4	LORD, spurned the **H** One of Israel,
Is	5:16	God the **H** shall be shown **h** by his
Is	6: 3	"**H**, **h**, **h** is the LORD of hosts!"
Is	6:13	fallen. [**H** offspring is the trunk.]
Is	29:23	They shall keep my name **h**; they shall reverence the **H** One
Is	40:25	me as an equal? says the **H** One.
Is	43: 3	the **H** One of Israel, your savior.
Is	52:10	The LORD has bared his **h** arm

Is	54: 5	Your redeemer is the H One
Is	57:15	eternally, whose name is the H One:
Is	58:13	and the Lord's h day honorable;
Jer	17:22	but keep h the sabbath, as I
Ez	22:26	my law and profane what is h to me;
Ez	36:20	they served to profane my h name,
Dn	3:52	blessed is your h and glorious name,
Dn	8:13	I heard a h one speaking,
Dn	9:24	for your people and for your h city:
Dn	9:24	and a most h will be anointed.
Dn	11:28	his mind set against the h covenant;
Jon	2: 5	I again look upon your h temple."
Hb	2:20	But the Lord is in his h temple;
Zec	8: 3	the Lord of hosts, the h mountain.
Zec	14: 5	come, and all his h ones with him.
Zec	14:20	bells of the horses, "H to the Lord."
Mt	1:18	with child through the h Spirit.
Mt	3:11	He will baptize you with the h Spirit
Mt	4: 5	the devil took him to the h city,
Mt	24:15	in the h place (let the reader
Mt	28:19	and of the Son, and of the h Spirit,
Mk	1:24	I know who you are—the H One
Mk	3:29	blasphemes against the h Spirit will
Lk	1:15	will be filled with the h Spirit even
Lk	1:35	"The h Spirit will come upon you,
Lk	1:35	the child to be born will be called h,
Lk	1:49	things for me, and h is his name.
Lk	3:22	the h Spirit descended upon him
Lk	4: 1	Filled with the h Spirit,
Lk	10:21	moment he rejoiced [in] the h Spirit
Lk	11:13	in heaven give the h Spirit to those
Jn	6:69	that you are the H One of God."
Jn	14:26	the h Spirit that the Father will send
Jn	20:22	said to them, "Receive the h Spirit.
Acts	1: 5	will be baptized with the h Spirit."
Acts	2: 4	they were all filled with the h Spirit
Acts	2:27	nor will you suffer your h one to see
Acts	2:38	will receive the gift of the h Spirit.
Acts	4:27	this city against your h servant Jesus
Acts	5: 3	heart so that you lied to the h Spirit
Acts	8:15	that they might receive the h Spirit,
Acts	10:44	the h Spirit fell upon all who were
Acts	13:35	'You will not suffer your h one
Acts	15: 8	granting them the h Spirit just as he
Acts	19: 2	"Did you receive the h Spirit
Acts	19: 2	even heard that there is a h Spirit."
Rom	1: 2	his prophets in the h scriptures,
Rom	7:12	So then the law is h, and the commandment is h
Rom	11:16	If the firstfruits are h, so is
Rom	11:16	and if the root is h, so are
Rom	12: 1	sacrifice, h and pleasing to God,
Rom	15:16	sanctified by the h Spirit.
Rom	16:16	Greet one another with a h kiss.
1 Cor	7:14	husband is made h through his wife,
1 Cor	7:14	wife is made h through the brother.
1 Cor	16:20	Greet one another with a h kiss.
Eph	1: 4	to be h and without blemish before
Eph	3: 5	now been revealed to his h apostles
Eph	4:30	do not grieve the h Spirit of God,
Col	1:22	to present you h, without blemish,
Col	3:12	God's chosen ones, h and beloved,
1 Tm	2: 8	lifting up h hands, without anger
2 Tm	1: 9	He saved us and called us to a h life,
Ti	3: 5	rebirth and renewal by the h Spirit,
Heb	2: 4	the gifts of the h Spirit according
Heb	6: 4	gift and shared in the h Spirit
Heb	7:26	h, innocent, undefiled,
Heb	9: 2	offering; this is called the H Place.
1 Pt	1:15	but, as he who called you is h, be h
1 Pt	1:16	it is written, "Be h because I [am] h."
1 Pt	2: 5	be a h priesthood to offer spiritual
1 Pt	2: 9	a royal priesthood, a h nation,
1 Pt	3: 5	how the h women who hoped
2 Pt	1:21	by the h Spirit spoke under
1 Jn	2:20	that comes from the h one, and you
Jude	1:14	has come with his countless h ones
Jude	1:20	yourselves up in your most h faith; pray in the h Spirit.
Rv	3: 7	write this: " 'The h one, the true,

Rv	4: 8	"H, h, h is the Lord God almighty,
Rv	11: 2	who will trample the h city
Rv	15: 4	For you alone are h. All the nations
Rv	20: 6	h is the one who shares in the first
Rv	21: 2	I also saw the h city, a new
Rv	21:10	and showed me the h city Jerusalem
Rv	22:11	still do right, and the h still be h."
Rv	22:19	in the h city described in this book."

HOME → HOMELAND, HOMELESS, HOMES

Dt	6: 7	Speak of them at h and abroad,
Dt	11:19	speaking of them at h and abroad,
1 Chr	16:43	each to his own h, and David
Ps	68: 7	Who gives a h to the forsaken,
Ps	84: 4	As the sparrow finds a h
Ps	113: 9	Gives the childless wife a h,
Prv	7:11	unruly, in her h her feet cannot rest;
Prv	27: 8	nest is a man who is far from his h.
Eccl	12: 5	Because man goes to his lasting h,
Hg	1: 9	and what you brought h, I blew
Mk	2:11	rise, pick up your mat, and go h."
Mk	5:19	"Go h to your family and announce
Jn	19:27	hour the disciple took her into his h.
Acts	16:15	come and stay at my h," and she
1 Cor	11:34	he should eat at h, so that your
2 Cor	5: 8	leave the body and go h to the Lord.

HOMELAND → HOME, LAND

Heb	11:14	thus show that they are seeking a h.

HOMELESS → HOME

Is	58: 7	sheltering the oppressed and the h;
1 Cor	4:11	roughly treated, we wander about h

HOMES → HOME

Nm	32:18	not return to our h until every one
Neh	4: 8	daughters, your wives and your h."
Ps	49:12	Tombs are their h forever,
Hos	11:11	And I will resettle them in their h,

HOMICIDE

Dt	4:42	that a h might take refuge there if he

HONEST → HONESTY

Lv	19:36	weights, an h ephah and an h hin.

HONESTY → HONEST

Gn	30:33	of mine, let my h testify against me:

HONEY → HONEYCOMB

Ex	3: 8	a land flowing with milk and h,
Ex	16:31	it tasted like wafers made with h.
Nm	14: 8	a land flowing with milk and h.
Jgs	14: 8	of bees and h in the lion's carcass.
Ps	19:11	Sweeter also than h or drippings
Ps	119:103	sweeter than h to my mouth!
Prv	5: 3	lips of an adulteress drip with h,
Prv	25:16	If you find h, eat only what you
Song	4:11	Your lips drip h, my bride,
Is	7:15	h by the time he learns to reject
Ez	3: 3	it was as sweet as h in my mouth.
Mt	3: 4	His food was locusts and wild h.
Rv	10: 9	mouth it will taste as sweet as h."

HONEYCOMB → HONEY

Prv	16:24	Pleasing words are a h,

HONOR → HONORABLE, HONORED, HONORING, HONORS

Ex	20:12	"H your father and your mother,
Dt	5:16	'H your father and your mother,
1 Sm	2:30	for I will h those who h me,
1 Chr	29:12	"Riches and h are from you, and you
Tb	4: 3	H your mother, and do not abandon
Ps	8: 6	crowned them with glory and h.
Ps	112: 9	their horn shall be exalted in h.
Prv	3: 9	H the Lord with your wealth,
Prv	3:35	H is the possession of wise men,
Prv	22: 4	fear of the Lord is riches, h and life.
Prv	25:27	is not good; nor to seek h after h.
Prv	29:23	he who is humble of spirit obtains h.
Sir	7:31	H God and respect the priest;
Mal	1: 6	a father, where is the h due to me?

Mt	13:57	"A prophet is not without **h** except
Mt	15: 4	said, 'H your father and your mother,'
Mt	19:19	**h** your father and your mother';
Mt	23: 6	They love places of **h** at banquets, seats of **h** in synagogues,
Mk	6: 4	"A prophet is not without **h** except
Lk	14: 8	not recline at table in the place of **h**.
Jn	4:44	that a prophet has no **h** in his native
Jn	5:23	all may **h** the Son just as they **h**
Jn	5:23	Whoever does not **h** the Son does not **h** the Father who
Jn	8:49	I **h** my Father, but you dishonor me.
Jn	12:26	The Father will **h** whoever serves
Rom	12:10	anticipate one another in showing **h**.
Rom	13: 7	respect is due, **h** to whom **h** is due.
1 Cor	12:23	we surround with greater **h**, and our
Eph	6: 2	"H your father and mother." This is
1 Tm	5:17	who preside well deserve double **h**,
Heb	2: 7	you crowned him with glory and **h**,
Heb	3: 3	a house has more "**h**" than the house
1 Pt	1: 7	**h** at the revelation of Jesus Christ.
2 Pt	1:17	For he received **h** and glory
Rv	4: 9	the living creatures give glory and **h**
Rv	4:11	to receive glory and **h** and power,
Rv	5:12	strength, **h** and glory and blessing."
Rv	7:12	thanksgiving, **h**, power, and might

HONORABLE →HONOR
Phil	4: 8	true, whatever is **h**, whatever is just,

HONORED →HONOR
Prv	13:18	but he who heeds reproof is **h**.
1 Cor	12:26	if one part is **h**, all the parts share its

HONORING →HONOR
2 Sm	10: 3	"Do you think that David is **h** your father

HONORS →HONOR
Prv	15:33	and humility goes before **h**.
Prv	18:12	haughty, but humility goes before **h**.
Sir	3: 3	He who **h** his father atones for sins;
Is	· 29:13	only and **h** me with their lips alone,
Mal	1: 6	A son **h** his father, and a servant
Mt	15: 8	This people **h** me with their lips,

HOOFS
Lv	11: 3	any animal that has **h** you may eat,
Dt	14: 6	Any animal that has **h** you may eat,

HOOK →HOOKS
Is	37:29	ears, I will put my **h** in your nose
Mt	17:27	drop in a **h**, and take the first fish

HOOKS →HOOK
Ex	26:37	with gold, with their **h** of gold;
Is	2: 4	and their spears into pruning **h**;
Jl	4:10	and your pruning **h** into spears;
Am	4: 2	they shall drag you away with **h**,
Mi	4: 3	and their spears into pruning **h**;

HOPE →HOPED, HOPES, HOPING
Ezr	10: 2	Yet even now there remains a **h**
Jdt	9:11	the savior of those without **h**.
Jb	17:15	Where then is my **h**, and my
Ps	9:19	nor will the **h** of the afflicted ever
Ps	33:18	those who **h** for his gracious help,
Ps	39: 8	do I have? You are my only **h**.
Ps	62: 6	alone, from whom comes my **h**.
Ps	65: 6	The **h** of all the ends of the earth
Ps	71:14	I will always **h** in you and add to all
Ps	119:43	mouth, for in your edicts is my **h**.
Ps	146: 5	whose **h** is in the LORD, their God,
Prv	11: 7	a wicked man dies his **h** perishes,
Prv	13:12	H deferred makes the heart sick,
Prv	23:18	and your **h** will not be cut off.
Prv	24:14	and your **h** will not be cut off.
Prv	26:12	There is more **h** for a fool than
Eccl	9: 4	for any among the living there is **h**;
Sir	34:13	for they put their **h** in their savior;
Jer	14: 8	O H of Israel, O LORD, our savior
Jer	29:11	plans to give you a future full of **h**.
Lam	3:21	to mind, as my reason to have **h**:
Ez	37:11	"Our bones are dried up, our **h** is lost,

Dn	13:60	blessing God who saves those that **h**
Mt	12:21	And in his name the Gentiles will **h**."
Jn	5:45	in whom you have placed your **h**.
Acts	2:26	my flesh, too, will dwell in **h**,
Acts	23: 6	am on trial for **h** in the resurrection
Rom	4:18	hoping against **h**, that he would
Rom	5: 4	character, and proven character, **h**,
Rom	5: 5	and **h** does not disappoint,
Rom	8:20	of the one who subjected it, in **h**
Rom	8:24	For in **h** we were saved. Now **h** that sees for itself is not **h**.
Rom	12:12	Rejoice in **h**, endure in affliction,
Rom	15: 4	of the scriptures we might have **h**.
Rom	15:12	in him shall the Gentiles **h**."
Rom	15:13	May the God of **h** fill you with all
Rom	15:13	you may abound in **h** by the power
1 Cor	13:13	So faith, **h**, love remain, these three;
2 Cor	1:10	him we have put our **h** [that] he will
2 Cor	3:12	since we have such **h**, we act very
Eph	2:12	without **h** and without God
Eph	4: 4	also called to the one **h** of your call;
Col	1: 5	because of the **h** reserved for you
Col	1:23	not shifting from the **h** of the gospel
Col	1:27	it is Christ in you, the **h** for glory.
1 Thes	1: 3	endurance in **h** of our Lord Jesus
1 Thes	4:13	grieve like the rest, who have no **h**.
1 Thes	5: 8	the helmet that is **h** for salvation.
2 Thes	2:16	and good **h** through his grace,
1 Tm	1: 1	our savior and of Christ Jesus our **h**,
1 Tm	4:10	because we have set our **h**
Ti	1: 2	in the **h** of eternal life that God,
Ti	2:13	as we await the blessed **h**,
Ti	3: 7	become heirs in **h** of eternal life.
Heb	3: 6	to our confidence and pride in our **h**.
Heb	6:11	for the fulfillment of **h** until the end,
Heb	7:19	other hand, a better **h** is introduced,
Heb	10:23	to our confession that gives us **h**,
1 Pt	1: 3	a living **h** through the resurrection
1 Pt	1:21	so that your faith and **h** are in God.
1 Pt	3:15	asks you for a reason for your **h**,
1 Jn	3: 3	Everyone who has this **h** based

HOPED →HOPE
Heb	11: 1	is the realization of what is **h**
1 Pt	3: 5	how the holy women who **h** in God

HOPES →HOPE
Ru	1:12	And even if I could offer any **h**,
Rom	8:24	For who **h** for what one sees?
1 Cor	13: 7	believes all things, **h** all things,

HOPHNI
A wicked priest (1 Sm 1:3; 2:34; 4:4-17).

HOPING →HOPE
Rom	4:18	He believed, **h** against hope, that he

HOR
Nm	33:38	[Aaron the priest ascended Mount H
Dt	32:50	brother Aaron died on Mount H

HOREB → =SINAI
Ex	3: 1	he came to H, the mountain of God.
Ex	17: 6	in front of you on the rock in H.
Dt	5: 2	God, made a covenant with us at H;
1 Kgs	19: 8	nights to the mountain of God, H.
Ps	106:19	At H they fashioned a calf,

HORMAH
Nm	14:45	them, beating them back as far as H.
Nm	21: 3	Hence that place was named H.

HORN →HORNS
1 Sm	16: 1	Fill your **h** with oil, and be on your
Ps	18: 3	shield, my saving **h**, my stronghold!
Ps	148:14	The LORD has lifted high the **h** of his
Dn	7: 8	a little **h**, sprang out of their midst,
Dn	8: 5	with a prominent **h** on its forehead

HORNETS
Jos	24:12	And I sent the **h** ahead of you

HORNS →HORN
Gn	22:13	a ram caught by its **h** in the thicket.

Ex	27: 2	At the four corners there are to be **h**,
Jos	6: 4	seven priests carrying ram's **h** ahead
Dn	7:24	The ten **h** shall be ten kings
Dn	8: 3	by the river a ram with two great **h**,
Zec	2: 1	eyes and looked: there were four **h**.
Rv	5: 6	He had seven **h** and seven eyes;
Rv	9:13	the [four] **h** of the gold altar before
Rv	12: 3	with seven heads and ten **h**,
Rv	13: 1	beast come out of the sea with ten **h**
Rv	13: 1	on its **h** were ten diadems, and on its
Rv	13:11	it had two **h** like a lamb's but spoke
Rv	17: 3	names, with seven heads and ten **h**.

HORRIBLE → HORROR
Jer	5:30	A shocking, **h** thing has happened
Jer	18:13	ever heard the like? Truly **h** things
Hos	6:10	of Israel I have seen a **h** thing:

HORROR → HORRIBLE
Jer	15: 4	I will make them an object of **h**

HORSE → HORSE'S, HORSEMEN, HORSES
Ex	15: 1	**h** and chariot he has cast
Est	6: 8	the **h** on which the king rode
Ps	33:17	Useless is the **h** for safety; its great
Prv	26: 3	The whip for the **h**, the bridle
Jer	51:21	With you I shatter **h** and rider,
Zec	1: 8	There appeared the driver of a red **h**,
Rv	6: 2	and there was a white **h**, and its
Rv	19:11	opened, and there was a white **h**;

HORSE'S → HORSE
Rv	14:20	wine press to the height of a **h** bridle

HORSEMEN → HORSE, MAN
2 Kgs	18:24	you do on Egypt for chariots and **h**?
Is	31: 1	and in **h** because of their combined
Hos	1: 7	by sword or bow, by horses or **h**.

HORSES → HORSE
Gn	47:17	sold them food in return for their **h**,
Ex	14:23	all Pharaoh's **h** and chariots
Dt	17:16	shall not have a great number of **h**;
Jos	11: 6	You must hamstring their **h**
1 Kgs	5: 6	for his twelve thousand chariot **h**.
2 Kgs	2:11	and flaming **h** came between them,
2 Kgs	6:17	saw the mountainside filled with **h**
Ps	20: 8	Some rely on chariots, others on **h**,
Ps	32: 9	Do not be senseless like **h** or mules;
Ps	147:10	takes no delight in the strength of **h**,
Is	31: 3	not God, their **h** are flesh, not spirit;
Jer	12: 5	how will you race against **h**?
Jl	2: 4	Their appearance is that of **h**;
Zec	6: 2	The first chariot had red **h**, the second chariot black **h**,
Rv	9: 7	was like that of **h** ready for battle.
Rv	19:14	mounted on white **h** and wearing

HOSANNA
Mt	21: 9	and saying: "**H** to the Son of David;
Mt	21: 9	name of the Lord; **h** in the highest."
Mt	21:15	temple area, "**H** to the Son of David,"
Mk	11: 9	those following kept crying out: "**H**!
Mk	11:10	that is to come! **H** in the highest!"
Jn	12:13	out to meet him, and cried out: "**H**!

HOSEA
Prophet whose wife and family pictured the unfaithfulness of Israel (Hos 1-3).

HOSHEA → =JOSHUA
1. Original name of Joshua (Nm 13:8, 16).
2. Last king of Israel (2 Kgs 15:30; 17:1-6).

HOSPITABLE → HOSPITALITY
1 Tm	3: 2	decent, **h**, able to teach,
Ti	1: 8	but **h**, a lover of goodness,
1 Pt	4: 9	Be **h** to one another without

HOSPITALITY → HOSPITABLE
Rom	12:13	needs of the holy ones, exercise **h**.
1 Tm	5:10	practiced **h**, washed the feet
Heb	13: 2	Do not neglect **h**, for through it

HOST → HOSTS
1 Kgs	22:19	with the whole **h** of heaven standing
2 Kgs	17:16	and worshiped all the **h** of heaven,
2 Kgs	23: 5	and to the whole **h** of heaven.
Neh	9: 6	the highest heavens and all their **h**,
Is	34: 4	and all their **h** shall wither away,
Dn	8:10	power extended to the **h** of heaven,
Dn	8:10	it cast down to earth some of the **h**
Lk	2:13	of the heavenly **h** with the angel,

HOSTILE → HOSTILITY
Col	1:21	and **h** in mind because of evil deeds

HOSTILITY → HOSTILE
Hos	9: 8	his ways, **h** in the house of his God.

HOSTS → HOST
Dt	4:19	or any star among the heavenly **h**,
1 Sm	1: 3	his city to worship the Lord of **h**
1 Kgs	19:10	the God of **h**, but the Israelites have
Ps	46: 8	The Lord of **h** is with us;
Ps	59: 6	Lord of **h**, are the God of Israel!
Ps	103:21	Bless the Lord, all you **h**,
Is	48: 2	Israel, whose name is the Lord of **h**.
Jer	23:36	living God, the Lord of **h**, our God.

HOT → HOTHEADED
Ex	11: 8	left Pharaoh's presence in **h** anger.
Rv	3:15	that you are neither cold nor **h**. I wish you were either cold or **h**.

HOTHEADED → HEAD, HOT
Prv	22:24	Be not friendly with a **h** man,
Prv	29:22	a **h** man is the cause of many sins.

HOUR
Mt	8:13	that very **h** [his] servant was healed.
Mt	24:36	"But of that day and **h** no one knows,
Mk	14:35	it were possible the **h** might pass
Mk	14:37	you not keep watch for one **h**?
Lk	12:40	for at an **h** you do not expect,
Jn	2: 4	affect me? My **h** has not yet come."
Jn	7:30	because his **h** had not yet come.
Jn	8:20	because his **h** had not yet come.
Jn	12:23	"The **h** has come for the Son of Man
Jn	12:27	'Father, save me from this **h**'?
Jn	12:27	this purpose that I came to this **h**.
Jn	13: 1	Jesus knew that his **h** had come
Jn	17: 1	and said, "Father, the **h** has come.
1 Jn	2:18	Children, it is the last **h**; and just as
1 Jn	2:18	Thus we know this is the last **h**.
Rv	8: 1	in heaven for about half an **h**.
Rv	17:12	along with the beast for one **h**.
Rv	18:10	In one **h** your judgment has come."

HOUSE → HOUSEHOLD, HOUSES, HOUSETOP, HOUSETOPS, STOREHOUSE
Gn	19: 2	into your servant's **h** for the night,
Gn	24:23	there room in your father's **h** for us
Ex	20:17	shall not covet your neighbor's **h**.
Nm	12: 7	Throughout my **h** he bears my trust:
Dt	5:21	shall not desire your neighbor's **h**
Jos	2: 1	into the **h** of a harlot named Rahab,
Jos	6:22	"Go into the harlot's **h** and bring
2 Sm	3: 1	stronger, but the **h** of Saul weaker.
2 Sm	7: 5	Should you build me a **h** to dwell
2 Sm	7:11	that he will establish a **h** for you.
2 Sm	23: 5	Is not my **h** firm before God?
2 Kgs	15: 5	He lived in a **h** apart, while Jotham,
1 Chr	9:23	Lord, the **h** which was then a tent.
1 Chr	17:12	He it is who shall build me a **h**,
Ezr	1: 5	to go up to build the **h** of the Lord
Ezr	3:11	of the Lord's **h** had been laid.
Neh	10:40	We will not neglect the **h** of our
1 Mc	7:37	"You have chosen this **h** to bear your
1 Mc	7:37	to be a **h** of prayer and petition
Ps	23: 6	I will dwell in the **h** of the Lord
Ps	27: 4	To dwell in the Lord's **h** all the days
Ps	52:10	like an olive tree in the **h** of God,
Ps	69:10	zeal for your **h** consumes me, I am
Ps	84:11	the threshold of the **h** of my God
Ps	122: 1	me, "Let us go to the **h** of the Lord."

Ps	127: 1	Unless the LORD build the h,
Prv	7:27	Her h is made up of ways
Prv	9: 1	Wisdom has built her h, she has set
Prv	14: 1	Wisdom builds her h, but Folly
Prv	14:11	The h of the wicked will be
Prv	21: 9	in a roomy h with a quarrelsome
Eccl	10:18	when hands are slack, the h leaks.
Is	5: 8	Woe to you who join h to h,
Is	7:13	Then he said: Listen, O h of David!
Is	56: 7	and make joyful in my h of prayer;
Is	56: 7	altar, For my h shall be called a h
Jer	3:18	those days the h of Judah will join the h of Israel;
Jer	7:11	Has this h which bears my name
Jer	18: 2	Rise up, be off to the potter's h;
Jer	31:31	a new covenant with the h of Israel and the h of Judah.
Jer	32:34	They defiled the h named after me
Ez	2: 8	you: be not rebellious like this h
Ez	33: 7	watchman for the h of Israel;
Ez	39:29	out my spirit upon the h of Israel,
Jl	4:18	shall issue from the h of the LORD,
Hg	1: 4	houses, while this h lies in ruins?
Hg	2: 7	And I will fill this h with glory,
Zec	8: 9	the foundation of the h of the LORD
Zec	13: 6	wounded in the h of my dear ones."
Mt	7:24	be like a wise man who built his h
Mt	12:29	can anyone enter a strong man's h
Mt	12:29	Then he can plunder his h.
Mt	13:57	in his native place and in his own h."
Mt	21:13	written: 'My h shall be a h of prayer,'
Mk	3:25	And if a h is divided against itself,
Mk	3:25	that h will not be able to stand.
Lk	6:48	one is like a person building a h,
Lk	6:48	the river burst against that h
Lk	10: 7	Stay in the same h and eat and drink
Lk	11:17	laid waste and h will fall against h.
Lk	15: 8	not light a lamp and sweep the h,
Lk	19: 9	to this h because this man too is
Jn	2:16	making my Father's h a marketplace."
Jn	2:17	"Zeal for your h will consume me."
Jn	12: 3	the h was filled with the fragrance
Jn	14: 2	In my Father's h there are many
Rom	16: 5	greet also the church at their h.
Heb	3: 2	as Moses was "faithful in [all] his h."
Heb	8: 8	a new covenant with the h of Israel and the h of Judah.
Heb	10:21	we have "a great priest over the h
1 Pt	2: 5	a spiritual h to be a holy priesthood
2 Jn	1:10	do not receive him in your h or even

HOUSEHOLD →HOUSE

Gn	7: 1	you and all your h, for you alone
Gn	31:19	appropriated her father's h idols.
Ex	12: 3	itself a lamb, one apiece for each h.
Jos	24:15	As for me and my h, we will serve
Prv	31:21	She fears not the snow for her h;
Prv	31:27	She watches the conduct of her h,
Mi	7: 6	a man's enemies are those of his h.
Mt	10:36	one's enemies will be those of his h.'
Jn	4:53	he and his whole h came to believe.
Acts	16:31	and you and your h will be saved."
Eph	2:19	ones and members of the h of God,
1 Tm	3: 4	He must manage his own h well,
1 Tm	3:15	how to behave in the h of God,
1 Pt	4:17	to begin with the h of God; if it

HOUSES →HOUSE

Ex	12:27	LORD, who passed over the h
Ex	12:27	the Egyptians, he spared our h.' "
1 Mc	1:31	demolished its h and its surrounding
Is	65:21	They shall live in the h they build,
Jer	29:28	be a long time; build h to live in;
Ez	11: 3	not," they say, "be building h soon?
Mt	19:29	everyone who has given up h
Mk	12:40	They devour the h of widows and,
Acts	4:34	property or h would sell them,

HOUSETOP →HOUSE

Mt	24:17	a person on the h must not go down

HOUSETOPS →HOUSE

Is	37:27	like the scorched grass on the h.
Mt	10:27	hear whispered, proclaim on the h.

HOVERING

Dt	32:11	by h over its brood,
Is	31: 5	Like h birds, so the LORD of hosts

HOW

Gn	6:15	This is h you shall build it:
Gn	28:17	cried out: "H awesome is this shrine!
Ex	12:11	"This is h you are to eat it: with your
Nm	23: 8	H can I curse whom God has not
Nm	23: 8	H denounce whom the LORD has not
Dt	31:27	For I already know h rebellious
2 Sm	1:19	h can the warriors have fallen!
1 Kgs	3: 7	youth, not knowing at all h to act.
2 Chr	6:18	h much less this temple which I
Jb	25: 4	H can a man be just in God's sight,
Ps	6: 4	my soul— and you, LORD, h long . . . ?
Ps	8: 2	h awesome is your name through all
Ps	31:20	H great is your goodness, LORD,
Ps	36: 8	H precious is your love, O God!
Ps	92: 6	H great are your works, LORD!
Ps	119: 9	H can the young walk without fault?
Ps	147: 1	H good to celebrate our God
Prv	15:23	a word in season, h good it is!
Is	1:21	H has she turned adulteress,
Is	14:12	H have you fallen from the heavens,
Jer	1: 6	said, "I know not h to speak; I am too
Lam	1: 1	H lonely she is now, the once
Ez	33:10	because of them. H can we survive?"
Hos	11: 8	H could I give you up, O Ephraim,
Mal	1: 2	but you say, "H have you loved us?"
Mk	10:23	"H hard it is for those who have
Lk	12:27	Notice h the flowers grow. They do
Lk	20:44	calls him 'lord,' h can he be his son?"
Jn	3: 4	"H can a person once grown old be
Jn	7:15	"H does he know scripture without
Eph	5:15	Watch carefully then h you live,
1 Tm	3: 5	if a man does not know h to manage
1 Tm	3: 5	h can he take care of the church
Heb	2: 3	h shall we escape if we ignore so
2 Pt	2: 9	then the Lord knows h to rescue

HUGE

Rv	16:21	hailstones like h weights came

HULDAH

Prophetess inquired by Hilkiah for Josiah (2 Kgs 22; 2 Chr 34:14-28).

HUMAN →HUMANS

Nm	19:16	or who touches a h bone or a grave,
1 Kgs	13: 2	he shall burn h bones upon you.' "
2 Kgs	23:14	where they had been with h bones.
Jdt	8:16	nor h, that he may be given
Ps	22: 7	But I am a worm, hardly h,
Ps	33:13	and observes the whole h race,
Is	37:19	not gods but the work of h hands,
Dn	5: 5	the fingers of a h hand appeared,
Hos	11: 4	I drew them with h cords,
Mt	9: 8	given such authority to h beings.
Mt	15: 9	teaching as doctrines h precepts.' "
Lk	16:15	what is of h esteem is an abomination
Lk	20: 6	'Of h origin,' then all the people will
Jn	5:41	"I do not accept h praise;
Jn	5:34	accept testimony from a h being,
Acts	5:38	or this activity is of h origin, it will
1 Cor	1:26	of you were wise by h standards,
1 Cor	2:13	not with words taught by h wisdom,
Phil	2: 7	coming in h likeness; and found h
Col	2: 8	philosophy according to h tradition,
Col	2:22	they accord with h precepts
1 Thes	4: 8	disregards not a h being but God,
1 Tm	2: 5	one mediator between God and the h race, Christ Jesus, himself h,
Rv	4: 7	had a face like that of a h being,
Rv	9: 7	gold; their faces were like h faces,
Rv	14: 4	as the firstfruits of the h race

HUMANS →HUMAN
Ps 8: 5 What are **h** that you are mindful

HUMBLE →HUMBLED, HUMBLES, HUMBLY
2 Chr 7:14 pronounced, **h** themselves and pray,
2 Chr 33:23 he did not **h** himself before the Lord
2 Chr 36:12 and he did not **h** himself before
Jb 22:29 but the man of **h** mien he saves.
Ps 18:28 **H** people you save; haughty eyes
Ps 25: 9 Guides the **h** rightly, and teaches the **h** the way.
Ps 55:20 will hear me and **h** them. For they
Prv 3:34 but to the **h** he shows kindness.
Prv 11: 2 comes; but with the **h** is wisdom.
Dn 10:12 and **h** yourself before God,
Zep 2: 3 the Lord, all you **h** of the earth,
Zep 3:12 in your midst a people **h** and lowly,
Mt 11:29 me, for I am meek and **h** of heart;
Jas 4: 6 the proud, but gives grace to the **h**."
Jas 4:10 **H** yourselves before the Lord and he
1 Pt 3: 8 one another, compassionate, **h**.
1 Pt 5: 5 proud but bestows favor on the **h**."
1 Pt 5: 6 So **h** yourselves under the mighty

HUMBLED →HUMBLE
Lv 26:41 their uncircumcised hearts are **h**
1 Kgs 21:29 that Ahab has **h** himself before me?
2 Kgs 22:19 and have **h** yourself before the Lord
2 Chr 12: 7 saw that they had **h** themselves,
2 Chr 33:12 He **h** himself abjectly before
2 Chr 34:27 and have **h** yourself before God
Dn 5:22 Belshazzar, have not **h** your heart,
Mt 23:12 Whoever exalts himself will be **h**;
Lk 14:11 who exalts himself will be **h**,
Phil 2: 8 he **h** himself, becoming obedient

HUMBLES →HUMBLE
Lk 14:11 but the one who **h** himself will be

HUMBLY →HUMBLE
Mi 6: 8 and to walk **h** with your God.

HUMILIATION →HUMILITY
Prv 29:23 Man's pride causes his **h**, but he who
Acts 8:33 In [his] **h** justice was denied him.

HUMILITY →HUMILIATION
Prv 15:33 wisdom, and **h** goes before honors.
Prv 18:12 haughty, but **h** goes before honors.
Prv 22: 4 The reward of **h** and fear
Sir 3:17 My son, conduct your affairs with **h**,
Zep 2: 3 Seek justice, seek **h**; perhaps you
Acts 20:19 I served the Lord with all **h**
Eph 4: 2 with all **h** and gentleness,
Col 3:12 kindness, **h**, gentleness,
1 Pt 5: 5 clothe yourselves with **h** in your

HUNDRED →HUNDREDFOLD
Gn 6: 3 His days shall comprise one **h**
Gn 15:13 and oppressed for four **h** years.
Gn 17:17 born to a man who is a **h** years old?
1 Kgs 18:13 Lord—that I hid a **h** of the prophets
Is 65:20 youth who reaches but a **h** years,
Is 65:20 of a **h** shall be thought accursed.
Mt 13: 8 fruit, a **h** or sixty or thirtyfold.
Mt 18:12 If a man has a **h** sheep and one
Lk 7:41 one owed five **h** days' wages
Acts 1:15 (there was a group of about one **h**
Rom 4:19 (for he was almost a **h** years old)
1 Cor 15: 6 to more than five **h** brothers at once,
Rv 7: 4 seal, one **h** and forty-four thousand
Rv 13:18 His number is six **h** and sixty-six.

HUNDREDFOLD →HUNDRED
Gn 26:12 region and reaped a **h** the same year.

HUNG →HANG
Ps 137: 2 of that land we **h** up our harps.

HUNGER →HUNGRY
Dt 8: 3 therefore let you be afflicted with **h**,
Neh 9:15 heaven you gave them in their **h**,
Is 49:10 They shall not **h** or thirst, nor shall
Mt 5: 6 Blessed are they who **h** and thirst

Rv 7:16 They will not **h** or thirst anymore,

HUNGRY →HUNGER
Tb 4:16 "Give to the **h** some of your bread,
Ps 50:12 Were I **h**, I would not tell you,
Ps 107: 9 thirsty, filled the **h** with good things.
Ps 146: 7 gives food to the **h**. The Lord sets
Prv 25:21 If your enemy be **h**, give him food
Sir 4: 2 A **h** man grieve not, a needy man
Is 29: 8 when a **h** man dreams he is eating
Is 58: 7 Sharing your bread with the **h**,
Ez 18: 7 if he gives food to the **h** and clothes
Mt 12: 1 His disciples were **h** and began
Mt 15:32 I do not want to send them away **h**,
Mt 25:35 For I was **h** and you gave me food,
Mt 25:42 For I was **h** and you gave me no
Mk 11:12 were leaving Bethany he was **h**.
Lk 1:53 The **h** he has filled with good
Rom 12:20 "if your enemy is **h**, feed him; if he is
1 Cor 4:11 To this very hour we go **h**
1 Cor 11:34 If anyone is **h**, he should eat
Phil 4:12 of being well fed and of going **h**,

HUNT →HUNTED, HUNTER
Gn 27: 3 the country to **h** some game for me.

HUNTED →HUNT
Lam 3:52 cause **h** me down like a bird;

HUNTER →HUNT
Gn 10: 9 He was a mighty **h** by the grace of the Lord."
Gn 25:27 up, Esau became a skillful **h**, a man

HUR
Ex 17:12 Aaron and **H** supported his hands,

HURAM →=HIRAM
2 Chr 4:11 **H** also made the pots, the shovels
2 Chr 4:11 **H** thus completed the work he had

HURAMABI →=HIRAM
2 Chr 2:12 you a craftsman of great skill, **H**,

HURRY
Gn 19:22 **H**, escape there! I cannot do

HURT
Eccl 8: 9 tyrannizes over another to his **h**.
Dn 6:23 mouths so that they have not **h** me.

HUSBAND →HUSBAND'S, HUSBANDS
Gn 3: 6 and she also gave some to her **h**,
Gn 3:16 Yet your urge shall be for your **h**,
Gn 16: 3 gave her to her **h** Abram to be his
Nm 30: 9 learns of it her **h** expresses to her his
Dt 24: 4 then her former **h**, who dismissed
Prv 7:19 For my **h** is not at home, he has
Prv 31:11 Her **h**, entrusting his heart to her,
Prv 31:23 Her **h** is prominent at the city gates
Prv 31:28 praise her; her **h**, too, extols her:
Sir 26: 1 Happy the **h** of a good wife,
Is 54: 5 has become your **h** is your Maker;
Hos 2:18 She shall call me "My **h**," and never
Mt 1:19 Joseph her **h**, since he was
Mk 10:12 if she divorces her **h** and marries
Jn 4:17 and said to him, "I do not have a **h**."
Jn 4:17 right in saying, 'I do not have a **h**."
Rom 7: 2 is bound by law to her living **h**; but if her **h** dies, she is released
1 Cor 7: 2 wife, and every woman her own **h**.
1 Cor 7: 3 The **h** should fulfill his duty toward
1 Cor 7: 3 and likewise the wife toward her **h**.
1 Cor 7:10 wife should not separate from her **h**
1 Cor 7:11 a **h** should not divorce his wife.
1 Cor 7:14 For the unbelieving **h** is made holy
1 Cor 7:39 is bound to her **h** as long as he lives.
1 Cor 7:39 But if her **h** dies, she is free to be
2 Cor 11: 2 to one **h** to present you as a chaste
Eph 5:23 For the **h** is head of his wife just as
Eph 5:33 and the wife should respect her **h**.
Rv 21: 2 as a bride adorned for her **h**.

HUSBAND'S →HUSBAND
Dt 25: 5 her **h** brother shall go to her

Prv	6:34	For vindictive is the **h** wrath,

HUSBANDS → HUSBAND

Tb	3: 8	she had been married to seven **h**,
Tb	3: 8	are the one who strangles your **h**!
Jn	4:18	For you have had five **h**,
1 Cor	14:35	they should ask their **h** at home.
Eph	5:22	should be subordinate to their **h** as
Eph	5:25	**H**, love your wives, even as Christ
Eph	5:28	**h** should love their wives as their
Col	3:18	be subordinate to your **h**, as is
Col	3:19	**H**, love your wives, and avoid any
Ti	2: 4	train younger women to love their **h**
Ti	2: 5	under the control of their **h**,
1 Pt	3: 1	be subordinate to your **h** so that,
1 Pt	3: 7	you **h** should live with your wives

HUSHAI
Wise man of David who frustrated Ahithophel's advice and foiled Absalom's revolt (2 Sm 15:32-37; 16:15-17:16; 1 Chr 27:33).

HUT

Is	24:20	and it will sway like a **h**;

HYMENAEUS
A false teacher (1 Tm 1:20; 2 Tm 2:17).

HYMN → HYMNS

Sir	39:14	the sweet odor of your **h** of praise;
Mt	26:30	after singing a **h**, they went
Mk	14:26	after singing a **h**, they went

HYMNS → HYMN

Tb	13:18	Jerusalem shall sing **h** of gladness,
Jdt	15:13	wearing garlands and singing **h**.
1 Mc	4:24	they were singing **h** and glorifying
Acts	16:25	singing **h** to God as the prisoners
Eph	5:19	one another [in] psalms and **h**
Col	3:16	singing psalms, **h**, and spiritual

HYPOCRISY → HYPOCRITE, HYPOCRITES

Mt	23:28	but inside you are filled with **h**
Mk	12:15	Knowing their **h** he said to them,
1 Tm	4: 2	through the **h** of liars with branded

HYPOCRITE → HYPOCRISY

Sir	32:15	masters it, but the **h** finds it a trap.
Mt	7: 5	You **h**, remove the wooden beam
Lk	6:42	You **h**! Remove the wooden beam

HYPOCRITES → HYPOCRISY

Ps	26: 4	deceivers, nor with **h** do I mingle.
Mt	6: 2	as the **h** do in the synagogues
Mt	6: 5	do not be like the **h**, who love
Mt	6:16	fast, do not look gloomy like the **h**.
Mt	15: 7	**H**, well did Isaiah prophesy
Mt	22:18	"Why are you testing me, you **h**?
Mt	23:13	to you, scribes and Pharisees, you **h**.
Mt	23:15	to you, scribes and Pharisees, you **h**.
Mt	23:23	to you, scribes and Pharisees, you **h**.
Mt	23:25	to you, scribes and Pharisees, you **h**.
Mt	23:27	to you, scribes and Pharisees, you **h**.
Mt	23:29	to you, scribes and Pharisees, you **h**.
Mt	24:51	and assign him a place with the **h**,
Mk	7: 6	did Isaiah prophesy about you **h**.
Lk	12:56	You **h**! You know how to interpret
Lk	13:15	The Lord said to him in reply, "**H**!

HYSSOP

Ex	12:22	Then take a bunch of **h**, and dipping
Nm	19: 6	**h** and scarlet yarn and throw them
Ps	51: 9	Cleanse me with **h**, that I may be
Jn	19:29	soaked in wine on a sprig of **h**
Heb	9:19	with water and crimson wool and **h**,

I

I AM

Gn	15: 1	"Fear not, Abram! **I am** your shield;
Gn	17: 1	"**I am** God Almighty; walk before me
Ex	3:14	God replied, "**I am** who am."
Ps	46:11	and confess that **I am** God!
Is	41:10	not dismayed; **I am** your God.
Is	43: 3	**I am** the Lord, your God,
Is	43:15	**I am** the Lord, your Holy One,
Is	44: 6	**I am** the first and **I am** the last;
Jer	3:14	**I am** your Master; I will take you,
Jer	32:27	**I am** the Lord, the God of all
Mt	16:15	"But who do you say that **I am**?"
Mt	28:20	behold, **I am** with you always,
Mk	8:29	"But who do you say that **I am**?"
Mk	14:62	Then Jesus answered, "**I am**; and
Jn	6:35	"**I am** the bread of life;
Jn	6:41	"**I am** the bread that came down
Jn	6:51	**I am** the living bread that came
Jn	8:12	"**I am** the light of the world.
Jn	8:24	if you do not believe that **I AM**,
Jn	8:28	then you will realize that **I AM**,
Jn	8:58	before Abraham came to be, **I AM**."
Jn	9: 5	**I am** the light of the world."
Jn	10: 7	**I am** the gate for the sheep.
Jn	10: 9	**I am** the gate. Whoever enters
Jn	10:11	**I am** the good shepherd.
Jn	10:36	I said, '**I am** the Son of God'?
Jn	11:25	"**I am** the resurrection and the life;
Jn	13:19	you may believe that **I AM**.
Jn	14: 6	"**I am** the way and the truth and
Jn	14:10	**I am** in the Father and the Father
Jn	15: 1	"**I am** the true vine,
Jn	15: 5	**I am** the vine, you are the branches.
Jn	18: 5	He said to them, "**I AM**."
Acts	9: 5	"**I am** Jesus, whom you are persecuting.
Acts	18:10	for **I am** with you.
Rv	1: 8	"**I am** the Alpha and the Omega,"
Rv	1:17	**I am** the first and the last,
Rv	1:18	now **I am** alive forever and ever.
Rv	3:11	**I am** coming quickly.
Rv	21: 6	I [am] the Alpha and the Omega,
Rv	22: 7	"Behold, **I am** coming soon."
Rv	22:12	"Behold, **I am** coming soon.
Rv	22:13	**I am** the Alpha and the Omega,
Rv	22:16	**I am** the root and offspring of David,
Rv	22:20	"Yes, **I am** coming soon."

IBZAN
Judge of Israel (Jgs 12:8-10).

ICHABOD

1 Sm	4:21	[She named the child **I**, saying,

ICONIUM

Acts	14: 1	I they entered the Jewish synagogue
2 Tm	3:11	as happened to me in Antioch, **I**,

IDDO

2 Chr	9:29	in the visions of **I** the seer
2 Chr	12:15	and of **I** the seer [his family record].
2 Chr	13:22	in the midrash of the prophet **I**.

IDLE → IDLENESS

Eccl	11: 6	at evening let not your hand be **i**:
Sir	33:28	Force him to work that he be not **i**,
1 Thes	5:14	admonish the **i**, cheer the fainthearted,
Ti	1:10	many rebels, **i** talkers and deceivers,

IDLENESS → IDLE

Prv	31:27	and eats not her food in **i**.
Sir	33:28	for **i** is an apt teacher of mischief.

IDOL → IDOLATER, IDOLATERS, IDOLATRY, IDOLS

Dt	27:15	or molten **i** —an abomination
Wis	14: 8	but the handmade **i** is accursed,
Is	40:19	An **i**, cast by a craftsman,
Is	44:17	god, his **i**, and prostrate before it
Dn	14: 3	Babylonians had an **i** called Bel,
1 Cor	8: 4	know that "there is no **i** in the world,"
1 Cor	10:19	anything? Or that an **i** is anything?

IDOLATER → IDOL

1 Cor	5:11	greedy, an **i**, a slanderer, a drunkard,
Eph	5: 5	is, an **i**, has any inheritance

IDOLATERS → IDOL

1 Cor	5:10	or the greedy and robbers or **i**;
1 Cor	6: 9	fornicators nor **i** nor adulterers nor
1 Cor	10: 7	And do not become **i**, as some

IDOLATRY →IDOL

1 Sm	15:23	and presumption is the crime of i.
Ez	23:49	and you shall pay for your sins of i.
Col	3: 5	evil desire, and the greed that is i.
1 Pt	4: 3	orgies, carousing, and wanton i.

IDOLS →IDOL

Ex	20: 4	You shall not carve i for yourselves
Dt	7: 5	poles, and destroy their i by fire.
1 Kgs	15:12	and removing all the i his father had
1 Mc	1:43	they sacrificed to i and profaned
Ps	31: 7	hate those who serve worthless i,
Ps	78:58	places; with their i they goaded him.
Ps	115: 4	Their i are silver and gold, the work
Wis	14:12	of wantonness is the devising of i;
Is	2: 8	Their land is full of i; they worship
Is	42: 8	give to no other, nor my praise to i.
Ez	14: 3	have the memory of their i fresh
Ez	23:37	committed adultery with their i,
Ez	23:39	they slew their children for their i,
Dn	14: 5	"Because I worship not i made
Hb	2:18	should trust in it, and make dumb i?
Acts	15:20	by letter to avoid pollution from i,
1 Cor	8: 1	in regard to meat sacrificed to i;
2 Cor	6:16	has the temple of God with i?
1 Thes	1: 9	to God from i to serve the living
1 Jn	5:21	be on your guard against i.
Rv	2:14	to eat food sacrificed to i

IF

Gn	4: 7	I you do well, you can hold up your
Gn	4: 7	but i not, sin is a demon lurking
Ex	19: 5	i you hearken to my voice and keep
Ex	33:15	"I you are not going yourself, do not
1 Kgs	18:21	I the LORD is God, follow him;
1 Chr	28: 9	I you seek him, he will let himself
1 Chr	28: 9	but i you abandon him, he will cast
Jer	18: 8	i that nation which I have threatened
Ez	18:21	i the wicked man turns away
Ez	18:21	i he keeps all my statutes and does
Mt	4: 3	to him, "I you are the Son of God,
Mt	27:40	yourself, i you are the Son of God,
Mk	3:24	I a kingdom is divided against itself,
Mk	5:28	She said, "I I but touch his clothes,
Lk	6:32	For i you love those who love you,
Jn	13:17	I you understand this, blessed are you i you do it.
Jn	14:15	"I you love me, you will keep my
Jn	15:10	I you keep my commandments,
Rom	6: 8	I, then, we have died with Christ,
Rom	8:31	I God is for us, who can be against
Jas	1: 5	But i any of you lacks wisdom,
1 Jn	1: 9	I we acknowledge our sins, he is
Rv	3:20	I anyone hears my voice and opens

IGNORANCE →IGNORE

Acts	3:17	that you acted out of i, just as your
Acts	17:30	God has overlooked the times of i,
1 Tm	1:13	I acted out of i in my unbelief.
1 Pt	2:15	doing good you may silence the i

IGNORANT →IGNORE

Heb	5: 2	is able to deal patiently with the i
2 Pt	3:16	things hard to understand that the i

IGNORE →IGNORANCE, IGNORANT, IGNORED

2 Pt	3: 5	They deliberately i the fact

IGNORED →IGNORE

Prv	1:25	my counsel, and my reproof you i—

ILL →ILLNESS

Jn	11: 1	Now a man was i,
1 Cor	11:30	That is why many among you are i

ILLEGITIMATE

Hos	5: 7	for they have begotten i children;
Jn	8:41	[So] they said to him, "We are not i.

ILLNESS →ILL

Jn	11: 4	he said, "This i is not to end in death,

ILLUSIONS

Is	30:10	speak flatteries to us, conjure up i.

IMAGE →IMAGES

Gn	1:26	"Let us make man in our i, after our
Gn	1:27	God created man in his i;
Gn	1:27	in the divine i he created him;
Gn	9: 6	For in the i of God has man been
Ps	106:20	God for the i of a grass-eating bull.
Wis	2:23	of his own nature he made
Rom	8:29	to be conformed to the i of his Son,
1 Cor	11: 7	because he is the i and glory
1 Cor	15:49	Just as we have borne the i
1 Cor	15:49	also bear the i of the heavenly one.
2 Cor	4: 4	glory of Christ, who is the i of God.
Col	1:15	He is the i of the invisible God,
Col	3:10	knowledge, in the i of its creator.
Rv	13:14	to make an i for the beast who had
Rv	14:11	its i or accept the mark of its name."
Rv	20: 4	or its i nor had accepted its mark

IMAGES →IMAGE

Nm	33:52	all their stone figures and molten i,
Is	42:17	Who say to molten i, "You are our

IMAGINATION →IMAGINE

Acts	17:29	silver, or stone by human art and i.

IMAGINE →IMAGINATION

Eph	3:20	far more than all we ask or i,

IMITATE →IMITATORS

Dt	18: 9	shall not learn to i the abominations
Heb	13: 7	of their way of life and i their faith.
3 Jn	1:11	Beloved, do not i evil but i good.

IMITATORS →IMITATE

1 Cor	4:16	Therefore, I urge you, be i of me.
1 Cor	11: 1	Be i of me, as I am of Christ.
Eph	5: 1	So be i of God, as beloved children,
1 Thes	1: 6	And you became i of us
1 Thes	2:14	have become i of the churches
Heb	6:12	but i of those who, through faith

IMMANUEL →=EMMANUEL

Is	7:14	bear a son, and shall name him I.
Is	8: 8	wings the full width of your land, I!

IMMORAL →IMMORALITY

1 Cor	5: 9	letter not to associate with i people,
1 Cor	5:10	at all referring to the i of this world,
1 Cor	5:11	named a brother, is i, greedy,
Heb	12:16	that no one be an i or profane

IMMORALITY →IMMORAL

Tb	4:12	against every form of i, and above all,
1 Cor	5: 1	reported that there is i among you,
1 Cor	5: 1	i of a kind not found even among
1 Cor	6:13	The body, however, is not for i,
1 Cor	7: 2	of i every man should have his own
1 Cor	10: 8	Let us not indulge in i as some
2 Cor	12:21	have not repented of the impurity, i,
Gal	5:19	of the flesh are obvious: i, impurity,
Eph	5: 3	I or any impurity or greed must not
Col	3: 5	that are earthly: i, impurity,
1 Thes	4: 3	holiness: that you refrain from i,

IMMORTAL →IMMORTALITY

Wis	4: 1	with virtue; for i is its memory:
Sir	17:25	for not i is any son of man.
Rom	1:23	exchanged the glory of the i God

IMMORTALITY →IMMORTAL

Wis	8:13	for her sake I should have i
Rom	2: 7	and i through perseverance in good
1 Cor	15:53	is mortal must clothe itself with i.
1 Cor	15:54	which is mortal clothes itself with i,
1 Tm	6:16	who alone has i, who dwells
2 Tm	1:10	life and i to light through the gospel,

IMPALED

Ezr	6:11	and he is to be lifted up and i on it;

IMPARTIALLY

1 Pt	1:17	Father him who judges i according

IMPEDIMENT

Mk	7:32	him a deaf man who had a speech i

IMPENITENT
Rom 2: 5 By your stubbornness and **i** heart,

IMPERISHABLE
Wis 18: 4 through whom the **i** light of the law
Mk 16: S **i** proclamation of eternal salvation.
1 Cor 9:25 a perishable crown, but we an **i** one.
1 Pt 1: 4 to an inheritance that is **i**, undefiled,
1 Pt 1:23 not from perishable but from **i** seed,

IMPLORE → IMPLORED
Mal 1: 9 So now if you **i** God for mercy

IMPLORED → IMPLORE
Ex 32:11 But Moses **i** the LORD, his God,

IMPORTANCE → IMPORTANT
1 Cor 15: 3 handed on to you as of first **i** what I

IMPORTANT → IMPORTANCE
Ex 18:22 More **i** cases they should refer

IMPOSSIBLE
Zec 8: 6 if this should seem **i** in the eyes
Mt 17:20 Nothing will be **i** for you."
Mt 19:26 "For human beings this is **i**,
Mk 10:27 "For human beings it is **i**, but not
Lk 1:37 for nothing will be **i** for God."
Lk 18:27 said, "What is **i** for human beings is
Acts 2:24 because it was **i** for him to be held
Heb 6: 4 For it is **i** in the case of those who
Heb 6:18 in which it was **i** for God to lie,
Heb 10: 4 for it is **i** that the blood of bulls
Heb 11: 6 without faith it is **i** to please him,

IMPOSTOR
Mt 27:63 that this **i** while still alive said,

IMPRINT
Heb 1: 3 of his glory, the very **i** of his being,

IMPRISONMENT → PRISON
Acts 23:29 of any charge deserving death or **i**.
Acts 26:31 [at all] that deserves death or **i**."
Heb 11:36 scourging, even chains and **i**.

IMPRISONMENTS → PRISON
2 Cor 6: 5 beatings, **i**, riots, labors, vigils,
2 Cor 11:23 far more **i**, far worse beatings,

IMPUDENT
Prv 7:13 him, and with an **i** look says to him:

IMPURE → IMPURITY
Eph 5: 5 this, that no immoral or **i** or greedy
1 Thes 2: 3 was not from delusion or **i** motives,

IMPURITY → IMPURE
Rom 1:24 them over to **i** through the lusts
Rom 6:19 parts of your bodies as slaves to **i**
2 Cor 12:21 and have not repented of the **i**,
Gal 5:19 immorality, **i**, licentiousness,
Eph 4:19 practice of every kind of **i** to excess.
Eph 5: 3 or any **i** or greed must not even be
Col 3: 5 immorality, **i**, passion, evil desire,
1 Thes 4: 7 For God did not call us to **i**

IMPUTES
Ps 32: 2 those to whom the LORD **i** no guilt,

INCENSE → FRANKINCENSE
Ex 25: 6 anointing oil and for the fragrant **i**;
Ex 30: 1 burning **i** you shall make an altar
Ex 40: 5 Put the golden altar of **i** in front
Nm 16:17 shall take his own censer, put **i** in it,
2 Chr 26:16 to make an offering on the altar of **i**.
Ps 141: 2 Let my prayer be **i** before you;
Is 1:13 offerings; your **i** is loathsome to me.
Hos 2:15 for whom she burnt **i** While she
Lk 1:10 outside at the hour of the **i** offering,
Heb 9: 4 in which were the gold altar of **i**
Rv 5: 8 a harp and gold bowls filled with **i**,
Rv 8: 4 The smoke of the **i** along

INCITED
Acts 13:50 **i** the women of prominence who

INCLINE
Prv 4:20 attentive, to my sayings **i** your ear;
Is 37:17 **I** your ear, O LORD, and listen!

INCREASE → INCREASED, INCREASES
Dt 1:11 fathers, **i** you a thousand times over,
Ps 62:11 Though wealth **i**, do not set your
Mt 24:12 and because of the **i** of evildoing,
Lk 17: 5 apostles said to the Lord, "**I** our faith."
Jn 3:30 He must **i**; I must decrease."
1 Thes 3:12 and may the Lord make you **i**

INCREASED → INCREASE
Gn 7:17 As the waters **i**, they lifted the ark,
Acts 6: 7 the disciples in Jerusalem **i** greatly;
Rom 5:20 where sin **i**, grace overflowed all

INCREASES → INCREASE
Prv 16:21 yet pleasing speech **i** his
Prv 29:16 When the wicked prevail, crime **i**;

INCUR
Lv 19:17 man, do not **i** sin because of him.
Nm 18:22 tent; else they will **i** guilt deserving
1 Tm 5:12 will **i** condemnation for breaking

INCURABLE
2 Chr 21:18 LORD afflicted him with an **i** disease
Jer 15:18 my wound **i**, refusing to be healed?
Jer 30:12 thus says the LORD: **I** is your wound,

INDEPENDENT
1 Cor 11:11 Woman is not **i** of man or man

INDESCRIBABLE
2 Cor 9:15 Thanks be to God for his **i** gift!

INDIA
Est 1: 1 twenty-seven provinces from **I**

INDICTMENT
Jer 25:31 LORD has an **i** against the nations,

INDIGNANT
Mk 10:14 When Jesus saw this he became **i**
Lk 13:14 **i** that Jesus had cured

INDULGE → INDULGED, SELF-INDULGENCE
1 Cor 10: 8 Let us not **i** in immorality as some

INDULGED → INDULGE
Jude 1: 7 as they, **i** in sexual promiscuity

INFANT → INFANTS
Is 65:20 in it an **i** who lives but a few days,

INFANTS → INFANT
Ps 8: 3 Out of the mouths of babes and **i**
Mt 21:16 'Out of the mouths of **i** and nurslings
1 Cor 3: 1 but as fleshly people, as **i** in Christ.
1 Cor 14:20 In respect to evil be like **i**,
1 Pt 2: 2 like newborn **i**, long for pure

INFERIOR
2 Cor 12:11 in no way **i** to these "superapostles,"

INFIRMITIES
Is 53: 4 Yet it was our **i** that he bore,
Mt 8:17 "He took away our **i** and bore our
Lk 8: 2 had been cured of evil spirits and **i**,

INHABITANTS → INHABITED
Nm 33:55 out the **i** of the land before you,
Jos 9:24 that all its **i** be destroyed before you.
1 Mc 1:28 land was shaken on account of its **i**,
Is 6:11 without **i**, Houses, without a man,
Rv 6:10 our blood on the **i** of the earth?"
Rv 8:13 Woe to the **i** of the earth
Rv 13: 8 All the **i** of the earth will worship it,

INHABITED → INHABITANTS
Jer 17:25 This city will remain **i** forever.

INHERIT → INHERITANCE, INHERITED
Prv 3:35 of wise men, but fools **i** shame.
Sir 4:16 his descendants too will **i** her.
Mt 5: 5 the meek, for they will **i** the land.
Mt 19:29 times more, and will **i** eternal life.

Mk	10:17	what must I do to i eternal life?"
Lk	10:25	what must I do to i eternal life?"
Lk	18:18	what must I do to i eternal life?"
1 Cor	6: 9	the unjust will not i the kingdom
1 Cor	15:50	blood cannot i the kingdom of God,
1 Cor	15:50	nor does corruption i incorruption.
Heb	1:14	sake of those who are to i salvation?
1 Pt	3: 9	called, that you might i a blessing.
Rv	21: 7	The victor will i these gifts, and I

INHERITANCE → INHERIT

Prv	13:22	The good man leaves an i to his
Eccl	7:11	Wisdom and an i are good,
Lk	12:13	my brother to share the i with me."
Gal	3:18	For if the i comes from the law, it is
Gal	4:30	slave woman shall not share the i
Eph	1:14	of our i toward redemption as God's
Eph	5: 5	has any i in the kingdom of Christ
Col	1:12	to share in the i of the holy ones
Col	3:24	the Lord the due payment of the i;
Heb	9:15	may receive the promised eternal i.
1 Pt	1: 4	to an i that is imperishable,

INHERITED → INHERIT

Heb	1: 4	the name he has i is more excellent

INIQUITIES

Lv	16:22	is to carry off their i to an isolated
Rom	4: 7	are they whose i are forgiven

INJURED → INJURY

Ez	34:16	will bring back, the i I will bind up,

INJURY → INJURED

Lv	24:20	The same i that a man gives another

INJUSTICE

Prv	16: 8	virtue, than a large income with i.
Sir	7: 3	Sow not in the furrows of i, lest you
Rom	9:14	to say? Is there i on the part of God?

INK

Jer	36:18	"and I wrote them down with i
2 Cor	3: 3	written not in i but by the Spirit
2 Jn	1:12	I do not intend to use paper and i.
3 Jn	1:13	do not wish to write with pen and i.

INMOST → INNER

Prv	20:27	it searches through all his i being.

INN

Lk	2: 7	there was no room for them in the i.
Lk	10:34	took him to an i and cared for him.

INNER → INMOST, INWARDLY

Ez	10: 3	entered, the cloud filled the i court,
Mt	24:26	'He is in the i rooms,' do not believe
2 Cor	4:16	our i self is being renewed day
Eph	3:16	through his Spirit in the i self,

INNOCENCE → INNOCENT

Ps	26: 6	I will wash my hands in i and walk
Hos	8: 5	they be unable to attain i in Israel?

INNOCENT → INNOCENCE

Ex	23: 7	The i and the just you shall not put
Dt	19:10	i blood will not be shed and you
1 Mc	1:37	And they shed i blood around
Jb	34: 5	For Job has said, "I am i, but God
Ps	19:14	shall I be blameless, i of grave sin.
Prv	6:17	tongue, and hands that shed i blood;
Prv	17:26	It is wrong to fine an i man,
Is	59: 7	and they are quick to shed i blood;
Dn	13:53	condemning the i, and freeing
Mt	27: 4	"I have sinned in betraying i blood."
Mt	27:24	saying, "I am i of this man's blood.
Lk	23:47	said, "This man was i beyond doubt."
Phil	2:15	that you may be blameless and i,

INQUIRE

Dt	12:30	Do not i regarding their gods,
2 Kgs	1: 2	"Go and i of Baalzebub, the god

INSCRIBE → INSCRIBED, INSCRIPTION

Is	30: 8	tablet they can keep, i it in a record;

INSCRIBED → INSCRIBE

Dn	5:25	"This is the writing that was i: MENE,
Rv	19:12	He had a name i that no one knows

INSCRIPTION → INSCRIBE

Mk	15:26	The i of the charge against him
2 Tm	2:19	bearing this i, "The Lord knows

INSCRUTABLE

Rom	11:33	How i are his judgments and how

INSECTS

Dt	14:19	All winged i, too, are unclean

INSIDE

Gn	6:14	it, and cover it i and out with pitch.
Dn	14: 7	"it is only clay i and bronze outside;
Mt	23:26	cleanse first the i of the cup,
Mt	23:27	but i are full of dead men's bones

INSIGHT

Eph	1: 8	upon us. In all wisdom and i,

INSINCERITY

1 Pt	2: 1	of all malice and all deceit, i, envy,

INSIST

Ti	3: 8	I want you to i on these points,

INSOLENT

Rom	1:30	They are i, haughty, boastful,

INSPIRED

2 Tm	3:16	All scripture is i by God and is

INSTALLMENT

2 Cor	1:22	the Spirit in our hearts as a first i.

INSTANT

Lk	4: 5	kingdoms of the world in a single i.

INSTEAD

Is	60:17	I will bring gold, i of iron, silver;
Mk	15:11	him release Barabbas for them i.

INSTITUTION

1 Pt	2:13	to every human i for the Lord's sake,

INSTRUCT → INSTRUCTED, INSTRUCTION, INSTRUCTIONS, INSTRUCTORS

Ps	32: 8	I will i you and show you the way
Ps	105:22	To i his princes by his word,
1 Cor	14:19	mind, so as to i others also, than ten

INSTRUCTED → INSTRUCT

Prv	21:11	when the wise man is i, he gains
Is	40:13	LORD, or has i him as his counselor?
Acts	18:25	He had been i in the Way

INSTRUCTION → INSTRUCT

Ex	24:12	commandments intended for their i."
Prv	1: 8	Hear, my son, your father's i,
Prv	4: 1	Hear, O children, a father's i,
Prv	4:13	Hold fast to i, never let her go;
Prv	8:10	Receive my i in preference to silver,
Prv	8:33	i and wisdom do not reject!
Prv	19:20	Listen to counsel and receive i,
Prv	23:12	Apply your heart to i, and your ears
Wis	3:11	despises wisdom and i is doomed.
Is	29:24	those who find fault shall receive i.
Mi	4: 2	For from Zion shall go forth i,
Rom	15: 4	previously was written for our i,
Eph	6: 4	with the training and i of the Lord.
1 Tm	1: 5	The aim of this i is love from a pure

INSTRUCTIONS → INSTRUCT

Acts	1: 2	after giving i through the holy Spirit

INSTRUCTORS → INSTRUCT

Prv	5:13	teachers, nor to my i incline my ear!

INSTRUMENT → INSTRUMENTS

Acts	9:15	for this man is a chosen i of mine

INSTRUMENTS → INSTRUMENT

1 Chr	15:16	to play on musical i, harps, lyres,
1 Chr	23: 5	with the i which David had devised

INSULT →INSULTED, INSULTS
Prv   12:16   the shrewd man passes over an i.

INSULTED →INSULT
Lk   18:32   he will be mocked and i and spat

INSULTS →INSULT
Rom   15: 3   "The i of those who insult you fall
2 Cor 12:10   I am content with weaknesses, i,

INTEGRITY
Jb   4: 6   and your i of life your hope?
Ps   41:13   For my i you have supported me
Ps   101: 2   I follow the way of i; when will you
Prv   19: 1   a poor man who walks in his i
Prv   20: 7   When a man walks in i and justice,
Prv   28: 6   a poor man who walks in his i
Sir   7: 6   favor to the ruler and mar your i.
Mal   2: 6   his lips; He walked with me in i
Ti   2: 7   respect, with i in your teaching,

INTELLIGENT
Prv   11:12   no sense, but the i man keeps silent.
Prv   18:15   The mind of the i gains knowledge,

INTELLIGIBLE
1 Cor 14: 9   do not utter i speech, how will

INTENT
Ex   32:12   'With evil i he brought them out,

INTENTLY
Acts   6:15   sat in the Sanhedrin looked i at him

INTERCEDE →INTERCEDES, INTERCESSION
1 Sm   2:25   one can i for him with the LORD;
1 Sm   2:25   against the LORD, who can i for him?"
Jer   7:16   You, now, do not i for this people;

INTERCEDES →INTERCEDE
Rom   8:26   the Spirit itself i with inexpressible
Rom   8:27   Spirit, because it i for the holy ones
Rom   8:34   hand of God, who indeed i for us.

INTERCESSION →INTERCEDE
Heb   7:25   he lives forever to make i for them.

INTEREST →INTERESTS
Ex   22:24   him by demanding i from him.
Dt   23:20   "You shall not demand i from your
Dt   23:21   You may demand i
Ps   15: 5   lends no money at i, accepts no
Lk   19:23   I would have collected it with i.'

INTERESTS →INTEREST
Is   58:13   seeking your own i, or speaking
Phil   2: 4   each looking out not for his own i,
Phil   2:21   For they all seek their own i,

INTERMARRY →MARRY
Dt   7: 3   You shall not i with them,

INTERMARRYING →MARRY
Jos   23:12   by i and intermingling with them,
Ezr   9:14   violate your commandments by i

INTERPRET →INTERPRETATION, INTERPRETATIONS,
   INTERPRETED, INTERPRETS
Gn   41:15   certain dreams that no one can i.
Gn   41:15   you are told a dream you can i it."
Dn   5:16   I have heard that you can i dreams
1 Cor 12:30   Do all speak in tongues? Do all i?
1 Cor 14:13   a tongue should pray to be able to i.
1 Cor 14:27   and each in turn, and one should i.

INTERPRETATION →INTERPRET
Gn   40:16   Joseph had given this favorable i,
1 Cor 12:10   of tongues; to another i of tongues.
1 Cor 14:26   a revelation, a tongue, or an i.
2 Pt   1:20   that is a matter of personal i,

INTERPRETATIONS →INTERPRET
Gn   40: 8   to them, "Surely, i come from God.

INTERPRETED →INTERPRET
Lk   24:27   he i to them what referred to him

INTERPRETS →INTERPRET
1 Cor 14: 5   unless he i, so that the church may

INVADED
Jl   1: 6   For a people has i my land,

INVISIBLE
Rom   1:20   his i attributes of eternal power
Col   1:15   He is the image of the i God,
Col   1:16   earth, the visible and the i,
1 Tm   1:17   ages, incorruptible, i, the only God,
Heb   11:27   as if seeing the one who is i.

INVITE →INVITED, INVITES
Jdt   12:10   he did not i any of the officers.
Mt   22: 9   i to the feast whomever you find.'
Lk   14:13   you hold a banquet, i the poor,

INVITED →INVITE
Lk   11:37   a Pharisee i him to dine at his home.
Lk   14:10   when you are i, go and take

INVITES →INVITE
1 Cor 10:27   If an unbeliever i you and you want

INVOKE →INVOKED
Gn   4:26   that time men began to i the LORD
Is   48: 1   LORD and i the God of Israel
1 Pt   1:17   if you i as Father him who judges

INVOKED →INVOKE
Gn   12: 8   to the LORD and i the LORD by name.

INWARDLY →INNER
Ps   62: 5   their mouths, but i they curse.
Rom   2:29   one is a Jew i, and circumcision is

IRON
Gn   4:22   forge instruments of bronze and i.
2 Kgs   6: 6   and brought the i to the surface.
Ps   2: 9   an i rod you shall shepherd them,
Prv   27:17   As i sharpens i, so man sharpens his
Is   60:17   I will bring gold, instead of i, silver;
Dn   2:33   the legs i, its feet partly i and partly
Dn   7: 7   it had great i teeth with which it
Rv   2:27   He will rule them with an i rod.
Rv   12: 5   to rule all the nations with an i rod.
Rv   19:15   He will rule them with an i rod,

IRRATIONAL
2 Pt   2:12   like i animals born by nature
Jude   1:10   they know by nature like i animals.

IRREVOCABLE
Rom   11:29   the gifts and the call of God are i.

ISAAC
   Son of Abraham by Sarah (Gn 17:19; 21:1-7; 1 Chr 1:28). Abrahamic covenant perpetuated with (Gn 17:21; 26:2-5). Offered up by Abraham (Gn 22; Heb 11:17-19). Rebekah taken as wife (Gn 24). Inherited Abraham's estate (Gn 25:5). Father of Esau and Jacob (Gn 25:19-26; 1 Chr 1:34). Nearly lost Rebekah to Abimelech (Gn 26:1-11). Covenant with Abimelech (Gn 26:12-31). Tricked into blessing Jacob (Gn 27). Death (Gn 35:27-29). Father of Israel (Ex 3:6; Dt 29:12; Rom 9:10).

ISAIAH
   Prophet to Judah (Is 1:1). Called by the LORD (Is 6). Announced judgment to Ahaz (Is 7), deliverance from Assyria to Hezekiah (2 Kgs 19; Is 36-37), deliverance from death to Hezekiah (2 Kgs 20:1-11; Is 38). Chronicler of Judah's history (2 Chr 26:22; 32:32).

ISCARIOT
Mt   10: 4   and Judas I who betrayed him.
Lk   22: 3   Judas, the one surnamed I, who was

ISHBAAL
   Son of Saul who attempted to succeed him as king (2 Sm 2:8-4:12).

ISHMAEL →ISHMAELITES
   Son of Abraham by Hagar (Gn 16; 1 Chr 1:28). Blessed, but not son of covenant (Gn 17:18-21; Gal 4:21-31). Sent away by Sarah (Gn 21:8-21). Children (Gn 25:12-18; 1 Chr 1:29-31). Death (Gn 25:17).

ISHMAELITES → ISHMAEL
Gn   37:27   let us sell him to these I,

ISLAND
Rv   1: 9   on the i called Patmos because I
Rv   16:20   Every i fled, and mountains

ISRAEL → ISRAELITE, ISRAELITES, =JACOB
1. Name given to Jacob (Gn 32:29; 35:10; see Jacob).
2. Corporate name of Jacob's descendants; often specifically Northern Kingdom.
Gn   49:24   of the Shepherd, the Rock of I,
Gn   49:28   All these are the twelve tribes of I,
Ex   28:11   with the names of the sons of I
Ex   28:29   of the sons of I on the breastpiece
Nm   19:13   the LORD and shall be cut off from I.
Nm   24:17   and a staff shall rise from I,
Dt   6: 4   "Hear, O I! The LORD is our God,
Dt   10:12   "And now, I, what does the LORD,
Dt   18: 1   have no share in the heritage with I;
Jos   4:22   'I crossed the Jordan here on dry
Jos 24:31   I served the LORD during the entire
Jgs 17: 6   In those days there was no king in I;
Jgs 21: 3   God of I, why has it come to pass
Ru   4:14   May I become famous in I!
1 Sm 3:20   Thus all I from Dan to Beer-sheba
1 Sm 4:21   "Gone is the glory from I,"
1 Sm 14:23   Thus the LORD saved I that day.
1 Sm 15:26   the LORD rejects you as king of I."
1 Sm 17:46   land shall learn that I has a God.
1 Sm 18:16   hand, all I and Judah loved him,
2 Sm 5: 2   'You shall shepherd my people I
2 Sm 5: 3   all the elders of I came to David
2 Sm 5: 3   and they anointed him king of I.
2 Sm 7:26   'The LORD of hosts is God of I,'
2 Sm 14:25   all I there was not a man who could
1 Kgs 1:35   I designate him ruler of I
1 Kgs 8:25   God of I, keep the further promise
1 Kgs 8:25   to sit before me on the throne of I,
1 Kgs 10: 9   to place you on the throne of I.
1 Kgs 12:19   I went into rebellion against David's
1 Kgs 18:17   to him, "Is it you, you disturber of I?"
2 Kgs 5: 8   the king of I had torn his garments,
2 Kgs 5: 8   find out that there is a prophet in I."
2 Kgs 17:20   LORD rejected the whole race of I.
1 Chr 17:22   You made your people I your own
1 Chr 21: 1   A satan rose up against I, and he
1 Chr 21: 1   David into taking a census of I.
1 Chr 29:25   by any king over I before him.
2 Chr 9: 8   Because your God has so loved I as
Tb   1: 4   a young man in my own country, I,
Jdt   8:33   the LORD will rescue I by my hand.
Jdt 15:10   You have done good to I, and God
1 Mc 4:25   Thus I had a great deliverance
Ps   22: 4   Holy One; you are the glory of I.
Ps   78:21   Jacob; anger flared up against I.
Ps   81: 9   If only you will obey me, I!
Ps   98: 3   toward the house of I. All the ends
Ps 125: 5   with the wicked. Peace upon I!
Is   1: 3   But I does not know, my people has
Is   11:12   and gather the outcasts of I;
Is   27: 6   root, I shall sprout and blossom,
Is   44:21   you, O I, who are my servant!
Is   46:13   within Zion, and give to I my glory.
Jer   2: 3   Sacred to the LORD was I, the first
Jer 23: 6   be saved, I shall dwell in security.
Jer 31: 2   As I comes forward to be given his
Jer 31:10   He who scattered I, now gathers
Jer 31:31   a new covenant with the house of I
Jer 33:17   on the throne of the house of I,
Lam   2: 5   he has consumed I: Consumed all
Ez   3:17   you a watchman for the house of I.
Ez   33: 7   watchman for the house of I;
Ez   34: 2   prophesy against the shepherds of I,
Ez   36: 1   prophesy to the mountains of I:
Ez   37:28   LORD, who make I holy, when my
Ez   39:23   of its sins the house of I went
Dn   9:20   my sin and the sin of my people I,
Hos   7: 1   when I would heal I, The guilt
Hos 11: 1   When I was a child I loved him,

Am   4:12   you, prepare to meet your God, O I:
Am   7:11   and I shall surely be exiled from its
Am   8: 2   ripe to have done with my people I;
Am   9:14   about the restoration of my people I;
Mi   5: 1   one who is to be ruler in I;
Zep   3:13   the remnant of I. They shall do no
Zec 11:14   brotherhood between Judah and I.
Mal   1: 5   the LORD, even beyond the land of I."
Mt   2: 6   who is to shepherd my people I.' "
Mt   10: 6   to the lost sheep of the house of I.
Mt   15:24   to the lost sheep of the house of I."
Mk   12:29   replied, "The first is this: 'Hear, O I!
Mk   15:32   the King of I, come down now
Lk   1:54   He has helped I his servant,
Lk   2:34   for the fall and rise of many in I,
Lk   22:30   judging the twelve tribes of I.
Jn   12:13   of the Lord, [even] the king of I."
Acts 1: 6   going to restore the kingdom to I?"
Rom   9: 6   failed. For not all who are of I are I,
Rom   9:31   but that I, who pursued the law
Rom 11: 7   What I was seeking it did not attain,
Rom 11:26   and thus all I will be saved, as it is
Eph   2:12   alienated from the community of I
Heb   8: 8   house of I and the house of Judah.

ISRAELITE → ISRAEL
Ex   35:29   Every I man and woman brought
Neh   9: 2   of I descent separated themselves
Jn   1:47   and said of him, "Here is a true I.
Rom 11: 1   For I too am an I, a descendant

ISRAELITES → ISRAEL
Ex   1: 7   But the I were fruitful and prolific.
Ex   2:23   Still the I groaned and cried
Ex   3: 9   the cry of the I has reached me,
Ex   12:35   The I did as Moses had
Ex   14:22   the I marched into the midst
Ex   16:12   "I have heard the grumbling of the I.
Ex   16:35   The I ate this manna for forty years,
Ex   28:30   the decisions for the I over his heart
Ex   29:45   I will dwell in the midst of the I
Ex   31:16   So shall the I observe the sabbath,
Ex   33: 5   The LORD said to Moses, "Tell the I:
Ex   39:42   The I had carried out all the work
Nm   2:32   This was the census of the I taken
Nm   6:23   This is how you shall bless the I.
Nm   9: 2   "Tell the I to celebrate the Passover
Nm   9:17   the tent, the I would break camp;
Nm   14: 2   All the I grumbled against Moses
Nm   20:12   forth my sanctity before the I,
Nm   27:12   the land that I am giving to the I.
Nm   33: 3   Passover morrow the I went forth
Nm   35:10   "Tell the I: When you go across
Dt   4:44   law which Moses set before the I.
Dt   33: 1   upon the I before he died.
Jos   1: 2   into the land I will give the I.
Jos   5: 6   Now the I had wandered forty years
Jos   7: 1   But the I violated the ban; Achan,
Jos   8:32   in the presence of the I.
Jos 18: 1   community of the I assembled
Jos 21: 3   the I gave the Levites the following
Jos 22: 9   Manasseh left the other I at Shiloh
Jgs   2:11   the I offended the LORD by serving
Jgs   3:12   Again the I offended the LORD,
Jgs   4: 1   the I again offended the LORD.
Jgs   6: 1   The I offended the LORD,
Jgs 10: 6   The I again offended the LORD,
Jgs 13: 1   The I again offended the LORD,
1 Sm 17: 2   Saul and the I also gathered
1 Kgs 9:22   Solomon enslaved none of the I,
1 Kgs 12:17   reigned over the I who lived
1 Chr 9: 2   and dwell there were certain lay I,
2 Cor 11:22   So am I. Are they I? So am I.

ISSACHAR
Son of Jacob by Leah (Gn 30:18; 35:23; 1 Chr 2:1). Tribe of blessed (Gn 49:14-15; Dt 33:18-19), numbered (Nm 1:29; 26:25), allotted land (Jos 19:17-23; Ez 48:25), assisted Deborah (Jgs 5:15), 12,000 from (Rv 7:7).

ISSUE
Gn   15: 4   heir; your own i shall be your heir."

ITALICA → ITALY
Acts   10: 1   a centurion of the Cohort called the I,

ITALY → ITALICA
Acts   27: 1   was decided that we should sail to I,
Heb   13:24   Those from I send you greetings.

ITHAMAR
Son of Aaron (Ex 6:23; 1 Chr 5:29). Duties at tabernacle (Ex 38:21; Nm 4:21-33; 7:8).

ITTAI
2 Sm   15:19   he said to I the Gittite: "Why should

IVORY
1 Kgs   10:22   with a cargo of gold, silver, i, apes,
1 Kgs   22:39   including the i palace and all
Am   3:15   The i apartments shall be ruined,
Rv   18:12   all articles of i and all articles

IVY
2 Mc   6: 7   procession, wearing wreaths of i.

J

JABBOK
Gn   32:23   and crossed the ford of the J.
Dt   3:16   bed and its banks—and to the Wadi J,

JABESH
1 Sm   11: 1   All the men of J begged Nahash,
1 Sm   31:12   and brought them to J, where they
1 Chr   10:12   their bones under the oak of J,

JABIN
Jos   11: 1   When J, king of Hazor,
Jgs   4:23   God humbled the Canaanite king, J,

JACKALS
Ps   63:11   the sword and become the prey of j!
Is   35: 7   The abode where j lurk will be
Mal   1: 3   a waste, his heritage a desert for j.

JACOB → =ISRAEL
1. Son of Isaac, younger twin of Esau (Gn 26:21-26; 1 Chr 1:34). Bought Esau's birthright (Gn 26:29-34); tricked Isaac into blessing him (Gn 27:1-37). Fled to Haran (Gn 28:1-5). Abrahamic covenant perpetuated through (Gn 28:13-15; Mal 1:2). Vision at Bethel (Gn 28:10-22). Served Laban for Rachel and Leah (Gn 29:1-30). Children (Gn 29:31-30:24; 35:16-26; 1 Chr 2-9). Flocks increased (Gn 30:25-43). Returned to Canaan (Gn 31). Wrestled with God; name changed to Israel (Gn 32:23-33). Reconciled to Esau (Gn 33). Returned to Bethel (Gn 35:1-15). Favored Joseph (Gn 37:3). Sent sons to Egypt during famine (Gn 42-43). Settled in Egypt (Gn 46). Blessed Ephraim and Manasseh (Gn 48). Blessed sons (Gn 49:1-28; Heb 11:21). Death (Gn 49:29-33). Burial (Gn 50:1-14).
2. Corporate name of Jacob's descendants; often specifically Northern Kingdom.
1 Mc   1:28   all the house of J was covered
Ps   53: 7   That J may rejoice and Israel be
Ps   59:14   people will know God rules over J,
Ps   135: 4   For the LORD has chosen J, Israel as
Sir   36:10   Gather all the tribes of J, that they
Is   44: 1   Hear then, O J, my servant, Israel,
Jer   30:10   But you, my servant J, fear not,
Jer   30:10   land of exile; J shall again find rest,
Ez   39:25   Now I will restore the fortunes of J
Mi   7:20   You will show faithfulness to J,
Rom   9:13   is written: "I loved J but hated Esau."

JAEL
Woman who killed Canaanite general, Sisera (Jgs 4:17-22; 5:6, 24-27).

JAILER
Gn   39:21   the chief j well-disposed toward
Acts   16:27   When the j woke up and saw

JAIR
Judge from Gilead (Jgs 10:3-5).

JAIRUS
Synagogue ruler whose daughter Jesus raised (Mk 5:22-43; Lk 8:41-56).

JAMBRES
2 Tm   3: 8   as Jannes and J opposed Moses,

JAMES
1. Apostle; brother of John (Mt 4:21-22; 10:2; Mk 3:17; Lk 5:1-10). At transfiguration (Mt 17:1-13; Mk 9:1-13; Lk 9:28-36). Killed by Herod (Acts 12:2).
2. Apostle; son of Alphaeus (Mt 10:3; Mk 3:18; Lk 6:15).
3. Brother of Jesus (Mt 13:55; Mk 6:3; Lk 24:10; Gal 1:19) and Judas (Jude 1). With believers before Pentecost (Acts 1:13). Leader of church at Jerusalem (Acts 12:17; 15; 21:18; Gal 2:9, 12). Author of epistle (Jas 1:1).

JANNES
2 Tm   3: 8   Just as J and Jambres opposed

JAPHETH
Son of Noah (Gn 5:32; 1 Chr 1:4-5). Blessed (Gn 9:18-28). Sons of (Gn 10:2-5).

JAR → JARS
1 Kgs   17:14   The j of flour shall not go empty,
Mk   14: 3   She broke the alabaster j and poured
Lk   22:10   a man will meet you carrying a j

JARS → JAR
Jgs   7:19   and broke the j they were holding.
Jn   2: 6   there were six stone water j there

JASHAR
Jos   10:13   this not recorded in the Book of J?
2 Sm   1:18   in the Book of J to be taught

JASON
2 Mc   4: 7   Onias' brother J obtained the high
Acts   17: 7   and J has welcomed them. They all

JASPER
Ex   28:20   row, a chrysolite, an onyx and a j.
Ez   28:13   onyx, and j, sapphire, garnet,
Rv   4: 3   whose appearance sparkled like j
Rv   21:19   the first course of stones was j,

JAWBONE
Jgs   15:15   Near him was the fresh j of an ass;

JAZER
Nm   21:32   Moses sent spies to J;
Nm   32: 1   Noticing that the land of J

JEALOUS → JEALOUSY
Ex   20: 5   am a j God, inflicting punishment
Ex   34:14   for the LORD is 'the J One'; a j God is he.
Nm   11:29   him, "Are you j for my sake?
Dt   4:24   God, is a consuming fire, a j God.
Dt   5: 9   am a j God, inflicting punishments
Dt   6:15   who is in your midst, is a j God.
Jos   24:19   he is a j God who will not forgive
Is   11:13   Ephraim shall not be j of Judah,
Ez   36: 6   With j fury I speak, because you
Ez   39:25   and I will be j for my holy name.
Na   1: 2   A j and avenging God is the LORD,
Zec   8: 2   I am intensely j for Zion, stirred to j
Acts   7: 9   "And the patriarchs, j of Joseph,
Acts   17: 5   But the Jews became j and recruited
Rom   10:19   "I will make you j of those who are
Rom   11:11   the Gentiles, so as to make them j.

JEALOUSY → JEALOUS
Nm   5:14   by a feeling of j that makes him
Prv   27: 4   but before j who can stand?
Ez   8: 3   stood the statue of j which stirs up j.
Acts   5:17   of the Sadducees, and, filled with j,
Acts   13:45   they were filled with j
Rom   13:13   licentiousness, not in rivalry and j.
1 Cor   3: 3   While there is j and rivalry among
2 Cor   11: 2   am jealous of you with the j of God,
2 Cor   12:20   that there may be rivalry, j, fury,
Gal   5:20   hatreds, rivalry, j, outbursts of fury,
Jas   4: 5   made to dwell in us tends toward j"?

JEBUS → =JERUSALEM, JEBUSITE, JEBUSITES
1 Chr 11: 4 that is, J, where the natives

JEBUSITE → JEBUS
2 Sm 24:18 the threshing floor of Araunah the J."
2 Chr 3: 1 the threshing-floor of Ornan the J.

JEBUSITES → JEBUS
Gn 15:21 the Girgashites, and the J."
Ex 3: 8 Amorites, Perizzites, Hivites and J.
Jos 15:63 the J who lived in Jerusalem
2 Sm 5: 6 against the J who inhabited

JECONIAH → =JEHOIACHIN
A form of Jehoiachin (Jer 24:1).

JEDIDIAH → =SOLOMON
2 Sm 12:25 the prophet Nathan to name him J,

JEDUTHUN
1 Chr 16:41 With them were Heman and J
2 Chr 35:15 Asaph, Heman and J, the king's seer.
Ps 39: 1 For the leader, for J. A psalm

JEERED
2 Kgs 2:23 came out of the city and j at him.

JEHOAHAZ
 1. Son of Jehu; king of Israel (2 Kgs 13:1-9).
 2. Son of Josiah; king of Judah (2 Kgs 23:31-34; 2 Chr 36:1-4).

JEHOASH → =JOASH
 1. Son of Ahaziah, king of Judah (2 Kgs 12). See Joash, 1.
 2. Son of Jehoahaz; king of Israel. Defeat of Aram prophesied by Elisha (2 Kgs 13:10-25). Defeated Amaziah in Jerusalem (2 Kgs 14:1-16). See Joash, 2.

JEHOIACHIN → =CONIAH, =JECONIAH
 Son of Jehoiakim; king of Judah exiled by Nebuchadnezzar (2 Kgs 24:8-17; 2 Chr 36:8-10; Ez 1:2). Raised from prisoner status (2 Kgs 25:27-30; Jer 52:31-34).

JEHOIADA
 Priest who sheltered Joash from Athaliah (2 Kgs 11-12; 2 Chr 22:11-24:16).

JEHOIAKIM → =ELIAKIM
 Son of Josiah; made king of Judah by Nebu-chadnezzar (2 Kgs 23:34-24:6; 2 Chr 36:4-8; Jer 22:18-23). Burned scroll of Jeremiah's prophecies (Jer 36).

JEHORAM → =JORAM
 1. Son of Jehoshaphat; king of Judah. Prophesied against by Elijah; killed by the LORD (2 Chr 21). See Joram, 1.
 2. Son of Ahab; king of Israel (2 Chr 22:5). With Jehoshaphat fought against Moab (2 Kgs 3). See Joram, 2.

JEHOSHAPHAT
 Son of Asa; king of Judah. Strengthened his kingdom (2 Chr 17). Joined with Ahab against Aram (2 Kgs 22; 2 Chr 18). Established judges (2 Chr 19). Joined Joram against Moab (2 Kgs 3; 2 Chr 20). Valley of judgment (Jl 4:2, 12).

JEHOZADAK
1 Chr 5:41 J was one of those who went
Hg 1:12 son of J, and all the remnant

JEHU
 1. Prophet against Baasha (2 Kgs 16:1-7).
 2. King of Israel. Anointed by Elijah to obliterate house of Ahab (1 Kgs 19:16-17); anointed by servant of Elisha (2 Kgs 9:1-13). Killed Joram and Ahaziah (2 Kgs 9:14-29; 2 Chr 22:7-9), Jezebel (2 Kgs 9:30-37), relatives of Ahab (2 Kgs 10:1-17; Hos 1:4), ministers of Baal (2 Kgs 10:18-29). Death (2 Kgs 10:30-36).

JEPHTHAH
 Judge from Gilead who delivered Israel from Ammon (Jgs 10:6-12:7). Made rash vow concerning his daughter (Jgs 11:30-40).

JEREMIAH
 Prophet to Judah (Jer 1:1-3). Called by the LORD (Jer 1). Put in stocks (Jer 20:1-3). Threatened for prophesying (Jer 11:18-23; 26). Opposed by Hananiah (Jer 28). Scroll burned (Jer 36). Imprisoned (Jer 37). Thrown into cistern (Jer 38). Forced to Egypt with those fleeing Babylonians (Jer 43).

JERICHO
Nm 22: 1 the other side of the J stretch
Dt 34: 3 of the Jordan with the lowlands at J,
Jos 3:16 the people crossed over opposite J.
Jos 5:10 at Gilgal on the plains of J,
Jos 6: 2 "I have delivered J and its king
Jos 6:26 who attempts to rebuild this city, J.
1 Kgs 16:34 his reign, Hiel from Bethel rebuilt J.
2 Kgs 25: 5 overtook him in the desert near J,
Lk 10:30 he went down from Jerusalem to J.
Lk 18:35 as he approached J a blind man was
Lk 19: 1 He came to J and intended to pass
Heb 11:30 faith the walls of J fell after being

JEROBOAM
 1. Official of Solomon; rebelled to become first king of Israel (1 Kgs 11:26-40; 12:1-20; 2 Chr 10). Idolatry (1 Kgs 12:25-33; Tb 1:5; Sir 47:23-25); judgment for (1 Kgs 13-14; 2 Chr 13).
 2. Son of Jehoash; king of Israel (1 Kgs 14:23-29).

JERUBBAAL → =GIDEON
Jgs 6:32 So on that day Gideon was called J,
1 Sm 12:11 Accordingly, the LORD sent J, Barak,

JERUSALEM → =JEBUS, JERUSALEM'S, =SALEM
Jos 10: 1 Adonizedek, king of J, heard that,
Jos 15: 8 flank of the Jebusites [that is, J],
Jgs 1: 8 [The Judahites fought against J
1 Sm 17:54 of the Philistine and brought it to J;
2 Sm 5: 5 thirty-three years in J over all Israel
2 Sm 9:13 But Meribbaal lived in J,
2 Sm 11: 1 David, however, remained in J.
2 Sm 15:29 took the ark of God back to J
2 Sm 24:16 stretched forth his hand toward J
1 Kgs 3: 1 of the LORD, and the wall around J.
1 Kgs 9:15 palace, Millo, the wall of J, Hazor,
1 Kgs 9:19 decided should be built in J,
1 Kgs 10:26 cities and to the king's service in J.
1 Kgs 10:27 silver as common in J as stones,
1 Kgs 11: 7 Ammonites, on the hill opposite J.
1 Kgs 11:13 sake of my servant David and of J,
1 Kgs 11:36 always have a lamp before me in J,
1 Kgs 14:25 Shishak, king of Egypt, attacked J.
2 Kgs 12:18 Hazael decided to go on to attack J.
2 Kgs 14:13 J where he tore down four hundred
2 Kgs 18:17 a great army to King Hezekiah at J.
2 Kgs 18:35 LORD then rescue J from my hand?' "
2 Kgs 19:31 For out of J shall come a remnant,
2 Kgs 21: 4 said, "I will establish my name in J"—
2 Kgs 21:12 'I will bring such evil on J and Judah
2 Kgs 23:27 I will reject this city, J, which I
2 Kgs 24:10 attacked J, and the city came under
2 Kgs 24:14 He deported all J: all the officers
2 Kgs 24:20 The LORD's anger befell J and Judah
2 Kgs 25: 1 his whole army advanced against J,
2 Kgs 25:10 down the walls that surrounded J.
1 Chr 11: 4 Then David and all Israel went to J,
1 Chr 21:16 in his hand stretched out against J.
2 Chr 1: 4 brought up from Kiriathjearim to J,
2 Chr 3: 1 of the LORD in J on Mount Moriah,
2 Chr 6: 6 but now I choose J, where I shall be
2 Chr 9: 1 she came to J to test him with subtle
2 Chr 20:15 of Judah, inhabitants of J, and King
2 Chr 20:27 turned back toward J celebrating
2 Chr 29: 8 LORD has come upon Judah and J;
2 Chr 36:19 tore down the walls of J, set all its
Ezr 1: 2 me to build him a house in J,
Ezr 2: 1 and who came back to J and Judah,
Ezr 3: 1 the people gathered at J as one man.
Ezr 4:12 up from you to us have arrived at J
Ezr 4:24 on the house of God in J was halted.
Ezr 6:12 or to destroy this house of God in J.
Ezr 7: 8 Ezra came to J in the fifth month
Ezr 9: 9 granted us a fence in Judah and J.
Ezr 10: 7 exiles should gather together in J,
Neh 1: 2 after the captivity, and about J,
Neh 1: 3 the wall of J lies breached, and its
Neh 2:17 how J lies in ruins and its gates
Neh 2:17 let us rebuild the wall of J,
Neh 2:20 share nor claim nor memorial in J."

Neh	3: 8	They restored J as far as the wall
Neh	4: 2	fight against J and thus to throw us
Neh	11: 1	bring one man in ten to reside in J,
Neh	12:27	At the dedication of the wall of J,
Neh	12:43	and the rejoicing at J could be heard
Tb	1: 6	make the pilgrimage alone to J
Jdt	4: 2	greatly alarmed for J and the temple
Jdt	15: 9	saying: "You are the glory of J,
1 Mc	1:14	built a gymnasium in J according
1 Mc	1:29	he came to J with a strong force.
1 Mc	6: 7	he had built upon the altar in J;
Ps	51:20	pleasure; rebuild the walls of J.
Ps	79: 1	holy temple, have laid J in ruins.
Ps	122: 2	are standing within your gates, J.
Ps	122: 6	For the peace of J pray: "May those
Ps	125: 2	As mountains surround J, the LORD
Ps	137: 5	If I forget you, J, may my right
Ps	147: 2	The LORD rebuilds J,
Ps	147:12	Glorify the LORD, J; Zion,
Eccl	1:12	Qoheleth, was king over Israel in J,
Song	6: 4	as lovely as J, as awe-inspiring as
Is	1: 1	Judah and J in the days of Uzziah,
Is	2: 1	Amoz, saw concerning Judah and J.
Is	3: 1	shall take away from J
Is	3: 8	J is crumbling, Judah is falling;
Is	4: 3	every one marked down for life in J.
Is	8:14	and a snare to those who dwell in J;
Is	27:13	the LORD on the holy mountain, in J.
Is	31: 5	hosts shall shield J, To protect
Is	33:20	let your eyes see J as a quiet abode,
Is	40: 2	Speak tenderly to J, and proclaim
Is	40: 9	your voice, J, herald of good news!
Is	52: 1	glorious garments, O J, holy city.
Is	52: 2	ascend to the throne, J;
Is	62: 6	Upon your walls, O J, I have
Is	62: 7	until he re-establishes J And makes
Is	65:18	For I create J to be a joy and its
Is	66:13	in J you shall find your comfort.
Jer	2: 2	cry out this message for J to hear!
Jer	3:17	they will call J the LORD's throne;
Jer	3:17	to honor the name of the LORD at J,
Jer	4: 5	Judah, make it heard in J;
Jer	4:14	Cleanse your heart of evil, O J,
Jer	5: 1	Roam the streets of J,
Jer	6: 6	throw up a siege mound against J.
Jer	9:10	I will turn J into a heap of ruins,
Jer	13:27	Woe to you, J, how long will it yet
Jer	26:18	a plowed field, J a heap of ruins,
Jer	32: 2	king of Babylon was besieging J,
Jer	33:10	in the streets of J that are now
Jer	39: 1	all his army marched against J
Jer	51:50	from afar, let J come to your minds.
Jer	52:14	all the walls that surrounded J.
Lam	1: 8	of which she is guilty, J is defiled;
Ez	8: 3	brought me in divine visions to J,
Ez	14:21	Even though I send J my four cruel
Ez	16: 2	make known to J her abominations.
Ez	21: 7	look toward J, preach against their
Ez	23: 4	is Oholah, and J is Oholibah.]
Dn	5: 3	of God in J had been brought in,
Dn	6:11	with the windows open toward J.
Dn	9: 2	of J seventy years must be fulfilled.
Dn	9:12	us in J the greatest calamity that has
Dn	9:25	of the word that J was to be rebuilt
Jl	4: 1	restore the fortunes of Judah and J,
Jl	4:16	and from J raises his voice;
Jl	4:17	my holy mountain; J shall be holy,
Am	2: 5	Judah, to devour the castles of J.
Mi	1: 5	of the house of Judah? Is it not J?
Mi	4: 2	and the word of the LORD from J.
Zep	3:16	On that day, it shall be said to J:
Zec	1:14	I am deeply moved for the sake of J
Zec	1:17	comfort Zion, and again choose J.
Zec	2: 6	"To measure J," he answered; "to see
Zec	2: 8	People will live in J as though
Zec	8: 3	and I will dwell within J; J shall be
Zec	8: 8	bring them back to dwell within J.
Zec	8:15	days I have determined to favor J
Zec	8:22	come to seek the LORD of hosts in J

Zec	9: 9	shout for joy, O daughter J! See,
Zec	9:10	and the horse from J; The warrior's
Zec	12: 3	day I will make J a weighty stone
Zec	12:10	the inhabitants of J a spirit of grace
Zec	14: 2	I will gather all the nations against J
Zec	14: 8	living waters shall flow from J,
Zec	14:16	that came against J shall come
Mt	2: 1	magi from the east arrived in J,
Mt	16:21	his disciples that he must go to J
Mt	20:18	we are going up to J, and the Son
Mt	21:10	he entered J the whole city was
Mt	23:37	"J, J, you who kill the prophets
Mk	10:33	we are going up to J, and the Son
Mk	15:41	who had come up with him to J.
Lk	2:22	they took him up to J to present him
Lk	2:41	Each year his parents went to J
Lk	2:43	the boy Jesus remained behind in J,
Lk	4: 9	Then he led him to J, made him
Lk	9:31	he was going to accomplish in J.
Lk	9:51	determined to journey to J,
Lk	18:31	we are going up to J and everything
Lk	21:20	you see J surrounded by armies,
Lk	21:24	J will be trampled underfoot
Lk	23:28	"Daughters of J, do not weep for me;
Lk	24:47	to all the nations, beginning from J.
Jn	1:19	When the Jews from J sent priests
Jn	4:20	say that the place to worship is in J."
Jn	5: 1	of the Jews, and Jesus went up to J.
Jn	10:22	was then taking place in J. It was
Acts	1: 4	enjoined them not to depart from J,
Acts	1: 8	and you will be my witnesses in J,
Acts	6: 7	the disciples in J increased greatly;
Acts	9:13	he has done to your holy ones in J,
Acts	9:28	moved about freely with them in J,
Acts	11:27	some prophets came down from J
Acts	15: 2	should go up to J to the apostles
Acts	20:22	by the Spirit, I am going to J.
Acts	21: 4	the Spirit not to embark for J.
Acts	23:11	borne witness to my cause in J,
Rom	15:19	so that from J all the way around
Gal	4:25	it corresponds to the present J,
Heb	12:22	the heavenly J, and countless angels
Rv	3:12	the new J, which comes down
Rv	21: 2	city, a new J, coming down
Rv	21:10	me the holy city J coming down

JERUSALEM'S → JERUSALEM

Is	62: 1	for J sake I will not be quiet,

JESHUA → =JOSHUA

Ezr	4: 3	But Zerubbabel, J, and the rest
Ezr	10:18	Of the sons of J, son of Jozadak,
Neh	12: 1	Zerubbabel, son of Shealtiel, and J:
Sir	49:12	And J, Jozadak's son? In their time

JESSE
Father of David (Ru 4:17-22; 1 Sm 16; 1 Chr 2:12-17).

JESUS → =JUSTUS
1. Jesus the Messiah.
LIFE: Genealogy (Mt 1:1-17; Lk 3:21-37). Birth announced (Mt 1:18-25; Lk 1:26-45). Birth (Mt 2:1-12; Lk 2:1-40). Escape to Egypt (Mt 2:13-23). As a boy in the temple (Lk 2:41-52). Baptism (Mt 3:13-17; Mk 1:9-11; Lk 3:21-22; Jn 1:32-34). Temptation (Mt 4:1-11; Mk 1:12-13; Lk 4:1-13). Ministry in Galilee (Mt 4:12-18:35; Mk 1:14-9:50; Lk 4:14-13:9; Jn 1:35-2:11; 4; 6), Transfiguration (Mt 17:1-8; Mk 9:2-8; Lk 9:28-36), on the way to Jerusalem (Mt 19-20; Mk 10; Lk 13:10-19:27), in Jerusalem (Mt 21-25; Mk 11-13; Lk 19:28-21:38; Jn 2:13-3:36; 5; 7-12). Last supper (Mt 26:17-35; Mk 14:12-31; Lk 22:1-38; Jn 13-17). Arrest and trial (Mt 26:36-27:31; Mk 14:43-15:20; Lk 22:39-23:25; Jn 18:1-19:16). Crucifixion (Mt 27:32-66; Mk 15:21-47; Lk 23:26-55; Jn 19:28-42). Resurrection and appearances (Mt 28; Mk 16; Lk 24; Jn 20-21; Acts 1:1-11; 7:56; 9:3-6; 1 Cor 15:1-8; Rv 1:1-20).
MIRACLES. *Healings:* official's son (Jn 4:43-54), demoniac in Capernaum (Mk 1:23-26; Lk 4:33-35), Peter's mother-in-law (Mt 8:14-17; Mk 1:29-31; Lk 4:38-39), leper (Mt 8:2-4; Mk 1:40-45; Lk 5:12-16), paralytic (Mt 9:1-8; Mk 2:1-12; Lk 5:17-26), cripple (Jn 5:1-9), shriveled hand (Mt 12:10-13; Mk 3:1-5; Lk 6:6-11), centurion's servant (Mt 8:5-13; Lk 7:1-10), widow's son raised (Lk 7:11-17), demoniac (Mt 12:22-23; Lk 11:14), Gadarene demoni-

acs (Mt 8:28-34; Mk 5:1-20; Lk 8:26-39), woman's bleeding and Jairus' daughter (Mt 9:18-26; Mk 5:21-43; Lk 8:40-56), blind man (Mt 9:27-31), mute man (Mt 9:32-33), Canaanite woman's daughter (Mt 15:21-28; Mk 7:24-30), deaf man (Mk 7:31-37), blind man (Mk 8:22-26), demoniac boy (Mt 17:14-18; Mk 9:14-29; Lk 9:37-43), ten lepers (Lk 17:11-19), man born blind (Jn 9:1-7), Lazarus raised (Jn 11), crippled woman (Lk 13:11-17), man with dropsy (Lk 14:1-6), two blind men (Mt 20:29-34; Mk 10:46-52; Lk 18:35-43), Malchus' ear (Lk 22:50-51). *Other Miracles:* water to wine (Jn 2:1-11), catch of fish (Lk 5:1-11), storm stilled (Mt 8:23-27; Mk 4:37-41; Lk 8:22-25), 5,000 fed (Mt 14:15-21; Mk 6:35-44; Lk 9:10-17; Jn 6:1-14), walking on water (Mt 14:25-33; Mk 6:48-52; Jn 6:15-21), 4,000 fed (Mt 15:32-39; Mk 8:1-9), money from fish (Mt 17:24-27), fig tree cursed (Mt 21:18-22; Mk 11:12-14), catch of fish (Jn 21:1-14).

MAJOR TEACHING: Sermon on the Mount (Mt 5-7; Lk 6:17-49), to Nicodemus (Jn 3), to Samaritan woman (Jn 4), Bread of Life (Jn 6:22-59), at Feast of Tabernacles (Jn 7-8), woes to Pharisees (Mt 23; Lk 11:37-54), Good Shepherd (Jn 10:1-18), Olivet Discourse (Mt 24-25; Mk 13; Lk 21:5-36), Upper Room Discourse (Jn 13-16).

PARABLES: Sower (Mt 13:3-23; Mk 4:3-25; Lk 8:5-18), seed's growth (Mk 4:26-29), wheat and weeds (Mt 13:24-30, 36-43), mustard seed (Mt 13:31-32; Mk 4:30-32), yeast (Mt 13:33; Lk 13:20-21), hidden treasure (Mt 13:44), valuable pearl (Mt 13:45-46), net (Mt 13:47-51), house owner (Mt 13:52), good Samaritan (Lk 10:25-37), unmerciful servant (Mt 18:15-35), lost sheep (Mt 18:10-14; Lk 15:4-7), lost coin (Lk 15:8-10), prodigal son (Lk 15:11-32), dishonest manager (Lk 16:1-13), rich man and Lazarus (Lk 16:19-31), persistent widow (Lk 18:1-8), Pharisee and tax collector (Lk 18:9-14), payment of workers (Mt 20:1-16), tenants and the vineyard (Mt 21:28-46; Mt 12:1-12; Lk 20:9-19), wedding banquet (Mt 22:1-14), faithful servant (Mt 24:45-51), ten virgins (Mt 25:1-13), talents (Mt 25:1-30; Lk 19:12-27).

DISCIPLES see APOSTLES. Call (Jn 1:35-51; Mt 4:18-22; 9:9; Mk 1:16-20; 2:13-14; Lk 5:1-11, 27-28). Named Apostles (Mk 3:13-19; Lk 6:12-16). Twelve sent out (Mt 10; Mk 6:7-11; Lk 9:1-5). Seventy sent out (Lk 10:1-24). Defection of (Jn 6:60-71; Mt 26:56; Mk 14:50-52). Final commission (Mt 28:16-20; Jn 21:15-23; Acts 1:3-8).

Acts	2:32	God raised this J; of this we are all
Acts	9: 5	"I am J, whom you are persecuting.
Acts	9:34	to him, "Aeneas, J Christ heals you.
Acts	15:11	through the grace of the Lord J,
Acts	16:31	"Believe in the Lord J and you
Acts	20:24	that I received from the Lord J,
Rom	3:24	through the redemption in Christ J,
Rom	5:17	life through the one person J Christ.
Rom	8: 1	for those who are in Christ J.
1 Cor	1: 7	the revelation of our Lord J Christ.
1 Cor	2: 2	I was with you except J Christ,
1 Cor	6:11	in the name of the Lord J Christ
1 Cor	8: 6	and one Lord, J Christ,
1 Cor	12: 3	spirit of God says, "J be accursed."
1 Cor	12: 3	And no one can say, "J is Lord,"
2 Cor	4: 5	as your slaves for the sake of J.
2 Cor	13: 5	Do you not realize that J Christ is
Eph	1: 5	to himself through J Christ,
Eph	2:10	in Christ J for the good works
Eph	2:20	Christ J himself as the capstone.
Phil	1: 6	complete it until the day of Christ J.
Phil	2: 5	that is also yours in Christ J,
Phil	2:10	that at the name of J every knee
Col	3:17	in the name of the Lord J,
1 Thes	1:10	whom he raised from [the] dead, J,
1 Thes	4:14	For if we believe that J died
1 Thes	5:23	for the coming of our Lord J Christ.
2 Thes	1: 7	of the Lord J from heaven with his
2 Thes	2: 1	to the coming of our Lord J Christ
1 Tm	1:15	Christ J came into the world to save
2 Tm	1:10	appearance of our savior Christ J,
2 Tm	2: 3	me like a good soldier of Christ J.
2 Tm	3:12	in Christ J will be persecuted.
Ti	2:13	God and of our savior J Christ,
Heb	2: 9	but we do see J "crowned with glory
Heb	3: 1	reflect on J, the apostle and high
Heb	4:14	has passed through the heavens, J,
Heb	6:20	where J has entered on our behalf as
Heb	7:22	to that same degree has J

Heb	12: 2	while keeping our eyes fixed on J,
Heb	12:24	and J, the mediator of a new
Heb	13: 8	J Christ is the same yesterday,
1 Pt	1: 3	through the resurrection of J Christ
2 Pt	1:16	and coming of our Lord J Christ,
1 Jn	1: 7	the blood of his Son J cleanses us
1 Jn	2: 1	Father, J Christ the righteous one.
1 Jn	4:15	acknowledges that J is the Son
Rv	1: 1	The revelation of J Christ,
Rv	12:17	and bear witness to J.
Rv	17: 6	on the blood of the witnesses to J.
Rv	22:16	"I, J, sent my angel to give you this
Rv	22:20	coming soon." Amen! Come, Lord J!

2. Disciple, also called Justus (Col 4:11).

3. Writer of Sirach or Ecclesiasticus (Sir Pr:1; 50:27; 51:1).

JETHRO

Father-in-law and adviser of Moses (Ex 3:1; 4:18; 18). Also known as Reuel (Ex 2:18).

JEW → JEWISH, JEWS, JUDAISM

Est	2: 5	of Susa a certain J named Mordecai,
Est	10: 3	The J Mordecai was next in rank
Dn	14:28	"The king has become a J," they said;
Zec	8:23	take hold of every J by the edge
Jn	4: 9	to him, "How can you, a J, ask me,
Jn	18:35	Pilate answered, "I am not a J, am I?
Acts	21:39	"I am a J, of Tarsus in Cilicia,
Rom	1:16	believes: for J first, and then Greek.
Rom	2: 9	does evil, J first and then Greek.
Rom	2:29	Rather, one is a J inwardly,
Rom	10:12	For there is no distinction between J
1 Cor	9:20	To the Jews I became like a J to win
Col	3:11	Here there is not Greek and J,

JEWELS

Is	61:10	like a bride bedecked with her j.
Zec	9:16	For they are the j in a crown

JEWISH → JEW

Est	6:13	is of the J race, you will not prevail
1 Mc	8:29	an agreement with the J people.
Jn	2: 6	there for J ceremonial washings,
Acts	13: 6	who was a J false prophet.
Acts	24:24	with his wife Drusilla, who was J.
Ti	1:14	of paying attention to J myths

JEWS → JEW

Ezr	5: 5	watched over the elders of the J so
Neh	3:33	much incensed. He ridiculed the J,
Est	3:13	that all the J, young and old,
Est	4:14	come to the J from another source;
Est	8:17	were seized with a fear of the J.
Est	10: 3	in high standing among the J,
Dn	3: 8	Chaldeans came and accused the J
Mt	2: 2	"Where is the newborn king of the J?
Mt	27:11	him, "Are you the king of the J?"
Mt	27:37	him: This is Jesus, the King of the J.
Lk	23: 3	him, "Are you the king of the J?"
Jn	4: 9	(For J use nothing in common
Jn	4:22	because salvation is from the J.
Jn	7:13	because they were afraid of the J.
Jn	9:22	because they were afraid of the J,
Jn	19: 3	to him and said, "Hail, King of the J!"
Jn	19:21	"Do not write 'The King of the J,'
Acts	20:21	I earnestly bore witness for both J
Acts	21:20	there are from among the J,
Rom	3:29	Does God belong to J alone?
Rom	9:24	not only from the J
1 Cor	1:22	For J demand signs and Greeks look
1 Cor	9:20	To the J I became like a Jew to win over J;
1 Cor	12:13	into one body, whether J or Greeks,
1 Thes	2:14	compatriots as they did from the J,
Rv	2: 9	slander of those who claim to be J
Rv	3: 9	of Satan who claim to be J and are

JEZEBEL

Sidonian wife of Ahab (1 Kgs 16:31). Promoted Baal worship (1 Kgs 16:32-33). Killed prophets of the LORD (1 Kgs 18:4, 13). Opposed Elijah (1 Kgs 19:1-2). Had Naboth killed (1 Kgs 21). Death prophesied (1 Kgs 21:17-24). Killed by Jehu (2 Kgs 9:30-37). Metaphor of immorality (Rv 2:20).

JEZREEL →JEZREELITE
1 Kgs 21:23 devour Jezebel in the district of J.")
2 Kgs 9:36 confines of J dogs shall eat the flesh
2 Kgs 10: 7 baskets, and sent them to Jehu in J.
Hos 1: 4 Give him the name J, for in a little
Hos 2: 2 for great shall be the day of J.
Hos 2:24 and oil, and these shall respond to J.

JEZREELITE →JEZREEL
1 Kgs 21: 1 as Naboth the J had a vineyard
2 Kgs 9:25 him into the field of Naboth the J.

JOAB
Nephew of David (1 Chr 2:16). Commander of his army (2 Sm 8:16). Victorious over Ammon (2 Sm 10; 1 Chr 19), Rabbah (2 Sm 11; 1 Chr 20), Jerusalem (1 Chr 11:6), Absalom (2 Sm 18), Sheba (2 Sm 20). Killed Abner (2 Sm 3:22-39), Amasa (2 Sm 20:1-13). Numbered David's army (2 Sm 24; 1 Chr 21). Sided with Adonijah (1 Kgs 1:17, 19). Killed by Benaiah (1 Kgs 2:5-6, 28-35).

JOANNA
Lk 8: 3 J, the wife of Herod's steward
Lk 24:10 women were Mary Magdalene, J,

JOASH →=JEHOASH
1. Son of Ahaziah; king of Judah. Sheltered from Athaliah by Jehoiada (2 Kgs 11; 2 Chr 22:10-23:21). Repaired temple (2 Chr 24). See Jehoash, 1.
2. Son of Jehoahaz, king of Israel (2 Kgs 13; 2 Chr 25:17-25). See Jehoash, 2.

JOB
Wealthy man from Uz; feared God (Jb 1:1-5). Integrity tested by disaster (Jb 1:6-22), personal affliction (Jb 2). Maintained innocence in debate with three friends (Jb 3-31), Elihu (Jb 32-37). Rebuked by the LORD (Jb 38-41). Vindicated and restored to greater stature by the LORD (Jb 42). Example of righteousness (Sir 49:9; Ez 14:14, 20).

JOCHEBED
Mother of Moses, Aaron and Miriam (Ex 6:20; Nm 26:59).

JOEL
1. Son of Samuel (1 Sm 8:2; 1 Chr 6:13).
2. Prophet (Jl 1:1; Acts 2:16).

JOHANAN
1. First high priest in Solomon's temple (1 Chr 5:36-37).
2. Jewish leader who tried to save Gedaliah from assassination (Jer 40:13-14); took Jews, including Jeremiah, to Egypt (Jer 40-43).

JOHN
1. Son of Zechariah and Elizabeth (Lk 1). Called the Baptist (Mt 3:1-12; Mk 1:2-8). Witness to Jesus (Mt 3:11-12; Mk 1:7-8; Lk 3:15-18; Jn 1:6-35; 3:27-30; 5:33-36). Doubts about Jesus (Mt 11:2-6; Lk 7:18-23). Arrest (Mt 4:12; Mk 1:14). Execution (Mt 14:1-12; Mk 6:14-29; Lk 9:7-9). Ministry compared to Elijah (Mt 11:7-19; Mk 9:11-13; Lk 7:24-35).
2. Apostle; brother of James (Mt 4:21-22; 10:2; Mk 3:17; Lk 5:1-10). At transfiguration (Mt 17:1-13; Mk 9:1-13; Lk 9:28-36). Desire to be greatest (Mk 10:35-45). Leader of church at Jerusalem (Acts 4:1-3; Gal 2:9). Elder who wrote epistles (2 Jn 1; 3 Jn 1). Prophet who wrote Revelation (Rv 1:1; 22:8).
3. Cousin of Barnabas, co-worker with Paul, (Acts 12:12-13:13; 15:37; see Mark).
4. Son of Simon Maccabeus; a high priest (1 Mc 13:53; 16).

JOIN →JOINED
Ex 1:10 war they too may j our enemies
Neh 10:30 j with their brethren who are their
Jer 3:18 the house of Judah will j the house
Ez 37:17 Then j the two sticks together,
Dn 11:34 many shall j them out of treachery.
Acts 5:13 None of the others dared to j them,
Acts 9:26 Jerusalem he tried to j the disciples,
Rom 15:30 to j me in the struggle by your

JOINED →JOIN
Mt 19: 6 what God has j together, no human
Mk 10: 9 Therefore what God has j together,
Eph 4:16 body, j and held together by every

JOINT →JOINTS
Rom 8:17 heirs of God and j heirs with Christ,

JOINTS →JOINT
Heb 4:12 soul and spirit, j and marrow,

JOKING
Prv 26:19 and then says, "I was only j."

JONADAB
2 Sm 13: 3 Now Amnon had a friend named J,
Jer 35: 8 Now we have heeded J,

JONAH
Prophet in days of Jeroboam II (2 Kgs 14:25). Called to Nineveh; fled to Tarshish (Jon 1:1-3). Cause of storm; thrown into sea (Jon 1:4-16). Swallowed by fish (Jon 2:1). Prayer (Jon 2). Preached to Nineveh (Jon 3). Attitude reproved by the LORD (Jon 4). Sign of (Mt 12:39-41; Lk 11:29-32).

JONATHAN
1. Son of Saul (1 Sm 13:16; 1 Chr 8:33). Valiant warrior (1 Sm 14). Relation to David (1 Sm 18:1-4; 19-20; 23:16-18). Killed at Gilboa (1 Sm 31). Mourned by David (2 Sm 1).
2. Brother and successor of Judas Maccabeus (1 Mc 2:5; 9:28-31).

JOPPA
2 Chr 2:15 them down to you at the port of J,
Ezr 3: 7 from the Lebanon to the port of J,
Jon 1: 3 He went down to J, found a ship
Acts 9:43 And he stayed a long time in J

JORAM →=JEHORAM
1. Son of Jehoshaphat; king of Judah (2 Kgs 8:16-24). See Jehoram, 1.
2. Son of Ahab; king of Israel. Killed with Ahaziah by Jehu (2 Kgs 8:25-29; 9:14-26; 2 Chr 22:5-9). See Jehoram, 2.

JORDAN
Gn 13:10 watered the whole J Plain was as far
Nm 22: 1 side of the Jericho stretch of the J.
Nm 34:12 boundary shall continue along the J
Dt 1: 1 to all Israel beyond the J [
Dt 3:27 well, for you shall not cross this J.
Jos 1: 2 So prepare to cross the J here,
Jos 3:11 earth will precede you into the J.
Jos 3:17 of the J until the whole nation had
Jos 4: 8 the bed of the J as there were tribes
Jos 4:22 'Israel crossed the J here on dry
Jos 23: 4 as those I destroyed] between the J
2 Kgs 2: 7 and when the two stopped at the J,
2 Kgs 2:13 back and stood at the bank of the J.
2 Kgs 5:10 "Go and wash seven times in the J,
2 Kgs 6: 4 they arrived at the J they began
Ps 114: 3 beheld and fled; the J turned back.
Is 8:23 the land west of the J, the District
Jer 12: 5 will you do in the thickets of the J?
Mt 3: 6 in the J River as they acknowledged
Mt 4:15 the way to the sea, beyond the J,
Mk 1: 9 and was baptized in the J by John.
Jn 1:28 happened in Bethany across the J,

JOSEPH →=BARNABAS, =BARSABBAS
1. Son of Jacob by Rachel (Gn 30:24; 1 Chr 2:2). Favored by Jacob, hated by brothers (Gn 37:3-4). Dreams (Gn 37:5-11). Sold by brothers (Gn 37:12-36). Served Potiphar; imprisoned by false accusation (Gn 39). Interpreted dreams of Pharaoh's servants (Gn 40), of Pharaoh (Gn 41:4-40). Made greatest in Egypt (Gn 41:41-57). Sold grain to brothers (Gn 42-45). Brought Jacob and sons to Egypt (Gn 46-47). Sons Ephraim and Manasseh blessed (Gn 48). Blessed (Gn 49:22-26; Dt 33:13-17). Death (Gn 50:22-26; Ex 13:19; Heb 11:22). 12,000 from (Rv 7:8).
2. Husband of Mary mother of Jesus (Mt 1:16-24; 2:13-19; Lk 1:27; 2; Jn 1:45).
3. Disciple from Arimathea; buried Jesus in his tomb (Mt 27:57-61; Mk 15:43-47; Lk 24:50-52).
4. Original name of Barnabas (Acts 4:36).

JOSHUA →=HOSHEA, =JESHUA
1. Son of Nun; name changed from Hoshea (Nm 13:8, 16; 1 Chr 7:27). Fought Amalekites under Moses (Ex 17:9-14). Servant of Moses on Sinai (Ex 24:13; 32:17). Spied Canaan (Nm 13). With Caleb, allowed to enter land (Nm 14:6, 30). Succeeded Moses (Dt 1:38; 31:1-8; 34:9).
Charged Israel to conquer Canaan (Jos 1). Crossed Jordan (Jos 3-4). Circumcised sons of wilderness wanderings (Jos 5). Con-

quered Jericho (Jos 6), Ai (Jos 7-8), five kings at Gibeon (Jos 10:1-28), southern Canaan (Jos 10:29-43), northern Canaan (Jos 11-12). Defeated at Ai (Jos 7). Deceived by Gibeonites (Jos 9). Renewed covenant (Jos 8:30-35; 24:1-27). Divided land among tribes (Jos 13-22). Last words (Jos 23). Death (Jos 24:28-31).
2. High priest during rebuilding of temple (Hg 1-2; Zec 3:1-9; 6:11). See Jeshua.

JOSIAH
Son of Amon; king of Judah (2 Kgs 21:26; 1 Chr 3:14). Prophesied (1 Kgs 13:2). Book of the Law discovered during his reign (2 Kgs 22; 2 Chr 34:14-31). Reforms (2 Kgs 23:1-25; 2 Chr 34:1-13; 35:1-19; Sir 49:1-4). Killed by Pharaoh Neco (2 Kgs 23:29-30; 2 Chr 35:20-26).

JOTHAM
1. Son of Gideon (Jgs 9).
2. Son of Azariah (Uzziah); king of Judah (2 Kgs 15:32-38; 2 Chr 26:21-27:9).

JOURNEY
Ex	3:18	to go a three-days' **j** in the desert,
Ezr	8:21	from him a safe **j** for ourselves,
Mt	25:14	a man who was going on a **j** called
Lk	9: 3	them, "Take nothing for the **j**,

JOY → JOYFULLY, OVERJOYED
1 Chr	16:27	praise and **j** are in his holy place.
Ezr	3:12	lifted up their voices in shouts of **j**,
Ezr	6:16	of this house of God with **j**.
Ezr	6:22	the Lord had filled them with **j**
1 Mc	3:45	**J** had disappeared from Jacob,
1 Mc	4:58	There was great **j** among the people
Jb	20: 5	and the **j** of the impious
Jb	38: 7	all the sons of God shouted for **j**?
Ps	5:12	and forever shout for **j**. Protect them
Ps	16:11	life, abounding **j** in your presence.
Ps	20: 6	May we shout for **j** at your victory,
Ps	21: 7	him with the **j** of your presence.
Ps	27: 6	sacrifices with shouts of **j**; I will
Ps	35:27	just cause shout for **j** and be glad.
Ps	43: 4	to God, my **j**, my delight. Then I
Ps	48: 3	of heights, the **j** of all the earth,
Ps	51:10	Let me hear sounds of **j**
Ps	51:14	Restore my **j** in your salvation;
Ps	65: 9	and west you make resound with **j**.
Ps	65:14	with grain; they cheer and sing for **j**.
Ps	67: 5	the nations be glad and shout for **j**;
Ps	71:23	will shout for **j** as I sing your praise;
Ps	92: 5	works of your hands I shout for **j**.
Ps	98: 8	the mountains shout with them for **j**,
Ps	105:43	He brought his people out with **j**,
Ps	107:22	declare his works with shouts of **j**.
Ps	119:111	forever; they are the **j** of my heart.
Ps	126: 2	our tongues sang for **j**. Then it was
Ps	126: 5	sow in tears will reap with cries of **j**.
Ps	126: 6	Will return with cries of **j**,
Ps	132: 9	justice; your faithful will shout for **j**."
Ps	132:16	its faithful shall shout for **j**.
Ps	149: 5	glory, cry out for **j** at their banquet,
Prv	12:20	but those who counsel peace have **j**.
Prv	14:10	and in its **j** no one else shares.
Prv	14:13	sad and the end of **j** may be sorrow.
Prv	15:23	There is **j** for a man in his utterance;
Prv	17:21	the father of a numskull has no **j**.
Prv	21:15	To practice justice is a **j** for the just,
Sir	26: 2	A worthy wife brings **j** to her
Is	9: 2	You have brought them abundant **j**
Is	12: 3	With **j** you will draw water
Is	16:10	are taken away **j** and gladness,
Is	24:11	lack of wine; all **j** has disappeared
Is	35:10	crowned with everlasting **j**;
Is	48:20	With shouts of **j** proclaim this,
Is	51: 3	**J** and gladness shall be found in her,
Is	51:11	crowned with everlasting **j**;
Is	52: 8	together they shout for **j**, For they
Is	55:12	Yes, in **j** you shall depart, in peace
Is	60:15	a **j** to generation after generation.
Is	61: 7	land, everlasting **j** shall be theirs.
Is	65:18	For I create Jerusalem to be a **j**
Is	66: 5	that we may see your **j**"; but they

Jer	15:16	they became my **j** and the happiness
Jer	31:13	I will turn their mourning into **j**,
Jer	33: 9	Then Jerusalem shall be my **j**,
Jer	48:33	**J** and jubilation are at an end
Jer	51:48	shall shout over Babylon with **j**,
Lam	2:15	city, the **j** of the whole earth?"
Lam	5:15	The **j** of our hearts has ceased,
Bar	5: 9	For God is leading Israel in **j**
Ez	24:25	their glorious **j**, the delight of their
Jl	1:12	Yes, **j** has withered away
Jl	1:16	house of our God, **j** and gladness?
Mt	13:20	word and receives it at once with **j**.
Mt	13:44	out of **j** goes and sells all that he has
Mk	4:16	the word, receive it at once with **j**.
Lk	1:14	And you will have **j** and gladness,
Lk	1:44	the infant in my womb leaped for **j**.
Lk	2:10	good news of great **j** that will be
Lk	6:23	Rejoice and leap for **j** on that day!
Lk	8:13	receive the word with **j**, but they
Lk	24:41	they were still incredulous for **j**
Lk	24:52	returned to Jerusalem with great **j**,
Jn	3:29	So this **j** of mine has been made
Jn	15:11	told you this so that my **j** might be
Jn	16:20	grieve, but your grief will become **j**.
Jn	16:22	no one will take your **j** away
Jn	16:24	so that your **j** may be complete.
Jn	17:13	they may share my **j** completely.
Acts	8: 8	There was great **j** in that city.
Acts	13:52	The disciples were filled with **j**
Rom	14:17	peace, and **j** in the holy Spirit;
Rom	15:13	the God of hope fill you with all **j**
Rom	15:32	I may come to you with **j** by the will
2 Cor	1:24	we work together for your **j**, for you
2 Cor	2: 3	all of you that my **j** is that of all
Gal	5:22	the fruit of the Spirit is love, **j**,
Phil	1: 4	praying always with **j** in my every
Phil	1:25	for your progress and **j** in the faith,
Phil	2: 2	complete my **j** by being of the same
Phil	4: 1	I love and long for, my **j** and crown,
1 Thes	1: 6	with **j** from the holy Spirit,
1 Thes	2:19	For what is our hope or **j** or crown
1 Thes	2:20	For you are our glory and **j**.
1 Thes	3: 9	for all the **j** we feel on your account
2 Tm	1: 4	tears, so that I may be filled with **j**,
Phlm	1: 7	For I have experienced much **j**
Heb	12: 2	the **j** that lay before him he endured
Heb	13:17	that they may fulfill their task with **j**
Jas	1: 2	Consider it all **j**, my brothers,
Jas	4: 9	mourning and your **j** into dejection.
1 Pt	1: 8	with an indescribable and glorious **j**,
1 Jn	1: 4	this so that our **j** may be complete.
2 Jn	1:12	face so that our **j** may be complete.
3 Jn	1: 4	Nothing gives me greater **j** than

JOYFULLY → JOY
1 Mc	4:56	of the altar and **j** offered holocausts

JUBILANT → JUBILATION
Is	24: 8	ended the shouts of the **j**, stilled is

JUBILATION → JUBILANT
Prv	11:10	when the wicked perish, there is **j**.

JUBILEE
Lv	25:10	It shall be a **j** for you, when every
Nm	36: 4	the Israelites celebrate the **j** year,

JUDAH → JUDEA
1. Son of Jacob by Leah (Gn 29:35; 35:23; 1 Chr 2:1). Did not want to kill Joseph (Gn 37:26-27). Among Canaanites, fathered Perez by Tamar (Gn 38). Tribe of blessed as ruling tribe (Gn 49:8-12; Dt 33:7), numbered (Nm 1:27; 26:22), allotted land (Jos 15; Ez 48:7), failed to fully possess (Jos 15:63; Jgs 1:1-20).
2. Name used for people and land of Southern Kingdom.
Ru	1: 7	on the road back to the land of **J**,
2 Sm	2: 4	Then the men of **J** came there
2 Sm	5: 5	and six months in Hebron over **J**,
2 Sm	5: 5	in Jerusalem over all Israel and **J**.
2 Sm	24: 1	him to number Israel and **J**.
1 Chr	28: 4	For he chose **J** as leader, then one
Neh	6: 7	to proclaim you king of **J**. Now,

1 Mc	2: 6	that were being committed in J
1 Mc	7:50	a short time the land of J was quiet.
1 Mc	9:57	and the land of J was quiet for two
Sir	49: 4	these kings of J, right to the very
Is	1: 1	Ahaz and Hezekiah, kings of J.
Is	3: 8	Jerusalem is crumbling, J is falling;
Jer	2:28	are your gods, O J! And as many as
Jer	13:19	to relieve them; All J is banished
Jer	30: 3	the lot of my people (of Israel and J,
Jer	31:31	house of Israel and the house of J.
Lam	1: 3	J has fled into exile from oppression
Hos	1: 7	Yet for the house of J I feel pity;
Jl	4: 1	the fortunes of J and Jerusalem,
Mi	5: 1	small to be among the clans of J,
Zec	2: 2	"These are the horns that scattered J
Zec	8:15	favor Jerusalem and the house of J;
Zec	11:14	off the brotherhood between J
Mal	2:11	J has broken faith; an abominable
Mal	2:11	J has profaned the temple
Mt	2: 6	'And you, Bethlehem, land of J,
Mt	2: 6	means least among the rulers of J;
Heb	7:14	is clear that our Lord arose from J,
Heb	8: 8	house of Israel and the house of J.
Rv	5: 5	The lion of the tribe of J, the root

JUDAISM →JEW

Acts	13:43	were converts to J followed Paul
Gal	1:13	heard of my former way of life in J,

JUDAS → =BARSABBAS, =JUDE, =THADDAEUS, MACCABEUS
1. Apostle; son of James (Lk 6:16; Jn 14:22; Acts 1:13). Probably also called Thaddaeus (Mt 10:3; Mk 3:18).
2. Brother of James and Jesus (Mt 13:55; Mk 6:3), also called Jude (Jude 1).
3. Christian prophet (Acts 15:22-32).
4. Apostle, also called Iscariot, who betrayed Jesus (Mt 10:4; 26:14-56; Mk 3:19; 14:10-50; Lk 6:16; 22:3-53; Jn 6:71; 12:4; 13:2-30; 18:2-11). Suicide of (Mt 27:3-5; Acts 1:16-25).
5. Leader of the Maccabean revolt (1 Mc 2:4, 66). Recaptured Jerusalem and rededicated the temple and altar (1 Mc 4:36-61). Death of (1 Mc 9).

JUDE → =JUDAS

Jude	1: 1	J, a slave of Jesus Christ

JUDEA →JUDAH, JUDEAN

Jdt	4: 7	since these offered access to J.
1 Mc	5:23	and brought them to J with great
Dn	14:33	In J there was a prophet, Habakkuk;
Mt	2: 1	Jesus was born in Bethlehem of J,
Mt	3: 1	preaching in the desert of J
Mt	24:16	then those in J must flee
Lk	1: 5	King of J, there was a priest named
Lk	3: 1	Pontius Pilate was governor of J,
Lk	7:17	him spread through the whole of J
Acts	1: 8	throughout J and Samaria,
Acts	8: 1	throughout the countryside of J
Acts	9:31	The church throughout all J,
1 Thes	2:14	of God that are in J in Christ Jesus.

JUDEAN →JUDEA

Mk	1: 5	People of the whole J countryside

JUDGE →JUDGE'S, JUDGED, JUDGES, JUDGING, JUDGMENT, JUDGMENTS

Gn	18:25	Should not the j of all the world act
Ex	2:14	appointed you ruler and j over us?
Dt	17: 9	to the j who is in office at that time.
Jgs	2:18	he would be with the j and save
Jgs	2:18	their enemies as long as the j lived;
Jgs	11:27	who is j, decide this day between
1 Sm	24:13	The Lord will j between me
Tb	3: 2	and truth; you are the j of the world.
Ps	7: 9	O Lord, j of the nations. Grant me
Ps	7:12	God is a just j, who rebukes
Ps	50: 6	justice, for God alone is the j.
Ps	75: 3	"I will choose the time; I will j fairly.
Ps	82: 8	Arise, O God, j the earth, for yours
Ps	94: 2	Rise up, j of the earth;
Sir	7: 6	Seek not to become a j if you have
Is	2: 4	He shall j between the nations,
Is	11: 3	Not by appearance shall he j,

Is	33:22	yes, the Lord our j, the Lord our
Jer	11:20	But, you, O Lord of hosts, O just J,
Ez	7: 3	and j you according to your conduct
Ez	7:27	to their judgments I will j them;
Ez	18:30	Therefore I will j you,
Ez	22: 2	would you j, would you j the bloody
Ez	33:20	I will j every one of you according
Ez	34:17	God, I will j between one sheep
Mi	4: 3	He shall j between many peoples
Lk	12:14	who appointed me as your j
Lk	18: 2	"There was a j in a certain town who
Jn	5:30	I j as I hear, and my judgment is
Jn	7:24	judging by appearances, but j justly."
Jn	8:15	You j by appearances, but I do not j
Jn	8:16	And even if I should j, my judgment
Jn	12:48	my words has something to j him:
Jn	18:31	and j him according to your law."
Acts	7:27	appointed you ruler and j over us?
Acts	10:42	appointed by God as j of the living
Rom	2: 1	which you j another you condemn
Rom	2: 1	you, the j, do the very same things.
Rom	2:16	God will j people's hidden works
Rom	3: 6	For how else is God to j the world?
1 Cor	5:12	not your business to j those within?
1 Cor	6: 2	that the holy ones will j the world?
1 Cor	6: 3	you not know that we will j angels?
2 Tm	4: 1	who will j the living and the dead,
2 Tm	4: 8	the just j, will award to me
Heb	10:30	again: "The Lord will j his people."
Heb	12:23	and God the j of all, and the spirits
Heb	13: 4	for God will j the immoral
Jas	4:12	lawgiver and j who is able to save
Jas	4:12	then are you to j your neighbor?
Jas	5: 9	the J is standing before the gates.
1 Pt	4: 5	him who stands ready to j the living

JUDGE'S →JUDGE

Jn	19:13	and seated him on the j bench

JUDGED →JUDGE

1 Sm	7:15	Samuel j Israel as long as he lived.
Ps	9:20	let the nations be j in your presence.
Mt	7: 1	"Stop judging, that you may not be j.
Rom	2:12	all who sin under the law will be j
1 Cor	4: 3	me in the least that I be j by you
Jas	2:12	so act as people who will be j
Jas	3: 1	that we will be j more strictly,
Jas	5: 9	one another, that you may not be j.
Rv	20:12	The dead were j according to their

JUDGES →JUDGE

Dt	1:16	I charged your j at that time,
Jgs	2:16	the Lord raised up j to deliver them
Ru	1: 1	the time of the j there was a famine
1 Sm	2:10	The Lord j the ends of the earth.
1 Sm	8: 1	appointed his sons j over Israel.
Jb	9:24	he covers the faces of its j. If it is
Sir	16:12	he j men, each according to his
Lk	11:19	Therefore they will be your j.
Acts	4:19	you rather than God, you be the j.
1 Cor	4: 4	the one who j me is the Lord.
Jas	4:11	j his brother speaks evil of the law and j the law.
1 Pt	1:17	him who j impartially according
1 Pt	2:23	himself over to the one who j justly.
Rv	18: 8	mighty is the Lord God who j her."
Rv	19:11	and True." He j and wages war

JUDGING →JUDGE

Mt	19:28	thrones, j the twelve tribes of Israel.

JUDGMENT →JUDGE

Ex	6: 6	arm and with mighty acts of j.
Dt	1:17	alike, fearing no man, for j is God's.
Jdt	9: 6	your j is made with foreknowledge.
Ps	1: 5	the wicked will not survive j,
Ps	9: 8	forever, has set up a throne for j.
Ps	82: 1	gives j in the midst of the gods.
Ps	143: 2	Do not enter into j with your
Eccl	11: 9	all this God will bring you to j.
Eccl	12:14	God will bring to j every work,
Is	3:14	The Lord enters into j with his

Is	28: 6	to him who sits in j, And strength
Jer	25:31	he is to pass j upon all mankind:
Ez	20:35	where I will enter into j with you
Dn	7:22	j was pronounced in favor
Jl	4: 2	I will enter into j with them there
Hb	1:12	O LORD, you have marked him for j,
Zep	3: 5	Morning after morning he renders j
Mal	3: 5	I will draw near to you for j, and I
Mt	5:21	and whoever kills will be liable to j.'
Mt	5:22	with his brother will be liable to j,
Mt	10:15	Gomorrah on the day of j than
Mt	11:24	Sodom on the day of j than for you."
Mt	12:36	of j people will render an account
Mt	12:41	At the j, the men of Nineveh will
Jn	5:22	but he has given all j to his Son,
Jn	5:30	and my j is just, because I do not
Jn	9:39	"I came into this world for j,
Jn	12:31	Now is the time of j on this world;
Acts	24:25	and self-restraint and the coming j,
Rom	2: 1	every one of you who passes j.
Rom	2: 2	We know that the j of God on those
Rom	5:16	one sin there was the j that brought
Rom	14:10	we shall all stand before the j seat
1 Cor	11:29	body, eats and drinks j on himself.
2 Cor	5:10	we must all appear before the j seat
2 Thes	1: 5	This is evidence of the just j of God,
Heb	6: 2	of the dead and eternal j.
Heb	9:27	beings die once, and after this the j,
Heb	10:27	a fearful prospect of j and a flaming
Jas	2:13	For the j is merciless to one who has
Jas	2:13	mercy triumphs over j.
1 Pt	4:17	it is time for the j to begin
2 Pt	2: 4	handed them over to be kept for j;
2 Pt	2: 9	under punishment for the day of j,
2 Pt	3: 7	for fire, kept for the day of j
1 Jn	4:17	on the day of j because as he is,
Jude	1: 6	in gloom, for the j of the great day.
Rv	14: 7	for his time has come to sit in j.
Rv	17: 1	I will show you the j on the great
Rv	18:10	In one hour your j has come."

JUDGMENTS →JUDGE

1 Chr	16:14	throughout the earth his j prevail.
Tb	3: 5	"Yes, your j are many and true
Wis	17: 1	For great are your j, and hardly
Rom	11:33	How inscrutable are his j and how
Rv	16: 7	almighty, your j are true and just."
Rv	19: 2	for true and just are his j. He has

JUDITH
Virtuous widow and heroine of the book of Judith (Jdt 8-16).

JUG

1 Kgs	17:12	in my jar and a little oil in my j.

JUICE

Nm	6: 3	or any kind of grape j, nor eat either

JUMPED →JUMPING

Jn	21: 7	was lightly clad, and j into the sea.

JUMPING →JUMPED

Acts	3: 8	walking and j and praising God.

JUST →JUSTICE, JUSTIFICATION, JUSTIFIED, JUSTIFIES, JUSTIFY, JUSTLY

Dt	32: 4	deceit, how j and upright he is!
Neh	9:33	has come upon us you have been j,
Tb	3: 2	and all your deeds are j; All your
Jb	35: 2	right to say, "I am j rather than God"?
Ps	119:121	I have fulfilled your j edict; do not
Ps	145:17	You, LORD, are j in all your ways,
Prv	12: 5	The plans of the j are legitimate;
Is	26: 7	The way of the j is smooth; the path
Ez	45: 9	and do what is right and j!
Jn	5:30	and my judgment is j, because I do
2 Thes	1: 6	For it is surely j on God's part
Heb	2: 2	received its j recompense,
1 Jn	1: 9	he is faithful and j and will forgive
Rv	15: 3	almighty. J and true are your ways,
Rv	16: 5	waters say: "You are j, O Holy One,
Rv	16: 7	your judgments are true and j."
Rv	19: 2	for true and j are his judgments.

JUSTICE →JUST

Ex	23: 2	side with the many in perverting j.
Dt	16:19	You shall not distort j; you must be
Dt	16:20	J and j alone shall be your aim,
1 Sm	8: 3	and accepted bribes, perverting j.
2 Sm	15: 4	to me and I would render him j."
1 Kgs	10: 9	king to carry out judgment and j."
2 Chr	9: 8	as king to administer right and j."
Jb	8: 3	and does the Almighty distort j?
Jb	29:14	j was my robe and my turban.
Jb	34:12	the Almighty cannot violate j.
Jb	34:17	Can an enemy of justice indeed be
Jb	37:23	his great j owes no one
Ps	33: 5	The LORD loves j and right and fills
Ps	72: 1	the king; your j to the son of kings;
Ps	72: 2	he may govern your people with j,
Ps	82: 3	render j to the afflicted and needy.
Ps	89:15	J and judgment are the foundation
Ps	99: 4	O mighty king, lover of j, you alone
Ps	101: 1	I sing of love and j; to you, LORD,
Ps	103: 6	deeds, brings j to all the oppressed.
Ps	112: 5	who conduct their affairs with j.
Ps	140:13	j for the needy, their rights
Prv	8:20	of duty I walk, along the paths of j,
Prv	17:23	bribe to pervert the course of j.
Prv	19:28	An unprincipled witness perverts j,
Prv	21:15	To practice j is a joy for the just,
Prv	28: 5	Evil men understand nothing of j,
Prv	29: 4	By j a king gives stability
Eccl	3:16	and in the seat of j, iniquity.
Eccl	5: 7	of rights and j in the realm, do not
Is	1:17	Make j your aim:
Is	1:21	upright! J used to lodge within her,
Is	1:27	and her repentant ones by j.
Is	5: 7	for j, but hark, the outcry!
Is	5:16	Holy shall be shown holy by his j.
Is	9: 6	By judgment and j, both now
Is	16: 5	upholding right and prompt to do j.
Is	28: 6	A spirit of j to him who sits
Is	28:17	of j a level.— Hail shall sweep away
Is	30:18	For the LORD is a God of j:
Is	32:16	the desert and j abide in the orchard.
Is	33: 5	high; he fills Zion with right and j.
Is	42: 1	he shall bring forth j to the nations,
Is	42: 4	Until he establishes j on the earth;
Is	56: 1	to come, my j, about to be revealed.
Is	59: 9	and j does not reach us. We look
Is	59:14	and j stands far off; For truth
Jer	9:23	j and uprightness on the earth;
Jer	21:12	Each morning dispense j,
Hos	2:21	I will espouse you in right and in j,
Am	5: 7	wormwood and cast j to the ground!
Am	5:15	and let j prevail at the gate; Then it
Am	5:24	then let j surge like water,
Am	6:12	and the fruit of j into wormwood.
Mt	12:18	he will proclaim j to the Gentiles.
Mt	12:20	quench, until he brings j to victory.
Lk	18: 8	to it that j is done for them speedily.
Acts	8:33	[his] humiliation j was denied him.
Acts	28: 4	sea, J has not let him remain alive."

JUSTIFICATION →JUST

Rom	4:25	and was raised for our j.
Rom	5:21	might reign through j for eternal life
Gal	2:21	for if j comes through the law,

JUSTIFIED →JUST

Jb	40: 8	you condemn me that you may be j?
Lk	18:14	you, the latter went home j,
Rom	2:13	those who observe the law will be j.
Rom	3: 4	"That you may be j in your words,
Rom	3:20	since no human being will be j
Rom	3:24	They are j freely by his grace
Rom	3:28	that a person is j by faith apart
Rom	4: 2	if Abraham was j on the basis of his
Rom	5: 1	since we have been j by faith,
Rom	5: 9	since we are now j by his blood,

Rom	8:30	and those he called he also **j**; and those he **j** he also glorified.
Rom	10:10	believes with the heart and so is **j**,
1 Cor	6:11	you were **j** in the name of the Lord
Gal	2:16	know that a person is not **j** by works
Gal	2:16	Jesus that we may be **j** by faith
Gal	2:16	works of the law no one will be **j**.
Gal	2:17	if, in seeking to be **j** in Christ,
Gal	3:11	no one is **j** before God by the law is
Gal	3:24	Christ, that we might be **j** by faith.
Gal	5: 4	you who are trying to be **j** by law;
Ti	3: 7	so that we might be **j** by his grace
Jas	2:21	Was not Abraham our father **j**
Jas	2:24	See how a person is **j** by works
Jas	2:25	**j** by works when she welcomed

JUSTIFIES →JUST

Rom	4: 5	in the one who **j** the ungodly,

JUSTIFY →JUST

Lk	10:29	But because he wished to **j** himself,
Lk	16:15	"You **j** yourselves in the sight
Rom	3:30	will **j** the circumcised on the basis
Gal	3: 8	that God would **j** the Gentiles

JUSTLY →JUST

Wis	9:12	and I shall judge your people **j**
Jer	7: 5	of you deals **j** with his neighbor;
Lk	23:41	we have been condemned **j**,
1 Pt	2:23	over to the one who judges **j**.

JUSTUS → =BARSABBAS, =JESUS

Acts	1:23	who was also known as **J**,
Acts	18: 7	belonging to a man named Titus **J**,
Col	4:11	who is called **J**, who are

K

KADESH →KADESH-BARNEA

Nm	20: 1	month, and the people settled at **K**.
Dt	1:46	had to stay as long as you did at **K**.

KADESH-BARNEA → KADESH

Nm	32: 8	I sent them from **K** to reconnoiter

KEDESH

Jos	12:22	**K**, Jokneam (at Carmel),
Jgs	4: 6	of Abinoam, from **K** of Naphtali.

KEEP → KEEPER, KEEPING, KEEPS, KEPT

Gn	6:19	that you may **k** them alive with you.
Gn	17: 9	you must **k** my covenant throughout
Ex	15:26	and **k** all his precepts, I will not
Ex	19: 5	to my voice and **k** my covenant,
Ex	20: 6	love me and **k** my commandments.
Nm	6:24	The LORD bless you and **k** you!
Dt	5:10	love me and **k** my commandments.
Dt	6:17	**k** the commandments of the LORD,
Dt	7: 9	love him and **k** his commandments,
Jos	22: 5	faithfully; **k** his commandments;
1 Kgs	8:25	**k** the further promise you made
1 Kgs	8:58	in everything and **k** the commands,
2 Kgs	17:19	did not **k** the commandments
1 Chr	29:18	**k** such thoughts in the hearts
Neh	1: 5	you and **k** your commandments,
Jb	14:16	steps, and not **k** watch for sin in me.
Ps	19:14	But from willful sins **k** your servant,
Ps	37:34	and **k** to the way; God will raise you
Ps	78:10	They did not **k** God's covenant;
Prv	4:21	sight, **k** them within your heart;
Prv	7: 2	**K** my commands and live,
Prv	7: 5	they may **k** you from another's wife,
Eccl	3: 6	a time to **k**, and a time to cast away.
Eccl	12:13	Fear God and **k** his commandments,
Sir	1:26	before men; over your lips **k** watch.
Is	26: 3	of firm purpose you **k** in peace,
Mt	19:17	into life, **k** the commandments."
Jn	10:24	"How long are you going to **k** us
2 Cor	12: 7	me, to **k** me from being too elated.
1 Tm	5:22	in another's sins. **K** yourself pure.
1 Pt	3:10	days must **k** the tongue from evil
2 Pt	1: 8	they will **k** you from being idle
Jude	1: 6	who did not **k** to their own domain

Jude	1:21	**K** yourselves in the love of God
Jude	1:24	the one who is able to **k** you
Rv	3:10	I will **k** you safe in the time of trial
Rv	22: 9	of those who **k** the message of this

KEEPER →KEEP

Gn	4: 9	"I do not know. Am I my brother's **k**?"

KEEPING →KEEP

Dt	13:19	**k** all his commandments which I
Ps	119: 9	fault? Only by **k** your words.
Prv	15: 3	**k** watch on the evil and the good.
Lk	2: 8	**k** the night watch over their flock.

KEEPS →KEEP

Prv	11:13	a trustworthy man **k** a confidence.
Sir	21:11	He who **k** the law controls his
Is	26: 2	a nation that is just, one that **k** faith.
Is	56: 2	to it; Who **k** the sabbath free
Jn	7:19	Yet none of you **k** the law. Why are
Jn	8:51	whoever **k** my word will never see
Jas	2:10	For whoever **k** the whole law,
Rv	22: 7	is the one who **k** the prophetic

KEILAH

1 Sm	23: 5	thus rescued the inhabitants of **K**.

KENITE

Jgs	1:16	The descendants of the **K**,
Jgs	4:17	wife of the **K** Heber, since Jabin,

KEPT →KEEP

Nm	17:25	to be **k** there as a warning
2 Sm	22:22	For I **k** the ways of the LORD
Jn	17: 6	to me, and they have **k** your word.
2 Tm	4: 7	finished the race; I have **k** the faith.
Heb	13: 4	and the marriage bed be **k** undefiled,
1 Pt	1: 4	and unfading, **k** in heaven for you
2 Pt	3: 7	**k** for the day of judgment
Rv	3: 8	yet you have **k** my word and have
Rv	3:10	Because you have **k** my message

KETTLES

Mk	7: 4	of cups and jugs and **k** [and beds].)

KETURAH

Wife of Abraham (Gn 25:1-4; 1 Chr 1:32-33).

KEY →KEYS

Is	22:22	I will place the **k** of the House
Lk	11:52	You have taken away the **k**
Rv	3: 7	the true, who holds the **k** of David,
Rv	9: 1	It was given the **k** for the passage
Rv	20: 1	in his hand the **k** to the abyss

KEYS →KEY

Mt	16:19	I will give you the **k** to the kingdom
Rv	1:18	I hold the **k** to death

KICK

Acts	26:14	is hard for you to **k** against the goad.'

KIDNAPER

Ex	21:16	"A **k**, whether he sells his victim or
Dt	24: 7	sell him, the **k** shall be put to death.

KIDRON

2 Sm	15:23	the king crossed the **K** Valley
Jn	18: 1	his disciples across the **K** valley

KILL →KILLED, KILLS

Gn	4:14	the earth, anyone may **k** me at sight."
Gn	12:12	then they will **k** me, but let you live.
Gn	20:11	so they would **k** me on account
Gn	26: 7	of the place would **k** him on account
Gn	37:18	up to them, they plotted to **k** him.
Ex	4:23	I warn you, I will **k** your son,
Eccl	3: 3	A time to **k**, and a time to heal;
Mt	10:28	be afraid of those who **k** the body but cannot **k** the soul;
Mt	17:23	and they will **k** him, and he will be
Mk	9:31	over to men and they will **k** him,
Jn	7:19	Why are you trying to **k** me?"
Rv	11: 7	them and conquer them and **k** them.

KILLED →KILL

Gn	4: 8	attacked his brother Abel and **k** him.
Ex	13:15	go, the LORD **k** every first-born
1 Kgs	11:40	have Jeroboam **k** for his rebellion,
1 Mc	2:24	forward and **k** him upon the altar.
Dn	14:28	"he has destroyed Bel, **k** the dragon,
Mk	8:31	and be **k**, and rise after three days.
Lk	11:48	for they **k** them and you do
Acts	23:12	to eat or drink until they had **k** Paul.
Rom	11: 3	"Lord, they have **k** your prophets,
Rv	9:18	a third of the human race was **k**.
Rv	19:21	The rest were **k** by the sword

KILLS →KILL

Gn	4:15	"If anyone **k** Cain, Cain shall be
Prv	1:32	the self-will of the simple **k** them,

KIND →KINDNESS, KINDS

Gn	1:11	every **k** of plant that bears seed
Prv	14:21	but happy is he who is **k** to the poor!
Prv	14:31	he who is **k** to the needy glorifies
Lk	6:35	for he himself is **k** to the ungrateful
Jn	18:32	he said indicating the **k** of death he
Jn	21:19	by what **k** of death he would glorify
1 Cor	13: 4	Love is patient, love is **k**. It is not
1 Cor	15:35	With what **k** of body will they come
Eph	4:32	[And] be **k** to one another,

KINDNESS →KIND

2 Sm	9: 3	house to whom I may show God's **k**?"
Prv	21:21	He who pursues justice and **k**
Sir	3:14	For **k** to a father will not be
Rom	2: 4	that the **k** of God would lead you
Rom	11:22	See, then, the **k** and severity of God:
Rom	11:22	but God's **k** to you, provided you remain in his **k**;
2 Cor	6: 6	patience, **k**, in a holy spirit,
Gal	5:22	joy, peace, patience, **k**, generosity,
Eph	2: 7	of his grace in his **k** to us in Christ
Col	3:12	heartfelt compassion, **k**, humility,
Ti	3: 4	But when the **k** and generous love

KINDRED →KINSMAN

Gn	24:40	from my own **k** of my father's house.

KINDS →KIND

Gn	1:24	"Let the earth bring forth all **k**
Gn	6:20	Of all **k** of birds, of all **k** of beasts,
Lv	19:19	yours with two different **k** of seed;
Lv	19:19	with two different **k** of thread.
Sir	25: 2	Three **k** of men I hate; their manner
Jer	15: 3	Four **k** of scourge I have decreed

KING →KING'S, KINGDOM, KINGDOMS, KINGS, KINGSHIP

Gn	14:18	Melchizedek, **k** of Salem,
Gn	20: 2	So Abimelech, **k** of Gerar,
Gn	26: 8	Abimelech, **k** of the Philistines,
Ex	1: 8	Then a new **k**, who knew nothing
Nm	21:26	capital of Sihon, **k** of the Amorites,
Nm	21:33	But Og, **k** of Bashan,
Nm	22:10	son of Zippor, **k** of Moab, sent me
Nm	23:21	with him is the triumph of his **K**.
Dt	17:14	to have a **k** over you like all
Jgs	9: 8	went to anoint a **k** over themselves.
Jgs	17: 6	those days there was no **k** in Israel;
Jgs	18: 1	At that time there was no **k** in Israel.
Jgs	19: 1	when there was no **k** in Israel,
Jgs	21:25	those days there was no **k** in Israel;
1 Sm	8: 5	your example, appoint a **k** over us,
1 Sm	8: 7	they are rejecting me as their **k**.
1 Sm	11:15	of the LORD, they made Saul **k**.
1 Sm	12:12	but a **k** must rule us,' even though the LORD your God is your **k**.
1 Sm	15:11	"I regret having made Saul **k**, for he
1 Sm	16: 1	whom I have rejected as **k** of Israel?
1 Sm	16: 1	I have chosen my **k** from among his
2 Sm	2: 4	anointed David **k** of the Judahites.
Tb	10:14	of heaven and earth, the **K** of all,
Jdt	9:12	waters, **K** of all you have created,
Ps	2: 6	"I myself have installed my **k**
Ps	10:16	The LORD is **k** forever; the nations
Ps	24: 7	that the **k** of glory may enter.
Ps	33:16	A **k** is not saved by a mighty army,

Ps	44: 5	You are my **k** and my God,
Ps	47: 8	God is **k** over all the earth;
Ps	48: 3	of Zaphon, the city of the great **k**.
Is	6: 5	yet my eyes have seen the **K**,
Is	32: 1	See, a **k** will reign justly and princes
Is	43:15	One, the creator of Israel, your **K**.
Jer	10:10	he is the living God, the eternal **K**,
Jer	30: 9	their **k**, whom I will raise
Hos	3: 5	and David, their **k**; They shall come
Mi	2:13	Their **k** shall go through before
Zep	3:15	The **K** of Israel, the LORD, is in your
Zec	9: 9	See, your **k** shall come to you; a just
Zec	14: 9	LORD shall become **k** over the whole
Mal	1:14	For a great **K** am I, says the LORD
Mt	2: 2	"Where is the newborn **k**
Mt	21: 5	'Behold, your **k** comes to you,
Mt	27:11	him, "Are you the **k** of the Jews?"
Mt	27:37	This is Jesus, the **K** of the Jews.
Mk	15:32	Let the Messiah, the **K** of Israel,
Lk	19:38	"Blessed is the **k** who comes
Lk	23: 3	him, "Are you the **k** of the Jews?"
Jn	1:49	Son of God; you are the **K** of Israel."
Jn	12:13	of the Lord, [even] the **k** of Israel."
Jn	18:37	Pilate said to him, "Then you are a **k**?"
Jn	18:37	Jesus answered, "You say I am a **k**.
Jn	19:15	said to them, "Shall I crucify your **k**?"
Jn	19:15	answered, "We have no **k** but Caesar."
Jn	19:21	"Do not write 'The **K** of the Jews,'
Acts	17: 7	claim instead that there is another **k**,
1 Tm	1:17	To the **k** of ages, incorruptible,
1 Tm	6:15	the **K** of kings and Lord of lords,
Heb	7: 1	**k** of Salem and priest of God Most
Rv	15: 3	are your ways, O **k** of the nations.
Rv	17:14	he is Lord of lords and **k** of kings,
Rv	19:16	thigh, "**K** of kings and Lord of lords."

KING'S →KING

2 Sm	9:13	because he always ate at the **k** table.
Prv	21: 1	Like a stream is the **k** heart in the hand
Jer	52:33	ate at the **k** table as long as he lived.
Heb	11:23	they were not afraid of the **k** edict.

KINGDOM →KING

Ex	19: 6	You shall be to me a **k** of priests,
Dt	17:18	When he is enthroned in his **k**,
1 Sm	13:14	things are, your **k** shall not endure.
1 Sm	28:17	he has torn the **k** from your grasp
2 Sm	7:12	loins, and I will make his **k** firm.
1 Kgs	11:31	says: 'I will tear away the **k**
1 Chr	17:11	own sons, and I will establish his **k**.
Wis	10:10	ways, Showed him the **k** of God
Is	9: 6	From David's throne, and over his **k**,
Jer	18: 7	down and destroy a nation or a **k**.
Dn	2:39	Another **k** shall take your place,
Dn	2:44	up a **k** that shall never be destroyed
Dn	3:00	wonders; his **k** is an everlasting **k**,
Dn	5:28	your **k** has been divided and given
Dn	7:27	High, Whose **k** shall be everlasting:
Mt	3: 2	for the **k** of heaven is at hand!"
Mt	4:17	for the **k** of heaven is at hand."
Mt	4:23	proclaiming the gospel of the **k**,
Mt	5: 3	spirit, for theirs is the **k** of heaven.
Mt	5:10	for theirs is the **k** of heaven.
Mt	5:19	be called least in the **k** of heaven.
Mt	5:19	be called greatest in the **k** of heaven.
Mt	5:20	will not enter into the **k** of heaven.
Mt	6:10	your **k** come, your will be done,
Mt	6:33	But seek first the **k** [of God] and his
Mt	7:21	Lord,' will enter the **k** of heaven,
Mt	8:12	the children of the **k** will be driven
Mt	9:35	proclaiming the gospel of the **k**,
Mt	10: 7	'The **k** of heaven is at hand.'
Mt	11:11	in the **k** of heaven is greater than he.
Mt	11:12	the **k** of heaven suffers violence,
Mt	12:25	"Every **k** divided against itself will
Mt	12:28	the **k** of God has come upon you.
Mt	13:11	of the **k** of heaven has been granted
Mt	13:19	of the **k** without understanding it,
Mt	13:24	"The **k** of heaven may be likened
Mt	13:31	"The **k** of heaven is like a mustard

Mt	13:33	"The **k** of heaven is like yeast
Mt	13:38	the good seed the children of the **k**.
Mt	13:44	"The **k** of heaven is like a treasure
Mt	13:45	the **k** of heaven is like a merchant
Mt	13:47	the **k** of heaven is like a net thrown
Mt	13:52	in the **k** of heaven is like the head
Mt	16:19	you the keys to the **k** of heaven.
Mt	16:28	see the Son of Man coming in his **k**."
Mt	18: 1	is the greatest in the **k** of heaven?"
Mt	18: 3	you will not enter the **k** of heaven.
Mt	18: 4	is the greatest in the **k** of heaven.
Mt	18:23	That is why the **k** of heaven may be
Mt	19:12	for the sake of the **k** of heaven.
Mt	19:14	for the **k** of heaven belongs to such
Mt	19:23	who is rich to enter the **k** of heaven.
Mt	20: 1	"The **k** of heaven is like a landowner
Mt	20:21	and the other at your left, in your **k**."
Mt	21:31	prostitutes are entering the **k** of God
Mt	21:43	the **k** of God will be taken away
Mt	22: 2	"The **k** of heaven may be likened
Mt	23:13	You lock the **k** of heaven before
Mt	24:14	of the **k** will be preached throughout
Mt	25: 1	"Then the **k** of heaven will be like ten
Mt	25:34	Inherit the **k** prepared for you
Mt	26:29	with you new in the **k** of my Father."
Mk	1:15	fulfillment. The **k** of God is at hand.
Mk	3:24	If a **k** is divided against itself, that **k**
Mk	4:11	of the **k** of God has been granted
Mk	4:26	"This is how it is with the **k** of God;
Mk	6:23	you ask of me, even to half of my **k**."
Mk	9: 1	they see that the **k** of God has come
Mk	9:47	enter into the **k** of God with one eye
Mk	10:14	for the **k** of God belongs to such as
Mk	10:15	whoever does not accept the **k**
Mk	10:23	have wealth to enter the **k** of God!"
Mk	10:24	how hard it is to enter the **k** of God!
Mk	11:10	Blessed is the **k** of our father David
Mk	12:34	"You are not far from the **k** of God."
Mk	13: 8	rise against nation and **k** against **k**.
Mk	14:25	when I drink it new in the **k** of God."
Mk	15:43	who was himself awaiting the **k**
Lk	1:33	and of his **k** there will be no end."
Lk	4:43	the good news of the **k** of God,
Lk	6:20	are poor, for the **k** of God is yours.
Lk	7:28	in the **k** of God is greater than he."
Lk	8: 1	the good news of the **k** of God,
Lk	8:10	of the **k** of God has been granted
Lk	9: 2	sent them to proclaim the **k** of God
Lk	9:11	spoke to them about the **k** of God,
Lk	9:27	not taste death until they see the **k**
Lk	9:60	you, go and proclaim the **k** of God."
Lk	9:62	left behind is fit for the **k** of God!"
Lk	10: 9	The **k** of God is at hand for you.'
Lk	10:11	know this: the **k** of God is at hand.
Lk	11: 2	be your name, your **k** come.
Lk	11:20	the **k** of God has come upon you.
Lk	12:31	seek his **k**, and these other things
Lk	12:32	Father is pleased to give you the **k**.
Lk	13:18	he said, "What is the **k** of God like?
Lk	13:29	will recline at table in the **k** of God.
Lk	14:15	one who will dine in the **k** of God."
Lk	16:16	then on the **k** of God is proclaimed,
Lk	17:20	when the **k** of God would come,
Lk	17:21	behold, the **k** of God is among you.'
Lk	18:16	for the **k** of God belongs to such as
Lk	18:24	have wealth to enter the **k** of God!
Lk	18:29	children for the sake of the **k** of God
Lk	19:11	the **k** of God would appear there
Lk	21:31	know that the **k** of God is near.
Lk	22:16	there is fulfillment in the **k** of God."
Lk	22:18	the vine until the **k** of God comes."
Lk	22:29	and I confer a **k** on you, just as my
Lk	22:30	eat and drink at my table in my **k**;
Lk	23:42	me when you come into your **k**."
Lk	23:51	and was awaiting the **k** of God.
Jn	3: 3	no one can see the **k** of God without
Jn	3: 5	you, no one can enter the **k** of God
Jn	18:36	"My **k** does not belong to this world.
Acts	1: 3	and speaking about the **k** of God.

Acts	1: 6	time going to restore the **k** to Israel?"
Acts	8:12	the good news about the **k** of God
Acts	14:22	hardships to enter the **k** of God."
Acts	19: 8	arguments about the **k** of God.
Acts	20:25	I preached the **k** during my travels
Acts	28:23	bearing witness to the **k** of God
Acts	28:31	hindrance he proclaimed the **k**
Rom	14:17	For the **k** of God is not a matter
1 Cor	4:20	For the **k** of God is not a matter
1 Cor	6: 9	the unjust will not inherit the **k**
1 Cor	15:24	when he hands over the **k** to his God
1 Cor	15:50	blood cannot inherit the **k** of God,
Eph	5: 5	any inheritance in the **k** of Christ
Col	1:13	us to the **k** of his beloved Son,
Col	4:11	are my co-workers for the **k** of God,
1 Thes	2:12	of the God who calls you into his **k**
2 Thes	1: 5	considered worthy of the **k** of God
2 Tm	4:18	will bring me safe to his heavenly **k**.
Heb	1: 8	scepter is the scepter of your **k**.
Heb	12:28	the unshakable **k** should have
Jas	2: 5	heirs of the **k** that he promised
2 Pt	1:11	entry into the eternal **k** of our Lord
Rv	1: 6	who has made us into a **k**,
Rv	1: 9	the **k**, and the endurance we have
Rv	5:10	You made them a **k** and priests
Rv	11:15	"The **k** of the world now belongs
Rv	12:10	come, and the **k** of our God
Rv	16:10	Its **k** was plunged into darkness,

KINGDOMS →KING

Dt	3:21	all the **k** which you will encounter
1 Kgs	5: 1	Solomon ruled over all the **k**
2 Kgs	19:15	You alone are God over all the **k**
2 Kgs	19:19	that all the **k** of the earth may know
2 Chr	20: 6	do you not rule over all the **k**
Ps	68:33	You **k** of the earth, sing to God;
Ez	37:22	shall they be divided into two **k**.
Dn	2:44	it shall break in pieces all these **k**
Zep	3: 8	to assemble the **k**, In order to pour
Lk	4: 5	showed him all the **k** of the world
Heb	11:33	who by faith conquered **k**, did what

KINGS →KING

Gn	14: 9	king of Ellasar—four **k** against five.
Gn	17: 6	of you; **k** shall stem from you.
Jos	12: 1	The **k** of the land east of the Jordan,
2 Sm	11: 1	year, when **k** go out on campaign,
1 Kgs	10:23	and wisdom all the **k** of the earth.
1 Mc	2:48	of the **k** and did not let the sinner
Ps	2: 2	**K** on earth rise up and princes plot
Ps	68:30	that **k** may bring you tribute.
Ps	72:11	May all **k** bow before him,
Ps	89:28	Most High over the **k** of the earth.
Ps	110: 5	who crushes **k** on the day of wrath,
Ps	138: 4	All the **k** of earth will praise you,
Ps	149: 8	To bind their **k** with chains,
Prv	8:15	By me **k** reign, and lawgivers
Prv	16:12	**K** have a horror of wrongdoing,
Prv	31: 4	It is not for **k**, O Lemuel, not for **k**
Is	24:21	and the **k** of the earth on the earth.
Is	52:15	of him **k** shall stand speechless;
Is	60:11	nations, and their **k**, in the vanguard.
Dn	2:21	makes **k** and unmakes them.
Dn	2:47	gods and Lord of **k** and a revealer
Dn	7:24	The ten horns shall be ten **k**
Lk	10:24	and **k** desired to see what you see,
Lk	21:12	they will have you led before **k**
Acts	4:26	The **k** of the earth took their stand
1 Cor	4: 8	rich; you have become **k** without us!
1 Tm	2: 2	for **k** and for all in authority, that we
1 Tm	6:15	the King of **k** and Lord of lords,
Rv	1: 5	dead and ruler of the **k** of the earth.
Rv	17: 2	The **k** of the earth have had
Rv	17:12	saw represent ten **k** who have not
Rv	17:14	for he is Lord of lords and king of **k**,
Rv	19:16	thigh, "King of **k** and Lord of lords."
Rv	19:19	I saw the beast and the **k** of the earth
Rv	21:24	it the **k** of the earth will bring their

KINGSHIP → KING
Dn	7:14	He received dominion, glory, and **k**;
Dn	7:14	away, his **k** shall not be destroyed.

KINSMAN → KINDRED
Tb	5:14	So it turns out that you are a **k**,

KISH
1 Sm	10:21	finally Saul, son of **K**, was chosen.

KISHON
Jgs	5:21	The Wadi **K** swept them away;
1 Kgs	18:40	them brought down to the brook **K**
Ps	83:10	Sisera and Jabin at the torrent **K**,

KISS → KISSED, KISSES, KISSING
Gn	27:26	to him, "Come closer, son, and **k** me."
Gn	31:28	did not even allow me a parting **k**
2 Sm	15: 5	his hand, hold him, and **k** him.
2 Sm	20: 9	held Amasa's beard as if to **k** him.
1 Kgs	19:20	let me **k** my father and mother
Ps	85:11	will meet; justice and peace will **k**.
Prv	24:26	He gives a **k** on the lips who makes
Song	1: 2	Let him **k** me with kisses of his
Song	8: 1	met you out of doors, I would **k** you
Mt	26:48	saying, "The man I shall **k** is the one;
Mk	14:44	saying, "The man I shall **k** is the one;
Lk	7:45	You did not give me a **k**, but she has
Lk	22:47	He went up to Jesus to **k** him.
Lk	22:48	betraying the Son of Man with a **k**?"
Rom	16:16	Greet one another with a holy **k**.
1 Cor	16:20	Greet one another with a holy **k**.
2 Cor	13:12	Greet one another with a holy **k**.
1 Thes	5:26	Greet all the brothers with a holy **k**.
1 Pt	5:14	Greet one another with a loving **k**.

KISSED → KISS
Gn	27:27	As Jacob went up and **k** him,
Gn	29:11	Then Jacob **k** Rachel and burst
Gn	32: 1	Laban **k** his grandchildren and his
Gn	33: 4	on his neck, **k** him as he wept.
Gn	45:15	Joseph then **k** all his brothers,
Gn	48:10	to him, he **k** and embraced them.
Gn	50: 1	face and wept over him as he **k** him.
Ex	4:27	the mountain of God, Aaron **k** him.
Ex	18: 7	bowed down before him, and **k** him.
Ru	1: 9	She **k** them good-by, but they wept
1 Sm	10: 1	Saul's head; he also **k** him, saying:
1 Sm	20:41	They **k** each other and wept aloud
2 Sm	14:33	the king. Then the king **k** him.
2 Sm	19:40	he **k** Barzillai and bade him
1 Kgs	19:18	who have not knelt to Baal or **k** him."
Tb	5:17	Tobiah **k** his father and mother.
Tb	7: 6	Raguel sprang up and **k** him,
Tb	10:12	Then he **k** his daughter Sarah
Tb	10:13	She **k** them both and sent them
Est	C: 6	Gladly would I have **k** the soles
Mt	26:49	and said, "Hail, Rabbi!" and he **k** him.
Mk	14:45	him and said, "Rabbi." And he **k** him.
Lk	15:20	to his son, embraced him and **k** him.
Acts	20:37	their arms around Paul and **k** him,

KISSES → KISS
Prv	7:13	When she seizes him, she **k** him,
Song	1: 2	Let him kiss me with **k** of his
Sir	29: 5	he borrows, he **k** the lender's hand

KISSING → KISS
Lk	7:45	she has not ceased **k** my feet since

KNEADING
Dt	28: 5	be your grain bin and your **k** bowl!
Dt	28:17	be your grain bin and your **k** bowl!

KNEE → KNEES
Is	45:23	To me every **k** shall bend; by me
Rom	14:11	Lord, every **k** shall bend before me,
Phil	2:10	name of Jesus every **k** should bend,

KNEEL → KNELT
Ps	95: 6	let us **k** before the Lord who made

KNEES → KNEE
Is	35: 3	make firm the **k** that are weak,

Lk	5: 8	he fell at the **k** of Jesus and said,
Heb	12:12	drooping hands and your weak **k**.

KNELT → KNEEL
2 Chr	6:13	it, Solomon **k** in the presence
Mt	9:18	came forward, **k** down before him,
Mt	17:14	approached, **k** down before him,
Acts	20:36	he had finished speaking he **k** down

KNEW → KNOW
Dt	34:10	whom the Lord **k** face to face.
Jer	1: 5	I formed you in the womb I **k** you,
Jon	4: 2	I **k** that you are a gracious
Mt	7:23	to them solemnly, 'I never **k** you.
Mt	12:25	But he **k** what they were thinking
Lk	4:41	speak because they **k** that he was
Jn	2:24	to them because he **k** them all,
Jn	4:10	"If you **k** the gift of God and who is
Jn	8:19	If you **k** me, you would know my
Jn	13: 1	Jesus **k** that his hour had come
Jn	13:11	For he **k** who would betray him;
Rom	1:21	for although they **k** God they did not

KNIFE → KNIVES
Gn	22:10	and took the **k** to slaughter his son.
Prv	23: 2	And put a **k** to your throat if you

KNIT
Jb	10:11	bones and sinews **k** me together.
Ps	139:13	you **k** me in my mother's womb.

KNIVES → KNIFE
Jos	5: 2	"Make flint **k** and circumcise
Prv	30:14	whose teeth are **k**,

KNOCK → KNOCKING, KNOCKS
Mt	7: 7	**k** and the door will be opened
Lk	11: 9	**k** and the door will be opened
Rv	3:20	" ' "Behold, I stand at the door and **k**.

KNOCKING → KNOCK
Song	5: 2	I heard my lover **k**: "Open to me,
Lk	13:25	will you stand outside **k** and saying,

KNOCKS → KNOCK
Mt	7: 8	and to the one who **k**, the door will
Lk	12:36	immediately when he comes and **k**.

KNOW → FOREKNEW, FOREKNOWLEDGE, KNEW, KNOWING, KNOWLEDGE, KNOWN, KNOWS
Gn	15: 8	"how am I to **k** that I shall possess it?"
Gn	22:12	I **k** now how devoted you are
Ex	3:19	"Yet I **k** that the king of Egypt will
Ex	6: 7	You will **k** that I, the Lord, am your
Ex	14: 4	the Egyptians will **k** that I am
Ex	18:11	Now I **k** that the Lord is a deity
Ex	33:12	have not let me **k** whom you will
Ex	33:13	you, do let me **k** your ways so that,
Nm	16:28	"This is how you shall **k** that it was
Jos	3: 7	that they may **k** I am with you, as I
1 Kgs	8:39	You who alone **k** the hearts of all
Est	C: 5	You **k** all things. You **k**, O Lord,
Jb	19:25	for me, I **k** that my Vindicator lives,
Jb	42: 2	I **k** that you can do all things,
Jb	42: 3	wonderful for me, which I cannot **k**.
Ps	100: 3	**K** that the Lord is God, our maker
Ps	139:23	Probe me, God, **k** my heart; try me, **k** my concerns.
Prv	27: 1	you **k** not what any day may bring
Prv	30: 4	what is his son's name, if you **k** it?"
Eccl	8:16	I applied my heart to **k** wisdom
Is	1: 3	But Israel does not **k**, my people has
Jer	4:22	Fools my people are, they **k** me not;
Jer	4:22	in evil, but **k** not how to do good.
Jer	6:15	ashamed, they **k** not how to blush.
Jer	31:34	and kinsmen how to **k** the Lord. All,
Jer	31:34	from least to greatest, shall **k** me,
Ez	2: 5	are a rebellious house—they shall **k**
Ez	6:10	they shall **k** that it was not in vain
Mt	6: 3	let your left hand **k** what your right
Mt	7:11	**k** how to give good gifts to your
Mt	9: 6	that you may **k** that the Son of Man
Mt	22:29	because you do not **k** the scriptures

Mt	24:42	For you do not k on which day your
Mt	26:74	and to swear, "I do not k the man."
Mk	12:24	because you do not k the scriptures
Lk	11:13	k how to give good gifts to your
Lk	13:25	'I do not k where you are from.'
Lk	18:20	You k the commandments,
Lk	21:31	k that the kingdom of God is near.
Lk	22:34	will deny three times that you k me."
Lk	23:34	them, they k not what they do."]
Jn	3:11	you, we speak of what we k and we
Jn	4:42	we k that this is truly the savior
Jn	7:28	"You k me and also k where I am
Jn	7:28	sent me, whom you do not k, is true.
Jn	8:14	But you do not k where I come
Jn	8:19	"You k neither me nor my Father.
Jn	8:19	me, you would k my Father also."
Jn	8:32	and you will k the truth,
Jn	8:55	You do not k him, but I k him.
Jn	8:55	But I do k him and I keep his word.
Jn	9:25	replied, "If he is a sinner, I do not k.
Jn	9:25	One thing I do k is that I was blind
Jn	10:14	and I k mine and mine k me,
Jn	10:27	voice; I k them, and they follow me.
Jn	12:35	in the dark does not k where he is
Jn	13:35	This is how all will k that you are
Jn	14:17	But you k it, because it remains
Jn	15:21	because they do not k the one who
Jn	16:30	we realize that you k everything
Jn	17: 3	that they should k you, the only true
Jn	17:23	the world may k that you sent me,
Jn	21:15	"Yes, Lord, you k that I love you."
Jn	21:24	and we k that his testimony is true.
Acts	1: 7	"It is not for you to k the times
Acts	1:24	Lord, who k the hearts of all,
Rom	6: 6	We k that our old self was crucified
Rom	6:16	Do you not k that if you present
Rom	7:14	We k that the law is spiritual; but I
Rom	7:18	For I k that good does not dwell
Rom	8:26	for we do not k how to pray as we
Rom	8:28	We k that all things work for good
1 Cor	1:21	not come to k God through wisdom,
1 Cor	2: 2	I resolved to k nothing while I was
1 Cor	3:16	Do you not k that you are the temple
1 Cor	5: 6	Do you not k that a little yeast
1 Cor	6: 2	Do you not k that the holy ones will
1 Cor	6:15	Do you not k that your bodies are
1 Cor	6:16	do you not k that anyone who joins
1 Cor	6:19	Do you not k that your body is
1 Cor	8: 2	he does not yet k as he ought to k.
1 Cor	8: 4	we k that "there is no idol
1 Cor	9:13	Do you not k that those who
1 Cor	9:24	Do you not k that the runners
1 Cor	12: 2	You k how, when you were pagans,
1 Cor	13: 9	For we k partially and we prophesy
1 Cor	13:12	At present I k partially; then I shall k fully as I am fully known.
1 Cor	14: 9	how will anyone k what is being
2 Cor	5: 1	For we k that if our earthly
2 Cor	5: 6	although we k that while we are
2 Cor	8: 9	For you k the gracious act of our
2 Cor	12: 2	body or out of the body I do not k,
Eph	1:18	that you may k what is the hope
Eph	3:19	to k the love of Christ that surpasses
Phil	3:10	to k him and the power of his
Phil	4:12	I k indeed how to live in humble
Phil	4:12	I k also how to live with abundance.
Col	4: 6	that you k how you should respond
1 Thes	3: 3	For you yourselves k that we are
1 Thes	5: 2	For you yourselves k very well
2 Thes	2: 6	And now you k what is restraining,
1 Tm	3: 5	a man does not k how to manage his
1 Tm	3:15	you should k how to behave
2 Tm	1:12	for I k him in whom I have believed
2 Tm	2:23	for you k that they breed quarrels.
Ti	1:16	They claim to k God, but by their
Heb	8:11	and kinsman, saying, "K the Lord,"
Heb	8:11	for all shall k me, from least
Jas	1: 3	for you k that the testing of your
Jas	4: 4	Do you not k that to be a lover

2 Pt	1:12	even though you already k them
1 Jn	2: 3	we may be sure that we k him is
1 Jn	2: 4	Whoever says, "I k him," but does not
1 Jn	2:11	and does not k where he is going
1 Jn	2:18	Thus we k this is the last hour.
1 Jn	2:29	you also k that everyone who acts
1 Jn	3: 1	reason the world does not k us is that it did not k him.
1 Jn	3: 2	We do k that when it is revealed we
1 Jn	3:14	We k that we have passed
1 Jn	3:16	The way we came to k love was
1 Jn	3:19	[Now] this is how we shall k that we
1 Jn	3:24	the way we k that he remains in us
1 Jn	4: 8	is without love does not k God,
1 Jn	4:13	This is how we k that we remain
1 Jn	5: 2	In this way we k that we love
1 Jn	5:13	you may k that you have eternal life,
1 Jn	5:15	if we k that he hears us in regard
1 Jn	5:18	We k that no one begotten by God
1 Jn	5:20	also k that the Son of God has come
1 Jn	5:20	to k the one who is true.
2 Jn	1: 1	only I but also all who k the truth—
3 Jn	1:12	and you k our testimony is true.
Rv	2: 2	"I k your works, your labor, and your
Rv	2: 9	"I k your tribulation and poverty,
Rv	2:13	"I k that you live where Satan's
Rv	2:19	"I k your works, your love, faith,
Rv	3: 3	you will never k at what hour I will
Rv	3: 8	" ' "I k your works (behold, I have left
Rv	3:15	"I k your works; I k that you are

KNOWING →KNOW

Gn	3:22	us, k what is good and what is bad!
Jn	18: 4	k everything that was going
1 Cor	15:58	k that in the Lord your labor is not
2 Cor	4:14	k that the one who raised the Lord
Phil	3: 8	good of k Christ Jesus my Lord.
Phlm	1:21	k that you will do even more than I
2 Pt	2:21	righteousness than after k it to turn

KNOWLEDGE →KNOW

Gn	2: 9	the tree of the k of good and bad.
Gn	2:17	except the tree of k of good and bad.
2 Chr	1:10	wisdom and k to lead this people,
Jb	21:22	Can anyone teach God k,
Ps	19: 3	one night to the next imparts that k.
Ps	73:11	"Does the Most High have any k?"
Ps	94:10	who teaches humans not have k?
Ps	119:66	Teach me wisdom and k, for in your
Ps	139: 6	Such k is beyond me, far too lofty
Prv	1: 4	to the young man k and discretion.
Prv	1: 7	of the Lord is the beginning of k;
Prv	1:29	Because they hated k, and chose not
Prv	2: 5	the Lord; the k of God you will find;
Prv	2: 6	from his mouth come k
Prv	2:10	your heart, k will please your soul,
Prv	3:20	By his k the depths break open,
Prv	8:10	silver, and k rather than choice gold.
Prv	8:12	experience, and judicious k I attain.
Prv	9:10	k of the Holy One is understanding.
Prv	10:14	Wise men store up k, but the mouth
Prv	11: 9	through their k the just make their
Prv	12: 1	He who loves correction loves k,
Prv	12:23	A shrewd man conceals his k,
Prv	14: 6	k is easy to the man of intelligence.
Prv	15: 7	The lips of the wise disseminate k,
Prv	15:14	mind of the intelligent man seeks k,
Prv	18:15	The mind of the intelligent gains k, and the ear of the wise seeks k.
Prv	19: 2	Without k even zeal is not good;
Prv	19:25	an intelligent man, he gains k.
Prv	23:12	and your ears to words of k.
Prv	24: 4	And by k are its rooms filled
Prv	24: 5	and a man of k than a man of might;
Eccl	1:18	he who stores up k stores up grief.
Eccl	2:26	he sees fit he gives wisdom and k
Eccl	7:12	the advantage of k is that wisdom
Is	11: 2	a spirit of k and of fear of the Lord,
Is	11: 9	the earth shall be filled with k
Is	40:14	Whom did he consult to gain k?

Dn	1:17	these four young men God gave **k**
Hos	4: 6	My people perish for want of **k**!
Hb	2:14	with the **k** of the Lord's glory
Mal	2: 7	the lips of the priest are to keep **k**,
Lk	1:77	to give his people **k** of salvation
Lk	11:52	You have taken away the key of **k**.
Rom	2:20	law you have the formulation of **k**
Rom	11:33	riches and wisdom and **k** of God!
Rom	15:14	filled with all **k**, and able
1 Cor	8: 1	we realize that "all of us have **k**";
1 Cor	8:10	with your **k**, reclining at table
1 Cor	8:11	Thus through your **k**, the weak
1 Cor	12: 8	the expression of **k** according
1 Cor	13: 2	comprehend all mysteries and all **k**;
1 Cor	13: 8	if **k**, it will be brought to nothing.
2 Cor	4: 6	to bring to light the **k** of the glory
2 Cor	8: 7	faith, discourse, **k**, all earnestness,
2 Cor	10: 5	raising itself against the **k** of God,
2 Cor	11: 6	in speaking, I am not so in **k**;
Eph	3:19	the love of Christ that surpasses **k**,
Eph	4:13	of faith and **k** of the Son of God,
Phil	1: 9	and more in **k** and every kind
Col	1:10	fruit and growing in the **k** of God,
Col	2: 3	all the treasures of wisdom and **k**.
Col	3:10	for **k**, in the image of its creator.
1 Tm	2: 4	saved and to come to **k** of the truth.
1 Tm	6:20	and the absurdities of so-called **k**.
Heb	10:26	after receiving **k** of the truth,
2 Pt	1: 3	through the **k** of him who called us
2 Pt	1: 5	your faith with virtue, virtue with **k**,
2 Pt	3:18	in the **k** of our Lord and savior Jesus
1 Jn	2:20	the holy one, and you all have **k**.

KNOWN →KNOW

Ex	6: 3	Lord, I did not make **k** to them.
Dt	13: 3	whom you have not **k**, and to serve
Ps	67: 3	So shall your rule be **k**
Ps	98: 2	The Lord has made his victory **k**;
Ps	105: 1	make **k** among the peoples his
Sir	4:24	speech that wisdom becomes **k**,
Is	12: 4	the nations make **k** his deeds,
Ez	38:23	make myself **k** in the sight of many
Ez	39: 7	my holy name **k** among my people
Zec	14: 7	one continuous day, **k** to the Lord,
Mt	10:26	nor secret that will not be **k**.
Mt	24:43	of the house had **k** the hour of night
Lk	6:44	For every tree is **k** by its own fruit.
Jn	17:26	I made **k** to them your name and I will make it **k**,
Acts	2:28	You have made **k** to me the paths
Rom	· 1:19	what can be **k** about God is evident
Rom	9:22	his wrath and make **k** his power,
Rom	11:34	"For who has **k** the mind of the Lord
Rom	16:26	made **k** to all nations to bring
1 Cor	2:16	for "who has **k** the mind of the Lord,
1 Cor	8: 3	if one loves God, one is **k** by him.
1 Cor	13:12	I shall know fully as I am fully **k**.
2 Cor	3: 2	on our hearts, **k** and read by all,
Eph	1: 9	he has made **k** to us the mystery
Eph	3: 3	that] the mystery was made **k** to me
Eph	6:19	to make **k** with boldness the mystery
2 Tm	3:15	infancy you have **k** [the] sacred
2 Pt	2:21	for them not to have **k** the way
Rv	1: 1	He made it **k** by sending his angel

KNOWS →KNOW

Gn	3: 5	God **k** well that the moment you eat
Est	4:14	Who **k** but that it was for a time like
Jb	23:10	Yet he **k** my way; if he proved me,
Ps	44:22	God who **k** the secrets of the heart?
Ps	103:14	For he **k** how we are formed,
Prv	14:10	The heart **k** its own bitterness,
Eccl	2:19	who **k** whether he will be a wise
Eccl	8: 5	and the wise man's heart **k** times
Wis	9:11	For she **k** and understands all things,
Jon	3: 9	Who **k**, God may relent and forgive,
Mt	6: 8	Your Father **k** what you need before
Mt	11:27	No one **k** the Son except the Father,
Mt	11:27	no one **k** the Father except the Son
Mt	24:36	"But of that day and hour no one **k**,
Lk	12:30	your Father **k** that you need them.

Lk	16:15	of others, but God **k** your hearts;
Acts	15: 8	And God, who **k** the heart,
Rom	8:27	who searches hearts **k** what is
1 Cor	2:11	who **k** what pertains to a person
1 Cor	2:11	no one **k** what pertains to God
1 Cor	3:20	"The Lord **k** the thoughts of the wise,
2 Tm	2:19	"The Lord **k** those who are his"; and,
Jas	4:17	So for one who **k** the right thing
2 Pt	2: 9	the Lord **k** how to rescue the devout
1 Jn	4: 6	and anyone who **k** God listens to us,
1 Jn	4: 7	loves is begotten by God and **k** God.
Rv	2:17	which no one **k** except the one who
Rv	19:12	that no one **k** except himself.

KOHATH →KOHATHITES

Gn	46:11	of Levi: Gershon, **K** and Merari.
Nm	26:58	the descendants of **K** was Amram,
1 Chr	23: 6	of Levi: Gershon, **K**, and Merari.

KOHATHITES →KOHATH

Nm	4:15	meeting tent that the **K** shall carry.
2 Chr	34:12	of the **K**, who directed them.

KORAH →KORAHITES

1. Levite who led rebellion against Moses and Aaron (Nm 16; Jude 11).
2. Psalms of the sons of Korah: See Korahites.

KORAHITES →KORAH
Psalms of the Korahites: Pss 42; 44-49; 84; 85; 87; 88.

L

LABAN
Brother of Rebekah (Gn 24:29), father of Rachel and Leah (Gn 29:16). Received Abraham's servant (Gn 24:29-51). Provided daughters as wives for Jacob in exchange for Jacob's service (Gn 29:1-30). Provided flocks for Jacob's service (Gn 30:25-43). After Jacob's departure, pursued and covenanted with him (Gn 31).

LABOR →LABORER, LABORERS

Ex	1:11	to oppress them with forced **l**.
Ex	20: 9	Six days you may **l** and do all your
Dt	5:13	Six days you may **l** and do all your
Ps	48: 7	there, anguish, like a woman's **l**,
Ps	127: 1	the house, they **l** in vain who build.
Is	54: 1	song, you who were not in **l**,
1 Cor	3: 8	receive wages in proportion to his **l**.
1 Cor	15:58	that in the Lord your **l** is not in vain.
Phil	2:16	that I did not run in vain or **l** in vain.
1 Thes	1: 3	your work of faith and **l** of love

LABORER →LABOR

Lv	19:13	overnight the wages of your day **l**.
Lk	10: 7	you, for the **l** deserves his payment.

LABORERS →LABOR

Lk	10: 2	is abundant but the **l** are few; so ask
Lk	10: 2	harvest to send out **l** for his harvest.

LACHISH

Jos	10:32	The Lord delivered **L** into the power
2 Chr	25:27	in Jerusalem; hence he fled to **L**.

LACK →LACKING, LACKS

Dt	8: 9	stint and where you will **l** nothing,
Ps	34:11	who seek the Lord **l** no good thing.
Prv	5:23	He will die from **l** of discipline,
1 Cor	7: 5	may not tempt you through your **l**

LACKING →LACK

Col	1:24	filling up what is **l** in the afflictions
Jas	1: 4	perfect and complete, **l** in nothing.

LACKS →LACK

Jas	1: 5	But if any of you **l** wisdom,
2 Pt	1: 9	Anyone who **l** them is blind

LADY

2 Jn	1: 1	The Presbyter to the chosen **L**
2 Jn	1: 5	But now, **L**, I ask you, not as though

LAID →LAY

Nm	27:23	he **l** his hands on him and gave him
Dt	34: 9	since Moses had **l** his hands

1 Kgs	6:37	of the LORD's temple were l
Ezr	3:11	of the LORD's house had been l.
1 Mc	2:12	and our glory l waste,
Ps	102:26	Of old you l the earth's foundations;
Is	14: 8	"Now that you are l to rest, there will
Is	44:28	the temple, "Let its foundations be l."
Is	53: 6	But the LORD l upon him the guilt
Zec	4: 9	Zerubbabel have l the foundations
Mk	6:29	and took his body and l it in a tomb.
Mk	16: 6	Behold, the place where they l him.
Lk	6:48	deeply and l the foundation on rock;
Jn	19:42	So they l Jesus there because
Acts	6: 6	who prayed and l hands on them.
Acts	7:58	The witnesses l down their cloaks
1 Jn	3:16	love was that he l down his life

LAKE
Lk	8:33	down the steep bank into the l

LAMB → LAMB'S, LAMBS
2 Sm	12: 6	restore the ewe l four-fold because
Is	11: 6	the wolf shall be a guest of the l,
Is	53: 7	mouth; Like a l led to the slaughter
Is	65:25	The wolf and the l shall graze alike,
Jer	11:19	Yet I, like a trusting l led to slaughter,
Mk	14:12	when they sacrificed the Passover l,
Jn	1:29	"Behold, the L of God, who takes
Acts	8:32	and as a l before its shearer is silent,
1 Cor	5: 7	For our paschal l, Christ, has been
1 Pt	1:19	as of a spotless unblemished l.
Rv	5:12	"Worthy is the L that was slain
Rv	6: 1	watched while the L broke open
Rv	7:14	them white in the blood of the L.
Rv	12:11	conquered him by the blood of the L
Rv	13: 8	belongs to the L who was slain.
Rv	14: 1	there was the L standing on Mount
Rv	15: 3	of God, and the song of the L:
Rv	17:14	They will fight with the L, but the L
Rv	19: 7	the wedding day of the L has come,
Rv	21: 9	you the bride, the wife of the L."
Rv	21:14	of the twelve apostles of the L.
Rv	21:23	gave it light, and its lamp was the L.
Rv	22: 1	from the throne of God and of the L

LAMB'S → LAMB
Rv	21:27	names are written in the L book of life.

LAMBS → LAMB
Ex	12:21	"Go and procure l for your families,
Ex	29:38	altar: two yearling l as the sacrifice
Ps	114: 4	rams; the hills, like l of the flock.
Is	40:11	flock; in his arms he gathers the l,
Lk	10: 3	sending you like l among wolves.
Jn	21:15	love you." He said to him, "Feed my l."

LAME
2 Sm	4: 4	hasty flight, he fell and became l.]
2 Sm	5: 6	blind and the l will drive you away!"
Is	33:23	and the l will carry off the loot.
Is	35: 6	Then will the l leap like a stag,
Mi	4: 6	LORD, I will gather the l, And I will
Zep	3:19	I will save the l, and assemble
Mt	11: 5	blind regain their sight, the l walk,
Mt	15:31	made whole, the l walking,
Lk	14:13	poor, the crippled, the l, the blind;
Jn	5: 3	number of ill, blind, l, and crippled.

LAMECH
Gn	4:19	L took two wives; the name

LAMENT
Jl	1: 8	L like a virgin girt with sackcloth

LAMP → LAMPS, LAMPSTAND, LAMPSTANDS
1 Sm	3: 3	The l of God was not yet
2 Sm	22:29	You are my l, O LORD! O my God,
1 Kgs	11:36	may always have a l before me
1 Kgs	15: 4	his God, gave him a l in Jerusalem,
2 Kgs	8:19	he would leave him a l in the LORD's
Ps	18:29	You, LORD, give light to my l;
Ps	119:105	Your word is a l for my feet, a light
Ps	132:17	line; I will set a l for my anointed.
Prv	6:23	For the bidding is a l,

Prv	20:27	A l from the LORD is the breath
Prv	31:18	at night her l is undimmed.
Mt	5:15	Nor do they light a l and then put it
Mt	6:22	"The l of the body is the eye. If your
Lk	8:16	"No one who lights a l conceals it
Jn	5:35	He was a burning and shining l,
Rv	21:23	gave it light, and its l was the Lamb.
Rv	22: 5	nor will they need light from l

LAMPS → LAMP
Ex	25:37	You shall then make seven l for it
Ex	25:37	set up the l that they shed their light
1 Mc	4:50	and lighted the l on the lampstand,
2 Mc	1: 8	we lighted the l and set
Mt	25: 1	be like ten virgins who took their l
Lk	12:35	"Gird your loins and light your l

LAMPSTAND → LAMP
Ex	25:31	"You shall make a l of pure beaten
Nm	3:31	ark, the table, the l, the altars,
1 Mc	4:50	altar and lighted the lamps on the l,
Zec	4: 2	"I see a l all of gold, with a bowl
Zec	4:11	two olive trees at each side of the l?"
Heb	9: 2	one, in which were the l, the table,
Rv	2: 5	and remove your l from its place,

LAMPSTANDS → LAMP
2 Chr	4: 7	He made the l of gold, ten of them
Rv	1:12	when I turned, I saw seven gold l
Rv	1:20	right hand, and of the seven gold l:
Rv	1:20	the seven l are the seven churches.
Rv	11: 4	the two l that stand before the Lord

LAND → COASTLANDS, HOMELAND, LANDMARK, LANDOWNER, LANDS
Gn	1:10	God called the dry l "the earth,"
Gn	7:22	on dry l with the faintest breath
Gn	12: 1	"Go forth from the l of your kinsfolk
Gn	12: 1	house to a l that I will show you.
Gn	12: 7	your descendants I will give this l."
Gn	12:10	There was famine in the l;
Gn	13:15	all the l that you see I will give
Gn	15:18	"To your descendants I give this l,
Gn	17: 8	now staying, the whole l of Canaan,
Gn	24: 7	made to me, 'I will give this l to your
Gn	26: 1	There was a famine in the l (distinct
Gn	28:15	you go, and bring you back to this l.
Gn	31:13	Leave this l and return to the l
Gn	40:15	kidnaped from the l of the Hebrews,
Gn	41:30	When the famine has ravaged the l,
Gn	50:24	out of this l to the l that he promised
Ex	1: 7	and strong that the l was filled
Ex	3: 8	lead them out of that l into a good and spacious l, a l flowing with milk and honey,
Ex	6: 8	bring you into the l which I swore
Ex	8:18	an exception of the l of Goshen:
Ex	20: 2	brought you out of the l of Egypt,
Ex	20:12	a long life in the l which the Lord,
Ex	34:12	inhabitants of the l that you are
Nm	13: 2	men to reconnoiter the l of Canaan,
Nm	14: 9	not be afraid of the people of that l;
Nm	14:30	shall enter the l where I solemnly
Nm	26:55	But the l shall be divided by lot,
Nm	35:33	not desecrate the l where you live.
Nm	35:33	Since bloodshed desecrates the l,
Dt	1: 8	occupy the l I swore to your fathers,
Dt	8: 7	country, a l with streams of water,
Dt	11:10	and occupy is not like the l of Egypt
Dt	28:21	you from the l you are entering
Dt	29:23	has the LORD dealt thus with this l?
Jos	1: 6	possession of the l which I swore
Jos	2: 1	"Go, reconnoiter the l and Jericho."
Jos	5:12	they ate of the produce of the l,
Jos	11:23	the tribes. And the l enjoyed peace.
Jos	13: 2	This additional l includes all Geshur
Jos	14: 4	no share of the l except cities to live
Jos	14: 9	"The l where you have set foot shall
Ru	1: 1	judges there was a famine in the l;
2 Sm	21:14	out, God granted relief to the l.
1 Kgs	8:34	back to the l you gave their fathers.
1 Kgs	17: 7	because no rain had fallen in the l.

2 Kgs	17: 5	occupied the whole l and attacked
2 Kgs	25:21	Thus was Judah exiled from her l.
2 Chr	7:14	pardon their sins and revive their l.
2 Chr	7:20	the people from the l I gave them;
2 Chr	36:21	"Until the l has retrieved its lost
Ezr	9:11	as your possession is a l unclean
Neh	9:36	for the l which you gave our fathers
Tb	14: 7	dwell forever in the l of Abraham,
Tb	14: 7	completely disappear from the l.
1 Mc	1:44	to follow customs foreign to their l:
1 Mc	14:11	He brought peace to the l, and Israel
Ps	25:13	and their descendants inherit the l.
Ps	37:11	But the poor will possess the l,
Ps	37:29	The just will possess the l and live
Ps	44: 4	own swords did they conquer the l,
Ps	142: 6	my portion in the l of the living.
Prv	2:21	For the upright will dwell in the l,
Prv	12:11	He who tills his own l has food
Sir	46: 8	the l flowing with milk and honey.
Is	2: 8	Their l is full of idols; they worship
Is	9: 1	those who dwelt in the l of gloom
Is	36:18	the nations ever rescued his l
Is	53: 8	was cut off from the l of the living,
Jer	2: 7	I brought you into the garden l
Jer	2: 7	You entered and defiled my l,
Jer	22:29	O l, l, l, hear the word of the LORD—
Ez	7:23	for the l is filled with bloodshed
Ez	36:24	and bring you back to your own l.
Ez	39:28	will gather them back on their l,
Dn	11:41	He shall enter the glorious l
Hos	2:25	I will sow him for myself in the l, .
Zec	3: 9	away the guilt of the l in one day.
Mal	3:24	I come and strike the l with doom.
Mk	15:33	came over the whole l until three
Heb	11: 9	in the promised l as in a foreign
Rv	10: 2	on the sea and his left foot on the l,

LANDMARK → LAND
Prv	22:28	Remove not the ancient l

LANDOWNER → LAND, OWN
Mt	20: 1	of heaven is like a l who went
Mt	20:11	it they grumbled against the l,
Mt	21:33	There was a l who planted

LANDS → LAND
Gn	26: 3	descendants l will give all these l,
Ps	105:44	He gave them the l of the nations,
Ps	106:27	nations, disperse them in foreign l.
Ps	107: 3	Those gathered from foreign l,
Ps	136:21	And made their l a heritage,
Ez	20: 6	milk and honey, a jewel among all l.

LANGUAGE → LANGUAGES
Gn	11: 1	The whole world spoke the same l,
Jer	5:15	a people whose l you know not,
Acts	2: 6	heard them speaking in his own l.
Col	3: 8	and obscene l out of your mouths.

LANGUAGES → LANGUAGE
Neh	13:24	to the l of the various other peoples.

LANTERNS
Jn	18: 3	the Pharisees and went there with l,

LAODICEA
Col	4:16	you yourselves read the one from L.
Rv	3:14	"To the angel of the church in L,

LAP
Prv	16:33	When the lot is cast into the l,
Lk	6:38	will be poured into your l.

LARGE → ENLARGE, ENLARGES
Dt	6:10	fine, l cities that you did not build,
Dt	25:13	your bag, one l and the other small;
Jon	2: 1	But the LORD sent a l fish,
Gal	6:11	See with what l letters I am writing

LASHES
2 Cor	11:24	Jews l received forty l minus one.

LAST → EVERLASTING, LASTING, LASTS
2 Sm	23: 1	These are the l words of David:

Is	41: 4	first, and with the l I will also be.
Is	44: 6	I am the first and I am the l; there is
Is	48:12	am the first, and also the l am I.
Mt	19:30	But many who are first will be l, and the l will be first.
Mt	20: 8	beginning with the l and ending
Mt	27:64	This l imposture would be worse
Mk	9:35	first, he shall be the l of all
Mk	15:37	gave a loud cry and breathed his l.
Jn	6:40	and I shall raise him [on] the l day."
Jn	7:37	On the l and greatest day
Jn	11:24	rise, in the resurrection on the l day."
Acts	2:17	'It will come to pass in the l days,'
1 Cor	15: 8	L of all, as to one born abnormally,
1 Cor	15:26	The l enemy to be destroyed is
1 Cor	15:45	the l Adam a life-giving spirit.
1 Cor	15:52	the blink of an eye, at the l trumpet.
1 Tm	4: 1	in the l times some will turn away
2 Tm	3: 1	will be terrifying times in the l days.
Heb	1: 2	in these l days, he spoke to us
2 Pt	2:20	their l condition is worse than their
2 Pt	3: 3	in the l days scoffers will come
1 Jn	2:18	Children, it is the l hour; and just as
Jude	1:18	"In [the] l time there will be scoffers
Rv	1:17	be afraid. I am the first and the l,
Rv	2: 8	" 'The first and the l, who once died
Rv	15: 1	angels with the seven l plagues,
Rv	21: 9	filled with the seven l plagues came
Rv	22:13	the first and the l, the beginning

LASTING → LAST
Heb	10:34	you had a better and l possession.

LASTS → LAST
Tb	13: 1	because his kingdom l for all ages.

LATE → LATER, LATTER
Jas	5: 7	it receives the early and the l rains.

LATER → LATE
Jn	13: 7	now, but you will understand l."

LATIN
Jn	19:20	and it was written in Hebrew, L,

LATTER → LATE
Jb	42:12	Thus the LORD blessed the l days

LAUGH → LAUGHED, LAUGHINGSTOCK, LAUGHS, LAUGHTER
Gn	18:13	"Why did Sarah l and say, 'Shall I
Gn	21: 6	"God has given me cause to l, and all who hear of it will l with me.
Ps	59: 9	You, LORD, l at them; you deride all
Eccl	3: 4	A time to weep, and a time to l;
Lk	6:21	are now weeping, for you will l.

LAUGHED → LAUGH
Gn	17:17	himself and l as he said to himself,
Gn	18:12	So Sarah l to herself and said,

LAUGHINGSTOCK → LAUGH
Jdt	5:21	we shall become the l of the whole
Lam	3:14	I have become a l for all nations,

LAUGHS → LAUGH
Ps	2: 4	The one enthroned in heaven l;
Ps	37:13	But the LORD l at them,

LAUGHTER → LAUGH
Ps	126: 2	Our mouths were filled with l;
Prv	14:13	Even in l the heart may be sad
Eccl	7: 3	Sorrow is better than l,
Jas	4: 9	Let your l be turned into mourning

LAVISHED
Eph	1: 8	that he l upon us. In all wisdom

LAW → LAWFUL, LAWGIVER, LAWLESS, LAWLESSNESS, LAWS, LAWSUIT, LAWSUITS
Nm	5:29	"This, then, is the l for jealousy:
Dt	1: 5	began to explain the l in the land
Dt	17:18	he shall have a copy of this l made
Dt	27:26	fulfill any of the provisions of this l!'
Dt	31: 9	Moses had written down this l,

Dt	31:11	you shall read this l aloud
Dt	31:26	"Take this scroll of the l and put it
Jos	1: 7	to observe the entire l which my
Jos	1: 8	Keep this book of the l on your lips.
Jos	8:32	the stones a copy of the l written
2 Kgs	22: 8	found the book of the l in the temple
2 Chr	6:16	as always to live according to my l,
2 Chr	17: 9	them the book containing the l
2 Chr	34:14	of the l of the LORD given through
Ezr	7: 6	well-versed in the l of Moses
Neh	8: 2	the priest brought the l before
Neh	8: 8	from the book of the l of God,
1 Mc	1:56	of the l which they found they tore
1 Mc	2:21	forbid that we should forsake the l
1 Mc	2:48	They saved the l from the hands
Ps	1: 2	Rather, the l of the LORD is their joy;
Ps	1: 2	God's l they study day and night.
Ps	19: 8	The l of the LORD is perfect,
Ps	40: 9	my God, your l is in my heart!"
Ps	89:31	If his descendants forsake my l,
Prv	28: 9	away his ear from hearing the l,
Prv	29:18	but happy is he who keeps the l.
Sir	2:16	who love him are filled with his l.
Sir	33: 2	who hates the l is without wisdom,
Jer	2: 8	who dealt with the l knew me not:
Jer	8: 8	are wise, we have the l of the LORD"?
Jer	31:33	I will place my l within them,
Bar	4: 1	of God, the l that endures forever;
Dn	9:11	all Israel transgressed your l
Hos	4: 6	Since you have ignored the l of your
Hb	1: 4	This is why the l is benumbed,
Mt	5:17	that I have come to abolish the l
Mt	5:17	This is the l and the prophets.
Mt	7:12	This is the l and the prophets.
Mt	22:36	in the l is the greatest?"
Mt	22:40	The whole l and the prophets
Mt	23:23	the weightier things of the l:
Lk	2:23	as it is written in the l of the Lord,
Lk	2:39	prescriptions of the l of the Lord,
Lk	10:25	There was a scholar of the l who stood
Lk	10:26	said to him, "What is written in the l?
Lk	11:46	"Woe also to you scholars of the l!
Lk	16:17	of a letter of the l to become invalid.
Lk	24:44	written about me in the l of Moses
Jn	1:17	because while the l was given
Jn	7:19	Did not Moses give you the l? Yet none of you keeps the l.
Jn	18:31	and judge him according to your l."
Acts	6:13	against [this] holy place and the l.
Acts	15: 5	direct them to observe the Mosaic l."
Acts	28:23	about Jesus from the l of Moses
Rom	2:12	All who sin outside the l will
Rom	2:12	who sin under the l will be judged
Rom	2:13	who observe the l will be justified.
Rom	2:15	the demands of the l are written
Rom	2:20	in the l you have the formulation
Rom	2:25	has value if you observe the l;
Rom	3:19	that what the l says is addressed to those under the l,
Rom	3:20	in his sight by observing the l;
Rom	3:20	through the l comes consciousness
Rom	3:21	been manifested apart from the l, though testified to by the l
Rom	3:28	by faith apart from works of the l.
Rom	3:31	then annulling the l by this faith?
Rom	3:31	contrary, we are supporting the l.
Rom	4:13	It was not through the l
Rom	4:15	For the l produces wrath; but where there is no l, neither is
Rom	5:13	is not accounted when there is no l.
Rom	5:20	The l entered in so
Rom	6:14	since you are not under the l
Rom	6:15	sin because we are not under the l
Rom	7: 1	the l has jurisdiction over one as
Rom	7: 4	to death to the l through the body
Rom	7: 5	awakened by the l, worked in our
Rom	7: 6	But now we are released from the l,
Rom	7: 7	That the l is sin? Of course not!
Rom	7: 7	not know sin except through the l,
Rom	7: 8	Apart from the l sin is dead.

Rom	7: 9	I once lived outside the l,
Rom	7:12	So then the l is holy,
Rom	7:14	We know that the l is spiritual; but I
Rom	7:22	For I take delight in the l of God,
Rom	7:25	my mind, serve the l of God but, with my flesh, the l of sin.
Rom	8: 2	Jesus has freed you from the l of sin
Rom	8: 3	For what the l,
Rom	8: 4	decree of the l might be fulfilled
Rom	8: 7	it does not submit to the l of God,
Rom	9: 4	the giving of the l, the worship,
Rom	9:31	who pursued the l of righteousness,
Rom	10: 4	the end of the l for the justification
Rom	13: 8	loves another has fulfilled the l.
Rom	13:10	love is the fulfillment of the l.
1 Cor	9: 9	It is written in the l of Moses,
1 Cor	9:20	to win over those under the l.
1 Cor	9:21	though I am not outside God's l
1 Cor	9:21	win over those outside the l.
1 Cor	15:56	is sin, and the power of sin is the l.
Gal	2:19	For through the l I died to the l,
Gal	3:11	before God by the l is clear,
Gal	3:19	Why, then, the l? It was added
Gal	4: 4	born of a woman, born under the l,
Gal	5: 4	who are trying to be justified by l;
Gal	5:23	Against such there is no l.
Gal	6: 2	so you will fulfill the l of Christ.
Eph	2:15	abolishing the l with its
Phil	3: 5	in observance of the l a Pharisee,
Phil	3: 9	of my own based on the l
1 Tm	1: 8	We know that the l is good, provided that one uses it as l,
Ti	3: 9	and quarrels about the l, for they are
Heb	7:12	is necessarily a change of l as well.
Heb	7:19	for the l brought nothing
Heb	10: 1	Since the l has only a shadow
Jas	1:25	peers into the perfect l of freedom
Jas	2: 8	if you fulfill the royal l according
Jas	2:10	For whoever keeps the whole l,
Jas	4:11	speaks evil of the l and judges the l.
Jas	4:11	If you judge the l, you are not a doer of the l

LAWFUL →LAW

Mt	12:12	So it is l to do good on the sabbath."
Mt	19: 3	"Is it l for a man to divorce his wife
Lk	14: 3	"Is it l to cure on the sabbath or not?"
1 Cor	6:12	"Everything is l for me," but not
1 Cor	10:23	"Everything is l," but not everything

LAWGIVER →GIVE, LAW

Jas	4:12	There is one l and judge who is able

LAWLESS →LAW

2 Thes	2: 8	And then the l one will be revealed,

LAWLESSNESS →LAW

Wis	5:23	Thus l shall lay the whole earth
2 Cor	6:14	do righteousness and l have?
2 Thes	2: 7	the mystery of l is already at work.
1 Jn	3: 4	who commits sin commits l, for sin is l.

LAWS →LAW

Neh	9:13	gave them just ordinances, firm l,
1 Mc	3:21	are fighting for our lives and our l.
Ps	105:45	That they might keep his l
Heb	8:10	Lord: I will put my l in their minds
Heb	10:16	Lord: "I will put my l in their hearts,

LAWSUIT →LAW

Ex	23: 2	when testifying in a l,

LAWSUITS →LAW

1 Cor	6: 7	that you have l against one another.

LAY →LAID, LAYING, LAYS

Gn	22:12	"Do not l your hand on the boy,"
Ex	7: 4	Therefore I will l my hand on Egypt
Ex	29:10	his sons shall l their hands on its
Nm	8:10	the Israelites shall l their hands
Nm	27:18	of spirit, and l your hand upon him.
Dt	9:25	nights, I l prostrate before the LORD,
Jb	22:22	and l up his words in your heart.
Mt	28: 6	Come and see the place where he l.

Jn	10:15	I will l down my life for the sheep.
Jn	10:18	but I l it down on my own. I have power to l it down,
Jn	13:37	I will l down my life for you."
Jn	15:13	to l down one's life for one's friends.
Acts	8:19	whom I l my hands may receive
1 Cor	3:11	no one can l a foundation other than
1 Jn	3:16	so we ought to l down our lives

LAYING →LAY

Is	28:16	See, I am l a stone in Zion, a stone
Acts	8:18	the Spirit was conferred by the l
Heb	6: 1	without l the foundation all over
Heb	6: 2	about baptisms and l on of hands,
1 Pt	2: 6	"Behold, I am l a stone in Zion,

LAYS →LAY

Jn	10:11	A good shepherd l down his life

LAZARUS
1. Poor man in Jesus' parable (Lk 16:19-31).
2. Brother of Mary and Martha whom Jesus raised from the dead (Jn 11:1-12:19).

LAZINESS →LAZY

Prv	19:15	L plunges a man into deep sleep,

LAZY →LAZINESS

Ex	5: 8	They are l; that is why they are
Ex	5:17	"It is just because you are l that you
Mt	25:26	him in reply, 'You wicked, l servant!
Ti	1:12	liars, vicious beasts, and l gluttons."

LEAD →LEADER, LEADERS, LEADS, LED

Ex	15:10	them; like l they sank in the mighty
Ex	32:34	l the people whither I have told you.
Ps	23: 2	to safe waters you l me;
Ps	27:11	me your way; l me on a level path
Ps	139:24	then l me in the ancient paths.
Jer	31: 9	I will l them to brooks of water,
Dn	12: 3	And those who l the many to justice
Rom	2: 4	of God would l you to repentance?

LEADER →LEAD

1 Chr	28: 4	For he chose Judah as l, then one

LEADERS →LEAD

Is	3:12	O my people, your l mislead,
Lk	19:47	and the l of the people, meanwhile,
Heb	13: 7	Remember your l who spoke
Heb	13:17	Obey your l and defer to them,

LEADS →LEAD

Ps	68: 7	who l prisoners out to prosperity,
Prv	12:26	the way of the wicked l them astray.
Prv	21: 5	all rash haste l certainly to poverty.
Is	49:10	For he who pities them l them
Mt	7:14	constricted the road that l to life.
Jn	10: 3	own sheep by name and l them out.
Rom	6:16	either of sin, which l to death,
Rom	6:16	which l to righteousness?
2 Cor	2:14	who always l us in triumph in Christ

LEAF →LEAVES

Gn	8:11	in its bill was a plucked-off olive l!

LEAH
Wife of Jacob (Gn 29:16-30); bore six sons and one daughter (Gn 29:31-30:21; 34:1; 35:23; Ru 4:11).

LEAP →LEAPED, LEAPING, LEAPS

2 Sm	22:30	the help of my God I l over a wall.
Is	35: 6	Then will the lame l like a stag,
Lk	6:23	Rejoice and l for joy on that day!

LEAPED →LEAP

Lk	1:41	greeting, the infant l in her womb,

LEAPING →LEAP

1 Chr	15:29	and when she saw King David l

LEAPS →LEAP

Jb	37: 1	heart trembles and l out of its place,

LEARN →LEARNED, LEARNING

Dt	4:10	that they may l to fear me as long as

Dt	5: 1	that you may l them and take care
Dt	18: 9	you, you shall not l to imitate
Dt	31:12	they may hear it and l it, and so fear
Prv	19:25	arrogant man, the simple l a lesson;
Is	1:17	l to do good. Make justice your aim:
Is	26: 9	the world's inhabitants l justice.
Mt	11:29	my yoke upon you and l from me,
Mk	13:28	"L a lesson from the fig tree.
1 Tm	5: 4	let these first l to perform their
Ti	3:14	too, l to devote themselves to good
Rv	14: 3	No one could l this hymn except

LEARNED →LEARN

Eph	4:20	That is not how you l Christ,
Phil	4: 9	Keep on doing what you have l
Phil	4:11	for I have l, in whatever situation I
2 Tm	3:14	remain faithful to what you have l
2 Tm	3:14	you know from whom you l it,
Heb	5: 8	he was, he l obedience from what he

LEARNING →LEARN

Prv	1: 5	by hearing them will advance in l,
Prv	9: 9	a just man, and he advances in l.
Acts	26:24	Paul; much l is driving you mad."

LEAST →LESS

1 Sm	9:21	is not my clan the l among the clans
Mt	2: 6	are by no means l among the rulers
Mt	5:19	one of the l of these commandments
Mt	5:19	do so will be called l in the kingdom
Mt	25:40	for one of these l brothers of mine,
Lk	7:28	yet the l in the kingdom of God is
Lk	9:48	the one who is l among all of you is
1 Cor	15: 9	For I am the l of the apostles, not fit
Eph	3: 8	me, the very l of all the holy ones,

LEATHER

2 Kgs	1: 8	"with a l girdle about his loins." "It is
Mt	3: 4	and had a l belt around his waist.

LEAVE →LEAVES, LEFT

Ex	11: 8	they shall beg me, 'L us, you and all
Nm	11:20	wailed, 'Why did we ever l Egypt?' "
Jl	2:14	relent and l behind him a blessing,
Mt	5:24	your gift there at the altar, go first
Mk	10: 7	this reason a man shall l his father
Jn	14:18	I will not l you orphans; I will come
Jn	14:27	Peace I l with you; my peace I give
Eph	5:31	this reason a man shall l [his] father

LEAVEN →LEAVENED, LEAVENS

Ex	12:15	shall have your houses clear of all l.
Mt	16: 6	beware of the l of the Pharisees and

LEAVENED →LEAVEN

Ex	12:20	Nothing l may you eat;
Dt	16: 4	Nothing l may be found in all your
Mt	13:33	flour until the whole batch was l."

LEAVENS →LEAVEN

1 Cor	5: 6	that a little yeast l all the dough?
Gal	5: 9	A little yeast l the whole batch

LEAVES →LEAF, LEAVE

Gn	3: 7	so they sewed fig l together
Ps	1: 3	its fruit in season; Its l never wither;
Jer	17: 8	heat when it comes, its l stay green;
Ez	47:12	their l shall not fade, nor their fruit
Ez	47:12	for food, and their l for medicine."
Mk	11:13	he reached it he found nothing but l;
Rv	22: 2	the l of the trees serve as medicine

LEBANON

Dt	11:24	from the desert and from L,
1 Kgs	5:13	from the cedar on L to the hyssop
2 Kgs	14: 9	"The thistle of L sent word to the cedar of L,
Ps	29: 6	Makes L leap like a calf, and Sirion
Ps	92:13	tree, shall grow like a cedar of L.
Is	40:16	L would not suffice for fuel, nor its
Hb	2:17	violence done to L shall cover you,

LECTURE

Acts	19: 9	hold daily discussions in the l hall

LED →LEAD

Neh	9:12	column of cloud you l them by day,
Ps	78:52	God l forth his people like sheep;
Is	53: 7	Like a lamb l to the slaughter
Jer	11:19	Yet I, like a trusting lamb l to slaughter,
Am	2:10	and who l you through the desert
Mt	4: 1	Jesus was l by the Spirit
Mt	27:31	and l him off to crucify him.
Acts	8:32	reading: "Like a sheep he was l
Rom	8:14	For those who are l by the Spirit

LEECH
Prv 30:15 The two daughters of the l are,

LEEKS
Nm 11: 5 the melons, the l, the onions,

LEFT →LEAVE, LEFT-HANDED

Gn	7:23	those with him in the ark were l.
Gn	13: 9	If you prefer the l, I will go
Gn	13: 9	prefer the right, I will go to the l."
Nm	26:65	not one of them was l except Caleb,
Dt	28:14	the right or to the l from any
Jos	1: 7	from it either to the right or to the l,
Prv	4:27	Turn neither to right nor to l,
Is	30:21	would turn to the right or to the l.
Mt	6: 3	do not let your l hand know what
Mt	25:33	on his right and the goats on his l.
Mk	8: 8	the fragments l over—seven baskets.
Mk	10:40	right or at my l is not mine to give
Lk	17:34	one will be taken, the other l.
1 Thes	4:15	who are l until the coming
Rv	10: 2	on the sea and his l foot on the land,

LEFT-HANDED →HAND, LEFT
Jgs 3:15 Ehud, son of Gera, who was l.
Jgs 20:16 hundred picked men who were l,

LEGION →LEGIONS
Lk 8:30 name?" He replied, "L," because many

LEGIONS →LEGION
Mt 26:53 with more than twelve l of angels?

LEGS
Dn 2:33 the l iron, its feet partly iron
Jn 19:33 dead, they did not break his l,

LEMA
Mt 27:46 a loud voice, "Eli, Eli, l sabachthani?"
Mk 15:34 voice, "Eloi, Eloi, l sabachthani?"

LEMUEL
Prv 31: 1 The words of L, king of Massa.
Prv 31: 4 It is not for kings, O L, not for kings

LEND →LENDER, LENDS
Dt 28:12 so that you will l to many nations
Dt 28:44 He will l to you, not you to him.
Sir 8:12 L not to one more powerful than
Sir 8:12 and whatever you l, count it as lost.
Lk 6:34 If you l money to those from whom
Lk 6:34 Even sinners l to sinners, and get

LENDER →LEND
Prv 22: 7 the borrower is the slave of the l.
Is 24: 2 as the seller, The l as the borrower,

LENDS →LEND
Prv 19:17 on the poor l to the Lord, and he

LENGTH →LONG
Gn 13:17 the land, through its l and breadth,
Ps 21: 5 you gave it to him, l of days forever.

LEOPARD
Is 11: 6 and the l shall lie down with the kid;
Jer 13:23 his skin? the l his spots?
Dn 7: 6 and saw another beast, like a l;
Rv 13: 2 The beast I saw was like a l, but it

LEPER →LEPROSY
Nm 12:10 there was Miriam, a snow-white l!
2 Kgs 5: 1 as he was, the man was a l.
Mt 8: 2 And then a l approached, did him
Mt 26: 6 Bethany in the house of Simon the l,

LEPERS →LEPROSY
Lk 7:22 the lame walk, l are cleansed,

LEPROSY →LEPER, LEPERS, LEPROUS
Mt 8: 3 His l was cleansed immediately.

LEPROUS →LEPROSY
Ex 4: 6 it, to his surprise his hand was l,

LESS →LEAST
Ex 30:15 nor shall the poor give l,
2 Chr 6:18 how much l this temple which I
2 Chr 32:15 how much the l shall your god save
Ezr 9:13 have made l of our sinfulness than it

LESSON
Mk 13:28 "Learn a l from the fig tree. When its

LET

Gn	1: 3	Then God said, "L there be light,"
Gn	1: 6	"L there be a dome in the middle
Gn	1: 9	said, "L the water under the sky be
Gn	1:11	"L the earth bring forth vegetation:
Gn	1:14	"L there be lights in the dome
Gn	1:14	L them mark the fixed times,
Gn	1:20	"L the water teem with an abundance
Gn	1:20	on the earth l birds fly beneath
Gn	1:24	"L the earth bring forth all kinds
Gn	1:26	"L us make man in our image,
Gn	1:26	L them have dominion over the fish
Gn	11: 7	L us then go down and there
Ex	5: 1	L my people go, that they may
Ex	5: 2	I should heed his plea to l Israel go?
Ex	5: 2	even if I did, I would not l Israel go."
Ex	13:17	when Pharaoh l the people go,
1 Mc	4:36	l us go up to purify the sanctuary
Ps	22: 9	if he loves you, l him rescue you."
Ps	25: 2	I trust; do not l me be disgraced;
Ps	25: 2	do not l my enemies gloat over me.
Ps	33: 8	L all the earth fear the Lord; l all
Ps	95: 1	Come, l us sing joyfully to the Lord;
Ps	118:24	made; l us rejoice in it and be glad.
Jer	9:23	But rather, l him who glories,
Lam	3:40	L us search and examine our ways
Dn	3:74	L the earth bless the Lord,
Jl	4:10	l the weak man say, "I am a warrior!"
Mt	5:37	L your 'Yes' mean 'Yes,' and your 'No'
Mt	27:43	l him deliver him now if he wants
Jn	7:37	"L anyone who thirsts come to me
Jn	14: 1	"Do not l your hearts be troubled.
Eph	4:26	do not l the sun set on your anger,
Col	3:15	l the peace of Christ control your
Col	3:16	L the word of Christ dwell in you
Heb	10:22	l us approach with a sincere heart
Jas	5:12	but l your "Yes" mean "Yes" and your
1 Jn	4: 7	Beloved, l us love one another,
Rv	22:17	say, "Come." L the hearer say, "Come."
Rv	22:17	L the one who thirsts come forward,

LETTER →LETTERS
Mt 5:18 not the smallest l or the smallest part of a l will pass
Acts 15:23 This is the l delivered by them:
2 Cor 3: 2 You are our l, written on our hearts,
2 Cor 3: 6 new covenant, not of l but of spirit;
2 Cor 3: 6 for the l brings death, but the Spirit
2 Thes 3:14 obey our word as expressed in this l,

LETTERS →LETTER
2 Chr 32:17 he had written l to deride the Lord,
2 Cor 3: 7 of death, carved in l on stone,
2 Cor 10:10 say, "His l are severe and forceful,
2 Pt 3:16 these things as he does in all his l.

LEVEL
Ps 143:10 spirit guide me on ground that is l.
Is 26: 7 the path of the just you make l.
Is 45: 2 and l the mountains; Bronze doors I
Lk 6:17 and stood on a stretch of l ground.

LEVI →LEVITE, LEVITES, LEVITICAL, =MATTHEW
1. Son of Jacob by Leah (Gn 29:34; 46:11; 1 Chr 2:1). With Simeon avenged rape of Dinah (Gn 34). Tribe of blessed (Gn

49:5-7; Dt 33:8-11), chosen as priests (Nm 3-4), numbered (Nm 3:39; 26:62), given cities, but not land (Nm 18; 35; Dt 10:9; Jos 13:14; 21), land (Ez 48:8-22), 12,000 from (Rv 7:7).
  2. See Matthew.

LEVIATHAN
Jb	3: 8	sea, the appointed disturbers of L!
Jb	40:25	Can you lead about L with a hook,
Ps	74:14	You crushed the heads of L,
Ps	104:26	course; here L, your creature, plays.
Is	27: 1	and strong, L the fleeing serpent,

LEVITE → LEVI
Ex	4:14	you not your brother, Aaron the L?
Jgs	19: 1	there was a L residing in remote
Acts	4:36	a L, a Cypriot by birth,

LEVITES → LEVI
Nm	1:53	the L shall camp around
Nm	1:53	The L, then, shall have charge
Nm	3:12	"It is I who have chosen the L
Nm	3:12	The L, therefore, are mine,
Nm	8: 6	"Take the L from among
Nm	16: 7	is the holy one. Enough from you L!"
Nm	18:21	"To the L, however, I hereby assign
Nm	35: 7	pasture lands to be assigned the L.
Jos	14: 4	The L themselves received no share
1 Chr	15: 2	carry the ark of God except the L,
2 Chr	31: 2	and the L according to their former
Ezr	6:18	and the L in their divisions
Neh	8: 9	[and the L who were instructing

LEVITICAL → LEVI
Heb	7:11	came through the l priesthood,

LEWDNESS
Ez	16:58	The penalty of your l and your
Ez	23:48	Thus I will put an end to l
Ez	23:48	will be warned not to imitate your l.

LIABLE
Mt	5:22	'You fool,' will be l to fiery Gehenna.

LIAR → LIE
Prv	19:22	rather be a poor man than a l.
Jn	8:44	because he is a l and the father
Jn	8:55	know him, I would be like you a l.
Rom	3: 4	though every human being is a l,
1 Jn	1:10	we make him a l, and his word is
1 Jn	2: 4	not keep his commandments is a l,
1 Jn	2:22	Who is the l? Whoever denies
1 Jn	5:10	not believe God has made him a l

LIARS → LIE
Ps	63:12	for the mouths of l will be shut!
Sir	15: 8	is she, not to be spoken of by l.
Is	44:25	who bring to nought the omens of l,
1 Tm	1:10	kidnapers, l, perjurers, and whatever
1 Tm	4: 2	through the hypocrisy of l
Ti	1:12	"Cretans have always been l,

LIBATION → LIBATIONS
Phil	2:17	out as a l upon the sacrificial service
2 Tm	4: 6	already being poured out like a l,

LIBATIONS → LIBATION
Jer	19:13	and poured out l to strange gods.

LIBERTY
Lv	25:10	sacred by proclaiming l in the land
Is	61: 1	To proclaim l to the captives
1 Cor	8: 9	make sure that this l of yours in no

LICENTIOUS → LICENTIOUSNESS
2 Pt	2: 2	Many will follow their l ways,

LICENTIOUSNESS → LICENTIOUS
Mk	7:22	malice, deceit, l, envy, blasphemy,
Rom	13:13	not in promiscuity and l,
2 Cor	12:21	immorality, and l they practiced.
Gal	5:19	are obvious: immorality, impurity, l,
Eph	4:19	have handed themselves over to l
Jude	1: 4	pervert the grace of our God into l

LICK
Ps	72: 9	before him, his enemies l the dust.
Is	49:23	and l the dust at your feet. Then you
Mi	7:17	They shall l the dust like

LIE → LIAR, LIARS, LIES, LYING
Gn	19:32	with wine and then l with him,
Gn	39: 7	fondly at him and said, "L with me."
Lv	18:22	You shall not l with a male as
Ru	3: 4	a place at his feet, and l down.
Ps	4: 9	In peace I shall both l down
Prv	3:24	When you l down, you need not be
Prv	14: 5	A truthful witness does not l,
Sir	7:13	Delight not in telling l after l, for it
Is	11: 6	the leopard shall l down
Ez	34:14	There they shall l down on good
Dn	13:20	give in to our desire, and l with us.
Rom	1:25	exchanged the truth of God for a l
1 Jn	1: 6	we l and do not act in truth.
1 Jn	2:21	because every l is alien to the truth.

LIES → LIE
Ex	22:18	"Anyone who l with an animal shall
Lv	20:13	If a man l with a male as
Ps	12: 3	Those who tell l to one another
Jer	14:14	L these prophets utter in my name,
Jer	27:10	For they prophesy l to you, in order
Hos	12: 1	Ephraim has surrounded me with l,
Zep	3:13	and speak no l; Nor shall there be
Jn	8:44	he is a liar and the father of l.
Phil	3:13	thing: forgetting what l behind
Phil	3:13	straining forward to what l ahead,

LIFE → LIVE
Gn	2: 7	blew into his nostrils the breath of l,
Gn	2: 9	with the tree of l in the middle
Gn	6:17	in which there is the breath of l;
Gn	9: 5	demand an accounting for human l.
Ex	21:23	injury ensues, you shall give l for l,
Nm	35:31	the l of a murderer who deserves
Dt	12:23	for blood is l, and you shall not
Dt	19:21	L for l, eye for eye, tooth for tooth,
Dt	30:15	I have today set before you l
Dt	30:19	I have set before you l and death,
Dt	30:19	Choose l, then, that you and your
Dt	32:47	you are to enjoy a long l on the land
1 Sm	19: 5	When he took his l in his hands
Neh	9: 6	To all of them you give l,
Jdt	13:20	because you risked your l
Jb	2: 6	is in your power; only spare his l."
Jb	10: 1	I loathe my l. I will give myself
Ps	16:11	You will show me the path to l,
Ps	23: 6	all the days of my l; I will dwell
Ps	34:13	Who among you loves l,
Ps	36:10	For with you is the fountain of l,
Ps	49: 9	Too high the price to redeem a l;
Ps	63: 4	For your love is better than l;
Ps	119:50	your promise that gives me l.
Prv	3: 2	For many days, and years of l,
Prv	3:16	Long l is in her right hand, in her
Prv	3:18	She is a tree of l to those who grasp
Prv	4:23	heart, for in it are the sources of l.
Prv	6:23	and a way to l are the reproofs
Prv	6:26	she is a trap for your precious l.
Prv	7:23	a snare, unaware that its l is at stake.
Prv	8:35	For he who finds me finds l,
Prv	10:11	A fountain of l is the mouth
Prv	10:27	The fear of the LORD prolongs l,
Prv	11:30	The fruit of virtue is a tree of l,
Prv	13:12	but a wish fulfilled is a tree of l.
Prv	13:14	of the wise is a fountain of l,
Prv	14:27	fear of the LORD is a fountain of l,
Prv	15: 4	A soothing tongue is a tree of l,
Prv	16:22	Good sense is a fountain of l to its
Prv	18:21	and l are in the power of the tongue;
Prv	19:23	The fear of the LORD is an aid to l;
Prv	21:21	and kindness will find l and honor.
Eccl	2:17	Therefore I loathed l, since for me
Eccl	7:12	wisdom preserves the l of its owner.
Eccl	9: 9	Enjoy l with the wife whom you

Sir	4:12	He who loves her loves l; those who
Sir	30:22	of heart is the very l of man,
Sir	31:27	Wine is very l to man if taken
Is	53:10	If he gives his l as an offering
Lam	3:58	mortal danger, you redeemed my l.
Ez	18:27	and just, he shall preserve his l;
Jon	2: 7	you brought up my l from the pit,
Mal	2: 5	My covenant with him was one of l
Mt	6:25	do not worry about your l, what you
Mt	6:25	Is not l more than food and the body
Mt	7:14	constricted the road that leads to l.
Mt	10:39	Whoever finds his l will lose it,
Mt	10:39	whoever loses his l for my sake will
Mt	16:25	wishes to save his l will lose it,
Mt	16:25	whoever loses his l for my sake will
Mt	19:16	good must I do to gain eternal l?"
Mt	19:29	more, and will inherit eternal l.
Mt	20:28	to give his l as a ransom for many."
Mt	25:46	but the righteous to eternal l."
Mk	3: 4	to save l rather than to destroy it?"
Mk	9:43	to enter into l maimed than with two
Mk	10:30	and eternal l in the age to come.
Mk	10:45	to give his l as a ransom for many."
Lk	6: 9	to save l rather than to destroy it?"
Lk	12:15	be rich, one's l does not consist
Lk	12:22	do not worry about your l and what
Jn	1: 4	through him was l, and this l was
Jn	3:15	believes in him may have eternal l."
Jn	3:36	believes in the Son has eternal l,
Jn	3:36	disobeys the Son will not see l,
Jn	4:14	of water welling up to eternal l."
Jn	5:21	Father raises the dead and gives l,
Jn	5:21	does the Son give l to whomever he
Jn	5:24	in the one who sent me has eternal l
Jn	5:24	but has passed from death to l.
Jn	5:39	you have eternal l through them;
Jn	5:40	do not want to come to me to have l.
Jn	6:27	the food that endures for eternal l,
Jn	6:35	said to them, "I am the bread of l;
Jn	6:47	you, whoever believes has eternal l.
Jn	6:48	I am the bread of l.
Jn	6:51	is my flesh for the l of the world."
Jn	6:63	It is the spirit that gives l,
Jn	6:63	I have spoken to you are spirit and l.
Jn	6:68	You have the words of eternal l.
Jn	8:12	but will have the light of l."
Jn	10:10	I came so that they might have l
Jn	10:11	A good shepherd lays down his l
Jn	10:28	I give them eternal l, and they shall
Jn	11:25	her, "I am the resurrection and the l;
Jn	12:25	Whoever loves his l loses it,
Jn	12:25	whoever hates his l in this world
Jn	12:50	that his commandment is eternal l.
Jn	13:37	I will lay down my l for you."
Jn	14: 6	"I am the way and the truth and the l.
Jn	15:13	to lay down one's l for one's friends.
Jn	17: 3	Now this is eternal l, that they
Jn	20:31	through this belief you may have l
Acts	2:28	made known to me the paths of l;
Acts	3:15	The author of l you put to death,
Acts	13:48	were destined for eternal l came
Rom	2: 7	eternal l to those who seek glory,
Rom	5:10	will we be saved by his l.
Rom	5:18	act acquittal and l came to all.
Rom	5:21	eternal l through Jesus Christ our
Rom	6: 4	we too might live in newness of l.
Rom	6:13	to God as raised from the dead to l
Rom	6:22	and its end is eternal l.
Rom	6:23	God is eternal l in Christ Jesus our
Rom	7:10	that was for l turned out to be death
Rom	8: 2	of the spirit of l in Christ Jesus has
Rom	8: 6	but the concern of the spirit is l
Rom	8:11	the dead will give l to your mortal
Rom	8:38	that neither death, nor l, nor angels,
1 Cor	15:19	If for this l only we have hoped
1 Cor	15:36	is not brought to l unless it dies.
2 Cor	2:16	to the former an odor of l that leads to l.
2 Cor	3: 6	brings death, but the Spirit gives l.
2 Cor	4:10	so that the l of Jesus may also be
2 Cor	5: 4	is mortal may be swallowed up by l.
Gal	6: 8	the spirit will reap eternal l
Phil	1:20	my body, whether by l or by death.
Phil	2:16	as you hold on to the word of l,
Phil	4: 3	whose names are in the book of l.
Col	3: 3	your l is hidden with Christ in God.
1 Tm	1:16	to believe in him for everlasting l.
1 Tm	4: 8	since it holds a promise of l both
1 Tm	6:12	Lay hold of eternal l, to which you
1 Tm	6:19	so as to win the l that is true l.
2 Tm	1:10	brought l and immortality to light
Ti	1: 2	in the hope of eternal l that God,
Ti	3: 7	become heirs in hope of eternal l.
Heb	7:16	of a l that cannot be destroyed.
Jas	1:12	he will receive the crown of l
Jas	3:13	works by a good l in the humility
1 Pt	3: 7	we are joint heirs of the gift of l,
1 Pt	3:10	"Whoever would love l and see good
1 Pt	4: 2	what remains of one's l in the flesh
2 Pt	1: 3	on us everything that makes for l
1 Jn	1: 1	our hands concerns the Word of l—
1 Jn	2:25	promise that he made us: eternal l.
1 Jn	3:14	to l because we love our brothers.
1 Jn	3:16	was that he laid down his l for us;
1 Jn	5:11	God gave us eternal l, and this l is
1 Jn	5:20	He is the true God and eternal l.
Jude	1:21	Jesus Christ that leads to eternal l.
Rv	2: 7	to eat from the tree of l that is
Rv	2: 8	who once died but came to l,
Rv	2:10	and I will give you the crown of l.
Rv	3: 5	erase his name from the book of l
Rv	11:11	days, a breath of l from God entered
Rv	13: 8	of the world in the book of l,
Rv	17: 8	in the book of l from the foundation
Rv	20: 4	They came to l and they reigned
Rv	20:12	scroll was opened, the book of l.
Rv	20:15	in the book of l was thrown
Rv	21:27	are written in the Lamb's book of l.
Rv	22: 2	of the river grew the tree of l
Rv	22:14	so as to have the right to the tree of l
Rv	22:19	take away his share in the tree of l

LIFE-GIVING → GIVE, LIVE
1 Cor 15:45 being," the last Adam a l spirit.

LIFETIME → LIVE
Ps 30: 6 divine favor lasts a l. At dusk
Lk 16:25 good during your l while Lazarus

LIFT → LIFTED, LIFTING, LIFTS
Ps 24: 7 L up your heads, O gates; rise up,
Ps 25: 1 wait for you, O LORD; I l up my soul
Ps 63: 5 I will l up my hands, calling on your
Ps 134: 2 L up your hands toward
Is 40:26 L up your eyes on high and see who
Lam 2:19 of the Lord; L up your hands to him
Lk 11:46 you yourselves do not l one finger

LIFTED → LIFT
Nm 9:21 Or if the cloud l during the day,
Ez 3:12 Then spirit l me up, and I heard
Ez 8: 3 Spirit l me up in the air and brought
Ez 11: 1 Spirit l me up and brought me
Mt 21:21 'Be l up and thrown into the sea,'
Jn 3:14 just as Moses l up the serpent
Jn 3:14 so must the Son of Man be l up,
Jn 12:34 that the Son of Man must be l up?

LIFTING → LIFT
Ps 28: 2 l my hands toward your holy place.
1 Tm 2: 8 men should pray, l up holy hands,

LIFTS → LIFT
1 Sm 2: 8 from the ash heap he l up the poor,
Ps 113: 7 dust, l the poor from the ash heap,

LIGAMENT → LIGAMENTS
Eph 4:16 held together by every supporting l,

LIGAMENTS → LIGAMENT
Col 2:19 and held together by its l and bonds,

LIGHT →DAYLIGHT, ENLIGHTENED, ENLIGHTENING,
  ENLIGHTENS, LIGHTED, LIGHTEN, LIGHTENED, LIGHTS

Gn	1: 3	said, "Let there be l," and there was l.
Gn	1: 5	God called the l "day,"
Ex	13:21	of a column of fire to give them l.
Ex	25:37	that they shed their l on the space
Jb	3:20	Why is l given to the toilers,
Jb	38:19	is the way to the dwelling place of l,
Ps	4: 7	LORD, show us the l of your face!"
Ps	18:29	You, LORD, give l to my lamp;
Ps	27: 1	The LORD is my l and my salvation;
Ps	36:10	of life, and in your l we see l.
Ps	56:14	before God in the l of the living.
Ps	104: 2	robed in l as with a cloak.
Ps	119:105	a lamp for my feet, a l for my path.
Ps	119:130	revelation of your words sheds l,
Ps	139:12	the day. Darkness and l are but one.
Prv	4:18	the path of the just is like shining l,
Prv	13: 9	The l of the just shines gaily.
Eccl	2:13	folly as much as l has the advantage
Wis	7:26	she is the refulgence of eternal l,
Is	2: 5	let us walk in the l of the LORD!
Is	9: 1	have seen a great l; Upon those who
Is	9: 1	in the land of gloom a l has shone.
Is	42: 6	of the people, a l for the nations,
Is	45: 7	I form the l, and create the darkness,
Is	49: 6	I will make you a l to the nations,
Is	53:11	he shall see the l in fullness of days;
Is	58:10	I shall rise for you in the darkness,
Is	60: 1	up in splendor! Your l has come,
Is	60:19	shall the sun be your l by day,
Is	60:19	The LORD shall be your l forever,
Bar	5: 9	by the l of his glory, with his mercy
Am	5:18	mean for you? Darkness and not l!
Mi	7: 8	I sit in darkness, the LORD is my l.
Mt	4:16	have seen a great l, on those
Mt	4:16	overshadowed by death l has arisen."
Mt	5:14	You are the l of the world. A city
Mt	5:16	so, your l must shine before others,
Mt	6:22	whole body will be filled with l;
Mt	11:30	my yoke is easy, and my burden l."
Mk	13:24	and the moon will not give its l,
Lk	2:32	a l for revelation to the Gentiles,
Lk	8:16	that those who enter may see the l.
Lk	11:33	that those who enter might see the l.
Jn	1: 4	this life was the l of the human race;
Jn	1: 5	the l shines in the darkness,
Jn	1: 7	to testify to the l, so that all might
Jn	1: 9	The true l, which enlightens
Jn	3:19	that the l came into the world,
Jn	3:19	but people preferred darkness to l,
Jn	5:35	you were content to rejoice in his l.
Jn	8:12	saying, "I am the l of the world.
Jn	8:12	darkness, but will have the l of life."
Jn	9: 5	in the world, I am the l of the world."
Jn	12:35	"The l will be among you only a little
Jn	12:35	Walk while you have the l,
Jn	12:46	I came into the world as l,
Acts	9: 3	a l from the sky suddenly flashed
Acts	13:47	'I have made you a l to the Gentiles,
Rom	13:12	[and] put on the armor of l;
2 Cor	4: 6	said, "Let l shine out of darkness,"
2 Cor	4: 6	to bring to l the knowledge
2 Cor	6:14	Or what fellowship does l have
2 Cor	11:14	Satan masquerades as an angel of l.
Eph	5: 8	but now you are l in the Lord. Live as children of l,
Eph	5: 9	for l produces every kind
Col	1:12	the inheritance of the holy ones in l.
1 Thes	5: 5	For all of you are children of the l
1 Tm	6:16	who dwells in unapproachable l.
1 Pt	2: 9	out of darkness into his wonderful l.
1 Jn	1: 5	you: God is l, and in him there is no
1 Jn	1: 7	if we walk in the l as he is in the l,
1 Jn	2: 8	and the true l is already shining.
1 Jn	2: 9	Whoever says he is in the l,
Rv	8:12	The day lost its l for a third
Rv	21:23	it, for the glory of God gave it l,
Rv	22: 5	nor will they need l from lamp
Rv	22: 5	for the Lord God shall give them l,

LIGHTED →LIGHT

1 Mc	4:50	and l the lamps on the lampstand,

LIGHTEN →LIGHT

2 Chr	10: 9	me to l the yoke my father imposed
Jon	1: 5	To l the ship for themselves,

LIGHTENED →LIGHT

Acts	27:38	they l the ship by throwing

LIGHTNING →LIGHTNINGS

Ex	19:16	there were peals of thunder and l,
Ex	20:18	people witnessed the thunder and l,
2 Sm	22:15	flight; he flashed l and routed them.
Ez	1:13	and from it came forth flashes of l.
Dn	10: 6	his face shone like l, his eyes were
Mt	24:27	For just as l comes from the east
Mt	28: 3	His appearance was like l and his
Lk	10:18	"I have observed Satan fall like l
Rv	4: 5	From the throne came flashes of l,
Rv	8: 5	flashes of l, and an earthquake.
Rv	11:19	There were flashes of l, rumblings,
Rv	16:18	Then there were l flashes,

LIGHTNINGS →LIGHTNING

Dn	3:73	L and clouds, bless the Lord;

LIGHTS →LIGHT

Gn	1:14	"Let there be l in the dome
Gn	1:16	God made the two great l,
Ps	136: 7	Who made the great l, God's love
Jas	1:17	coming down from the Father of l,

LIKE →ALIKE, LIKENESS

Gn	3: 5	you will be l gods who know what
Gn	3:22	The man has become l one of us,
Gn	13:16	make your descendants l the dust
Ex	8: 6	learn that there is none l the LORD,
Ex	15:11	Who is l to you among the gods,
Ex	34: 1	"Cut two stone tablets l the former,
Nm	11: 7	Manna was l coriander seed and had
Nm	13:33	we felt l mere grasshoppers, and so
Dt	8:20	L the nations which the LORD
Dt	18:15	"A prophet l me will the LORD,
Dt	32:31	Indeed, their "rock" is not l our Rock,
1 Sm	2: 2	There is no Holy One l the LORD; there is no Rock l our God.
2 Sm	7:22	There is none l you and there is no
1 Kgs	8:23	there is no God l you in heaven
1 Kgs	14: 8	have not been l my servant David,
1 Chr	17:21	"Is there, l your people Israel,
Jb	1: 8	that there is no one on earth l him,
Jb	40: 9	Have you an arm l that of God,
Jb	40: 9	can you thunder with a voice l his?
Ps	1: 3	They are l a tree planted near
Ps	1: 4	They are l chaff driven by the wind.
Ps	22:15	L water my life drains away; all my
Ps	22:15	My heart has become l wax, it melts
Ps	35:10	"O LORD, who is l you, Who rescue
Ps	48:11	L your name, O God, your praise
Ps	103:15	Our days are l the grass; l flowers
Ps	113: 5	Who is l the LORD, our God
Ps	114: 4	The mountains skipped l rams; the hills, l lambs of the flock.
Ps	144: 4	their days are l a passing shadow.
Prv	7:22	l an ox that is led to slaughter;
Prv	11:22	L a golden ring in a swine's snout
Prv	25:11	L golden apples in silver settings
Eccl	12:11	The sayings of the wise are l goads;
Eccl	12:11	l fixed spikes are the topics given
Sir	9:10	A new friend is l new wine
Sir	21:14	A fool's mind is l a broken jar—
Is	1: 9	Sodom, we should be l Gomorrah.
Is	1:18	Though your sins be l scarlet,
Is	11: 7	rest; the lion shall eat hay l the ox.
Is	40: 6	and all their glory l the flower
Is	46: 9	other; I am God, there is none l me.
Is	53: 2	He grew up l a sapling before him,
Is	53: 6	We had all gone astray l sheep,
Is	64: 5	of us have become l unclean men,
Is	64: 5	our good deeds are l polluted rags;
Jer	10: 6	No one is l you, O LORD, great are

Jer	23:29	Is not my word l fire, says the LORD, l a hammer shattering rocks?
Lam	1:12	is any suffering l my suffering,
Ez	1: 4	fire] something gleamed l electrum.
Ez	1:26	their heads something l a throne
Dn	7: 4	The first was l a lion,
Dn	7: 4	ground to stand on two feet l a man,
Dn	7:13	I saw One l a son of man coming,
Dn	10: 6	his face shone l lightning, his eyes
Hos	2: 1	Israelites shall be l the sand of the sea,
Hos	6: 4	Your piety is l a morning cloud,
Hos	14: 6	I will be l the dew of Israel: he shall
Hos	14: 6	he shall blossom l the lily; He shall
Mi	7:18	Who is there l you, the God who
Na	1: 6	His fury is poured out l fire,
Zec	1: 4	Be not l your fathers whom
Mt	9:36	l sheep without a shepherd.
Mt	10:16	I am sending you l sheep
Lk	6:48	one is l a person building a house,
Lk	13:18	said, "What is the kingdom of God l?
Acts	3:22	'A prophet l me will the Lord,
Rom	5:15	the gift is not l the transgression.
Rom	9:29	we would have become l Sodom
Rom	9:29	and have been made l Gomorrah."
Jas	1:24	promptly forgets what he looked l.
1 Pt	1:24	"All flesh is l grass, and all its glory l
2 Pt	3: 8	Lord one day is l a thousand years
2 Pt	3: 8	and a thousand years l one day.
2 Pt	3:10	day of the Lord will come l a thief,
Rv	1:13	the lampstands one l a son of man,
Rv	2:18	whose eyes are l a fiery flame
Rv	3: 3	I will come l a thief, and you will
Rv	4: 7	the second was l a calf, the third had
Rv	10: 1	his face was l the sun and his feet
Rv	16:15	("Behold, I am coming l a thief."
Rv	19:12	His eyes were [l] a fiery flame,

LIKENESS → LIKE

Gn	1:26	make man in our image, after our l.
Gn	5: 1	man, he made him in the l of God;
Ez	1:28	was the vision of the l of the glory
Rom	8: 3	his own Son in the l of sinful flesh
Phil	2: 7	coming in human l; and found
Jas	3: 9	who are made in the l of God.

LILIES → LILY

Song	2:16	l to him; he browses among the l.

LILITH

Is	34:14	There shall the l repose, and find

LILY → LILIES

Song	2: 1	a flower of Sharon, a l of the valley.
Song	2: 2	As a l among thorns, so is my
Hos	14: 6	he shall blossom like the l; He shall

LIMITS

Ex	19:23	us to set l around the mountain
2 Cor	10:13	to the l God has apportioned us,

LIMPED

Gn	32:32	Jacob l along because of his hip.

LINE

Is	28:17	I will make of right a measuring l,

LINEN

Ex	26: 1	out of sheets woven of fine l twined
Ex	28:39	tunic of fine l shall be brocaded.
Ex	28:39	The miter shall be made of fine l.
Prv	31:22	fine l and purple are her clothing.
Jer	13: 1	Go buy yourself a l loincloth.
Ez	9: 2	their midst was a man dressed in l,
Dn	10: 5	I saw a man dressed in l with a belt
Mk	15:46	Having bought a l cloth, he took
Mk	15:46	wrapped him in the l cloth and laid
Rv	15: 6	They were dressed in clean white l,
Rv	19: 8	a bright, clean l garment." (The l

LINGER

Prv	23:30	Those who l long over wine,

LION → LION'S, LIONS, LIONS'

Gn	49: 9	He crouches like a l recumbent,

Jgs	14: 6	he tore the l in pieces as one tears
1 Sm	17:34	whenever a l or bear came to carry
Ps	91:13	viper, trample the l and the dragon.
Eccl	27:28	a live dog is better off than a dead l.
Sir	27:28	lies in wait for them like a l.
Is	11: 7	rest; the l shall eat hay like the ox.
Is	65:25	and the l shall eat hay like the ox
Jer	4: 7	Up comes the l from his lair,
Jer	25:38	The l leaves his lair, and their land
Ez	1:10	on the right side was the face of a l,
Ez	10:14	the third that of a l, and the fourth
Dn	7: 4	The first was like a l,
Hos	13: 7	Therefore, I will be like a l to them,
1 Pt	5: 8	around like a roaring l looking
Rv	4: 7	The first creature resembled a l,
Rv	5: 5	The l of the tribe of Judah, the root

LION'S → LION

Gn	49: 9	Judah, like a l whelp,
2 Tm	4:17	I was rescued from the l mouth.

LIONS → LION

Dn	6:21	been able to save you from the l?"

LIONS' → LION

Dn	14:31	They threw Daniel into a l den,
Na	2:12	Where is the l cave, the young l den,
Rv	9: 8	Their teeth were like l teeth,

LIPS

Jb	27: 4	My l shall not speak falsehood,
Ps	12: 4	May the LORD cut off all deceiving l,
Ps	40:10	I did not restrain my l; you, LORD,
Ps	63: 4	than life; my l I offer you worship!
Ps	119:171	May my l pour forth your praise,
Ps	140: 4	venom of asps upon their l.
Ps	141: 3	my mouth, a gatekeeper at my l.
Prv	5: 3	The l of an adulteress drip
Prv	10:13	On the l of the intelligent is found
Prv	10:18	It is the l of the liar that conceal
Prv	10:21	The just man's l nourish many,
Prv	10:32	The l of the just know how
Prv	12:22	Lying l are an abomination
Prv	13: 3	to open wide one's l brings downfall.
Prv	15: 7	The l of the wise disseminate
Prv	24:26	He gives a kiss on the l who makes
Prv	26:23	are smooth l with a wicked heart.
Prv	27: 2	mouth; someone else—not your own l.
Eccl	10:12	favor, but the fool's l consume him.
Song	4:11	Your l drip honey, my bride,
Sir	12:16	With his l an enemy speaks sweetly,
Is	6: 5	For I am a man of unclean l,
Is	6: 5	living among a people of unclean l;
Is	29:13	and honors me with their l alone,
Mal	2: 7	For the l of the priest are to keep
Mt	15: 8	'This people honors me with their l,
Rom	3:13	the venom of asps on their l;
1 Cor	14:21	and by the l of foreigners I will
Heb	13:15	the fruit of l that confess his name.
1 Pt	3:10	evil and the l from speaking deceit,

LIST

1 Chr	27: 1	This is the l of the Israelite family

LISTEN → LISTENED, LISTENING, LISTENS

Ex	4: 1	not believe me, nor l to my plea?
Ex	6:30	can it be that Pharaoh will l to me?"
Ex	7:13	obstinate and would not l to them,
Ex	15:26	"If you really l to the voice
2 Kgs	17:40	They did not l, however,
2 Kgs	21: 9	But they did not l, and Manasseh
Ps	34:12	Come, children, l to me; I will teach
Ps	81: 9	l, my people, I give you warning!
Sir	6:33	If you are willing to l, you will
Is	1:10	l to the instruction of our God,
Mk	9: 7	"This is my beloved Son. L to him."
Lk	16:31	'If they will not l to Moses
Acts	3:22	to him you shall l in all that he may

LISTENED → LISTEN

Gn	3:17	"Because you l to your wife and ate
Dt	9:19	Yet once again the LORD l to me.

LISTENING →LISTEN
1 Sm 3:10 "Speak, for your servant is l."

LISTENS →LISTEN
Prv 17: 4 l to falsehood from a mischievous
Lk 10:16 Whoever l to you l to me.
Jn 18:37 belongs to the truth l to my voice."
1 Jn 4: 6 and anyone who knows God l to us,

LITTLE
Ex 16:18 a small amount did not have too l.
Ex 23:30 I will drive them out l by l before
1 Kgs 17:12 flour in my jar and a l oil in my jug.
Ps 8: 6 you have made them l less than
Prv 6:10 A l sleep, a l slumber, a l folding
Prv 13:11 away, but amassed l by l, it grows.
Prv 15:16 Better a l with fear of the LORD
Prv 16: 8 Better a l with virtue, than a large
Eccl 10: 1 than wisdom or wealth is a l folly!
Sir 29:23 Be it l or much, be content
Sir 51:28 Acquire but a l instruction; you will
Is 11: 6 with a l child to guide them.
Mt 6:30 provide for you, O you of l faith?
Mt 8:26 are you terrified, O you of l faith?"
Mt 14:31 him, "O you of l faith, why did you
Mt 16: 8 "You of l faith, why do you conclude
Mt 17:20 to them, "Because of your l faith.
Lk 7:47 one to whom l is forgiven, loves l."
1 Cor 5: 6 that a l yeast leavens all the dough?
2 Cor 8:15 and whoever had l did not have less."
Gal 5: 9 A l yeast leavens the whole batch
1 Tm 5:23 have a l wine for the sake of your
Heb 2: 7 for a l while lower than the angels;
1 Pt 5:10 you after you have suffered a l.

LIVE →ALIVE, LIFE, LIFE-GIVING, LIFETIME, LIVED, LIVES, LIVING
Gn 3:22 also, and thus eat of it and l forever."
Gn 12:12 then they will kill me, but let you l.
Ex 1:16 kill him; but if it is a girl, she may l."
Dt 4: 1 that you may l, and may enter
Dt 5:24 that a man can still l after God has
Dt 8: 3 that not by bread alone does man l,
Dt 30: 6 and all your soul, and so may l.
Jb 14:14 a man has died, were he to l again,
Ps 24: 1 the world and those who l there.
Ps 63: 5 I will bless you as long as I l; I will
Ps 119:175 Let me l to praise you; may your
Prv 4: 4 keep my commands, that you may l!
Prv 15:27 but he who hates bribes will l.
Wis 5:15 But the just l forever,
Is 26:19 But your dead shall l, their corpses
Ez 18: 9 that man is virtuous—he shall surely l,
Ez 18:32 says the Lord GOD. Return and l!
Am 5: 6 Seek the LORD, that you may l,
Jon 4: 3 for it is better for me to die than to l."
Hb 2: 4 man, because of his faith, shall l.
Mt 4: 4 'One does not l by bread alone,
Lk 4: 4 'One does not l by bread alone.' "
Lk 10:28 correctly; do this and you will l."
Jn 6:51 eats this bread will l forever;
Jn 11:25 in me, even if he dies, will l,
Jn 14:19 see me, because I l and you will l.
Acts 17:28 For 'In him we l and move and have
Rom 1:17 one who is righteous by faith will l."
Rom 6: 8 that we shall also l with him.
Rom 14: 8 For if we l, we l for the Lord,
Rom 14: 8 so then, whether we l or die, we are
2 Cor 5:15 that those who l might no longer l
2 Cor 6:16 "I will l with them and move among
Gal 2:20 yet I l, no longer I, but Christ lives
Gal 3:12 "the one who does these things will l
Gal 5:25 If we l in the Spirit, let us
Eph 4:17 you must no longer l as the Gentiles
Eph 5: 8 in the Lord. L as children of light,
2 Tm 3:12 fact, all who want to l religiously
Ti 2:12 worldly desires and to l temperately,
Heb 10:38 But my just one shall l by faith,

LIVED →LIVE
Dt 26: 5 household and l there as an alien.

Mt 1:18 but before they l together, she was

LIVES →LIVE
Ex 30:16 LORD, of the forfeit paid for their l."
Ex 33:20 see, for no man sees me and still l.
Tb 13: 1 Blessed be God who l forever,
Jb 19:25 for me, I know that my Vindicator l,
Ps 18:47 The LORD l! Blessed be my rock!
Prv 14:25 The truthful witness saves l, but he
Is 65:20 in it an infant who l but a few days,
Dn 12: 7 him who l forever that it should be
Jn 11:26 everyone who l and believes in me
Rom 6:10 for all; as to his life, he l for God.
Gal 2:20 live, no longer I, but Christ l in me;
Heb 7:25 him, since he l forever to make
1 Jn 3:16 to lay down our l for our brothers.
Rv 4:10 him, who l forever and ever.
Rv 10: 6 swore by the one who l forever
Rv 15: 7 fury of God, who l forever and ever.

LIVESTOCK
Ex 34:19 opens the womb among all your l,

LIVING →LIVE
Gn 2: 7 life, and so man became a l being.
Gn 3:20 she became the mother of all the l.
Gn 6:19 all other l creatures you shall bring
Gn 8:21 I ever again strike down all l beings,
Dt 5:26 the voice of the l God speaking
Jos 3:10 that there is a l God in your midst,
1 Sm 17:26 insult the armies of the l God?"
2 Kgs 19: 4 sent to taunt the l God, and will
Ps 84: 3 heart and flesh cry out for the l God.
Ps 142: 6 my portion in the land of the l.
Eccl 9: 4 for any among the l there is hope;
Is 53: 8 he was cut off from the land of the l,
Jer 2:13 forsaken me, the source of l waters;
Jer 10:10 he is the l God, the eternal King,
Jer 17:13 the source of l waters [the LORD].
Ez 1: 5 figures resembling four l creatures
Ez 10:17 for the l creatures' spirit was
Dn 6:27 feared: "For he is the l God,
Hos 2: 1 They shall be called, "Children of the l God."
Zec 14: 8 l waters shall flow from Jerusalem,
Mt 16:16 the Messiah, the Son of the l God."
Mt 22:32 not the God of the dead but of the l."
Jn 4:10 he would have given you l water."
Jn 6:51 I am the l bread that came down
Jn 7:38 'Rivers of l water will flow
Rom 9:26 shall be called children of the l God."
Rom 12: 1 to offer your bodies as a l sacrifice,
Rom 14: 9 be Lord of both the dead and the l.
2 Cor 6:16 For we are the temple of the l God;
1 Tm 4:10 we have set our hope on the l God,
2 Tm 4: 1 who will judge the l and the dead,
Heb 4:12 the word of God is l and effective,
Heb 10:20 l way he opened for us through
Heb 10:31 to fall into the hands of the l God.
1 Pt 1:23 through the l and abiding word
1 Pt 2: 4 Come to him, a l stone,
Rv 4: 6 there were four l creatures covered

LOAD
Gal 6: 5 for each will bear his own l.

LOAF →LOAVES
Prv 6:26 may be scarcely a l of bread,
Mk 8:14 they had only one l with them

LOAN
Dt 24:10 "When you make a l of any kind
Sir 29: 2 your neighbor when a l falls due;

LOAVES →LOAF
Mk 6:41 taking the five l and the two fish
Mk 8: 6 taking the seven l he gave thanks,
Mk 8:19 when I broke the five l for the five
Lk 11: 5 'Friend, lend me three l of bread,

LOCK →LOCKED, LOCKS
Mt 23:13 You l the kingdom of heaven before

LOCKED → LOCK
Jn   20:19   when the doors were l,
Acts   5:23   "We found the jail securely l
Rv   20: 3   abyss, which he l over it and sealed,

LOCKS → LOCK
Jgs   16:19   a man who shaved off his seven l

LOCUST → LOCUSTS
Jl   2:25   the years which the l has eaten,
Am   4: 9   trees and olive trees the l devoured;
Mal   3:11   For your sake I will forbid the l

LOCUSTS → LOCUST
Ex   10: 4   tomorrow I will bring l into your
2 Chr   6:28   or mildew, or l, or caterpillars;
Mt   3: 4   His food was l and wild honey.
Rv   9: 3   L came out of the smoke onto

LODGE
Ru   1:16   go I will go, wherever you l I will l,

LOFTY
Is   26: 5   and the l city he brings down;

LOINS
Ex   12:11   with your l girt, sandals on your feet
Heb   7:10   his father's l when Melchizedek met

LOIS
Godly grandmother of Timothy (2 Tm 1:5).

LONELY → ALONE
Lam   1: 1   How l she is now, the once crowded

LONG → LENGTH, LONGED, LONGER, LONGING, LONGS
Ex   20:12   you may have a l life in the land
Nm   14:11   "How l will this people spurn me?
Nm   14:11   How l will they refuse to believe
Dt   6: 2   I enjoin on you, and thus have l life.
1 Kgs   18:21   "How l will you straddle the issue?
2 Chr   1:11   nor even for a l life for yourself,
Ps   13: 2   How l will you hide your face
Ps   63: 5   I will bless you as l as I live; I will
Ps   119:97   teaching, Lord! I study it all day l.
Ps   119:174 I l for your salvation, Lord;
Prv   3:16   L life is in her right hand, in her left
Is   6:11   "How l, O Lord?" I asked. And he
Is   48: 3   Things of the past I foretold l ago,
Lk   10:13   they would l ago have repented,
1 Cor   11:14   man wears his hair l it is a disgrace
1 Cor   11:15   if a woman has l hair it is her glory,
1 Cor   11:15   because l hair has been given [her]
Phil   1: 8   how I l for all of you
1 Pt   2: 2   l for pure spiritual milk so
Rv   6:10   out in a loud voice, "How l will it be,

LONGED → LONG
Mt   13:17   righteous people l to see what you
2 Tm   4: 8   to all who have l for his appearance.
1 Pt   1:12   things into which angels l to look.

LONGER → LONG
Gn   17: 5   No l shall you be called Abram;
Gn   32:29   said, "You shall no l be spoken of as
Ez   14:11   of Israel may no l stray from me
Ez   14:11   may no l be defiled by all their sins.
Mt   5:13   It is no l good for anything but to be
Mk   10: 8   So they are no l two but one flesh.
Jn   13:33   will be with you only a little while l.
Jn   15:15   I no l call you slaves,
Rom   6: 6   that we might no l be in slavery
Gal   2:20   yet I live, no l I, but Christ lives
Eph   2:19   So then you are no l strangers
Eph   4:14   so that we may no l be infants,

LONGING → LONG
Ps   119:20   soul is stirred with l for your edicts.
2 Cor   5: 2   l to be further clothed with our

LONGS → LONG
Ps   42: 2   As the deer l for streams of water, so my soul l for
                 you, O God.

LOOK → LOOKED, LOOKING, LOOKS
Gn   15: 5   "L up at the sky and count the stars,
Gn   19:17   Don't l back or stop anywhere
Ex   3: 6   face, for he was afraid to l at God.
Dt   3:27   top of Pisgah and l out to the west,
Dt   3:27   L well, for you shall not cross this
Dt   26:15   L down, then, from heaven,
Ps   34: 6   L to God that you may be radiant
Ps   80:15   hosts; l down from heaven and see;
Prv   4:25   Let your eyes l straight ahead
Is   3: 9   Their very l bears witness against
Is   17: 7   that day man shall l to his maker,
Is   31: 1   But l not to the Holy One of Israel
Is   42:18   listen, you who are blind, l and see!
Hb   1:13   Too pure are your eyes to l
Zec   12:10   they shall l on him whom they have
Mt   6:26   L at the birds in the sky; they do not
Mk   13:21   here is the Messiah! L, there he is!'
Lk   24:39   L at my hands and my feet, that it is
Jn   4:35   l up and see the fields ripe
Jn   13:33   You will l for me, and as I told
Jn   19:37   "They will l upon him whom they
1 Pt   1:12   things into which angels longed to l.

LOOKED → LOOK
Gn   19:26   But Lot's wife l back, and she was
Ps   102:20   "The Lord l down from the holy
Sir   16:27   Then the Lord l upon the earth,
Ez   10: 1   I l and saw in the firmament
Dn   8: 3   I l up and saw standing by the river
Dn   10: 5   As I l up, I saw a man dressed
Dn   13:35   Through her tears she l
Zec   2: 1   I raised my eyes and l: there were
Zec   2: 5   Again I raised my eyes and l:
Lk   22:61   and the Lord turned and l at Peter;
1 Jn   1: 1   what we l upon and touched
Rv   5:11   I l again and heard the voices
Rv   6: 2   I l, and there was a white horse,
Rv   14: 1   I l and there was the Lamb standing

LOOKING → LOOK
Mk   1:37   finding him said, "Everyone is l for you."
Mk   8:24   L up he replied, "I see people l like
Lk   2:49   he said to them, "Why were you l for me?
Acts   1:11   why are you standing there l
Phil   2: 4   each l out not for his own interests,
Heb   11:26   for he was l to the recompense.
1 Pt   5: 8   prowling around like a roaring lion l

LOOKS → LOOK
Nm   21: 8   if anyone who has been bitten l at it,
1 Sm   16: 7   but the Lord l into the heart."
Ps   14: 2   The Lord l down from heaven
Ps   33:13   From heaven the Lord l down
Sir   11: 2   Praise not a man for his l;
Mt   5:28   everyone who l at a woman
Lk   9:62   l to what was left behind is fit

LOOSE
Mt   16:19   and whatever you l on earth shall be
Mt   18:18   and whatever you l on earth shall be

LORD → LORD'S, LORDS
Gn   18:27   I am presuming to speak to my L,
Gn   45: 8   to Pharaoh, l of all his household,
Ex   4:10   "If you please, L, I have never been
Nm   12:11   "Ah, my l!" he said to Moses,
Nm   16:13   that you must now l it over us?
Dt   10:17   the L of lords, the great God,
Tb   4:19   At all times bless the L God,
Tb   4:19   the L himself gives all good things.
Tb   4:19   If the L chooses, he raises a man up;
Jdt   6: 4   Nebuchadnezzar, l of all the earth;
Ps   16: 2   you are my L, you are my only
Ps   35:23   in my cause, my God and my L.
Ps   38:23   to help me, my L and my salvation!
Ps   40:18   and poor, the L keeps me in mind.
Ps   54: 6   as my helper; the L sustains my life.
Ps   57:10   praise you among the peoples, L;
Ps   62:13   so too, L, does kindness, And you
Ps   73:28   to make the L God my refuge.

Ps	86: 5	L, you are kind and forgiving,
Ps	86: 8	among the gods can equal you, O L;
Ps	97: 5	LORD, before the L of all the earth.
Ps	110: 1	The LORD says to you, my l:
Ps	110: 5	At your right hand is the L,
Ps	130: 3	mark our sins, L, who can stand?
Ps	135: 5	great, our L is greater than all gods.
Ps	136: 3	Praise the L of lords; God's love
Ps	147: 5	Great is our L, vast in power,
Is	6: 1	I saw the L seated on a high
Is	7:14	Therefore the L himself will give
Is	25: 8	forever. The L GOD will wipe away
Is	40:10	Here comes with power the L GOD,
Is	49:14	my L has forgotten me."
Is	61: 1	The spirit of the L GOD is upon me,
Jer	2:19	of me, says the L, the GOD of hosts.
Jer	46:10	this is the day of the L GOD of hosts,
Ez	4:14	"Oh no, L GOD!" I protested.
Ez	36:23	says the L GOD, when in their sight I
Dn	2:47	is the God of gods and L of kings
Dn	3:57	Bless the L, all you works of the L,
Dn	5:23	you have rebelled against the L
Dn	9: 3	I turned to the L God,
Dn	9: 7	Justice, O L, is on your side; we are
Dn	9: 9	But yours, O L, our God,
Dn	9:19	O L, hear! O L, pardon! O L,
Am	8:11	days are coming, says the L GOD,
Am	9: 5	I, the L GOD of hosts. I melt
Zep	1: 7	in the presence of the L GOD!
Mt	1:20	the angel of the L appeared to him
Mt	3: 3	'Prepare the way of the L,
Mt	4: 7	'You shall not put the L, your God,
Mt	4:10	'The L, your God, shall you worship
Mt	7:22	'L, L, did we not prophesy in your
Mt	12: 8	the Son of Man is L of the sabbath."
Mt	20:25	rulers of the Gentiles l it over them,
Mt	21: 9	he who comes in the name of the L;
Mt	22:37	"You shall love the L, your God,
Mt	22:44	'The L said to my l, "Sit at my right
Mt	23:39	he who comes in the name of the L.' "
Mk	1: 3	'Prepare the way of the L,
Mk	5:19	all that the L in his pity has done
Mk	12:29	O Israel! The L our God is L alone!
Mk	12:30	You shall love the L your God
Mk	12:11	by the L has this been done,/ and it is wonderful in our eyes'?"
Mk	12:37	David himself calls him 'l'; so how is
Lk	1:11	the angel of the L appeared to him,
Lk	1:32	the L God will give him the throne
Lk	1:46	proclaims the greatness of the L;
Lk	2: 9	The angel of the L appeared to them
Lk	2: 9	glory of the L shone around them,
Lk	2:11	born for you who is Messiah and L.
Lk	4:18	"The Spirit of the L is upon me,
Lk	4:19	and to proclaim a year acceptable to the L."
Lk	5:12	with him, and said, "L, if you wish,
Lk	5:17	the power of the L was with him
Lk	6: 5	"The Son of Man is l of the sabbath."
Lk	6:46	"Why do you call me, 'L, L,' but not
Lk	10:21	Father, L of heaven and earth,
Lk	10:27	"You shall love the L, your God,
Lk	10:39	Mary [who] sat beside the L at his feet
Lk	19:38	in the name of the L
Lk	24:34	"The L has truly been raised and has
Jn	1:23	"Make straight the way of the L," '
Jn	9:38	"I do believe, L," and he worshiped
Jn	20:18	"I have seen the L," and what he told
Jn	20:28	and said to him, "My L and my God!"
Jn	21:17	and he said to him, "L, you know
Acts	2:21	who calls on the name of the L.'
Acts	2:34	he himself said: 'The L said to my L,
Acts	2:36	that God has made him both L
Acts	4:26	against the L and against his
Acts	5:19	the angel of the L opened the doors
Acts	7:59	he called out, "L Jesus, receive my
Acts	8:16	baptized in the name of the L Jesus.
Acts	9:31	up and walked in the fear of the L,
Acts	10:36	Jesus Christ, who is L of all,
Acts	11:23	remain faithful to the L in firmness
Acts	16:31	"Believe in the L Jesus and you
Acts	22:10	The L answered me, 'Get up and go
Rom	4:24	the one who raised Jesus our L
Rom	5: 1	God through our L Jesus Christ,
Rom	6:23	is eternal life in Christ Jesus our L.
Rom	8:39	love of God in Christ Jesus our L.
Rom	10: 9	with your mouth that Jesus is L
Rom	10:12	the same L is L of all, enriching all
Rom	10:13	on the name of the L will be saved."
Rom	12:11	zeal, be fervent in spirit, serve the L.
Rom	13:14	But put on the L Jesus Christ,
Rom	14: 4	for the L is able to make him stand.
Rom	14: 8	live, we live for the L, and if we die, we die for the L;
Rom	14: 9	that he might be L of both the dead
1 Cor	1:31	boasts, should boast in the L."
1 Cor	2: 8	they would not have crucified the L
1 Cor	2:16	"who has known the mind of the L,
1 Cor	3: 5	just as the L assigned each one.
1 Cor	4: 4	the one who judges me is the L.
1 Cor	6:13	but for the L, and the L is
1 Cor	6:14	God raised the L and will also raise
1 Cor	7:10	this instruction (not I, but the L):
1 Cor	7:12	To the rest, I say (not the L): If any
1 Cor	7:25	have no commandment from the L
1 Cor	7:32	is anxious about the things of the L, how he may please the L.
1 Cor	7:39	wishes, provided that it be in the L.
1 Cor	8: 6	we exist, and one L, Jesus Christ,
1 Cor	10:21	You cannot drink the cup of the L
1 Cor	10:21	cannot partake of the table of the L
1 Cor	11:23	For I received from the L what I
1 Cor	11:23	that the L Jesus, on the night he was
1 Cor	11:27	cup of the L unworthily will have
1 Cor	11:27	for the body and blood of the L.
1 Cor	12: 3	"Jesus is L," except by the holy Spirit.
1 Cor	15:57	victory through our L Jesus Christ.
1 Cor	15:58	fully devoted to the work of the L,
1 Cor	15:58	in the L your labor is not in vain.
1 Cor	16:22	If anyone does not love the L,
2 Cor	1:24	Not that we I it over your faith;
2 Cor	2:12	a door was opened for me in the L,
2 Cor	3:17	Now the L is the Spirit, and where
2 Cor	4: 5	ourselves but Jesus Christ as L,
2 Cor	5: 8	the body and go home to the L.
2 Cor	8: 5	they gave themselves first to the L
2 Cor	10:17	boasts, should boast in the L."
2 Cor	10:18	the one whom the L recommends.
2 Cor	13:10	authority that the L has given me
Gal	6:14	in the cross of our L Jesus Christ,
Eph	2:21	grows into a temple sacred in the L;
Eph	4: 5	one L, one faith, one baptism;
Eph	5: 8	but now you are light in the L.
Eph	5:10	to learn what is pleasing to the L.
Eph	5:19	and playing to the L in your hearts,
Eph	5:22	to their husbands as to the L.
Eph	6: 1	obey your parents [in the L], for this
Eph	6: 8	the L for whatever good he does,
Eph	6:10	draw your strength from the L
Phil	2:11	that Jesus Christ is L, to the glory
Phil	3: 1	my brothers, rejoice in the L.
Phil	3: 8	good of knowing Christ Jesus my L.
Phil	4: 1	in this way stand firm in the L,
Phil	4: 4	Rejoice in the L always. I shall say
Phil	4: 5	be known to all. The L is near.
Col	1:10	to live in a manner worthy of the L,
Col	2: 6	as you received Christ Jesus the L,
Col	3:13	as the L has forgiven you, so must
Col	3:17	in the name of the L Jesus,
Col	3:18	your husbands, as is proper in the L.
Col	3:20	for this is pleasing to the L.
Col	3:24	receive from the L the due payment
Col	3:24	be slaves of the L Christ.
Col	4:17	ministry that you received in the L."
1 Thes	1: 6	became imitators of us and of the L,
1 Thes	3: 8	now live, if you stand firm in the L.
1 Thes	3:12	and may the L make you increase
1 Thes	4: 1	and exhort you in the L Jesus that,
1 Thes	4: 6	for the L is an avenger in all these

1 Thes	4:15	are left until the coming of the L,
1 Thes	4:17	the clouds to meet the L in the air.
1 Thes	4:17	Thus we shall always be with the L.
1 Thes	5: 2	day of the L will come like a thief
1 Thes	5:23	the coming of our L Jesus Christ.
2 Thes	1: 7	at the revelation of the L Jesus
2 Thes	2: 1	to the coming of our L Jesus Christ
2 Thes	2: 8	whom the L [Jesus] will kill
2 Thes	3: 3	But the L is faithful; he will
2 Thes	3: 5	May the L direct your hearts
1 Tm	1:14	grace of our L has been abundant,
1 Tm	6:14	the appearance of our L Jesus Christ
1 Tm	6:15	the King of kings and L of lords,
2 Tm	1: 8	ashamed of your testimony to our L,
2 Tm	2:19	"The L knows those who are his";
2 Tm	2:19	upon the name of the L avoid evil."
2 Tm	4: 8	me, which the L, the just judge,
2 Tm	4:17	But the L stood by me and gave me
Phlm	1:25	The grace of the L Jesus Christ be
Heb	1:10	O L, you established the earth,
Heb	8: 2	and of the true tabernacle that the L,
Heb	8:11	and kinsman, saying, "Know the L,"
Heb	10:30	again: "The L will judge his people."
Heb	12: 6	for whom the L loves,
Heb	12:14	without which no one will see the L.
Heb	13: 6	confidence: "The L is my helper,
Jas	1: 7	he will receive anything from the L,
Jas	3: 9	With it we bless the L and Father,
Jas	4:10	Humble yourselves before the L
Jas	5:11	because "the L is compassionate
Jas	5:15	person, and the L will raise him up.
1 Pt	1:25	the word of the L remains forever."
1 Pt	2: 3	you have tasted that the L is good.
1 Pt	3:12	face of the L is against evildoers."
1 Pt	3:15	sanctify Christ as L in your hearts.
2 Pt	1:11	into the eternal kingdom of our L
2 Pt	1:16	and coming of our L Jesus Christ,
2 Pt	2: 9	then the L knows how to rescue
2 Pt	3: 9	The L does not delay his promise,
2 Pt	3:10	day of the L will come like a thief,
2 Pt	3:18	and in the knowledge of our L
Jude	1: 4	who deny our only Master and L,
Jude	1:14	the L has come with his countless
Rv	4: 8	holy, holy is the L God almighty,
Rv	11: 8	where indeed their L was crucified.
Rv	11:15	of the world now belongs to our L
Rv	11:17	give thanks to you, L God almighty,
Rv	14:13	dead who die in the L from now on."
Rv	15: 4	Who will not fear you, L, or glorify
Rv	17:14	for he is L of lords and king
Rv	19: 6	The L has established his reign,
Rv	19:16	thigh, "King of kings and L of lords."
Rv	21:22	for its temple is the L God almighty
Rv	22: 5	for the L God shall give them light,
Rv	22:20	Amen! Come, L Jesus!

*LORD → *GOD, *LORD'S [This is the proper name of God, Yahweh, and is Lord in the NAB]

Gn	2: 4	when the L God made the earth
Gn	2: 7	the L God formed man
Gn	2:16	The L God gave man this order:
Gn	2:22	The L God then built
Gn	3: 9	The L God then called to the man
Gn	3:13	The L God then asked the woman,
Gn	3:14	Then the L God said to the serpent:
Gn	3:23	The L God therefore banished him
Gn	4: 4	The L looked with favor on Abel
Gn	4:15	So the L put a mark on Cain,
Gn	4:26	men began to invoke the L by name.
Gn	6: 8	But Noah found favor with the L.
Gn	8:20	Then Noah built an altar to the L,
Gn	10: 9	mighty hunter by the grace of the L;
Gn	11: 9	because there the L confused
Gn	12: 1	The L said to Abram: "Go forth
Gn	12: 7	The L appeared to Abram and said,
Gn	13: 4	and there he invoked the L by name.
Gn	15: 6	Abram put his faith in the L,
Gn	15:18	occasion that the L made a covenant

Gn	17: 1	old, the L appeared to him and said:
Gn	18: 1	The L appeared to Abraham
Gn	18:14	too marvelous for the L to do?
Gn	18:19	way of the L by doing what is right
Gn	19:14	"the L is about to destroy the city."
Gn	21: 1	The L took note of Sarah as he had
Gn	22:14	say, "On the mountain the L will see."
Gn	24: 1	the L had blessed him in every way.
Gn	25:21	Isaac entreated the L on behalf
Gn	25:21	The L heard his entreaty.
Gn	26: 2	The L appeared to him and said:
Gn	26:25	there and invoked the L by name.
Gn	28:16	"Truly, the L is in this spot,
Gn	31:49	"May the L keep watch between you
Gn	39: 2	But since the L was with him,
Gn	39:23	since the L was with him
Ex	3: 2	There an angel of the L appeared
Ex	3:15	The L, the God of your fathers,
Ex	4:11	another blind? Is it not I, the L?
Ex	4:31	they heard that the L was concerned
Ex	5: 2	"Who is the L, that I should heed his
Ex	5: 2	I do not know the L; even if I did,
Ex	6: 2	God also said to Moses, "I am the L.
Ex	6: 7	the L, am your God when I free you
Ex	8: 6	learn that there is none like the L,
Ex	9:12	But the L made Pharaoh obstinate,
Ex	9:12	just as the L had foretold to Moses.
Ex	9:30	I know, do not yet fear the L God."
Ex	10:16	"I have sinned against the L,
Ex	12:27	is the Passover sacrifice of the L,
Ex	12:29	midnight the L slew every first-born
Ex	13: 9	thus the law of the L will ever be
Ex	13: 9	a strong hand the L brought you
Ex	13:12	shall dedicate to the L every son
Ex	13:12	your animals shall belong to the L.
Ex	14:13	will see the victory the L will win
Ex	14:30	Thus the L saved Israel on that day
Ex	15: 3	The L is a warrior, L is his name!
Ex	15:11	is like to you among the gods, O L?
Ex	15:26	really listen to the voice of the L,
Ex	15:26	for I, the L, am your healer."
Ex	16:12	know that I, the L, am your God."
Ex	16:29	The L has given you the sabbath.
Ex	17: 2	quarreled there and tested the L,
Ex	17: 7	saying, "Is the L in our midst or not?"
Ex	18:10	"Blessed be the L," he said, "who has
Ex	19: 8	together, "Everything the L has said,
Ex	19:20	When the L came down to the top
Ex	20: 2	"I, the L, am your God, who brought
Ex	20: 5	For I, the L, your God, am a jealous
Ex	20: 7	shall not take the name of the L,
Ex	20: 7	the L will not leave unpunished him
Ex	20:10	seventh day is the sabbath of the L,
Ex	20:11	In six days the L made the heavens
Ex	20:11	is why the L has blessed the sabbath
Ex	23:25	The L, your God, you shall worship;
Ex	24: 3	the words and ordinances of the L,
Ex	24: 3	do everything that the L has told us."
Ex	24:16	The glory of the L settled
Ex	28:36	on a seal engraving, "Sacred to the L."
Ex	30:11	The L also said to Moses,
Ex	32:11	But Moses implored the L, his God,
Ex	33: 9	its entrance while the L spoke
Ex	34: 5	the L stood with him there and proclaimed his name, "L."
Ex	34: 6	Thus the L passed before him and cried out, "The L, the L,
Ex	34:14	god, for the L is 'the Jealous One';
Ex	40:34	glory of the L filled the Dwelling.
Ex	40:38	the L was seen over the Dwelling.
Lv	1: 2	to bring an animal offering to the L,
Lv	1: 9	a sweet-smelling oblation to the L.
Lv	8:36	that the L had commanded through
Lv	9:23	the glory of the L was revealed
Lv	19: 2	for I, the L, your God, am holy.
Lv	20: 8	what I, the L, who make you holy,
Lv	20:26	for I, the L, am sacred, I, who have
Lv	23:40	you shall make merry before the L,
Lv	24:16	the name of the L shall be put

Nm	6:24	The L bless you and keep you!
Nm	8: 5	The L said to Moses:
Nm	10:29	the place which the L has promised
Nm	11: 1	complained in the hearing of the L;
Nm	11: 1	the fire of the L burned among them
Nm	14:14	O L, are in the midst of this people;
Nm	14:14	you, L, who plainly reveal yourself!
Nm	14:18	The L is slow to anger and rich
Nm	20:13	Israelites contended against the L,
Nm	21: 6	In punishment the L sent among
Nm	21:14	in the "Book of the Wars of the L" :
Nm	22:31	Then the L removed the veil
Nm	22:31	too saw the angel of the L standing
Nm	23:12	"Is it not what the L puts in my
Nm	30: 3	When a man makes a vow to the L
Nm	32:12	have followed the L unreservedly.'
Dt	1:21	The L, your God, has given this
Dt	2: 7	The L, your God, has blessed you
Dt	4:29	Yet there too you shall seek the L,
Dt	4:39	that the L is God in the heavens
Dt	5: 6	'I, the L, am your God, who brought
Dt	5: 9	For I, the L, your God, am a jealous
Dt	5:11	shall not take the name of the L,
Dt	5:11	the L will not leave unpunished him
Dt	5:14	seventh day is the sabbath of the L,
Dt	6: 4	The L is our God, the L alone!
Dt	6: 5	you shall love the L, your God,
Dt	6:16	"You shall not put the L, your God,
Dt	7: 6	you are a people sacred to the L,
Dt	7: 8	It was because the L loved you
Dt	7: 9	then, that the L, your God, is God
Dt	8: 5	So you must realize that the L,
Dt	9:10	till the L gave me the two tablets
Dt	9:10	all the words that the L spoke to you
Dt	10:12	Israel, what does the L, your God,
Dt	10:12	ask of you but to fear the L,
Dt	10:12	to love and serve the L, your God,
Dt	10:17	for the L, your God, is the God of gods, the L of lords,
Dt	10:20	The L, your God, shall you fear,
Dt	11: 1	"Love the L, your God, therefore,
Dt	11:13	loving and serving the L, your God,
Dt	13: 4	for the L, your God, is testing you
Dt	14: 1	"You are children of the L,
Dt	17:15	over you as your king whom the L,
Dt	18: 2	the L himself is his heritage, as he
Dt	18:15	"A prophet like me will the L,
Dt	28: 1	continue to heed the voice of the L,
Dt	28:15	do not hearken to the voice of the L,
Dt	28:69	which the L ordered Moses to make
Dt	30: 4	even from there will the L,
Dt	30: 6	The L, your God, will circumcise
Dt	30: 6	that you may love the L, your God,
Dt	30:10	if only you heed the voice of the L,
Dt	30:10	when you return to the L, your God,
Dt	30:16	obey the commandments of the L,
Dt	30:20	by loving the L, your God,
Dt	30:20	which the L swore he would give
Dt	31: 6	of them, for it is the L, your God,
Jos	1:13	the servant of the L,
Jos	2:11	of you, since the L, your God,
Jos	7:20	"I have indeed sinned against the L,
Jos	10:14	when the L obeyed the voice
Jos	10:14	of a man; for the L fought for Israel.
Jos	21:44	the L gave them peace on every
Jos	22: 5	the servant of the L,
Jos	22: 5	upon you: love the L, your God;
Jos	22:22	The L, the God of gods,
Jos	22:34	among them that the L is God.
Jos	23:11	however, to love the L, your God.
Jos	24:15	does not please you to serve the L,
Jos	24:15	my household, we will serve the L."
Jos	24:18	Therefore we also will serve the L,
Jgs	2:12	Abandoning the L, the God of their
Jgs	2:12	of these gods provoked the L.
Jgs	3: 9	the Israelites cried out to the L,
Ru	1: 8	May the L be kind to you as you
Ru	4:13	the L enabled her to conceive
1 Sm	1:11	"O L of hosts, if you look with pity

1 Sm	1:11	him to the L for as long as he lives;
1 Sm	1:19	they worshiped before the L,
1 Sm	1:19	Hannah, the L remembered her.
1 Sm	1:28	Now I, in turn, give him to the L;
1 Sm	2: 2	There is no Holy One like the L;
1 Sm	2:25	can intercede for him with the L;
1 Sm	2:25	but if a man sins against the L,
1 Sm	2:26	in worth in the estimation of the L
1 Sm	3: 1	was minister to the L under Eli,
1 Sm	3: 1	revelation of the L was uncommon
1 Sm	3: 8	The L called Samuel again,
1 Sm	3:19	up, and the L was with him,
1 Sm	4: 3	fetch the ark of the L from Shiloh
1 Sm	5: 3	the ground before the ark of the L.
1 Sm	7:12	"To this point has the L helped us."
1 Sm	10: 1	"The L anoints you commander over
1 Sm	11:15	peace offerings there before the L,
1 Sm	12: 5	"The L is witness against you this
1 Sm	12:18	Samuel then called to the L,
1 Sm	12:18	and the L sent thunder and rain
1 Sm	12:22	since the L himself chose to make
1 Sm	12:24	you must fear the L and worship
1 Sm	13:14	The L has sought out a man after his
1 Sm	14: 6	Perhaps the L will help us,
1 Sm	14: 6	to grant victory through a few
1 Sm	15:22	"Does the L so delight in holocausts
1 Sm	15:22	obedience to the command of the L?
1 Sm	15:28	him: "The L has torn the kingdom
1 Sm	16:13	on, the spirit of the L rushed
1 Sm	17:45	you in the name of the L of hosts,
2 Sm	6:14	came dancing before the L
2 Sm	8: 6	The L brought David victory in all
2 Sm	12:13	Nathan, "I have sinned against the L."
2 Sm	12:13	"The L on his part has forgiven your
2 Sm	22: 2	sang: "O L, my rock, my fortress,
2 Sm	22:29	You are my lamp, O L! O my God,
2 Sm	22:31	the promise of the L is fire-tried;
1 Kgs	3: 3	Solomon loved the L, and obeyed
1 Kgs	5:19	to build a temple in honor of the L,
1 Kgs	5:26	The L, moreover, gave Solomon
1 Kgs	8:11	glory had filled the temple of the L.
1 Kgs	8:61	must be wholly devoted to the L,
1 Kgs	10: 9	Blessed be the L, your God,
1 Kgs	10: 9	the L has made you king to carry
1 Kgs	11: 4	heart was not entirely with the L,
1 Kgs	18:21	If the L is God, follow him; if Baal,
1 Kgs	18:37	Answer me, L! Answer me, that this
1 Kgs	18:39	said, "The L is God! The L is God!"
1 Kgs	19:11	stand on the mountain before the L; the L will be passing by."
1 Kgs	19:11	the L was not in the earthquake.
1 Kgs	22: 5	"Seek the word of the L at once."
2 Kgs	3:18	since the L does not consider this
2 Kgs	13:23	But the L was merciful with Israel
2 Kgs	17:20	So the L rejected the whole race
2 Kgs	18: 6	Loyal to the L, Hezekiah never
2 Kgs	19:31	zeal of the L of hosts shall do this.'
2 Kgs	22: 8	of the law in the temple of the L."
2 Kgs	23: 3	king made a covenant before the L
2 Kgs	23:25	king who turned to the L as he did,
2 Kgs	24: 4	Jerusalem, the L would not forgive.
2 Kgs	25: 9	He burned the house of the L,
1 Chr	10:13	of his rebellion against the L
1 Chr	11: 9	for the L of hosts was with him.
1 Chr	13: 6	by the name "L enthroned
1 Chr	16:11	Look to the L in his strength;
1 Chr	17: 1	of the L dwells under tentcloth."
1 Chr	17:20	O L, there is no one like you
1 Chr	21:24	will not take what is yours for the L,
1 Chr	22:11	my son, the L be with you, and may
1 Chr	25: 7	were trained in singing to the L,
1 Chr	28: 9	for the L searches all hearts
1 Chr	29:11	yours, O L, is the sovereignty;
2 Chr	1: 1	on the kingdom, for the L, his God,
2 Chr	2:10	"Because the L loves his people,
2 Chr	6:17	Now, L, God of Israel, may this
2 Chr	7: 1	the glory of the L filled the house.
2 Chr	7:12	The L appeared to Solomon during
2 Chr	9: 8	Blessed be the L, your God,

2 Chr	9: 8	you on his throne as king for the L,
2 Chr	13:12	Do not battle against the L, the God
2 Chr	14: 5	because the L had given them peace.
2 Chr	15:15	the L gave them rest on every side.
2 Chr	16: 9	of the L roam over the whole earth,
2 Chr	17: 9	book containing the law of the L;
2 Chr	19: 9	wholeheartedly in the fear of the L.
2 Chr	20:20	Trust in the L, your God, and you
2 Chr	21: 7	the L would not destroy the house
2 Chr	26: 5	and as long as he sought the L,
2 Chr	30: 9	For when you return to the L,
2 Chr	30: 9	and compassionate is the L,
2 Chr	32: 8	flesh, but we have the L, our God,
2 Chr	33:13	The L let himself be won over:
2 Chr	33:13	understood that the L is indeed God.
2 Chr	36:22	the L inspired King Cyrus of Persia
Ezr	3:10	to praise the L in the manner laid
Ezr	7: 6	Because the hand of the L, his God,
Ezr	7:10	practice of the law of the L
Neh	4: 8	Keep in mind the L, who is great
Neh	8: 1	of Moses which the L prescribed
Neh	8:10	prepared; for today is holy to our L.
Neh	8:10	in the L must be your strength!"
Neh	9: 6	"It is you, O L, you are the only one;
Jb	1: 6	to present themselves before the L,
Jb	1:21	The L gave and the L has taken away; blessed be the name of the L!"
Jb	38: 1	the L addressed Job out of the storm
Jb	42:12	Thus the L blessed the latter days
Ps	1: 2	Rather, the law of the L is their joy;
Ps	2: 2	against the L and his anointed:
Ps	3: 9	Safety comes from the L!
Ps	4: 7	L, show us the light of your face!"
Ps	6: 2	Do not reprove me in your anger, L,
Ps	7: 2	L my God, in you I take refuge;
Ps	8:10	O L, our Lord, how awesome is
Ps	9:10	The L is a stronghold
Ps	9:20	Arise, L, let no mortal prevail;
Ps	10:16	The L is king forever; the nations
Ps	11: 5	The L tests the good and the bad,
Ps	12: 7	The promises of the L are sure,
Ps	13: 2	How long, L? Will you utterly
Ps	14: 6	the poor have the L as their refuge.
Ps	15: 4	but honors those who fear the L;
Ps	16: 2	I say to the L, you are my Lord,
Ps	16: 8	I keep the L always before me;
Ps	17: 1	Hear, L, my plea for justice;
Ps	18: 2	He said: I love you, L, my strength,
Ps	18:32	Truly, who is God except the L?
Ps	19: 8	The law of the L is perfect,
Ps	19: 8	The decree of the L is trustworthy,
Ps	19:15	you, L, my rock and my redeemer.
Ps	20: 6	The L grant your every prayer!
Ps	21:14	Arise, L, in your power! We will
Ps	23: 1	of David. The L is my shepherd;
Ps	23: 6	I will dwell in the house of the L
Ps	24: 3	may go up the mountain of the L?
Ps	25: 4	Make known to me your ways, L;
Ps	25:10	the paths of the L are faithful love
Ps	26: 2	Test me, L, and try me; search my
Ps	27: 1	The L is my light and my salvation;
Ps	27: 1	do I fear? The L is my life's refuge;
Ps	27: 4	One thing I ask of the L; this I seek:
Ps	28: 7	The L is my strength and my shield,
Ps	29: 4	The voice of the L is power;
Ps	29: 4	the voice of the L is splendor.
Ps	30: 5	Sing praise to the L, you faithful;
Ps	31: 6	you will redeem me, L,
Ps	32: 2	to whom the L imputes no guilt,
Ps	33:12	the nation whose God is the L,
Ps	34: 2	I will bless the L at all times;
Ps	34: 8	The angel of the L, who encamps
Ps	34: 9	Learn to savor how good the L is;
Ps	35:10	shall say, "O L, who is like you,
Ps	36: 7	all living creatures you sustain, L.
Ps	37: 4	Find your delight in the L who will
Ps	37: 5	Commit your way to the L;
Ps	38:22	Forsake me not, O L; my God,
Ps	40: 2	I waited, waited for the L; who bent

Ps	40:14	L, graciously rescue me! Come quickly to help me, L!
Ps	41:11	But you, L, have mercy and raise
Ps	46: 8	The L of hosts is with us;
Ps	47: 3	For the L, the Most High,
Ps	48: 2	Great is the L and highly praised
Ps	50: 1	of Asaph. The L, the God of gods,
Ps	55:23	Cast your care upon the L, who will
Ps	59: 9	You, L, laugh at them; you deride
Ps	68: 5	this God whose name is the L.
Ps	69:32	will please the L more than oxen,
Ps	70: 6	help and deliverer. L, do not delay!
Ps	71: 1	In you, L, I take refuge; let me
Ps	78: 4	and mighty deeds of the L,
Ps	81:11	I, the L, am your God, who brought
Ps	83:17	shame, till they pay you homage, L.
Ps	84:12	For a sun and shield is the L God,
Ps	84:12	The L withholds no good thing
Ps	85: 8	Show us, L, your love; grant us
Ps	86:11	Teach me, L, your way that I may
Ps	88: 2	L, my God, I call out by day;
Ps	89: 7	Who in the skies ranks with the L?
Ps	89: 7	Who is like the L among the gods?
Ps	91: 9	You have the L for your refuge;
Ps	92: 2	It is good to give thanks to the L,
Ps	92: 5	For you make me jubilant, L,
Ps	93: 1	The L is king, robed with majesty;
Ps	94: 1	L, avenging God, avenging God,
Ps	94:12	Happy those whom you guide, L,
Ps	95: 3	For the L is the great God, the great
Ps	96: 1	Sing to the L a new song; sing to the L, all the earth.
Ps	96: 5	but the L made the heavens.
Ps	97: 1	The L is king; let the earth rejoice;
Ps	97:10	The L loves those who hate evil,
Ps	98: 2	The L has made his victory known;
Ps	99: 1	The L is king, the peoples tremble;
Ps	100: 2	worship the L with cries
Ps	101: 1	and justice; to you, L, I sing praise.
Ps	102:13	But you, L, are enthroned forever;
Ps	103: 1	Of David. Bless the L, my soul;
Ps	103: 8	Merciful and gracious is the L,
Ps	104:24	How varied are your works, L!
Ps	104:33	I will sing to the L all my life; I will
Ps	105: 4	Rely on the mighty L;
Ps	106:47	Save us, L, our God; gather us
Ps	107: 8	Let them thank the L for such
Ps	108: 4	praise you among the peoples, L;
Ps	109:26	Help me, L, my God; save me
Ps	110: 1	The L says to you, my lord:
Ps	110: 4	The L has sworn and will not
Ps	111: 2	Great are the works of the L, to be
Ps	111: 4	gracious and merciful is the L.
Ps	112: 1	Happy are those who fear the L,
Ps	113: 1	Praise, you servants of the L, praise the name of the L.
Ps	113: 5	Who is like the L, our God
Ps	115: 1	Not to us, L, not to us but to your
Ps	115:18	It is we who bless the L, both now
Ps	116: 5	Gracious is the L and just; yes,
Ps	116:12	How can I repay the L for all
Ps	116:15	Too costly in the eyes of the L
Ps	117: 1	Praise the L, all you nations!
Ps	118: 7	The L is with me as my helper;
Ps	118:18	The L chastised me harshly, but did
Ps	118:24	This is the day the L has made;
Ps	118:26	he who comes in the name of the L.
Ps	119: 1	who walk by the teaching of the L.
Ps	119:64	The earth, L, is filled with your
Ps	119:89	Your word, L, stands forever; it is
Ps	119:126	It is time for the L to act; they have
Ps	120: 1	song of ascents. The L answered me
Ps	121: 2	My help comes from the L,
Ps	121: 5	The L is your guardian; the L is
Ps	122: 1	me, "Let us go to the house of the L."
Ps	123: 2	So our eyes are on the L our God,
Ps	124: 1	Had not the L been with us,
Ps	124: 8	Our help is the name of the L,
Ps	125: 2	the L surrounds his people both now

Ps	126: 3	The L had done great things for us;
Ps	127: 1	Unless the L build the house,
Ps	127: 1	Unless the L guard the city,
Ps	128: 1	Happy are all who fear the L,
Ps	129: 4	But the just L cut me free
Ps	130: 5	I wait with longing for the L,
Ps	131: 3	Israel, hope in the L,
Ps	132: 1	song of ascents. L, remember David
Ps	132:13	Yes, the L has chosen Zion,
Ps	133: 3	There the L has lavished blessings,
Ps	134: 3	May the L who made heaven
Ps	135: 3	Praise the L; the L is good!
Ps	135: 6	Whatever the L wishes he does
Ps	136: 1	Praise the L, who is so good;
Ps	138: 8	The L is with me to the end. L,
Ps	139: 1	L, you have probed me, you know
Ps	140: 2	Deliver me, L, from the wicked;
Ps	141: 3	Set a guard, L, before my mouth,
Ps	142: 6	I cry out to you, L, I say, You are
Ps	143: 9	Rescue me, L, from my foes,
Ps	144: 3	L, what are mortals that you notice
Ps	145: 8	The L is gracious and merciful,
Ps	145: 9	The L is good to all,
Ps	145:17	You, L, are just in all your ways,
Ps	145:18	You, L, are near to all who call
Ps	146: 5	whose hope is in the L, their God,
Ps	146: 7	hungry. The L sets prisoners free;
Ps	147: 2	The L rebuilds Jerusalem,
Ps	148: 1	Praise the L from the heavens;
Ps	148: 7	Praise the L from the earth, you sea
Ps	149: 4	For the L takes delight in his
Ps	150: 6	give praise to the L! Hallelujah!
Prv	1: 7	The fear of the L is the beginning
Prv	1:29	and chose not the fear of the L;
Prv	2: 5	you understand the fear of the L;
Prv	2: 6	For the L gives wisdom, from his
Prv	3: 5	Trust in the L with all your heart,
Prv	3: 7	fear the L and turn away from evil;
Prv	3: 9	Honor the L with your wealth,
Prv	3:12	For whom the L loves he reproves,
Prv	3:19	The L by wisdom founded the earth,
Prv	6:16	There are six things the L hates,
Prv	8:13	[The fear of the L is to hate evil;]
Prv	8:35	life, and wins favor from the L,
Prv	9:10	of wisdom is the fear of the L,
Prv	10:27	The fear of the L prolongs life,
Prv	11:20	in heart are an abomination to the L,
Prv	12: 2	good man wins favor from the L,
Prv	12:22	lips are an abomination to the L,
Prv	14: 2	He who walks uprightly fears the L,
Prv	14:26	the fear of the L is a strong defense;
Prv	14:27	The fear of the L is a fountain
Prv	15: 3	The eyes of the L are in every place,
Prv	15:16	Better a little with fear of the L
Prv	15:29	The L is far from the wicked,
Prv	15:33	The fear of the L is training
Prv	16: 1	what the tongue utters is from the L.
Prv	16: 2	but it is the L who proves the spirit.
Prv	16: 3	Entrust your works to the L,
Prv	16: 9	course, but the L directs his steps.
Prv	17: 3	but the tester of hearts is the L.
Prv	18:10	The name of the L is a strong tower;
Prv	18:22	it is a favor he receives from the L.
Prv	19:14	but a prudent wife is from the L.
Prv	19:17	on the poor lends to the L, and he
Prv	19:23	The fear of the L is an aid to life;
Prv	20:12	that sees— the L has made them both.
Prv	20:22	Trust in the L and he will help you.
Prv	20:24	Man's steps are from the L; how,
Prv	21: 2	but it is the L who proves hearts.
Prv	21: 3	acceptable to the L than sacrifice.
Prv	21:30	no counsel, against the L.
Prv	22: 2	bond: the L is the maker of them all.
Prv	22:19	That your trust may be in the L,
Prv	23:17	zealous for the fear of the L always;
Prv	24:21	My son, fear the L and the king;
Prv	25:22	head, and the L will vindicate you.
Prv	28: 5	those who seek the L understand all.
Prv	29:25	but he who trusts in the L is safe.

Prv	31:30	the woman who fears the L is to be
Is	1: 4	They have forsaken the L,
Is	1:18	says the L: Though your sins be like
Is	2: 3	the word of the L from Jerusalem.
Is	2:11	and the L alone will be exalted,
Is	3:13	The L rises to accuse,
Is	4: 2	The branch of the L will be luster
Is	5: 7	of the L of hosts is the house
Is	5:16	the L of hosts shall be exalted by his
Is	6: 3	"Holy, holy, holy is the L of hosts!"
Is	7:11	Ask for a sign from the L,
Is	9: 6	zeal of the L of hosts will do this!
Is	11: 2	The spirit of the L shall rest
Is	11: 9	be filled with knowledge of the L,
Is	12: 2	strength and my courage is the L,
Is	13: 9	Lo, the day of the L comes, cruel,
Is	24: 1	the L empties the land and lays it
Is	25: 1	O L, you are my God, I will extol
Is	26: 4	Trust in the L forever! For the L is
Is	26: 8	your way and your judgments, O L,
Is	26:13	O L, our God, other lords than
Is	27: 3	I, the L, am its keeper, I water it
Is	28: 5	On that day the L of hosts will be
Is	29: 6	shall be visited by the L of hosts,
Is	29:19	lowly will ever find joy in the L,
Is	30:18	Yet the L is waiting to show you
Is	30:18	For the L is a God of justice:
Is	30:26	the day the L binds up the wounds
Is	33: 2	O L, have pity on us, for you we
Is	33: 6	the fear of the L is her treasure.
Is	33:22	Indeed the L will be there with us,
Is	33:22	the L our king, he it is who will
Is	34: 2	The L is angry with all the nations
Is	35: 2	They will see the glory of the L,
Is	35:10	Those whom the L has ransomed
Is	37:15	he prayed to the L:
Is	38: 7	the L that he will do what he has
Is	40: 3	the desert prepare the way of the L!
Is	40: 5	the glory of the L shall be revealed,
Is	40: 5	for the mouth of the L has spoken.
Is	40:27	"My way is hidden from the L,
Is	40:28	not heard? The L is the eternal God,
Is	40:31	in the L will renew their strength,
Is	41:14	I will help you, says the L,
Is	41:20	the hand of the L has done this,
Is	42: 8	I am the L, this is my name;
Is	42:10	Sing to the L a new song, his praise
Is	43: 3	For I am the L, your God, the Holy
Is	43:11	It is I, I the L; there is no savior
Is	44: 6	Thus says the L, Israel's King
Is	44:23	For the L has redeemed Jacob,
Is	45: 5	I am the L and there is no other,
Is	45: 7	I, the L, do all these things.
Is	45:17	Israel, you are saved by the L,
Is	49:14	Zion said, "The L has forsaken me;
Is	51: 1	who seek the L; Look to the rock
Is	51:11	Those whom the L has ransomed
Is	51:15	For I am the L, your God, who stirs
Is	51:15	waves roar; the L of hosts by name.
Is	52:10	The L has bared his holy arm
Is	53: 1	has the arm of the L been revealed?
Is	53: 6	But the L laid upon him the guilt
Is	53:10	[But the L was pleased to crush him
Is	53:10	the L shall be accomplished through
Is	54: 5	Maker; his name is the L of hosts;
Is	55: 6	Seek the L while he may be found,
Is	55: 7	Let him turn to the L for mercy;
Is	56: 6	who join themselves to the L,
Is	56: 6	him, Loving the name of the L,
Is	58: 5	a fast, a day acceptable to the L?
Is	58:11	Then the L will guide you always
Is	60: 2	But upon you the L shines, and over
Is	60:19	The L shall be your light forever,
Is	61: 1	me, because the L has anointed me;
Is	61: 3	planted by the L to show his glory.
Is	61: 8	For I, the L, love what is right,
Is	62: 4	"Espoused." For the L delights in you,
Is	63: 7	The favors of the L I will recall,
Is	63: 7	the glorious deeds of the L,

Is	64: 7	Yet, O L, you are our father; we are
Is	65:23	For a race blessed by the L are they
Is	66:15	Lo, the L shall come in fire,
Jer	2:19	is your forsaking the L, your God,
Jer	3:12	Return, rebel Israel, says the L,
Jer	3:12	For I am merciful, says the L, I will
Jer	4: 4	For the sake of the L,
Jer	6:10	the word of the L has become
Jer	8: 7	do not know the ordinance of the L.
Jer	9:23	that I, the L, bring about kindness,
Jer	9:23	with such am I pleased, says the L.
Jer	10: 6	No one is like you, O L, great are
Jer	10:10	The L is true God, he is the living
Jer	10:21	as cattle, the L they sought not;
Jer	12: 1	You would be in the right, O L, if I
Jer	14:20	We recognize, O L, our wickedness,
Jer	16:19	O L, my strength, my fortress,
Jer	17: 7	is the man who trusts in the L, whose hope is the L.
Jer	17:10	I, the L, alone probe the mind
Jer	17:13	O hope of Israel, O L! all who
Jer	23: 6	they give him: "The L our justice."
Jer	24: 7	which to understand that I am the L.
Jer	28: 9	as truly sent by the L only when his
Jer	31:11	The L shall ransom Jacob, he shall
Jer	31:22	The L has created a new thing
Jer	31:34	and kinsmen how to know the L.
Jer	32:27	I am the L, the God of all mankind!
Jer	33:16	shall call her: "The L our justice."
Jer	40: 3	because you sinned against the L
Jer	42: 4	I will pray to the L, your God,
Jer	42: 4	whatever the L answers you, I will
Jer	50: 4	they come, to seek the L, their God;
Lam	1: 5	are at ease; The L has punished her
Lam	3:24	My portion is the L, says my soul;
Lam	3:25	Good is the L to one who waits
Lam	3:26	silence for the saving help of the L.
Lam	3:40	ways that we may return to the L!
Ez	1: 3	the word of the L came to the priest
Ez	1: 3	the hand of the L came upon me.
Ez	1:28	of the likeness of the glory of the L.
Ez	3:23	I saw that the glory of the L was
Ez	10: 4	the glory of the L rose from over
Ez	10: 4	was bright with the glory of the L.
Ez	10:18	the glory of the L left the threshold
Ez	15: 7	you shall know that I am the L,
Ez	34:24	among them. I, the L, have spoken.
Ez	36:23	nations shall know that I am the L,
Ez	37: 4	Dry bones, hear the word of the L!
Ez	43: 4	glory of the L entered the temple
Ez	44: 4	of the L filling the Lord's temple,
Ez	48:35	shall henceforth be "The L is here."
Dn	9: 2	of which the L spoke to the prophet
Dn	9:14	so the L kept watch over
Dn	9:14	You, O L, our God, are just in all
Hos	1: 7	I will save them by the L, their God;
Hos	2:15	her lovers, forgot me, says the L.
Hos	2:22	fidelity, and you shall know the L.
Hos	3: 1	Even as the L loves the people
Hos	3: 5	turn back and seek the L, their God,
Hos	3: 5	They shall come trembling to the L
Hos	4: 1	Hear the word of the L, O people
Hos	4: 1	for the L has a grievance
Hos	6: 1	"Come, let us return to the L, For it
Hos	6: 3	us know, let us strive to know the L;
Hos	10:12	for it is time to seek the L, till he
Hos	12: 6	The L, the God of hosts, the L is his
Hos	14: 2	O Isreal, to the L, your God;
Jl	1:15	for near is the day of the L, and it
Jl	2:11	For great is the day of the L,
Jl	2:13	and return to the L, your God.
Jl	2:21	for the L has done great things.
Jl	3: 4	At the coming of the day of the L,
Jl	3: 5	who calls on the name of the L;
Jl	3: 5	survivors whom the L shall call.
Jl	4:14	For near is the day of the L
Jl	4:16	The L roars from Zion,
Jl	4:16	but the L is a refuge to his people,
Am	1: 2	The L will roar from Zion,

Am	4:13	The L, the God of hosts by name.
Am	5: 6	Seek the L, that you may live,
Am	5:18	who yearn for the day of the L!
Am	5:18	What will this day of the L mean
Am	7:15	The L took me from following
Am	8:11	but for hearing the word of the L.
Ob	1:15	For near is the day of the L for all
Jon	1: 3	to flee to Tarshish away from the L.
Jon	2:10	will pay: deliverance is from the L.
Mi	4: 2	let us climb the mount of the L,
Mi	4: 2	the word of the L from Jerusalem.
Mi	5: 3	flock by the strength of the L, in the majestic name of the L,
Mi	6: 2	O mountains, the plea of the L,
Mi	6: 8	and what the L requires of you:
Mi	7: 7	But as for me, I will look to the L,
Na	1: 2	jealous and avenging God is the L, an avenger is the L, and angry;
Na	1: 3	The L is slow to anger, yet great
Na	1: 3	and the L never leaves the guilty
Hb	1:12	Are you not from eternity, O L,
Hb	2:20	But the L is in his holy temple;
Zep	1: 7	for near is the day of the L,
Zep	1: 7	the L has prepared a slaughter feast,
Zep	1:14	Near is the great day of the L,
Zep	1:14	Hark, the day of the L! bitter, then,
Zep	3:17	The L, your God, is in your midst,
Hg	1:12	people listened to the voice of the L,
Hg	1:12	the people feared because of the L.
Zec	1: 2	The L was indeed angry with your
Zec	1:17	the L will again comfort Zion;
Zec	3: 1	standing before the angel of the L,
Zec	3: 2	the angel of the L said to Satan,
Zec	3: 2	to Satan, "May the L rebuke you,
Zec	6:12	he shall build the temple of the L.
Zec	8:21	go to implore the favor of the L"; and, "I too will go to seek the L."
Zec	9:16	And the L, their God, shall save
Zec	14: 5	Then the L, my God, shall come,
Zec	14: 7	known to the L, not day and night,
Zec	14: 9	The L shall become king over
Zec	14: 9	that day the L shall be the only one,
Zec	14:20	bells of the horses, "Holy to the L."
Zec	14:20	the L shall be as the libation bowls
Mal	1: 2	I have loved you, says the L;
Mal	3: 6	Surely I, the L, do not change,
Mal	3:23	Before the day of the L comes,

LORD'S →LORD

Sir	11:17	The L gift remains with the just;
Lam	3:31	For the L rejection/ does not last forever;
Mal	1:12	the L table and its offering may be
Acts	21:14	rest, saying, "The L will be done."
Rom	14: 8	whether we live or die, we are the L.
1 Cor	10:26	"the earth and its fullness are the L."
1 Cor	11:20	then, it is not to eat the L supper,
1 Pt	2:13	human institution for the L sake,
Rv	1:10	was caught up in spirit on the L day

*LORD'S →*LORD [This is the proper name of God, *Yahweh*, and is Lord's in the NAB]

Ex	9:29	shall learn that the earth is the L.
Nm	11:23	Moses, "Is this beyond the L reach?
Dt	32: 9	While the L own portion was Jacob,
1 Sm	17:47	For the battle is the L, and he shall
1 Sm	24:11	for he is the L anointed and a father
2 Sm	1:16	said, 'I dispatched the L anointed.' "
2 Sm	19:22	for this. He cursed the L anointed."
Ps	11: 4	temple; the L throne is in heaven.
Ps	24: 1	The earth is the L and all it holds,
Is	2: 2	The mountain of the L house
Jer	13:17	for the L flock, led away to exile.
Ob	1:21	and the kingship shall be the L.
Hb	2:16	revert the cup from the L right hand,
Zep	2: 3	sheltered on the day of the L anger.

LORDS →LORD

Dt	10:17	gods, the Lord of l, the great God,
Ps	136: 3	Praise the Lord of l; God's love
Is	26:13	O Lord, our God, other l than

1 Cor	8: 5	to be sure, many "gods" and many "l"),
1 Tm	6:15	the King of kings and Lord of l,
Rv	17:14	for he is Lord of l and king of kings,
Rv	19:16	thigh, "King of kings and Lord of l."

LOSE →LOSES, LOSS, LOST

Mk	8:35	wishes to save his life will l it,
Lk	9:25	for one to gain the whole world yet l
Jn	6:39	I should not l anything of what he
Heb	12: 3	may not grow weary and l heart.
Heb	12: 5	or l heart when reproved by him;
2 Jn	1: 8	that you do not l what we worked

LOSES →LOSE

Jn	12:25	Whoever loves his life l it,

LOSS →LOSE

1 Cor	3:15	is burned up, that one will suffer l;
Phil	3: 8	consider everything as a l because
Phil	3: 8	his sake I have accepted the l of all

LOST →LOSE

Nm	17:27	are perishing; we are l, we are all l!
Ps	119:176	I have wandered like a l sheep;
Jer	50: 6	L sheep were my people,
Ez	34: 4	back the strayed nor seek the l,
Ez	34:16	The l I will seek out, the strayed I
Mt	10: 6	Go rather to the l sheep of the house
Mt	15:24	"I was sent only to the l sheep
Mt	18:14	that one of these little ones be l.
Lk	15: 4	go after the l one until he finds it?
Lk	15: 6	because I have found my l sheep.'
Lk	15: 9	I have found the coin that I l.'
Lk	15:24	again; he was l, and has been found.'
Lk	19:10	to seek and to save what was l."
Jn	17:12	none of them was l except the son

LOT →LOT'S, LOTS

1. Nephew of Abraham (Gn 11:27; 12:5). Chose to live in Sodom (Gn 13). Rescued from four kings (Gn 14). Rescued from Sodom (Gn 19:1-29; 2 Pt 2:7). Fathered Moab and Ammon by his daughters (Gn 19:30-38).
2. Object cast to make decisions.

Nm	33:54	the land among yourselves by l,
Est	3: 7	or l, was cast in Haman's presence,
Est	9:24	or l, for the time of their defeat
Prv	16:33	When the l is cast into the lap,
Prv	18:18	The l puts an end to disputes, and is
Eccl	3:22	rejoice in his work; for this is his l.
Eccl	5:18	so that he receives his l and finds
Wis	2: 9	for this our portion is, and this our l.
Lk	17:32	Remember the wife of L.
Acts	1:26	and the l fell upon Matthias, and he

LOT'S →LOT

Gn	19:26	But L wife looked back,

LOTS →LOT

Jos	18:10	casting l for them before the LORD
1 Sm	14:42	said, "Cast l between me and my son
1 Chr	25: 8	They cast l for their functions
Est	F: 7	For this purpose he arranged two l:
Ps	22:19	them; for my clothing they cast l.
Jl	4: 3	Over my people they have cast l,
Jon	1: 7	let us cast l to find out on whose
Jon	1: 7	So they cast l, and thus singled
Mt	27:35	divided his garments by casting l;
Acts	1:26	Then they gave l to them,

LOUD →ALOUD

Ex	12:30	and there was l wailing throughout
Ex	19:16	and a very l trumpet blast, so that all
Jdt	9: 1	prayed to the LORD with a l voice:
Prv	27:14	greets his neighbor with a l voice
Ez	9: 1	Then he cried l for me to hear:
Mk	15:34	o'clock Jesus cried out in a l voice,
Jn	11:43	he cried out in a l voice, "Lazarus,
Rv	1:10	behind me a voice as l as a trumpet,
Rv	21: 3	I heard a l voice from the throne

LOVE →BELOVED, LOVED, LOVER, LOVERS, LOVES, LOVING

Gn	22: 2	whom you l, and go to the land

Gn	29:20	a few days because of his l for her.
Gn	29:32	misery; now my husband will l me.' "
Ex	20: 6	on the children of those who l me
Lv	19:18	You shall l your neighbor as
Lv	19:34	have the same l for him as
Dt	5:10	on the children of those who l me
Dt	6: 5	Therefore, you shall l the LORD,
Dt	7: 9	generation toward those who l him
Dt	7:13	He will l and bless and multiply
Dt	10:12	exactly, to l and serve the LORD,
Dt	10:15	his l for your fathers the LORD was
Dt	11: 1	"L the LORD, your God, therefore,
Dt	13: 4	learn whether you really l him
Dt	30: 6	that you may l the LORD, your God,
Jos	22: 5	upon you: l the LORD, your God;
Jos	23:11	however, to l the LORD, your God.
Jgs	14:16	you do not l me, for you have
Jgs	16: 4	that he fell in l with a woman
Jgs	16:15	him, "How can you say that you l me
1 Sm	18:22	of you, and all his officers l you.
1 Sm	20:17	And in his l for David,
2 Sm	1:26	More precious have I held l for you than l for women.
2 Sm	13: 4	said to him, "I am in l with Tamar,
2 Sm	19: 7	you and hating those who l you.
2 Chr	19: 2	and l those who hate the LORD?
Neh	1: 5	of mercy toward those who l you
Tb	4:13	Therefore, my son, l your kinsmen.
Tb	14: 7	Those who sincerely l God shall
1 Mc	4:33	by the sword of those who l you,
2 Mc	6:20	is unlawful to taste even for l of life.
Ps	4: 3	l what is worthless, chase after lies?
Ps	5: 8	house because of your great l. I can
Ps	5:12	the joy of those who l your name.
Ps	17: 7	Show your wonderful l, you who
Ps	18: 2	He said: I l you, LORD, my strength,
Ps	21: 8	stands firm through the l
Ps	25: 6	Remember your compassion and l,
Ps	25: 7	remember me only in light of your l.
Ps	25:10	the paths of the LORD are faithful l
Ps	26: 3	Your l is before my eyes; I walk
Ps	26: 8	LORD, I l the house where you dwell,
Ps	31: 8	I will rejoice and be glad in your l,
Ps	31:22	who has shown me wondrous l,
Ps	31:24	L the LORD, all you faithful.
Ps	32:10	l surrounds those who trust
Ps	36: 6	LORD, your l reaches to heaven;
Ps	36: 8	How precious is your l, O God!
Ps	42: 9	dawn may the LORD bestow faithful l
Ps	44:27	Redeem us as your l demands.
Ps	45: 1	A *maskil* of the Korahites. A l song.
Ps	45: 8	You l justice and hate wrongdoing;
Ps	48:10	temple we ponder your steadfast l.
Ps	52: 5	You l evil rather than good,
Ps	52: 6	You l any word that destroys,
Ps	52:10	God, trust in God's faithful l forever.
Ps	57: 4	May God send fidelity and l,
Ps	57:11	For your l towers to the heavens;
Ps	59:17	your strength, extol your l at dawn,
Ps	61: 8	may your l and fidelity preserve him"—
Ps	63: 4	For your l is better than life; my lips
Ps	69:17	me, LORD, in your generous l;
Ps	69:37	those who l God's name shall dwell
Ps	77: 9	Has God's l ceased forever?
Ps	85: 8	Show us, LORD, your l; grant us your
Ps	85:11	L and truth will meet;
Ps	86:13	Your l for me is great; you have
Ps	88:12	Is your l proclaimed in the grave,
Ps	89: 3	said, "My l is established forever;
Ps	89:15	l and loyalty march before you.
Ps	89:25	My loyalty and l will be with him;
Ps	89:29	Forever I will maintain my l
Ps	89:34	But I will not take my l from him,
Ps	90:14	Fill us at daybreak with your l,
Ps	92: 3	To proclaim your l in the morning,
Ps	94:18	slipping," your l, LORD, holds me up.
Ps	98: 3	Has remembered faithful l
Ps	100: 5	the LORD, Whose l endures forever,
Ps	103: 4	the pit, surrounds you with l

Ps	103:11	so God's l towers over the faithful.
Ps	106: 1	is good, whose l endures forever.
Ps	106: 7·	They did not remember your great l;
Ps	106:45	and relented in his abundant l,
Ps	107: 1	is good, whose l endures forever!"
Ps	108: 5	For your l towers to the heavens,
Ps	109: 4	In return for my l they slander me,
Ps	109: 5	hatred for my l. My enemies say
Ps	115: 1	because of your faithfulness and l.
Ps	116: 1	I l the LORD, who listened to my
Ps	117: 2	The LORD's l for us is strong;
Ps	118: 1	is good, whose l endures forever.
Ps	118: 2	Israel say: God's l endures forever.
Ps	118: 3	Aaron say, God's l endures forever.
Ps	118: 4	LORD say, God's l endures forever.
Ps	118:29	is good, whose l endures forever.
Ps	119:41	Let your l come to me, LORD,
Ps	119:47	in your commands, which I dearly l.
Ps	119:48	I study your laws, which I l.
Ps	119:64	earth, LORD, is filled with your l;
Ps	119:76	May your l comfort me in accord
Ps	119:97	How I l your teaching, LORD! I study
Ps	119:113	every hypocrite; your teaching I l.
Ps	119:119	on earth; therefore I l your decrees.
Ps	119:127	Truly I l your commands more than
Ps	119:149	Hear my voice in your l, O LORD;
Ps	119:159	See how I l your precepts, LORD;
Ps	119:163	I hate and abhor; your teaching I l.
Ps	119:167	your decrees; I l them very much.
Ps	122: 6	pray: "May those who l you prosper!
Ps	136: 1	is so good; God's l endures forever;
Ps	136: 2	of gods; God's l endures forever;
Ps	136: 3	of lords; God's l endures forever;
Ps	136: 4	wonders, God's l endures forever;
Ps	136: 5	the heavens, God's l endures forever;
Ps	136: 6	the waters, God's l endures forever;
Ps	136: 7	great lights, God's l endures forever;
Ps	136: 8	the day, God's l endures forever;
Ps	136: 9	the night, God's l endures forever;
Ps	136:10	of Egypt, God's l endures forever;
Ps	136:11	their midst, God's l endures forever;
Ps	136:12	arm, God's l endures forever;
Ps	136:13	the Red Sea God's l endures forever;
Ps	136:14	through, God's l endures forever;
Ps	136:15	Red Sea, God's l endures forever;
Ps	136:16	the desert, God's l endures forever;
Ps	136:17	great kings, God's l endures forever;
Ps	136:18	kings, God's l endures forever;
Ps	136:19	Amorites, God's l endures forever;
Ps	136:20	of Bashan, God's l endures forever;
Ps	136:21	a heritage, God's l endures forever;
Ps	136:22	servant, God's l endures forever.
Ps	136:23	our misery, God's l endures forever;
Ps	136:24	our foes, God's l endures forever.
Ps	136:25	to all flesh, God's l endures forever.
Ps	136:26	of heaven, God's l endures forever.
Ps	138: 2	your name for your fidelity and l.
Ps	138: 8	LORD, your l endures forever.
Ps	145: 8	slow to anger and abounding in l.
Ps	145:20	LORD, watch over all who l you,
Prv	1:22	you simple ones, will you l inanity,
Prv	4: 6	l her, and she will safeguard you;
Prv	5:19	Her l will invigorate you always,
Prv	5:19	through her l you will flourish
Prv	7:18	"Come, let us drink our fill of l, until morning, let us feast on l!
Prv	8:17	"Those who l me I also l, and those
Prv	8:21	Granting wealth to those who l me,
Prv	8:36	himself; all who hate me l death."
Prv	9: 8	a wise man, and he will l you.
Prv	10:12	disputes, but l covers all offenses.
Prv	15:17	Better a dish of herbs where l is
Prv	20:13	L not sleep, lest you be reduced
Prv	27: 5	rebuke than a l that remains hidden.
Eccl	3: 8	A time to l, and a time to hate;
Eccl	9: 1	L from hatred man cannot tell;
Eccl	9: 6	l and hatred and rivalry have long
Eccl	9: 9	life with the wife whom you l,
Song	1: 2	More delightful is your l than wine!

Song	1: 3	that is why the maidens l you.
Song	1: 4	we extol your l; it is beyond wine:
Song	2: 4	hall and his emblem over me is l.
Song	2: 5	with apples, for I am faint with l.
Song	2: 7	field, Do not arouse, do not stir up l
Song	3: 5	field, Do not arouse, do not stir up l
Song	4:10	How beautiful is your l, my sister,
Song	4:10	more delightful is your l than wine,
Song	5: 1	friends; drink! Drink freely of l!
Song	5: 8	you tell him?— that I am faint with l.
Song	7:13	There will I give you my l.
Song	8: 4	field, Do not arouse, do not stir up l,
Song	8: 6	For stern as death is l, relentless as
Song	8: 7	Deep waters cannot quench l,
Song	8: 7	to offer all he owns to purchase l,
Wis	1: 1	L justice, you who judge the earth;
Wis	3: 9	faithful shall abide with him in l:
Wis	6:12	perceived by those who l her,
Wis	6:17	then, care for discipline is l of her;
Wis	6:18	l means the keeping of her laws;
Wis	11:24	For you l all things that are
Sir	Pr: 1	that those who l wisdom might,
Sir	2:15	those who l him keep his ways.
Sir	2:16	those who l him are filled with his
Sir	4:14	those who l her the LORD loves.
Sir	7:30	all your strength, l your Creator,
Sir	34:16	the LORD are upon those who l him;
Sir	40:20	but better than either, conjugal l.
Is	43: 4	and glorious, and because I l you.
Is	54: 8	with enduring l I take pity on you,
Is	54:10	shaken, My l shall never leave you
Is	61: 8	For I, the LORD, l what is right,
Is	63: 9	Because of his l and pity
Is	66:10	all you who l her; Exult,
Jer	31: 3	With age-old l I have loved you;
Ez	16: 8	that you were now old enough for l.
Ez	23:17	to the l couch, and defiled her
Dn	9: 4	covenant toward those who l you
Dn	14:38	have not forsaken those who l you."
Hos	2:21	and in justice, in l and in mercy;
Hos	3: 1	said to me: Give your l to a woman
Hos	4:18	in their arrogance they l shame.
Hos	6: 6	For it is l that I desire, not sacrifice,
Hos	9:15	my house. I will l them no longer;
Hos	11: 4	with bands of l; I fostered them like
Hos	14: 5	their defection, I will l them freely;
Am	4: 5	For so you l to do, O men of Israel,
Am	5:15	Hate evil and l good, and let justice
Mi	3: 2	who hate what is good, and l evil?
Mi	6: 8	to do the right and to l goodness,
Zep	3:17	and renew you in his l, He will sing
Zec	8:17	in his heart, nor l a false oath.
Zec	8:19	Judah; only l faithfulness and peace.
Mt	5:43	'You shall l your neighbor and hate
Mt	5:44	But I say to you, l your enemies,
Mt	5:46	For if you l those who l you,
Mt	6: 5	who l to stand and pray
Mt	6:24	will either hate one and l the other,
Mt	19:19	and 'you shall l your neighbor as
Mt	22:37	said to him, "You shall l the Lord,
Mt	22:39	like it: You shall l your neighbor as
Mt	23: 6	They l places of honor at banquets,
Mt	24:12	the l of many will grow cold.
Mk	12:30	You shall l the Lord your God
Mk	12:31	is this: 'You shall l your neighbor as
Mk	12:33	And 'to l him with all your heart,
Mk	12:33	l your neighbor as yourself' is worth
Lk	6:27	you who hear l say, l your enemies,
Lk	6:32	For if you l those who l you,
Lk	6:32	Even sinners l those who l them.
Lk	6:35	l your enemies and do good to them,
Lk	7:42	Which of them will l him more?"
Lk	7:47	hence, she has shown great l.
Lk	10:27	said in reply, "You shall l the Lord,
Lk	11:42	to judgment and to l for God.
Lk	11:43	Pharisees! You l the seat of honor
Lk	16:13	will either hate one and l the other,
Lk	20:46	and l greetings in marketplaces,
Jn	5:42	that you do not have the l of God

Jn	8:42	you would l me, for I came
Jn	11: 3	saying, "Master, the one you l is ill."
Jn	13:34	A new commandment: l one another.
Jn	13:34	so you also should l one another.
Jn	13:35	if you have l for one another."
Jn	14:15	"If you l me, you will keep my
Jn	14:21	and I will l him and reveal myself
Jn	14:23	and my Father will l him, and we
Jn	14:24	Whoever does not l me does not
Jn	14:31	world must know that I l the Father
Jn	15: 9	the Father loves me, so I also l you. Remain in my l.
Jn	15:10	you will remain in my l, just as I
Jn	15:10	commandments and remain in his l.
Jn	15:12	l one another as I l you.
Jn	15:13	No one has greater l than this, to lay
Jn	15:17	This I command you: l one another.
Jn	15:19	world, the world would l its own;
Jn	17:26	that the l with which you loved me
Jn	21:15	John, do you l me more than these?"
Jn	21:15	"Yes, Lord, you know that I l you."
Jn	21:16	"Simon, son of John, do you l me?"
Jn	21:16	"Yes, Lord, you know that I l you."
Jn	21:17	"Simon, son of John, do you l me?"
Jn	21:17	to him a third time, "Do you l me?"
Jn	21:17	everything; you know that I l you."
Rom	5: 5	because the l of God has been
Rom	5: 8	God proves his l for us in that while
Rom	8:28	work for good for those who l God,
Rom	8:35	separate us from the l of Christ?
Rom	8:39	to separate us from the l of God
Rom	12: 9	Let l be sincere; hate what is evil,
Rom	12:10	l one another with mutual affection;
Rom	13: 8	to anyone, except to l one another;
Rom	13: 9	[namely] "You shall l your neighbor
Rom	13:10	L does no evil to the neighbor;
Rom	13:10	hence, l is the fulfillment of the law.
Rom	14:15	is no longer in accord with l. Do not
Rom	15:30	Christ and by the l of the Spirit,
1 Cor	2: 9	has prepared for those who l him,"
1 Cor	4:21	a rod, or with l and a gentle spirit?
1 Cor	8: 1	inflates with pride, but l builds up.
1 Cor	13: 1	but do not have l, I am a resounding
1 Cor	13: 2	but do not have l, I am nothing.
1 Cor	13: 3	but do not have l, I gain nothing.
1 Cor	13: 4	L is patient, l is kind. It is not jealous, [l] is not pompous,
1 Cor	13: 8	L never fails. If there are
1 Cor	13:13	So faith, hope, l remain, these three; but the greatest of these is l.
1 Cor	14: 1	Pursue l, but strive eagerly
1 Cor	16:14	every act should be done with l.
1 Cor	16:22	If anyone does not l the Lord,
1 Cor	16:24	My l to all of you in Christ Jesus.
2 Cor	2: 4	might know the abundant l I have
2 Cor	2: 8	urge you to reaffirm your l for him.
2 Cor	5:14	For the l of Christ impels us,
2 Cor	6: 6	in a holy spirit, in unfeigned l,
2 Cor	8: 7	and in the l we have for you,
2 Cor	8: 8	of your l by your concern for others.
2 Cor	8:24	proof before the churches of your l
2 Cor	11:11	Because I do not l you? God knows
2 Cor	12:15	If I l you more, am I to be loved
2 Cor	13:11	the God of l and peace will be
2 Cor	13:13	Lord Jesus Christ and the l of God
Gal	5: 6	but only faith working through l.
Gal	5:13	rather, serve one another through l.
Gal	5:14	"You shall l your neighbor as
Gal	5:22	the fruit of the Spirit is l, joy, peace,
Eph	1: 4	without blemish before him. In l
Eph	1:15	and of your l for all the holy ones,
Eph	2: 4	because of the great l he had for us,
Eph	3:17	that you, rooted and grounded in l,
Eph	3:19	and to know the l of Christ
Eph	4: 2	bearing with one another through l,
Eph	4:15	living the truth in l, we should grow
Eph	4:16	growth and builds itself up in l.
Eph	5: 2	and live in l, as Christ loved us
Eph	5:25	Husbands, l your wives, even as
Eph	5:28	husbands should l their wives as
Eph	5:33	of you should l his wife as himself,
Eph	6:23	and l with faith, from God
Eph	6:24	with all who l our Lord Jesus Christ
Phil	1: 9	that your l may increase ever more
Phil	1:16	The latter act out of l, aware that I
Phil	2: 1	any solace in l, any participation
Phil	2: 2	with the same l, united in heart,
Phil	4: 1	my brothers, whom I l and long for,
Col	1: 4	the l that you have for all the holy
Col	1: 8	also told us of your l in the Spirit.
Col	2: 2	as they are brought together in l,
Col	3:14	And over all these put on l, that is,
Col	3:19	Husbands, l your wives, and avoid
1 Thes	1: 3	labor of l and endurance in hope
1 Thes	3: 6	the good news of your faith and l,
1 Thes	3:12	and abound in l for one another
1 Thes	4: 9	been taught by God to l one another.
1 Thes	5: 8	on the breastplate of faith and l
1 Thes	5:13	them with special l on account
2 Thes	1: 3	the l of every one of you for one
2 Thes	2:10	because they have not accepted the l
2 Thes	3: 5	direct your hearts to the l of God
1 Tm	1: 5	of this instruction is l from a pure
1 Tm	1:14	faith and l that are in Christ Jesus.
1 Tm	2:15	women persevere in faith and l
1 Tm	4:12	in speech, conduct, l, faith,
1 Tm	6:10	For the l of money is the root of all
1 Tm	6:11	devotion, faith, l, patience,
2 Tm	1: 7	but rather of power and l
2 Tm	1:13	faith and l that are in Christ Jesus.
2 Tm	2:22	righteousness, faith, l, and peace,
2 Tm	3:10	faith, patience, l, endurance,
Ti	2: 2	sound in faith, l, and endurance.
Ti	2: 4	younger women to l their husbands
Ti	3:15	Greet those who l us in the faith.
Phlm	1: 5	as I hear of the l and the faith you
Phlm	1: 7	joy and encouragement from your l,
Phlm	1: 9	I rather urge you out of l, being as I
Heb	6:10	the l you have demonstrated for his
Heb	10:24	how to rouse one another to l
Heb	13: 1	Let mutual l continue.
Heb	13: 5	Let your life be free from l
Jas	1:12	that he promised to those who l him.
Jas	2: 5	he promised to those who l him?
Jas	2: 8	"You shall l your neighbor as
1 Pt	1: 8	you have not seen him you l him;
1 Pt	1:22	to the truth for sincere mutual l,
1 Pt	2:17	Give honor to all, l the community,
1 Pt	4: 8	let your l for one another be intense,
1 Pt	4: 8	because l covers a multitude of sins.
2 Pt	1: 7	affection, mutual affection with l.
1 Jn	2: 5	the l of God is truly perfected
1 Jn	2:15	Do not l the world or the things
1 Jn	2:15	the l of the Father is not in him.
1 Jn	3: 1	See what l the Father has bestowed
1 Jn	3:10	anyone who does not l his brother.
1 Jn	3:11	beginning: we should l one another,
1 Jn	3:14	to life because we l our brothers.
1 Jn	3:14	Whoever does not l remains
1 Jn	3:16	The way we came to know l was
1 Jn	3:17	how can the l of God remain
1 Jn	3:18	let us l not in word or speech
1 Jn	3:23	l one another just as he commanded
1 Jn	4: 7	Beloved, let us l one another, because l is of God;
1 Jn	4: 8	Whoever is without l does not know God, for God is l.
1 Jn	4: 9	this way the l of God was revealed
1 Jn	4:10	In this is l: not that we have loved
1 Jn	4:11	us, we also must l one another.
1 Jn	4:12	if we l one another, God remains
1 Jn	4:12	his l is brought to perfection in us.
1 Jn	4:16	to believe in the l God has for us.
1 Jn	4:16	God is l, and whoever remains in l
1 Jn	4:17	this is l brought to perfection among
1 Jn	4:18	There is no fear in l, but perfect l
1 Jn	4:18	one who fears is not yet perfect in l.
1 Jn	4:19	We l because he first loved us.
1 Jn	4:20	If anyone says, "I l God," but hates his

1 Jn	4:20	whoever does not l a brother whom
1 Jn	4:20	he has seen cannot l God whom he
1 Jn	4:21	loves God must also l his brother.
1 Jn	5: 2	we know that we l the children of God when we l God
1 Jn	5: 3	For the l of God is this, that we keep
2 Jn	1: 1	to her children whom I l
2 Jn	1: 3	Christ the Father's Son in truth and l.
2 Jn	1: 5	the beginning: let us l one another.
2 Jn	1: 6	For this is l, that we walk according
3 Jn	1: 1	the beloved Gaius whom I l in truth.
3 Jn	1: 6	testified to your l before the church.
Jude	1: 2	peace, and l be yours in abundance.
Jude	1:12	These are blemishes on your l feasts,
Jude	1:21	Keep yourselves in the l of God
Rv	2: 4	you have lost the l you had at first.
Rv	2:19	"I know your works, your l, faith,
Rv	3:19	Those whom I l, I reprove

LOVED →LOVE

Gn	29:30	also, and he l her more than Leah.
Gn	37: 3	Israel l Joseph best of all his sons,
Gn	37: 4	saw that their father l him best of all
Dt	7: 8	It was because the LORD l you
1 Sm	1: 5	portion to Hannah because he l her,
1 Sm	18: 1	on him; he l him as he l himself.
1 Sm	18: 3	David, because he l him as himself.
1 Sm	18:16	all Israel and Judah l him, since he
1 Sm	18:20	Saul's daughter Michal l David,
1 Sm	18:28	his own daughter Michal l David.
1 Sm	20:17	because he l him as his very self.]
2 Sm	12:24	named Solomon. The LORD l him
1 Kgs	3: 3	Solomon l the LORD, and obeyed
1 Kgs	11: 1	King Solomon l many foreign
2 Chr	9: 8	Because your God has so l Israel as
2 Chr	11:21	Rehoboam l Maacah,
Est	2:17	The king l Esther more than all
Jb	19:19	those whom I l have turned against
Ps	109:17	He l cursing; may it come
Wis	4:10	He who pleased God was l; he who
Wis	7:10	health and comeliness I l her, And I
Wis	8: 2	Her I l and sought after from my
Wis	16:26	your sons whom you l might learn,
Sir	3:17	you will be l more than a giver
Sir	7:35	sick— for these things you will be l.
Sir	47: 8	With his whole being he l his Maker
Jer	8: 2	of heaven, which they l and served,
Jer	31: 3	With age-old love I have l you; so l
Ez	16:37	whether you l them or l them not;
Hos	9:10	as abhorrent as the thing they l.
Hos	11: 1	When Israel was a child I l him,
Mal	1: 2	I have l you, says the LORD; but you say, "How have you l us?"
Mk	10:21	at him, l him and said to him,
Jn	3:16	For God so l the world that he gave
Jn	11: 5	Now Jesus l Martha and her sister
Jn	11:36	So the Jews said, "See how he l him."
Jn	13: 1	He l his own in the world and he l
Jn	13:23	the one whom Jesus l, was reclining
Jn	13:34	As I have l you, so you also should
Jn	14:21	whoever loves me will be l by my
Jn	14:28	If you l me, you would rejoice that l
Jn	16:27	because you have l me and have
Jn	17:23	that you l them even as you l me.
Jn	17:24	me, because you l me before
Jn	17:26	which you l me may be in them
Jn	19:26	and the disciple there whom he l,
Jn	20: 2	to the other disciple whom Jesus l,
Jn	21: 7	So the disciple whom Jesus l said
Jn	21:20	the disciple following whom Jesus l,
Rom	8:37	through him who l us.
Rom	9:13	As it is written: "I l Jacob but hated
2 Cor	12:15	If I love you more, am I to be l less?
Gal	2:20	in the Son of God who has l me
Eph	5: 2	as Christ l us and handed himself
Eph	5:25	even as Christ l the church
2 Thes	2:16	Father, who has l us and given us
Heb	1: 9	You l justice and hated wickedness;
2 Pt	2:15	who l payment for wrongdoing,

1 Jn	4:10	not that we have l God, but that he l
1 Jn	4:11	if God so l us, we also must love
1 Jn	4:19	We love because he first l us.

LOVELY

Gn	29:17	Leah had l eyes, but Rachel was
Gn	49:21	loose, which brings forth l fawns.
Jdt	8: 7	beautifully formed and l to behold.
Ps	84: 2	How l your dwelling, O LORD
Prv	5:19	your l hind, your graceful doe.
Song	1:16	yes, you are l. Our couch, too,
Song	2:14	your voice is sweet, and you are l."
Song	4: 3	your mouth is l. Your cheek is like
Jer	6: 2	O l and delicate daughter Zion,

LOVER →LOVE

Ps	99: 4	O mighty king, l of justice,
Eccl	5: 9	the l of wealth reaps no fruit from it;
1 Tm	3: 3	not contentious, not a l of money.
Ti	1: 8	but hospitable, a l of goodness,

LOVERS →LOVE

Wis	15: 6	L of evil things, and worthy of such
Sir	Pr: 1	themselves but, as l of wisdom,
Jer	3: 1	But you have sinned with many l,
Jer	4:30	yourself in vain? Your l spurn you,
Jer	22:20	Abarim, for all your l are crushed.
Jer	22:22	shepherds, your l shall go into exile.
Jer	30:14	All your l have forgotten you,
Lam	1:19	"I cried out to my l, but they failed
Ez	16:33	bestowed your gifts on all your l,
Ez	16:36	in your harlotry with your l
Ez	16:37	together all your l whom you tried
Ez	23: 5	she lusted after her l, the Assyrians,
Ez	23: 9	Therefore I handed her over to her l,
Ez	23:22	I will now stir up your l against you,
Hos	2: 7	"I will go after my l," she said,
Hos	2: 9	If she runs after her l, she shall not
Hos	2:12	before the eyes of her l, and no one
Hos	2:14	are the hire my l have given me";
Hos	2:15	and, in going after her l, forgot me,
Hos	8: 9	on its own— Ephraim bargained for l.
2 Tm	3: 2	be self-centered and l of money,
2 Tm	3: 4	l of pleasure rather than l of God,

LOVES →LOVE

Ru	4:15	is the daughter-in-law who l you.
2 Chr	2:10	"Because the LORD l his people,
2 Mc	15:14	who l his brethren and fervently
Ps	11: 7	The LORD is just and l just deeds;
Ps	33: 5	The LORD l justice and right and fills
Ps	37:28	For the LORD l justice and does not
Ps	87: 2	L the gates of Zion more than any
Ps	97:10	The LORD l those who hate evil,
Ps	119:140	Your servant l your promise; it has
Ps	146: 8	down; the LORD l the righteous.
Prv	3:12	For whom the LORD l he reproves,
Prv	12: 1	He who l correction l knowledge,
Prv	13: 1	A wise son l correction,
Prv	13:24	he who l him takes care to chastise
Prv	15: 9	but he l the man who pursues virtue.
Prv	16:13	man who speaks what is right he l.
Prv	17:19	He who l strife l guilt; he who
Prv	21:17	He who l pleasure will suffer want;
Prv	21:17	he who l wine and perfume will not
Prv	22:11	The LORD l the pure of heart;
Prv	29: 3	He who l wisdom makes his father
Song	1: 7	Tell me, you whom my heart l,
Song	3: 1	whom my heart l— I sought him but I
Song	3: 2	Him whom my heart l. I sought him
Song	3: 3	you seen him whom my heart l?
Song	3: 4	when I found him whom my heart l.
Wis	7:28	For there is nought God l, be it not
Wis	8: 7	Or if one l justice, the fruits of her
Sir	4:12	He who l her l life; those who seek
Sir	4:14	those who love her the LORD l.
Sir	30: 1	He who l his son chastises him
Is	1:23	Each one of them l a bribe
Hos	3: 1	Even as the LORD l the people
Hos	12: 8	a false balance, who l to defraud!
Mal	2:11	the temple which the LORD l, and has

Mt	10:37	"Whoever l father or mother more
Mt	10:37	and whoever l son or daughter more
Lk	7: 5	for he l our nation and he built
Lk	7:47	to whom little is forgiven, l little."
Jn	3:35	The Father l the Son and has given
Jn	5:20	For the Father l his Son and shows
Jn	10:17	This is why the Father l me,
Jn	12:25	Whoever l his life loses it,
Jn	16:27	For the Father himself l you,
Rom	13: 8	the one who l another has fulfilled
1 Cor	8: 3	But if one l God, one is known
2 Cor	9: 7	for God l a cheerful giver.
Eph	5:28	bodies. He who l his wife l himself.
Heb	12: 6	for whom the Lord l, he disciplines;
1 Jn	2:10	Whoever l his brother remains
1 Jn	4: 7	everyone who l is begotten by God
1 Jn	5: 1	and everyone who l the father l
Rv	1: 5	To him who l us and has freed us

LOVING →LOVE

Dt	11:13	you today, l and serving the LORD,
Dt	11:22	l enjoin on you, l the LORD,
Dt	19: 9	l enjoin on you today, l the LORD,
Dt	30:16	which l enjoin on you today, l him,
Dt	30:20	by l the LORD, your God, heeding his
Wis	7:22	Not baneful, l the good, keen,
Is	56:10	as they lie there, l their sleep.

LOW →LOWER, LOWERED, LOWEST, LOWING, LOWLY

| Is | 40: 4 | mountain and hill shall be made l; |
| Lk | 3: 5 | mountain and hill shall be made l. |

LOWER →LOW

Dt	28:43	above you, while you sink l and l.
Eph	4: 9	descended into the l [regions]
Heb	2: 7	for a little while l than the angels;

LOWERED →LOW

| Acts | 10:11 | l to the ground by its four corners. |

LOWEST →LOW

| Gn | 9:25 | "Cursed be Canaan! The l of slaves |
| Lk | 14:10 | and take the l place so |

LOWING →LOW

| 1 Sm | 15:14 | ears, and the l of oxen that l hear?" |

LOWLY →LOW

Jdt	9:11	but you are the God of the l,
Jb	5:11	He sets up on high the l, and those
Ps	138: 6	LORD is on high, but cares for the l
Lk	1:52	from their thrones but lifted up the l.
Rom	12:16	be haughty but associate with the l;

LOYAL

| Dn | 11:32 | but those who remain l to their God |

LUKE

Associate of Paul (Col 4:14; 2 Tm 4:11; Phlm 24).

LUKEWARM →WARM

| Rv | 3:16 | because you are l, neither hot nor |

LUMP

| Rom | 9:21 | of the same l one vessel for a noble |

LUNATIC →LUNATICS

| Mt | 17:15 | for he is a l and suffers severely; |

LUNATICS →LUNATIC

| Mt | 4:24 | who were possessed, l and paralytics, |

LURE

| Mt | 13:22 | and the l of riches choke the word |

LUST →LUSTED, LUSTFUL, LUSTS

| Dn | 13: 8 | for her walk, they began to l for her. |
| Mt | 5:28 | l has already committed adultery |

LUSTED →LUST

| Ez | 23: 5 | she l after her lovers, the Assyrians, |

LUSTFUL →LUST

Sir	23: 6	Let not the l cravings of the flesh
Ez	16:26	the Egyptians, your l neighbors,
1 Thes	4: 5	l passion as do the Gentiles who do

LUSTS →LUST

| Rom | 1:24 | impurity through the l of their hearts |

LUXURY

| Prv | 19:10 | L is not befitting a fool; much less |
| Jas | 5: 5 | You have lived on earth in l |

LUZ →=BETHEL

| Gn | 28:19 | name of the town had been L. |
| Gn | 48: 3 | appeared to me at L in the land |

LYDDA

| Acts | 9:32 | down to the holy ones living in L. |

LYDIA →LYDIA'S

| Acts | 16:14 | them, a woman named L, a dealer |

LYDIA'S →LYDIA

| Acts | 16:40 | they went to L house where they saw |

LYING →LIE

Ru	3: 8	around to find a woman l at his feet.
1 Sm	5: 4	broken off and l on the threshold,
1 Kgs	22:23	the LORD has put a l spirit
Ps	31:19	Strike dumb their l lips, proud lips
Ps	120: 2	LORD, deliver me from l lips,
Prv	6:17	Haughty eyes, a l tongue, and hands
Prv	12:19	the l tongue, for only a moment.
Prv	12:22	L lips are an abomination
Prv	21: 6	who makes a fortune by a l tongue
Prv	26:28	The l tongue is its owner's enemy,
Wis	1:11	and a l mouth slays the soul.
Hos	4: 2	False swearing, l, murder,
Mt	8:14	saw his mother-in-law l in bed
Mk	7:30	she found the child l in bed
Lk	2:12	clothes and l in a manger."
Jn	5: 6	When Jesus saw him l there

LYRE →LYRES

Gn	4:21	the ancestor of all who play the l
Ps	33: 2	on the ten-stringed l offer praise.
Ps	57: 9	awake, l and harp! I will wake

LYRES →LYRE

1 Chr	15:16	instruments, harps, l, and cymbals,
1 Chr	25: 6	harps and l, serving in the house
Neh	12:27	the music of cymbals, harps, and l.

LYSIAS

| 1 Mc | 3:32 | He left L, a nobleman of royal |
| Acts | 23:26 | "Claudius L to his excellency |

LYSTRA

| Acts | 14: 8 | At L there was a crippled man, |
| 2 Tm | 3:11 | and L, persecutions that I endured. |

M

MACCABEUS →JUDAS

| 1 Mc | 2: 4 | Judas, who was called M; |
| 1 Mc | 2:66 | And Judas M, a warrior from his |

MACEDONIA

Acts	16: 9	words, "Come over to M and help us."
Acts	18: 5	and Timothy came down from M,
Acts	20: 3	he decided to return by way of M.

MACHPELAH

Gn	23: 9	sell me the cave of M that he owns;
Gn	49:30	the cave in the field of M,
Gn	50:13	him in the cave in the field of M,

MAD →MADMEN, MADNESS

| Dt | 28:34 | until you are driven m by what your |
| Jer | 51: 7 | wine, with this they have become m. |

MADE →MAKE

Gn	1: 7	God m the dome, and it separated
Gn	1:16	God m the two great lights,
Gn	1:16	govern the night; and he m the stars.
Gn	1:25	God m all kinds of wild animals,
Gn	1:31	God looked at everything he had m,
Gn	3:21	the LORD God m leather garments,
Gn	6: 6	that he had m man on the earth,
Gn	9: 6	the image of God has man been m.
Gn	15:18	occasion that the LORD m a covenant

Gn	24:21	or not the LORD had **m** his errand
Gn	45: 9	God has **m** me lord of all Egypt;
Ex	7: 1	I have **m** you as God to Pharaoh,
Ex	20:11	In six days the LORD **m** the heavens
Ex	20:11	the sabbath day and **m** it holy.
Ex	24: 8	which the LORD has **m** with you
Ex	36: 8	**m** the Dwelling with its ten sheets
Ex	37: 1	Bezalel **m** the ark of acacia wood,
Ex	37:10	The table was **m** of acacia wood,
Ex	37:17	The lampstand was **m** of pure
Ex	37:25	of incense was **m** of acacia wood,
Ex	38: 9	The court was **m** as follows.
Nm	21: 2	Israel then **m** this vow to the LORD:
Nm	21: 9	Moses accordingly **m** a bronze
Dt	1:28	Our kinsmen have **m** us fainthearted
Dt	5: 2	**m** a covenant with us at Horeb;
Dt	32: 6	Has he not **m** you and established
Jos	24:25	So Joshua **m** a covenant
Jgs	11:30	Jephthah **m** a vow to the LORD.
1 Sm	1:11	and she **m** a vow, promising:
1 Sm	15:11	"I regret having **m** Saul king, for he
2 Sm	23: 5	He has **m** an eternal covenant
1 Kgs	12:28	the king **m** two calves of gold
2 Kgs	17:38	The covenant which I **m** with you,
2 Kgs	18: 4	Nehushtan which Moses had **m**,
2 Kgs	19:15	You have **m** the heavens
2 Chr	2:11	of Israel, who **m** heaven and earth,
2 Chr	3:10	holy of holies he **m** two cherubim
2 Chr	4:19	Solomon had all these articles **m**
Neh	9: 6	you **m** the heavens, the highest
Neh	9:10	thus you **m** for yourself a name even
Tb	8: 6	You **m** Adam and you gave him his
1 Mc	4:49	They **m** new sacred vessels
Jb	31: 1	If I have **m** an agreement with my
Jb	33: 4	For the spirit of God has **m** me,
Ps	8: 6	Yet you have **m** them little less than
Ps	33: 6	the LORD's word the heavens were **m**;
Ps	95: 5	who **m** them, formed them by hand.
Ps	96: 5	but the LORD **m** the heavens.
Ps	98: 2	The LORD has **m** his victory known;
Ps	118:24	This is the day the LORD has **m**;
Ps	136: 7	Who **m** the great lights, God's love
Ps	139:14	you, so wonderfully you **m** me;
Prv	8:26	the earth and the fields were not **m**,
Eccl	3:11	He has **m** everything appropriate
Eccl	7:13	straight what he has **m** crooked?
Is	43: 7	my glory, whom I formed and **m**.
Is	45:12	It was I who **m** the earth and created
Is	66: 2	My hand **m** all these things when all
Jer	10:12	He who **m** the earth by his power,
Jer	27: 5	It was I who **m** the earth, and man
Jer	31:32	It will not be like the covenant I **m**
Jer	33: 2	Thus says the LORD who **m** the earth
Jer	51:15	He has sworn who **m** the earth
Dn	3: 1	had a golden statue **m**, sixty cubits
Am	5: 8	He who **m** the Pleiades and Orion,
Jon	1: 9	who **m** the sea and the dry land."
Mk	2:27	them, "The sabbath was **m** for man,
Lk	19:46	but you have **m** it a den of thieves.' "
Jn	9: 6	ground and **m** clay with the saliva,
Acts	2:36	that God has **m** him both Lord
Acts	10:15	"What God has **m** clean, you are not
Acts	17:24	The God who **m** the world and all
Acts	17:24	in sanctuaries **m** by human hands,
1 Cor	1:20	Has not God **m** the wisdom
2 Cor	5:21	our sake he **m** him to be sin who did
2 Cor	12: 9	for power is **m** perfect in weakness."
Eph	2:14	he who **m** both one and broke down
Heb	2: 7	You **m** him for a little while lower
Heb	8: 9	It will not be like the covenant I **m**
Jas	3: 9	it we curse human beings who are **m**
Rv	5:10	You **m** them a kingdom and priests
Rv	14: 7	Worship him who **m** heaven
Rv	19: 7	come, his bride has **m** herself ready.

MADMEN → MAD, MAN

1 Sm	21:16	Do I not have enough **m**, that you

MADNESS → MAD

Dt	28:28	the LORD will strike you with **m**,

Eccl	7:25	wickedness is foolish and folly is **m**.
Eccl	9: 3	and **m** is in their hearts during life;
2 Pt	2:16	voice and restrained the prophet's **m**.

MAGDALENE

Mt	27:56	Among them were Mary **M**
Mk	16: 1	sabbath was over, Mary **M**, Mary,
Lk	8: 2	called **M**, from whom seven demons

MAGIC → MAGICIAN, MAGICIANS

Acts	8:11	them by his **m** for a long time,

MAGICIAN → MAGIC

Dn	2:10	asked such a thing of any **m**,
Acts	13: 6	they met a **m** named Bar-Jesus who

MAGICIANS → MAGIC

Gn	41: 8	So he summoned all the **m**
Ex	7:11	and they also, the **m** of Egypt,
Ex	7:22	But the Egyptian **m** did the same
Ex	8: 3	the **m** did the same by their magic
Ex	8:14	Though the **m** tried to bring forth
Ex	9:11	The **m** could not stand in Moses'
Ex	9:11	were boils on the **m** no less than
Dn	2: 2	So he ordered that the **m**,
Dn	5:11	father, made him chief of the **m**,

MAGNIFY

Ps	34: 4	**M** the LORD with me; let us exalt his

MAGOG

Ez	38: 2	turn toward Gog [the land of **M**],
Ez	39: 6	I will send fire upon **M**
Rv	20: 8	Gog and **M**, to gather them

MAHANAIM

Gn	32: 3	So he named that place **M**.
2 Sm	17:24	Now David had gone to **M**

MAHER-SHALAL-HASH-BAZ

Is	8: 3	The LORD said to me: Name him **M**,

MAHLON

Ru	1: 5	both **M** and Chilion died also,

MAID → MAIDS

Ps	123: 2	Like the eyes of a **m** on the hand
Is	24: 2	and master, The **m** as her mistress,

MAIDENS

Song	1: 3	perfume— that is why the **m** love you.

MAIDS → MAID

Gn	24:61	Rebekah and her **m** started out;
1 Sm	25:42	her five **m** following in attendance
Est	2: 9	picking out seven **m** for her
Est	2: 9	her **m** to the best place in the harem.

MAIMED

Mk	9:43	to enter into life **m** than with two

MAJESTIC → MAJESTY

Jb	37: 4	roars— the **m** sound of his thunder.
2 Pt	1:17	came to him from the **m** glory,

MAJESTY → MAJESTIC

Ex	15: 7	In your great **m** you overthrew your
1 Chr	16:27	Splendor and **m** go before him;
1 Chr	29:11	and power, **m**, splendor, and glory.
Jb	37:22	surrounding God's awesome **m**!
Jb	40:10	yourself with grandeur and **m**,
Ps	21: 6	**m** and splendor you confer
Ps	45: 4	splendor and **m** ride on triumphant!
Ps	68:35	of God, whose **m** protects Israel,
Ps	93: 1	The LORD is king, robed with **m**;
Ps	104: 1	You are clothed with **m** and glory,
Is	2:10	the LORD and the splendor of his **m**!
Is	2:19	and the splendor of his **m**, when he
Is	2:21	and the splendor of his **m**, when he
Is	24:14	the sea they proclaim the **m**
Is	26:10	and sees not the **m** of the LORD.
Heb	1: 3	at the right hand of the **M** on high,
Heb	8: 1	of the throne of the **M** in heaven,
2 Pt	1:16	we had been eyewitnesses of his **m**.
Jude	1:25	Jesus Christ our Lord be glory, **m**,

MAKE → MADE, MAKER, MAKES, MAKING, TENTMAKERS
Gn	1:26	"Let us **m** man in our image,
Gn	2:18	I will **m** a suitable partner for him."
Gn	6:14	"M yourself an ark of gopherwood,
Gn	11: 4	sky, and so **m** a name for ourselves;
Gn	12: 2	"I will **m** of you a great nation, and I
Gn	12: 2	bless you; I will **m** your name great,
Gn	13:16	I will **m** your descendants like
Gn	17: 6	fertile; I will **m** nations of you;
Gn	21:18	for I will **m** of him a great nation."
Gn	22:17	**m** your descendants as countless as
Gn	24:40	you and **m** your errand successful,
Gn	26: 4	I will **m** your descendants as
Gn	28: 3	bless you and **m** you fertile,
Gn	46: 3	for there I will **m** you a great nation.
Gn	48: 4	'I will **m** you fertile and numerous
Ex	6: 3	Lord, I did not **m** known to them.
Ex	20:23	Do not **m** anything to rank with me;
Ex	25: 9	you shall **m** exactly according
Ex	25:10	"You shall **m** an ark of acacia wood,
Ex	25:23	shall also **m** a table of acacia wood,
Ex	25:31	"You shall **m** a lampstand of pure
Ex	25:40	See that you **m** them according
Ex	32: 1	**m** us a god who will be our leader;
Ex	32:10	Then I will **m** of you a great nation."
Nm	21: 8	"M a saraph and mount it on a pole,
Dt	7: 2	M no covenant with them and show
Jos	9: 7	can we **m** an alliance with you?"
2 Sm	7: 9	I will **m** you famous like the great
1 Mc	1:11	**m** an alliance with the Gentiles all
Jb	7:17	is man, that you **m** much of him,
Ps	4: 9	for you alone, Lord, **m** me secure.
Ps	110: 1	hand, while I **m** your enemies your
Prv	3: 6	and he will **m** straight your paths.
Eccl	5: 3	When you **m** a vow to God,
Sir	2: 6	**m** straight your ways and hope
Is	6:10	You are to **m** the heart of this people
Is	40: 3	Lord! M straight in the wasteland
Is	61: 8	a lasting covenant I will **m**
Is	66:22	which I will **m** Shall endure before
Jer	10:11	Let the gods that did not **m** heaven
Jer	16:20	Can man **m** for himself gods?
Jer	31:31	when I will **m** a new covenant
Jer	32:40	I will **m** with them an eternal
Ez	34:25	I will **m** a covenant of peace
Ez	37:26	I will **m** with them a covenant
Ez	39: 7	I will **m** my holy name known
Hos	2:20	I will **m** a covenant for them
Mt	3: 3	of the Lord, **m** straight his paths.' "
Mt	28:19	and **m** disciples of all nations,
Mk	1:17	me, and I will **m** you fishers of men."
Jn	1:23	"M straight the way of the Lord," '
Acts	2:35	until I **m** your enemies your
Rom	14: 4	for the Lord is able to **m** him stand.
Heb	1:13	hand until I **m** your enemies your
2 Pt	1: 5	**m** every effort to supplement your
1 Jn	1:10	have not sinned," we **m** him a liar,

MAKER → MAKE
Jb	4:17	mortal be blameless against his M?
Jb	32:22	my M would soon take me away.
Jb	35:10	Saying, "Where is God, my M,
Jb	36: 3	and to my M I will accord the right.
Ps	149: 2	Let Israel be glad in their **m**,
Prv	14:31	the poor blasphemes his M, but he
Prv	17: 5	mocks the poor blasphemes his M;
Prv	22: 2	bond: the Lord is the **m** of them all.
Sir	38:15	He who is a sinner toward his M
Is	17: 7	On that day man shall look to his **m**,
Is	29:16	what is made should say of its **m**,
Is	45: 9	to him who contends with his M;
Is	45:11	the Holy One of Israel, his **m**:
Is	51:13	And forget the Lord, your **m**,
Is	54: 5	become your husband is your M;
Hos	8:14	Israel has forgotten his **m** and built
Hb	2:18	that its **m** should carve it?
Hb	2:18	that its very **m** should trust in it,

MAKES → MAKE
Ex	4:11	one man speech and **m** another deaf

Ex	4:11	sight to one and **m** another blind?
Prv	13:12	Hope deferred **m** the heart sick,
Mk	7:37	He **m** the deaf hear and [the] mute

MAKING → MAKE
Eccl	12:12	Of the **m** of many books there is no
Mt	21:13	but you are **m** it a den of thieves."
Jn	5:18	own father, **m** himself equal to God.
Eph	5:16	**m** the most of the opportunity,
Col	1:20	**m** peace by the blood of his cross

MALACHI
Post-exilic prophet (Mal 1:1).

MALE → MALES
Gn	1:27	**m** and female he created them.
Gn	5: 2	he created them **m** and female.
Gn	6:19	into the ark, one **m** and one female,
Gn	17:10	keep: every **m** among you shall be
Lv	20:13	If a man lies with a **m** as
Mt	19: 4	beginning the Creator 'made them **m**
Lk	2:23	"Every **m** that opens the womb shall
Rv	12: 5	She gave birth to a son, a **m** child,

MALES → MALE
Ex	12:48	all the **m** among them must first be

MALICE → MALICIOUS
Rom	1:29	of wickedness, evil, greed, and **m**;
1 Cor	5: 8	the yeast of **m** and wickedness,
Eph	4:31	from you, along with all **m**.
Col	3: 8	anger, fury, **m**, slander, and obscene
Ti	3: 3	and pleasures, living in **m** and envy,
1 Pt	2: 1	Rid yourselves of all **m** and all

MALICIOUS → MALICE
Ps	35:11	M witnesses come forward,

MALIGNED
1 Pt	3:16	when you are **m**, those who defame

MAMRE → =HEBRON
Gn	13:18	on to settle near the terebinth of M,
Gn	25:. 9	of Zohar the Hittite, which faces M,

MAN → FISHERMEN, HORSEMEN, MADMEN, MAN'S, MEN
Gn	1:26	God said: "Let us make **m** in our image,
Gn	2: 7	the Lord God formed **m**
Gn	2: 7	and so **m** became a living being.
Gn	2:15	took the **m** and settled him
Gn	2:18	"It is not good for the **m** to be alone.
Gn	2:20	The **m** gave names to all the cattle,
Gn	2:20	to be the suitable partner for the **m**.
Gn	2:23	the **m** said: "This one, at last, is bone
Gn	2:23	of 'her **m**' this one has been taken."
Gn	2:25	The **m** and his wife were both
Gn	3: 9	then called to the **m** and asked him,
Gn	3:22	The **m** has become like one of us,
Gn	4: 1	The **m** had relations with his wife
Gn	4: 1	"I have produced a **m** with the help
Gn	32:25	some **m** wrestled with him until
Lv	20:10	If a **m** commits adultery with his
Lv	20:13	If a **m** lies with a male as
Nm	23:19	God is not **m** that he should speak falsely,
Dt	22: 5	not wear an article proper to a **m**, nor shall a **m** put on a woman's
Jgs	8:21	for a man's strength is like the **m**."
1 Sm	13:14	sought out a **m** after his own heart
Est	6: 7	"For the **m** whom the king wishes
Jb	38: 3	Gird up your loins now, like a **m**;
Jb	40: 7	Gird up your loins now, like a **m**.
Ps	90: 1	A prayer of Moses, the **m** of God.
Prv	30:19	and the way of a **m** with a maiden.
Sir	33:10	of clay, for from earth **m** was formed;
Is	53: 3	a **m** of suffering,
Ez	1:10	each of the four had the face of a **m**,
Ez	8: 2	and saw a form that looked like a **m**.
Dn	7:13	I saw One like a son of **m** coming,
Zec	6:12	Here is a **m** whose name is Shoot,
Mt	9: 6	the Son of M has authority on earth
Mt	19: 5	this reason a **m** shall leave his father
Mk	2:27	"The sabbath was made for **m**, not **m** for the sabbath.

Mk	9:12	is it written regarding the Son of M
Lk	6: 5	"The Son of M is lord of the sabbath."
Jn	3:14	so must the Son of M be lifted up,
Jn	9:35	"Do you believe in the Son of M?"
Acts	7:56	the Son of M standing at the right
1 Cor	7: 1	"It is a good thing for a m not
1 Cor	7: 2	immorality every m should have his
1 Cor	11: 3	that Christ is the head of every m,
1 Cor	11: 7	A m, on the other hand, should not
1 Cor	11: 7	God, but woman is the glory of m.
1 Cor	11:14	that if a m wears his hair long it is
1 Cor	13:11	when I became a m, I put aside childish
1 Cor	15:47	The first m was from the earth,
1 Cor	15:47	the second m, from heaven.
Eph	5:31	"For this reason a m shall leave [his]
Rv	1:13	the lampstands one like a son of m,
Rv	14:14	one who looked like a son of m,

MAN'S → MAN
Nm 17:17 Mark each **m** name on his staff;

MANAGE

1 Tm	3: 4	He must m his own household well,
1 Tm	3: 5	know how to m his own household,
1 Tm	3:12	only once and must m their children
1 Tm	5:14	and m a home, so as to give

MANASSEH
1. Firstborn of Joseph (Gn 41:51; 46:20). Blessed by Jacob but not as firstborn (Gn 48). Tribe of blessed (Dt 33:17), numbered (Nm 1:35; 26:34), half allotted land east of Jordan (Nm 32; Jos 13:8-33), half west (Jos 16; Ez 48:4), failed to fully possess (Jos 17:12-13; Jgs 1:27), 12,000 from (Rv 7:6).
2. Son of Hezekiah; king of Judah (2 Kgs 21:1-18; 2 Chr 33:1-20). Judah exiled for his detestable sins (2 Kgs 21:10-15). Repentance (2 Chr 33:12-19).

MANDRAKES

Gn	30:14	some m which he brought home
Gn	30:14	let me have some of your son's m."
Song	7:14	The m give forth fragrance,

MANGER
Lk 2:12 swaddling clothes and lying in a **m.**"

MANIFESTATION

1 Cor	12: 7	each individual the m of the Spirit is
2 Thes	2: 8	powerless by the m of his coming,

MANNA

Ex	16:31	The Israelites called this food m.
Nm	11: 6	we see nothing before us but this m."
Dt	8:16	and fed you in the desert with m,
Jos	5:12	produce of the land, the m ceased.
Jos	5:12	No longer was there m
Ps	78:24	God rained m upon them for food;
Jn	6:49	Your ancestors ate the m
Heb	9: 4	were the gold jar containing the m,
Rv	2:17	I shall give some of the hidden m;

MANOAH
Father of Samson (Jgs 13:2-21; 16:31).

MANTLE

Gn	25:25	his whole body was like a hairy m;
Jos	7:21	I saw a beautiful Babylonian m,
2 Kgs	2: 8	Elijah took his m, rolled it
2 Kgs	2:13	up Elijah's m which had fallen
Zec	13: 4	neither shall he assume the hairy m

MANY

Dt	15: 6	you will lend to m nations,
Dt	15: 6	you will rule over m nations,
1 Kgs	8: 5	ark sheep and oxen too m to number
1 Kgs	11: 1	Solomon loved m foreign women
1 Mc	1:62	But m in Israel were determined
Ps	32:10	M are the sorrows of the wicked,
Ps	106:43	M times did he rescue them,
Prv	10:19	Where words are m, sin is not
Prv	15:22	succeed when counselors are m.
Prv	31:29	"M are the women of proven worth,
Eccl	5: 2	For nightmares come with m cares,
Eccl	5: 2	and a fool's utterance with m words.
Eccl	12:12	making of m books there is no end,

Sir	27: 1	For the sake of profit m sin,
Is	52:15	So shall he startle m nations,
Is	53:11	my servant shall justify m, and their
Is	53:12	he shall take away the sins of m,
Jer	11:13	And as m as the streets of Jerusalem
Dn	9:27	a firm compact with the m;
Dn	12: 3	And those who lead the m to justice
Mt	6: 7	be heard because of their m words.
Mt	10:31	are worth more than m sparrows.
Mt	18:21	I forgive him? As m as seven times?"
Mt	22:14	M are invited, but few are chosen."
Mt	24: 5	For m will come in my name,
Mt	24: 5	Messiah,' and they will deceive m.
Mt	26:28	on behalf of m for the forgiveness
Mk	10:31	But m that are first will be last,
Mk	10:45	to give his life as a ransom for m."
Lk	2:34	for the fall and rise of m in Israel,
Lk	10:41	anxious and worried about m things.
Jn	2:23	m began to believe in his name
Jn	20:30	Now Jesus did m other signs
Jn	21:25	also m other things that Jesus did,
Acts	1: 3	to them by m proofs after he had
Acts	5:12	M signs and wonders were done
Acts	14:22	us to undergo m hardships to enter
Rom	5:19	of one the m will be made righteous.
Rom	12: 5	though m, are one body in Christ
1 Cor	1:26	Not m of you were wise by human standards, not m were powerful, not m were of noble birth.
1 Cor	12:12	a body is one though it has m parts,
1 Cor	12:12	the body, though m, are one body,
Heb	2:10	in bringing m children to glory,
Heb	9:28	once to take away the sins of m,
Jas	3: 1	Not m of you should become
1 Jn	2:18	so now m antichrists have appeared.
2 Jn	1: 7	M deceivers have gone
Rv	5:11	m angels who surrounded the throne
Rv	19:12	and on his head were m diadems.

MAON
1 Sm 23:24 his men were in the desert below **M,**

MARA → =NAOMI
Ru 1:20 Call me **M,** for the Almighty has

MARAH

Ex	15:23	they arrived at M, where they could
Ex	15:23	Hence this place was called M.

MARCH → MARCHING
Jos 6: 4 the seventh day **m** around the city

MARCHING → MARCH
2 Sm 5:24 you hear a sound of **m** in the tops

MARK → MARKED, MARKS
1. Cousin of Barnabas (Acts 12:12; 15:37-39; Col 4:10; 2 Tm 4:11; Phlm 24; 1 Pt 5:13), see John.
2. Brand or symbol:

Gn	4:15	So the LORD put a m on Cain,
Rv	9: 4	or accepts its m on forehead
Rv	16: 2	on those who had the m of the beast
Rv	19:20	astray those who had accepted the m
Rv	20: 4	its image nor had accepted its m

MARKED → MARK

Ez	9: 6	But do not touch any m with the X;
Hb	1:12	LORD, you have m him for judgment,

MARKET → MARKETPLACE, MARKETPLACES
1 Cor 10:25 Eat anything sold in the **m,**

MARKETPLACE → MARKET

Lk	7:32	are like children who sit in the m
Jn	2:16	stop making my Father's house a m."

MARKETPLACES → MARKET
Mt 23: 7 greetings in **m,** and the salutation

MARKS → MARK
Gal 6:17 for I bear the **m** of Jesus on my

MARRED
Is 52:14 so **m** was his look beyond

MARRIAGE → MARRY
Sir	23:18	the man who dishonors his **m** bed
Mt	22:30	neither marry nor are given in **m**
Mt	24:38	marrying and giving in **m**,
Heb	13: 4	Let **m** be honored among all and the **m** bed be kept undefiled,

MARRIED → MARRY
Dt	24: 5	to bring joy to the wife he has **m**.
Mal	2:11	and has **m** an idolatrous woman.
Mk	12:23	For all seven had been **m** to her."
Rom	7: 2	Thus a **m** woman is bound by law
1 Cor	7:10	To the **m**, however, I give this
1 Cor	7:33	a **m** man is anxious about the things
1 Tm	3: 2	be irreproachable, **m** only once,
1 Tm	3:12	Deacons may be **m** only once
1 Tm	5: 9	than sixty years old, **m** only once,
Ti	1: 6	a man be blameless, **m** only once,

MARRIES → MARRY
Mt	5:32	and whoever **m** a divorced woman
Mt	19: 9	and **m** another commits adultery."
Mk	10:11	**m** another commits adultery against
Lk	16:18	and **m** another commits adultery,
Lk	16:18	the one who **m** a woman divorced
1 Cor	7:28	an unmarried woman sin if she **m**;
1 Cor	7:38	the one who **m** his virgin does well;

MARROW
Heb	4:12	joints and **m**, and able to discern

MARRY → INTERMARRY, INTERMARRYING, MARRIAGE, MARRIED, MARRIES, MARRYING
Mt	19:10	with his wife, it is better not to **m**."
Mt	22:30	resurrection they neither **m** nor are
1 Cor	7: 9	exercise self-control they should **m**, for it is better to **m** than to be
1 Cor	7:28	If you **m**, however, you do not sin,
1 Tm	5:14	I would like younger widows to **m**,

MARRYING → MARRY
Neh	13:27	our God by **m** foreign women?"
Mt	24:38	drinking, **m** and giving in marriage,
Lk	17:27	**m** and giving in marriage

MARTHA
Sister of Mary and Lazarus (Lk 10:38-42; Jn 11; 12:2).

MARVELED → MARVELOUS
Jdt	10:19	They **m** at her beauty,
Jdt	11:20	servants; they **m** at her wisdom
2 Thes	1:10	and to be **m** at on that day among all

MARVELOUS → MARVELED, MARVELS
Jb	9:10	past finding out, **m** things beyond reckoning.
Ps	96: 3	among all peoples, God's **m** deeds.
Ps	98: 1	who has done **m** deeds, have won

MARVELS → MARVELOUS
Ex	34:10	I will work such **m** as have never

MARY
1. Mother of Jesus (Mt 1:16-25; Lk 1:27-56; 2:1-40). With Jesus at temple (Lk 2:41-52), at the wedding in Cana (Jn 2:1-5), questioning his sanity (Mk 3:21), at the cross (Jn 19:25-27). Among disciples after Ascension (Acts 1:14).
2. Magdalene; former demoniac (Lk 8:2). Helped support Jesus' ministry (Lk 8:1-3). At the cross (Mt 27:56; Mk 15:40; Jn 19:25), burial (Mt 27:61; Mk 15:47). Saw angel after resurrection (Mt 28:1-10; Mk 16:1-9; Lk 24:1-12); also Jesus (Jn 20:1-18).
3. Sister of Martha and Lazarus (Jn 11). Washed Jesus' feet (Jn 12:1-8).
4. Mother of James and Joses; witnessed crucifixion (Mt 27:56; Mk 15:40) and empty tomb (Mk 16:1; Lk 24:10).

MASONS
1 Chr	22:15	stonecutters, **m**, carpenters,
2 Chr	24:12	who hired **m** and carpenters

MASSAH
Ex	17: 7	The place was called **M**
Dt	33: 8	For you put him to the test at **M**
Ps	95: 8	as on the day of **M** in the desert.

MASTER → MASTER'S, MASTERS, TASKMASTERS
Gn	4: 7	is toward you, yet you can be his **m**."
Gn	24:12	God of my **m** Abraham, let it turn
Ex	21: 5	'I am devoted to my **m** and my wife
Sir	23: 1	LORD, Father and **M** of my life,
Mal	1: 6	and a servant fears his **m**; If then I
Mal	1: 6	And if I am a **m**, where is
Mt	10:24	his teacher, no slave above his **m**.
Mt	24:46	servant whom his **m** on his arrival
Mt	25:21	His **m** said to him, 'Well done,
Mt	25:23	His **m** said to him, 'Well done,
Jn	13:16	slave is greater than his **m** nor any
Jn	15:20	you, 'No slave is greater than his **m**.'
Eph	6: 9	they and you have a **M** in heaven
Col	4: 1	that you too have a **M** in heaven.
2 Pt	2: 1	and even deny the **M** who ransomed

MASTER'S → MASTER
Gn	39: 7	his **m** wife began to look fondly

MASTERS → MASTER
Mt	6:24	"No one can serve two **m**. He will
Lk	16:13	No servant can serve two **m**. He will
Eph	6: 5	obedient to your human **m** with fear
Eph	6: 9	**M**, act in the same way towards
Col	3:22	obey your human **m** in everything,
Col	4: 1	**M**, treat your slaves justly
1 Tm	6: 1	must regard their **m** as worthy
1 Tm	6: 2	Those whose **m** are believers must
Ti	2: 9	the control of their **m** in all respects,
1 Pt	2:18	subject to your **m** with all reverence,

MAT → MATS
Mk	2: 9	say, 'Rise, pick up your **m** and walk'?
Jn	5: 8	"Rise, take up your **m**, and walk."

MATCH → MATCHED
Lk	5:36	from it will not **m** the old cloak.

MATCHED → MATCH
2 Cor	8:11	your eager willingness may be **m**

MATERIAL
Rom	15:27	also to serve them in **m** blessings.
1 Cor	9:11	that we reap a **m** harvest from you?

MATS → MAT
Mk	6:55	in the sick on **m** to wherever they
Acts	5:15	and **m** so that when Peter came by,

MATTANIAH → =ZEDEKIAH
Original name of King Zedekiah (2 Kgs 24:17).

MATTATHIAS
Priest who started the Maccabean revolt (1 Mc 2).

MATTHEW → =LEVI
Apostle; former tax collector (Mt 9:9-13; 10:3; Mk 3:18; Lk 6:15; Acts 1:13). Also called Levi (Mk 2:14-17; Lk 5:27-32).

MATTHIAS
Disciple chosen to replace Judas (Acts 1:23-26).

MATURE
Lk	8:14	life, and they fail to produce **m** fruit.
1 Cor	2: 6	speak a wisdom to those who are **m**,
Phil	3:15	then, who are "perfectly **m**" adopt this
Heb	5:14	But solid food is for the **m**, for those

MEAL
Heb	12:16	sold his birthright for a single **m**.

MEAN → MEANING, MEANINGLESS, MEANS
Ex	12:26	you, 'What does this rite of yours **m**?'
Jos	4: 6	ask you what these stones **m** to you,

MEANING → MEAN
Gn	40: 5	night, each dream with its own **m**.

MEANINGLESS → MEAN
1 Tm	1: 6	from these and turned to **m** talk,

MEANS → MEAN
Sir	8:13	Go not surety beyond your **m**;

MEASURE → MEASURED, MEASURES, MEASURING
Dt	25:15	and a true and just **m**, that you may

Ps	147: 5	in power, with wisdom beyond **m**.
Ez	45: 3	Also from this sector **m** off a strip,
Zec	2: 6	"To **m** Jerusalem," he answered;
Mk	4:24	The **m** with which you **m** will be
Lk	6:38	a good **m**, packed together,
Lk	6:38	For the **m** with which you **m** will
Rv	11: 1	"Come and **m** the temple of God

MEASURED →MEASURE
Jer	31:37	If the heavens on high can be **m**,

MEASURES →MEASURE
Dt	25:14	nor shall you keep two different **m**
Prv	20:10	Varying weights, varying **m**,

MEASURING →MEASURE
Ez	40: 3	holding a linen cord and a **m** rod.
Zec	2: 5	there was a man with a **m** line in his
Rv	11: 1	I was given a **m** rod like a staff and I
Rv	21:15	me held a gold **m** rod to measure

MEAT
Nm	11:13	Where can I get **m** to give to all this
Prv	23:20	nor with those who eat **m** to excess;
Ez	11: 3	city is the kettle, and we are the **m**."
Rom	14:21	it is good not to eat **m** or drink wine
1 Cor	8:13	I will never eat **m** again, so that I

MEDAD
Nm	11:27	and **M** are prophesying in the camp,"

MEDDLES
Prv	26:17	ears is he who **m** in a quarrel not his

MEDE →MEDIA
Dn	6: 1	And Darius the **M** succeeded
Dn	6: 9	irrevocable under **M** and Persian law."

MEDES →MEDIA
Dn	5:28	and given to the **M** and Persians."
Dn	8:20	the kings of the **M** and Persians.
Acts	2: 9	We are Parthians, **M**, and Elamites,

MEDIA →MEDE, MEDES
Ezr	6: 2	the stronghold in the province of **M**,
Tb	1:14	of Gabri, who lived at Rages, in **M**.

MEDIATOR
Jb	33:23	one out of a thousand, a **m**, To show
Gal	3:19	by angels at the hand of a **m**.
1 Tm	2: 5	There is also one **m** between God
Heb	8: 6	more excellent a ministry as he is **m**
Heb	9:15	For this reason he is **m** of a new
Heb	12:24	and Jesus, the **m** of a new covenant,

MEDITATE →MEDITATES, MEDITATING
Ps	77: 7	In the night I **m** in my heart;
Ps	119:148	watches as I **m** on your promise.

MEDITATES →MEDITATE
Sir	14:20	Happy the man who **m** on wisdom,
Sir	39: 7	counsel, as he **m** upon his mysteries.

MEDITATING →MEDITATE
1 Kgs	18:27	for he is a god and may be **m**,

MEDIUM →MEDIUMS
Lv	20:27	man or a woman who acts as a **m**
1 Sm	28: 7	"Find me a woman who is a **m**,
1 Sm	28: 7	is a woman in Endor who is a **m**."

MEDIUMS →MEDIUM
Lv	19:31	"Do not go to **m** or consult
1 Sm	28: 3	Meanwhile Saul had driven **m**

MEEK
Mt	5: 5	Blessed are the **m**, for they will

MEET →MEETING, MET
Ex	19:17	people out of the camp to **m** God,
Ex	30:36	the meeting tent where I will **m** you.
Ps	85:11	Love and truth will **m**;
Am	4:12	prepare to **m** your God, O Israel:
1 Thes	4:17	the clouds to **m** the Lord in the air.

MEETING →MEET
Ex	27:21	them before the Lord in the **m** tent,

Ex	29:44	Thus I will consecrate the **m** tent
Ex	33: 7	which was called the **m** tent,
Ex	40:34	Then the cloud covered the **m** tent,
Jos	18: 1	Shiloh, where they set up the **m** tent.

MEGIDDO
Jos	12:21	Taanach, **M**,
Jgs	1:27	towns, or those of **M** and its towns.

MELCHIZEDEK
Gn	14:18	**M**, king of Salem, brought out bread
Ps	110: 4	"Like **M** you are a priest forever."
Heb	5:10	priest according to the order of **M**.
Heb	6:20	forever according to the order of **M**.
Heb	7: 1	This "**M**, king of Salem and priest
Heb	7:11	to arise according to the order of **M**,

MELONS
Nm	11: 5	and the cucumbers, the **m**, the leeks,

MELT →MELTED, MELTS
Ps	97: 5	The mountains **m** like wax before
Ps	147:18	Again he sends his word and they **m**;
Mi	1: 4	The mountains **m** under him

MELTED →MELT
2 Pt	3:12	flames and the elements **m** by fire.

MELTS →MELT
Ps	22:15	like wax, it **m** away within me.

MEMBER →MEMBERS
Mk	15:43	a distinguished **m** of the council,

MEMBERS →MEMBER
Rom	7:23	I see in my **m** another principle
Rom	7:23	the law of sin that dwells in my **m**.
1 Cor	6:15	that your bodies are **m** of Christ?
Eph	2:19	and **m** of the household of God,
Eph	3: 6	are coheirs, **m** of the same body,
Eph	4:25	for we are **m** one of another.
Eph	5:30	because we are **m** of his body.

MEMORIAL →MEMORY
Jos	4: 7	are to serve as a perpetual **m**

MEMORY →MEMORIAL
Jb	18:17	His **m** perishes from the land,
Prv	10: 7	The **m** of the just will be blessed,
Sir	10:17	and effaces the **m** of them

MEN →MAN
Gn	18: 2	up, he saw three **m** standing nearby.
Nm	13: 2	"Send **m** to reconnoiter the land
Jgs	15:15	it, and with it killed a thousand **m**.
1 Kgs	12:10	The young **m** who had grown
Tb	7:11	given her in marriage to seven **m**,
Ps	148:12	Young **m** and women too,
Sir	44: 1	Now will I praise those godly **m**,
Dn	1:17	To these four young **m** God gave
Dn	3:92	"I see four **m** unfettered and unhurt,
Mk	6:44	the loaves] were five thousand **m**.
Lk	9:30	two **m** were conversing with him,
Acts	4:13	ordinary **m**, they were amazed,
1 Tm	2: 8	in every place the **m** should pray,
Ti	2: 2	that older **m** should be temperate,
Ti	2: 6	Urge the younger **m**, similarly,

MENAHEM
King of Israel (2 Kgs 15:14-23).

MENE
Dn	5:25	was inscribed: **M**, Tekel, and Peres.
Dn	5:26	**M**, God has numbered your

MENTION →MENTIONED
Am	6:10	for no one must **m** the name
Eph	5:12	shameful even to **m** the things done

MENTIONED →MENTION
Eph	5: 3	must not even be **m** among you,

MEPHIBOSHETH
Son of Jonathan shown kindness by David (2 Sm 4:4; 9; 21:7).
Accused of siding with Absalom (2 Sm 16:1-4; 19:24-30).

MERAB
Daughter of Saul (1 Sm 14:49; 18:17-19; 2 Sm 21:8).

MERARI
Gn	46:11	of Levi: Gershon, Kohath and **M**.
1 Chr	6: 4	The sons of **M** were Mahli
2 Chr	34:12	Levites of the line of **M**,

MERCHANDISE → MERCHANT
Neh	10:32	the peoples of the land bring in **m**

MERCHANT → MERCHANDISE, MERCHANTS
Prv	31:14	Like **m** ships, she secures her
Mt	13:45	heaven is like a **m** searching for fine

MERCHANTS → MERCHANT
Rv	18:11	The **m** of the earth will weep

MERCIES → MERCY
Lam	3:22	not exhausted, his **m** are not spent;

MERCIFUL → MERCY
Dt	4:31	is a **m** God, he will not abandon
1 Kgs	20:31	of the land of Israel are **m** kings.
Neh	9:31	them, for you are a kind and **m** God.
Ps	111: 4	deeds; gracious and **m** is the Lord.
Ps	145: 8	The Lord is gracious and **m**,
Sir	2:11	Compassionate and **m** is the Lord;
Jer	3:12	with you; For I am **m**, says the Lord,
Mt	5: 7	Blessed are the **m**, for they will be
Lk	6:36	Be **m**, just as [also] your Father is **m**.
Lk	18:13	prayed, 'O God, be **m** to me a sinner.'
Heb	2:17	that he might be a **m** and faithful

MERCY → MERCIES, MERCIFUL
Ex	33:19	will, I who grant **m** to whom I will.
Dt	7: 2	with them and show them no **m**.
Jos	11:20	destruction and thus receive no **m**,
1 Chr	21:13	of the Lord, whose **m** is very great,
Tb	3: 2	just; All your ways are **m** and truth;
Jdt	13:14	who has not withdrawn his **m**
Ps	51: 3	Have **m** on me, God, in your
Ps	69:17	love; in your great **m** turn to me.
Prv	28:13	and forsakes them obtains **m**.
Wis	3: 9	grace and **m** are with his holy ones,
Sir	2: 7	who fear the Lord, wait for his **m**,
Sir	17:24	How great the **m** of the Lord,
Is	47: 6	but you showed them no **m**,
Is	55: 7	Let him turn to the Lord for **m**;
Dn	2:18	that they might implore the **m**
Hb	1:17	sword to slay peoples without **m**?
Zec	1:12	how long will you be without **m**
Mt	5: 7	merciful, for they will be shown **m**.
Mt	9:13	the words, 'I desire **m**, not sacrifice.'
Mt	12: 7	this meant, 'I desire **m**, not sacrifice,'
Mt	23:23	law: judgment and **m** and fidelity.
Lk	1:50	His **m** is from age to age to those
Lk	1:58	had shown his great **m** toward her,
Lk	1:72	to show **m** to our fathers and to be
Lk	1:78	because of the tender **m** of our God
Lk	10:37	"The one who treated him with **m**."
Rom	9:15	"I will show **m** to whom I will, I will
Rom	9:18	he has **m** upon whom he wills,
Rom	9:23	of his glory to the vessels of **m**,
Rom	11:30	but have now received **m** because
Rom	11:31	by virtue of the **m** shown to you,
Rom	11:31	they too may [now] receive **m**.
Rom	15: 9	might glorify God for his **m**. As it is
1 Cor	7:25	who by the Lord's **m** is trustworthy.
2 Cor	4: 1	ministry through the **m** shown us,
Eph	2: 4	who is rich in **m**,
Phil	2:27	but God had **m** on him, not just
1 Tm	1: 2	grace, **m**, and peace from God
2 Tm	1: 2	grace, **m**, and peace from God
2 Tm	1:16	May the Lord grant **m** to the family
2 Tm	1:18	grant him to find **m** from the Lord
Ti	3: 5	but because of his **m**, he saved us
Heb	4:16	the throne of grace to receive **m**
Jas	2:13	to one who has not shown **m**;
Jas	3:17	compliant, full of **m** and good fruits;
1 Pt	1: 3	in his great **m** gave us a new birth

1 Pt	2:10	you "had not received **m**" but now you have received **m**.
2 Jn	1: 3	Grace, **m**, and peace will be with us
Jude	1:21	for the **m** of our Lord Jesus Christ
Jude	1:23	the fire; on others have **m** with fear,

MERIBAH
Ex	17: 7	place was called Massah and **M**,
Nm	20:13	These are the waters of **M**,
Dt	33: 8	with him at the waters of **M**.
Ps	95: 8	Do not harden your hearts as at **M**,
Ps	106:32	the waters of **M** they angered God,

MERRY
Eccl	9: 7	and drink your wine with a **m** heart,
Lk	12:19	many years, rest, eat, drink, be **m**!" '

MESHACH → =MISHAEL
Hebrew exiled to Babylon; name changed from Mishael (Dn 1:6-7). Refused defilement by food (Dn 1:8-20). Refused to worship idol (Dn 3:1-18); saved from furnace (Dn 3:19-97).

MESHECH
Ps	120: 5	Alas, I was an alien in **M**, I lived·
Ez	38: 3	Gog, chief prince of **M** and Tubal.
Ez	39: 1	Gog, chief prince of **M** and Tubal.

MESOPOTAMIA
Acts	2: 9	inhabitants of **M**,
Acts	7: 2	father Abraham while he was in **M**,

MESSAGE → MESSENGER, MESSENGERS
Jgs	3:20	said, "I have a **m** from God for you."
Is	28: 9	To whom would he convey the **m**?
Acts	2:41	who accepted his **m** were baptized,
1 Cor	1:18	The **m** of the cross is foolishness
2 Cor	5:19	to us the **m** of reconciliation.
1 Jn	1: 5	Now this is the **m** that we have
1 Jn	3:11	For this is the **m** you have heard

MESSENGER → MESSAGE
Is	42:19	servant, or deaf like the **m** I send?
Hg	1:13	And the Lord's **m**, Haggai,
Mal	2: 7	because he is the **m** of the Lord
Mal	3: 1	Lo, I am sending my **m** to prepare
Mal	3: 1	the **m** of the covenant whom you
Mt	11:10	I am sending my **m** ahead of you;

MESSENGERS → MESSAGE
2 Chr	36:15	of their fathers, send his **m** to them,
Ps	104: 4	You make the winds your **m**;
Is	44:26	out the plan announced by my **m**;

MESSIAH → CHRIST, MESSIAHS
Mt	16:16	"You are the **M**, the Son of the living
Mt	26:63	living God whether you are the **M**
Mk	13:21	to you then, 'Look, here is the **M**!
Lk	2:11	has been born for you who is **M**
Lk	23:35	he is the chosen one, the **M** of God."
Jn	1:20	it, but admitted, "I am not the **M**."
Jn	1:41	"We have found the **M**" (which is
Jn	4:25	"I know that the **M** is coming,
Jn	10:24	If you are the **M**, tell us plainly."
Acts	2:36	has made him both Lord and **M**,
Acts	3:20	send you the **M** already appointed
Rom	9: 5	according to the flesh, is the **M**.

MESSIAHS → MESSIAH
Mt	24:24	False **m** and false prophets will
Mk	13:22	False **m** and false prophets will arise

MET → MEET
Mt	28: 9	Jesus **m** them on their way
Jn	18: 2	because Jesus had often **m** there

METHUSELAH
Gn	5:27	lifetime of **M** was nine hundred

MICAH
1. Idolater from Ephraim (Jgs 17-18).
2. Prophet from Moresheth (Jer 26:18-19; Mi 1:1).

MICAIAH
Prophet of the Lord who spoke against Ahab (1 Kgs 22:1-28; 2 Chr 18:1-27).

MICHAEL
Archangel (Jude 9); warrior in angelic realm, protector of Israel (Dn 10:13, 21; 12:1; Rv 12:7).

MICHAL
Daughter of Saul, wife of David (1 Sm 14:49; 18:20-28). Warned David of Saul's plot (1 Sm 19). Saul gave her to Palti (1 Sm 25:43); David retrieved her (2 Sm 3:13-16). Criticized David for dancing before the ark (2 Sm 6:16-23; 1 Chr 15:29).

MIDDLE → MIDST
Gn	3: 3	the tree in the **m** of the garden
Acts	1:18	he burst open in the **m**, and all his
Rv	22: 2	down the **m** of its street. On either

MIDIAN → MIDIANITE, MIDIANITES
Ex	2:15	him and stayed in the land of **M**.
Ex	18: 1	the priest of **M**, heard of all
Ps	83:10	Deal with them as with **M**;

MIDIANITE → MIDIAN
Gn	37:28	Some **M** traders passed by, and they
Nm	25: 6	and brought in a **M** woman to his

MIDIANITES → MIDIAN
Gn	37:36	The **M**, meanwhile, sold Joseph
Nm	31: 2	"Avenge the Israelites on the **M**,

MIDNIGHT → NIGHT
Ex	11: 4	At **m** I will go forth through Egypt.
Ex	12:29	At **m** the LORD slew every first-born
Ps	119:62	At **m** I rise to praise you
Acts	16:25	About **m**, while Paul and Silas were

MIDST → MIDDLE
Dt	13: 6	you purge the evil from your **m**.
Mt	10:16	you like sheep in the **m** of wolves;

MIDWIVES
Ex	1:17	The **m**, however, feared God;

MIGHT → ALMIGHTY, MIGHTY
Dt	5:29	Would that they **m** always be
2 Chr	20: 6	In your hand is power and **m**,
Is	63:15	is your zealous care and your **m**,
Mi	3: 8	LORD, with authority and with **m**;
Zec	4: 6	an army, nor by **m**, but by my spirit,
Mk	14:35	it were possible the hour **m** pass
Jn	1: 7	so that all **m** believe through him.
2 Cor	8: 9	by his poverty you **m** become rich.
1 Pt	2:24	sin, we **m** live for righteousness.
1 Jn	4: 9	so that we **m** have life through him.

MIGHTY → MIGHT
Gn	10: 9	He was a **m** hunter by the grace of the LORD."
Gn	49:24	the power of the **M** One of Jacob,
Ex	6: 1	Forced by my **m** hand, he will send
Dt	3:24	can perform deeds as **m** as yours?
Dt	10:17	the great God, **m** and awesome,
Neh	9:32	God, great, **m**, and awesome God,
Ps	24: 8	The LORD, a **m** warrior, the LORD,
Ps	45: 4	sword upon your hip, **m** warrior!
Ps	68:34	whose voice is thunder, **m** thunder.
Ps	71:16	I will speak of the **m** works
Ps	89: 9	**M** LORD, your loyalty is always
Ps	99: 4	O **m** king, lover of justice,
Ps	106: 2	Who can tell the **m** deeds
Ps	145: 4	next and proclaims your **m** works.
Ps	150: 1	give praise in the **m** dome
Sir	15:18	he is **m** in power, and all-seeing.
Is	49:26	your redeemer, the **m** one of Jacob.
Is	60:16	your redeemer, the **m** one of Jacob.
Is	63: 1	vindication, I who am **m** to save."
Jer	32:19	great in counsel, **m** in deed,
Bar	2:11	the land of Egypt with your **m** hand,
Ez	20:33	with a **m** hand and outstretched arm,
Dn	3:00	are his signs, how **m** his wonders;
Lk	1:49	The **M** One has done great things
1 Pt	5: 6	yourselves under the **m** hand
Rv	18: 8	**m** is the Lord God who judges her."

MILCAH
Gn	11:29	the name of Nahor's wife was **M**,

MILCOM → =MOLECH
1 Kgs	11:33	and **M**, god of the Ammonites;
Jer	49: 3	yourselves; For **M** goes into exile
Zep	1: 5	who adore the LORD but swear by **M**;

MILDEW
2 Chr	6:28	or blight, or **m**, or locusts,

MILE
Mt	5:41	press you into service for one **m**,

MILETUS
2 Tm	4:20	while I left Trophimus sick at **M**.

MILK
Ex	3: 8	a land flowing with **m** and honey,
Ex	23:19	shall not boil a kid in its mother's **m**.
Prv	30:33	the stirring of **m** brings forth curds,
Song	4:11	and **m** are under your tongue;
Is	55: 1	and without cost, drink wine and **m**!
Jl	4:18	and the hills shall flow with **m**;
1 Cor	3: 2	I fed you **m**, not solid food,
Heb	5:12	You need **m**, [and] not solid food.
1 Pt	2: 2	pure spiritual **m** so that through it

MILLSTONE → STONE
Jgs	9:53	cast the upper part of a **m** down
Lk	17: 2	him if a **m** were put around his neck

MIND → MINDFUL, MINDS
Nm	23:19	human, that he should change his **m**.
Dt	29: 3	day has the LORD yet given you a **m**
Ps	26: 2	and try me; search my heart and **m**.
Eccl	2: 3	though my **m** was concerned
Sir	21:14	A fool's **m** is like a broken jar—
Sir	37:17	The root of all conduct is the **m**;
Jer	17:10	I, the LORD, alone probe the **m**
Lam	3:21	But I will call this to **m**, as my
Mt	22:37	all your soul, and with all your **m**.
Mk	3:21	for they said, "He is out of his **m**."
Mk	5:15	there clothed and in his right **m**.
Mk	12:30	with all your **m**, and with all your
Lk	10:27	and with all your **m**, and your
Rom	1:28	their undiscerning **m** to do what is
Rom	7:25	with my **m**, serve the law of God
Rom	11:34	who has known the **m** of the Lord
1 Cor	1:10	but that you be united in the same **m**
1 Cor	2:16	"who has known the **m** of the Lord,
1 Cor	2:16	But we have the **m** of Christ.
1 Cor	14:14	at prayer but my **m** is unproductive.
1 Thes	4:11	to **m** your own affairs, and to work
2 Tm	3: 8	the truth—people of depraved **m**,

MINDFUL → MIND
Ps	8: 5	are humans that you are **m** of them,
Ps	111: 5	you, **m** of your covenant forever.
Heb	2: 6	"What is man that you are **m** of him,

MINDS → MIND
Ps	7:10	of justice, who tries hearts and **m**.
Lk	24:45	he opened their **m** to understand
2 Cor	4: 4	of this age has blinded the **m**
2 Cor	5:13	For if we are out of our **m**, it is
Eph	4:23	be renewed in the spirit of your **m**,
Phil	4: 7	your hearts and **m** in Christ Jesus.
Heb	8:10	I will put my laws in their **m** and I
Heb	10:16	and I will write them upon their **m**,' "
Rv	2:23	I am the searcher of hearts and **m**

MINGLED
Ps	106:35	But **m** with the nations and imitated

MINISTER → MINISTERS, MINISTRY
Ex	28:43	tent or approach the altar to **m**
Dt	10: 8	before the LORD and to **m** to him,
1 Chr	15: 2	of the LORD and to **m** to him forever."
Rom	15:16	to be a **m** of Christ Jesus
Rom	16: 1	Phoebe our sister, who is [also] a **m**

MINISTERS → MINISTER
Ps	103:21	all you hosts, **m** who do God's will.
2 Cor	3: 6	who has indeed qualified us as **m**
2 Cor	11:15	masquerade as **m** of righteousness.
Phil	1: 1	Philippi, with the overseers and **m**:

MINISTRY → MINISTER
Acts	1:17	and was allotted a share in this **m**.
Rom	11:13	to the Gentiles, I glory in my **m**
Rom	12: 7	if **m**, in ministering; if one is
2 Cor	3: 7	Now if the **m** of death,
2 Cor	4: 1	we have this **m** through the mercy
2 Cor	5:18	and given us the **m** of reconciliation,
2 Cor	6: 3	no fault may be found with our **m**;
Eph	4:12	the holy ones for the work of **m**,
2 Tm	4: 5	of an evangelist; fulfill your **m**.
Heb	8: 6	so much more excellent a **m** as he is

MIRACLES
Sir	45: 3	God wrought swift **m** at his words

MIRE
Ps	69:15	Rescue me from the **m**; do not let

MIRIAM
Sister of Moses and Aaron (Nm 26:59). Led dancing at Red Sea (Ex 15:20-21). Struck with leprosy for criticizing Moses (Nm 12). Death (Nm 20:1).

MIRROR
Jb	37:18	of the skies, hard as a brazen **m**?
1 Cor	13:12	as in a **m**, but then face to face.
Jas	1:23	who looks at his own face in a **m**.

MISCARRIAGE → MISCARRY
Ex	21:22	so that she suffers a **m**, but no

MISCARRY → MISCARRIAGE
Ex	23:26	in your land will be barren or **m**;

MISERY
Rom	3:16	ruin and **m** are in their ways,

MISFORTUNE
Nm	23:21	**M** is not observed in Jacob,
Prv	13:21	**M** pursues sinners, but the just shall

MISHAEL → =MESHACH
Original name of Meshach (Dn 1:6-19; 2:17; 3:88).

MISLEAD → MISLEADS, MISLED
Is	3:12	O my people, your leaders **m**,

MISLEADS → MISLEAD
Dt	27:18	'Cursed be he who **m** a blind man

MISLED → MISLEAD
2 Kgs	21: 9	Manasseh **m** them into doing even

MISSING
Jgs	20:16	to sling a stone at a hair without **m**.
Is	40:26	of his power not one of them is **m**!

MISSION
Acts	12:25	and Saul completed their relief **m**,

MIST → MISTS
Is	44:22	your sins like a **m**; return to me,
Acts	13:11	Immediately a dark **m** fell

MISTAKE
Eccl	5: 5	"It was a **m**," lest God be angered

MISTRESS
Gn	16: 4	she looked on her **m** with disdain.
Ps	123: 2	on the hand of her **m**, So our eyes
Is	47: 7	a sovereign **m** forever!" But you did
Na	3: 4	and charming, a **m** of witchcraft,

MISTS → MIST
2 Pt	2:17	springs and **m** driven by a gale;

MIXED → MIXING
Ex	29: 2	flour make unleavened cakes **m**
Prv	9: 5	and drink of the wine I have **m**!
Dn	2:41	As you saw the iron **m** with clay
Rv	8: 7	came hail and fire **m** with blood,

MIXING → MIXED
Is	5:22	wine, the valiant at **m** strong drink!

MIZPAH
Gn	31:49	and also **M**, for he said:
1 Sm	7: 6	When they were gathered at **M**,
1 Sm	7: 6	It was at **M** that Samuel began

1 Mc	3:46	and went to **M** near Jerusalem,
1 Mc	3:46	there was formerly at **M** a place
Jer	41: 1	they were together at table in **M**,

MOAB → MOABITE, MOABITES
Gn	19:37	birth to a son whom she named **M**,
Nm	22: 3	**M** feared the Israelites greatly
Dt	34: 5	So there, in the land of **M**, Moses,
Jgs	3:12	Eglon, king of **M**, against Israel.
Ru	1: 1	sons to reside on the plateau of **M**.
1 Sm	22: 4	He left them with the king of **M**,
2 Kgs	1: 1	death, **M** rebelled against Israel.
Is	15: 1	Oracle on **M**: Laid waste in a night,
Jer	48: 1	Concerning **M**, thus says the LORD
Ez	25:11	I will execute judgment upon **M**,
Am	2: 1	For three crimes of **M**, and for four,
Zep	2: 9	Israel, **M** shall become like Sodom,

MOABITE → MOAB
Dt	23: 4	or **M** may ever be admitted
Ru	1:22	with the **M** daughter-in-law, Ruth,
Ru	4:10	I also take Ruth the **M**, the widow
Neh	13: 1	or **M** may ever be admitted

MOABITES → MOAB
Gn	19:37	He is the ancestor of the **M** of today.

MOAN
Is	59:11	like doves we **m** without ceasing.

MOCK → MOCKED, MOCKS
Ps	22: 8	All who see me **m** me; they curl
Prv	1:26	I will **m** when terror overtakes you;
Mk	10:34	who will **m** him, spit upon him,

MOCKED → MOCK
Neh	2:19	Geshem the Arab **m** us and ridiculed
Mt	27:29	kneeling before him, they **m** him,
Lk	23:11	him contemptuously and **m** him,
Gal	6: 7	God is not **m**, for a person will reap

MOCKS → MOCK
Prv	30:17	The eye that **m** a father, or scorns

MODEIN
1 Mc	2:23	the altar in **M** according to the king's

MODEL
Ti	2: 7	showing yourself as a **m** of good

MODERATE → MODERATION
Sir	31:22	In whatever you do, be **m**, and no

MODERATION → MODERATE
Sir	31:27	if taken in **m**. Does he really live

MODEST
Sir	26:15	Choicest of blessings is a **m** wife,

MOLDED
Wis	7: 1	in my mother's womb I was **m**
Sir	33:13	to be **m** according to his pleasure,

MOLECH → =MILCOM
Lv	18:21	offspring to be immolated to **M**,
2 Kgs	23:10	or daughters by fire in honor of **M**.
Jer	32:35	their sons and daughters to **M**,

MOMENT → MOMENTARY
Ex	33: 5	up in your company even for a **m**,
Jb	20: 5	the joy of the impious but for a **m**?
Ps	30: 6	For divine anger lasts but a **m**;
Prv	12:19	the lying tongue, for only a **m**.
Is	54: 7	For a brief **m** I abandoned you,
Is	66: 8	or a nation be born in a single **m**?

MOMENTARY → MOMENT
2 Cor	4:17	this **m** light affliction is producing

MONEY
Ex	22:24	"If you lend **m** to one of your poor
Ex	30:16	you receive this forfeit **m**
2 Kgs	12: 5	tax, personal redemption **m**,
Tb	5:19	I hope more **m** is not your chief
Ps	15: 5	lends no **m** at interest, accepts no
Eccl	5: 9	man is never satisfied with **m**,
Eccl	7:12	of wisdom is as the protection of **m**;

Eccl	10:19	glad, but **m** answers for everything.
Sir	7:18	Barter not a friend for **m**, nor a dear
Is	55: 1	You who have no **m**, come,
Mi	3:11	her prophets divine for **m**,
Mk	11:15	the tables of the **m** changers
Lk	9: 3	nor **m**, and let no one take a second
1 Tm	3: 3	not contentious, not a lover of **m**.
1 Tm	6:10	the love of **m** is the root of all evils,
2 Tm	3: 2	be self-centered and lovers of **m**,
Heb	13: 5	Let your life be free from love of **m**

MONSTERS

Gn	1:21	God created the great sea **m** and all
Ps	148: 7	you sea **m** and all deep waters;

MONTH → MONTHS

Ex	12: 2	"This **m** shall stand at the head
Ex	12: 2	you shall reckon it the first **m**
Ex	40: 2	day of the first **m** you shall erect
Nm	3:15	registering every male of a **m**
Nm	11:21	them meat to eat for a whole **m**.'
Ezr	6:19	on the fourteenth day of the first **m**.
Neh	8: 2	On the first day of the seventh **m**,
Est	9:21	and the fifteenth of the **m** of Adar
1 Mc	1:59	day of each **m** they sacrificed
1 Mc	4:59	twenty-fifth day of the **m** Chislev.
Ez	47:12	Every **m** they shall bear fresh fruit,
Rv	9:15	day, **m**, and year to kill a third
Rv	22: 2	twelve times a year, once each **m**;

MONTHS → MONTH

Ex	2: 2	child, she hid him for three **m**.
Jgs	11:37	Spare me for two **m**, that I may go
1 Sm	6: 1	the land of the Philistines seven **m**
1 Chr	13:14	with his family for three **m**,
Jn	4:35	'In four **m** the harvest will be here'?
Rv	9: 5	but only to torment them for five **m**;
Rv	11: 2	the holy city for forty-two **m**.
Rv	13: 5	authority to act for forty-two **m**.

MOON → MOONS

Gn	37: 9	the **m** and eleven stars were bowing
Dt	17: 3	the **m** or any of the host of the sky,
Jos	10:13	and the **m** stayed, while the nation
Ps	8: 4	the **m** and stars that you set in place—
Ps	72: 7	great bounty, till the **m** be no more.
Ps	89:38	Like the **m** it will stand eternal,
Ps	104:19	You made the **m** to mark
Ps	121: 6	harm you, nor the **m** by night.
Ps	136: 9	The **m** and stars to rule the night,
Ps	148: 3	Praise him, sun and **m**; give praise,
Song	6:10	as beautiful as the **m**, as resplendent
Sir	27:11	man, like the **m**, is inconstant.
Is	13:10	the light of the **m** does not shine.
Jer	31:35	day, **m** and stars to light the night;
Ez	32: 7	and the **m** shall not give its light.
Dn	3:62	Sun and **m**, bless the Lord;
Jl	3: 4	and the **m** to blood, At the coming
Hb	3:11	the **m** remains in its shelter,
Mt	24:29	and the **m** will not give its light,
Acts	2:20	and the **m** to blood,
1 Cor	15:41	the brightness of the **m** another,
Rv	6:12	and the whole **m** became like blood.
Rv	8:12	a third of the **m**, and a third
Rv	12: 1	with the **m** under her feet,
Rv	21:23	no need of sun or **m** to shine on it,

MOONS → MOON

2 Chr	8:13	at the new **m**, and on the fixed
2 Chr	31: 3	on sabbaths, new **m** and festivals,

MORALS

1 Cor	15:33	"Bad company corrupts good **m**."

MORDECAI

Benjamite exile who raised Esther (Est 2:5-15). Exposed plot to kill Xerxes (Est 2:19-23). Refused to honor Haman (Est 3:1-6; 5:9-14). Charged Esther to foil Haman's plot against the Jews (Est 4). Xerxes forced Haman to honor Mordecai (Est 6). Mordecai exalted (Est 8-10). Established Purim (Est 9:18-32). See also Additions to Esther.

MORE → MOST

Ex	1:12	Yet the **m** they were oppressed,
Ex	1:12	the **m** they multiplied and spread.
Jos	10:11	M died from these hailstones than
Jgs	16:30	his death were **m** than those he had
2 Sm	18: 8	thickets consumed **m** combatants
1 Kgs	16:33	He did **m** to anger the LORD, the God
Jb	42:12	days of Job **m** than his earlier ones.
Ps	19:11	M desirable than gold, than a hoard
Ps	37:10	a little, and the wicked will be no **m**;
Ps	69:32	will please the LORD **m** than oxen,
Ps	119:127	commands **m** than the finest gold.
Ps	130: 6	M than sentinels for daybreak,
Prv	21: 3	just is **m** acceptable to the LORD than
Is	54: 1	For **m** numerous are the children
Jer	31:34	and remember their sin no **m**.
Lam	5: 7	Our fathers, who sinned, are no **m**;
Jon	3: 4	"Forty days **m** and Nineveh shall be
Mt	2:18	be consoled, since they were no **m**."
Mk	4:25	the one who has, **m** will be given;
Mk	12:43	in **m** than all the other contributors
Lk	12:23	For life is **m** than food and the body **m** than clothing.
Jn	21:15	John, do you love me **m** than these?"
Acts	17:11	Jews were **m** fair-minded than those
Rom	5: 9	How much **m** then, since we are
1 Cor	12:31	show you a still **m** excellent way.
2 Cor	3: 9	righteousness will abound much **m**
Heb	8:12	and remember their sins no **m**."
Heb	10:17	evildoing I will remember no **m**."
Rv	10: 6	in them, "There shall be no **m** delay.
Rv	21: 4	and there shall be no **m** death
Rv	22: 5	Night will be no **m**, nor will they

MORIAH

Gn	22: 2	you love, and go to the land of M.
2 Chr	3: 1	the LORD in Jerusalem on Mount M,

MORNING → MORNINGS

Gn	1: 5	came, and **m** followed—the first day.
Ex	12:10	it must be kept beyond the next **m**;
Ex	12:10	over in the **m** shall be burned up.
Ex	16:12	in the **m** you shall have your fill
Ex	29:39	one lamb in the **m** and the other
Dt	28:67	In the **m** you will say, 'Would that it
Dt	28:67	you will say, 'Would that it were **m**!'
2 Sm	23: 4	Is like the **m** light at sunrise
Ezr	3: 3	the LORD on it, both **m** and evening.
Jb	38: 7	While the **m** stars sang in chorus
Prv	27:14	with a loud voice in the early **m**,
Eccl	11: 6	In the **m** sow your seed,
Is	50: 4	that will rouse them. M after **m**
Lam	3:23	They are renewed each **m**, so great
Hos	6: 4	Your piety is like a **m** cloud,
Hos	13: 3	they shall be like a **m** cloud or like
Zep	3: 5	M after **m** he renders judgment
Lk	24:22	they were at the tomb early in the **m**
Acts	2:15	for it is only nine o'clock in the **m**.
2 Pt	1:19	and the **m** star rises in your hearts.
Rv	2:28	And to him I will give the **m** star.
Rv	22:16	of David, the bright **m** star."

MORNINGS → MORNING

Dn	8:14	three hundred evenings and **m**;
Dn	8:26	vision of the evenings and the **m**

MORTAL → MORTALS

Is	51:12	Can you then fear **m** man, who is
Rom	1:23	the likeness of an image of **m** man
Rom	6:12	not reign over your **m** bodies so
Rom	8:11	will give life to your **m** bodies also,
1 Cor	15:53	this which is **m** must clothe itself
2 Cor	5: 4	so that what is **m** may be swallowed
Rv	13: 3	but this **m** wound was healed.

MORTALS → MORTAL

Ps	8: 5	mere **m** that you care for them?
Ps	56:12	What can mere **m** do to me?
Ps	118: 6	afraid; what can **m** do against me?
Is	52:14	and his appearance beyond that of **m**—

MOSES

Levite; brother of Aaron (Ex 6:20; 1 Chr 5:29). Put in basket into Nile; discovered and raised by Pharaoh's daughter (Ex 2:1-10). Fled to Midian after killing Egyptian (Ex 2:11-15). Married to Zipporah, fathered Gershom (Ex 2:16-22).

Called by the LORD to deliver Israel (Ex 3-4). Pharaoh's resistance (Ex 5). Ten plagues (Ex 7-11). Passover and Exodus (Ex 12-13). Led Israel through Red Sea (Ex 14). Song of deliverance (Ex 15:1-21). Brought water from rock (Ex 17:1-7). Raised hands to defeat Amalekites (Ex 17:8-16). Delegated judges (Ex 18; Dt 1:9-18).

Received Law at Sinai (Ex 19-23; 25-31; Jn 1:17). Announced Law to Israel (Ex 19:7-8; 24; 35). Broke tablets because of golden calf (Ex 32; Dt 9). Saw glory of the LORD (Ex 33-34). Supervised building of tabernacle (Ex 36-40). Set apart Aaron and priests (Lv 8-9). Numbered tribes (Nm 1-4; 26). Opposed by Aaron and Miriam (Nm 12). Sent spies into Canaan (Nm 13). Announced forty years of wandering for failure to enter land (Nm 14). Opposed by Korah (Nm 16). Forbidden to enter land for striking rock (Nm 20:1-13; Dt 1:37). Lifted bronze snake for healing (Nm 21:4-9; Jn 3:14). Final address to Israel (Dt 1-33). Succeeded by Joshua (Nm 27:12-23; Dt 34). Death and burial by God (Dt 34:5-12). Praise of (Sir 45).

"Law of Moses" (1 Kgs 2:3; Ezr 3:2; Mk 12:26; Lk 24:44). "Book of Moses" (2 Chr 25:12; Neh 13:1). "Song of Moses" (Ex 15:1-21; Rv 15:3). "Prayer of Moses" (Ps 90).

MOST → MORE

Gn	14:18	and being a priest of God **M** High,
Nm	4: 4	tent concerns the **m** sacred objects.
Nm	24:16	and knows what the **M** High knows,
Ps	46: 5	the holy dwelling of the **M** High.
Ps	78:35	rock, God **M** High, their redeemer.
Ps	91: 1	dwell in the shelter of the **M** High,
Wis	5:15	thought of them is with the **M** High.
Is	14:14	clouds; I will be like the **M** High!"
Jer	3:19	a heritage **m** beautiful among
Dn	7:25	He shall speak against the **M** High
Dn	7:25	the holy ones of the **M** High,
Mk	5: 7	me, Jesus, Son of the **M** High God?
Lk	1:32	will be called Son of the **M** High,
Lk	1:76	be called prophet of the **M** High,
1 Cor	10: 5	Yet God was not pleased with **m**
Eph	5:16	making the **m** of the opportunity,
Col	4: 5	making the **m** of the opportunity.
Jude	1:20	yourselves up in your **m** holy faith;

MOTH → MOTHS

| Mt | 6:19 | earth, where **m** and decay destroys, |

MOTHER → GRANDMOTHER, MOTHER'S,
MOTHER-IN-LAW, MOTHERHOOD, MOTHERS

Gn	2:24	why a man leaves his father and **m**
Gn	3:20	because she became the **m** of all
Ex	20:12	"Honor your father and your **m**,
Ex	21:15	his father or **m** shall be put to death.
Ex	21:17	his father or **m** shall be put to death.
Dt	5:16	'Honor your father and your **m**,
Dt	21:18	will not listen to his father or **m**,
Dt	22: 6	and the **m** bird is sitting on them,
Dt	22: 6	shall not take away the **m** bird along
Dt	27:16	who dishonors his father or his **m**!'
Jgs	5: 7	rose, when I rose, a **m** in Israel,
1 Sm	2:19	His **m** used to make a little garment
2 Sm	20:19	down a city that is a **m** in Israel.
1 Kgs	19:20	me kiss my father and **m** goodbye,
Tb	4: 3	Honor your **m**, and do not abandon
Ps	27:10	Even if my father and **m** forsake me,
Ps	51: 7	sinner, even as my **m** conceived me.
Ps	113: 9	a home, the joyful **m** of children.
Prv	20:20	If one curses his father or **m**,
Prv	23:22	despise not your **m** when she is old.
Prv	23:25	Let your father and **m** have joy;
Prv	29:15	left to his whims disgraces his **m**.
Prv	30:17	father, or scorns an aged **m**, Will be
Prv	31: 1	The advice which his **m** gave him:
Sir	3: 6	LORD who brings comfort to his **m**.
Is	8: 4	how to call his father or **m** by name,
Is	66:13	As a **m** comforts her son, so will I
Jer	20:17	my **m** would have been my grave,
Hos	2: 4	Protest against your **m**, protest!

Mi	7: 6	the daughter rises up against her **m**,
Mt	2:11	they saw the child with Mary his **m**.
Mt	10:35	a daughter against her **m**,
Mt	10:37	or **m** more than me is not worthy
Mt	12:48	one who told him, "Who is my **m**?
Mt	19: 5	a man shall leave his father and **m**
Mt	19:19	honor your father and your **m**';
Mk	7:10	'Honor your father and your **m**,'
Mk	7:10	curses father or **m** shall die.'
Mk	10:19	honor your father and your **m**.' "
Lk	12:53	a **m** against her daughter
Lk	12:53	and a daughter against her **m**,
Lk	14:26	me without hating his father and **m**,
Lk	18:20	honor your father and your **m**.' "
Jn	19:27	said to the disciple, "Behold, your **m**."
Eph	5:31	shall leave [his] father and [his] **m**
Eph	6: 2	"Honor your father and **m**." This is
2 Tm	1: 5	and in your **m** Eunice and that I am
Heb	7: 3	Without father, **m**, or ancestry,
Rv	17: 5	the great, the **m** of harlots

MOTHER'S → MOTHER

Ex	23:19	not boil a kid in its **m** milk.
Jb	1:21	"Naked I came forth from my **m** womb,
Prv	1: 8	and reject not your **m** teaching;
Prv	6:20	and reject not your **m** teaching;
Eccl	5:14	As he came forth from his **m** womb,
Eccl	11: 5	fashions the human frame in the **m** womb,
Jn	3: 4	Surely he cannot reenter his **m** womb

MOTHER-IN-LAW → MOTHER

Dt	27:23	be he who has relations with his **m**!'
Ru	2:11	your **m** after your husband's death;
Tb	10:12	your father-in-law and your **m**,
Mi	7: 6	The daughter-in-law against her **m**,
Mt	10:35	a daughter-in-law against her **m**;
Mk	1:30	Simon's **m** lay sick with a fever.

MOTHERHOOD → MOTHER

| 1 Tm | 2:15 | But she will be saved through **m**, |

MOTHERS → MOTHER

Hos	10:14	war, smashing **m** and their children.
Mk	10:30	and sisters and **m** and children
1 Tm	5: 2	older women as **m**, and younger

MOTHS → MOTH

| Is | 51: 8 | shall be like a garment eaten by **m**, |

MOTIONED

| Acts | 12:17 | He **m** to them with his hand to be |

MOTIVES

| 1 Thes | 2: 3 | was not from delusion or impure **m**, |

MOUNT → MOUNTAIN, MOUNTAINS

Ex	19:20	came down to the top of **M** Sinai
Ex	34:29	As Moses came down from **M** Sinai
Nm	33:39	years old when he died on **M** Hor.
Dt	11:29	the blessing on **M** Gerizim, the curse on **M** Ebal.
Dt	34: 1	from the plains of Moab to **M** Nebo,
Jos	8:30	LORD, the God of Israel, on **M** Ebal,
1 Chr	10: 8	where they had fallen on **M** Gilboa.
2 Chr	3: 1	the LORD in Jerusalem on **M** Moriah,
Ps	74: 2	Remember **M** Zion where you
Ps	78:68	of Judah, **M** Zion which he favored.
Is	14:13	take my seat on the **M** of Assembly,
Mi	4: 7	shall be king over them on **M** Zion,
Zec	14: 4	feet shall rest upon the **M** of Olives,
Zec	14: 4	The **M** of Olives shall be cleft
Mk	13: 3	the **M** of Olives opposite the temple
Heb	12:22	you have approached **M** Zion
Rv	14: 1	was the Lamb standing on **M** Zion,

MOUNTAIN → MOUNT

Ex	3: 1	he came to Horeb, the **m** of God.
Ex	19: 2	encamped here in front of the **m**,
Ex	19:20	Moses to the top of the **m**,
Ex	24:18	of the cloud as he went up on the **m**;
Ex	32:19	broke them on the base of the **m**.
Dt	5: 4	face on the **m** from the midst
Jb	14:18	But as a **m** falls at last and its rock is
Ps	48: 2	in the city of our God: The holy **m**,

Ps   68:17   at the **m** where God has chosen
Is   2: 2   to come, The **m** of the Lord's house
Is   2: 2   shall be established as the highest **m**
Is   11: 9   no harm or ruin on all my holy **m**;
Is   40: 4   every **m** and hill shall be made low;
Is   65:25   on all my holy **m**, says the Lord.
Dn   2:45   from the **m** without a hand being put
Mt   4: 8   devil took him up to a very high **m**,
Mt   17:20   you will say to this **m**,
Mk   9: 2   up a high **m** apart by themselves.
Lk   3: 5   every **m** and hill shall be made low.
Jn   4:21   the Father neither on this **m** nor
2 Pt   1:18   we were with him on the holy **m**.
Rv   6:14   every **m** and island was moved
Rv   8: 8   like a large burning **m** was hurled
Rv   21:10   high **m** and showed me the holy city

MOUNTAINS →MOUNT
Gn   7:20   cubits higher than the submerged **m**.
Gn   8: 4   ark came to rest on the **m** of Ararat.
Ps   36: 7   Your justice is like the highest **m**;
Ps   46: 3   **m** quake to the depths of the sea,
Ps   90: 2   Before the **m** were born, the earth
Ps   97: 5   The **m** melt like wax before
Ps   125: 2   As **m** surround Jerusalem, the Lord
Sir   43:16   before his might the **m** quake.
Is   52: 7   How beautiful upon the **m**
Is   54:10   Though the **m** leave their place
Is   55:12   M and hills shall break out in song
Ez   34: 6   wandered over all the **m** and high
Ez   39: 4   Upon the **m** of Israel you shall fall,
Dn   3:75   M and hills, bless the Lord;
Hos   10: 8   Then they shall cry out to the **m**,
Mi   4: 1   be established higher than the **m**;
Na   2: 1   See, upon the **m** there advances
Mk   13:14   those in Judea must flee to the **m**,
Lk   23:30   that time people will say to the **m**,
1 Cor   13: 2   if I have all faith so as to move **m**,
Rv   6:16   They cried out to the **m**
Rv   16:20   island fled, and **m** disappeared.

MOURN →MOURNING, MOURNS
Eccl   3: 4   a time to **m**, and a time to dance.
Sir   7:34   who weep, but **m** with those who **m**;
Is   61: 2   by our God, to comfort all who **m**;
Zec   12:10   they shall **m** for him as one mourns
Mt   5: 4   Blessed are they who **m**, for they
Mt   9:15   the wedding guests **m** as long as

MOURNING →MOURN
Gn   23: 2   performed the customary **m** rites
Est   4: 3   the Jews went into deep **m**,
Est   9:22   into joy, from **m** into festivity.
1 Mc   1:39   her feasts were turned into **m**,
Ps   30:12   You changed my **m** into dancing;
Eccl   7: 2   It is better to go to the house of **m**
Is   61: 3   them oil of gladness in place of **m**,
Jer   31:13   as well. I will turn their **m** into joy,
Lam   5:15   ceased, our dance has turned into **m**;
Rv   21: 4   there shall be no more death or **m**,

MOURNS →MOURN
Zec   12:10   for him as one **m** for an only son,

MOUTH →MOUTHS
Ex   4:15   then, and put the words in his **m**.
Nm   16:30   new, and the ground opens its **m**
Nm   22:38   speak only what God puts in my **m**."
Dt   8: 3   comes forth from the **m** of the Lord.
Dt   18:18   and will put my words into his **m**;
2 Kgs   4:34   placing his **m** upon the child's **m**,
Jb   23:12   the words of his **m** I have treasured
Jb   40: 4   I put my hand over my **m**.
Ps   17: 3   My **m** has not transgressed
Ps   19:15   Let the words of my **m** meet
Ps   40: 4   And put a new song in my **m**,
Ps   71: 8   My **m** shall be filled with your
Ps   78: 2   I will open my **m** in story,
Ps   119:103 sweeter than honey to my **m**!
Ps   141: 3   Set a guard, Lord, before my **m**,
Prv   2: 6   from his **m** come knowledge

Prv   8: 7   Yes, the truth my **m** recounts,
Prv   10:11   fountain of life is the **m** of the just,
Prv   10:11   but the **m** of the wicked conceals
Prv   10:31   The **m** of the just yields wisdom,
Prv   26:28   and the flattering **m** works ruin.
Prv   27: 2   another praise you—not your own **m**;
Eccl   6: 7   All man's toil is for his **m**, yet his
Song   1: 2   him kiss me with kisses of his **m**!
Wis   1:11   and a lying **m** slays the soul.
Is   40: 5   for the **m** of the Lord has spoken.
Is   48: 3   they went forth from my **m**, I let
Is   51:16   I have put my words into your **m**
Is   53: 7   he was silent and opened not his **m**.
Is   55:11   that goes forth from my **m**; It shall
Is   59:21   words that I have put into your **m**
Jer   1: 9   his hand and touched my **m**, saying,
Jer   1: 9   See, I place my words in your **m**!
Ez   3: 2   So I opened my **m** and he gave me
Dn   7: 8   man, and a **m** that spoke arrogantly.
Hos   6: 5   I slew them by the words of my **m**;
Mal   2: 7   is to be sought from his **m**,
Mt   4: 4   comes forth from the **m** of God.' "
Mt   12:34   fullness of the heart the **m** speaks.
Mt   15:11   It is not what enters one's **m**
Mt   15:11   out of the **m** is what defiles one."
Lk   6:45   fullness of the heart the **m** speaks.
Acts   8:32   is silent, so he opened not his **m**.
2 Thes   2: 8   will kill with the breath of his **m**
Jas   3:10   From the same **m** come blessing
1 Pt   2:22   and no deceit was found in his **m**."
Rv   1:16   two-edged sword came out of his **m**,
Rv   2:16   them with the sword of my **m**.
Rv   3:16   cold, I will spit you out of my **m**.
Rv   10:10   In my **m** it was like sweet honey,
Rv   13: 6   It opened its **m** to utter blasphemies
Rv   19:15   Out of his **m** came a sharp sword

MOUTHS →MOUTH
Dt   30:14   already in your **m** and in your
Ps   73: 9   They set their **m** against
Ps   78:36   But they deceived him with their **m**,
Ps   115: 5   They have **m** but do not speak,
Ps   135:17   but hear not; no breath is in their **m**.
Sir   21:26   Fools' thoughts are in their **m**,
Dn   6:23   closed the lion's **m** so that they have
Rom   3:14   their **m** are full of bitter cursing.
Eph   4:29   should come out of your **m**, but only
Heb   11:33   they closed the **m** of lions,
Jas   3: 3   If we put bits into the **m** of horses
Rv   9:17   and out of their **m** came fire, smoke,

MOVE →MOVED, MOVES
Dt   19:14   "You shall not **m** your neighbor's
Is   46: 7   stays, and does not **m** from the spot.
Mt   17:20   this mountain, 'M from here to there,' and it will
                 m

Acts   17:28   For 'In him we live and **m** and have

MOVED →MOVE
1 Chr   16:30   made the world firm, not to be **m**.
Ps   93: 1   surely stand in place, never to be **m**.
Ez   1:19   When the living creatures **m**, the wheels **m** with
                 them;

MOVES →MOVE
Dt   27:17   'Cursed be he who **m** his neighbor's

MUCH
Ex   16:18   a large amount did not have too **m**,
Dt   28:38   "Though you spend **m** seed on your
1 Kgs   8:27   how **m** less this temple which I have
Jb   7:17   is man, that you make **m** of him,
Jb   42:10   to Job twice as **m** as he had before.
Prv   16:16   How **m** better to acquire wisdom
Eccl   1:18   For in **m** wisdom there is **m** sorrow,
Eccl   9:18   a single slip can ruin **m** that is good."
Eccl   12:12   in **m** study there is weariness
Hg   1: 9   You expected **m**, but it came
Mt   12:12   How **m** more valuable a person is
Mt   23:15   Gehenna twice as **m** as yourselves.
Lk   12:48   M will be required of the person entrusted with **m**,

Jn 8:26 I have **m** to say about you
Jn 12:24 but if it dies, it produces **m** fruit.
Jn 15: 5 in me and I in him will bear **m** fruit,
2 Cor 3:11 how **m** more will what endures be
2 Cor 8:15 "Whoever had **m** did not have more,
Heb 9:14 how **m** more will the blood

MUD
Is 57:20 And its waters cast up **m** and filth.
Jer 38: 6 only **m**, and Jeremiah sank into the **m**.

MULBERRY
Lk 17: 6 you would say to [this] **m** tree,

MULE
2 Sm 18: 9 He was mounted on a **m**, and,
2 Sm 18: 9 as the **m** passed under the branches
1 Kgs 1:38 Solomon on King David's **m**,

MULTIPLIED → MULTIPLY
Ex 11: 9 my wonders may be **m** in the land

MULTIPLIES → MULTIPLY
Sir 6: 5 A kind mouth **m** friends.

MULTIPLY → MULTIPLIED, MULTIPLIES
Gn 1:28 "Be fertile and **m**; fill the earth
Gn 9: 7 Be fertile, then, and **m**;

MULTITUDE
Dn 10: 6 voice sounded like the roar of a **m**.
Jas 5:20 death and will cover a **m** of sins.
1 Pt 4: 8 because love covers a **m** of sins.
Rv 7: 9 this I had a vision of a great **m**,
Rv 19: 6 like the sound of a great **m**

MURDER → MURDERED, MURDERER, MURDERERS, MURDERS
Hos 4: 2 lying, **m**, stealing and adultery!
Mt 15:19 the heart come evil thoughts, **m**,
Lk 23:25 imprisoned for rebellion and **m**,
Rom 1:29 full of envy, **m**, rivalry, treachery,

MURDERED → MURDER
Mt 23:31 of those who **m** the prophets;

MURDERER → MURDER
Nm 35:16 he is a **m** and shall be put to death.
Nm 35:31 a **m** who deserves the death penalty;
Jn 8:44 He was a **m** from the beginning
Acts 3:14 asked that a **m** be released to you.

MURDERERS → MURDER
1 Tm 1: 9 who kill their fathers or mothers, **m**,
Rv 21: 8 the depraved, **m**, the unchaste,
Rv 22:15 the **m**, the idol-worshipers, and all

MURDERS → MURDER
Rv 9:21 Nor did they repent of their **m**,

MUSIC → MUSICAL
Sir 40:20 Wine and **m** delight the soul,
Lam 5:14 the gate, the young men their **m**.
Lk 15:25 house, he heard the sound of **m**

MUSICAL → MUSIC
1 Chr 15:16 to play on **m** instruments, harps,
2 Chr 23:13 their **m** instruments were leading
Neh 12:36 with the **m** instruments of David,

MUST
Dt 18:13 **m** be altogether sincere toward
Mt 16:21 to show his disciples that he **m** go
Mt 17:10 scribes say that Elijah **m** come first?"
Mk 10:17 what **m** I do to inherit eternal life?"
Mk 13: 7 such things **m** happen, but it will not
Lk 9:22 "The Son of Man **m** suffer greatly
Jn 3: 7 you, 'You **m** be born from above.'
Jn 3:14 so **m** the Son of Man be lifted up,
Jn 3:30 He **m** increase; I **m** decrease."
Jn 4:24 those who worship him **m** worship
2 Cor 5:10 we **m** all appear before the judgment
Gal 6: 4 Each one **m** examine his own work,
1 Tm 3: 2 a bishop **m** be irreproachable,
1 Tm 3: 8 Similarly, deacons **m** be dignified
Heb 11: 6 who approaches God **m** believe

Rv 4: 1 you what **m** happen afterwards."
Rv 22: 6 his servants what **m** happen soon."

MUSTARD
Mt 13:31 heaven is like a **m** seed that a person
Mt 17:20 you have faith the size of a **m** seed,
Mk 4:31 It is like a **m** seed that, when it is
Lk 13:19 It is like a **m** seed that a person took
Lk 17: 6 you have faith the size of a **m** seed,

MUTE
Mt 9:33 was driven out the **m** person spoke.
Mk 7:37 the deaf hear and [the] **m** speak."

MUTILATION
Phil 3: 2 evil-workers! Beware of the **m**!

MUTTER
Is 8:19 fortunetellers (who chirp and **m**!);

MUTUAL → MUTUALLY
Rom 12:10 love one another with **m** affection;
Heb 13: 1 Let **m** love continue.
2 Pt 1: 7 devotion with **m** affection,

MUTUALLY → MUTUAL
Rom 1:12 and I may be **m** encouraged by one

MUZZLE
Dt 25: 4 "You shall not **m** an ox when it is
1 Cor 9: 9 "You shall not **m** an ox while it is
1 Tm 5:18 "You shall not **m** an ox when it is

MYRRH
Ps 45: 9 With **m**, aloes, and cassia your robes
Song 1:13 My lover is for me a sachet of **m**
Mt 2:11 gifts of gold, frankincense, and **m**.
Mk 15:23 gave him wine drugged with **m**,
Jn 19:39 came bringing a mixture of **m**
Rv 18:13 spice, incense, **m**, and frankincense;

MYRTLE
Is 55:13 instead of nettles, the **m**. This shall
Zec 1: 8 standing among **m** trees in a shady

MYSTERIES → MYSTERY
Wis 14:23 sacrifices or clandestine **m**,
Sir 39: 7 counsel, as he meditates upon his **m**.
Dn 2:28 is a God in heaven who reveals **m**,
Dn 2:29 he who reveals **m** showed you what
Dn 2:47 Lord of kings and a revealer of **m**;
1 Cor 13: 2 and comprehend all **m** and all
1 Cor 14: 2 no one listens; he utters **m** in spirit.

MYSTERY → MYSTERIES
Dn 2:18 God of heaven in regard to this **m**,
Dn 2:19 During the night the **m** was revealed
Dn 2:27 "The **m** about which the king has
Dn 2:30 me also this **m** has been revealed;
Dn 2:47 why you were able to reveal this **m**."
Rom 11:25 want you to be unaware of this **m**,
Rom 16:25 to the revelation of the **m** kept secret
1 Cor 2: 1 brothers, proclaiming the **m** of God,
1 Cor 15:51 Behold, I tell you a **m**. We shall not
Eph 1: 9 made known to us the **m** of his will
Eph 3: 3 that] the **m** was made known to me
Eph 3: 4 my insight into the **m** of Christ,
Eph 3: 9 all] what is the plan of the **m** hidden
Eph 5:32 This is a great **m**, but I speak
Eph 6:19 with boldness the **m** of the gospel
Col 1:26 the **m** hidden from ages
Col 1:27 glory of this **m** among the Gentiles;
Col 2: 2 for the knowledge of the **m** of God,
Col 4: 3 to speak of the **m** of Christ,
2 Thes 2: 7 For the **m** of lawlessness is already
1 Tm 3: 9 holding fast to the **m** of the faith
1 Tm 3:16 Undeniably great is the **m**
Rv 17: 5 which is a **m**, "Babylon the great,
Rv 17: 7 explain to you the **m** of the woman

MYTHS
1 Tm 1: 4 to concern themselves with **m**
1 Tm 4: 7 Avoid profane and silly **m**.
2 Tm 4: 4 the truth and will be diverted to **m**.
Ti 1:14 of paying attention to Jewish **m**

2 Pt 1:16 did not follow cleverly devised **m**

N

NAAMAN
Aramean general whose leprosy was cleansed by Elisha (2 Kgs 5; Lk 4:27).

NABAL
Wealthy Carmelite the Lord killed for refusing to help David (1 Sm 25). David married Abigail, his widow (1 Sm 25:39-43).

NABOTH
Jezreelite killed by Jezebel for his vineyard (1 Kgs 21). Ahab's family destroyed for this (1 Kgs 21:17-24; 2 Kgs 9:21-37).

NADAB
1. Firstborn of Aaron (Ex 6:23); killed with Abihu for offering unauthorized fire (Lv 10; Nm 3:4).
2. Son of Jeroboam I; king of Israel (1 Kgs 15:25-32).

NAHASH
1 Sm	11: 1	**N** the Ammonite went up and laid
1 Sm	11: 1	All the men of Jabesh begged **N**,

NAHOR
Gn	11:26	the father of Abram, **N** and Haran.
Gn	22:23	Milcah bore to Abraham's brother **N**.
Gn	24:15	of Abraham's brother **N**) came

NAHUM
Prophet against Nineveh (Tb 14:4; Na 1:1).

NAILING → NAILS
Col	2:14	it from our midst, **n** it to the cross;

NAILS → NAILING
Is	41: 7	and he fastens it with **n** to steady it.
Jn	20:25	I see the mark of the **n** in his hands

NAKED → NAKEDNESS
Gn	2:25	The man and his wife were both **n**,
Jb	1:21	"**N** I came forth from my mother's
Jb	1:21	and **n** shall I go back again.
Eccl	5:14	again shall he depart, **n** as he came,
Is	58: 7	Clothing the **n** when you see them,
Mk	14:52	left the cloth behind and ran off **n**.
2 Cor	5: 3	taken it off, we shall not be found **n**.
Rv	3:17	pitiable, poor, blind, and **n**.

NAKEDNESS → NAKED
Gn	9:22	saw his father's **n**, and he told his
Ez	16: 8	my cloak over you to cover your **n**;
Rom	8:35	or famine, or **n**, or peril,
Rv	3:18	so that your shameful **n** may not be

NAME → NAME'S, NAMED, NAMES
Gn	2:19	called each of them would be its **n**.
Gn	4:26	men began to invoke the Lord by **n**.
Gn	11: 4	sky, and so make a **n** for ourselves;
Gn	12: 2	I will make your **n** great, so that you
Gn	12: 8	the Lord and invoked the Lord by **n**.
Gn	13: 4	and there he invoked the Lord by **n**.
Gn	17: 5	your **n** shall be Abraham, for I am
Gn	21:33	and there he invoked by **n** the Lord,
Gn	26:25	there and invoked the Lord by **n**.
Gn	32:30	him, "Do tell me your **n**, please."
Gn	32:30	should you want to know my **n**?"
Ex	3:15	"This is my **n** forever; this is my title
Ex	6: 3	Isaac and Jacob, but my **n**, Lord,
Ex	20: 7	"You shall not take the **n** of the Lord,
Ex	20: 7	unpunished him who takes his **n**
Ex	33:19	presence I will pronounce my **n**,
Ex	34: 5	him there and proclaimed his **n**,
Nm	17:17	Mark each man's **n** on his staff;
Dt	5:11	'You shall not take the **n** of the Lord,
Dt	5:11	unpunished him who takes his **n**
Dt	10: 8	and to give blessings in his **n**,
Dt	12:11	for his **n** you shall bring all
Dt	18: 5	to minister in the **n** of the Lord.
Dt	25: 6	that his **n** may not be blotted
Dt	28:58	and awesome **n** of the Lord,
Jos	7: 9	us and efface our **n** from the earth.
Jos	7: 9	What will you do for your great **n**?"
Jgs	13:17	"What is your **n**, that we may honor

1 Sm	17:45	against you in the **n** of the Lord
1 Sm	25:25	man Nabal, for he is just like his **n**. Fool is his **n**, and he acts the fool.
2 Sm	6: 2	which bears the **n** of the Lord
1 Chr	17: 8	I will make your **n** great like
2 Chr	7:14	whom my **n** has been pronounced,
Ezr	6:12	may the God who causes his **n**
Neh	9:10	for yourself a **n** even to this day.
Tb	11:14	God, and praised be his great **n**,
Tb	11:14	May his holy **n** be praised
Jdt	16: 1	a new song, exalt and acclaim his **n**.
Ps	5:12	be the joy of those who love your **n**.
Ps	8: 2	awesome is your **n** through all
Ps	9: 6	their **n** you blotted out for all time.
Ps	9:11	Those who honor your **n** trust
Ps	20: 8	we on the **n** of the Lord our God.
Ps	23: 3	for the sake of your **n**.
Ps	29: 2	to the Lord the glory due God's **n**.
Ps	34: 4	with me; let us exalt his **n** together.
Ps	44:21	we had forgotten the **n** of our God,
Ps	54: 3	O God, by your **n** save me. By your
Ps	66: 2	sing of his glorious **n**; give him
Ps	68: 5	Sing to God, praise the divine **n**;
Ps	68: 5	before this God whose **n** is the Lord.
Ps	74:10	Shall the foe revile your **n** forever?
Ps	74:21	the poor and needy praise your **n**.
Ps	79: 9	for the glory of your **n**. Deliver us,
Ps	96: 8	give to the Lord the glory due his **n**!
Ps	103: 1	soul; all my being, bless his holy **n**!
Ps	113: 1	of the Lord, praise the **n** of the Lord.
Ps	115: 1	but to your **n** give glory
Ps	124: 8	Our help is the **n** of the Lord,
Ps	138: 2	I praise your **n** for your fidelity
Ps	138: 2	over all your **n** and your promise.
Ps	145: 1	and king; I will bless your **n** forever.
Ps	149: 3	Let them praise his **n** in festive
Prv	10: 7	but the **n** of the wicked will rot.
Prv	18:10	The **n** of the Lord is a strong tower;
Prv	22: 1	A good **n** is more desirable than
Prv	30: 4	What is his **n**, what is his son's **n**,
Eccl	7: 1	A good **n** is better than good
Song	1: 3	Your **n** spoken is a spreading
Sir	41:13	days, but a good **n**, for days without
Is	12: 4	thanks to the Lord, acclaim his **n**;
Is	12: 4	proclaim how exalted is his **n**.
Is	26: 8	look to you; Your **n** and your title
Is	40:26	calling them all by **n**. By his great
Is	42: 8	I am the Lord, this is my **n**;
Is	50:10	Trusting in the **n** of the Lord
Is	56: 5	my walls, a monument and a **n**
Is	56: 5	imperishable **n** will I give them.
Is	57:15	eternally, whose **n** is the Holy One:
Is	63:14	people, bringing glory to your **n**.
Jer	7:11	bears my **n** become in your eyes
Jer	10: 6	are you, great and mighty is your **n**.
Jer	15:16	Because I bore your **n**, O Lord,
Jer	27:15	but they prophesy falsely in my **n**,
Ez	36:22	but for the sake of my holy **n**,
Ez	48:35	The **n** of the City shall henceforth
Dn	2:20	"Blessed be the **n** of God forever
Hos	12: 6	the God of hosts, the Lord is his **n**!
Jl	3: 5	who calls on the **n** of the Lord;
Am	9:12	all the nations that shall bear my **n**,
Mi	5: 3	in the majestic **n** of the Lord,
Mi	6: 9	[It is wisdom to fear your **n**!] Hear,
Zep	3: 9	all may call upon the **n** of the Lord,
Zec	6:12	Here is a man whose **n** is Shoot,
Zec	13: 9	They shall call upon my **n**, and I
Zec	14: 9	the only one, and his **n** the only one.
Mal	1: 6	who despise his **n**. But you ask, "How have we despised your **n**?"
Mal	3:20	But for you who fear my **n**,
Mt	1:21	a son and you are to **n** him Jesus,
Mt	6: 9	in heaven, hallowed be your **n**,
Mt	7:22	did we not prophesy in your **n**?
Mt	7:22	we not drive out demons in your **n**?
Mt	7:22	we not do mighty deeds in your **n**?'
Mt	12:21	And in his **n** the Gentiles will hope."
Mt	18:20	three are gathered together in my **n**,

Mt	24: 5	For many will come in my **n**,
Mt	28:19	them in the **n** of the Father,
Mk	11: 9	he who comes in the **n** of the Lord!
Lk	1:31	a son, and you shall **n** him Jesus.
Lk	11: 2	Father, hallowed be your **n**,
Lk	19:38	comes in the **n** of the Lord.
Jn	1:12	God, to those who believe in his **n**,
Jn	5:43	I came in the **n** of my Father,
Jn	5:43	yet if another comes in his own **n**,
Jn	10: 3	as he calls his own sheep by **n**
Jn	12:28	Father, glorify your **n**." Then a voice
Jn	14:13	And whatever you ask in my **n**,
Jn	15:16	the Father in my **n** he may give you.
Jn	16:23	the Father in my **n** he will give you.
Jn	16:24	have not asked anything in my **n**;
Jn	17:11	in your **n** that you have given me,
Jn	20:31	belief you may have life in his **n**.
Acts	2:21	who calls on the **n** of the Lord.'
Acts	3:16	And by faith in his **n**, this man,
Acts	3:16	and know, his **n** has made strong,
Acts	4:12	is there any other **n** under heaven
Acts	4:17	again to speak to anyone in this **n**."
Acts	5:40	to stop speaking in the **n** of Jesus,
Acts	15:17	Gentiles on whom my **n** is invoked.
Rom	10:13	on the **n** of the Lord will be saved."
1 Cor	6:11	in the **n** of the Lord Jesus Christ
Phil	2: 9	and bestowed on him the **n** that is above every **n**,
Phil	2:10	that at the **n** of Jesus every knee
Col	3:17	in the **n** of the Lord Jesus,
2 Tm	2:19	upon the **n** of the Lord avoid evil."
Heb	1: 4	as the **n** he has inherited is more
Heb	13:15	is, the fruit of lips that confess his **n**.
Jas	5:14	[him] with oil in the **n** of the Lord,
1 Pt	4:16	but glorify God because of the **n**.
1 Jn	3:23	should believe in the **n** of his Son,
1 Jn	5:13	you who believe in the **n** of the Son
Rv	2: 3	and have suffered for my **n**, and you
Rv	2:13	yet you hold fast to my **n** and have
Rv	2:17	upon which is inscribed a new **n**,
Rv	3: 5	and I will never erase his **n**
Rv	3: 5	but will acknowledge his **n**
Rv	3: 8	my word and have not denied my **n**.
Rv	3:12	him I will inscribe the **n** of my God
Rv	3:12	and the **n** of the city of my God,
Rv	3:12	from my God, as well as my new **n**.
Rv	11:18	ones and those who fear your **n**,
Rv	13:17	the stamped image of the beast's **n** or the number that stood for its **n**.
Rv	14: 1	who had his **n** and his Father's **n** written
Rv	16: 9	blasphemed the **n** of God who had
Rv	19:12	He had a **n** inscribed that no one
Rv	19:13	his **n** was called the Word of God.
Rv	19:16	He has a **n** written on his cloak
Rv	20:15	Anyone whose **n** was not found
Rv	22: 4	and his **n** will be on their foreheads.

NAME'S → NAME

Ps	79: 9	pardon our sins for your **n** sake;
Ps	106: 8	Yet he saved them for his **n** sake
Ez	20:44	I deal with you thus, for my **n** sake,

NAMED → NAME

Gn	5:29	and **n** him Noah, saying,
Gn	27:36	"He has been well **n** Jacob! He has
1 Sm	4:21	[She **n** the child Ichabod, saying,
1 Sm	7:12	he **n** it Ebenezer, explaining, "To this

NAMES → NAME

Gn	2:20	The man gave **n** to all the cattle,
Ex	28: 9	engrave on them the **n** of the sons
Hos	2:19	from her mouth the **n** of the Baals,
Mt	10: 2	The **n** of the twelve apostles are
Lk	10:20	rejoice because your **n** are written
Phil	4: 3	whose **n** are in the book of life.
Rv	17: 3	was covered with blasphemous **n**,
Rv	17: 8	of the earth whose **n** have not been
Rv	21:12	and on which **n** were inscribed,
Rv	21:12	[the **n**] of the twelve tribes
Rv	21:14	were inscribed the twelve **n**

NAOMI → =MARA

Wife of Elimelech, mother-in-law of Ruth (Ru 1:2, 4). Left Bethlehem for Moab during famine (Ru 1:1). Returned a widow, with Ruth (Ru 1:6-22). Advised Ruth to seek marriage with Boaz (Ru 2:17-3:4). Cared for Ruth's son Obed (Ru 4:13-17).

NAPHTALI

Son of Jacob by Bilhah (Gn 30:8; 35:25; 1 Chr 2:2). Tribe of blessed (Gn 49:21; Dt 33:23), numbered (Nm 1:43; 26:50), allotted land (Jos 19:32-39; Ez 48:3), failed to fully possess (Jgs 1:33), supported Deborah (Jgs 4:10; 5:18), David (1 Chr 12:35), 12,000 from (Rv 7:6).

NARD

Jn	12: 3	oil made from genuine aromatic **n**

NARROW

Nm	22:24	stand in a **n** lane between vineyards
Mt	7:13	"Enter through the **n** gate;
Lk	13:24	"Strive to enter through the **n** gate,

NATHAN

Prophet and chronicler of Israel's history (1 Chr 29:29; 2 Chr 9:29). Announced the Davidic covenant (2 Sm 7; 1 Chr 17). Denounced David's sin with Bathsheba (2 Sm 12). Supported Solomon (1 Kgs 1).

NATHANAEL → =BARTHOLOMEW?

Apostle (Jn 1:45-49; 21:2). Probably also called Bartholomew (Mt 10:3).

NATION → NATIONS

Gn	12: 2	"I will make of you a great **n**, and I
Gn	15:14	judgment on the **n** they must serve,
Gn	35:11	A **n**, indeed an assembly of nations,
Ex	19: 6	me a kingdom of priests, a holy **n**.
Ex	32:10	Then I will make of you a great **n**."
Nm	14:12	I will make of you a **n** greater
Dt	4: 7	For what great **n** is there that has
Jos	4: 1	the entire **n** had crossed the Jordan,
Jos	5: 8	the whole **n** remained in camp
2 Sm	7:23	What other **n** on earth is there like
1 Chr	16:20	Wandering from **n** to **n**, from one
Ps	33:12	Happy the **n** whose God is the Lord,
Prv	14:34	Virtue exalts a **n**, but sin is
Is	2: 4	One **n** shall not raise the sword
Is	26: 2	to let in a **n** that is just,
Is	65: 1	To a **n** that did not call upon my
Is	66: 8	or a **n** be born in a single moment?
Jer	2:11	Does any other **n** change its gods?—
Jer	18: 8	that **n** which I have threatened turns
Ez	37:22	I will make them one **n**
Mi	4: 3	One **n** shall not raise the sword
Mal	3: 9	for you, the whole **n**, rob me.
Mt	24: 7	**N** will rise against **n**, and kingdom
Jn	11:50	so that the whole **n** may not perish."
1 Pt	2: 9	a holy **n**, a people of his own,
Rv	5: 9	tribe and tongue, people and **n**.
Rv	7: 9	one could count, from every **n**, race,
Rv	14: 6	dwell on earth, to every **n**, tribe,

NATIONS → NATION

Gn	17: 4	to become the father of a host of **n**.
Gn	18:18	and all the **n** of the earth are to find
Gn	22:18	in your descendants all the **n**
Gn	25:23	her: "Two **n** are in your womb,
Ex	34:24	I will drive out the **n** before you
Dt	7: 1	and dislodges great **n** before
Dt	7: 1	seven **n** more numerous
Dt	15: 6	you will lend to many **n**, and borrow
Dt	15: 6	you will rule over many **n**, and none
Jos	23: 7	these **n** while they survive among
Jgs	3: 1	The following are the **n**
1 Sm	8:20	We too must be like other **n**,
1 Kgs	5:14	hear Solomon's wisdom from all **n**,
2 Kgs	17:15	the surrounding **n** whom the Lord
2 Chr	20: 6	rule over all the kingdoms of the **n**?
Ps	2: 1	Why do the **n** protest
Ps	2: 8	I will make your inheritance the **n**,
Ps	9: 6	You rebuked the **n**, you destroyed
Ps	22:29	to the Lord, the ruler over the **n**.
Ps	33:10	The Lord foils the plan of **n**,

Ps	46:11	I am exalted among the **n**,
Ps	47: 9	God rules over the **n**; God sits
Ps	66: 7	Whose eyes are fixed upon the **n**.
Ps	67: 3	your saving power among all the **n**.
Ps	72:17	may all the **n** regard him as favored.
Ps	106:35	But mingled with the **n** and imitated
Ps	110: 6	Who, robed in splendor, judges **n**,
Ps	113: 4	High above all **n** is the LORD;
Ps	147:20	God has not done this for other **n**;
Sir	44:21	in his descendants the **n** would be
Is	2: 2	All **n** shall stream toward it;
Is	11:10	set up as a signal for the **n**,
Is	12: 4	among the **n** make known his deeds,
Is	40:15	the **n** count as a drop of the bucket,
Is	42: 1	he shall bring forth justice to the **n**,
Is	52:15	So shall he startle many **n**,
Is	60: 3	**N** shall walk by your light,
Is	60:12	those **n** shall be utterly destroyed.
Is	66:18	come to gather **n** of every language;
Jer	1: 5	a prophet to the **n** I appointed you.
Jer	3:17	there all **n** will be gathered together
Jer	31:10	Hear the word of the LORD, O **n**,
Jer	33: 9	glory, before all the **n** of the earth,
Jer	46:28	I will make an end of all the **n**
Lam	1: 1	is she who was mistress over **n**;
Ez	22: 4	make you an object of scorn to the **n**
Ez	36:23	profaned among the **n**, in whose
Ez	36:23	Thus the **n** shall know that I am
Ez	37:22	Never again shall they be two **n**,
Ez	39:21	I will display my glory among the **n**,
Ez	39:21	all the **n** shall see the judgment I
Jl	2:17	with the **n** ruling over them!
Jl	4: 2	I will assemble all the **n** and bring
Jl	4: 2	have scattered them among the **n**,
Am	9:12	all the **n** that shall bear my name,
Zep	3: 8	decision to gather together the **n**,
Hg	2: 7	I will shake all the **n**,
Hg	2: 7	treasures of all the **n** will come in,
Zec	8:13	as you were a curse among the **n**,
Zec	9:10	and he shall proclaim peace to the **n**.
Zec	14: 2	gather all the **n** against Jerusalem
Mal	1:11	my name is great among the **n**;
Mal	3:12	Then all **n** will call you blessed,
Mt	24: 9	You will be hated by all **n** because
Mt	24:14	the world as a witness to all **n**,
Mt	25:32	all the **n** will be assembled before
Mt	28:19	and make disciples of all **n**,
Rom	4:18	would become "the father of many **n**,"
Rv	2:26	end, I will give authority over the **n**.
Rv	12: 5	to rule all the **n** with an iron rod.
Rv	15: 4	alone are holy. All the **n** will come
Rv	18:23	all **n** were led astray by your magic
Rv	19:15	came a sharp sword to strike the **n**.
Rv	20: 8	to deceive the **n** at the four corners
Rv	21:24	The **n** will walk by its light, and to it
Rv	22: 2	the trees serve as medicine for the **n**.

NATIVE

Ex	12:49	for the resident alien as for the **n**."
Acts	2: 8	us hear them in his own **n** language?

NATURAL →NATURE

Rom	1:26	Their females exchanged **n** relations
Rom	11:21	if God did not spare the **n** branches,

NATURE →NATURAL

1 Cor	11:14	Does not **n** itself teach you
Eph	2: 3	and we were by **n** children of wrath,
2 Pt	1: 4	may come to share in the divine **n**,

NAZARETH

Mt	2:23	went and dwelt in a town called **N**,
Mk	1:24	have you to do with us, Jesus of **N**?
Lk	1:26	God to a town of Galilee called **N**,
Lk	4:16	He came to **N**, where he had grown
Jn	1:46	"Can anything good come from **N**?"
Acts	10:38	how God anointed Jesus of **N**

NAZIRITE →NAZIRITES

Nm	6: 2	a woman) solemnly takes the **n** vow

NAZIRITES →NAZIRITE

Am	2:12	But you gave the **n** wine to drink,

NAZOREAN

Mt	2:23	be fulfilled, "He shall be called a **N**."

NEAR →NEARER

Dt	30:14	No, it is something very **n** to you,
Ps	73:28	As for me, to be **n** God is my good,
Ps	145:18	LORD, are **n** to all who call upon you,
Is	55: 6	be found, call him while he is **n**.
Ez	7: 7	The time has come, **n** is the day:
Jl	1:15	the day! for **n** is the day of the LORD,
Zep	1:14	**N** is the great day of the LORD,
Mal	3: 5	I will draw **n** to you for judgment,
Rom	10: 8	"The word is **n** you, in your mouth
Phil	4: 5	be known to all. The Lord is **n**.
Jas	4: 8	Draw **n** to God, and he will draw **n**
Rv	1: 3	in it, for the appointed time is **n**.
Rv	22:10	book, for the appointed time is **n**.

NEARER →NEAR

Rom	13:11	our salvation is **n** now than

NEBO

Dt	34: 1	the plains of Moab to Mount **N**,
Is	46: 1	Bel bows down, **N** stoops,

NEBUCHADNEZZAR

Babylonian king, also spelled Nebuchadrezzar. Subdued and exiled Judah (2 Kgs 24-25; 2 Chr 36; Jer 39). Dreams interpreted by Daniel (Dn 2; 4). Worshiped God (Dn 3:98-100; 4:34-37).

NEBUZARADAN

2 Kgs	25: 8	king of Babylon), **N**,
Jer	52:12	king of Babylon), **N**,

NECESSARY

Lk	24:26	Was it not **n** that the Messiah should
Acts	15: 5	"It is **n** to circumcise them and direct
2 Cor	9: 5	So I thought it **n** to encourage
Phil	1:24	the flesh is more **n** for your benefit.
Heb	9:23	it was **n** for the copies

NECK →NECKS, STIFF-NECKED

Gn	27:16	hands and the hairless parts of his **n**.
Prv	1: 9	for your head; a torque for your **n**.
Prv	3:22	soul, and an adornment for your **n**.
Prv	6:21	always, put them around your **n**;
Song	7: 5	Your **n** is like tower of ivory.
Sir	51:26	Submit your **n** to her yoke, that your
Jer	28:10	from the **n** of the prophet Jeremiah,
Hos	10:11	upon her fair **n**; Ephraim was to be
Mt	18: 6	a great millstone hung around his **n**

NECKS →NECK

Jos	10:24	your feet on the **n** of these kings."
Jos	10:24	and put their feet upon their **n**.
Is	3:16	and walk with **n** outstretched
Jer	7:26	they have stiffened their **n** and done

NECO

Pharaoh who killed Josiah (2 Kgs 23:29-30; 2 Chr 35:20-24), deposed Jehoahaz (2 Kgs 23:33-35; 2 Chr 36:3-4).

NEED →NEEDS, NEEDY

Mt	3:14	saying, "I **n** to be baptized by you,
Mt	6: 8	knows what you **n** before you ask
Mt	21: 3	reply, 'The master has **n** of them.'
Mk	2:17	who are well do not **n** a physician,
Lk	12:30	your Father knows that you **n** them.
Lk	15:14	and he found himself in dire **n**.
Acts	2:45	among all according to each one's **n**.
Acts	4:35	distributed to each according to **n**.
1 Cor	12:21	"I do not **n** you," nor again the head to the feet, "I do not **n** you."
1 Thes	5: 1	you have no **n** for anything to be
1 Jn	2:27	you do not **n** anyone to teach you.
1 Jn	3:17	worldly means sees a brother in **n**
Rv	21:23	The city had no **n** of sun or moon
Rv	22: 5	nor will they **n** light from lamp

NEEDLE

Lk	18:25	pass through the eye of a **n** than

NEEDS → NEED
2 Cor	8:14	present time should supply their **n**,
2 Cor	8:14	surplus may also supply your **n**,

NEEDY → NEED
Dt	15:11	The **n** will never be lacking
Dt	15:11	poor and **n** kinsman in your country.
1 Sm	2: 8	He raises the **n** from the dust;
Jb	29:16	I was a father to the **n**; the rights
Ps	9:19	The **n** will never be forgotten,
Ps	35:10	afflicted and **n** from the despoiler?"
Ps	74:21	the poor and **n** praise your name.
Ps	113: 7	The Lord raises the **n** from the dust,
Ps	140:13	justice for the **n**, their rights
Prv	14:31	who is kind to the **n** glorifies him.
Prv	31: 9	is just, defend the **n** and the poor!
Prv	31:20	poor, and extends her arms to the **n**.
Sir	4: 3	delay not to give to the **n**.
Am	8: 4	this, you who trample upon the **n**

NEGEB
Gn	13: 1	went up to the **N** with his wife
Gn	24:62	was living in the region of the **N**.
Jos	11:16	the entire **N**, all the land of Goshen,
Ps	126: 4	like the dry stream beds of the **N**.

NEGLECT → NEGLECTED
Dt	12:19	you do not **n** the Levite as long as
Dt	14:27	do not **n** the Levite who belongs
Neh	10:40	We will not **n** the house of our God.
Sir	7:10	and **n** not the giving of alms.
Acts	6: 2	not right for us to **n** the word of God
1 Tm	4:14	Do not **n** the gift you have,

NEGLECTED → NEGLECT
Mt	23:23	have **n** the weightier things

NEHEMIAH
Cupbearer of Artaxerxes (Neh 2:1); governor of Israel (Neh 8:9). Returned to Jerusalem to rebuild walls (Neh 2-6). With Ezra, reestablished worship (Neh 8). Prayer confessing nation's sin (Neh 9). Dedicated wall (Neh 12). Story of the miraculous fire (2 Mc 1).

NEHUSHTAN
2 Kgs	18: 4	smashed the bronze serpent called **N**

NEIGHBOR → NEIGHBOR'S, NEIGHBORS
Ex	3:22	Every woman shall ask her **n**
Ex	20:16	bear false witness against your **n**.
Lv	19:18	You shall love your **n** as yourself.
Dt	5:20	dishonest witness against your **n**.
Prv	3:29	Plot no evil against your **n**,
Prv	24:28	a witness against your **n** without just
Prv	25:18	bears false witness against his **n**.
Prv	27:10	Better is a **n** near at hand than
Prv	27:14	one greets his **n** with a loud voice
Prv	29: 5	The man who flatters his **n**
Sir	29:20	Go surety for your **n** according
Is	19: 2	war against brother, **N** against **n**,
Mt	5:43	'You shall love your **n** and hate your
Mt	19:19	'you shall love your **n** as yourself.' "
Mk	12:31	'You shall love your **n** as yourself.'
Lk	10:27	your mind, and your **n** as yourself."
Lk	10:29	he said to Jesus, "And who is my **n**?"
Rom	13: 9	"You shall love your **n** as yourself."
Rom	13:10	Love does no evil to the **n**; hence,
Rom	15: 2	each of us please our **n** for the good,
Jas	2: 8	"You shall love your **n** as yourself,"

NEIGHBOR'S → NEIGHBOR
Ex	20:17	"You shall not covet your **n** house.
Ex	22:25	If you take your **n** cloak as a pledge,
Dt	5:21	'You shall not covet your **n** wife.
Dt	19:14	"You shall not move your **n** landmarks
Dt	27:17	'Cursed be he who moves his **n** landmarks!'
Prv	25:17	Let your foot be seldom in your **n** house,

NEIGHBORS → NEIGHBOR
2 Kgs	4: 3	"borrow vessels from all your **n**—
Ezr	1: 6	All their **n** gave them help in every
Ps	79: 4	have become the reproach of our **n**,
Ps	80: 7	left us to be fought over by our **n**;

NEPHEW
Gn	14:14	heard that his **n** had been captured,
Tb	1:22	He was a close relative—in fact, my **n**.

NEPHILIM
Gn	6: 4	time the **N** appeared on earth (as

NEST → NESTS
Dt	22: 6	upon a bird's **n** with young birds
Ob	1: 4	and your **n** be set among the stars,
Hb	2: 9	his household, setting his **n** on high

NESTS → NEST
Mt	8:20	dens and birds of the sky have **n**,

NET → NETS
Prv	1:17	It is in vain that a **n** is spread
Lam	1:13	frame; He spread a **n** for my feet,
Hb	1:15	he hauls them away with his **n**,
Mt	13:47	of heaven is like a **n** thrown
Jn	21: 6	"Cast the **n** over the right side

NETS → NET
Ps	141:10	their own **n** let all the wicked fall,
Mt	4:20	At once they left their **n**
Mk	1:16	his brother Andrew casting their **n**
Lk	5: 4	water and lower your **n** for a catch."

NEVER
Gn	8:21	"**N** again will I doom the earth
Dt	32:17	of whom their fathers had **n** stood
Ps	15: 5	acts like this shall **n** be shaken.
Ps	30: 7	I once said, "I shall **n** be shaken."
Ps	119:93	I will **n** forget your precepts;
Prv	10:30	The just man will **n** be disturbed,
Prv	27:20	world and the abyss are **n** satisfied;
Prv	30:15	Three things are **n** satisfied, four **n**
Sir	4:25	**N** gainsay the truth, and struggle not
Is	51: 6	and my justice shall **n** be dismayed.
Jer	33:17	**N** shall David lack a successor
Dn	2:44	a kingdom that shall **n** be destroyed
Mt	7:23	to them solemnly, 'I **n** knew you.
Mk	3:29	holy Spirit will **n** have forgiveness,
Jn	4:14	the water I shall give will **n** thirst;
Jn	6:35	whoever comes to me will **n** hunger,
Jn	6:35	whoever believes in me will **n** thirst.
Jn	8:51	keeps my word will **n** see death."
Jn	10:28	eternal life, and they shall **n** perish.
Jn	11:26	lives and believes in me will **n** die.
1 Cor	13: 8	Love **n** fails. If there are prophecies,
Heb	13: 5	"I will **n** forsake you or abandon you."
2 Pt	1:10	for, in doing so, you will **n** stumble.

NEW → ANEW, NEWBORN, NEWNESS
Ex	1: 8	Then a **n** king, who knew nothing
Jgs	5: 8	**N** gods were their choice;
Ezr	9: 9	Thus he has given us **n** life to raise
Jdt	16: 1	Sing to him a **n** song,
1 Mc	4:47	built a **n** altar like the former one.
Ps	33: 3	Sing to God a **n** song; skillfully play
Ps	40: 4	And put a **n** song in my mouth,
Ps	98: 1	A psalm. Sing a **n** song to the Lord,
Eccl	1: 9	be done. Nothing is **n** under the sun.
Sir	9:10	for the **n** one cannot equal him.
Sir	9:10	A **n** friend is like a **n** wine which you
Is	42: 9	come to pass, **n** ones I now foretell";
Is	42:10	Sing to the Lord a **n** song, his praise
Is	43:19	See, I am doing something **n**!
Is	62: 2	You shall be called by a **n** name
Is	65:17	I am about to create **n** heavens and a **n** earth;
Is	66:22	As the **n** heavens and the **n** earth
Jer	31:31	I will make a **n** covenant
Ez	11:19	I will give them a **n** heart and put a **n** spirit within them;
Ez	18:31	make for yourselves a **n** heart and a **n** spirit.
Ez	36:26	I will give you a **n** heart and place a **n** spirit within you,
Mt	9:17	People do not put **n** wine into old
Mt	9:17	Rather, they pour **n** wine into fresh
Mt	13:52	from his storeroom both the **n**
Mk	1:27·	is this? A **n** teaching with authority.
Lk	5:39	been drinking old wine desires **n**,

Lk	22:20	"This cup is the **n** covenant in my
Jn	13:34	I give you a **n** commandment:
Acts	17:19	we learn what this **n** teaching is
1 Cor	11:25	"This cup is the **n** covenant in my
2 Cor	3: 6	us as ministers of a **n** covenant,
2 Cor	5:17	whoever is in Christ is a **n** creation:
2 Cor	5:17	behold, **n** things have come.
Gal	6:15	but only a **n** creation.
Eph	2:15	in himself one **n** person in place
Eph	4:24	and put on the **n** self,
Col	3:10	and have put on the **n** self, which is
Heb	8: 8	I will conclude a **n** covenant
Heb	9:15	he is mediator of a **n** covenant:
Heb	10:20	by the **n** and living way he opened
Heb	12:24	the mediator of a **n** covenant,
1 Pt	1: 3	his great mercy gave us a **n** birth
2 Pt	3:13	to his promise we await **n** heavens and a **n** earth in which righteousness
1 Jn	2: 7	I am writing no **n** commandment
2 Jn	1: 5	I were writing a **n** commandment
Rv	2:17	upon which is inscribed a **n** name,
Rv	3:12	the city of my God, the **n** Jerusalem,
Rv	3:12	my God, as well as my **n** name.
Rv	5: 9	They sang a **n** hymn: "Worthy are
Rv	14: 3	to be] a **n** hymn before the throne,
Rv	21: 1	Then I saw a **n** heaven and a **n** earth.
Rv	21: 2	saw the holy city, a **n** Jerusalem,
Rv	21: 5	said, "Behold, I make all things **n**."

NEWBORN → BEAR, NEW
1 Pt	2: 2	like **n** infants, long for pure spiritual

NEWNESS → NEW
Rom	6: 4	we too might live in **n** of life.

NEWS
2 Kgs	7: 9	This is a day of good **n**, and we are
Prv	15:30	heart; good **n** invigorates the bones.
Prv	25:25	thirst is good **n** from a far country.
Is	52: 7	Announcing peace, bearing good **n**,
Mt	11: 5	poor have the good **n** proclaimed
Lk	1:19	and to announce to you this good **n**.
Lk	2:10	proclaim to you good **n** of great joy
Lk	3:18	he preached good **n** to the people.
Lk	4:43	I must proclaim the good **n**
Lk	8: 1	and proclaiming the good **n**
Acts	14: 7	continued to proclaim the good **n**.
Acts	14:21	they had proclaimed the good **n**
Rom	10:15	of those who bring [the] good **n**!"

NICANOR'S
1 Mc	7:43	N army was crushed, and he himself
2 Mc	15:37	Since N doings ended in this way,

NICODEMUS
Pharisee who visted Jesus at night (Jn 3). Argued for fair treatment of Jesus (Jn 7:50-52). With Joseph, prepared Jesus for burial (Jn 19:38-42).

NICOLAITANS
Rv	2: 6	you hate the works of the N, which I
Rv	2:15	who hold to the teaching of [the] N.

NIGER
Acts	13: 1	Symeon who was called N,

NIGHT → MIDNIGHT, NIGHTS
Gn	1: 5	"day," and the darkness he called "n."
Gn	1:16	and the lesser one to govern the **n**;
Gn	8:22	and day and **n** shall not cease."
Ex	13:21	at **n** by means of a column of fire
Ex	13:21	they could travel both day and **n**.
Ex	40:38	whereas at **n**, fire was seen
Dt	28:66	and stand in dread both day and **n**,
Jos	1: 8	Recite it by day and by **n**, that you
Jb	35:10	who has given visions in the **n**,
Ps	1: 2	God's law they study day and **n**.
Ps	16: 7	even at **n** my heart exhorts me.
Ps	19: 3	one **n** to the next imparts
Ps	42: 9	that I may sing praise through the **n**,
Ps	63: 7	through the **n** watches I will recall
Ps	74:16	Yours the day and yours the **n**;
Ps	77: 7	In the **n** I meditate in my heart;

Ps	91: 5	You shall not fear the terror of the **n**
Ps	119:55	Even at **n** I remember your name
Ps	121: 6	harm you, nor the moon by **n**.
Ps	136: 9	The moon and stars to rule the **n**,
Prv	31:18	at **n** her lamp is undimmed.
Eccl	2:23	even at **n** his mind is not at rest.
Is	21:11	"Watchman, how much longer the **n**?
Jer	33:20	and my covenant with **n**, so that day
Mt	24:43	the house had known the hour of **n**
Lk	2: 8	and keeping the **n** watch over their
Lk	6:12	and he spent the **n** in prayer to God.
Jn	3: 2	He came to Jesus at **n** and said
Jn	9: 4	N is coming when no one can work.
Jn	11:10	But if one walks at **n**, he stumbles,
1 Cor	11:23	on the **n** he was handed over,
1 Thes	5: 2	the Lord will come like a thief at **n**.
1 Thes	5: 5	We are not of the **n** or of darkness.
Rv	8:12	for a third of the time, as did the **n**.
Rv	20:10	will be tormented day and **n** forever
Rv	21:25	be shut, and there will be no **n** there.
Rv	22: 5	N will be no more, nor will they

NIGHTS → NIGHT
Gn	7:12	forty **n** heavy rain poured down
Ex	24:18	he stayed for forty days and forty **n**.
1 Kgs	19: 8	and forty **n** to the mountain of God,
Jon	2: 1	of the fish three days and three **n**.
Mt	4: 2	He fasted for forty days and forty **n**,
Mt	12:40	of the whale three days and three **n**,
Mt	12:40	of the earth three days and three **n**.

NILE
Gn	41: 2	up out of the N came seven cows,

NIMROD
Gn	10: 9	"Like N, a mighty hunter

NINE
Nm	34:13	has commanded to be given to the **n**
Jos	13: 7	apportion among the **n** tribes
Mk	15:25	It was **n** o'clock in the morning
Acts	2:15	it is only **n** o'clock in the morning.

NINETY
Gn	17:17	Or can Sarah give birth at **n**?"

NINETY-NINE
Gn	17: 1	When Abram was **n** years old,
Lk	15: 4	of them would not leave the **n**

NINEVEH
Tb	1:10	Now after I had been deported to N,
Jon	1: 2	"Set out for the great city of N,
Na	1: 1	Oracle about N. The book
Mt	12:41	the men of N will arise with this

NOAH
Righteous man (Ez 14:14, 20) called to build ark (Gn 6-8; Heb 11:7; 1 Pt 3:20; 2 Pt 2:5). God's covenant with (Gn 9:1-17). Drunkenness of (Gn 9:18-23). Blessed sons, cursed Canaan (Gn 9:24-27). Praised (Sir 44:17-18).

NOB
1 Sm	21: 2	the priest of N, who came trembling

NOBLE → NOBLES
Is	32: 8	But the **n** man plans **n** things, and by **n** things he stands.
1 Cor	1:26	powerful, not many were of **n** birth.
1 Tm	3: 1	the office of bishop desires a **n** task.

NOBLES → NOBLE
Prv	8:16	govern, and **n**; all the rulers of earth.

NOISE
Ex	32:17	Joshua heard the **n** of the people
Is	29: 6	thunder, earthquake, and great **n**,

NONE
Nm	14:23	N of these who have spurned me
Ps	86: 8	N among the gods can equal you,

NOON → AFTERNOON
Mk	15:33	At **n** darkness came over the whole

NORTH
Is	41:25	I have stirred up one from the **n**,
Jer	4: 6	Evil I bring from the **n**, and great
Ez	1: 4	a stormwind came from the **N**,
Dn	11: 6	to the king of the **n** in the interest
Zec	2:10	Flee from the land of the **n**,

NOSE →NOSES
2 Kgs	19:28	I will put my hook in your **n** and my

NOSES →NOSE
Ps	115: 6	but do not hear, **n** but do not smell.

NOSTRILS
Gn	2: 7	blew into his **n** the breath of life,
Gn	7:22	breath of life in its **n** died out.
Ps	18:16	at the storming breath of his **n**.
Is	2:22	alone, in whose **n** is but a breath;

NOTHING
2 Sm	24:24	L**ORD** my God holocausts that cost **n**."
2 Chr	9: 2	and there remained **n** hidden
Jb	1: 9	"Is it for **n** that Job is God-fearing?
Eccl	1: 9	be done. **N** is new under the sun.
Eccl	3:22	that there is **n** better for a man than
Eccl	8:15	because there is **n** good for man
Sir	32:19	Do **n** without counsel, and then you
Sir	39:20	ages; to him there is **n** unexpected.
Is	44: 9	Idol makers all amount to **n**,
Jer	32:17	**n** is impossible to you.
Mt	17:20	**N** will be impossible for you."
Lk	1:37	for **n** will be impossible for God."
Lk	8:17	For there is **n** hidden that will not
Lk	8:17	and **n** secret that will not be known
Lk	12: 2	"There is **n** concealed that will not be
Jn	15: 5	because without me you can do **n**.
1 Cor	2: 2	I resolved to know **n** while I was
1 Cor	13: 2	but do not have love, I am **n**.
1 Tm	6: 7	For we brought **n** into the world,
Heb	7:19	for the law brought **n** to perfection;

NOTORIOUS
Mt	27:16	they had a **n** prisoner called [Jesus]

NOW
Gn	22:12	I know **n** how devoted you are
Ezr	9: 8	"And **n**, but a short time ago,
Ps	20: 7	**N** I know victory is given
Lk	1:48	from **n** on will all ages call me
Jn	2:10	you have kept the good wine until **n**."
Jn	5:25	is **n** here when the dead will hear
Jn	9:25	know is that I was blind and **n** I see."
Jn	13:19	From **n** on I am telling you before it
Jn	13:36	you cannot follow me **n**, though you
Jn	16:12	to tell you, but you cannot bear it **n**.
Rom	3:21	**n** the righteousness of God has been
Rom	5: 9	then, since we are **n** justified by his
Rom	8: 1	**n** there is no condemnation for those
Rom	13:11	it is the hour for you to awake
Rom	13:11	our salvation is nearer **n** than
2 Cor	6: 2	Behold, **n** is a very acceptable time;
2 Cor	6: 2	behold, **n** is the day of salvation.
Eph	2: 2	air, the spirit that is **n** at work
Eph	3: 5	generations as it has **n** been revealed
Col	1:26	**n** it has been manifested to his holy
1 Pt	1: 8	you do not see him **n** yet believe
1 Pt	2:10	but **n** you are God's people; you "had
1 Pt	2:10	but **n** you have received mercy.
1 Jn	2:18	coming, so **n** many antichrists have

NOWHERE →WHERE
Lk	9:58	Son of Man has **n** to rest his head."

NULLIFY
Rom	3: 3	Will their infidelity **n** the fidelity
Gal	2:21	I do not **n** the grace of God;

NUMBER →NUMBERED, NUMBERS, NUMEROUS
Nm	1:45	The total **n** of the Israelites
Dt	32: 8	after the **n** of the sons of God;
Ps	105:12	When they were few in **n**, a handful,
Acts	2:47	their **n** those who were being saved.
Acts	6: 1	as the **n** of disciples continued

Acts	11:21	a great **n** who believed turned
Rom	11:25	part, until the full **n** of the Gentiles
Rv	6:11	while longer until the **n** was filled
Rv	7: 4	I heard the **n** of those who had been
Rv	13:18	who understands can calculate the **n**
Rv	13:18	for it is a **n** that stands for a person.
Rv	13:18	His **n** is six hundred and sixty-six.

NUMBERED →NUMBER
2 Sm	24:10	David regretted having **n** the people,
Dn	5:26	God has **n** your kingdom and put

NUMBERS →NUMBER
Ps	147: 4	**N** all the stars, calls each of them
Acts	9:31	of the holy Spirit it grew in **n**.

NUMEROUS →NUMBER
Ex	1: 9	"Look how **n** and powerful
Zec	10: 8	them they will be as **n** as before.

NURSE →NURSED, NURSING
Gn	21: 7	added, "that Sarah would **n** children!
Ex	2: 7	of the Hebrew women to **n** the child
Ru	4:16	him on her lap, and became his **n**.
Is	66:11	That you may **n** with delight at her

NURSED →NURSE
Ex	2: 9	therefore took the child and **n** it.
Lk	11:27	you and the breasts at which you **n**."
Lk	23:29	bore and the breasts that never **n**.'

NURSING →NURSE
Lk	21:23	women and **n** mothers in those days,

O

OAK →OAKS
Ez	6:13	every green tree and leafy **o**,

OAKS →OAK
Ps	29: 9	The voice of the L**ORD** twists the **o**

OATH
Gn	21:31	the two of them took an **o** there.
Gn	26: 3	in fulfillment of the **o** that I swore
Nm	30: 3	binds himself under **o** to a pledge
Dt	7: 8	his fidelity to the **o** he had sworn
Jos	2:17	we will fulfill the **o** you made us
1 Sm	14:24	Saul swore a very rash **o** that day,
Ps	15: 4	Who keeps an **o** despite the cost,
Ps	132:11	The L**ORD** swore an **o** to David,
Eccl	8: 2	king, and in view of your **o** to God,
Mt	26:72	Again he denied it with an **o**, "I do
Heb	7:20	others became priests without an **o**,

OBADIAH
1. Believer who sheltered 100 prophets from Jezebel (1 Kgs 18:1-16).
2. Prophet against Edom (Ob 1).

OBED
Ru	4:22	**O** was the father of Jesse, and Jesse
Lk	3:32	Jesse, the son of **O**, the son of Boaz,

OBED-EDOM
2 Sm	6:12	blessed the family of **O** and all that
1 Chr	13:13	instead to the house of **O** the Gittite.

OBEDIENCE →OBEY
Rom	1: 5	to bring about the **o** of faith,
Rom	5:19	so through the **o** of one the many
Rom	6:16	to death, or of **o**, which leads
Rom	15:18	me to lead the Gentiles to **o** by word
Rom	16:19	For while your **o** is known to all,
Rom	16:26	nations to bring about the **o** of faith,
2 Cor	7:15	as he remembers the **o** of all of you,
2 Cor	10: 6	once your **o** is complete.
Heb	5: 8	he learned **o** from what he suffered;
1 Pt	1:22	you have purified yourselves by **o**

OBEDIENT →OBEY
Ps	103:20	and attentive, **o** to every command.
Lk	2:51	to Nazareth, and was **o** to them;
Acts	6: 7	priests were becoming **o** to the faith.
Rom	6:16	yourselves to someone as **o** slaves,

Rom	6:17	you have become **o** from the heart
2 Cor	2: 9	whether you were **o** in everything.
Phil	2: 8	himself, becoming **o** to death,
Ti	3: 1	to be **o**, to be open to every good
1 Pt	1:14	Like **o** children, do not act

OBEY → OBEDIENCE, OBEDIENT, OBEYED, OBEYING, OBEYS

Dt	21:18	will not **o** them even though they
Jos	24:24	the LORD, our God, and **o** his voice."
Jgs	3: 4	they would **o** the commandments
Ezr	7:26	Whoever does not **o** the law of your
1 Mc	2:22	We will not **o** the words of the king
Jer	11: 7	I warned your fathers to **o** my voice,
Jer	42: 6	we will **o** the command of the LORD,
Mt	8:27	even the winds and the sea **o**?"
Acts	5:29	"We must **o** God rather than men.
Acts	5:32	God has given to those who **o** him."
Rom	6:12	bodies so that you **o** their desires.
Rom	6:16	you are slaves of the one you **o**,
Eph	6: 1	**o** your parents [in the Lord], for this
Col	3:20	**o** your parents in everything,
Col	3:22	Slaves, **o** your human masters
2 Thes	3:14	If anyone does not **o** our word as
Heb	5: 9	eternal salvation for all who **o** him,
Heb	13:17	**O** your leaders and defer to them,
1 Pt	4:17	for those who fail to **o** the gospel

OBEYED → OBEY

Gn	22:18	this because you **o** my command."
Gn	26: 5	this because Abraham **o** me,
Heb	11: 8	faith Abraham **o** when he was called
1 Pt	3: 6	thus Sarah **o** Abraham, calling him

OBEYING → OBEY

Dt	11:27	a blessing for **o** the commandments

OBEYS → OBEY

Sir	3: 6	he **o** the LORD who brings comfort

OBSCENITY

Eph	5: 4	no **o** or silly or suggestive talk,

OBSERVE → OBSERVING

Lv	20: 8	therefore, to **o** what I, the LORD,
Dt	4: 6	**O** them carefully, for thus will you
Dt	11:22	**o** all these commandments I enjoin
Dt	26:16	commands you to **o** these statutes
Dt	26:16	to **o** them with all your heart
1 Mc	2:67	gather about you all who **o** the law,

OBSERVING → OBSERVE

Gal	4:10	You are **o** days, months, seasons,

OBSOLETE

Heb	8:13	covenant, he declares the first one **o**.
Heb	8:13	what has become **o** and has grown

OBSTACLE

1 Cor	9:12	so as not to place an **o** to the gospel

OBSTINATE

Ex	4:21	I will make him **o**, however, so that
Ex	7:13	Pharaoh, however, was **o** and would not
Ex	7:22	So Pharaoh remained **o** and would not
Ex	8:15	Yet Pharaoh remained **o** and would not
Ex	9:12	But the LORD made Pharaoh **o**,
Ex	10:20	the LORD made Pharaoh **o**,
Ex	10:27	But the LORD made Pharaoh **o**,
Ex	11:10	the LORD made Pharaoh **o**,
Ex	14: 4	Thus will I make Pharaoh so **o** that
Ex	14:17	But I will make the Egyptians so **o** that

OBTAIN → OBTAINED, OBTAINING

2 Tm	2:10	they too may **o** the salvation that is

OBTAINED → OBTAIN

Heb	8: 6	Now he has **o** so much more

OBTAINING → OBTAIN

Heb	9:12	blood, thus **o** eternal redemption.

OBVIOUS

Gal	5:19	Now the works of the flesh are **o**:

OCCUPY

Dt	11:31	enter and **o** the land which the LORD,

Neh	2: 8	wall and the house that I shall **o**."

ODED

2 Chr	28: 9	of the LORD by the name of **O**.

ODOR

Gn	8:21	When the LORD smelled the sweet **o**,
Tb	8: 3	repelled by the **o** of the fish,

OFFEND → OFFENSE, OFFENSES

Jb	34:31	"I was misguided; I will **o** no more.

OFFENSE → OFFEND

Dt	19:15	or any **o** of which he may be guilty;
Prv	19:11	and it is his glory to overlook an **o**.
Mt	11: 6	blessed is the one who takes no **o**
Mk	6: 3	with us?" And they took **o** at him.

OFFENSES → OFFEND

Prv	10:12	up disputes, but love covers all **o**.

OFFER → OFFERED, OFFERING, OFFERINGS

Gn	22: 2	There you shall **o** him up as
Ex	29:38	this is what you shall **o** on the altar:
Dt	12:14	but **o** them up in the place
1 Mc	2:23	sight of all to **o** sacrifice on the altar
Ps	4: 6	**O** fitting sacrifice and trust
Sir	38:11	**O** your sweet-smelling oblation
Mt	5:24	and then come and **o** your gift.
Heb	9:25	that he might **o** himself repeatedly,
Heb	13:15	let us continually **o** God a sacrifice

OFFERED → OFFER

Gn	22:13	**o** it up as a holocaust in place of his
Ex	40:29	tent, and **o** holocausts and cereal
1 Sm	13: 9	offerings," and he **o** up the holocaust.
1 Mc	4:53	**o** sacrifice according to the law
Heb	5: 7	he **o** prayers and supplications
Heb	7:27	that once for all when he **o** himself.
Heb	9:14	eternal spirit **o** himself unblemished
Heb	11: 4	By faith Abel **o** to God a sacrifice
Heb	11:17	when put to the test, **o** up Isaac,

OFFERING → OFFER

Gn	4: 4	with favor on Abel and his **o**,
Ex	29:14	the camp, since this is a sin **o**.
Ex	29:24	them as a wave **o** before the LORD.
Ps	40: 7	Sacrifice and **o** you do not want;
Ps	51:18	a burnt **o** you would not accept.
Sir	30:19	What good is an **o** to an idol
Sir	35: 1	commandments sacrifices a peace **o**.
Is	53:10	If he gives his life as an **o** for sin,
Eph	5: 2	over for us as a sacrificial **o** to God
Heb	10:14	one **o** he has made perfect forever

OFFERINGS → OFFER

1 Sm	13: 9	"Bring me the holocaust and peace **o**,"
1 Chr	21:26	offered up holocausts and peace **o**.
Is	1:13	Bring no more worthless **o**;
Mal	3: 8	do we rob you?" In tithes and in **o**!
Mk	12:33	is worth more than all burnt **o**
Heb	10: 6	and sin **o** you took no delight in.

OFFICERS

Ex	15: 4	the elite of his **o** were submerged

OFFSPRING

Gn	3:15	and between your **o** and hers;
Is	44: 3	will pour out my spirit upon your **o**,
Dn	13:56	"**O** of Canaan, not of Judah,"
Mal	2:15	does that one require but godly **o**?
Acts	17:29	Since therefore we are the **o** of God,

OFTEN

Jn	18: 2	because Jesus had **o** met there

OG

Nm	21:33	But **O**, king of Bashan,
Dt	31: 4	just as he dealt with Sihon and **O**,
Ps	136:20	**O**, king of Bashan, God's love

OHOLIAB

Craftsman who worked on the tabernacle (Ex 31:6; 35:34; 36:1-2; 38:23).

OIL

Gn	28:18	stone, and poured o on top if it.
Gn	35:14	he made a libation and poured out o.
Ex	25: 6	o for the light;
Ex	25: 6	spices for the anointing o
Ex	29: 7	take the anointing o and anoint him
Ex	30:25	blend them into sacred anointing o,
Dt	14:23	wine and o, as well as the firstlings
1 Sm	10: 1	Samuel poured o on Saul's head;
1 Sm	16:13	with the horn of o in hand,
1 Kgs	17:16	nor the jug of o run dry, as the LORD
2 Kgs	4: 6	And then the o stopped.
Ps	23: 5	You anoint my head with o; my cup
Ps	45: 8	with the o of gladness above your
Ps	104:15	hearts, O to make our faces gleam,
Prv	5: 3	and her mouth is smoother than o;
Is	61: 3	To give them o of gladness in place
Jl	2:24	vats shall overflow with wine and o.
Mt	25: 3	their lamps, brought no o with them,
Heb	1: 9	with the o of gladness above your
Jas	5:14	anoint [him] with o in the name

OLD →OLDER

Gn	17:12	when he is eight days o, shall be
Gn	17:17	to a man who is a hundred years o?
Gn	21: 7	I have borne him a son in his o age."
Dt	32: 7	Think back on the days of o,
Ps	71: 9	Do not cast me aside in my o age;
Ps	74:12	you, God, are my king from of o,
Prv	22: 6	even when he is o, he will not
Sir	8: 6	Insult no man when he is o, for some of us, too, will grow o.
Sir	9:10	Discard not an o friend, for the new
Lam	5:21	us anew such days as we had of o.
Jl	3: 1	your o men shall dream dreams,
Mi	5: 1	Whose origin is from of o,
Mk	2:22	pours new wine into o wineskins.
Jn	3: 4	person once grown o be born again?
Acts	2:17	your o men shall dream dreams.
Rom	4:19	he was almost a hundred years o)
1 Cor	5: 7	Clear out the o yeast, so that you
2 Cor	5:17	the o things have passed away;
Eph	4:22	you should put away the o self
1 Jn	2: 7	but an o commandment that you had
1 Jn	2: 7	The o commandment is the word

OLDER →OLD

1 Tm	5: 1	Do not rebuke an o man, but appeal
1 Tm	5: 2	o women as mothers, and younger
Ti	2: 2	that o men should be temperate,
Ti	2: 3	o women should be reverent in their

OLIVE →OLIVES

Gn	8:11	in its bill was a plucked-off o leaf!
Jgs	9: 8	So they said to the o tree,
Ps	52:10	I, like an o tree in the house of God,
Jer	11:16	A spreading o tree,
Hb	3:17	Though the yield of the o fail
Zec	4: 3	and beside it are two o trees,
Rom	11:17	a wild o shoot, were grafted in their
Rom	11:17	to share in the rich root of the o tree,
Rom	11:24	from what is by nature a wild o tree,
Rom	11:24	grafted back into their own o tree.
Rv	11: 4	These are the two o trees

OLIVES →OLIVE

Zec	14: 4	feet shall rest upon the Mount of O,
Zec	14: 4	The Mount of O shall be cleft
Mt	24: 3	he was sitting on the Mount of O,
Jas	3:12	produce o, or a grapevine figs?

OMEGA

Rv	1: 8	"I am the Alpha and the O,"
Rv	21: 6	I [am] the Alpha and the O,
Rv	22:13	I am the Alpha and the O, the first

OMENS

Sir	34: 5	o and dreams all are unreal;

OMRI

King of Israel (1 Kgs 16:21-26).

ONAN

Gn	38: 8	Then Judah said to O,
Gn	46:12	O had died in the land of Canaan;

ONCE →ONE

Ex	30:10	O a year Aaron shall perform
Ex	30:10	atonement is to be made o a year
Jb	40: 5	Though I have spoken o, I will not
Lam	1: 1	she is now, the o crowded city!
Rom	6:10	death, he died to sin o and for all;
Rom	7: 9	I o lived outside the law,
Eph	5: 8	For you were o darkness, but now
Heb	7:27	he did that o for all when he offered
Heb	9:12	he entered o for all
Heb	9:27	appointed that human beings die o,
1 Pt	2:10	O you were "no people" but now you
1 Pt	3:18	For Christ also suffered for sins o,

ONE →EVERYONE, FIRST, ONCE, ONES

Gn	2:24	and the two of them become o body.
Jos	23:10	O of you puts to flight a thousand,
Ps	14: 3	Not o does what is right, not even o.
Eccl	4: 9	Two are better than o: they get
Is	30:17	shall tremble at the threat of o;
Ez	34:23	I will appoint o shepherd over them
Ez	37:22	I will make them o nation
Ez	37:22	there shall be o prince for them all.
Zec	14: 9	the LORD shall be the only o, and his name the only o.
Mal	2:10	Have we not all the o Father?
Mal	2:10	Has not the o God created us?
Mk	10: 8	and the two shall become o flesh.'
Mk	10: 8	they are no longer two but o flesh.
Mk	10:21	to him, "You are lacking in o thing.
Lk	10:42	There is need of only o thing.
Jn	1:18	No o has ever seen God. The only
Jn	10:16	voice, and there will be o flock,
Jn	10:30	The Father and I are o."
Jn	17:22	so that they may be o, as we are o,
Rom	3:10	is written: "There is no o just, not o,
Rom	5:15	o person's transgression the many
Rom	5:15	the o person Jesus Christ overflow
1 Cor	6:16	to a prostitute becomes o body
1 Cor	6:16	"the two," it says, "will become o flesh."
1 Cor	8: 4	and that "there is no God but o."
1 Cor	10:17	Because the loaf of bread is o, we, though many, are o body, for we all partake of the o loaf.
1 Cor	12:13	in o Spirit we were all baptized into o body,
1 Cor	12:13	were all given to drink of o Spirit.
Eph	4: 5	o Lord, o faith, o baptism;
1 Tm	2: 5	For there is o God. There is also o
2 Pt	3: 8	But do not ignore this o fact,
2 Pt	3: 8	the Lord o day is like a thousand
2 Pt	3: 8	and a thousand years like o day.

ONES →ONE

Dt	33: 3	But all his holy o were in his hand;
1 Chr	16:13	sons of Jacob, his chosen o!
Mt	18: 6	one of these little o who believe
Jude	1:14	has come with his countless holy o

ONESIMUS

Col	4: 9	together with O, a trustworthy
Phlm	1:10	I urge you on behalf of my child O,

ONIAS

1 Mc	12: 7	sent to the high priest O from Arius,
2 Mc	3: 1	of the piety of the high priest O
2 Mc	4:36	to see him about the murder of O.

ONIONS

Nm	11: 5	the leeks, the o, and the garlic.

ONLY

Gn	7:23	O Noah and those with him
Gn	22: 2	"Take your son Isaac, your o one,
1 Kgs	18:22	"I am the o surviving prophet
Ps	37: 8	not be provoked; it brings o harm.
Mk	13:32	nor the Son, but o the Father.
Jn	1:14	the glory as of the Father's o Son,
Jn	1:18	The o Son, God, who is
Jn	3:16	the world that he gave his o Son,

1 Tm   1:17   invisible, the o God,
1 Jn   4: 9   God sent his o Son into the world so

ONYX
Ex   28: 9   "Get two o stones and engrave

OPEN →OPENED, OPENLY, OPENS
Dt   28:12   The LORD will o up for you his rich
Ps   51:17   Lord, o my lips; my mouth will
Ps   78: 2   I will o my mouth in story,
Ps   118:19   O the gates of victory; I will enter
Ps   145:16   You o wide your hand and satisfy
Prv   15:11   and the abyss lie o before the LORD;
Prv   27: 5   Better is an o rebuke than a love
Song   5: 2   "O to me, my sister, my beloved,
Is   42: 7   To o the eyes of the blind, to bring
Mal   3:10   Shall I not o for you the floodgates
Mt   13:35   "I will o my mouth in parables, I will
Mt   17:27   O its mouth and you will find a coin
Rv   3: 8   I have left an o door before you,
Rv   4: 1   this I had a vision of an o door
Rv   5: 2   "Who is worthy to o the scroll

OPENED →OPEN
Gn   3: 7   the eyes of both of them were o,
Nm   16:32   and the earth o its mouth
Neh   8: 5   Ezra o the scroll so that all
Neh   8: 5   and, as he o it, all the people rose.
Is   35: 5   Then will the eyes of the blind be o,
Is   53: 7   and o not his mouth; Like a lamb
Is   53: 7   he was silent and o not his mouth.
Dn   7:10   convened, and the books were o.
Mt   3:16   the heavens were o [for him],
Lk   11: 9   knock and the door will be o to you.
Lk   24:45   he o their minds to understand
Acts 10:11   He saw heaven o and something
Heb   10:20   living way he o for us through
Rv   11:19   Then God's temple in heaven was o,
Rv   20:12   the throne, and scrolls were o.
Rv   20:12   Then another scroll was o, the book

OPENLY →OPEN
Jn   7:26   look, he is speaking o and they say

OPENS →OPEN
Rv   3: 7   who o and no one shall close,

OPHIR
1 Kgs 10:11   which used to bring gold from O,
Is   13:12   than pure gold, men, than gold of O.

OPPONENTS
2 Tm   2:25   correcting o with kindness. It may

OPPORTUNITY
Mt   26:16   he looked for an o to hand him over.
Rom   7: 8   finding an o in the commandment,
2 Cor   5:12   but giving you an o to boast of us,
Gal   5:13   do not use this freedom as an o
Phil   1:22   about me but lacked an o.
Heb   11:15   they would have had o to return.

OPPOSE →OPPOSED, OPPOSES
2 Tm   3: 8   o the truth—people of depraved mind,

OPPOSED →OPPOSE
Gal   3:21   then o to the promises [of God]?
Gal   5:17   these are o to each other, so that you
2 Tm   3: 8   as Jannes and Jambres o Moses,

OPPOSES →OPPOSE
2 Thes 2: 4   who o and exalts himself
1 Pt   5: 5   one another, for: "God o the proud

OPPRESS →OPPRESSED, OPPRESSES, OPPRESSING,
     OPPRESSION, OPPRESSOR
Ex   1:11   set over the Israelites to o them
Ex   22:20   "You shall not molest or o an alien,
Ps   105:14   He let no one o them; for their sake
Zec   7:10   Do not o the widow or the orphan,

OPPRESSED →OPPRESS
Gn   15:13   and o for four hundred years.
Ex   1:12   Yet the more they were o, the more
Jdt   9:11   the helper of the o, the supporter

Ps   9:10   The LORD is a stronghold for the o,
Ps   103: 6   deeds, brings justice to all the o.
Ps   146: 7   secures justice for the o, gives food
Sir   4: 9   Deliver the o from the hand
Lk   4:18   to the blind, to let the o go free,

OPPRESSES →OPPRESS
Prv   28: 3   A rich man who o the poor is like
Ez   18:12   o the poor and needy,

OPPRESSING →OPPRESS
Jas   2: 6   Are not the rich o you? And do they

OPPRESSION →OPPRESS
Dt   26: 7   our affliction, our toil and our o.
Ps   119:134 Free me from human o, that I may
Ez   45: 9   Put away violence and o, and do

OPPRESSOR →OPPRESS
Ps   72: 4   save the poor and crush the o.
Is   51:13   of the fury of the o; But when he
Jer   22: 3   the victim from the hand of his o.

ORACLE
Nm   23: 7   Then Balaam gave voice to his o:

ORDAIN →FOREORDAINED, ORDAINED, ORDINATION
Ex   29: 9   thus shall you o Aaron and his sons.

ORDAINED →ORDAIN
Nm   3: 3   the anointed priests who were o

ORDER →ORDERLY, ORDERS
Mk   7: 9   God in o to uphold your tradition!
Jn   10:17   because I lay down my life in o
Rom   7: 4   the dead in o that we might bear
Heb   5:10   according to the o of Melchizedek.
Heb   7:11   according to the o of Melchizedek.
Heb   7:11   according to the o of Aaron?

ORDERLY →ORDER
Lk   1: 3   write it down in an o sequence

ORDERS →ORDER
Acts   5:28   "We gave you strict o [did we not?]

ORDINARY
Acts   4:13   them to be uneducated, o men,

ORDINATION →ORDAIN
Ex   29:22   right thigh, since this is the o ram;

OREB
Jgs   7:25   two princes of Midian, O and Zeeb,
Jgs   7:25   killing O at the rock of O and Zeeb
Ps   83:12   Make their nobles like O and Zeeb,

ORIGIN
Mt   21:26   say, "Of human o," we fear the crowd,
Acts   5:38   or this activity is of human o, it will

ORNAMENTS
Ex   33: 6   the Israelites laid aside their o.

ORNAN →=ARAUNAH
1 Chr 21:15   threshing floor of O the Jebusite.
2 Chr 3: 1   threshing-floor of O the Jebusite.

ORPAH
Ru   1: 4   one named O, the other Ruth.

ORPHAN →ORPHANS
Ex   22:21   shall not wrong any widow or o.
Hos   14: 4   for in you the o finds compassion."

ORPHANS →ORPHAN
Jn   14:18   I will not leave you o;
Jas   1:27   to care for o and widows in their

OTHER →OTHERS
Ex   20: 3   shall not have o gods besides me.
Ex   23:13   mention the name of any o god;
Dt   4:35   the LORD is God and there is no o.
Jgs   2:19   following o gods in service
1 Sm   8:20   We too must be like o nations,
2 Kgs 17: 7   and because they venerated o gods.
2 Chr 2: 4   our God is greater than all o gods.
Ps   147:20   God has not done this for o nations;

Is	45: 5	I am the LORD and there is no o,
Dn	3:96	there is no o God who can rescue
Mt	6:24	will either hate one and love the o,
Mt	6:24	be devoted to one and despise the o.
Lk	17:34	one will be taken, the o left.
Jn	20:30	Now Jesus did many o signs
Jn	21:25	also many o things that Jesus did,
1 Cor	3:11	can lay a foundation o than the one
2 Pt	3:16	just as they do the o scriptures.

OTHERS → OTHER
Mt	7:12	o whatever you would have them do
Lk	6:31	Do to o as you would have them do
Phil	2: 3	humbly regard o as more important

OTHNIEL
Nephew of Caleb (Jos 15:15-19; Jgs 1:12-15). Judge who freed Israel from Aram (Jgs 3:7-11).

OUGHT
Rom	8:26	do not know how to pray as we o,
Rom	12: 3	himself more highly than one o
2 Pt	3:11	what sort of persons o [you] to be,
1 Jn	3:16	so we o to lay down our lives
3 Jn	1: 8	we o to support such persons,

OUTCOME → COME
Is	41:22	And know their o; or declare to us
Heb	13: 7	Consider the o of their way of life

OUTSIDE → OUTSIDERS
Prv	22:13	The sluggard says, "A lion is o;
Dn	14: 7	"it is only clay inside and bronze o;
Lk	11:39	Although you cleanse the o
Lk	13:33	a prophet should die o of Jerusalem.'
1 Cor	5:13	God will judge those o.
Heb	13:12	Jesus also suffered o the gate,
Rv	22:15	O are the dogs, the sorcerers,

OUTSIDERS → OUTSIDE
Col	4: 5	yourselves wisely toward o,
1 Thes	4:12	yourselves properly toward o
1 Tm	3: 7	have a good reputation among o,

OUTSTRETCHED → STRETCH
Ex	6: 6	I will rescue you by my o arm
Dt	4:34	with his strong hand and o arm,
1 Kgs	8:42	your mighty hand and your o arm),
Ps	136:12	With mighty hand and o arm,
Is	3:16	and walk with necks o
Jer	27: 5	by my great power, with my o arm;
Jer	32:17	your great might, with your o arm;
Ez	20:33	with a mighty hand and o arm,

OUTWARDLY
Rom	2:28	One is not a Jew o.

OVER
Ex	12:13	Seeing the blood, I will pass o you;
Ex	12:23	the LORD will pass o that door
Ps	1: 6	The LORD watches o the way
Ps	8: 7	have given them rule o the works
Ps	145:20	LORD, watch o all who love you,
Mk	15:15	handed him o to be crucified.

OVERCOME
Jn	1: 5	and the darkness has not o it.

OVERFLOW → OVERFLOWS
Jl	2:24	and the vats shall o with wine

OVERFLOWS → OVERFLOW
Ps	23: 5	anoint my head with oil; my cup o.

OVERJOYED → JOY
Acts	12:14	She was so o when she recognized

OVERLOOK → OVERLOOKED
Prv	19:11	and it is his glory to o an offense.
Heb	6:10	is not unjust so as to o your work

OVERLOOKED → OVERLOOK
Acts	17:30	God has o the times of ignorance,

OVERSEERS
Acts	20:28	the holy Spirit has appointed you o,

Phil	1: 1	in Philippi, with the o and ministers:

OVERSHADOW → OVERSHADOWING
Lk	1:35	power of the Most High will o you.

OVERSHADOWING → OVERSHADOW
Heb	9: 5	the cherubim of glory o the place

OVERTAKE
Sir	7: 1	Do no evil, and evil will not o you;

OVERTHREW
Gn	19:25	He o those cities and the whole

OVERTURNED
Mk	11:15	He o the tables of the money

OVERWHELMED → OVERWHELMING
2 Cor	2: 7	or else the person may be o

OVERWHELMING → OVERWHELMED
Prv	27: 4	Anger is relentless, and wrath o—
Is	28:15	When the o scourge passes, it will

OWE → OWES
Mt	18:28	demanding, 'Pay back what you o.'
Rom	13: 8	O nothing to anyone, except to love

OWES → OWE
Phlm	1:18	you any injustice or o you anything,

OWN → LANDOWNER, OWNER
Gn	15: 4	heir; your o issue shall be your heir."
Ex	32:13	you swore to them by your o self,
Dt	18:15	you from among your o kinsmen;
Dt	24:16	for his o guilt shall a man be put
1 Sm	13:14	sought out a man after his o heart
Ps	141:10	their o nets let all the wicked fall,
Prv	3: 7	Be not wise in your o eyes,
Prv	26:12	You see a man wise in his o eyes?
Is	48:11	my sake, for my o sake, I do this;
Is	53: 6	each following his o way;
Jer	31:30	but through his o fault only shall
Ez	33: 4	shall be responsible for his o death.
Lk	6:42	the wooden beam in your o eye?
Jn	1:11	He came to what was his o, but his o people did not accept him.
Jn	10:18	from me, but I lay it down on my o.
Rom	8:32	He who did not spare his o Son
1 Cor	6:19	God, and that you are not your o?
Phil	2: 4	looking out not for his o interests,

OWNER → OWN
Mt	21:40	What will the o of the vineyard do

OX → OXEN
Ex	20:17	or female slave, nor his o or ass,
Dt	22:10	You shall not plow with an o
Dt	25: 4	"You shall not muzzle an o when it is
Prv	7:22	like an o that is led to slaughter;
Is	11: 7	rest; the lion shall eat hay like the o.
Is	65:25	and the lion shall eat hay like the o
Ez	1:10	and on the left side the face of an o,
Lk	13:15	of you on the sabbath untie his o
1 Cor	9: 9	shall not muzzle an o while it is
1 Tm	5:18	"You shall not muzzle an o when it is

OXEN → OX
1 Kgs	19:20	Elisha left the o, ran after Elijah,
Lk	14:19	'I have purchased five yoke of o
1 Cor	9: 9	the grain." Is God concerned about o,

P

PAGANS
1 Cor	12: 2	how, when you were p, you were

PAID → PAY
Mt	26:15	They p him thirty pieces of silver,

PAIN → PAINFUL, PAINS
Gn	3:16	in p shall you bring forth children.
Jb	6:10	could exult through unremitting p,
Jb	33:19	a man is chastened on his bed by p
Jer	15:18	Why is my p continuous, my wound
Jn	16:21	no longer remembers the p because

1 Pt	2:19	For whenever anyone bears the **p**
Rv	21: 4	wailing or **p**, [for] the old order has

PAINFUL →PAIN
2 Cor	2: 1	to you again in **p** circumstances.

PAINS →PAIN
Rom	8:22	groaning in labor **p** even until now;
1 Thes	5: 3	them, like labor **p** upon a pregnant

PAIRS
Gn	7: 2	take with you seven **p**, a male

PALACES
2 Chr	36:19	set all its **p** afire, and destroyed all
Hos	8:14	and built **p**. Judah, too, has fortified
Lk	7:25	sumptuously are found in royal **p**.

PALE
Is	29:22	of, nor shall his face grow **p**.
Jer	30: 6	all their faces turned deathly **p**?
Rv	6: 8	and there was a **p** green horse.

PALM →PALMS
Ex	15:27	springs of water and seventy **p** trees,
Jgs	4: 5	used to sit under Deborah's **p** tree,
1 Kgs	6:29	carved figures of cherubim, **p** trees,
Ps	92:13	just shall flourish like the **p** tree,
Jn	12:13	they took **p** branches and went
Rv	7: 9	holding **p** branches in their hands.

PALMS →PALM
Is	49:16	the **p** of my hands I have written

PANELED
Hg	1: 4	you to dwell in your own **p** houses,

PANGS
Gn	3:16	he said: "I will intensify the **p** of your
Is	13: 8	**P** and sorrows take hold of them,

PANIC
1 Sm	14:15	Then **p** spread to the army
1 Sm	14:15	the **p** was beyond human endurance.
Jdt	14: 3	do not find him, **p** will seize them,

PAPER
2 Jn	1:12	I do not intend to use **p** and ink.

PAPYRUS
Ex	2: 3	she took a **p** basket, daubed it

PARABLE →PARABLES
Mt	13:18	"Hear then the **p** of the sower.
Mt	15:15	him in reply, "Explain [this] **p** to us."
Mt	21:33	"Hear another **p**. There was
Lk	20:19	that he had addressed this **p** to them.

PARABLES →PARABLE; See also JESUS: PARABLES
Mt	13:35	"I will open my mouth in **p**, I will
Lk	8:10	they are made known through **p** so

PARADISE
Lk	23:43	you, today you will be with me in **P**."
2 Cor	12: 4	was caught up into **P** and heard

PARALYTIC →PARALYZED
Mt	9: 2	to him a **p** lying on a stretcher.
Mt	9: 2	their faith, he said to the **p**, "Courage,

PARALYZED →PARALYTIC
Acts	8: 7	many **p** and crippled people were

PARAN
Gn	21:21	his home in the wilderness of **P**.
Nm	10:12	came to rest in the desert of **P**.
Hb	3: 3	the Holy One from Mount **P**.

PARCHED
Ps	143: 6	I thirst for you like a **p** land.

PARCHMENTS
2 Tm	4:13	papyrus rolls, and especially the **p**.

PARDON
Ex	34: 9	yet **p** our wickedness and sins,
Nm	14:19	**P**, then, the wickedness of this people
Dt	29:19	LORD will never consent to **p** him.
2 Chr	30:18	the LORD, who is good, grant **p**

Jb	7:21	Why do you not **p** my offense,

PARENTS
Prv	19:14	are an inheritance from **p**,
Mk	13:12	children will rise up against **p**
Lk	2:27	and when the **p** brought in the child
Lk	18:29	or brothers or **p** or children
Lk	21:16	You will even be handed over by **p**,
Jn	9: 3	"Neither he nor his **p** sinned; it is so
Rom	1:30	and rebellious toward their **p**.
2 Cor	12:14	ought not to save for their **p**, but **p**
Eph	6: 1	Children, obey your **p** [in the Lord],
Col	3:20	Children, obey your **p** in everything,
1 Tm	5: 4	and to make recompense to their **p**,
2 Tm	3: 2	disobedient to their **p**, ungrateful,

PARTAKE
1 Cor	10:17	body, for we all **p** of the one loaf.

PARTIAL →PARTIALITY, PARTLY, PARTS
Prv	18: 5	It is not good to be **p** to the guilty,
1 Cor	13:10	perfect comes, the **p** will pass away.

PARTIALITY →PARTIAL
2 Chr	19: 7	no injustice, no **p**, no bribe-taking."
Jb	13: 8	Is it for him that you show **p**?
Jb	13:10	you if even in secret you show **p**.
Prv	24:23	To show **p** in judgment is not good.
Prv	28:21	To show **p** is never good: for even
Wis	6: 7	For the Lord of all shows no **p**,
Mal	2: 9	ways, but show **p** in your decisions.
Rom	2:11	There is no **p** with God.
Gal	2: 6	God shows no **p** of repute made me
Eph	6: 9	and that with him there is no **p**.
Jas	2: 1	show no **p** as you adhere to the faith

PARTLY →PART
Dn	2:33	legs iron, its feet **p** iron and **p** tile.

PARTNERSHIP
2 Cor	6:14	For what **p** do righteousness

PARTS →PARTIAL
Nm	18:29	and from the best **p**, you are

PASHHUR
Priest; opponent of Jeremiah (Jer 20:1-6).

PASS →PASSED, PASSING
Ex	12:13	Seeing the blood, I will **p** over you;
Ex	12:23	the LORD will **p** over that door
Ex	33:19	make all my beauty **p** before you,
Nm	20:17	Kindly let us **p** through your
Nm	21:22	"Let us **p** through your country.
Ps	105:19	Till his prediction came to **p**,
Is	43: 2	When you **p** through the water,
Jer	22: 8	Many people will **p** by this city
Lam	1:12	"Come, all you who **p** by the way,
Am	5:17	when I **p** through your midst,
Mt	24:35	Heaven and earth will **p** away,
Mt	24:35	but my words will not **p** away.
Mk	14:35	it were possible the hour might **p**
2 Pt	3:10	then the heavens will **p** away

PASSED →PASS
Gn	15:17	which **p** between those pieces.
Ex	12:27	LORD, who **p** over the houses
Ex	33:22	you with my hand until I have **p** by.
Ex	34: 6	Thus the LORD **p** before him
Ps	37:36	When I **p** by again, they were gone;
Lk	10:32	him, he **p** by on the opposite side.
1 Cor	10: 1	the cloud and all **p** through the sea,
2 Cor	5:17	the old things have **p** away; behold,
1 Jn	3:14	We know that we have **p** from death
Rv	21: 1	and the former earth had **p** away,
Rv	21: 4	pain, [for] the old order has **p** away."

PASSING →PASS
1 Kgs	19:11	the LORD; the LORD will be **p** by."
Wis	2: 5	our lifetime is the **p** of a shadow;
1 Cor	7:31	world in its present form is **p** away.
1 Jn	2: 8	for the darkness is **p** away,
1 Jn	2:17	and its enticement are **p** away.

PASSION →PASSIONS
Col   3: 5   immorality, impurity, **p**, evil desire,

PASSIONS →PASSION
Rom   7: 5   our sinful **p**, awakened by the law,
Gal   5:24   have crucified their flesh with its **p**

PASSOVER
Ex   12:11   are in flight. It is the **P** of the LORD.
Nm   9: 2   to celebrate the **P** at the prescribed
Dt   16: 1   Abib by keeping the **P** of the LORD,
Jos   5:10   they celebrated the **P** on the evening
2 Kgs 23:21   people to observe the **P** of the LORD,
2 Chr 30: 1   to celebrate the **P** in honor
Ezr   6:19   The exiles kept the **P**
Mk   14:12   when they sacrificed the **P** lamb,
Mk   14:12   go and prepare for you to eat the **P**?"
Lk   22: 8   preparations for us to eat the **P**."
Heb   11:28   By faith he kept the **P** and sprinkled

PAST
Acts   14:16   In **p** generations he allowed all
2 Pt   1: 9   of the cleansing of his **p** sins.

PASTORS
Eph   4:11   others as **p** and teachers,

PASTURE →PASTURES
Ps   79:13   your people, the sheep of your **p**,
Jer   23: 1   and scatter the flock of my **p**,
Jn   10: 9   will come in and go out and find **p**.

PASTURES →PASTURE
Ps   23: 2   In green **p** you let me graze; to safe

PATH →PATHS
Ps   16:11   You will show me the **p** to life,
Ps   27:11   lead me on a level **p** because of my
Ps   119:105 a lamp for my feet, a light for my **p**.
Prv   2: 9   and justice, honesty, every good **p**;
Prv   12:28   In the **p** of justice there is life,
Prv   15:19   the **p** of the diligent is a highway.
Prv   15:24   The **p** of life leads the prudent man
Is   26: 7   the **p** of the just you make level.
Mt   13: 4   some seed fell on the **p**, and birds

PATHS →PATH
Ps   17: 5   My steps have kept to your **p**;
Ps   25: 4   your ways, LORD; teach me your **p**.
Prv   2:13   Who leave the straight **p** to walk
Prv   3: 6   and he will make straight your **p**.
Prv   4:11   I lead you on straightforward **p**.
Prv   5:21   LORD's sight; all their **p** he surveys;
Prv   8:20   duty I walk, along the **p** of justice,
Is   2: 3   and we may walk in his **p**."
Mi   4: 2   that we may walk in his **p**."
Mt   3: 3   of the Lord, make straight his **p**.' "
Heb   12:13   Make straight **p** for your feet,

PATIENCE →PATIENT
Prv   25:15   By **p** is a ruler persuaded, and a soft
Mi   2: 7   "Is the LORD short of **p**, or are such
Rom   2: 4   and **p** in low esteem,
Rom   9:22   has endured with much **p** the vessels
2 Cor   6: 6   by purity, knowledge, **p**, kindness,
Gal   5:22   joy, peace, **p**, kindness, generosity,
Col   1:11   for all endurance and **p**, with joy
Col   3:12   humility, gentleness, and **p**,
1 Tm   1:16   display all his **p** as an example
2 Tm   3:10   purpose, faith, **p**, love, endurance,
2 Tm   4: 2   encourage through all **p**
Heb   6:12   through faith and **p**, are inheriting
Jas   5:10   as an example of hardship and **p**,
2 Pt   3:15   And consider the **p** of our Lord as

PATIENT →PATIENCE, PATIENTLY
Neh   9:30   You were **p** with them for many
Jb   6:11   what is my limit that I should be **p**?
Eccl   7: 8   better is the **p** spirit than the lofty
1 Cor 13: 4   Love is **p**, love is kind. It is
1 Thes 5:14   support the weak, be **p** with all.
Jas   5: 7   Be **p**, therefore, brothers,
Jas   5: 7   being **p** with it until it receives
Jas   5: 8   You too must be **p**. Make your

2 Pt   3: 9   but he is **p** with you, not wishing

PATIENTLY →PATIENT
2 Mc   6:14   the LORD **p** waits until they reach
Acts   26: 3   And therefore I beg you to listen **p**.
1 Pt   3:20   disobedient while God **p** waited

PATMOS
Rv   1: 9   on the island called **P** because I

PATRIARCH →PATRIARCHS
Heb   7: 4   whom the **p** "Abraham [indeed] gave

PATRIARCHS →PATRIARCH
Acts   7: 9   "And the **p**, jealous of Joseph,
Rom   9: 5   theirs the **p**, and from them,
Rom   15: 8   to confirm the promises to the **p**,

PATTERN
Ex   25:40   them according to the **p** shown you
Nm   8: 4   to the **p** which the LORD had shown
Heb   8: 5   according to the **p** shown you

PAUL →=SAUL
   Also called Saul (Acts 13:9). Pharisee from Tarsus (Acts 9:11; Phil 3:5). Apostle (Gal 1). At stoning of Stephen (Acts 8:1). Persecuted Church (Acts 9:1-2; Gal 1:13). Vision of Jesus on road to Damascus (Acts 9:4-9; 26:12-18). In Arabia (Gal 1:17). Preached in Damascus; escaped death through the wall in a basket (Acts 9:19-25). In Jerusalem; sent back to Tarsus (Acts 9:26-30).
   Brought to Antioch by Barnabas (Acts 11:22-26). First missionary journey to Cyprus and Galatia (Acts 13-14). Stoned at Lystra (Acts 14:19-20). At Jerusalem council (Acts 15). Split with Barnabas over Mark (Acts 15:36-41).
   Second missionary journey with Silas (Acts 16-20). Called to Macedonia (Acts 16:6-10). Freed from prison in Philippi (Acts 16:16-40). In Thessalonica (Acts 17:1-9). Speech in Athens (Acts 17:16-33). In Corinth (Acts 18). In Ephesus (Acts 19). Return to Jerusalem (Acts 20). Farewell to Ephesian elders (Acts 20:13-38). Arrival in Jerusalem (Acts 21:1-26). Arrested (Acts 21:27-36). Addressed crowds (Acts 22), Sanhedrin (Acts 23:1-11). Sent to Caesarea (Acts 23:12-35). Trial before Felix (Acts 24), Festus (Acts 25:1-12). Before Agrippa (Acts 25:13-26:32). Voyage to Rome; shipwreck (Acts 27). Arrival in Rome (Acts 28).
   Letters: Romans, 1 and 2 Corinthians, Galatians, Ephesians, Philippians, Colossians, 1 and 2 Thessalonians, 1 and 2 Timothy, Titus, Philemon.

PAVEMENT
Jn   19:13   bench in the place called Stone **P**,

PAY →PAID, PAYS, REPAID, REPAY, REPAYS
Dt   24:15   You shall **p** him each day's wages
1 Mc   2:68   **P** back the Gentiles what they
Prv   6:31   be caught he must **p** back sevenfold;
Mt   22:17   Is it lawful to **p** the census tax
Rom   13: 6   This is why you also **p** taxes,
Rom   13: 7   **P** to all their dues, taxes to whom

PAYS →PAY
Prv   19:19   man of violent temper **p** the penalty;

PEACE →PEACEABLE, PEACEFUL, PEACEMAKERS
Lv   26: 6   I will establish **p** in the land,
Nm   6:26   upon you kindly and give you **p**!
Dt   20:10   attack a city, first offer it terms of **p**.
Jos   11:19   no city made with the Israelites;
1 Sm   1:17   "Go in **p**, and may the God of Israel
1 Sm   7:14   there was **p** between Israel
2 Sm   10:19   then made **p** with the Israelites
1 Kgs   2:33   But there shall be the **p** of the LORD
1 Chr 19:19   they made **p** with David and became
1 Chr 22: 9   and in his time I will bestow **p**
1 Mc   14:11   He brought **p** to the land, and Israel
Jb   22:21   Come to terms with him to be at **p**.
Ps   29:11   the LORD bless his people with **p**!
Ps   34:15   and do good; seek **p** and pursue it.
Ps   85: 9   surely the LORD will proclaim **p**
Ps   85:11   will meet; justice and **p** will kiss.
Ps   119:165 of your teaching have much **p**;
Ps   120: 7   When I spoke of **p**, they were
Ps   122: 6   For the **p** of Jerusalem pray:
Ps   147:14   Brought **p** to your borders,
Prv   3:17   ways, and all her paths are **p**;

Prv	12:20	but those who counsel **p** have joy.
Prv	16: 7	he makes even his enemies be at **p**
Eccl	3: 8	hate; a time of war, and a time of **P**.
Is	9: 5	Father-Forever, Prince of **P**.
Is	26: 3	of firm purpose you keep in **p**; in **p**,
Is	32:17	Justice will bring about **p**; right will
Is	48:22	[There is no **p** for the wicked,
Is	52: 7	Announcing **p**, bearing good news,
Is	54:10	nor my covenant of **p** be shaken,
Is	55:12	in **p** you shall be brought back;
Is	57: 2	enters into **p**; There is rest on his
Is	57:19	**P**, **p** to the far and the near,
Is	57:21	No **p** for the wicked! says my God.
Is	59: 8	The way of **p** they know not,
Is	59: 8	whoever threads them knows no **p**.
Jer	6:14	"**P**, **p**!" they say, though there is no **p**.
Jer	8:11	"**P**, **p**!" they say, though there is no **p**.
Lam	3:17	My soul is deprived of **p**, I have
Ez	13:10	led my people astray, saying, "**P**!" when there was no **p**,
Ez	34:25	I will make a covenant of **p**
Ez	37:26	make with them a covenant of **p**;
Mi	5: 4	he shall be **p**. If Assyria invades our
Na	2: 1	bearer of good news, announcing **p**!
Zec	8:19	Judah; only love faithfulness and **p**.
Zec	9:10	he shall proclaim **p** to the nations.
Mt	10:13	is worthy, let your **p** come upon it; if not, let your **p** return to you.
Mt	10:34	come to bring **p** upon the earth.
Mt	10:34	I have come to bring not **p**
Mk	9:50	you will have **p** with one another."
Lk	1:79	to guide our feet into the path of **p**."
Lk	2:14	and on earth **p** to those on whom his
Lk	7:50	"Your faith has saved you; go in **p**."
Lk	19:38	the name of the Lord. **P** in heaven
Jn	14:27	**P** I leave with you; my **p** I give
Jn	16:33	this so that you might have **p** in me.
Acts	10:36	as he proclaimed **p** through Jesus
Rom	2:10	and **p** for everyone who does good,
Rom	3:17	and the way of **p** they know not.
Rom	5: 1	we have **p** with God through our
Rom	8: 6	concern of the spirit is life and **p**.
Rom	14:19	then pursue what leads to **p**
Rom	16:20	of **p** will quickly crush Satan under
1 Cor	7:15	such cases; God has called you to **p**.
1 Cor	14:33	is not the God of disorder but of **p**.
2 Cor	13:11	live in **p**, and the God of love and **p**
Gal	5:22	of the Spirit is love, joy, **p**, patience,
Eph	2:14	For he is our **p**, he who made both
Eph	2:15	place of the two, thus establishing **p**,
Eph	2:17	preached **p** to you who were far off and **p** to those who were near,
Eph	4: 3	of the spirit through the bond of **p**:
Eph	6:15	in readiness for the gospel of **p**.
Phil	4: 7	Then the **p** of God that surpasses all
Col	1:20	making **p** by the blood of his cross
Col	3:15	And let the **p** of Christ control your
Col	3:15	the **p** into which you were
1 Thes	5: 3	people are saying, "**P** and security,"
1 Thes	5:13	Be at **p** among yourselves.
1 Thes	5:23	**p** himself make you perfectly holy
2 Thes	3:16	the Lord of **p** himself give you **p**
2 Tm	2:22	and **p**, along with those who call
Heb	7: 2	"king of Salem," that is, king of **p**.
Heb	12:14	Strive for **p** with everyone,
Heb	13:20	May the God of **p**, who brought
Jas	3:18	righteousness is sown in **p** for those who cultivate **p**.
1 Pt	3:11	do good, seek **p** and follow after it.
2 Pt	3:14	spot or blemish before him, at **p**.
Rv	6: 4	was given power to take **p** away

PEACEABLE →PEACE

Jas	3:17	is first of all pure, then **p**, gentle,

PEACEFUL →PEACE

Heb	12:11	pain, yet later it brings the **p** fruit

PEACEMAKERS →PEACE

Mt	5: 9	Blessed are the **p**, for they will be

PEARL →PEARLS

Mt	13:46	When he finds a **p** of great price,
Rv	21:21	of the gates made from a single **p**;

PEARLS →PEARL

Jb	28:18	be thought of; it surpasses **p**
Mt	7: 6	or throw your **p** before swine,
Mt	13:45	like a merchant searching for fine **p**.
1 Tm	2: 9	or **p**, or expensive clothes,
Rv	21:21	The twelve gates were twelve **p**,

PEBBLE

Am	9: 9	sieve, letting no **p** fall to the ground.

PEG

Jgs	4:21	got a tent **p** and took a mallet in her
Jgs	4:21	and drove the **p** through his temple
Is	22:23	I will fix him like a **p** in a sure spot,

PEKAH

King of Israel (2 Kgs 15:25-31; 2 Chr 28:6; Is 7:1).

PEKAHIAH

Son of Menahem; king of Israel (2 Kgs 15:22-26).

PELETHITES

2 Sm	20: 7	the Cherethites and **P** and all
1 Chr	18:17	of the Cherethites and the **P**;

PEN

Ps	45: 2	My tongue is the **p** of a nimble
3 Jn	1:13	but I do not wish to write with **p**

PENALTY

Prv	19:19	man of violent temper pays the **p**;
Ez	23:49	on you the **p** of your lewdness,
Rom	1:27	their own persons the due **p** for their

PENIEL

Gn	32:31	Jacob named the place **P**, "Because I

PENINNAH

1 Sm	1: 2	one named Hannah, the other **P**;

PENNY

Mt	5:26	until you have paid the last **p**.
Lk	12:59	until you have paid the last **p**."

PENTECOST

2 Mc	12:32	After this feast called **P**, they lost no
Acts	2: 1	When the time for **P** was fulfilled,
Acts	20:16	if at all possible, for the day of **P**.
1 Cor	16: 8	I shall stay in Ephesus until **P**,

PEOPLE →PEOPLE'S, PEOPLES

Gn	11: 6	while they are one **p**, all speaking
Ex	3:10	send you to Pharaoh to lead my **p**,
Ex	5: 1	Israel: Let my **p** go, that they may
Ex	6: 7	I will take you as my own **p**,
Ex	8:19	make this distinction between my **p** and your **p**.
Ex	13:17	when Pharaoh let the **p** go, God did
Ex	15:13	mercy you led the **p** you redeemed;
Ex	15:24	As the **p** grumbled against Moses,
Ex	19: 8	the **p** all answered together,
Ex	32: 3	When Moses came to the **p**
Ex	32: 1	When the **p** became aware of Moses'
Ex	32: 9	I see how stiff-necked this **p** is,"
Ex	32:12	down; relent in punishing your **p**.
Ex	33:13	this nation is, after all, your own **p**."
Nm	11:11	that you burden me with all this **p**?
Nm	14:11	"How long will this **p** spurn me?
Nm	14:19	the wickedness of this **p** in keeping
Nm	21: 7	Then the **p** came to Moses and said,
Nm	21: 7	from us." So Moses prayed for the **p**,
Nm	22: 5	"A **p** has come here from Egypt who
Dt	4: 6	is truly a wise and intelligent **p**.'
Dt	4:20	that you might be his very own **p**,
Dt	5:28	the words these **p** have spoken
Dt	7: 6	For you are a **p** sacred to the LORD,
Dt	7: 6	earth to be a **p** peculiarly his own.
Dt	26:18	you are to be a **p** peculiarly his own,
Dt	31: 7	you must bring this **p** into the land
Dt	31:16	this **p** will take to rendering wanton
Jos	1: 6	you may give this **p** possession
Jos	3:16	Thus the **p** crossed over opposite

Jos	24:25	made a covenant with the **p** that day
Jgs	2: 7	The **p** served the LORD during
Ru	1:16	I will lodge, your **p** shall be my **p**,
1 Sm	10:24	Samuel said to all the **p**, "Do you see
1 Sm	10:24	is none like him among all the **p**!"
1 Sm	12:22	the LORD will not abandon his **p**,
1 Sm	12:22	himself chose to make you his **p**.
2 Sm	5: 2	'You shall shepherd my **p** Israel
2 Sm	7:10	I will fix a place for my **p** Israel;
2 Sm	7:23	on earth is there like your **p** Israel,
2 Sm	7:23	God has led, redeeming it as his **p**;
2 Sm	7:23	their gods out of the way of your **p**,
2 Sm	24:17	the angel who was striking the **p**,
1 Kgs	3: 8	of the **p** whom you have chosen, a **p**
1 Kgs	8:30	of your **p** Israel which they offer
1 Kgs	8:56	who has given rest to his **p** Israel,
1 Kgs	18:39	this, all the **p** fell prostrate and said,
2 Kgs	23: 3	all the **p** stood as participants
2 Kgs	25:11	exile the last of the **p** remaining
1 Chr	29:17	joy I have seen your **p** here present
2 Chr	2:10	"Because the LORD loves his **p**, he has
2 Chr	7:14	and if my **p**, upon whom my name
2 Chr	36:16	LORD against his **p** was so inflamed
Ezr	3: 1	the **p** gathered at Jerusalem as one
Neh	1:10	your **p**, whom you freed by your
Neh	3:38	its height. The **p** worked with a will.
Neh	8: 1	the whole **p** gathered as one man
Jdt	13:17	All the **p** were greatly astonished.
Jdt	13:17	to nought the enemies of your **p**."
Est	3: 6	Mordecai's **p**, throughout the realm
Est	7: 3	beg that you spare the lives of my **p**.
1 Mc	3:43	"Let us restore our **p** from their
1 Mc	3:43	fight for our **p** and our sanctuary!"
Ps	3: 9	Your blessing for your **p**!
Ps	29:11	May the LORD give might to his **p**; may the LORD bless his **p**
Ps	33:12	LORD, the **p** chosen as his very own.
Ps	50: 4	the earth to the judgment of his **p**:
Ps	53: 7	be glad when God restores the **p**!
Ps	81:14	But even now if my **p** would listen,
Ps	94:14	You, LORD, will not forsake your **p**,
Ps	95: 7	For this is our God, whose **p** we are,
Ps	125: 2	the LORD surrounds his **p** both now
Ps	135:14	For the LORD defends his **p**,
Ps	144:15	Happy the **p** so blessed; happy the **p**
Ps	149: 4	For the LORD takes delight in his **p**,
Prv	29: 2	When the just prevail, the **p** rejoice;
Prv	29: 2	when the wicked rule, the **p** groan.
Prv	29:18	Without prophecy the **p** become
Is	1: 3	not know, my **p** has not understood.
Is	1: 4	nation, **p** laden with wickedness,
Is	5:13	Therefore my **p** go into exile,
Is	6:10	to make the heart of this **p** sluggish,
Is	9: 1	The **p** who walked in darkness
Is	19:25	it: "Blessed be my **p** Egypt,
Is	25: 8	reproach of his **p** he will remove
Is	29:13	Since this **p** draws near with words
Is	40: 1	Comfort, give comfort to my **p**,
Is	40: 7	upon it. [So then, the **p** is the grass.]
Is	42: 6	as a covenant of the **p**, a light
Is	49:13	For the LORD comforts his **p**
Is	51: 4	Be attentive to me, my **p**; my folk,
Is	52: 6	day my **p** shall know my renown,
Is	53: 8	and smitten for the sin of his **p**,
Is	60:21	Your **p** shall all be just, they shall
Is	62:12	They shall be called the holy **p**,
Is	65: 2	to a rebellious **p**, Who walk in evil
Jer	2:11	But my **p** have changed their glory
Jer	2:13	Two evils have my **p** done:
Jer	2:32	Yet my **p** have forgotten me
Jer	4:22	Fools my **p** are, they know me not;
Jer	5:14	And this **p** is the wood that it shall
Jer	5:31	they wish; Yet my **p** will have it so;
Jer	6:27	tester among my **p** I have appointed
Jer	7:16	now, do not intercede for this **p**;
Jer	7:23	be your God and you shall be my **p**.
Jer	18:15	Yet my **p** have forgotten me:
Jer	23: 2	the shepherds who shepherd my **p**:
Jer	30: 3	change the lot of my **p** (of Israel
Jer	31:33	their God, and they shall be my **p**.
Jer	50: 6	Lost sheep were my **p**,
Ez	13:23	I will rescue my **p** from your power.
Ez	36: 8	and bear fruit for my **p** Israel,
Ez	36:28	you shall be my **p**, and I will be
Ez	37:13	have you rise from them, O my **p**!
Ez	38:14	When my **p** Israel are dwelling
Ez	39: 7	name known among my **p** Israel;
Dn	7:27	to the holy **p** of the Most High,
Dn	9:19	this city and your **p** bear your name!"
Dn	9:24	for your **p** and for your holy city:
Dn	10:14	shall happen to your **p** in the days
Dn	12: 1	guardian of your **p**; It shall be a time
Dn	12: 1	At that time your **p** shall escape,
Hos	2:25	will say to Lo-ammi, "You are my **p**,"
Hos	4:14	So must a **p** without understanding
Jl	2:18	for his land and took pity on his **p**.
Jl	4:16	but the LORD is a refuge to his **p**,
Am	9:14	about the restoration of my **p** Israel;
Mi	3: 5	who lead my **p** astray; Who,
Mi	6: 2	the LORD has a plea against his **p**,
Mi	7:14	Shepherd your **p** with your staff,
Zep	2: 9	remnant of my **p** shall plunder them,
Hg	1:12	all the remnant of the **p** listened
Hg	1:12	the **p** feared because of the LORD.
Zec	2:15	and they shall be his **p**, and he will
Zec	8: 7	I will rescue my **p** from the land
Zec	13: 9	I will say, "They are my **p**," and they
Mt	1:21	because he will save his **p**
Mt	2: 6	who is to shepherd my **p** Israel.' "
Mt	4:16	the **p** who sit in darkness have seen
Mk	7: 6	'This **p** honors me with their lips,
Mk	8:27	disciples, "Who do **p** say that I am?"
Lk	1:17	to prepare a **p** fit for the Lord."
Lk	1:68	and brought redemption to his **p**.
Lk	2:10	of great joy that will be for all the **p**.
Lk	21:23	a wrathful judgment upon this **p**.
Jn	11:50	one man should die instead of the **p**,
Jn	18:14	man should die rather than the **p**.
Acts	2:47	and enjoying favor with all the **p**.
Acts	5:13	join them, but the **p** esteemed them.
Acts	15:14	from among the Gentiles a **p** for his
Acts	18:10	you, for I have many **p** in this city."
Rom	9:25	who were not my **p** I will call 'my **p**,"
Rom	11: 1	I ask, then, has God rejected his **p**?
Rom	15:10	"Rejoice, O Gentiles, with his **p**."
2 Cor	6:16	be their God and they shall be my **p**.
Ti	2:14	cleanse for himself a **p** as his own,
Heb	2:17	God to expiate the sins of the **p**.
Heb	4: 9	rest still remains for the **p** of God.
Heb	5: 3	for himself as well as for the **p**.
Heb	8:10	their God, and they shall be my **p**.
Heb	10:30	again: "The Lord will judge his **p**."
Heb	13:12	consecrate the **p** by his own blood.
1 Pt	2: 9	a holy nation, a **p** of his own,
1 Pt	2:10	Once you were "no **p**" but now you are God's **p**;
2 Pt	2: 1	also false prophets among the **p**,
Rv	18: 4	"Depart from her, my **p**, so as not

PEOPLE'S →PEOPLE
2 Chr	25:15	"Why have you had recourse to this **p** gods

PEOPLES →PEOPLE
Gn	17:16	and rulers of **p** shall issue from him."
Gn	25:23	two **p** are quarreling while still
Gn	27:29	"Let **p** serve you, and nations pay
Gn	28: 3	you may become an assembly of **p**.
Jos	4:24	that all the **p** of the earth may learn
1 Kgs	8:43	all the **p** of the earth may know your
2 Chr	7:20	proverb and a byword among all **p**.
Ezr	3: 3	their fear of the **p** of the land,
Ezr	10: 2	foreign women of the **p** of the land.
Neh	10:31	our daughters to the **p** of the land,
Ps	2: 1	protest and the **p** grumble in vain?
Ps	9: 9	who judges the **p** with fairness.
Ps	67: 4	May the **p** praise you, God; may all the **p** praise you!
Ps	87: 6	LORD notes in the register of the **p**:
Ps	96:10	God rules the **p** with fairness.
Ps	117: 1	you nations! Give glory, all you **p**!

Is	2: 4	and impose terms on many **p**.
Is	17:12	the roaring of many **p** that roar like
Is	25: 6	will provide for all **p** A feast of rich
Is	34: 1	be attentive, O **p**! Let the earth
Is	49:22	and raise my signal to the **p**;
Is	55: 4	As I made him a witness to the **p**,
Dn	7:14	and **p** of every language serve him.
Dn	8:24	He shall destroy powerful **p**;
Mi	4: 1	the hills, And **p** shall stream to it:
Mi	5: 6	be in the midst of many **p**, Like dew
Zep	3: 9	the lips of the **p**, That they all may
Zep	3:20	praise, among all the **p** of the earth,
Zec	8:20	of hosts: There shall yet come **p**,
Zec	12: 2	a bowl to stupefy all **p** round about.
Acts	4:25	rage and the **p** entertain folly?
Rv	10:11	must prophesy again about many **p**,

PEOR

Nm	25: 3	submitted to the rites of Baal of **P**,
Dt	4: 3	that followed the Baal of **P**;
Jos	22:17	For the sin of **P**, a plague came

PERCEIVE

Prv	24:12	does not he who tests hearts **p** it?

PERES

Dn	5:25	inscribed: MENE, TEKEL, and **P**.
Dn	5:28	**P**, your kingdom has been divided

PEREZ

Gn	38:29	for yourself!" So he was called **P**.
Ru	4:12	house become like the house of **P**,
Mt	1: 3	Judah became the father of **P**
Mt	1: 3	**P** became the father of Hezron,

PERFECT → PERFECTER, PERFECTION

Jb	36: 4	the one **p** in knowledge I set before
Jb	37:16	of him who is **p** in knowledge?
Ps	19: 8	The law of the LORD is **p**,
Song	6: 9	One alone is my dove, my **p** one,
Ez	16:14	nations for your beauty, **p** as it was,
Ez	27: 3	you said, "I am a ship, **p** in beauty.
Ez	28:12	of complete wisdom and **p** beauty.
Mt	5:48	So be **p**, just as your heavenly Father is **p**.
Mt	19:21	said to him, "If you wish to be **p**, go,
Rom	12: 2	what is good and pleasing and **p**.
2 Cor	7: 1	making holiness **p** in the fear
2 Cor	12: 9	for power is made **p** in weakness."
Heb	2:10	their salvation **p** through suffering.
Heb	5: 9	and when he was made **p**,
Heb	7:28	a son, who has been made **p** forever.
Heb	9: 9	offered that cannot **p** the worshiper
Heb	9:11	and more **p** tabernacle not made
Heb	10: 1	it can never make **p** those who come
Heb	10:14	For by one offering he has made **p**
Heb	11:40	us they should not be made **p**.
Heb	12:23	and the spirits of the just made **p**,
Jas	1:17	and every **p** gift is from above,
Jas	1:25	the one who peers into the **p** law
Jas	3: 2	he is a **p** man, able to bridle his
1 Jn	4:18	**p** love drives out fear because fear
1 Jn	4:18	and so one who fears is not yet **p**

PERFECTER → PERFECT

Heb	12: 2	on Jesus, the leader and **p** of faith.

PERFECTION → PERFECT

Ps	119:96	I have seen the limits of all **p**,
Ez	28:12	were stamped with the seal of **p**,
Heb	7:11	If, then, **p** came through the levitical
1 Jn	4:12	his love is brought to **p** in us.

PERFORMED

Ex	4:30	and he **p** the signs before the people.
Jn	10:41	to him and said, "John **p** no sign,
Rv	19:20	it the false prophet who had **p** in its

PERFUME

Song	1: 3	Your name spoken is a spreading **p**—

PERGAMUM

Rv	1:11	to Ephesus, Smyrna, **P**, Thyatira,
Rv	2:12	"To the angel of the church in **P**,

PERIL

Rom	8:35	or nakedness, or **p**, or the sword?

PERISH → PERISHABLE, PERISHED, PERISHES, PERISHING

Jos	23:13	until you **p** from this good land
Est	4:16	king, contrary to the law. If I **p**, I **p**!"
Ps	37:20	The wicked **p**, the enemies
Ps	73:27	But those who are far from you **p**;
Ps	102:27	They **p**, but you remain; they all
Prv	11:10	and when the wicked **p**, there is
Prv	19: 9	and he who utters lies will **p**.
Prv	21:28	The false witness will **p**, but he who
Is	29:14	The wisdom of its wise men shall **p**
Is	60:12	For the people or kingdom shall **p**
Jer	51:18	work, that will **p** in their time
Jon	1: 6	mindful of us so that we may not **p**."
Jon	3: 9	wrath, so that we shall not **p**."
Lk	13: 3	repent, you will all **p** as they did!
Jn	3:16	who believes in him might not **p**
Jn	10:28	eternal life, and they shall never **p**.
Acts	8:20	him, "May your money **p** with you,
Rom	2:12	will also **p** without reference to it,
Col	2:22	These are all things destined to **p**
Heb	1:11	They will **p**, but you remain;
2 Pt	3: 9	not wishing that any should **p**

PERISHABLE → PERISH

1 Cor	9:25	They do it to win a **p** crown, but we
1 Pt	1:18	not with **p** things like silver or gold
1 Pt	1:23	not from **p** but from imperishable

PERISHED → PERISH

Dt	2:14	of soldiers had **p** from the camp,
Ps	119:92	I would have **p** in my affliction.

PERISHES → PERISH

Jn	6:27	Do not work for food that **p**

PERISHING → PERISH

1 Cor	1:18	is foolishness to those who are **p**,
2 Cor	2:15	saved and among those who are **p**,
2 Cor	4: 3	it is veiled for those who are **p**,

PERIZZITES

Gn	13: 7	and the **P** were occupying the land.)
Ex	3: 8	Amorites, **P**, Hivites and Jebusites.

PERJURERS

1 Tm	1:10	liars, **p**, and whatever else is

PERMIT

1 Tm	2:12	I do not **p** a woman to teach

PERPETUAL

Ex	29: 9	the priesthood be theirs by **p** law,

PERPLEXED

2 Cor	4: 8	**p**, but not driven to despair;

PERSECUTE → PERSECUTED, PERSECUTING, PERSECUTION, PERSECUTIONS

Mt	5:11	you when they insult you and **p** you
Mt	5:44	and pray for those who **p** you,
Lk	11:49	some of them they will kill and **p**'
Lk	21:12	they will seize and **p** you, they will
Jn	15:20	persecuted me, they will also **p** you.
Rom	12:14	Bless those who **p** [you],

PERSECUTED → PERSECUTE

Mt	5:10	Blessed are they who are **p**
Mt	5:12	Thus they **p** the prophets who were
Jn	15:20	master.' If they **p** me, they will
Acts	22: 4	I **p** this Way to death, binding both
1 Cor	4:12	we bless; when **p**, we endure;
1 Cor	15: 9	because I **p** the church of God.
2 Cor	4: 9	**p**, but not abandoned; struck down,
Phil	3: 6	in zeal I **p** the church,
2 Tm	3:12	religiously in Christ Jesus will be **p**.

PERSECUTING → PERSECUTE

Acts	9: 5	came, "I am Jesus, whom you are **p**.
Acts	22: 8	the Nazorean whom you are **p**.'
Acts	26:15	replied, 'I am Jesus whom you are **p**.

PERSECUTION → PERSECUTE
Mt	13:21	or **p** comes because of the word,
Acts	8: 1	broke out a severe **p** of the church
Rom	8:35	or distress, or **p**, or famine,

PERSECUTIONS → PERSECUTE
Mk	10:30	with **p**, and eternal life in the age
2 Cor	12:10	hardships, **p**, and constraints,
2 Thes	1: 4	faith in all your **p** and the afflictions
2 Tm	3:11	**p**, and sufferings, such as happened
2 Tm	3:11	and Lystra, **p** that I endured.

PERSEVERE → PERSEVERED, PERSEVERES
Rom	12:12	endure in affliction, **p** in prayer.

PERSEVERED → PERSEVERE
Sir	2:10	Has anyone **p** in his fear and been
Heb	11:27	for he **p** as if seeing the one who is

PERSEVERES → PERSEVERE
Dn	12:12	and **p** until the one thousand three

PERSIA → PERSIANS
Ezr	1: 1	king of **P**, in order to fulfill
Ezr	1: 1	the Lord inspired King Cyrus of **P**
Dn	10:20	I must fight the prince of **P** again.

PERSIANS → PERSIA
Jdt	16:10	"The **P** were dismayed at her daring,

PERSISTENCE → PERSISTENT
Lk	11: 8	whatever he needs because of his **p**.

PERSISTENT → PERSISTENCE
2 Tm	4: 2	be **p** whether it is convenient

PERSUADE → PERSUADED, PERSUASIVENESS
Acts	26:28	soon **p** me to play the Christian."
2 Cor	5:11	fear of the Lord, we try to **p** others;

PERSUADED → PERSUADE
Prv	25:15	By patience is a ruler **p**, and a soft
Mt	27:20	the elders **p** the crowds to ask

PERSUASIVENESS → PERSUADE
Prv	16:21	yet pleasing speech increases his **p**.
Prv	16:23	and augments the **p** of his lips.

PERVERSE → PERVERT, PERVERTED, PERVERTING
Prv	3:32	To the Lord the **p** man is
Prv	17:20	He who is **p** in heart finds no good,
Wis	1: 3	For **p** counsels separate a man
Lk	9:41	"O faithless and **p** generation,

PERVERT → PERVERSE
Jb	8: 3	Does God **p** judgment, and does
Prv	17:23	bribe to **p** the course of justice.
Gal	1: 7	and wish to **p** the gospel of Christ.

PERVERTED → PERVERSE
Jer	3:21	Because they have **p** their ways

PERVERTING → PERVERSE
Ex	23: 2	side with the many in **p** justice.
1 Sm	8: 3	and accepted bribes, **p** justice.

PESTILENCE
Dt	32:24	and bitter **p**, And the teeth of wild
Ps	91: 6	Nor the **p** that roams in darkness,
Rv	18: 8	in one day, **p**, grief, and famine;

PETER → =CEPHAS, =SIMON
Apostle, brother of Andrew, also called Simon (Mt 10:2; Mk 3:16; Lk 6:14; Acts 1:13), and Cephas (Jn 1:42). Confession of Christ (Mt 16:13-20; Mk 8:27-30; Lk 9:18-27). At transfiguration (Mt 17:1-8; Mk 9:2-8; Lk 9:28-36; 2 Pt 1:16-18). Caught fish with coin (Mt 17:24-27). Denial of Jesus predicted (Mt 26:31-35; Mk 14:27-31; Lk 22:31-34; Jn 13:31-38). Denied Jesus (Mt 26:69-75; Mk 14:66-72; Lk 22:54-62; Jn 18:15-27). Commissioned by Jesus to shepherd his flock (Jn 21:15-23).

Speech at Pentecost (Acts 2). Healed beggar (Acts 3:1-10). Speech at temple (Acts 3:11-26), before Sanhedrin (Acts 4:1-22). In Samaria (Acts 8:14-25). Sent by vision to Cornelius (Acts 10). Announced salvation of Gentiles in Jerusalem (Acts 11; 15). Freed from prison (Acts 12). Inconsistency at Antioch (Gal 2:11-21). At Jerusalem Council (Acts 15).

Letters: 1 and 2 Peter.

PHARAOH → PHARAOH'S
Gn	12:15	saw her, they praised her to **P**.
Gn	41:14	**P** therefore had Joseph summoned,
Gn	47:10	Jacob bade **P** farewell and withdrew
Ex	1:22	**P** then commanded all his subjects,
Ex	2:15	**P**, too, heard of the affair
Ex	3:11	"Who am I that I should go to **P**
Ex	5: 2	**P** answered, "Who is the Lord, that I
Ex	11: 1	more plague will I bring upon **P**
Ex	14:17	I will receive glory through **P**
Dt	7: 8	ransomed you from the hand of **P**,
Is	36: 6	That is what **P**, king of Egypt,
Rom	9:17	For the scripture says to **P**, "This is

PHARAOH'S → PHARAOH
Ex	11:10	these various wonders in **P** presence,
Heb	11:24	to be known as the son of **P** daughter;

PHARISEE → PHARISEES
Lk	11:37	a **P** invited him to dine at his home.
Jn	3: 1	there was a **P** named Nicodemus,
Acts	5:34	But a **P** in the Sanhedrin named
Acts	23: 6	I am a **P**, the son of Pharisees;
Phil	3: 5	in observance of the law a **P**,

PHARISEES → PHARISEE
Mt	5:20	surpasses that of the scribes and **P**,
Mt	16: 6	beware of the leaven of the **P**
Mt	23:13	you, scribes and **P**, you hypocrites.
Mk	2:18	John and the disciples of the **P** fast,
Lk	11:42	Woe to you **P**! You pay tithes
Acts	23: 7	a dispute broke out between the **P**

PHILADELPHIA
Rv	1:11	Thyatira, Sardis, **P**, and Laodicea."
Rv	3: 7	"To the angel of the church in **P**,

PHILEMON
Phlm	1: 1	brother, to **P**, our beloved and our

PHILIP
1. Apostle (Mt 10:3; Mk 3:18; Lk 6:14; Jn 1:43-48; 14:8; Acts 1:13).
2. Deacon (Acts 6:1-7); evangelist in Samaria (Acts 8:4-25), to Ethiopian (Acts 8:26-40).
3. Herod Philip I (Mt 14:3; Mk 6:17).
4. Herod Philip II (Lk 3:1).

PHILIPPI
Mt	16:13	Caesarea **P** he asked his disciples,
Acts	16:12	and from there to **P**, a leading city
Phil	1: 1	ones in Christ Jesus who are in **P**,

PHILISTIA → PHILISTINE, PHILISTINES
Ex	15:14	anguish gripped the dwellers in **P**.
Ps	60:10	my sandal. I will triumph over **P**."

PHILISTINE → PHILISTIA
1 Sm	14: 1	let us go over to the **P** outpost
1 Sm	17:23	talking with them, the **P** champion,
1 Sm	17:37	me safe from the clutches of this **P**."

PHILISTINES → PHILISTIA
Gn	21:34	in the land of the **P** for many years.
Gn	26: 1	Abimelech, king of the **P** in Gerar.
Ex	23:31	the Red Sea to the sea of the **P**,
Jgs	10: 7	them to fall into the power of [the **P**
Jgs	13: 1	the power of the **P** for forty years.
Jgs	16: 5	The lords of the **P** came to her
Jgs	16:30	Samson said, "Let me die with the **P**!"
1 Sm	4: 1	the **P** gathered for an attack on Israel.
1 Sm	5: 1	The **P**, having captured the ark
1 Sm	13:20	to the **P** to sharpen their plowshares,
1 Sm	17: 1	The **P** rallied their forces for battle
1 Sm	17:51	hero was dead, the **P** took to flight.
1 Sm	23: 1	that the **P** were attacking Keilah
1 Sm	27: 1	but to escape to the land of the **P**;
2 Sm	5:17	When the **P** heard that David had
2 Sm	8: 1	After this David attacked the **P**
2 Sm	21:15	was another battle between the **P**
2 Kgs	18: 8	and walled cities of the **P**,
Jer	47: 4	Yes, the Lord is destroying the **P**,
Ez	25:16	out my hand against the **P**; I will cut
Am	1: 8	and the last of the **P** shall perish,

PHILOSOPHERS → PHILOSOPHY
Acts   17:18   Stoic **p** engaged him in discussion.

PHILOSOPHY → PHILOSOPHERS
Col   2: 8   seductive **p** according to human

PHINEHAS
1. Grandson of Aaron (Ex 6:25; Jos 22:30-32). Zeal for the LORD stopped plague (Nm 25:7-13; Ps 106:30).
2. Son of Eli; a wicked priest (1 Sm 1:3; 2:12-17; 4:1-19).

PHOEBE
Rom   16: 1   I commend to you **P** our sister,

PHYLACTERIES
Mt   23: 5   They widen their **p** and lengthen

PHYSICAL
1 Tm   4: 8   while **p** training is of limited value,

PHYSICIAN
Sir   38: 1   Hold the **p** in honor, for he is
Jer   8:22   there no balm in Gilead, no **p** there?
Mt   9:12   "Those who are well do not need a **p**,
Lk   4:23   this proverb, 'P, cure yourself,'
Col   4:14   Luke the beloved **p** sends greetings,

PIECE → BREASTPIECE, PIECES
Ex   15:25   out to him a certain **p** of wood.
Mk   2:21   No one sews a **p** of unshrunken
Jn   19:23   woven in one **p** from the top down.

PIECES → PIECE
Gn   15:17   which passed between those **p**.
1 Kgs   11:30   his new cloak, tore it into twelve **p**,
Mi   1: 7   All her idols shall be broken to **p**,
Lk   20:18   on that stone will be dashed to **p**;

PIERCE → PIERCED
Ex   21: 6   he shall **p** his ear with an awl,
Lk   2:35   you yourself a sword will **p**) so

PIERCED → PIERCE
Nm   25: 8   his retreat where he **p** the pair
Jn   19:37   look upon him whom they have **p**."
1 Tm   6:10   have **p** themselves with many pains.
Rv   1: 7   him, even those who **p** him.

PIETY
Acts   3:12   him walk by our own power or **p**?

PIG
Dt   14: 8   and the **p**, which indeed has hoofs

PIGEON → PIGEONS
Lv   12: 6   a **p** or a turtledove for a sin offering.

PIGEONS → PIGEON
Lk   2:24   "a pair of turtledoves or two young **p**,"

PILATE
Governor of Judea. Questioned Jesus (Mt 27:1-26; Mk 15:15; Lk 22:66-23:25; Jn 18:28-19:16); sent him to Herod (Lk 23:6-12); consented to his crucifixion when crowds chose Barabbas (Mt 27:15-26; Mk 15:6-15; Lk 23:13-25; Jn 19:1-10).

PILLAR → PILLARS
Gn   19:26   and she was turned into a **p** of salt.
Wis   10: 7   soul, a standing **p** of salt.
1 Tm   3:15   God, the **p** and foundation of truth.
Rv   3:12   I will make into a **p** in the temple

PILLARS → PILLAR
Ex   24: 4   and twelve **p** for the twelve tribes
2 Kgs   25:13   The bronze **p** that belonged
Ps   75: 4   but I have firmly set its **p**."
Rv   10: 1   sun and his feet were like **p** of fire.

PINE
Is   60:13   the cypress, the plane and the **p**,

PINIONS
Dt   32:11   them and bore them up on his **p**.
Ps   91: 4   Will shelter you with **p**,
Ez   17: 3   eagle, with great wings, with long **p**,

PISGAH
Dt   3:27   Go up to the top of **P** and look

PIT
Ps   7:16   but fall into the **p** they have dug.
Ps   40: 3   Drew me out of the **p** of destruction,
Ps   103: 4   Delivers your life from the **p**,
Prv   23:27   ditch, and the adulteress a narrow **p**;
Prv   26:27   He who digs a **p** falls into it;
Is   24:17   Terror, **p**, and trap are upon you,
Is   38:17   from the **p** of destruction, When you
Ez   19: 4   in their **p** he was caught; They took
Jon   2: 7   you brought up my life from the **p**,
Mt   15:14   blind person, both will fall into a **p**."

PITCH
Gn   6:14   and cover it inside and out with **p**.
Ex   2: 3   daubed it with bitumen and **p**,
Dn   14:27   Then Daniel took some **p**, fat,

PITY
Dt   7:16   You are not to look on them with **p**,
Jb   19:21   **P** me, **p** me, O you my friends,
Ps   72:13   He shows **p** to the needy
Ez   7: 4   upon you with **p** nor have mercy;
Hos   1: 6   I no longer feel **p** for the house
Hos   2:25   and I will have **p** on Lo-ruhama.
Jl   2:18   his land and took **p** on his people.

PLACE → PLACES
Gn   50:19   no fear. Can I take the **p** of God?
Ex   3: 5   for the **p** where you stand is holy
Ex   26:33   divides the holy **p** from the holy
Dt   12: 5   shall resort to the **p** which the LORD,
Jos   5:15   for the **p** on which you are standing
2 Chr   6:21   which they direct toward this **p**.
Ezr   9: 8   and gave us a stake in his holy **p**;
Ps   24: 3   LORD? Who can stand in his holy **p**?
Ps   132:14   "This is my resting **p** forever; here I
Eccl   6: 6   do not both go to the same **p**?
Hg   2: 9   And in this **p** I will give peace,
Mt   27:33   they came to a **p** called Golgotha
Mt   27:33   (which means **P** of the Skull),
Jn   14: 3   And if I go and prepare a **p** for you,
2 Pt   1:19   it, as to a lamp shining in a dark **p**,
Rv   20:11   and there was no **p** for them.

PLACES → PLACE
Lv   26:30   I will demolish your high **p**,
1 Kgs   3: 2   were sacrificing on the high **p**,
2 Kgs   18: 4   It was he who removed the high **p**,
Ps   78:58   They enraged him with their high **p**;
Jer   19: 5   They have built high **p** for Baal
Jn   14: 2   house there are many dwelling **p**.

PLAGUE → PLAGUES
Ex   11: 1   "One more **p** will I bring
Nm   11:33   he struck them with a very great **p**.
2 Chr   6:28   whenever there is a **p** or sickness
Zec   14:12   this shall be the **p**
Rv   11: 6   with any **p** as often as they wish.
Rv   16:21   the **p** of hail because this **p** was so

PLAGUES → PLAGUE
Hos   13:14   death? Where are your **p**, O death!
Rv   9:18   By these three **p** of fire, smoke,
Rv   15: 1   seven angels with the seven last **p**,
Rv   21: 9   filled with the seven last **p** came
Rv   22:18   to him the **p** described in this book,

PLAIN
Gn   13:12   settled among the cities of the **P**,
Gn   19:29   God destroyed the Cities of the **P**,
Is   40: 4   The rugged land shall be made a **p**,

PLANNED → PLANS
Is   23: 9   The LORD of hosts has **p** it,
Is   46:11   I have **p** it, and I will do it.

PLANS → PLANNED
Tb   4:19   success to all your endeavors and **p**.
Prv   15:22   **P** fail when there is no counsel,
Prv   16: 3   the LORD, and your **p** will succeed.
Prv   19:21   Many are the **p** in a man's heart,
Prv   20:18   **P** made after advice succeed;
Jer   29:11   I know well the **p** I have in mind

PLANT

Jer	29:11	says the LORD, **p** for your welfare,
Jer	29:11	**p** to give you a future full of hope.
2 Cor	1:17	do I make my **p** according to human

PLANT →PLANTED, PLANTS, REPLANTED

Gn	1:29	you every seed-bearing **p** all over
Gn	9:20	soil, was the first to **p** a vineyard.
Eccl	3: 2	a time to **p**, and a time to uproot the **p**.
Am	9:15	I will **p** them upon their own
Mt	15:13	"Every **p** that my heavenly Father

PLANTED →PLANT

Gn	2: 8	the LORD God **p** a garden in Eden,
Ps	1: 3	like a tree **p** near streams of water,
Ps	92:14	**P** in the house of the LORD,
Jer	17: 8	He is like a tree **p** beside the waters
Mt	15:13	Father has not **p** will be uprooted.
Mt	21:33	was a landowner who **p** a vineyard,
Lk	13: 6	was a person who had a fig tree **p**
1 Cor	3: 6	I **p**, Apollos watered, but God

PLANTS →PLANT

Gn	9: 3	them all to you as I did the green **p**.
Ps	144:12	May our sons be like **p**
Prv	31:16	out of her earnings she **p** a vineyard.
1 Cor	3: 7	neither the one who **p** nor the one
1 Cor	9: 7	Who **p** a vineyard without eating its

PLASTER

Dt	27: 2	large stones and coat them with **p**.
Dn	5: 5	writing on the **p** of the wall

PLATES

Ex	25:29	Of pure gold you shall make its **p**

PLATFORM

2 Chr	6:13	made a bronze **p** five cubits long,
Neh	8: 4	on a wooden **p** that had been made

PLATTER

Mk	6:25	at once on a **p** the head of John

PLAY →PLAYED, PLAYING

Ps	33: 3	song; skillfully **p** with joyful chant.
Is	11: 8	The baby shall **p** by the cobra's den,

PLAYED →PLAY

Mt	11:17	'We **p** the flute for you, but you did
1 Cor	14: 7	how will what is being **p** on flute

PLAYING →PLAY

1 Sm	18:10	**p** the harp as at other times,
1 Sm	19: 9	and David was **p** the harp nearby.
Zec	8: 5	with boys and girls **p** in her streets.
Rv	14: 2	like that of harpists **p** their harps.

PLEASANT

Gn	49:15	and how **p** the country, He bent his
Ps	16: 6	**P** places were measured out for me;
Ps	133: 1	How good it is, how **p**,

PLEASE →PLEASED, PLEASES, PLEASING, PLEASURE, PLEASURES

Ps	69:32	My song will **p** the LORD more than
Sir	2:16	who fear the LORD seek to **p** him,
Rom	8: 8	who are in the flesh cannot **p** God.
Rom	15: 1	of the weak and not to **p** ourselves;
Rom	15: 3	For Christ did not **p** himself; but,
1 Cor	7:32	of the Lord, how he may **p** the Lord.
1 Cor	7:33	the world, how he may **p** his wife,
1 Cor	10:33	just as I try to **p** everyone in every
2 Cor	5: 9	we aspire to **p** him, whether we are
1 Thes	2: 4	not as trying to **p** human beings,
1 Thes	4: 1	you should conduct yourselves to **p**
Heb	11: 6	faith it is impossible to **p** him,

PLEASED →PLEASE

Nm	14: 8	If the LORD is **p** with us, he will
Nm	24: 1	that the LORD was **p** to bless Israel,
1 Kgs	3:10	The LORD was **p** that Solomon made
Is	42:21	Though it **p** the LORD in his justice
Dn	8: 4	it did what it **p** and became very
Mi	6: 7	Will the LORD be **p** with thousands
Mt	3:17	Son, with whom I am well **p**."
Mt	17: 5	Son, with whom I am well **p**;

Mk	1:11	beloved Son; with you I am well **p**."
Lk	3:22	beloved Son; with you I am well **p**."
1 Cor	10: 5	Yet God was not **p** with most
Col	1:19	him all the fullness was **p** to dwell,
Heb	11: 5	up, he was attested to have **p** God.
2 Pt	1:17	beloved, with whom I am well **p**."

PLEASES →PLEASE

Dn	11: 3	rule with great might, doing as he **p**.
Dn	11:36	"The king shall do as he **p**,
1 Jn	3:22	commandments and do what **p** him.

PLEASING →PLEASE

Ezr	6:10	offer sacrifices of **p** odor to the God
Ps	104:34	May my theme be **p** to God; I will
Eph	5:10	Try to learn what is **p** to the Lord.
Phil	4:18	an acceptable sacrifice, **p** to God.
1 Tm	5: 4	to their parents, for this is **p** to God.
Heb	13:21	you what is **p** to him through Jesus

PLEASURE →PLEASE

Gn	18:12	is so old, am I still to have sexual **p**?"
Ps	147:10	of horses, no **p** in the runner's stride.
Prv	21:17	He who loves **p** will suffer want;
Ez	18:32	For I have no **p** in the death
Ez	33:11	I swear I take no **p** in the death
Hg	1: 8	That I may take **p** in it and receive
2 Tm	3: 4	lovers of **p** rather than lovers

PLEASURES →PLEASE

Lk	8:14	anxieties and riches and **p** of life,
Ti	3: 3	slaves to various desires and **p**,

PLEDGE

Gn	38:17	you leave a **p** until you send it."
Nm	30: 3	under oath to a **p** of abstinence,
Dt	24: 6	even its upper stone as a **p** for debt,
Dt	24: 6	taking the debtor's sustenance as a **p**.
Dt	24:17	take the clothing of a widow as a **p**.
Prv	6: 1	given your hand in **p** to another,
Ez	18: 7	gives back the **p** received for a debt,

PLENTY

Prv	12:11	who tills his own land has food in **p**,

PLOW →PLOWED, PLOWS, PLOWSHARES

Dt	22:10	You shall not **p** with an ox
Lk	9:62	"No one who sets a hand to the **p**

PLOWED →PLOW

Jgs	14:18	"If you had not **p** with my heifer,
Ps	129: 3	Upon my back the plowers **p**,

PLOWS →PLOW

Prv	20: 4	In seedtime the sluggard **p** not;

PLOWSHARES →PLOW

Is	2: 4	They shall beat their swords into **p**
Jl	4:10	Beat your **p** into swords, and your
Mi	4: 3	They shall beat their swords into **p**,

PLUCK

Dt	23:26	you may **p** some of the ears

PLUNDER

Jer	30:16	All who **p** you shall be plundered,
Ez	39:10	Thus they shall **p** those who
Zep	2: 9	remnant of my people shall **p** them,

PLUNGE

1 Tm	6: 9	desires, which **p** them into ruin

PODS

Lk	15:16	to eat his fill of the **p**

POETS

Acts	17:28	as even some of your **p** have said,

POINT

Heb	12: 4	resisted to the **p** of shedding blood.

POISON

Jas	3: 8	It is a restless evil, full of deadly **p**.

POLE →POLES

Nm	21: 8	"Make a saraph and mount it on a **p**,
Dt	16:21	"You shall not plant a sacred **p**

Jgs 6:25 cut down the sacred **p** that is by it.
1 Kgs 16:33 and also made a sacred **p**. He did

POLES → POLE
Ex 25:13 Then make **p** of acacia wood
Dt 12: 3 destroy by fire their sacred **p**,
2 Kgs 17:10 sacred **p** for themselves on every

POLISHED
Is 49: 2 He made me a **p** arrow, in his quiver

POLLUTED
Prv 25:26 a troubled fountain or a **p** spring

POMEGRANATES
Ex 28:33 hem at the bottom you shall make **p**,
Dt 8: 8 of vines and fig trees and **p**, of olive
1 Kgs 7:18 Four hundred **p** were also cast;

PONDER → PONDERING
Ps 48:10 temple we **p** your steadfast love.

PONDERING → PONDER
Ps 64:10 God's deed, **p** what has been done.

PONTIUS
Lk 3: 1 when **P** Pilate was governor

POOL → POOLS
2 Sm 2:13 and met them at the **p** of Gibeon.
1 Kgs 22:38 was washed at the **p** of Samaria,
Jn 5: 2 at the Sheep [Gate] a **p** called
Jn 9: 7 "Go wash in the **P** of Siloam"
Rv 19:20 the fiery **p** burning with sulfur.
Rv 20:10 into the **p** of fire and sulfur,
Rv 20:14 into the **p** of fire. (This **p** of fire is the second death.)

POOLS → POOL
Ps 107:35 He changed the desert into **p**
Ps 114: 8 Who turned rock into **p** of water,

POOR → POVERTY
Ex 23: 3 You shall not favor a **p** man in his
Dt 15:11 you to open your hand to your **p**
Dt 24:12 If he is a **p** man, you shall not sleep
Dt 24:14 "You shall not defraud a **p** and needy
1 Sm 2: 8 from the ash heap he lifts up the **p**,
2 Sm 12: 1 were two men, one rich, the other **p**.
Jb 24: 4 all the **p** of the land are driven
Ps 14: 6 would crush the hopes of the **p**,
Ps 14: 6 the **p** have the Lord as their refuge.
Ps 40:18 Though I am afflicted and **p**,
Ps 112: 9 Lavishly they give to the **p**;
Ps 113: 7 dust, lifts the **p** from the ash heap,
Ps 140:13 for the needy, their rights for the **p**.
Prv 13: 7 another pretends to be **p**, yet has
Prv 14:20 by his neighbor the **p** man is hated,
Prv 14:31 who oppresses the **p** blasphemes his
Prv 17: 5 He who mocks the **p** blasphemes his
Prv 19: 1 Better a **p** man who walks in his
Prv 19:17 who has compassion on the **p** lends
Prv 19:22 shame; rather be a **p** man than a liar.
Prv 21:13 who shuts his ear to the cry of the **p**
Prv 22: 2 Rich and **p** have a common bond:
Prv 22: 9 he gives of his sustenance to the **p**.
Prv 22:22 Injure not the **p** because they are **p**,
Prv 28: 6 Better a **p** man who walks in his
Prv 28:27 who gives to the **p** suffers no want,
Prv 29: 7 has a care for the rights of the **p**;
Prv 31: 9 is just, defend the needy and the **p**!
Prv 31:20 She reaches out her hands to the **p**,
Eccl 4:13 Better is a **p** but wise youth than
Sir 4: 8 Give a hearing to the **p** man,
Sir 7:32 To the **p** man also extend your hand,
Is 3:14 the loot wrested from the **p** is
Is 10: 2 and robbing my people's **p** of their
Is 14:30 In my pastures the **p** shall eat,
Is 25: 4 For you are a refuge to the **p**,
Is 32: 7 How to ruin the **p** with lies,
Jer 22:16 justice to the weak and the **p**,
Ez 18:12 oppresses the **p** and needy,
Zec 7:10 or the orphan, the alien or the **p**;
Mt 5: 3 "Blessed are the **p** in spirit, for theirs

Mt 11: 5 and the **p** have the good news
Mk 10:21 give to [the] **p** and you will have
Mk 12:42 A **p** widow also came and put
Mk 14: 7 The **p** you will always have
Lk 4:18 to bring glad tidings to the **p**. He has
Lk 6:20 "Blessed are you who are **p**,
Lk 14:13 a banquet, invite the **p**, the crippled,
Lk 19: 8 I shall give to the **p**, and if I have
Lk 21: 2 he noticed a **p** widow putting in two
Jn 12: 8 You always have the **p** with you,
Rom 15:26 for the **p** among the holy ones
2 Cor 6:10 rejoicing; as **p** yet enriching many;
2 Cor 8: 9 sake he became **p** although he was
2 Cor 9: 9 scatters abroad, he gives to the **p**;
Jas 2: 2 and a **p** person in shabby clothes
Jas 2: 5 Did not God choose those who are **p**
Rv 3:17 you are wretched, pitiable, **p**, blind,

PORCIUS
Acts 24:27 Felix was succeeded by **P** Festus.

PORTENT
Ps 71: 7 I have become a **p** to many, but you
Is 20: 3 years as a sign and **p** against Egypt

PORTION → APPORTION
Dt 32: 9 While the Lord's own **p** was Jacob,
1 Sm 1: 5 a double **p** to Hannah because he
Ps 16: 5 Lord, my allotted **p** and my cup,
Ps 73:26 the rock of my heart, my **p** forever.
Ps 119:57 My **p** is the Lord; I promise to keep
Ps 142: 6 my **p** in the land of the living.
Sir 17:14 but the Lord's own **p** is Israel.
Is 53:12 will give him his **p** among the great,
Is 61: 7 disgrace and spittle were their **p**,
Jer 10:16 Not like these is the **p** of Jacob:
Lam 3:24 My **p** is the Lord, says my soul;
Zec 2:16 Lord will possess Judah as his **p**

POSSESS → POSSESSED, POSSESSING, POSSESSION, POSSESSIONS
Is 14: 2 and **p** them as male and female
Is 60:21 they shall always **p** the land, They,
Dn 7:18 kingship, to **p** it forever and ever."

POSSESSED → POSSESS
Mt 8:16 they brought him many who were **p**

POSSESSING → POSSESS
2 Cor 6:10 having nothing and yet **p** all things.

POSSESSION → POSSESS
Ex 19: 5 you shall be my special **p**,
Jos 1:11 take **p** of the land which the Lord,
Ps 2: 8 nations, your **p** the ends of the earth.
Ps 135: 4 Jacob, Israel as a treasured **p**.
Mal 3:17 my own special **p**, on the day I take

POSSESSIONS → POSSESS
Lk 12:15 rich, one's life does not consist of **p**."
Lk 19: 8 "Behold, half of my **p**, Lord, I shall
Acts 4:32 that any of his **p** was his own,

POSSIBLE
Mt 19:26 but for God all things are **p**."
Mt 26:39 if it is **p**, let this cup pass from me;
Mk 10:27 for God. All things are **p** for God."
Mk 14:35 if it were **p** the hour might pass
Lk 18:27 for human beings is **p** for God."

POSTERITY
Tb 4:12 that their **p** shall inherit the land.

POT → FLESHPOTS, POTSHERD, POTTER, POTTER'S
2 Kgs 4:40 of God, there is poison in the **p**!"

POTIPHAR
Egyptian who bought Joseph (Gn 37:36), set him over his house (Gn 39:1-6), sent him to prison (Gn 39:7-30).

POTSHERD → POT
Jb 2: 8 And he took a **p** to scrape himself,
Ps 22:16 As dry as a **p** is my throat;

POTTER → POT

Sir	33:13	Like clay in the hands of a **p**, to be
Is	29:16	Your perversity is as though the **p**
Is	29:16	Or the vessel should say of the **p**,
Is	64: 7	we are the clay and you the **p**:
Jer	18: 6	house of Israel, as this **p** has done?
Jer	18: 6	like clay in the hand of the **p**, so are
Rom	9:21	does not the **p** have a right over

POTTER'S → POT

Jer	18: 2	Rise up, be off to the **p** house;
Mt	27: 7	to buy the **p** field as a burial place

POUR → POURED, POURING

Dt	12:16	but must **p** it out on the ground like
Ps	62: 9	**P** out your hearts to God our refuge!
Ps	79: 6	**P** out your wrath on nations
Is	44: 3	I will **p** out water upon the thirsty
Is	44: 3	I will **p** out my spirit upon your
Jl	3: 1	Then afterward I will **p** out
Zec	12:10	I will **p** out on the house of David
Mal	3:10	to **p** down blessing upon you
Acts	2:17	'that I will **p** out a portion of my
Rv	16: 1	**p** out the seven bowls of God's fury

POURED → POUR

Gn	28:18	stone, and **p** oil on top if it.
Gn	35:14	it he made a libation and **p** out oil.
2 Sm	23:16	it, and instead **p** it out to the LORD,
Is	32:15	spirit from on high is **p** out on us.
Lam	4:11	his anger, **p** out his blazing wrath;
Ez	39:29	for I have **p** out my spirit
Mk	14: 3	alabaster jar and **p** it on his head.
Acts	2:33	Spirit from the Father and **p** it forth,
Acts	10:45	the holy Spirit should have been **p**
Rom	5: 5	the love of God has been **p**
Phil	2:17	even if I am **p** out as a libation
2 Tm	4: 6	For I am already being **p** out like
Ti	3: 6	whom he richly **p** out on us
Rv	14:10	**p** full strength into the cup of his
Rv	16: 2	and **p** out his bowl on the earth.

POURING → POUR

1 Sm	1:15	I was only **p** out my troubles
Ez	20: 8	I thought of **p** out my fury on them

POVERTY → POOR

Prv	6:11	Then will **p** come upon you like
Prv	10:15	the ruination of the lowly is their **p**.
Prv	13:18	**P** and shame befall the man who
Prv	24:34	Then will **p** come upon you like
Prv	28:19	idle pursuits a man has his fill of **p**.
Prv	30: 8	me, give me neither **p** nor riches;
Sir	10:30	Honored in **p**, how much more so in wealth!
		Dishonored in wealth, in **p** how much the more!
Sir	11:14	**p** and riches, are from the LORD.
Mk	12:44	from her **p**, has contributed all she
Lk	21: 4	from her **p**, has offered her whole
2 Cor	8: 2	their profound **p** overflowed
2 Cor	8: 9	by his **p** you might become rich.
Rv	2: 9	"I know your tribulation and **p**,

POWDER

Ex	32:20	fire and then ground it down to **p**,

POWER → POWERFUL, POWERS

Ex	9:16	to show you my **p** and to make my
Ex	15: 6	hand, O LORD, magnificent in **p**,
Ex	32:11	the land of Egypt with such great **p**
Dt	8:17	'It is my own **p** and the strength
Dt	34:12	the terrifying **p** that Moses exhibited
1 Chr	29:11	"Yours, O LORD, are grandeur and **p**,
2 Chr	20: 6	In your hand is **p** and might, and no
Jdt	9:14	clearly that you are the God of all **p**
Jb	36:22	Behold, God is sublime in his **p**.
Jb	37:23	pre-eminent in **p** and judgment;
Ps	63: 3	sanctuary to see your **p** and glory.
Ps	68:35	Confess the **p** of God,
Ps	68:35	Israel, whose **p** is in the sky.
Ps	147: 5	Great is our Lord, vast in **p**,
Prv	3:27	when it is in your **p** to do it for him.
Prv	18:21	and life are in the **p** of the tongue;

Is	40:26	great might and the strength of his **p**
Jer	10:12	He who made the earth by his **p**,
Jer	27: 5	by my great **p**, with my outstretched
Dn	2:20	and ever, for wisdom and **p** are his.
Dn	6:28	delivered Daniel from the lions' **p**."
Hos	13:14	from the **p** of the nether world?
Mi	3: 8	But as for me, I am filled with **p**,
Na	1: 3	LORD is slow to anger, yet great in **p**,
Mt	22:29	know the scriptures or the **p** of God.
Mt	24:30	upon the clouds of heaven with **p**
Mk	9: 1	the kingdom of God has come in **p**."
Mk	13:26	coming in the clouds' with great **p**
Lk	1:17	and **p** of Elijah to turn the hearts
Lk	1:35	you, and the **p** of the Most High will
Lk	4:14	to Galilee in the **p** of the Spirit,
Lk	6:19	to touch him because **p** came forth
Lk	8:46	for I know that **p** has gone
Lk	9: 1	gave them **p** and authority over all
Lk	10:19	I have given you the **p** 'to tread
Lk	21:27	of Man coming in a cloud with **p**
Lk	24:49	the city until you are clothed with **p**
Jn	19:11	"You would have no **p** over me if it
Acts	1: 8	you will receive **p** when the holy
Acts	4:33	great **p** the apostles bore witness
Acts	8:10	"This man is the 'P of God' that is
Acts	10:38	Nazareth with the holy Spirit and **p**.
Acts	26:18	and from the **p** of Satan to God,
Rom	1:16	It is the **p** of God for the salvation
Rom	1:20	his invisible attributes of eternal **p**
Rom	9:17	to show my **p** through you that my
Rom	15:13	in hope by the **p** of the holy Spirit.
Rom	15:19	by the **p** of signs and wonders,
Rom	15:19	by the **p** of the Spirit [of God],
1 Cor	1:18	us who are being saved it is the **p**
1 Cor	1:24	Christ the **p** of God and the wisdom
1 Cor	2: 4	with a demonstration of spirit and **p**
1 Cor	6:14	Lord and will also raise us by his **p**.
1 Cor	15:24	and every authority and **p**.
1 Cor	15:56	is sin, and the **p** of sin is the law.
2 Cor	4: 7	that the surpassing **p** may be of God
2 Cor	6: 7	in truthful speech, in the **p** of God;
2 Cor	12: 9	for **p** is made perfect in weakness."
2 Cor	12: 9	order that the **p** of Christ may dwell
2 Cor	13: 4	but he lives by the **p** of God.
2 Cor	13: 4	shall live with him by the **p** of God.
Gal	3:22	confined all things under the **p**
Eph	1:19	of his **p** for us who believe,
Eph	1:21	authority, **p**, and dominion,
Eph	3:16	with **p** through his Spirit in the inner
Eph	3:20	imagine, by the **p** at work within us,
Eph	6:10	the Lord and from his mighty **p**.
Phil	3:10	him and the **p** of his resurrection
Phil	3:21	body by the **p** that enables him
Col	1:11	strengthened with every **p**, in accord
1 Thes	1: 5	also in **p** and in the holy Spirit
2 Tm	1: 7	cowardice but rather of **p** and love
2 Tm	3: 5	a pretense of religion but deny its **p**.
Heb	2:14	might destroy the one who has the **p**
Heb	7:16	but by the **p** of a life that cannot be
1 Pt	1: 5	by the **p** of God are safeguarded
2 Pt	1: 3	His divine **p** has bestowed on us
2 Pt	1: 3	called us by his own glory and **p**.
2 Pt	1:16	when we made known to you the **p**
Jude	1:25	majesty, **p**, and authority from ages
Rv	4:11	to receive glory and honor and **p**,
Rv	5:12	to receive **p** and riches,
Rv	7: 2	the four angels who were given **p**
Rv	11:17	For you have assumed your great **p**
Rv	12:10	"Now have salvation and **p** come,
Rv	13: 2	To it the dragon gave its own **p**
Rv	20: 6	second death has no **p** over these;

POWERFUL → POWER

Ex	1: 9	**p** the Israelite people are growing,
Est	9: 4	Mordecai was **p** in the royal palace,
1 Cor	1:26	not many were **p**, not many were
Jas	5:16	of a righteous person is very **p**.

POWERS → POWER

Mt	14: 2	that is why mighty **p** are at work

Rom	8:38	things, nor future things, nor **p**,
Eph	6:12	with the **p**, with the world rulers
Col	1:16	or dominions or principalities or **p**;
Heb	6: 5	of God and the **p** of the age to come,
1 Pt	3:22	authorities, and **p** subject to him.

PRACTICE → PRACTICED, PRACTICES

Sir	50:29	If he puts them into **p**, he can cope
Ez	13:23	see false visions and **p** divination,
Mt	23: 3	For they preach but they do not **p**.

PRACTICED → PRACTICE

Acts	19:19	of those who had **p** magic collected

PRACTICES → PRACTICE

Jgs	2:19	relinquishing none of their evil **p**
Ps	101: 7	No one who **p** deceit can hold a post
Col	3: 9	have taken off the old self with its **p**

PRAISE → PRAISED, PRAISES, PRAISING

Ex	15: 2	He is my God, I **p** him; the God
Dt	26:19	then raise you high in **p** and renown
1 Chr	23: 5	four thousand were to **p** the LORD
1 Chr	23: 5	which David had devised for **p**.
2 Chr	20:21	to **p** the holy Appearance as it went
Ezr	3:10	the cymbals to **p** the LORD
Neh	9: 5	exalted above all blessing and **p**."
Tb	12: 6	Give him the **p** and the glory.
Jdt	15:14	the people swelled this hymn of **p**:
Ps	22:24	"You who fear the LORD, give **p**!
Ps	33: 1	LORD; **p** from the upright is fitting.
Ps	34: 2	**p** shall be always in my mouth.
Ps	42: 6	Wait for God, whom I shall **p** again,
Ps	43: 5	Wait for God, whom I shall **p** again,
Ps	45:18	thus nations shall **p** you forever.
Ps	51:17	my mouth will proclaim your **p**.
Ps	56: 5	God, I **p** your promise; in you I
Ps	65: 2	To you we owe our hymn of **p**,
Ps	66: 2	glorious name; give him glorious **p**.
Ps	66: 8	you peoples; loudly sound his **p**,
Ps	69:31	That I may **p** God's name in song
Ps	69:35	Let the heavens and the earth sing **p**,
Ps	71: 8	mouth shall be filled with your **p**,
Ps	71:14	hope in you and add to all your **p**.
Ps	71:22	That I may **p** you with the lyre
Ps	74:21	the poor and needy **p** your name.
Ps	89: 6	The heavens **p** your marvels, LORD,
Ps	100: 4	Enter the temple gates with **p**,
Ps	102:19	yet born, that they may **p** the LORD:
Ps	106: 2	the LORD, proclaim in full God's **p**?
Ps	111:10	live by it. Your **p** endures forever.
Ps	113: 1	**P**, you servants of the LORD,
Ps	117: 1	**P** the LORD, all you nations!
Ps	119:175	Let me live to **p** you; may your
Ps	135: 1	Hallelujah! **P** the name of the LORD! **P**, you servants of the LORD,
Ps	139:14	I **p** you, so wonderfully you made
Ps	147: 1	in song; how sweet to give fitting **p**.
Ps	148: 1	**P** the LORD from the heavens; give **p**
Ps	148:13	Let them all **p** the LORD's name,
Ps	150: 2	Give **p** for his mighty deeds, give **p**
Ps	150: 6	that has breath give **p** to the LORD!
Prv	27: 2	Let another **p** you—not your own
Prv	31:31	let her works **p** her at the city gates.
Sir	11: 2	**P** not a man for his looks;
Sir	44: 1	Now will I **p** those godly men,
Is	42:10	his **p** from the end of the earth:
Jer	33: 9	shall be my joy, my **p**, my glory,
Dn	3:57	**p** and exalt him above all forever.
Hb	3: 3	and with his **p** the earth is filled.
Mt	21:16	nurslings you have brought forth **p**'?"
Lk	19:37	his disciples began to **p** God aloud
Rom	2:29	his **p** is not from human beings
Rom	15:11	again: "**P** the Lord, all you Gentiles,
Rom	15:11	and let all the peoples **p** him."
1 Cor	14:15	I will sing **p** with the spirit, but I
1 Cor	14:15	but I will also sing **p** with the mind.
Eph	1: 6	for the **p** of the glory of his grace
Eph	1:12	might exist for the **p** of his glory,
Eph	1:14	possession, to the **p** of his glory.
1 Thes	2: 6	nor did we seek **p** from human

Heb	13:15	offer God a sacrifice of **p**, that is,
Jas	5:13	in good spirits? He should sing **p**.
Rv	19: 5	"**P** our God, all you his servants,

PRAISED → PRAISE

Gn	12:15	saw her, they **p** her to Pharaoh.
Jgs	16:24	people saw him, they **p** their god.
2 Sm	14:25	was not a man who could so be **p**
Ps	18: 4	**P** be the LORD, I exclaim! I have
Ps	48: 2	Great is the LORD and highly **p**
Prv	31:30	who fears the LORD is to be **p**.
Dn	5: 4	they **p** their gods of gold and silver,

PRAISES → PRAISE

2 Chr	29:30	the Levites to sing the **p** of the LORD
2 Chr	29:30	They sang **p** till their joy was full,
Ps	9:15	Then I will declare all your **p**,
Ps	18:50	I will sing the **p** of your name.
Ps	145:21	My mouth will speak your **p**, LORD;
Sir	24: 1	Wisdom sings her own **p**, before her
Is	38:18	nor death that **p** you; Neither do

PRAISING → PRAISE

Lk	2:13	with the angel, **p** God and saying:
Lk	2:20	and **p** God for all they had heard
Acts	2:47	**p** God and enjoying favor with all
Acts	3: 8	walking and jumping and **p** God.

PRAY → PRAYED, PRAYER, PRAYERS, PRAYING, PRAYS

Ex	8: 5	the time when I am to **p** for you
Nm	21: 7	**P** the LORD to take the serpents
1 Sm	12:23	the LORD by ceasing to **p** for you
2 Chr	6:38	when they **p** in the direction of their
2 Chr	7:14	humble themselves and **p**, and seek
Ezr	6:10	heaven and **p** for the life of the king
Jb	42: 8	and let my servant Job **p** for you;
Ps	5: 3	king, my God! To you I **p**, O LORD;
Ps	122: 6	For the peace of Jerusalem **p**:
Sir	37:15	Most important of all, **p** to God
Jer	29: 7	**p** for it to the LORD, for upon its
Jer	29:12	when you go to **p** to me, I will listen
Mt	5:44	and **p** for those who persecute you,
Mt	6: 5	"When you **p**, do not be like
Mt	6: 5	to stand and **p** in the synagogues
Mt	6: 9	"This is how you are to **p**: Our Father
Mt	14:23	up on the mountain by himself to **p**.
Mt	19:13	might lay his hands on them and **p**.
Mt	26:36	"Sit here while I go over there and **p**."
Lk	6:28	you, **p** for those who mistreat you.
Lk	11: 1	to **p** just as John taught his disciples."
Lk	18: 1	**p** always without becoming weary.
Lk	18:10	went up to the temple area to **p**;
Lk	22:40	"**P** that you may not undergo the test."
Rom	8:26	do not know how to **p** as we ought,
1 Cor	11:13	is it proper for a woman to **p** to God
1 Cor	14:13	in a tongue should **p** to be able
1 Cor	14:15	I will **p** with the spirit, but I will also **p** with the mind.
Eph	6:18	**p** at every opportunity in the Spirit.
1 Thes	5:17	**P** without ceasing.
2 Thes	1:11	To this end, we always **p** for you,
Jas	5:13	He should **p**. Is anyone in good
Jas	5:16	one another and **p** for one another,
1 Jn	5:16	he should **p** to God and he will give
1 Jn	5:16	I do not say that you should **p**.
Jude	1:20	most holy faith; **p** in the holy Spirit.

PRAYED → PRAY

Nm	11: 2	he **p** to the LORD and the fire died
Nm	21: 7	from us." So Moses **p** for the people,
1 Sm	1:27	I **p** for this child, and the LORD
2 Kgs	6:17	Then he **p**, "O LORD, open his eyes,
2 Chr	30:18	for Hezekiah **p** for them, saying,
Neh	4: 3	We **p** to our God and posted a watch
Jb	42:10	of Job, after he had **p** for his friends;
Dn	9: 4	I **p** to the LORD, my God,
Mk	1:35	off to a deserted place, where he **p**.
Mk	14:35	**p** that if it were possible the hour
Lk	22:41	throw from them and kneeling, he **p**,
Acts	4:31	As they **p**, the place where they
Acts	6: 6	these men to the apostles who **p**

Acts	8:15	who went down and **p** for them,
Jas	5:17	yet he **p** earnestly that it might not

PRAYER → PRAY

2 Chr	7:12	him: "I have heard your **p**, and I have
2 Chr	30:27	heard and their **p** reached heaven,
2 Chr	33:19	His **p** and how his supplication was
1 Mc	3:46	at Mizpah a place of **p** for Israel.
Jb	42: 8	for his **p** I will accept, not to punish
Ps	4: 2	a way; show me favor; hear my **p**.
Ps	6:10	The LORD has heard my **p**; the LORD
Ps	17: 1	A **p** of David. Hear, LORD, my plea
Ps	17: 1	Listen to my **p** spoken without
Ps	55: 2	Listen, God, to my **p**; do not hide
Ps	66:20	me the kindness I sought in **p**.
Prv	15: 8	the **p** of the upright is his delight.
Prv	15:29	but the **p** of the just he hears.
Sir	4: 6	you, his Creator will hear his **p**.
Is	56: 7	and make joyful in my house of **p**;
Is	56: 7	called a house of **p** for all peoples.
Hb	3: 1	[**P** of Habakkuk, the prophet.
Mt	21:13	'My house shall be a house of **p**,'
Mt	21:22	you ask for in **p** with faith, you will
Mk	9:29	kind can only come out through **p**."
Mk	11:24	all that you ask for in **p**,
Acts	1:14	themselves with one accord to **p**,
Acts	6: 4	we shall devote ourselves to **p**
Acts	10:31	your **p** has been heard and your
Acts	16:13	thought there would be a place of **p**.
Rom	10: 1	and **p** to God on their behalf is
Rom	12:12	endure in affliction, persevere in **p**.
1 Cor	7: 5	to be free for **p**, but then return
Phil	1: 9	And this is my **p**: that your love
Phil	4: 6	but in everything, by **p** and petition,
Col	4: 2	Persevere in **p**, being watchful in it
1 Tm	4: 5	holy by the invocation of God in **p**.
Jas	5:15	and the **p** of faith will save the sick
Jas	5:16	The fervent **p** of a righteous person
1 Pt	3:12	and his ears turned to their **p**,

PRAYERS → PRAY

Ps	65: 3	you who hear our **p**. To you all flesh
Mk	12:40	and, as a pretext, recite lengthy **p**.
Acts	2:42	breaking of the bread and to **p**.
2 Cor	1:11	the gift granted us through the **p**
1 Tm	2: 1	I ask that supplications, **p**, petitions,
Heb	5: 7	he offered **p** and supplications
1 Pt	3: 7	so that your **p** may not be hindered.
Rv	5: 8	which are the **p** of the holy ones.
Rv	8: 3	with the **p** of all the holy ones,

PRAYING → PRAY

1 Sm	1:13	for Hannah was **p** silently;
Dn	6:12	found Daniel **p** and pleading before
Lk	3:21	also had been baptized and was **p**,
Lk	9:29	While he was **p** his face changed
Acts	9:11	Tarsus named Saul. He is there **p**,
Acts	16:25	Silas were **p** and singing hymns

PRAYS → PRAY

Sir	3: 5	children, and when he **p** he is heard.
Sir	34:24	If one man **p** and another curses,
1 Cor	11: 4	Any man who **p** or prophesies

PREACHING

1 Tm	5:17	especially those who toil in **p**

PRECEDE

1 Thes	4:15	will surely not **p** those who have

PRECEPTS

Ps	19: 9	The **p** of the LORD are right,
Ps	119: 4	command to keep your **p** with care.
Ps	119:15	I will ponder your **p** and consider
Ps	119:27	me understand the way of your **p**;
Ps	119:40	See how I long for your **p**; in your
Ps	119:45	space because I cherish your **p**.
Ps	119:56	fortune, for I have observed your **p**.
Ps	119:63	fear you, of all who keep your **p**.
Ps	119:69	I observe your **p** with all my heart.
Ps	119:78	unjustly, that I may study your **p**.
Ps	119:87	earth, but I do not forsake your **p**.

Ps	119:93	I will never forget your **p**;
Ps	119:94	yours; save me, for I cherish your **p**.
Ps	119:100	my elders, because I observe your **p**.
Ps	119:104	Through your **p** I gain insight;
Ps	119:110	me, but from your **p** I do not stray.
Ps	119:128	Thus I follow all your **p**;
Ps	119:134	oppression, that I may keep your **p**.
Ps	119:141	and despised, I do not forget your **p**.
Ps	119:159	See how I love your **p**, LORD;
Ps	119:168	I observe your **p** and decrees; all my
Ps	119:173	help me, for I have chosen your **p**.
Mt	15: 9	me, teaching as doctrines human **p**.' "
Mk	7: 7	me, teaching as doctrines human **p**.'

PRECIOUS

1 Sm	26:21	you have held my life **p** today.
2 Chr	3: 6	the building with **p** stones.
Ps	72:14	for **p** is their blood in his sight.
Prv	3:15	She is more **p** than corals, and none
Is	28:16	tested, A **p** cornerstone as a sure
Ez	28:13	every **p** stone was your covering
1 Pt	1:19	with the **p** blood of Christ as
1 Pt	2: 4	chosen and **p** in the sight of God,
1 Pt	2: 6	a cornerstone, chosen and **p**,
2 Pt	1: 4	he has bestowed on us the **p**

PREDESTINED

Rom	8:29	**p** to be conformed to the image
Rom	8:30	And those he **p** he also called;

PREDICTED

Acts	11:28	**p** by the Spirit that there would be

PREGNANT

Gn	19:36	of Lot's daughters became **p** by their
Ex	21:22	have a fight and hurt a **p** woman,
Ps	7:15	conceive iniquity; **p** with mischief,
Mt	24:19	Woe to **p** women and nursing
1 Thes	5: 3	like labor pains upon a **p** woman,

PREPARATION → PREPARE

Mt	27:62	the one following the day of **p**,
Jn	19:14	It was **p** day for Passover, and it

PREPARE → PREPARATION, PREPARED

Is	40: 3	In the desert **p** the way of the LORD!
Am	4:12	you, **p** to meet your God, O Israel:
Mal	3: 1	to **p** the way before me;
Mt	3: 3	in the desert, 'P the way of the Lord,
Mt	11:10	he will **p** your way before you.'
Jn	14: 2	that I am going to **p** a place for you?

PREPARED → PREPARE

Ex	23:20	and bring you to the place I have **p**.
1 Chr	15: 1	and **p** a place for the ark of God,
Mt	20:23	whom it has been **p** by my Father."
Mt	25:34	Inherit the kingdom **p** for you
Rom	9:23	which he has **p** previously for glory,
1 Cor	2: 9	what God has **p** for those who love
Eph	2:10	works that God has **p** in advance,
Heb	10: 5	not desire, but a body you **p** for me;
Heb	11:16	God, for he has **p** a city for them.
Rv	12: 6	the desert where she had a place **p**
Rv	21: 2	God, **p** as a bride adorned for her

PRESBYTER → PRESBYTERS

1 Tm	5:19	not accept an accusation against a **p**
1 Pt	5: 1	as a fellow **p** and witness to the
2 Jn	1: 1	The **P** to the chosen Lady and to her
3 Jn	1: 1	The **P** to the beloved Gaius whom I

PRESBYTERS → PRESBYTER

Acts	11:30	sending it to the **p** in care of
Acts	14:23	They appointed **p** for them in each
Acts	15: 2	to Jerusalem to the apostles and **p**
Acts	15: 6	The apostles and the **p** met together
Acts	15:23	"The apostles and the **p**, your brothers,
Acts	16: 4	decisions reached by the apostles and **p**
Acts	20:17	the **p** of the church at Ephesus summoned.
Acts	21:18	to James, and all the **p** were present.
1 Tm	5:17	**P** who preside well deserve double
Ti	1: 5	and appoint **p** in every town,
Jas	5:14	He should summon the **p** of the church,

1 Pt	5: 1	So I exhort the **p** among you,
1 Pt	5: 5	younger members, be subject to the **p**.

PRESCRIBED
2 Kgs	23:21	God, as it was **p** in that book
Ezr	3: 4	the feast of Booths in the manner **p**,

PRESENCE → PRESENT
Nm	4: 7	the **P** they shall spread a violet cloth
1 Sm	21: 7	had been removed from the Lord's **p**
2 Kgs	24:20	till he cast them out from his **p**.
Jb	1:12	went forth from the **p** of the Lord.
Jb	2: 7	went forth from the **p** of the Lord
Ps	16:11	to life, abounding joy in your **p**,
Ps	21: 7	gladden him with the joy of your **p**.
Ps	31:21	hide them in the shelter of your **p**,
Ps	41:13	and let me stand in your **p** forever.
Ps	51:13	Do not drive me from your **p**,
Ps	139: 7	From your **p**, where can I flee?
Jn	8:38	what I have seen in the Father's **p**;
Acts	2:28	you will fill me with joy in your **p**.'
2 Thes	1: 9	separated from the **p** of the Lord
Jude	1:24	and exultant, in the **p** of his glory,
Rv	20:11	the sky fled from his **p** and there

PRESENT → PRESENCE, PRESENTED
Jb	1: 6	to **p** themselves before the Lord,
Jb	2: 1	to **p** themselves before the Lord,
Lk	2:22	to Jerusalem to **p** him to the Lord,
Rom	6:13	do not **p** the parts of your bodies
Rom	6:13	**p** yourselves to God as raised
Rom	8:18	this **p** time are as nothing compared
Rom	8:38	nor principalities, nor **p** things,
1 Cor	3:22	life or death, or the **p** or the future:
1 Cor	7:31	world in its **p** form is passing away.
2 Cor	11: 2	husband to **p** you as a chaste virgin
Eph	5:27	he might **p** to himself the church
Col	1:22	to **p** you holy, without blemish,
1 Tm	4: 8	a promise of life both for the **p**
2 Tm	2:15	Be eager to **p** yourself as acceptable
2 Pt	3: 7	The **p** heavens and earth have been

PRESENTED → PRESENT
Acts	1: 3	He **p** himself alive to them by many

PRESERVE → PRESERVES
Prv	14: 3	but the lips of the wise **p** them.

PRESERVES → PRESERVE
Sir	32:24	He who keeps the law **p** himself;

PRESS → PRESSURE
Rv	14:20	The wine **p** was trodden outside
Rv	19:15	in the wine **p** the wine of the fury

PRESSURE → PRESS
2 Cor	11:28	there is the daily **p** upon me of my

PRESUMES → PRESUMPTUOUSLY
Dt	18:20	if a prophet **p** to speak in my name

PRESUMPTUOUSLY → PRESUMES
Dt	18:22	The prophet has spoken it **p**,

PRETEXT
1 Thes	2: 5	or with a **p** for greed—God is witness—
1 Pt	2:16	yet without using freedom as a **p**

PREVAIL → PREVAILED, PREVAILS
Gn	32:26	saw that he could not **p** over him,
1 Sm	2: 9	For not by strength does man **p**;
2 Chr	14:10	our God; let no man **p** against you."
Jdt	11:10	nor does the sword **p** against them,

PREVAILED → PREVAIL
Gn	32:29	and human beings and have **p**."

PREVAILS → PREVAIL
Wis	7:30	but wickedness **p** not over Wisdom.

PREY
Gn	15:11	Birds of **p** swooped down

PRICE
Gn	23: 9	at its full **p**, for a burial place."
1 Chr	21:22	Sell it to me at its full **p**,

Sir	6:15	A faithful friend is beyond **p**,
Zec	11:13	the handsome **p** at which they
Mt	13:46	When he finds a pearl of great **p**,
Mt	27: 9	value of a man with a **p** on his head,
Mt	27: 9	a **p** set by some of the Israelites,
1 Cor	6:20	For you have been purchased at a **p**.
1 Cor	7:23	You have been purchased at a **p**.

PRIDE → PROUD
Prv	8:13	evil;] **P**, arrogance, the evil way,
Prv	11: 2	When **p** comes, disgrace comes;
Prv	16:18	**P** goes before disaster,
Prv	29:23	Man's **p** causes his humiliation,
Sir	10:13	For **p** is the reservoir of sin,
Is	25:11	He will bring low their **p** as his
Am	8: 7	Lord has sworn by the **p** of Jacob:
2 Cor	7: 4	in you, I have great **p** in you; I am

PRIEST → PRIESTHOOD, PRIESTS
Gn	14:18	and being a **p** of God Most High,
Ex	2:16	daughters of a **p** of Midian came
Ex	18: 1	Jethro, the **p** of Midian, heard of all
Nm	5:10	of the **p** to whom he gives them."
Jgs	17:10	"Be father and **p** to me, and I will
1 Sm	2:11	service of the Lord under the **p** Eli.
1 Sm	2:35	will choose a faithful **p** who shall do
1 Sm	21: 7	So the **p** gave him holy bread,
2 Chr	13: 9	seven rams becomes a **p** of no-gods.
Ps	110: 4	Melchizedek you are a **p** forever."
Sir	7:31	Honor God and respect the **p**;
Jer	23:11	Both prophet and **p** are godless!
Ez	1: 3	of the Lord came to the **p** Ezekiel,
Zec	6:13	The **p** shall be at his right hand,
Mk	14:63	At that the high **p** tore his garments
Heb	2:17	and faithful high **p** before God
Heb	3: 1	and high **p** of our confession,
Heb	4:14	have a great high **p** who has passed
Heb	4:15	do not have a high **p** who is unable
Heb	5: 6	"You are a **p** forever
Heb	6:20	becoming high **p** forever according
Heb	7: 3	Son of God, he remains a **p** forever.
Heb	7:15	more obvious if another **p** is raised
Heb	7:26	that we should have such a high **p**:
Heb	8: 1	we have such a high **p**, who has
Heb	9:11	Christ came as high **p** of the good
Heb	10:21	we have "a great **p** over the house
Heb	13:11	whose blood the high **p** brings

PRIESTHOOD → PRIEST
Ex	29: 9	Thus shall the **p** be theirs
Nm	16:10	and yet you now seek the **p** too.
Nm	25:13	him the pledge of an everlasting **p**,
Ezr	2:62	they were degraded from the **p**,
2 Mc	11: 3	to put the high **p** up for sale every
Heb	7:24	has a **p** that does not pass away.
1 Pt	2: 5	to be a holy **p** to offer spiritual
1 Pt	2: 9	race, a royal **p**, a holy nation,

PRIESTS → PRIEST
Ex	19: 6	You shall be to me a kingdom of **p**,
Ex	28: 1	to you, that they may be my **p**.
Ex	40:15	father, anoint them also as my **p**.
Dt	31: 9	it to the livitical **p** who carry the ark
Jos	6: 4	seven **p** carrying ram's horns ahead
Jos	6: 4	and have the **p** blow the horns.
1 Sm	22:17	a hand to strike the **p** of the Lord.
2 Chr	5: 7	The **p** brought the ark
2 Chr	31: 2	reestablished the classes of the **p**
2 Chr	34: 5	the bones of the **p** he burned
Ezr	6:20	for their brethren the **p**,
Ezr	10: 5	an oath from the chiefs of the **p**,
Neh	3:28	the Horse Gate the **p** carried
Neh	13:30	the various functions for the **p**
1 Mc	4:42	He chose blameless **p**,
Ps	99: 6	and Aaron were among his **p**,
Jer	5:31	and the **p** teach as they wish;
Ez	22:26	Her **p** violate my law and profane
Dn	14:28	the dragon, and put the **p** to death."
Mi	3:11	her **p** give decisions for a salary,
Mal	1: 6	says the Lord of hosts to you, O **p**,
Mt	20:18	will be handed over to the chief **p**

Mt	27: 3	thirty pieces of silver to the chief **p**
Mk	2:26	that only the **p** could lawfully eat,
Mk	15: 3	The chief **p** accused him of many
Jn	19:15	The chief **p** answered, "We have no
Acts	6: 7	group of **p** were becoming obedient
Heb	7:27	as did the high **p**, to offer sacrifice
Rv	1: 6	kingdom, **p** for his God and Father,
Rv	5:10	them a kingdom and **p** for our God,
Rv	20: 6	they will be **p** of God and of Christ,

PRINCE → PRINCES

Dt	33:16	brow of the **p** among his brothers,
Is	9: 5	Father-Forever, **P** of Peace.
Ez	34:24	David shall be **p** among them. I,
Ez	37:25	my servant David their **p** forever.
Ez	45:17	of the **p** to provide the holocausts,
Ez	46: 8	The **p** shall always enter and depart
Dn	8:11	It boasted even against the **p**
Dn	8:25	he rises against the **p** of princes,
Dn	10:20	Soon I must fight the **p** of Persia
Dn	10:20	I leave, the **p** of Greece will come;
Dn	10:21	all these except Michael, your **p**.
Dn	11:22	and even the **p** of the covenant.
Dn	12: 1	Michael, the great **p**,

PRINCES → PRINCE

Ps	2: 2	Kings on earth rise up and **p** plot
Ps	113: 8	Seats them with **p**, the **p**
Ps	118: 9	the LORD than to put one's trust in **p**.
Ps	146: 3	Put no trust in **p**, in mere mortals
Ps	148:11	**p** and all who govern on earth;
Prv	31: 4	strong drink is not for **p**!
Is	40:23	He brings **p** to nought and makes
Dn	8:25	he rises against the prince of **p**,
Dn	10:13	one of the chief **p**, came to help me.

PRISCA See PRISCILLA

PRISCILLA
Wife of Aquila, also called Prisca; co-worker with Paul (Acts 18; Rom 16:3; 1 Cor 16:19; 2 Tm 4:19); instructor of Apollos (Acts 18:24-28).

PRISON → IMPRISONMENT, IMPRISONMENTS, PRISONER, PRISONERS

Gn	39:20	But even while he was in **p**,
Jgs	16:25	So they called Samson from the **p**,
2 Kgs	25:29	Jehoiachin took off his **p** garb
Ps	107:10	in **p**, bound with chains,
Ps	142: 8	Lead me out of my **p**, that I may
Mt	14:10	and he had John beheaded in the **p**.
Mt	25:36	for me, in **p** and you visited me.'
Lk	22:33	I am prepared to go to **p** and to die
Acts	12: 5	Peter thus was being kept in **p**,
1 Pt	3:19	went to preach to the spirits in **p**,
Rv	2:10	devil will throw some of you into **p**,
Rv	20: 7	Satan will be released from his **p**.

PRISONER → PRISON

Mk	15: 6	to them one **p** whom they requested.
Eph	3: 1	I, Paul, a **p** of Christ [Jesus] for you

PRISONERS → PRISON

Ps	68: 7	who leads **p** out to prosperity,
Ps	79:11	the groans of **p** come before you;
Ps	146: 7	to the hungry. The LORD sets **p** free;
Is	42: 7	to bring out **p** from confinement,
Is	61: 1	to the captives and release to the **p**,
Zec	9:12	of the waiting **p**, This very day,
Heb	13: 3	Be mindful of **p** as if sharing their

PRIVATE → PRIVATELY

Mk	4:34	he explained everything in **p**.
Mk	9:28	his disciples asked him in **p**,

PRIVATELY → PRIVATE

Mk	13: 3	John, and Andrew asked him **p**,

PRIZE

1 Cor	9:24	in the race, but only one wins the **p**?
Phil	3:14	goal, the **p** of God's upward calling,

PROCESSION

Ps	42: 5	When I went in **p** with the crowd,

Ps	118:27	Join in **p** with leafy branches

PROCLAIM → PROCLAIMED, PROCLAIMING, PROCLAIMS, PROCLAMATION

Dt	32: 3	Oh, **p** the greatness of our God!
Ps	22:32	they may **p** to a people yet unborn
Ps	97: 6	The heavens **p** God's justice;
Is	12: 4	deeds, **p** how exalted is his name.
Is	61: 1	To **p** liberty to the captives
Jer	7: 2	the LORD, and there **p** this message:
Mt	10:27	hear whispered, **p** on the housetops.
Mt	12:18	and he will **p** justice to the Gentiles.
Lk	4:19	to **p** a year acceptable to the Lord."
Lk	9:60	you, go and **p** the kingdom of God."
Acts	17:23	unknowingly worship, I **p** to you.
1 Cor	11:26	you **p** the death of the Lord until he
Col	1:28	It is he whom we **p**,

PROCLAIMED → PROCLAIM

Ex	34: 5	with him there and **p** his name,
Lk	16:16	then on the kingdom of God is **p**,
Rom	9:17	my name may be **p** throughout

PROCLAIMING → PROCLAIM

Mk	1:14	Jesus came to Galilee **p** the gospel
Acts	4: 2	**p** in Jesus the resurrection

PROCLAIMS → PROCLAIM

Ps	19: 2	of God; the sky **p** its builder's craft.

PROCLAMATION → PROCLAIM

Rom	16:25	my gospel and the **p** of Jesus Christ,

PROCONSUL

Acts	13:12	the **p** saw what had happened,

PRODUCE → PRODUCED, PRODUCES

Jos	5:11	they ate of the **p** of the land
Prv	3: 9	wealth, with first fruits of all your **p**;

PRODUCED → PRODUCE

Rom	7: 8	**p** in me every kind of covetousness.

PRODUCES → PRODUCE

Lk	6:45	of goodness in his heart **p** good,
Lk	6:45	person out of a store of evil **p** evil;
Rom	5: 3	knowing that affliction **p** endurance,
2 Cor	7:10	For godly sorrow **p** a salutary
2 Cor	7:10	regret, but worldly sorrow **p** death.
Heb	6: 8	But if it **p** thorns and thistles, it is
Jas	1: 3	testing of your faith **p** perseverance.

PROFANE → PROFANED

Lv	22:32	and do not **p** my holy name;
1 Mc	1:45	to **p** the sabbaths and feast days,
Ez	20:39	never again **p** my holy name

PROFANED → PROFANE

Jdt	4:12	or the sanctuary to be **p** and mocked
1 Mc	1:43	sacrificed to idols and **p** the sabbath.
Jer	34:16	and **p** my name by taking back your
Ez	20: 9	that it should not be **p** in the sight
Ez	39: 7	longer allow my holy name to be **p**.

PROFESS → PROFESSES, PROFESSING

1 Tm	2:10	as befits women who **p** reverence

PROFESSES → PROFESS

Wis	2:13	He **p** to have knowledge of God

PROFESSING → PROFESS

1 Tm	6:21	By **p** it, some people have deviated

PROFIT

Prv	14:23	In all labor there is **p**, but mere talk
Sir	29:11	that will **p** you more than the gold.
Mt	16:26	What **p** would there be for one

PROGRESS

Phil	1:25	the service of all of you for your **p**
1 Tm	4:15	so that your **p** may be evident

PROMISE → PROMISED, PROMISES

1 Kgs	6:12	will fulfill toward you the **p** I made
1 Kgs	8:20	now the LORD has fulfilled the **p**
Neh	5:13	every man who fails to keep this **p**,
Ps	106:24	land; they did not believe the **p**.

Ps	119:41	salvation in accord with your **p**.
Ps	119:50	affliction, your **p** that gives me life.
Ps	119:58	mercy on me in accord with your **p**.
Ps	119:172	May my tongue sing of your **p**,
Acts	2:39	For the **p** is made to you and to your
Acts	26: 7	**p** as they fervently worship God day
Rom	4:13	through the law that the **p** was made
Rom	4:20	He did not doubt God's **p**
Rom	9: 8	of the **p** are counted as descendants.
Gal	3:18	the law, it is no longer from a **p**;
Gal	3:18	it on Abraham through a **p**.
Gal	4:28	like Isaac, are children of the **p**.
Eph	2:12	and strangers to the covenants of **p**,
Eph	6: 2	is the first commandment with a **p**,
1 Tm	4: 8	since it holds a **p** of life both
2 Tm	1: 1	God for the **p** of life in Christ Jesus,
Heb	4: 1	on our guard while the **p** of entering
Heb	6:13	When God made the **p** to Abraham,
2 Pt	2:19	They **p** them freedom, though they
2 Pt	3: 9	The Lord does not delay his **p**,
2 Pt	3:13	to his **p** we await new heavens

PROMISED → PROMISE

Gn	21: 1	he would; he did for her as he had **p**.
Gn	28:15	you until I have done what I **p** you."
Ex	32:13	and all this land that I **p**, I will give
Nm	10:29	which the LORD has **p** to give us.
Nm	10:29	for the LORD has **p**,
Dt	1:11	times over, and bless you as he **p**!
Dt	15: 6	your God, will bless you as he **p**.
Dt	26:18	peculiarly his own, as he **p** you;
Jos	23: 5	land as the LORD, your God, **p** you.
1 Kgs	9: 5	as I **p** your father David when I
Acts	13:32	you that what God **p** our ancestors
Rom	4:21	that what he had **p** he was also able
Eph	1:13	were sealed with the **p** holy Spirit,
Ti	1: 2	does not lie, **p** before time began,
Heb	10:36	of God and receive what he has **p**.
Jas	1:12	life that he **p** to those who love him.
Jas	2: 5	that he **p** to those who love him?

PROMISES → PROMISE

Neh	9: 8	These **p** of yours you fulfilled,
Ps	12: 7	The **p** of the LORD are sure,
Wis	12:21	the sworn covenants of goodly **p**!
Rom	9: 4	of the law, the worship, and the **p**;
Rom	15: 8	to confirm the **p** to the patriarchs.
2 Cor	1:20	For however many are the **p** of God,
2 Cor	7: 1	Since we have these **p**, beloved,
Gal	3:21	law then opposed to the **p** [of God]?
Heb	8: 6	better covenant, enacted on better **p**.
2 Pt	1: 4	on us the precious and very great **p**,

PROMPTED → PROMPTS

Mt	14: 8	**P** by her mother, she said, "Give me

PROMPTS → PROMPTED

Ex	25: 2	that his heart **p** him to give me.

PROOF → PROVE

2 Cor	8:24	So give **p** before the churches

PROOFS → PROVE

Acts	1: 3	by many **p** after he had suffered,

PROPER

Sir	31:28	are wine drunk freely at the **p** time.
1 Cor	11:13	is it **p** for a woman to pray to God
Jude	1: 6	but deserted their **p** dwelling, he has

PROPERTY

Gn	23: 4	your holdings a piece of **p**
Lv	25:10	one of you shall return to his own **p**,
Mt	12:29	a strong man's house and steal his **p**,
Lk	15:12	father divided the **p** between them.
Acts	5: 1	his wife Sapphira, sold a piece of **p**.

PROPHECIES → PROPHESY

Tb	14: 4	word of the **p** shall prove false.
1 Cor	13: 8	If there are **p**, they will be brought

PROPHECY → PROPHESY

Prv	29:18	Without **p** the people become
Acts	21: 9	four virgin daughters gifted with **p**.

1 Cor	12:10	to another **p**; to another discernment
1 Cor	14: 6	or knowledge, or **p**, or instruction?
1 Cor	14:22	whereas **p** is not for unbelievers
2 Pt	1:20	that there is no **p** of scripture that is
Rv	19:10	Witness to Jesus is the spirit of **p**."

PROPHESIED → PROPHESY

Nm	11:25	spirit came to rest on them, they **p**.
Jer	2: 8	against me. The prophets **p** by Baal,
Jer	26:11	he has **p** against this city, as you
Mt	11:13	and the law **p** up to the time of John.
Jn	11:51	he **p** that Jesus was going to die
Acts	19: 6	and they spoke in tongues and **p**.
Jude	1:14	**p** also about them when he said,

PROPHESIES → PROPHESY

2 Chr	18: 7	for he **p** not good but always evil
Jer	28: 9	But the prophet who **p** peace is
Ez	12:27	way off; he **p** of the distant future!"
1 Cor	11: 4	or **p** with his head covered brings
1 Cor	14: 5	One who **p** is greater than one who

PROPHESY → PROPHECIES, PROPHECY, PROPHESIED, PROPHESIES, PROPHESYING, PROPHET, PROPHET'S, PROPHETESS, PROPHETIC, PROPHETS

Jer	5:31	The prophets **p** falsely,
Ez	13: 2	**p** against the prophets of Israel, **p**!
Ez	13: 2	to those who **p** their own thought:
Ez	13:17	of your people who **p** their own
Ez	13:17	against these, **p**: Thus says the Lord
Ez	34: 2	**p** against the shepherds of Israel,
Ez	37: 4	**P** over these bones, and say to them:
Jl	3: 1	Your sons and daughters shall **p**,
Am	2:12	commanded the prophets not to **p**.
Am	7:16	You say: **p** not against Israel,
Mt	7:22	Lord, did we not **p** in your name?
Lk	22:64	him and questioned him, saying, "**P**!
Acts	2:17	sons and your daughters shall **p**,
1 Cor	13: 9	know partially and we **p** partially,
1 Cor	14: 5	in tongues, but even more to **p**.
1 Cor	14:39	strive eagerly to **p**, and do not forbid
Rv	11: 3	commission my two witnesses to **p**

PROPHESYING → PROPHESY

Nm	11:27	"Eldad and Medad are **p** in the camp,"
Rv	11: 6	can fall during the time of their **p**.

PROPHET → PROPHESY

Ex	7: 1	your brother shall act as your **p**.
Dt	18:18	for them a **p** like you from among
Dt	18:22	even though a **p** speaks in the name
Dt	34:10	no **p** has arisen in Israel like Moses,
1 Sm	3:20	Samuel was an accredited **p**
1 Sm	9: 9	is now called **p** was formerly called
1 Kgs	1: 8	Nathan the **p**, and Shimei and his
1 Kgs	18:36	the **p** Elijah came forward and said,
1 Kgs	22: 7	"Is there no other **p** of the LORD here
2 Kgs	5: 8	find out that there is a **p** in Israel."
2 Kgs	6:12	"The Israelite **p** Elisha can tell
2 Kgs	20: 1	was mortally ill, the **p** Isaiah,
2 Chr	35:18	since the time of the **p** Samuel,
2 Chr	36:12	himself before the **p** Jeremiah,
1 Mc	4:46	until a **p** should come and decide
1 Mc	14:41	and high priest until a true **p** arises.
Jer	1: 5	a **p** to the nations I appointed you.
Jer	23:11	Both **p** and priest are godless! In my
Jer	28: 1	of the fourth year, the **p** Hananiah,
Ez	2: 5	know that a **p** has been among them.
Ez	33:33	that there was a **p** among them.
Dn	3:38	We have in our day no prince, **p**,
Dn	9: 2	the LORD spoke to the **p** Jeremiah:
Hos	9: 7	Let Israel know it! "The **p** is a fool,
Am	7:14	"I was no **p**, nor have I belonged
Hb	1: 1	Habakkuk the **p** received in vision.
Hg	1: 1	the LORD came through the **p** Haggai
Zec	1: 1	of the LORD came to the **p** Zechariah,
Mal	3:23	Elijah, the **p**, Before the day
Mt	10:41	Whoever receives a **p** because he is a **p** will receive
Mt	11: 9	To see a **p**? Yes, I tell you, and more than a **p**.
Mt	12:39	it except the sign of Jonah the **p**.
Lk	1:76	will be called **p** of the Most High,

Lk	4:24	no **p** is accepted in his own native
Lk	7:16	"A great **p** has arisen in our midst,"
Lk	20: 6	are convinced that John was a **p**."
Lk	24:19	who was a **p** mighty in deed
Jn	1:21	"Are you the P?" He answered, "No."
Jn	7:40	these words said, "This is truly the P."
Acts	7:37	your own kinsfolk, a **p** like me.'
Acts	13: 6	Bar-Jesus who was a Jewish false **p**.
Acts	21:10	a **p** named Agabus came down
1 Cor	14:37	If anyone thinks that he is a **p**
Rv	16:13	and from the mouth of the false **p**.
Rv	19:20	it the false **p** who had performed
Rv	20:10	the beast and the false **p** were.

PROPHET'S → PROPHESY
Mt	10:41	a prophet will receive a **p** reward,

PROPHETESS → PROPHESY
Jgs	4: 4	At this time the **p** Deborah,
2 Kgs	22:14	where the **p** Huldah resided.
Neh	6:14	keep in mind as well Noadiah the **p**
Is	8: 3	I went to the **p** and she conceived

PROPHETIC → PROPHESY
1 Sm	10:10	that he joined them in their **p** state.
1 Sm	19:23	in a **p** condition until he reached
2 Pt	1:19	we possess the **p** message that is

PROPHETS → PROPHESY
Nm	11:29	all the people of the LORD were **p**!
1 Sm	10:11	in a prophetic state among the **p**,
1 Sm	10:11	of Kish? Is Saul also among the **p**?"
1 Sm	19:24	they say, "Is Saul also among the **p**?"
1 Sm	28: 6	dreams or by the Urim or through **p**.
1 Kgs	18: 4	Jezebel was murdering the **p**
1 Kgs	18: 4	Obadiah took a hundred **p**, hid them
1 Kgs	18:40	said to them, "Seize the **p** of Baal.
1 Kgs	19:10	altars, and put your **p** to the sword.
2 Kgs	17:23	through all his servants, the **p**;
1 Chr	16:22	anointed, and to my **p** do no harm."
2 Chr	18:22	spirit in the mouths of these your **p**,
Ezr	6:14	supported by the message of the **p**;
Neh	9:30	your spirit, by means of your **p**;
1 Mc	9:27	in Israel since the time **p** ceased
Ps	105:15	my anointed, to my **p** do no harm."
Jer	5:13	The **p** have become wind,
Jer	14:14	Lies these **p** utter in my name,
Jer	23: 9	Concerning the **p**: My heart within
Jer	23:30	Therefore I am against the **p**,
Lam	2: 9	And her **p** have not received
Ez	13: 2	prophesy against the **p** of Israel,
Hos	6: 5	reason I smote them through the **p**,
Mi	3: 6	The sun shall go down upon the **p**,
Zep	3: 4	Her **p** are insolent, treacherous men;
Zec	1: 5	And the **p**, can they live forever?
Mt	5:17	come to abolish the law or the **p**.
Mt	7:12	do to you. This is the law and the **p**.
Mt	7:15	"Beware of false **p**, who come to you
Mt	22:40	law and the **p** depend on these two
Mt	24:24	messiahs and false **p** will arise,
Lk	6:23	For their ancestors treated the **p**
Lk	10:24	many **p** and kings desired to see
Lk	11:49	'I will send to them **p** and apostles;
Lk	16:29	replied, 'They have Moses and the **p**.
Lk	24:25	heart to believe all that the **p** spoke!
Lk	24:44	and in the **p** and psalms must be
Acts	3:24	Moreover, all the **p** who spoke,
Acts	10:43	To him all the **p** bear witness,
Acts	13: 1	were in the church at Antioch **p**
Acts	26:22	nothing different from what the **p**
Acts	28:23	from the law of Moses and the **p**.
Rom	1: 2	promised previously through his **p**
Rom	3:21	testified to by the law and the **p**,
Rom	11: 3	they have killed your **p**, they have
1 Cor	12:28	apostles; second, **p**; third, teachers;
1 Cor	12:29	Are all **p**? Are all teachers? Do all
1 Cor	14:32	spirits of **p** are under the **p**' control,
Eph	2:20	the foundation of the apostles and **p**,
Eph	3: 5	his holy apostles and **p** by the Spirit,
Eph	4:11	others as **p**, others as evangelists,
1 Thes	2:15	Jesus and the **p** and persecuted us;
Heb	1: 1	ways to our ancestors through the **p**;
1 Pt	1:10	**p** who prophesied about the grace
2 Pt	2: 1	were also false **p** among the people,
2 Pt	3: 2	previously spoken by the holy **p**
1 Jn	4: 1	because many false **p** have gone
Rv	11:10	because these two **p** tormented
Rv	16: 6	the blood of the holy ones and the **p**,
Rv	18:20	you holy ones, apostles, and **p**.

PROPORTION
Dt	16:10	own freewill offering shall be in **p**
Rom	12: 6	them: if prophecy, in **p** to the faith;

PROPOSED
Acts	1:23	So they **p** two, Joseph called

PROSPER → PROSPERED, PROSPERITY, PROSPERS
Ps	25:13	They live well and **p**, and their
Jer	12: 1	Why does the way of the godless **p**,

PROSPERED → PROSPER
1 Chr	29:23	he **p**, and all Israel obeyed him.
2 Chr	14: 6	on every side." So they built and **p**.
2 Chr	31:21	did this wholeheartedly, and he **p**.

PROSPERITY → PROSPER
Dt	30: 9	will again take delight in your **p**,
Dt	30:15	have today set before you life and **p**,
Jb	36:11	they spend their days in **p**,
Ps	73: 3	when I saw the **p** of the wicked.
Prv	8:18	and honor, enduring wealth and **p**.
Sir	12: 8	our **p** we cannot know our friends;
Is	48:18	your **p** would be like a river,

PROSPERS → PROSPER
Ps	1: 3	never wither; whatever they do **p**.
Prv	28:13	He who conceals his sins **p** not,

PROSTITUTE → PROSTITUTES
Dt	23:18	nor a temple **p** among the Israelite
1 Cor	6:15	and make them the members of a **p**?
1 Cor	6:16	himself to a **p** becomes one body

PROSTITUTES → PROSTITUTE
1 Kgs	14:24	There were also cult **p** in the land.
1 Kgs	15:12	banishing the temple **p**
Mt	21:31	**p** are entering the kingdom of God
Lk	15:30	swallowed up your property with **p**,
1 Cor	6: 9	adulterers nor boy **p** nor practicing

PROSTRATE
Dt	9:18	I lay **p** before the LORD for forty
Dn	8:17	I was standing, I fell **p** in terror.

PROTECT → PROTECTED, PROTECTION, PROTECTS
Ps	12: 8	LORD, **p** us always; preserve us

PROTECTED → PROTECT
Jos	24:17	and **p** us along our entire journey
Jn	17:12	with them I **p** them in your name

PROTECTION → PROTECT
Eccl	7:12	For the **p** of wisdom is as the **p**

PROTECTS → PROTECT
Jdt	9:14	there is no other who **p** the people
Ps	116: 6	The LORD **p** the simple; I was

PROTEST
Acts	13:51	from their feet in **p** against them

PROUD → PRIDE
2 Chr	32:25	of gratitude, for he had become **p**.
Ps	94: 2	earth; give the **p** what they deserve.
Prv	16:19	than to share plunder with the **p**.
Prv	21: 4	Haughty eyes and a **p** heart—
Sir	10: 9	Why are dust and ashes **p**?
Is	2:12	against all that is **p** and arrogant,
Hos	13: 6	when filled, they became **p** of heart
Jas	4: 6	"God resists the **p**, but gives grace
1 Pt	5: 5	for: "God opposes the **p** but bestows

PROVE → PROOF, PROOFS, PROVING
Ezr	2:59	Immer were unable to **p** that their

PROVERB → PROVERBS
Prv	26: 7	A **p** in the mouth of a fool

Prv	26: 9	is a **p** in the mouth of fools.
Ez	18: 3	among you who will repeat this **p**
Lk	4:23	"Surely you will quote me this **p**,

PROVERBS → PROVERB

1 Kgs	5:12	also uttered three thousand **p**,
Prv	1: 1	The **p** of Solomon, the son
Prv	10: 1	The **P** of Solomon: A wise son
Prv	25: 1	These also are **p** of Solomon.
Eccl	12: 9	scrutinized and arranged many **p**.

PROVIDE → PROVIDED, PROVIDES, PROVISION

Gn	22: 8	"God himself will **p** the sheep
1 Cor	10:13	the trial he will also **p** a way out,
1 Tm	5: 8	whoever does not **p** for relatives

PROVIDED → PROVIDE

1 Kgs	8:21	I have **p** in it a place for the ark
Rom	11:22	you, **p** you remain in his kindness;

PROVIDES → PROVIDE

1 Tm	6:17	who richly **p** us with all things

PROVING → PROVE

Acts	9:22	**p** that this is the Messiah.

PROVISION → PROVIDE

Rom	13:14	and make no **p** for the desires

PROVOCATION → PROVOKE

Prv	27: 3	but a fool's **p** is heavier than both.

PROVOKE → PROVOCATION, PROVOKED

Dt	32:21	I will **p** them with a 'no-people';
Jer	25: 6	lest you **p** me with your handiwork,

PROVOKED → PROVOKE

Jgs	2:12	worship of these gods **p** the LORD.
Ps	78:41	God, **p** the Holy One of Israel.
Bar	4: 7	For you **p** your Maker

PROWLING

1 Pt	5: 8	Your opponent the devil is **p** around

PRUDENCE → PRUDENT

Wis	8: 7	For she teaches moderation and **p**,

PRUDENT → PRUDENCE

Prv	19:14	but a **p** wife is from the LORD.
Jer	49: 7	has counsel perished from the **p**,
Am	5:13	Therefore the **p** man is silent at this

PRUNES → PRUNING

Jn	15: 2	does he **p** so that it bears more fruit.

PRUNING → PRUNES

Is	2: 4	and their spears into **p** hooks;
Jl	4:10	and your **p** hooks into spears;
Mi	4: 3	and their spears into **p** hooks;

PSALM → PSALMS

Acts	13:33	as it is written in the second **p**,

PSALMS → PSALM

Lk	20:42	himself in the Book of **P** says:
Lk	24:44	the prophets and **p** must be fulfilled."
Acts	1:20	For it is written in the Book of **P**:
Eph	5:19	addressing one another [in] **p**
Col	3:16	one another, singing **p**, hymns,

PTOLEMY

1 Mc	1:18	to make war on **P**, king of Egypt.
1 Mc	10:51	Alexander sent ambassadors to **P**,

PUBLIC → PUBLICLY

Col	2:15	he made a **p** spectacle of them,

PUBLICLY → PUBLIC

Gal	3: 1	eyes Jesus Christ was **p** portrayed as
Heb	10:33	times you were **p** exposed to abuse

PUL → =TIGLATH-PILESER

2 Kgs	15:19	**P**, king of Assyria,

PULLED → PULLS

Neh	13:25	of them beaten and their hair **p** out;

PULLS → PULLED

Mt	9:16	its fullness **p** away from the cloak

PUNISH → PUNISHMENT

Ex	32:34	When it is time for me to **p**, I will **p**
Is	13:11	Thus I will **p** the world for its evil
Jer	2:19	your own infidelities **p** you.
Jer	21:14	I will **p** you, says the LORD, as your
Zep	1:12	I will **p** the men who thicken
Acts	4:21	them, finding no way to **p** them,

PUNISHMENT → PUNISH

Gn	4:13	the LORD: "My **p** is too great to bear.
Ps	91: 8	the **p** of the wicked you will see.
Lam	4: 6	The **p** of the daughter of my people
Hos	9: 7	They have come, the days of **p**!
Mt	25:46	And these will go off to eternal **p**,
2 Pt	2: 9	keep the unrighteous under **p**
1 Jn	4:18	fear because fear has to do with **p**,
Jude	1: 7	by undergoing a **p** of eternal fire.

PUR → PURIM

Est	3: 7	of King Ahasuerus, the **p**, or lot,

PURE → PURIFICATION, PURIFIED, PURIFY, PURITY

Ex	25:11	it inside and outside with **p** gold,
Ex	25:31	lampstand of **p** beaten gold —its shaft
Ex	37: 6	propitiatory was made of **p** gold,
1 Kgs	6:21	interior of the temple with **p** gold.
Tb	8:15	with every holy and **p** blessing!
Ps	19:10	The fear of the LORD is **p**,
Ps	24: 4	"The clean of hand and **p** of heart,
Prv	15:26	the **p** speak what is pleasing to him.
Wis	7:25	and a **p** effusion of the glory
Hb	1:13	Too **p** are your eyes to look
Phil	1:10	so that you may be **p** and blameless
Phil	4: 8	whatever is **p**, whatever is lovely,
1 Tm	1: 5	instruction is love from a **p** heart,
1 Tm	5:22	in another's sins. Keep yourself **p**.
Heb	10:22	and our bodies washed in **p** water.
Jas	1:27	Religion that is **p** and undefiled
Jas	3:17	wisdom from above is first of all **p**,
1 Jn	3: 3	hope based on him makes himself **p**, as he is **p**.
Rv	21:18	while the city was **p** gold, clear as

PURGE

Dt	13: 6	Thus shall you **p** the evil from your
Dt	13:19	Thus shall you **p** the evil from your

PURIFICATION → PURE

2 Mc	1:18	We shall be celebrating the **p**
Lk	2:22	completed for their **p** according
Heb	1: 3	he had accomplished **p** from sins,

PURIFIED → PURE

Ezr	6:20	one of whom had **p** himself
Neh	12:30	and Levites first **p** themselves,
Neh	12:30	then they **p** the people, the gates,
Ps	12: 7	in a crucible, silver **p** seven times.
Dn	12:10	Many shall be refined, **p**, and tested,
1 Pt	1:22	Since you have **p** yourselves

PURIFY → PURE

Nm	19:12	he shall **p** himself with the water
Nm	19:12	if he fails to **p** himself on the third
Mal	3: 3	and he will **p** the sons of Levi,
Jas	4: 8	and **p** your hearts, you of two

PURIM → PUR

Est	9:26	so these days have been named **P**

PURITY → PURE

2 Cor	6: 6	by **p**, knowledge, patience,
1 Tm	4:12	speech, conduct, love, faith, and **p**.
1 Tm	5: 2	women as sisters with complete **p**.

PURPLE

Ex	25: 4	violet, **p** and scarlet yarn; fine linen
Prv	31:22	fine linen and **p** are her clothing.
Dn	5:29	Belshazzar they clothed Daniel in **p**,
Mk	15:17	They clothed him in **p** and,
Rv	17: 4	The woman was wearing **p**
Rv	18:16	wearing fine linen, **p** and scarlet,

PURPOSE

Is	46:10	stand, I accomplish my every **p**.
Rom	8:28	who are called according to his **p**.

Eph	1:11	the **p** of the One who accomplishes
Eph	3:11	the eternal **p** that he accomplished
Heb	6:17	of the immutability of his **p**,
Rv	17:17	it into their minds to carry out his **p**

PURSUE →PURSUED, PURSUES

Dt	19: 6	the heat of his anger **p** the homicide
Ps	34:15	and do good; seek peace and **p** it.
Is	51: 1	Listen to me, you who **p** justice,
Rom	14:19	Let us then **p** what leads to peace
1 Cor	14: 1	**P** love, but strive eagerly
1 Tm	6:11	Instead, **p** righteousness, devotion,
2 Tm	2:22	desires and **p** righteousness, faith,

PURSUED →PURSUE

Ps	18:38	I **p** my enemies and overtook them;

PURSUES →PURSUE

Lv	26:17	take to flight though no one **p** you.
Prv	11:19	he who **p** evil does so to his death.
Prv	13:21	Misfortune **p** sinners, but the just
Prv	21:21	He who **p** justice and kindness
Prv	28: 1	man flees although no one **p** him;
Sir	31: 5	for he who **p** wealth is led astray

PUT →PUTS, PUTTING

Gn	3:15	I will **p** enmity between you
Gn	4:15	So the LORD **p** a mark on Cain,
Gn	24: 2	"**P** your hand under my thigh,
Gn	47:29	**p** your hand under my thigh as
Ex	4: 6	to him, "**P** your hand in your bosom."
Ex	4: 6	He **p** it in his bosom, and when he
Nm	17:25	"**P** back Aaron's staff in front
1 Sm	7: 4	So the Israelites **p** away their Baals
Ps	40: 4	And **p** a new song in my mouth,
Is	42: 1	Upon whom I have **p** my spirit;
Is	59:17	He **p** on justice as his breastplate,
Jer	32:14	and **p** them in an earthen jar,
Ez	36:27	I will **p** my spirit within you
Ez	37:14	I will **p** my spirit in you that you
Mt	4: 7	'You shall not **p** the Lord, your God,
Jn	20:25	and **p** my finger into the nailmarks
Jn	20:25	and **p** my hand into his side, I will
Rom	8:13	the spirit you **p** to death the deeds
Rom	9:33	in him shall not be **p** to shame."
Rom	10:11	believes in him will be **p** to shame."
1 Cor	13:11	a man, I **p** aside childish things.
1 Cor	15:25	reign until he has **p** all his enemies
Eph	6:11	**P** on the armor of God so that you
Heb	8:10	I will **p** my laws in their minds and I
1 Pt	3:18	**P** to death in the flesh, he was

PUTS →PUT

Nm	23:12	"Is it not what the LORD **p** in my

PUTTING →PUT

Eph	4:25	Therefore, **p** away falsehood,

Q

QUAIL

Ex	16:13	In the evening **q** came up and covered
Nm	11:31	drove in **q** from the sea and brought
Ps	105:40	They asked and he brought them **q**;
Wis	16: 2	by providing **q** for their food;

QUAKE →EARTHQUAKE, EARTHQUAKES, QUAKED

Na	1: 5	The mountains **q** before him,

QUAKED →QUAKE

2 Sm	22: 8	"The earth swayed and **q**;

QUARREL →QUARRELED, QUARRELS

Prv	17:14	check a **q** before it begins!
Prv	20: 3	strife, while every fool starts a **q**.
Prv	26:17	he who meddles in a **q** not his own.

QUARRELED →QUARREL

Ex	17: 7	because the Israelites **q** there

QUARRELS →QUARREL

Sir	28:11	and insistent **q** provoke bloodshed.
2 Tm	2:23	for you know that they breed **q**.
Ti	3: 9	and **q** about the law, for they are

QUEEN

1 Kgs	10: 1	The **q** of Sheba, having heard
2 Chr	15:16	he deposed as **q** mother because she
Est	1:12	But **Q** Vashti refused to come
Est	2:17	and made her **q** in place of Vashti.
Jer	7:18	to make cakes for the **q** of heaven,
Ez	16:13	beautiful, with the dignity of a **q**.
Mt	12:42	the judgment the **q** of the south will
Acts	8:27	that is, the **q** of the Ethiopians,
Rv	18: 7	'I sit enthroned as **q**; I am no widow,

QUENCH →QUENCHED

Song	8: 7	Deep waters cannot **q** love,
Is	1:31	there shall be none to **q** the flames.
Jer	4: 4	and burn till none can **q** it,

QUENCHED →QUENCH

Jer	7:20	earth; it will burn without being **q**.
Mk	9:48	does not die, and the fire is not **q**.'

QUESTION →QUESTIONS

Jb	38: 3	I will **q** you, and you tell me
Jb	40: 7	I will **q** you, and you tell me
Mk	11:29	said to them, "I shall ask you one **q**.

QUESTIONS →QUESTION

2 Chr	9: 1	Jerusalem to test him with subtle **q**,
Mt	22:46	anyone dare to ask him any more **q**.

QUICK →QUICK-TEMPERED, QUICKLY

Eccl	5: 1	let not your heart be **q** to make
Jas	1:19	everyone should be **q** to hear,

QUICK-TEMPERED →QUICK, TEMPER

Prv	14:17	The **q** man makes a fool of himself,
Prv	14:29	but the **q** man displays folly at its
Sir	8:16	Provoke no quarrel with a **q** man

QUICKLY →QUICK

Jos	23:16	and you will **q** perish from the good
Ps	22:20	my strength, come **q** to help me.
Mt	28: 7	Then go **q** and tell his disciples,
Jn	13:27	"What you are going to do, do **q**."
Rom	9:28	**q** will the Lord execute sentence
Gal	1: 6	you are so **q** forsaking the one who

QUIET →QUIETLY

Eccl	9:17	"The **q** words of the wise are better
1 Tm	2: 2	that we may lead a **q** and tranquil

QUIETLY →QUIET

Mt	1:19	to shame, decided to divorce her **q**.

QUIRINIUS

Lk	2: 2	when **Q** was governor of Syria.

QUIVER →QUIVERS

Is	49: 2	a polished arrow, in his **q** he hid me.

QUIVERS →QUIVER

Ps	127: 5	Blessed are they whose **q** are full.

QUOTE

Lk	4:23	"Surely you will **q** me this proverb,

R

RAAMESES

Ex	1:11	the supply cities of Pithom and **R**.

RABBI →RABBOUNI

Mt	23: 8	As for you, do not be called '**R**.'
Mt	26:49	went over to Jesus and said, "Hail, **R**!"
Jn	1:38	to him, "**R**" (which translated means

RABBOUNI →RABBI

Jn	20:16	and said to him in Hebrew, "**R**,"

RACE

Eccl	9:11	under the sun that the **r** is not won
1 Cor	9:24	in the stadium all run in the **r**,
2 Tm	4: 7	I have finished the **r**; I have kept
Heb	12: 1	in running the **r** that lies before us
1 Pt	2: 9	But you are "a chosen **r**, a royal

RACHEL
Daughter of Laban (Gn 29:16); wife of Jacob (Gn 29:28); bore

two sons (Gn 30:22-24; 35:16-24; 46:19). Stole Laban's gods (Gn 31:19, 32-35). Death (Gn 35:19-20).

RADIANCE →RADIANT
Rv	21:11	Its r was like that of a precious

RADIANT →RADIANCE
Ps	34: 6	to God that you may be r with joy
Song	5:10	My lover is r and ruddy;
Is	60: 5	Then you shall be r at what you see,

RAGE →RAGING
Acts	4:25	'Why did the Gentiles r

RAGING →RAGE
Jon	1:15	into the sea, and the sea's r abated.

RAGS
Jer	38:12	tattered r between your armpits

RAGUEL'S
Tb	3:17	to marry R daughter Sarah to Tobit's son
Tb	14:13	Then he inherited R estate as well as

RAHAB
Prostitute of Jericho who hid Israelite spies (Jos 2; 6:22-25; Heb 11:31; Jas 2:25). Mother of Boaz (Mt 1:5).

RAIN →RAINED, RAINS
Gn	2: 5	the LORD God had sent no r
Gn	7: 4	now I will bring r down on the earth
Ex	16: 4	"I will now r down bread
Lv	26: 4	I will give you r in due season,
Dt	11:14	I will give the seasonal r to your land, the early r and the late r,
1 Kgs	17: 1	be no dew or r except at my word."
1 Kgs	18: 1	"that I may send r upon the earth."
2 Chr	6:26	sky is closed so that there is no r,
Jb	38:28	Has the r a father; or who has
Ps	147: 8	with clouds, provides r for the earth,
Is	45: 8	like gentle r let the skies drop it
Jer	14:22	idols is there any that gives r?
Zec	14:17	of hosts, no r shall fall upon them.
Mt	5:45	and causes r to fall on the just
Mt	7:25	The r fell, the floods came,
Jas	5:17	prayed earnestly that it might not r,
Jas	5:17	and six months it did not r
Rv	11: 6	so that no r can fall during the time

RAINED →RAIN
Gn	19:24	time the LORD r down sulphurous
Ex	9:23	the LORD r down hail upon the land
Ps	78:24	God r manna upon them for food;
Ps	78:27	He r meat upon them like dust,
Lk	17:29	brimstone r from the sky to destroy

RAINS →RAIN
Jas	5: 7	it receives the early and the late r.

RAISE →RISE
Dt	18:15	r up for you from among your own
Prv	8: 1	call, and Understanding r her voice?
Is	11:12	He shall r a signal to the nations
Mt	3: 9	God can r up children to Abraham
Jn	2:19	and in three days I will r it up."
Jn	6:39	that I should r it [on] the last day.
Acts	3:22	the Lord, your God, r up for you
1 Cor	6:14	and will also r us by his power.
2 Cor	4:14	who raised the Lord Jesus will r us
Heb	11:19	God was able to r even

RAISED →RISE
Jgs	2:18	Whenever the LORD r up judges
Mt	17:23	and he will be r on the third day."
Lk	7:22	the dead are r, the poor have
Lk	24:34	"The Lord has truly been r
Acts	2:24	But God r him up, releasing him
Acts	10:40	This man God r [on] the third day
Acts	13:30	But God r him from the dead,
Rom	4:25	and was r for our justification.
Rom	6: 4	just as Christ was r from the dead
Rom	8:11	the one who r Jesus from the dead
Rom	9:17	"This is why I have r you up,
Rom	10: 9	your heart that God r him

1 Cor	15: 4	that he was r on the third day
1 Cor	15:20	But now Christ has been r
2 Cor	5:15	who for their sake died and was r.
Eph	2: 6	r us up with him, and seated us
Col	2:12	also r with him through faith
Col	2:12	of God, who r him from the dead.

RAISES →RISE
1 Sm	2: 8	He r the needy from the dust;
Ps	113: 7	The LORD r the needy from the dust,
Jn	5:21	For just as the Father r the dead

RAM →RAMS, RAMS'
Gn	22:13	he spied a r caught by its horns
Gn	22:13	and took the r and offered it up as
Ex	29:22	since this is the ordination r;
Dn	8: 3	the river a r with two great horns,

RAMAH
Jer	31:15	In R is heard the sound of moaning,
Mt	2:18	"A voice was heard in R,

RAMPARTS
Ps	48:14	Consider the r, examine its citadels,

RAMS →RAM
1 Sm	15:22	and submission than the fat of r.
Ps	114: 4	The mountains skipped like r;
Mi	6: 7	be pleased with thousands of r,

RAMS' →RAM
Ex	25: 5	r skins dyed red, and tahash
Jos	6: 4	with seven priests carrying r horns

RAN →RUN
Gn	39:12	he got away from her and r outside.
1 Kgs	18:46	and r before Ahab as far as
Lk	24:12	But Peter got up and r to the tomb,

RANGE
Zec	4:10	the LORD that r over the whole earth.

RANK →RANKS
Est	10: 3	The Jew Mordecai was next in r

RANKS →RANK
1 Sm	17:10	"I defy the r of Israel today. Give me
Jn	1:15	one who is coming after me r ahead

RANSOM →RANSOMED
Mt	20:28	and to give his life as a r for many."
Mk	10:45	and to give his life as a r for many."
Gal	4: 5	to r those under the law,
1 Tm	2: 6	who gave himself as r for all.

RANSOMED →RANSOM
Is	35:10	whom the LORD has r will return
Is	51:11	whom the LORD has r will return

RAPHAEL
Tb	3:17	So R was sent to heal them both:
Tb	5: 4	found the angel R standing before
Tb	12:15	I am R, one of the seven angels who

RASH →RASHLY
Ps	106:33	spirit that r words crossed his lips.

RASHLY →RASH
Prv	20:25	R to pledge a sacred gift is a trap

RATHER
Jb	32: 2	for considering himself r than God
Mt	10: 6	Go r to the lost sheep of the house
Acts	5:29	"We must obey God r than men.
1 Cor	14:19	church I would r speak five words

RAVEN →RAVENS
Gn	8: 7	and he sent out a r, to see

RAVENS →RAVEN
1 Kgs	17: 6	R brought him bread and meat
Jb	38:41	Who provides nourishment for the r
Ps	147: 9	their food and r what they cry for.
Lk	12:24	Notice the r: they do not sow

RAW
Ex	12: 9	It shall not be eaten r or boiled,
1 Sm	2:15	boiled meat from you, only r meat."

RAZOR
Jgs   16:17   told her, "No r has touched my head,
1 Sm   1:11   and no r shall ever touch his head."

REACHED →REACHES
Ps   18:17   He r down from on high and seized

REACHES →REACHED
Prv   31:20   She r out her hands to the poor,

READ →READER, READING, READS
Ex   24: 7   he r it aloud to the people,
Dt   17:19   r it all the days of his life that he
Jos   8:34   were r aloud all the words
2 Kgs 23: 2   temple of the LORD, r out to them.
Neh   8: 8   Ezra r plainly from the book
Neh   8: 8   all could understand what was r.
Is   34:16   Look in the book of the LORD and r:
Jer   36: 6   r publicly in the LORD's house
Dn   5:16   if you are able to r the writing
Mk   12:10   Have you not r this scripture
Lk   4:16   on the sabbath day. He stood up to r
2 Cor 3: 2   on our hearts, known and r by all,
2 Cor 3:15   whenever Moses is r, a veil lies

READER →READ
Mt   24:15   the holy place (let the r understand),
Mk   13:14   he should not (let the r understand),

READING →READ
Jer   36:23   Each time Jehudi finished r three
Acts   8:30   and heard him r Isaiah the prophet
Acts   8:30   "Do you understand what you are r?"
1 Tm   4:13   I arrive, attend to the r, exhortation,

READS →READ
Rv   1: 3   Blessed is the one who r aloud

READY
Ps   119:173 Keep your hand r to help me, for I
Mt   25:10   and those who were r went
1 Pt   1: 5   a salvation that is r to be revealed
1 Pt   3:15   Always be r to give an explanation
Rv   19: 7   come, his bride has made herself r.

REAFFIRM
2 Cor 2: 8   I urge you to r your love for him.

REAP →REAPER, REAPS
Lv   19: 9   "When you r the harvest of your
Jb   4: 8   and sow trouble, r the same.
Ps   126: 5   sow in tears will r with cries of joy.
Hos   8: 7   the wind, they shall r the whirlwind;
Hos   10:12   justice, r the fruit of piety;
Lk   12:24   they do not sow or r; they have
Jn   4:38   to r what you have not worked for;
1 Cor 9:11   thing that we r a material harvest
2 Cor 9: 6   sows sparingly will also r sparingly,
2 Cor 9: 6   bountifully will also r bountifully.
Gal   6: 7   a person will r only what he sows,
Rv   14:15   "Use your sickle and r the harvest,
Rv   14:15   for the time to r has come,

REAPER →REAP
Am   9:13   plowman shall overtake the r,
Jn   4:36   The r is already receiving his
Jn   4:36   the sower and r can rejoice together.

REAPS →REAP
Jn   4:37   that 'One sows and another r.'

REAR
Nm   10:25   Finally, as r guard for all the camps,
Is   52:12   your r guard is the God of Israel.

REASON
Mt   19: 5   this r a man shall leave his father
Rom   4:16   For this r, it depends on faith,
Heb   9:15   For this r he is mediator of a new
2 Pt   1: 5   For this very r, make every effort

REBEKAH
Sister of Laban, secured as bride for Isaac (Gn 24). Mother of Esau and Jacob (Gn 25:19-26). Taken by Abimelech as sister of Isaac;

returned (Gn 26:1-11). Encouraged Jacob to trick Isaac out of blessing (Gn 27:1-17).

REBEL →REBELLED, REBELLION, REBELLIOUS, REBELS
Ex   23:21   Do not r against him, for he will not
Nm   14: 9   But do not r against the LORD!
1 Sm 12:14   him and do not r against the LORD's

REBELLED →REBEL
Nm   20:24   because you both r against my
Ps   78:56   tested, r against God Most High,
Is   63:10   But they r, and grieved his holy

REBELLION →REBEL
1 Sm 15:23   For a sin like divination is r,
Heb   3: 8   'Harden not your hearts as at the r

REBELLIOUS →REBEL
Ps   78: 8   a r and defiant generation,
Ez   2: 5   they are a r house—they shall know

REBELS →REBEL
Jos   1:18   If anyone r against your orders

REBIRTH →BEAR
Ti   3: 5   he saved us through the bath of r

REBUILD →BUILD
Neh   2:17   let us r the wall of Jerusalem,
Tb   14: 5   They shall r the temple, but it will
Tb   14: 5   and they shall r Jerusalem
Am   9:14   they shall r and inhabit their ruined
Acts 15:16   and r the fallen hut of David;
Acts 15:16   from its ruins I shall r it and raise it

REBUILT →BUILD
Ezr   6: 3   The house is to be r as a place
Ez   36:36   have r what was destroyed

REBUKE →REBUKED, REBUKES
Ps   50: 8   Not for your sacrifices do I r you,
Ps   119:21   With a curse you r the proud
Prv   27: 5   Better is an open r than a love
Eccl   7: 5   better to hearken to the wise man's r
Is   54: 9   to be angry with you, or to r you.
Zec   3: 2   Satan, "May the LORD r you, Satan;
Zec   3: 2   who has chosen Jerusalem r you!
Mk   8:32   took him aside and began to r him.
Lk   17: 3   If your brother sins, r him; and if he
Jude   1: 9   him but said, "May the Lord r you!"

REBUKED →REBUKE
Mt   8:26   he got up, r the winds and the sea,
Mt   17:18   Jesus r him and the demon came
Lk   4:39   He stood over her, r the fever, and it

REBUKES →REBUKE
Prv   28:23   He who r a man gets more thanks

RECEDED
Gn   8: 3   Gradually the waters r

RECEIVE →RECEIVED, RECEIVES
Gn   4:11   its mouth to r your brother's blood
Dt   9: 9   the mountain to r the stone tablets
Ps   24: 5   They will r blessings from the LORD,
Mt   10:41   a prophet will r a prophet's reward,
Mt   10:41   is righteous will r a righteous man's
Mk   10:30   who will not r a hundred times
Jn   16:24   ask and you will r, so that your joy
Jn   20:22   and said to them, "R the holy Spirit.
Acts   1: 8   But you will r power when the holy
Acts   2:38   you will r the gift of the holy Spirit.
Acts 19: 2   "Did you r the holy Spirit when you
Acts 20:35   'It is more blessed to give than to r.' "
Rom   11:31   to you, they too may [now] r mercy.
1 Cor 4: 5   everyone will r praise from God.
Heb   4:16   the throne of grace to r mercy
Jas   1: 7   he will r anything from the Lord,
Jas   1:12   has been proved he will r the crown
1 Jn   3:22   and r from him whatever we ask,
Rv   4:11   to r glory and honor and power,
Rv   5:12   to r power and riches,

RECEIVED → RECEIVE
Jos   14: 1   which the Israelites r in the land
Ps   68:19   you took captives, r slaves as tribute.
Mt   6: 2   say to you, they have r their reward.
Mt   10: 8   Without cost you have r;
Jn   1:16   From his fullness we have all r,
Acts   8:17   on them and they r the holy Spirit.
Acts   10:47   who have r the holy Spirit even as
Rom   8:15   fear, but you r a spirit of adoption,
Rom   11:30   have now r mercy because of their
1 Cor   2:12   We have not r the spirit of the world
1 Cor 11:23   For I r from the Lord what I
Col   2: 6   So, as you r Christ Jesus the Lord,
Col   4:17   the ministry that you r in the Lord."
1 Tm   4: 4   is to be rejected when r
1 Pt   2:10   you "had not r mercy" but now you have r mercy.
1 Pt   4:10   As each one has r a gift, use it
2 Pt   1: 1   to those who have r a faith of equal
2 Pt   1:17   For he r honor and glory from God

RECEIVES → RECEIVE
Lk   11:10   For everyone who asks, r;
Jn   13:20   you, whoever r the one I send r me,
Jn   13:20   whoever r me r the one who sent

RECENT
1 Tm   3: 6   He should not be a r convert,

RECHABITE
Jer   35: 5   these R men bowls full of wine

RECITE → RECITED
Ex   17:14   and r it in the ears of Joshua. I will

RECITED → RECITE
Dt   31:30   Moses r the words of this song

RECKLESS
2 Tm   3: 4   traitors, r, conceited,

RECLINING
Est   7: 8   on the couch on which Esther was r;
Jn   13:23   Jesus loved, was r at Jesus' side.

RECOGNITION → RECOGNIZE
1 Cor 16:18   as yours. So give r to such people.

RECOGNIZE → RECOGNITION, RECOGNIZED,
    RECOGNIZING
Gn   42: 8   although they did not r him,
Jb   2:12   up their eyes and did not r him,
Lk   19:44   you because you did not r the time

RECOGNIZED → RECOGNIZE
Gn   42: 8   When Joseph r his brothers,
Lk   24:31   eyes were opened and they r him,

RECOGNIZING → RECOGNIZE
Lk   24:16   eyes were prevented from r him.

RECOMMENDATION
2 Cor   3: 1   do, letters of r to you or from you?

RECOMPENSE
Is   40:10   reward with him, his r before him.
Is   62:11   reward with him, his r before him.

RECONCILE → RECONCILED, RECONCILIATION,
    RECONCILING
Acts   7:26   and tried to r them peacefully,
Eph   2:16   and might r both with God, in one
Col   1:20   through him to r all things for him,

RECONCILED → RECONCILE
Mt   5:24   go first and be r with your brother,
Rom   5:10   we were r to God through the death
Rom   5:10   once r, will we be saved by his life.
1 Cor   7:11   remain single or become r to her
2 Cor   5:18   who has r us to himself through
2 Cor   5:20   you on behalf of Christ, be r to God.
Col   1:22   he has now r in his fleshly body

RECONCILIATION → RECONCILE
Rom   5:11   whom we have now received r.
Rom   11:15   their rejection is the r of the world,
2 Cor   5:18   and given us the ministry of r,

2 Cor   5:19   entrusting to us the message of r.

RECONCILING → RECONCILE
2 Cor   5:19   God was r the world to himself

RECORDED → RECORDS
Est   9:20   Mordecai r these events and sent
Ps   56: 9   stored in your vial, r in your book?

RECORDS → RECORDED
Ezr   2:62   These men searched their family r,

RECOVER
Is   38: 1   you are about to die; you shall not r."
Jn   4:52   He asked them when he began to r.

RED
Ex   15: 4   were submerged in the R Sea.
Nm   19: 2   procure for you a r heifer that is free
2 Kgs   3:22   the water at a distance as r as blood.
1 Mc   4: 9   our fathers were saved in the R Sea,
Ps   106: 9   He roared at the R Sea and it dried
Prv   23:31   Look not on the wine when it is r,
Is   1:18   Though they be crimson r, they may
Zec   1: 8   appeared the driver of a r horse,
Zec   6: 2   The first chariot had r horses,
Mt   16: 3   for the sky is r and threatening.'
Heb   11:29   faith they crossed the R Sea as if it
Rv   6: 4   Another horse came out, a r one.
Rv   12: 3   it was a huge r dragon, with seven

REDEEM → REDEEMED, REDEEMER, REDEEMS, REDEMPTION
Ex   13:13   of an ass you shall r with a sheep.
Ex   13:13   Every first-born son you must r.
Lv   25:25   who has the right to r it, may go
Ps   26:11   blame; r me, be gracious to me!
Ps   44:27   help us! R us as your love demands.
Ps   130: 8   And God will r Israel from all their
Hos   13:14   shall I r them from death?
Lk   24:21   that he would be the one to r Israel;

REDEEMED → REDEEM
Ex   15:13   mercy you led the people you r;
2 Sm   7:23   which you r for yourself
Ps   107: 2   Let that be the prayer of the LORD's r,
Ps   107: 2   those r from the hand of the foe,
Is   1:27   Zion shall be r by judgment, and her
Is   35: 9   to make, and on it the r will walk.
Is   44:22   mist; return to me, for I have r you.
Is   63: 9   his love and pity he r them himself,

REDEEMER → REDEEM
Ps   19:15   you, LORD, my rock and my r.
Ps   78:35   their rock, God Most High, their r.
Is   44: 6   King and r, the LORD of hosts: I am
Is   48:17   Thus says the LORD, your r, the Holy
Is   59:20   He shall come to Zion a r to those

REDEEMS → REDEEM
1 Mc   4:11   shall know that there is One who r
Ps   34:23   The LORD r loyal servants; no one is

REDEMPTION → REDEEM
Lk   2:38   to all who were awaiting the r
Lk   21:28   raise your heads because your r is
Rom   3:24   by his grace through the r in Christ
Rom   8:23   for adoption, the r of our bodies.
1 Cor   1:30   righteousness, sanctification, and r,
Eph   1: 7   In him we have r by his blood,
Eph   1:14   of our inheritance toward r as God's
Eph   4:30   you were sealed for the day of r.
Col   1:14   in whom we have r, the forgiveness
Heb   9:12   own blood, thus obtaining eternal r.

REED → REEDS
2 Kgs 18:21   in fact a broken r which pierces
Is   42: 3   A bruised r he shall not break,
Mt   12:20   A bruised r he will not break,
Lk   7:24   to the desert to see—a r swayed

REEDS → REED
Ex   2: 3   it, placed it among the r on the river

REELED
Ps   107:27   They r, staggered like drunkards;

REFINE → REFINED, REFINING
Zec 13: 9 and I will **r** them as silver is refined,

REFINED → REFINE
Ps 12: 7 Lord are sure, silver **r** in a crucible,
Is 48:10 See, I have **r** you like silver,
Dn 12:10 Many shall be **r**, purified,

REFINING → REFINE
Mal 3: 3 He will sit **r** and purifying [silver],

REFLECT → REFLECTING
Sir 6:37 **R** on the precepts of the Lord, let his

REFLECTING → REFLECT
Lk 2:19 these things, **r** on them in her heart.

REFRESH → REFRESHMENT
Phlm 1:20 in the Lord. **R** my heart in Christ.

REFRESHMENT → REFRESH
Acts 3:20 the Lord may grant you times of **r**

REFUGE
Nm 35:11 unintentionally may take **r**.
Ru 2:12 whose wings you have come for **r**."
2 Sm 22: 3 my God, my rock of **r**! My shield,
2 Sm 22: 3 my stronghold, my **r**, my savior,
2 Sm 22:31 is a shield to all who take **r** in him."
Ps 2:11 Happy are all who take **r** in God!
Ps 5:12 all who take **r** in you will be glad
Ps 11: 1 In the Lord I take **r**; how can you
Ps 16: 1 me safe, O God; in you I take **r**.
Ps 17: 7 those who seek **r** from their foes.
Ps 31: 3 Be my rock of **r**, a stronghold
Ps 34: 9 happy are those who take **r** in him.
Ps 36: 8 We take **r** in the shadow of your
Ps 46: 2 God is our **r** and our strength,
Ps 59:17 my fortress, my **r** in time of trouble.
Ps 62: 9 Pour out your hearts to God our **r**!
Ps 71: 1 In you, Lord, I take **r**; let me never
Ps 91: 2 Say to the Lord, "My **r** and fortress,
Ps 118: 8 Better to take **r** in the Lord
Prv 14:26 for one's children he will be a **r**.
Prv 14:32 the just man finds a **r** in his honesty.
Prv 30: 5 a shield to those who take **r** in him.
Is 25: 4 For you are a **r** to the poor, a **r**
Jer 16:19 fortress, my **r** in the day of distress!
Na 1: 7 is good, a **r** on the day of distress;

REFULGENCE
Wis 7:26 For she is the **r** of eternal light,
Heb 1: 3 who is the **r** of his glory,

REFUSE → REFUSED
Ex 7:27 If you **r** to let them go, I warn you,
Nm 14:11 How long will they **r** to believe

REFUSED → REFUSE
Ex 13:15 Pharaoh stubbornly **r** to let us go,
Jer 5: 3 laid them low, but they **r** correction;
Jer 5: 3 than stone, and **r** to return to you.
Heb 12:25 they **r** the one who warned them

REFUTE → REFUTED
Ti 1: 9 sound doctrine and to **r** opponents.

REFUTED → REFUTE
Acts 18:28 He vigorously **r** the Jews in public,

REGAIN → REGAINED
Acts 9:17 that you may **r** your sight and be

REGAINED → REGAIN
Acts 22:13 at that very moment I **r** my sight

REGARD
Phil 2: 6 of God, did not **r** equality with God

REGRET
1 Sm 15:11 "I **r** having made Saul king, for he
2 Cor 7:10 a salutary repentance without **r**,

REGULATIONS
Col 2:20 why do you submit to **r** as if you
Heb 9:10 **r** concerning the flesh,

REHOBOAM
Son of Solomon (1 Kgs 11:43; 1 Chr 3:10). Harsh treatment of subjects caused divided kingdom (1 Kgs 12:1-24; 14:21-31; 2 Chr 10-12).

REIGN → REIGNED
Ex 15:18 The Lord shall **r** forever and ever.
Dt 17:20 his descendants will enjoy a long **r**
Ps 146:10 The Lord shall **r** forever, your God,
Prv 8:15 By me kings **r**, and lawgivers
Is 24:23 pale, For the Lord of hosts will **r**
Is 32: 1 See, a king will **r** justly and princes
Jer 23: 5 As king he shall **r** and govern
1 Cor 15:25 For he must **r** until he has put all his
2 Tm 2:12 we shall also **r** with him. But if we
Rv 5:10 our God, and they will **r** on earth."
Rv 11:15 and he will **r** forever and ever."
Rv 11:17 power and have established your **r**.
Rv 20: 6 and they will **r** with him
Rv 22: 5 and they shall **r** forever and ever.

REIGNED → REIGN
Rv 20: 4 they **r** with Christ for a thousand

REJECT → REJECTED, REJECTION, REJECTS
Is 30:12 of Israel: Because you **r** this word,
Hos 4: 6 I will **r** you from my priesthood;

REJECTED → REJECT
1 Sm 15:23 Because you have **r** the command
1 Sm 15:23 he, too, has **r** you as a ruler."
2 Kgs 17:20 So the Lord **r** the whole race
Ps 60: 3 O God, you **r** us, broke our
Ps 118:22 The stone the builders **r** has become
Jer 8: 9 Since they have **r** the word
Mt 21:42 'The stone that the builders **r**
Acts 4:11 He is 'the stone **r** by you,
1 Tm 4: 4 and nothing is to be **r** when received
1 Pt 2: 4 **r** by human beings but chosen
1 Pt 2: 7 "The stone which the builders **r**

REJECTION → REJECT
Rom 11:15 if their **r** is the reconciliation

REJECTS → REJECT
Lk 10:16 listens to me. Whoever **r** you **r** me.
Lk 10:16 whoever **r** me **r** the one who sent
Jn 12:48 Whoever **r** me and does not accept

REJOICE → REJOICED, REJOICES, REJOICING
1 Chr 16:10 **r**, O hearts that seek the Lord!
1 Chr 16:31 the heavens be glad and the earth **r**;
2 Chr 6:41 may your faithful ones **r** in good
Ps 14: 7 That Jacob may **r**, and Israel be glad
Ps 31: 8 I will **r** and be glad in your love,
Ps 51:10 let the bones you have crushed **r**.
Ps 63:12 But the king shall **r** in God; all who
Ps 64:11 The just will **r** and take refuge
Ps 97: 1 The Lord is king; let the earth **r**;
Ps 105: 3 **r**, O hearts that seek the Lord!
Ps 118:24 has made; let us **r** in it and be glad.
Ps 119:162 I **r** at your promise, as one who has
Ps 149: 2 the people of Zion **r** in their king.
Prv 24:17 **R** not when your enemy falls,
Prv 29: 2 When the just prevail, the people **r**;
Sir 8: 7 **R** not when a man dies; remember,
Is 9: 2 As they **r** before you as
Is 35: 1 exult; the steppe will **r** and bloom.
Is 62: 5 his bride so shall your God **r** in you.
Hb 3:18 Yet will I **r** in the Lord and exult
Zep 3:17 He will **r** over you with gladness,
Zec 9: 9 **R** heartily, O daughter Zion,
Lk 6:23 **R** and leap for joy on that day!
Lk 10:20 do not **r** because the spirits are
Lk 10:20 **r** because your names are written
Lk 15: 6 '**R** with me because I have found my
Lk 15: 9 '**R** with me because I have found
Rom 12:15 **R** with those who **r**, weep with those
Phil 2:17 I **r** and share my joy with all of you.
Phil 3: 1 Finally, my brothers, **r** in the Lord.
Phil 4: 4 **R** in the Lord always. I shall say it again: **r**!
1 Thes 5:16 **R** always.

1 Pt	4:13	r to the extent that you share
1 Pt	4:13	revealed you may also r exultantly.
Rv	18:20	R over her, heaven, you holy ones,
Rv	19: 7	Let us r and be glad and give him

REJOICED → REJOICE

Ex	18: 9	Jethro r over all the goodness
1 Chr	29: 9	The people r over these free-will
1 Chr	29: 9	King David also r greatly.
Jb	31:25	Or had I r that my wealth was great,
Jn	8:56	Abraham your father r to see my

REJOICES → REJOICE

Ps	16: 9	my heart is glad, my soul r;
Prv	11:10	When the just prosper, the city r;
Is	62: 5	And as a bridegroom r in his bride
Lk	1:47	my spirit r in God my savior.
1 Cor	13: 6	wrongdoing but r with the truth.

REJOICING → REJOICE

2 Cor	6:10	as sorrowful yet always r; as poor

RELATIONS → RELATIVE

Lv	18:20	You shall not have carnal r
Lv	20:15	a man has carnal r with an animal,
Mt	1:25	He had no r with her until she bore

RELATIVE → RELATIONS, RELATIVES

Ru	2:20	and she continued, "He is a r of ours,

RELATIVES → RELATIVE

Lk	21:16	by parents, brothers, r, and friends,
1 Tm	5: 8	whoever does not provide for r

RELEASE → RELEASED

Is	61: 1	the captives and r to the prisoners,
Mt	27:15	the governor was accustomed to r
Rv	9:14	"R the four angels who are bound

RELEASED → RELEASE

Mk	15:15	the crowd, r Barabbas to them and,
Rv	20: 7	Satan will be r from his prison.

RELENT → RELENTING

Jl	2:14	Perhaps he will again r and leave
Jon	3: 9	knows, God may r and forgive,
Zec	8:14	the LORD of hosts, and I did not r,

RELENTING → RELENT

Jl	2:13	in kindness, and r in punishment.

RELIED → RELY

2 Chr	13:18	were victorious because they r
2 Chr	16: 8	And yet, because you r on the LORD,

RELIEF

Est	4:14	r and deliverance will come

RELIGION → RELIGIOUS

1 Mc	1:43	Israelites were in favor of his r;
1 Mc	2:19	each forsakes the r of his fathers
Acts	25:19	issues with him about their own r
Acts	26: 5	Pharisee, the strictest party of our r.
Jas	1:26	but deceives his heart, his r is vain.
Jas	1:27	R that is pure and undefiled before

RELIGIOUS → RELIGION

Acts	17:22	that in every respect you are very r.
1 Tm	5: 4	to perform their r duty to their own
Jas	1:26	If anyone thinks he is r and does not

RELY → RELIED

2 Kgs	18:20	do you r, that you rebel against me?
2 Chr	14:10	for we r on you, and in your name
Prv	3: 5	on your own intelligence r not;
Sir	5: 1	R not on your wealth; say not:
Rom	2:17	call yourself a Jew and r on the law

REMAIN → REMAINED, REMAINS

Gn	6: 3	"My spirit shall not r in man forever,
Nm	33:55	you allow to r will become as barbs
Mk	14:34	to death. R here and keep watch."
Jn	15: 4	R in me, as I in you.
Jn	15: 7	If you r in me and my words r in you,
1 Cor	7:20	Everyone should r in the state
1 Cor	13:13	So faith, hope, love r, these three;

Heb	1:11	They will perish, but you r;
1 Jn	2:28	And now, children, r in him,
1 Jn	3:24	who keep his commandments r in him,
2 Jn	1: 9	not to r in the teaching of the Christ

REMAINED → REMAIN

2 Sm	11: 1	David, however, r in Jerusalem.
1 Jn	2:19	been, they would have r with us.

REMAINS → REMAIN

2 Tm	2:13	If we are unfaithful he r faithful,
Heb	4: 9	a sabbath rest still r for the people
Heb	7: 3	Son of God, he r a priest forever.
Heb	10:26	there no longer r sacrifice for sins

REMEDY

2 Chr	36:16	was so inflamed that there was no r.

REMEMBER → REMEMBERED, REMEMBERS, REMEMBRANCE

Ex	20: 8	"R to keep holy the sabbath day.
Dt	5:15	For r that you too were once slaves
Dt	8:18	R then, it is the LORD, your God,
Jos	1:13	"R what Moses, the servant
Neh	13:31	R this in my favor, O my God!
1 Mc	4:10	us, r his covenant with our fathers,
Jb	10: 9	r that you fashioned me from clay!
Jb	36:24	R, you should extol his work,
Ps	74: 2	R your flock that you gathered
Ps	74: 2	R Mount Zion where you dwell.
Ps	77:12	I will r the deeds of the LORD; yes, your wonders of old I will r.
Eccl	12: 1	R your Creator in the days of your
Is	46: 8	R this and be firm, bear it well
Is	46: 8	r the former things, those long ago:
Jer	31:34	evildoing and r their sin no more.
Lam	5: 1	R, O LORD, what has befallen us,
Ez	36:31	Then you shall r your evil conduct,
Hos	7: 2	that I r all their wickedness
Hb	3: 2	known; in your wrath r compassion!
Mk	8:18	and not hear? And do you not r,
Lk	17:32	R the wife of Lot.
Lk	23:42	r me when you come into your
2 Tm	2: 8	R Jesus Christ, raised from the dead,
Heb	8:12	evildoing and r their sins no more."
Jude	1:17	r the words spoken beforehand
Rv	3: 3	R then how you accepted and heard;

REMEMBERED → REMEMBER

Gn	8: 1	and then God r Noah and all
Gn	30:22	Then God r Rachel; he heard her
1 Sm	1:19	his wife Hannah, the LORD r her.
Ps	78:35	They r that God was their rock,
Ps	98: 3	Has r faithful love toward the house
Ps	106:45	For their sake he r his covenant
Ps	136:23	The LORD r us in our misery,
Is	17:10	and r not the Rock, your strength.
Is	65:17	The things of the past shall not be r
Ez	18:22	he committed shall be r against him;
Ez	33:13	of his virtuous deeds shall be r;
Mt	26:75	Then Peter r the word that Jesus had
Rv	16:19	But God r great Babylon, giving it

REMEMBERS → REMEMBER

Ps	103:14	we are formed, r that we are dust.

REMEMBRANCE → REMEMBER

1 Cor	11:24	that is for you. Do this in r of me."
Heb	10: 3	there is only a yearly r of sins,

REMIND → REMINDER

Jn	14:26	and r you of all that [I] told you.

REMINDER → REMIND

Ex	13: 9	hand and as a r on your forehead;

REMNANT

Gn	45: 7	of you to ensure for you a r on earth
2 Kgs	19:31	For out of Jerusalem shall come a r,
Ezr	9: 8	who left us a r and gave us a stake
Is	10:21	A r will return, the r of Jacob,
Is	11:11	to reclaim the r of his people that is
Jer	23: 3	I myself will gather the r of my
Jer	50:20	for I will forgive the r I preserve.
Zep	3:13	the r of Israel. They shall do no

Zec	8:12	all these things I will have the **r**
Rom	9:27	of the sea, only a **r** will be saved;
Rom	11: 5	also at the present time there is a **r**,

REMOVAL → REMOVED
Is	27: 9	the whole fruit of the **r** of his sin:
1 Pt	3:21	It is not a **r** of dirt from the body

REMOVED → REMOVAL
Jn	20: 1	and saw the stone **r** from the tomb.

REND
Jl	2:13	**R** your hearts, not your garments,

RENEW → RENEWAL, RENEWED
Is	40:31	in the LORD will **r** their strength,
Zep	3:17	and **r** you in his love, He will sing

RENEWAL → RENEW
Rom	12: 2	be transformed by the **r** of your mind,
Ti	3: 5	of rebirth and **r** by the holy Spirit,

RENEWED → RENEW
Ps	103: 5	your youth is **r** like the eagle's.
2 Cor	4:16	our inner self is being **r** day by day.
Eph	4:23	and be **r** in the spirit of your minds,
Col	3:10	which is being **r**, for knowledge,

RENOUNCED
Ps	89:40	You **r** the covenant with your
2 Cor	4: 2	we have **r** shameful, hidden things;

RENOWN
Gn	6: 4	were the heroes of old, the men of **r**.
Ps	135:13	is forever, your **r**, from age to age!

REPAID → PAY
Lk	14:14	For you will be **r** at the resurrection

REPAIR → REPAIRED, REPAIRER
2 Chr	24: 5	all Israel that you may **r** the house

REPAIRED → REPAIR
2 Chr	29: 3	of the LORD's house and **r** them.

REPAIRER → REPAIR
Is	58:12	"**R** of the breach," they shall call you,

REPAY → PAY
Ps	28: 4	**R** them for their deeds, for the evil
Ps	28: 4	For the work of their hands **r** them;
Ps	35:12	They **r** me evil for good and I am all
Jer	25:14	thus I will **r** them according to their
Jer	51:56	God who requites, he will surely **r**.
Jl	2:25	And I will **r** you for the years
Rom	12:17	Do not **r** anyone evil for evil;
Rom	12:19	is mine, I will **r**, says the Lord."
Heb	10:30	"Vengeance is mine; I will **r**,"

REPAYS → PAY
Is	59:18	He **r** his enemies their deserts,
Sir	35:10	For the LORD is one who always **r**,

REPENT → REPENTANCE, REPENTED, REPENTS
1 Kgs	8:47	may they **r** in the land of their
Jb	42: 6	I have said, and **r** in dust and ashes.
Jer	4:28	I have spoken, I will not **r**,
Ez	24:14	I will not have pity nor **r**.
Mt	3: 2	[and] saying, "**R**, for the kingdom
Mt	4:17	Jesus began to preach and say, "**R**,
Lk	13: 3	if you do not **r**, you will all perish as
Acts	2:38	[said] to them, "**R** and be baptized,
Acts	3:19	**R**, therefore, and be converted,
Acts	17:30	that all people everywhere **r**
Acts	26:20	I preached the need to **r** and turn
Rv	2: 5	**R**, and do the works you did at first.
Rv	2:21	I have given her time to **r**, but she refuses to **r** of her harlotry.
Rv	9:20	did not **r** of the works of their
Rv	16: 9	but they did not **r** or give him glory.

REPENTANCE → REPENT
Mt	3: 8	good fruit as evidence of your **r**.
Mk	1: 4	desert proclaiming a baptism of **r**
Mk	6:12	So they went off and preached **r**.
Lk	3: 8	good fruits as evidence of your **r**;

Lk	5:32	not come to call the righteous to **r**
Lk	24:47	and that **r**, for the forgiveness
Acts	5:31	and savior to grant Israel **r**
Acts	11:18	granted life-giving **r** to the Gentiles
Acts	20:21	Greeks to **r** before God and to faith
Acts	26:20	to do works giving evidence of **r**.
Rom	2: 4	of God would lead you to **r**?
2 Cor	7:10	produces a salutary **r** without regret,
Heb	6: 1	**r** from dead works and faith in God,
2 Pt	3: 9	perish but that all should come to **r**.

REPENTED → REPENT
Am	7: 3	And the LORD **r** of this.
Am	7: 6	The LORD **r** of this.
Zec	1: 6	Then they **r** and admitted: "The LORD
Mt	11:21	they would long ago have **r**
Lk	11:32	at the preaching of Jonah they **r**,

REPENTS → REPENT
Jer	8: 6	true; No one **r** of his wickedness,
Lk	15: 7	over one sinner who **r** than over
Lk	15:10	of God over one sinner who **r**."

REPHAIM
Gn	15:20	the Hittites, the Perizzites, the **R**,
Jos	12: 4	a survivor of the **R**, who lived

REPLANTED → PLANT
Ez	36:36	destroyed and **r** what was desolate.

REPORT → REPORTS
1 Kgs	10: 7	I did not believe the **r** until I came
1 Kgs	10: 7	and prosperity surpass the **r** I heard.

REPORTS → REPORT
Gn	37: 2	he brought his father bad **r**
Nm	13:32	spread discouraging **r** among

REPROACH
Jb	27: 6	my heart does not **r** me for any
Is	51: 7	at heart: Fear not the **r** of men,
Jer	20: 8	me derision and **r** all the day.

REPROOF → REPROVE
Prv	3:11	my son, disdain not; spurn not his **r**;
Prv	13:18	but he who heeds **r** is honored.
Sir	32:17	The sinner turns aside **r** and distorts

REPROVE → REPROOF, REPROVES
Rv	3:19	Those whom I love, I **r** and chastise.

REPROVES → REPROVE
Jb	5:17	Happy is the man whom God **r**!
Prv	3:12	For whom the LORD loves he **r**,

REQUESTS
Phil	4: 6	make your **r** known to God.

REQUIRE → REQUIRED, REQUIRES
Ps	40: 7	Holocausts and sin-offerings you do not **r**;

REQUIRED → REQUIRE
1 Cor	4: 2	Now it is of course **r** of stewards

REQUIRES → REQUIRE
Mi	6: 8	and what the LORD **r** of you:

RESCUE → RESCUED, RESCUES
Ps	22: 9	if he loves you, let him **r** you."
Ps	31: 3	make haste to **r** me! Be my rock
Ps	69:15	**R** me from the mire; do not let me sink. **R** me from my enemies
Ps	82: 4	**R** the lowly and poor; deliver them
Is	31: 5	protect and deliver, to spare and **r** it.
2 Cor	1:10	death, and he will continue to **r** us;
2 Cor	1:10	hope [that] he will also **r** us again,
2 Pt	2: 9	the Lord knows how to **r** the devout

RESCUED → RESCUE
Ps	81: 8	In distress you called and I **r** you;
Acts	12:11	and **r** me from the hand of Herod
2 Pt	2: 7	and if he **r** Lot, a righteous man

RESCUES → RESCUE
Ps	37:40	The LORD helps and **r** them,
Sir	40:24	but better than either, charity that **r**.

RESERVED
2 Pt	2:17	the gloom of darkness has been r.
2 Pt	3: 7	earth have been r by the same word

RESIST → RESISTED, RESISTS
Jas	4: 7	R the devil, and he will flee
1 Pt	5: 9	R him, steadfast in faith,

RESISTED → RESIST
Heb	12: 4	against sin you have not yet r

RESISTS → RESIST
Rom	13: 2	whoever r authority opposes what

RESOLVED
1 Mc	1:62	r in their hearts not to eat anything
Dn	1: 8	Daniel was r not to defile himself

RESPECT → RESPECTED
Mk	12: 6	of all, thinking, 'They will r my son.'
Rom	13: 7	toll is due, r to whom r is due,
Eph	5:33	and the wife should r her husband.
1 Thes	5:12	r those who are laboring among you

RESPECTED → RESPECT
Acts	5:34	of the law, r by all the people,
Heb	12: 9	to discipline us, and we r them.

RESPOND
Hos	2:17	She shall r there as in the days

REST → RESTED, RESTING
Gn	8: 4	the ark came to r on the mountains
Ex	16:23	Tomorrow is a day of complete r,
Ex	31:15	day is the sabbath of complete r,
Ex	33:14	"will go along, to give you r."
Lv	25: 4	the land shall have a complete r,
Nm	10:36	And when it came to r, he would
Dt	12:10	he has given you r from all your
2 Sm	7:11	I will give you r from all your
Jb	3:17	troubling, there the weary are at r.
Ps	95:11	anger: "They shall never enter my r."
Prv	6:10	a little folding of the arms to r—
Is	11: 2	spirit of the Lord shall r upon him:
Jer	6:16	thus you will find r for your souls.
Jer	47: 6	how long till you find r?
Mt	11:28	are burdened, and I will give you r.
Mk	6:31	to a deserted place and r a while."
1 Cor	2: 5	your faith might r not on human
Heb	3:11	"They shall not enter into my r." ' "
Heb	4: 3	we who believed enter into [that] r,
Heb	4: 3	"They shall not enter into my r,' "
Heb	4:10	And whoever enters into God's r,
Rv	14:13	"let them find r from their labors,

RESTED → REST
Gn	2: 2	he r on the seventh day from all
Ex	16:30	that the people r on the seventh day.
Ex	20:11	them; but on the seventh day he r.
Heb	4: 4	God r on the seventh day from all

RESTING → REST
Ps	132:14	"This is my r place forever; here I

RESTITUTION
Ex	21:36	in, he must make full r, an ox

RESTLESS
Jas	3: 8	It is a r evil, full of deadly poison.

RESTORE → RESTORED, RESTORES
2 Chr	24: 4	Joash decided to r the Lord's temple.
1 Mc	3:43	"Let us r our people from their
Ps	51:14	R my joy in your salvation;
Ps	80: 4	O Lord of hosts, r us; Let your face
Ps	126: 4	R again our fortunes, Lord,
Is	49: 6	and r the survivors of Israel; I will
Mt	17:11	will indeed come and r all things;
Acts	1: 6	this time going to r the kingdom
1 Pt	5:10	Christ [Jesus] will himself r,

RESTORED → RESTORE
Ps	85: 2	land, r the good fortune of Jacob.
Mk	3: 5	stretched it out and his hand was r.
Mk	8:25	his sight was r and he could see

RESTORES → RESTORE
Ps	14: 7	be glad when the Lord r his people!
Ps	53: 7	be glad when God r the people!

RESTRAINED → RESTRAINING
2 Pt	2:16	voice and r the prophet's madness.

RESTRAINING → RESTRAINED
2 Thes	2: 6	And now you know what is r,

RESURRECTION
2 Mc	7:14	for you, there will be no r to life."
2 Mc	12:43	inasmuch as he had the r of the dead
Mt	22:23	him, saying that there is no r.
Mt	22:28	Now at the r, of the seven,
Mt	22:30	At the r they neither marry nor are
Mt	22:31	And concerning the r of the dead,
Mt	27:53	forth from their tombs after his r,
Mk	12:18	who say there is no r, came to him
Mk	12:23	the r [when they arise] whose wife
Lk	14:14	be repaid at the r of the righteous."
Lk	20:27	those who deny that there is a r,
Lk	20:33	Now at the r whose wife will
Lk	20:35	the r of the dead neither marry nor
Jn	5:29	done good deeds to the r of life,
Jn	5:29	deeds to the r of condemnation.
Jn	11:24	he will rise, in the r on the last day."
Jn	11:25	told her, "I am the r and the life;
Acts	1:22	become with us a witness to his r."
Acts	2:31	and spoke of the r of the Messiah,
Acts	4: 2	in Jesus the r of the dead.
Acts	4:33	witness to the r of the Lord Jesus,
Acts	17:18	he was preaching about 'Jesus' and 'R.'
Acts	17:32	they heard about r of the dead,
Acts	23: 6	on trial for hope in the r of the dead."
Acts	23: 8	the Sadducees say that there is no r
Acts	24:15	that there will be a r of the righteous
Acts	24:21	you today for the r of the dead.' "
Rom	1: 4	of holiness through r from the dead,
Rom	6: 5	also be united with him in the r.
1 Cor	15:12	some among you say there is no r
1 Cor	15:13	If there is no r of the dead,
1 Cor	15:21	the r of the dead came also through
1 Cor	15:42	So also is the r of the dead. It is
Phil	3:10	the power of his r and [the] sharing
Phil	3:11	if somehow I may attain the r
2 Tm	2:18	that [the] r has already taken place
Heb	6: 2	r of the dead and eternal judgment.
Heb	11:35	received back their dead through r.
Heb	11:35	in order to obtain a better r.
1 Pt	1: 3	a living hope through the r of Jesus
1 Pt	3:21	through the r of Jesus Christ,
Rv	20: 5	years were over. This is the first r.
Rv	20: 6	is the one who shares in the first r.

RETAIN
Nm	36: 7	but all the Israelites will r their own
Jn	20:23	and whose sins you r are retained."

RETIRE
Nm	8:25	he shall r from the required service

RETRIBUTION
Rom	11: 9	a stumbling block and a r for them;

RETURN → RETURNED, RETURNS
Gn	3:19	to eat, Until you r to the ground,
Gn	3:19	you are dirt, and to dirt you shall r."
Gn	18:10	"I will surely r to you about this time
Nm	10:36	"R, O Lord, you who ride
Dt	30: 2	you and your children r to the Lord,
2 Sm	12:23	go to him, but he will not r to me."
2 Chr	30: 9	For when you r to the Lord,
2 Chr	30: 9	with their captors and r to this land;
2 Chr	30: 9	his face from you if you r to him."
Neh	1: 9	but should you r to me and carefully
Jb	10:21	Before I go whence I shall not r,
Jb	16:22	a journey from which I shall not r.
Jb	22:23	If you r to the Almighty, you will
Ps	51:15	ways, that sinners may r to you.
Ps	104:29	r to the dust from which they came.
Is	10:21	A remnant will r, the remnant

Is	35:10	whom the Lord has ransomed will r
Is	44:22	r to me, for I have redeemed you.
Is	55:11	my mouth; It shall not r to me void,
Jer	3:12	say: R, rebel Israel, says the Lord,
Jer	4: 1	If you wish to r, O Israel, says the Lord, r to me.
Jer	24: 7	for they shall r to me with their
Jer	31: 8	they shall r as an immense throng.
Lam	3:40	our ways that we may r to the Lord!
Hos	5: 4	do not allow them to r to their God;
Hos	6: 1	"Come, let us r to the Lord, For it is
Hos	12: 7	You shall r by the help of your God,
Hos	14: 2	R, O Isreal, to the Lord, your God;
Jl	2:12	r to me with your whole heart,
Zec	1: 3	R to me, says the Lord of hosts,
Zec	1: 3	and I will r to you, says the Lord
Zec	10: 9	they shall rear their children and r.
Mal	3: 7	R to me, and I will r to you,
Mal	3: 7	Yet you say, "How must we r?"
Rom	9: 9	"About this time I shall r and Sarah

RETURNED → RETURN

Gn	8: 9	and it r to him in the ark, for there
Nm	13:25	the land for forty days they r,
Ezr	2: 1	of the province who r
Neh	7: 6	of the province who r
Jdt	4: 3	Now, they had lately r from exile,
Am	4: 6	your dwellings, Yet you r not to me,
1 Pt	2:25	but you have now r to the shepherd

RETURNS → RETURN

Prv	26:11	As the dog r to his vomit,
Eccl	12: 7	the dust r to the earth as it once was,
Eccl	12: 7	the life breath r to God who gave it.
Sir	40:11	All that is of earth r to earth,
Sir	40:11	and what is from above r above.
1 Thes	5:15	See that no one r evil for evil;

REUBEN → REUBENITES

Firstborn of Jacob by Leah (Gn 29:32; 46:8; 1 Chr 2:1). Attempted to rescue Joseph (Gn 37:21-30). Lost birthright for sleeping with Bilhah (Gn 35:22; 49:4). Tribe of blessed (Gn 49:3-4; Dt 33:6), numbered (Nm 1:21; 26:7), allotted land east of Jordan (Nm 32; 34:14; Jos 13:15), west (Ez 48:6), failed to help Deborah (Jgs 5:15-16), supported David (1 Chr 12:38), 12,000 from (Rv 7:5).

REUBENITES → REUBEN

Nm	32: 1	Now the R and Gadites had a very
Dt	29: 7	we then gave as a heritage to the R,
Jos	13: 8	as well as the R and Gadites,

REVEAL → REVEALED, REVEALS, REVELATION, REVELATIONS

Est	2:10	Esther did not r her nationality
Sir	1:28	For then the Lord will r your secrets
Mt	11:27	to whom the Son wishes to r him.

REVEALED → REVEAL

Dt	29:28	what has already been r concern us
Is	40: 5	the glory of the Lord shall be r,
Is	53: 1	has the arm of the Lord been r?
Dn	2:19	During the night the mystery was r
Mt	11:25	the learned you have r them
Mt	16:17	and blood has not r this to you,
Lk	17:30	be on the day the Son of Man is r.
Jn	2:11	Cana in Galilee and so r his glory,
Jn	12:38	has the might of the Lord been r?"
Rom	1:17	in it is r the righteousness of God
Rom	8:18	with the glory to be r for us.
1 Cor	2:10	this God has r to us through
1 Cor	3:13	It will be r with fire, and the fire
Eph	3: 5	generations as it has now been r
2 Thes	2: 3	comes first and the lawless one is r,
1 Pt	1:20	world but r in the final time for you,
1 Pt	4:13	so that when his glory is r you may
1 Jn	3: 2	what we shall be has not yet been r.
1 Jn	3: 2	when it is r we shall be like him,
Rv	15: 4	for your righteous acts have been r."

REVEALS → REVEAL

Dn	2:22	He r deep and hidden things
Dn	2:28	is a God in heaven who r mysteries,

REVELATION → REVEAL

2 Sm	7:27	who said in a r to your servant,
Lk	2:32	a light for r to the Gentiles,
Rom	16:25	to the r of the mystery kept secret
1 Cor	14: 6	if I do not speak to you by way of r,
1 Cor	14:26	another an instruction, a r, a tongue,
1 Cor	14:30	But if a r is given to another person
Gal	1:12	it came through a r of Jesus Christ.
Gal	2: 2	I went up in accord with a r, and I
Eph	1:17	r resulting in knowledge of him.
Eph	3: 3	was made known to me by r, as I
Rv	1: 1	The r of Jesus Christ, which God

REVELATIONS → REVEAL

2 Cor	12: 1	go on to visions and r of the Lord.
2 Cor	12: 7	because of the abundance of the r.

REVELRY

2 Pt	2:13	Thinking daytime r a delight,

REVERE → REVERENCE, REVERENT

Neh	1:11	willing servants who r your name.

REVERENCE → REVERE

Eph	5:21	to one another out of r for Christ.
Heb	5: 7	he was heard because of his r.
1 Pt	1:17	conduct yourselves with r during

REVERENT → REVERE

Ti	2: 3	older women should be r in their
1 Pt	3: 2	observe your r and chaste behavior.

REVILE

Ex	22:27	"You shall not r God, nor curse
Ps	74:10	Shall the foe r your name forever?

REVIVE

Is	57:15	To r the spirits of the dejected, to r
Hos	6: 2	He will r us after two days;

REVOKED

Est	8: 8	the royal signet ring cannot be r.

REWARD → REWARDED, REWARDS

Gn	15: 1	I will make your r very great."
1 Sm	24:20	May the Lord r you generously
1 Sm	26:23	The Lord will r each man
Ps	19:12	obeying them brings much r.
Ps	127: 3	the Lord, the fruit of the womb, a r.
Prv	11:18	but he who sows virtue has a sure r.
Is	40:10	strong arm; Here is his r with him,
Is	49: 4	strength, Yet my r is with the Lord,
Is	62:11	comes! Here is his r with him,
Mt	5:12	for your r will be great in heaven.
Mt	6: 5	to you, they have received their r.
Mt	10:41	a prophet will receive a prophet's r,
Mt	10:41	will receive a righteous man's r.
Lk	6:23	Behold, your r will be great
Lk	6:35	then your r will be great and you

REWARDED → REWARD

2 Sm	22:21	"The Lord r me according to my
2 Chr	15: 7	not relax, for your work shall be r."
Prv	13:13	reveres the commandment will be r.

REWARDS → REWARD

Heb	11: 6	and that he r those who seek him.

REZIN

Is	7: 1	son of Uzziah, R, king of Aram,

RHODA

Acts	12:13	a maid named R came to answer it.

RIB → RIBS

Gn	2:22	into a woman the r that he had taken

RIBLAH

2 Kgs	25: 6	brought to R to the king of Babylon,

RIBS → RIB

Gn	2:21	he took out one of his r and closed

RICH → ENRICHED, RICHES, RICHLY

2 Sm	12: 1	were two men, one r, the other poor.
Jb	34:19	nor respects the r more than
Ps	49:17	Do not fear when others become r,

Prv	13: 7	One man pretends to be **r**, yet has
Prv	21:17	wine and perfume will not be **r**.
Prv	22: 2	**R** and poor have a common bond:
Prv	28:20	to grow **r** will not go unpunished.
Eccl	5:11	the **r** man's abundance allows him
Sir	8: 2	Quarrel not with a **r** man, lest he
Ez	34:14	in **r** pastures shall they be pastured
Mt	19:23	one who is **r** to enter the kingdom
Lk	1:53	the **r** he has sent away empty.
Lk	6:24	But woe to you who are **r**, for you
Lk	12:21	but is not **r** in what matters to God."
Lk	16: 1	"A **r** man had a steward who was
Lk	16:19	"There was a **r** man who dressed
2 Cor	8: 9	he became poor although he was **r**,
2 Cor	8: 9	by his poverty you might become **r**.
Eph	2: 4	But God, who is **r** in mercy,
1 Tm	6: 9	Those who want to be **r** are falling
1 Tm	6:17	Tell the **r** in the present age not
1 Tm	6:18	good, to be **r** in good works, to be
Jas	1:10	and the **r** one in his lowliness, for he
Jas	2: 5	are poor in the world to be **r** in faith
Jas	5: 1	you **r**, weep and wail over your
Rv	2: 9	and poverty, but you are **r**. I know
Rv	3:17	say, 'I am **r** and affluent and have no
Rv	3:18	refined by fire so that you may be **r**,

RICHES →RICH

1 Kgs	3:13	such **r** and glory that among kings
1 Kgs	10:23	Thus King Solomon surpassed in **r**
Ps	49: 7	and boast of their abundant **r**?
Ps	119:14	of your decrees more than in all **r**.
Prv	3:16	hand, in her left are **r** and honor;
Prv	11:28	He who trusts in his **r** will fall,
Prv	22: 1	name is more desirable than great **r**,
Prv	30: 8	me, give me neither poverty nor **r**;
Lk	8:14	are choked by the anxieties and **r**
Rom	9:23	to make known the **r** of his glory
Rom	11:33	the depth of the **r** and wisdom
Eph	2: 7	he might show the immeasurable **r**
Eph	3: 8	to the Gentiles the inscrutable **r**
Col	1:27	to make known the **r** of the glory

RICHLY →RICH

Col	3:16	the word of Christ dwell in you **r**,
1 Tm	6:17	who **r** provides us with all things
Ti	3: 6	whom he **r** poured out on us

RID

| 1 Pt | 2: 1 | **R** yourselves of all malice and all |

RIDDLE →RIDDLES

| Jgs | 14:12 | to them, "Let me propose a **r** to you. |
| Ez | 17: 2 | propose a **r**, and speak this proverb |

RIDDLES →RIDDLE

| Nm | 12: 8 | plainly and not in **r**. The presence |
| Prv | 1: 6 | the words of the wise and their **r**. |

RIDE →RIDER, RIDERS, RIDES, RIDING

| Ps | 45: 4 | In splendor and majesty **r** on triumphant! |

RIDER →RIDE

Ps	68: 5	exalt the **r** of the clouds.
Rv	6: 2	a white horse, and its **r** had a bow.
Rv	19:11	its **r** was [called] "Faithful and True."

RIDERS →RIDE

| Rv | 9:17 | is how I saw the horses and their **r**. |

RIDES →RIDE

| Dt | 33:26 | who **r** the heavens in his power, |
| Dt | 33:26 | and **r** the skies in his majesty; |

RIDING →RIDE

| Zec | 9: 9 | Meek, and **r** on an ass, on a colt, |

RIGGING

| Is | 33:23 | The **r** hangs slack; it cannot hold |

RIGHT →BIRTHRIGHT, RIGHTLY, RIGHTS

Gn	13: 9	you prefer the left, I will go to the **r**; if you prefer the **r**, I will go
Gn	48:13	Ephraim with his **r** hand, to Israel's
Gn	48:13	to Israel's **r**, and led them to him.

Ex	14:22	with the water like a wall to their **r**
Ex	15: 6	your **r** hand, O LORD, has shattered
Ex	15:26	them, "and do what is **r** in his eyes:
Dt	5:32	not turning aside to the **r**
Dt	6:18	Do what is **r** and good in the sight
Dt	13:19	today, doing what is **r** in his sight.
Dt	28:14	not turning aside to the **r**
Jos	1: 7	Do not swerve from it either to the **r**
1 Sm	12:23	to teach you the good and **r** way.
Jb	40:14	that your own **r** hand can save you.
Ps	16: 8	with the Lord at my **r**, I shall never
Ps	16:11	the delights at your **r** hand forever.
Ps	17: 7	you who deliver with your **r** arm
Ps	18:36	shield; your **r** hand has upheld me;
Ps	19: 9	The precepts of the LORD are **r**,
Ps	44: 4	It was your **r** hand, your own arm,
Ps	45: 5	justice may your **r** hand show you
Ps	63: 9	fast to you; your **r** hand upholds me.
Ps	73:23	you take hold of my **r** hand.
Ps	80:18	help be with the man at your **r** hand,
Ps	89:14	hand, your **r** hand is ever exalted.
Ps	91: 7	ten thousand at your **r** hand,
Ps	110: 1	lord: "Take your throne at my **r** hand,
Ps	110: 5	At your **r** hand is the Lord,
Ps	118:15	"The LORD's **r** hand strikes
Ps	137: 5	Jerusalem, may my **r** hand wither.
Ps	139:10	guide me, your **r** hand hold me fast.
Prv	3:16	Long life is in her **r** hand, in her left
Prv	4:27	Turn neither to **r** nor to left,
Prv	12:15	of the fool seems **r** in his own eyes,
Prv	14:12	Sometimes a way seems **r** to a man,
Prv	16:25	Sometimes a way seems **r** to a man,
Prv	18:17	his case first seems to be in the **r**;
Prv	21: 2	of a man may be **r** in his own eyes,
Is	30:10	"Do not descry for us what is **r**;
Is	30:21	when you would turn to the **r**
Is	41:10	and uphold you with my **r** hand
Is	41:13	who grasp your **r** hand; It is I who
Is	48:13	my **r** hand spread out the heavens
Is	64: 4	that you might meet us doing **r**,
Ez	1:10	on the **r** side was the face of a lion,
Ez	18: 5	a man is virtuous—if he does what is **r**
Ez	18:21	statutes and does what is **r** and just,
Ez	33:14	his sin and does what is **r** and just,
Am	3:10	they know not how to do what is **r**,
Jon	4:11	who cannot distinguish their **r** hand
Zec	3: 1	while Satan stood at his **r** hand
Mt	5:29	If your **r** eye causes you to sin,
Mt	6: 3	left hand know what your **r** is doing,
Mt	22:44	"Sit at my **r** hand until I place your
Mt	25:33	He will place the sheep on his **r**
Mk	14:62	seated at the **r** hand of the Power
Acts	2:34	said to my Lord, "Sit at my **r** hand
Acts	7:55	Jesus standing at the **r** hand of God,
Rom	8:34	who also is at the **r** hand of God,
Rom	9:21	not the potter have a **r** over the clay,
1 Cor	9: 4	Do we not have the **r** to eat
Eph	1:20	and seating him at his **r** hand
Eph	6: 1	parents [in the Lord], for this is **r**.
Col	3: 1	where Christ is seated at the **r** hand
Heb	1: 3	he took his seat at the **r** hand
Heb	1:13	"Sit at my **r** hand until I make your
Heb	10:12	took his seat forever at the **r** hand
1 Pt	3:22	heaven and is at the **r** hand of God,
Rv	1:16	In his **r** hand he held seven stars.
Rv	22:11	The righteous must still do **r**,
Rv	22:14	robes so as to have the **r** to the tree

RIGHTEOUS →RIGHTEOUSNESS

Tb	3: 2	"You are **r**, O Lord, and all your
Jb	4:17	"Can a man be **r** as against God?
Ps	55:23	will never allow the **r** to stumble.
Ps	119:137	You are **r**, LORD, and just are your
Ps	146: 8	bowed down; the LORD loves the **r**.
Jer	23: 5	I will raise up a **r** shoot to David;
Mt	13:43	the **r** will shine like the sun
Mt	13:49	and separate the wicked from the **r**
Mt	25:37	Then the **r** will answer him and say,
Mt	25:46	punishment, but the **r** to eternal life."

Mk	2:17	I did not come to call the r
Acts	3:14	You denied the Holy and **R** One
Acts	24:15	there will be a resurrection of the r
Rom	1:17	"The one who is r by faith will live."
Rom	5:19	of one the many will be made r.
Jas	5:16	of a r person is very powerful.
1 Pt	3:12	For the eyes of the Lord are on the r
1 Pt	3:18	the r for the sake of the unrighteous,
1 Pt	4:18	"And if the r one is barely saved,
2 Pt	2: 7	a r man oppressed by the licentious
1 Jn	2: 1	the Father, Jesus Christ the r one.
1 Jn	3: 7	who acts in righteousness is r, just as he is r.
Rv	19: 8	(The linen represents the r deeds

RIGHTEOUSNESS → RIGHTEOUS

Gn	15: 6	who credited it to him as an act of r.
Tb	12: 8	is almsgiving accompanied by r.
Tb	12: 8	little with r is better than abundance
Ps	18:21	The Lord acknowledged my r,
Prv	16:12	for by r the throne endures.
Mt	3:15	thus it is fitting for us to fulfill all r."
Mt	5: 6	are they who hunger and thirst for r,
Mt	5:10	they who are persecuted for the sake of r,
Mt	5:20	unless your r surpasses
Mt	6:33	first the kingdom [of God] and his r,
Jn	16: 8	the world in regard to sin and r
Rom	1:17	in it is revealed the r of God
Rom	3:22	the r of God through faith in Jesus
Rom	4: 3	God, and it was credited to him as r."
Rom	4: 5	ungodly, his faith is credited as r.
Rom	4: 6	to whom God credits r apart
Rom	4: 9	"faith was credited to Abraham as r."
Rom	4:13	through the r that comes from faith.
Rom	4:22	is why "it was credited to him as r."
Rom	6:13	bodies to God as weapons for r.
Rom	6:16	or of obedience, which leads to r?
Rom	6:18	sin, you have become slaves of r.
Rom	6:19	so now present them as slaves to r
Rom	8:10	sin, the spirit is alive because of r.
Rom	9:30	who did not pursue r, have achieved it, that is, r that comes from faith;
Rom	10: 3	unawareness of the r that comes
Rom	10: 3	attempt to establish their own [r],
Rom	10: 3	they did not submit to the r of God.
Rom	14:17	of food and drink, but of r, peace,
1 Cor	1:30	God, as well as r, sanctification,
2 Cor	5:21	that we might become the r of God
2 Cor	6: 7	with weapons of r at the right
2 Cor	6:14	For what partnership do r
2 Cor	9: 9	to the poor; his r endures forever."
2 Cor	9:10	and increase the harvest of your r.
2 Cor	11:15	also masquerade as ministers of r.
Gal	3: 6	God, and it was credited to him as r."
Eph	4:24	self, created in God's way in r
Eph	6:14	truth, clothed with r as a breastplate,
Phil	1:11	the fruit of r that comes through
Phil	3: 6	church, in r based on the law I was
Phil	3: 9	not having any r of my own based
Phil	3: 9	faith in Christ, the r from God,
1 Tm	6:11	Instead, pursue r, devotion, faith,
2 Tm	2:22	from youthful desires and pursue r,
2 Tm	3:16	for correction, and for training in r,
2 Tm	4: 8	now on the crown of r awaits me,
Heb	5:13	lacks experience of the word of r,
Heb	11: 7	inherited the r that comes through
Heb	12:11	later it brings the peaceful fruit of r
Jas	2:23	and it was credited to him as r,"
Jas	3:18	the fruit of r is sown in peace
1 Pt	2:24	free from sin, we might live for r.
2 Pt	2:21	have known the way of r than
2 Pt	3:13	and a new earth in which r dwells.
Rv	19:11	He judges and wages war in r.

RIGHTLY → RIGHT

Lk	7:43	He said to him, "You have judged r."

RIGHTS → RIGHT

Ex	21:10	food, her clothing, or her conjugal r.
Prv	31: 8	dumb, and for the r of the destitute;
Lam	3:35	When he distorts men's r in the very

1 Cor	9:15	I have not used any of these r,

RING → EARRINGS

Gn	41:42	Pharaoh took off his signet r
Est	3:12	and sealed with the royal signet r.
Est	8:10	and sealed with the royal signet r,
Prv	11:22	Like a golden r in a swine's snout
Jer	22:24	are a signet r on my right hand,
Hg	2:23	And I will set you as a signet r; for I
Lk	15:22	put a r on his finger and sandals

RIOT → RIOTS

Mk	14: 2	there may be a r among the people."

RIOTS → RIOT

2 Cor	6: 5	beatings, imprisonments, r, labors,

RIPE

Jl	4:13	for the harvest is r; Come and tread,
Mk	4:29	And when the grain is r, he wields
Jn	4:35	and see the fields r for the harvest.
Rv	14:15	because the earth's harvest is fully r."

RISE → ARISE, ARISEN, ARISES, RAISE, RAISED, RAISES, RISES, RISING, ROSE

Nm	24:17	and a staff shall r from Israel,
Ps	7: 7	**R** up, Lord, in your anger; r against
Ps	94: 2	**R** up, judge of the earth;
Is	26:19	dead shall live, their corpses shall r;
Dn	12:13	you shall r for your reward
Am	8:14	those shall fall, never to r again.
Mt	5:45	for he makes his sun r on the bad
Mk	8:31	and be killed, and r after three days.
Mk	13: 8	Nation will r against nation
Lk	18:33	him, but on the third day he will r."
Jn	20: 9	that he had to r from the dead.
Acts	17: 3	had to suffer and r from the dead,
1 Thes	4:16	and the dead in Christ will r first.

RISES → RISE

Eccl	1: 5	The sun r and the sun goes down;
2 Pt	1:19	the morning star r in your hearts.

RISING → RISE

Ps	113: 3	From the r of the sun to its setting
Mt	2: 2	We saw his star at its r and have
Mk	9:10	questioning what r from the dead

RIVALRY

Phil	1:15	preach Christ from envy and r,

RIVER → RIVERS

Gn	2:10	A r rises in Eden to water
Gn	15:18	to the Great **R** [the Euphrates],
Dt	1: 7	far as the Great **R** [the Euphrates].
Dt	11:24	the Euphrates **R** to the Western Sea,
Ps	46: 5	Streams of the r gladden the city
Is	48:18	your prosperity would be like a r,
Is	66:12	spread prosperity over her like a r,
Ez	47:12	Along both banks of the r,
Mt	3: 6	the Jordan **R** as they acknowledged
Rv	22: 1	Then the angel showed me the r

RIVERS → RIVER

Ps	78:16	from crags, drew out r of water.
Ps	78:44	God changed their r to blood;
Ps	137: 1	By the r of Babylon we sat
Rv	8:10	It fell on a third of the r
Rv	16: 4	angel poured out his bowl on the r

ROAD → CROSSROADS

Nm	22:22	the r to hinder him as he was riding
Mt	7:13	the r broad that leads to destruction,
Mk	11: 8	people spread their cloaks on the r,

ROAR → ROARING, ROARS

Am	1: 2	The Lord will r from Zion,

ROARING → ROAR

Ps	65: 8	You still the r of the seas, the r
1 Pt	5: 8	around like a r lion looking

ROARS → ROAR

Jer	25:30	to them: The Lord r from on high,
Jer	25:30	Mightily he r over the range,

Hos 11:10 follow the L<small>ORD</small>, who **r** like a lion;
Hos 11:10 When he **r**, his sons shall come
Jl 4:16 The L<small>ORD</small> **r** from Zion,

ROASTED
Ex 12: 8 same night they shall eat its **r** flesh

ROB →ROBBER, ROBBERS, ROBBERY
Mal 3: 8 Dare a man **r** God? Yet you are
Mal 3: 8 And you say, "How do we **r** you?"
Rom 2:22 who detest idols, do you **r** temples?

ROBBER →ROB
1 Cor 5:11 or a **r**, not even to eat with such

ROBBERS →ROB
Lk 10:30 fell victim to **r** as he went down
1 Cor 6:10 nor slanderers nor **r** will inherit

ROBBERY →ROB
Is 61: 8 what is right, I hate **r** and injustice;
Ez 22:29 practice extortion and commit **r**;

ROBE →ROBED, ROBES
Ex 28: 4 an ephod, a **r**, a brocaded tunic,
Is 61:10 has clothed me with a **r** of salvation,
Lk 15:22 'Quickly bring the finest **r** and put it
Rv 1:13 wearing an ankle-length **r**,
Rv 6:11 Each of them was given a white **r**,

ROBED →ROBE
Ps 93: 1 The L<small>ORD</small> is king, **r** with majesty;
Ps 93: 1 the L<small>ORD</small> is **r**, girded with might.

ROBES →ROBE
Ps 45: 9 aloes, and cassia your **r** are fragrant.
Mk 12:38 who like to go around in long **r**
Rv 22:14 are they who wash their **r** so as

ROCK →ROCKS, ROCKY
Gn 49:24 of the Shepherd, the **R** of Israel,
Ex 17: 6 in front of you on the **r** in Horeb.
Ex 17: 6 Strike the **r**, and the water will flow
Ex 33:22 I will set you in the hollow of the **r**
Nm 20: 8 the **r** you shall bring forth water
Dt 32: 4 The **R**—how faultless are his deeds,
Dt 32:15 them and scorned their saving **R**.
Dt 32:31 Indeed, their "**r**" is not like our **R**,
1 Sm 2: 2 the L<small>ORD</small>; there is no **R** like our God.
2 Sm 22: 2 sang: "O L<small>ORD</small>, my **r**, my fortress,
Ps 18: 3 L<small>ORD</small>, my **r**, my fortress,
Ps 18: 3 My God, my **r** of refuge, my shield,
Ps 19:15 you, L<small>ORD</small>, my **r** and my redeemer.
Ps 27: 3 his tent; and set me high upon a **r**.
Ps 40: 3 Set my feet upon **r**, steadied my
Ps 61: 3 Raise me up, set me on a **r**,
Ps 62: 3 God alone is my **r** and salvation,
Ps 78:15 He split **r** in the desert,
Ps 92:16 our **r**, in whom there is no wrong."
Wis 11: 4 was given them from the sheer **r**,
Is 26: 4 For the L<small>ORD</small> is an eternal **R**.
Is 44: 8 Is there a God or any **R** besides me?
Is 48:21 Water from the **r** he set flowing
Is 48:21 he cleft the **r**, and waters welled
Is 51: 1 Look to the **r** from which you were
Mt 7:24 wise man who built his house on **r**.
Mt 16:18 upon this **r** I will build my church,
Mk 15:46 that had been hewn out of the **r**.
Rom 9:33 and a **r** that will make them fall,
1 Cor 10: 4 a spiritual **r** that followed them, and the **r** was the Christ.
1 Pt 2: 8 and a **r** that will make them fall."

ROCKS →ROCK
Dt 32:13 them honey to suck from its **r**
Is 2:19 Men will go into caves in the **r**
Na 1: 6 the **r** are rent asunder before him.
Mt 27:51 The earth quaked, **r** were split,

ROCKY →ROCK
Mk 4: 5 on **r** ground where it had little soil.

ROD →RODS
2 Sm 7:14 I will correct him with the **r** of men

Ps 2: 9 an iron **r** you shall shepherd them,
Ps 23: 4 your **r** and staff give me courage.
Prv 13:24 He who spares his **r** hates his son,
Prv 14: 3 mouth of the fool is a **r** for his back,
Prv 22:15 the **r** of discipline will drive it far
Prv 23:13 if you beat him with the **r**, he will
Prv 29:15 The **r** of correction gives wisdom,
Is 11: 4 the ruthless with the **r** of his mouth,
Rv 2:27 He will rule them with an iron **r**.
Rv 19:15 He will rule them with an iron **r**,

RODS →ROD
2 Cor 11:25 Three times I was beaten with **r**,

ROLL →ROLLED
Mk 16: 3 "Who will **r** back the stone for us
Heb 1:12 You will **r** them up like a cloak,

ROLLED →ROLL
Lk 24: 2 They found the stone **r** away

ROMAN →ROME
Acts 16:37 even though we are **R** citizens
Acts 22:25 to scourge a man who is a **R** citizen

ROMANS →ROME
1 Mc 8: 1 had heard of the reputation of the **R**.
1 Mc 14:24 to confirm the alliance with the **R**.
Jn 11:48 and the **R** will come and take away

ROME →ROMAN, ROMANS
Acts 18: 2 had ordered all the Jews to leave **R**.
Acts 28:14 seven days. And thus we came to **R**.
Rom 1:15 preach the gospel also to you in **R**.

ROOF
Gn 19: 8 come under the shelter of my **r**."
Jos 2: 6 Now, she had led them to the **r**,
2 Sm 11: 2 strolled about on the **r** of the palace.
2 Sm 11: 2 the **r** he saw a woman bathing,
Mt 8: 8 to have you enter under my **r**;
Mk 2: 4 they opened up the **r** above him.
Acts 10: 9 went up to the **r** terrace to pray

ROOM →ROOMS
Mt 6: 6 go to your inner **r**, close the door,
Mk 14:15 show you a large upper **r** furnished
Rom 12:19 revenge but leave **r** for the wrath;
2 Cor 7: 2 Make **r** for us; we have not wronged
Eph 4:27 and do not leave **r** for the devil.

ROOMS →ROOM
Mt 24:26 'He is in the inner **r**,' do not believe

ROOT →ROOTED, ROOTS
Prv 12:12 but the **r** of the just is enduring.
Sir 47:22 to David a **r** from his own family.
Is 11:10 On that day, The **r** of Jesse,
Mt 3:10 now the ax lies at the **r** of the trees.
Mt 13:21 he has no **r** and lasts only for a time.
Rom 11:18 that you do not support the **r**; the **r**
Rom 15:12 says: "The **r** of Jesse shall come,
1 Tm 6:10 love of money is the **r** of all evils,
Rv 5: 5 of the tribe of Judah, the **r** of David,
Rv 22:16 I am the **r** and offspring of David,

ROOTED →ROOT
Eph 3:17 that you, **r** and grounded in love,
Col 2: 7 **r** in him and built upon him

ROOTS →ROOT
Is 11: 1 and from his **r** a bud shall blossom.
Jer 17: 8 that stretches out its **r** to the stream:
Ez 17: 9 Will he not rather tear it out by the **r**
Ez 17: 9 wither when he pulls it up by the **r**?

ROSE →RISE
Acts 10:41 with him after he **r** from the dead.
1 Thes 4:14 if we believe that Jesus died and **r**,

ROT →ROTTED
Prv 10: 7 but the name of the wicked will **r**.
Zec 14:12 their flesh shall **r** while they stand
Zec 14:12 their eyes shall **r** in their sockets,
Zec 14:12 their tongues shall **r** in their mouths.

ROTTED → ROT
Jas 5: 2 Your wealth has r away,

ROUGH
Is 40: 4 plain, the r country, a broad valley.
Bar 4:26 children have trodden r roads,
Lk 3: 5 and the r ways made smooth,

ROUNDS
Eccl 1: 6 again and again, resuming its r.

ROYAL
2 Chr 22:10 to kill off all the r offspring
Est 4:14 this that you obtained the r dignity?"
Is 62: 3 LORD, a r diadem held by your God.
Jas 2: 8 you fulfill the r law according
1 Pt 2: 9 are "a chosen race, a r priesthood,

RUBBISH
1 Cor 4:13 We have become like the world's r,
Phil 3: 8 and I consider them so much r,

RUDDER
Jas 3: 4 a very small r wherever the pilot's

RUDDY
1 Sm 16:12 He was r, a youth handsome
Song 5:10 My lover is radiant and r;

RUDE
1 Cor 13: 5 it is not r, it does not seek its own

RUIN → RUINS
Prv 10:14 the mouth of a fool is imminent r.
Prv 19:13 The foolish son is r to his father,
Prv 26:28 and the flattering mouth works r.
Is 25: 2 the fortified city a r; The castle
Hos 4:14 without understanding come to r.
1 Tm 6: 9 which plunge them into r

RUINS → RUIN
Ezr 9: 9 house of our God and restore its r,
Neh 2:17 how Jerusalem lies in r and its gates
Jer 9:10 will turn Jerusalem into a heap of r,
Am 9:11 raise up its r, and rebuild it as
Acts 15:16 from its r I shall rebuild it and raise

RULE → RULER, RULERS, RULES
Dt 15: 6 you will r over many nations,
Dt 15: 6 and none will r over you,
Jgs 8:22 then said to Gideon, "R over us—you,
Ps 110: 2 LORD says: "R over your enemies!
Prv 17: 2 An intelligent servant will r over
Is 32: 1 justly and princes will r rightly.
Rom 15:12 raised up to r the Gentiles; in him
Rv 2:27 He will r them with an iron rod.
Rv 12: 5 destined to r all the nations
Rv 19:15 He will r them with an iron rod,

RULER → RULE
Ex 2:14 "Who has appointed you r and judge
Prv 23: 1 When you sit down to dine with a r,
Prv 25:15 By patience is a r persuaded,
Prv 29:12 If a r listens to lying words,
Prv 29:26 Many curry favor with the r,
Eccl 9:17 than the shout of a r of fools"—!
Mt 2: 6 since from you shall come a r,
Acts 7:27 'Who appointed you r and judge
Eph 2: 2 following the r of the power
Rv 1: 5 dead and r of the kings of the earth.

RULERS → RULE
Sir 4:27 man, nor refuse to do so before r.
Is 40:23 makes the r of the earth as nothing.
Mt 2: 6 by no means least among the r
Mt 20:25 that the r of the Gentiles lord it over
Rom 13: 3 For r are not a cause of fear to good
1 Cor 2: 6 of the r of this age who are passing
Eph 6:12 the world r of this present darkness,

RULES → RULE
2 Sm 23: 3 said, 'He that r over men in justice, that r in the fear of God,
Ps 66: 7 who r by might forever,
Ps 103:19 God's royal power r over all.

RUMOR → RUMORS
Ez 7:26 be disaster after disaster, r after r.

RUMORS → RUMOR
Jer 51:46 for fear of r spread in the land;

RUN → FORERUNNER, RAN, RUNNERS, RUNNING, RUNS
Ps 119:32 I will r the way of your commands,
Prv 4:12 and should you r, you will not
Is 40:31 They will r and not grow weary,
1 Cor 9:24 in the stadium all r in the race,
1 Cor 9:24 one wins the prize? R so as to win.
Gal 2: 2 not be running, or have r, in vain.
Phil 2:16 May be that I did not r in vain

RUNNERS → RUN
1 Cor 9:24 that the r in the stadium all run

RUNNING → RUN
Ps 133: 2 on the head, r down upon the beard,
Gal 5: 7 You were r well; who hindered you
Heb 12: 1 in r the race that lies before us

RUNS → RUN
Prv 18:10 the just man r to it and is safe.
Jn 10:12 and leaves the sheep and r away,

RUTH
Moabitess; widow who went to Bethlehem with mother-in-law Naomi (Ru 1). Gleaned in field of Boaz; shown favor (Ru 2). Proposed marriage to Boaz (Ru 3). Married (Ru 4:1-12); bore Obed, ancestor of David (Ru 4:13-22), Jesus (Mt 1:5).

RUTHLESS
Rom 1:31 are senseless, faithless, heartless, r.

S

SABACHTHANI
Mt 27:46 out in a loud voice, *"Eli, Eli, lema s?"*
Mk 15:34 in a loud voice, *"Eloi, Eloi, lema s?"*

SABBATH → SABBATHS
Ex 16:23 rest, the s, sacred to the LORD.
Ex 20: 8 "Remember to keep holy the s day.
Ex 31:14 you must keep the s as something
Nm 15:32 gathering wood on the s day.
Dt 5:12 to keep holy the s day as the LORD,
Neh 13:17 you are doing, profaning the s day?
1 Mc 1:43 to idols and profaned the s.
1 Mc 2:38 and soldiers attacked them on the s,
Is 56: 2 to it; Who keeps the s free
Is 58:13 If you hold back your foot on the s
Is 58:13 If you call the s a delight,
Jer 17:21 not to carry burdens on the s day,
Mt 12: 1 through a field of grain on the s.
Mk 2:28 the Son of Man is lord even of the s."
Lk 6: 9 to do good on the s rather than to do
Lk 13:10 teaching in a synagogue on the s.
Lk 14: 3 "Is it lawful to cure on the s or not?"

SABBATHS → SABBATH
Ex 31:13 Take care to keep my s, for that is
2 Chr 36:21 the land has retrieved its lost s,
1 Mc 1:45 to profane the s and feast days,
Ez 20:12 I also gave them my s to be a sign

SACKCLOTH → CLOTH
1 Chr 21:16 clothed in s, prostrated themselves
Jdt 4:10 also girded themselves with s.
Jdt 8: 5 She put s about her loins and wore
1 Mc 2:14 put on s, and mourned bitterly.
Ps 30:12 you took off my s and clothed me
Dn 9: 3 prayer, with fasting, s, and ashes.
Jl 1:13 altar! Come, spend the night in s,
Jon 3: 5 of them, great and small, put on s.
Mt 11:21 would long ago have repented in s
Rv 6:12 the sun turned as black as dark s

SACRED
Ex 28: 2 you shall have s vestments made.
Ex 34:13 smash their s pillars, and cut down their s poles.

Lam   4: 1   metal; How the **s** stones lie strewn

SACRIFICE → SACRIFICED, SACRIFICES

Ex	5:17	'Let us go and offer **s** to the LORD.'
Ex	12:27	'This is the Passover **s** of the LORD,
1 Sm	2:13	When someone offered a **s**,
1 Sm	15:22	Obedience is better than **s**,
1 Mc	1:47	to **s** swine and unclean animals,
1 Mc	4:53	offered **s** according to the law
Ps	40: 7	**S** and offering you do not want;
Ps	50:14	Offer praise as your **s** to God;
Ps	51:18	For you do not desire **s**; a burnt
Ps	54: 8	Then I will offer you generous **s**
Ps	141: 2	my uplifted hands an evening **s**.
Prv	15: 8	The **s** of the wicked is
Prv	21: 3	more acceptable to the LORD than **s**.
Prv	21:27	The **s** of the wicked is
Sir	35: 2	when he gives alms he presents his **s** of praise.
Dn	8:11	from whom it removed the daily **s**,
Dn	9:27	he shall abolish **s** and oblation;
Dn	11:31	abolishing the daily **s** and setting
Dn	12:11	the time that the daily **s** is abolished
Hos	6: 6	For it is love that I desire, not **s**,
Mt	9:13	of the words, 'I desire mercy, not **s**.'
1 Cor	10:20	I mean that what they **s**, [they **s**]
Phil	4:18	an acceptable **s**, pleasing to God.
Heb	9:26	of the ages to take away sin by his **s**.
Heb	11: 4	to God a **s** greater than Cain's.
Heb	13:15	let us continually offer God a **s**

SACRIFICED → SACRIFICE

Acts	15:29	to abstain from meat **s** to idols,
1 Cor	5: 7	paschal lamb, Christ, has been **s**.
1 Cor	8: 1	Now in regard to meat **s** to idols:
Rv	2:14	to eat food **s** to idols and to play
Rv	2:20	the harlot and to eat food **s** to idols.

SACRIFICES → SACRIFICE

Ex	22:19	"Whoever **s** to any god,
2 Chr	7: 1	consumed the holocaust and the **s**,
Ezr	6: 3	to be rebuilt as a place for offering **s**
Ps	50: 8	Not for your **s** do I rebuke you,
Is	1:11	care I for the number of your **s**?
Is	56: 7	Their holocausts and **s** will be
Jer	6:20	favor with me, your **s** please me not.
Am	5:25	Did you bring me **s** and offerings
Mk	12:33	more than all burnt offerings and **s**."
Heb	9:23	themselves by better **s** than these.
Heb	13:16	God is pleased by **s** of that kind.
1 Pt	2: 5	to offer spiritual **s** acceptable to God

SAD

Neh	2: 1	As I had never before been **s** in his
Lk	18:23	he heard this he became quite **s**,

SADDUCEES

Mt	16: 1	The Pharisees and **S** came and,
Mt	16: 6	of the leaven of the Pharisees and **S**."
Mt	22:34	heard that he had silenced the **S**,
Mk	12:18	Some **S**, who say there is no
Acts	23: 7	out between the Pharisees and **S**,

SAFE → SAFEGUARD, SAFETY

Ezr	8:21	from him a **s** journey for ourselves,
Prv	18:10	the just man runs to it and is **s**.
Prv	28:18	He who walks uprightly is **s**, but he

SAFEGUARD → GUARD, SAFE

Phil   3: 1   no burden for me but is a **s** for you.

SAFETY → SAFE

Is   14:30   and the needy lie down in **s**; But I

SAKE → SAKES

1 Sm	12:22	For the **s** of his own great name
1 Kgs	11:12	for the **s** of your father David; it is
Ps	23: 3	right path for the **s** of your name.
Ps	25:11	For the **s** of your name, LORD,
Ps	69: 8	For your **s** I bear insult,
Ps	106: 8	Yet he saved them for his name's **s**
Ps	109:21	kindly with me for your name's **s**;
Ps	132:10	For the **s** of David your servant,
Is	43:25	out, for my own **s**, your offenses;

Is	48: 9	For the **s** of my name I restrain my
Is	48: 9	the **s** of my renown I hold it back
Is	48:11	For my **s**, for my own **s**, I do this;
Is	62: 1	For Zion's **s** I will not be silent,
Is	62: 1	for Jerusalem's **s** I will not be quiet,
Jer	14:21	For your name's **s** spurn us not,
Bar	2:14	and deliver us for your own **s**:
Ez	20: 9	but I acted for my name's **s**, that it
Ez	20:14	but I acted for my name's **s**, that it
Ez	20:22	acting for my name's **s**, lest it be
Dn	3:34	For your name's **s**, do not deliver us
Dn	9:17	and for your own **s**, O Lord, let your
Mt	10:39	loses his life for my **s** will find it.
Mt	19:29	for the **s** of my name will receive
Mk	13:20	the **s** of the elect whom he chose,
Rom	8:36	"For your **s** we are being slain all
Rom	9: 3	from Christ for the **s** of my brothers,
Rom	14:20	For the **s** of food, do not destroy
1 Cor	9:23	All this I do for the **s** of the gospel,
2 Cor	4:11	given up to death for the **s** of Jesus,
2 Cor	12:10	and constraints, for the **s** of Christ;
1 Pt	2:13	human institution for the Lord's **s**,
3 Jn	1: 7	have set out for the **s** of the Name

SAKES → SAKE

Ez   36:32   Not for your **s** do I act,

SALE → SELL

Dt   28:68   there you will offer yourselves for **s**

SALEM → =JERUSALEM

Gn	14:18	king of **S**, brought out bread
Heb	7: 2	and he was also "king of **S**," that is,

SALIVA

Jn   9: 6   ground and made clay with the **s**,

SALT → SALTED

Gn	19:26	and she was turned into a pillar of **s**.
2 Kgs	2:20	bowl," Elisha said, "and put **s** into it."
Mt	5:13	"You are the **s** of the earth. But if **s**
Mk	9:50	**S** is good, but if **s** becomes insipid,
Mk	9:50	Keep **s** in yourselves and you will
Lk	14:34	"**S** is good, but if **s** itself
Col	4: 6	seasoned with **s**, so that you know

SALTED → SALT

Mk   9:49   "Everyone will be **s** with fire.

SALVATION → SAVE

2 Sm	22: 3	My shield, the horn of my **s**,
2 Sm	22:47	Extolled be my God, Rock of my **s**.
1 Chr	16:23	earth, announce his **s**, day after day.
2 Chr	6:41	priests, LORD God, be clothed with **s**,
Jb	13:16	And this shall be my **s**, that no
Ps	27: 1	The LORD is my light and my **s**;
Ps	35: 3	Say to my heart, "I am your **s**."
Ps	37:39	The **s** of the just is from the LORD,
Ps	38:23	to help me, my Lord and my **s**!
Ps	50:23	to the obedient I will show the **s**
Ps	51:14	Restore my joy in your **s**;
Ps	62: 2	God alone, from whom comes my **s**.
Ps	62: 3	God alone is my rock and **s**,
Ps	62: 7	God alone is my rock and my **s**,
Ps	68:20	God, our **s**, who carries us.
Ps	85: 8	us, LORD, your love; grant us your **s**.
Ps	85:10	Near indeed is **s** for the loyal;
Ps	95: 1	LORD; cry out to the rock of our **s**.
Ps	96: 2	name; announce his **s** day after day.
Ps	116:13	I will raise the cup of **s** and call
Ps	119:41	LORD, **s** in accord with your promise.
Ps	119:81	My soul longs for your **s**; I put my
Ps	119:123	My eyes long to see your **s**
Ps	119:155	**S** is far from sinners because they
Ps	119:166	I look for your **s**, LORD, and I fulfill
Ps	119:174	I long for your **s**, LORD;
Wis	5: 2	and amazed at the unlooked-for **s**.
Is	12: 3	will draw water at the fountain of **s**,
Is	33: 2	morning, our **s** in time of trouble!
Is	45: 8	Let the earth open and **s** bud forth;
Is	46:13	it is not far off, my **s** shall not tarry;
Is	46:13	I will put **s** within Zion, and give

Is	49: 6	that my **s** may reach to the ends
Is	49: 8	you, on the day of **s** I help you,
Is	51: 5	come speedily; my **s** shall go forth
Is	51: 6	like flies, My **s** shall remain forever
Is	51: 8	and my **s**, for all generations.
Is	52: 7	announcing **s**, and saying to Zion,
Is	52:10	earth will behold the **s** of our God.
Is	56: 1	is just; for my **s** is about to come,
Is	59:11	not there; for **s**, and it is far from us.
Is	59:17	**s**, as the helmet on his head;
Is	60:18	You shall call your walls "**S**" and your
Is	61:10	he has clothed me with a robe of **s**,
Jer	3:23	our God, alone is the **s** of Israel.
Bar	4:24	so shall they soon see God's **s** come
Mk	16: S	proclamation of eternal **s**. Amen.]
Lk	1:77	to give his people knowledge of **s**
Lk	2:30	for my eyes have seen your **s**,
Lk	3: 6	and all flesh shall see the **s** of God.' "
Lk	19: 9	him, "Today **s** has come to this house
Jn	4:22	because **s** is from the Jews.
Acts	4:12	There is no **s** through anyone else,
Acts	13:26	to us this word of **s** has been sent.
Acts	13:47	you may be an instrument of **s**
Acts	16:17	who proclaim to you a way of **s**."
Acts	28:28	you that this **s** of God has been sent
Rom	1:16	for the **s** of everyone who believes:
Rom	11:11	their transgression **s** has come
Rom	13:11	For our **s** is nearer now than
2 Cor	1: 6	it is for your encouragement and **s**;
2 Cor	6: 2	and on the day of **s** I helped you."
2 Cor	6: 2	behold, now is the day of **s**.
Eph	1:13	truth, the gospel of your **s**, and have
Eph	6:17	take the helmet of **s** and the sword
Phil	1:28	them of destruction, but of your **s**.
Phil	2:12	work out your **s** with fear
1 Thes	5: 8	and the helmet that is hope for **s**.
1 Thes	5: 9	but to gain **s** through our Lord Jesus
2 Thes	2:13	for **s** through sanctification
2 Tm	2:10	that they too may obtain the **s** that is
2 Tm	3:15	you wisdom for **s** through faith
Heb	1:14	sake of those who are to inherit **s**?
Heb	2: 3	we escape if we ignore so great a **s**?
Heb	2:10	to their **s** perfect through suffering.
Heb	5: 9	of eternal **s** for all who obey him,
Heb	6: 9	of better things related to **s**,
1 Pt	1: 5	to a **s** that is ready to be revealed
1 Pt	1: 9	of [your] faith, the **s** of your souls.
1 Pt	1:10	Concerning this **s**, prophets who
1 Pt	2: 2	that through it you may grow into **s**,
2 Pt	3:15	the patience of our Lord as **s**, as our
Jude	1: 3	to write to you about our common **s**,
Rv	7:10	"**S** comes from our God, who is
Rv	12:10	say: "Now have **s** and power come,
Rv	19: 1	**S**, glory, and might belong to our

SAMARIA → SAMARITAN, SAMARITANS, SHEMER

1 Kgs	16:24	bought the hill of **S** from Shemer
1 Kgs	16:24	hill, naming the city he built **S**
1 Kgs	16:32	temple of Baal which he built in **S**,
1 Kgs	20:43	of Israel went off homeward and entered **S**.
2 Kgs	17: 6	the king of Assyria took **S**,
Is	36:19	Where are the gods of **S**? Have they
Is	36:19	Have they saved **S** from my hand?
Ez	23: 4	**S** is Oholah, and Jerusalem is
Hos	8: 5	Cast away your calf, O **S**! my wrath
Am	6: 1	overconfident on the mount of **S**,
Mi	1: 6	I will make **S** a stone heap
Jn	4: 4	He had to pass through **S**.
Acts	1: 8	throughout Judea and **S**,
Acts	8: 1	the countryside of Judea and **S**,
Acts	8:14	heard that **S** had accepted the word

SAMARITAN → SAMARIA

Lk	10:33	But a **S** traveler who came upon him
Lk	17:16	Jesus and thanked him. He was a **S**.
Jn	8:48	not right in saying that you are a **S**
Acts	8:25	the good news to many **S** villages.

SAMARITANS → SAMARIA

Jn	4: 9	use nothing in common with **S**.)

SAME

Ex	5: 8	them the **s** quota of bricks as they
Ex	7:22	the Egyptian magicians did the **s**
Ex	8: 3	But the magicians did the **s** by their
Dt	7:19	The **s** also will he do to all
1 Sm	2:34	both shall die on the **s** day.
Ps	102:28	but you are the **s**, your years have
Eccl	9: 3	that things turn out the **s** for all.
Sir	42:21	he is from all eternity one and the **s**,
Acts	1:11	in the **s** way as you have seen him
Acts	11:17	God gave them the **s** gift he gave
Rom	2: 1	you, the judge, do the very **s** things.
Rom	10:12	the **s** Lord is Lord of all,
Rom	12: 4	the parts do not have the **s** function,
1 Cor	10: 3	All ate the **s** spiritual food,
1 Cor	12: 4	of spiritual gifts but the **s** Spirit;
1 Cor	12: 5	forms of service but the **s** Lord;
Phil	2: 5	among yourselves the **s** attitude
Heb	1:12	But you are the **s**, and your years
Heb	13: 8	Jesus Christ is the **s** yesterday,

SAMSON

Danite judge. Birth promised (Jgs 13). Married a Philistine, but his wife given away (Jgs 14). Vengeance on the Philistines (Jgs 15). Betrayed by Delilah (Jgs 16:1-22). Death (Jgs 16:23-31). Feats of strength: killed lion (Jgs 14:6), 30 Philistines (Jgs 14:19), 1, 000 Philistines with jawbone (Jgs 15:13-17), carried off gates of Gaza (Jgs 16:3), pushed down temple of Dagon (Jgs 16:25-30; Heb 11:32).

SAMUEL

Ephraimite judge and prophet (Heb 11:32). Birth prayed for (1 Sm 1:10-18). Dedicated to temple by Hannah (1 Sm 1:21-28). Raised by Eli (1 Sm 2:11, 18-26). Called as prophet (1 Sm 3). Led Israel to victory over Philistines (1 Sm 7). Asked by Israel for a king (1 Sm 8). Anointed Saul as king (1 Sm 9-10). Farewell speech (1 Sm 12). Rebuked Saul for sacrifice (1 Sm 13). Announced rejection of Saul (1 Sm 15). Anointed David as king (1 Sm 16). Protected David from Saul (1 Sm 19:18-24). Death (1 Sm 25:1). Returned from dead to condemn Saul (1 Sm 28).

SANBALLAT

Led opposition to Nehemiah's rebuilding of Jerusalem (Neh 2:10, 19; 4: 6).

SANCTIFICATION → SANCTIFY

Rom	6:19	as slaves to righteousness for **s**.
Rom	6:22	the benefit that you have leads to **s**,
1 Cor	1:30	as well as righteousness, **s**,
2 Thes	2:13	for salvation through **s** by the Spirit

SANCTIFIED → SANCTIFY

1 Chr	15:14	the Levites **s** themselves to bring
Rom	15:16	be acceptable, **s** by the holy Spirit.
1 Cor	1: 2	to you who have been **s** in Christ
1 Cor	6:11	you were **s**, you were justified

SANCTIFY → SANCTIFICATION, SANCTIFIED

1 Pt	3:15	but **s** Christ as Lord in your hearts.

SANCTUARIES → SANCTUARY

Lv	26:31	your cities and devastate your **s**,
Am	7: 9	and the **s** of Israel made desolate;

SANCTUARY → SANCTUARIES

Ex	15:17	the **s**, O LORD, which your hands
Ex	25: 8	"They shall make a **s** for me, that I
Nm	3:28	hundred. They had charge of the **s**.
Nm	18: 1	house shall be responsible for the **s**;
1 Kgs	6:19	of the temple was located the **s**
1 Chr	22:19	to build the **s** of the LORD God,
1 Mc	1:21	He insolently invaded the **s** and took
1 Mc	4:36	let us go up to purify the **s**
Ps	60: 8	In the **s** God promised: "I will exult,
Ps	63: 3	So I look to you in the **s** to see your
Ps	73:17	Till I entered the **s** of God and came
Ps	74: 7	They set your **s** on fire; the abode
Ps	150: 1	Praise God in his holy **s**; give praise
Lam	1:10	enter her **s** Whom you forbade
Ez	5:11	because you have defiled my **s**
Ez	37:26	and put my **s** among them forever.
Dn	8:11	sacrifice, and whose **s** it cast down,
Dn	9:26	shall destroy the **s**. Then the end

Heb	8: 2	a minister of the **s** and of the true
Heb	8: 5	copy and shadow of the heavenly **s**,
Heb	9:24	Christ did not enter into a **s** made

SAND →SANDS

Ex	2:12	the Egyptian and hid him in the **s**.
Hos	2: 1	Israelites shall be like the **s** of the sea,
Mt	7:26	like a fool who built his house on **s**.
Rom	9:27	the Israelites were like the **s**

SANDS →SAND

Gn	22:17	of the sky and the **s** of the seashore,
Gn	32:13	make your descendants like the **s**
Gn	41:49	in quantities like the **s** of the sea,
1 Kgs	4:20	were as numerous as the **s** by the sea;
Heb	11:12	sky and as countless as the **s**

SANDAL →SANDALS

Dt	25: 9	to him and strip his **s** from his foot
Ru	4: 7	one party would take off his **s**
Jn	1:27	whose **s** strap I am not worthy

SANDALS →SANDAL

Ex	3: 5	Remove the **s** from your feet,
Ex	12:11	girt, **s** on your feet and your staff
Dt	29: 4	in tatters nor your **s** from your feet;
Jos	5:15	"Remove your **s** from your feet,
Mt	3:11	I am not worthy to carry his **s**.

SANG →SING

Ex	15: 1	the Israelites **s** this song to the LORD:
Nm	21:17	Then it was that Israel **s** this song:
Jgs	5: 1	Barak, son of Abinoam] **s** this song:
1 Sm	18: 7	The women played and **s**: "Saul has
2 Chr	29:30	They **s** praises till their joy was full,
Jb	38: 7	While the morning stars **s** in chorus
Ps	106:12	his words and **s** songs of praise.

SANK →SINK

Jer	38: 6	mud, and Jeremiah **s** into the mud.

SAPPHIRA

Acts	5: 1	with his wife **S**, sold a piece

SAPPHIRE

Ex	24:10	feet there appeared to be **s** tilework,
Ex	28:18	row, a garnet, a **s** and a beryl;
Ez	1:26	throne could be seen, looking like **s**.
Ez	10: 1	what appeared to be **s** stone;
Rv	21:19	the second, the third chalcedony,

SARAH → =SARAI

Wife of Abraham, originally named Sarai; barren (Gn 11:29-31; 1 Pt 3:6). Taken by Pharaoh as Abraham's sister; returned (Gn 12:10-20). Gave Hagar to Abraham; sent her away in pregnancy (Gn 16). Name changed; Isaac promised (Gn 17:15-21; 18:10-15; Heb 11:11). Taken by Abimelech as Abraham's sister; returned (Gn 20). Isaac born; Hagar and Ishmael sent away (Gn 21:1-21; Gal 4:21-31). Death (Gn 23).

SARAI → =SARAH

Gn	17:15	"As for your wife **S**, do not call her **S**;

SARDIS

Rv	3: 1	"To the angel of the church in **S**,

SASH

Ex	28: 4	a brocaded tunic, a miter and a **s**.
Rv	1:13	robe, with a gold **s** around his chest.

SAT →SIT

Gn	48: 2	rallied his strength and **s** up in bed.
1 Kgs	19: 4	to a broom tree and **s** beneath it.
Ps	137: 1	we **s** mourning and weeping
Mt	5: 1	and after he had **s** down,
Mt	13: 2	that he got into a boat and **s** down,
Mt	28: 2	rolled back the stone, and **s** upon it.
Lk	7:15	The dead man **s** up and began
Lk	10:39	named Mary [who] **s** beside
Jn	12:14	Jesus found an ass and **s** upon it,

SATAN

1 Chr	21: 1	A **s** rose up against Israel, and he
Jb	1: 6	the LORD, **S** also came among them.
Jb	2: 1	LORD, and **S** also came with them.

Zec	3: 2	And the angel of the LORD said to **S**, "May the LORD rebuke you, **S**;
Mt	4:10	this, Jesus said to him, "Get away, **S**!
Mt	12:26	And if **S** drives out **S**, he is divided
Mt	16:23	and said to Peter, "Get behind me, **S**!
Mk	4:15	**S** comes at once and takes away
Lk	10:18	"I have observed **S** fall like lightning
Lk	22: 3	Then **S** entered into Judas, the one
Jn	13:27	he took the morsel, **S** entered him.
Acts	5: 3	why has **S** filled your heart so
Acts	26:18	and from the power of **S** to God,
Rom	16:20	will quickly crush **S** under your feet.
1 Cor	5: 5	are to deliver this man to **S**
1 Cor	7: 5	**S** may not tempt you through your
2 Cor	2:11	not be taken advantage of by **S**,
2 Cor	11:14	for even **S** masquerades as an angel
2 Cor	12: 7	to me, an angel of **S**, to beat me,
2 Thes	2: 9	the power of **S** in every mighty deed
1 Tm	1:20	whom I have handed over to **S** to be
1 Tm	5:15	already turned away to follow **S**.
Rv	2: 9	are members of the assembly of **S**.
Rv	2:13	martyred among you, where **S** lives.
Rv	2:24	of the so-called deep secrets of **S**:
Rv	3: 9	the assembly of **S** who claim to be
Rv	12: 9	who is called the Devil and **S**,
Rv	20: 2	which is the Devil or **S**, and tied it
Rv	20: 7	**S** will be released from his prison.

SATISFACTION →SATISFY

Ti	2: 9	giving them **s**, not talking back

SATISFIED →SATISFY

Ps	107: 9	For he **s** the thirsty, filled
Prv	27:20	world and the abyss are never **s**;
Prv	30:15	Three things are never **s**, four never
Eccl	5: 9	The covetous man is never **s**
Mi	6:14	You shall eat, without being **s**,

SATISFY →SATISFACTION, SATISFIED

Ps	91:16	With length of days I will **s** them
Prv	6:30	to **s** his appetite when he is hungry;
Is	55: 2	your wages for what fails to **s**?
Is	58:10	and **s** the afflicted; Then light shall
Mk	15:15	wishing to **s** the crowd,

SATRAPS

Est	3:12	Haman, an order to the royal **s**,
Dn	6: 2	kingdom one hundred and twenty **s**,

SAUL → =PAUL

1. Benjamite; anointed by Samuel as first king of Israel (1 Sm 9-10). Defeated Ammonites (1 Sm 11). Rebuked for offering sacrifice (1 Sm 13:1-15). Defeated Philistines (1 Sm 14). Rejected as king for failing to annihilate Amalekites (1 Sm 15). Soothed from evil spirit by David (1 Sm 16:14-23). Sent David against Goliath (1 Sm 17). Jealousy and attempted murder of David (1 Sm 18:1-11). Gave David Michal as wife (1 Sm 18:12-30). Second attempt to kill David (1 Sm 19). Anger at Jonathan (1 Sm 20:26-34). Pursued David: killed priests at Nob (1 Sm 22), went to Keilah and Ziph (1 Sm 23), life spared by David at En Gedi (1 Sm 24) and in his tent (1 Sm 26). Rebuked by Samuel's spirit for consulting witch at Endor (1 Sm 28). Wounded by Philistines; took his own life (1 Sm 31; 1 Chr 10). Lamented by David (2 Sm 1:17-27). Children (1 Sm 14:49-51; 1 Chr 8).
2. See Paul.

SAVAGE

Acts	20:29	my departure **s** wolves will come

SAVE →SALVATION, SAVED, SAVES, SAVING, SAVIOR, SAVIORS

1 Chr	16:35	And say, "**S** us, O God, our savior,
Jdt	6: 2	the earth. Their God will not **s** them;
Ps	6: 5	Turn, LORD, **s** my life; in your mercy
Ps	28: 9	**S** your people, bless your
Ps	31:17	your servant; **s** me in your kindness.
Ps	54: 3	O God, by your name **s** me. By your
Ps	71: 2	deliver me; listen to me and **s** me!
Ps	86: 2	**s** your servant who trusts in you.
Ps	119:94	I am yours; **s** me, for I cherish your
Is	33:22	LORD our king, he it is who will **s** us.
Is	35: 4	recompense he comes to **s** you.

Is	36:20	then s Jerusalem from my hand?' "
Is	45:20	idols and pray to gods that cannot s.
Is	59: 1	of the LORD is not too short to s,
Is	63: 1	vindication, I who am mighty to s."
Jer	17:14	healed; s me, that I may be saved,
Lam	4:17	for a nation that could not s us.
Ez	7:19	gold cannot s them on the day
Ez	14:14	they could s only themselves
Ez	33:12	a man has practiced will not s him
Ez	34:22	I will s my sheep so that they may
Hos	1: 7	I will s them by the LORD, their God;
Hos	1: 7	But I will not s them by war,
Zep	1:18	shall be able to s them on the day
Mt	1:21	because he will s his people
Mt	16:25	wishes to s his life will lose it,
Mt	27:42	saved others; he cannot s himself.
Lk	6: 9	to s life rather than to destroy it?"
Lk	19:10	come to seek and to s what was lost."
Lk	23:37	are King of the Jews, s yourself."
Jn	12:27	'Father, s me from this hour'? But it
Jn	12:47	the world but to s the world.
Acts	2:40	them, "S yourselves from this corrupt
Rom	11:14	jealous and thus s some of them.
1 Cor	7:16	whether you will s your husband;
1 Cor	7:16	whether you will s your wife?
1 Cor	9:22	all things to all, to s at least some.
1 Tm	1:15	came into the world to s sinners.
Heb	7:25	s those who approach God through
Jas	2:14	have works? Can that faith s him?
Jas	5:20	of his way will s his soul from death
Jude	1:23	s others by snatching them

SAVED → SAVE

Ex	14:30	Thus the LORD s Israel on that day
2 Chr	32:22	Thus the LORD s Hezekiah
Est	F: 6	Israel, who cried to God and was s.
Est	F: 6	"The LORD s his people and delivered
1 Mc	2:59	for their faith, were s from the fire.
Ps	33:16	A king is not s by a mighty army,
Ps	34: 7	heard and s me from all distress.
Ps	106: 8	Yet he s them for his name's sake
Ps	116: 6	I was helpless, but God s me.
Is	45:17	Israel, you are s by the LORD,
Jer	4:14	that you may be s. How long must
Jer	17:14	save me, that I may be s, for it is
Dn	3:88	and s us from the power of death;
Mt	10:22	endures to the end will be s.
Mt	19:25	and said, "Who then can be s?"
Mt	24:13	who perseveres to the end will be s.
Mk	15:31	themselves and said, "He s others;
Lk	7:50	to the woman, "Your faith has s you;
Lk	13:23	"Lord, will only a few people be s?"
Jn	10: 9	enters through me will be s, and will
Acts	2:21	everyone shall be s who calls on
Acts	2:47	number those who were being s.
Acts	4:12	human race by which we are to be s."
Acts	15:11	that we are s through the grace
Acts	16:30	said, "Sirs, what must I do to be s?"
Rom	5: 9	will we be s through him
Rom	8:24	For in hope we were s. Now hope
Rom	9:27	of the sea, only a remnant will be s;
Rom	10: 9	him from the dead, you will be s.
Rom	10:13	on the name of the Lord will be s."
Rom	11:26	and thus all Israel will be s, as it is
1 Cor	1:18	to us who are being s it is the power
1 Cor	3:15	the person will be s, but only as
1 Cor	5: 5	so that his spirit may be s on the day
1 Cor	10:33	that of the many, that they may be s.
1 Cor	15: 2	Through it you are also being s,
Eph	2: 5	Christ (by grace you have been s),
Eph	2: 8	grace you have been s through faith,
2 Thes	2:10	love of truth so that they may be s.
1 Tm	2: 4	who wills everyone to be s
1 Tm	2:15	she will be s through motherhood,
2 Tm	1: 9	He s us and called us to a holy life,
Ti	3: 5	he s us through the bath of rebirth
1 Pt	4:18	"And if the righteous one is barely s,

SAVES → SAVE

Ps	7:11	me is God who s the honest heart.

Ps	34:19	s those whose spirit is crushed.
Prv	14:25	The truthful witness s lives, but he
Sir	2:11	sins, he s in time of trouble.
Sir	51: 8	For he s those who take refuge
Dn	13:60	blessing God who s those that hope
1 Pt	3:21	baptism, which s you now. It is not

SAVING → SAVE

Ps	78:22	in God, did not trust in his s power.

SAVIOR → SAVE

2 Sm	22: 3	my s, from violence you keep me
2 Kgs	13: 5	So the LORD gave Israel a s,
Jdt	9:11	the s of those without hope.
Est	D: 2	invoking the all-seeing God and s,
Est	E:13	our s and constant benefactor,
1 Mc	4:30	"Blessed are you, O S of Israel,
1 Mc	9:21	one has fallen, the s of Israel!"
Wis	16: 7	he saw, but by you, the s of all.
Sir	46: 1	the great s of God's chosen ones,
Sir	51: 1	I praise you, O God my s! I will
Is	19:20	and he sends them a s to defend
Is	43: 3	the Holy One of Israel, your s.
Is	43:11	is I, the LORD; there is no s but me.
Is	45:15	is hidden, the God of Israel, the s!
Is	49:26	that I, the LORD, am your s,
Is	60:16	know that I, the LORD, am your s,
Is	63: 8	not disloyal; So he became their s
Jer	14: 8	O LORD, our s in time of need!
Bar	4:22	reach you from your eternal s.
Hos	13: 4	me, and there is no s but me.
Lk	1:47	my spirit rejoices in God my s.
Lk	2:11	the city of David a s has been born
Jn	4:42	that this is truly the s of the world."
Acts	5:31	and s to grant Israel repentance
Acts	13:23	has brought to Israel a s, Jesus.
Eph	5:23	church, he himself the s of the body.
Phil	3:20	and from it we also await a s,
1 Tm	1: 1	Jesus by command of God our s
1 Tm	2: 3	is good and pleasing to God our s,
1 Tm	4:10	the living God, who is the s of all,
2 Tm	1:10	the appearance of our s Christ Jesus,
Ti	1: 3	by the command of God our s,
Ti	1: 4	the Father and Christ Jesus our s.
Ti	2:10	doctrine of God our s in every way.
Ti	2:13	great God and of our s Jesus Christ,
Ti	3: 4	love of God our s appeared,
Ti	3: 6	out on us through Jesus Christ our s,
2 Pt	1: 1	of our God and s Jesus Christ:
2 Pt	1:11	and s Jesus Christ will be richly
2 Pt	2:20	of [our] Lord and s Jesus Christ,
2 Pt	3: 2	Lord and s through your apostles.
2 Pt	3:18	of our Lord and s Jesus Christ.
1 Jn	4:14	the Father sent his Son as s
Jude	1:25	our s, through Jesus Christ our Lord

SAVIORS → SAVE

Neh	9:27	to your great mercy give them s

SAW → SEE

Gn	1: 4	God s how good the light was.
Gn	3: 6	The woman s that the tree was good
Gn	6: 2	sons of heaven s how beautiful
Gn	6:12	God s how corrupt the earth had
Ex	2:11	he s an Egyptian striking a Hebrew,
Nm	22:23	When the ass s the angel of the LORD
Dt	4:15	"You s no form at all on the day
Dt	32:19	When the LORD s this, he was filled
2 Sm	11: 2	the roof he s a woman bathing,
Ps	73: 3	when I s the prosperity
Eccl	2:13	I s that wisdom has the advantage
Is	6: 1	I s the Lord seated on a high
Ez	1: 1	opened, and I s divine visions.
Dn	8: 2	my vision I s myself in the fortress
Dn	10: 7	I alone, Daniel, s the vision;
Am	9: 1	I s the Lord standing beside
Mt	3:16	he s the Spirit of God descending
Mt	9: 2	When Jesus s their faith, he said
Mk	1:10	of the water he s the heavens being
Mk	3:11	whenever unclean spirits s him they
Lk	9:32	they s his glory and the two men

Jn	1:29	next day he **s** Jesus coming toward
Jn	20: 1	**s** the stone removed from the tomb.
Jn	20: 8	tomb first, and he **s** and believed.
Acts	7:55	to heaven and **s** the glory of God
Acts	10:11	He **s** heaven opened and something
Rv	1: 2	Jesus Christ by reporting what he **s**.
Rv	1:12	I turned, I **s** seven gold lampstands
Rv	5: 6	Then I **s** standing in the midst
Rv	21: 1	Then I **s** a new heaven and a new
Rv	21:22	I **s** no temple in the city, for its
Rv	22: 8	who heard and **s** these things,
Rv	22: 8	**s** them I fell down to worship

SAWED

Heb	11:37	They were stoned, **s** in two,

SAY →SAYING, SAYINGS, SAYS

Gn	12:19	Why did you **s**, 'She is my sister,'
Gn	18:13	"Why did Sarah laugh and **s**, 'Shall I
Sir	11:23	**S** not: "What do I need? What further
Mt	10:19	are to speak or what you are to **s**.
Mt	10:19	at that moment what you are to **s**.
Mt	16:15	them, "But who do you **s** that I am?"
Mk	2: 9	Which is easier, to **s** to the paralytic,
Mk	2: 9	'Your sins are forgiven,' or to **s**, 'Rise,
Mk	8:27	"Who do people **s** that I am?"
Lk	11:54	catch him at something he might **s**.
Jn	8:26	I have much to **s** about you
Jn	12:49	sent me commanded me what to **s**
1 Cor	15:12	can some among you **s** there is no
Rv	22:17	The Spirit and the bride **s**, "Come." Let the hearer **s**, "Come."

SAYING →SAY

Jn	8:43	do you not understand what I am **s**?
1 Tm	1:15	This **s** is trustworthy and deserves
1 Tm	3: 1	This **s** is trustworthy:
1 Tm	4: 9	This **s** is trustworthy and deserves
2 Tm	2:11	This **s** is trustworthy: If we have
Ti	3: 8	This **s** is trustworthy. I want you

SAYINGS →SAY

Eccl	12:11	The **s** of the wise are like goads;

SAYS →SAY

1 Sm	9: 6	all that he **s** is sure to come true.
Ps	110: 1	The Lord **s** to you, my lord:
Eccl	1: 2	Vanity of vanities, **s** Qoheleth,
Eccl	12: 8	Vanity of vanities, **s** Qoheleth,
Rom	3:19	what the law **s** is addressed to those
1 Tm	4: 1	Now the Spirit explicitly **s**

SCABBARD

Jer	47: 6	Return into your **s**; stop, be still!

SCALES

Prv	16:11	Balance and **s** belong to the Lord;
Dn	5:27	you have been weighed on the **s**
Acts	9:18	Immediately things like **s** fell

SCARLET

Is	1:18	Though your sins be like **s**,
Mt	27:28	threw a **s** military cloak about him.
Rv	17: 3	I saw a woman seated on a **s** beast

SCATTER →SCATTERED, SCATTERS

Dt	4:27	The Lord will **s** you among
Neh	1: 8	I will **s** you among the nations;
Jer	9:15	I will **s** them among nations whom
Bar	2:29	the nations to which I will **s** them.

SCATTERED →SCATTER

Gn	11: 4	otherwise we shall be **s** all over
Nm	10:35	O Lord, that your enemies may be **s**,
Dt	30: 3	all the nations wherein he has **s** you.
2 Chr	18:16	"I see all Israel **s** on the mountains,
Tb	13: 5	among whom you have been **s**.
Ps	89:11	blow; your strong arm **s** your foes.
Jer	31:10	He who **s** Israel, now gathers them
Ez	34:12	he finds himself among his **s** sheep,
Ez	34:12	every place where they were **s**
Zec	2: 2	"These are the horns that **s** Judah
Acts	8: 1	and all were **s** throughout
Acts	8: 4	Now those who had been **s** went

SCATTERS →SCATTER

Mt	12:30	whoever does not gather with me **s**.
Jn	10:12	and the wolf catches and **s** them.

SCEPTER

Gn	49:10	The **s** shall never depart from Judah,
Est	4:11	king extends to him the golden **s**,
Ps	45: 7	your royal **s** is a **s** for justice.
Ps	125: 3	The **s** of the wicked will not prevail
Heb	1: 8	and a righteous **s** is the **s** of your

SCHEMES →SCHEMING

Ps	10: 2	they trap them by their cunning **s**.

SCHEMING →SCHEMES

Eph	4:14	in the interests of deceitful **s**.

SCOFFERS

Ps	1: 1	sinners, nor sit in company with **s**.
2 Pt	3: 3	the last days **s** will come [to] scoff,

SCORCHED →SCORCHING

Mk	4: 6	it was **s** and it withered for lack

SCORCHING →SCORCHED

Jas	1:11	For the sun comes up with its **s** heat

SCORNED

Ps	22: 7	**s** by everyone,

SCORPION →SCORPIONS

Lk	11:12	Or hand him a **s** when he asks
Rv	9: 5	that of a **s** when it stings a person.

SCORPIONS →SCORPION

1 Kgs	12:11	whips, but I will beat you with **s**.' "
Rv	9:10	They had tails like **s**, with stingers;

SCOUNDRELS

1 Kgs	21:10	get two **s** to face him and accuse

SCOURGE →SCOURGED

Is	28:18	When the overwhelming **s** passes,
Mt	10:17	and **s** you in their synagogues,
Mk	10:34	will mock him, spit upon him, **s** him,
Acts	22:25	"Is it lawful for you to **s** a man who

SCOURGED →SCOURGE

Jn	19: 1	Then Pilate took Jesus and had him **s**.

SCRIBE →SCRIBES

Neh	8: 1	Ezra the **s** to bring forth the book
Neh	12:36	[Ezra the **s** was at their head.]
Mk	12:32	The **s** said to him, "Well said,

SCRIBES →SCRIBE

Mt	7:29	having authority, and not as their **s**.
Mt	23:13	"Woe to you, **s** and Pharisees,
Mk	12:38	said, "Beware of the **s**, who like to go
Acts	4: 5	and **s** were assembled in Jerusalem,

SCRIPTURE →SCRIPTURES

Mk	12:10	Have you not read this **s** passage:
Lk	4:21	"Today this **s** passage is fulfilled
Jn	2:22	they came to believe the **s**
Jn	7:42	Does not **s** say that the Messiah will
Jn	10:35	came, and **s** cannot be set aside,
Acts	1:16	the **s** had to be fulfilled
Acts	8:32	This was the **s** passage he was
2 Tm	3:16	All **s** is inspired by God and is
2 Pt	1:20	there is no prophecy of **s** that is

SCRIPTURES →SCRIPTURE

Mt	22:29	because you do not know the **s**
Mk	14:49	but that the **s** may be fulfilled."
Lk	24:27	what referred to him in all the **s**.
Lk	24:45	their minds to understand the **s**.
Jn	5:39	You search the **s**, because you think
Acts	17:11	examined the **s** daily to determine
Acts	18:28	from the **s** that the Messiah is Jesus.
1 Cor	15: 3	our sins in accordance with the **s**;
1 Cor	15: 4	third day in accordance with the **s**;
2 Pt	3:16	just as they do the other **s**.

SCROLL

Dt	31:24	Moses had finished writing out on a **s**
1 Mc	1:57	was found with a **s** of the covenant,

Ps	40: 8	for me are written in the s.
Is	34: 4	heavens shall be rolled up like a s,
Jer	36: 4	who wrote down on a s, as Jeremiah
Bar	1:14	publicly this s which we send you,
Ez	3: 1	eat this s, then go,
Zec	5: 1	my eyes again and saw a s flying.
Lk	4:17	and was handed a s of the prophet
Lk	4:17	He unrolled the s and found
Heb	10: 7	I said, "As is written of me in the s,
Rv	1:11	"Write on a s what you see
Rv	5: 2	"Who is worthy to open the s
Rv	6:14	was divided like a torn s curling up,
Rv	10: 8	take the s that lies open in the hand

SEA → SEAS, SEASHORE

Gn	1:26	dominion over the fish of the s,
Gn	32:13	descendants like the sands of the s,
Gn	41:49	in quantities like the sands of the s,
Ex	14:16	with hand outstretched over the s, split the s in two,
Ex	14:27	stretched out his hand over the s,
Ex	14:27	and at dawn the s flowed back to its
Ex	14:27	were fleeing head on toward the s,
Ex	15: 1	and chariot he has cast into the s.
Nm	11:31	that drove in quail from the s
Nm	34: 6	boundary you shall have the Great S
Dt	11:24	Euphrates River to the Western S,
Dt	30:13	Nor is it across the s, that you
Dt	30:13	'Who will cross the s to get it for us
1 Kgs	7:23	The s was then cast; it was made
2 Kgs	25:13	and the bronze s in the house
Neh	9:11	The s you divided before them,
Neh	9:11	passed through the midst of the s;
Jb	11: 9	in measure, and broader than the s.
Ps	46: 3	quake to the depths of the s,
Ps	74:13	You stirred up the s in your might;
Ps	93: 4	powerful than the breakers of the s,
Ps	95: 5	The s and dry land belong to God,
Ps	106: 7	defied the Most High at the Red S.
Ps	139: 9	of dawn and alight beyond the s,
Eccl	1: 7	All rivers go to the s, yet never does the s become full.
Is	10:22	were like the sand of the s,
Is	48:18	vindication like the waves of the s;
Is	57:20	But the wicked are like the tossing s
Bar	3:30	Who has crossed the s and found
Jon	1: 4	hurled a violent wind upon the s,
Jon	2: 4	the deep, into the heart of the s,
Mi	7:19	into the depths of the s all our sins;
Hb	2:14	LORD's glory as water covers the s.
Zec	9:10	his dominion shall be from s to s,
Mt	18: 6	to be drowned in the depths of the s.
Mk	11:23	'Be lifted up and thrown into the s,'
1 Cor	10: 1	cloud and all passed through the s,
Heb	11:29	faith they crossed the Red S as if it
Jas	1: 6	is like a wave of the s that is driven
Jude	1:13	They are like wild waves of the s,
Rv	4: 6	resembled a s of glass like crystal.
Rv	8: 8	mountain was hurled into the s. A third of the s turned to blood,
Rv	10: 2	He placed his right foot on the s
Rv	12:18	its position on the sand of the s.
Rv	13: 1	come out of the s with ten horns
Rv	15: 2	I saw something like a s of glass
Rv	15: 2	the s of glass were standing those
Rv	20:13	The s gave up its dead; then Death
Rv	21: 1	away, and the s was no more.

SEAL → SEALED, SEALS

Est	8: 8	and s the letter with the royal signet
Song	8: 6	Set me as a s on your heart, as a s
Sir	22:27	and upon my lips an effective s,
Mt	27:66	secured the tomb by fixing a s
Jn	6:27	him the Father, God, has set his s."
1 Cor	9: 2	for you are the s of my apostleship
2 Cor	1:22	he has also put his s upon us
Rv	6: 3	When he broke open the second s,
Rv	6: 5	When he broke open the third s,
Rv	6: 7	When he broke open the fourth s,
Rv	6: 9	When he broke open the fifth s,

Rv	6:12	while he broke open the sixth s,
Rv	7: 2	holding the s of the living God.
Rv	7: 3	or the trees until we put the s
Rv	8: 1	When he broke open the seventh s,
Rv	9: 4	those people who did not have the s
Rv	10: 4	"S up what the seven thunders have
Rv	22:10	"Do not s up the prophetic words

SEALED → SEAL

Is	8:16	and the s instruction kept among my
Is	29:11	become like the words of a s scroll.
Is	29:11	he replies, "I cannot; it is s."
Dn	6:18	the king s with his own ring
Dn	12: 9	kept secret and s until the end time.
Eph	1:13	him, were s with the promised holy
Rv	5: 1	sides and was s with seven seals.
Rv	20: 3	which he locked over it and s,

SEALS → SEAL

Rv	5: 2	to open the scroll and break its s?"
Rv	6: 1	broke open the first of the seven s,

SEAMLESS

Jn	19:23	but the tunic was s, woven in one

SEARCH → SEARCHED, SEARCHES, SEARCHING

Dt	4:29	find him when you s after him
Ezr	5:17	let a s be made in the royal archives
Prv	2: 4	and like hidden treasures s her out:
Mt	2: 8	"Go and s diligently for the child.

SEARCHED → SEARCH

Jb	5:27	Lo, this we have s out; so it is!

SEARCHES → SEARCH

1 Chr	28: 9	soul, for the LORD s all hearts
Rom	8:27	the one who s hearts knows what is

SEARCHING → SEARCH

Lk	15: 8	house, s carefully until she finds it?

SEAS → SEA

Ps	65: 8	You still the roaring of the s,

SEASHORE → SEA, SHORE

Gn	22:17	of the sky and the sands of the s;
Jos	11: 4	numerous as the sands on the s,
1 Kgs	5: 9	as vast as the sand on the s.
Heb	11:12	as countless as the sands on the s.

SEASON → SEASONED, SEASONS

Dt	28:12	to give your land rain in due s,
Ps	1: 3	that yields its fruit in s; Its leaves

SEASONED → SEASON

Col	4: 6	always be gracious, s with salt,

SEASONS → SEASON

Ps	104:19	You made the moon to mark the s,
Gal	4:10	days, months, s, and years.
1 Thes	5: 1	Concerning times and s, brothers,

SEAT → SEATED

Mt	23: 2	the Pharisees have taken their s
Rom	14:10	shall all stand before the judgment s
2 Cor	5:10	all appear before the judgment s

SEATED → SEAT

Lk	22:69	of Man will be s at the right hand
Eph	2: 6	and s us with him in the heavens
Col	3: 1	where Christ is s at the right hand

SECLUSION

Lk	1:24	and she went into s for five months,

SECOND → TWO

Ex	4: 8	should believe the message of the s.
Nm	9:11	But he shall keep it in the s month,
1 Kgs	9: 2	the LORD appeared to him a s time,
Ez	10:14	that of an ox, the s that of a man,
Dn	7: 5	The s was like a bear; it was raised
Jon	3: 1	of the LORD came to Jonah a s time:
Hg	2:20	of the LORD came a s time to Haggai
Mt	22:39	The s is like it: You shall love your
1 Cor	12:28	to be, first, apostles; s, prophets;
1 Cor	15:47	earthly; the s man, from heaven.

Ti	3:10	After a first and s warning,
Heb	9:28	will appear a s time, not to take
Rv	2:11	shall not be harmed by the s death." '
Rv	4: 7	a lion, the s was like a calf, the third
Rv	6: 3	When he broke open the s seal,
Rv	6: 3	I heard the s living creature cry out,
Rv	8: 8	When the s angel blew his trumpet,
Rv	11:14	The s woe has passed, but the third
Rv	16: 3	The s angel poured out his bowl
Rv	20: 6	The s death has no power over
Rv	20:14	(This pool of fire is the s death.)
Rv	21: 8	fire and sulfur, which is the s death."

SECRET → SECRETLY, SECRETS

Ps	139:15	you, When I was being made in s,
Prv	21:14	A s gift allays anger,
Jer	23:24	Can a man hide in s without my
Mt	6: 4	so that your almsgiving may be s.
Mt	6: 4	Father who sees in s will repay you.
Mt	6: 6	door, and pray to your Father in s.
Mt	6: 6	Father who sees in s will repay you.
Jn	18:20	gather, and in s I have said nothing.
Phil	4:12	in all things I have learned the s

SECRETLY → SECRET

Dt	13: 7	entices you s to serve other gods,
Mt	2: 7	Then Herod called the magi s

SECRETS → SECRET

Ps	44:22	God who knows the s of the heart?
Prv	11:13	A newsmonger reveals s,
1 Cor	14:25	the s of his heart will be disclosed,

SECT

Acts	24: 5	ringleader of the s of the Nazoreans.

SECURE → SECURELY, SECURITY

Ps	16: 9	rejoices; my body also dwells s,

SECURELY → SECURE

Prv	10: 9	He who walks honestly walks s,

SECURITY → SECURE

1 Thes	5: 3	"Peace and s," then sudden disaster

SEDUCES

Ex	22:15	"When a man s a virgin who is not

SEE → FORESAW, SAW, SEEING, SEEN, SEER, SEERS, SEES, SIGHT

Gn	2:19	man to s what he would call them;
Gn	8: 8	to s if the waters had lessened
Gn	9:16	I will s it and recall the everlasting
Gn	13:15	all the land that you s I will give
Ex	14:13	you will s the victory the LORD will
Ex	14:13	Egyptians whom you s today you will never s
Ex	33:20	But my face you cannot s, for no
Nm	14:23	not one shall s the land which I
Nm	14:23	who have spurned me shall s it.
Tb	2:10	I went to s some doctors for a cure,
Tb	2:10	became, until I could s no more.
Tb	11: 8	will again be able to s the light
Jb	19:26	And from my flesh I shall s God;
Ps	16:10	let your faithful servant s the pit.
Ps	115: 5	but do not speak, eyes but do not s.
Is	40: 5	and all mankind shall s it together;
Is	53:10	he shall s his descendants in a long
Is	53:11	he shall s the light in fullness
Ez	8:12	"The LORD cannot s us; the LORD has
Dn	3:92	"I s four men unfettered and unhurt,
Jl	3: 1	your young men shall s visions;
Mi	·7: 9	forth to the light; I will s his justice.
Mt	5: 8	clean of heart, for they will s God.
Mt	7: 5	you will s clearly to remove
Mt	13:16	eyes, because they s, and your ears,
Mk	8:18	Do you have eyes and not s,
Mk	14:62	"I am; and 'you will s the Son of Man
Lk	3: 6	and all flesh shall s the salvation
Jn	9:25	is that I was blind and now I s."
Jn	14:19	while the world will no longer s me,
Jn	14:19	but you will s me, because I live
Jn	16:16	while and you will no longer s me,

Jn	16:16	little while later and you will s me."
Acts	2:17	your young men shall s visions,
1 Cor	13:12	At present we s indistinctly,
2 Cor	13: 5	to s whether you are living in faith.
Heb	12:14	which no one will s the Lord.
1 Jn	3: 2	like him, for we shall s him as he is.
Rv	1: 7	and every eye will s him, even those

SEED → SEEDS, SEEDTIME

Gn	1:11	every kind of plant that bears s
Gn	1:11	earth that bears fruit with its s in it."
Eccl	11: 6	In the morning sow your s,
Is	55:10	fruitful, Giving s to him who sows
Mt	13:31	of heaven is like a mustard s
Mt	17:20	have faith the size of a mustard s,
Mk	4:31	It is like a mustard s that, when it is
Lk	8:11	parable. The s is the word of God.
2 Cor	9:10	The one who supplies s to the sower
2 Cor	9:10	and multiply your s and increase
1 Pt	1:23	perishable but from imperishable s,
1 Jn	3: 9	sin, because God's s remains in him;

SEEDS → SEED

Mk	4:31	the smallest of all the s on the earth.

SEEDTIME → SEED

Gn	8:22	long as the earth lasts, s and harvest,

SEEING → SEE

Ex	12:13	S the blood, I will pass over you;

SEEK → SEEKING, SEEKS, SOUGHT

Dt	4:29	Yet there too you shall s the LORD,
1 Chr	28: 9	If you s him, he will let himself be
2 Chr	7:14	and s my presence and turn
2 Chr	15: 2	if you s him he will be present
Ps	9:11	you never forsake those who s you,
Ps	24: 6	that s the face of the God of Jacob."
Ps	34:11	those who s the LORD lack no good
Ps	105: 3	rejoice, O hearts that s the LORD!
Ps	105: 4	mighty LORD; constantly s his face.
Ps	119: 2	who s the LORD with all their heart.
Ps	119:10	With all my heart I s you; do not let
Ps	119:176	like a lost sheep; s out your servant,
Prv	8:17	love, and those who s me find me.
Prv	25:27	not good; nor to s honor after honor.
Prv	28: 5	those who s the LORD understand all.
Sir	2:16	Those who fear the LORD s to please
Sir	24:34	Before you are judged, s merit for yourself,
Is	55: 6	S the LORD while he may be found,
Jer	29:13	when you s me with all your heart,
Hos	10:12	for it is time to s the LORD, till he
Am	5: 6	S the LORD, that you may live,
Zep	2: 3	S the LORD, all you humble
Zep	2: 3	his law; S justice, s humility;
Lk	19:10	For the Son of Man has come to s
Jn	5:30	because I do not s my own will
Acts	15:17	rest of humanity may s out the Lord,
1 Cor	7:27	to a wife? Do not s a separation.
1 Cor	10:24	No one should s his own advantage,
Heb	11: 6	that he rewards those who s him.
1 Pt	3:11	do good, s peace and follow after it.

SEEKING → SEEK

Rom	10:20	[by] those who were not s me;
1 Cor	10:33	not s my own benefit

SEEKS → SEEK

Prv	11:27	He who s the good commands
Prv	14: 6	The senseless man s in vain
Prv	15:14	of the intelligent man s knowledge,
Jn	4:23	indeed the Father s such people
Rom	3:11	there is no one who s God.

SEEM → SEEMED, SEEMS

Zec	8: 6	this should s impossible in the eyes

SEEMED → SEEM

Gn	29:20	yet they s to him but a few days
Nm	13:33	and so we must have s to them."
Lk	24:11	but their story s like nonsense
Rv	13: 3	of its heads s to have been mortally

SEEMS → SEEM
Prv	14:12	Sometimes a way **s** right to a man,
Prv	16:25	Sometimes a way **s** right to a man,
Heb	12:11	all discipline **s** a cause not for joy

SEEN → SEE
Gn	16:13	"Have I really **s** God and remained
Ex	33:23	my back; but my face is not to be **s**."
Dt	4: 9	things which your own eyes have **s**,
Jos	23: 3	You have **s** all that the LORD,
Jgs	6:22	that I have **s** the angel of the LORD
Jgs	13:22	certainly die, for we have **s** God."
Ezr	3:12	men who had **s** the former house,
Ps	37:25	age have I ever **s** the just abandoned
Ps	37:35	I have **s** ruthless scoundrels,
Ps	98: 3	All the ends of the earth have **s**
Is	6: 5	yet my eyes have **s** the King,
Is	9: 1	in darkness have **s** a great light;
Is	64: 3	ear has ever heard, no eye ever **s**,
Mt	2: 9	that they had **s** at its rising preceded
Mt	4:16	sit in darkness have **s** a great light,
Lk	2:30	for my eyes have **s** your salvation,
Jn	1:18	No one has ever **s** God. The only
Jn	6:46	anyone has **s** the Father except
Jn	6:46	is from God; he has **s** the Father.
Jn	14: 9	Whoever has **s** me has **s** the Father.
Jn	20:25	said to him, "We have **s** the Lord."
Jn	20:29	to believe because you have **s** me?
Jn	20:29	Blessed are those who have not **s**
1 Cor	2: 9	"What eye has not **s**, and ear has not
Phil	4: 9	and received and heard and **s** in me.
1 Tm	3:16	vindicated in the spirit, **s** by angels,
1 Pt	1: 8	you have not **s** him you love him;
1 Jn	1: 3	what we have **s** and heard
1 Jn	4:12	No one has ever **s** God. Yet, if we
3 Jn	1:11	does what is evil has never **s** God.
Rv	1:19	what you have **s**, and what is

SEER → SEE
1 Sm	9: 9	used to say, "Come, let us go to the **s**."
1 Sm	9: 9	prophet was formerly called **s**.)
2 Sm	24:11	the prophet Gad, David's **s**, saying:
1 Chr	29:29	in the history of Samuel the **s**,
1 Chr	29:29	and the history of Gad the **s**,
2 Chr	9:29	Iddo the **s** which concern Jeroboam,
2 Chr	29:30	words of David and of Asaph the **s**.

SEERS → SEE
2 Chr	33:19	written down in the history of his **s**.
Mi	3: 7	Then shall the **s** be put to shame,

SEES → SEE
Is	47:10	and said, "No one **s** me."
Mt	6: 4	your Father who **s** in secret will
Mt	6: 6	your Father who **s** in secret will
Mt	6:18	your Father who **s** what is hidden
Jn	5:19	but only what he **s** his father doing;
1 Jn	3:17	who has worldly means **s** a brother

SEIR
Gn	32: 4	to his brother Esau in the land of **S**,
Dt	2: 4	descendants of Esau, who live in **S**.
Ez	35: 2	set your face against Mount **S**,

SELECT
Acts	6: 3	**s** from among you seven reputable

SELF → SELFISH, SELFISHNESS
Rom	6: 6	know that our old **s** was crucified
Eph	4:22	you should put away the old **s**
Col	3:10	and have put on the new **s**, which is

SELF-ABASEMENT
Col	2:18	you, delighting in **s** and worship

SELF-CONDEMNED → CONDEMN
Ti	3:11	is perverted and sinful and stands **s**.

SELF-CONTROL → CONTROL
1 Cor	7: 5	tempt you through your lack of **s**.
2 Pt	1: 6	knowledge with **s**, **s** with endurance,

SELF-CONTROLLED → CONTROL
Ti	1: 8	temperate, just, holy, and **s**,

Ti	2: 5	to be **s**, chaste, good homemakers,

SELF-INDULGENCE → INDULGE
Mt	23:25	inside they are full of plunder and **s**.

SELFISH → SELF
Phil	1:17	proclaim Christ out of **s** ambition,
Jas	3:14	and **s** ambition in your hearts,
Jas	3:16	where jealousy and **s** ambition exist,

SELFISHNESS → SELF
2 Cor	12:20	jealousy, fury, **s**, slander, gossip,

SELL → SALE, SELLING, SELLS, SOLD
Prv	23:23	Get the truth, and **s** it not— wisdom,
Mk	10:21	Go, **s** what you have, and give
Acts	2:45	they would **s** their property
Rv	13:17	**s** except one who had the stamped

SELLING → SELL
Mk	11:15	area he began to drive out those **s**
Lk	17:28	eating, drinking, buying, **s**, planting,

SELLS → SELL
Prv	31:24	She makes garments and **s** them,
Mt	13:44	out of joy goes and **s** all that he has

SEND → SENDING, SENT
Ex	33: 2	I will **s** an angel before you
1 Sm	5:11	"**S** away the ark of God of Israel.
Ps	43: 3	**S** your light and fidelity, that they
Ps	57: 4	May God **s** help from heaven
Ps	57: 4	May God **s** fidelity and love.
Ps	104:30	When you **s** forth your breath,
Is	6: 8	of the Lord saying, "Whom shall I **s**?
Is	6: 8	go for us?" "Here I am;" I said; "**s** me!"
Mal	3:23	Lo, I will **s** you Elijah, the prophet,
Mt	9:38	of the harvest to **s** out laborers
Mt	24:31	And he will **s** out his angels
Lk	11:49	said, 'I will **s** to them prophets
Lk	20:13	I shall **s** my beloved son;
Jn	3:17	God did not **s** his Son into the world
Jn	14:26	the Father will **s** in my name—he will
Jn	15:26	Advocate comes whom I will **s** you
Jn	16: 7	But if I go, I will **s** him to you.
Acts	3:20	**s** you the Messiah already appointed
1 Cor	1:17	For Christ did not **s** me to baptize

SENDING → SEND
Mt	10:16	I am **s** you like sheep in the midst
Rom	8: 3	by **s** his own Son in the likeness
Rv	1: 1	He made it known by **s** his angel

SENNACHERIB
Assyrian king whose siege of Jerusalem was overthrown by the LORD following prayer of Hezekiah and Isaiah (2 Kgs 18:13-19:37; 2 Chr 32:1-21; Is 36-37).

SENSELESS
Rom	1:21	and their **s** minds were darkened.

SENSIBLE
Tb	6:12	Now the girl is **s**, courageous,
Sir	25: 8	is he who dwells with a **s** wife,

SENSUALITY
1 Tm	5:11	their **s** estranges them from Christ,

SENT → SEND
Gn	8: 8	Then he **s** out a dove, to see
Gn	45: 5	lives that God **s** me here ahead
Ex	3:14	tell the Israelites: I AM **s** me to you."
Nm	16:29	then it was not the LORD who **s** me.
Nm	21: 6	In punishment the LORD **s** among
Jos	2: 1	Nun, secretly **s** out two spies
Jos	24:12	I **s** the hornets ahead of you
2 Sm	24:15	then **s** a pestilence over Israel
2 Kgs	14: 9	King Jehoash of Israel **s** this reply
2 Kgs	14: 9	"The thistle of Lebanon **s** word
Ps	107:20	**S** forth the word to heal them,
Is	55:11	achieving the end for which I **s** it.
Is	61: 1	He has **s** me to bring glad tidings
Jer	28: 9	peace is recognized as truly **s**
Dn	3:95	who **s** his angel to deliver
Dn	6:23	My God has **s** his angel and closed

Mt	10:40	me receives the one who **s** me.
Lk	1:26	the angel Gabriel was **s** from God
Lk	4:18	He has **s** me to proclaim liberty
Lk	9: 2	he **s** them to proclaim the kingdom
Lk	10:16	rejects me rejects the one who **s** me."
Lk	13:34	prophets and stone those **s** to you,
Jn	1: 6	A man named John was **s** from God.
Jn	3:28	but that I was **s** before him.
Jn	4:34	is to do the will of the one who **s** me
Jn	5:24	in the one who has eternal life
Jn	8:16	but it is I and the Father who **s** me.
Jn	9: 4	of the one who **s** me while it is day.
Jn	16: 5	I am going to the one who **s** me,
Jn	17: 3	God, and the one whom you **s**,
Jn	17:18	As you **s** me into the world, so I **s**
Jn	20:21	As the Father has **s** me, so I send
Rom	10:15	can people preach unless they are **s**?
Gal	4: 4	of time had come, God **s** his Son,
Gal	4: 6	God **s** the spirit of his Son into our
1 Jn	4:10	**s** his Son as expiation for our sins.
Rv	22:16	"I, Jesus, **s** my angel to give you this

SENTENCE → SENTENCED

Eccl	8:11	Because the **s** against evildoers is
Acts	13:28	they found no grounds for a death **s**,
2 Cor	1: 9	had accepted within ourselves the **s**

SENTENCED → SENTENCE

1 Cor	4: 9	the last of all, like people **s** to death,

SEPARATE → SEPARATED, SEPARATES

Mt	19: 6	together, no human being must **s**."
Rom	8:35	What will **s** us from the love
1 Cor	7:10	Lord): A wife should not **s** from her
2 Cor	6:17	from them and be **s**," says the Lord,

SEPARATED → SEPARATE

Gn	1: 4	then **s** the light from the darkness.
Gn	1: 7	it **s** the water above the dome
Neh	13: 3	law, they **s** from Israel every foreign
Heb	7:26	undefiled, **s** from sinners,

SEPARATES → SEPARATE

Prv	16:28	and a talebearer **s** bosom friends.
Mt	25:32	as a shepherd **s** the sheep
1 Cor	7:15	If the unbeliever **s**, however, let him

SERAPHIM

Is	6: 2	**S** were stationed above; each of them
Is	6: 6	Then one of the **s** flew to me, holding

SERIOUS

1 Pt	4: 7	be **s** and sober for prayers.

SERPENT → SERPENTS

Gn	3: 1	Now the **s** was the most cunning
Gn	3: 1	The **s** asked the woman, "Did God
Gn	3:13	answered, "The **s** tricked me into it,
Gn	3:14	Then the LORD God said to the **s**:
Nm	21: 9	Moses accordingly made a bronze **s**
Nm	21: 9	who had been bitten by a **s** looked at the bronze **s**,
2 Kgs	18: 4	the bronze **s** called Nehushtan
Is	27: 1	Leviathan the fleeing **s**,
Is	27: 1	Leviathan the coiled **s**; and he will
2 Cor	11: 3	that, as the **s** deceived Eve by his
Rv	12: 9	the ancient **s**, who is called
Rv	20: 2	the ancient **s**, which is the Devil

SERPENTS → SERPENT

Nm	21: 6	sent among the people saraph **s**,
Mt	10:16	so be shrewd as **s** and simple as
1 Cor	10: 9	them did, and suffered death by **s**.

SERVANT → SERVANT'S, SERVANTS

Ex	14:31	believed in him and in his **s** Moses.
Nm	12: 7	Not so with my **S** Moses!
1 Sm	3:10	"Speak, for your **s** is listening."
1 Kgs	3: 7	your **s**, king to succeed my father
1 Kgs	8:56	he made through his **s** Moses.
1 Kgs	8:66	the LORD had given to his **s** David
1 Kgs	20:40	But while your **s** was looking here
Jb	1: 8	"Have you noticed my **s** Job,
Jb	2: 3	"Have you noticed my **s** Job,
Jb	42: 8	and let my **s** Job pray for you;

Jb	42: 8	concerning me, as has my **s** Job."
Ps	19:12	By them your **s** is instructed;
Ps	19:14	But from willful sins keep your **s**;
Ps	31:17	Let your face shine on your **s**;
Ps	78:70	He chose David his **s**, took him
Ps	89: 4	I have sworn to David my **s**:
Ps	105:26	He sent his **s** Moses, Aaron whom
Ps	119:135	Let your face shine upon your **s**;
Ps	136:22	A heritage for Israel, God's **s**,
Prv	14:35	The king favors the intelligent **s**,
Is	41: 8	But you, Israel, my **s**, Jacob,
Is	42: 1	Here is my **s** whom I uphold,
Is	44: 1	Hear then, O Jacob, my **s**, Israel,
Is	45: 4	For the sake of Jacob, my **s**,
Is	48:20	"The LORD has redeemed his **s** Jacob.
Is	49: 3	You are my **s**, he said to me, Israel,
Is	52:13	See, my **s** shall prosper, he shall be
Is	53:11	suffering, my **s** shall justify many,
Jer	30:10	But you, my **s** Jacob, fear not,
Jer	33:21	can my covenant with my **s** David
Ez	34:24	my **s** David shall be prince among
Zec	3: 8	Yes, I will bring my **s** the Shoot.
Mt	8:13	at that very hour [his] **s** was healed.
Mt	20:26	be great among you shall be your **s**;
Lk	1:54	He has helped Israel his **s**,
Lk	1:69	within the house of David his **s**,
Jn	12:26	where I am, there also will my **s** be.
Acts	3:13	has glorified his **s** Jesus whom you
Rom	13: 4	for it is a **s** of God for your good.
Rom	13: 4	it is the **s** of God to inflict wrath
Heb	3: 5	in all his house" as a "**s**" to testify
Rv	15: 3	the song of Moses, the **s** of God,
Rv	19:10	I am a fellow **s** of yours and of your

SERVANT'S → SERVANT

Ps	119:122	Guarantee your **s** welfare;

SERVANTS → SERVANT

Dt	32:36	on his **s** he shall have pity. When he
2 Kgs	17:23	as he had foretold through all his **s**,
Ezr	5:11	'We are the **s** of the God of heaven
Jb	4:18	Lo, he puts no trust in his **s**,
Ps	34:23	The LORD redeems loyal **s**; no one is
Ps	90:13	How long? Have pity on your **s**!
Ps	113: 1	Praise, you **s** of the LORD,
Is	43:10	the LORD, my **s** whom I have chosen
Is	65: 8	Thus will I do with my **s**: I will not
Is	65:14	My **s** shall shout for joy of heart,
Jer	7:25	you untiringly all my **s** the prophets.
Dn	3:33	we, your **s**, who revere you,
Dn	9: 6	not obeyed your **s** the prophets,
Acts	4:29	enable your **s** to speak your word
Rv	7: 3	the foreheads of the **s** of our God."
Rv	19: 2	avenged on her the blood of his **s**."
Rv	22: 3	be in it, and his **s** will worship him.

SERVE → SERVED, SERVES, SERVICE, SERVING

Gn	15:14	judgment on the nation they must **s**,
Gn	25:23	and the older shall **s** the younger.
Dt	6:13	him shall you **s**, and by his name
Dt	10:12	to love and **s** the LORD, your God,
Dt	28:47	Since you would not **s** the LORD,
Jos	22: 5	and **s** him with your whole heart
Jos	24:14	fear the LORD and **s** him completely
Jos	24:14	River and in Egypt, and **s** the LORD.
Jos	24:15	it does not please you to **s** the LORD,
Jos	24:15	decide today whom you will **s**,
Jos	24:15	my household, we will **s** the LORD."
Jos	24:18	Therefore we also will **s** the LORD,
2 Kgs	17:35	nor worship them, nor **s** them,
Neh	9:35	they did not **s** you nor did they turn
Jb	36:11	If they obey and **s** him, they spend
Ps	2:11	**S** the LORD with fear; with trembling
Is	60:12	that does not **s** you; those nations
Jer	2:20	your bonds. "I will not **s**," you said.
Jer	25: 6	Do not follow strange gods to **s**
Dn	3:17	whom we **s**, can save us
Mt	4:10	worship and him alone shall you **s**.' "
Mt	6:24	"No one can **s** two masters. He will
Mt	6:24	You cannot **s** God and mammon.

Mk	10:45	to **s** and to give his life as a ransom
Lk	16:13	No servant can **s** two masters.
Lk	16:13	You cannot **s** God and mammon."
Rom	12:11	zeal, be fervent in spirit, **s** the Lord.
1 Thes	1: 9	to God from idols to **s** the living
1 Pt	4:10	it to **s** one another as good stewards

SERVED → SERVE

Gn	29:20	So Jacob **s** seven years for Rachel,
Jos	24:15	the gods your fathers **s** beyond
Mt	20:28	the Son of Man did not come to be **s**
Jn	12: 2	and Martha **s**, while Lazarus was
Acts	17:25	nor is he **s** by human hands because

SERVES → SERVE

Jn	12:26	Whoever **s** me must follow me,
Jn	12:26	Father will honor whoever **s** me.
Rom	14:18	whoever **s** Christ in this way is
1 Pt	4:11	whoever **s**, let it be with the strength

SERVICE → SERVE

Nm	3: 8	Israelites in the **s** of the Dwelling.
Nm	8:25	he shall retire from the required **s**
1 Cor	16:15	themselves to the **s** of the holy ones—
Rv	2:19	your love, faith, **s**, and endurance,

SERVING → SERVE

1 Pt	1:12	that they were **s** not themselves

SET → SETS

Gn	9:13	I **s** my bow in the clouds to serve as
Gn	28:18	head, **s** it up as a memorial stone,
Gn	31:45	and **s** it up as a memorial stone.
Gn	35:14	him, Jacob **s** up a memorial stone,
Ex	40:18	placed its pedestals, **s** up its boards,
Ex	40:18	put in its bars, and **s** up its columns.
Nm	9:23	and at his bidding that they **s** out;
Dt	27: 2	you, **s** up some large stones and coat
Dt	30:15	I have today **s** before you life
Jos	4: 9	had twelve stones **s** up in the bed
Ps	8: 2	You have **s** your majesty
Is	50: 7	I have **s** my face like flint,
Dn	11:28	riches, his mind **s** against the holy
Rom	1: 1	and **s** apart for the gospel of God,
1 Pt	1:13	and **s** your hopes completely

SETH

Gn	4:25	birth to a son whom she called **S**.
1 Chr	1: 1	Adam, **S**, Enosh,

SETS → SET

Jb	5:11	He **s** up on high the lowly,
Ps	146: 7	hungry. The LORD **s** prisoners free;

SETTLE → SETTLED

Gn	47: 4	let your servants **s** in the region
Nm	33:53	possession of the land and **s** in it,

SETTLED → SETTLE

Ex	24:16	of the LORD **s** upon Mount Sinai.
Ex	40:35	because the cloud **s** down upon it
Dt	19: 1	their place and are **s** in their cities
2 Kgs	18:11	to Assyria and **s** them in Halah,

SEVEN → SEVENFOLD, SEVENTH

Gn	7: 2	take with you **s** pairs, a male and its
Gn	21:28	set apart **s** ewe lambs of the flock,
Gn	29:18	"I will serve you **s** years for your
Gn	41: 2	up out of the Nile came **s** cows,
Gn	41: 5	He saw **s** ears of grain,
Ex	2:16	**s** daughters of a priest of Midian
Ex	12:15	For **s** days you must eat unleavened
Ex	25:37	You shall then make **s** lamps for it
Ex	29:35	"**S** days you shall spend in ordaining
Nm	23: 1	"Build me **s** altars, and prepare **s**
Nm	23: 1	**s** bullocks and **s** rams for me here."
Dt	7: 1	**s** nations more numerous
Jos	6: 4	**s** priests carrying ram's horns ahead
Jos	6: 4	day march around the city **s** times,
Jgs	16:13	"If you weave my **s** locks of hair
1 Sm	2: 5	The barren wife bears **s** sons,
1 Kgs	19:18	Yet I will leave **s** thousand men
2 Kgs	5:10	"Go and wash **s** times in the Jordan,

Tb	3: 8	she had been married to **s** husbands,
Ps	119:164	**S** times a day I praise you
Prv	6:16	yes, **s** are an abomination to him;
Prv	9: 1	house, she has set up her **s** columns;
Prv	24:16	For the just man falls **s** times
Prv	26:25	for **s** abominations are in his heart.
Sir	40: 8	beast, but for sinners **s** times more.
Is	4: 1	**S** women will take hold of one man
Dn	3:19	to be heated **s** times more than usual
Dn	9:25	there shall be **s** weeks.
Zec	3: 9	Joshua, one stone with **s** facets.
Zec	4: 2	"on it are **s** lamps with their tubes,
Mt	18:22	"I say to you, not **s** times but **s** times.
Mk	12:20	Now there were **s** brothers. The first
Mk	16: 9	of whom he had driven **s** demons.
Lk	11:26	and brings back **s** other spirits more
Rom	11: 4	myself **s** thousand men who have
Rv	1: 4	John, to the **s** churches in Asia:
Rv	1: 4	from the **s** spirits before his throne,
Rv	1:12	I turned, I saw **s** gold lampstands
Rv	1:16	In his right hand he held **s** stars.
Rv	3: 1	" 'The one who has the **s** spirits
Rv	3: 1	of God and the **s** stars says this:
Rv	4: 5	**S** flaming torches burned in front
Rv	4: 5	which are the **s** spirits of God.
Rv	5: 1	sides and was sealed with **s** seals.
Rv	6: 1	broke open the first of the **s** seals,
Rv	8: 2	the **s** angels who stood before God
Rv	8: 2	before God were given **s** trumpets.
Rv	10: 4	When the **s** thunders had spoken,
Rv	12: 3	dragon, with **s** heads and ten horns,
Rv	12: 3	and on its heads were **s** diadems.
Rv	15: 1	**s** angels with the **s** last plagues,
Rv	15: 7	creatures gave the **s** angels **s** gold
Rv	16: 1	from the temple to the **s** angels,
Rv	16: 1	pour out the **s** bowls of God's fury
Rv	17: 9	The **s** heads represent **s** hills
Rv	17: 9	They also represent **s** kings:

SEVENFOLD → SEVEN

Gn	4:15	kills Cain, Cain shall be avenged **s**."
Gn	4:24	If Cain is avenged **s**, then Lamech **s**."
Lv	26:18	the chastisement for your sins **s**,
Prv	6:31	if he be caught he must pay back **s**;

SEVENTH → SEVEN

Gn	2: 2	Since on the **s** day God was finished
Gn	2: 2	he rested on the **s** day from all
Ex	16:30	that the people rested on the **s** day.
Ex	20:10	the **s** day is the sabbath of the LORD,
Ex	23:11	the **s** year you shall let the land lie
Ex	23:12	but on the **s** day you must rest,
Jos	6:16	The **s** time around, the priests blew
1 Mc	6:53	because it was the **s** year,
Heb	4: 4	spoken somewhere about the **s** day
Heb	4: 4	God rested on the **s** day from all his
Jude	1:14	of the **s** generation from Adam,
Rv	8: 1	When he broke open the **s** seal,
Rv	11:15	Then the **s** angel blew his trumpet.
Rv	16:17	The **s** angel poured out his bowl

SEVENTY → SEVENTY-SEVEN

Gn	46:27	Egypt amounted to **s** persons in all.
Ex	24: 1	Abihu, and **s** of the elders of Israel.
Nm	11:25	he bestowed it on the **s** elders;
2 Chr	36:21	have rest while **s** years are fulfilled."
Ps	90:10	**S** is the sum of our years, or eighty,
Jer	25:12	but when the **s** years have elapsed,
Dn	9: 2	Jerusalem **s** years must be fulfilled.
Dn	9:24	"**S** weeks are decreed for your people

SEVENTY-SEVEN → SEVENTY

Mt	18:22	to you, not seven times but **s** times.

SEVERE

Gn	12:10	since the famine in the land was **s**.
Lk	4:25	a **s** famine spread over the entire
Lk	15:14	a **s** famine struck that country,
Acts	11:28	there would be a **s** famine all over
2 Cor	8: 2	for in a **s** test of affliction,

SEWED
Gn   3: 7   so they **s** fig leaves together

SEX → SEXUAL
1 Pt   3: 7   honor to the weaker female **s**,

SEXUAL → SEX
Jude   1: 7   they, indulged in **s** promiscuity

SHADE
Ps   121: 5   the LORD is your **s** at your right
Is   25: 4   from the rain, **s** from the heat.
Ez   31: 6   in its **s** dwelt numerous peoples
Jon   4: 6   giving **s** that relieved him of any
Mk   4:32   birds of the sky can dwell in its **s**."

SHADOW → SHADOWS
2 Kgs 20:11   who made the **s** retreat the ten steps
1 Chr 29:15   earth is like a **s** that does not abide.
Jb   14: 2   swift as a **s** that does not abide.
Ps   17: 8   hide me in the **s** of your wings
Ps   36: 8   take refuge in the **s** of your wings.
Ps   57: 2   In the **s** of your wings I seek shelter
Ps   63: 8   in the **s** of your wings I shout
Ps   91: 1   who abide in the **s** of the Almighty,
Is   49: 2   concealed me in the **s** of his arm.
Is   51:16   shielded you in the **s** of my hand, I,
Lk   1:79   who sit in darkness and death's **s**,
Acts   5:15   by, at least his **s** might fall on one
Heb   8: 5   and **s** of the heavenly sanctuary,
Heb   10: 1   Since the law has only a **s**

SHADOWS → SHADOW
Col   2:17   These are **s** of things to come;

SHADRACH → =HANANIAH
Hebrew exiled to Babylon; name changed from Hananiah (Dn 1:6-7). Refused defilement by food (Dn 1:8-20). Refused to worship idol (Dn 3:1-18); saved from furnace (Dn 3:19-97).

SHAKE → SHAKEN, SHAKING, SHOOK
Ps   64: 9   all who see them will **s** their heads.
Hg   2: 6   and I will **s** the heavens
Hg   2:21   I will **s** the heavens and the earth;
Mk   6:11   **s** the dust off your feet in testimony
Heb   12:26   "I will once more **s** not only earth

SHAKEN → SHAKE
Mt   24:29   the powers of the heavens will be **s**.
Lk   6:38   packed together, **s** down,

SHAKING → SHAKE
Mt   27:39   passing by reviled him, **s** their heads
Mk   15:29   him, **s** their heads and saying, "Aha!

SHALLUM
King of Israel (2 Kgs 15:10-16).

SHALMANESER
King of Assyria; conquered and deported Israel (2 Kgs 17:3-4; 18:9; Tb 1:2).

SHAME → ASHAMED, SHAMEFUL, SHAMELESS
Ps   97: 7   All who serve idols are put to **s**,
Prv   18:13   he hears — his is the folly and the **s**.
Is   30: 5   nor benefit, but only **s** and reproach.
Is   45:17   You shall never be put to **s**
Is   61: 7   Since their **s** was double
Dn   3:42   Do not let us be put to **s**, but deal
Hos   4: 7   me, exchanging their glory for **s**.
Jl   2:26   people shall nevermore be put to **s**.
Rom   9:33   believes in him shall not be put to **s**."
Rom   10:11   who believes in him will be put to **s**."
1 Cor   1:27   foolish of the world to **s** the wise,
1 Cor   1:27   weak of the world to **s** the strong,
Phil   3:19   stomach; their glory is in their "**s**."
Heb   12: 2   despising its **s**, and has taken his
1 Pt   2: 6   believes in it shall not be put to **s**."
1 Jn   2:28   not be put to **s** by him at his coming.

SHAMEFUL → SHAME
2 Cor   4: 2   we have renounced **s**, hidden things;
Eph   5:12   for it is **s** even to mention the things

SHAMELESS → SHAME
Sir   23: 6   me, surrender me not to **s** desires.
Jer   13:27   your neighings, your **s** prostitutions:

SHAMGAR
Judge; killed 600 Philistines (Jgs 3:31; 5:6).

SHAPHAN
2 Kgs 22: 8   Hilkiah gave the book to **S**,

SHARE → SHARED, SHARING
2 Sm   20: 1   David, nor any **s** in the son of Jesse.
2 Chr 10:16   the king, "What **s** have we in David?
Neh   2:20   be neither **s** nor claim nor memorial
Lk   3:11   "Whoever has two cloaks should **s**
Lk   15:12   give me the **s** of your estate
Acts   8:21   You have no **s** or lot in this matter,
Rom   1:11   I may **s** with you some spiritual gift
Rom   15:27   the Gentiles have come to **s** in their
2 Cor   1: 7   know that as you **s** in the sufferings,
2 Cor   1: 7   you also **s** in the encouragement.
Eph   4:28   he may have something to **s**
Col   1:12   who has made you fit to **s**
1 Tm   6:18   works, to be generous, ready to **s**,
2 Tm   2: 6   ought to have the first **s** of the crop.
Heb   12:10   in order that we may **s** his holiness.
Heb   13:16   to do good and to **s** what you have;
Rv   18: 4   sins and receive a **s** in her plagues,
Rv   22:19   God will take away his **s** in the tree

SHARED → SHARE
Heb   2:14   and flesh, he likewise **s** in them,
Heb   6: 4   heavenly gift and **s** in the holy Spirit

SHARING → SHARE
Phil   3:10   [the] **s** of his sufferings by being

SHARON
Song   2: 1   I am a flower of **S**, a lily

SHARP → SHARPENED, SHARPENS, SHARPER
Prv   5: 4   as **s** as a two-edged sword.
Is   5:28   Their arrows are **s**, and all their
Acts   15:39   So **s** was their disagreement
Rv   1:16   A **s** two-edged sword came
Rv   2:12   the **s** two-edged sword says this:
Rv   14:14   his head and a **s** sickle in his hand.
Rv   19:15   his mouth came a **s** sword to strike

SHARPENED → SHARP
Ez   21:14   A sword, a sword has been **s**,

SHARPENS → SHARP
Prv   27:17   As iron **s** iron, so man **s** his fellow

SHARPER → SHARP
Heb   4:12   **s** than any two-edged sword,

SHATTERED
Ex   15: 6   right hand, O LORD, has **s** the enemy.
1 Sm   2:10   the LORD's foes shall be **s**.

SHAVE → SHAVED
Nm   6:18   tent the nazirite shall **s** his dedicated
Dt   14: 1   not gash yourselves nor **s** the hair

SHAVED → SHAVE
Nm   6:19   the nazirite has **s** off his dedicated
Jgs   16:17   If I am **s**, my strength will leave me,
1 Cor 11: 5   thing as if she had had her head **s**.

SHEAF → SHEAVES
Gn   37: 7   suddenly my **s** rose to an upright
Gn   37: 7   sheaves formed a ring around my **s**
Lv   23:11   shall wave the **s** before the LORD
Dt   24:19   in your field and overlook a **s** there,

SHEAR → SHEARER, SHEARERS
Dt   15:19   nor **s** the firstlings of your flock.

SHEARER → SHEAR
Acts   8:32   and as a lamb before its **s** is silent,

SHEARERS → SHEAR
Is   53: 7   or a sheep before the **s**, he was

SHEAVES → SHEAF
Gn   37: 7   we were, binding **s** in the field,
Gn   37: 7   and your **s** formed a ring around my
Ru   2:15   among the **s** themselves without
Ps   126: 6   of joy, carrying their bundled **s**.

SHEBA
1. Benjamite; rebelled against David (2 Sm 20).
2. Queen of Sheba (1 Kgs 10; 2 Chr 9). Queen of the South (Mt 12:42; Lk 11:31).

SHECHEM
1. Raped Jacob's daughter Dinah; killed by Simeon and Levi (Gn 34).
2. City where Joshua renewed the covenant (Jos 24). Abimelech as king (Jgs 9).

SHED → BLOODSHED, SHEDDING, SHEDS
Gn   9: 6   by man shall his blood be **s**;
Nm   35:33   the blood **s** on it except through the blood of him who **s** it.
Dt   19:10   innocent blood will not be **s** and you
1 Mc   1:24   great arrogance and **s** much blood.
Prv   6:17   and hands that **s** innocent blood;
Is   59: 7   they are quick to **s** innocent blood;
Ez   22:12   in you who take bribes to **s** blood.
Mt   23:35   you all the righteous blood **s**
Rom   3:15   Their feet are quick to **s** blood;
Rv   16: 6   For they have **s** the blood

SHEDDING → SHED
Heb   9:22   without the **s** of blood there is no
Heb   12: 4   yet resisted to the point of **s** blood.

SHEDS → SHED
Gn   9: 6   If anyone **s** the blood of man,

SHEEP → SHEEP'S
Nm   27:17   not be like **s** without a shepherd."
1 Sm 15:14   of this bleating of **s** that comes
1 Kgs 22:17   like **s** without a shepherd,
Ps   44:23   day long, considered only as **s** to be
Ps   74: 1   does your anger burn against the **s**
Ps   78:52   God led forth his people like **s**;
Ps   119:176 I have wandered like a lost **s**;
Is   53: 6   We had all gone astray like **s**,
Is   53: 7   or a **s** before the shearers, he was
Jer   50: 6   Lost **s** were my people,
Ez   34:15   I myself will pasture my **s**; I myself
Zec   13: 7   that the **s** may be dispersed, and I
Mt   9:36   like **s** without a shepherd.
Mt   10: 6   Go rather to the lost **s** of the house
Mt   10:16   I am sending you like **s** in the midst
Mt   12:11   one of you who has a **s** that falls
Mt   25:32   as a shepherd separates the **s**
Lk   15: 4   man among you having a hundred **s**
Jn   10: 3   and the **s** hear his voice, as he calls
Jn   10: 3   as he calls his own **s** by name
Jn   10: 7   I say to you, I am the gate for the **s**.
Jn   10:11   lays down his life for the **s**.
Jn   10:15   I will lay down my life for the **s**.
Jn   10:27   My **s** hear my voice; I know them,
Jn   21:17   [Jesus] said to him, "Feed my **s**.
Acts   8:32   "Like a **s** he was led to the slaughter,
Rom   8:36   looked upon as **s** to be slaughtered."
Heb   13:20   great shepherd of the **s** by the blood
1 Pt   2:25   For you had gone astray like **s**,

SHEEP'S → SHEEP
Mt   7:15   false prophets, who come to you in **s** clothing,

SHEET
Acts 10:11   resembling a large **s** coming down,
Acts 11: 5   resembling a large **s** coming down,

SHEKEL → SHEKELS
Ex   30:13   to the standard of the sanctuary **s**, twenty gerahs to the **s**.

SHEKELS → SHEKEL
1 Chr 21:25   So David paid Ornan six hundred **s**

SHELAH
Gn   38:11   father's house until my son **S** grows

SHELTER
Ps   27: 5   For God will hide me in his **s**
Ps   31:21   hide them in the **s** of your presence,
Ps   55: 9   I would soon find a **s**
Ps   61: 5   take refuge in the **s** of your wings.
Ps   91: 1   dwell in the **s** of the Most High,
Sir   6:14   A faithful friend is a sturdy **s**;
Is   4: 6   his glory will be **s** and protection:
Is   25: 4   needy in distress; **S** from the rain,
Rv   7:15   who sits on the throne will **s** them.

SHEM
Son of Noah (Gn 5:32; 6:10). Blessed (Gn 9:26). Descendants (Gn 10:21-31; 11:10-32; Lk 3:36).

SHEMAIAH
1 Kgs 12:22   the LORD spoke to **S**, a man of God:
2 Chr 12: 5   **S** the prophet came to Rehoboam
Jer   29:31   Thus says the LORD concerning **S**,
Jer   29:31   Because **S** prophesies to you

SHEMER → SAMARIA
1 Kgs 16:24   the city he built Samaria after **S**,

SHEOL
Ps   6: 6   Who praises you in **S**?
Ps   16:10   For you will not abandon me to **S**,
Ps   55:16   let them go down alive to **S**, for evil
Ps   139: 8   if I lie down in **S**, you are there too.

SHEPHERD → SHEPHERDS
Gn   48:15   The God who has been my **s**
Gn   49:24   because of the **S**, the Rock of Israel,
Nm   27:17   may not be like sheep without a **s**.
1 Kgs 22:17   like sheep without a **s**, and the LORD
1 Chr 11: 2   'You shall **s** my people Israel and be
Ps   23: 1   The LORD is my **s**; there is nothing I
Ps   78:71   brought him, to **s** Jacob, his people,
Ps   80: 2   **S** of Israel, listen, guide of the flock
Is   40:11   Like a **s** he feeds his flock; in his
Jer   31:10   he guards them as a **s** his flock.
Ez   34: 5   they were scattered for lack of a **s**,
Zec   10: 2   sheep, wretched: they have no **s**.
Zec   11:17   Woe to my foolish **s** who forsakes
Zec   13: 7   Awake, O sword, against my **s**,
Zec   13: 7   Strike the **s** that the sheep may be
Mt   2: 6   ruler, who is to **s** my people Israel.' "
Mt   25:32   as a **s** separates the sheep
Mt   26:31   'I will strike the **s**, and the sheep
Mk   6:34   for they were like sheep without a **s**;
Jn   10:11   I am the good **s**. A good **s** lays down
Jn   10:14   I am the good **s**, and I know mine
Jn   10:16   and there will be one flock, one **s**.
Heb   13:20   the dead the great **s** of the sheep
1 Pt   2:25   you have now returned to the **s**
1 Pt   5: 4   And when the chief **S** is revealed,
Rv   7:17   the center of the throne will **s** them

SHEPHERDS → SHEPHERD
Gn   46:34   since all **s** are abhorrent
Ex   2:19   us from the interference of the **s**.
Is   56:11   These are the **s** who know no
Jer   3:15   I will appoint over you **s** after my
Jer   23: 1   Woe to the **s** who mislead
Jer   50: 6   my people, their **s** misled them,
Ez   34: 2   prophesy against the **s** of Israel,
Ez   34: 2   Should not **s**, rather, pasture sheep?
Zec   10: 3   My wrath is kindled against the **s**,
Lk   2: 8   Now there were **s** in that region

SHESHBAZZAR
Ezr   1: 8   and counted out to **S**, the prince
Ezr   5:16   Then this same **S** came and laid

SHIBBOLETH → SIBBOLETH
Jgs   12: 6   they would ask him to say "**S**." If he

SHIELD → SHIELDED
Gn   15: 1   I am your **s**; I will make your
Dt   33:29   The LORD is your saving **s**, and his
2 Sm 22:36   "You have given me your saving **s**,
Ps   3: 4   But you, LORD, are a **s** around me;

Gn   46:12   Onan, **S**, Perez and Zerah—but Er

Ps	5:13	surround them with favor like a **s**.
Ps	7:11	A **s** before me is God who saves
Ps	18: 3	of refuge, my **s**, my saving horn,
Ps	28: 7	The LORD is my strength and my **s**,
Ps	33:20	for the LORD, who is our help and **s**.
Ps	84:12	For a sun and **s** is the LORD God,
Ps	91: 4	God's faithfulness is a protecting **s**.
Ps	115: 9	in the LORD, who is their help and **s**.
Ps	119:114	You are my refuge and **s**; in your
Ps	144: 2	my deliverer, My **s**, in whom I trust,
Prv	2: 7	he is the **s** of those who walk
Prv	30: 5	he is a **s** to those who take refuge
Zec	12: 8	the LORD will **s** the inhabitants
Eph	6:16	hold faith as a **s**, to quench all

SHIELDED → SHIELD
Dt	32:10	He **s** them and cared for them,

SHIFTING
Col	1:23	not **s** from the hope of the gospel

SHILOH
Jos	18: 1	of the Israelites assembled at **S**,
1 Sm	1:24	him at the temple of the LORD in **S**.
1 Sm	3:21	The LORD continued to appear at **S**;
1 Sm	3:21	to Samuel at **S** through his word,
Ps	78:60	He forsook the shrine at **S**, the tent

SHIMEI
Cursed David (2 Sm 16:5-14); spared (2 Sm 19:17-24). Killed by Solomon (1 Kgs 2:8-9, 36-46).

SHINAR
Gn	11: 2	came upon a valley in the land of **S**
Dn	1: 2	he carried off to the land of **S**,

SHINE → SHINES, SHINING, SHONE
Nm	6:25	The LORD let his face **s** upon you,
Ps	37: 6	make your integrity **s** like the dawn,
Ps	67: 2	bless us; may God's face **s** upon us.
Ps	94: 1	God, avenging God, **s** forth!
Dn	12: 3	But the wise shall **s** brightly
Mt	5:16	your light must **s** before others,
Mt	13:43	the righteous will **s** like the sun
2 Cor	4: 6	said, "Let light **s** out of darkness,"
Phil	2:15	among whom you **s** like lights
Rv	21:23	no need of sun or moon to **s** on it,

SHINES → SHINE
Ps	50: 2	From Zion God **s** forth,
Is	60: 1	the glory of the Lord **s** upon you.
Is	62: 1	Until her vindication **s** forth like
Jn	1: 5	the light **s** in the darkness,

SHINING → SHINE
Jn	5:35	He was a burning and **s** lamp,
2 Pt	1:19	as to a lamp **s** in a dark place,
1 Jn	2: 8	away, and the true light is already **s**.

SHIP → SHIPS, SHIPWRECK, SHIPWRECKED
Jon	1: 4	that arose the **s** was on the point
Acts	27:22	one of you will be lost, only the **s**.

SHIPS → SHIP
1 Kgs	22:49	Jehoshaphat made Tarshish **s** to go
1 Kgs	22:49	but in fact the **s** did not go,
Ps	107:23	Some went off to sea in **s**,
Prv	31:14	Like merchant **s**, she secures her
Jas	3: 4	It is the same with **s**: even though
Rv	8: 9	and a third of the **s** were wrecked.

SHIPWRECK → SHIP
1 Tm	1:19	have made a **s** of their faith,

SHIPWRECKED → SHIP
2 Cor	11:25	three times I was **s**, I passed a night

SHISHAK
2 Chr	12: 2	the fifth year of King Rehoboam, **S**,

SHONE → SHINE
Mt	17: 2	them; his face **s** like the sun and his
Lk	2: 9	the glory of the Lord **s** around them,
2 Cor	4: 6	has **s** in our hearts to bring to light

SHOOK → SHAKE
Is	6: 4	cry, the frame of the door **s**
Acts	13:51	So they **s** the dust from their feet
Acts	18: 6	he **s** out his garments and said
Heb	12:26	His voice **s** the earth at that time,

SHOOT → SHOOTS
Is	11: 1	a **s** shall sprout from the stump
Rom	11:17	a wild olive **s**, were grafted in their

SHOOTS → SHOOT
Hos	14: 7	and put forth his **s**. His splendor

SHORE → SEASHORE
Lk	5: 3	put out a short distance from the **s**.

SHORT
Is	59: 1	hand of the LORD is not too **s** to save,
Lk	19: 3	of the crowd, for he was **s** in stature.
Rv	12:12	for he knows he has but a **s** time."

SHOULDER → SHOULDERS
Is	22:22	key of the House of David on his **s**;

SHOULDERS → SHOULDER
Ex	28:12	his **s** as a reminder before the LORD.
Mt	23: 4	to carry] and lay them on people's **s**,
Lk	15: 5	it, he sets it on his **s** with great joy

SHOUT → SHOUTED, SHOUTS
Jos	6:16	"Now **s**, for the LORD has given you
Ezr	3:11	all the people raised a great **s** of joy,
Ps	20: 6	May we **s** for joy at your victory,
Ps	35:27	my just cause **s** for joy and be glad.
Ps	47: 2	hands; **s** to God with joyful cries.
Is	12: 6	**S** with exultation, O city of Zion,
Is	44:23	done this; **s**, you depths of the earth.
Zec	9: 9	**s** for joy, O daughter Jerusalem!

SHOUTED → SHOUT
1 Sm	17: 8	stood and **s** to the ranks of Israel:
Jb	38: 7	and all the sons of God **s** for joy?
Mk	15:13	They **s** again, "Crucify him."

SHOUTS → SHOUT
Ps	27: 6	in his tent sacrifices with **s** of joy;

SHOW → SHOWED, SHOWING, SHOWN, SHOWS
Gn	12: 1	house to a land that I will **s** you.
Ex	9:16	to **s** you my power and to make my
Ex	25: 9	to the pattern that I will now **s** you.
Dt	7: 2	with them and **s** them no mercy.
1 Sm	20:14	may you **s** me the kindness
2 Sm	9: 1	whom I may **s** kindness for the sake
Ps	17: 7	**S** your wonderful love, you who
Ps	85: 8	**S** us, LORD, your love; grant us your
Prv	28:21	To **s** partiality is never good:
Is	30:18	the LORD is waiting to **s** you favor,
Mi	7:20	You will **s** faithfulness to Jacob,
Zec	7: 9	and **s** kindness and compassion
Mt	22:19	**S** me the coin that pays the census
Jn	2:18	"What sign can you **s** us for doing
Jn	14: 8	"Master, **s** us the Father, and that will
1 Cor	12:31	I shall **s** you a still more excellent
2 Cor	11:30	of the things that **s** my weakness.
Eph	2: 7	come he might **s** the immeasurable
Rv	1: 1	to **s** his servants what must happen
Rv	4: 1	and I will **s** you what must happen
Rv	17: 1	I will **s** you the judgment
Rv	21: 9	I will **s** you the bride, the wife

SHOWED → SHOW
Gn	39:21	he **s** him kindness by making
Dt	34: 1	the LORD **s** him all the land—Gilead,
Mt	4: 8	**s** him all the kingdoms of the world
Lk	24:40	he **s** them his hands and his feet.
Jn	20:20	he **s** them his hands and his side.
Rv	21:10	**s** me the holy city Jerusalem coming
Rv	22: 1	Then the angel **s** me the river

SHOWERS
Jer	3: 3	Therefore the **s** were withheld,

SHOWING → SHOW
Ti	2: 7	**s** yourself as a model of good deeds

SHOWN → SHOW
Ex	25:40	the pattern s you on the mountain.
1 Kgs	3: 6	"You have s great favor to your
Ps	78:11	the wondrous deeds he had s them.
Jn	10:32	"I have s you many good works

SHOWS → SHOW
Prv	3:34	but to the humble he s kindness.
Prv	12:16	The fool immediately s his anger,
Rom	9:16	but upon God, who s mercy.

SHREWDLY
Ex	1:10	let us deal s with them to stop their

SHUDDER
Ez	32:10	their kings shall s over you in horror

SHUH
Jb	2:11	Bildad from S, and Zophar from

SHULAMMITE
Song	7: 1	Turn, turn, O S, turn, turn,
Song	7: 1	Why would you look at the S

SHUNAMITE
1 Kgs	1: 3	and found Abishag the S,

SHUNAMMITE
2 Kgs	4:12	servant Gehazi, "Call this S woman."

SHUT
Gn	7:16	Then the LORD s him in.
Gn	19: 6	When he had s the door behind him,
Is	22:22	when he opens, no one shall s,
Rv	21:25	the day its gates will never be s,

SIBBOLETH → SHIBBOLETH
Jgs	12: 6	If he said "S," not being able to give

SICK → SICKBED, SICKNESS
Prv	13:12	Hope deferred makes the heart s,
Sir	7:35	Neglect not to visit the s— for these
Ez	34: 4	the weak nor heal the s nor bind
Mt	8:16	spirits by a word and cured all the s,
Mt	9:12	not need a physician, but the s do.
Mt	10: 8	Cure the s, raise the dead,
Acts	19:12	his skin were applied to the s,
2 Tm	4:20	I left Trophimus s at Miletus.
Jas	5:14	Is anyone among you s? He should

SICKBED → BED, SICK
Ps	41: 4	The LORD sustains them on their s,

SICKLE
Jl	4:13	Apply the s, for the harvest is ripe;
Mk	4:29	grain is ripe, he wields the s at once,
Rv	14:14	his head and a sharp s in his hand.

SICKNESS → SICK
Ex	23:25	I will remove all s from your midst;

SIDE → ASIDE, SIDES
1 Chr	22: 9	rest from all his enemies on every s.
Ps	91: 7	Though a thousand fall at your s,
Ez	1:10	on the right s was the face of a lion,
Ez	1:10	and on the left s the face of an ox,
Ez	1:10	on the right s was the face of a lion,
Ez	1:10	and on the left s the face of an ox,
Ez	4: 4	Then you shall lie on your left s,
Jn	19:18	one on either s, with Jesus
Jn	19:34	soldier thrust his lance into his s,
Jn	20:20	he showed them his hands and his s.
Rv	22: 2	On either s of the river grew the tree

SIDES → SIDE
Ex	29:16	and splash on all the s of the altar.
Nm	33:55	in your eyes and thorns in your s,
Jos	23:13	a scourge for your s and thorns

SIDON
Jgs	1:31	inhabitants of Acco or those of S,
1 Kgs	17: 9	"Move on to Zarephath of S and stay
Mt	11:21	midst had been done in Tyre and S,
Mk	7:31	and went by way of S to the Sea
Lk	4:26	widow in Zarephath in the land of S.

SIEGE → BESIEGED
2 Kgs	25: 1	it, and built s walls on every side.
Ez	4: 2	Raise a s against it: build a tower,

SIEVE
Sir	27: 4	When a s is shaken, the husks
Am	9: 9	As one sifts with a s, letting no

SIFT
Lk	22:31	behold Satan has demanded to s all

SIGHED → SIGHING
Mk	8:12	He s from the depth of his spirit

SIGHING → SIGHED
Ps	5: 2	my words, O LORD; listen to my s.

SIGHT → SEE
Ex	3: 3	go over to look at this remarkable s,
Ps	51: 6	I have done such evil in your s
Ps	72:14	for precious is their blood in his s.
Mt	11: 5	the blind regain their s, the lame
Acts	1: 9	and a cloud took him from their s.
Acts	4:19	"Whether it is right in the s of God
2 Cor	5: 7	for we walk by faith, not by s.
1 Pt	3: 4	which is precious in the s of God.

SIGN → SIGNS
Gn	9:12	"This is the s that I am giving for all
Ex	13:16	then, be as a s on your hand and as
Nm	17: 3	In this way they shall serve as a s
Jgs	6:17	give me a s that you are speaking
1 Kgs	13: 3	He gave a s that same day and said:
1 Kgs	13: 3	said: "This is the s that the LORD has
Is	7:14	Lord himself will give you this s:
Is	55:13	an everlasting imperishable s.
Ez	20:12	my sabbaths to be a s between me
Ez	24:24	Ezekiel shall be a s for you:
Mt	12:38	we wish to see a s from you."
Mt	16: 1	him to show them a s from heaven.
Mt	24: 3	what s will there be of your coming,
Mt	24:30	the s of the Son of Man will appear
Mk	8:12	"Why does this generation seek a s?
Mk	8:12	no s will be given to this generation."
Lk	2:12	And this will be a s for you:
Lk	11:29	it seeks a s, but no s will be given it, except the s of Jonah.
Jn	2:18	"What s can you show us for doing
Rom	4:11	he received the s of circumcision as
1 Cor	11:10	a woman should have a s of authority
1 Cor	14:22	tongues are a s not for those who

SIGNET
Gn	41:42	Pharaoh took off his s ring and put
Est	3:10	The king took the s ring from his
Est	8: 2	The king removed his s ring
Jer	22:24	Judah, are a s ring on my right hand,
Hg	2:23	And I will set you as a s ring; for I

SIGNS → SIGN
Ex	4: 9	will not believe even these two s,
Ex	7: 3	despite the many s and wonders
Ps	105:27	They worked his s in Egypt
Is	8:18	we are s and portents in Israel
Dn	6:28	working s and wonders in heaven
Mt	16: 3	you cannot judge the s of the times.]
Mt	24:24	they will perform s and wonders so
Mk	13:22	will perform s and wonders in order
Jn	3: 2	no one can do these s that you are
Jn	7:31	will he perform more s that this man
Jn	9:16	"How can a sinful man do such s?"
Jn	20:30	Now Jesus did many other s
Acts	2:19	and s on the earth below: blood,
Acts	5:12	Many s and wonders were done
1 Cor	1:22	For Jews demand s and Greeks look
2 Cor	12:12	The s of an apostle were performed
2 Cor	12:12	with all endurance, s and wonders,
2 Thes	2: 9	deed and in s and wonders that lie,
Heb	2: 4	God added his testimony by s,
Rv	13:13	It performed great s, even making
Rv	16:14	demonic spirits who performed s.
Rv	19:20	had performed in its sight the s

SIHON
Nm	21:21	Now Israel sent men to **S**,
Dt	31: 4	with them just as he dealt with **S**
Ps	136:19	**S**, king of the Amorites, God's love

SILAS
Prophet (Acts 15:22-32); co-worker with Paul on second missionary journey (Acts 16-18; 2 Cor 1:19). Co-writer with Paul (1 Thes 1:1; 2 Thes 1:1); Peter (1 Pt 5:12).

SILENCE → SILENCED, SILENT
Ps	8: 3	your foes, to **s** enemy and avenger.
1 Pt	2:15	doing good you may **s** the ignorance
Rv	8: 1	there was **s** in heaven for about half

SILENCED → SILENCE
| Mt | 22:34 | heard that he had **s** the Sadducees, |
| Rom | 3:19 | so that every mouth may be **s** |

SILENT → SILENCE
Ps	39: 3	Dumb and **s** before the wicked,
Prv	17:28	if he keeps **s**, is considered wise;
Is	53: 7	he was **s** and opened not his mouth.
Is	62: 1	For Zion's sake I will not be **s**,
Mk	14:61	But he was **s** and answered nothing.
Acts	8:32	and as a lamb before its shearer is **s**,
1 Cor	14:34	women should keep **s**

SILOAM
| Jn | 9: 7 | in the Pool of **S**" (which means Sent). |

SILVER → SILVERSMITH
Gn	37:28	Ishmaelites for twenty pieces of **s**.
Ex	11: 2	for **s** and gold articles
Ex	20:23	neither gods of **s** nor gods of gold
Ex	25: 3	from them: gold, **s** and bronze;
Dt	17:17	he accumulate a vast amount of **s**
Jos	7:21	two hundred shekels of **s**, and a bar
2 Chr	1:15	The king made **s** and gold as
1 Mc	1:23	took away the gold and **s**
Ps	12: 7	are sure, **s** refined in a crucible,
Ps	66:10	us, O God, tried us as **s** tried by fire.
Ps	115: 4	Their idols are **s** and gold, the work
Prv	2: 4	If you seek her like **s**, and like
Prv	3:14	her profit is better than profit in **s**,
Prv	8:10	my instruction in preference to **s**,
Prv	22: 1	and high esteem, than gold and **s**.
Prv	25: 4	Remove the dross from **s**, and it
Prv	25:11	Like golden apples in **s** settings
Is	48:10	See, I have refined you like **s**,
Ez	22:18	dross from **s** have they become.
Dn	2:32	its chest and arms were **s**, its belly
Dn	5: 4	praised their gods of gold and **s**,
Hg	2: 8	Mine is the **s** and mine the gold,
Zec	11:12	out my wages, thirty pieces of **s**.
Zec	13: 9	I will refine them as **s** is refined,
Mal	3: 3	will sit refining and purifying [**s**],
Mal	3: 3	Refining them like gold or like **s**
Mt	26:15	They paid him thirty pieces of **s**,
Acts	3: 6	"I have neither **s** nor gold, but what I
1 Cor	3:12	on this foundation with gold, **s**,
2 Tm	2:20	are vessels not only of gold and **s**
1 Pt	1:18	not with perishable things like **s**

SILVERSMITH → SILVER
| Acts | 19:24 | There was a **s** named Demetrius |

SIMEON → =SIMON
1. Son of Jacob by Leah (Gn 29:33; 35:23; 1 Chr 2:1). With Levi killed Shechem for rape of Dinah (Gn 34:25-29). Held hostage by Joseph in Egypt (Gn 42:24-43:23). Tribe of blessed (Gn 49:5-7), numbered (Nm 1:23; 26:14), allotted land (Jos 19:1-9; Ez 48:24), 12, 000 from (Rv 7:7).
2. Godly Jew who blessed the infant Jesus (2:25-35).
3. See Peter (Acts 15:14; 2 Pt 1:1).

SIMON → =PETER, =SIMEON
1. See Peter.
2. Apostle, called the Zealot (Mt 10:4; Mk 3:18; Lk 6:15; Acts 1:13).
3. Samaritan sorcerer (Acts 8:9-24).

SIMPLE
| Ps | 19: 8 | trustworthy, giving wisdom to the **s**. |

Ps	119:130	light, gives understanding to the **s**.
Prv	1:22	"How long, you **s** ones, will you love
Prv	8: 5	You **s** ones, gain resource,

SIN → SINFUL, SINNED, SINNER, SINNERS, SINS
Gn	4: 7	**s** is a demon lurking at the door:
Ex	32:32	If you would only forgive their **s**!
Ex	34: 7	wickedness and crime and **s**; yet not
Nm	32:23	do this, you will **s** against the LORD,
Nm	32:23	escape the consequences of your **s**.
1 Sm	12:23	me to **s** against the LORD by ceasing
1 Sm	15:23	For a **s** like divination is rebellion,
1 Kgs	8:46	"When they **s** against you (for there is no man who does not **s**),
1 Kgs	13:34	This was a **s** on the part of the house
Neh	13:26	king of Israel, **s** because of them?
Neh	13:26	Israel, yet even he was made to **s**
Tb	12:10	of **s** are their own worst enemies.
Jb	1:22	In all this Job did not **s**, nor did he
Ps	4: 5	Tremble and do not **s**; upon your
Ps	32: 5	Then I declared my **s** to you;
Ps	32: 5	you took away the guilt of my **s**.
Ps	38:19	my guilt and grieve over my **s**.
Ps	39: 2	my ways, lest I **s** with my tongue;
Ps	51: 4	all my guilt; from my **s** cleanse me.
Ps	119:11	that I may not **s** against you.
Prv	5:22	of his own **s** he will be held fast;
Prv	20: 9	heart clean, I am cleansed of my **s**"?
Wis	10:13	was sold, but delivered him from **s**.
Sir	7: 8	Do not plot to repeat a **s**; not even
Sir	42: 1	lest you **s** through human respect:
Is	3: 9	them; their **s** like Sodom they vaunt:
Is	6: 7	is removed, your **s** purged."
Jer	16:18	their **s** of profaning my land
Dn	9:20	confessing my **s** and the **s** of my
Mi	6: 7	of my body for the **s** of my soul?
Mt	5:29	If your right eye causes you to **s**,
Mk	3:29	but is guilty of an everlasting **s**."
Jn	1:29	who takes away the **s** of the world.
Jn	8: 7	you who is without **s** be the first
Jn	8:34	everyone who commits **s** is a slave of **s**.
Jn	8:46	Can any of you charge me with **s**?
Jn	16: 9	**s**, because they do not believe
Acts	7:60	do not hold this **s** against them";
Rom	4: 8	is the man whose **s** the Lord does
Rom	5:12	as through one person **s** entered the world, and through **s**, death,
Rom	5:20	increase but, where **s** increased,
Rom	6: 2	How can we who died to **s** yet live
Rom	6:11	of yourselves as [being] dead to **s**
Rom	6:14	For **s** is not to have any power over
Rom	6:23	For the wages of **s** is death,
Rom	7: 7	That the law is **s**? Of course not!
Rom	7: 7	I did not know **s** except through
Rom	7:25	but, with my flesh, the law of **s**.
Rom	8: 2	has freed you from the law of **s**
Rom	14:23	for whatever is not from faith is **s**.
1 Cor	8:12	When you **s** in this way against your
1 Cor	15:56	The sting of death is **s**, and the power of **s** is the law.
2 Cor	5:21	him to be **s** who did not know **s**,
Eph	4:26	Be angry but do not **s**; do not let
1 Tm	5:20	Reprimand publicly those who do **s**,
Heb	4:15	tested in every way, yet without **s**.
Heb	9:26	ages to take away **s** by his sacrifice.
Heb	10:18	there is no longer offering for **s**.
Heb	11:25	than enjoy the fleeting pleasure of **s**.
Heb	12: 1	every burden and **s** that clings to us
Jas	1:15	desire conceives and brings forth **s**,
Jas	1:15	**s** reaches maturity it gives birth
1 Pt	2:22	"He committed no **s**, and no deceit
1 Jn	1: 7	his Son Jesus cleanses us from all **s**.
1 Jn	1: 8	say, "We are without **s**," we deceive
1 Jn	2: 1	you so that you may not commit **s**. But if anyone does **s**, we have
1 Jn	3: 4	Everyone who commits **s** commits lawlessness, for **s** is lawlessness.
1 Jn	3: 5	away sins, and in him there is no **s**.
1 Jn	3: 9	who is begotten by God commits **s**,

1 Jn	3: 9	he cannot **s** because he is begotten
1 Jn	5:16	if the **s** is not deadly, he should pray
1 Jn	5:16	only for those whose **s** is not deadly.
1 Jn	5:16	There is such a thing as deadly **s**,
1 Jn	5:17	All wrongdoing is **s**, but there is **s**

SINAI →=HOREB

Ex	19: 1	Israelites came to the desert of **S**.
Ex	19:20	came down to the top of Mount **S**,
Ex	31:18	speaking to Moses on Mount **S**,
Nm	1:19	census as taken in the desert of **S**.
Ps	68:18	**S** the Lord entered the holy place.
Gal	4:25	Hagar represents **S**, a mountain

SINCERE → SINCERELY, SINCERITY

2 Cor	11: 3	thoughts may be corrupted from a **s**
1 Tm	1: 5	a good conscience, and a **s** faith.
2 Tm	1: 5	as I recall your **s** faith that first lived

SINCERELY → SINCERE

Jb	33: 3	my lips shall utter knowledge **s**;

SINCERITY → SINCERE

1 Cor	5: 8	with the unleavened bread of **s**
2 Cor	1:12	with the simplicity and **s** of God,
2 Cor	2:17	but as out of **s**, indeed as from God

SINEWS

Ez	37: 6	I will put **s** upon you, make flesh

SINFUL → SIN

1 Mc	1:10	sprang from these a **s** offshoot,
Is	1: 4	**s** nation, people laden
Lk	5: 8	from me, Lord, for I am a **s** man."
Rom	7: 5	we were in the flesh, our **s** passions,
Rom	8: 3	own Son in the likeness of **s** flesh

SING → SANG, SINGER, SINGERS, SINGING, SONG, SONGS

Ex	15: 1	Lord: I will **s** to the Lord, for he is
1 Sm	21:12	During their dances do they not **s**,
Jdt	16:13	"A new hymn I will **s** to my God.
Ps	13: 6	That I may **s** of the Lord, "How good
Ps	30: 5	**S** praise to the Lord, you faithful;
Ps	33: 3	**S** to God a new song; skillfully play
Ps	47: 7	**S** praise to God, **s** praise; **s** praise to our king, **s** praise.
Ps	57: 8	steadfast. I will **s** and chant praise.
Ps	59:17	But I shall **s** of your strength,
Ps	66: 2	**s** of his glorious name; give him
Ps	68: 5	**S** to God, praise the divine name;
Ps	89: 2	of the Lord I will **s** forever,
Ps	95: 1	Come, let us **s** joyfully to the Lord;
Ps	96: 1	**S** to the Lord a new song;
Ps	98: 1	A psalm. **S** a new song to the Lord,
Ps	101: 1	I **s** of love and justice; to you, Lord, I **s** praise.
Ps	108: 2	steadfast. I will **s** and chant praise.
Ps	119:172	May my tongue **s** of your promise,
Ps	137: 3	joyful song: "**S** for us a song of Zion!"
Ps	149: 1	**S** to the Lord a new song, a hymn
Is	5: 1	Let me now **s** of my friend,
Is	27: 2	The pleasant vineyard, **s** about it!
1 Cor	14:15	I will **s** praise with the spirit,
1 Cor	14:15	I will also **s** praise with the mind.
Jas	5:13	in good spirits? He should **s** praise.

SINGED

Dn	3:94	not a hair of their heads had been **s**,

SINGER → SING

Ez	33:32	For them you are only a ballad **s**,

SINGERS → SING

Ezr	2:70	but the **s**, the gatekeepers,
Ps	68:26	The **s** go first, the harpists follow;

SINGING → SING

Is	35:10	and enter Zion **s**,
Is	51:11	and enter Zion **s**,
Acts	16:25	and **s** hymns to God as the prisoners
Eph	5:19	**s** and playing to the Lord in your
Col	3:16	admonish one another, **s** psalms,

SINGLE

Nm	13:23	cut down a branch with a **s** cluster

Mt	6:27	by worrying add a **s** moment to your
Heb	12:16	who sold his birthright for a **s** meal.
Rv	21:21	of the gates made from a **s** pearl;

SINK → SANK

Jer	51:64	and say: Thus shall Babylon **s**.

SINNED → SIN

1 Sm	15:24	"I have **s**, for I have disobeyed
2 Sm	12:13	to Nathan, "I have **s** against the Lord."
2 Sm	24:10	"I have **s** grievously in what I have
2 Chr	6:37	say, 'We have **s** and done wrong;
Jb	1: 5	"It may be that my sons have **s**
Jb	33:27	men and say, "I **s** and did wrong,
Ps	51: 6	Against you alone have I **s**; I have
Jer	2:35	on that word of yours, "I have not **s**."
Jer	14:20	fathers; that we have **s** against you.
Lam	5: 7	Our fathers, who **s**, are no more;
Dn	9: 5	We have **s**, been wicked and done
Mi	7: 9	because I have **s** against him,
Mt	27: 4	"I have **s** in betraying innocent
Lk	15:18	I have **s** against heaven and against
Jn	9: 2	who **s**, this man or his parents,
Rom	3:23	all have **s** and are deprived
Rom	5:12	death came to all, inasmuch as all **s**—
2 Pt	2: 4	not spare the angels when they **s**,
1 Jn	1:10	"We have not **s**," we make him a liar,

SINNER → SIN

Ps	51: 7	a **s**, even as my mother conceived
Lk	15: 7	heaven over one **s** who repents than
Lk	18:13	'O God, be merciful to me a **s**.'
Jas	5:20	whoever brings back a **s**

SINNERS → SIN

Ps	1: 1	Nor go the way of **s**, nor sit
Ps	25: 8	is the Lord, who shows **s** the way,
Ps	51:15	your ways, that **s** may return to you.
Prv	1:10	My son, should **s** entice you,
Prv	23:17	Let not your heart emulate **s**, but be
Is	1:28	Rebels and **s** alike shall be crushed,
Mt	9:13	not come to call the righteous but **s**."
Mk	14:41	of Man is to be handed over to **s**.
Lk	6:33	is that to you? Even **s** do the same.
Lk	15: 2	"This man welcomes **s** and eats
Rom	5: 8	while we were still **s** Christ died
1 Tm	1:15	Jesus came into the world to save **s**.
Heb	7:26	separated from **s**, higher than
Heb	12: 3	he endured such opposition from **s**,

SINS → SIN

1 Sm	2:25	If a man **s** against another man,
1 Sm	2:25	but if a man **s** against the Lord,
2 Kgs	17:22	Jeroboam in all the **s** he committed,
2 Chr	7:14	pardon their **s** and revive their land.
Ps	51:11	Turn away your face from my **s**;
Ps	79: 9	Deliver us, pardon our **s** for your
Ps	103:10	Has not dealt with us as our **s** merit,
Sir	2:11	he forgives **s**, he saves in time
Sir	3: 3	who honors his father atones for **s**;
Sir	34:26	So with a man who fasts for his **s**,
Is	1:18	Lord: Though your **s** be like scarlet,
Is	38:17	you cast behind your back all my **s**.
Is	40: 2	of the Lord double for all her **s**.
Is	43:25	your **s** I remember no more.
Is	53:12	he shall take away the **s** of many,
Is	59: 2	It is your **s** that make him hide his
Lam	3:39	any mortal, in the face of his **s**?
Ez	18: 4	mine; only the one who **s** shall die.
Ez	33:10	crimes and our **s** weigh us down;
Mi	7:19	into the depths of the sea all our **s**;
Mt	1:21	he will save his people from their **s**."
Mt	9: 6	has authority on earth to forgive **s**
Mt	18:15	"If your brother **s** [against you],
Mt	26:28	of many for the forgiveness of **s**.
Mk	1: 5	River as they acknowledged their **s**.
Lk	5:24	on earth to forgive **s** said to the man
Lk	11: 4	and forgive us our **s** for we
Lk	17: 3	If your brother **s**, rebuke him;
Jn	8:24	told you that you will die in your **s**.
Jn	8:24	that I AM, you will die in your **s**."

Jn	20:23	Whose **s** you forgive are forgiven
Jn	20:23	and whose **s** you retain are retained."
Acts	2:38	Christ for the forgiveness of your **s**;
Acts	3:19	that your **s** may be wiped away,
Acts	10:43	forgiveness of **s** through his name."
Acts	22:16	baptized and your **s** washed away,
Acts	26:18	they may obtain forgiveness of **s**
Rom	4: 7	forgiven and whose **s** are covered.
1 Cor	6:18	but the immoral person **s** against his
1 Cor	15: 3	Christ died for our **s** in accordance
Eph	2: 1	dead in your transgressions and **s**
1 Tm	5:22	and do not share in another's **s**.
Heb	1: 3	accomplished purification from **s**,
Heb	2:17	God to expiate the **s** of the people.
Heb	7:27	first for his own **s** and then for those
Heb	8:12	and remember their **s** no more."
Heb	9:28	once to take away the **s** of many,
Heb	10: 4	of bulls and goats take away **s**.
Heb	10:12	this one offered one sacrifice for **s**,
Heb	10:26	no longer remains sacrifice for **s**
Jas	5:16	confess your **s** to one another
Jas	5:20	and will cover a multitude of **s**.
1 Pt	2:24	He himself bore our **s** in his body
1 Pt	3:18	For Christ also suffered for **s** once,
1 Pt	4: 8	love covers a multitude of **s**.
1 Jn	1: 9	If we acknowledge our **s**, he is
1 Jn	1: 9	will forgive our **s** and cleanse us
1 Jn	2: 2	He is expiation for our **s**, and not for our **s** only but for those
1 Jn	3: 5	that he was revealed to take away **s**,
1 Jn	4:10	sent his Son as expiation for our **s**.
Rv	1: 5	freed us from our **s** by his blood,

SISERA

Jgs	4: 2	The general of his army was **S**,
Jgs	5:26	She hammered **S**, crushed his head;

SISTER → SISTERS

Gn	12:13	that you are my **s**, so that it may go
Gn	20: 2	said of his wife Sarah, "She is my **s**."
Gn	26: 7	his wife, he answered, "She is my **s**."
Prv	7: 4	Say to Wisdom, "You are my **s**!"
Song	4: 9	ravished my heart, my **s**, my bride;
Jer	3: 7	even though her traitor **s** Judah saw
Ez	16:46	Your elder **s** was Samaria with her
Ez	16:46	and your younger **s**,
Mk	3:35	the will of God is my brother and **s**
Lk	10:40	you not care that my **s** has left me
Jn	11: 5	loved Martha and her **s** and Lazarus.
Rom	16: 1	I commend to you Phoebe our **s**,
2 Jn	1:13	of your chosen **s** send you greetings.

SISTERS → SISTER

Mt	19:29	up houses or brothers or **s** or father
Mk	6: 3	And are not his **s** here with us?"
1 Tm	5: 2	younger women as **s** with complete

SIT → SAT, SITS, SITTING

Ex	18:14	Why do you **s** alone while all
1 Kgs	8:25	from your line to **s** before me
Ps	1: 1	nor **s** in company with scoffers.
Ps	26: 5	with the wicked I do not **s**.
Ps	139: 2	you know when I **s** and stand;
Is	16: 5	and on it shall **s** in fidelity
Mi	4: 4	Every man shall **s** under his own
Mal	3: 3	He will **s** refining and purifying
Mt	20:23	but to **s** at my right and at my left [,
Mt	22:44	said to my lord, "**S** at my right hand
Mk	14:32	to his disciples, "**S** here while I pray."
Lk	22:30	you will **s** on thrones judging
Acts	2:34	said to my Lord, "**S** at my right hand
Heb	1:13	has he ever said: "**S** at my right hand

SITS → SIT

Ps	29:10	The Lord **s** enthroned
Is	28: 6	to him who **s** in judgment,
Is	40:22	He **s** enthroned above the vault

SITTING → SIT

Lk	8:35	whom the demons had come out **s**

SIX → SIXTH

Ex	20: 9	**S** days you may labor and do all
1 Chr	20: 6	who had **s** fingers to each hand and **s** toes to each foot;
Prv	6:16	There are **s** things the Lord hates,
Is	6: 2	each of them had **s** wings: with two
Rv	4: 8	each of them with **s** wings,
Rv	13:18	His number is **s** hundred and **s**.

SIXTH → SIX

Rv	6:12	while he broke open the **s** seal,
Rv	16:12	The **s** angel emptied his bowl

SIXTY

Mt	13: 8	fruit, a hundred or **s** or thirtyfold.

SIXTY-SIX

Rv	13:18	His number is six hundred and **s**.

SIZE

Mt	17:20	if you have faith the **s** of a mustard

SKIES → SKY

Ps	89: 7	Who in the **s** ranks with the Lord?

SKILL → SKILLFULLY

Ex	28: 3	whom I have endowed with **s**,
1 Kgs	7:14	from Tyre. He was endowed with **s**,

SKILLFULLY → SKILL

Ps	33: 3	new song; **s** play with joyful chant.

SKIN → SKINS, WINESKINS

Ex	34:30	noticed how radiant the **s** of his face
Jb	2: 4	answered the Lord and said, "**S** for **s**!
Jb	19:20	My bones cleave to my **s**, and I
Jer	13:23	Can the Ethiopian change his **s**?
Ez	37: 6	cover you with **s**, and put spirit

SKINS → SKIN

Ex	25: 5	rams' **s** dyed red, and tahash **s**;
Lk	5:37	the new wine will burst the **s**, and it
Lk	5:37	be spilled, and the **s** will be ruined.

SKIRT

Lam	1: 9	Her filth is on her **s**;

SKULL

2 Kgs	9:35	they found nothing of her but the **s**,
Mt	27:33	(which means Place of the **S**),

SKY → SKIES

Gn	1: 8	God called the dome "the **s**."
Dt	28:23	The **s** over your heads will be like
Mt	16: 3	for the **s** is red and threatening.'
Mt	16: 3	to judge the appearance of the **s**,
Rv	6:13	The stars in the **s** fell to the earth
Rv	6:14	the **s** was divided like a torn scroll
Rv	11: 6	close up the **s** so that no rain can fall

SLACK

Prv	18: 9	The man who is **s** in his work

SLAIN

1 Chr	10: 1	of them fell, **s** on Mount Gilboa.
Ez	37: 9	into these **s** that they may come

SLANDER → SLANDERED, SLANDERERS, SLANDERS

Ps	15: 3	Who does not **s** a neighbor, does no
2 Cor	12:20	fury, selfishness, **s**, gossip, conceit,
Col	3: 8	malice, **s**, and obscene language
1 Pt	2: 1	deceit, insincerity, envy, and all **s**;

SLANDERED → SLANDER

1 Cor	4:13	when **s**, we respond gently.

SLANDERERS → SLANDER

1 Tm	3:11	not **s**, but temperate and faithful
Ti	2: 3	not **s**, not addicted to drink,

SLANDERS → SLANDER

Ps	101: 5	Whoever **s** another in secret

SLAPPED

2 Chr	18:23	up and **s** Micaiah on the cheek,
Mt	26:67	and struck him, while some **s** him,

SLAUGHTER → SLAUGHTERED

Ex	29:11	Then **s** the bullock before the Lord,
Dt	12:15	any of your communities you may **s**
Prv	7:22	like an ox that is led to **s**;
Is	53: 7	Like a lamb led to the **s** or a sheep
Jer	11:19	Yet I, like a trusting lamb led to **s**,
Acts	8:32	"Like a sheep he was led to the **s**,

SLAUGHTERED → SLAUGHTER

Ex	12: 6	it shall be **s** during the evening
Nm	14:16	that is why he **s** them in the desert.'
Zec	11: 4	my God: Shepherd the flock to be **s**.
Rom	8:36	we are looked upon as sheep to be **s**."
Rv	6: 9	those who had been **s** because

SLAVE → ENSLAVE, SLAVERY, SLAVES

Gn	9:26	God of Shem! Let Canaan be his **s**.
Gn	21:10	"Drive out that **s** and her son! No son of that **s** is going to share
Mk	10:44	be first among you will be the **s**
Jn	8:34	everyone who commits sin is a **s**
1 Cor	7:21	Were you a **s** when you were
1 Cor	9:19	I have made myself a **s** to all so as
Gal	3:28	there is neither **s** nor free person,
Gal	4:30	"Drive out the **s** woman and her son!
Gal	4:30	of the **s** woman shall not share
Phil	2: 7	taking the form of a **s**,
Col	3:11	barbarian, Scythian, **s**, free;
Phlm	1:16	no longer as a **s** but more than a **s**,
Rv	13:16	free and **s**, to be given a stamped

SLAVERY → SLAVE

Ex	2:23	and cried out because of their **s**.
Ex	20: 2	of the land of Egypt, that place of **s**.
Dt	7: 8	his strong hand from the place of **s**,
Rom	7:14	but I am carnal, sold into **s** to sin.
Gal	5: 1	do not submit again to the yoke of **s**.
1 Tm	6: 1	of **s** must regard their masters as

SLAVES → SLAVE

Gn	9:25	The lowest of **s** shall he be to his
Eccl	10: 7	I have seen **s** on horseback,
Eccl	10: 7	princes walked on the ground like **s**.
Jer	34: 9	Everyone was to free his Hebrew **s**,
Rom	6:16	to someone as obedient **s**, you are **s**
1 Cor	7:23	Do not become **s** to human beings.
1 Cor	12:13	Jews or Greeks, **s** or free persons,
Eph	6: 5	**S**, be obedient to your human
Col	3:22	**S**, obey your human masters
Col	4: 1	treat your **s** justly and fairly,
Ti	2: 9	**S** are to be under the control of their
2 Pt	2:19	though they themselves are **s**

SLAYS

Jb	5: 2	and indignation **s** the simpleton.

SLEEP → ASLEEP, SLEEPER, SLEEPING, SLEEPLESS, SLEEPS

Gn	2:21	So the Lord God cast a deep **s**
Ex	22:26	What else has he to **s** in? If he cries
Dt	24:13	at sunset that he himself may **s** in it.
Ps	4: 9	In peace I shall both lie down and **s**,
Ps	13: 4	light to my eyes lest I **s** in death,
Ps	76: 6	bold warriors; they **s** their final **s**;
Ps	78:65	Then the Lord awoke as from **s**,
Ps	121: 3	your guardian does not **s**.
Ps	127: 2	this God gives to his beloved in **s**.
Ps	132: 4	I will give my eyes no **s**, my eyelids
Prv	6: 9	when will you rise from your **s**?
Prv	6:10	A little **s**, a little slumber, a little
Eccl	5:11	**S** is sweet to the laboring man,
Eccl	5:11	man's abundance allows him no **s**.
Is	29:10	a spirit of deep **s**. He has shut your
Dn	12: 2	Many of those who **s** in the dust
Acts	20: 9	sinking into a deep **s** as Paul talked
Acts	20: 9	Once overcome by **s**, he fell down
1 Thes	5: 7	Those who **s** go to **s** at night,

SLEEPER → SLEEP

Eph	5:14	"Awake, O **s**, and arise

SLEEPING → SLEEP

Mt	9:24	The girl is not dead but **s**." And they

SLEEPLESS → SLEEP

2 Cor	11:27	through many **s** nights,

SLEEPS → SLEEP

Ps	121: 4	of Israel never slumbers nor **s**.

SLING

Jgs	20:16	of them able to **s** a stone at a hair
1 Sm	17:50	overcame the Philistine with **s**
Prv	26: 8	one who entangles the stone in the **s**

SLIP → SLIPPED, SLIPPERY, SLIPPING

Dt	4: 9	nor let them **s** from your memory as

SLIPPED → SLIP

Ps	73: 2	I lost my balance; my feet all but **s**,

SLIPPERY → SLIP

Ps	35: 6	Make their way **s** and dark,
Ps	73:18	You set them, indeed, on a **s** road;
Jer	23:12	shall become for them **s** ground.

SLIPPING → SLIP

Ps	94:18	When I say, "My foot is **s**," your love,

SLOW

Ex	4:10	but I am **s** of speech and tongue."
Ex	34: 6	**s** to anger and rich in kindness
Nm	14:18	The Lord is **s** to anger and rich
Neh	9:17	**s** to anger and rich in mercy;
Ps	86:15	**s** to anger, most loving and true.
Ps	103: 8	**s** to anger, abounding in kindness.
Ps	145: 8	**s** to anger and abounding in love.
Prv	19:11	sense in a man to be **s** to anger,
Jl	2:13	is he, **s** to anger, rich in kindness,
Jon	4: 2	and merciful God, **s** to anger,
Na	1: 3	The Lord is **s** to anger, yet great
Lk	24:25	How **s** of heart to believe all
Jas	1:19	quick to hear, **s** to speak, **s** to wrath,

SLUGGISH

Heb	6:12	so that you may not become **s**,

SLUMBER → SLUMBERS

Prv	6:10	A little sleep, a little **s**, a little

SLUMBERS → SLUMBER

Ps	121: 4	of Israel never **s** nor sleeps.
Prv	10: 5	a son who **s** during harvest, a disgrace.

SMALL → SMALLEST

Nm	26:54	to a **s** group a **s** heritage, each group
Mk	12:42	in two **s** coins worth a few cents.
Lk	19:17	been faithful in this very **s** matter;
Jas	3: 5	same way the tongue is a **s** member
Jas	3: 5	Consider how **s** a fire can set a huge

SMALLEST → SMALL

Mk	4:31	is the **s** of all the seeds on the earth.

SMASH

Dt	12: 3	their altars, **s** their sacred pillars,

SMEAR

Ps	119:69	The arrogant **s** me with lies, but I

SMELL

Dt	4:28	see nor hear, neither eat nor **s**.
Ps	115: 6	but do not hear, noses but do not **s**.
Dn	3:94	there was not even a **s** of fire

SMOKE → SMOKING

Ex	19:18	Mount Sinai was all wrapped in **s**,
Ex	19:18	The **s** rose from it as though
Ps	68: 3	The wind will disperse them like **s**;
Ps	104:32	God touches the mountains, they **s**!
Is	6: 4	and the house was filled with **s**.
Jl	3: 3	earth, blood, fire, and columns of **s**;
Rv	8: 4	The **s** of the incense along
Rv	9: 2	**s** came up out of the passage like **s**
Rv	15: 8	so filled with the **s** from God's glory

SMOKING → SMOKE

Gn	15:17	there appeared a **s** brazier
Ex	20:18	trumpet blast and the mountain **s**,

SMOLDERING
Mt 12:20 break, a s wick he will not quench,

SMOOTH →SMOOTHER
1 Sm 17:40 David selected five s stones
Prv 6:24 from the s tongue of the adulteress.
Prv 7:21 with her s lips she leads him astray;
Lk 3: 5 straight, and the rough ways made s,

SMOOTHER →SMOOTH
Ps 55:22 hearts. S than oil are their words,
Prv 5: 3 honey, and her mouth is s than oil;

SMYRNA
Rv 2: 8 "To the angel of the church in S,

SNAKE
Ex 7:10 and it was changed into a s.
Lk 11:11 among you would hand his son a s

SNARE →ENSNARED, SNARES
Jgs 2: 3 their gods shall become a s for you."
Ps 69:23 Make their own table a s for them,
Ps 91: 3 will rescue you from the fowler's s,
Prv 29:25 The fear of man brings a s, but he
Rom 11: 9 "Let their table become a s

SNARES →SNARE
Ps 18: 6 the s of death lay in wait for me.
Prv 13:14 that a man may avoid the s of death.

SNATCHED
Acts 8:39 the Spirit of the Lord s Philip away,

SNEEZED
2 Kgs 4:35 who now s seven times and opened

SNOUT
Prv 11:22 Like a golden ring in a swine's s

SNOW
Ex 4: 6 his hand was leprous, like s.
2 Kgs 5:27 left Elisha, a leper white as s.
Ps 51: 9 wash me, make me whiter than s.
Is 1:18 they may become white as s;
Dn 7: 9 His clothing was s bright,
Mt 28: 3 and his clothing was white as s.
Rv 1:14 was as white as white wool or as s,

SO-CALLED →CALL
1 Cor 8: 5 even though there are s gods
2 Thes 2: 4 exalts himself above every s god

SOAP
Jer 2:22 Though you scour it with s, and use

SOBER
1 Thes 5: 6 rest do, but let us stay alert and s.

SOCKET
Gn 32:26 he struck Jacob's hip at its s,
Gn 32:26 that the hip s was wrenched as they

SODOM
Gn 13:12 the Plain, pitching his tents near S.
Gn 13:13 inhabitants of S were very wicked
Gn 18:20 "The outcry against S and Gomorrah
Gn 19:24 rained down sulphurous fire upon S
Is 1: 9 We had become as S, we should be
Ez 16:49 look at the guilt of your sister S:
Lk 10:12 it will be more tolerable for S
Rom 9:29 we would have become like S
Jude 1: 7 Likewise, S, Gomorrah,
Rv 11: 8 which has the symbolic names "S"

SOFT
Prv 25:15 and a s tongue will break a bone.

SOIL →SOILED
Gn 9:20 a man of the s, was the first to plant
Mt 13:23 rich s is the one who hears the word

SOILED →SOIL
Rv 3: 4 who have not s their garments;

SOLD →SELL
Gn 37:28 They s Joseph to the Ishmaelites
Dt 32:30 it was because their Rock s them

1 Mc 1:15 and s themselves to wrongdoing.
Mt 10:29 Are not two sparrows s for a small
Acts 5: 1 wife Sapphira, s a piece of property.
Rom 7:14 but I am carnal, s into slavery to sin.
1 Cor 10:25 Eat anything s in the market,
Heb 12:16 who s his birthright for a single

SOLDIER →SOLDIERS
2 Tm 2: 3 me like a good s of Christ Jesus.

SOLDIERS →SOLDIER
Mt 27:27 the s of the governor took Jesus
Mt 28:12 gave a large sum of money to the s,
Jn 19:23 When the s had crucified Jesus,

SOLE
Is 1: 6 From the s of the foot to the head

SOLID
1 Cor 3: 2 I fed you milk, not s food,
Heb 5:14 But s food is for the mature,

SOLOMON → =JEDIDIAH
Son of David by Bathsheba; king of Judah (2 Sm 12:24; 1 Chr 3:5, 10). Appointed king by David (1 Kgs 1); adversaries Adonijah, Joab, Shimei killed by Benaiah (1 Kgs 2). Asked for wisdom (1 Kgs 3; 2 Chr 1). Judged between two prostitutes (1 Kgs 3:16-28). Built temple (1 Kgs 5-7; 2 Chr 2-5); prayer of dedication (1 Kgs 8; 2 Chr 6). Visited by Queen of Sheba (1 Kgs 10; 2 Chr 9). Wives turned his heart from God (1 Kgs 11:1-13). Jeroboam rebelled against (1 Kgs 11:26-40). Death (1 Kgs 11:41-43; 2 Chr 9:29-31).
Proverbs of (1 Kgs 5:12; Prv 1:1; 10:1; 25:1); psalms of (Ps 72; 127); song of (Song 1:1).

SOLVE
Dn 5:16 interpret dreams and s difficulties;

SOME
Gn 3: 6 So she took s of its fruit and ate it;
Gn 3: 6 and she also gave s to her husband,
1 Cor 9:22 all things to all, to save at least s.
Eph 4:11 And he gave s as apostles, others as
Phil 1:15 s preach Christ from envy
1 Tm 4: 1 in the last times s will turn away
2 Tm 2:20 s for lofty and others for humble
2 Pt 3:16 In them there are s things hard

SOMEONE
Ex 4:13 "If you please, Lord, send s else!"
Lk 16:31 they be persuaded if s should rise
Rom 10:14 And how can they hear without s

SOMETHING
Nm 16:30 But if the Lᴏʀᴅ does s entirely new,
Acts 3: 5 expecting to receive s from them.
Phil 2: 6 equality with God s to be grasped.
Rv 8: 8 s like a large burning mountain was

SON →SONS
Gn 5: 3 when he begot a s in his likeness,
Gn 17:19 your wife Sarah is to bear you a s,
Gn 21: 2 bore Abraham a s in his old age,
Gn 21:10 "Drive out that slave and her s! No s
Gn 21:10 the inheritance with my s Isaac!"
Gn 22: 2 "Take your s Isaac, your only one,
Gn 22:12 from me your own beloved s."
Gn 25:11 God blessed his s Isaac, who made
Ex 4:23 Let my s go, that he may serve me.
Ex 4:23 I will kill your s, your first-born."
Dt 18:10 you anyone who immolates his s
Dt 21:18 unruly s who will not listen to his
2 Sm 7:14 to him, and he shall be a s to me.
1 Kgs 8:19 but the s who will spring from you,
2 Kgs 6:29 So we boiled my s and ate him.
2 Kgs 6:29 give up your s that we may eat him.'
1 Chr 22:10 he shall be a s to me, and I will be
Prv 1: 8 Hear, my s, your father's instruction,
Prv 2: 1 My s, if you receive my words
Ps 2: 7 who said to me, "You are my s;
Prv 3: 1 My s, forget not my teaching,
Prv 3:12 and he chastises the s he favors.
Prv 4:10 Hear, my s, and receive my words,
Prv 5: 1 My s, to my wisdom be attentive,
Prv 7: 1 My s, keep my words,

Prv	10: 1	A wise **s** makes his father glad, but a foolish **s** is a grief to his mother.
Prv	13: 1	A wise **s** loves correction,
Prv	23:26	My **s**, give me your heart,
Sir	4:10	Thus will you be like a **s**
Sir	6:18	My **s**, from youth embrace discipline;
Is	7:14	and bear a **s**, and shall name him
Is	8: 3	and she conceived and bore a **s**.
Is	9: 5	a child is born to us, a **s** is given us;
Is	66:13	As a mother comforts her **s**,
Jer	31:20	Is Ephraim not my favored **s**,
Hos	11: 1	him, out of Egypt I called my **s**.
Mal	1: 6	A **s** honors his father, and a servant
Mt	1: 1	of Jesus Christ, the **s** of David, the **s**
Mt	1:23	shall be with child and bear a **s**,
Mt	2:15	fulfilled, "Out of Egypt I called my **s**."
Mt	3:17	"This is my beloved **S**, with whom I
Mt	4: 3	"If you are the **S** of God,
Mt	8:20	the **S** of Man has nowhere to rest his
Mt	11:27	one knows the **S** except the Father,
Mt	11:27	one knows the Father except the **S**
Mt	11:27	to whom the **S** wishes to reveal him.
Mt	12: 8	For the **S** of Man is Lord
Mt	12:32	speaks a word against the **S** of Man
Mt	12:40	so will the **S** of Man be in the heart
Mt	13:55	Is he not the carpenter's **s**? Is not his
Mt	14:33	saying, "Truly, you are the **S** of God."
Mt	16:16	Messiah, the **S** of the living God."
Mt	16:27	For the **S** of Man will come with his
Mt	17: 5	"This is my beloved **S**, with whom I
Mt	19:28	when the **S** of Man is seated on his
Mt	20:18	the **S** of Man will be handed over
Mt	20:28	so, the **S** of Man did not come to be
Mt	21: 9	"Hosanna to the **S** of David;
Mt	22:42	about the Messiah? Whose **s** is he?"
Mt	24:27	will the coming of the **S** of Man be.
Mt	24:30	the sign of the **S** of Man will appear
Mt	24:30	they will see the **S** of Man coming
Mt	24:44	not expect, the **S** of Man will come.
Mt	25:31	"When the **S** of Man comes in his
Mt	26:63	you are the Messiah, the **S** of God."
Mt	27:54	said, "Truly, this was the **S** of God!"
Mt	28:19	and of the **S**, and of the holy Spirit,
Mk	1:11	the heavens, "You are my beloved **S**;
Mk	2:28	is why the **S** of Man is lord even
Mk	8:38	the **S** of Man will be ashamed
Mk	9: 7	came a voice, "This is my beloved **S**.
Mk	10:45	For the **S** of Man did not come to be
Mk	13:32	nor the **S**, but only the Father.
Mk	14:62	"I am; and 'you will see the **S** of Man
Mk	15:39	"Truly this man was the **S** of God!"
Lk	1:32	will be called **S** of the Most High,
Lk	1:35	will be called holy, the **S** of God.
Lk	2: 7	and she gave birth to her firstborn **s**.
Lk	3:22	heaven, "You are my beloved **S**;
Lk	9:35	voice that said, "This is my chosen **S**;
Lk	9:58	the **S** of Man has nowhere to rest his
Lk	12: 8	me before others the **S** of Man will
Lk	15:21	His **s** said to him, 'Father, I have
Lk	15:21	longer deserve to be called your **s**.'
Lk	18: 8	But when the **S** of Man comes,
Lk	18:31	about the **S** of Man will be fulfilled.
Lk	19:10	For the **S** of Man has come to seek
Lk	20:44	calls him 'lord,' how can he be his **s**?"
Jn	1:34	and testified that he is the **S** of God."
Jn	1:49	him, "Rabbi, you are the **S** of God;
Jn	3:14	so must the **S** of Man be lifted up,
Jn	3:16	the world that he gave his only **S**,
Jn	3:36	believes in the **S** has eternal life,
Jn	3:36	whoever disobeys the **S** will not see
Jn	5:19	a **s** cannot do anything on his own,
Jn	5:19	for what he does, his **s** will also do.
Jn	6:40	that everyone who sees the **S**
Jn	11: 4	that the **S** of God may be glorified
Jn	12:34	that the **S** of Man must be lifted up? Who is this **S** of Man?"
Jn	13:31	said, "Now is the **S** of Man glorified,
Jn	17: 1	Give glory to your **s**, so that your **s**
Acts	7:56	the **S** of Man standing at the right
Acts	13:33	in the second psalm, 'You are my **s**;
Rom	1: 4	established as **S** of God in power
Rom	5:10	to God through the death of his **S**,
Rom	8: 3	by sending his own **S** in the likeness
Rom	8:29	be conformed to the image of his **S**,
Rom	8:32	He who did not spare his own **S**
1 Cor	15:28	then the **S** himself will [also] be
Col	1:13	us to the kingdom of his beloved **S**,
1 Thes	1:10	and to await his **S** from heaven,
Heb	1: 2	he spoke to us through a **s**, whom he
Heb	1: 5	say: "You are my **s**; this day I have
Heb	1: 5	to him, and he shall be a **s** to me"?
Heb	4:14	Jesus, the **S** of God, let us hold fast
Heb	5: 5	him: "You are my **s**; this day I have
Heb	7:28	appoints a **s**, who has been made
Heb	10:29	who has contempt for the **S** of God,
Heb	12: 6	he scourges every **s** he acknowledges."
Jas	2:21	when he offered his **s** Isaac
2 Pt	1:17	glory, "This is my **S**, my beloved,
1 Jn	1: 3	Father and with his **S**, Jesus Christ.
1 Jn	1: 7	the blood of his **S** Jesus cleanses us
1 Jn	2:23	one who denies the **S** has the Father,
1 Jn	2:23	but whoever confesses the **S** has
1 Jn	3: 8	the **S** of God was revealed
1 Jn	4: 9	God sent his only **S** into the world
1 Jn	4:14	the Father sent his **S** as savior
1 Jn	5: 5	believes that Jesus is the **S** of God?
1 Jn	5:11	eternal life, and this life is in his **S**.
Rv	1:13	the lampstands one like a **s** of man,
Rv	2:18	" The **S** of God, whose eyes are like
Rv	12: 5	She gave birth to a **s**, a male child,
Rv	14:14	the cloud one who looked like a **s**

SONG →SING

Ex	15: 1	the Israelites sang this **s** to the LORD:
Dt	31:21	this **s**, which their descendants will
Dt	32:44	all the words of this **s** for the people
Ps	33: 3	Sing to God a new **s**; skillfully play
Ps	40: 4	And put a new **s** in my mouth,
Ps	69:31	That I may praise God's name in **s**
Ps	96: 1	Sing to the LORD a new **s**;
Ps	98: 4	the earth; break into **s**; sing praise.
Ps	149: 1	Sing to the LORD a new **s**, a hymn
Is	5: 1	my friend's **s** concerning his vineyard.
Is	54: 1	break forth in jubilant **s**, you who
Is	55:12	hills shall break out in **s** before you,
Rv	15: 3	and they sang the **s** of Moses,
Rv	15: 3	of God, and the **s** of the Lamb:

SONGS →SING

1 Kgs	5:12	and his **s** numbered a thousand
1 Mc	4:54	day it was reconsecrated with **s**,
Eph	5:19	psalms and hymns and spiritual **s**,
Col	3:16	and spiritual **s** with gratitude in your

SONS →SON

Gn	6: 2	the **s** of heaven saw how beautiful
Gn	9: 1	Noah and his **s** and said to them:
Gn	10:32	These are the groupings of Noah's **s**,
Gn	35:22	The **s** of Jacob were now twelve.
Ex	13:15	I redeem every first-born of my **s**.'
Ex	28: 9	on them the names of the **s** of Israel:
Nm	18: 8	and to your **s** as your priestly share.
Dt	7: 3	to their **s** nor taking their daughters for your **s**.
Ru	4:15	is worth more to you than seven **s**!"
1 Sm	1: 8	Am I not more to you than ten **s**?"
1 Mc	1:48	to leave their **s** uncircumcised,
1 Mc	2: 2	He had five **s**: John, who was called
Ps	132:12	If your **s** observe my covenant,
Ps	132:12	I shall teach them, Their **s**, in turn,
Jl	3: 1	Your **s** and daughters shall
Acts	2:17	Your **s** and your daughters shall
2 Cor	6:18	you shall be **s** and daughters to me,

SOON

Ps	106:13	But they **s** forgot all he had done;
Rv	1: 1	his servants what must happen **s**.
Rv	22: 7	"Behold, I am coming **s**." Blessed is
Rv	22:12	"Behold, I am coming **s**. I bring
Rv	22:20	testimony says, "Yes, I am coming **s**."

SOOTHSAYER → SOOTHSAYERS
Dt   18:10   fire, nor a fortune-teller, **s**, charmer,

SOOTHSAYERS → SOOTHSAYER
Is   2: 6   and **s**, like the Philistines;
Mi   5:11   shall no longer be **s** among you.

SORCERERS → SORCERY
Ex   7:11   summoned wise men and **s**,
Jer   27: 9   to your soothsayers and **s**, who say
Dn   2: 2   enchanters, **s**, and Chaldeans be
Rv   21: 8   the unchaste, **s**, idol-worshipers,
Rv   22:15   are the dogs, the **s**, the unchaste,

SORCERIES → SORCERY
Is   47: 9   you For your many **s** and the great

SORCERY → SORCERERS, SORCERIES
Gal   5:20   idolatry, **s**, hatreds, rivalry,

SORDID
Ti   1:11   for **s** gain what they should not.

SOREK
Jgs   16: 4   in the Wadi **S** whose name was

SORES
Lk   16:20   named Lazarus, covered with **s**,

SORROW → SORROWFUL, SORROWS
Est   9:22   was turned for them from **s** into joy,
Eccl   1:18   in much wisdom there is much **s**.
Is   35:10   gladness, **s** and mourning will flee.
Is   51:11   gladness, **s** and mourning will flee.
Rom   9: 2   that I have great **s** and constant

SORROWFUL → SORROW
2 Cor   6:10   as **s** yet always rejoicing; as poor

SORROWS → SORROW
Ps   16: 4   They multiply their **s** who court

SOUGHT → SEEK
1 Sm   13:14   The LORD has **s** out a man after his
2 Chr 26: 5   and as long as he **s** the LORD,
Ps   34: 5   I **s** the LORD, who answered me,
Sir   51:13   young and innocent, I **s** wisdom.

SOUL → SOULS
Dt   6: 5   and with all your **s**, and with all
Dt   10:12   with all your heart and all your **s**,
Dt   30: 6   with all your heart and all your **s**,
Jos   22: 5   him with your whole heart and **s**."
2 Kgs 23:25   his whole **s**, and his whole strength,
Ps   16: 9   my heart is glad, my **s** rejoices;
Ps   19: 8   refreshing the **s**. The decree
Ps   25: 1   I wait for you, O LORD; I lift up my **s**
Ps   33:20   Our **s** waits for the LORD, who is our
Ps   34: 3   My **s** will glory in the LORD
Ps   42: 2   so my **s** longs for you, O God.
Ps   42:12   Why are you downcast, my **s**,
Ps   62: 6   My **s**, be at rest in God alone,
Ps   63: 9   My **s** clings fast to you; your right
Ps   103: 1   Bless the LORD, my **s**; all my being,
Ps   116: 7   Return, my **s**, to your rest; the LORD
Ps   130: 5   the LORD, my **s** waits for his word.
Prv   13:19   Lust indulged starves the **s**,
Prv   24:14   must know, is wisdom to your **s**.
Sir   7:29   With all your **s**, fear God, revere his
Lam   3:20   leaves my **s** downcast within me.
Mi   6: 7   fruit of my body for the sin of my **s**?
Mt   10:28   kill the body but cannot kill the **s**;
Mt   10:28   of the one who can destroy both **s**
Mt   22:37   with all your **s**, and with all your
Lk   1:46   "My **s** proclaims the greatness
1 Thes 5:23   you entirely, spirit, **s**, and body,
Heb   4:12   penetrating even between **s**
Heb   6:19   This we have as an anchor of the **s**,
Jas   5:20   his way will save his **s** from death
1 Pt   2:11   desires that wage war against the **s**.
3 Jn   1: 2   health, just as your **s** is prospering.

SOULS → SOUL
Jer   6:16   thus you will find rest for your **s**.
1 Pt   1: 9   [your] faith, the salvation of your **s**.

1 Pt   2:25   the shepherd and guardian of your **s**.
Rv   6: 9   I saw underneath the altar the **s**
Rv   20: 4   saw the **s** of those who had been

SOUND
Gn   3: 8   they heard the **s** of the LORD God
Ex   32:18   "It does not **s** like cries of victory,
Ex   32:18   nor does it **s** like cries of defeat;
Dt   4:12   You heard the **s** of the words,
Ps   66: 8   you peoples; loudly **s** his praise,
Ps   115: 7   and no **s** rises from their throats.
Ez   1:24   Then I heard the **s** of their wings,
Jl   2: 1   **s** the alarm on my holy mountain!
Jn   3: 8   and you can hear the **s** it makes,
1 Cor 14: 8   if the bugle gives an indistinct **s**,
1 Cor 15:52   For the trumpet will **s**, the dead will
1 Tm   1:10   else is opposed to **s** teaching,
1 Tm   6: 3   does not agree with the **s** words
2 Tm   1:13   Take as your norm the **s** words
2 Tm   4: 3   will not tolerate **s** doctrine but,
Ti   1: 9   able both to exhort with **s** doctrine
Ti   2: 1   what is consistent with **s** doctrine,
Rv   1:15   his voice was like the **s** of rushing
Rv   19: 6   I heard something like the **s**
Rv   19: 6   multitude or the **s** of rushing water

SOURCE
Heb   5: 9   he became the **s** of eternal salvation

SOUTH
Dn   11: 5   "The king of the **s** shall grow strong,
Mt   12:42   the queen of the **s** will arise

SOVEREIGN
Acts   4:24   with one accord and said, "S Lord,

SOW → SOWED, SOWER, SOWN, SOWS
Ex   23:10   "For six years you may **s** your land
Jb   4: 8   and **s** trouble, reap the same.
Ps   126: 5   Those who **s** in tears will reap
Eccl 11: 6   In the morning **s** your seed,
Hos   8: 7   When they **s** the wind, they shall
Hos   10:12   "S for yourselves justice,
Mt   6:26   they do not **s** or reap, they gather
Mt   13: 3   saying: "A sower went out to **s**.
1 Cor 15:36   What you **s** is not brought to life
2 Pt   2:22   "A bathed **s** returns to wallowing

SOWED → SOW
Mt   13:24   a man who **s** good seed in his field.

SOWER → SOW
Mt   13:18   "Hear then the parable of the **s**.
Jn   4:36   so that the **s** and reaper can rejoice
2 Cor   9:10   The one who supplies seed to the **s**

SOWN → SOW
Mk   4:15   on the path where the word is **s**.
Mk   4:15   and takes away the word **s** in them.
1 Cor   9:11   If we have **s** spiritual seed for you,
1 Cor 15:42   It is **s** corruptible; it is raised

SOWS → SOW
Prv   22: 8   He who **s** iniquity reaps calamity,
Mk   4:14   The sower **s** the word.
Jn   4:37   the saying is verified that 'One **s**
2 Cor   9: 6   whoever **s** sparingly will also reap
2 Cor   9: 6   and whoever **s** bountifully will

SPAN
Is   40:12   marked off the heavens with a **s**?

SPARE → SPARED, SPARINGLY
Ps   78:50   anger; he did not **s** them from death;
Rom   11:21   God did not **s** the natural branches,
Rom   11:21   [perhaps] he will not **s** you either.
2 Pt   2: 4   God did not **s** the angels when they

SPARED → SPARE
Gn   12:13   and my life may be **s** for your sake."
Jos   6:25   Joshua **s** her with her family and all

SPARINGLY → SPARE
2 Cor   9: 6   whoever sows **s** will also reap **s**,

SPARROW → SPARROWS
Ps	84: 4	As the **s** finds a home

SPARROWS → SPARROW
Mt	10:29	Are not two **s** sold for a small coin?
Lk	12: 7	You are worth more than many **s**.

SPAT → SPIT
Lk	18:32	be mocked and insulted and **s** upon;
Jn	9: 6	he **s** on the ground and made clay

SPEAK → SPEAKER, SPEAKING, SPEAKS, SPEECH, SPOKE, SPOKEN
Gn	18:27	"See how I am presuming to **s** to my
Ex	33:11	The Lord used to **s** to Moses face
Nm	12: 8	face to face I **s** to him,
Nm	12: 8	fear to **s** against my servant Moses?"
Dt	18:20	a prophet presumes to **s** in my name
Dt	18:20	that I have not commanded him to **s**,
1 Sm	3: 9	and if you are called, reply, 'S, Lord,
2 Kgs	18:26	Do not **s** to us in Judean within
Jb	13: 3	But I would **s** with the Almighty;
Ps	49: 4	My mouth shall **s** wisdom, my heart
Ps	135:16	They have mouths but **s** not;
Prv	23: 9	S not for the fool's hearing; he will
Eccl	3: 7	a time to be silent, and a time to **s**.
Is	28:11	language he will **s** to this people
Is	40: 2	S tenderly to Jerusalem,
Jer	10: 5	they cannot **s**; They must be carried
Ez	3:18	or **s** out to dissuade him from his
Dn	7:25	He shall **s** against the Most High
Mt	13:13	This is why I **s** to them in parables,
Mk	7:37	the deaf hear and [the] mute **s**."
Jn	12:49	because I did not **s** on my own,
Jn	12:49	commanded me what to say and **s**.
Acts	2: 4	and began to **s** in different tongues,
Acts	4:18	ordered them not to **s** or teach at all
1 Cor	12:30	of healing? Do all **s** in tongues?
1 Cor	13: 1	If I **s** in human and angelic tongues,
1 Cor	14: 2	a tongue does not **s** to human beings
1 Cor	14:19	church I would rather **s** five words
Eph	4:25	putting away falsehood, **s** the truth,
Jas	1:19	to hear, slow to **s**, slow to wrath,

SPEAKER → SPEAK
Ex	6:30	"Since I am a poor **s**, how can it be

SPEAKING → SPEAK
Ex	4:12	It is I who will assist you in **s**
Dt	5:26	of the living God **s** from the midst
Mt	10:20	Spirit of your Father **s** through you.
Acts	2: 6	because each one heard them **s**
Acts	10:46	they could hear them **s** in tongues
1 Cor	14:39	and do not forbid **s** in tongues,

SPEAKS → SPEAK
Ex	33:11	to face, as one man **s** to another.
Mt	12:32	whoever **s** a word against the Son
Mt	12:32	whoever **s** against the holy Spirit
Lk	6:45	the fullness of the heart the mouth **s**.
1 Cor	14: 5	prophesies is greater than one who **s**
Heb	11: 4	through this, though dead, he still **s**.

SPEAR → SPEARS
1 Sm	19:10	to nail David to the wall with the **s**,
1 Sm	19:10	so that the **s** struck only the wall,
1 Sm	20:33	this Saul brandished his **s** to strike
Ps	46:10	breaks the bow, splinters the **s**,

SPEARS → SPEAR
Is	2: 4	and their **s** into pruning hooks;
Jl	4:10	and your pruning hooks into **s**;
Mi	4: 3	and their **s** into pruning hooks;

SPECTACLE
1 Cor	4: 9	since we have become a **s**

SPEECH → SPEAK
Ex	4:10	but I am slow of **s** and tongue."
Prv	4:24	talk, deceitful **s** put far from you.
Sir	4:29	Be not surly in your **s**, nor lazy
Jn	10: 6	Although Jesus used this figure of **s**,
1 Tm	4:12	for those who believe, in **s**, conduct,

1 Jn	3:18	let us love not in word or **s**

SPELLS
Dt	18:11	or caster of **s**, nor one who consults

SPEND → SPENT
Jgs	19:20	and do not **s** the night in the public
Is	55: 2	Why **s** your money for what is not
2 Cor	12:15	I will most gladly **s** and be utterly

SPENT → SPEND
Mk	5:26	doctors and had **s** all that she had.
Lk	6:12	and he **s** the night in prayer to God.
Lk	15:14	When he had freely **s** everything,

SPICES
Ex	25: 6	**s** for the anointing oil
1 Kgs	10:10	a very large quantity of **s**,
1 Kgs	10:10	such an abundance of **s** as the queen
Jn	19:40	with burial cloths along with the **s**,

SPIED → SPYING
Jos	6:22	directed the two men who had **s**

SPIES → SPYING
Gn	42: 9	He said to them: "You are **s**.
Jos	2: 1	secretly sent out two **s** from Shittim,
Heb	11:31	for she had received the **s** in peace.

SPIN
Mt	6:28	They do not work or **s**.

SPIRIT → SPIRITS, SPIRITUAL, SPIRITUALLY
Gn	6: 3	said: "My **s** shall not remain in man
Ex	31: 3	filled him with a divine **s** of skill
Nm	11:25	Taking some of the **s** that was
Nm	11:25	and as the **s** came to rest on them,
Nm	24: 2	tribe, the **s** of God came upon him,
Dt	34: 9	was filled with the **s** of wisdom,
Jgs	6:34	The **s** of the Lord enveloped
Jgs	11:29	The **s** of the Lord came
Jgs	13:25	the **s** of the Lord first stirred him
Jgs	14: 6	But the **s** of the Lord came
Jgs	15:14	the **s** of the Lord came upon him:
1 Sm	10: 6	The **s** of the Lord will rush
1 Sm	16:13	on, the **s** of the Lord rushed
1 Sm	16:14	The **s** of the Lord had departed
1 Sm	16:14	by an evil **s** sent by the Lord.
1 Sm	16:15	An evil **s** from God is tormenting
2 Sm	23: 2	The **s** of the Lord spoke through
2 Kgs	2: 9	I receive a double portion of your **s**."
2 Kgs	2:15	said, "The **s** of Elijah rests on Elisha."
2 Chr	18:21	become a lying **s** in the mouths
Neh	9:20	"Your good **s** you bestowed on them,
Jb	33: 4	For the **s** of God has made me,
Ps	31: 6	Into your hands I commend my **s**;
Ps	34:19	saves those whose **s** is crushed.
Ps	51:12	me, God; renew in me a steadfast **s**.
Ps	51:13	nor take from me your holy **s**.
Ps	51:19	My sacrifice, God, is a broken **s**;
Ps	106:33	They so embittered his **s** that rash
Ps	139: 7	Where can I hide from your **s**?
Ps	143:10	May your kind **s** guide me
Prv	16:18	and a haughty **s** before a fall.
Prv	29:23	who is humble of **s** obtains honor.
Wis	1: 6	For wisdom is a kindly **s**, yet she
Is	11: 2	The **s** of the Lord shall rest
Is	11: 2	a **s** of wisdom and of understanding,
Is	11: 2	A **s** of counsel and of strength,
Is	32:15	Until the **s** from on high is poured
Is	42: 1	Upon whom I have put my **s**;
Is	44: 3	pour out my **s** upon your offspring,
Is	48:16	the Lord God has sent me, and his **s**."
Is	57:15	with the crushed and dejected in **s**,
Is	59:21	the Lord: My **s** which is upon you
Is	61: 1	The **s** of the Lord God is upon me,
Is	63:10	his holy **s**; So he turned on them
Ez	3:12	Then **s** lifted me up, and I heard
Ez	11:19	heart and put a new **s** within them;
Ez	13: 3	who follow their own **s** and have
Ez	36:26	heart and place a new **s** within you,
Jl	3: 1	pour out my **s** upon all mankind.
Zec	4: 6	but by my **s**, says the Lord of hosts.

Mt	1:18	found with child through the holy **S**.
Mt	3:11	He will baptize you with the holy **S**
Mt	3:16	he saw the **S** of God descending like
Mt	4: 1	was led by the **S** into the desert
Mt	5: 3	"Blessed are the poor in **s**, for theirs
Mt	10:20	but the **S** of your Father speaking
Mt	12:31	blasphemy against the **S** will not be
Mt	26:41	The **s** is willing, but the flesh is
Mt	28:19	and of the Son, and of the holy **S**,
Mk	1: 8	he will baptize you with the holy **S**."
Lk	1:15	the holy **S** even from his mother's
Lk	1:35	"The holy **S** will come upon you,
Lk	1:80	child grew and became strong in **s**,
Lk	3:16	He will baptize you with the holy **S**
Lk	4: 1	Filled with the holy **S**,
Lk	4: 1	and was led by the **S** into the desert
Lk	4:18	"The **S** of the Lord is upon me,
Lk	11:13	heaven give the holy **S** to those who
Lk	23:46	into your hands I commend my **s**";
Jn	1:33	whomever you see the **S** come down
Jn	1:33	who will baptize with the holy **S**.'
Jn	3: 5	without being born of water and **S**.
Jn	3: 6	is flesh and what is born of **s** is **s**.
Jn	3:34	He does not ration his gift of the **S**.
Jn	4:24	God is **S**, and those who worship him must worship in **S**
Jn	6:63	It is the **s** that gives life,
Jn	6:63	words I have spoken to you are **s**
Jn	7:39	to the **S** that those who came
Jn	7:39	of course, no **S** yet, because Jesus
Jn	14:17	the **S** of truth, which the world
Jn	14:26	the holy **S** that the Father will send
Jn	15:26	the **S** of truth that proceeds
Jn	16:13	But when he comes, the **S** of truth,
Jn	20:22	said to them, "Receive the holy **S**.
Acts	1: 5	will be baptized with the holy **S**."
Acts	1: 8	when the holy **S** comes upon you,
Acts	2: 4	they were all filled with the holy **S**
Acts	2: 4	as the **S** enabled them to proclaim.
Acts	2:17	'that I will pour out a portion of my **s**
Acts	2:38	will receive the gift of the holy **S**.
Acts	4:31	they were all filled with the holy **S**
Acts	5: 3	heart so that you lied to the holy **S**
Acts	6: 3	men, filled with the **S** and wisdom,
Acts	7:51	ears, you always oppose the holy **S**;
Acts	8:15	that they might receive the holy **S**,
Acts	9:17	sight and be filled with the holy **S**."
Acts	11:16	will be baptized with the holy **S**.'
Acts	13: 2	the holy **S** said, "Set apart for me
Acts	19: 2	"Did you receive the holy **S**
Acts	19: 2	even heard that there is a holy **S**."
Rom	7: 6	may serve in the newness of the **s**
Rom	8: 4	to the flesh but according to the **s**.
Rom	8: 5	according to the **s** with the things of the **s**.
Rom	8: 9	you are in the **s**, if only the **S** of God
Rom	8: 9	Whoever does not have the **S**
Rom	8:13	by the **s** you put to death the deeds
Rom	8:15	you did not receive a **s** of slavery
Rom	8:15	but you received a **s** of adoption,
Rom	8:16	The **S** itself bears witness with our **s**
Rom	8:23	who have the firstfruits of the **S**,
Rom	8:26	the **S** too comes to the aid of our
Rom	8:26	but the **S** itself intercedes
1 Cor	2:10	has revealed to us through the **S**. For the **S** scrutinizes everything,
1 Cor	2:14	what pertains to the **S** of God,
1 Cor	5: 3	absent in body but present in **s**,
1 Cor	6:17	to the Lord becomes one **s** with him.
1 Cor	6:19	is a temple of the holy **S** within you,
1 Cor	12: 4	of spiritual gifts but the same **S**;
1 Cor	12:13	in one **S** we were all baptized
1 Cor	12:13	we were all given to drink of one **S**.
2 Cor	1:22	given the **S** in our hearts as a first
2 Cor	3: 3	ink but by the **S** of the living God,
2 Cor	3: 6	new covenant, not of letter but of **s**;
2 Cor	3: 6	brings death, but the **S** gives life.
2 Cor	3:17	Now the Lord is the **S**, and where the **S** of the Lord is,
2 Cor	5: 5	who has given us the **S** as a first

2 Cor	7: 1	every defilement of flesh and **s**,
Gal	3: 2	did you receive the **S** from works
Gal	3:14	the promise of the **S** through faith.
Gal	5:16	live by the **S** and you will certainly
Gal	5:22	the fruit of the **S** is love, joy, peace,
Gal	5:25	If we live in the **S**, let us also follow the **S**.
Gal	6: 8	sows for the **s** will reap eternal life from the **s**.
Eph	1:13	sealed with the promised holy **S**,
Eph	2:18	have access in one **S** to the Father.
Eph	4: 3	the unity of the **s** through the bond
Eph	4: 4	one body and one **S**, as you were
Eph	4:30	do not grieve the holy **S** of God,
Eph	5:18	debauchery, but be filled with the **S**,
Eph	6:17	of salvation and the sword of the **S**,
Col	2: 5	yet I am with you in **s**, rejoicing as I
1 Thes	5:19	Do not quench the **S**.
1 Thes	5:23	holy and may you entirely, **s**, soul,
2 Thes	2:13	through sanctification by the **S**
1 Tm	3:16	vindicated in the **s**, seen by angels,
2 Tm	1: 7	For God did not give us a **s**
2 Tm	4:22	The Lord be with your **s**. Grace be
Heb	2: 4	of the holy **S** according to his will.
Heb	4:12	even between soul and **s**,
Heb	6: 4	gift and shared in the holy **S**
Heb	10:29	and insults the **s** of grace?
1 Pt	1: 2	through sanctification by the **S**,
2 Pt	1:21	the holy **S** spoke under the influence
1 Jn	3:24	in us is from the **S** that he gave us.
1 Jn	4: 1	do not trust every **s** but test
1 Jn	4:13	in us, that he has given us of his **S**.
Jude	1:20	most holy faith; pray in the holy **S**.
Rv	1:10	was caught up in **s** on the Lord's day
Rv	2: 7	ought to hear what the **S** says
Rv	4: 2	At once I was caught up in **s**.

SPIRITS → SPIRIT

Nm	16:22	God of the **s** of all mankind,
Nm	27:16	the God of the **s** of all mankind,
Dt	18:11	nor one who consults ghosts and **s**
Mt	12:45	itself seven other **s** more evil than
Lk	4:36	power he commands the unclean **s**,
Acts	8: 7	For unclean **s**, crying out in a loud
1 Cor	12:10	to another discernment of **s**;
1 Cor	14:32	the **s** of prophets are under
Heb	12: 9	all the more to the Father of **s**
1 Pt	3:19	went to preach to the **s** in prison,
1 Jn	4: 1	test the **s** to see whether they belong
Rv	1: 4	from the seven **s** before his throne,
Rv	16:13	saw three unclean **s** like frogs come
Rv	22: 6	the God of prophetic **s**, sent his

SPIRITUAL → SPIRIT

Rom	1:11	I may share with you some **s** gift so
Rom	7:14	We know that the law is **s**; but I am
Rom	12: 1	pleasing to God, your **s** worship.
Rom	15:27	come to share in their **s** blessings,
1 Cor	2:13	describing **s** realities in **s** terms.
1 Cor	3: 1	I could not talk to you as **s** people,
1 Cor	9:11	If we have sown **s** seed for you, is it
1 Cor	10: 3	All ate the same **s** food,
1 Cor	12: 1	Now in regard to **s** gifts, brothers,
1 Cor	14: 1	but strive eagerly for the **s** gifts,
1 Cor	15:44	a natural body; it is raised a **s** body.
1 Cor	15:44	a natural body, there is also a **s** one.
1 Cor	15:46	But the **s** was not first;
1 Cor	15:46	rather the natural and then the **s**.
Eph	1: 3	Christ with every **s** blessing
Eph	5:19	[in] psalms and hymns and **s** songs,
Col	1: 9	of his will through all **s** wisdom
Col	3:16	**s** songs with gratitude in your hearts
1 Pt	2: 2	long for pure **s** milk so that through
1 Pt	2: 5	let yourselves be built into a **s** house
1 Pt	2: 5	to offer **s** sacrifices acceptable

SPIRITUALLY → SPIRIT

1 Cor	2:14	understand it, because it is judged **s**.

SPIT → SPAT

Dt	25: 9	from his foot and **s** in his face,
Mk	14:65	Some began to **s** on him.
Rv	3:16	cold, I will **s** you out of my mouth.

SPLENDOR

Jb	37:22	From the North the s comes,
Ps	21: 6	majesty and s you confer upon him.
Ps	29: 2	Bow down before the Lord's holy s!
Ps	145: 5	of the s of your majestic glory,
Ps	145:12	power, the glorious s of your rule.
Eph	5:27	present to himself the church in s,

SPLIT

Nm	16:31	the ground beneath them s open,
Mt	27:51	The earth quaked, rocks were s,
Rv	16:19	The great city was s into three parts,

SPOIL → SPOILS

Ps	119:162	as one who has found rich s.

SPOILS → SPOIL

Ex	15: 9	I will divide the s and have my fill

SPOKE → SPEAK

Gn	16:13	To the Lord who s to her she gave
Dt	4:12	the Lord s to you from the midst
Dt	5: 4	The Lord s with you face to face
Ps	99: 7	the pillar of cloud God s to them;
Mt	9:33	was driven out the mute person s.
Mk	4:33	many such parables he s the word
2 Cor	4:13	therefore I s," we too believe
Heb	1: 1	God s in partial and various ways
Heb	13: 7	your leaders who s the word of God
2 Pt	1:21	the holy Spirit s under the influence

SPOKEN → SPEAK

Dt	18:22	prophet has s it presumptuously,
Jb	42: 7	the Lord had s these words to Job,
Jb	42: 7	you have not s rightly concerning
Prv	25:11	are words s at the proper time.

SPONGE

Jn	19:29	So they put a s soaked in wine

SPOT → SPOTS, SPOTTED

Eph	5:27	without s or wrinkle or any such
2 Pt	3:14	be eager to be found without s

SPOTS → SPOT

Jer	13:23	the leopard his s? As easily would

SPOTTED → SPOT

Gn	30:32	every s or speckled one among
Zec	6: 3	and the fourth chariot s horses—

SPRANG → SPRING

Mt	13: 5	It s up at once because the soil was
Mk	4: 5	It s up at once because the soil was

SPREAD → SPREADING

Ex	37: 9	The cherubim had their wings s
Ps	78:19	"Can God s a table in the desert?
Is	48:13	my right hand s out the heavens.
Ez	1:11	Each had two wings s out above so
Mk	11: 8	Many people s their cloaks
Mk	11: 8	others s leafy branches that they had
Jn	21:23	So the word s among the brothers
Acts	6: 7	The word of God continued to s,
Acts	13:49	to s through the whole region.
2 Tm	2:17	their teaching will s like gangrene.

SPREADING → SPREAD

1 Sm	2:24	the people of the Lord s about you.
Prv	29: 5	neighbor is s a net under his feet.

SPRING → SPRANG, SPRINGS

Gn	16: 7	found her by a s in the wilderness,
Ps	85:12	Truth will s from the earth;
Is	45: 8	let justice also s up! I, the Lord,
Is	58:11	like a s whose water never fails.
Jer	8:23	Oh, that my head were a s of water,
Jn	4:14	become in him a s of water welling
Rv	21: 6	gift from the s of life-giving water.

SPRINGS → SPRING

Is	49:10	and guides them beside s of water.
2 Pt	2:17	These people are waterless s
Rv	7:17	lead them to s of life-giving water,

SPRINKLE → SPRINKLED

Nm	8: 7	S them with the water of remission;
2 Mc	1:21	Nehemiah ordered the priests to s
Ez	36:25	I will s clean water upon you

SPRINKLED → SPRINKLE

Lv	8:11	he s some of this oil seven times
Heb	10:22	with our hearts s clean from an evil
Heb	11:28	he kept the Passover and s the blood,

SPROUT

Nm	17:20	of the man of my choice shall s.

SPURN

Jer	14:21	For your name's sake s us not,

SPYING → SPIED, SPIES

Gn	42:30	custody as if we were s on the land.

SQUANDERED

Lk	15:13	country where he s his inheritance

SQUARE → SQUARES

Gn	19: 2	shall pass the night in the town s."
Ex	27: 1	on a s, five cubits long and five
Ex	28:16	It is to be s when folded double,
Ex	30: 2	with a s surface, a cubit long,
Jgs	19:20	not spend the night in the public s."

SQUARES → SQUARE

Prv	1:20	in the open s she raises her voice;

STABILITY

Prv	29: 4	By justice a king gives s to the land;

STAFF → STAFFS

Gn	38:25	seal and cord and whose s these are."
Ex	4: 4	of it, and it became a s in his hand.
Ex	7:12	Each one threw down his s, and it
Ex	7:12	But Aaron's s swallowed their staffs.
Ex	14:16	you, lift up your s and, with hand
Nm	17:21	prince; and Aaron's s was with them.
Nm	20:11	struck the rock twice with his s,
Ps	23: 4	your rod and s give me courage.
Mi	7:14	Shepherd your people with your s,
Zec	11:10	I took my s "Favor" and snapped it

STAFFS → STAFF

Nm	17:22	Moses laid the s down before

STAGES

Nm	33: 1	The following are the s

STAGGER → STAGGERED

Is	28: 7	But these also s from wine
Is	28: 7	and prophet s from strong drink,
Is	29: 9	wine, s, but not from strong drink!

STAGGERED → STAGGER

Ps	107:27	They reeled, s like drunkards;

STAIN

Jer	2:22	The s of your guilt is still before

STAIRWAY

Gn	28:12	a dream: a s rested on the ground,

STAKES

Is	54: 2	your ropes and make firm your s.

STALK → STALKS

Gn	41: 5	and healthy, growing on a single s.

STALKS → STALK

Jos	2: 6	hidden them among her s of flax

STALL → STALLS

Mal	3:20	will gambol like calves out of the s

STALLS → STALL

1 Kgs	5: 6	Solomon had four thousand s for his
Hb	3:17	fold and there be no herd in the s,

STAND → STANDING, STANDS, STOOD

Ex	9:11	The magicians could not s in Moses'
Ex	14:13	S your ground, and you will see
Dt	11:25	None shall s up against you;
Jos	10:12	of Israel: S still, O sun, at Gibeon,
2 Chr	20:17	Take your places, s firm, and see

Jb	19:25	he will at last **s** forth upon the dust;
Ps	10: 1	Why, Lord, do you **s** at a distance
Ps	24: 3	Lord? Who can **s** in his holy place?
Ps	76: 8	who can **s** before you and your great
Ps	130: 3	mark our sins, Lord, who can **s**?
Ez	22:30	or **s** in the breach before me to keep
Mi	5: 3	He shall **s** firm and shepherd his
Mal	3: 2	And who can **s** when he appears?
Mt	12:25	house divided against itself will **s**.
Rom	5: 2	faith] to this grace in which we **s**,
Rom	14: 4	for the Lord is able to make him **s**.
Rom	14:10	we shall all **s** before the judgment
1 Cor	16:13	on your guard, **s** firm in the faith,
2 Cor	1:24	your joy, for you **s** firm in the faith.
Eph	6:11	be able to **s** firm against the tactics
2 Thes	2:15	**s** firm and hold fast to the traditions

STANDARDS
1 Cor	1:26	many of you were wise by human **s**,

STANDING → STAND
Gn	18:22	Lord remained **s** before Abraham.
Nm	22:23	the angel of the Lord **s** on the road
2 Chr	18:18	the whole host of heaven **s** by to his
Am	7: 7	this: he was **s** by a wall,
Am	9: 1	I saw the Lord **s** beside the altar,
Zec	1: 8	**s** among myrtle trees in a shady
Zec	3: 1	the high priest **s** before the angel
Acts	7:55	and Jesus **s** at the right hand of God,
1 Cor	10:12	thinks he is **s** secure should take
1 Tm	3:13	serve well as deacons gain good **s**
Jas	5: 9	the Judge is **s** before the gates.
Rv	20:12	and the lowly, **s** before the throne,

STANDS → STAND
1 Kgs	7:27	Ten **s** were also made of bronze,
Ps	26:12	My foot is **s** on level ground;
2 Tm	2:19	God's solid foundation **s**,

STAR → STARS
Nm	24:17	near: A **s** shall advance from Jacob,
Sir	50: 6	Like a **s** shining among the clouds,
Is	14:12	O morning **s**, son of the dawn!
Mt	2: 2	We saw his **s** at its rising and have
2 Pt	1:19	the morning **s** rises in your hearts.
Rv	2:28	to him I will give the morning **s**.
Rv	8:11	The **s** was called "Wormwood,"
Rv	9: 1	I saw a **s** that had fallen
Rv	22:16	of David, the bright morning **s**."

STARS → STAR
Gn	1:16	govern the night; and he made the **s**.
Gn	15: 5	"Look up at the sky and count the **s**,
Gn	37: 9	eleven **s** were bowing down to me."
Dt	1:10	you are now as numerous as the **s**
Jb	38: 7	While the morning **s** sang in chorus
Ps	148: 3	and moon; give praise, all shining **s**.
Is	14:13	Above the **s** of God I will set up my
Dn	3:63	S of heaven, bless the Lord;
Dn	12: 3	to justice shall be like the **s** forever.
Jl	2:10	and the **s** withhold their brightness.
Mk	13:25	the **s** will be falling from the sky,
Rv	1:16	In his right hand he held seven **s**.
Rv	6:13	The **s** in the sky fell to the earth like
Rv	8:12	and a third of the **s** were struck,
Rv	12: 1	on her head a crown of twelve **s**.
Rv	12: 4	away a third of the **s** in the sky

STATE
1 Cor	7:20	remain in the **s** in which he was called.

STATUE
Dn	2:31	O king, you saw a **s**, very large
Dn	3: 1	had a golden **s** made, sixty cubits

STATURE
1 Sm	2:26	young Samuel was growing in **s**

STATUTES
Dt	4: 1	hear the **s** and decrees which I am
1 Kgs	3: 3	obeyed the **s** of his father David;
1 Kgs	11:33	is pleasing to me according to my **s**
Neh	9:13	laws, good **s**, and commandments;

Is	24: 5	have transgressed laws, violated **s**,

STAY
Ex	16:29	seventh day everyone is to **s** home

STEADFAST
Ps	57: 8	My heart is **s**, God, my heart is **s**.
Ps	108: 2	My heart is **s**, God; my heart is **s**.
1 Pt	5: 9	Resist him, **s** in faith,

STEADY
Ex	17:12	that his hands remained **s** till sunset.

STEAL → STEALING, STOLE, STOLEN
Gn	31:30	house, why did you **s** my gods?"
Ex	20:15	"You shall not **s**.
Dt	5:19	'You shall not **s**.
Jer	23:30	who **s** my words from each other.
Mt	6:19	destroys, and thieves break in and **s**.
Mt	19:18	you shall not **s**; you shall not bear
Jn	10:10	A thief comes only to **s**
Rom	2:21	preach against stealing, do you **s**?
Rom	13: 9	you shall not **s**; you shall not covet,"

STEALING → STEAL
Rom	2:21	You who preach against **s**, do you

STEPHEN
Early church leader (Acts 6:5). Arrested (Acts 6:8-15). Speech to Sanhedrin (Acts 7). Stoned (Acts 7:54-60; 8:2; 11:19; 22:20).

STEPS
Ex	20:26	You shall not go up by **s** to my altar,
Ps	37:23	Those whose **s** are guided
Prv	5: 5	to the nether world her **s** attain;
Prv	14:15	but the shrewd man measures his **s**.
Prv	16: 9	course, but the Lord directs his **s**.
Prv	20:24	Man's **s** are from the Lord; how,

STEW
Gn	25:29	when Jacob was cooking a **s**,
2 Kgs	4:39	pot of vegetable **s** without anybody's

STEWARD → STEWARDS, STEWARDSHIP
Ti	1: 7	bishop as God's **s** must be blameless,

STEWARDS → STEWARD
1 Cor	4: 2	of course required of **s** that they be
1 Pt	4:10	serve one another as good **s** of God's

STEWARDSHIP → STEWARD
1 Cor	9:17	I have been entrusted with a **s**.
Eph	3: 2	heard of the **s** of God's grace
Col	1:25	minister in accordance with God's **s**

STICK
2 Kgs	6: 6	Elisha cut off a **s**, threw it
Ez	37:16	man, take a single **s**, and write on it:
Ez	37:16	Then take another **s** and write on it:

STIFF-NECKED → NECK, STIFFENED
Ex	32: 9	I see how **s** this people is,"
Ex	34: 9	This is indeed a **s** people;
Bar	2:30	me, because they are a **s** people.
Acts	7:51	"You **s** people,

STIFFENED → STIFF-NECKED
Jer	19:15	because they have **s** their necks

STILL → STILLBORN
Ex	14:14	for you; you have only to keep **s**."
Jos	10:13	And the sun stood **s**, and the moon
Ps	37: 7	Be **s** before the Lord; wait for God.
Ps	46:11	"Be **s** and confess that I am God!
Ps	83: 2	silent; God, be not **s** and unmoved!
Ps	89:10	raging sea; you **s** its swelling waves.
Dn	11:35	the end time which is **s** appointed
Mk	4:39	Be **s**!" The wind ceased and there
Rom	5: 8	while we were **s** sinners Christ died
Heb	11: 4	this, though dead, he **s** speaks.
Rv	22:11	Let the wicked **s** act wickedly, and the filthy **s** be filthy.
Rv	22:11	The righteous must **s** do right, and the holy **s** be holy."

STILLBORN →BEAR, STILL
Nm   12:12   Let her not thus be like the **s** babe

STING
1 Cor 15:55   victory? Where, O death, is your **s**?"

STIR →STIRRED, STIRS
Ps   80: 3   **S** up your power, come to save us.
Song   2: 7   Do not arouse, do not **s** up love

STIRRED →STIR
Sir   51:21   My whole being was **s** as I learned
Hg   1:14   Then the LORD **s** up the spirit
Acts   13:50   **s** up a persecution against Paul

STIRS →STIR
Prv   10:12   Hatred **s** up disputes, but love
Prv   15: 1   wrath, but a harsh word **s** up anger.
Prv   28:25   The greedy man **s** up disputes,
Prv   29:22   An ill-tempered man **s** up disputes,

STOIC
Acts   17:18   and **S** philosophers engaged him

STOLE →STEAL
Mt   28:13   and **s** him while we were asleep.'

STOLEN →STEAL
Prv   9:17   **S** water is sweet, and bread gotten

STOMACH
Ez   3: 3   and fill your **s** with this scroll I am
Mk   7:19   the **s** and passes out into the latrine?"
1 Cor   6:13   "Food for the **s** and the **s** for food,"
1 Tm   5:23   a little wine for the sake of your **s**
Rv   10: 9   It will turn your **s** sour, but in your

STONE →CORNERSTONE, MILLSTONE, STONED, STONES,
STONING
Gn   28:18   the next morning Jacob took the **s**
Gn   28:18   head, set it up as a memorial **s**,
Gn   31:45   Jacob took a **s** and set it up as a memorial **s**.
Gn   35:14   Jacob set up a memorial **s**,
Ex   17: 4   A little more and they will **s** me!"
Ex   28:10   six of their names on one **s**, and the other six on
                the other **s**,
Ex   31:18   the **s** tablets inscribed by God's own
Ex   34: 1   "Cut two **s** tablets like the former,
Dt   4:13   which he wrote on two tablets of **s**.
Dt   28:36   serve strange gods of wood and **s**,
1 Sm   7:12   then took a **s** and placed it between
1 Sm   17:50   the Philistine with sling and **s**;
Ps   91:12   lest you strike your foot against a **s**.
Ps   118:22   The **s** the builders rejected
Is   8:14   snare, an obstacle and a stumbling **s**
Is   28:16   See, I am laying a **s** in Zion, a **s**
Jer   3: 9   committing adultery with **s**
Zec   3: 9   at the **s** that I have placed before
Zec   3: 9   Joshua, one **s** with seven facets.
Mt   4: 6   lest you dash your foot against a **s**.' "
Mt   7: 9   you would hand his son a **s** when he
Mt   24: 2   there will not be left here a **s**
Mk   12:10   The **s** that the builders rejected
Mk   16: 3   "Who will roll back the **s** for us
Lk   4: 3   command this **s** to become bread."
Lk   20:18   on that **s** will be dashed to pieces;
Jn   8: 7   sin be the first to throw a **s** at her."
Jn   10:32   of these are you trying to **s** me?"
Jn   19:13   in the place called **S** Pavement,
Acts   4:11   He is 'the **s** rejected by you,
Rom   9:32   They stumbled over the **s**
2 Cor   3: 3   not on tablets of **s** but on tablets
1 Pt   2: 4   a living **s**, rejected by human beings
1 Pt   2: 6   "Behold, I am laying a **s** in Zion,

STONED →STONE
Nm   15:36   outside the camp and **s** him to death,
Jos   7:25   us!" And all Israel **s** him to death
1 Kgs 21:13   out of the city and **s** him to death.
2 Chr 24:21   the king's order they **s** him to death
Acts   14:19   They **s** Paul and dragged him
Heb   11:37   They were **s**, sawed in two,

STONES →STONE
Ex   28: 9   "Get two onyx **s** and engrave
Dt   27: 2   set up some large **s** and coat them
Jos   4: 3   to take up twelve **s** from this spot
1 Sm   17:40   David selected five smooth **s**
1 Kgs 18:31   He took twelve **s**, for the number
Ps   102:15   Its **s** are dear to your servants;
Eccl   3: 5   A time to scatter **s**, and a time
Sir   21:10   The path of sinners is smooth **s**
Mt   3: 9   children to Abraham from these **s**.
Mt   4: 3   that these **s** become loaves of bread."
Mk   13: 1   teacher, what **s** and what buildings!"
Lk   19:40   they keep silent, the **s** will cry out!"
1 Cor   3:12   gold, silver, precious **s**, wood, hay,
1 Pt   2: 5   like living **s**, let yourselves be built

STONING →STONE
1 Sm   30: 6   for the men spoke of **s** him, so bitter
Acts   7:59   As they were **s** Stephen, he called

STOOD →STAND
Ex   15: 8   the flowing waters **s** like a mound,
Jos   10:13   And the sun **s** still, and the moon
Lk   10:25   was a scholar of the law who **s**
Lk   22:28   It is you who have **s** by me in my
Jn   20:19   Jesus came and **s** in their midst
2 Tm   4:17   But the Lord **s** by me and gave me

STOOP
Mk   1: 7   I am not worthy to **s** and loosen

STOP →STOPPED
Gn   19:17   back or **s** anywhere on the Plain.

STOPPED →STOP
2 Kgs   4: 6   he answered her. And then the oil **s**.

STORE →SHOREHOUSE, STORING
Sir   29:12   **S** up almsgiving in your treasure
Mt   6:19   "Do not **s** up for yourselves treasures
Lk   12:17   I do not have space to **s** my harvest?'

STOREHOUSE →HOUSE, STORE
Mal   3:10   into the **s**, That there may be food

STORING →STORE
Rom   2: 5   you are **s** up wrath for yourself

STORM
Ps   107:29   Hushed the **s** to a murmur;
Jer   30:23   See, the **s** of the LORD! His wrath
Jer   30:23   In a whirling **s** that bursts
Jon   1:12   me that this violent **s** has come

STRAIGHT
Prv   3: 6   him, and he will make **s** your paths.
Prv   4:25   Let your eyes look **s** ahead and your
Prv   11: 5   honest man's virtue makes his way **s**,
Prv   15:21   of understanding goes the **s** way.
Eccl   7:29   God made mankind **s**, but men
Sir   2: 6   make **s** your ways and hope in him.
Is   40: 3   Make **s** in the wasteland a highway
Mt   3: 3   way of the Lord, make **s** his paths.' "
Lk   3: 5   The winding roads shall be made **s**,
Jn   1:23   desert, "Make **s** the way of the Lord," '
Acts   9:11   go to the street called **S** and ask
2 Pt   2:15   Abandoning the **s** road, they have

STRAIN →STRAINING
Mt   23:24   who **s** out the gnat and swallow

STRAINING →STRAIN
Phil   3:13   but **s** forward to what lies ahead,

STRANGE →STRANGER, STRANGERS
Dt   32:16   They provoked him with **s** gods
1 Cor 14:21   "By people speaking **s** tongues
Heb   13: 9   away by all kinds of **s** teaching. It is
1 Pt   4:12   as if something **s** were happening

STRANGER →STRANGE
Mt   25:35   drink, a **s** and you welcomed me,
Jn   10: 5   But they will not follow a **s**;

STRANGERS →STRANGE
1 Chr 16:19   in number, a handful, and **s** there,

1 Mc	1:38	and she became the abode of s.
Prv	5:17	yours alone, not one shared with s;
Eph	2:12	and s to the covenants of promise,
Heb	11:13	acknowledged themselves to be s
3 Jn	1: 5	do for the brothers, especially for s;

STRAW

Ex	5:10	I will not provide you with s.
1 Cor	3:12	precious stones, wood, hay, or s,

STRAY → ASTRAY, STRAYED

Ps	119:10	seek you; do not let me s from your

STRAYED → STRAY

Wis	5: 6	then, have s from the way of truth,
Hos	7:13	Woe to them, they have s from me!

STREAM → STREAMS

Is	2: 2	All nations shall s toward it;
Am	5:24	and goodness like an unfailing s.
Mi	4: 1	the hills, And peoples shall s to it:

STREAMS → STREAM

Ps	1: 3	like a tree planted near s of water,
Ps	42: 2	As the deer longs for s of water,
Ps	46: 5	S of the river gladden the city
Is	35: 6	S will burst forth in the desert,

STREET → STREETS

Prv	1:20	Wisdom cries aloud in the s,
Mt	6: 5	on s corners so that others may see
Acts	9:11	go to the s called Straight and ask
Rv	21:21	the s of the city was of pure gold,
Rv	22: 2	down the middle of its s. On either

STREETS → STREET

Ps	144:14	walls, no exile, no outcry in our s.
Zec	8: 5	with boys and girls playing in her s.
Mt	12:19	will anyone hear his voice in the s.

STRENGTH → STRONG

Ex	15: 2	My s and my courage is the LORD,
Dt	33:25	may your s endure through all your
Jgs	16:15	told me the secret of your great s!"
1 Sm	2: 9	For not by s does man prevail;
2 Sm	22:33	The God who girded me with s
1 Chr	16:11	Look to the LORD in his s;
1 Chr	29:12	yours to give grandeur and s to all.
Neh	8:10	in the LORD must be your s!"
Jdt	9:11	"Your s is not in numbers, nor does
1 Mc	3:19	but on s that comes from Heaven.
Ps	18: 2	He said: I love you, LORD, my s,
Ps	28: 7	The LORD is my s and my shield,
Ps	46: 2	God is our refuge and our s,
Ps	59:10	My s, for you I watch; you, God,
Ps	59:18	My s, your praise I will sing; you,
Ps	118:14	The LORD, my s and might,
Ps	147:10	takes no delight in the s of horses,
Prv	31:25	She is clothed with s and dignity,
Is	12: 2	My s and my courage is the LORD,
Is	40:26	great might and the s of his power
Is	40:31	hope in the LORD will renew their s,
Mi	5: 3	by the s of the LORD, in the majestic
Hb	3:19	GOD, my Lord, is my s; he makes
Mk	12:30	all your mind, and with all your s.'
Lk	10:27	with all your s, and with all your
1 Cor	1:25	of God is stronger than human s.
2 Tm	4:17	Lord stood by me and gave me s,
1 Pt	4:11	it be with the s that God supplies,

STRENGTHEN → STRONG

Jgs	16:28	S me, O God, this last time
Ps	119:28	in accord with your word to s me.
Is	35: 3	S the hands that are feeble,
Is	41:10	I will s you, and help you,
Lk	22:32	back, you must s your brothers."
1 Thes	3:13	so as to s your hearts, to be
2 Thes	2:17	and s them in every good deed
Heb	12:12	So s your drooping hands and your
1 Pt	5:10	confirm, s, and establish you

STRENGTHENED → STRONG

Acts	15:32	and s the brothers with many words.

Heb	13: 9	is good to have our hearts s by grace

STRETCH → OUTSTRETCHED, STRETCHED

Ex	3:20	I will s out my hand, therefore,
Ps	138: 7	enemies rage. You s out your hand;
Zep	1: 4	I will s out my hand against Judah,
Mk	3: 5	he said to the man, "S out your hand."
Acts	4:30	as you s forth [your] hand to heal,

STRETCHED → STRETCH

Ex	14:21	Moses s out his hand over the sea,
2 Sm	24:16	the angel s forth his hand toward
1 Kgs	13: 4	he s forth his hand from the altar
1 Kgs	13: 4	But the hand he s forth against him
Is	45:12	It was my hands that s
Jer	10:12	and s out the heavens by his skill.
Mt	12:13	He s it out, and it was restored as

STRICKEN → STRIKE

Is	53: 4	While we thought of him as s,

STRICT → STRICTEST

Acts	5:28	"We gave you s orders [did we not?]

STRICTEST → STRICT

Acts	26: 5	Pharisee, the s party of our religion.

STRIFE

Prv	17: 1	than a house full of feasting with s.
Prv	18: 6	The fool's lips lead him into s,
Prv	20: 3	It is honorable for a man to shun s,
Prv	22:10	discord goes out; s and insult cease.
Prv	23:29	Who have s? Who have anxiety?

STRIKE → STRICKEN, STRIKES, STRUCK

Gn	3:15	He will s at your head, while you s at his heel."
Ex	17: 6	S the rock, and the water will flow
Is	11: 4	He shall s the ruthless with the rod
Zec	13: 7	the LORD of hosts: S the shepherd
Mal	3:24	Lest I come and s the land
Mk	14:27	it is written: 'I will s the shepherd,
Rv	19:15	came a sharp sword to s the nations.

STRIKES → STRIKE

Ex	21:12	"Whoever s a man a mortal blow
Mt	5:39	When someone s you on [your]

STRIPPED

Gn	37:23	they s him of the long tunic he had
Mt	27:28	They s off his clothes and threw
Acts	16:22	and the magistrates had them s

STRIVE

1 Cor	12:31	S eagerly for the greatest spiritual

STRONG → STRENGTH, STRENGTHEN, STRENGTHENED, STRONGER, STRONGHOLD

Ps	140: 8	My revered LORD, my s helper,
Prv	18:10	The name of the LORD is a s tower;
Is	35: 4	hearts are frightened: Be s, fear not!
Jer	50:34	S is their avenger, whose name is
Dn	2:40	shall be a fourth kingdom, s as iron;
Zec	8: 9	Let your hands be s, you who
Mt	12:29	can anyone enter a s man's house
Mt	12:29	unless he first ties up the s man?
Lk	1:80	child grew and became s in spirit,
Lk	2:40	The child grew and became s,
Rom	15: 1	We who are s ought to put
1 Cor	1:27	weak of the world to shame the s,
1 Cor	16:13	in the faith, be courageous, be s.
2 Cor	12:10	for when I am weak, then I am s.
2 Tm	2: 1	be s in the grace that is in Christ

STRONGER → STRONG

2 Sm	3: 1	in which David grew s,
1 Cor	1:25	of God is s than human strength.

STRONGHOLD → STRONG

Ps	9:10	The LORD is a s for the oppressed, a s in times of trouble.
Ps	18: 3	my shield, my saving horn, my s!
Ps	144: 2	and my fortress, my s, my deliverer,

STRUCK → STRIKE

Gn	32:26	him, he s Jacob's hip at its socket,

Nm	20:11	Moses s the rock twice with his
1 Sm	17:49	and s the Philistine on the forehead.
Ps	78:20	True, when he s the rock,
Dn	2:34	put to it, s its iron and tile feet,
Acts	23: 3	of the law order me to be s?"

STRUGGLE
Eph	6:12	For our s is not with flesh and blood
Heb	12: 4	your s against sin you have not yet

STUBBLE
Ex	15: 7	your wrath to consume them like s.
Is	33:11	conceive dry grass, bring forth s;
Mal	3:19	the proud and all evildoers will be s,

STUBBORN → STUBBORNLY, STUBBORNNESS
Hos	4:16	For Israel is as s as a heifer;

STUBBORNLY → STUBBORN
Ex	13:15	When Pharaoh s refused to let us

STUBBORNNESS → STUBBORN
Dt	9:27	not upon the s of this people nor

STUDY
Ezr	7:10	Ezra had set his heart on the s
Eccl	12:12	in much s there is weariness

STUMBLE → STUMBLED, STUMBLING
Ps	37:24	May s, but they will never fall,
Prv	3:23	go your way; your foot will never s;
Prv	4:12	and should you run, you will not s.
Jer	13:16	Before your feet s on darkening
Jer	31: 9	on a level road, so that none shall s.
Hos	14:10	the just walk, but sinners s in them.
Jn	11: 9	he does not s, because he sees
Rom	9:33	that will make people s and a rock
1 Pt	2: 8	"A stone that will make people s,
1 Pt	2: 8	They s by disobeying the word, as is

STUMBLED → STUMBLE
Rom	9:32	They s over the stone that causes

STUMBLING → STUMBLE
Rom	9:32	over the stone that causes s,
Rom	11: 9	a s block and a retribution for them;
Rom	14:13	rather resolve never to put a s block
1 Cor	1:23	a s block to Jews and foolishness
1 Cor	8: 9	in no way becomes a s block

STUMP
Is	11: 1	shall sprout from the s of Jesse,

STUPID
Prv	12: 1	but he who hates reproof is s.

SUBDUE
Gn	1:28	and multiply; fill the earth and s it.
1 Chr	17:10	Israel. And I will s all your enemies.

SUBJECTED
Rom	8:20	but because of the one who s it,
1 Cor	15:28	When everything is s to him,
1 Cor	15:28	be s to the One who s everything

SUBMIT
Rom	8: 7	it does not s to the law of God,
Gal	5: 1	and do not s again to the yoke
Col	2:20	why do you s to regulations as
Jas	4: 7	So s yourselves to God.

SUCCEED → SUCCESS, SUCCESSFUL
1 Kgs	2: 3	that you may s in whatever you do,
1 Kgs	22:22	'You shall s in deceiving him.
Prv	15:22	they s when counselors are many.

SUCCESS → SUCCEED
Gn	39: 3	and brought him s in whatever he did,
Gn	39:23	with him and brought s to all he did.
Neh	2:20	God of heaven who will grant us s.
Tb	4: 6	your good works will bring s,
1 Mc	4:55	praised Heaven, who had given them s.

SUCCESSFUL → SUCCEED
Gn	24:56	that the LORD has made my errand s;

SUCCOTH
Gn	33:17	Jacob journeyed to S. There he built
Gn	33:17	That is why the place was called S.
Jgs	8:16	ground these men of S into them.

SUCH
Ps	139: 6	S knowledge is beyond me, far too
Jer	5: 9	On a nation s as this shall I not take
Mt	8:10	no one in Israel have I found s faith.
Jn	9:16	"How can a sinful man do s signs?"
2 Cor	3: 4	S confidence we have through
Gal	5:23	Against s there is no law.
Heb	7:26	that we should have s a high priest:
Heb	12: 3	how he endured s opposition
2 Jn	1: 7	flesh; s is the deceitful one
3 Jn	1: 8	we ought to support s persons,

SUDDEN → SUDDENLY
Prv	3:25	Be not afraid of s terror, of the ruin
1 Thes	5: 3	then s disaster comes upon them,

SUDDENLY → SUDDEN
Mal	3: 1	And s there will come to the temple
Mk	13:36	May he not come s and find you
Acts	9: 3	from the sky s flashed around him.

SUFFER → SUFFERED, SUFFERING, SUFFERINGS, SUFFERS
Lk	22:15	this Passover with you before I s,
Lk	24:26	the Messiah should s these things
Lk	24:46	is written that the Messiah would s
Acts	3:18	prophets, that his Messiah would s.
1 Cor	3:15	is burned up, that one will s loss;
Heb	9:26	he would have had to s repeatedly
1 Pt	3:17	For it is better to s for doing good,
1 Pt	4:16	whoever is made to s as a Christian
Rv	2:10	of anything that you are going to s.

SUFFERED → SUFFER
Heb	2:18	was tested through what he s, he is
Heb	5: 8	learned obedience from what he s;
1 Pt	2:21	because Christ also s for you,
1 Pt	4: 1	since Christ s in the flesh,

SUFFERING → SUFFER
Jb	2:13	for they saw how great was his s.
Is	53: 3	a man of s, accustomed to infirmity,

SUFFERINGS → SUFFER
Rom	8:18	that the s of this present time are as
2 Cor	1: 5	For as Christ's s overflow to us,
2 Cor	1: 7	we know that as you share in the s,
Phil	3:10	sharing of his s by being conformed
1 Pt	1:11	advance to the s destined for Christ
1 Pt	4:13	that you share in the s of Christ,

SUFFERS → SUFFER
1 Cor	12:26	If [one] part s, all the parts suffer

SUFFICIENT
2 Cor	12: 9	he said to me, "My grace is s for you,

SULFUR
Rv	9:17	mouths came fire, smoke, and s.
Rv	14:10	in burning s before the holy angels
Rv	19:20	into the fiery pool burning with s.
Rv	20:10	thrown into the pool of fire and s,
Rv	21: 8	is in the burning pool of fire and s,

SUMMED
Rom	13: 9	there may be, are s up in this saying,

SUMMER
Prv	6: 8	She procures her food in the s,
Mk	13:28	leaves, you know that s is near.

SUMMON
Ps	68:29	S again, O God, your power,

SUN
Jos	10:13	And the s stood still, and the moon
Jos	10:13	The s halted in the middle
Jgs	5:31	your friends be as the s rising in its
Ps	72: 5	he live as long as the s endures,
Ps	84:12	For a s and shield is the LORD God,
Ps	113: 3	From the rising of the s to its setting
Ps	121: 6	By day the s cannot harm you,

Ps	136: 8	The **s** to rule the day, God's love
Ps	148: 3	Praise him, **s** and moon; give praise,
Eccl	1: 9	Nothing is new under the **s**.
Song	6:10	as the moon, as resplendent as the **s**,
Is	60:19	No longer shall the **s** be your light
Dn	3:62	**S** and moon, bless the Lord;
Jl	3: 4	The **s** will be turned to darkness,
Jl	4:15	**S** and moon are darkened,
Mi	3: 6	The **s** shall go down
Mal	3:20	the **s** of justice with its healing rays;
Mt	5:45	for he makes his **s** rise on the bad
Mt	13:43	the righteous will shine like the **s**
Mt	17: 2	his face shone like the **s** and his
Mk	13:24	tribulation the **s** will be darkened,
Acts	2:20	The **s** shall be turned to darkness,
Eph	4:26	do not let the **s** set on your anger,
Rv	1:16	and his face shone like the **s** at its
Rv	8:12	a third of the **s**, a third of the moon,
Rv	9: 2	The **s** and the air were darkened
Rv	10: 1	his face was like the **s** and his feet
Rv	12: 1	a woman clothed with the **s**,
Rv	19:17	I saw an angel standing on the **s**.
Rv	21:23	The city had no need of **s** or moon
Rv	22: 5	will they need light from lamp or **s**,

SUPERAPOSTLES →APOSTLE
2 Cor	11: 5	not in any way inferior to these "**s**."
2 Cor	12:11	in no way inferior to these "**s**,"

SUPERIOR
Heb	1: 4	as far **s** to the angels as the name he

SUPPER
1 Cor	11:25	way also the cup, after **s**, saying,

SUPPLICATION →SUPPLICATIONS
Eph	6:18	With all prayer and **s**, pray at every
Eph	6:18	and **s** for all the holy ones

SUPPLICATIONS →SUPPLICATION
1 Tm	2: 1	then, I ask that **s**, prayers, petitions,
Heb	5: 7	offered prayers and **s** with loud cries

SUPPLIES
2 Cor	9:10	The one who **s** seed to the sower

SUPPORT →SUPPORTS
Ps	18:19	distress, but the Lord came to my **s**.
Mk	7:11	"Any **s** you might have had from me
Rom	11:18	consider that you do not **s** the root;

SUPPORTS →SUPPORT
Rom	11:18	not support the root; the root **s** you.

SUPPRESS
Rom	1:18	wickedness of those who **s** the truth

SURE →SURELY, SURETY
Nm	32:23	and you can be **s** that you will not
Prv	4:26	your feet, and let all your ways be **s**.
Is	28:16	cornerstone as a **s** foundation;
Eph	5: 5	Be **s** of this, that no immoral
Heb	6:19	as an anchor of the soul, **s** and firm,
1 Jn	2: 3	The way we may be **s** that we know

SURELY →SURE
Gn	50:24	God will **s** take care of you and lead
Prv	23:18	For you will **s** have a future,
Ez	33:15	he shall **s** live, he shall not die.
Mk	14:19	say to him, one by one, "**S** it is not I?"

SURETY →SURE
Gn	43: 9	I myself will stand **s** for him.
Prv	17:18	who becomes **s** for his neighbor.
Sir	8:13	Go not **s** beyond your means;

SURPASSES →SURPASSING
Sir	25:11	Fear of the Lord **s** all else,
Eph	3:19	the love of Christ that **s** knowledge,
Phil	4: 7	**s** all understanding will guard your

SURPASSING →SURPASSES
2 Cor	9:14	because of the **s** grace of God

SURPRISED
1 Pt	4:12	do not be **s** that a trial by fire is

SURROUND →SURROUNDED, SURROUNDS
Ps	22:13	Many bulls **s** me; fierce bulls
Ps	125: 2	As mountains **s** Jerusalem, the Lord

SURROUNDED →SURROUND
Jgs	19:22	**s** the house and beat on the door.
Ps	118:11	They **s** me on every side;
Lk	21:20	you see Jerusalem **s** by armies,
Heb	12: 1	since we are **s** by so great a cloud
Rv	20: 9	and **s** the camp of the holy ones

SURROUNDS →SURROUND
Ps	32:10	love **s** those who trust in the Lord.
Ps	125: 2	Jerusalem, the Lord **s** his people

SURVIVORS
Ez	14:22	still some **s** shall be left in it who

SUSA
Neh	1: 1	year, I was in the citadel of **S**
Est	1: 2	royal throne in the stronghold of **S**,

SUSANNA
Righteous woman wrongly accused of immorality (Dn 13:1-44); vindicated by Daniel (Dn 13:45-64).

SUSPENSE
Jn	10:24	long are you going to keep us in **s**?

SUSPICIONS
1 Tm	6: 4	come envy, rivalry, insults, evil **s**,

SUSTAIN →SUSTAINED, SUSTAINS
Ps	51:14	salvation; **s** in me a willing spirit.

SUSTAINED →SUSTAIN
Neh	9:21	Forty years in the desert you **s** them:

SUSTAINS →SUSTAIN
Heb	1: 3	who **s** all things by his mighty word.

SWALLOW →SWALLOWED
Nm	16:34	saying, "The earth might **s** us too!"
Ps	84: 4	and the **s** a nest to settle her young,
Mt	23:24	strain out the gnat and **s** the camel!

SWALLOWED →SWALLOW
Gn	41: 7	the seven thin ears **s** up the seven
Nm	16:32	earth opened its mouth and **s** them
Ps	106:17	The earth opened and **s** Dathan,
Jon	2: 1	Lord sent a large fish, that **s** Jonah;
1 Cor	15:54	about: "Death is **s** up in victory.
2 Cor	5: 4	so that what is mortal may be **s**

SWEAR →SWEARING, SWEARS, SWORE, SWORN
Dt	10:20	hold fast to him and **s** by his name.
Dt	32:40	the heavens I raise my hand and **s**:
Jos	2:12	Now then, **s** to me by the Lord that,
Jos	23: 7	gods, or **s** by them, or serve them,
Is	45:23	By myself I **s**, uttering my just
Is	45:23	bend; by me every tongue shall **s**,
Mt	5:34	But I say to you, do not **s** at all;
Heb	6:13	he had no one greater by whom to **s**,
Jas	5:12	do not **s**, either by heaven

SWEARING →SWEAR
Hos	4: 2	False **s**, lying, murder,

SWEARS →SWEAR
Sir	23:11	A man who often **s** heaps
Sir	23:11	If he **s** in error, he incurs guilt; if he
Sir	23:11	If he **s** without reason he cannot be
Mt	23:20	One who **s** by the altar **s** by it

SWEAT
Gn	3:19	By the **s** of your face shall you get
Lk	22:44	that his **s** became like drops

SWEEP →SWEPT
Gn	18:23	"Will you **s** away the innocent
Lk	15: 8	not light a lamp and **s** the house,

SWEET →SWEETER
Jb	20:12	Though wickedness is **s** in his
Ps	119:103	How **s** to my tongue is your
Prv	9:17	Stolen water is **s**, and bread gotten
Prv	20:17	The bread of deceit is **s** to a man,

SWEETER

Eccl	5:11	Sleep is s to the laboring man,
Is	5:20	who change bitter into s, and s
Ez	3: 3	it was as s as honey in my mouth.
Rv	10:10	In my mouth it was like s honey,

SWEETER → SWEET

Jgs	14:18	said to him, "What is s than honey,
Ps	19:11	of purest gold, S also than honey
Ps	119:103	promise, s than honey to my mouth!

SWELL

Dt	8: 4	nor did your feet s these forty years.

SWEPT → SWEEP

Ps	88:17	Your wrath has s over me;
Mt	12:44	it finds it empty, s clean, and put
Rv	12: 4	Its tail s away a third of the stars

SWIFT → SWIFTLY

Eccl	9:11	sun that the race is not won by the s,
Jer	46: 6	The s cannot flee, nor the hero
2 Pt	2: 1	them, bringing s destruction

SWIFTLY → SWIFT

Ps	147:15	command to earth; his word runs s!

SWINE

1 Mc	1:47	to sacrifice s and unclean animals,
Mt	7: 6	or throw your pearls before s,
Mk	5:12	with him, "Send us into the s. Let us

SWORD → SWORDS

Gn	3:24	cherubim and the fiery revolving s,
Ex	18: 4	he has rescued me from Pharaoh's s."
Nm	14: 3	land only to have us fall by the s?
Dt	32:41	I will sharpen my flashing s, and my
Jos	5:13	stood facing him, drawn s in hand.
1 Sm	17:45	"You come against me with s
1 Sm	17:47	shall learn that it is not by s or spear
1 Sm	31: 4	"Draw your s and run me through,
1 Sm	31: 4	So Saul took his own s and fell
2 Sm	12:10	the s shall never depart from your
1 Chr	21:30	he was fearful of the s of the angel
Neh	4:12	he worked, had his s girt at his side.
Ps	22:21	Deliver me from the s, my forlorn
Ps	44: 7	nor does my s bring me victory.
Ps	45: 4	Gird your s upon your hip,
Ps	57: 5	their tongue, a sharpened s.
Prv	5: 4	as sharp as a two-edged s.
Prv	12:18	of some men is like s thrusts,
Sir	21: 3	Every offense is a two-edged s;
Is	2: 4	shall not raise the s against another,
Is	49: 2	He made of me a sharp-edged s
Jer	15: 2	whoever is marked for the s, to the s;
Lam	1:20	In the streets the s bereaves,
Ez	5: 2	the city and strike it with the s;
Ez	5: 2	in the wind, and pursue it with the s.
Hos	2:20	on the ground. Bow and s and war
Mi	4: 3	shall not raise the s against another,
Mt	10:34	come to bring not peace but the s.
Mt	26:52	him, "Put your s back into its sheath,
Mt	26:52	all who take the s will perish by the s.
Lk	2:35	you yourself a s will pierce) so
Acts	12: 2	the brother of John, killed by the s,
Rom	13: 4	does not bear the s without purpose;
Eph	6:17	of salvation and the s of the Spirit,
Heb	4:12	sharper than any two-edged s,
Heb	11:34	fires, escaped the devouring s;
Rv	1:16	A sharp two-edged s came
Rv	6: 4	another. And he was given a huge s.
Rv	13:14	who had been wounded by the s
Rv	19:15	his mouth came a sharp s to strike

SWORDS → SWORD

Ps	44: 4	their own s did they conquer
Ps	64: 4	They sharpen their tongues like s,
Is	2: 4	peoples. They shall beat their s
Jl	4:10	Beat your plowshares into s,
Mi	4: 3	nations; They shall beat their s
Mk	14:48	against a robber, with s and clubs,

SWORE → SWEAR

Gn	26: 3	oath that I s to your father Abraham.

Ex	6: 8	into the land which I s to give
Ex	32:13	and how you s to them by your own
Nm	14:30	enter the land where I solemnly s
Dt	6:10	the land which he s to your fathers,
Ps	132:11	The LORD s an oath to David,
Lk	1:73	the oath he s to Abraham our father,
Heb	3:11	As I s in my wrath, "They shall not
Heb	6:13	by whom to swear, "he s by himself,"
Rv	10: 6	and s by the one who lives forever

SWORN → SWEAR

Ps	110: 4	The LORD has s and will not waver:
Am	4: 2	The Lord GOD has s by his holiness:
Heb	7:21	him: "The Lord has s, and he will not

SYCAMORE

Lk	19: 4	and climbed a s tree in order to see

SYCHAR

Jn	4: 5	came to a town of Samaria called S,

SYMBOL

Heb	11:19	and he received Isaac back as a s.

SYMPATHIZE

Heb	4:15	have a high priest who is unable to s

SYNAGOGUE → SYNAGOGUES

Mt	13:54	and taught the people in their s.
Lk	4:16	into the s on the sabbath day.
Lk	8:41	an official of the s, came forward.
Acts	13:14	the sabbath they entered [into] the s
Acts	14: 1	they entered the Jewish s together
Acts	18: 4	he entered into discussions in the s,
Acts	18:26	He began to speak boldly in the s;

SYNAGOGUES → SYNAGOGUE

Mt	4:23	teaching in their s,
Mt	6: 2	as the hypocrites do in the s
Mt	10:17	to courts and scourge you in their s,
Lk	12:11	When they take you before s
Acts	13: 5	the word of God in the Jewish s.

SYNTYCHE

Phil	4: 2	and I urge S to come to a mutual

SYRIA → SYRIAN, SYROPHOENICIAN

Mt	4:24	His fame spread to all of S, and they

SYRIAN → SYRIA

Lk	4:27	cleansed, but only Naaman the S."

SYROPHOENICIAN → SYRIA

Mk	7:26	woman was a Greek, a S by birth,

T

TABERNACLE → TABERNACLES

Heb	9:11	more perfect t not made by hands,

TABERNACLES → TABERNACLE

Jn	7: 2	But the Jewish feast of T was near.

TABITHA → =DORCAS

Disciple, also known as Dorcas, whom Peter raised from the dead (Acts 9:36-42).

TABLE → TABLES

Ex	25:23	shall also make a t of acacia wood,
Nm	3:31	to the ark, the t, the lampstand,
Ps	23: 5	You set a t before me as my
Ps	78:19	"Can God spread a t in the desert?
1 Cor	10:21	cannot partake of the t of the Lord and of the t of demons.

TABLES → TABLE

Mk	11:15	He overturned the t of the money
Jn	2:15	and overturned their t,

TABLET → TABLETS

Prv	7: 3	write them on the t of your heart.
Is	30: 8	come, write it on a t they can keep,
Lk	1:63	He asked for a t and wrote, "John is

TABLETS → TABLET

Ex	31:18	Sinai, he gave him the two t
Ex	31:18	the stone t inscribed by God's own

Ex	32:19	up, so that he threw the t down
Dt	10: 5	placed the t in the ark I had made.
2 Cor	3: 3	not on t of stone but on t that are

TAIL → TAILS

Dt	28:13	not the t, and you will always mount
Jgs	15: 4	Turning them t to t, he tied between
Rv	12: 4	Its t swept away a third of the stars

TAILS → TAIL

Rv	9:10	They had t like scorpions,
Rv	9:10	with their t they had power to harm
Rv	9:19	is in their mouths and in their t; for their t are like snakes,

TAKE → TAKEN, TAKES, TAKING, TOOK

Gn	22: 2	"T your son Isaac, your only one,
Ex	6: 7	I will t you as my own people,
Nm	1: 2	"T a census of the whole community
Dt	31:26	"T this scroll of the law and put it
1 Sm	8:11	He will t your sons and assign them
1 Kgs	11:34	Yet I will not t any of the kingdom
1 Kgs	19: 4	T my life, for I am no better than
Ps	2:12	Happy are all who t refuge in God!
Ps	27:14	Wait for the LORD, t courage;
Ps	31:25	Be strong and t heart, all you who
Ps	51:13	nor t from me your holy spirit.
Ps	118: 8	Better to t refuge in the LORD
Hos	1: 2	t a harlot wife and harlot's children,
Hos	14: 3	T with you words, and return
Mt	1:20	do not be afraid to t Mary your wife
Mt	2:13	"Rise, t the child and his mother,
Mt	2:20	t the child and his mother and go
Mt	11:29	T my yoke upon you and learn
Mt	16:24	must deny himself, t up his cross.
Mt	17:27	and t the first fish that comes up.
Mt	26:26	it to his disciples said, "T and eat;
Mk	8:34	must deny himself, t up his cross.
Acts	1:20	And: 'May another t his office.'
1 Tm	3: 5	how can he t care of the church

TAKEN → TAKE

Gn	2:23	out of 'her man' this one has been t."
Gn	27:36	and now he has t away my blessing."
Nm	8:16	I have t them for myself in place
Jos	7:11	They have stealthily t goods subject
Sir	44:16	walked with the LORD and was t up,
Jer	38:28	guard till the day Jerusalem was t.
Dn	5: 2	had t from the temple in Jerusalem,
Mt	13:12	even what he has will be t away.
Mt	24:40	one will be t, and one will be left.
Jn	20:13	said to them, "They have t my Lord,
1 Tm	3:16	throughout the world, t up in glory.
Heb	11: 5	By faith Enoch was t up so that he
Heb	11: 5	no more because God had t him."
Heb	11: 5	Before he was t up, he was attested

TAKES → TAKE

Ps	149: 4	For the LORD t delight in his people,
Mk	4:15	and t away the word sown in them.
Lk	6:30	the one who t what is yours do not
Jn	1:29	who t away the sin of the world.
Jn	10:18	No one t it from me, but I lay it
Rv	22:19	if anyone t away from the words

TAKING → TAKE

Phil	2: 7	himself, t the form of a slave,

TALENT → TALENTS

Mt	25:25	off and buried your t in the ground.

TALENTS → TALENT

Mt	25:15	To one he gave five t; to another,

TALITHA

Mk	5:41	the hand and said to her, "T koum,"

TALK

1 Cor	4:20	kingdom of God is not a matter of t

TALL → TALLER

1 Chr	11:23	Egyptian, a huge man five cubits t.

TALLER → TALL

Dt	1:28	people are stronger and t than we,

TAMAR

1. Wife of Judah's sons Er and Onan (Gn 38:1-10). Tricked Judah into fathering children when he refused her his third son (Gn 38:11-30; Mt 1:3).
   2. Daughter of David, raped by Amnon (2 Sm 13).

TAMARISK

Gn	21:33	Abraham planted a t at Beer-sheba,

TAMBOURINE → TAMBOURINES

Ex	15:20	Aaron's sister, took a t in her hand,

TAMBOURINES → TAMBOURINE

Ps	150: 4	Give praise with t and dance,
Jer	31: 4	Carrying your festive t, you shall go

TAME

Jas	3: 8	no human being can t the tongue.

TANNER

Acts	9:43	long time in Joppa with Simon, a t.

TARGET

Jb	16:12	to pieces. He has set me up for a t;

TARSHISH

Ps	48: 8	the east wind wrecks the ships of T!
Is	60: 9	with the ships of T in the lead,
Jon	1: 3	to flee to T away from the LORD.
Jon	1: 3	found a ship going to T,
Jon	4: 2	This is why I fled at first to T.

TARSUS

Acts	9:11	Judas for a man from T named Saul.
Acts	11:25	Then he went to T to look for Saul,

TASK → TASKMASTERS

Ex	18:18	The t is too heavy for you;
Acts	6: 3	whom we shall appoint to this t,
1 Tm	3: 1	office of bishop desires a noble t.

TASKMASTERS → MASTER, TASK

Ex	1:11	t were set over the Israelites

TASTE → TASTED

Prv	24:13	if virgin honey is sweet to your t;
Mt	16:28	here who will not t death until they
Col	2:21	not handle! Do not t! Do not touch!"
Heb	2: 9	God he might t death for everyone.

TASTED → TASTE

Heb	6: 4	enlightened and t the heavenly gift
1 Pt	2: 3	for you have t that the Lord is good.

TATTOO

Lv	19:28	the dead, and do not t yourselves.

TAUGHT → TEACH

Dt	31:22	day, and he t it to the Israelites.
2 Kgs	17:28	t them how to venerate the LORD.
2 Chr	17: 9	They t in Judah, having with them
2 Chr	17: 9	of Judah and t among the people.
Ps	119:102	not turn, for you have t them to me.
Prv	4: 4	He t me, and said to me: "Let your
Is	40:14	Who t him the path of judgment,
Is	54:13	All your sons shall be t by the LORD,
Hos	11: 3	Yet it was I who t Ephraim to walk,
Mt	7:29	he t them as one having authority,
Jn	6:45	prophets: 'They shall all be t by God.'
1 Cor	2:13	not with words t by human wisdom,
1 Cor	2:13	but with words t by the Spirit,
1 Jn	2:27	false; just as it t you, remain in him.

TAUNT

Ps	102: 9	All day long my enemies t me;
Jer	24: 9	and a byword, a t and a curse, in all

TAX → TAXES

2 Chr	24: 6	Jerusalem the t levied by Moses,
Mt	5:46	Do not the t collectors do the same?
Mt	11:19	a friend of t collectors and sinners.'
Mt	17:24	of the temple t approached Peter
Mt	17:24	your teacher pay the temple t?"
Mt	22:17	pay the census t to Caesar or not?"

Lk   18:10   and the other was a **t** collector.

TAXES → TAX
Rom   13: 7   all their dues, **t** to whom **t** are due,

TEACH → TAUGHT, TEACHER, TEACHERS, TEACHES,
     TEACHING, TEACHINGS
Ex   4:12   and will **t** you what you are to say."
Dt   11:19   T them to your children,
Jb   6:24   T me, and I will be silent;
Jb   21:22   Can anyone **t** God knowledge,
Ps   25: 4   your ways, LORD; **t** me your paths.
Ps   34:12   I will **t** you the fear of the LORD.
Ps   51:15   I will **t** the wicked your ways,
Ps   78: 5   they were to **t** their children;
Ps   90:12   T us to count our days aright,
Ps   143:10   T me to do your will, for you are my
Prv   9: 9   **t** a just man, and he advances
Jer   31:34   will they have need to **t** their friends
Lk   11: 1   **t** us to pray just as John taught his
Lk   12:12   For the holy Spirit will **t** you
Jn   14:26   in my name—he will **t** you everything
Rom   2:21   then you who **t** another, are you failing to **t**
               yourself?
1 Cor 11:14   Does not nature itself **t** you
Col   3:16   richly, as in all wisdom you **t**
1 Tm   1: 3   people not to **t** false doctrines
1 Tm   2:12   I do not permit a woman to **t**
2 Tm   2: 2   have the ability to **t** others as well.
Heb   5:12   have someone **t** you again the basic
Heb   8:11   And they shall not **t**, each one his
1 Jn   2:27   you do not need anyone to **t** you.

TEACHER → TEACH
Mt   10:24   No disciple is above his **t**, no slave
Mt   22:36   "T, which commandment in the law
Lk   6:40   No disciple is superior to the **t**;
Lk   6:40   every disciple will be like his **t**.
Jn   1:38   "Rabbi" (which translated means **T**),
Jn   3: 2   know that you are a **t** who has come
Jn   13:14   the master and **t**, have washed your
Rom   12: 7   if one is a **t**, in teaching;
2 Tm   1:11   preacher and apostle and **t**.

TEACHERS → TEACH
Ps   119:99   more understanding than all my **t**,
Prv   5:13   did I not listen to the voice of my **t**,
1 Cor 12:28   third, **t**; then, mighty deeds;
Eph   4:11   evangelists, others as pastors and **t**,
2 Tm   4: 3   curiosity, will accumulate **t**
Heb   5:12   Although you should be **t** by this
Jas   3: 1   Not many of you should become **t**,
2 Pt   2: 1   as there will be false **t** among you,

TEACHES → TEACH
Ps   25: 9   rightly, and **t** the humble the way.
Ps   94:10   The one who **t** humans not have
Mt   5:19   **t** others to do so will be called least
1 Tm   6: 3   Whoever **t** something different
1 Jn   2:27   his anointing **t** you about everything

TEACHING → TEACH
1 Kgs   8:36   **t** them the right way to live
Ps   78: 1   Attend, my people, to my **t**;
Prv   1: 8   and reject not your mother's **t**;
Prv   3: 1   My son, forget not my **t**,
Prv   6:23   bidding is a lamp, and the **t** a light,
Prv   13:14   The **t** of the wise is a fountain
Mt   28:20   **t** them to observe all that I have
Mk   1:27   is this? A new **t** with authority.
Mk   11:18   crowd was astonished at his **t**.
Lk   19:47   every day he was **t** in the temple
Jn   7:17   his will shall know whether my **t** is
Acts   2:42   themselves to the **t** of the apostles
Acts   5:28   to stop **t** in that name[.]
Acts   5:28   have filled Jerusalem with your **t**
Rom   12: 7   ministering; if one is a teacher, in **t**;
Col   1:28   and **t** everyone with all wisdom,
1 Tm   4:13   to the reading, exhortation, and **t**.
1 Tm   5:17   those who toil in preaching and **t**.
1 Tm   6: 3   Lord Jesus Christ and the religious **t**
2 Tm   3:16   inspired by God and is useful for **t**,

Ti   1:11   are upsetting whole families by **t**
Ti   2: 7   with integrity in your **t**, dignity,
2 Jn   1: 9   in the **t** of the Christ does not have
2 Jn   1: 9   remains in the **t** has the Father

TEACHINGS → TEACH
Col   2:22   accord with human precepts and **t**.

TEAR → TEARS, TORE, TORN
Mk   2:21   from the old, and the **t** gets worse.
Rv   7:17   God will wipe away every **t**
Rv   21: 4   He will wipe every **t** from their

TEARS → TEAR
Ps   42: 4   My **t** have been my food day
Ps   126: 5   Those who sow in **t** will reap
Is   25: 8   will wipe away the **t** from all faces;
Jer   8:23   my eyes a fountain of **t**, That I
Jer   31:16   wipe the **t** from your eyes.
Lam   1:16   my eyes run with **t**: Far from me are
Dn   13:35   Through her **t** she looked
Lk   7:38   began to bathe his feet with her **t**.
2 Cor   2: 4   of heart I wrote to you with many **t**,
Phil   3:18   told you and now tell you even in **t**,
Heb   5: 7   **t** to the one who was able to save

TEETH → TOOTH
Nm   11:33   the meat was still between their **t**,
Jb   19:20   with my flesh between my **t**.
Ps   3: 8   you will break the **t** of the wicked.
Ps   35:16   me, gnashed their **t** against me.
Sir   21: 2   if you go near it; Its are lion's **t**,
Jer   31:29   and the children's **t** are set on edge,"
Dn   7: 7   it had great iron **t** with which it
Jl   1: 6   number; His **t** are the **t** of a lion,
Mt   8:12   will be wailing and grinding of **t**.
Acts   7:54   and they ground their **t** at him.
Rv   9: 8   Their **t** were like lions' **t**,

TEKEL
Dn   5:25   was inscribed: MENE, T, and PERES.
Dn   5:27   T, you have been weighed

TEKOA
2 Sm   14: 4   So the woman of **T** went to the king
Am   1: 1   Amos, a shepherd from **T**, which he

TELL → FORETOLD, FORTUNE-TELLING, TOLD
Ex   6:11   "Go and **t** Pharaoh, king of Egypt,
Nm   22:35   but you may say only what I **t** you."
Ru   3: 4   lie down. He will **t** you what to do."
1 Sm   3:15   LORD. He feared to **t** Eli the vision,
2 Chr 18:15   must I adjure you to **t** me nothing
Ps   50:12   Were I hungry, I would not **t** you,
Dn   2: 4   T your servants the dream and we
Jn   20:15   him away, **t** me where you laid him,
1 Cor 15:51   Behold, I **t** you a mystery. We shall

TEMAN
Jb   2:11   Eliphaz from **T**, Bildad from Shuh,

TEMPER → QUICK-TEMPERED, TEMPERATE
Prv   16:32   and he who rules his **t**, than he who

TEMPERATE → TEMPER
1 Tm   3: 2   irreproachable, married only once, **t**,
1 Tm   3:11   but **t** and faithful in everything.
Ti   2: 2   that older men should be **t**,

TEMPLE → TEMPLES
Jgs   4:21   drove the peg through his **t** down
1 Sm   3: 3   in the **t** of the LORD where the ark
1 Kgs   6: 7   (The **t** was built of stone dressed
Ezr   3:10   laid the foundation of the LORD's **t**,
Tb   14: 5   They shall rebuild the **t**, but it will
Tb   14: 5   In her the **t** of God shall also be
1 Mc   2: 8   "Her **t** has become like a man
1 Mc   4:48   the interior of the **t** and purified
Ps   11: 4   The LORD is in his holy **t**; the LORD's
Ps   27: 4   on the LORD's beauty, to visit his **t**.
Ps   30: 1   A song for the dedication of the **t**.
Is   6: 1   the train of his garment filling the **t**.
Jer   7: 4   words: "This is the **t** of the LORD!
Ez   8:16   and there at the door of the LORD's **t**,

Ez	8:16	men with their backs to the LORD's t
Ez	43: 4	of the LORD entered the t by way
Dn	5: 2	had taken from the t in Jerusalem,
Mi	1: 2	you, the LORD from his holy t!
Hb	2:20	But the LORD is in his holy t;
Mt	4: 5	him stand on the parapet of the t,
Mt	12: 6	something greater than the t is here.
Mt	26:61	said, 'I can destroy the t of God
Lk	21: 5	about how the t was adorned
Jn	2:14	in the t area those who sold oxen,
Jn	2:21	speaking about the t of his body.
Acts	2:46	to meeting together in the t area
Acts	5:42	both at the t and in their homes,
1 Cor	3:16	not know that you are the t of God,
1 Cor	6:19	your body is a t of the holy Spirit
2 Cor	6:16	What agreement has the t of God
2 Cor	6:16	For we are the t of the living God;
Eph	2:21	grows into a t sacred in the Lord;
2 Thes	2: 4	so as to seat himself in the t of God,
Rv	3:12	into a pillar in the t of my God,
Rv	11:19	Then God's t in heaven was opened,
Rv	11:19	his covenant could be seen in the t.
Rv	21:22	I saw no t in the city, for its t is

TEMPLES →TEMPLE
Rom	2:22	You who detest idols, do you rob t?

TEMPT →TEMPTATION, TEMPTED, TEMPTER, TEMPTS
1 Cor	7: 5	Satan may not t you through your

TEMPTATION →TEMPT
1 Tm	6: 9	who want to be rich are falling into t
Jas	1:12	is the man who perseveres in t,

TEMPTED →TEMPT
Mt	4: 1	into the desert to be t by the devil.
Mk	1:13	the desert for forty days, t by Satan.
Lk	4: 2	for forty days, to be t by the devil.
Gal	6: 1	so that you also may not be t.
Jas	1:13	should say, "I am being t by God";
Jas	1:14	each person is t when he is lured

TEMPTER →TEMPT
Mt	4: 3	The t approached and said to him,
1 Thes	3: 5	fear that somehow the t had put you

TEMPTS →TEMPT
Jas	1:13	to evil, and he himself t no one.

TEN →TENTH
Gn	18:32	What if there are at least t there?"
Gn	18:32	"For the sake of those t," he replied,
Ex	34:28	the covenant, the t commandments.
Dt	4:13	the t commandments, which he
Dt	10: 4	the t commandments which he
1 Sm	1: 8	Am I not more to you than t sons?"
2 Kgs	20: 9	shadow go forward or back t steps?"
Ps	91: 7	side; t thousand at your right hand,
Dn	1:12	"Please test your servants for t days.
Dn	7:24	The t horns shall be t kings
Mt	25: 1	will be like t virgins who took their
Mt	25:28	him and give it to the one with t.
Lk	15: 8	"Or what woman having t coins
Rv	12: 3	with seven heads and t horns,
Rv	17:12	The t horns that you saw represent t

TENANTS
Mt	21:34	to the t to obtain his produce.

TEND
Jn	21:16	He said to him, "T my sheep."

TENDER →TENDERLY
Lk	1:78	because of the t mercy of our God

TENDERLY →TENDER
Is	40: 2	Speak t to Jerusalem, and proclaim

TENT →TENTMAKERS, TENTS
Ex	27:21	before the LORD in the meeting t,
Ex	33: 7	The t, which was called the meeting t,
Ex	40: 2	erect the Dwelling of the meeting t.
2 Sm	7: 2	while the ark of God dwells in a t!"
Ps	61: 5	Then I will ever dwell in your t,

Is	33:20	as a quiet abode, a t not to be struck,
Is	54: 2	Enlarge the space for your t,
2 Cor	5: 1	dwelling, a t, should be destroyed,

TENTH →TEN
Gn	14:20	Abram gave him a t of everything.
Is	6:13	If there be still a t part in it,
Heb	7: 4	patriarch "Abraham [indeed] gave a t"

TENTMAKERS →MAKE, TENT
Acts	18: 3	worked, for they were t by trade.

TENTS →TENT
Ps	84:11	than a home in the t of the wicked.

TERAH
Gn	11:27	the record of the descendants of T.

TEREBINTH
Is	6:13	be laid waste; As with a t or an oak

TERRIFIED →TERROR
Mt	14:26	him walking on the sea they were t.
Heb	12:21	Moses said, "I am t and trembling."
Rv	11:13	the rest were t and gave glory

TERRIFYING →TERROR
Gn	15:12	a deep, t darkness enveloped him.

TERROR →TERRIFIED, TERRIFYING, TERRORS
Ps	91: 5	You shall not fear the t of the night
Is	2:19	earth, From the t of the LORD
Is	24:17	T, pit, and trap are upon you,
Jer	20:10	of many: "T on every side!

TERRORS →TERROR
Jb	6: 4	the t of God are arrayed against me.
Ps	31:14	of the crowd; t are all around me.
Ps	55: 5	within me; death's t fall upon me.

TERTIUS
Rom	16:22	I, T, the writer of this letter,

TEST →TESTED, TESTER, TESTING
Ex	16: 4	thus will I t them, to see whether
Dt	6:16	God, to the t, as you did at Massah.
1 Kgs	10: 1	came to t him with subtle questions.
Jdt	8:12	have put God to the t this day,
Ps	26: 2	T me, LORD, and try me; search my
Jer	9: 6	I will smelt them and t them;
Lk	4:12	not put the Lord, your God, to the t.' "
Lk	10:25	of the law who stood up to t him
Acts	5: 9	"Why did you agree to t the Spirit
1 Cor	3:13	the fire [itself] will t the quality
1 Cor	10: 9	Let us not t Christ as some of them
2 Cor	13: 5	you are living in faith. T yourselves.
2 Cor	13: 5	unless, of course, you fail the t.
1 Thes	5:21	T everything; retain what is good.
Heb	11:17	when put to the t, offered up Isaac,
1 Jn	4: 1	but t the spirits to see whether they
Rv	3:10	the whole world to t the inhabitants

TESTED →TEST
Ex	17: 7	quarreled there and t the LORD,
Ps	66:10	You t us, O God, tried us as silver
Ps	78:41	Again and again they t God,
Prv	27:21	gold, so a man is t by the praise he
Sir	44:20	and when t he was found loyal.
Is	28:16	a stone that has been t, A precious
Is	48:10	t you in the furnace of affliction.
Dn	1:14	this request, and t them for ten days;
1 Tm	3:10	Moreover, they should be t first;
Heb	2:18	he himself was t through what he
Heb	2:18	able to help those who are being t.
Heb	3: 9	where your ancestors t and tried me
Heb	4:15	but one who has similarly been t

TESTER →TEST
Jer	6:27	A t among my people I have

TESTIFIED →TESTIFY
Jn	1:15	John t to him and cried out, saying,
Jn	5:37	the Father who sent me has t on my
1 Pt	1:11	them indicated when it t in advance

TESTIFIES → TESTIFY
Jn	5:32	there is another who t on my behalf,
1 Jn	5: 6	The Spirit is the one that t,

TESTIFY → TESTIFIED, TESTIFIES, TESTIMONY
Jn	1: 7	came for testimony, to t to the light,
Jn	5:39	them; even they t on my behalf.
Jn	7: 7	because I t to it that its works are
Jn	15:26	from the Father, he will t to me.
1 Jn	4:14	and t that the Father sent his Son as
1 Jn	5: 7	So there are three that t,

TESTIMONY → TESTIFY
Mk	14:59	Even so their t did not agree.
Lk	22:71	"What further need have we for t?
Jn	8:17	the t of two men can be verified.
Jn	21:24	them, and we know that his t is true.
Heb	2: 4	God added his t by signs, wonders,
1 Jn	5: 9	If we accept human t, the t of God is
1 Jn	5: 9	Now the t of God is this, that he has
Rv	1: 9	God's word and gave t to Jesus.
Rv	12:11	and by the word of their t;

TESTING → TEST
Dt	13: 4	is t you to learn whether you really
Heb	3: 8	in the day of t in the desert,
Jas	1: 3	that the t of your faith produces

THADDAEUS → =JUDAS
Apostle (Mt 10:3; Mk 3:18); probably also known as Judas son of James (Lk 6:16; Acts 1:13).

THANK → THANKFULLY, THANKS, THANKSGIVING
2 Chr	29:31	t offerings for the house of the LORD."
Ps	107: 8	Let them t the LORD for such
Lk	18:11	I t you that I am not like the rest
Jn	11:41	said, "Father, I t you for hearing me.

THANKFULLY → THANK
1 Cor	10:30	If I partake t, why am I reviled

THANKS → THANK
1 Chr	16: 8	Give t to the LORD, invoke his name;
Ps	30:13	my God, forever will I give you t.
Ps	75: 2	We thank you, God, we give t;
Ps	107: 1	"Give t to the LORD who is good,
Ps	118:28	You are my God, I give you t;
Sir	51: 1	I give you t, O God of my father;
Is	38:18	the nether world that gives you t,
Is	38:19	The living, the living give you t, as I
Dn	3:89	Give t to the Lord, for he is good,
Rom	1:21	him glory as God or give him t.
Rom	14: 6	the Lord, since he gives t to God;
1 Cor	11:24	and after he had given t, broke it
1 Cor	15:57	t be to God who gives us the victory
2 Cor	2:14	But t be to God, who always leads
2 Cor	9:15	T be to God for his indescribable
Phil	1: 3	I give t to my God at every
1 Thes	5:18	In all circumstances give t, for this
Rv	4: 9	t to the one who sits on the throne,
Rv	4:11	said: "We give t to you, Lord God

THANKSGIVING → THANK
Lv	7:12	anyone makes a peace offering in t,
Lv	7:12	with his t sacrifice he shall offer
Jdt	15:14	Judith led all Israel in this song of t,
Ps	100: 1	A psalm of t. Shout joyfully
Ps	100: 4	its courts with t. Give thanks
Ps	147: 7	Sing to the LORD with t;
2 Cor	9:11	which through us produces t to God,
Phil	4: 6	with t, make your requests known
1 Tm	4: 3	to be received with t by those who
Rv	7:12	Blessing and glory, wisdom and t,

THEFT → THIEF
Mt	15:19	adultery, unchastity, t, false witness,
Mk	7:21	evil thoughts, unchastity, t, murder,

THEME
Ps	45: 2	My heart is stirred by a noble t, as I

THEOPHILUS
Lk	1: 3	sequence for you, most excellent T,
Acts	1: 1	In the first book, T, I dealt with all

THESSALONICA
Acts	17: 1	they reached T, where there was
Phil	4:16	I was at T you sent me something

THICK
Zep	1:15	and gloom, A day of t black clouds,

THICKET
Gn	22:13	a ram caught by its horns in the t.

THIEF → THEFT, THIEVES
Lk	12:39	the hour when the t was coming,
Jn	10:10	A t comes only to steal
1 Thes	5: 2	the Lord will come like a t at night.
1 Pt	4:15	as a murderer, a t, an evildoer, or as
Rv	16:15	("Behold, I am coming like a t."

THIEVES → THIEF
Mt	6:19	destroys, and t break in and steal.
Jn	10: 8	All who came [before me] are t
1 Cor	6:10	nor t nor the greedy nor drunkards

THIGH → THIGHS
Gn	24: 2	"Put your hand under my t,
Gn	47:29	put your hand under my t as a sign
Rv	19:16	written on his cloak and on his t,

THIGHS → THIGH
Dn	2:32	were silver, its belly and t bronze,

THIN
Gn	41: 7	the seven t ears swallowed

THING → ANYTHING, EVERYTHING, THINGS
Gn	18:25	Far be it from you to do such a t,
Ps	27: 4	One t I ask of the LORD; this I seek:
Ps	84:12	The LORD withholds no good t
Jer	31:22	The LORD has created a new t
Mk	10:21	to him, "You are lacking in one t.
Lk	10:42	There is need of only one t.
Jn	9:25	One t I do know is that I was blind
Phil	3:13	Just one t: forgetting what lies

THINGS → THING
Ps	71:19	You have done great t; O God,
Ps	87: 3	Glorious t are said of you, O city
Prv	6:16	There are six t the LORD hates, yes,
Is	42: 9	See, the earlier t have come to pass,
Is	66: 2	My hand made all these t when all
Jer	10:16	he is the creator of all t; Israel is his
Jl	2:21	for the LORD has done great t.
Mt	19:26	but for God all t are possible."
Mk	11:33	you by what authority I do these t."
Jn	1: 3	All t came to be through him,
Jn	1:50	You will see greater t than this."
Jn	21:25	are also many other t that Jesus did,
Eph	1:22	And he put all t beneath his feet
Eph	1:22	gave him as head over all t
Col	1:17	He is before all t, and in him all t
Heb	1: 3	and who sustains all t by his mighty
1 Pt	4: 7	The end of all t is at hand.
Rv	4:11	for you created all t;

THINK → THINKING, THINKS, THOUGHT, THOUGHTS
Ps	63: 7	When I t of you upon my bed,
Jn	5:39	because you t you have eternal life
Rom	12: 3	I tell everyone among you not to t
Rom	12: 3	more highly than one ought to t, but to t soberly,
Phil	4: 8	of praise, t about these things.

THINKING → THINK
Mt	12:25	he knew what they were t and said
1 Cor	14:20	stop being childish in your t.
1 Cor	14:20	like infants, but in your t be mature.

THINKS → THINK
1 Cor	10:12	Therefore whoever t he is standing

THIRD → THREE
Ez	5:12	A t of your people shall die
Ez	5:12	another t shall fall by the sword all
Ez	5:12	a t I will scatter in every direction,
Ez	10:14	that of a man, the t that of a lion,
Dn	5: 7	and be t in the government
Hos	6: 2	on the t day he will raise us up,

Mt	26:44	withdrew again and prayed a t time,
Mk	14:41	He returned a t time and said
Lk	18:33	him, but on the t day he will rise."
Jn	21:17	He said to him the t time, "Simon,
Jn	21:17	that he had said to him a t time,
2 Cor	12: 2	was caught up to the t heaven.
Rv	4: 7	the t had a face like that of a human
Rv	6: 5	When he broke open the t seal,
Rv	6: 5	I heard the t living creature cry out,
Rv	8:10	When the t angel blew his trumpet,
Rv	8:10	It fell on a t of the rivers
Rv	12: 4	Its tail swept away a t of the stars

THIRST → THIRSTS, THIRSTY

Ex	17: 3	then, in their t for water, the people
Dt	28:48	therefore in hunger and t,
Ps	69:22	for my t they gave me vinegar.
Mt	5: 6	who hunger and t for righteousness,
Rv	7:16	They will not hunger or t anymore,

THIRSTS → THIRST

Ps	42: 3	My being t for God, the living God.
Ps	63: 2	for you my soul t, Like a land

THIRSTY → THIRST

Ps	107: 9	For he satisfied the t,
Prv	25:21	to eat, if he be t, give him to drink;
Mt	25:35	I was t and you gave me drink,
Rom	12:20	if he is t, give him something
Rv	21: 6	To the t I will give a gift

THIRTY

Gn	41:46	Joseph was t years old when he
2 Sm	23:24	Among the T were: Elhanan,
Prv	22:20	Have I not written for you the "T,"
Mk	4:20	accept it and bear fruit t and sixty
Lk	3:23	his ministry he was about t years

THISTLE → THISTLES

2 Kgs	14: 9	"The t of Lebanon sent word to

THISTLES → THISTLE

Gn	3:18	and t shall it bring forth to you,
Hos	10: 8	and t shall overgrow their altars.
Heb	6: 8	But if it produces thorns and t, it is

THOMAS

  Apostle (Mt 10:3; Mk 3:18; Lk 6:15; Jn 11:16; 14:5; 21:2; Acts 1:13). Doubted resurrection (Jn 20:24-28).

THONGS

Lk	3:16	to loosen the t of his sandals.

THORN → THORNBUSH, THORNS

Mi	7: 4	the most upright like a t hedge.
2 Cor	12: 7	a t in the flesh was given to me,

THORNBUSH → BUSH, THORN

Is	55:13	In place of the t, the cypress

THORNS → THORN

Gn	3:18	T and thistles shall it bring forth
Nm	33:55	in your eyes and t in your sides,
Jer	12:13	They have sown wheat and reaped t,
Mt	13: 7	Some seed fell among t, and the t
Jn	19: 2	the soldiers wove a crown out of t
Heb	6: 8	But if it produces t and thistles, it is

THOUGH

Is	1:18	the Lord: T your sins be like scarlet,
Hb	3:17	For t the fig tree blossom not
Hb	3:17	T the yield of the olive fail
Hb	3:17	T the flocks disappear from the fold

THOUGHT → THINK

2 Cor	10: 5	take every t captive in obedience

THOUGHTS → THINK

Is	55: 8	For my t are not your t, nor are your
Mt	9: 4	and said, "Why do you harbor evil t?
Rom	2:15	their conflicting t accuse or even
1 Cor	3:20	"The Lord knows the t of the wise,
Heb	4:12	reflections and t of the heart.

THOUSAND → THOUSANDS

Dt	32:30	"How could one man rout a t, or two men put ten t to flight,
Jos	23:10	One of you puts to flight a t,
Jgs	15:16	of an ass I have slain a t men."
Ps	84:11	courts than a t elsewhere.
Ps	90: 4	A t years in your eyes are merely
Ps	91: 7	Though a t fall at your side, ten t
Ps	105: 8	the pact imposed for a t generations,
Mt	14:21	who ate were about five t men,
Mt	15:38	Those who ate were four t men,
2 Pt	3: 8	the Lord one day is like a t years and a t years like one day.
Rv	20: 4	reigned with Christ for a t years.

THOUSANDS → THOUSAND

1 Sm	18: 7	"Saul has slain his t, and David his ten t."
Ps	50:10	beasts by the t on my mountains.
Ps	68:18	chariots were myriad, t upon t;
Song	5:10	and ruddy; he stands out among t.
Dn	7:10	T upon t were ministering to him,
Mi	6: 5	Will the Lord be pleased with t

THREAT → THREATEN, THREATS

Is	30:17	shall tremble at the t of one; if five
Lam	2:17	he has fulfilled the t He set forth

THREATEN → THREAT

1 Pt	2:23	when he suffered, he did not t;

THREATS → THREAT

Bar	2:24	and you fulfilled the t you had made
Acts	9: 1	breathing murderous t against

THREE → THIRD

Gn	6:10	he walked with God, begot t sons:
Gn	18: 2	up, he saw t men standing nearby.
Ex	23:14	"T times a year you shall celebrate
Dt	19:15	the testimony of two or t witnesses.
1 Sm	31: 8	his t sons lying on Mount Gilboa.
2 Sm	23: 9	among the T warriors, was Eleazar,
Jb	2:11	Now when t of Job's friends heard
Prv	30:15	T things are never satisfied,
Prv	30:18	T things are too wonderful for me,
Prv	30:21	Under t things the earth trembles,
Prv	30:29	T things are stately in their stride,
Sir	25: 1	With t things I am delighted,
Sir	25: 2	T kinds of men I hate; their manner
Dn	3:91	"Did we not cast t men bound
Dn	7: 5	the teeth in its mouth were t tusks.
Am	1: 3	For t crimes of Damascus,
Jon	2: 1	in the belly of the fish t days and t
Zec	11: 8	I did away with the t shepherds.
Mt	12:40	in the belly of the whale t days and t nights,
Mt	12:40	in the heart of the earth t days and t nights.
Mt	17: 4	I will make t tents here, one for you,
Mt	18:20	t are gathered together in my name,
Mt	26:34	crows, you will deny me t times."
Mt	26:75	crows you will deny me t times."
Mt	27:63	said, 'After t days I will be raised up."
Mk	8:31	and be killed, and rise after t days.
Mk	14:30	twice you will deny me t times."
Jn	2:19	and in t days I will raise it up."
1 Cor	13:13	So faith, hope, love remain, these t;
1 Cor	14:27	let it be two or at most t, and each
2 Cor	12: 8	T times I begged the Lord
2 Cor	13: 1	of two or t witnesses a fact shall be
1 Jn	5: 7	So there are t that testify,

THRESH → THRESHING

Mi	4:13	Arise and t, O daughter Zion;

THRESHING → THRESH

Ru	3: 3	attire and go down to the t floor.
2 Sm	24:18	the Lord on the t floor of Araunah
Hos	9: 1	a harlot's hire upon every t floor.
Lk	3:17	fan is in his hand to clear his t floor
1 Tm	5:18	shall not muzzle an ox when it is t,"

THRESHOLD

1 Sm	5: 4	hands broken off and lying on the t,
Ez	10:18	of the Lord left the t of the temple
Ez	47: 1	beneath the t of the temple toward

THREW → THROW

Ex	7:10	Aaron t his staff down before
Ex	15:25	When he t this into the water,
Ex	32:19	up, so that he t the tablets down
2 Kgs	6: 6	cut off a stick, t it into the water,
Dn	14:31	They t Daniel into a lions' den,
Jon	1:15	took Jonah and t him into the sea,
Rv	20: 3	and t it into the abyss, which he

THROATS

Ps	5:10	are corrupt. Their t are open graves;
Ps	115: 7	and no sound rises from their t.
Rom	3:13	Their t are open graves;

THRONE → ENTHRONED, THRONES

2 Sm	7:13	I will make his royal t firm forever.
1 Chr	17:12	and I will establish his t forever.
Ps	11: 4	temple; the LORD's t is in heaven.
Ps	45: 7	Your t, O god, stands forever;
Ps	47: 9	nations; God sits upon his holy t.
Ps	89:15	are the foundation of your t;
Prv	20:28	and he upholds his t by justice.
Is	6: 1	Lord seated on a high and lofty t,
Is	66: 1	The heavens are my t, the earth is
Jer	33:21	not have a son to be king upon his t,
Ez	1:26	something like a t could be seen,
Dn	7: 9	and the Ancient One took his t.
Dn	7: 9	as wool; His t was flames of fire,
Mt	5:34	not by heaven, for it is God's t;
Mt	19:28	of Man is seated on his t of glory,
Lk	1:32	the Lord God will give him the t
Acts	7:49	'The heavens are my t, the earth is
Heb	1: 8	"Your t, O God, stands forever
Heb	4:16	So let us confidently approach the t
Heb	12: 2	his seat at the right of the t of God.
Rv	2:13	that you live where Satan's t is,
Rv	3:21	the right to sit with me on my t, as I
Rv	3:21	and sit with my Father on his t.
Rv	4: 2	A t was there in heaven, and on the t
Rv	4:10	before the one who sits on the t
Rv	4:10	down their crowns before the t,
Rv	5:13	"To the one who sits on the t
Rv	20:11	Next I saw a large white t
Rv	22: 1	flowing from the t of God
Rv	22: 3	The t of God and of the Lamb will

THRONES → THRONE

Ps	122: 5	Here are the t of justice, the t
Dn	7: 9	As I watched, T were set up
Mt	19:28	will yourselves sit on twelve t,
Col	1:16	invisible, whether t or dominions
Rv	4: 4	the throne I saw twenty-four other t
Rv	20: 4	Then I saw t; those who sat on them

THRONG

Ps	35:18	will praise you before the mighty t.

THROUGH

Gn	21:12	it is t Isaac that descendants shall
Ex	15:19	had marched on dry land t the midst
Is	43: 2	When you pass t the water, I will be
Is	43: 2	When you walk t fire, you shall not
Jn	14: 6	comes to the Father except t me.
Rom	5: 1	with God t our Lord Jesus Christ,
1 Cor	8: 6	t whom all things are and t whom
Gal	2:19	For t the law I died to the law, that I
Eph	2: 8	grace you have been saved t faith,
Col	1:16	all things were created t him
Heb	1: 2	he spoke to us t a son, whom he
Heb	1: 2	and t whom he created the universe,

THROW → THREW, THROWN

Ex	1:22	"T into the river every boy that is
Ex	4: 3	LORD then said, "T it on the ground."
Zec	11:13	LORD said to me, "T it in the treasury,
Mt	5:30	you to sin, cut it off and t it away.
Mt	7: 6	or t your pearls before swine,
Jn	8: 7	is without sin be the first to t a stone

THROWN → THROW

Mk	11:23	'Be lifted up and t into the sea,'
Rv	12: 9	whole world, was t down to earth,

Rv	12: 9	and its angels were t down with it.
Rv	19:20	The two were t alive into the fiery
Rv	20:10	Devil who had led them astray was t
Rv	20:14	Hades were t into the pool of fire.

THUMMIM

Ex	28:30	you shall put the Urim and T,
Ezr	2:63	be a priest bearing the Urim and T.

THUNDER → THUNDERED, THUNDERS

Ex	9:23	LORD sent forth hail and peals of t.
Ex	20:18	When the people witnessed the t
Jb	40: 9	or can you t with a voice like his?
Mk	3:17	named Boanerges, that is, sons of t;
Rv	4: 5	lightning, rumblings, and peals of t.
Rv	6: 1	creatures cry out in a voice like t,
Rv	16:18	and peals of t, and a great

THUNDERED → THUNDER

Ps	18:14	The LORD t from heaven; the Most

THUNDERS → THUNDER

Ps	29: 3	the God of glory t, the LORD,
Rv	10: 3	out, the seven t raised their voices,
Rv	10: 4	When the seven t had spoken, I was
Rv	10: 4	what the seven t have spoken,

THYATIRA

Acts	16:14	from the city of T, a worshiper
Rv	2:18	"To the angel of the church in T,

TIBERIAS

Jn	6: 1	across the Sea of Galilee [of T].

TIBERIUS

Lk	3: 1	year of the reign of T Caesar,

TIBNI

King of Israel (1 Kgs 16:21-22).

TIDINGS

Is	40: 9	Zion, herald of glad t;
Is	41:27	I will pick out a bearer of the glad t."

TIE → TIED

Mt	23: 4	They t up heavy burdens [hard

TIED → TIE

Jos	2:21	she t the scarlet cord in the window.
Jn	13: 4	a towel and t it around his waist.

TIGLATH-PILESER → =PUL

2 Kgs	16: 7	Ahaz sent messengers to T,

TIGRIS

Gn	2:14	The name of the third river is the T;
Dn	10: 4	on the bank of the great river, the T.

TILES

Lk	5:19	the stretcher through the t

TILL

Gn	4:12	If you t the soil, it shall no longer

TIME → TIMES

Gn	4:26	that t men began to invoke the LORD
Dt	32:35	against the t they lose their footing?"
Est	4:14	that it was for a t like this that you
Ps	119:126	It is t for the LORD to act; they have
Eccl	3: 1	There is an appointed t
Eccl	3: 1	and a t for every affair under
Eccl	3:11	made everything appropriate to its t,
Dn	12: 1	"At that t there shall arise Michael,
Dn	12: 1	It shall be a t unsurpassed in distress
Hos	10:12	for it is t to seek the LORD, till he
Lk	21: 8	'I am he,' and 'The t has come.' Do not
Rom	5: 6	at the appointed t for the ungodly.
1 Cor	4: 5	judgment before the appointed t,
1 Cor	7:29	you, brothers, the t is running out.
2 Cor	6: 2	"In an acceptable t I heard you,
2 Cor	6: 2	Behold, now is a very acceptable t;
Gal	4: 4	when the fullness of t had come,
Heb	9:28	will appear a second t, not to take
1 Pt	4:17	For it is t for the judgment to begin
Rv	1: 3	in it, for the appointed t is near.
Rv	2:21	I have given her t to repent, but she
Rv	22:10	book, for the appointed t is near.

TIMES → TIME
Ex	23:14	"Three t a year you shall celebrate
Jos	6: 4	day march around the city seven t,
Ps	9:10	a stronghold in t of trouble.
Ps	31:16	My t are in your hands; rescue me
Ps	62: 9	Trust God at all t, my people!
Prv	24:16	For the just man falls seven t
Eccl	8: 5	the wise man's heart knows t
Mt	16: 3	you cannot judge the signs of the t.]
Mt	18:22	you, not seven t but seventy-seven t.
Mk	14:30	twice you will deny me three t."
Lk	17: 4	if he wrongs you seven t in one day
Lk	17: 4	and returns to you seven t saying,
Acts	1: 7	"It is not for you to know the t
1 Tm	4: 1	that in the last t some will turn away
2 Tm	3: 1	there will be terrifying t in the last

TIMOTHY
Believer from Lystra (Acts 16:1). Joined Paul on second missionary journey (Acts 16-20). Sent to settle problems at Corinth (1 Cor 4:17; 16:10). Led church at Ephesus (1 Tm 1:3). Co-writer with Paul (1 Thes 1:1; 2 Thes 1:1; Phlm 1).

TIP
Jgs	6:21	out the t of the staff he held,

TIRED
Jn	4: 6	Jesus, t from his journey, sat down

TIRZAH
1 Kgs	15:33	reign over Israel in T.

TISHBITE
1 Kgs	17: 1	Elijah the T, from Tishbe in Gilead,
2 Kgs	1: 8	"It is Elijah the T!" he exclaimed.

TITHE → TITHES
Nm	18:26	them to the LORD, a t of the tithes;
Dt	12:17	partake of your t of grain or wine
Mal	3:10	Bring the whole t

TITHES → TITHE
Mal	3: 8	we rob you?" In t and in offerings!
Mt	23:23	You pay t of mint and dill

TITUS
Gentile co-worker of Paul (Gal 2:1-3; 2 Tm 4:10); sent to Corinth (2 Cor 2:13; 7-8; 12:18), Crete (Ti 1:4-5).

TOBIAH
Enemy of Nehemiah and the exiles (Neh 2:10-19; 4; 6; 13:4-9). Son of Tobit:
Tb	1: 9	By her I had a son whom I named T.
Tb	3:17	daughter Sarah to Tobit's son T,

TOBIJAH
Zec	6:14	of the LORD in favor of Heldai, T,

TOBIT
Tb	1: 1	This book tells the story of T,
Tb	1: 3	I, T, have walked all the days of my
Tb	3:17	In the very moment that T returned
Tb	7: 4	said, "Do you know our kinsman T?"
Tb	11:16	T went out to the gate of Nineveh

TODAY
Ex	14:13	victory the LORD will win for you t.
Ex	14:13	whom you see t you will never see
Ex	34:11	commandments I am giving you t.
Dt	30:15	then, I have t set before you life
Ps	2: 7	"You are my son; t I am your father.
Ps	95: 7	Oh, that t you would hear his voice:
Lk	4:21	"T this scripture passage is fulfilled
Lk	19: 9	"T salvation has come to this house
Lk	23:43	t you will be with me in Paradise."
Heb	3: 7	"Oh, that t you would hear his voice,
Heb	3:13	yourselves daily while it is still "t,"
Heb	4: 7	he once more set a day, "t," when long
Heb	4: 7	"Oh, that t you would hear his voice:
Heb	13: 8	Jesus Christ is the same yesterday, t,

TOES
Dn	2:42	and the t partly iron and partly tile,

TOGETHER
Gn	3: 7	so they sewed fig leaves t and made

Dt	22:10	with an ox and an ass harnessed t.
Ps	2: 2	and princes plot t against the LORD
Ps	34: 4	with me; let us exalt his name t.
Is	11: 6	and the young lion shall browse t,
Ez	37: 7	it was a rattling as the bones came t,
Mt	19: 6	what God has joined t, no human
Acts	2:44	All who believed were t and had all
Acts	4:26	and the princes gathered t
Acts	5:12	They were all t in Solomon's

TOIL
Gn	3:17	In t shall you eat its yield
Gn	5:29	our work and the t of our hands."

TOLA
A judge of Israel (Jgs 10:1-2).

TOLD → TELL
Gn	3:11	"Who t you that you were naked?
Jgs	16:17	into his confidence and t her,
Ps	44: 2	our ancestors have t us The deeds
Lk	2:20	seen, just as it had been t to them.
Jn	14:29	And now I have t you this before it

TOLERABLE → TOLERATE
Lk	10:12	it will be more t for Sodom
Lk	10:14	But it will be more t for Tyre

TOLERATE → TOLERABLE
Rv	2: 2	and that you cannot t the wicked;

TOMB → TOMBS
Mk	15:46	laid him in a t that had been hewn
Mk	15:46	a stone against the entrance to the t.
Lk	24: 2	the stone rolled away from the t;

TOMBS → TOMB
Mt	23:29	You build the t of the prophets
Mt	27:52	t were opened, and the bodies

TOMORROW
Prv	27: 1	Boast not of t, for you know not
Is	22:13	wine: "Eat and drink, for t we die!"
Mt	6:34	Do not worry about t; t will take
1 Cor	15:32	"Let us eat and drink, for t we die."
Jas	4:14	no idea what your life will be like t.

TONGUE → DOUBLE-TONGUED, TONGUES
Ex	4:10	but I am slow of speech and t."
Jb	33: 2	my t and my voice form words.
Ps	34:14	Keep your t from evil, your lips
Ps	39: 2	lest I sin with my t; I will set a curb
Ps	51:16	that my t may praise your healing
Ps	52: 6	word that destroys, you deceitful t.
Ps	71:24	Yes, my t shall recount your justice
Ps	119:172	May my t sing of your promise,
Ps	137: 6	May my t stick to my palate if I do
Ps	139: 4	Even before a word is on my t,
Prv	6:17	Haughty eyes, a lying t, and hands
Prv	12:18	but the t of the wise is healing.
Prv	15: 4	A soothing t is a tree of life,
Prv	18:21	and life are in the power of the t;
Prv	25:15	and a soft t will break a bone.
Prv	26:28	The lying t is its owner's enemy,
Prv	28:23	the end than one with a flattering t.
Prv	31:26	and on her t is kindly counsel.
Song	4:11	and milk are under your t;
Is	45:23	bend; by me every t shall swear,
Is	50: 4	a well-trained t, That I might know
Is	59: 3	falsehood, and your t utters deceit.
Mk	7:33	ears and, spitting, touched his t;
Lk	16:24	of his finger in water and cool my t,
Rom	14:11	and every t shall give praise to God."
1 Cor	14: 2	who speaks in a t does not speak
1 Cor	14: 4	speaks in a t builds himself up,
1 Cor	14:13	one who speaks in a t should pray
1 Cor	14:19	also, than ten thousand words in a t.
1 Cor	14:26	a revelation, a t, or an interpretation.
1 Cor	14:27	If anyone speaks in a t, let it be two
Phil	2:11	and every t confess that Jesus Christ
Jas	3: 5	In the same way the t is a small
Jas	3: 8	but no human being can tame the t.

TONGUES → TONGUE

Ps	12: 5	Those who say, "By our t we prevail;
Acts	2: 3	there appeared to them t as of fire,
Acts	10:46	they could hear them speaking in t
Acts	19: 6	and they spoke in t and prophesied.
Rom	3:13	they deceive with their t; the venom
1 Cor	12:10	to another varieties of t; to another interpretation of t.
1 Cor	12:28	administration, and varieties of t.
1 Cor	12:30	Do all speak in t? Do all interpret?
1 Cor	13: 1	If I speak in human and angelic t,
1 Cor	13: 8	to nothing; if t, they will cease;
1 Cor	14: 5	I should like all of you to speak in t,
1 Cor	14: 5	is greater than one who speaks in t,
1 Cor	14: 9	because of speaking in t, do not
1 Cor	14:18	I speak in t more than any of you,
1 Cor	14:21	"By people speaking strange t
1 Cor	14:22	Thus, t are a sign not for those who
1 Cor	14:39	and do not forbid speaking in t,

TOOK → TAKE

Gn	2:21	he t out one of his ribs and closed
Gn	3: 6	So she t some of its fruit and ate it;
Gn	5:24	was no longer here, for God t him.
1 Mc	1:23	and t away the gold and silver
1 Mc	1:23	t all the hidden treasures he could
1 Mc	4:47	Then they t uncut stones,
Ps	78:70	servant, t him from the sheepfold.
Dn	7: 9	up and the Ancient One t his throne.
Mt	4: 5	the devil t him to the holy city,
Mt	4: 8	the devil t him up to a very high
Mt	8:17	prophet: "He t away our infirmities
Mt	26:26	they were eating, Jesus t bread,
Mt	26:27	Then he t a cup, gave thanks,
1 Cor	11:23	night he was handed over, t bread,

TOOTH → TEETH

Ex	21:24	eye for eye, t for t, hand for hand,
Mt	5:38	'An eye for an eye and a t for a t.'

TOP → TOPS

Gn	28:12	with its t reaching to the heavens;
Ex	19:20	came down to the t of Mount Sinai,
Ex	19:20	Moses to the t of the mountain,
Mt	27:51	was torn in two from t to bottom.
Jn	19:23	in one piece from the t down.

TOPHETH

2 Kgs	23:10	king also defiled T in the Valley
Jer	19:12	Lord; I will make this city like T.

TOPS → TOP

Gn	8: 5	day of the tenth month the t

TORCH → TORCHES

Gn	15:17	a smoking brazier and a flaming t,
Is	62: 1	and her victory like a burning t.
Rv	8:10	a large star burning like a t fell

TORCHES → TORCH

Ez	1:13	they seemed like t,
Dn	10: 6	his eyes were like fiery t, his arms
Rv	4: 5	Seven flaming t burned in front

TORE → TEAR

1 Mc	1:56	the law which they found they t
1 Mc	4:45	defiled it; so they t down the altar.
Mt	26:65	the high priest t his robes and said,

TORMENT → TORMENTED, TORMENTORS

Lk	16:28	lest they too come to this place of t.'

TORMENTED → TORMENT

1 Sm	16:14	he was t by an evil spirit sent
Rv	20:10	There they will be t day and night

TORMENTORS → TORMENT

Ps	137: 3	of a song; Our t, for a joyful song:
Is	51:23	I will put it into the hands of your t,

TORN → TEAR

Gn	37:33	Joseph has been t to pieces!"
1 Sm	28:17	me: he has t the kingdom from your
Mk	1:10	he saw the heavens being t open

Lk	23:45	the temple was t down the middle.
Gal	4:15	you would have t out your eyes

TORTURED

Heb	11:35	Some were t and would not accept

TOSSED → TOSSING

Eph	4:14	t by waves and swept along
Jas	1: 6	is driven and t about by the wind.

TOSSING → TOSSED

Is	57:20	But the wicked are like the t sea

TOUCH → TOUCHED, TOUCHES

Gn	3: 3	'You shall not eat it or even t it,
Ex	19:12	the mountain, or even to t its base.
Nm	4:15	they shall not t the sacred objects;
Ps	105:15	"Do not t my anointed, to my
Wis	3: 1	of God, and no torment shall t them.
Is	52:11	forth from there, t nothing unclean!
Ez	9: 6	But do not t any marked with the X;
Mt	9:21	"If only I can t his cloak, I shall be
Lk	18:15	infants to him that he might t them,
Lk	24:39	T me and see, because a ghost does
2 Cor	6:17	"and t nothing unclean; then I will
Col	2:21	not handle! Do not taste! Do not t!"
Heb	11:28	of the firstborn might not t them.

TOUCHED → TOUCH

1 Sm	10:26	whose hearts the Lord had t.
Is	6: 7	He t my mouth with it. "See," he said,
Is	6: 7	"now that this has t your lips,
Jer	1: 9	extended his hand and t my mouth,
Dn	10:16	like a man's hand t my lips; I opened
Mt	8: 3	He stretched out his hand, t him,
Mt	14:36	and as many as t it were healed.
Mk	5:30	and asked, "Who has t my clothes?"
Acts	19:12	aprons that t his skin were applied
1 Jn	1: 1	and t with our hands

TOUCHES → TOUCH

Ps	104:32	if God t the mountains, they smoke!
Zec	2:12	Whoever t you t the apple of my
Heb	12:20	"If even an animal t the mountain,

TOWER → TOWERS, WATCHTOWER

Gn	11: 4	a city and a t with its top in the sky,
Ps	61: 4	of strength against the foe.
Prv	18:10	The name of the Lord is a strong t;
Lk	14:28	construct a t does not first sit down

TOWERS → TOWER

Ps	48:13	around it, note the number of its t.
Ps	122: 7	ramparts, prosperity within your t."

TOWN

Mt	2:23	and dwelt in a t called Nazareth,
Mt	10:11	Whatever t or village you enter,
Lk	2: 3	to be enrolled, each to his own t.

TRADE

Rv	18:22	No craftsmen in any t will ever be

TRADITION

Mt	15: 2	"Why do your disciples break the t
Mk	7:13	of your t that you have handed on.
Col	2: 8	philosophy according to human t,

TRAIN → TRAINED, TRAINING, TRAINS

Prv	22: 6	T a boy in the way he should go;
1 Tm	4: 7	silly myths. T yourself for devotion,

TRAINED → TRAIN

Heb	5:14	for those whose faculties are t
Heb	12:11	to those who are t by it.

TRAINING → TRAIN

1 Tm	4: 8	while physical t is of limited value,
2 Tm	3:16	and for t in righteousness,
Ti	2:12	and t us to reject godless ways

TRAINS → TRAIN

Ps	144: 1	my rock, who t my hands for battle,

TRAITOR → TREASON

Lk	6:16	and Judas Iscariot, who became a t.

TRAMPLE → TRAMPLED
Ps	91:13	the viper, t the lion and the dragon.
Am	2: 7	They t the heads of the weak
Am	8: 4	Hear this, you who t upon the needy
Mt	7: 6	swine, lest they t them underfoot,
Rv	11: 2	Gentiles, who will t the holy city

TRAMPLED → TRAMPLE
1 Mc	3:45	The sanctuary was t on,
Is	63: 6	I t down the peoples in my anger,
Dn	8: 7	it, to the ground, and t upon it;
Dn	8:10	and some of the stars and t on them.
Mt	5:13	to be thrown out and t underfoot.
Lk	21:24	Jerusalem will be t underfoot

TRANCE
Acts	10:10	making preparations he fell into a t.
Acts	11: 5	of Joppa when in a t I had a vision,
Acts	22:17	praying in the temple, I fell into a t

TRANSFIGURED
Mt	17: 2	And he was t before them; his face
Mk	9: 2	And he was t before them,

TRANSFORMED
Rom	12: 2	be t by the renewal of your mind,
2 Cor	3:18	are being t into the same image

TRANSGRESS → TRANSGRESSED, TRANSGRESSION, TRANSGRESSIONS, TRANSGRESSOR
Jos	23:16	If you t the covenant of the Lord,

TRANSGRESSED → TRANSGRESS
Dn	9:11	Because all Israel t your law

TRANSGRESSION → TRANSGRESS
Dn	9:24	Then t will stop and sin will end,
Gal	6: 1	even if a person is caught in some t,

TRANSGRESSIONS → TRANSGRESS
Gal	3:19	the law? It was added for t,

TRANSGRESSOR → TRANSGRESS
Gal	2:18	down, then I show myself to be a t.
Jas	2:11	kill, you have become a t of the law.

TRANSPARENT
Rv	21:21	the city was of pure gold, t as glass.

TRAP → ENTRAP
Jos	23:13	they will be a snare and a t for you,
Ps	69:23	snare for them, a t for their friends.
Is	8:14	the houses of Israel, A t and a snare
Lk	20:20	to be righteous who were to t him
Rom	11: 9	their table become a snare and a t,

TRAVEL → TRAVELER
Ex	13:21	Thus they could t both day

TRAVELER → TRAVEL
Jer	14: 8	like a t who has stopped

TREAD → TREADING
Ps	91:13	You shall t upon the asp
Lk	10:19	I have given you the power 'to t
Rv	19:15	and he himself will t out in the wine

TREADING → TREAD
Dt	25: 4	muzzle an ox when it is t out grain.
Mi	7:19	on us, t underfoot our guilt?
1 Cor	9: 9	shall not muzzle an ox while it is t

TREASON → TRAITOR
2 Kgs	11:14	tore her garments and cried out, "T,

TREASURE → TREASURED, TREASURES, TREASURIES, TREASURY
Ps	119:11	In my heart I t your promise, that I
Sir	29:12	Store up almsgiving in your t house,
Is	33: 6	the fear of the Lord is her t.
Mt	6:21	For where your t is, there also will
Mt	13:44	heaven is like a t buried in a field,
Mt	19:21	poor, and you will have t in heaven.
Lk	12:33	an inexhaustible t in heaven that no
2 Cor	4: 7	we hold this t in earthen vessels,
1 Tm	6:19	thus accumulating as t a good

TREASURED → TREASURE
Jb	23:12	of his mouth I have t in my heart.

TREASURES → TREASURE
Dt	33:19	seas and the hidden t of the sand."
2 Kgs	24:13	He carried off all the t of the temple
Prv	10: 2	Ill-gotten t profit nothing, but virtue
Is	45: 3	I will give you t out of the darkness,
Mt	6:19	store up for yourselves t on earth,
Col	2: 3	in whom are hidden all the t
Heb	11:26	Anointed greater wealth than the t

TREASURIES → TREASURE
Prv	8:21	who love me, and filling their t.

TREASURY → TREASURE
Mt	27: 6	to deposit this in the temple t, for it
Mk	12:43	all the other contributors to the t.

TREE → TREES
Gn	1:29	every t that has seed-bearing fruit
Gn	2: 9	with the t of life in the middle
Gn	2: 9	and the t of the knowledge of good
Gn	3:24	to guard the way to the t of life.
Dt	21:23	shall not remain on the t overnight.
Dt	21:23	curse rests on him who hangs on a t,
1 Kgs	14:23	high hill and under every green t.
1 Kgs	19: 4	until he came to a broom t and sat
Ps	52:10	like an olive t in the house of God,
Ps	92:13	just shall flourish like the palm t,
Prv	3:18	She is a t of life to those who grasp
Prv	11:30	The fruit of virtue is a t of life,
Prv	27:18	He who tends a fig t eats its fruit,
Is	65:22	As the years of a t, so the years
Jer	17: 8	He is like a t planted beside
Ez	17:24	Bring low the high t, lift high the lowly t,
Ez	17:24	Wither up the green t, and make the withered t bloom.
Hos	9:10	first fruits of the fig t in its prime,
Hos	14: 7	His splendor shall be like the olive t
Hb	3:17	For though the fig t blossom not
Mt	3:10	Therefore every t that does not bear
Mt	12:33	"Either declare the t good and its
Mt	12:33	or declare the t rotten and its fruit is
Mt	12:33	rotten, for a t is known by its fruit.
Mk	11:13	from a distance a fig t in leaf,
Lk	19: 4	climbed a sycamore t in order to see
Acts	5:30	him killed by hanging him on a t.
Rom	11:24	what is by nature a wild olive t,
Rom	11:24	grafted back into their own olive t.
Jas	3:12	Can a fig t, my brothers,
Rv	2: 7	right to eat from the t of life that is
Rv	22: 2	side of the river grew the t of life
Rv	22:14	so as to have the right to the t of life
Rv	22:19	take away his share in the t of life

TREES → TREE
Gn	3: 1	eat from any of the t in the garden?"
Gn	3: 2	eat of the fruit of the t in the garden;
Dt	20:19	you shall not destroy its t by putting
Dt	20:19	but you must not cut down the t.
Dt	20:19	After all, are the t of the field men,
Jgs	9: 8	Once the t went to anoint a king
1 Chr	14:15	marching in the tops of the mastic t,
Ps	96:12	Then let all the t of the forest rejoice
Is	55:12	all the t of the countryside shall clap
Ez	47:12	fruit t of every kind shall grow;
Zec	4:11	another under your vines and fig t."
Zec	4:11	"What are these two olive t at each
Mt	3:10	now the ax lies at the root of the t.
Mk	8:24	"I see people looking like t
Jude	1:12	by winds, fruitless t in late autumn,
Rv	8: 7	up, along with a third of the t and all
Rv	11: 4	These are the two olive t

TREMBLE → TREMBLED, TREMBLES, TREMBLING
1 Chr	16:30	T before him, all the earth; he has
Ps	99: 1	The Lord is king, the peoples t;
Ps	114: 7	T, earth, before the Lord,
Jer	5:22	should you not t before me? I made
Jl	2: 1	Let all who dwell in the land t,
Hb	3: 6	his look makes the nations t.

TREMBLED → TREMBLE
Ex	19:16	so that all the people in the camp t.
Ex	20:18	smoking, they all feared and t.
2 Sm	22: 8	the foundations of the heavens t

TREMBLES → TREMBLE
Ps	97: 4	the world; the earth sees and t.
Ps	104:32	If God glares at the earth, it t;
Is	66: 2	and afflicted man who t at my word.

TREMBLING → TREMBLE
Ps	2:11	fear; with t bow down in homage,
Phil	2:12	out your salvation with fear and t.

TRENCH
1 Kgs	18:38	and it lapped up the water in the t.

TRESPASSES
2 Cor	5:19	not counting their t against them

TRIAL → TRIALS
2 Pt	2: 9	how to rescue the devout from t
Rv	3:10	safe in the time of t that is going

TRIALS → TRIAL
Lk	22:28	you who have stood by me in my t;
Jas	1: 2	when you encounter various t,
1 Pt	1: 6	have to suffer through various t,

TRIBE → HALF-TRIBE, TRIBES
Nm	1: 4	there shall be a man from each t,
Nm	36: 9	can pass from one t to another,
Jos	13:14	to the t of Levi Moses assigned no
1 Kgs	11:13	I will leave your son one t
Ps	78:68	God chose the t of Judah,
Heb	7:13	are said belonged to a different t,
Rv	5: 5	The lion of the t of Judah, the root
Rv	5: 9	God those from every t and tongue,
Rv	14: 6	on earth, to every nation, t, tongue,

TRIBES → TRIBE
Gn	49:28	All these are the twelve t of Israel,
Ex	24: 4	pillars for the twelve t of Israel.
Ex	39:14	the name of one of the twelve t.
Jgs	21: 6	of the t of Israel has been cut off.
1 Kgs	11:31	grasp and will give you ten of the t.
1 Kgs	18:31	for the number of t of the sons
Ps	122: 4	Here the t have come, the t
Is	49: 6	to raise up the t of Jacob,
Mt	19:28	judging the twelve t of Israel.
Jas	1: 1	to the twelve t in the dispersion,
Rv	21:12	of the twelve t of the Israelites.

TRIBUTE
1 Kgs	5: 1	they paid Solomon t and were his

TRIED → TRY
Ex	8:14	Though the magicians t to bring
Jn	19:12	Pilate t to release him; but the Jews
Gal	1:23	is now preaching the faith he once t

TRIMMED
Mt	25: 7	virgins got up and t their lamps.

TRIUMPH → TRIUMPHS
Ps	118: 7	helper; I shall look in t on my foes.
2 Cor	2:14	who always leads us in t in Christ
Col	2:15	leading them away in t by it.

TRIUMPHS → TRIUMPH
Jas	2:13	mercy; mercy t over judgment.

TROPHIMUS
2 Tm	4:20	while I left T sick at Miletus.

TROUBLE → TROUBLED, TROUBLES
Jb	14: 1	woman is short-lived and full of t,
Ps	9:10	a stronghold in times of t.
Ps	22:12	for t is near, and there is no one
Ps	27: 5	in time of t, Will conceal me
Ps	86: 7	In this time of t I call, for you will
Prv	11: 8	The just man escapes t,
Prv	12:13	but the just comes free of t.
Prv	25:19	on] a faithless man in time of t.
Sir	51:10	Do not abandon me in time of t,
Is	33: 2	morning, our salvation in time of t!

TROUBLED → TROUBLE
Jn	14: 1	"Do not let your hearts be t.
Jn	14:27	Do not let your hearts be t or afraid.

TROUBLES → TROUBLE
Jb	5:19	Out of six t he will deliver you,
Ps	25:17	Relieve the t of my heart; bring me

TRUE → TRUTH
1 Sm	9: 6	all that he says is sure to come t.
1 Kgs	10: 6	your deeds and your wisdom is t,"
2 Chr	15: 3	For a long time Israel had no t God,
Jer	10:10	The LORD is t God, he is the living
Lk	16:11	who will trust you with t wealth?
Jn	1: 9	The t light, which enlightens
Jn	4:23	t worshipers will worship the Father
Jn	6:32	my Father gives you the t bread
Jn	7:28	me, whom you do not know, is t.
Jn	15: 1	"I am the t vine, and my Father is
Jn	17: 3	the only t God, and the one whom
Jn	19:35	has testified, and his testimony is t;
Jn	21:24	and we know that his testimony is t.
Rom	3: 4	God must be t, though every human
Phil	4: 8	brothers, whatever is t, whatever is
1 Thes	1: 9	idols to serve the living and t God
1 Jn	2: 8	which holds t in him and among
1 Jn	2: 8	and the t light is already shining.
1 Jn	5:20	to know the one who is t. And we are in the one who is t,
1 Jn	5:20	He is the t God and eternal life.
3 Jn	1:12	and you know our testimony is t.
Rv	3: 7	" 'The holy one, the t, who holds
Rv	3:14	the faithful and t witness, the source
Rv	6:10	holy and t master, before you sit
Rv	15: 3	Just and t are your ways, O king
Rv	16: 7	your judgments are t and just."
Rv	19: 2	for t and just are his judgments.
Rv	19: 9	he said to me, "These words are t;
Rv	19:11	its rider was [called] "Faithful and T."
Rv	21: 5	for they are trustworthy and t."
Rv	22: 6	"These words are trustworthy and t,

TRUMPET → TRUMPETERS, TRUMPETS
Ex	19:16	and a very loud t blast, so that all
Nm	29: 1	a day on which you sound the t.
Is	27:13	On that day, A great t shall blow,
Ez	33: 5	He heard the t blast yet refused
Jl	2:15	Blow the t Zion! proclaim a fast,
Zec	9:14	The LORD God shall sound the t,
Mt	24:31	send out his angels with a t blast,
1 Cor	15:52	in the blink of an eye, at the last t. For the t will sound, the dead will
1 Thes	4:16	an archangel and with the t of God,
Rv	1:10	behind me a voice as loud as a t,
Rv	8: 7	When the first one blew his t,

TRUMPETERS → TRUMPET
2 Chr	5:13	When the t and singers were heard

TRUMPETS → TRUMPET
Nm	10: 2	"Make two t of beaten silver,
Rv	8: 2	before God were given seven t.

TRUST → ENTRUST, ENTRUSTED, TRUSTED, TRUSTS, TRUSTWORTHY
Dt	1:32	you would not t the LORD, your God,
1 Chr	9:22	them in their position of t
Jb	4:18	Lo, he puts no t in his servants,
Jb	31:24	Had I put my t in gold or called fine
Ps	4: 6	fitting sacrifice and t in the LORD.
Ps	9:11	Those who honor your name t
Ps	25: 2	my God. In you I t; do not let me be
Ps	31: 7	worthless idols, but I t in the LORD.
Ps	31:15	But I t in you, LORD; I say, "You are
Ps	32:10	love surrounds those who t
Ps	33:21	rejoice; in your holy name we t.
Ps	37: 3	T in the LORD and do good that you
Ps	37: 5	way to the LORD; t that God will act
Ps	40: 4	in awe and they shall t in the LORD.
Ps	40: 5	Happy those whose t is the LORD,
Ps	44: 7	Not in my bow do I t, nor does my
Ps	49: 7	Those who t in their wealth

Ps	52:10	God, t in God's faithful love forever.
Ps	55:24	their days, but I put my t in you.
Ps	56: 4	I am afraid, in you I place my t.
Ps	56: 5	promise; in you I t, I do not fear.
Ps	56:12	in you I t, I do not fear. What can
Ps	62: 9	T God at all times, my people!
Ps	71: 5	Lord; my t, GOD, from my youth.
Ps	78:22	God, did not t in his saving power.
Ps	84:13	happy are those who t in you!
Ps	91: 2	and fortress, my God in whom I t."
Ps	115: 8	shall be like them, all who t in them.
Ps	115:11	Those who fear the LORD t
Ps	119:42	with a word, for I t in your word.
Ps	125: 1	Zion are they who t in the LORD,
Ps	135:18	shall be like them, all who t in them.
Ps	143: 8	for in you I t. Show me the path I
Ps	146: 3	Put no t in princes, in mere mortals
Prv	3: 5	T in the LORD with all your heart,
Prv	22:19	That your t may be in the LORD,
Sir	2: 6	T God and he will help you;
Is	26: 4	T in the LORD forever! For the LORD
Is	30:15	in quiet and in t your strength lies.
Is	31: 1	Who put their t in chariots because
Is	42:17	back in utter shame who t in idols;
Jer	2:37	has rejected those in whom you t,
Jer	5:17	the fortified city in which you t.
Jer	7: 4	Put not your t in the deceitful
Jer	7: 8	putting your t in deceitful words
Jer	7:14	me, in which you t, and to this place
Jer	9: 3	neighbor; put no t in any brother.
Jer	49:11	your widows, let them t in me.
Mi	7: 5	Put no t in a friend, have no
Heb	2:13	and again: "I will put my t in him";

TRUSTED → TRUST

1 Sm	27:12	And Achish t David, thinking,
Jb	12:20	He silences the t adviser, and takes
Ps	22: 5	In you our ancestors t; they t
Ps	22: 6	escaped; in you they t and were not
Ps	26: 1	In the LORD I have t; I have not
Ps	52: 9	but t in great wealth,
Jer	13:25	forgotten me, and t in the lying idol,
Dn	3:95	to deliver the servants that t in him;
Dn	6:24	den, unhurt because he t in his God.
Dn	13:35	she t in the Lord wholeheartedly.
Zep	3: 2	In the LORD she has not t, to her God

TRUSTS → TRUST

Ps	21: 8	For the king t in the LORD,
Ps	86: 2	save your servant who t in you.
Ps	115: 9	The house of Israel t in the LORD,
Ps	115:10	The house of Aaron t in the LORD,
Prv	16:20	happy is he who t in the LORD!
Prv	28:25	he who t in the LORD will prosper.
Prv	29:25	but he who t in the LORD is safe.
Jer	17: 7	Blessed is the man who t

TRUSTWORTHY → TRUST

Ex	18:21	men, t men who hate dishonest gain,
Tb	5: 3	find yourself a t man who will make
Tb	5: 9	and whether he is t enough to travel
Tb	10: 6	man who is traveling with him is t,
Prv	11:13	but a t man keeps a confidence.
Sir	46:15	As a t prophet he was sought out
1 Cor	4: 2	of stewards that they be found t.
1 Cor	7:25	as one who by the Lord's mercy is t.
Rv	21: 5	words down, for they are t and true."
Rv	22: 6	to me, "These words are t and true,

TRUTH → TRUE, TRUTHFUL

Gn	42:16	your words be tested for their t;
1 Kgs	22:16	but the t in the name of the LORD?"
2 Chr	18:15	but the t in the name of the LORD?"
Tb	3: 2	All your ways are mercy and t;
Ps	15: 2	is right, speaking t from the heart;
Ps	25: 5	Guide me in your t and teach me,
Ps	45: 5	In the cause of t and justice
Ps	86:11	your way that I may walk in your t,
Ps	119:43	Do not take the word of t from my
Ps	145:18	you, to all who call upon you in t.
Prv	23:23	Get the t, and sell it not— wisdom,

Sir	4:25	Never gainsay the t, and struggle
Is	59:14	For t stumbles in the public square,
Jer	9: 2	with lying, and not with t, they hold
Jer	9: 4	no one speaks the t. They have
Jer	26:15	in t it was the LORD who sent me
Dn	8:12	It cast t to the ground, and was
Am	5:10	and abhor him who speaks the t.
Zec	8:16	do: Speak the t to one another;
Mk	5:33	Jesus and told him the whole t.
Lk	20:21	of God in accordance with the t.
Jn	1:14	only Son, full of grace and t.
Jn	1:17	and t came through Jesus Christ.
Jn	4:23	worship the Father in Spirit and t;
Jn	4:24	him must worship in Spirit and t."
Jn	5:33	to John, and he testified to the t.
Jn	8:32	and you will know the t, and the t
Jn	8:40	a man who has told you the t that I
Jn	8:44	does not stand in t, because there is no t in him.
Jn	8:45	But because I speak the t, you do
Jn	14: 6	"I am the way and the t and the life.
Jn	14:17	the Spirit of t, which the world
Jn	15:26	the Spirit of t that proceeds
Jn	16:13	the Spirit of t, he will guide you to all t.
Jn	17:17	Consecrate them in the t. Your word is t.
Jn	18:37	into the world, to testify to the t.
Jn	18:37	who belongs to the t listens to my
Jn	18:38	Pilate said to him, "What is t?"
Jn	19:35	he knows that he is speaking the t,
Acts	20:30	will come forward perverting the t
Rom	1:18	of those who suppress the t by their
Rom	1:25	They exchanged the t of God
Rom	2: 8	to those who selfishly disobey the t
Rom	2:20	the formulation of knowledge and t—
Rom	9: 1	I speak the t in Christ, I do not lie;
1 Cor	5: 8	unleavened bread of sincerity and t.
1 Cor	13: 6	wrongdoing but rejoices with the t.
2 Cor	4: 2	of the t we commend ourselves
2 Cor	11:10	By the t of Christ in me, this boast
2 Cor	12: 6	foolish, for I would be telling the t.
2 Cor	13: 8	we cannot do anything against the t, but only for the t.
Gal	5: 7	you from following [the] t?
Eph	1:13	who have heard the word of t,
Eph	4:15	Rather, living the t in love,
Eph	4:21	were taught in him, as t is in Jesus,
Eph	6:14	fast with your loins girded in t,
Col	1: 5	already heard through the word of t,
2 Thes	2:10	have not accepted the love of t so
2 Thes	2:13	by the Spirit and belief in t.
1 Tm	2: 4	and to come to knowledge of the t.
1 Tm	2: 7	and apostle (I am speaking the t,
1 Tm	2: 7	teacher of the Gentiles in faith and t.
1 Tm	3:15	God, the pillar and foundation of t,
1 Tm	4: 3	those who believe and know the t.
1 Tm	6: 5	who are deprived of the t,
2 Tm	2:15	the word of t without deviation.
2 Tm	2:18	have deviated from the t by saying
2 Tm	2:25	that leads to knowledge of the t,
2 Tm	3: 7	able to reach a knowledge of the t.
2 Tm	4: 4	will stop listening to the t and will
Ti	1: 1	and the recognition of religious t,
Ti	1:14	of people who have repudiated the t.
Heb	10:26	after receiving knowledge of the t,
Jas	1:18	the word of t that we may be a kind
Jas	3:14	do not boast and be false to the t.
Jas	5:19	among you should stray from the t
1 Pt	1:22	to the t for sincere mutual love,
2 Pt	1:12	are established in the t you have.
2 Pt	2: 2	of them the way of t will be reviled.
1 Jn	1: 8	ourselves, and the t is not in us.
1 Jn	2: 4	is a liar, and the t is not in him.
1 Jn	2:21	not because you do not know the t
1 Jn	2:21	because every lie is alien to the t.
1 Jn	3:18	in word or speech but in deed and t.
1 Jn	3:19	shall know that we belong to the t
1 Jn	4: 6	This is how we know the spirit of t
1 Jn	5: 6	one that testifies, and the Spirit is t.
2 Jn	1: 1	only I but also all who know the t—
2 Jn	1: 2	because of the t that dwells in us

2 Jn	1: 3	Jesus Christ the Father's Son in t
2 Jn	1: 4	in the t just as we were commanded
3 Jn	1: 1	the beloved Gaius whom I love in t.
3 Jn	1: 3	to how truly you walk in the t.
3 Jn	1: 4	my children are walking in the t.
3 Jn	1: 8	that we may be co-workers in the t.
3 Jn	1:12	from all, even from the t itself.

TRUTHFUL → TRUTH
Prv	12:19	T lips endure forever, the lying
Prv	14:25	The t witness saves lives, but he
2 Cor	6: 7	in t speech, in the power of God;

TRY → TRIED
Ps	26: 2	Test me, LORD, and t me; search my
1 Cor	10:33	just as I t to please everyone
2 Cor	5:11	of the Lord, we t to persuade others;
Eph	5:10	T to learn what is pleasing

TRYPHO
1 Mc	11:39	When a certain T, who had
1 Mc	13:31	T dealt treacherously

TUNIC → TUNICS
Ex	28: 4	a brocaded t, a miter and a sash.
Lk	9: 3	and let no one take a second t.
Jn	19:23	They also took his t, but the t was

TUNICS → TUNIC
Ex	28:40	of Aaron's sons you shall have t

TURN → TURNED, TURNING, TURNS
Ex	23:27	I will make all your enemies t
Nm	32:15	If you t away from following him,
2 Chr	7:14	presence and t from their evil ways,
2 Chr	30: 9	he will not t away his face from you
Ps	6: 5	T, LORD, save my life; in your mercy
Ps	119:132	T to me and be gracious, your edict
Prv	7:25	Let not your heart t to her ways,
Is	6:10	and they will t and be healed.
Is	28: 6	who t back the battle at the gate.
Is	30:21	when you would t to the right
Is	45:22	T to me and be safe, all you ends
Jer	31:13	I will t their mourning into joy,
Ez	33: 9	man, trying to t him from his way,
Ez	33: 9	and he refuses to t from his way,
Ez	33:11	T, t from your evil ways!
Mal	3:24	To t the hearts of the fathers to their
Mt	5:39	t the other one to him as well.
Lk	1:17	of Elijah to t the hearts of fathers
Acts	26:18	eyes that they may t from darkness
Gal	4: 9	how can you t back again
1 Pt	3:11	must t from evil and do good,

TURNED → TURN
Dt	23: 6	t this curse into a blessing for you,
1 Kgs	11: 4	was old his wives had t his heart
2 Chr	15: 4	in their distress they t to the LORD,
Est	9:22	as the month which was t for them
Ps	114: 3	beheld and fled; the Jordan t back.
Is	9:11	For all this, his wrath is not t back,
Jl	3: 4	The sun will be t to darkness,
Jon	3:10	their actions how they t from their
Zec	7:11	they stubbornly t their backs
Lk	22:32	and once you have t back, you must

TURNING → TURN
Dt	5:32	not t aside to the right or to the left,
Dt	28:14	not t aside to the right or to the left

TURNS → TURN
2 Cor	3:16	whenever a person t to the Lord

TURTLEDOVES
Lv	5: 7	as the sin offering for his sin two t
Lv	12: 8	she may take two t or two pigeons,
Lk	2:24	to offer the sacrifice of "a pair of t

TWELVE
Gn	35:22	The sons of Jacob were now t.
Gn	49:28	All these are the t tribes of Israel,
Ex	24: 4	and t pillars for the t tribes of Israel.
Ex	28:21	t of them to match the names
Ex	28:21	with the name of one of the t tribes.

Jos	4: 3	to take up t stones from this spot
1 Kgs	11:30	his new cloak, tore it into t pieces,
1 Kgs	18:31	He took t stones, for the number
Mt	10: 1	he summoned his t disciples
Lk	9:17	up, they filled t wicker baskets.
Jas	1: 1	to the t tribes in the dispersion,
Rv	12: 1	and on her head a crown of t stars.
Rv	21:12	with t gates where t angels were
Rv	21:12	[the names] of the t tribes
Rv	21:14	the city had t courses of stones as its
Rv	21:14	were inscribed the t names of the t
Rv	21:21	The t gates were t pearls,
Rv	22: 2	that produces fruit t times a year,

TWENTY
Nm	1: 3	all the men in Israel of t years

TWICE → TWO
Ex	16: 5	let it be t as much as they gather
Nm	20:11	Moses struck the rock t with his
1 Sm	18:11	the wall, but t David escaped him.]
1 Kgs	11: 9	of Israel, who had appeared to him t
Jb	42:10	to Job t as much as he had before.
Mk	14:30	the cock crows t you will deny me

TWILIGHT
Ex	12: 6	be slaughtered during the evening t.
Ex	16:12	In the evening t you shall eat flesh,

TWINS
Gn	25:24	came, there were t in her womb.

TWO → SECOND, TWICE, TWO-EDGED
Gn	1:16	God made the t great lights,
Gn	4:19	Lamech took t wives; the name
Gn	6:19	living creatures you shall bring t
Ex	31:18	he gave him the t tablets
Ex	34: 1	"Cut t stone tablets like the former,
Dt	4:13	which he wrote on t tablets of stone.
Dt	17: 6	The testimony of t or three
Dt	25:13	shall not keep t differing weights
1 Kgs	3:16	t harlots came to the king and stood
Prv	30: 7	T things I ask of you, deny them not
Prv	30:15	The t daughters of the leech are,
Eccl	4: 9	T are better than one: they get
Is	6: 2	with t they veiled their faces,
Is	6: 2	feet, and with t they hovered aloft.
Ez	1:11	Each had t wings spread
Ez	1:11	while the other t wings of each
Dn	8: 3	the river a ram with t great horns,
Zec	4:11	"What are these t olive trees at each
Zec	14: 4	of Olives shall be cleft in t from east
Mt	6:24	"No one can serve t masters. He will
Mt	18:16	take one or t others along with you,
Mt	18:16	be established on the testimony of t
Mt	19: 5	and the t shall become one flesh'?
Mk	6: 7	began to send them out t by t
Mk	12:42	in t small coins worth a few cents.
Mk	15:27	him they crucified t revolutionaries,
Lk	9:30	t men were conversing with him,
Lk	17:35	there will be t women grinding meal
Lk	18:10	"T people went up to the temple area
1 Cor	6:16	For "the t," it says, "will become one
Gal	4:24	These women represent t covenants.
Eph	5:31	and the t shall become one flesh."
Rv	11: 3	I will commission my t witnesses
Rv	19:20	The t were thrown alive

TWO-EDGED → EDGE, TWO
Sir	21: 3	Every offense is a t sword; when it
Heb	4:12	effective, sharper than any t sword,
Rv	1:16	A sharp t sword came out of his
Rv	2:12	one with the sharp t sword says this:

TYCHICUS
Companion of Paul (Acts 20:4; Eph 6:21; Col 4:7; 2 Tm 4:12; Ti 3:12).

TYPE
Rom	5:14	who is the t of the one who was

TYRANNUS
Acts	19: 9	discussions in the lecture hall of T.

TYRE

1 Kgs	5:15	king of **T**, heard that Solomon had
Ps	45:13	honor him, daughter of **T**.
Is	23: 1	Oracle on **T**: Wail, O ships
Ez	27: 2	son of man, utter a lament over **T**,
Ez	28:12	utter a lament over the king of **T**,
Mt	11:22	it will be more tolerable for **T**

U

UGLY

Gn	41: 3	them seven other cows, **u** and gaunt,

UNAPPROACHABLE

1 Tm	6:16	who dwells in **u** light, and whom no

UNBELIEF → UNBELIEVER, UNBELIEVERS, UNBELIEVING

Mk	9:24	cried out, "I do believe, help my **u**!"
Rom	11:20	They were broken off because of **u**,
Rom	11:23	if they do not remain in **u**, will be
1 Tm	1:13	I acted out of ignorance in my **u**.

UNBELIEVER → UNBELIEF

1 Cor	7:12	any brother has a wife who is an **u**,
1 Cor	7:13	woman has a husband who is an **u**,
1 Cor	10:27	If an **u** invites you and you want
1 Cor	14:24	an **u** or uninstructed person should
2 Cor	6:15	a believer in common with an **u**?
1 Tm	5: 8	the faith and is worse than an **u**.

UNBELIEVERS → UNBELIEF

1 Cor	6: 6	against brother, and that before **u**?
1 Cor	14:22	not for those who believe but for **u**, whereas prophecy is not for **u**
1 Cor	14:23	people or **u** should come in,
2 Cor	4: 4	age has blinded the minds of the **u**,
2 Cor	6:14	with those who are different, with **u**.

UNBELIEVING → UNBELIEF

1 Cor	7:14	the **u** husband is made holy through
1 Cor	7:14	the **u** wife is made holy through
Ti	1:15	are defiled and **u** nothing is clean;

UNCIRCUMCISED → UNCIRCUMCISION

Ex	12:48	no man who is **u** may partake of it.
1 Sm	17:26	Who is this **u** Philistine in any case,
1 Mc	1:48	to leave their sons **u**, and to let
Jer	9:25	whole house of Israel, are **u** in heart.
Acts	7:51	people, **u** in heart and ears,
Rom	3:30	of faith and the **u** through faith.
Rom	4:11	through faith while he was **u**.
Rom	4:11	the father of all the **u** who believe,
1 Cor	7:18	Was an **u** person called? He should
Gal	2: 7	entrusted with the gospel to the **u**,

UNCIRCUMCISION → UNCIRCUMCISED

Rom	2:25	your circumcision has become **u**.
1 Cor	7:19	nothing, and **u** means nothing;
Gal	5: 6	neither circumcision nor **u** counts
Gal	6:15	nor does **u**, but only a new creation.
Col	2:13	and the **u** of your flesh, he brought
Col	3:11	not Greek and Jew, circumcision and **u**,

UNCLEAN → UNCLEANNESS

Lv	5: 2	touches any **u** thing, as the carcass of an **u** wild animal,
Lv	5: 2	and thus becomes **u** and guilty;
1 Mc	1:47	to sacrifice swine and **u** animals,
Is	6: 5	For I am a man of **u** lips,
Is	6: 5	living among a people of **u** lips;
Is	52:11	touch nothing **u**! Out from there!
Mk	3:11	whenever **u** spirits saw him they
Mk	6: 7	gave them authority over **u** spirits.
Acts	10:14	have I eaten anything profane and **u**."
Rom	14:14	Lord Jesus that nothing is **u** in itself;
Rom	14:14	it is **u** for someone who thinks it **u**.
2 Cor	6:17	"and touch nothing **u**; then I will
Rv	21:27	but nothing **u** will enter it,

UNCLEANNESS → UNCLEAN

Lv	5: 3	it, touches some human **u**,
Lv	5: 3	whatever kind of **u** this may be,

UNCLOTHED

2 Cor	5: 4	because we do not wish to be **u**

UNCOVER → UNCOVERED

Ru	3: 4	Then go, **u** a place at his feet,

UNCOVERED → UNCOVER

Ru	3: 7	she stole up, **u** a place at his feet,

UNDER

Gn	24: 2	"Put your hand **u** my thigh,
Gn	47:29	put your hand **u** my thigh as a sign
1 Kgs	5: 5	every man **u** his vine or **u** his fig
Jer	3:13	yon to strangers [**u** every green tree]
Mi	4: 4	Every man shall sit **u** his own vine
Mi	4: 4	or **u** his own fig tree, undisturbed;
Mt	5:15	and then put it **u** a bushel basket;
Mt	22:44	I place your enemies **u** your feet" '?
Lk	13:34	a hen gathers her brood **u** her wings,
Acts	4:12	any other name **u** heaven given
Rom	6:14	since you are not **u** the law but **u**
1 Cor	15:27	"he subjected everything **u** his feet."
Gal	3:10	on works of the law are **u** a curse;
Gal	4: 4	born of a woman, born **u** the law,

UNDERSTAND → UNDERSTANDING, UNDERSTANDS, UNDERSTOOD

Gn	11: 7	one will not **u** what another says."
Jb	42: 3	with great things that I do not **u**;
Ps	73:16	Though I tried to **u** all this, it was
Ps	119:27	Make me **u** the way of your
Prv	2: 5	will you **u** the fear of the LORD;
Prv	2: 9	you will **u** rectitude and justice,
Prv	30:18	for me, yes, four I cannot **u**:
Is	44:18	their hearts so that they cannot **u**.
Jer	17: 9	heart, beyond remedy; who can **u** it?
Dn	9:25	Know and **u** this:
Hos	14:10	Let him who is wise **u** these things;
Mt	13:15	ears and **u** with their heart and be
Mt	24:15	in the holy place (let the reader **u**),
Mk	4:13	to them, "Do you not **u** this parable?
Mk	4:13	how will you **u** any of the parables?
Lk	24:45	their minds to **u** the scriptures.
Jn	13: 7	you do not **u** now, but you will **u**
Acts	8:30	"Do you **u** what you are reading?"
Rom	7:15	What I do, I do not **u**. For I do not
Rom	15:21	have never heard of him shall **u**."
1 Cor	2:12	we may **u** the things freely given us
1 Cor	2:14	and he cannot **u** it, because it is
Eph	5:17	try to **u** what is the will of the Lord.
Heb	11: 3	By faith we **u** that the universe was
2 Pt	3:16	them there are some things hard to **u**

UNDERSTANDING → UNDERSTAND

Ex	36: 1	**u** in knowing how to execute all
Dt	32:28	devoid of reason, having no **u**.
1 Kgs	5: 9	and exceptional **u** and knowledge,
Jb	12:12	wisdom, and with length of days **u**.
Jb	28:12	and where is the place of **u**?
Jb	28:28	is wisdom; and avoiding evil is **u**.
Jb	32: 8	of the Almighty, that gives him **u**.
Ps	119:130	sheds light, gives **u** to the simple.
Prv	2: 2	wisdom, inclining your heart to **u**;
Prv	2: 6	his mouth come knowledge and **u**;
Prv	3:13	finds wisdom, the man who gains **u**!
Prv	15:21	the man of **u** goes the straight way.
Prv	15:32	but he who heeds reproof gains **u**.
Prv	16:16	To acquire **u** is more desirable than
Prv	18: 2	The fool takes no delight in **u**,
Prv	19: 8	he who keeps **u** will be successful.
Prv	23:23	sell it not— wisdom, instruction and **u**.
Is	11: 2	a spirit of wisdom and of **u**, A spirit
Is	40:14	or showed him the way of **u**?
Dn	10:12	you made up your mind to acquire **u**
Hos	4:11	and new deprive my people of **u**.
Mk	12:33	heart, with all your **u**, with all your
Lk	2:47	heard him were astounded at his **u**
Phil	4: 7	that surpasses all **u** will guard your
Col	1: 9	through all spiritual wisdom and **u**
Col	2: 2	all the richness of fully assured **u**,
2 Tm	2: 7	for the Lord will give you **u**

Jas   3:13   Who among you is wise and **u**?

UNDERSTANDS → UNDERSTAND
1 Chr 28: 9   hearts and **u** all the mind's thoughts.
Mt   13:23   the one who hears the word and **u** it,

UNDERSTOOD → UNDERSTAND
Neh   8:12   for they **u** the words that had been
Is   40:21   Have you not **u**? Since the earth was
Rom   1:20   divinity have been able to be **u**

UNDERTAKEN
Lk   1: 1   Since many have **u** to compile
1 Mc   4:51   finished all the work they had **u**.

UNFAIR
Ez   18:25   Is it my way that is **u**, or rather, are not your ways
                u?

UNFAITHFUL
Nm   5:12   goes astray and becomes **u** to him
Rom   3: 3   What if some were **u**? Will their

UNGODLINESS → UNGODLY
Jer   23:15   **u** has gone forth into the whole

UNGODLY → UNGODLINESS
Rom   5: 6   died at the appointed time for the **u**.

UNGRATEFUL
Lk   6:35   for he himself is kind to the **u**
2 Tm   3: 2   disobedient to their parents, **u**,

UNHOLY
1 Tm   1: 9   and sinful, the **u** and profane,

UNITED → UNITY
Rom   6: 5   be **u** with him in the resurrection.
1 Cor   1:10   that you be **u** in the same mind

UNITY → UNITED
Eph   4: 3   preserve the **u** of the spirit through
Eph   4:13   until we all attain to the **u** of faith

UNJUST
Rom   3: 5   Is God **u**, humanly speaking,
Heb   6:10   God is not **u** so as to overlook your

UNKNOWN
Acts   17:23   an altar inscribed, 'To an **U** God.'

UNLEAVENED
Ex   12:17   then, this custom of the **u** bread.
Dt   16:16   at the feast of **U** Bread, at the feast
Mt   26:17   first day of the Feast of **U** Bread,

UNLESS
Ps   127: 1   **U** the LORD build the house,
Ps   127: 1   **U** the LORD guard the city,
Jn   4:48   to him, "**U** you people see signs
Jn   12:24   you, **u** a grain of wheat falls
Acts   8:31   "How can I, **u** someone instructs me?"

UNMARRIED
1 Cor   7: 8   Now to the **u** and to widows, I say:
1 Cor   7:32   An **u** man is anxious

UNNATURAL
Rom   1:26   exchanged natural relations for **u**,
Jude   1: 7   promiscuity and practiced **u** vice,

UNPRODUCTIVE
1 Cor   14:14   spirit is at prayer but my mind is **u**.
Ti   3:14   needs, so that they may not be **u**.

UNPUNISHED
Prv   6:29   none who touches her shall go **u**.
Prv   11:21   Truly the evil man shall not go **u**,
Prv   19: 5   The false witness will not go **u**,
Prv   28:20   in haste to grow rich will not go **u**.

UNQUENCHABLE
Lk   3:17   the chaff he will burn with **u** fire."

UNRIGHTEOUS
1 Pt   3:18   the righteous for the sake of the **u**,
2 Pt   2: 9   to keep the **u** under punishment

UNSEARCHABLE
Rom   11:33   his judgments and how **u** his ways!

UNSHRUNKEN
Mt   9:16   an old cloak with a piece of **u** cloth,

UNSPIRITUAL
Jas   3:15   down from above but is earthly, **u**,

UNSTABLE
2 Pt   3:16   **u** distort to their own destruction,

UNTIE
Lk   13:15   one of you on the sabbath **u** his ox
Lk   19:30   has ever sat. **U** it and bring it here.

UNVEILED
1 Cor   11: 5   with her head **u** brings shame
2 Cor   3:18   gazing with **u** face on the glory

UNWASHED
Mt   15:20   to eat with **u** hands does not defile."
Mk   7: 2   meals with unclean, that is, **u**, hands.

UNWILLING
2 Thes   3:10   you that if anyone was **u** to work,

UNWORTHILY
1 Cor   11:27   drinks the cup of the Lord **u** will have

UPHELD → UPHOLD
Rom   14: 4   And he will be **u**, for the Lord is

UPHOLD → UPHELD, UPHOLDS
Is   41:10   **u** you with my right hand of justice.
Is   42: 1   Here is my servant whom I **u**,

UPHOLDS → UPHOLD
Ps   63: 9   fast to you; your right hand **u** me.

UPRIGHT → UPRIGHTLY
Gn   37: 7   my sheaf rose to an **u** position,
Dt   32: 4   without deceit, how just and **u** he is!
Jb   1: 1   a blameless and **u** man named Job,
Jb   1: 8   blameless and **u**, fearing God
Jb   2: 3   faultless and **u**, fearing God
Ps   11: 7   just deeds; the **u** shall see his face.
Ps   25: 8   Good and **u** is the LORD, who shows
Ps   33: 1   the LORD; praise from the **u** is fitting.
Ps   64:11   all the **u** will glory in their God.
Ps   112: 4   the darkness, a light for the **u**;
Prv   2: 7   He has counsel in store for the **u**,
Prv   2:21   For the **u** will dwell in the land,
Prv   3:32   but with the **u** is his friendship.
Prv   11: 3   The honesty of the **u** guides them;
Prv   15: 8   but the prayer of the **u** is his delight.
Prv   21:29   the **u** man pays heed to his ways.

UPRIGHTLY → UPRIGHT
Prv   14: 2   He who walks **u** fears the LORD,

UPROOTED
Lk   17: 6   tree, 'Be **u** and planted in the sea,'
Jude   1:12   in late autumn, twice dead and **u**.

UR
Gn   15: 7   the LORD who brought you from **U**
Neh   9: 7   him out from **U** of the Chaldeans,

URGED
Gn   19:15   was breaking, the angels **u** Lot on,
Ex   12:33   The Egyptians likewise **u** the people

URIAH
    Hittite husband of Bathsheba, killed at David's order (2 Sm 11).

URIM
Ex   28:30   of decision you shall put the **U**
1 Sm   28: 6   or by the **U** or through prophets.
Ezr   2:63   should be a priest bearing the **U**

USE → USED, USEFUL, USELESS, USES
Sir   14: 3   and to the miser, of what **u** is gold?
Gal   5:13   But do not **u** this freedom as
2 Tm   2:20   for lofty and others for humble **u**.

USED → USE
Jn   10: 6   Although Jesus **u** this figure
1 Cor   6:11   That is what some of you **u** to be;

USEFUL → USE
2 Tm   3:16   by God and is **u** for teaching,

Phlm 1:11 to you but is now **u** to [both] you
Heb 6: 7 and brings forth crops **u** to those

USELESS →USE
Phlm 1:11 who was once **u** to you but is now

USES →USE
1 Tm 1: 8 good, provided that one **u** it as law,

UTTER →UTTERANCE, UTTERING
Lv 5: 4 as men are accustomed to **u** rashly,
Mt 5:11 and **u** every kind of evil against you
Rv 13: 6 to **u** blasphemies against God,

UTTERANCE →UTTER
Prv 6: 2 been snared by the **u** of your lips,

UTTERING →UTTER
Rv 13: 5 was given a mouth **u** proud boasts

UZ
Jb 1: 1 the land of **U** there was a blameless

UZZAH
2 Sm 6: 6 **U** reached out his hand to the ark
1 Chr 13: 9 **U** stretched out his hand to steady

UZZIAH →=AZARIAH
Son of Amaziah; king of Judah also known as Azariah (2 Kgs 15:1-7; 2 Chr 26). Struck with leprosy because of pride (2 Chr 26:16-23).

V

VAIN →VANITIES, VANITY
Lv 26:16 You will sow your seed in **v**,
Ps 2: 1 and the peoples grumble in **v**?
Ps 73:13 Is it in **v** that I have kept my heart
Ps 127: 1 they labor in **v** who build.
Ps 127: 1 city, in **v** does the guard keep watch.
Is 65:23 They shall not toil in **v**, nor beget
Ez 6:10 shall know that it was not in **v** that I,
Mt 15: 9 in **v** do they worship me, teaching as
1 Cor 15: 2 to you, unless you believed in **v**.
1 Cor 15:58 in the Lord your labor is not in **v**.
2 Cor 6: 1 not to receive the grace of God in **v**.
Gal 2: 2 not be running, or have run, in **v**.
Phil 2:16 may be that I did not run in **v** or labor in **v**.

VALLEY →VALLEYS
Jos 7:26 is why the place is called the **V**
Jos 10:12 O moon, in the **v** of Aijalon!
1 Sm 17: 3 hill, with a **v** between them.
2 Kgs 23:10 Topheth in the **V** of Ben-hinnom,
2 Chr 33: 6 by fire in the **V** of Ben-hin-nom.
Ps 23: 4 Even when I walk through a dark **v**,
Is 22: 1 Oracle of the **V** of Vision: What is
Is 40: 4 Every **v** shall be filled in,
Is 40: 4 plain, the rough country, a broad **v**.
Hos 2:17 the **v** of Achor as a door of hope.
Jl 4:14 day of the Lord in the **v** of decision.
Lk 3: 5 Every **v** shall be filled and every

VALLEYS →VALLEY
Dt 8: 7 welling up in the hills and **v**,
Song 2: 1 of Sharon, a lily of the **v**.

VALUE
Rom 3: 1 Or what is the **v** of circumcision?
1 Tm 4: 8 physical training is of limited **v**,

VANISH →VANISHED
Ps 37:20 Like the beauty of meadows they **v**;

VANISHED →VANISH
Lk 24:31 him, but he **v** from their sight.

VANITIES →VAIN
Eccl 1: 2 Vanity of **v**, says Qoheleth,
Eccl 1: 2 vanity of **v**! All things are vanity!
Eccl 12: 8 Vanity of **v**, says Qoheleth,

VANITY →VAIN
Eccl 1: 2 **V** of vanities, says Qoheleth,
Eccl 1: 2 **v** of vanities! All things are **v**!
Eccl 12: 8 **V** of vanities, says Qoheleth, all things are **v**!

VARIOUS
Mk 1:34 who were sick with **v** diseases,
Heb 1: 1 **v** ways to our ancestors through
1 Pt 1: 6 may have to suffer through **v** trials,

VASHTI
Queen of Persia replaced by Esther (Est 1-2).

VAST
Ps 139:17 O God; how **v** the sum of them!

VATS
Prv 3:10 with new wine your **v** will overflow.
Jl 2:24 and the **v** shall overflow with wine

VEGETABLES
Dn 1:12 Give us **v** to eat and water to drink.
Rom 14: 2 while the weak person eats only **v**.

VEGETATION
Gn 1:11 said, "Let the earth bring forth **v**:

VEIL →VEILED
Ex 26:31 "You shall have a **v** woven of violet,
Ex 34:33 with them, he put a **v** over his face.
Lv 4:17 before the Lord, toward the **v**.
2 Chr 3:14 He made the **v** of violet,
Is 40:22 He stretches out the heavens like a **v**,
Mt 27:51 the **v** of the sanctuary was torn in two
Mk 15:38 The **v** of the sanctuary was torn in two
Lk 23:45 the **v** of the temple was torn down the
2 Cor 3:13 who put a **v** over his face so
2 Cor 3:15 is read, a **v** lies over their hearts,
Heb 6:19 reaches into the interior behind the **v**,
Heb 9: 3 Behind the second **v** was the tabernacle
Heb 10:20 way he opened for us through the **v**,

VEILED →VEIL
2 Cor 4: 3 And even though our gospel is **v**, it is **v** for those who are perishing,

VENGEANCE →AVENGE, AVENGED, AVENGER, AVENGES, AVENGING
Nm 31: 3 and execute the Lord's **v** on them.
Sir 28: 1 vengeful will suffer the Lord's **v**,
Is 34: 8 For the Lord has a day of **v**, a year
Jer 50:15 are torn down: **V** of the Lord is this!
Na 1: 2 and angry; The Lord brings **v** on his

VENOM
Dt 32:33 Their wine is the **v** of dragons

VENT
Prv 29:11 The fool gives **v** to all his anger;

VERDICT
Lk 23:24 The **v** of Pilate was that their

VERY
Gn 1:31 had made, and he found it **v** good.
Gn 15: 1 I will make your reward **v** great."
Dt 30:14 No, it is something **v** near to you,
Mt 4: 8 took him up to a **v** high mountain,

VICTORIES →VICTORY
Ps 44: 5 my God, who bestows **v** on Jacob.

VICTORY →VICTORIES
1 Sm 2: 1 I rejoice in my **v**.
2 Sm 8: 6 The Lord brought David **v** in all his
Prv 21:31 the day of battle, but **v** is the Lord's.
Prv 24: 6 war, and the **v** is due to a wealth
1 Cor 15:54 about: "Death is swallowed up in **v**.
1 Cor 15:57 who gives us the **v** through our Lord
1 Jn 5: 4 the **v** that conquers the world is our

VIEW
Dt 32:49 and **v** the land of Canaan, which I

VILLAGE
Mt 10:11 Whatever town or **v** you enter,

VINDICATED →VINDICATION
Mt 11:19 But wisdom is **v** by her works."
1 Tm 3:16 in the flesh, **v** in the spirit,

VINDICATION →VINDICATED
Is 54:17 their **v** from me, says the Lord.

VINE → GRAPEVINE, VINES, VINEYARD, VINEYARDS
Ps	80: 9	You brought a **v** out of Egypt;
Ps	128: 3	Like a fruitful **v** your wife within
Is	36:16	each of you will eat of his own **v**
Jer	2:21	I had planted you, a choice **v**
Jer	2:21	out obnoxious to me, a spurious **v**?
Ez	17: 6	To sprout and grow up a **v**,
Ez	17: 6	Thus it became a **v**,
Hos	10: 1	Israel is a luxuriant **v** whose fruit
Mk	14:25	again the fruit of the **v** until the day
Jn	15: 1	"I am the true **v**, and my Father is the **v** grower.

VINEGAR
Nm	6: 3	he may neither drink wine **v**,
Nm	6: 3	other **v**, or any kind of grape juice,
Ps	69:22	food; for my thirst they gave me **v**.
Prv	10:26	As **v** to the teeth, and smoke

VINES → VINE
Hb	3:17	not nor fruit be on the **v**,
Rv	14:18	cut the clusters from the earth's **v**,

VINEYARD → VINE
Gn	9:20	of the soil, was the first to plant a **v**.
Dt	22: 9	"You shall not sow your **v** with two
Dt	22: 9	have sown and the yield of the **v**.
1 Kgs	21: 1	as Naboth the Jezreelite had a **v**
Prv	31:16	out of her earnings she plants a **v**.
Song	1: 6	my own **v** I have not cared for.
Is	5: 1	my friend's song concerning his **v**. My friend had a **v** on a fertile
Is	27: 2	day— The pleasant **v**, sing about it!
Mt	21:33	was a landowner who planted a **v**,
1 Cor	9: 7	Who plants a **v** without eating its

VINEYARDS → VINE
Nm	22:24	in a narrow lane between **v**
Dt	6:11	with **v** and olive groves that you did
Song	2:15	that damage the **v**; for our **v** are

VIOLENCE → VIOLENT, VIOLENTLY
Ps	7:17	their **v** falls on their own heads.
Ps	73: 6	a necklace; **v** clothes them as a robe.
Is	60:18	No longer shall **v** be heard
Ez	45: 9	Put away **v** and oppression, and do
Jl	4:19	Because of **v** done to the people
Jon	3: 8	way and from the **v** he has in hand.
Hb	2:17	For the **v** done to Lebanon shall
Hb	2:17	and **v** done to the land, to the city
Zep	3: 4	what is holy, and do **v** to the law.

VIOLENT → VIOLENCE
Mt	11:12	and the **v** are taking it by force.

VIOLENTLY → VIOLENCE
Ex	19:18	and the whole mountain trembled **v**.

VIOLET
Ex	25: 4	**v**, purple and scarlet yarn;
Ex	26:31	"You shall have a veil woven of **v**,
Ex	28:31	you shall make entirely of **v** material.
2 Chr	3:14	He made the veil of **v**, purple, crimson

VIPER → VIPERS
Acts	28: 3	was putting it on the fire when a **v**,

VIPERS → VIPER
Mt	12:34	You brood of **v**, how can you say
Mt	23:33	you brood of **v**, how can you flee
Lk	3: 7	be baptized by him, "You brood of **v**!

VIRGIN → VIRGINS
1 Kgs	1: 2	"Let a young **v** be sought to attend
Sir	9: 5	Entertain no thoughts against a **v**,
Jer	31:21	Turn back, O **v** Israel, turn back
Lam	2:13	for your comfort, **v** daughter Zion?
Mt	1:23	the **v** shall be with child and bear
1 Cor	7:36	he is behaving improperly toward his **v**,
2 Cor	11: 2	present you as a chaste **v** to Christ.

VIRGINS → VIRGIN
Est	2: 2	"Let beautiful young **v** be sought
1 Cor	7:25	Now in regard to **v**, I have no

VISIBLE
Eph	5:13	exposed by the light becomes **v**,
Col	1:16	and on earth, the **v** and the invisible,
Heb	11: 3	what is **v** came into being through

VISION → VISIONS
Gn	15: 1	of the LORD came to Abram in a **v**:
Gn	16:13	a name, saying, "You are the God of **V**";
1 Sm	3:15	the LORD. He feared to tell Eli the **v**,
Ps	89:20	Once you spoke in **v**; to your
Is	22: 1	Oracle of the Valley of **V**: What is
Dn	7: 2	In the **v** I saw during the night,
Dn	8: 1	After this first **v**, I, Daniel,
Dn	8:26	The **v** of the evenings
Dn	8:26	however, keep this **v** undisclosed,
Dn	9:24	introduced, **v** and prophecy ratified,
Dn	10: 7	I alone, Daniel, saw the **v**; but great
Dn	10: 7	although they did not see the **v**.
Lk	1:22	he had seen a **v** in the sanctuary.
Acts	9:10	and the Lord said to him in a **v**,
Acts	10:17	the meaning of the **v** he had seen,
Acts	16: 9	During [the] night Paul had a **v**.
Acts	26:19	not disobedient to the heavenly **v**.
Rv	9:17	in my **v** this is how I saw the horses

VISIONS → VISION
Nm	12: 6	you, in **v** will I reveal myself to him,
Jer	23:16	**V** of their own fancy they speak,
Lam	2:14	false and specious **v**; They did not
Ez	1: 1	heavens opened, and I saw divine **v**.
Dn	1:17	to Daniel the understanding of all **v**
Jl	3: 1	dreams, your young men shall see **v**;
Acts	2:17	your young men shall see **v**,

VOICE → VOICES
Dt	4:33	Did a people ever hear the **v** of God
Jb	40: 9	or can you thunder with a **v** like his?
Ps	29: 3	The **v** of the LORD is over the waters;
Ps	95: 7	Oh, that today you would hear his **v**:
Prv	1:20	in the open squares she raises her **v**;
Prv	8: 1	call, and Understanding raise her **v**?
Is	40: 3	A **v** cries out: In the desert prepare
Dn	9:14	done, for we did not listen to your **v**.
Mt	2:18	"A **v** was heard in Ramah,
Mt	3:17	And a **v** came from the heavens,
Mk	1: 3	A **v** of one crying out in the desert:
Jn	1:23	"I am 'the **v** of one crying
Jn	5:25	the dead will hear the **v** of the Son
Jn	10: 3	and the sheep hear his **v**, as he calls
Jn	12:28	Then a **v** came from heaven, "I have
Rom	10:18	for "Their **v** has gone forth to all
Heb	3: 7	"Oh, that today you would hear his **v**,
Rv	3:20	If anyone hears my **v** and opens

VOICES → VOICE
Rv	11:15	There were loud **v** in heaven,

VOID
Rom	4:14	faith is null and the promise is **v**.

VOMIT
Lv	18:28	otherwise the land will **v** you
Prv	26:11	As the dog returns to his **v**,
Is	28: 8	are covered with filthy **v**, with no
2 Pt	2:22	"The dog returns to its own **v**,"

VOTIVE
Lv	7:16	if the sacrifice is a **v** or a free-will
Dt	12: 6	your **v** and freewill offerings,

VOW → VOWED, VOWS
Gn	28:20	Jacob then made this **v**: "If God
Nm	6: 2	solemnly takes the nazirite **v**
Nm	21: 2	Israel then made this **v** to the LORD:
Nm	30: 3	When a man makes a **v** to the LORD
Dt	23:22	"When you make a **v** to the LORD,
Jgs	11:30	Jephthah made a **v** to the LORD.
1 Sm	1:11	and she made a **v**, promising:
Eccl	5: 3	When you make a **v** to God,
Sir	18:23	Before making a **v** have the means
Acts	18:18	hair cut because he had taken a **v**.

VOWED →VOW
Jon 2:10 to you; What I have **v** I will pay:

VOWS →VOW
Ps 22:26 my **v** I will fulfill before those who
Ps 50:14 fulfill your **v** to the Most High.
Ps 116:14 I will pay my **v** to the LORD
Jon 1:16 offered sacrifice and made **v** to him.

VULTURES
Mt 24:28 the corpse is, there the **v** will gather.

W

WADI
Nm 34: 5 from Azmon to the **W** of Egypt,
2 Kgs 24: 7 of Egypt from the **w** of Egypt

WAFERS
Ex 16:31 it tasted like **w** made with honey.

WAGE →WAGES
Rom 4: 4 A worker's **w** is credited not as a

WAGES →WAGE
Mi 1: 7 all her **w** shall be burned in the fire,
Mi 1: 7 As the **w** of a harlot they were
Mi 1: 7 to the **w** of a harlot shall they return.
Mal 3: 5 who defraud the hired man of his **w**,
Jn 6: 7 "Two hundred days' **w** worth of food
Rom 6:23 For the **w** of sin is death, but the gift

WAIL →WAILING
Mi 1: 8 For this reason I lament and **w**, I go

WAILING →WAIL
Mt 8:12 there will be **w** and grinding of teeth."
Mt 13:42 there will be **w** and grinding of teeth.
Mt 22:13 there will be **w** and grinding of teeth.'
Mt 24:51 there will be **w** and grinding of teeth.
Mt 25:30 there will be **w** and grinding of teeth.'

WAIST
Is 11: 5 shall be the band around his **w**,
Mt 3: 4 and had a leather belt around his **w**.

WAIT →WAITED
Ps 27:14 **W** for the LORD, take courage;
Ps 27:14 be stouthearted, **w** for the LORD!
Ps 37:34 **W** eagerly for the LORD, and keep
Ps 130: 5 I **w** with longing for the LORD,
Prv 1:18 These men lie in **w** for their own
Sir 2: 7 who fear the LORD, **w** for his mercy,
Is 30:18 blessed are all who **w** for him!
Hb 2: 3 If it delays, **w** for it, it will surely
Acts 1: 4 to **w** for "the promise of the Father
Rom 8:23 groan within ourselves as we **w**

WAITED →WAIT
Ps 40: 2 I **w**, **w** for the LORD; who bent down

WALK →WALKED, WALKING, WALKS
Gn 17: 1 **W** in my presence and be blameless.
Dt 26:17 God and you are to **w** in his ways
Dt 28: 9 and **w** in his ways, he will establish
Ps 23: 4 when I **w** through a dark valley,
Ps 84:12 from those who **w** without reproach.
Ps 89:16 who **w** in the radiance of your face.
Ps 115: 7 feel, feet but do not **w**, and no sound
Ps 119:45 I will **w** freely in an open space
Prv 4:12 When you **w**, your step will not be
Prv 13:20 **W** with wise men and you will become
Is 2: 3 and we may **w** in his paths."
Is 2: 5 let us **w** in the light of the LORD!
Is 30:21 "This is the way; **w** in it," when you
Is 40:31 grow weary, **w** and not grow faint.
Is 43: 2 When you **w** through fire, you shall
Jer 6:16 Which is the way to good, and **w** it;
Jer 6:16 But they said, "We will not **w** it."
Am 3: 3 Do two **w** together unless they have
Mi 4: 5 For all the peoples **w**
Mi 4: 5 we will **w** in the name of the LORD,
Mi 6: 8 and to **w** humbly with your God.
Zec 10:12 and they shall **w** in his name,
Mk 2: 9 say, 'Rise, pick up your mat and **w**'?
Jn 8:12 Whoever follows me will not **w**
2 Cor 5: 7 for we **w** by faith, not by sight.
1 Jn 1: 7 if we **w** in the light as he is
2 Jn 1: 6 is love, that we **w** according to his
2 Jn 1: 6 beginning, in which you should **w**.
3 Jn 1: 3 to how truly you **w** in the truth.
Rv 9:20 which cannot see or hear or **w**.
Rv 21:24 The nations will **w** by its light,

WALKED →WALK
Gn 5:24 Then Enoch **w** with God, and he
Acts 3: 8 and **w** around, and went

WALKING →WALK
Dt 8: 6 by **w** in his ways and fearing him.
Dn 3:92 unfettered and unhurt, **w** in the fire,
Mt 14:26 the disciples saw him **w** on the sea
Acts 3: 8 **w** and jumping and praising God.
2 Jn 1: 4 your children **w** in the truth just as
3 Jn 1: 4 that my children are **w** in the truth.

WALKS →WALK
Ps 15: 2 Whoever **w** without blame,
Prv 10: 9 He who **w** honestly **w** securely,

WALL →WALLS
Ex 14:22 with the water like a **w** to their right
Jos 2:15 lived in a house built into the city **w**.
Jos 6:20 The **w** collapsed, and the people
Neh 1: 3 the **w** of Jerusalem lies breached,
Neh 2:17 let us rebuild the **w** of Jerusalem,
Neh 12:27 dedication of the **w** of Jerusalem,
Dn 5: 5 plaster of the **w** in the king's palace.
Zec 2: 9 be for her an encircling **w** of fire,
Acts 9:25 down through an opening in the **w**,
2 Cor 11:33 a basket through a window in the **w**
Eph 2:14 and broke down the dividing **w**
Rv 21:12 high **w**, with twelve gates where

WALLOWING
2 Pt 2:22 "A bathed sow returns to **w**

WALLS →WALL
2 Kgs 25: 4 the city **w** were breached.
Neh 2:13 observing how the **w** of Jerusalem
Ps 51:20 rebuild the **w** of Jerusalem.
Is 26: 1 he sets up **w** and ramparts to protect
Is 60:18 You shall call your **w** "Salvation"
Jer 52:14 of the guard tore down all the **w**
Heb 11:30 By faith the **w** of Jericho fell

WANDER →WANDERED, WANDERER, WANDERING
Nm 32:13 the Israelites the LORD made them **w**

WANDERED →WANDER
Ez 34: 6 and **w** over all the mountains

WANDERER →WANDER
Gn 4:12 You shall become a restless **w**

WANDERING →WANDER
Dt 26: 5 father was a **w** Aramean who went

WANT →WANTED, WANTING, WANTS
Lk 18:41 "What do you **w** me to do for you?"
Lk 19:14 'We do not **w** this man to be our
Rom 7:15 For I do not do what I **w**, but I do
2 Cor 12:14 for I **w** not what is yours, but you.

WANTED →WANT
Mt 14: 5 Although he **w** to kill him, he feared

WANTING →WANT
Dn 5:27 weighed on the scales and found **w**;

WANTS →WANT
Mt 5:42 your back on one who **w** to borrow.
Mt 27:43 him deliver him now if he **w** him.

WAR →WARRIOR, WARRIORS, WARS
Ex 17:16 the LORD will **w** against Amalek
Ps 68:31 scatter the nations that delight in **w**.
Ps 120: 7 I spoke of peace, they were for **w**.
Ps 144: 1 hands for battle, my fingers for **w**;
Eccl 3: 8 a time of **w**, and a time of peace.

Is	2: 4	nor shall they train for **w** again.
Dn	7:21	horn made **w** against the holy ones
Dn	9:26	until the end there shall be **w**,
Rom	7:23	my members another principle at **w**
1 Pt	2:11	desires that wage **w** against the soul.
Rv	12: 7	Then **w** broke out in heaven;
Rv	19:11	and wages **w** in righteousness.

WARM →LUKEWARM, WARMED, WARMING, WARMS
Eccl	4:11	they keep each other **w**. How can one alone keep **w**?
Jas	2:16	"Go in peace, keep **w**, and eat well,"

WARMED →WARM
Hg	1: 6	clothed yourselves, but not been **w**;

WARMING →WARM
Mk	14:67	Seeing Peter **w** himself, she looked

WARMS →WARM
Is	44:15	a part of their wood he **w** himself,

WARN →FOREWARNED, WARNED, WARNING, WARNINGS, WARNS
Ex	19:21	**w** the people not to break through
1 Sm	8: 9	**w** them solemnly and inform them
Ez	3:18	you do not **w** him or speak
Ez	33: 9	But if you **w** the wicked man,
Lk	16:28	so that he may **w** them, lest they too
Rv	22:18	I **w** everyone who hears

WARNED →WARN
2 Kgs	17:13	though the Lord **w** Israel and Judah
Ez	3:19	hand, you have **w** the wicked man,
Ez	3:21	you have a **w** virtuous man not
Mt	2:12	having been **w** in a dream not
Mt	2:22	because he had been **w** in a dream,
Mt	3: 7	Who **w** you to flee from the coming
Heb	11: 7	**w** about what was not yet seen,
Heb	12:25	they refused the one who **w** them

WARNING →WARN
Ez	33: 5	trumpet blast yet refused to take **w**;
Ez	33: 5	for had he taken **w** he would have
Acts	4:17	us give them a stern **w** never again

WARNS →WARN
Heb	12:25	from the one who **w** from heaven.

WARRIOR →WAR
Ex	15: 3	The Lord is a **w**, Lord is his name!
1 Mc	2:66	Maccabeus, a **w** from his youth,

WARRIORS →WAR
2 Sm	23:22	He was listed among the Thirty **w**

WARS →WAR
Nm	21:14	in the "Book of the **W** of the Lord" :
Ps	46:10	Who stops **w** to the ends
Mt	24: 6	You will hear of **w** and reports of **w**;

WASH →WASHED, WASHING
2 Kgs	5:10	"Go and **w** seven times in the Jordan,
Ps	51: 9	**w** me, make me whiter than snow.
Jn	9: 7	"Go **w** in the Pool of Siloam"
Jn	13: 5	began to **w** the disciples' feet and dry
Rv	22:14	are they who **w** their robes so as

WASHED →WASH
Ps	73:13	clean, **w** my hands in innocence?
Jn	9:11	So I went there and **w** and was able
1 Cor	6:11	but now you have had yourselves **w**,
Heb	10:22	and our bodies **w** in pure water.
Rv	7:14	they have **w** their robes and made

WASHING →WASH
Lk	11:38	observe the prescribed **w** before

WASTE →WASTING
Lv	26:31	I will lay **w** your cities
1 Mc	2:12	and our glory laid **w**,
Is	6:11	a man, and the earth is a desolate **w**.
Jer	2:15	They have made his land a **w**;
Ez	4:17	and **w** away because of his sins.

WASTING →WASTE
2 Cor	4:16	although our outer self is **w** away,

WATCH →WATCHER, WATCHES, WATCHING, WATCHTOWER
Gn	31:49	"May the Lord keep **w** between you
Ps	59:10	My strength, for you I **w**; you, God,
Prv	6:22	When you lie down she will **w** over you,
Lk	2: 8	keeping the night **w** over their flock.
Heb	13:17	for they keep **w** over you and will

WATCHER →WATCH
Jb	7:20	what can I do to you, O **w** of men?

WATCHES →WATCH
Ps	1: 6	The Lord **w** over the way of the just,
Ps	63: 7	bed, through the night **w** I will recall

WATCHING →WATCH
Jer	1:12	seen, for I am **w** to fulfill my word.

WATCHTOWER → TOWER, WATCH
Is	5: 2	Within it he built a **w**, and hewed

WATER →WATERED, WATERLESS, WATERS
Ex	7:20	all the **w** of the river was changed
Ex	15:25	When he threw this into the **w**, the **w** became fresh.
Ex	17: 1	Here there was no **w** for the people
Nm	5:19	to the curse brought by this bitter **w**.
Nm	20: 2	As the community had no **w**,
Nm	21: 5	desert, where there is no food or **w**?
2 Kgs	2: 8	rolled it up and struck the **w**,
2 Kgs	6: 5	the iron axhead slipped into the **w**.
Ps	1: 3	tree planted near streams of **w**,
Ps	22:15	Like **w** my life drains away; all my
Ps	107:35	changed the desert into pools of **w**, arid land into springs of **w**,
Prv	5:15	Drink **w** from your own cistern,
Prv	5:15	running **w** from your own well.
Prv	9:17	Stolen **w** is sweet, and bread gotten
Sir	15: 3	give him the **w** of learning to drink.
Is	12: 3	With joy you will draw **w**
Is	30:20	and the **w** for which you thirst.
Is	32: 2	They will be like streams of **w**
Is	49:10	guides them beside springs of **w**.
Jer	2:13	broken cisterns, that hold no **w**.
Jer	31: 9	I will lead them to brooks of **w**,
Ez	36:25	I will sprinkle clean **w** upon you
Mt	14:29	to walk on the **w** toward Jesus.
Mk	1: 8	I have baptized you with **w**; he will
Mk	9:41	Anyone who gives you a cup of **w**
Lk	5: 4	"Put out into deep **w** and lower your
Jn	2: 9	the headwaiter tasted the **w** that had
Jn	2: 9	who had drawn the **w** knew),
Jn	3: 5	of God without being born of **w**
Jn	4:10	he would have given you living **w**."
Jn	7:38	'Rivers of living **w** will flow
Jn	19:34	blood and **w** flowed out.
Eph	5:26	her by the bath of **w** with the word,
Heb	10:22	and our bodies washed in pure **w**.
Jas	3:11	opening both pure and brackish **w**?
1 Jn	5: 6	This is the one who came through **w**
1 Jn	5: 6	not by **w** alone, but by **w** and blood.
Rv	7:17	them to springs of life-giving **w**,
Rv	21: 6	gift from the spring of life-giving **w**.
Rv	22: 1	me the river of life-giving **w**,
Rv	22:17	it receive the gift of life-giving **w**.

WATERED →WATER
1 Cor	3: 6	Apollos **w**, but God caused

WATERLESS →WATER
2 Pt	2:17	These people are **w** springs
Jude	1:12	They are **w** clouds blown

WATERS →WATER
Gn	1: 2	a mighty wind swept over the **w**.
Gn	7: 7	ark because of the **w** of the flood.
Jos	4: 7	'The **w** of the Jordan ceased to flow
Ps	18:17	drew me out of the deep **w**.
Ps	23: 2	let me graze; to safe **w** you lead me;
Ps	106:32	the **w** of Meribah they angered God,

Eccl	11: 1	Cast your bread upon the **w**;
Song	8: 7	Deep **w** cannot quench love,
Jer	17: 8	is like a tree planted beside the **w**
1 Cor	3: 7	nor the one who **w** is anything,

WAVE →WAVES
Jas	1: 6	for the one who doubts is like a **w**

WAVER
Jude	1:22	On those who **w**, have mercy;

WAVES →WAVE
Ps	89:10	raging sea; you still its swelling **w**.
Jude	1:13	They are like wild **w** of the sea,

WAX
Ps	22:15	My heart has become like **w**,
Ps	97: 5	mountains melt like **w** before

WAY →HIGHWAY, WAYS
Gn	3:24	to guard the **w** to the tree of life.
Ex	13:21	of cloud to show them the **w**,
Dt	1:33	the fire, to show the **w** you must go.
1 Sm	12:23	to teach you the good and right **w**.
2 Sm	22:31	God's **w** is unerring; the promise
1 Kgs	8:36	teaching them the right **w** to live
2 Chr	6:27	But teach them the right **w** to live,
Jb	23:10	Yet he knows my **w**; if he proved
Ps	1: 6	The LORD watches over the **w**
Ps	1: 6	the **w** of the wicked leads to ruin.
Ps	18:31	God's **w** is unerring; the LORD's
Ps	32: 8	show you the **w** you should walk,
Ps	37: 5	Commit your **w** to the LORD;
Ps	86:11	Teach me, LORD, your **w** that I may
Ps	139:24	See if my **w** is crooked, then lead
Prv	4:11	On the **w** of wisdom I direct you,
Prv	12:15	The **w** of the fool seems right in his
Prv	14:12	Sometimes a **w** seems right
Prv	16:17	to his **w** safeguards his life.
Prv	22: 6	Train a boy in the **w** he should go;
Prv	30:19	The **w** of an eagle in the air,
Prv	30:19	The **w** of a ship on the high seas,
Prv	30:19	and the **w** of a man with a maiden.
Is	30:21	your ears: "This is the **w**; walk in it,"
Is	35: 8	called the holy **w**; No one unclean
Is	40: 3	the desert prepare the **w** of the LORD!
Is	48:17	lead you on the **w** you should go.
Is	53: 6	each following his own **w**;
Is	55: 7	Let the scoundrel forsake his **w**,
Mal	3: 1	to prepare the **w** before me;
Mt	3: 3	desert, 'Prepare the **w** of the Lord,
Lk	7:27	he will prepare your **w** before you.'
Jn	14: 6	"I am the **w** and the truth and the life.
Acts	1:11	in the same **w** as you have seen him
Acts	9: 2	or women who belonged to the **W**,
Acts	19: 9	disparaged the **W** before
Acts	22: 4	I persecuted this **W** to death,
Acts	24:14	that according to the **W**, which they
1 Cor	10:13	trial he will also provide a **w** out,
1 Cor	12:31	show you a still more excellent **w**.
Heb	9: 8	In this **w** the holy Spirit shows
Heb	9: 8	the **w** into the sanctuary had not yet
Heb	10:20	living **w** he opened for us through
2 Pt	2:21	have known the **w** of righteousness

WAYS →WAY
Ex	33:13	do let me know your **w** so that,
Dt	10:12	your and follow his **w** exactly,
Dt	26:17	you are to walk in his **w** and observe
Dt	30:16	and walking in his **w**, and keeping
Dt	32: 4	how right all his **w**! A faithful God,
2 Kgs	17:13	"Give up your evil **w** and keep my
Jb	34:21	For his eyes are upon the **w** of man,
Ps	25: 4	Make known to me your **w**, LORD;
Ps	51:15	I will teach the wicked your **w**,
Ps	119:59	I have examined my **w** and turned
Ps	139: 3	with all my **w** you are familiar.
Ps	145:17	You, LORD, are just in all your **w**,
Prv	3: 6	In all your **w** be mindful of him,
Prv	3:17	Her **w** are pleasant **w**, and all her
Prv	4:26	your feet, and let all your **w** be sure.
Prv	5:21	For each man's **w** are plain

Prv	6: 6	study her **w** and learn wisdom;
Prv	7:25	Let not your heart turn to her **w**,
Prv	16: 2	All the **w** of a man may be pure
Prv	16: 7	the LORD is pleased with a man's **w**,
Sir	2:15	those who love him keep his **w**.
Is	2: 3	That he may instruct us in his **w**,
Is	42:24	In his **w** they refused to walk,
Is	55: 8	nor are your **w** my **w**, says the LORD.
Jer	18:11	reform your **w** and your deeds.
Ez	16:47	not only in their **w** did you walk,
Ez	16:47	corrupt in all your **w** than they.
Lk	3: 5	and the rough **w** made smooth,
Rv	15: 3	Just and true are your **w**, O king

WEAK →WEAKENED, WEAKER, WEAKNESS, WEAKNESSES
Jgs	16: 7	"I shall be as **w** as any other man."
Ez	34: 4	did not strengthen the **w** nor heal
Jl	4:10	let the **w** man say, "I am a warrior!"
Mt	26:41	spirit is willing, but the flesh is **w**."
Acts	20:35	of that sort we must help the **w**,
Rom	14: 1	Welcome anyone who is **w** in faith,
Rom	15: 1	to put up with the failings of the **w**
1 Cor	1:27	and God chose the **w** of the world
1 Cor	8: 9	becomes a stumbling block to the **w**.
1 Cor	9:22	To the **w** I became **w**, to win over the **w**.
2 Cor	12:10	for when I am **w**, then I am strong.
Gal	4: 9	can you turn back again to the **w**
1 Thes	5:14	support the **w**, be patient with all.
Heb	12:12	drooping hands and your **w** knees.

WEAKENED →WEAK
Rom	8: 3	For what the law, **w** by the flesh,

WEAKER →WEAK
2 Sm	3: 1	stronger, but the house of Saul **w**.
1 Cor	12:22	to be **w** are all the more necessary,
1 Pt	3: 7	showing honor to the **w** female sex,

WEAKNESS →WEAK
Rom	8:26	Spirit too comes to the aid of our **w**;
1 Cor	1:25	the **w** of God is stronger than human
1 Cor	2: 3	I came to you in **w** and fear
2 Cor	11:30	boast of the things that show my **w**.
2 Cor	12: 9	you, for power is made perfect in **w**."
2 Cor	13: 4	indeed he was crucified out of **w**,
Heb	5: 2	erring, for he himself is beset by **w**
Heb	7:28	the law appoints men subject to **w**
Heb	11:34	out of **w** they were made powerful,

WEAKNESSES →WEAK
2 Cor	12: 5	I will not boast, except about my **w**.
2 Cor	12: 9	rather boast most gladly of my **w**,
2 Cor	12:10	I am content with **w**, insults,
Heb	4:15	is unable to sympathize with our **w**,

WEALTH
Dt	8:18	gives you the power to acquire **w**,
Ps	49: 7	Those who trust in their **w** and boast
Ps	49:11	and must leave their **w** to others.
Ps	112: 3	**W** and riches shall be in their
Prv	13: 7	pretends to be poor, yet has great **w**.
Prv	13:11	**W** quickly gotten dwindles away,
Prv	13:22	the **w** of the sinner is stored
Prv	19: 4	**W** adds many friends, but the friend
Eccl	5: 9	the lover of **w** reaps no fruit from it;
Sir	5: 1	Rely not on your **w**; say not: "I have
Lk	16:11	not trustworthy with dishonest **w**, who will trust you with true **w**?

WEANED
1 Sm	1:22	"Once the child is **w**, I will take him
Ps	131: 2	hushed it like a **w** child. Like a **w**

WEAPON →WEAPONS
Neh	4:11	hand and held a **w** with the other.
Is	54:17	No **w** fashioned against you shall

WEAPONS →WEAPON
Jn	18: 3	there with lanterns, torches, and **w**.
2 Cor	6: 7	with **w** of righteousness at the right
2 Cor	10: 4	for the **w** of our battle are not

WEAR →WEARING, WEARS
Dt	22: 5	woman shall not **w** an article proper

Ps	102:27	they all **w** out like a garment;
Mt	6:31	we to drink?' or 'What are we to **w**?'

WEARIED →WEARY

Is	43:24	sins, and **w** me with your crimes.
Mal	2:17	You have **w** the LORD with your
Mal	2:17	yet you say, "How have we **w** him?"

WEARING →WEAR

1 Sm	18: 4	himself of the mantle he was **w**
Jn	19: 5	out, **w** the crown of thorns
Jas	2: 3	to the one **w** the fine clothes
1 Pt	3: 3	braiding the hair, **w** gold jewelry,

WEARS →WEAR

Is	51: 6	the earth **w** out like a garment

WEARY →WEARIED

Is	40:28	He does not faint nor grow **w**,
Is	40:31	They will run and not grow **w**,
Is	50: 4	I might know how to speak to the **w**
Heb	12: 3	in order that you may not grow **w**
Rv	2: 3	name, and you have not grown **w**.

WEDDING

Mt	22: 2	to a king who gave a **w** feast for his
Mt	22:11	there not dressed in a **w** garment.
Jn	2: 1	the third day there was a **w** in Cana

WEEDS

Mt	13:25	and sowed **w** all through the wheat,

WEEK →WEEKS

Mt	28: 1	the first day of the **w** was dawning,
Lk	18:12	I fast twice a **w**, and I pay tithes
1 Cor	16: 2	the first day of the **w** each of you

WEEKS →WEEK

Ex	34:22	"You shall keep the feast of **W**
Lv	23:15	sheaf, you shall count seven full **w**,
Lv	25: 8	"Seven **w** of years shall you
Dn	9:24	"Seventy **w** are decreed for your

WEEP →WEEPING, WEPT

Eccl	3: 4	A time to **w**, and a time to laugh;
Lam	1:16	"At this I **w**, my eyes run with tears:
Lk	23:28	of Jerusalem, do not **w** for me;
Rom	12:15	who rejoice, **w** with those who **w**.

WEEPING →WEEP

Ps	6: 9	do evil! The LORD has heard my **w**.
Ps	30: 6	At dusk **w** comes for the night;
Ps	126: 6	Those who go forth **w**,
Jer	31:15	of bitter **w**! Rachel mourns her
Mt	2:18	Rachel **w** for her children, and she
Lk	6:21	Blessed are you who are now **w**,

WEIGHED →WEIGHTS

Dn	5:27	you have been **w** on the scales

WEIGHTS →WEIGHED

Dt	25:13	"You shall not keep two differing **w**
Prv	20:23	Varying **w** are an abomination

WELL

Gn	4: 7	If you do **w**, you can hold up your
Gn	12:16	On her account it went very **w**
2 Chr	6: 8	a temple to my honor, you do **w**
Prv	5:15	running water from your own **w**.
Mt	3:17	Son, with whom I am **w** pleased."
Mt	17: 5	Son, with whom I am **w** pleased;
Mt	25:21	His master said to him, 'W done,
Jn	4: 6	Jacob's **w** was there.
Jn	4: 6	his journey, sat down there at the **w**.
Eph	6: 3	"that it may go **w** with you
2 Pt	1:17	with whom I am **w** pleased."

WEPT →WEEP

Is	38: 3	to you!" And Hezekiah **w** bitterly.
Lk	19:41	near, he saw the city and **w** over it,

WEST →WESTERN

Ps	103:12	As far as the east is from the **w**,
Ps	107: 3	from east and **w**, from north
Is	43: 5	from the **w** I will gather you.
Zec	14: 4	east to **w** by a very deep valley,

WESTERN →WEST

Nm	34: 6	this shall be your **w** boundary.
Dt	11:24	the Euphrates River to the **W** Sea,
Zec	14: 8	and half to the **w** sea, and it shall be

WHATEVER

Ps	135: 6	**W** the LORD wishes he does
Mt	16:19	**W** you bind on earth shall be bound
Mt	16:19	**w** you loose on earth shall be loosed
Mt	18:18	**w** you bind on earth shall be bound
Mt	18:18	**w** you loose on earth shall be loosed
Jn	14:13	And **w** you ask in my name, I will
Jn	15:16	so that **w** you ask the Father in my
Phil	4: 8	**w** is true, **w** is honorable, **w** is just, **w** is pure, **w** is lovely, **w** is gracious,
Phil	4:11	in **w** situation I find myself, to be
1 Jn	5:15	he hears us in regard to **w** we ask,

WHEAT

Ex	34:22	with the first of the **w** harvest;
Mt	3:12	floor and gather his **w** into his barn,
Mt	13:25	and sowed weeds all through the **w**,
Lk	22:31	demanded to sift all of you like **w**,
Jn	12:24	you, unless a grain of **w** falls
Jn	12:24	dies, it remains just a grain of **w**;

WHEEL →WHEELS

Ez	1:16	as though one **w** were within

WHEELS →WHEEL

Ex	14:25	he so clogged their chariot **w**
Ez	1:16	The **w** had the sparkling appearance
Dn	7: 9	of fire, with **w** of burning fire.

WHENEVER

Dt	4: 7	God, is to us **w** we call upon him?

WHERE → EVERYWHERE, NOWHERE, WHEREVER

Dt	32:37	He will say, "W are their gods
Jb	28:12	and **w** is the place of understanding?
Ps	26: 8	LORD, I love the house **w** you dwell,
Ps	42: 4	as they ask daily, "W is your God?"
Ps	121: 1	From **w** will my help come?
Ps	139: 7	**W** can I hide from your spirit?
Ps	139: 7	From your presence, **w** can I flee?
Hos	13:14	**W** are your plagues, O death!
Hos	13:14	**w** is your sting, O nether world!
Mal	1: 6	a father, **w** is the honor due to me?
Mal	1: 6	if I am a master, **w** is the reverence
Mt	6:21	For **w** your treasure is,
Mt	28: 6	Come and see the place **w** he lay.
Jn	3: 8	The wind blows **w** it wills, and you do not know **w** it comes from or **w** it goes;
Jn	13:33	the Jews, 'W I go you cannot come,'
1 Cor	15:55	**W**, O death, is your victory? **W**,
Col	3: 1	**w** Christ is seated at the right hand
2 Pt	3: 4	"W is the promise of his coming?

WHEREVER →WHERE

Jos	1: 7	that you may succeed **w** you go.
Mk	14: 9	**w** the gospel is proclaimed
Lk	9:57	to him, "I will follow you **w** you go."
Rv	14: 4	who follow the Lamb **w** he goes.

WHETHER

Rom	14: 8	so then, **w** we live or die, we are
1 Jn	4: 1	test the spirits to see **w** they belong

WHILE

Is	55: 6	Seek the LORD **w** he may be found, call him **w** he is near.
Is	65:24	**w** they are yet speaking, I will
Jn	12:35	will be among you only a little **w**.
Jn	12:35	Walk **w** you have the light,
Jn	16:16	"A little **w** and you will no longer see
Jn	16:16	again a little **w** later and you will
Rom	5: 8	**w** we were still sinners Christ died
2 Cor	5: 4	For **w** we are in this tent we groan

WHIP

Jn	2:15	He made a **w** out of cords and drove

WHIRLWIND →WIND

2 Kgs	2:11	and Elijah went up to heaven in a **w**.

Sir	48:12	O Elijah, enveloped in the **w**!
Hos	8: 7	they shall reap the **w**; The stalk

WHISPERED
Mt	10:27	what you hear **w**,

WHITE → WHITER, WHITEWASH, WHITEWASHED
Dn	7: 9	the hair on his head as **w** as wool;
Zec	1: 8	him were red, sorrel, and **w** horses.
Zec	6: 3	the third chariot **w** horses,
Mt	5:36	for you cannot make a single hair **w**
Mt	28: 3	and his clothing was **w** as snow.
Acts	1:10	in **w** garments stood beside them.
Rv	1:14	hair of his head was as **w** as **w** wool
Rv	2:17	also give a **w** amulet upon which is
Rv	3: 4	will walk with me dressed in **w**,
Rv	6: 2	and there was a **w** horse, and its
Rv	7:13	"Who are these wearing **w** robes,
Rv	14:14	I looked and there was a **w** cloud,
Rv	19:11	opened, and there was a **w** horse;
Rv	20:11	Next I saw a large **w** throne

WHITER → WHITE
Ps	51: 9	wash me, make me **w** than snow.

WHITEWASH → WHITE
Ez	13:10	a wall, they would cover it with **w**,
Ez	22:28	Her prophets cover them with **w**,

WHITEWASHED → WHITE
Mt	23:27	You are like **w** tombs, which appear
Acts	23: 3	"God will strike you, you **w** wall.

WHOEVER
Mt	12:50	For **w** does the will of my heavenly
Mk	3:29	But **w** blasphemes against the holy
Mk	9:40	For **w** is not against us is for us.
Jn	3:36	**W** believes in the Son has eternal
Jn	3:36	**w** disobeys the Son will not see life,

WHOLE → WHOLEHEARTED
Gn	11: 1	The **w** world spoke the same
Gn	18:28	Will you destroy the **w** city because
Ex	12:47	The **w** community of Israel must
Dt	13:17	all its spoils as a **w** burnt offering
1 Kgs	10:24	the **w** world sought audience
Is	1: 5	The **w** head is sick, the **w** heart faint.
Is	14:26	is the plan proposed for the **w** earth.
Ez	37:11	man, these bones are the **w** house
Dn	2:35	mountain and filled the **w** earth.
Mt	5:29	than to have your **w** body thrown
Mt	6:22	your **w** body will be filled
Mt	16:26	there be for one to gain the **w** world
Mk	15:33	came over the **w** land until three
Acts	17:26	made from one the **w** human race
Rom	3:19	the **w** world stand accountable
1 Cor	12:17	If the **w** body were an eye,
1 Cor	12:17	If the **w** body were hearing,
Gal	5: 9	A little yeast leavens the **w** batch
Gal	5:14	For the **w** law is fulfilled in one
Eph	2:21	Through him the **w** structure is held
Ti	1:11	as they are upsetting **w** families
Jas	2:10	For whoever keeps the **w** law,
1 Jn	2: 2	only but for those of the **w** world.
1 Jn	5:19	the **w** world is under the power
Rv	3:10	to come to the **w** world to test
Rv	12: 9	who deceived the **w** world,
Rv	13: 3	the **w** world followed

WHOLEHEARTED → HEART, WHOLE
Tb	1:12	Because of this **w** service of God,

WHY
Gn	4: 6	to Cain: "**W** are you so resentful
Gn	12:19	**W** did you say, 'She is my sister,'
Gn	32:30	"**W** should you want to know my
Jgs	13:18	him, "**W** do you ask my name,
Jb	24: 1	**W** are not times set
Jb	24: 1	**w** do his friends not see his days?
Ps	2: 1	**W** do the nations protest
Ps	10: 1	**W**, LORD, do you stand at a distance
Ps	22: 2	God, **w** have you abandoned me?
Ps	42: 6	**W** are you downcast, my soul; **w** do

Ps	79:10	**W** should the nations say, "Where is
Is	40:27	**W**, O Jacob, do you say,
Lam	5:20	**W**, then, should you forget us,
Mt	9:11	"**W** does your teacher eat with tax
Mt	17:19	said, "**W** could we not drive it out?"
Mt	27:46	my God, **w** have you forsaken me?"
Mk	10:18	him, "**W** do you call me good?
Acts	9: 4	Saul, **w** are you persecuting me?"

WICK
Is	42: 3	a smoldering **w** he shall not quench,
Mt	12:20	a smoldering **w** he will not quench,

WICKED → WICKEDNESS
Gn	13:13	Sodom were very **w** in the sins they
Ex	23: 1	Do not join the **w** in putting your
Nm	14:35	all this **w** community that conspired
2 Chr	19: 2	"Should you help the **w** and love
Jb	15:20	The **w** man is in torment all his
Jb	20:29	This is the portion of a **w** man,
Jb	27:13	This is the portion of a **w** man
Ps	1: 1	the counsel of the **w**, Nor go
Ps	1: 5	Therefore the **w** will not survive
Ps	7:10	Bring the malice of the **w** to an end;
Ps	10:13	Why should the **w** scorn God,
Ps	11: 6	And rains upon the **w** fiery coals
Ps	12: 9	On every side the **w** strut;
Ps	26: 5	of evildoers; with the **w** I do not sit.
Ps	32:10	Many are the sorrows of the **w**,
Ps	36: 2	Sin directs the heart of the **w**;
Ps	37:40	rescues and saves them from the **w**,
Ps	50:16	But to the **w** God says: "Why do you
Ps	58: 4	The **w** have been corrupt since birth;
Ps	73: 3	when I saw the prosperity of the **w**.
Ps	82: 2	and favor the cause of the **w**?
Ps	112:10	The **w** shall be angry to see this;
Ps	112:10	away; the desires of the **w** come
Ps	119:61	the snares of the **w** surround me,
Ps	140: 9	do not grant the desires of the **w**;
Ps	141:10	Into their own nets let all the **w** fall,
Ps	146: 9	but thwarts the way of the **w**.
Prv	4:14	The path of the **w** enter not,
Prv	5:22	his own iniquities the **w** man will be
Prv	6:18	A heart that plots **w** schemes,
Prv	9: 7	and he who reproves a **w** man incurs
Prv	10:20	the heart of the **w** is of little worth.
Prv	10:28	but the expectation of the **w**
Prv	11: 5	by his wickedness the **w** man falls.
Prv	11:10	and when the **w** perish, there is
Prv	12: 5	the designs of the **w** are deceitful.
Prv	12:10	but the heart of the **w** is merciless.
Prv	14:19	and the **w**, at the gates of the just.
Prv	21:10	The soul of the **w** man desires evil;
Prv	21:29	The **w** man is brazenfaced,
Prv	28: 1	The **w** man flees although no one
Prv	28: 4	abandon the law praise the **w** man,
Prv	29: 7	the **w** man has no such concern.
Prv	29:16	When the **w** prevail,
Prv	29:27	is an abomination to the **w**.
Eccl	7:15	justice, and a **w** one surviving in his
Eccl	8:14	**w** men treated as though they had
Is	11: 4	breath of his lips he shall slay the **w**.
Is	13:11	and the **w** for their guilt. I will put
Is	26:10	The **w** man, spared, does not learn
Is	48:22	[There is no peace for the **w**,
Is	53: 9	was assigned him among the **w**
Is	55: 7	and the **w** man his thoughts; Let him
Is	57:20	But the **w** are like the tossing sea
Ez	3:18	If I say to the **w** man, You shall
Ez	3:18	dissuade him from his **w** conduct so
Ez	3:18	that **w** man shall die for his sin, but I
Ez	13:22	have encouraged the **w** man not
Ez	18:21	if the **w** man turns away from all
Ez	18:23	pleasure from the death of the **w**?
Ez	21:30	depraved and **w** prince of Israel,
Ez	33: 8	I tell the **w** man that he shall surely
Ez	33: 8	to dissuade the **w** man from his way,
Ez	33: 8	way, he [the **w** man] shall die for his
Ez	33:11	pleasure in the death of the **w** man,
Ez	33:11	but rather in the **w** man's conversion,

Ez	33:19	But when a **w** man turns away
Dn	12:10	and tested, but the **w** shall prove **w**;
Lk	6:35	is kind to the ungrateful and the **w**.

WICKEDNESS → WICKED

Gn	6: 5	the LORD saw how great was man's **w**
Dt	9: 4	because of the **w** of these nations
Prv	11: 5	but by his **w** the wicked man falls.
Eccl	3:16	sun in the judgment place I saw **w**,
Wis	2:21	they erred; for their **w** blinded them,
Jer	8: 6	No one repents of his **w**,
Jer	14:20	We recognize, O LORD, our **w**,
Ez	18:20	as the wicked man's **w** shall be his
Ez	33:19	a wicked man turns away from **w**
Jon	1: 2	their **w** has come up before me."
Rom	1:18	**w** of those who suppress the truth by their **w**.
Heb	1: 9	You loved justice and hated **w**;

WIDE

Ps	81:11	Open **w** your mouth that I may fill
Mt	7:13	for the gate is **w** and the road broad

WIDOW → WIDOW'S, WIDOWED, WIDOWHOOD, WIDOWS

Ex	22:21	You shall not wrong any **w**
Dt	10:18	justice for the orphan and the **w**,
Ru	4: 5	the Moabite, the **w** of the late heir,
Ps	146: 9	sustains the orphan and the **w**,
Is	1:17	hear the orphan's plea, defend the **w**.
Lk	2:37	as a **w** until she was eighty-four.
Lk	18: 3	a **w** in that town used to come
Lk	21: 3	this poor **w** put in more than all
1 Tm	5: 4	if a **w** has children or grandchildren,
Rv	18: 7	I am no **w**, and I will never know

WIDOW'S → WIDOW

Gn	38:14	she took off her **w** garb, veiled
Jdt	8: 5	about her loins and wore **w** weeds.
Prv	15:25	he preserves intact the **w** landmark.

WIDOWED → WIDOW

Jdt	8: 4	The **w** Judith remained three years
Lam	1: 1	the once crowded city! **W** is she

WIDOWHOOD → WIDOW

Is	54: 4	of your **w** no longer remember.

WIDOWS → WIDOW

Ps	68: 6	of the fatherless, defender of **w**—
Lk	4:25	there were many **w** in Israel
Acts	6: 1	because their **w** were being
1 Cor	7: 8	Now to the unmarried and to **w**,
1 Tm	5: 3	Honor **w** who are truly **w**.
Jas	1:27	for orphans and **w** in their affliction

WIFE → WIVES

Gn	2:24	and mother and clings to his **w**,
Gn	3:20	The man called his **w** Eve,
Gn	12:18	didn't you tell me she was your **w**?
Gn	19:26	But Lot's **w** looked back, and she
Gn	20:11	would kill me on account of my **w**.
Gn	24:67	her, and thus she became his **w**.
Ex	20:17	shall not covet your neighbor's **w**,
Nm	5:12	them: If a man's **w** goes astray
Dt	5:21	shall not covet your neighbor's **w**.
Dt	24: 5	to bring joy to the **w** he has married.
Ru	4:13	they came together as man and **w**,
2 Sm	12:10	have taken the **w** of Uriah to be your.'
Tb	8: 6	Adam and you gave him his **w** Eve
Ps	128: 3	vine your **w** within your home,
Prv	5:18	have joy of the **w** of your youth,
Prv	6:24	keep you from your neighbor's **w**,
Prv	12: 4	A worthy **w** is the crown of her
Prv	18:22	He who finds a **w** finds happiness;
Prv	19:14	but a prudent **w** is from the LORD.
Prv	31:10	When one finds a worthy **w**,
Eccl	9: 9	life with the **w** whom you love,
Sir	7:19	Dismiss not a sensible **w**; a gracious **w** is more precious than
Sir	26: 1	Happy the husband of a good **w**,
Sir	26: 3	A good **w** is a generous gift
Hos	1: 2	take a harlot **w** and harlot's children,
Mal	2:14	you and the **w** of your youth,

Mal	2:14	your companion, your betrothed **w**.
Mt	1:20	take Mary your **w** into your home.
Mt	5:32	whoever divorces his **w** (unless
Mt	19: 3	a man to divorce his **w** for any cause
Mk	6:18	for you to have your brother's **w**."
Mk	10: 2	for a husband to divorce his **w**?"
Mk	12:23	they arise] whose **w** will she be?
Lk	17:32	Remember the **w** of Lot.
Lk	18:29	no one who has given up house or **w**
1 Cor	7: 2	every man should have his own **w**,
1 Cor	7:11	a husband should not divorce his **w**.
1 Cor	7:33	the world, how he may please his **w**,
Eph	5:23	head of his **w** just as Christ is head
Eph	5:28	He who loves his **w** loves himself.
Eph	5:33	of you should love his **w** as himself,
Eph	5:33	the **w** should respect her husband.
Rv	21: 9	you the bride, the **w** of the Lamb."

WILD

Gn	1:25	God made all kinds of **w** animals,
Gn	8: 1	and all the animals, **w** and tame,
Ex	32:25	Aaron had let the people run **w**,
Mk	1: 6	He fed on locusts and **w** honey.
Mk	1:13	He was among **w** beasts,
Rom	11:17	off, and you, a **w** olive shoot,
Jude	1:13	They are like **w** waves of the sea,

WILL → WILLING, WILLS

Ezr	7:18	conformably to the **w** of your God.
Ezr	10:11	God of your fathers, and do his **w**:
Tb	12:18	my part, but because it was God's **w**.
Est	C: 2	oppose you in your **w** to save Israel.
2 Mc	1: 3	to do his **w** readily and generously.
2 Mc	12:16	Capturing the city by the **w** of God,
Ps	27:12	not abandon me to the **w** of my foes;
Ps	40: 9	To do your **w** is my delight;
Ps	103:21	hosts, ministers who do God's **w**.
Ps	143:10	Teach me to do your **w**, for you are
Wis	14: 5	But you **w** that the products of your
Sir	41: 4	should you reject the **w** of the Most
Sir	42:15	they do his **w** as he has ordained
Is	53:10	life, and the **w** of the LORD shall be
Ez	16:27	you over to the **w** of your enemies,
Mt	6:10	kingdom come, your **w** be done,
Mt	7:21	only the one who does the **w** of my
Mt	11:26	such has been your gracious **w**.
Mt	12:50	whoever does the **w** of my heavenly
Mt	18:14	way, it is not the **w** of your heavenly
Mt	21:31	Which of the two did his father's **w**?"
Mt	26:42	my drinking it, your **w** be done!"
Mk	3:35	whoever does the **w** of God is my
Lk	10:21	such has been your gracious **w**.
Lk	22:42	still, not my **w** but yours be done."
Jn	4:34	to do the **w** of the one who sent me
Jn	5:30	because I do not seek my own **w** but the **w** of the one who sent me.
Jn	6:38	from heaven not to do my own **w** but the **w** of the one who sent me.
Jn	6:39	this is the **w** of the one who sent me,
Jn	6:40	For this is the **w** of my Father,
Jn	7:17	to do his **w** shall know whether my
Jn	9:31	but if one is devout and does his **w**,
Acts	21:14	rest, saying, "The Lord's **w** be done."
Acts	22:14	designated you to know his **w**,
Rom	2:18	know his **w** and are able to discern
Rom	8:27	the holy ones according to God's **w**.
Rom	9:16	So it depends not upon a person's **w**
Rom	9:19	For who can oppose his **w**?"
Rom	12: 2	you may discern what is the **w**
Rom	15:32	to you with joy by the **w** of God
1 Cor	1: 1	of Christ Jesus by the **w** of God,
2 Cor	1: 1	of Christ Jesus by the **w** of God,
Gal	1: 4	age in accord with the **w** of our God
Gal	3:15	even a human **w** once ratified.
Eph	1: 5	in accord with the favor of his **w**,
Eph	1: 9	to us the mystery of his **w** in accord
Eph	1:11	according to the intention of his **w**,
Eph	5:17	to understand what is the **w**
Eph	6: 6	doing the **w** of God from the heart,
Col	1: 9	his **w** through all spiritual wisdom

1 Thes	4: 3	This is the **w** of God, your holiness:
1 Thes	5:18	for this is the **w** of God for you
2 Tm	2:26	are entrapped by him, for his **w**.
Heb	2: 4	of the holy Spirit according to his **w**.
Heb	9:16	Now where there is a **w**, the death
Heb	9:17	For a **w** takes effect only at death;
Heb	10: 7	I come to do your **w**, O God.' "
Heb	10: 9	says, "Behold, I come to do your **w**."
Heb	10:10	By this "**w**," we have been
Heb	10:36	need endurance to do the **w** of God
Heb	13:21	that is good, that you may do his **w**.
1 Pt	2:15	For it is the **w** of God that by doing
1 Pt	3:17	if that be the **w** of God,
1 Pt	4: 2	human desires, but on the **w** of God.
1 Pt	4:19	with God's **w** hand their souls over
2 Pt	1:21	ever came through human **w**;
1 Jn	2:17	But whoever does the **w** of God remains forever.
1 Jn	5:14	if we ask anything according to his **w**, he hears us.
Rv	4:11	because of your **w** they came to be

WILLING →WILL

1 Chr	28: 9	with a perfect heart and a **w** soul,
Ps	51:14	salvation; sustain in me a **w** spirit.
Mt	26:41	The spirit is **w**, but the flesh is
Lk	22:42	if you are **w**, take this cup away

WILLS →WILL

1 Mc	3:60	Whatever Heaven **w**, he will do."

WIN →WON

1 Cor	9:19	so as to **w** over as many as possible.

WIND →WHIRLWIND, WINDS

Gn	1: 2	while a mighty **w** swept over
1 Kgs	19:11	heavy **w** was rending the mountains
1 Kgs	19:11	but the LORD was not in the **w**.
Ps	1: 4	They are like chaff driven by the **w**.
Ps	18:11	borne along on the wings of the **w**.
Ps	104: 3	you travel on the wings of the **w**.
Prv	30: 4	who has cupped the **w** in his hands?
Eccl	1:14	all is vanity and a chase after **w**.
Ez	5: 2	the final third strew in the **w**,
Hos	8: 7	When they sow the **w**, they shall
Jon	1: 4	hurled a violent **w** upon the sea,
Jon	4: 8	arose, God sent a burning east **w**;
Mk	4:41	is this whom even **w** and sea obey?"
Jn	3: 8	The **w** blows where it wills, and you
Acts	2: 2	sky a noise like a strong driving **w**,
Eph	4:14	along by every **w** of teaching arising
Jas	1: 6	is driven and tossed about by the **w**.

WINDOW →WINDOWS

Jos	2:21	she tied the scarlet cord in the **w**.
1 Sm	19:12	Michal let David down through a **w**,
Acts	20: 9	was sitting on the **w** sill was sinking
2 Cor	11:33	in a basket through a **w** in the wall

WINDOWS →WINDOW

2 Kgs	7: 2	the LORD were to make **w** in heaven,

WINDS →WIND

Ps	104: 4	You make the **w** your messengers;
Dn	3:65	All you **w**, bless the Lord;
Mt	7:25	and the **w** blew and buffeted
Mt	8:27	whom even the **w** and the sea obey?"
Mt	24:31	will gather his elect from the four **w**,
Heb	1: 7	says: "He makes his angels **w** and his

WINE →WINESKINS

Gn	9:21	When he drank some of the **w**,
Gn	19:32	let us ply our father with **w**
Nm	6: 3	he shall abstain from **w** and strong
Nm	6: 3	he may neither drink **w** vinegar,
Dt	7:13	your soil, your grain and **w** and oil,
Jgs	13: 4	be careful to take no **w** or strong
1 Sm	1:15	I have had neither **w** nor liquor;
Neh	13:12	brought in the tithes of grain, **w**,
Ps	4: 8	have when grain and **w** abound.
Ps	75: 9	hand, foaming **w**, fully spiced.
Ps	104:15	and **w** to gladden our hearts,
Prv	3:10	with new **w** your vats will overflow.
Prv	9: 2	has dressed her meat, mixed her **w**,
Prv	20: 1	**W** is arrogant, strong drink is

Prv	23:31	Look not on the **w** when it is red,
Prv	31: 4	not for kings to drink **w**;
Prv	31: 6	and **w** to the sorely depressed;
Eccl	2: 3	of beguiling my senses with **w**,
Eccl	9: 7	drink your **w** with a merry heart,
Eccl	10:19	and **w** makes the living glad,
Song	1: 2	More delightful is your love than **w**!
Song	7:10	And your mouth like an excellent **w**—
Sir	9:10	A new friend is like new **w**
Sir	31:28	are **w** drunk freely at the proper
Sir	31:29	is **w** drunk amid anger and strife.
Sir	40:20	**W** and music delight the soul,
Is	5:22	to the champions at drinking **w**,
Is	28: 7	But these also stagger from **w**
Is	28: 7	overpowered by **w**; Led astray
Is	29: 9	Be drunk, but not from **w**, stagger,
Is	51:21	afflicted one, drunk, but not with **w**,
Is	55: 1	and without cost, drink **w** and milk!
Dn	1: 8	himself with the king's food or **w**;
Jl	2:24	the vats shall overflow with **w**
Jl	4:18	the mountains shall drip new **w**,
Am	2:12	you gave the nazirites **w** to drink,
Mi	2:11	"I pour you **w** and strong drink as my
Mt	9:17	People do not put new **w** into old
Mt	9:17	the skins burst, the **w** spills out,
Mt	9:17	Rather, they pour new **w** into fresh
Mt	27:34	they gave Jesus **w** to drink mixed
Lk	23:36	As they approached to offer him **w**
Jn	2: 3	When the **w** ran short, the mother
Jn	2: 3	Jesus said to him, "They have no **w**."
Jn	2: 9	tasted the water that had become **w**,
Acts	2:13	"They have had too much new **w**."
Rom	14:21	drink **w** or do anything that causes
Eph	5:18	And do not get drunk on **w**,
1 Tm	5:23	have a little **w** for the sake of your
Rv	14: 8	the **w** of her licentious passion."
Rv	14:10	will also drink the **w** of God's fury,
Rv	18: 3	the **w** of her licentious passion.

WINESKINS →SKIN, WINE

Mt	9:17	do not put new wine into old **w**.
Mt	9:17	they pour new wine into fresh **w**,

WINGED →WINGS

Gn	1:21	teems, and all kinds of **w** birds.

WINGS →WINGED

Ex	19: 4	how I bore you up on eagle **w**
Ex	37: 9	The cherubim had their **w** spread
Ru	2:12	under whose **w** you have come
1 Kgs	8: 7	The cherubim had their **w** spread
2 Chr	3:11	The **w** of the cherubim spanned
Ps	17: 8	hide me in the shadow of your **w**
Ps	91: 4	spread **w** that you may take refuge;
Is	6: 2	each of them had six **w**: with two
Is	40:31	they will soar as with eagles' **w**;
Ez	1: 6	but each had four faces and four **w**,
Ez	1:11	Each had two **w** spread out above so
Ez	10:21	Each had four faces and four **w**;
Ez	10:21	human hands were under their **w**.
Zec	5: 9	forth with a wind ruffling their **w**,
Zec	5: 9	for they had **w** like the **w** of a stork.
Lk	13:34	a hen gathers her brood under her **w**,
Rv	4: 8	each of them with six **w**,

WINNOW →WINNOWING, WINNOWS

Is	41:16	When you **w** them, the wind shall

WINNOWING →WINNOW

Mt	3:12	His **w** fan is in his hand. He will

WINNOWS →WINNOW

Prv	20:26	A wise king **w** the wicked,

WINTER

Gn	8:22	Summer and **w**, and day and night
Ps	74:17	the earth; summer and **w** you made.
Mk	13:18	Pray that this does not happen in **w**.

WIPE →WIPED

Is	25: 8	The Lord GOD will **w** away the tears
Rv	7:17	God will **w** away every tear
Rv	21: 4	He will **w** every tear from their

WIPED →WIPE		
Acts	3:19	that your sins may be **w** away,

WISDOM →WISE

Dt	4: 6	will you give evidence of your **w**
1 Kgs	5: 9	God gave Solomon **w**
1 Kgs	10: 6	about your deeds and your **w** is true,"
2 Chr	1:10	**w** and knowledge to lead this
Jb	11: 6	And tell you that the secrets of **w**
Jb	12:13	With him are **w** and might; his are
Jb	28:12	But whence can **w** be obtained,
Jb	28:28	Behold, the fear of the LORD is **w**;
Ps	37:30	The mouths of the just utter **w**;
Ps	51: 8	in my inmost being teach me **w**.
Ps	111:10	of the LORD is the beginning of **w**;
Prv	1: 7	**w** and instruction fools despise.
Prv	1:20	**W** cries aloud in the street,
Prv	2: 6	For the LORD gives **w**, from his
Prv	3:13	Happy the man who finds **w**,
Prv	4: 5	"Get **w**, get understanding! Do not
Prv	4: 7	The beginning of **w** is: get **w**;
Prv	8:11	[For **W** is better than corals, and no
Prv	9: 1	**W** has built her house, she has set
Prv	9:10	The beginning of **w** is the fear
Prv	11: 2	comes; but with the humble is **w**.
Prv	13:10	with those who take counsel is **w**.
Prv	15:33	fear of the LORD is training for **w**,
Prv	23:23	**w**, instruction and understanding.
Prv	29: 3	He who loves **w** makes his father
Prv	29:15	The rod of correction gives **w**,
Prv	31:26	She opens her mouth in **w**,
Eccl	1:13	investigate in all things that are
Eccl	2: 3	my mind was concerned with **w**,
Eccl	2:13	**w** has the advantage over folly as
Eccl	7:12	protection of **w** is as the protection
Eccl	7:12	is that **w** preserves the life of its
Eccl	10: 1	More weighty than **w** or wealth is
Wis	6:12	Resplendent and unfading is **W**,
Wis	7: 7	and the spirit of **W** came to me.
Sir	1: 1	All **w** comes from the LORD
Sir	24: 1	**W** sings her own praises, before her
Is	11: 2	a spirit of **w** and of understanding,
Is	28:29	is his counsel and great his **w**.
Jer	9:22	Let not the wise man glory in his **w**,
Jer	10:12	established the world by his **w**,
Bar	3:12	have forsaken the fountain of **w**!
Ez	28:12	of complete **w** and perfect beauty.
Dn	5:14	knowledge and extraordinary **w**.
Mi	6: 9	the city. [It is **w** to fear your name!]
Mt	11:19	But **w** is vindicated by her works."
Mt	12:42	the earth to hear the **w** of Solomon;
Mt	13:54	"Where did this man get such **w**
Lk	2:40	and became strong, filled with **w**;
Lk	2:52	And Jesus advanced [in] **w** and age
Acts	6: 3	filled with the Spirit and **w**,
Rom	11:33	the depth of the riches and **w**
1 Cor	1:17	not with the **w** of human eloquence,
1 Cor	1:19	"I will destroy the **w** of the wise,
1 Cor	1:20	Has not God made the **w**
1 Cor	1:30	who became for us **w** from God,
1 Cor	2: 7	Rather we speak God's **w**,
1 Cor	3:19	the **w** of this world is foolishness
1 Cor	12: 8	the Spirit the expression of **w**;
Eph	1:17	may give you a spirit of **w**
Col	1: 9	of his will through all spiritual **w**
Col	1:28	and teaching everyone with all **w**,
Col	2: 3	are hidden all the treasures of **w**
Col	2:23	While they have a semblance of **w**
Jas	1: 5	But if any of you lacks **w**, he should
Jas	3:13	in the humility that comes from **w**.
Jas	3:17	the **w** from above is first of all pure,
Rv	5:12	power and riches, **w** and strength,
Rv	7:12	and glory, **w** and thanksgiving,
Rv	13:18	**W** is needed here; one who
Rv	17: 9	Here is a clue for one who has **w**.

WISE →WISDOM, WISELY, WISER

Gn	41:39	no one can be as **w** and discerning
Ex	7:11	summoned **w** men and sorcerers,
Dt	4: 6	'This great nation is truly a **w**
Dt	16:19	a bribe blinds the eyes even of the **w**
1 Kgs	3:12	I give you a heart so **w**
Jb	5:13	He catches the **w** in their own ruses,
Jb	32: 9	not those of many days who are **w**,
Ps	94: 8	You fools, when will you be **w**?
Ps	107:43	Whoever is **w** will take note of these
Prv	3: 7	Be not **w** in your own eyes,
Prv	9: 9	Instruct a **w** man, and he becomes
Prv	10: 1	A **w** son makes his father glad,
Prv	13: 1	A **w** son loves correction,
Prv	13:20	Walk with **w** men and you will become **w**,
Prv	16:23	of the **w** man makes him eloquent,
Prv	17:28	if he keeps silent, is considered **w**;
Prv	23:15	My son, if your heart be **w**, my own
Prv	24: 5	A **w** man is more powerful than
Prv	26: 5	lest he become **w** in his own eyes.
Prv	29:11	biding his time, the **w** man calms it.
Eccl	2:14	The **w** man has eyes in his head,
Eccl	7:19	for the **w** man than would be ten
Eccl	9:17	words of the **w** are better heeded
Eccl	12:11	The sayings of the **w** are like goads;
Is	29:14	wisdom of its **w** men shall perish
Jer	8: 9	The **w** are confounded,
Jer	9:22	LORD: Let not the **w** man glory in his
Dn	2:21	He gives wisdom to the **w**
Dn	11:35	Of the **w** men, some shall fall,
Dn	12: 3	But the **w** shall shine brightly
Mt	11:25	have hidden these things from the **w**
Mt	25: 2	them were foolish and five were **w**.
Rom	1:22	While claiming to be **w**,
Rom	16:27	to the only **w** God, through Jesus
1 Cor	1:19	"I will destroy the wisdom of the **w**,
1 Cor	1:26	of you were **w** by human standards,
1 Cor	3:18	among you considers himself **w**
1 Cor	3:18	become a fool, so as to become **w**.
1 Cor	3:19	"He catches the **w** in their own ruses,"
Eph	5:15	live, not as foolish persons but as **w**,
Jas	3:13	Who among you is **w**

WISELY →WISE

Jer	23: 5	king he shall reign and govern **w**,
Col	4: 5	Conduct yourselves **w** toward

WISER →WISE

1 Kgs	5:11	He was **w** than all other men—than
Prv	9: 9	a wise man, and he becomes still **w**;
Prv	26:16	The sluggard imagines himself **w**
1 Cor	1:25	of God is **w** than human wisdom.

WISH →WISHES

Rom	9: 3	For I could **w** that I myself were
Rv	3:15	I **w** you were either cold or hot.

WISHES →WISH

Est	6: 6	for the man whom the king **w**

WITHER →WITHERED, WITHERS

Ps	1: 3	Its leaves never **w**; whatever they do

WITHERED →WITHER

Mt	13: 6	scorched, and it **w** for lack of roots.
Mt	21:19	And immediately the fig tree **w**.

WITHERS →WITHER

Is	40: 7	The grass **w**, the flower wilts,
1 Pt	1:24	the grass **w**, and the flower wilts;

WITHHELD →WITHHOLD

Am	4: 7	Though I also **w** the rain from you
Hg	1:10	Therefore the heavens **w** from you

WITHHOLD →WITHHELD, WITHHOLDS

Neh	9:20	your manna you did not **w**
Ps	40:12	do not **w** your compassion from me;
Prv	23:13	**W** not chastisement from a boy;

WITHHOLDS →WITHHOLD

Ps	84:12	The LORD **w** no good thing

WITHIN

Ps	42: 6	why do you groan **w** me?
Ps	122: 7	May peace be **w** your ramparts, prosperity **w** your towers."
Prv	4:21	your sight, keep them **w** your heart;

Jer	31:33	I will place my law **w** them,
Zep	3: 5	The LORD **w** her is just, who does no
Zec	12: 1	and forms the spirit of man **w** him:
Mk	7:21	From **w** people, from their hearts,
1 Cor	2:11	the spirit of the person that is **w**?

WITHOUT

Nm	27:17	may not be like sheep **w** a shepherd."
2 Chr	18:16	mountains, like sheep **w** a shepherd,
Ps	26: 1	I have walked **w** blame. In the LORD
Ps	69: 5	are those who hate me **w** cause.
Prv	19: 2	**W** knowledge even zeal is not good;
Is	52: 3	**w** money you shall be redeemed.
Is	55: 1	Come, **w** paying and **w** cost,
Mt	9:36	abandoned, like sheep **w** a shepherd.
Mt	23:23	have done, **w** neglecting the others.
Jn	8: 7	among you who is **w** sin be the first
Eph	2:12	were at that time **w** Christ,
Eph	2:12	**w** hope and **w** God in the world.
Phil	2:14	Do everything **w** grumbling
Heb	4:15	been tested in every way, yet **w** sin.
Heb	9:22	**w** the shedding of blood there is no

WITHSTAND

2 Chr	20: 6	and might, and no one can **w** you.
Est	9: 2	and no one could **w** them, but all

WITNESS →EYEWITNESSES, WITNESSES

Gn	31:44	I; the LORD shall be a **w** between us."
Nm	35:30	of a single **w** is not sufficient
Dt	19:15	"One **w** alone shall not take the stand
Jgs	11:10	"The LORD is **w** between us that we
1 Sm	12: 5	"The LORD is **w** against you this day,
1 Sm	12: 5	"He is **w**," they agreed.
Jb	16:19	now, behold, my **w** is in heaven,
Prv	12:17	of, but a lying **w** speaks deceitfully.
Prv	14:25	The truthful **w** saves lives, but he
Prv	19: 9	The false **w** will not go unpunished,
Prv	21:28	The false **w** will perish, but he who
Rom	2:15	also bears **w** and their conflicting
1 Pt	5: 1	and **w** to the sufferings of Christ
Rv	1: 5	the faithful **w**, the firstborn
Rv	2:13	my faithful **w**, who was martyred
Rv	3:14	the faithful and true **w**, the source

WITNESSES →WITNESS

Dt	17: 6	or three **w** is required for putting
Dt	19:15	on the testimony of two or three **w**.
Jos	24:22	"You are your own **w** that you have
Ps	27:12	and lying **w** have risen against me.
Is	43:10	You are my **w**, says the LORD,
Mt	18:16	on the testimony of two or three **w**.'
Mt	26:60	though many false **w** came forward.
Mk	14:63	"What further need have we of **w**?
Acts	1: 8	and you will be my **w** in Jerusalem,
Acts	2:32	this Jesus; of this we are all **w**.
Acts	6:13	presented false **w** who testified,
Heb	12: 1	surrounded by so great a cloud of **w**,
Rv	11: 3	I will commission my two **w**

WIVES →WIFE

Gn	6:18	your wife and your sons' **w**, shall go
Dt	17:17	shall he have a great number of **w**,
Dt	21:15	"If a man with two **w** loves one
1 Kgs	11: 3	He had seven hundred **w** of princely
1 Kgs	11: 3	and his **w** turned his heart.
1 Chr	14: 3	David took other **w** in Jerusalem
Mt	19: 8	allowed you to divorce your **w**,
Eph	5:22	**W** should be subordinate to their
Eph	5:25	love your **w**, even as Christ loved
Col	3:18	**W**, be subordinate to your husbands,
1 Pt	3: 1	you **w** should be subordinate to your
1 Pt	3: 1	without a word by their **w**' conduct

WOE

Is	3:11	**W** to the wicked man! All goes ill,
Is	6: 5	Then I said, "**W** is me, I am doomed!
Jer	13:27	**W** to you, Jerusalem, how long will
Jer	23: 1	**W** to the shepherds who mislead
Lam	5:16	heads: **w** to us, for we have sinned!
Hos	9:12	till not one is left. **W** to them when I
Mt	18: 7	**W** to the world because of things

Mt	18: 7	but **w** to the one through whom they
Mt	23:13	"**W** to you, scribes and Pharisees,
Mt	23:16	"**W** to you, blind guides, who say,
Mk	14:21	**w** to that man by whom the Son
Lk	6:24	But **w** to you who are rich, for you
Lk	11:42	**W** to you Pharisees! You pay tithes
Lk	11:52	**W** to you, scholars of the law!
1 Cor	9:16	and **w** to me if I do not preach it!
Jude	1:11	**W** to them! They followed the way
Rv	8:13	cry out in a loud voice, "**W**! **W**!

WOLF →WOLVES

Is	11: 6	the **w** shall be a guest of the lamb,
Is	65:25	The **w** and the lamb shall graze
Jn	10:12	sees a **w** coming and leaves
Jn	10:12	and the **w** catches and scatters them.

WOLVES →WOLF

Ez	22:27	Her nobles within her are like **w**
Zep	3: 3	lions; Her judges are **w** of the night
Mt	7:15	but underneath are ravenous **w**.
Mt	10:16	you like sheep in the midst of **w**;
Acts	20:29	my departure savage **w** will come

WOMAN →WOMAN'S, WOMEN, WOMEN'S

Gn	2:22	up into a **w** the rib that he had taken
Gn	2:23	This one shall be called '**w**,'
Gn	3: 6	The **w** saw that the tree was good
Gn	3:12	"The **w** whom you put here
Gn	3:15	put enmity between you and the **w**,
Gn	3:16	To the **w** he said: "I will intensify
Gn	12:11	well how beautiful a **w** you are.
Gn	20: 3	because of the **w** you have taken,
Ex	3:22	Every **w** shall ask her neighbor
Ex	21:22	have a fight and hurt a pregnant **w**,
Nm	30: 4	"When a **w**, while still a maiden
Dt	20: 7	there anyone who has betrothed a **w**
Dt	21:11	see a comely **w** among the captives
Dt	22: 5	"A **w** shall not wear an article proper
Dt	24: 1	man, after marrying a **w** and having
Jgs	4: 9	Sisera fall into the power of a **w**."
Jgs	9:54	they say of me that a **w** killed me."
Jgs	14: 2	"There is a Philistine **w** I saw
Jgs	16: 4	a **w** in the Wadi Sorek whose name
Ru	3:11	know you for a worthy **w**.
1 Sm	1:15	"I am an unhappy **w**. I have had
1 Sm	25: 3	The **w** was intelligent and attractive,
1 Sm	28: 7	"Find me a **w** who is a medium,
1 Sm	28: 7	him, "There is a **w** in Endor who is
2 Sm	11: 2	From the roof he saw a **w** bathing,
2 Sm	14: 2	and brought from there a gifted **w**,
2 Sm	20:16	a wise **w** from the city stood
1 Kgs	17:24	man of God," the **w** replied to Elijah.
2 Kgs	4: 8	where there was a **w** of influence,
2 Kgs	8: 1	to the **w** whose son he had restored
2 Kgs	9:34	"Attend to that accursed **w** and bury
Jdt	8:31	now, God-fearing **w** that you are,
Jb	14: 1	Man born of **w** is short-lived
Prv	9:13	The **w** Folly is fickle, she is inane,
Prv	11:16	A gracious **w** wins esteem, but she
Prv	11:22	is a beautiful **w** with a rebellious
Prv	30:23	Under an odious **w** when she is wed,
Prv	31:30	the **w** who fears the LORD is to be
Sir	9: 3	Be not intimate with a strange **w**,
Dn	13: 2	a very beautiful and God-fearing **w**,
Mt	5:28	a **w** with lust has already committed
Mt	9:20	A **w** suffering hemorrhages
Mt	15:22	a Canaanite **w** of that district came
Mt	26: 7	a **w** came up to him
Mk	7:25	Soon a **w** whose daughter had
Lk	7:37	Now there was a sinful **w** in the city
Lk	10:38	village where a **w** whose name was
Lk	13:12	he called to her and said, "**W**, you are
Lk	15: 8	"Or what **w** having ten coins
Jn	2: 4	[And] Jesus said to her, "**W**,
Jn	4: 7	A **w** of Samaria came to draw water.
Jn	8: 4	this **w** was caught in the very act
Jn	19:26	he said to his mother, "**W**, behold,
Jn	20:15	Jesus said to her, "**W**, why are you
Acts	16:14	One of them, a **w** named Lydia,

Acts	17:34	the Areopagus, a **w** named Damaris,
Rom	7: 2	Thus a married **w** is bound by law
1 Cor	7: 2	wife, and every **w** her own husband.
1 Cor	7:34	An unmarried **w** or a virgin is
1 Cor	7:34	A married **w**, on the other hand,
1 Cor	11: 6	if a **w** does not have her head veiled,
1 Cor	11: 6	for a **w** to have her hair cut off
1 Cor	11: 7	of God, but **w** is the glory of man.
1 Cor	11:12	For just as **w** came from man, so man is born of **w**;
Gal	4: 4	born of a **w**, born under the law,
1 Tm	2:11	A **w** must receive instruction
1 Tm	5:16	If any **w** believer has widowed
Rv	2:20	that you tolerate the **w** Jezebel
Rv	12: 1	in the sky, a **w** clothed with the sun,
Rv	12: 4	the dragon stood before the **w**
Rv	12:13	it pursued the **w** who had given
Rv	17: 3	place where I saw a **w** seated
Rv	17:18	The **w** whom you saw represents

WOMAN'S →WOMAN
Dt	22: 5	nor shall a man put on a **w** dress;

WOMB
Gn	25:23	her: "Two nations are in your **w**,
Ex	13: 2	opens the **w** among the Israelites,
Dt	7:13	he will bless the fruit of your **w**
Jb	1:21	I came forth from my mother's **w**,
Ps	22:10	Yet you drew me forth from the **w**,
Ps	139:13	you knit me in my mother's **w**.
Prv	31: 2	what, O son of my **w**; what, O son
Eccl	11: 5	the human frame in the mother's **w**,
Jer	1: 5	I formed you in the **w** I knew you,
Lk	1:44	the infant in my **w** leaped for joy.
Jn	3: 4	he cannot reenter his mother's **w**
Rom	4:19	years old) and the dead **w** of Sarah.

WOMEN →WOMAN
Nm	25: 1	illicit relations with the Moabite **w**.
Jgs	5:24	Blessed among **w** be Jael,
Jgs	5:24	blessed among tent-dwelling **w**.
Ezr	10: 2	by taking as wives foreign **w**
Neh	13:26	he was made to sin by foreign **w**.
Jdt	15:13	and the other **w** crowned themselves
Jdt	15:13	people, she led the **w** in the dance,
Song	1: 8	O most beautiful among **w**,
Sir	19: 2	Wine and **w** make the mind giddy,
Is	3:12	and **w** will rule them! O my people,
Zec	5: 9	and saw two **w** coming forth
Mt	11:11	**w** there has been none greater than
Mt	24:41	Two **w** will be grinding at the mill;
Mt	28: 5	the angel said to the **w** in reply,
Mk	15:41	These **w** had followed him when he
Mk	15:41	many other **w** who had come
Lk	1:42	"Most blessed are you among **w**,
Lk	8: 2	some **w** who had been cured of evil
Lk	23:27	including many **w** who mourned
Lk	23:55	The **w** who had come from Galilee
Acts	1:14	together with some **w**, and Mary
Acts	8:12	men and **w** alike were baptized.
Acts	16:13	with the **w** who had gathered there.
Acts	17: 4	and not a few of the prominent **w**.
1 Cor	14:34	**w** should keep silent
1 Tm	2: 9	**w** should adorn themselves
1 Tm	5: 2	older **w** as mothers, and younger **w**
2 Tm	3: 6	make captives of **w** weighed down
Ti	2: 3	older **w** should be reverent in their
Ti	2: 4	they may train younger **w** to love
Heb	11:35	**W** received back their dead through
1 Pt	3: 5	how the holy **w** who hoped in God

WOMEN'S →WOMAN
Rv	9: 8	and they had hair like **w** hair.

WON →WIN
Est	2: 9	girl pleased him and **w** his favor.
1 Pt	3: 1	they may be **w** over without a word

WONDER →WONDERFUL, WONDERFULLY, WONDERS, WONDROUS
Ex	7: 9	demands that you work a sign or **w**,

WONDERFUL →WONDER
Jb	42: 3	things too **w** for me, which I cannot
Ps	119:129	**W** are your decrees; therefore I
Ps	139:14	you made me; **w** are your works!
Is	28:29	hosts; **w** is his counsel and great his

WONDERFULLY →WONDER
Ps	139:14	I praise you, so **w** you made me;

WONDERS →WONDER
Ex	11:10	Aaron performed these various **w**
Ex	15:11	O terrible in renown, worker of **w**,
Ps	78:32	they did not believe in his **w**.
Ps	136: 4	Who alone has done great **w**,
Dn	3t00	are his signs, how mighty his **w**;
Jn	4:48	"Unless you people see signs and **w**,
2 Cor	12:12	signs and **w**, and mighty deeds.
2 Thes	2: 9	deed and in signs and **w** that lie,
Heb	2: 4	added his testimony by signs, **w**,

WONDROUS →WONDER
Ps	26: 7	thanks, recounting all your **w** deeds.

WOOD →WOODEN, WOODS
Gn	22: 9	altar there and arranged the **w** on it.
Gn	22: 9	put him on top of the **w** on the altar.
Ex	15:25	out to him a certain piece of **w**.
Ex	25:10	"You shall make an ark of acacia **w**,
Ex	25:13	make poles of acacia **w** and plate
Ex	25:23	shall also make a table of acacia **w**,
Ex	26:15	make boards of acacia **w** as walls
Ex	27: 1	"You shall make an altar of acacia **w**,
Dt	28:64	you will serve strange gods of **w**
1 Kgs	18:23	and place it on the **w**, but start no
1 Kgs	18:23	the other and place it on the **w**,
Is	44:19	"Half of the **w** I burned in the fire,
Is	44:19	of the rest, or worship a block of **w**?"
Is	60:17	of iron, silver; In place of **w**, bronze,
Ez	20:32	foreign lands, serving **w** and stone."
Hos	4:12	They consult their piece of **w**,
Hb	2:19	Woe to him who says to **w**, "Awake!"
1 Cor	3:12	silver, precious stones, **w**, hay,

WOODEN →WOOD
Neh	8: 4	the scribe stood on a **w** platform

WOODS →WOOD
2 Kgs	2:24	two she-bears came out of the **w**

WOOL
Dt	22:11	kinds of thread, **w** and linen,
Prv	31:13	She obtains **w** and flax and makes
Is	1:18	red, they may become white as **w**.
Dn	7: 9	the hair on his head as white as **w**;
Rv	1:14	of his head was as white as white **w**

WORD →BYWORD, WORDS
Gn	15: 1	this **w** of the LORD came to Abram
Nm	30: 3	he shall not violate his **w**, but must
Dt	8: 3	by every **w** that comes forth
1 Kgs	8:56	Not a single **w** has gone unfulfilled
1 Chr	17: 3	that same night the **w** of God came
2 Chr	36:22	to fulfill the **w** of the LORD spoken
2 Chr	36:22	both by **w** of mouth and in writing:
Ps	33: 4	For the LORD's **w** is true; all his
Ps	107:20	Sent forth the **w** to heal them,
Ps	119:42	me answer my taunters with a **w**, for I trust in your **w**.
Ps	119:74	to see me, because I hope in your **w**.
Ps	119:89	Your **w**, LORD, stands forever; it is
Ps	119:105	Your **w** is a lamp for my feet, a light
Ps	139: 4	Even before a **w** is on my tongue,
Prv	12:25	it, but a kindly **w** makes it glad.
Prv	15: 1	wrath, but a harsh **w** stirs up anger.
Prv	15:23	a **w** in season, how good it is!
Prv	30: 5	Every **w** of God is tested; he is
Sir	3: 8	In **w** and deed honor your father
Sir	18:16	Sometimes the **w** means more than
Is	1:10	Hear the **w** of the LORD,
Is	40: 8	the **w** of our God stands forever."
Is	55:11	So shall my **w** be that goes forth
Jer	5:13	and the **w** is not in them. May their
Jer	23:29	Is not my **w** like fire, says the LORD,

Mt	4: 4	but by every **w** that comes forth
Mt	12:36	for every careless **w** they speak.
Mt	15: 6	You have nullified the **w** of God
Mk	4:14	The sower sows the **w**.
Lk	1: 2	of the **w** have handed them down
Jn	1: 1	In the beginning was the **W**, and the **W** was with God, and the **W**
Jn	1:14	And the **W** became flesh and made
Jn	8:37	because my **w** has no room among
Jn	17:17	them in the truth. Your **w** is truth.
Acts	4:31	continued to speak the **w** of God
Acts	6: 4	prayer and to the ministry of the **w**."
Rom	9: 6	it is not that the **w** of God has failed.
Rom	10: 8	what does it say? "The **w** is near you,
Rom	10: 8	the **w** of faith that we preach),
2 Cor	2:17	many who trade on the **w** of God;
2 Cor	4: 2	or falsifying the **w** of God,
Gal	6: 6	the **w** should share all good things
Eph	6:17	of the Spirit, which is the **w** of God.
Phil	2:16	as you hold on to the **w** of life,
Col	3:16	Let the **w** of Christ dwell in you
2 Tm	2:15	imparting the **w** of truth without
Heb	1: 3	sustains all things by his mighty **w**.
Heb	4:12	the **w** of God is living and effective,
Heb	6: 5	and tasted the good **w** of God
Jas	1:21	and humbly welcome the **w** that has
Jas	1:22	Be doers of the **w** and not hearers
1 Pt	1:23	the living and abiding **w** of God,
2 Pt	3: 5	and through water by the **w** of God;
1 Jn	1: 1	our hands concerns the **W** of life—
1 Jn	2: 5	But whoever keeps his **w**, the love
Rv	3: 8	yet you have kept my **w** and have
Rv	12:11	and by the **w** of their testimony;
Rv	19:13	his name was called the **W** of God.
Rv	20: 4	to Jesus and for the **w** of God,

WORDS →WORD

Ex	24: 3	related all the **w** and ordinances
Ex	34:28	on the tablets the **w** of the covenant,
Dt	11:18	take these **w** of mine into your heart
Dt	13: 4	pay no attention to the **w**
Dt	18:19	not listen to my **w** which he speaks
Dt	31:24	on a scroll the **w** of the law in their
Dt	32:45	had finished speaking all these **w**
Jos	8:34	were read aloud all the **w** of the law,
2 Sm	7:28	you are God and your **w** are truth;
2 Sm	23: 1	These are the last **w** of David:
Ps	5: 2	Hear my **w**, O Lord; listen to my
Ps	19:15	Let the **w** of my mouth meet
Ps	64: 4	their bows for arrows of poison **w**.
Ps	119: 9	fault? Only by keeping your **w**.
Ps	119:130	revelation of your **w** sheds light,
Prv	2: 1	My son, if you receive my **w**
Prv	2:16	the adulteress with her smooth **w**,
Prv	10:19	Where **w** are many, sin is not
Prv	16:24	Pleasing **w** are a honeycomb,
Prv	25:11	are **w** spoken at the proper time.
Prv	26:22	The **w** of a talebearer are like dainty
Prv	30: 6	Add nothing to his **w**, lest he
Eccl	5: 1	earth; therefore let your **w** be few.
Sir	32: 8	brief, but say much in those few **w**,
Jer	15:16	When I found your **w**, I devoured
Hos	6: 5	I slew them by the **w** of my mouth;
Zec	1: 6	But my **w** and my decrees, which I
Mt	7:24	who listens to these **w** of mine
Mt	12:37	By your **w** you will be acquitted,
Mt	12:37	by your **w** you will be condemned."
Mt	24:35	away, but my **w** will not pass away.
Lk	6:47	listens to my **w**, and acts on them.
Jn	6:68	You have the **w** of eternal life.
Jn	15: 7	in me and my **w** remain in you,
1 Cor	2:13	them not with **w** taught by human
1 Cor	2:13	but with **w** taught by the Spirit,
1 Cor	14:19	church I would rather speak five **w**
1 Cor	14:19	than ten thousand **w** in a tongue.
Rv	19: 9	he said to me, "These **w** are true;
Rv	22: 6	"These **w** are trustworthy and true,
Rv	22:19	from the **w** in this prophetic book,

WORK → CO-WORKER, CO-WORKERS, WORKED, WORKING, WORKMAN, WORKS

Gn	2: 2	with the **w** he had been doing,
Gn	2: 2	from all the **w** he had undertaken.
Ex	20:10	No **w** may be done then either
Ex	23:12	"For six days you may do your **w**,
Ex	40:33	Thus Moses finished all the **w**.
Dt	5:14	No **w** may be done then,
1 Chr	22:16	Set to **w**, therefore, and the Lord be
2 Chr	2: 6	send me men skilled at **w** in gold,
2 Chr	2: 6	who know how to do engraved **w**,
2 Chr	8:16	All of Solomon's **w** was carried
Ezr	4:24	Thus it was that the **w** on the house
Ezr	6: 7	elders of the Jews continue the **w**
Jb	1:10	You have blessed the **w** of his
Ps	8: 4	your heavens, the **w** of your fingers,
Ps	90:17	Prosper the **w** of our hands!
Eccl	11: 5	So you know not the **w** of God
Is	64: 7	we are all the **w** of your hands.
Jer	48:10	he who does the Lord's **w** remissly,
Lk	13:14	are six days when **w** should be done.
Jn	5:17	"My Father is at **w** until now, so I am at **w**."
Jn	6:27	Do not **w** for food that perishes
Jn	6:29	said to them, "This is the **w** of God,
Jn	9: 4	Night is coming when no one can **w**.
Jn	17: 4	accomplishing the **w** that you gave
Acts	13: 2	and Saul for the **w** to which I have
Rom	14:20	food, do not destroy the **w** of God.
1 Cor	3:13	the **w** of each will come to light,
1 Cor	3:13	will test the quality of each one's **w**.
Gal	6: 4	Each one must examine his own **w**,
Eph	3:20	by the power at **w** within us,
Phil	1: 6	the one who began a good **w** in you
Phil	2:12	**w** out your salvation with fear
1 Thes	4:11	and to **w** with your [own] hands,
2 Thes	2: 7	of lawlessness is already at **w**.
2 Thes	3:10	that if anyone was unwilling to **w**,
2 Tm	2:21	the house, ready for every good **w**.
2 Tm	3:17	equipped for every good **w**.
Heb	6:10	not unjust so as to overlook your **w**

WORKED →WORK

2 Thes	3: 8	night and day we **w**, so as not
2 Jn	1: 8	that you do not lose what we **w**

WORKING →WORK

1 Cor	4:12	and we toil, **w** with our own hands,
Gal	5: 6	but only faith **w** through love.

WORKMAN →WORK

2 Tm	2:15	to God, a **w** who causes no disgrace,

WORKS →WORK

Ps	8: 7	have given them rule over the **w**
Ps	46: 9	Come and see the **w** of the Lord,
Ps	77:13	I will recite all your **w**;
Ps	92: 6	How great are your **w**, Lord!
Prv	31:31	let her **w** praise her at the city gates.
Is	2: 8	they worship the **w** of their hands,
Rom	4: 6	credits righteousness apart from **w**:
Gal	2:16	a person is not justified by **w**
Gal	2:16	in Christ and not by **w** of the law,
Gal	2:16	because by **w** of the law no one will
Gal	5:19	Now the **w** of the flesh are obvious:
Eph	2: 9	it is not from **w**, so no one may
Eph	2:10	the good **w** that God has prepared
1 Tm	6:18	to be rich in good **w**, to be generous,

WORLD →WORLDLY

1 Chr	16:30	he has made the **w** firm, not to be
Ps	9: 9	It is God who governs the **w**
Ps	19: 5	their message, to the ends of the **w**.
Ps	50:12	for mine is the **w** and all that fills it.
Ps	96:13	To govern the **w** with justice
Is	13:11	Thus I will punish the **w** for its evil
Mt	4: 8	of the **w** in their magnificence,
Mt	5:14	You are the light of the **w**. A city set
Mt	16:26	there be for one to gain the whole **w**
Jn	1:10	He was in the **w**, and the **w** came
Jn	1:10	him, but the **w** did not know him.
Jn	1:29	who takes away the sin of the **w**.

Jn	3:16	God so loved the **w** that he gave his
Jn	3:17	Son into the **w** to condemn the **w**,
Jn	3:17	the **w** might be saved through him.
Jn	8:12	saying, "I am the light of the **w**.
Jn	9: 5	While I am in the **w**, I am the light of the **w**."
Jn	15:19	If you belonged to the **w**, the **w**
Jn	15:19	because you do not belong to the **w**,
Jn	15:19	and I have chosen you out of the **w**, the **w** hates you.
Jn	16:33	In the **w** you will have trouble,
Jn	16:33	courage, I have conquered the **w**."
Jn	17:18	As you sent me into the **w**, so I sent them into the **w**.
Jn	18:36	kingdom does not belong to this **w**.
Jn	18:36	If my kingdom did belong to this **w**,
Acts	17:31	he will 'judge the **w** with justice'
Rom	3:19	the whole **w** stand accountable
Rom	5:12	one person sin entered the **w**,
Rom	10:18	and their words to the ends of the **w**."
1 Cor	1:27	foolish of the **w** to shame the wise,
1 Cor	1:27	weak of the **w** to shame the strong,
1 Cor	3:19	the wisdom of this **w** is foolishness
1 Cor	6: 2	that the holy ones will judge the **w**?
1 Cor	6: 2	If the **w** is to be judged by you,
2 Cor	5:19	God was reconciling the **w**
Gal	6:14	which the **w** has been crucified to me, and I to the **w**.
1 Tm	1:15	came into the **w** to save sinners.
1 Tm	6: 7	For we brought nothing into the **w**,
Heb	1: 6	he leads the first born into the **w**,
Heb	11: 7	Through this he condemned the **w**
Heb	11:38	The **w** was not worthy of them.
Jas	1:27	to keep oneself unstained by the **w**.
Jas	4: 4	to be a lover of the **w** means enmity
Jas	4: 4	of the **w** makes himself an enemy
1 Pt	1:20	before the foundation of the **w**
1 Jn	2: 2	only but for those of the whole **w**.
1 Jn	2:15	Do not love the **w** or the things of the **w**.
1 Jn	5: 4	is begotten by God conquers the **w**.
1 Jn	5: 4	that conquers the **w** is our faith.
Rv	11:15	"The kingdom of the **w** now belongs
Rv	13: 8	the foundation of the **w** in the book

WORLDLY →WORLD

Ti	2:12	to reject godless ways and **w** desires

WORM →WORMS

Ps	22: 7	But I am a **w**, hardly human,
Is	41:14	Fear not, O **w** Jacob, O maggot
Mk	9:48	where 'their **w** does not die,

WORMS →WORM

Acts	12:23	he was eaten by **w** and breathed his

WORMWOOD

Am	5: 7	to those who turn judgment to **w**
Rv	8:11	The star was called "**W**," and a third of all the water turned to **w**.

WORRIED →WORRY

Lk	10:41	anxious and **w** about many things.

WORRY →WORRIED, WORRYING

Mt	6:25	I tell you, do not **w** about your life,
Mt	6:34	Do not **w** about tomorrow;
Mt	10:19	over, do not **w** about how you are

WORRYING →WORRY

Mt	6:27	of you by **w** add a single moment

WORSE →BAD

Mt	12:45	of that person is **w** than the first.
Mt	5:14	so that nothing **w** may happen
1 Tm	5: 8	faith and is **w** than an unbeliever.
2 Pt	2:20	last condition is **w** than their first.

WORSHIP →WORSHIPED, WORSHIPERS, WORSHIPING, WORSHIPS

Ex	20: 5	bow down before them or **w** them.
Ex	34:14	You shall not **w** any other god,
Dt	12: 4	is not how you are to **w** the Lord,
1 Chr	16:29	presence; **w** the Lord in holy attire.
Ps	95: 6	Enter, let us bow down in **w**; let us

Ps	100: 2	**w** the Lord with cries of gladness;
Dn	3:95	or **w** any god except their own God.
Jon	1: 9	"I **w** the Lord, the God of heaven,
Zec	14:17	come up to Jerusalem to **w** the King,
Mt	4: 9	will prostrate yourself and **w** me."
Lk	4: 8	'You shall **w** the Lord, your God,
Jn	4:24	those who **w** him must **w** in Spirit
Rom	12: 1	pleasing to God, your spiritual **w**.
Rv	4:10	who sits on the throne and **w** him,
Rv	13:12	and its inhabitants **w** the first beast,
Rv	14: 7	**W** him who made heaven and earth
Rv	22: 3	be in it, and his servants will **w** him.

WORSHIPED →WORSHIP

Rv	5:14	and the elders fell down and **w**.
Rv	13: 4	They **w** the dragon because it gave
Rv	13: 4	they also **w** the beast and said,
Rv	20: 4	who had not **w** the beast or its image

WORSHIPERS →WORSHIP

Jn	4:23	when true **w** will worship the Father

WORSHIPING →WORSHIP

Acts	13: 2	While they were **w** the Lord

WORSHIPS →WORSHIP

Is	44:15	he adores, an idol which he **w**.

WORTHLESS →WORTHY

Ps	31: 7	You hate those who serve **w** idols,
Ps	60:13	aid against the foe; **w** is human help.
Rom	3:12	have gone astray; all alike are **w**;

WORTHY →WORTHLESS

Mt	10:37	or mother more than me is not **w**
Mt	10:37	daughter more than me is not **w**
Mt	10:38	and follow after me is not **w** of me.
Lk	3:16	I am not **w** to loosen the thongs
Eph	4: 1	in a manner **w** of the call you have
Phil	1:27	yourselves in a way **w** of the gospel
Col	1:10	to live in a manner **w** of the Lord,
Heb	3: 3	he is **w** of more "glory" than Moses,
Heb	11:38	The world was not **w** of them.
3 Jn	1: 6	Please help them in a way **w** of God
Rv	3: 4	in white, because they are **w**.
Rv	4:11	"Are you, Lord our God, to receive
Rv	5: 2	"Who is **w** to open the scroll
Rv	5:12	voice: "**W** is the Lamb that was slain

WOUND →WOUNDS

Ex	21:25	burn for burn, **w** for **w**,
Jer	10:19	I am undone, my **w** is incurable;
Jer	10:19	if I make light of my **w**, I can bear
1 Cor	8:12	brothers and **w** their consciences,
Rv	13: 3	but this mortal **w** was healed.

WOUNDS →WOUND

Jb	5:18	For he **w**, but he binds up;
Ps	147: 3	the brokenhearted, binds up their **w**,
Prv	27: 6	**W** from a friend may be accepted as
Zec	13: 6	"What are these **w** on your chest?"
1 Pt	2:24	By his **w** you have been healed.

WOVEN

Jn	19:23	**w** in one piece from the top down.

WRAPPED

Mk	15:46	**w** him in the linen cloth and laid
Lk	2: 7	She **w** him in swaddling clothes

WRATH

Nm	17:11	for **w** has come forth from the Lord
1 Chr	27:24	for because of it **w** fell upon Israel.
1 Mc	7:38	the **w** of the Almighty that has justly fallen
1 Mc	3: 8	He turned away **w** from Israel
Ps	2: 5	to them in anger, terrifies them in **w**:
Ps	6: 2	Lord, nor punish me in your **w**.
Ps	37: 8	up your anger, abandon your **w**;
Prv	15: 1	A mild answer calms **w**, but a harsh
Sir	16:11	though on the wicked alights his **w**.
Is	13:13	place, At the **w** of the Lord of hosts
Is	51:17	the cup of his **w**; Who drained
Jer	6:11	Therefore my **w** brims up within
Lam	4:11	poured out his blazing **w**; He has

Zep	1:15	A day of **w** is that day, a day
Mt	3: 7	you to flee from the coming **w**?
Jn	3:36	but the **w** of God remains upon him.
Rom	1:18	The **w** of God is indeed being
Rom	2: 5	you are storing up **w** for yourself for the day of **w**
Rom	5: 9	be saved through him from the **w**.
Rom	9:22	wishing to show his **w** and make
Rom	9:22	patience the vessels of **w** made
Eph	2: 3	we were by nature children of **w**,
1 Thes	1:10	who delivers us from the coming **w**
1 Thes	5: 9	For God did not destine us for **w**,
Rv	6:17	the great day of their **w** has come
Rv	19:15	the fury and **w** of God the almighty.

WRESTLED

Gn	32:25	some man **w** with him until

WRETCHED

Rv	3:17	yet do not realize that you are **w**,

WRINKLE

Eph	5:27	without spot or **w** or any such thing,

WRISTS

Acts	12: 7	quickly." The chains fell from his **w**.

WRITE →WRITES, WRITING, WRITTEN, WROTE

Ex	17:14	"**W** this down in a document as
Ex	34:27	said to Moses, "**W** down these words,
Dt	6: 9	**W** them on the doorposts of your
Dt	10: 2	I will **w** upon the tablets
Prv	7: 3	**w** them on the tablet of your heart.
Jer	31:33	them, and **w** it upon their hearts;
Lk	1: 3	to **w** it down in an orderly sequence
Heb	8:10	and I will **w** them upon their hearts.
Rv	1:19	**W** down, therefore, what you have
Rv	21: 5	Then he said, "**W** these words down,

WRITES →WRITE

Dt	24: 1	therefore he **w** out a bill of divorce

WRITING →WRITE

Dt	31:24	When Moses had finished **w**
Dn	5: 7	"Whoever reads this **w** and tells me
1 Cor	14:37	that what I am **w** to you is
1 Jn	2: 7	I am **w** no new commandment
2 Jn	1: 5	you, not as though I were **w** a new

WRITTEN →WRITE

Ex	32:32	me out of the book that you have **w**."
Dt	28:58	of the law which is **w** in this book,
Jos	1: 8	observe carefully all that is **w** in it;
Jos	23: 6	all that is **w** in the book of the law
1 Kgs	2: 3	decrees as they are **w** in the law
Neh	8:14	They found it **w** in the law
Ps	40: 8	for me are **w** in the scroll.
Prv	22:20	Have I not **w** for you the "Thirty,"
Dn	12: 1	everyone who is found **w**
Mal	3:16	a record book was **w** before him
Mt	26:24	Man indeed goes, as it is **w** of him,
Lk	10:20	rejoice because your names are **w**
Lk	24:44	that everything **w** about me
Jn	20:31	these are **w** that you may [come
Jn	21:25	contain the books that would be **w**.
Rom	2:15	of the law are **w** in their hearts,
Rom	15: 4	whatever was **w** previously was **w**
1 Cor	4: 6	from us not to go beyond what is **w**,
1 Cor	10:11	and they have been **w** down as
2 Cor	3: 3	**w** not in ink but by the Spirit
Heb	10: 7	I said, "As is **w** of me in the scroll,
Rv	13: 8	it, all whose names were not **w**
Rv	14: 1	and his Father's name **w** on their
Rv	17: 5	On her forehead was **w** a name,
Rv	20:12	deeds, by what was **w** in the scrolls.
Rv	20:15	whose name was not found **w**
Rv	21:27	those will enter whose names are **w**

WRONG →WRONGDOER, WRONGDOING, WRONGED

Nm	5: 7	he shall confess the **w** he has done,
1 Kgs	8:47	say, 'We have sinned and done **w**;
Zep	3: 5	just, who does no **w**;
Zep	3:13	They shall do no **w** and speak no
Acts	23: 9	"We find nothing **w** with this man.

Col	3:25	recompense for the **w** he committed,

WRONGDOER →DO, WRONG

Col	3:25	For the **w** will receive recompense

WRONGDOING →DO, WRONG

1 Cor	13: 6	it does not rejoice over **w**
1 Jn	5:17	All **w** is sin, but there is sin that is

WRONGED →WRONG

Nm	5: 7	of their value to the one he has **w**.

WROTE →WRITE

Ex	24: 4	**w** down all the words of the LORD
Ex	34:28	he **w** on the tablets the words
Dt	10: 4	The LORD then **w** on them, as he had
Jer	36: 4	of Neriah, who **w** down on a scroll,
Dn	5: 5	king saw the wrist and hand that **w**,
Jn	1:45	about whom Moses **w** in the law,
Jn	5:46	me, because he **w** about me.
Jn	8: 8	he bent down and **w** on the ground.

Y

YARN

Ex	35:23	purple or scarlet **y**, fine linen or goat
Lv	14: 4	cedar wood, scarlet **y**, and hyssop.

YEAR →YEARS

Gn	17:21	shall bear to you by this time next **y**."
Ex	23:14	"Three times a **y** you shall celebrate
Ex	34:23	Three times a **y** all your men shall
Nm	14:34	for your crimes: one **y** for each day.
Dt	1: 3	In the fortieth **y**, on the first day
Neh	10:32	We will forgo the seventh **y**, as well
Is	6: 1	In the **y** king Uzziah died, I saw
Is	34: 8	a **y** of requital by Zion's defender.
Is	61: 2	To announce a **y** of favor
Is	63: 4	my **y** for redeeming was at hand.
Zec	14:16	against Jerusalem shall come up **y** after **y** to worship the King,
Lk	2:41	Each **y** his parents went
Lk	13: 8	leave it for this **y** also, and I shall
Jn	11:49	who was high priest that **y**,
Jn	18:13	who was high priest that **y**.
Heb	9: 7	goes into the inner one once a **y**,
Heb	10: 1	that they offer continually each **y**.

YEARNS

Is	26: 9	My soul **y** for you in the night, yes,

YEARS →YEAR

Gn	1:14	the fixed times, the days and the **y**,
Gn	41:26	The seven healthy cows are seven **y**,
Gn	41:30	be followed by seven **y** of famine,
Gn	47: 9	"The **y** I have lived as a wayfarer
Gn	47: 9	hard have been these **y** of my life,
Ex	12:40	was four hundred and thirty **y**.
Ex	16:35	Israelites ate this manna for forty **y**,
Nm	1: 3	all the men in Israel of twenty **y**
Nm	14:34	forty **y** shall you suffer for your
Dt	2: 7	It is now forty **y** that he has been
Dt	8: 4	nor did your feet swell these forty **y**.
2 Sm	21: 1	was a famine for three successive **y**.
2 Chr	36:21	rest while seventy **y** are fulfilled."
Ezr	5:11	the house built here long **y** ago,
Neh	9:21	Forty **y** in the desert you sustained
Jb	36:26	of his **y** is past searching out.
Ps	90: 4	A thousand **y** in your eyes
Ps	90:10	Seventy is the sum of our **y**,
Ps	95:10	Forty **y** I loathed that generation;
Prv	3: 2	For many days, and **y** of life,
Prv	9:11	and the **y** of your life increased."
Prv	10:27	but the **y** of the wicked are brief.
Eccl	6: 6	Should he live twice a thousand **y**
Jer	25:12	when the seventy **y** have elapsed,
Dn	9: 2	of Jerusalem seventy **y** must be
Jl	2:25	And I will repay you for the **y**
Mt	2:16	and its vicinity two **y** old and under,
Mt	9:20	hemorrhages for twelve **y** came
Lk	3:23	he was about thirty **y** of age. He was
Lk	13:16	Satan has bound for eighteen **y** now,
Jn	2:20	under construction for forty-six **y**,

YEAST

Gal	4:10	days, months, seasons, and y.
Heb	3:17	whom was he "provoked for forty y"?
2 Pt	3: 8	Lord one day is like a thousand y and a thousand y like one day.
Rv	20: 2	and tied it up for a thousand y

YEAST

1 Cor	5: 6	that a little y leavens all the dough?
Gal	5: 9	A little y leavens the whole batch

YES

Mt	5:37	Let your 'Y' mean 'Y,' and your 'No'
2 Cor	1:17	so that with me it is "y, y" and "no, no"?
2 Cor	1:20	promises of God, their Y is in him;
Jas	5:12	but let your "Y" mean "Y" and your "No"

YESTERDAY

Heb	13: 8	Jesus Christ is the same y, today,

YET

Am	4: 6	dwellings, Y you returned not to me,
Mt	6:26	y your heavenly Father feeds them.
Jn	2: 4	affect me? My hour has not y come."
Jn	6:70	twelve? Y is not one of you a devil?"
Jn	7: 6	"My time is not y here, but the time
Jn	7: 8	my time has not y been fulfilled."
Jn	7:39	no Spirit y, because Jesus had not y
Jn	8:20	because his hour had not y come.
Heb	12: 4	against sin you have not y resisted
Rv	17:10	and the last has not y come,

YIELDED

Is	5: 2	but what it y was wild grapes.

YOKE

Dt	28:48	He will put an iron y on your neck,
1 Kgs	12: 4	"Your father put on us a heavy y.
Sir	28:20	For its y is a y of iron and its chains
Mt	11:30	For my y is easy, and my burden
Gal	5: 1	not submit again to the y of slavery.

YOUNG → YOUNGER, YOUNGEST, YOUTH, YOUTHFUL, YOUTHS

Dt	22: 6	upon a bird's nest with y birds
1 Sm	2:17	Thus the y men sinned grievously
2 Chr	10:14	to the advice of the y men:
2 Chr	36:17	who slew their y men in their own
2 Chr	36:17	sparing neither y man nor maiden,
Ps	78:63	Fire consumed their y men; their y
Ps	119: 9	How can the y walk without fault?
Prv	7: 7	ones, I observed among the y men,
Prv	20:29	The glory of y men is their strength,
Eccl	11: 9	Rejoice, O y man, while you are y,
Dn	1: 4	y men without any defect,
Dn	1:17	To these four y men God gave
Jl	3: 1	your y men shall see visions;
Mk	14:51	Now a y man followed him wearing
Mk	16: 5	the tomb they saw a y man sitting
Lk	2:24	pair of turtledoves or two y pigeons,"
Acts	2:17	your y men shall see visions,
Acts	7:58	at the feet of a y man named Saul.
Acts	20: 9	a y man named Eutychus who was
1 Jn	2:13	I am writing to you, y men,

YOUNGER → YOUNG

Gn	19:35	then the y one went in and lay
Gn	25:23	and the older shall serve the y.
Rom	9:12	told, "The older shall serve the y."
1 Tm	5: 1	as a father. Treat y men as brothers,
1 Tm	5: 2	y women as sisters with complete
1 Tm	5:14	So I would like y widows to marry,
1 Pt	5: 5	Likewise, you y members,

YOUNGEST → YOUNG

Gn	9:24	learned what his y son had done
Gn	42:20	back to me with your y brother.
Jos	6:26	he shall lose his y son when he sets
1 Sm	17:14	David was the y. While the three
1 Kgs	16:34	foundation, and his y son, Segub,
Lk	22:26	the greatest among you be as the y,

YOUTH → YOUNG

1 Sm	17:33	for you are only a y, while he has been a warrior from his y."

Ps	71: 5	Lord; my trust, GOD, from my y.
Ps	103: 5	your y is renewed like the eagle's.
Ps	144:12	well nurtured from their y,
Prv	2:17	forsakes the companion of her y
Prv	5:18	And have joy of the wife of your y,
Eccl	4:13	is a poor but wise y than an old
Eccl	11:10	though the dawn of y is fleeting.
Eccl	12: 1	your Creator in the days of your y,
Is	65:20	He dies a mere y who reaches
Mal	2:14	between you and the wife of your y,

YOUTHFUL → YOUNG

2 Tm	2:22	So turn from y desires and pursue

YOUTHS → YOUNG

Is	40:30	grow weary, and y stagger and fall,

Z

ZACCHAEUS

Lk	19: 2	Now a man there named Z, who was

ZADOK

2 Sm	15:27	The king also said to the priest Z:
1 Kgs	1:26	nor Z the priest, nor Benaiah,
Neh	13:13	the priest Shelemiah, Z the scribe,

ZALMON

Jgs	9:48	up Mount Z with all his soldiers,
Ps	68:15	were scattered like snow on Z.

ZALMUNNA

Jgs	8: 5	and I am pursuing Zebah and Z,
Ps	83:12	all their princes like Zebah and Z,

ZAPHON

Jos	13:27	Succoth, Z, the other part

ZAREPHATH

1 Kgs	17: 9	"Move on to Z of Sidon and stay
Lk	4:26	only to a widow in Z in the land

ZEAL → ZEALOT, ZEALOUS

Nm	25:11	by his z for my honor among them;
2 Kgs	10:16	he said, "and see my z for the LORD."
2 Kgs	19:31	The z of the LORD of hosts shall do
1 Mc	2:26	Thus he showed his z for the law,
Ps	69:10	Because z for your house consumes
Is	37:32	The z of the LORD of hosts shall do
Jn	2:17	"Z for your house will consume me."
Rom	10: 2	to them that they have z for God,
Rom	12:11	Do not grow slack in z, be fervent
2 Cor	7:11	yearning, and z, and punishment.
Phil	3: 6	in z I persecuted the church,

ZEALOT → ZEAL

Lk	6:15	Simon who was called a Z,
Acts	1:13	Simon the Z, and Judas son
Gal	1:14	I was even more a z for my ancestral

ZEALOUS → ZEAL

Nm	25:13	because he was z on behalf of his
1 Kgs	19:10	"I have been most z for the LORD,
1 Kgs	19:14	"I have been most z for the LORD,
1 Mc	2:27	"Let everyone who is z for the law
2 Mc	4: 2	and a z defender of the laws.
Acts	21:20	they are all z observers of the law.

ZEBAH

Jgs	8: 5	and I am pursuing Z and Zalmunna,
Ps	83:12	Zeeb, all their princes like Z

ZEBEDEE

Mt	4:21	the son of Z, and his brother John.
Mt	4:21	with their father Z, mending their
Mt	26:37	along Peter and the two sons of Z,
Mk	1:20	So they left their father Z in the boat
Mk	10:35	the sons of Z, came to him and said
Lk	5:10	the sons of Z, who were partners

ZEBOIIM

Dt	29:22	Admah and Z, which the LORD
Hos	11: 8	or make you like Z? My heart is

ZEBUL

Jgs	9:30	had said, Z, the ruler of the city,

ZEBULUN
Son of Jacob by Leah (Gn 30:20; 35:23; 1 Chr 2:1). Tribe of blessed (Gn 49:13; Dt 33:18-19), numbered (Nm 1:31; 26:27), allotted land (Jos 19:10-16; Ez 48:26), failed to fully possess (Jgs 1:30), supported Deborah (Jgs 4:6-10; 5:14, 18), David (1 Chr 12:34), 12,000 from (Rv 7:8).

ZECHARIAH
1. Son of Jeroboam II; king of Israel (2 Kgs 15:8-12).
2. Post-exilic prophet who encouraged rebuilding of temple (Ezr 5:1; 6:14; Zec 1:1).

ZEDEKIAH → =MATTANIAH
1. False prophet (1 Kgs 22:11-24; 2 Chr 18:10-23).
2. Mattaniah, son of Josiah (1 Chr 3:15), made king of Judah by Nebuchadnezzar (2 Kgs 24:17-25:7; 2 Chr 36:10-14; Jer 37-39; 52:1-11).

ZEEB
Jgs	7:25	Oreb and Z at the wine press of Z.
Ps	83:12	Make their nobles like Oreb and Z,

ZELOPHEHAD
Nm	26:33	Z, son of Hepher, had no sons,
Jos	17: 3	Furthermore, Z, son of Hepher,

ZEPHANIAH
Prophet; descendant of Hezekiah (Zep 1:1).

ZERUBBABEL
Descendant of David (1 Chr 3:19; Mt 1:3). Led return from exile (Ezr 2:2; Neh 7:7). Governor of Israel; helped rebuild altar and temple (Ezr 3; Hg 1-2; Zec 4).

ZERUIAH
2 Sm	2:18	The three sons of Z were there—Joab,

ZEUS
2 Mc	6: 2	and dedicate it to Olympian Z,
2 Mc	6: 2	Mount Gerizim to Z the Hospitable,
Acts	14:12	They called Barnabas "Z" and Paul

ZIBA
2 Sm	9: 2	of the family of Saul named Z.
2 Sm	16: 1	gone a little beyond the top when Z,

ZIKLAG
1 Sm	27: 6	That same day Achish gave him Z,
1 Sm	30: 1	his men reached Z on the third day,
1 Sm	30: 1	had raided the Negeb and Z,
1 Sm	30:26	When David came to Z, he sent part

ZILPAH
Servant of Leah, mother of Jacob's sons Gad and Asher (Gn 30:9-12; 35:26; 46:16-18).

ZIMRI
King of Israel (1 Kgs 16:9-20).

ZIN
Nm	13:21	of Z as far as where Rehob adjoins

ZION
2 Sm	5: 7	David did take the stronghold of Z,
2 Kgs	19:31	and from Mount Z, survivors.
Ps	2: 6	my king on Z, my holy mountain."
Ps	9:12	hymns to the Lord enthroned on Z;
Ps	14: 7	Oh, that from Z might come
Ps	48: 3	Mount Z, the heights of Zaphon,
Ps	50: 2	From Z God shines forth,

Ps	65: 2	O God on Z; To you our vows must
Ps	74: 2	Remember Mount Z where you
Ps	78:68	Judah, Mount Z which he favored.
Ps	87: 2	Loves the gates of Z more than any
Ps	102:14	You will again show mercy to Z;
Ps	137: 3	joyful song: "Sing for us a song of Z!"
Sir	24:10	him, and in Z I fixed my abode.
Is	1:27	Z shall be redeemed by judgment,
Is	2: 3	from Z shall go forth instruction,
Is	14:32	"The Lord has established Z,
Is	28:16	God: See, I am laying a stone in Z,
Is	40: 9	mountain, Z, herald of glad tidings;
Is	51: 3	Yes, the Lord shall comfort Z
Is	51:11	and enter Z singing,
Is	52: 1	Put on your strength, O Z;
Is	52: 8	their eyes, the Lord restoring Z.
Jer	50: 5	goal in Z they shall ask the way.
Lam	2:13	virgin daughter Z? For great as
Jl	2: 1	Blow the trumpet in Z,
Jl	4:16	The Lord roars from Z,
Jl	4:21	it unpunished. The Lord dwells in Z.
Am	1: 2	The Lord will roar from Z,
Am	6: 1	Woe to the complacent in Z,
Mi	3:12	you, Z shall be plowed like a field,
Mi	4: 2	from Z shall go forth instruction,
Zec	1:17	the Lord will again comfort Z,
Zec	9: 9	Rejoice heartily, O daughter Z,
Mt	21: 5	"Say to daughter Z, 'Behold,
Rom	9:33	"Behold, I am laying a stone in Z
Rom	11:26	"The deliverer will come out of Z,
Heb	12:22	you have approached Mount Z
1 Pt	2: 6	"Behold, I am laying a stone in Z,
Rv	14: 1	was the Lamb standing on Mount Z,

ZIPH → ZIPHITES
1 Sm	23:14	or in the barren hill country near Z.
1 Sm	26: 1	Men from Z came to Saul in Gibeah,

ZIPHITES → ZIPH
1 Sm	23:19	Some of the Z went up to Saul

ZIPPOR'S
Nm	22: 4	Balak, Z son, who was king of Moab

ZIPPORAH
Daughter of Reuel; wife of Moses (Ex 2:21-22; 4:20-26; 18:1-6).

ZIV
1 Kgs	6: 1	in the month of Z, which is

ZOAN
Ps	78:43	Egypt, his marvels in the plain of Z.

ZOAR
Gn	19:22	That is why the town is called Z.
Gn	19:30	Since Lot was afraid to stay in Z,

ZOBAH
1 Sm	14:47	the king of Z, and the Philistines.
1 Chr	18: 3	king of Z toward Hamath,

ZOPHAR
One of Job's friends (Jb 2:11; 11; 20; 42:9).

ZORAH
Jgs	13: 2	There was a certain man from Z,